CW01023987

# *The Architecture of* SOUTHERN ENGLAND

# *The Architecture of* SOUTHERN ENGLAND

JOHN JULIUS NORWICH

PHOTOGRAPHY BY JORGE LEWINSKI AND MAYOTTE MAGNUS

MACMILLAN LONDON

*To the owners and occupiers*
*of all the houses*
*described in this book,*
*with grateful memories*
*of their kindness*
*and the warmth of*
*their welcomes.*



First published 1985 by
MACMILLAN LONDON LIMITED
4 Little Essex Street London WC2R 3LF
and Basingstoke

Associated companies in Auckland, Delhi, Dublin, Gaborone, Hamburg, Harare, Hong Kong, Johannesburg, Kuala Lumpur, Lagos, Manzini, Melbourne, Mexico City, Nairobi, New York, Singapore and Tokyo

Designed by Robert Updegraff

Filmset in Apollo by Filmtype Services Limited, Scarborough, North Yorkshire

Printed in Italy by Sagdos SpA, Milan

British Library Cataloguing in Publication Data

Norwich, John Julius
The architecture of southern England.
1. Architecture—England
I. Title
720'.9422 NA961

ISBN 0–333–22037–4

# Contents

# *How to Use the Book*

For every county except Oxfordshire and Cambridgeshire, there is a main selection of the best buildings – some of which are additionally distinguished by a star – followed by a Short List. This system of classification is further explained in the Introduction. Oxfordshire and Cambridgeshire have separate sections describing the buildings – of both Town and Gown – in Oxford and Cambridge respectively. The section on London has no Short List, the task of compilation having been quite difficult enough without one.

Entries are normally listed under place name, with specific buildings picked out in small capitals. The exceptions are when a single house stands alone, or when it is considerably better known than its nearest town or village.

In the line printed in italics immediately below each heading, the first figure is that by which the entry is marked on the relevant map, the entries in each county being numbered separately. There follows a brief indication of the whereabouts of the place or building in question – not precise in every case, but sufficiently so to enable the reader to locate it on any good road map (or, for London, Oxford and Cambridge, on a city atlas).

The letters *NT* at the beginning of the italic line signify that the building concerned is the property of the National Trust. Further details of these buildings, including the days and times of opening to the public, are given in publications available at any National Trust shop, or can be obtained from the National Trust, 36 Queen Anne's Gate, London SW1 (Telephone 01-222 9251). For buildings not belonging to the Trust, information can usually be found in the annually issued *Historic Houses, Castles and Gardens in Great Britain and Ireland,* published by British Leisure Publications, East Grinstead, and obtainable from most bookshops and bookstalls.

There are four area maps (pp. 684–92) on which every entry in the book is marked. Entries are numbered from *1* within their county and a key to the buildings of each county is provided.

# *Introduction*

The first thing to be said about this book is that it is an anthology and not – most emphatically *not* – a catalogue. If you are looking for a work in which you will find listed virtually every building of any architectural importance in the country, you must turn to the late Dr Nikolaus Pevsner's majestic series *The Buildings of England*, an almost unbelievable achievement for the lifetime of a single man and one which, either in its comprehensiveness or in the depth of its scholarship, I could never hope to match. But Dr Pevsner's work runs to some fifty volumes, and quite deliberately – except on those rare and magical occasions when he allows his excitement and enthusiasm momentarily to show through – makes no value judgements. Thus he tends to tell us everything that there is to be told about a given building except the one thing that many of us want to know: is it any good? My own brief was less ambitious. I was simply to tour England as exhaustively as I could and to produce a series of succinct but informative descriptions of all the buildings I liked – so long as I actually *liked* them. They might be old or new, religious or secular; they could range from a neo-classical town hall to an abandoned windmill, from a Gothic cathedral to a labourer's cottage. There was, throughout, to be only one overriding consideration: did the building in question appeal, personally, to me?

It was, I suppose, inevitable that at quite an early stage this initially somewhat amorphous programme should have begun to assume a more coherent shape. In the first few months of my task I would still find myself staring at new factory blocks or experimental secondary schools, vainly hoping for some inner response; before long, however, I began almost subconsciously to impose limitations, dictated not only by the time available but also by my own taste. I had learnt, in short, to accept the fact that although my eye for architecture is, I think, moderately acute – it certainly should be by now – my reactions to it remain almost depressingly orthodox. It was soon clear to me that despite occasional deviations in the direction of castles or follies, public monuments or village streets, this book was going to be primarily concerned with those classes of building in which the English architectural genius shows itself at its brilliant best: with churches and cathedrals on the one hand, and with country and manor houses on the other.

In the former category, most of my selections date from the Middle Ages. Not all, of course: it would be perverse not to include the cathedrals at Truro or Coventry, or such masterpieces as St Augustine's, Kilburn, or All Saints, Margaret Street. But the fact remains that the Victorians, in all their ecclesiastical architecture, looked backwards rather than forwards; and few indeed of their innumerable religious buildings give one the same sense of excitement and uplift as the humblest medieval church that has escaped nineteenth-century restoration. In the secular field, too, I have tended to concentrate on houses built before or during the Regency. Once again there are exceptions. Knightshayes is one, Standen another – and how could one possibly leave out St Pancras Station? I have also included several works by Lutyens, as well as his *tour de force* at Castle Drogo, simply because I love him. But most Victorian buildings I do not love, however much I may admire them; and if the following pages reflect the fact, then that is surely as it should be. The same, with even fewer exceptions, goes for the moderns. If, in future centuries, any amateur of antique *curiosa* were to come upon this book, he might almost conclude that in the twentieth century nobody actually built anything at all. *Mea culpa* – but, while I feel much genuine regret, I cannot feel repentance. If we are to play the anthology game, we must play it fairly; it is no good pretending to enthusiasms that do not exist.

By the same token, particular favourites should be properly singled out, and I have distinguished my own with the time-honoured accolade of a star. Once again let it be said that just as this is a very personal book, so the stars reflect very personal tastes: thus Salisbury Cathedral, which I admit – albeit reluctantly – to be one of the great cathedrals of England, is to me so lacking in charm that I could not bring myself to give it a star; while the tiny village church of Up Marden in Sussex, architecturally undistinguished as it may be, gives me such pleasure every time I enter it that I would willingly award it a dozen.

In one respect only, I think, could I be accused – not, perhaps, of breaking the rules but possibly of bending them a little. There are certain buildings – of which

Buckingham Palace is the most obvious example – which would never have made the grade on architectural merit alone but which are of such importance for other reasons that any purchaser of this book might reasonably expect to find them included and feel justifiably aggrieved if he did not. Included, therefore, they are – or at least some of them. If their descriptions sound a little lukewarm, that too is just as well; for the sad fact is that for every one of these buildings that is allowed in, another, better, one has had to be left out.

But there – England is so fantastically rich in superb architecture that, in most counties at any rate, any selection amounts to little more than a sample. In order to cover as much ground as possible I have added, after the principal entries for each county, a Short List of further buildings in that county for which there is room for only the very briefest of descriptions; but this is not for a moment to suggest that they would not have been given considerably longer ones had space permitted, nor that there are not a dozen or more others just as deserving that have been left out. I fully realise that one or two of the latter have occasionally received a passing mention in other entries. For these, just as for other buildings that I have ignored altogether, the reader will have to revert to Dr Pevsner – for whose great work, I repeat, this volume can never be a substitute.

'In that county ...' – how deceptively simple the words sound. When we decided, at the very beginning, to group our chosen buildings by counties, we little knew how much confusion this apparently simple decision was to cause. A quarter of a century ago, all would have been well; but in 1965 the local government of the London area was reorganised, to be followed by that of the rest of England nine years later. County boundaries were redrawn with carefree abandon, regardless of historical propriety or local traditions. Some counties, like Huntingdonshire and Rutland, were simply obliterated, after close on a thousand years' existence; others, like Berkshire and Somerset, were shorn of almost half their acres; yet others, like Herefordshire and Worcestershire, were merged. Families who had lived for centuries in Staffordshire and Cheshire were one day informed that they were thenceforth resident in previously unheard-of areas named, with singular infelicity, 'West Midlands' and 'Greater Manchester'. I would not presume to compare my own irritation with theirs; none the less, when all the best books of reference – including several which were first published *after* the boundary changes – adhere firmly to the ancient dispensation, when County Record Libraries find themselves in possession of records other than their own and others in possession of theirs, when in short it gradually dawns on the serious researcher how unpardonably the bureaucrats have ridden roughshod over English history, he begins to have fears for his blood pressure.

The next important point to be made – and it cannot be made too strongly, which is why it is repeated elsewhere – is that by no means all the houses described in this book are open to the public. A few – a very few – of the several hundred house owners to whom we wrote seeking permission to visit their houses refused, with varying degrees of politeness, outright, very reasonably pointing out that their houses were their private property and that they had no wish to have their peace – and, very often, their rare moments of weekend leisure – disturbed by unknown and uninvited visitors bearing this book in their hands. A good many others, while receiving us most warmly and taking endless trouble to show us round, expressed similar fears. It would be a poor return for their kindness were I not now to enter this most sincere plea: do not, I beg you, unless the owner is a personal friend, attempt to visit a house which is not open to the public or even one which, though open at other times, is closed on that particular day. Nice people hate saying no, and it is not fair to put them unnecessarily in a position where they have to do so.

But how, it may be asked, does one find out whether, and if so when, a house is open? The simplest answer to the difficulty is to buy, at any bookshop, the superbly comprehensive index entitled *Historic Houses, Castles and Gardens in Great Britain and Ireland*, published annually around Easter by British Leisure Publications, Windsor Court, East Grinstead House, East Grinstead, West Sussex, RH19 1XA. The 1985 edition costs £2.00, a sum that it is worth many times over. It naturally includes all the relevant National Trust properties – of which, however, a separate, still more informative catalogue can be bought for a mere 40p (in 1984) at any National Trust shop.

Churches can present a rather more intractable problem. Theoretically they should be open at all times during the day, and – especially in the country – a good many of them are. In most towns, however, and in such villages where there is thought to be a risk of robbery or vandalism and where it is not possible to keep a verger in constant attendance, the casual visitor may arrive only to discover the door firmly locked against him. He should accept this philosophically, but only provided that there is, prominently pinned to the notice-board in the porch, some clear indication of the rectory or vicarage – and, ideally, one or two other addresses as well – where the key may be obtained. If there is no such notice, he will have to initiate a chain of enquiries which may well take him half an hour or more, without any guarantee of success at the end. (Once, at Ockham in Surrey, I ran the vicar to earth in his house only to be met with a point-blank refusal either to entrust me with the key or to accompany me to the church himself; but this, I hope and believe, was an isolated instance.)

Were I a bishop, I should insist not only on those addresses on the notice-board but also on the proper disposition of switches for the electric light inside the building. How often does one arrive at a small parish church on a November afternoon, only to find one's relief at discovering the door to be unlocked rapidly changing to frustration at the impossibility of seeing anything at all amid the encircling gloom – a frustration much increased by the knowledge that the switches have almost certainly been concealed on purpose, to prevent thoughtless visitors from leaving them on and so wasting the electricity. Experience, it is true, gradually teaches one the usual hiding-places: behind the chancel or tower arches, inside the vestry or beside the organ are the old favourites. But why will parish councils not install those little coin-in-the-slot machines which – at a deliberately inflated price – will flood the building with light for five minutes or so and then automatically switch themselves off? Many churches, I suspect, could recover their initial outlay in a matter of months or even weeks, after which the machine would provide a steady supplement to parish funds. Meanwhile we church-lovers must continue to arm ourselves with the most powerful torch we can find, and never stir without it.

It should be clear from the last two paragraphs that there are a fair number of churches that I have either failed altogether to penetrate or have seen less thoroughly than I should have liked. These I have either omitted or – when I have been virtually certain of their quality – have described at second hand or from photographs. The same, *mutatis mutandis*, goes for houses. Of those described here, I have personally visited all but a very few. The exceptions are perhaps half a dozen to which I was refused admittance and about the same number again from which I received no answer to my letters. (Sometimes the owners were simply away; sometimes the house, when we got there, proved to be untenanted or even derelict.) As with churches, where and for whatever reason I have failed to get in I have decided each case on its merits insofar as I could judge them. When, however, a description is not based on a personal visit, I have been careful to say so.

Looking back, however, on the immense number of houses, large and small, that Mollie Philipps and I have visited in the past eight years – for she has accompanied me on virtually every field trip, and my debt to her is beyond computation – I am astonished at the kindness, generosity and hospitality that we have been shown. Whenever possible we have written well in advance (often simply to 'The Owner', since it sometimes proves quite extraordinarily difficult to discover to whom a particular house belongs), but on more occasions than I like to remember we have had to resort to a last-minute telephone call, or have even just turned up, unannounced and without warning, on the doorstep. (Yes, I know; but this was a *job*.) In very nearly every case, we have been welcomed, brought in, offered a cup of tea or a drink – or, quite often, both – and then been taken on a detailed and comprehensive tour of the house. Old photographs have been unearthed for our benefit, old plans and maps fetched down from attics. The briefing over, we have been invited to stay for lunch, for dinner, even occasionally for the night. It is clearly impossible for me to thank so many people at all adequately; as a small token, however, of my very deep gratitude, I am dedicating to them this book.

I do so fully conscious of its shortcomings. Most of them are simple reflections of my own. I have never studied architecture in any formal way and have no technical qualifications whatever. Moreover – particularly in the early days, when we were still feeling our way – I have been a good deal less methodical than I should have liked. But certain other flaws are inevitable. Incompleteness is one, out-of-dateness another. Many houses may have changed hands since we began researching in 1976, many churches may have been restored; some buildings may now be in better condition than when we saw them, some in worse. Books of this kind are therefore to some extent out of date even before they are published, even though the basic architectural information that they contain remains timeless. Inevitably, too, they will contain errors; but here the reader should be warned that architectural history is still far from being an exact science. Many houses have traditions – that they were designed by Inigo Jones or Sir Christopher Wren, that the overmantel is by Grinling Gibbons or the drawing room ceiling by Robert Adam – which simply do not stand up to close examination; in many others the experts themselves cannot agree on attributions or even on dating. Faced with problems such as these, I have always tried to follow the leading authority, who is not by any means invariably the owner of the house; where there is doubt about an attribution to any given architect I have wherever possible taken Howard Colvin's superb *Biographical Dictionary of British Architects* as my final arbiter.

The present volume covers only the South of England – those counties lying to the south, roughly speaking, of a line drawn from the Severn to the Wash. I had originally intended to cover the whole country, together with Scotland and Wales; but after a few years on the job I realised that I had been hopelessly over-ambitious. I was unwilling, in any case, to contemplate a task that might well take me the rest of my working life. Not, therefore, without a measure of relief, I have delegated the direct responsibility for the North – apart from a few small areas which are already written up – to my friend John Martin Robinson, who is travelling tirelessly through Yorkshire even as I write these words. He is himself a northerner, and already a very considerable architectural historian; and I know of no one more admirably qualified to carry on the job. I am more than grateful to him for doing so, and wish him an unbroken succession of open doors.

My final thanks go to two more old friends, Jorge Lewinski and Mayotte Magnus, who have worked indefatigably over the past year to provide photographs of such dazzling quality that, time and time again, I find them recapturing the poetry of the buildings concerned in a way that my words alone would never have been able to do. In a truly just world, this would have been a book of their photographs, to which I would have provided captions. I am all the more grateful to them for collaborating as willingly and enthusiastically as they have, and I feel sure that any distinction this book may be thought to possess will be due, in very large measure, to them.

*John Julius Norwich*
*London*
*November 1984*

# *Photographers' Note*

At one time architectural photographers considered only one kind of a camera – the large, cumbersome view camera initially used for plates and later for cut film. Superb images of cathedrals and sumptuous interiors could be created with this camera, but it demanded great patience and a leisurely approach as the photographer had to spend an interminable amount of time with his head under the black cloth, viewing, arranging and focusing. Although we took some of the photographs for this book – especially the interiors of cathedrals – in a similar way, with a 5 × 6 inch Linhof Technica, if we had used such a camera for all the shots it would have taken us perhaps five years to complete the project instead of one. Modern cameras, lenses and photographic materials, however, have improved so much that nowadays a smaller-sized negative provides an image of more than adequate quality. Consequently we chose two basic cameras for our task – the Pentax 6 × 7 cm and the Nikon FA, the latter often used with one of the excellent PC (Perspective Corrective) lenses.

The great advantage of a view camera such as our Linhof Technica is its flexibility. The lens is mounted on a panel that can be shifted in all directions (as can the back of the camera), which means that the photographer can virtually shoot around the corner of a building, so to speak. But its main advantage is that, from relatively close to the building, it allows the correction of optically distorted verticals so that they appear perfectly parallel in the photograph. Most ordinary modern cameras have to be tilted to include the higher parts of a building, and the resulting photographs show the verticals – towers or spires, say – converging towards the top. The effect can be dramatic – and in fact this is how the eye sees the building most of the time – but it is often preferable to avoid it. The view camera with its 'rising front' does just that, but it is a convenience that was denied owners of small cameras until the invention of the PC lens. Our Nikon PC lens is fitted with a movable front element: it can be shifted up or to the side without tilting the camera, and we have taken advantage of that feature in many of these photographs.

Yet in spite of the first-class sharpness and resolution that Nikon lenses always provide, there are a number of reasons why an architectural photographer may still prefer a larger format. For one thing, the 35mm format often calls for a fine grain, making it necessary to use slower negative and positive materials, and in a dark interior this may mean excessively long exposures. In addition, all the colour reproductions in a book or a magazine invariably come from colour transparencies and not from prints and so it is much more satisfactory to view relatively large 6 × 7cm rather than small 36mm colour slides. Similarly, the quality of a black-and-white negative is much easier to maintain on a large format than on a small one. Some photographers also prefer to use a short film (10–12 exposures) and then switch to a new roll for the next building, rather than rely on a long 35mm film, believing that with shorter rolls and fewer frames one tends to concentrate and shoot with more care – though this is arguable.

We have tried to cover every kind of architecture with these three types of camera. However, most, if not all, of the photographs in this book could have been taken reasonably adequately with just one camera and, had we been forced to make a choice, we would have opted for a light, portable Nikon with 28mm PC lens.

Finally a note about light. Because we had to cover so many buildings in such a relatively short time, unfortunately we could not always wait for the ideal moment or ideal light. But morning, with its low rays of soft, diffused light, is perhaps the most interesting and beautiful time for photography, especially for exterior shots. Hard, mid-day sun is certainly least suitable with its uncompromising contrast of deep shadows and burnt-out highlights. For general purposes, reasonably bright, overcast conditions are often best, allowing a building to be photographed successfully from many angles, and bringing out the texture of the fabric of the building.

*Jorge Lewinski and Mayotte Magnus*
*London*
*November 1984*

# Avon

As a county, Avon should not exist. Indeed, it would not do so if it had not been for the disastrous local government reorganisation of 1974, which killed off several counties altogether, invented a few new ones and generally rode roughshod over a thousand years of English history and tradition. Avon was one of the new inventions. It took a huge bite out of Somerset and a rather smaller one out of Gloucestershire, swallowing up not only Bath but also Bristol, which had until then enjoyed independent county status. These two cities, architecturally among the most important in England, are the greatest pearls in its crown, though it has managed to snatch several great houses into the bargain: Badminton, Dodington, Dyrham and Kings Weston, to name but four. All these, however, are described in their places; it is impossible to ascribe local characteristics to a region which, despite its present status, is in reality only a short-sighted piece of administrative opportunism. For what needs to be said about the northern parts, see the introduction to Gloucestershire; for the rest, turn to Somerset. And that, for Avon, will have to do.

## Badminton

*1; 5 miles E of Chipping Sodbury off A46*
*Includes Worcester Lodge**

The seat of ten successive Dukes of Beaufort, BADMINTON HOUSE was a long time a-building – from the Restoration of Charles II in 1660 for the next thirty years. The principal front is the entrance front, and faces north: a work of cool classicism by an architect unknown, somewhat on the lines of Petworth or Boughton – which it must have resembled still more before the pediment, the twin cupolas, the curved gables, the wings and massive side pavilions were added on by William Kent in about 1740.

The glorious Entrance Hall, where the game of badminton was invented, is also the work of Kent, so far as the decoration is concerned – redesigned by him in order to accommodate the five gigantic pictures by John Wootton, commissioned by the 3rd Duke. Just behind it is a ravishing little octagonal 'waiting-hall', all stuccoed delicacy, with a big marble chimneypiece intended, presumably, for the benefit of the powdered footman who was on duty here, until quite recent times, from morning till night. From here a door leads to the Oak Room, whose superb panelling came originally from Raglan Castle, the family's home until they were forced to leave during the Civil War. The overmantel in particular sticks in the memory, reminding one of the rood-screens in the little churches of the Welsh Borders.

It is fascinating to compare this woodwork with the staggering virtuosity of Grinling Gibbons's carvings in the Dining Room. They are of about 1683 (they include a ducal coronet, which was only granted to the family in 1682) and provide a most impressive illustration of the way the art developed in little more than a century. There, above the chimneypiece and between the windows on the opposite wall, are all the delicacies – game birds, fish, venison, fruit, even crustacea – that would, in various seasons, have found their way to the master's table. Of the other principal rooms, the Library and Great Drawing Room were remodelled by Wyatville in 1811. Another, known as the East Room, contains the wax figure of Bébé, the court dwarf of Louis XV's father-in-law, Stanislaus, King of Poland and Duke of Lorraine: oddly macabre.

Attached to the house is ST MICHAEL'S CHURCH (not a chapel), built in 1785 by Charles Evans on the model, we are told, of St Martin-in-the-Fields. The chancel and apse, however, are additions of 1875, designed to accommodate Gibbons's tremendous monument, now on the north side of the chancel (whither it was moved from St George's Chapel, Windsor) of the 1st Duke in his Garter robes. Do not, however, allow even this to blind you to the splendour of Rysbrack's remarkable monument, at the east end of the aisle, to the 2nd and 3rd Dukes, with the white marble drapery tumbling down over their sarcophagus.

Before leaving Badminton, make a point of visiting William Kent's WORCESTER LODGE* (technically in Gloucestershire), which stands at the end of a 3-mile ride directly to the north of the house. This exquisite little Palladian conceit, constructed over a heavily rusticated arch, with pediment and octagonal dome, has a threefold purpose: that of a gate, an eye-catcher and a banqueting room. On the first floor, above the arch, is as pretty a room as Kent ever designed, richly stuccoed with a deep plaster frieze. A candle-lit dinner here on a summer evening must have been something to remember.

The Abbey, Bath.

## Bath★

*2; 13 miles SE of Bristol on A4*
*Includes Assembly Rooms (NT)*

This is a city of superlatives. First of all, Bath is the most beautiful city in Britain. Next, it is the most appropriately named: had it not been for those extraordinary springs which, every day since the world began, have hurled forth a quarter of a million gallons of water heated to a constant 120 degrees Fahrenheit, the Romans would never have adopted it as they did or adorned it with buildings of which enough have survived to constitute the most important classical remains that we possess. Nine centuries later, Bath saw the coronation of the first king of all England. Finally, it is a city in which fine building and inspired town planning go hand in hand, together creating an atmosphere of Palladian elegance and civilised refinement which is quite without equal anywhere.

At the beginning of the eighteenth century Bath was still an unassuming little town, its ruins unexcavated, unremarkable except for the springs. Then Queen Anne went to take the waters. High society followed, and with it five architects who together span the century – the two John Woods, father and son, Thomas Baldwin, John Eveleigh and John Palmer. All, however, owed their inspiration to one man, the presiding genius of eighteenth-century Bath – a professional gambler called Richard Nash. Arriving penniless from London in 1703, 'Beau' Nash soon became Master of Ceremonies and within a few years had given his adopted home a social *cachet* that no other English provincial city has ever enjoyed before or since. Distinguished visitors were welcomed by peals of bells from the abbey, and soon found that Bath society during the high season, while marginally – and refreshingly – less exclusive than that of the capital, yielded nothing to it in sophistication. The price they had to pay was discipline. The Beau was a martinet, and for half a century he ruled the city with a rod of iron. Clothes to be worn in the public rooms were precisely regulated by his decree; offenders were asked to leave – and did so. He even laid down the pattern of daily life, always beginning with the required three glasses of spring water in the Pump Room.

The first PUMP ROOM opened in 1706, the joint brainchild of Nash and his doctor, William Oliver, inventor of the Bath Oliver biscuit. By the end of the century, however, it could no longer contain the number of visitors and a new one was designed by the City Architect, Thomas Baldwin. The main front has a giant Corinthian portico with a pediment; to one side, towards the abbey, there is a late Victorian extension by J.M. Brydon, to the other a nine-bay colonnade, Ionic this time, with another pediment over the centre. The interior is equally splendid: a long rectangular saloon lined with attached Corinthian columns supporting a coved ceiling. At each end is an apse framed by a broad segmental arch, beneath which a three-piece orchestra plays selections from *Rose Marie* as one sits in prim gentility over coffee and tea-cakes. A third apse, glazed, looks out from one of the longer sides on to the ROMAN BATHS below.

These are ranged in a line about 100 yards long. At the extreme west end is a small oval swimming bath; next comes a circular bath; then, most impressive of all, the Great Bath, occupying about a third of the whole area if we include the surrounding ambulatory. Originally open to the sky, it was later given a vast barrel vault. Beyond is the so-called Lucas Bath, rectangular again and apsed to north and south; and finally a complex of what were once *tepidaria* and *calidaria* known simply as the East Baths. Together they constitute the best preserved and by far the most spectacular Roman monument in Britain – with the possible exception of Hadrian's Wall.

Immediately to the east of the Baths is the ABBEY. There has been a monastic foundation in Bath since the eighth century, but the Saxon and Norman churches have disappeared (the latter leaving a single arch and column, still to be seen at the eastern end of the south chancel aisle) and the present building was begun as late as 1499; it was still incomplete at the time of the Dissolution. Having been built in a single campaign, it still looks almost exactly as its unknown architects intended. The nave roof was vaulted in the nineteenth century and there have been one or two inevitable restorations; but the only major addition to the structure is Sir Thomas Jackson's covered 'cloister' – in fact the choir vestry – built against the south aisle. The plan is cruciform, with a tall crossing-tower of which the east and west sides are broader than those to the north and south. It has four big crocketed corner turrets and more modest, remarkably slender pinnacles halfway between them. These are all linked by tall, perforated battlements similar to those which run along the roofs of chancel, nave and transepts. The three-bay chancel has aisles with big five-light windows and flying buttresses above, supporting the clerestory with still higher windows, also of five lights. The east end is, to all intents and purposes, just one enormous window: seven lights, three proper transoms and what amounts to a fourth where the tracery begins at the top. It is set, significantly for its date, in a square frame, with roundels and mouchettes filling the two small spandrels. Then come the transepts, their immensely tall end windows set between pairs of high-pinnacled buttresses emphasising still further their extreme narrowness. The five-bay nave carries on the same system as the chancel; what makes it memorable is its west front. The magnificently carved west door of 1617 is set within a broad arch with multiple mouldings and emblems of the Passion in the spandrels, and is flanked by statues in canopied niches. Immediately above it are more of those characteristic perforated battlements and in the middle another canopied statue, this time of Henry VII – the work, somewhat surprisingly, of Sir George Frampton, who was also responsible for the figure of Peter Pan in Kensington Gardens. Next comes a huge double-transomed, seven-light window, and above that a crowd of angels in high relief surrounding a representation (also Frampton's) of the seated Christ. Most enjoyable of all, however, are the polygonal buttresses to each side, the fronts of which are carved with ladders, and little angels climbing up and down them. This represents not Jacob's Ladder (as is often thought) but a dream of Bishop Oliver King, Chief Secretary to Henry VII, who was the prime mover in the rebuilding of the abbey.

The interior is indisputably fine, but somehow devoid of mystery. There is something boring, too, about a clerestory which is almost the same height as the arcade below – like a seascape with the horizon halfway up. Lofty as the whole thing is, it stubbornly refuses to soar. The best feature by far is the superb fan vault over nave (though this is nineteenth-century), aisles and chancel.

The next building to claim our attention is the GUILDHALL, immediately to the north of the abbey. It was built by Baldwin in 1766–75: Palladian, as one might expect, with a three-bay pedimented portico on giant Ionic columns. From the entrance a fine stuccoed staircase leads up to the Banqueting Hall, the finest room in the city. The attached Corinthian columns around the wall support, at measured intervals, blank arches interspersed with garlanded roundels. There follows a frieze, and a deeply coved ceiling above, from which hang three superb chandeliers. Halfway along the inner wall, a deep gallery rises up three tiers, each with its own wrought-iron railing – a wonderful effect.

The other public building of note is the ASSEMBLY ROOMS (NT); it occupies the block between Bennet Street and Alfred Street, just east of the Circus. Originally built by John Wood the Younger and first opened in 1771, it was badly damaged during the Second World War but was carefully restored by Sir Albert Richardson in the 1950s. The *pièce de résistance* is the Ball Room – a curious but most effective composition, divided horizontally into three, the lower stage containing only doors and fireplace, the middle featuring attached Corinthian columns framing square windows and, on the inner wall, round-headed niches, and the upper rising in a high cove to the ceiling. The Tea Room, with its two-storeyed screen of columns, is almost as impressive.

To walk through Bath is a constant joy, which is heightened by the warm, mellow stone of which the whole city is built. The worthwhile streets are too numerous to list, but no one should miss QUEEN SQUARE, a few hundred yards north-west of the abbey. This glorious enclosure was planned, all of a piece, by the elder John Wood, and built between 1729 and 1736. What was exciting and innovative about it, however, was the fact that Wood, probably for the first time in England, treated a whole side of the square as a single architectural composition; indeed, he did this on all four sides – though the west one is no longer as he designed it.

From Queen Square, walk up the unfortunately named GAY STREET – pausing at the corner of the Square to look for a moment at No. 41, which Wood built for himself. With its corner bow rising all three floors, its heavy Gibbs surrounds on the lower two and its general air of fantasy it makes an extraordinary contrast with the austere Palladianism of the rest of the Square. Gay Street is also John Wood's work – it was continued after his death by his son – but it serves principally to link the Square with his most ambitious conception of all, the CIRCUS. Even this was intended as part of something grander still. Wood had never seen the Roman Baths – in his day they still lay beneath several feet of earth and rubble – but he knew that the city was Roman in origin and, good Palladian that he was, he was determined to recreate the classical spirit. He therefore planned a Forum, a Circus and what he called an 'Imperial Gymnasium' for 'medicinal exercises'. We do not know what this last would have been like, because it never materialised; and the Forum fared very little better. But the Circus, with its three splendid superimposed arcades loosely based on the Roman Colosseum, is a triumph. Still unfinished when Wood died in 1754, it too was completed by his son, who went on to create an even grander concept – the ROYAL CRESCENT, first of its kind in England.

It is one of the paradoxes of eighteenth-century taste that, just at the time when Palladian architects were insisting on the merits of symmetry and proportion in buildings, the landscape gardeners were doing away with the formal, artificial compositions of the previous century and striving to obtain a 'natural' effect – however carefully contrived this effect might in fact be. In the work of the two Woods we can see both principles being followed. Thus, in the Circus, the streets leading in are carefully arranged *not* to bisect it. In the same way Royal Crescent, though less than 300 yards away from the Circus down a dead straight street – Brock Street – is actually invisible from it, which makes the surprise of its sudden revelation one of the great dramatic moments of European architecture. No. 1 Royal Crescent, the first house as you come in from Brock Street, is now the property of the Bath Preservation Trust and has been made into a delightful museum of eighteenth-century domestic interiors – well worth a visit.

That wonderful elliptical sweep of Royal Crescent, its giant Ionic columns supporting a continuous cornice over 200 yards long, looking down on to what is now Victoria Park but in the eighteenth century was a prospect of open fields, could not fail to start a fashion. Within the next half-century, crescents appeared across the whole country, from Buxton to Brighton. There are several in Bath; John Palmer's LANSDOWN CRESCENT, with its convexities at each end and its beautiful wrought-iron lamp-holders, is probably the most successful, though John Eveleigh's CAMDEN CRESCENT, unfinished though it is, seems to me to run it close.

*Sydney Place, Bath.*

Still further up the hill stands one of the most unexpected of Bath landmarks. LANSDOWN TOWER was built, by the successful Bath architect H.E. Goodridge, for William Beckford in 1825. Beckford was by this time an old man; he had left Fonthill three years before and had settled in Lansdown Crescent, but clearly could not resist the idea of one more folly before he died. The tower is 154 feet high and basically Italianate, although the octagonal lantern at the top was inspired by the Choragic monument of Lysicrates at Athens. The arrangement of the rooms in the two-storey building at its foot is no longer as it was in Beckford's day, having been much remodelled after a fire in 1931; but a spiral stair still winds up to the Belvidere (*sic*) from whose twelve windows Beckford maintained that he could enjoy 'the finest prospect in Europe'.

Returning now to the centre of the city, cross John Adam's PULTENEY BRIDGE to Bathwick. The bridge dates from 1770; with its three arches spanning the Avon and its line of shops along the top, carrying pilasters supporting a broken pediment on each side, it is quite a show-stopper in its way – one of the most photographed sights of Bath. It leads to a diagonally-set square known as Laura Place, from which there is a long straight vista to what was originally the Sydney Hotel but is now the HOLBURNE ART MUSEUM – in essence a small Palladian country house, *rus in urbe*, though somewhat altered by Sir Reginald Blomfield after the First World War.

Three more country houses should be mentioned, so near the city and so closely associated with it that it would be pedantic – and misleading – to list them separately. The first is WIDCOMBE MANOR, a ravishing house built by an unknown architect in 1727, with fluted Corinthian pilasters carrying a pediment with *oeil-de-boeuf* windows and garlands; the second is the Manor House at CLAVERTON, a most elegant villa in Bath stone by Sir Jeffrey Wyatville dating from 1820, now the American Museum. The third must be described at slightly greater length. It is PRIOR PARK, and was built by John Wood the Elder for Ralph Allen who, as owner of the Bath stone quarries on Combe Down, did more than anyone except Nash himself to make Bath what it is today. His magnificent Palladian mansion near the quarries was begun around 1735, and is described by Pevsner as 'the most ambitious and the most complete re-creation of Palladio's villas on English soil'. It is a building of considerable size: fifteen bays, the five centre ones marked by a vast Corinthian portico, and two main floors over a rusticated basement. It looks down a broad green hillside to a Palladian bridge, one of the three in England built according to Palladio's famous design now at the RIBA. (The other two are at Wilton and Stowe.) The original side pavilions are now much altered – the western one by the building of an enormous church, made necessary after the house was turned into a Roman Catholic boys' school in 1830. This proves to be a building, if anything, still more magnificent than the house itself – apsed, and with a coffered tunnel vault supported on giant Corinthian columns.

It is interesting to compare the classical grandeur of Prior Park – and, incidentally, of Allen's town house in Bath at NO. 2 OLD LILIPUT ALLEY (North Parade Passage) – with the Gothick fantasy of the sham castle, almost certainly designed by Sanderson Miller, that he built as an eye-catcher on BATHWICK HILL in 1762. It marks the first appearance of the Gothic Revival in Bath.

*Pulteney Bridge, Bath.*

There are many other houses in and around the city that would deserve a mention – if only space permitted. But the beauty of Bath, and its uniqueness, lies less in those individual triumphs than in the ensemble – in the squares, crescents and parades, ranging from the panache of the Circus to many a secluded, unpretentious little street behind. It is the quantity of fine houses that impresses, almost as much as their quality. The life they were built to sustain was vacuous, vapid and, one suspects, quite shatteringly dull; but they themselves embody very different values – strength, reason, humanity, permanence. This is the paradox of Bath. When the guide-books call it 'a monument to bygone elegance' they are wrong. Only the perishable has perished. The elegance remains.

## Blaise Hamlet

*NT; 3; 4 miles NW of Bristol*

The tiny MODEL HAMLET, the ultimate in the picturesque, lies in the great sweep of parkland that stretches across the hills immediately to the north-west of Bristol. This has its origins in two big private estates – Kings Weston (*q.v.*) and BLAISE CASTLE HOUSE. The latter, now a branch of the Bristol City Museum, was built in 1796 by William Paty, a local architect, for the banker J.S. Harford. (BLAISE CASTLE itself, the sham castle built to a triangular plan on a nearby hilltop, was already standing at that time, having been erected thirty years before by the previous owner of the estate to the designs of Robert Mylne.) Paty's mansion is austere – appropriately enough for the Quaker Harfords – and of no particular distinction architecturally; the Hamlet, however, which was designed by John Nash in 1811 to accommodate the family's old retainers when they retired, is quite the reverse. It consists of nine buildings – one of them originally a semi-detached pair – grouped around a broad green with a pump, which Nash was careful *not* to place in the centre.

All the cottages are different, though two of the façades are similar. They are completely irregular, in their spacing, in their architectural details, even in their orientation. Most of them do not even face the green, or each other. All they share is a tendency towards very tall chimneys and a determination to be picturesque at all costs. Some are thatched, some have slated roofs, some pantiles. As Pevsner points out, Blaise Hamlet is responsible for some of the worst sentimentalities of England; yet here, it has to be admitted, the effect is enchanting – even if we may be a little ashamed of ourselves for finding it so.

*Blaise Hamlet.*

## Bristol*

*4; 11 miles NW of Bath on A4*

Among the great cities of England, Bristol was a late developer. It had no importance in Roman days, and although by the time of the Norman Conquest it had become a rich and prosperous port it was only in the fourteenth and fifteenth centuries that it realised its full potential. In 1373 this fact was formally recognised when Edward III granted it county status, a privilege it enjoyed until the 1972 legislation. By then, however, its fortunes had long been on the decline. What had been a perfect harbour for the small ships of the Middle Ages – it was from Bristol that the Venetians John and Sebastian Cabot set sail for the New World – could not begin to accommodate the Leviathans of the Industrial Revolution. Gradually but inevitably, Liverpool took over. Bristol today is no longer what it was: it suffered badly in the last war, and post-war planning, while not as calamitous as, for example, at Gloucester or Worcester, could hardly be described as sensitive – as any would-be visitor to St Mary Redcliffe will discover to his cost. Elsewhere, however, it has retained much of its beauty, and the recent redevelopment of the old harbour area seems to me a model of its kind. There is a flourishing cultural life, too, led by a first-rate University. It remains a most agreeable place in which to be, and any walk through the city yields rich architectural rewards.

### THE CATHEDRAL AND IMMEDIATE ENVIRONS

We must start, naturally, with the cathedral – originally the church of the twelfth-century Augustinian abbey, and given cathedral status only in 1542 after the Dissolution. Some most remarkable Norman work still survives, particularly in the Chapter House, and there is an outstandingly fine Early English Lady Chapel; what makes Bristol uniquely exciting, however, is the work that was done there in the early Decorated period. As Pevsner writes: '. . . from the point of view of spatial imagination – which is after all the architectural point of view *par excellence* – [this work] is superior to anything else built in England and indeed in Europe at the same time. It proves incontrovertibly that English design surpassed that of all other countries during the first third of the 14th century.'

The best place from which to see the exterior of the cathedral – though this, it must be said at the outset, is not the most interesting part – is from College Green, immediately to the north. Reading from the east end, we have first of all two bays of the Eastern Lady Chapel, the second partially obscured by an eastward-projecting buttress at the end of the north chancel aisle; then the chancel aisle itself, five bays, its immensely tall windows traceried not only in the heads but also below the transoms. Here again, the western half is partly hidden, this time by the Elder Lady Chapel with its four bays of three stepped lancets. Next comes the north transept, with its big six-light Victorian end window occupying virtually the entire wall; and finally the four-bay nave with a fussy north porch, culminating in twin towers at the west end. This last section, comprising the whole cathedral west of the crossing, is the work of G.E. Street, done between 1868 and 1888. We are left with the beautiful late Perpendicular crossing-tower. It has two stages, each stage with five transomed two-light windows to each side.

The view from the south is essentially similar, except for the astonishing Berkeley Chapel – of which more later – which projects from the eastern end of the chancel aisle and, further to the west, what remains of the monastic buildings, including the Chapter House and Cloister. We can now enter and, temporarily ignoring the Victorian work, go straight up to the crossing.

The first thing to understand is that we are in the only example in England of a hall church – one in which the aisles rise to the same height as the nave, thus eliminating triforium and clerestory. The aisles are consequently of far more importance than they would otherwise be; the question also arises of how to convey the weight of the chancel vault to the outside walls. This, as we shall shortly see, is the problem which is solved at Bristol with such spectacular success; but since we are taking a chronological approach, let us first look at the oldest part of the cathedral proper, the Elder Lady Chapel.

This chapel, so called to distinguish it from the Eastern Lady Chapel which was added in the early fourteenth century, was built between *c.*1210 and 1220. It is a lovely room. The stepped lancets which we observed from the outside are now seen to be separated on the inside by slender detached shafts of Purbeck marble, and to be reflected, as it were, along the inner wall by similar shafts supporting recessed blank arches. Below, on both sides, run rows of blank arcading on shorter Purbeck shafts, also detached, the arches trefoiled. The capitals are deeply carved in stiff-leaf, and there is more foliage in some of the spandrels, the others being given little animal scenes – a fox with a goose, a goat carrying a rabbit, lizards, birds, St Michael and the dragon, and any number of monkeys. The arch leading into the transept is clearly contemporary with the chapel itself; but the two others in the south wall are clearly somewhat later, as is the delicately moulded rib vault and the five-light Decorated east window.

And so to the chancel, which must be taken together with the Eastern Lady Chapel beyond it, there being no structural separation between the two. The first surprise here is to find it lierne-vaulted – with the Lady Chapel at Wells (*q.v.*) the earliest lierne vault in the West of England. The architect was obviously acutely conscious of this, and proud of it: to make sure everybody noticed, he emphasised the areas framed by the liernes over the chancel with double cusping. (The reason why he did not do so over the Lady Chapel is almost certainly because he had not yet thought of it.) But the real excitement is provided by the sidelong views, above the choir stalls and screens, of the choir and chancel aisles. Here, at the level from which the vaults spring, we see soaring across the aisles what are in fact flying buttresses of moulded stone ribs. (Were they of timber rather than stone, one might be tempted to describe them as tie-beams, with pierced mouchettes in the spandrels.) Above them, what happens is more ingenious still: for the aisles are rib-vaulted on a sexpartite plan in such a way as to form two-bay tunnel vaults running north–south across each of the main bays, while the ridge ribs run east–west. Then, as a final virtuoso flourish, the panels of the vaults which would normally rest on the stone 'tie-beams' are left open, giving us tantalising views across from one vault to the other.

For our next trick, we pass on to the Berkeley Chapel, with its ante-chapel, off the eastern corner of the south choir aisle. We enter by the ante-chapel, and look up to the roof. Where in the choir aisles the Bristol Master – there can be no other name for him – left one of his panels open in each bay, here he has quite simply dispensed with them all. We are left with just the free-flying ribs – the skeleton without the flesh. The huge and intricately carved bosses at each intersection seem to emphasise, if anything, the airiness of the structure. Along the south side of the little room are three quite deep niches with ornate ogee canopies above them; in the north-east corner another niche, clearly intended as a cupboard, is set into the right-angle of the wall, a similar canopy rising above it quite unperturbed by the change of plane.

A tall, rather narrow doorway, with a hood-mould composed apparently of snail shells rising up to a leafy ogee, leads into the Chapel itself. Despite three more oddly shaped niches, it would be a good deal more restful than the ante-chapel – were it not for the framing of the tomb chest in the north wall. This is a recurring feature of the cathedral and a most memorable one, but we are meeting it here for the first time. The five upper sides of a vast octagon are depressed to form five inward-pointing semi-circles; within these is inscribed the upper half of a smaller octagon, its corners meeting each semi-circle at its halfway point; finally, three cusped outward-pointing semi-circles with a quarter-circle at each end meet the inner sides of the octagon at a tangent. The effect is breathtaking and somehow oriental, like an immensely elaborate Chinese head-dress. As a final touch, the outer semi-circles (which also finish with two quadrants) display normal Gothic crockets and finials in a most *insouciant* manner.

Three more of these recesses line the outer wall of the south choir aisle, and another three the walls of the Lady Chapel, whither we now come. In essence it is simply a two-bay extension of the choir, beyond the ambulatory. At the end is the great east window, of nine lights. It is not entirely successful, largely because the upper part of the traceried head is occupied by a vast spreading trefoil which, despite the more delicate tracery within it, contrives to look ungainly and brash. Fortunately the eye is at this point directed downwards, to the contemporary stone reredos. It consists of three ogee arches with cusps on the inside, ball-flower in the mouldings and crockets on the outside, rising to high finials which break into a frieze of large and rather threatening heads. In their spandrels are heraldic shields; between them, extremely narrow niches with steep gables, flanked by high canopied pinnacles. Above the frieze runs the elaborately crested parapet of a wall passage. All this would be striking enough without colour; it has,

*Bristol Cathedral.*

however, been painted to within an inch of its life by the celebrated Professor Tristram, who based his scheme on original scrapes. Along the south wall, above the sedilia, are four cusped arches surmounted by four more, upside-down – reminiscent, on a smaller scale, of those great strainer arches at Wells. Though largely of the nineteenth century, they too are said to be accurate representations of the originals.

Of the crossing and transepts there is little to be said. The walls are basically Norman, and there is one tiny Norman window above the arch into the Newton Chapel, off the south-west corner of the south choir aisle; but almost everything else visible is late Perpendicular. The crossing and both transepts are vaulted in much the same style as the chancel, though on close inspection all the schemes prove to be subtly different from each other. And so we come at last to Street. He had a hard act to follow – made harder still, one suspects, by his disapproval of the Bristol style, which would have seemed frivolous and not a little vulgar to any serious-minded Victorian ecclesiologist. Still, he did what he could, faithfully continuing the design of the hall church – careful, competent and, above all, safe.

Of the monastic buildings there remain of importance only part of the CLOISTER, the CHAPTER HOUSE and the ABBEY GATEHOUSE. The east walk of the Cloister still survives, with a little Norman masonry on the inner side, late fifteenth-century work on the outer. The door at the end with its depressed ogee gable and line of crockets obviously belongs to the period of the Berkeley Chapel. The Chapter House is a good deal more exciting. Here we find the best Norman work anywhere in the cathedral. It begins with a rib-vaulted vestibule, round-arched, three bays by two, supporting above it what used to be the Dormitory. From here a doorway, flanked by twin windows under a single round arch and separated by a single column of Purbeck marble, leads into the Chapter House proper. It has two deep bays and is also rib-vaulted, the ribs being deeply carved with zigzag; the north, south and west walls are decorated from top to bottom with various designs of blank arches, sometimes intersecting, with zigzag and trellis work in the lunettes. The east wall is of the nineteenth century and can safely be ignored.

The Abbey Gatehouse stands on the street a little further to the west. It consists of two late Norman gateways, one for carriages and one for pedestrians. Again, there is liberal decoration with zigzag and interlaced blind arcading, and more zigzag on the ribs of the vaulting within. The upper part, with its oriel framed by figures in canopied niches, is fairly obviously of the early sixteenth century, though now much restored.

### THE CITY

Just beyond the Gatehouse it is worth taking a close look, first, at the MUNICIPAL LIBRARY of 1906 – the work of Charles Holden, best known for his chain of suburban London Underground stations in the 1930s. The style here is very different – vaguely Tudorish, but clearly much influenced by Charles Rennie Mackintosh. Then walk northwards across College Green – trying not to notice Vincent Harris's enormous and shatteringly dull Council House to your left – to the LORD MAYOR'S CHAPEL, which was originally built in the thirteenth century as a chapel to the Hospital of St Mark. The body of the church has been enlarged and more than once restored; apart from some good monuments it gives little pleasure. In the south-east corner, however, you will find a ravishing little chantry chapel, exquisitely fan-vaulted, built in 1536 in memory of Sir Robert Poyntz. Here, and elsewhere in the church, there is some good medieval glass.

Emerging from the church, turn left and follow the road round to the Centre. To your right, beyond the eighteenth-century statue of Neptune, is part of the FLOATING HARBOUR; with its shops, pubs and an art gallery at the bottom, it is well worth a brief exploration. A little to the east of it is QUEEN SQUARE, named after Queen Anne and built during her reign. Most of the original brick houses still stand, though a number on the north and west sides were burnt during the dreadful Reform Riots of 1831. Rysbrack's fine equestrian statue of William III escaped the flames – but has disastrously fallen victim to the traffic, a main road having now been driven diagonally through the middle of the square. Such a thoughtless piece of vandalism seems hardly credible: how can it ever have been allowed to happen?

The continuation of this road to the south-east leads you across another bridge and another roundabout – the whole traffic system here is an unrelieved nightmare – to the finest parish church in Bristol and, arguably, in England: ST MARY REDCLIFFE. With its 300-foot spire and a length of 240 feet on the inside, it is bigger and taller than many cathedrals – and, in many respects, grander too. Parts of it go back to the early thirteenth century; from the outside, however, one is conscious only of the fourteenth and fifteenth – Decorated and Perpendicular in roughly equal proportions. The tower is to the north-west, and has much rather florid Decorated work on the upper stage – ogees, crockets and ball-flower in profusion. It is not particularly tall, which makes the spire look even loftier than it is. The top three stages of the latter actually date from the end of the last century: the original was struck by lightning in 1446 and can still be seen in its sadly truncated form in old photographs. It reached its full height again only in 1872.

The nave embraces the tower, and is consequently longer on the south side than on the north – six bays as opposed to four. Its high clerestory, supported by flying buttresses, has – like the aisles and virtually every other horizontal roof line on the building – an openwork frieze of cusped triangles. Next to the tower on the north side, and in the opposite position on the south, are porches, of which more later. The transepts are considerably wider than those of the cathedral itself, since they have their own aisles – a rare luxury for a parish church – from which more flying buttresses soar up to support them. Four more bays of the choir follow, and then finally a lower, two-bay ante-chapel. In general, the aisle windows are of four lights throughout, those of the clerestory six.

We enter by the north porch – the most remarkable single feature of the entire church. The main doorway is inescapably reminiscent of the star-shaped tomb recesses of the cathedral – those same concave curves swooping up to points; here, however, they are not semi-circles, only gentle arcs, and the effect, though still indisputably oriental, seems rather Indian than Chinese. (It has been suggested that Indian motifs may actually have been brought to Bristol by some of the foreign merchants who thronged the port; but in the early fourteenth century the discovery of the Cape Route was still nearly 200 years away in the future.) Three orders of intricate carving – mostly vegetable, but with a few small figures half-hiding within the foliage – surround the doorway, which is cusped and sub-cusped. To each side of the steps are blank niches, with nodding ogee canopies, heavily crocketed. They are empty, but their pedestals are still supported by curious monsters and grotesques, some of them renewed.

Inside, the porch proves to be a hexagon – a most unusual shape in medieval architecture. Octagons we have in plenty; they satisfy because they are, fundamentally, rectangles or squares with the corners chamfered. With a hexagon, on the other hand, if you look to either side you see not a flat wall but a corner; such a choice is another example of that strange wilfulness, that love of a challenge for its own sake, which is characteristic of the Bristol Master. Around it run niches, above them a wall passage. The three-light windows have curious tracery in a kite-like design, and the sexpartite vault has a central hexagon of liernes, heavily bossed. The door opposite the entrance leads into an inner porch, of about 1200 – earlier, that is, than anything visible from the outside. Here a door in the east wall leads up into the old Muniment Room, in which young Thomas Chatterton wrote his 'Rowley' poems; passing straight ahead, we enter the church itself.

The interior gives one an immediate thrill – the loftiness, the airiness, the clustered vertical shafts between the arches of the arcades soaring skyward without interruption, the verticality still further emphasised by the height of the clerestory windows, their mullions extended down below their sills to meet the tops of the arches below. And then the roof: the marvellous controlled intricacy of the liernes, cusped as in the cathedral, bursting into golden bosses at every intersection. (In the south aisle, the liernes surrounding the central panel of each bay are actually *curved* – a great rarity, appearing here for the first time in England.) The vault continues over the crossing and through the chancel – though the patterns are different.

*The church of St Mary Redcliffe, Bristol.*

The chancel ends, at its upper level, with a lovely reticulated east window of seven lights; at the lower level, however, it continues into the Lady Chapel, sumptuously vaulted like the rest and ending in another window, this time of six lights only but with tracery a good deal more complicated.

From the east end there is a wonderful vista back along the length of the church to the great transomed west window. Here a band of panels with nodding ogee heads rises, not just up each side, but around the curve too, forming a continuous border: a lovely touch that rounds off the whole design with a gentle flourish.

The church has many fine monuments, including three which are set into star-burst recesses similar to – though a little more restrained than – those in the cathedral. There is also a most enjoyable painted wooden statue of Queen Elizabeth I, now placed in St John's Chapel under the tower. It was originally a ship's figurehead, and was probably made immediately after the Queen's visit to Bristol in 1574. On that occasion she is said to have described St Mary Redcliffe as 'the fairest, goodliest and most famous parish church in England'. One can only agree.

After this, any other church in Bristol must come as something of a disappointment. The most noteworthy are ST JAMES'S in Whitson Street, which shows more Norman work than any other parish church in the city; ALL SAINTS, with a Norman west end, a Perpendicular centre, a Baroque tower and a largely Victorian chancel; the late Georgian CHRIST CHURCH at the end of Broad Street, with a most elegant and graceful interior; and ST STEPHEN'S in St Stephen's Avenue, whose tower with its high 'Gloucester crown' is one of the great features of the Bristol skyline.

Perhaps the greatest of all such features, however, is – contrary to all appearances – not ecclesiastical at all. It is the most exuberantly Gothic WILLS MEMORIAL TOWER of Bristol University, and it was completed by a somewhat obscure architect named Sir George Oatley in 1925. Walk straight up Park Street from College Green and you will see it directly in front of you. With its four turreted angle buttresses and its upper octagon it makes a truly astonishing affirmation, not of the pseudo-Gothic of the Victorians, but of the real medieval thing: as a piece of deliberate, unashamed archaism, there is nothing better in England. Nor is the exterior the whole story. Inside, the vast Entrance Hall rises over 70 feet; meanwhile two parallel flights of stairs, each of immense breadth, sweep back to an equally Gothic upper landing with quite sensational effect. Next to this magnificent building is the architecturally unremarkable (though in other respects highly rewarding) CITY MUSEUM AND ART GALLERY, and next to that the so-called UNIVERSITY REFECTORY of 1867 – a West Country version of the Doge's Palace. If, after this last, you would like something to take the taste away, you have only to cross the road at this point and walk one block to the south to BERKELEY SQUARE; for here is the equivalent of Queen Square 100 years later, a small and select oasis for the polite Bristol society of 1800, still virtually unspoilt. (John Addington Symonds was born at No. 7.)

Before completing this already overlong essay, I should like to recommend one more brief itinerary. It starts in KING STREET, which leads off the roundabout at the north-west corner of Queen Square. Beginning with a lovely old ALMSHOUSE of 1696, you pass William Halfpenny's GUILD HALL OF THE COOPERS and ST NICHOLAS'S ALMSHOUSES of 1652. Then, across Charlotte Street, comes the LLANDOGER TROW, a tremendous timber-framed house of the seventeenth century, now a pub. A block behind it stands an even more memorable building, a GRANARY of 1871, built in a style that can only be described as Bristol Byzantine.

Turning left up Welsh Back, cross Baldwin Street and go up the flight of steps opposite, past the Covered Market and so into Corn Street, where the building housing LLOYDS BANK is said to be another echo of Venice, this time Sansovino's Marciana Library (although it does not look much like it to me). Go right for a few yards, and then left into Broad Street, with Christ Church at the corner. Here, at NO. 37 BROAD STREET, is the most unexpected house in Bristol – a piece of wild and extravagant *art nouveau*, designed in 1900 by Henry Williams for the printer Edward Everard. On the front are portraits of William Morris and Gutenberg, irresistible. Just beyond stands ST JOHN'S GATE, the sole surviving medieval gateway into the city: much restored, and probably altered as well.

There is much more that could be written about this fascinating city, but this must suffice. The beauties of Clifton and the church of Redland are dealt with separately.

## Clevedon Court

*NT; 5; 11 miles W of Bristol on B3130*

There are not many manor houses dating from the reign of Edward II which still survive relatively unspoilt; of the few, Clevedon Court is one of the most remarkable. It was built around 1320 by Sir John de Clevedon, as an extension to even earlier buildings; these, too – or some of them – have been preserved. They seem to have formed part of a thirteenth-century fort erected as a protection against the Welsh, and consist of a small circular tower and a higher rectangular one with a pitched roof, the two being connected by a battlemented wall. To the south-west of the rectangular tower is a large room known as the Museum, which probably served as a Hall; to the west, two other rooms which would then have been kitchen and offices. All this older group stands askew to Sir John's house, forming a small triangular courtyard known as Pump Court and containing a medieval well.

Seen from the entrance front to the south, the manor house proper begins with the big projecting porch to the right, heavily buttressed at the corners and crowned with a deep, unadorned parapet. The heavily moulded doorway is clearly original, though the cross window above must be a sixteenth-century addition – probably of the same date as the remodelled bay to the right again, where the kitchen, buttery and pantry were replaced *c.*1575 by grander rooms (including a Justice Room) with tall transomed windows. These are on two storeys;

*Clevedon Court.*

above them, in the attic formed by an irregular gable, is a tiny little two-light window with an outsize pediment – an agreeably dotty touch.

Immediately to the left of the porch is the Hall, with its tall six-light south window. The round-headed lights suggest the early sixteenth century, but are in fact less than 100 years old, being replacements for a tall traceried Gothic Revival window inserted in Georgian times. At the western end, instead of the usual bow, a deep alcove projects forward in the style of Bingham's Melcombe or Lytes Cary, having on the ground floor a four-light window with transom; but it is what happens above that astonishes. Here, marking the Chapel, is a vast square window entirely filled with reticulated tracery, ogival in shape and heavily cusped. Another, smaller, window of the same kind can be seen round the corner to the east of the projection, which is buttressed and parapeted in a manner similar to the porch, though the buttresses here are diagonal.

Beyond the Hall to the left, the last bay represents Sir John's Great Chamber and solar and marks the limit of his original ground plan. To this was attached, until recently, a huge and hideous west wing, originally added in Tudor times but since then twice remodelled – most recently by Charles E. Davis, City Architect of Bath, in 1882. This was wisely demolished when the property came to the National Trust in 1961.

Inside the house, although the original domestic offices have gone, the screens passage still survives with its three fourteenth-century arches, linked by their hood-moulds. Opposite is the Hall, with its eighteenth-century coved ceiling and plaster screen, and a fine Elizabethan doorway in the north-west corner which was inserted early in the last century. None of the other rooms, apart from the Chapel, is of outstanding interest, though the Museum contains an extraordinary collection of 'Elton Ware' – a form of pottery invented by Sir Edmund Elton, who lived here from 1883 to 1920.

## Clifton

*6; just NW of Bristol*

There is no suburb of any English city that is quite like Clifton. Apart from the few 'very pretty lodging houses' mentioned by Pope in 1739 there was little building there before 1790 or so. Then a building boom began, only to grind to a halt a mere three years later in a flush of bankruptcies. It was 1810 before things were straightened out and development began again; but the next thirty years or so made Clifton the Regency and neo-classical – or, more precisely, Neo-Grecian – suburb *par excellence*. It seems invidious to single out individual felicities from the squares, terraces and crescents that climb around CLIFTON HILL and GRANBY HILL, though the size and scale of ROYAL YORK CRESCENT are unforgettable, as is the whole composition formed by the MALL, WEST MALL and VICTORIA PLACE. But, as in Bath or Brighton or Cheltenham, it is the ensemble that makes the point: the whole of Clifton is far greater than the sum of its parts.

Wherever you wander, though, you must on no account miss the SUSPENSION BRIDGE. Soaring some 250 feet over the Avon Gorge and spanning over 700 feet without any intermediate support, it is easily the most dramatic suspension bridge in the country. It is also, to my eye, one of the most beautiful. The design is by Isambard Kingdom Brunel, and the foundation stone was laid as early as 1836; but seven years later money ran out and work was interrupted, to be seriously resumed only in 1861, three years after Brunel's death. By now the work was under the direction of Sir John Hawkshaw and W.H. Barlow, who had considerably modified Brunel's original design. The bridge was finally opened on Thursday 8 December 1864.

## Combe Hay Manor

*7; 5 miles SW of Bath off A367*

A house of considerable elegance and mild eccentricity, Combe Hay Manor is beautifully sited in the valley of the Cam Brook. With the tower of the little parish church rising up directly behind it, its golden Bath stone glowing in the afternoon sun, it seems everything the smaller Georgian country house should be; and so, in a way, it is. Few such houses, however, have a large blank round-headed niche forming the ground-floor centre of the main front, with a big Baroque coat of arms above it at the level of the first-floor windows. This gives it a slightly blind look – an impression that is strengthened by the fact that the second bay from each end is also blind at both levels. What saves the day is the way in which the central niche is flanked by windows whose elaborate entablatures on Ionic pilasters extend inwards to cut into the mouldings of the niche itself, joining the three elements together in the manner of a Venetian window; the whole composition could almost be considered as a single bay were it not for the first floor, where the quite separate windows on each side of the heraldry lay the emphasis in the other direction. This centre, however many bays we may consider it to contain, is distinguished by two giant pilasters rising the whole height of the house and supporting a triangular pediment.

This west front must be of *c.*1730. The other principal front, to the south, is probably about forty years later. It too has an indeterminate number of bays – three or five, depending on whether or not you count the further niches, tall and round-headed below, circular above, which frame the centre. This is of three bays, the outer ones tripartite again but under broad triangular pediments, the centre a narrow doorway flanked by slender columns with an urn above, a semi-circular niche scooped out behind. The seven-bay east front, with its central doorway approached up a flight of steps – for the whole house stands raised on a just visible basement – could hardly be simpler.

The interiors are glorious. Nearly all the main rooms in the earlier part of the house have that same richly elaborate woodwork decoration that is such a feature of Frampton Court, Gloucestershire (*q.v.*); so close, indeed,

*The Suspension Bridge, Clifton.*

is the similarity that one suspects the same designing hand. (Gordon Nares, writing in *Country Life* of 9 March 1951, suggests the Bristol architect John Strahan, though the attribution is unlikely ever to be proved.) Pedimented, eared doorcases, richly framed panels for pictures or mirrors, classical friezes on fluted pilasters and high pedimented overmantels are the hallmarks of the style, and at Combe Hay they make a delightful contrast with the Adamish plasterwork of the later rooms – for which the name of George Steuart has been suggested.

Behind the house is an ornamental lake with a modern rotunda, most sensitively designed. One tries not to feel envious – but it's hard work.

## Compton Martin

*8; 20 miles SW of Bath on A368*

A splendid old Norman church is ST MICHAEL'S, constructed of reddish grey stone. It stands on high ground a little above the village's main – indeed, only – street, which gives even more emphasis than usual to its odd and not very successful Perpendicular west tower. But the tower is unimportant. It is only when you go in that the church makes its proper effect with its broad, round-arched arcades of four bays with circular piers – one of which is fluted barley-sugarwise. The arch immediately to the east of this is taller and Perpendicular; clearly there was an attempt to Gothicise the whole thing at the time the south chancel chapel was added. But structural problems arose – the other pier supporting this arch is quite alarmingly out of true – and the attempt was given up. We can only be thankful.

The chancel arch is much depressed, making room for a small three-light window above, with cusped lancets. The chancel beyond is rib-vaulted in two bays: three ribs spring from a three-lobed respond on each side, two of them transverse (to form the vaults) and one, zig-zagged, latitudinally spanning the altar rail.

The church has a Norman clerestory on both sides, of small lancets with broad splays. There is also a Norman font, and a Norman arched recess obviously intended for a side altar just to the north of the chancel arch. On your way out don't miss the good corbel table running along the north side.

## Dodington Park

*9; 10 miles N of Bath off A46*

It was in 1796 that Christopher Bethell Codrington, an enormously rich sugar baron with immense plantations in the West Indies, commissioned James Wyatt to build him a splendid new mansion, worthy of the great park that Capability Brown had designed round his old Tudor manor house thirty years before. Wyatt was at this time heavily engaged with another sugar baron, William Beckford, for whose Gothick fantasy at Fonthill he was at that moment employing over 500 workmen; and it was another two years before building at Dodington could begin. Once started, however, it continued without interruption for the next fifteen years; and the house was still unfinished in September 1813 when Wyatt was killed in a carriage accident while travelling with Codrington over the Marlborough Downs.

It must have been a relief for Wyatt, after the suffocating atmosphere of Fonthill, to turn to the cool classicism of Dodington; here at last he seems to sum up, effortlessly, a lifetime's experience in the style. He does not, however, repeat himself. Dodington bears no close resemblance to any of his other houses. It is not Palladian, for the main rooms are all on the ground floor; nor, within the accepted meaning of the term, is it neo-classical. The huge portico which takes up almost the entire entrance front is distinctly Greek in its proportions, in the shallowness of its pediment and in the absence of a plinth beneath its columns; but those columns are Corinthian, and the interior is clearly inspired less by Greece than by Rome. The garden front is Roman too, but seen through the eye of Sir William Chambers; of its seven bays, the three-bay centre is punctuated by a curious rhythm of pilasters and attached columns, above which stands a tall panelled parapet. To the back, towards the lake, the façade is surprisingly plain, apart from two generous bows rising the height of the house.

It is all very grand; and the interior is grander still. Entering beneath that tremendous portico – really an outsize *porte-cochère* – you at once find yourself in the centre of the Hall, which like the portico occupies the five central bays of the west front. At either end, three steps lead up to a screen of porphyry scagliola columns;

the ceiling is coffered, the floor equally ornate in black marble, red stone, Cotswold stone, and even brass inlays. Everywhere, the original decoration remains unchanged. The same is true of the Library on the south front, where the ebony and mahogany bookcases are fitted with delicate glazed brass grilles, their tiny diamond panes reflecting the afternoon sun. Along the top is a whole row of marvellous maps, invisible until they are rolled down to show the Codringtons' West Indian estates. The great bow of the Drawing Room commands a sublime eastward view to the lake; the room has tall, beautifully inlaid doors reaching right up to the gilded frieze of sphinxes. (All through the house, the doors are a particular joy.) The other bow belongs to a lovely elliptical Music Room, beyond which comes the Dining Room, with another glorious view.

In the centre of the house is the Great Staircase Hall, lit by a cupola with semi-circular windows below it. The staircase itself divides halfway up; the two branches then double back and ascend to an arcaded gallery – all is spaciousness and elegance. The Rococo ironwork came from Beckford's father's house at Fonthill.

The house is connected by means of a curving conservatory to ST MARY'S CHURCH, which was completely rebuilt by Wyatt in 1799. It is cruciform, with a central dome on pendentives supported by fluted Doric columns. In the park, it is also worth looking at Wyatt's dairy-cum-bathhouse a little way to the north of the house, his stables (now occupied by a carriage museum) and Capability Brown's cascade buildings, a pretty little Gothick fantasy on the lake.

## Dyrham Park

*NT; 10; 8 miles N of Bath off A46*

The distant prospect of Dyrham, looking west down the slopes of Humphry Repton's deer park, is the view that most of us remember best. Architecturally speaking, however, the important thing to remember about this lovely house is that it is really two houses, back to back; and that this entrance front that greets us as we wind our way down through the park is in fact the later of the two. It will therefore be no bad thing if on our arrival we walk straight through the house and out on to the lawn behind. From there we can see the first phase of William Blathwayt's transformation of the old Tudor house bequeathed to him by his wife.

Blathwayt was a self-made man who had raised himself through hard work and financial acumen to a high position in the service of King William III. It was presumably his business sense that caused him to employ, in 1691, the most obscure architect in England, a French Huguenot named Samuel Hauduroy. Hauduroy had, so far as we know, built nothing before in England or France; nor did he ever build anything again. But he was an expert painter and decorator as well as an architect – and, as a penniless refugee, he was cheap. Later he was to complain that for all his work on the house he had received only ten pounds, four of which he had had to spend on travelling. It was indeed an inadequate reward, for he did an admirable job. His front, of simple Cotswold stone, is of two storeys, divided up into fifteen rather narrow bays, the three outer ones on each side breaking slightly forward, the

*Dyrham Park.*

*Kings Weston.*

three central ones emphasised by a massive first-floor stone balcony on heavy scrolled consoles. From each side of the house, single-storey galleries come forward at right-angles and lead to two-storey square pavilions, the open courtyard thus formed providing a raised stone terrace. House and pavilions are all surmounted by a tall, rather Baroque balustrade with urns.

It is all beautifully proportioned, but at the same time unassuming and domestic. Seven years later, when Blathwayt decided to turn his attention to the east front, he was richer and grander; moreover, thanks to his exalted rank – he was by this time the King's Secretary of State – he had access to a royal architect; thus for his new east front he secured the services of the Comptroller of the Royal Works, William Talman. The result, it must be said, is a good deal more distinguished: Talman echoes Hauduroy's three-bay side projections, but broadens the bays a little (there are thirteen instead of fifteen) and adds an attic storey. He also emphasises the horizontals, and gives pediments to certain of the *piano nobile* rooms on the first floor – triangular to numbers 2, 7 and 12, segmental to numbers 5 and 9. Then, when the façade was completed, he threw out a greenhouse to the south – one of the first in England to be treated monumentally. Ideally, there should have been a companion range to the north, but there was no room; Talman had to content himself with a line of arcading which runs into the hillside.

One of the most agreeable things about Dyrham is the way it has been preserved, inside and out, virtually unchanged for nearly three centuries. If Blathwayt were to return today, he would recognise every room and a good deal of the furniture and pictures. Everywhere there is a strong Dutch influence – scarcely surprising in view of the fact that he accompanied the King to Holland every summer during the years that the building was in progress. The rooms themselves have nothing sensational or ostentatious about them; they are just quietly distinguished, as would befit a cultivated country gentleman.

Immediately to the north-west of the house, behind and above the north pavilion, stands ST PETER'S CHURCH. In itself it is of no outstanding architectural interest, but it is a vital element in the setting. Originally of the thirteenth century, it has an early fifteenth-century Perpendicular tower with a south porch – a curious arrangement, but easily explained by the fact that there would have been no room for one in the more usual place. There are many fine medieval encaustic tiles, probably from Hailes Abbey, in the floor of the south aisle.

## Kings Weston

*11; 5 miles NW of Bristol*

Sir John Vanbrugh designed Kings Weston for Sir Edward Southwell around 1710. The south-west front is so massive and monumental that one is surprised to find that it has only seven bays. The three-bay centre projects in the form of a portico with giant Corinthian pilasters, paired at the two ends; the triangular pediment contains a semi-circular window; the front door is also pedimented, while the five windows surrounding it are round-headed, with heavy sills on brackets. On the two bays to each side there is a deep string-course on the level of the base of the pediment and small attic windows above. These, and the larger windows below them on the ground and first floors, are all segment-headed, in simple frames but with the same prominent sills. There are urns on the corners of the roof and of the centre. Any other architect would have left it at that; Vanbrugh, however, has added a further flourish, so capricious as to be almost nonsensical: across the top of the roof runs an arcade of five arches, with prominent abaci and keystones, above the spandrels of which rise six chimneystacks, each supporting two squat, square chimneys. This arcade runs round three sides of the roof, making its impact on all three of the principal façades. It adds greatly to the apparent height of the house, especially on the north-west front where the ground falls steeply away towards the Severn, revealing virtually all of a deep basement. Despite the obvious importance of this front, it has no enrichment except a canted bay rising all four storeys.

The house was a police training college when I visited it, and consequently not looking its best; but its two principal features were being well looked after. The first is the Staircase Hall, containing an extraordinary 'hanging' staircase – one, that is to say, with no visible means of support – rising through a rectangular well lit by nine small skylights in three rows of three, all square except the central one which is a circular cupola on pendentives. The arcaded walls contain statues and urns cunningly painted in *trompe-l'oeil*.

The second memorable feature of the house is the Saloon, remodelled in 1767 by Robert Mylne to accommodate the superb Southwell collection of family portraits. Lely, Kneller and Allan Ramsay are all represented, and the thirty-six pictures are all set in individual stucco frames to quite splendid effect.

## Little Sodbury Manor

*12; 2½ miles NE of Chipping Sodbury off A46*

Clinging – almost precariously, it seems – to the side of a steep hill, Little Sodbury Manor looks out to the south and west across the broad valley to the Severn. It is, in its essentials, a fifteenth-century house, built in the middle of the Wars of the Roses; indeed it is said to have given shelter on 29 April 1471 to Henry VI's Queen, Margaret of Anjou, and two days later to her enemies, Edward IV and his brother the Duke of Gloucester (later Richard III), who on 4 May were to crush Margaret's army at the battle of Tewkesbury.

The Great Hall which, with the two-storey gabled porch, is the oldest part of the existing house, still looks much as it did in those days. Admittedly the west windows have been altered, and the western part of the screens is a later replacement; but that marvellous, tall, steeply pitched timber roof with its elaborately moulded purlins and no fewer than four tiers of wind-braces is still in place, as are the stone corbels with shield-bearing angels. Immediately above the screens a wall of timber framing rises to the roof, in a manner reminiscent of the much more modest and slightly later Hall at Buckland, Gloucestershire (*q.v.*).

South of the Hall we come to that part of the house which was added in the early sixteenth century by Sir John Walsh, who had acted as Henry VIII's champion at his coronation in 1509. He it was who engaged, as tutor to his children, the services of William Tyndale; it was at Little Sodbury that Tyndale uttered the famous words to a learned divine: 'Ere many years I will cause a boy that driveth the plough shall know more of the Scriptures than thou dost'; and it was in one of the attic bedrooms, in all probability, that he began his great translation of the Bible. The most distinguished feature of this sixteenth-century block is the charming oriel with an openwork parapet; it was from this window that King Henry and Anne Boleyn are said to have watched a tournament during their visit in 1535. The other windows are largely eighteenth-century replacements.

The next major building period occurred during the occupation of Thomas Stephens, High Sheriff of Gloucestershire, in the 1630s. His is the staircase to the south of the Hall, leading to two rooms – the Porch Room and the Passage Room – with contemporary panelling and four-centred stone fireplaces bearing his initials. (A similar fireplace in the Oriel Room bears his wife's initials as well as his own and a love knot.)

The great storm of 1703 did considerable damage to the house and was followed by a serious fire, as a result of which the early eighteenth century saw much rebuilding. The north wing was entirely remodelled, a new Entrance Hall was created in the centre of the north front, windows were changed, ceilings replaced and a second staircase constructed. The floor of the Great Hall was dropped to the level of the north wing, and the house, having been brought, as it were, up-to-date, served for a century as the country seat of Dr David Hartley, the philosopher, his son, the scientist and statesman, and his comparatively undistinguished grandson. Then, in the 1820s, it was stripped of many of its finest furnishings and decorations and abandoned to a tenant farmer. Gradually it fell into greater and greater disrepair, and was on the point of collapse when, on the eve of the First World War, it was bought by Lord Hugh Grosvenor and restored by Sir Harold Breakspear, who had recently completed work on Great Chalfield Manor in Wiltshire (*q.v.*). The house as we see it today is virtually as Breakspear left it. Much has been added to the house that King Edward and Queen Margaret saw, and much has been lost; but the beauty remains and, in the Great Hall at any rate, the old medieval spirit is still very much alive.

## Redland

*13; 1½ miles NW of Bristol*

REDLAND COURT AND CHAPEL were built between 1735 and 1743 for John Cossins, a prosperous London grocer. The former stood on the site of an Elizabethan mansion which was demolished to make room for it, and was designed by the Bristol architect John Strahan; the latter is also almost certainly Strahan's work, although it is sometimes ascribed to William Halfpenny. The truth seems to be that Strahan died in 1742 before it was finished, and the remaining work was given to Halfpenny to supervise.

The Court, of seven bays and two storeys over a half basement, is now occupied by the Redland High School for Girls. The main front is to the south; it has a three-bay centre with attached Ionic columns and pilasters at first-floor level and is crowned by a pediment with urns. The wings and interior are much altered, though the two fine staircases survive.

The Chapel – now Redland parish church – stands in what is now a public park, Redland having become a suburb of Bristol. It is a tall and imposing building of Bath stone, Baroque in feeling and distinctly old-fashioned for its date. The west front has four Ionic pilasters in two pairs, supporting an entablature and triangular pediment, in which is a semi-circular window. From behind this pediment rises the bell-tower, first square and then octagonal, which supports a lead umbrella dome. North and south elevations are identical, with four bays of tall round-headed windows with prominent dropped keystones. The east end has a slightly projecting chancel but no true east window – only a small blank arch containing a painted panel of the All-Seeing Eye and supported on two negro heads.

Going in, we first find ourselves in an octagonal entrance hall, and then in the nave itself, rectangular apart from a deeply coved ceiling and bounded on the west by an elaborate stone screen rising to the roof. On the ground floor each side contains a tall, round-headed arch of a design similar to that of the windows – that to the north has been filled in – and in the centre a doorway on the same model as the exterior west doorway of the church, eared and with a segmental head and garlands to each side of the keystone. On the upper level there are three more arched openings, slightly stepped, with two small recesses between them in which are busts by Rysbrack of John and Martha Cossins. The two side openings have blind balustrading.

To the east the nave leads to the barrel-vaulted chancel, the vault being supported on fluted Corinthian pilasters and elaborately coffered. The lunette beyond is framed by five winged cherub heads. Below, the whole apse is panelled in oak and most sumptuously carved, with flowers and foliage, by Thomas Paty of Bristol. Within the panels are the Lord's Prayer and the Decalogue, and in the centre a copy of Carracci's *Embalming of Christ*. Instead of the normal altar there is a marble-topped table supported by a gilded eagle. Pulpit and font are also by Paty – what a superb craftsman he was.

## Thornbury

*14; 12 miles N of Bristol on B4061*

A church and a castle stand close together at the edge of the town. The ironstone CHURCH OF ST MARY catches the visitor's eye at once with its remarkable tower, high-turreted and with pierced battlements. More fussy than beautiful, this explosion of ornament is all the odder in that the lower stages of the tower are simple to the point of dullness. Although there was a Norman church on the site, the present building has kept only its north and south doorways; for the rest, the chancel is Decorated of about 1340 (though it has been much restored) and just about everything else is Perpendicular – including that extraordinary tower, which seems to have been added last of all, in the second quarter of the sixteenth century. The aisle windows on the south side have most unusual tracery, characterised by inverted drop-shapes with the mullions running through the centre. The inside is of little interest.

The CASTLE was built by Edward Stafford, 3rd Duke of Buckingham – though he was executed in 1521, before it was finished. It is thus one of the earliest of the great Tudor palaces. The plan was for the buildings to surround a central court, with its entrance on the west; and this west front still stands much as the Duke left it. It has a central Gatehouse bearing the date 1511, and octagonal towers at either end. The south range was also completed by Stafford, and despite much meticulous restoration by Salvin in the 1850s has also retained its original elevation with three projecting bays east of the corner tower, the last of them cinquefoil in plan on the upper storeys. The high Tudor windows have many transoms, and cusped heads.

Relatively little of the interior has survived the restoration. At the time of writing the building has been converted into an extremely grand restaurant and is now surrounded by its own vineyards.

## Wrington

*15; 10 miles SW of Bristol off A38*

ALL SAINTS is the only church with one of the great west towers of Somerset to have fallen into the clutches of Avon. The tower is very tall, with the Somerset characteristic of prolonging the bell openings in blank form for most of the way down. The proportions are said to have been used by Sir Charles Barry when he was designing the Victoria Tower of the Palace of Westminster. At the top there is a parapet pierced with cusped triangles, a motif which recurs on aisles and clerestory. The east gable of the nave has a charming little bell-cote, still containing its original bell of *c.*1500. The chancel predates the rest of the church; judging from the east window – five lights with a circle in the head containing a cusped quatrefoil, a Victorian replica of the original – it must date from around 1300; the two little Perpendicular niches are obvious afterthoughts. Around the aisle walls and those of the tower are some particularly enjoyable gargoyles.

Inside, there is fan vaulting in the tall tower arch; indeed, the whole church gives a feeling of great height, accentuated by the relative shortness of the four-bay nave. From the rather curiously shaped arcade piers one shaft is carried up to clerestory level where it supports an angel, who in turn carries one of the arched braces for the roof. There are more angels on the eastern responds of the two arcades.

The reredos is by Barry, and much what one might expect. The splendid oak screen, however, is of about 1500, and runs the whole breadth of the church. According to the church guide, it 'almost became a victim of the Victorian "restorers" and was only saved by the intervention of the Rector'.

In the south porch are two busts, both nineteenth-century work, respectively of John Locke and Hannah More. The former was born at Wrington, while the latter lived and died there and is buried in the churchyard.

St Mary's Church, Yatton.

## Yatton

*16; 5 miles SE of Clevedon on B3133*

Most people remember ST MARY'S CHURCH for the octagonal spire which never got more than halfway up, but there is a good deal more to it than that. The building history starts around 1280, the date of the lancet or Y-traceried windows in the crossing-tower and the geometrical tracery of the end window of the south transept. Nothing much seems to have happened during the High Decorated period of the early fourteenth century, unless we count the two tomb recesses in the north transept. The rest is Perpendicular, though of different periods. Most spectacular of all is the south porch, the gift of Isobel of Cheddar, Lady Newton, which probably dates from the 1480s. Its four-centred doorway, decorated with a frieze of little leaves running all the way round, is given a swirling ogee gable whose sides, having met at the apex, swoop outwards again like a lyre to form the blank arcading that fills the spandrels. Inside the porch is a most delicate lierne vault; above it is a pinnacled parapet of pierced trefoils in triangles. Lady Newton was also responsible for the chantry chapel on the north side of the chancel, designed to contain the monument to her husband, Sir John, and herself. It has pretty traceried windows and, a little surprisingly, a single turret at the north-east corner.

The rest of the church is somewhat lacking in atmosphere. The nave and aisles are of *c.*1460, with five-bay arcades; they are of course a remodelling, but the clerestory must have been a new addition of that time, since one of the tower west windows can be seen from inside the nave. There is a good wagon roof, with little angels along the wall plates, and a large number of carved bosses.

The modern church hall which now adjoins the church to the north is a bit of an eyesore, even if there is something rather touching about the way in which the architect has tried to echo the effect of the truncated spire. To the south-east, however, the OLD RECTORY is a very handsome fifteenth-century house indeed.

# Short List

## Abbotsleigh

*17; 2 miles W of Bristol on A369*

LEIGH COURT is now a hospital, but even this cannot entirely disguise the fact that here, in 1814, Thomas Hopper built a neo-classical house of real distinction. It has a detached pedimented portico on both principal fronts, and a third, *in antis*, to one side. Within, the most memorable feature is a staircase rising in a wonderfully gentle slope up the long Staircase Hall to an Ionic gallery running all the way round.

## Hinton Charterhouse

*18; 4 miles S of Bath on B3110*

The Carthusian PRIORY was founded in 1232 and is the second oldest in England. The best survival is the three-bay rib-vaulted Chapter House with similarly vaulted Library above, its ribs descending to corbels only a couple of feet from the ground. Nearby to the west is the Refectory, with vaulted Undercroft. The fifteenth-century Gatehouse is now a residence, for which purpose it was much altered in Elizabethan times and again early in the present century. In the village, HINTON HOUSE has a fine Queen Anne front of 1701. The CHURCH OF ST JOHN THE BAPTIST has a Norman south doorway and a thirteenth-century chancel, but gives little pleasure.

## Horton Court

*NT; 19; ¾ mile N of Horton and 3 miles NE of Chipping Sodbury off A46*

Horton Court is essentially a Cotswold manor house: the north wing is in fact the hall of a manor house of *c.*1140 – a rare survival indeed, though it has inevitably been altered over the centuries. The rest of the house too has been much restored, and contains little of architectural interest except a pretty carved porch of 1521.

## Long Ashton

*20; 3½ miles W of Bristol off A370*

ASHTON COURT is indeed extremely long: the south front stretches about 100 yards. Some parts of it go back to the fifteenth century, while other parts are Elizabethan, dated to 1635, and of the early nineteenth century. To the last period belongs the whole south front to the right of the Gatehouse (itself a most suspicious feature). This thirteen-bay composition – the ground-floor windows with alternating pediments, those on the first floor with heavy hoods on corbels, and on the attic floor a row of small circular windows even more irregularly spaced than those below – has been attributed to Inigo Jones, who must be turning in his grave at the very idea.

## Midford Castle

*21; 3½ miles S of Bath off B3110*

The 'castle' was built in the 1770s in the shape of the Ace of Clubs to commemorate a prodigious gambling success by a Mr Roebuck. The design is by the ever-eccentric John Carter, who may not, however, have been directly involved in its erection. There are three floors, each with a lozenge-shaped hall and three rooms with apsed ends leading off it. The whole thing is embattled, with pretty plasterwork and quatrefoil windows. The entrance, with two small polygonal towers, is also embattled. It is all very Gothick, dotty and fun.

## Newton St Loe

*22; 3 miles W of Bath off A39*

NEWTON PARK – now the City of Bath Training College – was built by Stiff Leadbetter from 1761. It is noble, restrained, austere and just a little bit dull. Inside it has excellent stucco ceilings and fireplaces and a most elegant staircase. To the south-west is the old CASTLE KEEP, originally thirteenth-century but since much remodelled.

## Saltford Manor

*23; 5 miles NW of Bath off A4*

Immediately to the west of Saltford church is that rarest of survivals, a Norman manor house, one of the oldest still-inhabited dwellings in the whole country. A rectangular building of three storeys, it has inevitably been much altered over the centuries; but it still retains, between the two stout buttresses on the north front, a two-light Norman window with a zigzag frieze and hood-mould. Another similar window – that of the solar under the east gable – has been blocked but still has its original stone window seat on the inside. (The other two-light window in the north wall is fifteenth-century and not *in situ*.) There are immense ceiling beams in the Hall, and a segmental Norman arch below them; an upper room contains traces of a Wheel of Fortune wall painting of *c.*1200.

# Bedfordshire

Not a bore (though it could easily be mistaken for one) Bedfordshire inevitably suffers by its proximity to London, and tends to be thought of rather as the kind of county one drives through than as the kind one actually visits. Many people, indeed, see it as little more than a rather uninteresting verge of the M1. In fact, however, it remains predominantly agricultural; over half the population live in Bedford, Luton and Dunstable – the last two have now become, to all intents and purposes, a single town – and most of the county's remaining acres are accordingly left to the farmer.

The landscape itself could hardly be called exciting. True, Bedfordshire's most famous son, John Bunyan, is said to have had Dunstable Downs in mind when he wrote, in *The Pilgrim's Progress*, of the Delectable Mountains; but Bunyan was a man of vivid imagination. This abrupt scarp, where the Chilterns, as if suddenly realising that they have overstepped their natural Buckinghamshire boundary, quickly pull themselves up short – much to the delight of the gliding community – marks the beginning of the real Bedfordshire, quiet and rural, starting with a belt of rather soggy clay, then rising slowly and undramatically to a long sandstone ridge of woodland – and park – from Woburn right the way north-east across the county and into Cambridgeshire. North of this again, we are in the valley of the Great Ouse and its tributaries, flowing through the rich green pastureland, much of it beautiful in its modest Bedfordshire way, in which remarkably little ever seems to happen, or ever has – dotted with remote villages of brown ironstone houses, thatched roofs, and many fine churches with soaring stone spires, reminding us that Northamptonshire, the supreme spire county, is nearby.

This rather muted atmosphere is reflected in the architecture. Bedfordshire has no castles, no cathedrals, no great mansion of the sixteenth century. The single really important seventeenth-century one, Houghton House, is an empty shell; and it is consequently only with the beginning of the eighteenth, at Park House, also at Ampthill, that country house architecture gets into its stride. Even then, the treasures are few: Thomas Archer's Pavilion at Wrest stands out almost alone until we get to Flitcroft's Palladian west front of Woburn (1747) and Holland's still more distinguished work there forty years later – all too much of which was demolished after the Second World War. As for the ecclesiastical architecture, the two great monastic foundations, at Dunstable and Elstow, have been physical and even to some extent spiritual cripples ever since the Dissolution; we are left with the parish churches, among which Chalgrave, Eaton Bray and a few others remain to show what Bedfordshire could do when it really tried, and Felmersham stands supreme and inexplicable among its water-meadows.

---

## Ampthill

*1; 9 miles S of Bedford on A418*

In the eighteenth century Ampthill was reckoned 'the genteelest town in the county'. It is still one of the prettiest, with any number of fine seventeenth- and eighteenth-century houses. Among the best are the admirable ST JOHN'S ALMSHOUSES – more properly known as the Oxford Hospital – of 1697, which local tradition misguidedly attributes to Sir Christopher Wren; and, in Church Street, AVENUE HOUSE by Henry Holland. Open by appointment, it is restrained, exquisitely proportioned and endowed with an unexpectedly huge and magnificent garden. More remarkable still, however, are the two great country houses just outside the town. The earlier of these, HOUGHTON HOUSE, was built in 1615 for Sir Philip Sidney's sister, with frontispieces to the north and west added some twenty years later, possibly by Inigo Jones. Now a roofless ruin, it has managed somehow to preserve traces of its old splendour, and is not surprisingly identified with the Palace Beautiful of *The Pilgrim's Progress*. (The staircase, of 1688, is now in Henry Holland's admirable Swan Hotel, Bedford.) Access nowadays is on foot only, but the approach has little in common with Bunyan's Hill Difficulty and anyone prepared to undertake the five-minute walk will find himself well repaid.

*Houghton House, Ampthill.*

The other building, PARK HOUSE, gradually took shape between 1687 and 1707 on the site of an earlier mansion in which Henry VIII kept Catherine of Aragon while their divorce proceedings were being held at Dunstable Priory. Some of the credit for the original plan and elevations should probably go to one Robert Grumbold, a Cambridge builder who among many other commissions for the University had also been Wren's master mason for the Library at Trinity; but he seems to have given less than total satisfaction because he was paid off in 1689, well before the house was finished. In the 1690s we know that the owner, the 1st Lord Ashburnham, consulted Hawksmoor and perhaps even Wren himself, who in 1696 designed the family pew in the parish church (don't bother looking for it – it was demolished in 1877) and who may have advised on the house as well.

But Ashburnham was obviously still unhappy about his new house, and in 1704 called on the services of John Lumley of Northampton for extensive alterations. Since he was three years at Ampthill, it seems likely that most of what we see now is Lumley's work; just how much, we shall never know for sure. By the time he left in 1707, Ashburnham was employing yet another distinguished architect to advise him, William Winde; but Winde's involvement seems to have been confined to the interior, and to such questions as whether Jean Tijou (referred to as 'Tissue the french iron worker') should provide a new staircase.

In the wake of such confusion, it is remarkable that the house turned out as well as it did. It is of noble proportions – eleven bays, and two storeys above a basement – and with its three-bay pediment with coat of arms and its wide curving staircase up to the front door makes an impressive show, especially with the two wings and links added by Sir W. Chambers in the 1760s. After some years as a Cheshire Home, it is being converted into flats.

## Chalgrave

*2; 4 miles N of Dunstable on A5120*

The only remarkable thing about ALL SAINTS' CHURCH seen from the outside is that the tower now rises barely higher than the nave. This is because most of it collapsed in a gale in 1889 and was never rebuilt. But go in – at the time of writing the key was kept at Pond Farm in the neighbouring village of Wingfield – and you find yourself in a lovely unrestored country church of the thirteenth century. Almost as soon as it was consecrated, on Holy Cross Day, 1220, the parish began improvements, and these must have gone on till about 1300, the date of the rebuilt south arcade and chancel; but then construction stopped and the wall painting began. This continues all over the nave and aisles; much of it is faded, but there remains enough – particularly the life-size Apostles on the west wall and the little Annunciation in the former Lady Chapel at the east end of the north aisle – to give real pleasure. Still more of this same pleasure is afforded by the splendid carving on corbels and label stops, and there are two good tomb effigies, that on the north side being almost certainly that of Sir Nigel Loring, one of the original Knights of the Garter, immortalised in *The White Company* and *Sir Nigel* by Sir Arthur Conan Doyle. A more modest sepulchre, in the north-east corner of the churchyard, is that of Arnold Bennett.

## Dunstable Priory

*3; 12½ miles NW of St Albans on A5*

Despite a generous Norman four-ordered arch of 1170 or so, the exterior of Dunstable Priory – in which Henry VIII got his divorce from Catherine of Aragon – is too decayed on the one hand and too restored on the other to be of more than academic interest. For a brief period it boasted two towers: but they both collapsed on the same day in 1222. Inside, things are better. True, the east end, transepts and crossing have gone; but the sumptuous north-west doorway of the mid-thirteenth century and the seven western bays of the magnificently broad twelfth-century nave are still there – the latter retained after the Dissolution of the Monasteries because they also served as the parish church; so is the monumental Norman arcading with its triforium screen of the late eighteenth century. It is a pity that the truncated east end should have been treated quite so insensitively, with garishly painted figures in modern niches and rather bad glass. The Norman west wall is, not surprisingly, a great deal more interesting with its seven pointed lancets, stepped but only just. The first and last two have been awkwardly squashed; only numbers 3 and 5 are now glazed, the rest blank.

It all strikes me as rather sad; this is so nearly a great building, and somehow just misses it. But Bedfordshire is not rich in monuments of this scale and we must be grateful for what we can get.

## Eaton Bray

*4; 3½ miles SW of Dunstable off A4146*

Like Chalgrave, ST MARY'S at Eaton Bray gives little away from the outside. It is built of Totternhoe stone, has a short west tower and mainly Perpendicular windows. The first real sign of quality is the mid-thirteenth-century south door, with marvellous scrolly ironwork. This was very much a Bedfordshire speciality; we find it again at Turvey and also at Leighton Linslade. Its most distinguished exponent was one Thomas of Leighton, who was responsible for the railings round the monument of Queen Eleanor in Westminster Abbey; what we see here may well be from his workshop. The moment you enter the church the two arcades with their splendidly rich mouldings and carvings make their impact. The southern one is of about 1220, the northern some fifteen years or so later. In both, the stiff-leaf carving of the soft clunch capitals is masterly – free yet disciplined, sumptuous yet never exaggerated. On the north side in particular, the lavishness extends to the arches themselves – eight shafts, some detached, with no fewer than eleven rolls of moulding. There are also the beginnings of triple-roll arches across the aisle to the outer wall, but these seem never to have been completed. Perhaps those concerned felt that they would be overdoing it, in which case they were probably right. There is more glorious stiff-leaf on, of all things, the font.

But now for the bad news: the whole thing has recently been repainted, carvings and all, a particularly nasty dirty cream colour which has obscured much of the detail and totally robbed the church of its charm. We can admire it still, but no longer love it.

## Elstow

*5; 1½ miles S of Bedford on A6*

The CHURCH OF ST MARY AND ST HELENA began life around 1075 as a Benedictine abbey founded by William the Conqueror's niece, Judith. At the time of the Dissolution it was the eighth-richest nunnery out of a total of 106, with a régime that could hardly be classified as unduly strict: in 1530 the local bishop ordered the lady abbess to stop having breakfast and supper in the buttery with her steward, and added an injunction to the nuns 'that their gown and kirtles do close afore and are not so deep voided at the breast and no more to use red stomachers but other sadder colours'.

Ichabod! The once great abbey is now, like the priory at Dunstable, little more than a stump from which chancel, crossing, transepts and even the east end of the nave have been remorselessly lopped. What is left is, first of all, a curious and surely French panel above the north door, depicting Christ enthroned, surrounded by a mandorla and flanked by St Peter and St John. It must date from the early twelfth century. Then there is the arcade, very lofty and noble, three Norman bays to the east and two Early English ones, of 1220 or so, to the west. The Norman work has scarcely any decoration, the Early English rather more; but the general impression remains distinctly austere. Finally there is the thirteenth-century Chapter House, reached through a door in the south aisle. Its shape is that of a nearly square rectangle, vaulted throughout from a central pier of Purbeck marble, moulded along its entire length. The odd thing is that this pier and the others around the walls seem to be too short to take the vaulting properly; as a result, the vaults spring not from a normal abacus but from a sort of super-abacus nearly 2 feet higher than the top of the capital.

On the outside, the west front is a pretty good mess – some of it, like the central doorway, is early thirteenth-century, contemporary with the west end of the nave; but the west window is Elizabethan and much of the rest dates from the restoration by Sir Thomas Jackson in 1880. Most of the east end is Jackson's too. There is a separate fifteenth-century bell-tower.

Elstow was the birthplace of John Bunyan. The old timber-framed MOOT HALL on the green had been standing at least a century and a quarter by the time he was baptised in the church font in 1628, but it has now been restored as a museum of the village's most celebrated son and of seventeenth-century village life. The splendid upper hall runs almost the full length of the building and boasts a tremendous timber roof.

## Felmersham ★

*6; 6 miles NW of Bedford off A6*

Taken all in all, inside and out, ST MARY'S is the loveliest parish church in Bedfordshire. It is not particularly large, was never monastic or even collegiate, yet it radiates a quiet magnificence which is the last thing one might expect from the unassuming little village in which, and for which, it was built. It stands on a slight elevation just off the road, aligned in such a way that one is immediately brought face to face with its principal

*St Mary's Church, Felmersham.*

showpiece, the west front. This is purest Early English – but how often did the English church builders of the thirteenth century manage to bring off their west fronts with total success? Very seldom, especially when they tried to create major theatrical effects. At Salisbury the result was a fiasco; at Peterborough and Lichfield, near misses. Only Wells, to me, scores full marks among the cathedrals of that period. Among the parish churches, where less ostentation was called for, success rates were higher; and as a general rule it was the modest approach that paid off best. But not at Felmersham. Here we have three full stages, each taking up all the available space between the corner buttresses: the great central doorway, broad, high, with many shafts and rich mouldings, flanked by two more arches only a little narrower, each containing two trefoil-headed blank sub arches with a quatrefoil in their common spandrel. Above this comes a row of seven more blank arches, each supported on four detached shafts; and above this again a big west window of three lights within a big segmental arch, and a narrow, richly shafted arch containing a lancet to each side. The proportions are flawless, the harmony perfect.

The same music continues within. This time it is the crossing that first claims your attention, its arches exquisitely moulded, elegantly aristocratic. Then you look at the arcades, north and south for once of the same date and conceived as a single unit – note the alternation of circular piers with octagonal ones, zigzagging across the nave. Beyond the ravishing fifteenth-century screen the chancel takes up the Early English melody once more, with beautifully spaced lancets and a double piscina to remind one yet again, in the nicest possible way, that this is a church to be reckoned with. Finally, the east window: alas, where once three slender lancets rose behind the altar, there is now a five-light Decorated replacement. Elsewhere it might have made a fitting climax; in this context it strikes an almost jazzy note, like an added sixth after plainchant. When you look at the aisles, you see that they too are later additions; but being out of the axial line of vision they do not offend.

There is a predictably good roof, with shield-bearing angels, and splendidly grotesque figures on the corbels supporting the wall posts. Just to the south of the church a brave fifteenth-century TITHE BARN of stone looks as if it could stand for ever, and probably will.

## Luton Hoo

*7; 2 miles S of Luton off A6*

People do not normally go to Luton Hoo for the sake of its architecture. They go for the staggering collection of pictures, furniture, tapestries and *objets d'art* amassed by Sir Julius Wernher during the later part of the last century, to which was then added a remarkable Russian collection brought to the house by Sir Julius's daughter-in-law Lady Zia, a member of the Russian Imperial Family. That of course falls outside the scope of this book; but the building itself should not be ignored; particularly on the inside, it gives a good deal of pleasure.

On the outside, it is a curious palimpsest. The building history began in 1766, when the 3rd Earl of Bute, who had recently resigned the premiership, commissioned a new house on the estate he had purchased four years before. As his architect he chose Robert Adam, who after producing magnificent plans finally contented himself with remodelling much of the old house, adding a sumptuous new suite of rooms and enclosing the whole thing in an exterior ashlar shell in his usual late Palladian style. Among the new additions was a Library which Adam himself considered his '*chef d'oeuvre* both in point of elegance and contrivance'. Meanwhile Capability Brown was enlarging the park from 300 acres to 1,200, including two lakes which he formed by damming the River Lea.

Adam's house lasted unchanged for less than half a century. In 1814 Bute's great-grandson, the 2nd Marquess, ordered major alterations from Sir Robert Smirke, whose younger brother Sydney was called in for repairs and further alterations after a disastrous fire in 1843. Then, in 1903, the estate was purchased by Sir Julius Wernher and Luton Hoo entered its final phase of rebuilding. This time the architect was Charles Mewès, of Mewès and Davis, that splendid firm of turn-of-the-century architects who were responsible for the Ritz Hotels in both London and Paris and were leading exponents of the French Beaux-Arts school.

The exterior bears the imprint of all these transformations. On the entrance front, to the west, the giant hexastyle portico and pediment are Smirke's; to each side, within the four-bay recessed sections of the façade, the little Neo-Grecian compositions with tall Doric

*The church of St Mary, Marston Morteyne.*

pilasters and wreaths in the entablatures are Mewès's contribution; the angle bows are by Adam. To the south, where the fall in the ground gives the house a lovely sunken garden, the recessed centre with the Doric columns is Adam's again, while everything else is by Mewès. On the north front, the giant columns are thought to be by Sydney Smirke, as is the bow with attached columns facing the lakes to the east.

With the exception of the Chapel, which was designed in a rather curious Byzantine style by G.E. Street in 1875, virtually the whole interior is the work of Mewès, and quite spectacular it is. Money was clearly no object: the expanses of marble, the encrustations of stucco, the superb *boiseries*, the mirrors, the chandeliers, the dazzle of white and gold – what fun they must have had. Best of all is the Staircase Hall, an ellipse of snow-white walls rising to a high skylight and a beautiful wrought-iron balustrade snaking up in the most graceful of spirals around Borgonzoli's *L'Amore degli Angeli* at its foot and more sculptural groups in niches above. Few great collections can be seen in so luxurious a setting.

## Marston Morteyne

*8; 6 miles SW of Bedford off A5140*

There seem to be as many different spellings of this village's name as there are signposts to it, or chimneys of the London Brick Works which fence it off like some gigantic palisade. The CHURCH OF ST MARY is initially and chiefly remarkable for its huge late thirteenth-century detached bell-tower, a good distance away and quite formidable in its breadth and strength, accentuated by the four big cut-offs on the diagonal buttresses which give it an increasingly massive appearance as they descend. The ironstone chancel must be of very much the same period, though there was obviously a major effort to bring it up to date about a century later, fortunately sparing the impressive vaulted vestry. The body of the church is wholly Perpendicular, its tall and slender arcades surmounted by a good wooden roof with painted angels and bosses. The north arcade loses itself in a rather jolly little stair turret in the side of the chancel arch.

The chancel as it exists today is broad and bright, thanks to the clear glass in most of the windows. The exceptions are a distinctly camp Christ in the east window, beardless, looking like Rupert Brooke with stigmata, and a rather good Burne-Jones group (Morris & Co.) to the south. A Doom painting over the chancel arch is too faded for much comprehension, let alone enjoyment. Finally there are some lovely benches of about 1500, with tracery and linenfold; alas, all but the last three rows had been removed shortly before my visit to the aisles and replaced by most unsuitable modern chairs in bright blue leather. There was a notice saying that woodworm and dry rot were the cause – a very inadequate excuse nowadays.

## Southill*

*9; 9 miles NE of Ampthill off B658*

In the words of Christopher Hussey, 'Southill is a complete work of art to an extent that is true of few other great English homes of any period .... Above all, its exquisite internal decoration is of a quality that makes almost every other house appear a little overdone or a little barbaric in contrast.' Both architecture and decorations are, in their present form, the work of Henry Holland, who began the task of remodelling an earlier house (probably by Isaac Ware) for the second Samuel Whitbread in the year 1795, and for the next eleven years until his death remained intermittently engaged in bringing its interior to perfection. Southill therefore represents, more than any other existing building, Holland's final testament of taste and is, with Berrington in Hereford and Worcester, his masterpiece.

Samuel Whitbread was a brewer – as his great-great-great-grandson, the present owner of Southill, is today; he was also, however, a man of wide culture, and the house he built for himself is as austerely aristocratic as any in the kingdom. The north front, in particular, at first appears almost forbidding. It is very long – nearly 100 yards from end to end – and consists of a five-bay centre (with a three-bay pediment broken slightly forward) connected by straight links to three-bay rusticated angle pavilions. The centre is of three storeys, the pavilions two. Apart from the rustication, which also appears on the ground floor of the centre, there is no decoration of any kind; the only other salient feature is a polygonal bay, separately pedimented, where one might expect the front entrance. In fact, however, this marks the Dining Room; the entrance is a little further to the right and totally unemphasised.

On the south front the mood is considerably more relaxed. The system is the same, but the centre here has a three-bay colonnade beneath the pediment, with four pairs of Ionic columns supporting a long balustrade; and this motif is continued along the two links, where the columns are arranged in a pleasantly syncopated 1–2–2–1 rhythm with unusually broad spaces between the elements. Above these colonnades, on the other hand, there is the same restraint as before; one looks in vain for any decoration to the window frames, for quoins or dressings, for a coat of arms or even a round window in the pediment. Southill needs none of these things. It relies for its effect on the inherent quality firstly of the design itself, and secondly of its execution. Given its perfect proportions and superb craftsmanship, its statement is as cogent and as clear as anything could be. There is no need, in such circumstances, to shout.

The interior of the house shows everywhere the same refinement; and its contents – the pictures, the furniture, the sculpture and even the books – set it off to perfection. Virtually every object of importance was already in the house by the death of Samuel Whitbread II in 1815; yet there is no feeling of oppression or constraint. Cool it may be; cold, never. Of the individual rooms, one remembers the Drawing Room, behind the colonnade to the south, with its broad polished boards and walls hung with honey-coloured silk under a delicately stuccoed ceiling; Mrs Whitbread's Room, with its three doors gently curved to fit the apsidal end; the Dining Room, with its long, narrow vertical panels of sinuous tendrils, its west door flanked by a clock and barometer of mahogany and sumptuous ormolu which once belonged to Marie Antoinette; and – most perfect of all, perhaps – the Library, linked by a broad arch to the Ante-Library at one end, picked out with a narrow frieze above the shelves and again below the coving, many of its books dating from the days of the first Mr Whitbread. Up the purest and simplest of staircases, the first-floor passage shows how brilliantly Holland could make a virtue of necessity. Having raised the ceiling over the Drawing Room, he had similarly to raise the floors of the bedrooms above it; his solution was a charming short flight of wooden 'horseblock' steps, which serves the additional purpose of punctuating a long corridor that might otherwise have been monotonous.

Southill is not, at the time of writing, open to the public. It is, however, loved and cherished by its owners, thanks to whom the future of this wonderful house is assured.

*The Library, Southill.*

*The oak roof, church of St George, Toddington.*

## Toddington

*10; 4½ miles N of Dunstable on A5120*

This charming village is built around an enormous and irregular green called, with what can only be wilful perverseness, the Square. High at the north-east corner stands the CHURCH OF ST GEORGE, imposingly large and Perpendicular with a crossing-tower to match. Various animals, both natural and monstrous, scamper around a continuous frieze below the battlements, though many are now growing sadly defaced. The interior, like that of Eaton Bray, has been most ill-advisedly painted, a fact which must diminish its appeal; but it is nobly planned and proportioned, with aisles and transepts, a clerestory, and even, between north transept and chancel, a three-storeyed annex – vestry below, priest's dwelling above. Here one can see, as one could not have guessed from the outside, that all the Perpendicular work covers a thirteenth-century core; the crossing arches, the lancet above the western one and traces of the old roof line dating from before the clerestory was added, all give the game away; so does the double piscina. But the best feature of all is the indisputably Perpendicular roof – of oak, with big flowered quadripartite bosses and full-length angels in each bay, almost horizontal, looking down on to the congregation.

## Turvey

*11; 8 miles W of Bedford on A428*

The tower of ALL SAINTS' CHURCH is Anglo-Danish, but it does not impress in the manner of, say, Clapham. No matter: the church has other trump cards to play. There is, first of all, a wondrously wrought south door in the manner of Thomas of Leighton (see Eaton Bray) if not by his very hand. Within, the thirteenth- and fourteenth-century arcades sweep up to a magnificent chancel arch, leading to a Victorian chancel by Sir George Gilbert Scott. There are countless references to Scott in this book, all too many of them uncomplimentary; but here it must be admitted that he has done a superb job. Equally grand are the monuments and brasses – particularly those to the Mordaunt family. Best of all is the tomb of the 2nd Baron (who died in 1571) and his two wives, one on each side but at a conspicuously lower level. All are on pallets rolled at the bottom *à la suisse*, while His Lordship's feet rest most uncomfortably on his spurs. In the south aisle is a really exquisite early fourteenth-century fresco of the Crucifixion. Brought to light during Scott's restoration, it is still fresh and genuinely poignant – perhaps the best church fresco on this theme in the whole country. Beyond it are four stepped sedilia, the nearest with its seat only some 18 inches from the ground, the easternmost about 4 feet. The hieratical order of the seated deacons would have been made mercilessly clear, and only one could have preserved any dignity, let alone comfort. There is an excellent timber roof with carved figures over the nave.

Two fine country houses stand close by. TURVEY ABBEY is Jacobean; its pinnacles and balustrades, together with the two huge double-transomed windows towards the garden, were brought over from Easton Maudit in Northamptonshire in 1801. I have not been inside.

TURVEY HOUSE was built in 1794. The architect is unknown, but he was obviously a man of character and not given to false modesty. The garden front could hardly be more swagger if it tried. It is of seven bays, the centre one flanked by two fluted pilasters with capitals oddly oriental in design. The outer bays are also flanked, this time by Corinthian columns. These, together with the pilasters, support an extraordinary frieze of cavorting cherubs, very delicate, with occasional arms and legs projecting, three-dimensional and miraculously unbroken, from the bas-relief ground. Other relief panels are thought to be the work of Thorwaldsen. Above the entablature comes an attic floor of five low windows – the two outer bays have blank panels instead – and the centre is crowned with a large curly acroterion. The whole effect is that of a tiny palace rather than a quite modestly proportioned country house.

Inside, there is a similarly spectacular central Staircase Hall, surmounted by a deep coffered dome. This, curiously enough, is not supported on pendentives but simply rests on the four sides of the square base below. At the top of the stairs a small chamber with its own separate dome and apsed at the end makes a pretty climax. The Dining Room has a beautiful frieze in its original colours, the Library a lovely bookcase obviously made for it by the local carpenter; best of all is the Drawing Room, its windows set in big depressed arches, the western one broadened out into a shallow alcove, the ceiling panelled and with a big rosette in the middle. Two of the french windows on the side have charming little stone steps leading down to the garden level.

On the entrance front the central block comes forward with a pediment, while the stables opposite have blank arches and might just possibly be by Sir John Soane. (If so, could he perhaps have had a hand in the design of the bedroom corridor on the first floor?) To the east of the entrance courtyard the drive leads in through a short range which must date from the early nineteenth century, though its style looks vaguely Palladian – reminiscent, almost, of Kent's Horse Guards, though on an infinitely smaller scale.

## Woburn Abbey

*12; 8½ miles NW of Dunstable off A528*

Since a group of Cistercian monks from Fountains established their daughter-house there in 1145, Woburn Abbey has changed a good deal. Even if we leave aside the largest big game reserve in Europe, the playgrounds and the amusement parks, the art gallery and antiques centre – to say nothing of the 'Flying Duchess Buffet' – and fix our attention on the house itself, we are still faced with as supremely secular a building as any in England: a temple, perhaps, but a temple to the eighteenth-century virtues of reason, sensibility and civilised good living. (Even the glorious collection of pictures contains remarkably few on religious themes.)

The change came about as a result of two national disasters. The first was the Dissolution of the Monasteries by King Henry VIII in 1539 – an event for which no family has had greater cause for thanksgiving than that of the four Earls and thirteen Dukes of Bedford, since it was to John Russell, the 1st Earl, that the abbey was left in Henry's will, and it is to his direct descendants that, transmogrified, it still belongs. Monastic austerity never had much appeal for the early Russells, and for seventy-five years the crumbling ruins lay desolate; then, in 1625, came the second disaster, a plague that swept London and drove out most of its wealthier inhabitants, including Francis, the 4th Earl, who sought refuge at Woburn. Two years later he began rebuilding in earnest. His favourite architect, Inigo Jones, was already fully occupied on his London estate and Covent Garden; the contract almost certainly went to Jones's associate, Isaac de Caux. Of de Caux's house only the north wing survives, but it contains one outstanding feature – the Grotto, first of its kind in England and still one of the most sensational, a riot of stucco and seashells; the ideal setting for a masque on a marine theme by, say, Drayton and Purcell.

Another century passed. Earls became Dukes, but Woburn again began to crumble, the 3rd Duke – who preferred to spend his money at the gambling-tables – philosophically remarking that it would probably last his lifetime and proving himself right by dying, after the dissipation of an immense fortune, in 1732 at the age of twenty-four. Then, however, everything changed. For the next century there reigned (no other word will serve) three successive noblemen who combined impeccable taste and knowledge with almost limitless wealth; and it was they who made Woburn the treasure-house it is today, a repository of paintings and sculpture, of books

*Woburn Abbey.*

and furniture, of gold and silver and porcelain. Immediately on his succession, the 4th Duke began the Herculean task of restoring finances and fabric. By 1747 he was rich enough to order a new west front from 'Burlington Harry' Flitcroft.

Once again the house seems to have been saved in the nick of time: five years later Flitcroft's foreman reported: 'I Finnisht the Underpining the Libery . . . and I Bless God without Any Misfortens though one of the most Rottenest Walls I Ever Saw.' Then, in 1762, that same 'merry little Duke' (as Horace Walpole called him) was sent as Ambassador to France. He remained less than a year – during which he negotiated the Treaty of Paris which brought to an end the Seven Years' War – but he returned with much of the superb French furniture that is still one of the glories of Woburn, to say nothing of a magnificent Sèvres dinner service given to his wife by Louis XV in person. He it was, too, who commissioned the famous collection of twenty-four Canalettos – twenty-one now hanging in the Dining Room, three in private rooms upstairs. These are not, incidentally, Woburn's only importations from Venice: surviving documents tell of a substantial consignment of Venetian glass being shipped over in the seventeenth century on the good ship *Supply* (Capt. Haddock, master).

The 5th Duke carried on his father's work. A close friend of the Prince of Wales – later George IV – he had been much impressed by the reconstruction of the Prince's London residence, Carlton House, by Henry Holland; and in 1787 he persuaded Holland to do the same for Woburn. Of all the architects who have worked on the house, Holland has left the deepest stamp. His is the south front and the lovely Library behind it, the main staircase, the Sculpture Gallery, the enchanting Chinese Dairy, and any number of farm buildings, cottages and kennels. He gave Woburn a new lightness outside and a new brightness within, both of which, we may imagine, it needed.

Holland's work left the 6th Duke free to concentrate on the collections. He lost no time; within a year of his succession in 1802 he was in Paris, buying from Napoleon so many Italian antiquities that thirty-six enormous cases were needed to ship them back to England. Ten years later we find him at Pompeii where Queen Caroline of Naples presented him with a bronze satyr. No wonder Wyatville had to be summoned in 1818 to enlarge the Sculpture Gallery.

But the other arts were not neglected; one of the remarkable things about Woburn is its comprehensiveness. Like all true dilettanti, those dukes were all-rounders; they specialised only in the best, whatever the medium, the period or the country of origin. When their house could contain no more, they enlarged it; when it filled again, they caught the overspill in the dependent buildings until the whole park was transformed, and everything around them seemed designed for their pleasure – but it was a pleasure born of discipline and discernment. They were doubly fortunate – intellectually and financially – to be able to enjoy it.

Then things began once more to go downhill. The first half of the twentieth century saw Woburn in the hands of two successive eccentric dukes and one duchess, whose respective passions for revolutionary economic theories, ornithology and aviation left them little time – or love – for the house. By 1950 dry rot was rampant. Sir Albert Richardson was appointed executioner; and the entire east wing, together with parts of those on the north and south, were demolished. Among the casualties were Holland's eastern portico and entrance hall – though not, thank heaven, any of his south front, which extended only part of the way along the wing.

This reduction in space has merely added to the density of the wealth within. Pictures, furniture, porcelain, gold, silver – the country has few more magnificent private treasure-houses, and none, perhaps, where the treasure is more brilliantly displayed. It also numbers several ghosts among whom must surely be those of the monkish brethren who first settled there eight centuries ago. What, one wonders, can be their reaction? Disapproving, perhaps: Cistercian austerity was never like this. Bored? No, that they could never be.

## Wrest Park

*13; 10 miles N of Luton on A6*

You are driving northwards up the A6 between Luton and Bedford. You turn left into the little village of Silsoe and follow the sign to the National Institute for Agricultural Engineering. Crossing the A6 again over a bridge, you immediately see on your right a high wall, interrupted at intervals by elaborate gateways, and beyond it an enormous mansion. Suddenly, Bedfordshire has disappeared. You are in France. The building you see before you is, in every detail, a French château, with segmental-headed windows and a mansard roof. You enter, through a small stone hall with apsed ends and stucco *putti* gambolling about as *putti* will, and enter the great Staircase Hall, a blaze of white and gold, the staircase itself sweeping up two opposite sides to a central gallery with fluted columns, the balusters painted and gilded and coming to an oddly abrupt end at the bottom. Along the south front there is an enfilade of five most sumptuous rooms, all a riot of exuberant Louis XV – painted ceilings, gilded stucco, immensely elaborate doorcases, chimneypieces and window shutters; and, amid all the splendour, the wildly incongruous impedimenta of the agricultural engineers. Could any house in England have been more inappropriate?

Emerging on to the terrace, there before you is one of the great formal gardens of England – though still far more redolent of France; immense lawns, immaculately tended and without a single weed (bravo NIAE) lead down to a long, rectangular *pièce d'eau* at the far end of which, nearly half a mile from the house, stands the only work of architecture on the entire property worth a fig: the famous PAVILION by Thomas Archer. It was built between 1709 and 1711. What one sees as one approaches is a tall, narrow building with a central portico, above which a deep ribbed dome carries a graceful lantern topped by a golden ball. Two other porticoes can be seen to left and right; but only as one approaches does one realise that they are not at right-angles to the centre, but at 120 degrees, so that they are in fact facing diagonally backwards. The Pavilion thus reveals itself as having a basically triangular plan; between the three porticoes are little semi-circular apses. Thanks to the banked-up grassy causeway which leads to the entrance, the latter is at first-floor level; the other two porticoes actually contain windows rather than doors, as do the apses, and the entire building is set on a deep basement with blocked windows in each of the five remaining bays. Above these windows and the entrance door is a row of circular bulls-eye windows, below the pediment in the portico bays, but, in the intervening ones, above the apses and set directly in the drum below the dome. The inner portico of the entrance is painted with rustication and the two side walls have *trompe-l'oeil* figures in niches, not very good. There is however a fine stone doorcase with the two side jambs facing outwards at 30 degrees, thus picking up the three-part plan of the building. Inside there are more painted statues and a painted, coffered ceiling.

From the temple there is a fine view back to the house – which looks from this distance still more French than it did from the front. One is not surprised to learn that the architect, who built Wrest in 1834–6, was a Frenchman by the name of Cléphane, but rather more so that his patron, the 1st Earl de Grey, was also the first President of the (Royal) Institute of British Architects. Cléphane was also responsible for the Orangery. Behind it, the Bath House was ascribed by Horace Walpole to Capability Brown, while nearby BOWLING GREEN HOUSE is thought to be by Batty Langley.

### Wymington

*14; 11 miles NW of Bedford on A6*

ST LAWRENCE'S CHURCH is not, from a distance, particularly prepossessing, owing largely to its rather warty-looking spire sticking up from the middle of a much broader battlemented tower. It is only when you get close to it that you see it for what it is – a charming, stocky Decorated church, built at the end of the fourteenth century by a rich local merchant, John Curteys. There is fine detail almost everywhere you look – the bell openings in the tower, for example, with ogival arches below their transoms, or the south porch with its original stone benches, rib vaulting and a green man boss. The east end is nice, too, with its angle turrets; the lovely five-light east window between them is in fact a restoration of about 1850, but done 'after the exact pattern of the original'. The excellent tracery in all other windows is apparently genuine enough. Another quite remarkable feature is that the whole church – nave, aisles, south chapel, chancel and even the vestry – is spanned by a single roof; not bad considering it was built 600 years ago.

Inside, the point of the church is its unity as an unspoilt and essentially unchanged building of its date. Some of the furnishings are later, like the Jacobean pulpit and screen, but the benches are original and delightful, there are two lovely canopied piscinae, faded wall paintings and some unusually fine brasses. It is not in any way a pretentious church, but a very pretty one that lingers strangely in the memory.

## Short List

### Chicksands Priory

*15; 7 miles E of Ampthill off A507*

The medieval priory, remodelled in the 1740s by Isaac Ware and in 1813 by James Wyatt, now stands deserted in the middle of the vast American air base. The once magnificent house of the Osborns forms the south end of the monastic cloister, with a northern annex on the site of the former church. Most of the exterior is Ware's, together probably with the Gothick King James Room; Wyatt's the Inner Vestibule, and the principal first-floor rooms including the Library with painted ceiling, now supported on wire netting. A noble group of 'Friends' does what it can, but the present appearance and future prospects of an inherently fascinating building are grim indeed.

### Clapham

*16; 2 miles NW of Bedford on A6*

The CHURCH OF ST THOMAS OF CANTERBURY receives a mention here for one reason only: its magnificent Anglo-Danish tower, virtually untouched since the Normans added the top stage with its bell openings. The interior, or at least the west end of it, is thirteenth-century; but the heavy hand of George Gilbert Scott has had its baleful effect, for which the monument to Sir Thomas Taylor and a seventeenth-century collecting shovel provide wholly inadequate compensation.

### Haynes

*17; 12½ miles N of Luton on A6*

HAYNES PARK (also known as HAWNES) is now occupied by Clarendon School. The early eighteenth-century red-brick house – still unchanged on the west – was remodelled on the south in 1790 by James Lewis; it has seven bays, with a three-bay centre of four fluted pilasters, plus a deep semi-circular bay at each end. On this side the brick is white, but returns again to red on the east, where there is a Neo-Grecian porch of 1850 by Cubitt. Inside there is a delightful little Garden Hall with painted ceiling, with an equally pretty elliptical painted room behind. The staircase is splendid.

### Mogerhanger Park

*18; 5½ miles E of Bedford on A603*

Now an orthopaedic hospital, and nowhere near big enough for the purpose, Mogerhanger Park has been hedged around with countless hutlike outbuildings. No marks, then, for atmosphere; but if you ask the authorities nicely they will allow you on to the lawn from which you can still see, relatively unchanged, the small and elegant mansion built in 1809 by Sir John Soane. It has a very odd and superbly Soanish façade, in which a shallow pediment is supported on pairs of pilaster strips joined at the top like inverted tuning forks.

# Berkshire

From east to west, the Royal County of Berkshire is about 50 miles long – which is lucky, because it takes a good 15 of those miles to escape from the shadow of London and assert itself in its own right. The eastern part consequently tends to be fairly depressing – pretty enough along the reaches of the Thames, but most of it too heavily built over to give any real lift to the spirit. Only beyond Reading does one gradually grow conscious of a change in the prevailing atmosphere; only then, with the Stockbroker Tudor country clubs, the golf courses and the leisure centres, the sandy heaths and gloomy conifers all fading mercifully into the distance, does Berkshire become what Berkshire ought to be. There is a new freedom and lightness in the air. The ground begins first to roll gently and then to rise in earnest until, at Inkpen Beacon in the extreme south-west, it stops only just short of the thousand-foot mark – and we are at the summit of the highest chalk Downs in England.

The curious thing is that Berkshire's most glorious building – indeed, the only one in the county that belongs incontestably to the first division – is situated in its least glorious, easternmost, corner, crowning the high chalk bluff that rises unexpectedly from the flat fields around it. Windsor Castle is not, perhaps, as magnificently medieval as it may look at first sight, but it is a good deal more genuine than many people seem to think: a hotch-potch of many styles and periods – as any castle must be that has been continuously inhabited for almost a millennium – but none the less impressive for that. Apart from Windsor the county is, architecturally speaking, relatively undistinguished. It possesses no great cities and no town larger than Reading; no cathedral; and, though there is many a fine country house, it has no splendid stately homes on the scale of Longleat, or Holkham, or Chatsworth. Its other great deficiency, of a different order from these but just as significant to the architectural picture, is in building stone. The county used to be able to claim a narrow ridge of corallian limestone, running along its northern edge – the stone of which the town of Faringdon is largely built; but since the iniquitous boundary changes of 1974, which sacrificed age-old loyalties and traditions on the altar of administrative convenience, this ridge has now been allotted to Oxfordshire. Berkshire is thus, even more than it used to be, a county of brick; but though Berkshire brickwork in such towns as Hungerford or Newbury can be of a fairly high order, nowhere does it reach the superlative standards of, let us say, Kent or Sussex.

The nearest approach to a cathedral in the county is St George's Chapel, Windsor. Both in its architecture and in its monuments it is worthy to rank, if not with Lincoln or Durham or Canterbury, at least with Chichester, Rochester or Lichfield. As for the parish churches, which are mostly of flint – brick tended to come only later, after the great period of medieval church building was over – Avington and Shottesbrooke are to me the most interesting (now that Uffington has been lost to Oxfordshire) with an honourable mention to Wickham for those elephants.

The country houses are, on the whole, relatively small – I except Bear Wood, which is a law unto itself – and several which gave Berkshire some much-needed architectural distinction have passed, like the limestone, into the next county. These include Buscot, Faringdon, Buckland, Kingstone Lisle and those two buildings of haunting beauty, Ashdown and Compton Beauchamp. Fortunately there is still Basildon, and Farley Hill, and Donnington Grove, and Swallowfield Park; and, above all, that castle, proud and tremendous on its hill. Once it protected London from the barons of Berkshire; would that it could with equal success have protected Berkshire from the bureaucrats of London!

## Avington*

*1; 7 miles W of Newbury off A4*

The approach is lovely, for a start. You walk across a broad water-meadow beside the River Kennet (there is no road) to where the little Norman CHURCH OF ST MARK AND ST LUKE nestles under a huge cedar tree. There is nothing showy about it; the walls are rendered in buff plaster which, at the west end, even covers the stone surrounds of the two round-headed windows, one above the other, beneath the gable. There are two similar windows in the south wall of the nave and one in the north, which is unhappily encumbered with a late Victorian vestry; the south doorway, on the other hand, is original and richly ornamented in the Norman fashion. The two-bay chancel leads to an east end of three stepped round-headed windows – unchanged, like the others, since the day they were made.

Inside, the nave carries – the fact is unfortunate but must be faced – more than a trace of William Butterfield, who restored the church (but only gently) in 1848–53. His are most of the roof, the benches and the pulpit. But turn your attention now to the chancel arch. Ignore, if you can, its alarming sag – Butterfield's roof is a good deal lighter than its predecessor, so there is no danger – and concentrate on the wealth of its decoration: zigzag, beak-head, and heads of cats and unidentifiable monsters. There are even a few traces of the original colouring, with red-painted stars.

The chancel was once rib-vaulted; the springing still survives at the corners. (The corbels at the east end are carved with the heads of a lion and a bull, a fact which presumably accounts for the dedication – though the symbols of the other two Evangelists may once have been present as well.) In the south wall, piscina and sedilia are both simple Norman arches; the aumbry opposite has doors by Butterfield, who also seems to have been responsible for the encaustic tiles; the grey and black stone pavement, however, is eighteenth-century. Do not miss, on your way out, the curious and intriguing Norman font.

## Basildon Park

*NT; 2; 7 miles NW of Reading between Pangbourne and Streatley on A329*

The grandest Georgian house in Berkshire was built in 1776 by John Carr of York – his only building in the south of England – for the majestically rich Indian nabob Sir Francis Sykes. A century and a half later it had fallen on evil days: deserted in 1910, it ultimately came into the possession of an American entrepreneur who had plans to ship it stone by stone across the Atlantic. His scheme fortunately miscarried, but not before he had sold off some of the fittings and decorative detail, which can now be seen in the Basildon Room of New York's Waldorf Astoria Hotel. By 1952 the house was derelict, and would surely have been demolished had it not been the subject

*The Hall, Basildon Park.*

of a last-minute rescue by Lord and Lady Iliffe, who slowly brought it back to its old splendour. Recently they handed it over, together with its furniture and pictures, to the National Trust.

The main approach from the west reveals a magnificent Palladian front of yellow-grey Bath stone, made dramatic by the portico of four giant Ionic columns extending the height of the *piano nobile* and the half storey above it, and deeply recessed in such a way as to give a splendid *chiaroscuro* effect on a summer afternoon. This portico stands on another, rusticated, half storey, with three round-headed arches under the portico and small square windows in the two flanking bays. To each side of the central block this lower half storey is extended to form a three-bay link, beyond which is a two-storey pavilion of a further three bays. And even this is not all, for beyond that pavilion there runs a further screen wall identical with that of the link, cunningly concealing courtyards for the domestic offices. The complete composition thus comprises no fewer than seven elements, held together not only by Carr's immaculate proportions but also by a low balustrade running the entire length of the façade.

A second element of drama awaits you as you enter the house. You might have expected the usual Palladian front steps leading up to the portico, but the entrance to Basildon is a good deal more exciting than that. Going in under the central arch, you find yourself in a little vestibule supported on Doric columns and pilasters, from each side of which rises a staircase which turns back on itself before bringing you into the portico. Thus the abrupt transition from darkness to light, from a low ceiling to a dizzyingly high one, provides its own *coup de théâtre* as the great park stretches away before you in the afternoon sun.

Immediately behind the portico lies the Hall, formerly the Saloon; with its pairs of fluted pilasters, coved and elaborately stuccoed ceiling and more fine plasterwork on the walls and overdoors, it is architecturally the most splendid room in the house. Note, too, the doors in panelled mahogany and their superb ormolu fittings: everything in this room is designed for what Lord Hervey described as 'taste, expense, state and parade'. So also is the immense Staircase Hall immediately behind it – a masterly enclosure of space rising the whole height of the two upper floors. At the lower level it carries on the neo-classical decorative scheme of the Hall/Saloon with plasterwork a very little more restrained. The upper floor is taken up with two open galleries and broad arches leading through to the bedroom corridor. The only sadness is the disappearance of Carr's original groined vault and its replacement (by the Ministry of Works after the last war) by a flat roof above the lunette windows, slightly lower than its predecessor.

The central axis of the house continues to the Octagon Room, its shape having been dictated by the canted bay window which Carr made the centre of his east front. The decoration of this room was never completed by Sir Francis Sykes, and had to wait until the purchase of Basildon by James Morrison, MP, in 1838. It is the work of Morrison's close friend, J.B. Papworth, who gave it a deeply recessed ceiling in Italian Renaissance manner and a heavily ornate frieze below it – all this despite Mrs Morrison's protests: 'I own I always dread Mr Papworth's love of gold and loading in decoration.' The whole room is splendidly opulent; but it is impossible to forget that by the time it was completed Queen Victoria was already – just – on the throne.

Of the other principal rooms on the first floor, the Green Drawing Room has another plaster ceiling of outstanding quality; that of the Library, on the other hand, was a casualty of a fire during the last war, when Basildon was occupied by the army. Only the frieze survives. We are left with the Dining Room. Here, once again, is Carr at his inspired best. At one end is a screen of two scagliola columns supporting, above a beautifully detailed frieze, a shallow segmental pediment which gives its line to the gently tunnel-vaulted ceiling. This is another virtuoso exhibition by the unknown plasterer. (William Roberts of Oxford was paid over £150 by Sir Francis between 1777 and 1783 and may have been responsible; if so, Basildon is incontestably his masterpiece.)

The bedrooms upstairs are chiefly remarkable for two tremendous beds. That in the Crimson Bedroom, which came from the Ashburnham Place sale in 1953, has its original damask hangings; that in the Green Chintz Room is an extremely rare domed model from Ditchley. There is also a charming Shell Room and another room, above the Octagon, which houses a small exhibition illustrating the life and times of the eighteenth-century nabobs.

## Bear Wood

*3; 4 miles NW of Wokingham off B3030*

Nobody nowadays – and few people, I suspect, a century ago – would describe Bear Wood as great architecture. So stunning, however, is its impact, so complete is its summation of the wealthy Victorian bourgeois ideal of the Gentleman's House, so magnificent is it in its very monstrosity, that it cannot be denied a place in this book.

*The Gentleman's House* – that was the title of a book published in 1864, analysing the plans of the leading country house architects of the day. It was written by a rather unattractive Scotsman named Robert Kerr, whose talent for self-advertisement (rather than any outstanding qualities as an architect) had gained him the Professorship of the Arts of Construction at King's College, London. The book soon became required reading for any rich man thinking of building himself a country seat, and so impressed the chief proprietor of *The Times*, John Walter, that he immediately commissioned him. Walter's consequent withdrawal of the contract from William Burn, an architect infinitely superior to Kerr in every respect, was one of the great mistakes of his life.

Bear Wood is of red brick – 4,477,000 of them, all made in kilns established by Walter for the purpose – with copious dressings of grey stone. Its style was described by Kerr as 'irregular or Non-Classical', which was certainly true as far as it went; it could, I suppose, be called Elizabethan, were it not for the heavy hints of the French Renaissance. But no description does it justice.

The main body of the house, at the west end of the northward-facing entrance front, obviously started off as a symmetrical five-bay composition with a central tower and a large gable to each side; but then, with characteristic brashness, Kerr stuck – there is no other word for it – a huge square tower, twice the size of the other, across about a third of the left-hand gable, into which it cuts quite mercilessly, inserting a minute polygonal stair turret in a half-hearted attempt to conceal the wound. That this great tower contains the main staircase is deafeningly proclaimed by the lower windows, which follow the line of the stairs. Further on towards the east, the front becomes a little more restful, then turns at right-angles to the north, the angle being taken up by another small turret (round this time, with a conical roof) in which the windows indicate yet another staircase. Bear Wood has a total of six staircases altogether – the principal stairs, the back stairs, the men's stairs, the women's stairs, the bachelors' stairs and the young ladies' stairs.

The south front, overlooking the lake, is even more of a hotch-potch. Occasionally Kerr again nods in the direction of symmetry, then almost immediately breaks it in the way the Victorians loved to do. The garden entrance is crowned with some fake reticulated tracery and flanked by rather improbable angels holding babies. Turrets, balconies, porphyry columns, monogrammed labels, all crop up where least expected. And yet, in some extraordinary way, there is confidence amid the chaos, like the work of some mad space-fiction scientist who believes he has the power to conquer the world.

The interior has inevitably suffered to some extent in the seventy-odd years that it has been operated as a school for the Merchant Navy. The Hall, however, still keeps its original leather wall covering and an elaborate carved screen – made, like all the other woodwork, in John Walter's own carpenters' shops. There is a top-lit picture gallery (the pictures, alas, are gone), billiard room, gun room and domestic quarters that seem to go on for ever. The *pièce de résistance*, however, is the main staircase which runs up the whole height of the building. Standing in the stairwell, one can look straight up to the roof, 88 feet above, glowing gold – thanks to the tinted glass windows just below it – deeply coffered and covered with painted stars.

Walter's estate covered 7,500 acres. As well as his own brick kilns and sawmills, he had his private gasworks and an engine house that pumped water to his five bathrooms and twenty-two lavatories.

They don't come like that any more; and, gazing through aching eyes at Bear Wood, one cannot help reflecting that it is just as well.

## Donnington

*4; 2½ miles N of Newbury on A34*
*Includes Donnington Grove**

Of DONNINGTON CASTLE, built in 1386, there now survives only the tall and very beautiful Gatehouse that originally formed the centre of the east wall. The rest was destroyed by Cromwell's troops in the Civil War, when Colonel John Boys held out in an epic resistance for nearly two years, surviving not only a formidable and relentless bombardment but even the poisoning of one of his wells. What remains today constitutes a noble monument to his endurance.

DONNINGTON GROVE*, standing in its lovely park half a mile or so to the south, is a very different building indeed. It was designed in about 1760 by John Chute of The Vyne (*q.v.*), the friend of Horace Walpole and his collaborator at Strawberry Hill; and a more perfect example of mid-Georgian Gothick would be hard to find. Much of its success relies, paradoxically, on its underlying classicism: Chute was described by Walpole as an able geometrician – a fact which he proved conclusively with his staircase at The Vyne – and his design for Donnington was perfectly geometrical: essentially it is a simple cube, three bays by three bays by three storeys, with a square projection to the south and a half-octagonal one to the east. His formal Gothicism was in fact little more than an overlay, just as Pugin's was to be at the Palace of Westminster three-quarters of a century later.

The approach through the park, over a hump-backed bridge spanning the artificially widened River Lambourn, is a pleasure in itself, as the house is revealed above its broad sloping lawns, with dense beechwoods to the right. Its high parapet, pinnacled and embattled,

*Donnington Castle.*

makes it look tall for its breadth; but, like Ashdown, it is none the worse for that. The material is a reddish grey brick but, as one drives up to the entrance front, one can be forgiven for not noticing the fact: what strikes the eye is, first, the tall, separately embattled oriel at first-floor level; and secondly, below it, the porch. The front door has a tall pediment with concave sides, lending it a slightly oriental air, while to each side is a little square-topped *baldacchino* supported on thin Gothic shafts. This originally stretched right across the doorway, but the central portion was removed to show the underside of the oriel above it. It was probably not designed by Chute, but added towards the end of the century by William Brummell (father of the Beau), who acquired the house in the 1780s. On the east side of the porch projection there is a charming Gothick statue in a deep niche.

The Entrance Hall is another proof of Chute's ingenuity. It is vaulted, with depressed Gothic arches on clustered colonnettes, banquettes being set in the thickness of the arches. The space is low, and might easily have seemed cramped: Chute's treatment of it seems little short of inspired. It leads through into the Staircase Hall, rising the height of the house, lit by clerestory lights above the arcaded gallery that runs all round the second floor. *All* around, because the main staircase goes only as far as the first: those wishing to proceed further must use another, concealed, staircase of which, in the central Hall, there is no ostensible sign. What one does notice is the decoration of the doorcases: they are crowned with those same depressed arches, supported on colonnettes, that are already a *leitmotiv* of the house. Here, unlike those of the Entrance Hall, they have a pretty little line of painted panelling, in vaguely Perpendicular style, running across the top.

The ground-floor rooms are rather low, though not uncomfortably so – except for a big Saloon to the north, added by Brummell and consequently, alone of the principal rooms of the house, devoid of Gothick fancies. On the first floor the showpiece is the big three-bay central room with the oriel. Originally the Drawing Room, it was subsequently converted into the principal Bedroom, and most magnificent is the bed that occupies one end. It boasts no fewer than three pendants for chandeliers – one of them in the oriel – each with beautifully designed radiating plasterwork.

Donnington is not at present open to the public; being conceived on quite a small and intimate scale, there is no reason why it should be. But even if John Chute had never set foot in The Vyne this rare jewel of a house would, I suspect, have assured him a distinguished place among English architects.

*The wall paintings, Eton College Chapel.*

## Eton College

*5; 1 mile N of Windsor on B3026*

King Henry VI founded Eton in 1440, shortly before his twentieth birthday, and after at least one false start the present Chapel was begun in 1449. If the royal Founder had had his way, it would have been merely the chancel of a far larger building, stretching for another 100 yards or so to the west; even as it stands, however, it ranks with the Chapel of King's College, Cambridge and that of St George's, Windsor as one of the three greatest free-standing Perpendicular monuments in England. Inside, it cannot quite aspire to the majesty of King's. The scale is considerably smaller; except at the east end, the vault supports begin only at window level; and even the fan vaulting itself seems strangely lacking in magic – until one learns that it dates not from the 1450s but from the 1950s, when Sir W. Holford substituted it for its seventeenth-century wooden predecessor. Technically, in fact, it is not a vault at all, being suspended from steel frames and carrying no weight whatever. Elsewhere, post-war innovations have been more successful, notably in the great east window, designed by Evie Hone (possibly a descendant of King Henry's original glazier) to replace the Victorian glass mercifully shattered by a bomb on the eve of the College's 500th anniversary. From this, John Piper's eight windows in the chancel make a perfect transition to the *grisaille* of the nave.

Finally, the wall paintings. The work of two Englishmen, Gilbert and Baker, completed by 1488, it is hard to believe that they were whitewashed over by the college barber in 1560; more incredible still that after their rediscovery in 1847 they should have been immediately covered over again by Victorian Gothic stalls – the upper row being almost completely destroyed in the process. Only in 1923 were they finally revealed and seen for what they are – the finest fifteenth-century murals north of the Alps.

The Chapel forms the south side of School Yard. On the east side, facing you as you enter, rises Lupton's Tower, built of a lovely mellow brick, with a glorious two-storeyed stone oriel. But by the time it was begun in 1517 the college had been in existence for some thirty years, its unfortunate scholars living, studying and sleeping in Long Chamber and Lower School, both still to be seen along the north range of the Yard. The west range (that of the main entrance) contains Upper School. It is considerably later (1689–94) – the work of Wren's master carpenter Matthew Banckes – and was much damaged by the quinquecentennial bomb.

Behind Lupton's Tower lie the Cloisters, which were part of King Henry's original plan and begun in his time, though given an upper storey on the north and east by Stiff Leadbetter in the mid-eighteenth century. Around them, *inter alia*, are the Provost's Lodge, College Hall (heavily Victorianised and deeply disappointing), Election Hall and the ravishing eighteenth-century College Library.

Such is the nucleus from which, over the centuries, the College has spread until it has assumed the proportions of a large village of its own. Few of the later buildings, however, are of much architectural interest.

## Farley Hill

*6; 8 miles SE of Reading off A327*

It comes as something of a surprise to discover that FARLEY HILL PLACE, or FARLEY HALL, was completed as late as 1730. To look at this long, low house (twenty-one bays, not counting the stables at one end and the Orangery at the other, and only two storeys high) in typically Queen Anne brick, one would put it at 1700 or even a bit earlier. But its builder, John Walter – presumably a forebear of that other John Walter who perpetrated Bear Wood nearby – seems to have been a staunch Tory; as such he would have despised the new Palladianism that was all the rage in smart Whig circles. His house was simple and dignified, and that was enough; despite its length, it looks from the outside almost homely.

The second surprise comes when you walk in at the front door. The presence of a large central lantern above, with four big round-headed windows, admittedly suggests the existence of some top-lit central chamber; but that mild exterior certainly gives no warning of anything remotely sensational. Sensational, however, is the only word for what lies within. Despite the lantern, the room remains rather dark, owing to the rich wooden panelling around the walls, broken by handsome wooden doorcases, carved in a style at once sensitive and robust – Doric on the ground floor, Ionic around the first-floor gallery which runs along three sides, the only communication between the north and south ends of the house. This gallery is bordered with a low brass rail which, together with touches of gilding at all levels, affords a most satisfactory golden gleam. Above it, in the lunettes of the vaulted ceiling rising to the lantern, are painted immense mythological scenes, signed and dated by Lanscroon in 1729. On the upper wall, above the entrance into the Drawing Room, is another series of paintings – scenes of rural life this time, by the younger Nollekens. They are on panels, and relatively recent acquisitions, as is the Thornhill ceiling in the Dining Room.

There are several other fine rooms, but none to rival the Hall for splendour or exuberance. Fine chimneypieces abound, and the same careful craftsmanship is evident throughout. There is also a particularly pretty Print Room upstairs.

## Langley Marish*

*7; 2½ miles NE of Slough off A412*

Even the suburbs of Slough are not beyond redemption: ST MARY'S CHURCH, Langley Marish, is not as easy to find as once it was, but it is well worth the search. The outside is not particularly prepossessing: confronted with a peculiarly nasty plaster porch, the eye turns gratefully to the two ranges of seventeenth-century ALMSHOUSES to north and south. But take heart and enter: at once the charm becomes apparent. It's still a question of charm rather than beauty: every period from the twelfth century to the seventeenth seems to be represented: when Pevsner describes it as a 'happy jumble' he is not far wrong. The best, however, is still to come. Along the south side of the nave runs a long screen of painted wood; behind this is the family pew built in 1623 by Sir John Kedermister (Kiderminster, Kittermaster – the name seems never to be spelt twice in the same way) and beyond that lies the church's greatest glory, the Kedermister Library.

If pew and Library are locked, don't hesitate to ask at the vicarage opposite for the key; you won't have a chance like this every day. The pew is completely shut off from the body of the church; the family entered from the churchyard behind, and could have heard the service and caught an occasional glimpse of it only through wooden lattices of almost Arabian closeness and complexity. Wherever they looked, however, their eyes would have met the Eye of God, painted all over the inner walls, warning them sternly to behave themselves. At the end of the pew, a tiny door leads into the Library, still looking almost exactly as it did when Sir John built it in 1623, and when Milton used to come over regularly from nearby Horton to consult its 300-odd volumes. It is an enchanting little room, complete with a fireplace, its walls painted all over with local views, seascapes, portraits of the Apostles and, on the inside of the cupboard doors, open books in *trompe-l'oeil*. Here is one of those hidden pearls that make sight-seeing in England the fun it is.

*St Mary's Church, Langley Marish.*

## Ockwells Manor

*8; 1 mile W of Bray and 1½ miles SE of Maidenhead*

This is a difficult house to find – and, at the time of writing, a still more difficult one to penetrate. For any serious student of architecture, however, the effort must be made; for Ockwells, restored as it is, remains the earliest surviving, most sophisticated and most complete timber-framed medieval manor house in England. It was built between 1446 and 1466 by Sir John Norrys, Master of the Wardrobe to Henry VI, who somehow contrived to get himself accepted by the Yorkist Edward IV after the latter's succession and to remain in the royal favour. (The hastily carved representations of the Sun, the Yorkist emblem, in the spandrels of the hall chimneypiece tell their own story.)

At the entrance to the outer courtyard the old Gatehouse remains unaltered, gabled and timber-framed, with a six-light oriel projecting on the inner side, supported on high arching beams so that the horses and their equipages could pass directly beneath it. Opposite, at the northern end, stands the barn, a magnificent construction of similar date and style; to the left, forming the western side of the enclosure, the show front of the house itself. It is almost symmetrical, though not rigidly so, and – as was usual in the fifteenth century, when domestic architecture had not yet entirely rid itself of castle influence – has its points of interest not at the centre but at the ends. Here, to north and south, are two tall terminal gables, the southern one a little larger than the northern, which however redresses the balance with its more opulent fenestration – a huge six-light bay rising through two storeys. Abutting these gables on the inside are two more, smaller and lower, representing the porch and the bay window of the Hall. The recessed centre, by contrast, is relatively plain; just a timber-framed wall with brick nogging surmounted by ten closely set round-headed windows, uncusped. Some of the windows in the gabled bays date from the careful and sensitive restoration by Fairfax Wade early this century; but most of the rest – including the delicately carved bargeboards – survive much as Sir John left them over five centuries ago. There has been only one major loss: his chapel, which extended from the south-east corner of the house eastward towards the gateway. Of this there survives only the lower part of the north wall, containing a series of two- and four-light windows, now largely blocked in.

The house's interior is, if anything, still more impressive. The porch – which contains a porter's wicket door to the left of the principal one – leads, predictably, straight into the screens passage, from which the Hall goes off immediately to the right. It is, by any standards, spectacular – rising the entire two-storey height of the building to a noble timber roof with wind-braces, arched braces and tie-beams. The principal timbers are all deeply moulded. Halfway along the inner wall is the vast stone chimneypiece already mentioned; along virtually the whole length of the outer wall runs the row of windows which we saw from the outside, containing a famous set of fifteenth-century heraldic stained glass – a magnificent sight on a sunny summer morning.

*Ockwells Manor.*

The two doors in the screens passage led in the normal way to the buttery and the pantry; the kitchen, however, was situated some way away on the west side of the house beyond the central court; and Ockwells is particularly remarkable for the series of galleries that run around this court, along three sides and on both floors. The lower, now glazed, may originally have been an open cloister; the upper is one of the earliest examples in all England of a communication gallery – the alternative, not normally found till the mid-sixteenth century, to the old collegiate system of rooms grouped round a number of separate staircases. Just outside the former serving room next to the kitchen there still survives an enormous service hatch on iron hinges.

Of the other rooms on the ground floor, there is a fine panelled Parlour – more recently used as a dining room – with its original chamfered ceiling beams and, above a stone fireplace of about 1550, a carved overmantel with pilasters that looks Jacobean. Another Parlour, to the west, has a wonderful Elizabethan chimneypiece, far more ornate, and red and gold Spanish leather on the walls. The staircase is of about 1600, when Ockwells was occupied by William Day, former Provost of Eton. Day also added the oak screen and archway at its foot. Upstairs, the *pièce de résistance* is the so-called 'Queen Elizabeth's Room' – although, as with so many of its kind, it is extremely unlikely that she ever slept in it. No matter: it is a wonderful room – occupying the old solar, beneath the gable, at the north end beyond the top of the Hall – with moulded tie-beams, queenposts, collar-beams and wind-braces, sumptuously panelled, and lit by the canted bay numbering no fewer than ten tall lights. Fit for a Queen, anyway.

## Padworth

*9; 9 miles SW of Reading and 1½ miles off A4*

Now a girls' residential college, PADWORTH HOUSE was built in 1769 by John Hobcraft, who designed the Gothick Chapel at Audley End and drew out Chute's elevations for Donnington Grove which now hang at The Vyne. There is, however, nothing of that style here. As seen from the south (insofar as it is possible to do so through the tangle of creeper) it is just a nice, safe, mid-Georgian house of middle size, with seven bays – the three central ones pedimented and slightly projecting – and lower side wings. The north front somehow manages to cram in more bays and has a segmental instead of a triangular pediment, but is otherwise similar in style. The excitement comes only when one enters the main Staircase Hall, where Hobcraft suddenly lets himself go. The first-floor landing is carried on arches resting on fluted Doric columns, with a vault behind them, a design which it then repeats, precisely, at the upper level. On the side wall another similar arch, with pilasters this time, contains a smaller round-headed niche. All around, in panels on the wall, above and between the windows, and in the spandrels of the arches, is pretty stucco decoration of a vaguely Adamish kind. The main Saloon is similarly adorned; elsewhere, reticence returns.

Close by the house is the pebble-dashed twelfth-century CHURCH OF ST JOHN THE BAPTIST. Consisting of only a nave and an apsed chancel – there are no aisles – it is unspoilt Norman work, with the exception of the Perpendicular windows in the nave. There are remains of medieval wall paintings on the south side of the chancel arch.

## Shottesbrooke

*10; 3 miles SW of Maidenhead off B3024*

The CHURCH OF ST JOHN THE BAPTIST – a favourite dedication in this part of the world – stands in the private grounds of Shottesbrooke Park, but the public have full access. Built in about 1340, it is a near-perfect Decorated church of flint with a tall octagonal spire, four lucarnes set around its base. Inside, it is bare and beautiful, with a big central crossing and tall transepts; the chancel is bigger than the nave and dominated by a huge five-light window with flowing tracery, somewhat spoilt by Hardman's rather nasty Victorian glass. The stone floor is uncarpeted, showing off the magnificent brasses. There is also a memorable monument to William Throckmorton, a priest who died in 1535. He has a large moustache, and his stone effigy is carved inside what appears to be a stone coffin.

The church is all on one level: there are no chancel steps, only a very low dais for the altar itself. The Victorian pulpit (presumably a legacy of Street's otherwise harmless restoration of 1854) contrasts unfavourably with the fourteenth-century font; it is quite good of its kind, but surely a mistake here.

## Sonning

*11; 5 miles N of Reading on B481*

Deanery Gardens – now known simply as THE DEANERY – was built by Sir Edwin Lutyens in 1901 for his friend Edward Hudson, the founder of *Country Life*. The first surprise is the entrance: Lutyens was reluctant to break the ancient wall along Thames Street more than was absolutely necessary, and therefore provided only small arched doorways in it – one of which leads through a short vaulted passage to the front door. This proves to be part of the east wing of a square; opposite, across an open courtyard with a small pool, is the service wing to the west; the principal rooms are to the south, while the north side is of course the wall to the street. The show front, as one would expect, is that facing south. It has as its main accent a splendid bay window of forty-eight lights – twenty-four to the front in four rows of six, and four rows of three on each side – which is balanced to the east by a tall stack of three chimneys, set diagonally. Between the two is the door leading out into the garden, deeply recessed, with five semi-circular courses of brick. Brick is indeed the material used throughout, except for the tiled roof and the window frames, all of which – including that of the bay – are of wood.

Inside the house, the central focus is the Hall, which rises to the roof and is flooded with light by the bay – opposite which is a perfectly enormous fireplace. The walls are timber-framed, with huge S-shaped wind-braces which Lutyens plays for all they are worth. The general atmosphere is grand seventeenth-century rustic – very different from the Renaissance Mannerism of Marsh Court (*q.v.*) which followed two years later.

## Swallowfield Park

*12; 6 miles SE of Reading off A33*

When William and Mary succeeded to the throne of England in 1689, one of those who refused to take the oath of allegiance was Henry Hyde, 2nd Earl of Clarendon. As brother-in-law to the exiled King James II, he could be forgiven this apparent discourtesy; but it obliged him, nonetheless, to withdraw from public life and to retire to his wife's estate at Swallowfield Park. Once there, he decided almost at once to pull down the existing house and to erect in its place a new and grander one, and on 11 April he engaged William Talman to submit plans accordingly.

*Stone garden doorway, Swallowfield Park.*

*The face in the arch, St Laurence's Church, Tidmarsh.*

The house that we see today – it is now the property of the Mutual Households Association – is unfortunately not so much that of Talman as of William Atkinson, a one-time pupil of James Wyatt, who remodelled Swallowfield in 1823–4 for Sir Henry Russell, Bart, retired Chief Justice of Bengal. The result was not an improvement – a fact which becomes all too obvious when we look at one of the few traces of Talman's work still remaining inside, the little oval vestibule which links the entrance to the main Staircase Hall. Its walls are butter yellow; there is fine (if slightly heavy) stucco work around the top, and charming medallions over the four doors. Atkinson's work has nothing as good as this. On the outside, too, he made changes – replacing the tall hipped roof by a lower one surrounded by a parapet, rendering over the old brick with Roman cement, adding a *porte-cochère* on the south front and providing to the east what he described as 'a very handsome Grecian front'. This last is in fact his most successful creation: nine bays, with a three-bay centre whose giant pilasters, according to an old engraving, once supported a pediment. Had it not been for his words quoted above, one might well have thought it was Talman's own – compare his south front at Chatsworth.

Nothing remains of the great formal gardens which so impressed John Evelyn; but at the bottom of the present garden, at the end of a row of Irish yews, stands one of Talman's monumental doorways, rescued and re-erected. It looks a little tall for its breadth, now, but may well originally have had side extensions. Its carved stone decoration is very splendid indeed.

## Tidmarsh

*13; 6 miles W of Reading on A340*

ST LAURENCE'S CHURCH has been unattractively rendered and does not look anything very special from the outside – though the little shingled bell-turret, with the small quatrefoil set into its south wall, is pretty enough. It is only when you enter the south porch that you realise just how remarkable the building is. The magnificent Norman doorway has continuous orders, all richly ornamented – one in a most unusual pattern of plaited ropework – and is crowned by a semi-abstract representation of a face on the keystone, surely not that of Christ. Inside, everything of importance seems to be of the mid-thirteenth century; the doorway was obviously kept from a previous church on the site. Both east and west ends capture the attention: the east for the polygonal apse – rare indeed in medieval English churches – which has, however, been recently re-vaulted in plaster; the west for the magnificent wooden beams which support the bell-turret and which are decorated, with themes derived from the doorway, by the wife of a nineteenth-century rector. There are the remains of thirteenth-century wall paintings in the splays of two opposite lancets towards the east end, and three very fine brasses. Do not miss, either, the glorious medieval tiles, carefully retained (or replaced with others of similar age and kind) by John Oldrid Scott when he restored the church in 1897.

## Warfield

*14; 8 miles S of Maidenhead off A3095*

First impressions of ST MICHAEL'S CHURCH are not too good, owing largely to the peculiarly unattractive dark brown conglomerate in which much of it is built. The copious stone dressings should help, but many of them, especially around the east window, are preternaturally white and look somehow out of keeping with the rest. One can only hope that they will weather down. The tower is villainously low, the spire stumpy. Perhaps we had better forget the exterior – which is not, after all, what we have come to see.

The real splendour of the church is the chancel, which has defied all Street's efforts to ruin it in the 1870s. Its *pièce de résistance* is the great five-light east window, a masterpiece of flowing Decorated tracery, the best in the county. Most of the actual glass is, alas, rather second-rate Victorian, but there are a few fine fourteenth-century (that is, original) pieces at the top. On the south wall, the elaborate piscina and sedilia keep up the standard – and don't miss the jack-in-the-green in one of the spandrels. To the north, the Easter sepulchre must have been beautiful too; but it is now damaged beyond repair. The stone reredos is a Street reconstruction. Another stone screen divides the chancel from the north chapel – two bays of three lights each, with ogival canopies and cusps. But this dwindles to insignificance beside the wooden screen that separates the north chapel from its aisle, which has four-light divisions and fanned coving that still supports its broad and generous loft. Even this, it must be admitted, falls short of Devon or East Anglian standards; for Berkshire, however, it is a rare delight.

## Windsor

*15; 21 miles W of London off M4*
*Includes Windsor Castle**

THE CASTLE*
Windsor Castle is a world of its own. The largest castle in England and the largest inhabited castle in the world, it has existed in one form or another since 1070, when the first motte and bailey was constructed by William the Conqueror as one of the nine castles surrounding London, a day's march away, with the additional responsibility of guarding the middle reaches of the Thames. Forty years later, under King Henry I, it first became a royal residence. And as if that were not enough it also contains, in St George's Chapel, one of the most magnificent late Perpendicular buildings in existence. In this short survey, we shall take these three aspects one by one: the Precinct, the Chapel and its related buildings, and the State Apartments.

PRECINCT. Nothing now remains of Henry I's castle, which was probably timber-framed. The first stone buildings were erected by his grandson, Henry II, who in 1165 began work on two separate ranges of royal lodgings, one in the Upper Ward – the area to the east of the Round Tower, beyond the misleadingly named Norman Gate – and one along the north side of the Lower Ward, which extends from the present Deanery to the west. (There is also a Middle Ward, comprising the area around the Round Tower itself.) Later, faced with his sons' rebellion, he turned his attention to the outer defensive walls and the keep. Quite a lot of his work can still be seen, notably around the Winchester Tower (at the north-west corner of the Upper Ward), along the east side, and in the Round Tower – formerly the keep – which is virtually all twelfth-century work as far as the large windows.

The next major builder was Henry III, who completed the physical and spiritual defences of the Lower Ward with high curtain walls and a chapel, and built the whole western wall (above Thames Street) with its three massive round towers. He was also responsible for the tower that bears his name and, paradoxically, for that which is named after his great-grandson Edward III, both on the south side. Edward in his turn added a new range of State Apartments along the north side of the Upper Ward, and the 'Norman Gateway' which gave access to them. He also rebuilt the Lower Ward as the headquarters of the Order of the Garter, which he had founded in 1348; but it was another 130 years before his namesake Edward IV began work on the Order's own Chapel, which he dedicated to St George.

Tudor additions to the castle were relatively few. There are the buildings in the north-west corner of the Upper Ward, now part of the Royal Library, which were erected by Henry VII (east side) and Elizabeth I (west side); and in the Lower Ward there are the lodgings of the Military Knights (see below), dating from the 1550s. Apart from these, we need only concern ourselves with Henry VIII's great Gateway, the principal entrance to the castle. The Stuarts were responsible for one great burst of activity between 1675 and 1683, when Charles II

commissioned from Hugh May a Baroque mansion to replace Edward III's dilapidated old palace in the Upper Ward. What survives of the exterior has been altered out of all recognition, but May's magnificent suite of rooms still forms the nucleus of the State Apartments today.

And so we come to the last and most ambitious phase of Windsor's architectural history – that which gave the castle its present appearance. The work was begun by George III, but the real transformation was the achievement of George IV and his chief architect, Sir Jeffrey Wyatville. From the King's own point of view, the most radical change was the transfer of his private apartments away from the cold and cheerless north side to new buildings on the south and east; but he also set about a massive medievalisation of the whole precinct. Away went King Charles's Baroquery; back came the lancets and the battlements, the pinnacles and the turrets. Wherever a stretch of unbroken wall threatened to become monotonous, new towers were inserted; and the squat and stumpy old Round Tower itself, still essentially the same ancient keep that Henry II had left 650 years before, was almost doubled in height to provide a worthy focus for the grand design.

We enter through Henry VIII's Gateway and immediately find ourselves in the Lower Ward, with St George's Chapel in front of us, the Guard Room to our left – for this is also the Parade Ground – and, to our right, the lodgings of the Military Knights, a body of retired officers maintained in association with the Order of the

*Windsor Castle.*

Garter. Through an archway just to the left of the Chapel is the so-called Horseshoe Cloister, not really a cloister at all but a range of twenty-one small houses, timber-framed with brick nogging, built around 1480 for the Priest Vicars of the Chapel. Despite heavy restoration by George Gilbert Scott, it still possesses a good deal of charm, largely by reason of the contrast it provides with the formal magnificence around it. Beyond the cloister, in the extreme north-west corner of the castle, is the Curfew Tower, originally built by Henry III but topped off by Salvin in 1863 on the model of the Tour de la Peyre at Carcassonne.

All the remaining buildings of any note in the Lower Ward are ecclesiastical, and connected in a greater or a lesser degree with St George's Chapel. They will be dealt with below. We can meanwhile proceed to the Middle Ward, which is dominated by the Round Tower, set high on its artificial mound. It is the one feature of the castle that everybody knows, and even if the top 33 feet are by Wyatville it must be admitted that the job could scarcely have been better done. This nineteenth-century work goes down to the broad line of coving below the two upper rows of windows; the round-headed two-light windows immediately below it are also Wyatville's, though set in the old wall, but the straight-headed windows beneath them are original. Within the tower, Edward III's timber-framed building still survives, and houses the Royal Archives; it is not open to the public.

The curtain wall to our left as we approach the Norman Gateway is also of the twelfth century, though the little Magazine Tower halfway along dates from only the mid-fifteenth. And so to the Gateway itself, completed by Edward III in 1359, its portcullis still in place. Until some 200 years ago it served as a prison; it was here that King John II of France and his son, the future Philip the Bold of Burgundy, were held after their capture at the battle of Poitiers.

Next we come to the Upper Ward, past the Royal Library (see above) and into the Quadrangle – where, though a little earlier building remains, the overall character is that imposed by James Wyatt from 1796 to 1804 and his nephew Wyatville from 1820 to 1840. Where the windows have Portland stone surrounds, the work is Wyatt's; Wyatville used brown stone dressings throughout. Apart from this, there is little difference; both architects were perfectly at home in the medieval style required of them. But for all their efforts to avoid monotony – the change of roof levels, the various styles of battlements, the bays and the oriels, the towers and projecting porticoes, some square, some polygonal, these ranges still preserve a stubborn classical regularity as far removed as anything can be from the spirit of the Middle Ages. The entire quadrangle is presided over by an equestrian statue of Charles II on a high pedestal with reliefs by Grinling Gibbons – the gift, it appears, of the King's Yeoman of the Robes in 1680. Poor Charles: with his beloved Baroque all destroyed or hidden away, how he would have hated what has taken its place!

ST GEORGE'S CHAPEL AND RELATED BUILDINGS. The Chapel itself was begun by King Edward IV in 1475 and was over half a century in the building, the nave vault being completed only in 1528. It is thus the last of the three great Perpendicular Royal Chapels, more splendid and larger than Eton, although neither so large nor, it must be said, quite so beautiful as King's College, Cambridge. Seen from its show front to the south, however, it is considerably more impressive than either, the embattled aisles, corner chapels, flying buttresses and – most surprising of all – broad polygonal transepts giving it a liveliness somehow lacking in the others. Another curious feature is the placing of these transepts – not, as one would normally expect, towards the east end, but precisely halfway down the nave. The worship of symmetry would come only with the Renaissance, but St George's shows unmistakable signs that the Renaissance was not far away. The west front, dominated by an immense fifteen-light window, has been ruined by the addition, in 1866–72, of a broad flight of steps which might look all right in an eighteenth-century garden, but which is utterly out of keeping with a late medieval chapel. Fortunately, one normally enters by the door to the south.

Inside, there comes a further indication that the Perpendicular – indeed, Gothic as a whole – has almost run its course. Though the detail is orthodox enough, there is a feeling of breadth and expansiveness far removed from the soaring verticality usually associated with the style. Here, the proportions seem almost Palladian. The reason is not hard to find: the consistent *leitmotiv* of St George's Chapel is the four-centred arch – which is, in fact, the shape of the entire building in cross-section. The shafts of the nave arcades rise up unbroken to their point of springing, then branch out into palm fronds to form tiercerons; but instead of running straight to the central ridge to meet those from the other side, these ribs flatten out before they reach the centre, stopping short at the nearest of three longitudinal ribs. Thus the central section of the roof is flat, the palm fronds forming merely a coving along each side. The aisles are, by contrast, sumptuously fan-vaulted, as is the crossing. The transepts follow the same pattern as the nave, but the chancel dispenses with the central ridge rib and has instead a line of pendants. Here, above the two bays of the north-east corner, can be seen the Upper Chantry built by Edward IV over the site reserved for his tomb. It is marked by a stone oriel, with which its slightly smaller neighbour to the east provides a fascinating contrast. This second oriel, which is of wood, was added by Henry VIII as a royal pew for the use of Catherine of Aragon, whence she could conveniently watch the Garter ceremonies. Though its arches and panels are Gothic, the balusters are the purest Renaissance.

St George's Chapel is as full of monuments, chantry chapels and various splendid furnishings as any cathedral. It also contains the tombs of no fewer than ten British sovereigns (Henry VI, Edward IV, Henry VIII, Charles I, George III, George IV, William IV, Edward VII, George V and George VI). There is no space in this book to list everything worth seeing; but the first-class guide leaflet available in the Chapel is, in default of anything more detailed, warmly recommended. If I had to name three outstanding items I would choose the late fifteenth-century Garter Stalls with their heraldic plates, the sword of Edward III, 6 feet 8 inches long but intended (as Gibbon said of the concubines of the Emperor Gordian) 'for use rather than ostentation', and – best of all, in the little Urswick Chantry in the north-west corner of the nave – Matthew Cotes Wyatt's memorial to Princess Charlotte, the only daughter of George IV, who died in 1817 after giving birth to a still-born son. She lies on her side, completely covered by a sheet except for the fingers of one hand, which hang down to within an inch of the floor. Four mourning women, similarly shrouded, crouch around her, while above, before a slightly open curtain revealing part of a tomb, her soul – full-sized, diaphanously clad, one breast daringly bared – ascends to heaven between angels, one of whom is holding her baby. The whole thing is life-size, in dazzling white marble; a show-stopper if ever there was one.

We leave the Chapel by the north-east corner, and emerge into the Dean's Cloister – the southern side of which was formerly the side wall of Henry III's Chapel. In it is set a magnificent mid-thirteenth-century doorway with its original door. The Chapel itself, however, has gone – demolished either by Edward III or by Henry VII – nobody seems too sure. Henry, in any case, decided to provide a new chapel for the tomb of Henry VI (his mother's second cousin) and, incidentally, for his own. In fact, this plan never materialised. The chapel was unfinished at Henry's death and was appropriated by Cardinal Wolsey, who completed it for himself; but with Wolsey's fall from favour it remained without an occupant until Queen Victoria remodelled it as yet another memorial to the Prince Consort. The effect is breathtaking. Around the walls runs a series of narrative pictures in etched white marble, surmounting a dado of coloured marbles. Above this are the four-light windows (there are no aisles) with glass by Clayton and Bell; and the lierne-vaulted roof is inlaid with mosaics by Salviati of Venice. The decoration was all the work of Baron H. de Trinqueti, who was also responsible for the white marble tomb of the Prince. (It is actually a cenotaph, since he was buried in the Royal Mausoleum: see below.) This tomb, however, is completely overshadowed, as indeed the whole Chapel is dominated, by Alfred Gilbert's tremendous monument to the Duke of Clarence, the eldest son of the Prince of Wales (later Edward VII), who died in 1892. The monument itself is remarkable enough, owing to the immense size of the bronze angel, wings outspread, that holds a crown above the head of the recumbent effigy of the Duke; but even this takes second place to the surrounding grille – an almost unbelievable fantasy on the theme of the Tree of Jesse, executed in an exuberant *art nouveau* style that paralyses criticism. Owing to Gilbert's bankruptcy, he did not complete it till 1927; but most of it was done by 1898. Did Queen Victoria ever see it? And, if so, what must she have thought?

STATE APARTMENTS. As explained above, these apartments have as their nucleus the palace built by Hugh May for Charles II and his Queen, Catherine of Braganza, in the years around 1680. They have, however, been heavily overlaid by Wyatt and Wyatville – particularly the latter – and, more recently still, by Edward Blore and Anthony Salvin, who built the Grand Staircase for Queen Victoria in 1866. This was the sort of thing Salvin did best; but it must be said that he did not do it very well. It is indubitably grand, and the arms and armour (including the bull-like suit of armour built for Henry VIII which has been ill-advisedly placed immediately below Chantrey's heroic statue of George IV) add to the impression; but there is something leaden and unimaginative about it, especially when it is compared with Wyatt's vaulting of the Grand Vestibule to which it leads – a work of refreshing vitality and *brio*.

These qualities are even more apparent in the Waterloo Chamber, built by Wyatville for George IV in 1830. The King wanted a suitable setting for the series of portraits he had commissioned from Sir Thomas Lawrence of all the sovereigns, statesmen and soldiers who had contributed to the defeat of Napoleon; Wyatville's solution was to roof in an open courtyard enclosed by the walls of Henry II's castle, lighting it through a most individual clerestory in which the inner window frames are raked inwards like the outside of a galleon's poop. Apart from the marvellous pictures (don't miss the Archduke Charles of Austria on the west wall and Pope Pius VII on the south) there are some superb wood carvings by Grinling Gibbons. The rather fussy fretwork decoration of the upper walls is, however, Blore – and *not* a success.

More Gibbons carvings adorn the Garter Throne Room; they come, like those in the Waterloo Chamber, from Hugh May's famous chapel – 'the most Baroque interior in England', Pevsner calls it – demolished by Wyatville in 1829 to make St George's Hall. The adjoining Grand Reception Room, on the other hand, is a riot of Louis XV Rococo, less like Windsor than Versailles. I hope the Prince Regent liked it: I don't, though I find myself mesmerised by the gigantic vase of green malachite that occupies the window. It was the gift of Tsar Nicholas I to Queen Victoria, a stunning present for the woman who had everything.

With St George's Hall, we are back in the world of Gothic – impressive if a little monotonous, with suits of armour on heavy heraldic brackets and nearly a thousand escutcheons of Knights of the Garter filling the panels of the roof, which pretends to be timber but is in fact painted plaster. The same style prevails in the Queen's Guard Chamber, which George III used as his chapel (May's already having fallen into disuse) but which was converted by his son into a sort of military museum. It is a deceptive room, first because it was almost doubled in size by the addition of Wyatville's *porte-cochère*, and secondly because despite its appearance it is really, as its name implies, a part of the second of the two suites of rooms built by May for Charles II and Queen Catherine. It leads straight into the Queen's Presence Chamber, which, like the Queen's Audience Chamber beyond it, has remained essentially as it was in Stuart times – an extraordinary contrast after everything we have seen so far. These two rooms have almost identical decoration: Verrio ceilings, Gobelins tapestries of Esther and Ahasuerus, and Gibbons carvings. They even share the same shrieking anachronism – Adam fireplaces in snow-white marble, ill-advisedly brought by William IV from Buckingham Palace.

The blue silk Queen's Ball Room and the red silk Queen's Drawing Room are Wyatville again, more remarkable for their splendid ceilings and pictures (note the Canalettos in the first, the Van Dycks in the second) than for their architectural distinction; and the same can be said of all but one of the King's Suite which follows. It was, paradoxically, the King's Dressing Room in which Charles II actually slept; the State Bed Chamber was, however, used by Napoleon III and the Empress Eugénie, for whom Queen Victoria provided the tremendous French eighteenth-century bed when they paid a State Visit in 1855. It is only when we reach the King's Dining Room that we are allowed one final glimpse into the days of the Restoration. Here it was that Charles II would dine in public; in those days, the so-called Brick Court outside the windows had not been converted into a staircase and roofed over, so that spectators could actually have seen him without the aid of artificial light – something they would certainly find great difficulty in doing today.

### THE PARK

There are technically two parks, the Great Park and the Home Park, but the distinction is so subtle as to be negligible. Most of the Great Park is open to the public, though not its buildings; the Home Park is private, but contains one building which, though open on only three days a year (usually the first Wednesday and Thursday in May and the Wednesday nearest to 24 May) should on no account be missed.

This is the ROYAL MAUSOLEUM at Frogmore, built by Queen Victoria as a final resting-place for the Prince Consort and herself. They had decided on this dramatic break with royal tradition within two or three years of their marriage, and it was less than a month after the Prince's premature death (in 1861, aged forty-two) that his distracted widow commissioned Professor Ludwig Grüner of Dresden – whom he had appointed his official artistic adviser some years before – to draw up designs, and the architect A.J. Humbert to put them into effect. Work began at once, and within a year the building had been consecrated; but it was another decade before the decoration was complete.

The style chosen was Italian Romanesque, the materials granite (of several different colours) and Portland stone. The ground plan is that of an octagon with four arms, the intermediate sides rounded to provide a roughly circular ambulatory and the octagon itself marked by a short central tower, pyramidally capped on the outside, domed within. You enter through a three-arched portico and in doing so advance some 300 years, since the interior is High Renaissance in the style of Raphael – the Prince's favourite painter. In the centre under the dome stands the double sarcophagus designed by Baron Carlo Marochetti, surmounted by two recumbent effigies in white marble, with a sorrowing angel in bronze at each corner. The Queen is shown as a woman still young, the figure having been carved at the same time as that of her husband – though it was not set in place until after her own funeral. In the surrounding ambulatory and chapels are several other monuments of considerable interest. The most touching is that to the Queen's second daughter, Princess Alice of Hesse, and her own little daughter May, both of whom died of diphtheria within a few days of each other in 1878; the oddest by far an irresistibly funny group showing the Queen and Prince dressed as Anglo-Saxons. In the north-east ambulatory is a tablet to the memory of the Queen's Highland servant, John Brown. But it is the Mausoleum itself, rather than anything it contains, that holds one fascinated. The polychrome marble, the glittering mosaic, the stained glass (by Pace), the paintings a little distance after Raphael – all add up to one of the great ecclesiastical interiors of the High Victorian age.

There are two other buildings in the Park which are not normally open but which deserve brief mentions here. The first is PRINCE ALBERT'S DAIRY at Shaw Farm, to the south-south-west of Frogmore House. It is nothing much from the outside, but the interior is a blaze of coloured faience, with putti on panels – the whole thing very light-hearted and un-Albertian, the work of the Prince's favourite sculptor, the unfortunately named John Thomas. The second building is FORT BELVEDERE, near Virginia Water. This, originally a three-sided eighteenth-century folly, was enlarged by Wyatville in 1827–9 into a little Gothic castle – to become, just over a century later, the preferred residence of King Edward VIII (and Mrs Simpson) at the time of the abdication crisis in 1936.

THE TOWN

Windsor contains plenty of good Georgian houses, but is inevitably overshadowed, architecturally as well as physically, by the castle around which it has grown. The most notable building is the TOWN HALL in the High Street. Designed by Sir Thomas Fitch, its building was supervised after his death by Sir Christopher Wren. The Tuscan columns apparently supporting the first floor in fact stop a fraction of an inch short of it; the story goes that the Council feared for the safety of the structure, refusing to believe Wren's insistence that supports were unnecessary; he gave them their columns, but made them very slightly too short in order to prove his point.

*St George's Chapel, Windsor.*

Windsor Castle and Park.

## Short List

### Hurley

*16; Hall Place 5 miles SW of Marlow off A404*

HALL PLACE has an austere red-brick seven-bay entrance front of three storeys, *c.* 1730, with giant pilasters at the angles and one-storeyed links leading to projecting wings. The Drawing Room by contrast (now the Library of Berkshire Agricultural College) has splendidly exuberant stucco work on ceiling and walls, probably by the Italians Artari and Vassali. In the ante-room is a superb chimneypiece surmounted by plaster eagles.

### Hurst

*17; 4 miles E of Reading on A321*

HIGH CHIMNEYS is a red-brick house built in 1661 (the date is scratched on some of the bricks) and remarkably unaltered. It is on an H-plan, with a recessed and gabled Hall. The windows retain their wooden mullioned and transomed frames, and the doorways their canopies on scrolled brackets.

### Lambourn

*18; 7½ miles N of Hungerford on B4001*

ST MICHAEL'S CHURCH is another grand cruciform edifice, late Norman from the west end to the crossing, with a Norman west door and a round window in the gable. Inside, the capitals have scallops and Norman foliage. There is a Decorated south transept, but most of the rest of the church is Perpendicular, including two splendid chapels, as is the top of the tower. Look for a lively hunting scene carved in an arch between the south chapel and the transept.

### Monkey Island

*19; in River Thames at Bray, 1½ miles SE of Maidenhead on B4447*

Here the 3rd Duke of Marlborough built a Fishing Lodge and Pavilion in 1744. The Lodge has a raised octagon with lunette windows, and some charming paintings of monkeys engaged in sport (fishing, shooting, etc.) by Clermont, the monkey painter.

### Newbury

*20; 16 miles SW of Reading on A4*

ST NICHOLAS'S CHURCH was built in the first quarter of the sixteenth century, when Newbury was at its most prosperous; obviously no expense was spared to make it a fine and fitting focus for the life of the town. It is of course Perpendicular through and through. Like so many of its kind, it is a little soulless, and restoration has not been as sympathetic as one might have wished. But it remains a splendid building for all that. There is a most remarkable pulpit, presented in 1607.

## Sandleford Priory

*21; 2 miles SE of Newbury on A34*

A Gothick confection, the house was built by James Wyatt in 1780–1 for the bluestocking and wit, Mrs Elizabeth Montagu. It is now a girls' school run by Anglican nuns. Two storeys high, the centre has seven bays, with a triangular gable over numbers 1–2 and 6–7 and a square tower over number 4, all embattled. In the wing projecting backward, there is an oval room (octagonal on the outside) with Adamish decoration behind which is the old priory chapel. Wyatt transformed this into a Drawing Room, but it retains its fifteenth-century timber roof.

## Shaw House

*22; 1 mile N of Newbury on B4009*

The largest Elizabethan mansion in Berkshire, Shaw House was built for a clothier and completed in 1581. Of red brick, it has a gabled E-shape front. The Greek inscription over the porch translates as: 'Let no jealous man enter', while a Latin one on the stone surround of the window above says: 'The toothless man envies the eater's teeth, and the mole despises the eye of the goat.' The back façade has a projecting wing with an eighteenth-century arcade along the centre. It is now a school.

## Sulhamstead

*23; 6½ miles SW of Reading off A4*

FOLLY FARM represents two separate commissions undertaken by Sir Edwin Lutyens. He began in 1906 with a medieval timber-framed cottage which was already standing on the site; this he enlarged to form an H-shaped William and Mary house of red and silver brick, with a two-storey Hall. Six years later, for a different owner, he doubled the size of this house by adding a large new wing in his early Arts and Crafts Tudor style, featuring a vast tiled roof which comes sweeping down over a little brick cloister bordering a goldfish pool. The Hall had black walls with red balconies; the Dining Room had murals – now alas lost – by Lutyens's friend William Nicholson. The garden, of a particularly complex design, was laid out by Gertrude Jekyll.

## Theale

*24; 5½ miles SW of Reading on A4*

HOLY TRINITY CHURCH, built in 1820–2 by E.W. Garbett in the style of Salisbury Cathedral, is a most intriguing curiosity. It was entirely paid for by Mrs Sophia Sheppard, sister of the celebrated Dr Routh who was President of Magdalen College, Oxford, for sixty-three years – thanks to whom Bishop Waynflete's 'Chantry Chapel' was transferred here from Magdalen in 1830. Mrs Sheppard's cenotaph is also worth close inspection – particularly her portrait on top of it in mock medieval brass. The tower, separated from the south-east corner of the church by a library, is a later addition of 1827–8 by John Buckler; the apse, ill-advisedly added by John Oldrid Scott in the 1890s, contains glass by Kempe.

## Wickham

*25; 6 miles NW of Newbury on B4000*

ST SWITHIN'S CHURCH has an Anglo-Saxon tower of flint with Roman brick incorporated in it. It also boasts a richly ornate interior by Benjamin Ferrey, a friend and collaborator of the Pugins. But its over-riding charm is its elephants – eight of them, in *papier mâché* – supporting the roof of the north aisle. Four were exhibited at the Paris exhibition of 1862, and four more specially ordered to make up the numbers. They must serve as a reminder, the church guide piously admonishes us, 'of our duty to spread the Christian faith in other lands'.

# Buckinghamshire

On the map, Buckinghamshire looks an untidy sort of county, its boundaries a labyrinth of salients and re-entrants; again and again, the driver finds himself entering it when he never knew he had left it, and vice versa. What makes it untidier still is that whereas its axis runs more or less north–south, that of its most decisive geographical feature, the Chilterns, runs south-west–north-east. This means that there are effectively three different Buckinghamshires. The first is the comparatively flat land to the south-east, centred unalluringly on what, before it passed to Berkshire in 1974, was the largest and least inspiring of its towns, Slough. Although in the heart of the commuter belt, this region somehow contrives to preserve one or two of the loveliest villages in the whole country. Next come the Chilterns themselves, sloping upwards quite gently on the London side. Unlike other chalky downlands – those of Sussex or Berkshire, for example – they are magnificently forested, with glorious beechwoods far thicker and more peaceful than anyone has a right to expect so near the capital. On the north-west side they end abruptly with a steep escarpment – experienced with dramatic effect from the M40 just beyond Stokenchurch – giving way to the Vale of Aylesbury which runs on north to the Northamptonshire border.

These three natural divisions are united less by any common characteristics than by the things which they lack. From the architectural point of view, perhaps the most important deficiency is that of good building stone. There is the occasional little limestone quarry to the west of Aylesbury, and a small deposit further north of another rather inferior limestone optimistically known as Buckingham marble; but for the most part the county has had to rely on imports from Oxfordshire or the Cotswolds – or, alternatively, from Northamptonshire and Lincolnshire – whenever it has felt stone to be essential. Otherwise, it has wisely concentrated on brick – and very beautiful brick it can be.

Perhaps, if stone had been more plentiful, Buckingham might have built itself a cathedral. In fact, apart from some excellent parish churches and some good cottages, there is in the whole county comparatively little medieval building that survives unspoilt. Monastic remains are scanty, castles still more so. Eton College, once Buckinghamshire's grandest medieval monument, was lost in 1974 to Berkshire. It is only with the eighteenth century that the local architecture really gets into its stride. There follows a sudden explosion of talent, with the sumptuous Palladian *tours de force* of Stowe and West Wycombe, inspired eccentricities like those at Claydon, Wotton or the churches at West Wycombe again and at Gayhurst, and more sober but equally noble mansions such as Shardeloes or Harleyford. Inevitably, the nineteenth century suffers by comparison; but with such tremendous piles as Cliveden, Mentmore and Waddesdon it has unquestionably made its mark.

A survey of this kind cannot, alas, by its very nature include all those marvellous but minor buildings in which the county is so astonishingly rich. There is hardly a town or village in it that does not contain something worth looking at; the eye must be ever on the alert if good things are not to be missed. In short, Buckinghamshire is as beautiful architecturally as much of it is scenically. Just because it is so near London it must not – emphatically *not* – be taken for granted.

## Amersham

*1; 26 miles NW of London on A413*

Despite one of the most insensitively placed gasometers in England, Amersham remains a delightful small seventeenth- and eighteenth-century country town, most of the modern building having been mercifully relegated to Amersham-on-the-Hill. Its proudest feature is the TOWN HALL of 1682, with its open ground floor; but along the main street there are plenty of other buildings, mostly of good Georgian brick, to do it credit. ST MARY'S CHURCH is disappointing at first sight, having been calamitously Victorianised in 1890, though its interior is redeemed by some nice medieval work, especially in the Early English transepts; but what makes it ultimately worth a visit is its stunning collection of monuments – surpassed in all Buckinghamshire only by those of Chenies (*q.v.*). Most of them are in the Drake Chapel on the north side of the church which, like the Bedford Chapel at Chenies, is all too often locked. (Why must some church authorities make it quite so difficult for people to see their greatest treasures?)

A mile outside the town to the west stands the Palladian SHARDELOES, begun in stuccoed brick by Stiff Leadbetter in 1758 but completed in 1766 by Robert Adam, who added the Corinthian portico – rather fussy-looking in this context: Doric might have been happier. It has now been converted into high-class flats, the most desirable of which retain their elaborate plasterwork. The Library is by James Wyatt – an early work, with a stucco ceiling by Joseph Rose – and the grounds by Repton. They descend majestically to the River Misbourne, here artificially broadened out into a lake – a view which not even the A40 beyond entirely spoils.

## Beaconsfield

*2; 24 miles NW of London on A40*

It is quite extraordinary that the two Buckinghamshire towns which are situated nearest to London should also be among the most beautiful and the most unspoilt. Like Amersham, Beaconsfield has been saved by the decision, conscious or otherwise, to build the new town a mile away from the old, Georgian, one. The latter naturally contains a few buildings dating from earlier centuries – notably the OLD RECTORY, next to the church, which cannot be much later than 1500; but most of the good houses in the four main streets that radiate from the Market Place seem to date from the first half of the eighteenth century, and the best of them – like the other RECTORY in Wycombe End, and HIGHWAY HOUSE and BURKE HOUSE in London End – are very fine indeed. The CHURCH OF ST MARY AND ALL SAINTS is a Victorian rebuilding of remarkably little interest. In the churchyard, however, is the tomb chest of the poet Edmund ('Go, lovely rose . . .') Waller.

Just beyond the town to the south stands HALL BARN: not a barn at all, but the imposing if somewhat eccentric mansion built for Waller around 1670. (Sir John Summerson refers to its 'gallant but amateurish play with superimposed order'.) Inside, it contains little of its original decoration or furnishings, and is not open to the public; but one gets a good view of it from the drive, at the entrance to which the gloriously dotty Victorian Gatehouse – an absolute riot of wooden panels, Gothic, Renaissance, Jacobean, all higgledy-piggledy – is a delight in itself.

*Amersham.*

## Bledlow

*3; 2 miles SW of Princes Risborough off A4010*

If HOLY TRINITY is locked, you should get the keys from the rectory 50 yards to the north; for the lovely flint church with its thirteenth-century additions is well worth the effort. Its four-bay arcades, of about 1200, have piers which are still cylindrical but arches which are already pointed; there is early stiff-leaf carving on the capitals. The west tower is Early English, the chancel and great four-light window at the end of the south transept pointing the way to Decorated. The whole thing is beautifully proportioned and includes some faded wall paintings and a perfectly splendid Norman font.

But the outside is memorable too, both for its setting on the edge of a wooded ravine and for a robust, chunky quality which the decorated corbels round the tower, doors and windows do nothing to diminish. The village is worthy of its church, especially the MANOR HOUSE, of a wonderful pale brick, and the timber-framed and brick-nogged MANOR COTTAGE close by.

## Chequers

*4; 2 miles NE of Princes Risborough off A4010*

Presented to the Government by Sir Arthur Lee – later Lord Lee of Fareham – in 1917, as the official country residence of the Prime Minister, Chequers still performs this function. It was built on the foundations of an earlier house by one William Hawtrey, in good russet brick with dressings of local Buckinghamshire stone, and bears the date 1565; unfortunately, however, it was radically Gothicised in the 1820s and though the Gothic accretions were all removed in the first dozen years of this century – mostly by Sir Reginald Blomfield – only the north front, which had remained virtually intact beneath the stucco, can be described as original. It has eight bays, with canted bay windows on both its principal floors at the second and sixth (an asymmetrical composition unusual by the 1560s and probably explained by the pattern of the medieval foundations) and triangular gables above these, as also above the first, fourth and eighth. All the windows are of four lights and two transoms, the canted bays having an additional pair of lights on each side. There is also a two-light, single-transomed attic window within each of the gables.

In Hawtrey's day, entry was probably from an open courtyard to the south, but this was closed by Blomfield and largely filled in; one now enters through a two-storeyed porch added by him on the east side. It leads into the 'Stone Hall', now completely panelled but with a balustraded opening roughly opposite the front door, revealing the old timber-framed staircase behind it. Immediately to the right a four-centred stone doorway, bearing Hawtrey's initials in the spandrels, opens into the L-shaped room occupying the north-east corner, which may have been his Hall, but was later known as the Cromwell Room (the house was long occupied by the Proctector's descendants through his daughter, Frances). It too was wainscoted by Blomfield, as was the present Hall which he formed when he covered in the central courtyard. It rises through two floors, and has on its south side a wooden screen in Renaissance style, its three arches separated by pilasters and supporting an open gallery with paired Ionic columns.

*Holy Trinity, Bledlow.*

Most of the other rooms are also essentially by Blomfield, though several of them retain features which, for one reason or another, survived the Gothicising. The most distinguished are the Long Gallery, which occupies six of the first-floor bays on the north side and which Lord Lee converted into a library, and the Great Parlour above the Cromwell Room, whose superb panelling with pilasters and inlaid arcading was brought from a house in Ipswich. On the second floor, in the oak-beamed room occupying the north-east angle, Lady Mary Grey – sister of the unfortunate Lady Jane – was kept a prisoner for two years at the command of Queen Elizabeth, infuriated by an unauthorised *mésalliance*.

## Chetwode*

*5; 6 miles SW of Buckingham (turn S off A421 at Tingewick)*

You approach it across a broad field, and as those five great stepped lancets of the east window loom larger and larger, so you realise more and more clearly that ST MARY AND ST NICHOLAS is no ordinary church. And you are right; it is in fact the chancel of a mid-thirteenth-century Augustinian priory, adapted for parish purposes only in 1480, when a Perpendicular tower was added to the west end.

When you enter, those lancets reveal themselves as more magnificent still, framed as they are with a profusion of slender shafts. Occupying the walls to the north and south are other lancets in groups of three, similarly shafted, their capitals all intricately carved with stiff-leaf, through which from time to time little animals peep out. There is more stiff-leaf around the doorway in the chancel and the sedilia, whose moulding looks as if it had slipped out of its groove and then been tucked rather insecurely back in like an inner tube.

The nave – formerly the western half of the priory chancel – is rather less exciting. It has, however, a good late thirteenth-century north window with lovely foliage capitals. The west window – reset – is of the same date.

Finally, there is some really beautiful glass, of the mid-thirteenth (rare in England) and fourteenth centuries, in the south-east lancets of the chancel.

## Chicheley Hall

*6; 2 miles NE of Newport Pagnell on A422*

Built of brick between 1719 and 1721 for Sir John Chester by Francis Smith of Warwick (to whom Thomas Archer may have given last-minute inspiration), Chicheley is a curious – but surprisingly successful – marriage between early Georgian austerity and exuberant Baroque. Doors and windows are freely adapted from Bernini, Borromini and other leading architects of Baroque Rome; while to walk clockwise round the house on the outside, beginning with the west front opposite the car park, is to experience a steady crescendo of architectural effect. This west front is of variegated brick with asymmetrical windows; next comes the north front, with the same rough brickwork but with cornices, window surrounds and Tuscan pilasters of stone. The east or garden front is of finely laid, uniformly coloured brick; the windows have brick aprons, there is an elaborately carved cornice, and the Doric order is introduced. The climax comes with the extraordinary south front, where the rather strident orange brick is punctuated by six giant Corinthian pilasters, the façade is broken out into a three-bay projection, and the cornice beneath the attic floor simultaneously swept up to create a distinctly theatrical *trompe-l'oeil* effect, suggesting that the centre projects forward further than it really does. The frieze and oddly curved window surrounds are both richly sculpted.

Inside, Baroque gives way to Palladianism in the Great Hall, designed by Henry Flitcroft. The ceiling has a characteristically inept painting by another of Burlington's protégés, William Kent. (He could do everything but paint.) There is a glorious and magnificently carved early eighteenth-century oak and walnut staircase climbing up behind. The original decoration of the Sitting Room, Drawing Room and Study, with superb panelling and carving, is largely preserved. Sir John Chester's Library at the top of the house, in particular, is a masterpiece of subtle joinery – on the face of it a conventional panelled room, but with nearly every panel opening to reveal shelves; even the pilasters and the frieze above the door are on hinges. These rooms and the staircase were designed by Francis Smith; how he must have enjoyed it!

The CHURCH is fourteenth-century with an early eighteenth-century chancel. It is of much charm.

## Claydon House★

*NT; 7; 3½ miles SW of Winslow, near Middle Claydon*

The surviving west wing of a mansion formerly three times the size, Claydon House, faced with finely cut ashlar, was built between 1757 and 1771 by the 2nd Earl Verney when he decided to enlarge and remodel his old Jacobean manor house. This restrainedly classical wing was the first part to be built; for it, Verney seems to have been very largely his own architect – assisted, however, by one Luke Lightfoot, a builder and surveyor of fair ability but a carpenter and wood carver possessed of a fantasy of imagination approaching genius. After 1768 the two were joined by Sir Thomas Robinson, an eccentric Yorkshire squire who had been a friend of Lord Burlington and fancied himself – with some justification – as an amateur architect. Robinson it was who added first a central block which included a marble hall and a domed observatory, and then an east wing entirely given over to an enormous ballroom. It was all very magnificent; so magnificent indeed that Verney soon found himself bankrupt. By the end of the century much of the contents had been sold and Claydon had been reduced once again to the original wing, self-sufficient and self-contained except that it had – and still has – no proper front door.

Most of the decoration in this surviving wing is Lightfoot's, and is entirely executed in carved wood. On the ground floor he was responsible for the Pink Parlour

*The Entrance Hall, Chicheley Hall.*

*Claydon House.*

and for the adjoining North Hall, a double cube of 50 by 25 by 25 feet, to which the wildly elaborate carving on ceilings and cornices, panels and overmantels gives an effect of quite overwhelming exuberance. Unfortunately, their lack of inhibition so appalled the more austere Robinson that he was able to persuade Verney to restrain Lightfoot before he got his teeth into the Library and the Saloon; these two rooms, though decorated in impeccable taste by Joseph Rose, one of the leading stuccoists of his day, consequently strike one as a distinct anticlimax.

On the first floor, thank goodness, we re-enter the Lightfoot world in the Gothic Room, the Paper Room and the Chinese Room – all of which show once again both his incredible fertility of ideas and, as a wood carver, his quite breathtaking skill. The Chinese Room in particular marks the high point of the mid-eighteenth-century taste for *chinoiserie*, featuring what can only be described as a Rococo pagoda with a complete Chinese tea party carved in high relief in the ceiling.

And then there is the Staircase. Here Robinson may have been responsible for the overall design, but Lightfoot certainly had a hand in the construction. Rose's contribution was the superb plasterwork on the walls. The result of this collaboration is yet another of the marvels of Claydon; for my part, I know of no lovelier staircase in England. The exquisite inlay of mahogany, boxwood, ivory and ebony on treads, risers and soffits, the wrought-iron balustrade with its gilded ears of corn, the triumphant flourish at the foot where the bottom step sweeps out like a fan across the floor – all is done with a combined delicacy and panache that leaves one gasping.

Florence Nightingale's sister, Parthenope, was married to Sir Harry Verney, 2nd baronet, and Miss Nightingale herself was a regular visitor to Claydon. Her bedroom can still be seen, and there is a fascinating if motley collection of other memorabilia.

## Cliveden

*NT; 8; 2 miles N of Taplow on B476*

The site is what matters – that massive arcaded terrace dominating a great curve of the Thames and looking, therefore, not across the river but down it. Cliveden is essentially a house less for the spring or the autumn than for the hot, high summer, for cucumber sandwiches and strawberries and cream, while, far below, the pleasure boats ply between the lushest, greenest beechwood banks in England.

The terrace was built in the year of the Great Fire by the Duke of Buckingham's architect, William Winde, but Winde's house was itself burnt down and the present mansion – the third to occupy the site – was completed by Sir Charles Barry in 1851, in his favourite Italian Renaissance style. The interior, largely the work of J.L. Pearson in the 1890s, is distinctly disappointing, apart from some fine French Rococo panelling in the Dining Room; and the recent tenancy of Stanford University cannot be said to have enhanced the aristocratic atmosphere. But the gardens and grounds, on the right day, are sublime; and the two little eighteenth-century conceits by Giacomo Leoni (the Octagon Temple and the Blenheim Pavilion) are well worth seeking out.

At the time of writing the house is being converted into a luxury hotel.

## Denham Place

*9; 17 miles NW of London on A40*

It is hard to believe that any village as beautiful and as unspoilt as Denham can have been allowed to survive so close to central London. A pretty church with a Norman tower, a swiftly flowing stream – the Misbourne – a village green and a main street of delightful and occasionally distinguished houses, late medieval timber-framed mingling with seventeenth- and eighteenth-century brick: Denham seems to have everything. And it also possesses, within a few yards of that main street, a country house of considerable splendour.

Denham Place was begun within a few weeks of the Glorious Revolution of 1688, and was not completed until shortly before William III's death in March 1702. It was built for Sir Roger Hill, long the Member of Parliament for Amersham, by the master mason William Stanton, who had recently completed the house at Belton, Lincolnshire. The original designer of Belton is unknown, but the several striking similarities between the two houses suggest that the original drawings for Denham may have been Stanton's own, though Hill probably contributed some ideas. The elevations are classically symmetrical: to both east and west there is a five-bay centre, flanked by three-bay wings projecting one bay – eleven bays in all. There are two main storeys, and attic dormers in a 2–5–2 rhythm along the hipped roof. Only the chimneys are irregular. There are six bays to north and south.

The house has not quite managed to preserve its original appearance. Some time in the eighteenth century the windows were reshaped and given narrower glazing bars, a balustrade and cupola were removed from the roof, and the dormers were shorn of their alternating triangular and segmental pediments. At the same time the entrance was moved round from the west front to the east, together with the broad main doorway – a distinctly swagger affair with widely set Ionic columns and, above, a broken scrolly pediment with busts. The net result of all these changes was to give the house a rather more austere appearance than was originally intended; but the warm red brick throughout – there are no stone dressings, even the quoins being of brick though in a slightly different colour – mitigates the effect, so that the house itself never looks other than welcoming.

Unfortunately the Sheraton Management Corporation that now occupies it is rather less so, and I have twice been refused permission to see inside. By peering through the ground-floor windows, however, it is possible to see that the principal reception rooms are still essentially intact. They are remarkable above all for their astonishing plasterwork – particularly in the former Drawing Room and Tapestry Room, which occupy respectively the north-west corner and the second and third bays of the north wing. The ceilings themselves are sophisticated and urbane; the surprise comes with the broad plaster friezes in the covings below. In the Drawing Room, the frieze represents a panorama of field sports – the hunting of deer, foxes, rabbits and otters, the shooting of pigeons, and the catching of fish both by net and by rod; in its neighbour, we have a continuous landscape of forests and rivers, houses and castles, bridges and windmills, but with no human figures except above the chimneypiece, where a chubby *amorino* is impatiently and ineffectually flogging a tortoise. These friezes are almost certainly Dutch. Picked out as they are in brilliant colours, they are a good deal more naïve than the ceiling stucco; but even when only glimpsed through a window they are irresistible.

The eastern end of the north wing was taken up by a most elegant Chapel in seventeenth-century Gothic, with linenfold panelling, a fine gilt Tudor screen (brought in from some earlier house) and a beautifully carved gallery above; in the south wing was Sir Roger's pretty oak-panelled Library, with recessed shelves and inset pictures. Whether these and other rooms have been preserved, and if so to what degree, I have alas been unable to discover.

## Dorney

*10; 2 miles NW of Windsor off B3026*

ST JAMES'S CHURCH is a wholly satisfying jumble of every period from the Saxon – see the pothook-shaped stone in the outside south wall of the chancel – to the nineteenth century, all on a delightfully intimate scale, dominated by an early sixteenth-century tower of diapered brick, and covered with a beautifully undulating tiled roof.

*The Garrard tomb, St James's Church, Dorney.*

The interior is even better, with panelled box pews, and a seventeenth-century west gallery and pulpit. The chancel is on the same level as the nave, the only steps being *west* of the south door; its interior south wall slopes outwards as it rises, like the poop of a galleon. In a separate chapel in the north-east corner is the absolutely lovely tomb of Sir William Garrard and his wife, kneeling, attended by their fifteen children – five of whom, having died before their parents, carry skulls in their hands. Nearby is a faded wall painting of the Annunciation, the figures being placed one each side of the door opening into the Garrard Chapel.

DORNEY COURT, opposite, was begun in about 1510. It has survived many alterations and restorations, but the Great Hall has been preserved intact, including its fine canted timber roof with arched braces and wind-braces. The linenfold panelling was formerly in Faversham Abbey. The table at the dais end bears in the centre a vast model pineapple, to remind us that it was here at Dorney that the first pineapple was grown in England, to be subsequently presented to Charles II – an event commemorated by Danckaerts's famous picture, of which versions exist at Houghton and Ham (*qq.v.*). Of the other rooms, the Parlour has another good timber ceiling with moulded beams and a Jacobean overmantel, while the Great Chamber immediately above it is barrel-vaulted and has also retained its original panelling.

A hundred yards away, in curious contrast, is a building known as the HERMITAGE, in reality a *cottage orné* of stone and flint, with an octagonal tower.

## Dropmore

*11; 2½ miles N of Taplow off B476*

There was only a labourer's cottage standing in what is now the Dropmore Estate when it was bought in 1792 by Lord Grenville, later to be Prime Minister in George III's 'Government of All the Talents'. He immediately started building, his architect being almost certainly Samuel Wyatt. Quite apart from the fact that Wyatt was to design Grenville's London house in Cleveland Row only two years later, the south front of Dropmore bears an extremely close resemblance both to Herstmonceux Place in East Sussex and to Belmont in Kent (*qq.v.*). It has only two storeys, the principal features being three round bows topped by shallow domes – of which, however, only the right-hand two were part of the original composition, the westernmost being added somewhat as an afterthought around 1810. This seems also to be roughly the date of the north front, with its Tuscan portico and low three-storey towers behind.

It seems, therefore, as if Grenville's original house was only one room thick. What is certain is that the north and south fronts, as well as differing quite considerably in style, fit together too clumsily to have been conceived as a single design. Thus the great Gallery – the finest room in the house – which links the two Drawing Rooms occupying the ground floor of the two eastern bays is entered from the north, not centrally as one might have expected, but by a small jib door towards one end: a marked contrast to the splendid enfilade of the rooms along the south front, whose double doors are all so aligned as to give a seemingly endless vista the entire length of the house.

This Gallery, which possesses the best of Dropmore's several superb plaster ceilings and is flanked by a long verandah to the south, was, with its two immediate neighbours, part of Lord Grenville's famous Library. Beyond it was his Study, with which Wyatt's original house came to an end. The later extension contains, in its additional bow, the Dining Room; but although this completes the line of important rooms, the house continues along the south front with a pergola which extends a further 200 yards or so to the west. The general effect is enchanting: the pergola consists in essence of a long high wall, over which a wooden trellis represents arcades and pilasters, broken at intervals by little Doric temple fronts and, in the centre, by a vast aviary made of ornamental metalwork and pierced green Chinese tiles, crowned by a tall, domed hexagon.

In the grounds to the west of the lake is a stone alcove from Old London Bridge, bought and re-erected by Lord Grenville's widow in 1839 after its demolition.

The house is now occupied by the International University of San Diego.

## Gayhurst

*12; 4½ miles NW of Newport Pagnell on B526*

Basically Jacobean, Gayhurst has been much altered, first in the eighteenth century and then again by William Burges in the nineteenth. After two separate periods of service as a school the house has now been converted into flats.

But the joy of Gayhurst is its church – ST PETER'S – a hundred yards or so across Capability Brown's park. Here is one of the most enchanting examples of Georgian church architecture that you could ever hope to find. Begun in 1728, by an unknown architect of individuality and imagination, it is nothing if not wilful: thus it has a small pediment supported on giant Ionic half columns in the centre of the external south wall of the nave and *two*, superimposed, on the north. The broad, square tower has urns on the corners and an entrancing (and faintly oriental) little cupola in the middle.

The interior is almost unchanged; the eye is at once captivated by the fantasy of the plasterwork, especially on the ceiling – don't miss the books with the turned-down pages. The glowing Decalogue – personally restored by John Piper – begins with the surprising injunction: 'Thow shalt not have none other Gods but me', and there is a marvellous monument to Sir Nathan Wrighte – Keeper of the Great Seal under Queen Anne – and his son George. Opinion is divided about the traditional attribution to Roubiliac – oddly enough, there is no inscription of *any* kind – but there can be no denying that it is a masterpiece.

## Hartwell House

*13; 2 miles SW of Aylesbury on A418*

The sturdy austerity of the grey stone Jacobean north front of Hartwell House, together with the rather pompous-looking brackets which look as though they should be supporting far weightier loads than three quite modest bow windows, make one not entirely surprised to learn that the building is now the seat of an academy for young ladies until recently known as the House of Citizenship. The south front of mellow honey-coloured stone presents, however, a very different picture. Here we have the familiar story of an early seventeenth-century house being altered to conform with mid-eighteenth-century fashion, and we have documentary proof that the east front at least is the work of Henry Keene in 1755–6. If, as seems more than probable, Keene was also responsible for the south, Hartwell has come down to us as the best and most complete of all Keene's country house work. He shows again and again his respect for the earlier structure and carefully avoids any exaggerated Palladianism – which could only have produced an ugly clash of styles.

Within the house, the Hall and most of the principal rooms have been thoroughly Georgianised, with fine plasterwork and elaborate fireplaces. The one major Jacobean survival – and by far the most sensational feature of Hartwell – is the Grand Staircase with its twenty-four carved wooden figures, each two and a half feet high, spaced out along the newel posts. The balusters also are carved into caryatids, all different – some mythical, others grotesque. Two modern replacements include Sir Winston Churchill complete with cigar and, rather surprisingly, G.K. Chesterton. One searches in vain for Louis XVIII of France who, with his brother, the future Charles X, rented Hartwell during his exile.

*The octagonal church, Hartwell House.*

A little to the north-west of the house is Keene's beautiful octagonal CHURCH, built between 1754 and 1756, with mock fan vaulting in plaster. Keene was one of the first to exploit the fashion for Gothick, and this is his masterpiece in the style. More or less gutted during the Second World War, it has been rebuilt at great cost – rightly so, for it is a rare gem.

## Hillesden*

*14; 3 miles S of Buckingham off A421*

Here is a treasure indeed: ALL SAINTS' CHURCH, late Perpendicular, built all of a piece in the very last years of the fifteenth century, in one of the loveliest and loneliest spots in the whole county. Although restored by George Gilbert Scott, who had drawn it at the age of fifteen and whose love of Gothic architecture it is said to have inspired – his father was perpetual curate of Gawcott nearby – it bears no strong marks of his hand; rather, it looks exactly what it is, and very magnificent to boot. You approach it from the north, which is consequently the show front; there is a brave north aisle with generous windows of three lights and a wonderful clerestory above consisting of a continuous row of windows virtually touching each other. Four-light windows mark the north transept and chapel, and the vestry at the north-east corner has an enchanting little stair turret with crown. Everything is splendidly embattled, and the north porch by which you enter is actually fan-vaulted. Within it, the door still shows the bullet holes from the days of the Civil War when it was a Royalist outpost stormed by Cromwell's troops.

The interior shows no falling-off of quality: beautifully moulded arcades and chancel arch, and a really glorious north chapel and chancel with a rich frieze of angels bearing scrolls and musical instruments. There are some good tombs too – notably of the Denton family, whose house has long since disappeared. We should be all the more grateful that this wonderful church should have survived so well.

## Mentmore

*15; 5 miles S of Leighton Buzzard off B488*

'I do not believe', remarked Lady Eastlake of Mentmore House, 'that the Medicis were ever so lodged at the height of their glory.' She was right. Mentmore is more a palace than a house, built in 1854 by Joseph Paxton (of Great Exhibition fame) for Baron Meyer Amschel de Rothschild; it thus formed one of that astonishing group of Rothschild mansions in the Chilterns – together with Waddesdon (*q.v.*), Tring, Halton, Aston Clinton and Ascott (*q.v.*), of which only Waddesdon can hold a candle to it in magnificence. But whereas Waddesdon is a sort of misplaced château of the Loire, Mentmore is English through and through, avowedly inspired by Wollaton, Robert Smythson's masterpiece of the 1580s. Like Wollaton, it has four great angle towers with shaped gables and pinnacles galore; like Wollaton, too, its exterior is carved all over with quite exceptionally fine detailing in late Elizabethan motifs. Elsewhere, however, the hand of Paxton is in evidence, notably in the Grand Hall which rises the full height of the house

*Nether Winchendon.*

and which he roofed over in glass, using the ridge-and-furrow principle that he had developed for the Crystal Palace. This roof rests on a vast coving, sumptuously decorated, below which at first-floor level runs a vaguely Renaissance arcaded Gallery in pink alabaster and green marble. In the centre of the left-hand wall is a huge chimneypiece in black and white marble, brought from Rubens's house in Antwerp. Yet more marble, from Sicily this time, was imported to provide the Grand Staircase, which is conceived on a similarly gigantic scale. The doors at the foot of this staircase, and several others leading from the Grand Hall, consist of immense single sheets of plate glass – among the earliest anywhere – set in narrow walnut frames.

Of the main reception rooms, by far the most opulent today is the Dining Room, with its gilded *boiseries* originally designed in 1731 for one of the Hôtels de Villars in Paris, framing mirrors, painted panels and pieces of exquisite eighteenth-century Genoa velvet. Alas, virtually all the Rothschild furniture, pictures and works of art have gone, dispersed in the great sale of 1977 after the Government had refused to buy, for a derisory sum, the house and contents for the nation. Only the fittings remained, as is required by law in any house classified as Grade I. Mentmore was subsequently purchased by 'The World Government of the Age of Enlightenment' – the followers of the Maharishi Mahesh Yogi who practise the art of transcendental meditation and who have now converted the house into the Maharishi European Research University. They are caring for it quite beautifully and are gradually providing the main rooms with fittings and furniture worthy of their setting. Thanks to them, too, Mentmore is now open to the public once or twice a week.

## Nether Winchendon

*16; 6 miles SW of Aylesbury off A418*

A fascinating example of the smaller English country house at its idiosyncratic best, Nether Winchendon is medieval in its origins, but now predominantly Tudor with a light-hearted overlay of late eighteenth-century Gothick which suits it remarkably well. This overlay was added by Sir Scrope Barnard – a forebear of the present owners – who clad the original timber-framed house in stone, built the charming four-arched entrance screen across the courtyard in front of it – one of the arches is now blocked up – and the square tower immediately to the east, and added various pointed windows, buttresses and battlements. These combine with the tall ornamented Tudor brick chimneys and the seventeenth-century cupola in a wholly enchanting ensemble. The south or garden front is particularly picturesque with three square towers, an off-centre gable and a quantity of mullioned windows, some Tudor, some Gothick – and, at the eastern end, a delightful little first-floor verandah.

Inside, the Entrance Hall and Morning Room were added by Sir Scrope, who also replaced the ceiling of the Great Hall with one of his own design; but the Parlour and the Chamber above are both of about 1530. The Parlour – now the Drawing Room – is a particularly lovely room, with white-painted oak linenfold panelling and a narrow frieze carved in a most sophisticated Renaissance style with scrolls, arabesques, mythological figures, green men and a portrait head of the builder, Sir John Daunce. Intimate and unassuming, Nether Winchendon has, one feels, always been loved by its owners but never allowed to dominate them. It radiates an air of friendliness and charm.

*The church of St Michael and All Angels, Stewkley.*

## Notley Abbey

*17; 2 miles N of Thame off B4011*

This charming country house is built on the site of an early twelfth-century monastic foundation for Augustinian canons and incorporates the old Abbot's Lodging of the fourteenth and fifteenth centuries. Hall, parlour and solar are still identifiable, and despite a good deal of restoration and rebuilding – of all the Perpendicular windows, only one appears unchanged and in its original position – the overall ecclesiastical atmosphere has been retained to a surprising degree. A beautifully engineered spiral staircase winds up into a tremendous timber roof – now visible only from a loft – with traces of medieval paintings. It runs the entire length of the building.

Of the church itself, there remain only the south-east corner and three pier bases from the crossing; but parts of the cloister and refectory have survived. Moreover, in the barn nearby is a magnificent length of fourteenth-century arcading on a beautifully carved corbel table. If – which is by no means certain – this is in its original position, it would argue that the end of the barn was at some period part of a separate chapel. Such a chapel would almost certainly have been privately endowed, since the workmanship and detailing are quite exceptionally lavish.

## Stewkley*

*18; 4 miles SE of Winslow on B4032*

Of the 6,000 churches built in this country during the Norman period, three only have survived virtually unaltered. ST MICHAEL AND ALL ANGELS is one of them. It earns its star, however, not just for its rarity value; for it is also quite exceptionally rich in mid-twelfth-century decoration. Reading from west to east, it consists of a nave, a tower and a chancel; there are no aisles, nor – despite the position of the tower – are there any transepts. To this original Norman base the only additions have been a deep fourteenth-century buttress containing a stairway to the belfry, a Victorian south porch, and a modern vestry which is a disgrace.

The tower – massive, short and square – is given its great distinction by the tall row of interlaced arcading that runs round all four sides immediately above the roof ridge of the nave. Each individual arch is adorned with deeply cut zigzag, while the gargoyles projecting at a slightly higher level include the symbols of the four Evangelists. This already sets a high standard, which is fully maintained on the west front: here the basic composition is one of a central doorway with slightly lower blank arches, one on each side. The doorway is of two orders and an inner arch running uninterruptedly all the way round; all three are heavily zigzagged, as are the two side arches, and are surmounted by a continuous band of zigzag in the form of a string-course which encircles the church, rising to accommodate the doorway and then returning to its original level on the other side. Above this again is a tall round-headed window with yet more zigzag, on the general pattern of those along the north and south walls of nave and chancel. The small circular window in the gable is probably later; the decoration is similar to that of the rest, but a good deal less regular. So far, all this is orthodox enough; the surprise comes with the tympanum just above the west door. This has a long, narrow, dropped keystone at its centre, on each side of which the stone has been cut back in a deep segment. Thus the base of the tympanum, instead of being straight, assumes the shape of a cupid's bow, while what is left of it, divided into two by the keystone, is decorated with dragons. The east end is, predictably, a good deal simpler: a single window, with blind companion arches to either side, though these two have the ubiquitous zigzag.

The interior is dominated by the two tower arches. On them, the multiple orders of zigzag are joined by a new motif, that of beak-heads, carved with considerable imagination and much variety. Still more zigzag, but alas no more beak-head, continues around each of the deeply splayed windows and the ribs of the vaulted chancel. Here it alters very slightly to form a lozenge pattern, with tiny heads peeping out from the spaces.

All this may sound somewhat overpowering; I can only assure you that it is not. The general scheme of decoration is certainly ornate, but it is never fussy, and there is plenty of rest for the eye. This, in short, is one of the most memorable churches not only of Buckinghamshire but of all England.

## Stowe

*20; 3 miles NW of Buckingham off A422*

When Sir Richard Temple built the house in the first quarter of the eighteenth century, he was probably the richest man in England; yet the splendour of Stowe lies neither in its size nor in its magnificence. What really sets it apart is the grandeur of the overall conception; for Temple had sought to create not just a house but a world to enclose it: that ideal Palladian world in which the ancient virtues were revered, the ancient philosophers' truths illustrated, and in which Nature, no longer rigidly corseted as in the preceding century, was now 'educated' to provide ever-balanced compositions to delight the eye of gentlemen brought up on the landscapes of Poussin or Claude.

To enter any new world, some degree of preparation is advisable; and the approach to Stowe is every bit as important to the modern visitor as it was in Temple's day. Ignore, therefore, all instructions to the contrary and drive up the Grand Avenue which begins just outside Buckingham and leads north-west towards the house. Pass between the pair of Georgian lodges with their endearingly salacious reliefs; then, when the road turns sharp left, leave the car and walk up the hill to the Corinthian arch. Before you, a mile away across the lake, lies the house as you were meant to see it for the first time – the south front, designed by Robert Adam in 1771 but subtly modified by Thomas Pitt, 1st Lord Camelford, and the Italian architect Giovanni Battista Borra: three superb pavilions in honey-coloured stone connected by two galleries in stucco, simple enough as a scheme but carried out in breathtakingly flawless proportions.

Now, and only now, return to the main road and follow it round to the right until you reach the Oxford Avenue. It crosses an urn-topped bridge (which it is well worth leaving the car once again to admire), passes between two more pavilions and brings you at last to the north front. The pavilions are the work of another Italian, Vincenzo Valdrati, who designed several rooms at Stowe including the Saloon, State Drawing Room and Pompeian Music Room. He would not have earned a separate mention here but for an irresistible fact which I learn from Howard Colvin: 'While at Stowe he attended a wedding in the neighbourhood and, when the bridegroom failed to appear, chivalrously offered himself as a substitute – and was accepted.' The north front grew organically from the late seventeenth-century brick house of thirteen bays that still forms its core. First it was stuccoed, then given its brave portico and finally those long sweeping colonnades that impart lightness to the whole structure and make it sing. Who was responsible? Vanbrugh? Kent? Leoni? All worked at Stowe at different times and all, perhaps, played their part.

Of the interior of the house, all one can say is that it must have been lovely. In a way, it still is; the Entrance Hall with its ceiling painted by Kent and the Marble Saloon next to it are magnificent by any standards. But these, and the long suites of state rooms designed by Valdrati that stretch out on either side, are now mere shells; the furniture they once contained has given place to the sturdier impedimenta of Stowe School; and though we owe that school a debt of immeasurable gratitude for having saved the whole place from destruction and for cherishing it with such loving care, it is hard to think of its former elegance without regret.

But stand now beneath the south portico and look out across the park. Thanks to the combined genius of Vanbrugh, Bridgeman, Kent and Capability Brown, that Augustan dream world stretches out again before you with its obelisks and rotundas, its River Styx and its Elysian Fields, seemingly artless and yet in fact so rigidly conceived that a whole fourteenth-century village had to be eliminated, and the church – in which, incidentally, Brown was married – rendered invisible by a dense and deliberate screen of trees.

Of Temple's temples – the pun may be forgiven, since he incorporated it in his family crest – his follies and his fantasies, over thirty still remain in the settings for which they were intended. Several are the work of Kent, others are by Vanbrugh and Gibbs. Most perfect is the Palladian bridge of 1742, copied (with improvements) from that at Wilton; most enjoyable, Kent's Temple of British Worthies of 1735. All repay the effort of seeking them out; all contribute to the Grand Design. That is what counts. Through it, Stowe tells us more about the eighteenth century, its tastes and values and its underlying philosophies, than any other house in England.

## Tyringham House

*20; 2½ miles NW of Newport Pagnell on B526*

Built by Sir John Soane between 1793 and 1797, Tyringham House was cruelly transformed at the beginning of this century. The central bow with its attached giant columns, the incised Grecian decoration and the balustrade are much as Soane left them, but there is little else that he would recognise, far less acknowledge. The house is now a health clinic, and serve it right. The stables are still essentially Soane's, apart from a hideous slated roof; but by far the most interesting element still to be seen – and remaining absolutely untouched – is the entrance gateway. This extraordinary edifice of elephant-grey stone is described by Pevsner as being 'in spite of its small scale, a monument of European importance ... entirely independent of period precedent, a sign of daring only matched at that moment by what Ledoux was designing in France and Gilly in Germany'.

But is it also beautiful? Not, certainly, if you are looking for the elegance that one normally associates with the neo-classical – of Robert Adam, let us say, or Henry Holland. It is stark, assertive, eccentrically self-confident, and Soanish through and through. The horizontal grooves that take the place of mouldings and constitute virtually the sole surface adornment, the bare Tuscan columns, the statueless niches – somehow it seems to speak more of the 1930s than the 1790s. But there it is – not so much a milestone as a landmark. Admire it if you will, or execrate it; but do not pass it by without a second glance.

## Waddesdon Manor

*NT; 21; 10 miles SW of Bicester off A41*

Unlike the Tyringham gate, Waddesdon Manor could not conceivably be ignored. This gigantic, supremely bogus Loire château, plonked inappropriately down in the Chilterns by the French architect Gabriel-Hippolyte Destailleur (creator of the Empress Eugénie's abbey–mausoleum at Farnborough in Hampshire, *q.v.*) at the behest of Baron Ferdinand de Rothschild in the 1870s, amply makes up in *superbia* what it lacks in architectural purity. The greatest and grandest of the six tremendous mansions built by various members of that amazing family, all within 15 miles of each other in the Vale of Aylesbury – the others being Mentmore (*q.v.*), Aston Clinton, Halton, Ascott (*q.v.*, short list) and Tring – it is also, since the catastrophic Mentmore sale of 1977, the only major showplace of the *goût Rothschild* in the country, boasting the finest collection of paintings, sculpture, porcelain, glass, furniture, books and illuminated manuscripts outside a national museum.

The gardens were laid out by another Frenchman, Lainé, in an appropriately formal style.

## West Wycombe★

*NT; 22; 3 miles W of High Wycombe off A40*

First, the house. Elegant, cool and serenely Palladian – its double-tiered colonnade of 1775 was inspired by Palladio's Palazzo Chiericati in Vicenza, though its columns are of plastered wood rather than stone – it was built for Sir Francis Dashwood (Hell-Fire Francis) by John Donowell between 1745 and 1771 around the nucleus of

*Waddesdon Manor.*

an older house, in the middle of a park soon to be transformed into one of the great landscape gardens of England. But WEST WYCOMBE PARK is considerably more eccentric, both literally and figuratively, than appears at first sight: the north and south façades are not quite the same length, and Donowell's east portico has somehow missed the centre of the wall. It seems clear, in fact, that this obscure architect – who produced no other major building – was not really up to the job. He was eventually dismissed in 1764, one of Dashwood's friends commenting: 'I believe the Man is honest & does to the best of his Abilities, but these I am afraid from the experience I have had of him are not very extensive.'

Another curious feature is that having entered the house through the front door to the west (where the massive Ionic portico was added by Nicholas Revett in 1770–1, based on his own measured drawings of the Temple of Bacchus at Teos in Ionia) one has to re-emerge on to the lower terrace before making a second entrance, into the Hall. But that Hall, with its Tuscan screens at each end and its glorious staircase of inlaid mahogany, comes as no anti-climax; nor, indeed, do the ground-floor state rooms to which it leads. In the Library and Study, and over the staircase landing, are superb plaster ceilings, probably by Thomas Roberts of Oxford, dating from soon after 1750; in the Saloon, Blue Drawing Room and Music Room are fine Baroque paintings by Giuseppe Borgnis. William Hannan, a talented Scot, painted the ceilings of the Red Drawing Room and Tapestry Room, while those in the Dining Room and Hall are by Borgnis's son Giovanni, based on engravings in Robert Wood's *Ruins of Palmyra*, of 1752. All these rooms have fine furniture, noble fireplaces, and any number of Italian *seicento* paintings, for this is the world of the Whig aristocracy in the days of the Grand Tour. Sir Francis's fondness for archaeological models is evidence of his progressive taste, and the hypocaust heating system in the Hall is a good example of antiquarian interests being put to practical use. The landscape, too, with its garden buildings by Revett – in particular his enchanting Island Temple – and the several neo-classical experiments in garden planning, shows him to have been, there again, well in advance of his time. Thus the Temple of the Winds is – apart from the Doric Temple at Hagley – the earliest attempt in England to reproduce a monument of antiquity. By contrast, the Temple of Venus must surely be the most recent, having been completed by the present Sir Francis Dashwood in 1982.

Next, the church. Set high on the neighbouring hill and crowned with its famous golden ball which is large enough to accommodate four people seated, ST LAURENCE'S is one of the most prominent landmarks in Buckinghamshire. It began as a parish church, of the hilltop village of Haveringdon, long since disappeared; but little now remains, inside or out, to betray its medieval origins. The interior is a riot of opulent classical decoration: sixteen giant Corinthian columns, stucco garlands, cherubs, cornucopias, magnificent marble floors, the lot. All this is the result of a rebuilding by Sir Francis, carried out between 1751 and 1762 – probably with Revett as his architect; and it demonstrates, just as clearly as does the house itself, what a determined classicist he was. The very design of the nave, for example, is based on the Temple of Bel at Palmyra. Nothing in the main body of the church – except the altar, which is on castors – and little enough in the chancel suggests religion: even the font is disguised as a birdbath, and in place of pulpit and lectern there are wooden platforms each supporting a small reading desk and a large and commodious carved armchair. Here is the Age of Reason – or of cultivated frivolity – with a vengeance. Scarcely a House of God perhaps, but as an eighteenth-century drawing room hard to beat.

*St Laurence's Church, West Wycombe.*

Just to the east of the church is the DASHWOOD MAUSOLEUM, built in 1763–4: a huge hexagon of flint, open to the sky, with Tuscan columns and urns in appropriate positions. It proves, surprisingly enough, to be by John Bastard, the *genius loci* of Blandford Forum in Dorset. Directly beneath church and mausoleum are the caves, hewn into the chalk for a quarter of a mile or more in the 1750s, partly to furnish building materials for a new road, partly to relieve the plight of the local unemployed, and partly – if cherished legend is to be believed – to provide a meeting place for the notorious Hell-Fire Club, of which Sir Francis was a founder.

Finally, the village: another of those miraculous survivals in which Buckinghamshire is so rich – still more miraculous than most, indeed, since until the building of the M40 in the early 1970s the main London–Oxford road went right through the middle. That it has preserved so much of its beauty is due to the National Trust, who own it more or less *in toto*.

## Willen

*23; 2 miles S of Newport Pagnell on B488*

The CHURCH OF ST MARY MAGDALENE is at the time of writing almost impossible to reach, engulfed as it is among the tangle of expressways that make up the penumbra of Milton Keynes. But the situation – or at least the signposting – will perhaps improve, and anyway the effort is well worth while. The church is in fact the only original work still surviving virtually entire (with the arguable exceptions of Ramsbury Manor, Wiltshire, *q.v.*, and the Monument in the City of London, *q.v.*) by that remarkable polymath Robert Hooke – colleague of Wren, arch-enemy of Newton (who took the credit for many of Hooke's discoveries) and the nearest approximation that this country has ever produced to Leonardo da Vinci.

You approach from the west up a short avenue of limes, and there before you is the tower, its bottom stage faced in stone and almost entirely taken up with a deeply splayed doorway. Above this stage and everywhere else on the building, the material is darkish red and black brick with stone dressings. The tower continues upwards with a circular window on the second stage, and then with a third which actually contains two storeys but unites them with attached Corinthian pilasters. A high and somewhat complicated cornice is topped with finials at the corners; a lead cupola was unfortunately removed in 1867. The rest of the exterior is plain and symmetrical – single-storey side chambers flanking the tower to make up the breadth of the nave, which then rises behind to the height of the second stage. It has three bays of tall, round-headed windows, and a discreet eastern apse which, one is a little surprised to learn, was added as recently as 1861.

The interior is similarly modest, but is nevertheless a perfect example of its period (1680) – particularly since it has kept just about all its original furnishings. There is a fine barrel-vaulted plaster ceiling, good wooden panelling, and a marble font with a cover which is not, as the guide-book claims, by Grimling (*sic*) Gibbons but by a lesser-known stone carver named Bate.

## Wing

*24; 3 miles SW of Leighton Buzzard on A418*

Close your eyes to the Perpendicular west tower; ignore the fifteenth-century windows and the battlements. Focus instead on the seven-sided apse with its slender blind arches and, once you are inside, on the magnificent broad sweep of the chancel arch and the stark round arches of the nave arcades. For here you are at the CHURCH OF ALL SAINTS, Wing, one of the three or four most important tenth-century Anglo-Saxon churches in the whole country, and one of the best preserved. Moreover, unlike most of its contemporaries, it possesses not only age but real elegance; what other word is there for those external blind arches, with the ghosts of the typically Saxon triangular heads above them? (The roof above would originally have been a little higher.) Below the apse there is a small crypt with a narrow ambulatory; its proportions are equally elegant, its vaulting considerably less so. You will be lucky if you get in, since it is usually locked; but at least you can peer through the grille at the south-east corner.

Some time in the fifteenth century the nave was heightened and given a clerestory – without, fortunately, disturbing the great chancel arch (a deep segment, not quite a semi-circle) and the little two-light window above it. This, one feels, was no bad thing: the church must have been terribly dark before, since even now the wooden roof, whose tie-beams terminate in figures of saints and kings, is almost invisible. (Would not a coin-in-the-slot lighting system pay for itself in no time?)

For the rest, the north aisle remains essentially Saxon; the south is Decorated, and very nice too. Among the tombs of the Dormer family, take a long, hard look at that of Sir Robert, who died in 1552. Here, almost unbelievably, is a work of the purest and most sophisticated Italian Renaissance, with only the stone (which is local), the occasional touches of strapwork and the inscription to betray its Englishness. The church guide remarks that 'it seems strangely out-of-place in this setting', which is true in a way; it might have added with equal truth that few finer monuments of its date and style exist in all England.

## Winslow Hall★

*25; 10 miles N of Aylesbury on A413*

There can be little, if any, serious doubt that Winslow Hall is the work of Sir Christopher Wren. We know that its first owner, William Lowndes, Secretary to the Treasury from 1695 until his death in 1724, was a personal friend of his; furthermore the original accounts, which are still in the house, mention Wren's name as Surveyor of Her Majesty's Works and make it clear that he not only went through these accounts and approved them but also, on occasion, got certain items reduced – exactly what an architect would do. Most convincing of all, perhaps, is the stylistic evidence: the house is virtually identical on the outside to the Master's House of Middle Temple – only the chimneys are different – and the Governor's House of the Royal Hospital, Chelsea, has the same ingenious system of central flues as those described below.

It is a tall house, two and a half storeys with a steeply pitched roof standing on a high basement (fifteen steps up to the front door) and only seven bays in width; and the four high chimneystacks crowning the roof ridge add considerably to the effect. The predominant material is a rich, dark red brick – made, in fact, from mud dredged up from the bottom of the garden; contrast is provided by a paler rubbed brick, which frames the windows and must have come from further afield, and copious stone dressings. There is a three-bay centre, projecting only an inch or two but emphasised by its own lines of quoins, supporting a rather deep triangular pediment with a small round window in the middle. The north and south fronts are identical.

The interior plan is of considerable interest in that there are four principal rooms on each floor – on the top, attic, floor two of them have been run into one to form a sort of long gallery – all grouped around the central core which contains the four great chimney flues. As a result of this arrangement, no fewer than five fireplaces are set diagonally in the inner corners of their respective rooms. It also rules out any possibility of a central staircase, and Wren has consequently given the house two, of equal importance, one at each end of the house. On each floor there is a gallery landing running parallel to the flights, giving direct access to all the main rooms. These rooms all have small closets opening off them at the corners of the house; far from the fireplaces and with two outside walls and windows each, these closets must have been perishingly cold in winter.

For some two centuries of its existence, Winslow Hall served its owners only as a second, supplementary house, since they had also acquired the adjoining property of Whaddon. To this fortunate circumstance, probably, we owe the fact that its interior has come down to us virtually unchanged since 1700 – the date of the building itself. It is not lavish; you will find no exuberance of virtuoso plasterwork, metalwork or joinery. Winslow does not give itself airs. Only in one room on the first floor – his own – did Mr Secretary Lowndes let himself go a little, commissioning from some unknown painter – a follower, probably, of Daniel Marot – a charming series of four mural paintings of formal landscapes with fountains, surrounded by wildly extravagant frames of caryatids and curtains, scrolls and cartouches, garlands of fruit and flowers and countless other conceits that utterly overpower the central subjects. Everywhere else, quiet distinction rules.

Winslow Hall is privately owned, but is open to the public. For anyone interested in seeing how a well-to-do village squire lived in the reign of Queen Anne, this is the house to visit.

## Wotton Underwood

*26; 2 miles S of A41, halfway between Aylesbury and Bicester*

WOTTON HOUSE begins with a mystery. Who was its architect? John Keene, the obscure local stonemason who actually built it – together with its two enchanting side pavilions – in 1704, is most unlikely to have been capable of so grand a conception. Sir James Thornhill has been suggested, largely because there exists a drawing by him of the house with one of the pavilions; but the only major house for which Thornhill is known to have been responsible is Moor Park in Hertfordshire (*q.v.*), and there is anyway no evidence that he ever thought of abandoning decorative painting, even temporarily, in favour of architecture before 1715. By far the most likely candidate is William Winde, for Wotton bears a strong resemblance to old Buckingham House – precursor of the present Buckingham Palace – which was almost certainly Winde's work. Its pavilions, moreover, are strikingly similar to those at Ashdown in Oxfordshire (*q.v.*).

But we shall probably never know for sure; and what makes the problem still more difficult is the fact that these pavilions – they are of five by five bays, single-storeyed, with hipped roofs and lanterns – are the only elements of Wotton which are known to have remained unaltered, the main house having been gutted by fire in 1820. The task of rebuilding it was entrusted to Sir John Soane. According to the Thornhill drawing, he seems to have retained most of the outer shell of brick, with its stone dressings and its unorthodox arrangement of eleven bays on one front and nine on the other, except for the top, attic, floor, which he suppressed, leaving only a vestigial row of rather mean-looking little windows

*Winslow Hall.*

beneath the cornice. This may have in turn necessitated, for reasons of proportion, a slight lowering of the first-floor windows. Soane kept, of course, the four giant pilasters marking both the angles of the building and its five-bay centre; on the garden side, however, he added more of the same to form an impressive portico.

Certain it is that, for all its impressiveness, the exterior of Wotton is something less than a total success. Perhaps, in the circumstances, it could hardly have been otherwise. If we are to compare it with Ashdown, for example, we see at once how the suppression of hipped roof and pediment in favour of a flat horizontal roof line, with or without the full-size attic storey – an innovation in English architecture which can be safely attributed to Winde – inevitably involves a substitution of austere severity for informal domesticity: an impression which the side pavilions may soften, but do not altogether eliminate. The interior, however, is a different story. The present owner has managed to undo the effects of a disastrous remodelling of 1928, and Soane's work is once again everywhere visible. His master's hand is revealed in that marvellously sinuous staircase (though the balustrade is from the earlier building); in the sudden openings in the walls, displaying again and again some tantalising vista where it is least expected; in the use of similar cornices for different rooms, to give a feeling of unity; in the groove decoration such as we see at Tyringham (*q.v.*), always one of his hallmarks; in the delicate reeded mouldings; and above all, perhaps, in the first-floor landing, where the shallow dome, supported on high arches, could be by no one else. Here is a house of endless subtlety, imagination and delight.

---

# Short List

## Ascott

*NT; 27; 2 miles SW of Leighton Buzzard off A418*

Originally a quite modest timber-framed house of 1606 – the date is inscribed over the front door – it was considerably enlarged by George Devey towards the end of the last century and again in 1938, always in the same style. One of the six Rothschild houses in the area (see Mentmore and Waddesdon), it contains a superb collection of paintings, porcelain and furniture; great architecture, alas, it is not.

## Boarstall Tower

*NT; 28; 2 miles W of Brill off B4011*

The gatehouse of a fortified and moated house for which licence to crenellate was granted in 1312, Boarstall Tower is basically fourteenth-century. It underwent much alteration 300 years later, but retains its two polygonal angle towers with arrow slits and battlements.

## Chenies

*29; 4 miles NW of Rickmansworth on A404*

The Bedford Chapel in ST MICHAEL'S CHURCH contains the most astonishing collection of funerary monuments to be found in any parish church in the country. But be warned: it is almost invariably locked. If you want to do more than peep through the iron grille you will have to write to the Bedford Estate Office for permission. I can only say that you will be amply rewarded.

The MANOR HOUSE just beyond the church consists essentially of two wings, at right-angles to each other, facing respectively west and south. The west wing, with its short tower, dates from towards the end of the fifteenth century; the south was added in the 1520s by the 1st Earl of Bedford, who was also responsible for the twenty-two surviving ornamental chimneys. These, with the tall, crow-stepped brick gables, are the principal feature of the house. The material throughout is a rich brick, dark red but occasionally diapered in blue. The south range has six huge projections with curious little closets built into them; on the north, courtyard, side is a row of pretty corbelled-out oriels.

## Dinton

*30; 4 miles SW of Aylesbury off A418*

The CHURCH OF ST PETER AND ST PAUL is remarkable only for its Norman south doorway, which is of considerable splendour: the lintel and tympanum above both exuberantly carved, the latter with a diminutive St Michael defending himself with a cross against a very much larger dragon. Flanking the door is an order of spiral shafts and several rows of continuous mouldings. The inside of the church is a disappointment, sadly Victorianised.

## Fawley Court

*31; 1 mile N of Henley-on-Thames on A4155*

An H-plan William and Mary house, Fawley Court is now a Catholic boys' school. Though much Georgianised on the outside, it is considerably better within: the Saloon in particular has first-rate stucco work of 1691, and there is good decoration in the Library and 'Museum' by James Wyatt, who also designed the Island Temple in the grounds (technically over the border in Berkshire).

John Freeman, the house's second owner, was an amateur architect of some distinction. He refitted the nearby ST MARY'S CHURCH at his own expense and built the family mausoleum, domed and octagonal, which stands in its churchyard.

## Fingest

*32; 6 miles SW of High Wycombe off B482*

This charming little village at the edge of the Cotswolds is famous for the colossal Norman tower of ST BARTHOLOMEW'S CHURCH – 27 feet square, and topped by a twin saddleback roof of uncertain age. It has two round-headed bell openings quite separate from each other on each of the four sides, several tiny windows lower down, and a good but sadly inappropriate late thirteenth-century one at the bottom to the west. The nave and chancel, much smaller, have features of Norman, Early English, Decorated and Perpendicular, but are of no special interest.

## Gerrards Cross

*33; 20 miles W of London on A40*

The CHURCH OF ST JAMES is a most extraordinary work by Sir William Tite, architect of the Royal Exchange. Its style can best be described as Neo-Byzantine, with a healthy admixture of Victorian Gothic and just a touch of *chinoiserie*. The composition includes an unusually high north-west campanile and a dome with dormers.

## Hanslope

*34; 6 miles NE of Stony Stratford off A508*

The lovely white pinnacled tower of ST JAMES'S, its slender spire anchored by flying buttresses, is one of the glories of Buckinghamshire. The late Norman chancel with its blank arcading and corbel table is also worth a close look. Inside, there are good broad proportions and a fine chancel arch; but the walls have been hideously scraped, and insensitive restoration generally has taken away much of the atmosphere.

## Harleyford Manor

*35; 4 miles NE of Henley-on-Thames on A4155*

A lovely house on the banks of the Thames, it was built in 1755 by Sir Robert Taylor – his first country house; the grounds are said to be by Capability Brown. The room behind the great bow facing the river has fine plasterwork. The house would probably not have been relegated to this short list had it not been for several years a vast building site and caravan park. The intention is apparently to convert it into flats. How much of its beauty will ultimately be preserved is anybody's guess.

## High Wycombe

*36; 18 miles NE of Reading on A40*

The town is worth including for the sake of Henry Keene's GUILDHALL of 1757, its open ground floor raised on a Tuscan arcade, its roof crowned with an enchanting little colonnaded cupola. Robert Adam's rebuilding of the MARKET HALL opposite is disappointing in comparison – partly, perhaps, because of the shallow dome and lantern with which it was covered in about 1900.

## Hughenden Manor

*NT; 37; 1½ miles N of High Wycombe on A4128*

The simple Georgian house was 'quite ruthlessly dramatized' – I quote Pevsner – for Benjamin Disraeli in 1862. Here he lived until his death in 1881 and here, in the park, he is buried. Architecturally it is a bit of a joke; but as a monument to the High Victorian age shaped and symbolised by its owner, a joy.

## Ivinghoe

*38; 9½ miles NE of Aylesbury on B488*
*Includes Pitstone Windmill (NT)*

ST MARY'S is a large and impressive church, basically thirteenth-century, with a slightly later crossing-tower. It boasts beautifully Early English five-bay arcades with exquisite stiff-leaf carving, and fine timber roofs with angels and Apostles. If only Street had not got his hands on it in 1871 . . . .

Parts of PITSTONE WINDMILL (NT) nearby, which has recently been restored to full working order, go back as far as 1627.

## Long Crendon

*39; 2 miles N of Thame on B4011*
*Includes Long Crendon Courthouse (NT)*

ST MARY'S CHURCH is large and imposing, with a tall Perpendicular crossing-tower. Most of the rest is, however, Early English, and there is a Decorated north aisle – considerably broader than the Early English south one. There is a magnificent Decorated window in the north transept, too, of which the chancel east window is a nineteenth-century copy. Several fine old houses can be seen in the village, including the fifteenth-century COURTHOUSE (NT).

## Maids' Moreton

*40; 1 mile NE of Buckingham on A413*

The 'Maids' concerned were two spinster sisters of the Peover family, who are said to have endowed and built ST EDMUND'S CHURCH in the mid-fifteenth century. The immense transomed nave windows and still larger ones to east and west flood the church with light. There is some intricate and most unusual cusping in the windows on the upper stage of the tower and over the north door, and fan vaulting can be seen in both the tower and the porches.

## Marlow Place

*41; 4 miles N of Maidenhead on A4155*

Almost certainly by Thomas Archer, Marlow Place was built in 1720, probably for the future George II. Quietly eccentric like all Archer's work, particularly in the capitals of the angle pilasters and the front door surround, it is nevertheless a fine example of a noble provincial town house of the period.

## North Marston

*42; 3 miles NW of Whitchurch off A413*

The oldest parts of ST MARY'S CHURCH date from the twelfth and thirteenth centuries, but the outstanding features are all of the fifteenth, paid for by Edward IV in return for the relics of John Schorne, a miracle-working local vicar who had one day captured the Devil and imprisoned him in a boot. The church was restored – on the whole, well – by Sir Matthew Digby Wyatt at the expense of Queen Victoria.

## Twyford

*43; 5 miles NE of Reading on B3024*

The CHURCH OF THE ASSUMPTION, like St Peter and St Paul at Dinton, is chiefly remarkable for its Norman south doorway. There is no tympanum this time but a frieze of heads, seven stars rising in a row up the jambs, and lions fighting on the capitals of the three orders of supporting columns. Beak-head appears on the left-hand side of the chancel arch, now completely stylised into a simple triangular ornament. There is a fine Perpendicular timber roof with kingposts and good plain fifteenth-century benches.

# Cambridgeshire

The county was vastly increased in size in 1974 by the addition of Huntingdonshire, to which the Soke of Peterborough had been added only seven years before. It is consequently a good deal richer architecturally than it used to be, and still more heterogeneous; geographically, however, it remains – to me at any rate – a hard county to love. It is, for the most part, quite remarkably flat, and oddly featureless; and where it can provide a little relief – in both senses of the word – as in the Gog Magog Hills in the south, the land is too built up to give any real pleasure. There are those, I am aware, upon whom the Fens in the northern part of the county exert a curious spell, romantic and even exciting; and in the days of Hereward the Wake, or indeed at any time before the first great draining operations undertaken by the 5th Earl of Bedford and the Dutch engineer Cornelius Vermuyden in the 1630s, I suppose (though without much conviction) that I might have fallen under it myself. But not today. Those monotonous, misty expanses of nothing in particular under that immense Cambridgeshire sky seem to me at best boring and at worst quite unutterably bleak.

Thank God, then, for the buildings. The county, as circumscribed by its present boundaries, possesses wonderful things indeed. First of all comes the town and University of Cambridge itself, which in its ensemble is even lovelier than Oxford, thanks in large measure to the way it uses its river, an invaluable asset which Oxford seems virtually to ignore. Nor, among individual buildings, does the latter possess anything to compare with King's College Chapel, surely one of the most breathtaking monuments of all England. And King's is only a beginning: several other college chapels (Wren's at Emmanuel, for example, or that extraordinary achievement by an unknown architect at Peterhouse) remain stubbornly in the memory, as does the spacious neoclassicism of Downing, the sheer opulence of Trinity, or the irresistible Renaissance conceits of Dr Caius in the college which bears his name.

Cambridge University could of course always afford good building stone, most of it brought by water from Northamptonshire, Peterborough or Rutland. Few of its neighbouring towns, however, were so lucky: apart from a narrow belt of carstone – whose brown cobbles are never a very satisfactory material at the best of times – and the chalk in the south-east that yielded a certain amount of clunch, the county had to rely for the most part on other resources: timber, flint and, above all, brick. Brick came early – as early as the fourteenth century – to this part of England, and by the first half of the fifteenth we find the First Court of Queens' College faced entirely in it. From thenceforth it was almost *de rigueur* for important domestic architecture: the Bishop's Palace at Ely, Kirtling Tower, Madingley, Wimpole – these are all of brick, as is practically the whole town of Wisbech. One's only regret is that from time to time, in Cambridge and its neighbourhood, the builders should for some reason have decided to forsake the rich mellow red brick for that nasty, anaemic, dirty yellow stuff that detracts so much from the beauty of any building for which it is used.

The redrawing of the boundaries that took effect in 1974, deplorable as it was, enriched Cambridgeshire not only architecturally but geologically as well, by presenting it with the quarries of Barnack limestone, together with a quantity of superb parish churches built wholly or partly thereof. (Many more are of the very similar stone which comes from Ketton, just across the border of what is now Lincolnshire.) The county gained in addition Peterborough Cathedral, and two outstanding Anglo-Saxon monuments from the Soke of Peterborough – the tower at Barnack and that astonishing *coup de théâtre*, the chancel arch at Wittering.

It seems unfair that a single medium-sized county which can already boast King's College Chapel should also possess two of the dozen most spectacular cathedrals in England; but no one, surely, who has stood before the great west front of Peterborough or has gazed upward from the crossing into Alan of Walsingham's lantern at Ely would cavil at the claim. Together, the two provide a perfect illustration of the development of the Norman style – early as in the nave at Ely; middle as in that of the nave, and in particular the glorious transepts, at Peterborough; late, as at Ely again, in the infirmary and infirmary chapel. Some might regret the absence of vaulting in both naves; both, on the other hand, possess the immeasurable advantage of a vista right through to the east end, uninterrupted by organ or screen; and the painted wooden roofs of both cathedrals – but especially the medieval one at Peterborough – are in their own ways so successful that I for one would not wish for anything different.

Of the memorable parish churches in what must still, I think, be thought of as Greater Cambridgeshire, the choice has not been easy. There are some, however, which no list could possibly omit: of Norman churches, Castor and – despite the recent fire – Ickleton; of Early English, Etton, Somersham, Histon (for those extraordinary transepts) and Leighton Bromswold with its seventeenth-century additions by George Herbert. The Decorated style presents us with some problems: the crossing and Lady Chapel at Ely seem to have overshadowed everything else. But St Mary the Less at Cambridge certainly deserves a mention, together with several remarkable individual windows – Soham, Sutton, Yaxley, and the otherwise disappointing church of St Peter and St Paul at Wisbech – to say nothing of the lovely chancel at Fenstanton in which stands the tomb of Capability Brown. With the coming of the Perpendicular we get the miraculous timber roofs at Willingham and March and – to me the pearl of them all – the whole ensemble of Burwell, a symphony in clunch. Of post-Reformation churches there is not much to be said; Little Gidding has received a well-deserved star, but more for its atmosphere of peace and quiet serenity than for any architectural excellence.

Among secular buildings the county now includes that rarity of rarities, a Norman manor house with a twelfth-century upper hall, overlooking the Ouse at Hemingford Grey; and, at Burghley, one of the greatest of Elizabethan extravaganzas. Milton, just outside Peterborough, is also Tudor in its origins; but it was added to so much over the next three centuries that it could now stand as a three-dimensional history of English architecture. Milton is still, I am delighted to say, used for the purpose for which it was intended – as a private country house. Two of its principal companions, however, have been less fortunate: Peter Mills's Thorpe Hall and Vanbrugh's Kimbolton. But the latter is loved and cherished by the school which now occupies it and there is nothing, inside or out, to suggest that it has fallen on evil days. The other great Cambridgeshire mansion, Wimpole, is now the property of the National Trust and looks today as magnificent as it ever has – which is to say very magnificent indeed.

Apart from Cambridge, there is only one other town that deserves a mention for itself rather than for any individual buildings in it. That town is Wisbech. It is only a mile or two from Lincolnshire, and even nearer to Norfolk; and yet it remains, somehow, quintessentially Cambridgeshire – with the best approach, via the Brinks, to any English town I know. It is the first view of Wisbech, from the south-west, that invariably comes to my mind whenever I think of Cambridgeshire; together with the sight of King's, towering white above the Backs, and the distant view of Ely, looming over the Fens. Perhaps there is something to be said for so much flatness, after all.

---

## Alconbury

*1; 4½ miles NW of Huntingdon off A1*

ST PETER AND ST PAUL is a really lovely church, essentially of the late thirteenth century, built entirely of the fine local stone. The first thing one notices is the big central tower – which closer inspection actually reveals to be a little off-centre – carrying a tall broach spire with three tiers of lucarnes. The chancel is pure Early English with its three stepped lancets at the east end, and the nave must be more or less contemporary – note the Y-tracery in the clerestory. The south aisle too has a lancet and a thirteenth-century doorway, so the two later windows (one Decorated, one Perpendicular) must be later alterations; the north, on the other hand, is virtually all Decorated, so must be a generation or so after.

The interior is broad and spacious; but one's eye is immediately drawn to the chancel. The three eastern lancets are opulently shafted on the inside; but instead of leaving it at that, the medieval masons have continued the shafting all along the north and south walls, giving a wonderful feeling of richness and elegance. When I saw it in the summer of 1982, it was undergoing careful restoration; it should be looking glorious by the time this book is published.

## Barnack*

*2; 8 miles NW of Peterborough on B1443*

The CHURCH OF ST JOHN THE BAPTIST may not be the most beautiful church in Cambridgeshire; but it is unquestionably one of the most interesting. Its story begins with the tower – or at least its bottom two stages. It was

*Christ in Majesty, church of St John the Baptist, Barnack.*

probably begun half a century or so before the Norman Conquest, and reads like a text-book of Anglo-Saxon architecture: the long-and-short work at the corners, the lesenes (those thin pilaster strips that seem to serve no useful purpose), the triangular heads to the windows. Note, too, the little decorative plaques with birds carved on them in relief. Two centuries later, a third stage was added to the tower, with tall two-light windows under round containing arches, spirelets at the corners, and a stubby octagonal spire which must be one of the earliest in England. Beneath the tower stands an old Saxon throne, of stone like the church – the old quarries, known as the 'Hills and Holes', are just outside the village to the south – which was probably used by the local lord while administering justice.

The three-bay nave arcades make it clear that the north side is slightly earlier than the south: the former has round piers, the latter has ones with a quatrefoil section. This is further borne out by the two doorways, where the capitals have water-leaf carving on the north and stiff-leaf on the south. Later than either is the Decorated chancel, with its glorious east window of five steeply stepped lights and the most curious tracery – which Pevsner compares with that of Milan Cathedral. The Perpendicular style is represented by the south (Walcot) chapel: good, but hardly spectacular.

Before leaving, look long and hard at the late Saxon relief carving of Christ in Majesty. It is one of the most astonishingly assured and powerful works of its date in the country, and would alone make a visit to Barnack worthwhile.

## Bottisham

*3; 6 miles E of Cambridge on A45*

HOLY TRINITY CHURCH dominates the large but fairly undistinguished village around it, and looks splendid from a distance across the flat Fen country – especially its tall west tower, begun in the early-to-middle thirteenth century (the narrow lancet windows of the lower stage), continued in the fourteenth (the Decorated two-light bell openings) and finished off in the early fifteenth with the usual battlements and pinnacles. Attached to it is a galilee – a tall west porch obviously inspired by that of Ely Cathedral and, judging from its lancets, built very soon afterwards. Why its west door was deliberately and rather clumsily reduced in size by much flint in-filling remains a mystery.

Inside, the nave dates from 1310 or thereabouts – the reign of Edward II which, deeply unsatisfactory as it was in most other ways, coincided with that most exciting moment of English medieval church building when the Gothic style was in transition from the Early English to the Decorated, but had not yet lost its freshness and vigour and gone, as it were, over the top. The clerestory, which one would expect to be later – they nearly always are – is in this instance contemporary: a row of simple lancets, whose gentle cusps are the only hint of the luxuriance to come. The aisle windows, on the other hand, go a good deal further in this direction, and there is some pretty blank arcading, inside and out, on the walls. The roof, too, keeps up the general high standard, without being particularly showy. So does the chancel, though the east windows are Victorian. Two splendid fourteenth-century wooden parclose screens and several good tombs – don't miss that of the Allington children – complete one's pleasure.

## Burghley House

*4; 1 mile E of Stamford off B1443*

This great mansion is the creation of William Cecil, whom Queen Elizabeth appointed her Secretary of State within a year of her accession to the throne and whom she elevated to the peerage as Lord Burghley thirteen years later, in 1571. During four decades he was the greatest power in the land after the Queen herself, amassing an immense fortune – a good deal of which he spent on building. (As well as Burghley, he was also responsible for the even larger Theobalds in Hertfordshire, which his son was to make over to James I in exchange for Hatfield.)

It is, by any standards, a tremendous house. The size of a small village, it stands magnificently on a slight elevation, looking across Capability Brown's broad deer park to the lake beyond – that incredible skyline of towers and turrets and pinnacles and soaring chimney-stacks making it one of the most fantastically picturesque of all the great Elizabethan prodigy houses. The building took over thirty years (for ten of which, however, its owner was largely occupied with Theobalds) and the design seems to have been Burghley's own – at least as much as anybody else's. He began in 1556 with the east range, in which he sited the nucleus of the house – the kitchen and the Hall, whose immense bay window is the predominant feature of the elevation. The three other façades are later, and a good deal more showy; the west front in particular, which bears the date 1577, has a formidable Tudor Gatehouse in a style that was becoming a little old-fashioned, with high polygonal angle turrets; the archway is closed by a superb pair of wrought-iron gates by Tijou. The south front has what used to be an open loggia of nine bays which, like so many others of its kind, has now been closed. Finally the north front, of 1587, breaks forward twice to the main entrance and, at its east end, a long advancing projection ends in a five-stage tower with an ogival cap.

Of the rooms within, only the Hall and kitchen remain substantially unchanged since Burghley's day, the kitchen having preserved its high stone vault rising to the central louvre, the Hall its steeply pitched double hammer-beam roof. Note well, however, the vast fireplace. Where the outside of Burghley and most of the Hall itself remains entirely Gothic, this extraordinary piece is purely of the Renaissance. It set the scene for much that was to follow.

The present screens passage – it is not the original one – brings us out into the central courtyard, dominated by the most remarkable single feature in all Burghley: the immense frontispiece, crowned by what appears at first sight to be a church spire but is in fact a broad but tapering obelisk, supported by rampant lions. Each of the three storeys below it consists of pairs of flanking columns – rising Doric–Ionic–Corinthian in the approved style – separated by round-headed niches. The centre on the ground floor takes the form of a wide archway; above that is a deep niche framing a bust, and above that again a transomed bay window. All this dates from the 1560s; the obelisk and supporters, however, are an afterthought of 1585. The arcades on each side were originally open to form a loggia; but this, like that of the south front, has now been walled up.

One other feature of the house that has been preserved intact since the sixteenth century is the tunnel-vaulted 'Roman Staircase' just north of the Hall. The type is familiar enough in Italy, where it is to be found in scores of Renaissance *palazzi* in Rome, Florence and elsewhere, as well as in the *Scala d'Oro* of the Doge's Palace in Venice. What is surprising here, however, is the design of the landings, which have rib vaults and central pendants – an odd piece of vestigial Gothic amid the classicism.

The rest of the interior is largely due to the 5th Earl of Exeter, who transformed it during the last two decades of the seventeenth century. He certainly was responsible for the sumptuous series of rooms along the first floor of the west range – they had previously formed the Long Gallery – and the state rooms, known as the George Rooms, around the corner facing south. There are fine plaster ceilings by Edward Martin, fantastic wood carvings by Grinling Gibbons, and some marvellous French and English furniture including a stunning James II state bed. The painting of the George Rooms is largely the work of Verrio, and there is much too much of it; as so easily happens with Baroque architecture and decoration, the atmosphere becomes stiflingly oppressive and one longs for air. I prefer Laguerre's painted Ballroom in the north range and – best of all – the two great eighteenth-century Halls on the ground floor, whose comparative restraint comes like a cool breeze after the excesses upstairs. Near the top of the staircase is a charming Chapel which is also more eighteenth-century than anything else, despite more *tours de force* by Gibbons and an altarpiece by Veronese.

There is a vast quantity of pictures, collected principally by the 5th and 9th Earls, all wonderfully revealing of the English tastes of their time. Many of them are superb – they include a memorable Rembrandt of his mother and a Cranach of Martin Luther – and they deserve a good deal more attention than they usually get. They incurred, however, the stern disapproval of Celia Fiennes when she visited Burghley in May 1697:'very fine paint in pictures, but they were all without Garments or very little, that was the only fault, the immodesty of the Pictures especially in my Lords apartment . . . .'

Capability Brown first came to Burghley in 1756, and worked there on and off as both landscape gardener and architect for the next quarter of a century. Inside the house he seems to have been responsible, *inter alia*, for the Gothick ceiling of the Billiard Room; he also made minor alterations to the south front. In the park, his are the charming Gothick Orangery and Stables, the pretty three-arch bridge and the Neo-Jacobean Bath-house. But his grandest creation is the park itself, one of the loveliest in England.

## Burwell*

*5; 9½ miles NE of Cambridge on B1102*

Only a few miles from Suffolk, ST MARY'S CHURCH at Burwell is – together with that of St Mary the Great in Cambridge itself – Cambridgeshire's nearest equivalent to the splendid Perpendicular wool churches of the next county: Long Melford, Lavenham and the rest. It stands at the southern end of the long, straggling village, on high ground (or what passes for high in this part of the world). The material is the usual East Anglian flint, with dressings of brave Barnack limestone, and the long row of three-light clerestory windows, set so close together that there is virtually no space at all between them, leaves one in no doubt that here is no ordinary village church, but something rather special.

The west tower is at first a bit of a puzzle. For one thing, it is quite obviously a good deal older than the rest of the building, and a closer look at the north wall indeed reveals traces of Norman work – including a blocked Norman window just below the clock face. Clearly, the fifteenth-century architects kept at least part of the original tower, on to whose square base they proceeded to add an octagonal stage with diagonal buttresses, a stair turret to the south-west, battlements and pinnacles. The little open lantern, pretty enough in its way but distinctly out of place in this context, is a later addition.

Both north and south porches are rich – the north one is actually fan-vaulted – but even they hardly prepare one for the opulence of the interior. On entering the nave, one's first impression is of almost limitless light and space; then one's eyes are led upwards to the magnificent wooden roof of intricately carved arched braces, between which runs a wall plate, or wooden frieze, of affronted pairs of mythical beasts. Below this is the clerestory, two windows to each bay, and below these the entire wall space down to and including the spandrels of the arcade is covered with blank tracery. In a further virtuoso touch, the east wall of the nave, above the chancel arch, is pierced with a highly elaborate wheel window with mouchettes instead of spokes, giving it the appearance of a spinning Catherine wheel. Just below it, together with another splendid display of ornamental tracery, runs an inscription commemorating the benefactors and giving the date 1464.

The same design of roof continues across both the broad aisles and into the chancel – more palatial even than the nave, its pale green glass giving a slightly underwater effect. All round it, between the windows, are niches with high crocketed canopies, resting on angelic supporters; more angels, often with musical instruments, adorn the corbels supporting the braces of the roof; still more do a similar job in the aisles.

One final point: virtually the whole interior of this marvellous building is of the local clunch, a material too often unjustly disparaged. Externally used, it does indeed stand up badly to wind and weather; but if properly protected from the elements, as here, it lasts superbly well; much of the carving at Burwell has as fine an edge today as it did five centuries ago. The creamy whiteness, too, adds much to a Perpendicular more-glass-than-wall church like this one.

*The great gateway, Christ's College, Cambridge.*

## CAMBRIDGE
*49 miles N of London off M11*

### Christ's College
*6; St Andrew's Street*

Originally founded by the Rev. William Bingham in 1439, Christ's College was first named, with commendable modesty, God's House. A year or two later, however, the site was needed by Henry VI for his new foundation, King's. Bingham ultimately chose somewhere else, but building progress was slow and it was not till 1505 that Lady Margaret Beaufort, mother of Henry VII and Henry VI's second cousin, took matters in hand and refounded the College under its new name.

As you approach Christ's along St Andrew's Street, the first thing that strikes you is the great GATEWAY, with its outsize coat of arms. (The supporters are yales, rare animals even by mythical standards, with the still rarer ability to rotate their horns at will.) This is of Lady Margaret's time; all the rest of the long, low street frontage, however, is an early eighteenth-century remodelling, ashlar-faced, with crenellations and, to the north side, broad generous sash windows at first-floor level. The inside of FIRST COURT is also largely eighteenth-century, though a little later in date – the work of that admirable Cambridge architect James Essex. Its charm lies in its variety and its cheerful lack of any formal composition. The east side contains the MASTER'S LODGE, its pretty oriel repeating Lady Margaret's coat of arms, and the Hall – marked by the tall bay window. Inside, this proves a disappointment, having been almost completely rebuilt by G.G. Scott Jun. in the 1870s.

In the north range is the CHAPEL with its tall ashlared turret and pretty eighteenth-century top. Most of the fabric is original, as are the two vestries to the north and the mighty moulded beams of the ante-chapel. Original too is the ceiling, though it was restored and painted towards the end of the nineteenth century. But perhaps the best feature of all is the fifteenth- and sixteenth-century stained glass in the windows along the north side, almost certainly from the royal workshops.

After this First Court, the next building of any importance to be added to Christ's was FELLOWS' BUILDING, some way beyond it towards the gardens. It has three storeys, plus dormers in the hipped roof, and is eleven bays long – an important and ambitious building, therefore, with a firm statement to make. The date is 1640–3, and the design used to be attributed to Inigo Jones, all stylistic evidence to the contrary notwithstanding. In fact it is almost certainly the work of a local architect. Thomas Grumbold, perhaps? We shall never know.

The problem with Christ's is that as an architectural entity it is curiously shapeless. First Court is coherent enough, but Fellows' Building is already too far away from it to relate in any significant manner, and the nineteenth- and twentieth-century buildings (there are none of the eighteenth) have failed to pull the whole thing together. North-west of Fellows' Building, towards Hobson Street, two uninspired post-war blocks by Sir Albert Richardson were added to an equally boring nineteenth-century one to form another loosely knit court which provides little aesthetic pleasure. Far more exciting is Sir Denys Lasdun's spectacular new addition along King Street, with undergraduates' rooms arranged in seven tiers of terracing most sensitively landscaped. Seen from a distance to the south the effect is spectacular; but again it is all too far away to make any real contribution to the ensemble.

## Clare College

*7; Trinity Hall Lane*

If Christ's lacks cohesion, Clare is surely the most tightly knit of all Cambridge colleges. This statement was perhaps truer still before the building of Sir Giles Gilbert Scott's Memorial Court in the 1920s; but though the College now has two distinct sections, with the Cam flowing between them, each of these sections forms a complete and self-contained unit with the river less of a dividing line than an axis of symmetry. It is, moreover, spanned by the prettiest of all the Cambridge bridges and the earliest to be built in the classical idiom. The architect was Thomas Grumbold; the date 1640.

Since Clare has no medieval buildings one tends to forget that it is the oldest Cambridge college after Peterhouse. The University acquired the site as early as 1298, and the present College was actually founded forty years later by a granddaughter of Edward I, Lady Elizabeth de Clare. In those days – and indeed till 1856 – it was known as Clare Hall. All its original buildings are gone, destroyed in a fire in 1521; gone too are their successors, which seem to have been inadequate affairs from the start. It was only in 1638 that work began on the buildings as we know them today.

Four years later the east and south ranges were finished; but then came the Civil War and the Commonwealth, and the hiatus in building operations continued until 1669. By 1690 the court was complete except for the west range north of the gateway, and that followed in 1705–15. Thus the whole job was done in three-quarters of a century, with a uniform style maintained throughout. Of the old part of the College as we know it, only the Chapel remained unbuilt; that, in the form of an eastward projection from the north-east corner of the court up to Trinity Lane, had to wait another fifty years.

All four ranges share the same basic features, but there is enough development of style to avoid monotony. Thus in the earliest (east) range there are still a few Gothic features – notably the fan-vaulted GATEHOUSE, though plenty of classical motifs appear here as well – but these gradually die out as the work progresses. The south range with its broad central pediment is made even more impressive by its situation, looking out as it does over the lawn of King's – with such a proprietorial air that most visitors assume that it is part of King's and not Clare at all. But it is above all with the west range that this tremendous building comes into its own, for this is the view that one sees from the river, the bridge and the famous gardens, surely the loveliest in Cambridge. By the time this range was built, Wren had made his mark on the University, and his influence is there for all to see in the giant Ionic pilasters between the bays – just as it is in the north range, almost certainly the work of Robert Grumbold, Thomas's son. This range alone is of two storeys, since it contains the HALL. One would love to have seen it in its original form; alas, it was remodelled in 1870 by Sir Matthew Digby Wyatt – an intervention as disastrous as Scott Jun.'s at Christ's.

And so to the CHAPEL. It was designed by Sir James Burrough, Master of Gonville and Caius, who occupies a position at Cambridge as an amateur architect analogous to that held at Oxford by Dean Aldrich and Dr George Clarke; unfortunately, however, he never saw it completed, having died in 1764, only a year after the work was begun. The exterior – obviously derived on the east from Wren's design for Pembroke Chapel – is not particularly distinguished; inside, one is surprised (and enchanted) to find an octagonal ante-chapel, lit from a glazed cupola. The chapel itself is barrel-vaulted but of no special interest.

The new buildings erected across the river by Sir Giles Gilbert Scott between 1923 and 1934 to accommodate the huge influx of students after the First World War are perfectly agreeable in a nice, safe, Georgian way; but they can hardly be called exciting.

## Corpus Christi College

*8; Trumpington Street*

The only college in either Oxford or Cambridge to have been founded not by an individual but by two town guilds – those of Corpus Christi and of the Blessed Virgin Mary – it started in 1352 in a very small way, with just a Master, two scholars and two servants, a hall, kitchen, library, offices and the minimum of accommodation. There was no chapel, only the neighbouring church of St Benet's (*q.v.*) to which it was connected around 1500 by a two-storey brick passageway.

The miracle is that, in OLD COURT, these first buildings have survived, largely unaltered apart from some of the windows and the addition of buttresses and garrets in the very early sixteenth century. No other court in Cambridge is so redolent of the Middle Ages. (At Oxford, Mob Quad at Merton is the nearest counterpart.) The rubble walls are plastered on the sides towards the court – they have been left uncovered on the outside, facing the churchyard and Free School Lane – and though certain of the windows have been changed, a good many (for example on the ground floor of the west range) retain their original cusped lights, all dating from before 1377 when the court was completed. The Saxon tower of St Benet's peeks up, agreeably if asymmetrically, above the roof of multicoloured small tiles – a Cambridgeshire speciality. The original HALL, which was subsequently converted into the College kitchens, occupied the south side of the court, just east of the central doorway. It is marked by two four-light Perpendicular windows and an eighteenth-century bay. Next to it, in the corner, is the MASTER'S LODGE, with its pretty little seventeenth-century timber window.

NEW COURT lies to the south and west, and has its principal entrance on Trumpington Street. It is by William Wilkins and dates from 1823–7. The style is early Tudor, complete with GATEHOUSE – which looks a bit stunted since the addition of the extra attic floor to the rest of the range in 1920. Wilkins, we are told, was particularly proud of it, but it is hard to see why. The general effect seems far too symmetrical and ordered for the late Gothic idiom; something, somewhere, ought to ramble a bit, and absolutely nothing does. The HALL, with its William Morris wallpaper and tremendous Royal Arms, is to the north – on your left as you enter – and the CHAPEL opposite you to the east, its twin turrets echoing those of the Gatehouse; but in these, too, Wilkins's inspiration seems to have deserted him. Far more worth visiting is the LIBRARY, which occupies nearly all the embattled range to the south. It contains the greatest collection of Anglo-Saxon manuscripts in the world and a number of other, later, illuminated books of spellbinding beauty.

## Downing College

*9; Regent Street*

It was 1717 when Sir George Downing died; but such were the complications of his will and the length of the litigation which followed that the charter for the college he wished to establish was not granted till 1800 – and it was another seven years before work started on the Neo-Grecian composition designed by William Wilkins. The College as we see it today is not precisely as Wilkins intended. He died leaving it unfinished, and then the money ran out. (Most of it had gone on the litigation.) Edward Barry carried on the work in the 1870s, Sir Herbert Baker was called in in 1929, and the central range, with the apsed Chapel behind it, was completed only in 1953 by A.T. Scott. Yet although these last three all departed in greater or lesser degrees from Wilkins's initial conception, enough of it remains for us to see just how original it was.

For Downing College is nothing like any other college at either of the two ancient universities. It is built on the open campus plan, which Wilkins must take the credit for having invented: his design predates by a decade Jefferson's for the University of Virginia. Essentially, it consists of a long central range to the north and two even longer ranges, broken about a quarter of the way along their length, extending southwards from each end; the western range ending in the marble-pilastered HALL, the eastern in the MASTER'S LODGE. Wilkins actually envisaged a fourth range to the south, which would in theory have formed a quadrangle; but the dimensions are such – a good 100 yards across and perhaps 130 in length – that it would never have seemed like one. The impression with which one is left is that of smooth and spacious lawns framed by Ionic temples of pale honey-coloured stone against a backdrop of trees. The hubbub of central Cambridge suddenly seems far away.

## Emmanuel College

*10; St Andrew's Street*

Founded in 1584 by Sir Walter Mildmay, Chancellor of the Exchequer to Queen Elizabeth, Emmanuel was intended for the training of Protestant clergymen. Before the Dissolution of the Monasteries, the site had been occupied by the Cambridge house of the Dominican Friars, but their still-existing buildings offended Sir Walter's puritanical susceptibilities; he therefore built his Hall on the site of their old church, and his Chapel at right-angles to it, on a deliberately chosen north–south axis. These two buildings, constituting respectively the south and east ranges of what is misleadingly known as NEW COURT, are the oldest in the College, though neither is any longer of particular interest. The Hall still serves its original purpose, despite a drastic remodelling by

James Essex in the 1760s, which included an elegant plaster ceiling; the Chapel, however, became a Library when the College commissioned a new Chapel from Sir Christopher Wren in 1666, and was converted again by George Drysdale in 1932.

This new CHAPEL dominates FRONT COURT, which is separated from New Court by the Hall range. It stands in the centre of the east side, an unusual placing doubtless inspired by Wren's uncle's Chapel at Peterhouse (*q.v.*). It is thus the first building you see when you enter Emmanuel beneath its understated Ionic portico from St Andrew's Street, and it lifts the spirit at once. It consists essentially of a three-bay Corinthian portico with a broken pediment supported on pilasters and half columns. On the ground floor is an arcaded loggia, with cross-windows above and a frieze of garlands above them. The break of the pediment contains a clock, surmounted by a tall lantern with cupola; at the corners, acroteria with urns. The loggia and cross-windows are continued beneath hipped roofs for five bays on each side, until they meet the two side ranges – the HALL RANGE to the north, and the so-called WESTMORLAND BUILDING (1719–22) to the south. The result is a composition which is beautiful certainly, but is also, in its

*The Fitzwilliam Museum, Cambridge.*

surprisingly small scale, refreshingly light-hearted and unpompous; the Pembroke Chapel is solemn in comparison. The interior is much what one might expect, with a sumptuous plaster ceiling and a glorious communion rail by Wren's favourite carpenter, Edward Pearce.

One other ancient building deserves special mention. This is known as BRICK BUILDING, or OLD COURT – a curious description since it is a straight single range built in 1633–4. It runs for ten bays southward from the east end of Westmorland Building at a quite surprising height, since it is of three storeys with garrets and dormers above. It has a big shaped gable at the southern end. Beyond it, yet further to the south, is the Arts-and-Craftsy LIBRARY (of 1909, by Leonard Stokes) and, a little to the west, Tom Hancock's brick-faced SOUTH COURT, its plan a rather wonky H with the Junior Common Room taking up the cross-bar. At the other end of the College, across Emmanuel Street and approached through a depressingly lavatorial tiled tunnel, is Stokes's other contribution, NORTH COURT, which he completed just before the First World War. Its quirkish mixture of styles is not for the purist, but there is obviously an original and imaginative mind at work – and that alone gives us sufficient cause to be grateful.

## Fitzwilliam Museum

*11; Trumpington Street*

The wealth of the Fitzwilliam is so great, one's eagerness to get inside so pressing, that one seldom bothers to look at it very carefully. This is a pity; for though the building admittedly falls some way short of classical perfection, it has much to interest and even instruct. The architect, from its beginning in 1834 until he fell to his death from Ely Cathedral in 1845, was George Basevi; and in the Fitzwilliam he gives the perfect demonstration of how, at just about the time of Victoria's accession, neo-classicism lost its former purity and coolness, becoming more dramatic, restless, almost Baroque. Take, for example, the way the giant columns of the portico continue round the recessed bays on either side, only to be echoed once again in the fluted pilasters of the projecting wings.

After Basevi's death the work was carried on by C.R. Cockerell, and was only completed, by Edward Barry, in 1875. Barry's, it need hardly be said, is the great Staircase Hall, like that of a very grand London club.

## Gonville and Caius College

*12; Trinity Street*

The College is called after its two successive founders, Edmund Gonville and Dr John Kay – who, after the academic fashion of the time, Latinised his name. It is by this name (pronounced 'keys') that the College is almost universally known; and quite right too, for it was Dr Caius who in 1557 took up the obscure and impecunious Gonville Hall – originally founded in 1348 – obtained for it a new charter, became Master two years later, and continued to enlarge and enrich it until shortly before his death in 1573.

The buildings of the old foundation were all grouped round what is still known as GONVILLE COURT, apart from two small houses between it and Trinity Lane. The Chapel formed the south wing, and it was on the further side of this that Caius now began work on the court that bears his name, adding wings to the east and west but leaving the south open 'lest the air from being confined within a narrow space should become foul, and so do harm to us'. (As the foremost physician in England, one who had studied at Padua with the great Vesalius, his ideas on health and hygiene were far in advance of his time.) His two-storey stone wings are pleasant enough with their rows of three-light windows, though they could hardly be called exciting; but Dr Caius soon made up for this unadventurous display. He now turned his attention to a series of three allegorical Gateways, each intended to symbolise a step in the student's career through the University. The first, the GATE OF HUMILITY, was an appropriately simple affair which has since been moved from its original location on Trinity Street and now adorns the Master's garden; the other two, however, mark significant steps not just for Dr Caius's students, but for British architecture itself.

Having passed through the Gate of Humility, the student would cross what is now TREE COURT and come to the GATE OF VIRTUE. This is one of the earliest buildings in the country to have been inspired, not just in its decoration but in its whole architecture, by the Italian Renaissance. Caius designed it himself, and it was finished in 1567. The principal side, facing east, has three storeys, each composed of three bays separated by Ionic pilasters. At the base is a round-headed arch with figures of Victory in the spandrels; on each of the first and second floors is a single three-light window, square and very plain; and the whole thing is surmounted by a most curious attic with circles and lozenges set into a sort of grid and a little triangular pediment on top.

With the Gate of Virtue safely behind him, the student would now turn, as it were, sharp left and pass through the GATE OF HONOUR – and so into the Old Schools across Senate House Passage, where he would finally receive his degree. This third Gate is the most astonishing of all. A row of four Ionic columns – pilasters towards the south – enclose a four-centred arch and, at each side, odd rectangular niches with canted walls; these in turn support an entablature above which there stands, over the middle bay, a complete classical temple façade in miniature. On each side of this temple, curved sidepieces swoop down in traditional Italian style to end at four corner obelisks. To east and west, these sidepieces carry their own pediments – to somewhat ridiculous effect. So far, so classical; then, suddenly, Caius reverts to a more native style and tops his composition with a hexagonal tower – each side with its own sundial – and dome. The general effect is odd rather than beautiful; the whole building cannot be more than some 30 feet high, and far too many monumental motifs have been crammed into far too small a space. And yet, by reason of its very dottiness, the Gate of Honour is one of the memorable sights of Cambridge.

*The Gate of Honour, Gonville and Caius, Cambridge.*

Along the north side of Caius Court runs the CHAPEL. Originally part of the first foundation, it was completed before 1370 and was thus in all probability the first of all Cambridge college chapels; but it was radically remodelled by the local master builder John Westley in 1637, faced with ashlar by John James early in the eighteenth century, and finally given its eastern apse by Waterhouse, of whom more later. By far the best thing in it is Dr Caius's monument. At the time of the remodelling the rest of Gonville Court probably looked much as it always had; but in 1753 it too was taken in hand – by Sir James Burrough – and given its present character, respectable but dull. This character, alas, remained unaltered after the extension of the MASTER'S LODGE on the west side in 1795.

Dull is a word that can seldom be applied to Anthony Salvin and never to Alfred Waterhouse, whatever their other failings. Salvin was responsible, in the 1850s, for the massive brick block with the big south gable that occupies the space between Gonville Court and Trinity Lane. Into this he has ingeniously fitted both the LIBRARY and the HALL. Waterhouse had an even more challenging commission in 1870: to rebuild the whole of Tree Court. The College, one suspects, has been regretting it ever since. This court covers a considerable area – almost half the total area of the College – but even it cannot sustain Waterhouse's attempt to combine all the principal châteaux of the Loire around a single corner of it, with several pre-echoes of University College Hospital and the Prudential thrown in for good measure. To erect such an extraordinary assemblage, on so prodigious a scale, some 30 yards from the Senate House and in the very shadow of St Mary the Great, argues a degree of insensitivity difficult nowadays to conceive.

## Holy Sepulchre (The Round Church)

*13; Bridge Street*

The Round Church, as it is usually called, is a cruel disappointment. It was built on land granted to the Fraternity of the Holy Sepulchre (of whom nothing else is known) by Abbot Reinald of Ramsey (1114–30), and the nave, gallery and ambulatory are all of this date. Virtually all else, however, including the whole of the ostensibly Norman exterior, is the result of Salvin's pitiless restoration of 1841. To see just how pitiless, you have only to look at the chancel, which Salvin chose, for reasons best known to himself, to rebuild in Middle Pointed. The *Ecclesiologist* applauded him enthusiastically at the time; men have been shot for less.

Why, then, does the church find its way into this book? First of all because, restored or not, it is one of only five round churches in the country; and second, and more important, because the impact of those massive piers circling the nave, with the squat columns of the gallery above, the recarved heads of (presumably) crusaders gazing down from above their capitals, remains tremendous.

A slot machine by the door provides lighting for a limited but adequate period. Would that more churches would invest in such devices; they would be repaid a hundredfold.

## Jesus College

*14; Jesus Lane*

By 1496 the Benedictine convent of St Radegund had fallen on evil days. It had only two nuns left, one of whom was described as *infamis* and said to behave in a most unconventual manner in the Maid's Causeway not far off. Thus nobody can have been much surprised when John Alcock, Bishop of Ely, closed it down, took over its land, buildings and revenues, and built Jesus College in its place.

You approach Jesus in much the same way as visitors used to find themselves approaching Mussolini – at the far end of a long, straight walk calculated to induce proper feelings of respect and awe. High brick walls on each side of this walk – it is popularly known as the

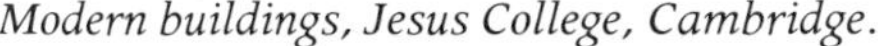

*Modern buildings, Jesus College, Cambridge.*

'chimney', from the French *cheminée* – block out the view of all but Bishop Alcock's red-brick GATEHOUSE, diapered, step-battlemented and liberally dressed in stone. It leads through into the OUTER COURT; opposite you stands a deliberately archaic block dating from *c.* 1640, and to your right are the old monastic buildings of St Radegund's – still the focus of the College today.

Let us begin with the old church which, in a somewhat truncated form, still serves Jesus for its CHAPEL – something of a surprise since that big, square, embattled tower with its slightly later Perpendicular bell openings looks most uncollegiate. The western end of the nave has gone, together with the aisles of both nave and chancel; what remains is the eastern end of the nave – now an ante-chapel – transepts, crossing and chancel. A good deal of this work goes back to the twelfth century; the Norman windows in the north transept and the old aisle piers on the north side of the nave are sufficient evidence for that. The beautiful chancel, on the other hand, is Early English. Its east end, with the five very gently stepped lancets (two of them blank) is in fact a reconstruction by Pugin of what had almost certainly been there before Alcock put in a big Perpendicular window; but it is scarcely less satisfying for that. The rows of tall lancets along the walls to north and south – the latter including a remarkable double piscina almost identical with that at Histon (*q.v.*) are original. Most of the furnishings are Pugin's too, though some of the wood carving of Alcock's time can be seen built into screen and stalls; Pugin also designed the east windows and the easternmost window in north and south chancel walls. The rest of the glass, and all the ceilings except those of the two transepts – which are Alcock's – are the work of Morris & Co. The glass is nearly all by Burne-Jones, but there are a few pieces by Ford Madox Brown and – in the south window of the south transept – by Morris himself.

Immediately north-west of the chapel crossing are the CLOISTERS. They too go back to the days of St Radegund's, though they were altered and enlarged when the College was founded – principally by the addition of a third storey to the surrounding buildings. It was Alcock too who gave the cloister walk its lovely timber roof. On a hot summer's afternoon there is much to be said for CLOISTER COURT, loud with birdsong and fragrant with the flowers that hang in little baskets from the top of the cloister arches, inserted by James Essex in the 1760s. In the east range, following on from the north transept of the Chapel, is the old CHAPTER HOUSE with its beautiful, delicate and typically Early English front towards the Cloisters; in the north, sensibly placed above the kitchens, is the HALL, formerly the refectory. Alcock would still recognise it as his, with its splendid timber roof and gloriously sumptuous oriel.

He would recognise his LIBRARY, too, upstairs in the west range. It has changed even less than the Hall, the only structural alteration being the seventeenth-century south doorway, inserted at the same time as the bookcases. The number of cocks in the eastern windows – they were repeated in the twentieth century in the western ones – suggests that the Bishop was particularly proud of this room, as well he might be.

Just to the north of the Library, during building operations connected with the westward extension of the Hall and the provision of a new Western Gallery, the room just behind this Gallery was discovered to have a similar roof and charmingly painted timbers. This is now known as the UPPER HALL and is well worth a special visit.

The south range of Cloister Court beyond the end of the Chapel, turning the corner of the court and extending as far as the Gatehouse, is now the MASTER'S LODGE. It includes most of the quarters formerly occupied by the Prioress of St Radegund's, including her little oratory with a pretty painted ceiling; most of it however is Alcock's work, dating from *c.*1500.

Of more recent buildings only two deserve special mention, both of them in the north-west corner of the College complex. The first is the range running east–west behind OUTER COURT with tower and spirelet. No prizes for attributing this to Alfred Waterhouse; it is a good deal less disastrous, at least, than what he perpetrated at Caius. The second is David Roberts's L-shaped building immediately to the west, whose zigzag outline betrays the skewed positioning of the students' rooms within: a most ingenious design, and one of the best of post-war residential blocks in Cambridge.

## King's College

*15; King's Parade*

The breathtaking impact of King's on all who see it for the first time is based on two factors: the spaciousness of its layout and the splendour of its Chapel. Both are due to that most hopeless of English monarchs, Henry VI. Henry's initial plans, dating from 1441, had been for something comparatively modest, north of the Chapel around what is now the West Court of the Old Schools (*q.v.*) where his original GATEHOUSE can still be seen; soon, however, he decided on a completely new concept, more ambitious than anything that Cambridge – or Oxford, for that matter – had ever seen. An entire parish of the town was ruthlessly swept away; in its place – according to a document drawn up by the King in 1448 and known, misleadingly, as his Will – there was to be an immense court, framed by the Chapel on the north, a gateway and chambers on the east, a Provost's Lodge and more chambers on the south, and Library and Hall on the west. Henry's projected great open space remains, as the FRONT COURT we see today; but of all the buildings he planned, only one was ever executed – the CHAPEL.

This is not only the most spectacular edifice in Cambridge; it is one of the great buildings of England, and indeed the world – the building in which the Perpendicular style was brought to the fullness of its flower. Its soaring verticals make it look considerably higher than its 94 feet, to which the angle turrets add some 40 more. When first built it must have totally dominated the little town clustered about its base; to a very large extent it continues to do so today.

The elevations could hardly be simpler: twelve virtually identical bays along each side, with a row of aisle chapels below them and an elaborate pierced parapet above, separated by deep buttresses with crocketed pinnacles. The east and west ends are largely taken up by vast windows of nine lights, the west having in addition a doorway flanked by empty canopied niches, with a coat of arms and crowned roses above. So unified is the design, so immaculate the symmetry, that it comes as a surprise to learn that the Chapel is in fact the work of three different architects at three different periods.

The King himself laid the foundation stone on 25 July 1446, and work continued under his master mason, Reginald Ely, for the next fifteen years. Then, in 1461, Henry was deposed and the half-finished building was abandoned. Not till 1476 did the new King, Edward IV, provide funds for its continuation under Ely's successor, Simon Clerk. (Interestingly enough, Clerk used a different sort of limestone – buff-coloured oolitic from Weldon and its surroundings – instead of the white magnesian limestone from Yorkshire with which the Chapel had been begun. The irregular line where the two stones meet is easily visible, particularly on the north side, and shows the approximate point that the building had reached at the time of the first interruption.) For the next seven years good progress was made; but in 1485 the death of Richard III at Bosworth interrupted the work again.

It was resumed only in 1508 by Henry VII, under John Wastell, who gave the Chapel its magical fan-vaulted roof instead of the lierne vault that the founder had intended. On the outside, the point where the Tudor work began can be seen from the buttresses. Previously, they had been of the plainest; but those towards the west, which date from the final phase, are copiously carved with Tudor emblems – crowned roses and portcullises and heraldic beasts. The general effect is not improved.

Nothing, however, can destroy the impression made by the interior. It is dazzlingly lit, thanks to the twenty-four mighty lateral windows, each of five lights, traceried and transomed, covering a good three-quarters of the total height of the building and an even greater proportion of its length, to the point where there appears to be hardly any wall left. Such as there is seems largely to be composed of a thousand slender shafts, all streaking up together like petrified fireworks before they simultaneously burst out into those huge radiating fans. The principal shafts dividing the bays, however, do not burst. Instead they curve round over the fans to the central ridge in vast four-centred arches, giving the whole vault a feeling of strength without in any way impairing its lightness.

The danger is that of monotony. For this building is too big for a chapel – too big to be just a long, tall, narrow box, with no transepts, clerestory or open aisles to add interest. Its length is almost exactly 100 yards; the same window tracery is repeated twenty-four times over; nave and choir would be virtually indistinguishable but for the wooden screen that divides them. That screen, however, is a major work of art – one which constitutes, with the choir stalls behind it, the most important example of early Renaissance woodwork in England. Opinions differ as to whether it is of French or Italian workmanship, but all are agreed on its quality. Nor is

*King's College Chapel, Cambridge.*

there any problem over its dating: the repeated cyphers H.R. and A.B. can only signify the period when Henry VIII was married to Anne Boleyn, from 1531 to 1536. (A door on the west side, surprisingly enough inscribed 'C.R. 1636', must be a later addition, and has enabled Pevsner to identify one of the earliest known cases of period imitation.)

The stalls are of similarly superb workmanship, doubtless – except for the unmistakably English misericords of the upper row – by the same continental hand. They are separated by turned balusters supporting an arcade, with ornamental cornice above, added in 1633 – the date also of the big carved coats of arms against the wall. Look particularly at the Provost's stall – the eastward-facing one immediately to your right as you pass under the screen. What a tragedy, one feels, that such a consummate artist should have left, so far as we can see, no other work in England outside this Chapel. England had plenty of good wood carvers in the mid-sixteenth century, but no one of this man's calibre.

The other chief glory of King's College Chapel is its glass. It, too, dates from the reign of Henry VIII; the east window, and perhaps several others, are the work of the King's glazier, Galyon Hone. As with so much of the work of this period, where the glass is more usually painted than stained and the leads tend to cut across the lines of the figures, the subjects are not always easy to identify; but the bold, brilliant colours, spread over so immense an area of wall space, fill the Chapel with so warm a radiance that it hardly seems to matter.

What *does* matter is the altarpiece. It is *The Adoration of the Magi*, painted by Rubens in 1633–4 and presented in 1961 to the College by Major A.E. Allnatt. No one would deny its greatness as a picture, but its placing here in the Chapel – whose entire east end was levelled the better to accommodate it – seems to me a disaster. Stylistically, its great swirling Baroque is as far removed as anything can be from the Gothic purity of its surroundings. Tonally, its colours belong to a totally different spectrum from those of the great east window above it. The whole beauty of the Chapel lies in its inner harmony; the Rubens destroys that harmony as cruelly as an F sharp in the middle of a C major chord. Equally cruelly, it is itself destroyed – by the glass above and also by the vast distance from which it is normally seen. Just what the right place is for it I cannot begin to tell; I do know that this is the wrong one.

Apart from the unpretentious little buildings left over, as it were, from Henry's first foundation and clustered behind it to the north, the Chapel stood by itself for over 200 years. Only at the beginning of the eighteenth century did the College finally decide to build that GREAT COURT for which the ground had been cleared in the 1440s. At the suggestion of the eighty-year-old Sir Christopher Wren, plans were commissioned in 1712 from Wren's old associate Nicholas Hawksmoor, who produced a model for a long and elaborate range running southward from near the west end of the Chapel, where the Founder had planned his Library and Hall. This was, however, rejected as being too grandiose – the College were fortunately able to cite Henry's 'Will', in which he had forbidden 'superfluite of too great curious works of *enteille* and besy moulding' – and Hawksmoor was asked to go back to his drawing board. The next model proved smaller (seventeen bays against twenty-three) and a good deal simpler (both can now be seen in one of the south aisle chapels) but had no greater success. Finally, in 1723, James Gibbs was called in; the result was the edifice that still bears his name – the GIBBS BUILDING. Gibbs retained – ill-advisedly, I think – Hawksmoor's semi-circular thermal window, but cut away almost all ornament except that of the pediment, the balustrade, the characteristically fussy window frames, the simple portico and the rusticated ground floor. His building is consequently one of the plainest and most austere that he ever designed: elegant – as is all his work – but a little dull. It is certainly not to be compared with his Senate House, not 200 yards away.

Two sides of the Great Court were now completed, but it was to be another century before it was fully enclosed. The man who did it was William Wilkins. His is the charming Gothic GATEHOUSE, with the open Perpendicular screen running off on each side, that separates the court from King's Parade; his, too, the HALL RANGE to the south. Of the two, the Gatehouse is the more successful: light-hearted without being playful, but with just a hint of fantasy. The screen, too, is an imaginative, even amusing, idea, and perfectly realised. The Hall range is, I fear, rather less inspired – though the HALL itself, with its high pendanted roof and its most uncanonical central bay window placed there to comply with Wilkins's passion for symmetry, is possessed of a certain splendour. The whole of Wilkins's work – which included an extension of the Hall range well beyond the Gibbs Building, to provide for a Library and Provost's Lodgings – was achieved in four years, from 1824 to 1828. After nearly four centuries, the court was finally complete.

But the College did not stop – not, at least, for long. In 1873 Sir Gilbert Scott added the so-called CHETWYND BUILDING on King's Parade, just south of the end of the Hall range; he was with difficulty prevented from demolishing the screen and Gatehouse, and carrying on all the way up to the Chapel in the same style. Twenty years later, G.F. Bodley began a new court down by the river, and early in the present century Sir Aston Webb formed yet another one between the two. Of all the pre- and post-war construction, however, there is only one resounding triumph; and that is the complex group of buildings and courts designed in the 1960s by Fello Atkinson, as a joint commission from King's and its neighbour to the south, St Catharine's. It was the first time two colleges had co-operated in this way; had they not done so, they would never have acquired an astonishing 160 sets for students in under 2 acres, to say nothing of a new Concert Hall for King's, a new Dining Hall for St Catharine's and an exciting – if labyrinthine – new building into the bargain. This is the best thing King's has done since the Chapel itself.

## Magdalene College

*16; Magdalene Street*

At Oxford three colleges (St John's, Trinity and Worcester) began life as monastic foundations; at Cambridge Magdalene – pronounced, like its Oxford near-namesake, Mawdlin – is the only one. Its original purpose was to serve as a hostel for young monks from the Benedictine abbey of Croyland, though these were joined in due course by others from Ely, Ramsey and Walden; then, after the Dissolution, it was taken over by Thomas, Lord Audley, Henry VIII's Lord Chancellor, who refounded it under its present name in 1542.

FIRST COURT dates almost entirely from monastic times; only the entrance gateway and the corner immediately to the right of it are later, *c.*1585. As might be expected, it is an attractively modest little court of two storeys with dormers, its paths and buildings agreeably asymmetrical. When you enter from Magdalene Street the HALL, with its delightful eighteenth-century Gothick louvre, occupies the left side of the range facing you. It dates from 1519; the interior, however, is nearly all Queen Anne, whose Royal Arms are emblazoned above the dais. Don't miss the particularly pretty wainscoting, carved with bunches of fruit, behind the high table; this is part of an earlier redecoration of 1585–7, further pieces of which remain in the delightful painted gallery above the screens passage.

The CHAPEL has also been altered, but a good deal less successfully. The best – and almost the only original – thing about it now is the roof, arch-braced and king-posted; there are also four canopied niches at the east end. For the rest, J.C. Buckler's restoration of 1847–50 put paid to just about the lot. The east window is by Pugin, but affords little real pleasure.

The south range – to your right as you enter – contained the Prior's, and later the Master's, Lodgings, which became a LIBRARY in 1835 when the Master was given a separate house for the first time. Passing out of the court by the passage leading between Hall and Chapel, we emerge in front of the pride of Magdalene – PEPYS BUILDING. Its history is uncertain, but it was most probably begun in *c.*1585 as the result of an endowment by the Lord Chief Justice, Sir Christopher Wray, who had also contributed towards the Gatehouse. At that time it seems to have been H-shaped; in the late 1670s, however – probably according to designs known to have been made for the College in 1677 by Robert Hooke – the area between the two uprights of the H on the side facing FRONT COURT was filled in. This would explain not only the obvious difference in style between the centre and the wings, but also the quoins on the inside of those wings, which now scarcely project at all. The in-fill is elegant in the extreme. Its ground floor consists of a five-bay arcade, the central arch being separated from the others by pilaster strips which support Ionic pilasters rising to the low parapet. The five windows above the arches are all heavily ornamented – numbers 1 and 5 with steep triangular pediments containing coats of arms, numbers 2 and 4 with straight heads like mantel-pieces, topped with busts, and the central one with a generous segmental pediment and another coat of arms, this time fringed with garlands. It also has a curious volute design along each side. There are decorative stone carvings below all these windows and in the spandrels of the arches; but these are eighteenth-century work.

The date, 1724, over the central arch refers not to any stage of the building itself but to the transfer to it in that year of Samuel Pepys's famous library of exactly 3,000 volumes – every time he acquired a new book, an old one was thrown out to make room for it. They are still there, in the original bookcases of red oak which Pepys ordered in 1666, each volume standing on its own little platform so that the tops are all at the same level. There too is the great Diary.

As you stand in front of Pepys Building, you see a two-storeyed brick range behind the wall to your right, towards the river; this is BRIGHT'S BUILDINGS, by Sir Aston Webb. The only other building of any note on this side of Magdalene Street is that which extends the other side of First Court, to the north-west. It is of no particular distinction; its interest lies in the fact that it was personally designed – as well as financed – by A.C. Benson, the novelist, essayist and diarist, while he was Master of the College. The large and rather sprawling court named after him on the other side of Magdalene Street principally consists of a long brick range built in 1931–2 by Sir Edwin Lutyens. It is characteristically playful – look at the dormers – but not one of his best.

## Old Schools

*17; Trinity Lane*

Built round an irregular court – or, to be more precise, two courts – immediately to the north of King's, the Old Schools were begun *c.*1350, and were for the next four centuries the only buildings belonging to the University, as opposed to its individual colleges. They are a heterogeneous bunch. The DIVINITY SCHOOL came first, forming the north range of the smaller, eastern court known as COBBLE COURT. It is vaguely Perpendicular in style, but of no special interest. West and south ranges followed, in the middle of the fifteenth century, round the same court – the south range, which was intended partly as a Library, being of brick rather than rubble, always an indication of rising fortunes. By this time, however, a new court had been begun to the west by King's College (founded in 1441) featuring a magnificent ornamental GATEHOUSE; the north range of this court, containing the original College Hall, even extended behind that of Cobble Court – an arrangement that must have been equally inconvenient for College and University alike. Then, in 1829, after the completion of William Wilkins's work at King's (*q.v.*), the University bought the whole of this western quadrangle, incorporated it into the Old Schools and shortly afterwards had the whole thing (except the Gatehouse) rebuilt – by Scott in 1862–7 and Pearson in 1890. Pearson's west range, not surprisingly, is by far the best.

Towards the end of the fifteenth century an east range was added to Cobble Court; but this was replaced in the 1750s by a lovely Palladian building, designed to complement Gibbs's Senate House (*q.v.*) which stands at right-angles to it. This is not, as is sometimes maintained, by Sir James Burrough – though Burrough did indeed submit designs for it – but by Stephen Wright, the protégé of the Duke of Newcastle, Chancellor of the University, for whom Wright had already worked at Claremont and at 22 Arlington Street in London, and for whom he later built Clumber. Burrough was furious at the Duke's intervention, but posterity should be grateful; for the resultant building, apart from its own considerable beauty, sets off the Senate House to perfection. The five-bay centre consists of an arched loggia with heavy Gibbs surrounds, supporting on the first floor pedimented windows (the middle one Venetian) set in deep round-headed arches with garlands above them. A balustrade with urns only partly conceals a low hipped roof. To each side is a single-bay wing, set somewhat back. If you go to the extreme northern end (by the corner of the Senate House) and look around the corner, you will see that this is merely a façade; the old Divinity School marches off behind it to the west just as it always did. The centre block, however, conceals a long room running the length of its five bays, with fine plasterwork and exquisite coffered apses at each end.

## Pembroke College

*18; Trumpington Street*

The College was founded in 1346 by Marie, daughter of Count Guy IV of Chatillon and St Pol, and widow of Aymer de Valence, 1st Earl of Pembroke, who had been one of the most powerful lords of England in the reign of Edward II. The north and west sides of her original court still stand, running respectively along Pembroke and Trumpington Streets; but there is little of them to be seen from the outside, owing to seventeenth-century brick refacing and eighteenth-century ashlaring. The best remaining features are the two oriels over the Trumpington Street gateway. A little to the south, inside the court, the big gable with the tall Perpendicular windows marks the end of the south range of OLD COURT, sadly demolished on the advice of Alfred Waterhouse in 1874.

The court is therefore now twice its original size, and the next part to be built was the new CHAPEL, a replacement for the old one at the west end of the north range, which was subsequently converted into a Library. The architect for this new Chapel was the thirty-one-year-old Christopher Wren, still Savilian Professor of Astronomy at Oxford; this was his first architectural work to be completed. The street frontage is the best, with its central round-headed window flanked by arched niches, its four Corinthian pilasters supporting a triangular pediment and, crowning all, a hexagonal lantern. It may not be a masterpiece; seen from the front gate of Peterhouse it looks distinctly top-heavy. But it is a distinguished building by any standards and it certainly did not deserve its lengthening in 1880 by George Gilbert Scott Jun. (All one can say about this is that Scott was a good deal more sensitive than his father would have been.) Wren's part has a superb plaster ceiling and some fine wood carving above the stalls.

*Pembroke College, Cambridge.*

At the time the Chapel went up it was free-standing; almost immediately, however, a short range was added to connect it with the existing buildings to the north. On the street side it maintains the medieval style of the latter; to the court there is a pretty classicising colonnade – hence its name, HITCHAM'S CLOISTER.

Sir Robert Hitcham, an early seventeenth-century benefactor of the College, also posthumously gave his name to the south range of the so-called IVY COURT, which was by now taking shape immediately to the east of Old Court. This range was designed in 1659 by Peter Mills. The two-storey north range had already been built in the second decade of the century, though it was to be extended eastward in 1670. Between the two courts ran the fourteenth-century Hall range of the original foundation, but this too was pulled down by Waterhouse to make room for something he considered more suitable. The block we see today is not as Waterhouse conceived it, having been altered twice in the present century. The existing emasculated version has little positive to recommend it, but at least it gives the rest of the court a bit more of a chance.

If we want an idea of what the Hall block would have been like before it was toned down, we have only to look at Waterhouse's other two principal contributions to Pembroke: his extension of the Trumpington Street frontage south of the Chapel, and the Library range opposite it to the east. Here, as at Caius, he has harked back to French Renaissance ideas; and once again, he has shown quite a majestic disregard for everything around him. His material is his favourite dark red brick, just as it was for the later University College Hospital in London, of which one is reluctantly but inescapably reminded. Only in his new MASTER'S LODGE, east of Ivy Court, has he shown any real restraint. (Presumably the Master of the day, knowing he would have to live there, took a strong line.) Less showy, but infinitely more distinguished, is the younger G.G. Scott's NEW BUILDING, further along Pembroke Street. The style is hard to define – it seems to include a touch of practically everything – but while there is plenty of interest and imagination we find none of Waterhouse's compulsive exhibitionism. It is the sort of thing that Sir Thomas Jackson was doing so brilliantly at Oxford at about the same time. How the College must have wished they had gone to Scott in the beginning; he would have spared them – and us – much pain.

## Peterhouse

*19; Trumpington Street*

The oldest college in Cambridge dates from 1280, when Hugh de Balsham, Bishop of Ely, founded a community of scholars at St John's Hospital 'living according to the rule of the scholars of Oxford called of Merton'. Unfortunately the scholars failed to get on with the regular canons of the Hospital, and in 1284 they moved into two hostels outside Trumpington Gate, next to St Peter's church – now St Mary the Less. Church and College are still connected by a gallery.

Balsham died in 1286, leaving money for the building of the HALL. It was begun at once, and still stands on the south side of PRINCIPAL COURT. It was heightened in the fifteenth century and – far more tragically – underwent some heavy-handed restoration by George Gilbert Scott Jun. in 1870; but an idea of what it must have looked like can be gained from the south side, where the original door and much of the masonry have been preserved. Inside, it actually gives considerable pleasure, though for the wrong reasons: the decoration of the walls and the tiling of the fireplace are by William Morris, whose firm also made the stained glass to the designs of Burne-Jones and Ford Madox Brown. There is more Pre-Raphaelite work by the same hands in the Combination Room next door. This, together with the western end of the MASTER'S LODGE beyond it, is in origin a fifteenth-century building – though the ashlar facing and general tidying-up by Sir James Burrough in 1754 successfully conceal the fact. Fortunately, however, the north and west ranges are also late medieval in date and have – although ashlared on the inside looking on to the court – on the outside been rather less altered; the original state of the former can be seen to good advantage from the churchyard of St Mary the Less.

In the sixteenth, and again in the seventeenth, century the south range of the court was extended further eastward, stopping only when it reached Trumpington Street and celebrating its arrival with a pleasant brick oriel. This now forms the Library range; it includes the PERNE LIBRARY, named after a sixteenth-century master whose see-saw changes of religion provided a useful precedent for the Vicar of Bray. It is still well worth visiting, though it must have been a good deal prettier before the bookcases were heightened. North of this range is the perversely named FIRST COURT. It is, most unusually, E-shaped, the central bar of the E being the CHAPEL.

Until the reign of Charles I, Peterhouse had no Chapel of its own, being apparently content to worship in St Mary the Less; it was only in 1628 that its first Chapel was begun by the then Master, Matthew Wren. Wren was a remarkable man. He was later to become, in quick succession, Bishop of Hertford, Norwich and Ely, and then to spend eighteen years in prison for his High Church opinions. Soon after his release he was to build another chapel – this time for his own old college, Pembroke (*q.v.*) – commissioning it from his nephew Christopher; but by then Peterhouse Chapel had already been consecrated for over thirty years.

Its architect is unknown. He was probably a local man, since no one with any formal training could conceivably have combined Gothic, Renaissance and Baroque motifs with such cheerful insouciance. (Brasenose Chapel at Oxford is the nearest parallel that springs to mind.) But he was full of good ideas, not the least of which was his placing of the Chapel so that its west end forms the centrepiece of Principal Court, where it stands halfway along the east side, being attached by open colonnades to the ranges to north and south. This west front consists, at ground-floor level, of three depressed blank arches – those of the loggias to each side are, since 1709, round-headed – with a smaller, four-centre-arched doorway let into the central one. Above is a tall three-light window with formalised Perpendicular tracery, flanked by round-headed niches with crocketed Gothic canopies; and, to cap it all, a sinuously curving skyline leading to a raised centre with more curly bits on top of that. This now contains a clock where originally there was a third niche. The east end, on Trumpington Street, is essentially the same except that its window has five lights instead of three, its centre is crowned by a restrained triangular pediment, and it has short side turrets to left and right. The interior is lovely, dominated by a panelled timber ceiling studded by elliptical Suns in Splendour; it retains its original balustered stalls and interesting contemporary Flemish stained glass in the east window, said – though I doubt it – to have been designed by Rubens. The late nineteenth-century German glass in the other windows is a pity, and makes the Chapel terribly dark. Its evening services are still, however, lit by candles, which is marvellous.

The nineteenth-century GISBORNE COURT, immediately west of Principal Court, is by W. McIntosh Brooks and is as dull as any court could possibly be. Further west still, Hughes and Bicknell's T-shaped building enclosing FEN COURT dates from 1939 and shows that there are worse things than dullness.

## Queens' College

*20; Queens' Lane*

Note, first of all, the position of the apostrophe. Queens' College was founded not by one queen, but by two. The first was Margaret of Anjou, wife of Henry VI, who in 1448 resolved to follow the example her husband was setting a few hundred yards away at King's; she therefore took over a small college dedicated to St Bernard which had been established by one Andrew Docket only two years before, renaming it Queen's College 'to laud and honneure of sexe feminine'. (She might have achieved this object a good deal more successfully by declaring it to be for women students; but the first true women's college, Girton, was not to be founded for over four more centuries.) The second queen was Elizabeth Woodville, the consort of Henry's Yorkist enemy Edward IV, who decided after her husband's accession to carry on where her predecessor had left off. She it was who gave the College its statutes and completed the buildings; and the apostrophe was shifted accordingly.

Queens' has a good claim to be the prettiest of Cambridge colleges; it is certainly the most unspoilt. The whole of its FIRST COURT was completed by 1449 and still looks much as it did then, its lovely mellow brick having mercifully escaped the eighteenth-century passion for ashlar. The great GATEHOUSE in Queens' Lane, with its two soaring polygonal turrets – owing to the narrowness of the Lane, it can best be seen from inside St Catharine's opposite – leads one to expect something corresponding-

*The Hall, Queens' College, Cambridge.*

ly grand within; in fact, however, the beauty of this court resides in its quiet informality, almost intimacy; it has no brave statements to make. Some of the windows have been altered, and the dormers are probably Jacobean; no matter. If you want to know what a Cambridge college looked like in the later Middle Ages, it is to Queens' that you should come.

The HALL is where it always was, in the western range; it can be identified by the traditional bay window at the dais end, which has kept its original lierne vaulting on the inside, though all else in it is later restoration. The interior of the Hall itself comes as a considerable surprise. The gallery, screen, wainscoting and the reredos behind the high table are all good mid-eighteenth-century work by James Essex, but this is almost lost in the blaze of Victorian Gothic. The architect here was Bodley, who was given the job in 1861; the brilliant painted decoration is by Morris, with figures of the months over the fireplace designed by Rossetti, Burne-Jones and Ford Madox Brown. The patchwork effect is exhilarating and unquestionably cheerful; one might never have ordered it in the first place, but now it is there one would be sorry to see it go.

Around the corner, on the upper floor of the north range at the end nearer the Hall, is the LIBRARY, its sixteenth-century bookcases regrettably heightened early in the seventeenth century but its original roof beams still in place. Then, on the outside wall, comes a formidably complicated sundial, and then Queen Margaret's original chapel, now a READING ROOM. It is quite pretty, but having been remodelled first by Bodley in the nineteenth century and then by Sir Albert Richardson in the twentieth, it need hardly detain us today. On the other side of the Hall, beyond the screens passage, old kitchen and buttery at the south-west corner of the court, is the tower in which Erasmus lived while he was Professor of Divinity and Reader in Greek from 1511 to 1514 and which is still called ERASMUS TOWER.

The screens passage leads through into CLOISTER COURT, of which the east, south and west sides were all complete before 1500. Their brick cloister arcades with narrow four-centred arches were the first to appear in any Cambridge college, and most delightful they are. The west range is occupied by the PRESIDENT'S LODGE, the outer walls of which sweep straight down into the river and can be seen only from the bridge, the other side, or a punt. This is all of about 1450, and virtually unchanged apart from the early eighteenth-century oriel marking the dining room. Note the bricked-up arches at water level; their origins remain a mystery, but the likeliest explanation is that they were originally open bays where the College provisions could be landed from the river lighters. In the Middle Ages and for a good three centuries afterwards, the state of the roads made heavy goods traffic by land impossible; if you were lucky enough to have a river at your door, you used it.

Back now into Cloister Court and to the range we have not yet mentioned – the most spectacular of all. This is the timber-framed PRESIDENT'S GALLERY, which runs the entire length of the north cloister. For its date, which must be somewhere around 1540, it has one or two quite surprising features. For one thing, it has made a very remarkable effort towards symmetry; for another, its oriels are supported on quite classical-looking consoles, and the lower ones even have pediments. The Renaissance, in short, may not have altogether arrived; but it is certainly not very far away. Inside, there is a good Elizabethan fireplace and some nice contemporary panelling, together with the so-called Chair of Erasmus. It is late fifteenth-century and distinctly professorial; the great man could well have sat in it.

At this point you could, if you wished, cross the Cam to see the quite wonderfully boring FISHER BUILDING, built in the mid-thirties with extreme caution. The visit is not recommended; you might, however, spare a moment for the MATHEMATICAL BRIDGE, which spans the river immediately behind the President's Lodge. It was originally constructed in 1749 by James Essex to a design by William Etheridge, based, he claimed, on such sound mathematical principles that no nails, bolts or other fastenings were required. Whether or not it was the principles that were at fault, the bridge has since twice had to be rebuilt, most recently in 1902. The present one is said to be an exact copy of the original, but the builder does not seem to have shared Mr Etheridge's confidence.

Between the President's Lodge and the Silver Street bridge stands another building by Essex in that rather unpleasing Cambridge white brick. It is actually L-shaped, returning along Silver Street to meet First Court at Erasmus Tower. It will not linger particularly long in the memory. We should now therefore retrace our steps into Cloister Court, leaving it by the north-east corner, where a short passage leads into WALNUT TREE COURT. To our left, it is open – apart from a short northward extension of the President's Gallery; facing us is a set of students' chambers built in 1617–19, though still in Tudor style; to the north, the new CHAPEL. It was built by Bodley, in a second burst of activity at Queens', in 1890–1 (thirty years after his work in the Hall) and it is hard to believe that it is the work of the same man. Gone are the ebullience and the colour; here all is austerity and restraint. Remembering the splendour of the Hall, was the College, I wonder, very disappointed to see how the architect had changed his ways? I know I was.

Beyond the Chapel, a further court contains a very dull Victorian building, a far from inspired Edwardian one and, to the west, the ERASMUS BUILDING erected in 1959–61 by Sir Basil Spence. There was a dreadful outcry at the time about the desecration of the atmosphere by modern monstrosities; twenty-odd years later it is hard to see what all the fuss was about.

## Round Church

See Holy Sepulchre.

## St Bene't's

*21; Bene't Street*

Connected by a covered passageway to Corpus Christi (*q.v.*) which for two centuries used it as a College Chapel, St Bene't's is the oldest church in Cambridgeshire, having probably been built soon after AD 1000. Much has been done to it over the centuries, but two Saxon features remain which are of outstanding interest. The first is the tower, three stages, with typical long-and-short quoins and double bell openings which have narrow arches and a stocky central baluster. (The flanking round-headed windows are Elizabethan.)

The second memorable thing about St Bene't's is the tower arch. This is really the most extraordinary affair. The masons obviously had some idea of the way things were done on the Continent, since they have flanked it with heavy continuous mouldings above primitive pilasters and half columns. But then, for the jambs themselves, they have given up and gone back – one suspects with relief – to their familiar old long-and-short work. Above the mouldings they have provided a couple of crouching animals of indeterminate species, through whose bodies the vertical shafts seem to pass as they continue up into the arch.

For the rest, though pieces of Saxon work remain elsewhere, the predominant feeling is of 1300 or so, with a Perpendicular clerestory. But none of this is in any way remarkable, though the painted corbels are fun, especially in the north aisle.

## St Catharine's College

*22; Queens' Lane*

Although St Catharine's was founded in 1473 – by Robert Woodlark, the third Provost of King's – every one of its original buildings has gone. Thus, when the rebuilding programme for the whole College was undertaken in 1674, it began virtually from scratch. Within thirteen years a court had been formed, consisting of the central (west) range of what is now PRINCIPAL COURT and the western sections of the north and south ranges. Of these, the west range was the last to go up, and could clearly only do so after some readjustment of the plans: the attentive observer will note that it is slightly lower than its two neighbours and has been brought a few inches forward so that it partly covers their quoins. The designer may have been a certain 'Mr Elder', surveyor, a payment for whose journey from London is recorded in the building accounts; but most of the credit should probably go to Robert Grumbold, the builder, whose work we have seen at Clare. The three-storey ranges in very dark brick are quite distinguished in an austere sort of way, with their tall, rather narrow cross windows and their rows of dormers with alternating triangular and semi-circular pediments. There is also an impressive Baroque frontispiece in the centre of the west range, providing a perfect focus for the view from Trumpington Street.

The north range was occupied by the HALL; we have, however, no very clear idea of what it was like, because it was radically remodelled in 1869 by W.M. Fawcett, who decided – with that baffling insensitivity to prevailing style and mood to which the Victorians were so disastrously subject – to Gothicise both it and the eighteenth-century Library above it, giving it quite unsuitable Gothic windows and even a ridiculously embattled Gothic bay. Now, since the provision of a new Dining Hall as part of the recent joint building operation by St Catharine's and King's (*q.v.*), the old Hall has been divided up – and a good job too.

The CHAPEL, which stands immediately east of the Hall, was built between 1694 and 1697. Once again, the design seems to have been principally Grumbold's own, though William Talman was apparently consulted in 1696. It is basically a continuation of the Hall range, with such alterations (for instance, a single row of much larger windows, of the same cross pattern but with pediments above and blank panels below) as the purpose of the building demanded. The east end, facing the street, is clearly inspired by the west end of Wren's Pembroke Chapel a little further along. But it is only when one gets inside that there is much real scope for admiration. Though most of the interior is austere and simple enough, the screen, reredos and organ gallery are all superb pieces of Baroque wood carving, as fine as anything of their kind in Cambridge.

After Grumbold, the next architect to have a hand in the development of St Catharine's was another familiar Cambridge figure, James Essex, who in 1757 extended the south wing just as its companion to the north had been extended sixty years before. The result was what is now known as the RAMSDEN BUILDING, which – though the point where it joins the earlier wing is plainly marked – follows the design of the latter in every detail, excepting only for the dormers which (as on Grumbold's Chapel opposite) all have triangular pediments instead of alternating ones. At the same time the east side was closed off by the iron gates and railings, virtually guaranteeing that the often proposed east range would never be built. Trumpington Street gains much from this decision.

Apart from Fawcett's ill-advised work on the Hall and Library and his relatively inoffensive MASTER'S LODGE of 1875, there was fortunately no Victorian building at St Catharine's. The twentieth-century buildings to north and south of Principal Court are uninspired – or were until Fello Atkinson came along. His work is described under King's College (*q.v.*).

## St John's College

*23; St John's Street*

To look up at the great GATEHOUSE on St John's Street is to have an immediate sense of *déjà vu*. That vast coat of arms, with its two dappled beasts – yales – climbing, as it were, up the crocketed sides of an ogee which in turn rises above a four-centred arch, is almost (though not quite) identical to that which proclaims the entry into Christ's; and not surprisingly, since St John's was founded by that same Lady Margaret Beaufort who had refounded Christ's in 1505. Sadly, she never saw it; by the time building began in 1511 she was dead. But St John's remains her college, and the most beautiful of all Cambridge gatehouses ensures that she is not forgotten.

Above the climbing yales is a statue of St John himself – the Evangelist rather than the Baptist, for it was on the site of an earlier Hospital of his that Lady Margaret founded the College. He is flanked, on the outside, by two-light windows on two storeys, on each side of which are polygonal angle turrets dressed in stone, in the traditional early Tudor fashion. The ground floor is fan-vaulted and has preserved its original massive door with linenfold panelling. The whole ensemble impresses one with its sumptuous grandeur and fills one with high expectations for what lies within.

These expectations, however, are not fulfilled. Lady Margaret's FIRST COURT must have looked fine indeed – like a rather later, richer, Queens' – until the last century; alas in 1863 it was decided to enlarge the court in order to provide room for a longer Hall along its west side. This entailed the wholesale demolition of the north range, which included the Chapel, and the building of a new CHAPEL some 50 yards to the north. The architect of this work was, somehow inevitably, George Gilbert Scott; and his effect proved, as usual where the universities are concerned, disastrous. Scott built his Chapel in the Early Decorated style of about 1300, which had nothing to do with the early Tudor brickwork of the east and west ranges and still less with the eighteenth-century ashlaring of the south; worse still, he gave it a French-inspired apse at the east end – a form obviously, one would have thought, unsuited to quadrangular courts. In an attempt to resolve this difficulty, he added a short extension to the northern end of the frontage on St John's Street; but the break in this frontage – to say nothing of the damage to the shape of the court itself – remains painful and induces no small measure of irritation. The outline of the old Chapel, still visible on the lawn, ensures that the wound is not allowed to close.

The additional space gained on the west side of the court is not left open, but is taken up with the northward extension of the Hall and the transverse ante-chapel

*The Bridge of Sighs, St John's College, Cambridge.*

which Scott provided on the Oxford pattern. Of the Chapel interior there is little to be said except that it is exactly what one might expect. The HALL is more interesting, in that the south end of it – as far as the first of the bay windows – preserves its original hammer-beam roof and much of its original panelling. The northern end is a competent copy, but the dead hand of Scott remains all too evident.

SECOND COURT was built between 1598 and 1602 with an endowment from Mary, Countess of Shrewsbury, daughter of the celebrated Bess of Hardwick. It shares the same east–west axis as its predecessor, being entered through the service passage between Hall and kitchens, but it is almost perfectly preserved and consequently a good deal more satisfactory. Despite the lapse of almost a century there is little change in style; even the GATEHOUSE in the centre of the west range echoes the older one, and the three-light windows with their hood-moulds are deliberate copies of those on the east side, which forms, of course, the back of the Hall range. The principal indications of the later date are the central oriels to north and south, with their strapwork cresting – apart from the statue of the Countess above the western gateway which, as its setting in an arched niche suggests, is later still (1671). When first built, the entire first floor of the north range – all 50 yards of it – was taken up by a Long Gallery known as the Master's Gallery. Of this, rather more than a third was lopped off to provide a staircase and lobby for the Library and, later, a small Combination (Common) Room. The remainder, which now serves as the main COMBINATION ROOM, has a splendid plaster ceiling of 1601.

And so to the LIBRARY, the gift of John Williams, Bishop of Lincoln and Lord Keeper of the Great Seal – functions worth bearing in mind if only to explain the letters 'J.L.C.S.' on the gable facing the river: *Johannes Lincolniensis Custos Sigilli*. Building began in 1623, continuing the north range of Second Court towards the west, the Library itself occupying the upper floor, students' chambers the lower. Stylistically it is extraordinary, since the style selected is a deliberately archaic early fourteenth-century Gothic, with appropriate tracery. The square frames to the middle-pointed windows give the game away a little, as do the curiously shaped battlements; nonetheless, as an early essay in Gothic Revival architecture St John's Library takes some beating. Only inside the 100-foot-long room does the later Gothic four-centred arch make its appearance, supporting a fine panelled roof.

Later in the seventeenth century, a THIRD COURT was formed by adding a west range along the Cam and a south one continuing the range of First and Second Courts. Once again the same central axis was preserved; but the court is perforce irregular and somewhat cramped since it has to follow the river bank. The date, proudly emblazoned on the south gable, is 1671; and this time the buildings act their age: four storeys (including dormers) with battlements, following the example set by the Library. The west range has a sort of cloister walk behind a series of round-headed arches separated by pilasters, above the centre of which rises a most improbable frontispiece towering to the roof and featuring more pilasters bearing empty oval frames and emblems at their centres. The composition is crowned by a broken segmental pediment. As late seventeenth-century English Baroque goes, it is all a bit tentative and fumbly, and the lopsidedness of the court itself hardly helps; but it is not without charm. Immediately behind it is St John's most famous and best-loved landmark – Henry Hutchinson's so-called BRIDGE OF SIGHS, leading across the river to New Court. Built in 1831, it in no way resembles its Venetian namesake; with its five unglazed three-light Perpendicular windows, its nearest equivalent is probably William Wilkins's screen along King's Parade, which predates it by only five years or so.

NEW COURT, designed by Hutchinson and his partner Thomas Rickman, is a vast Neo-Gothic fantasy inspired, one imagines, more by Sir Walter Scott than anyone else. It belongs, however, to that period of early nineteenth-century Gothic Revival – the dates are 1825–31 – that found it almost impossible to break free from classical symmetry. In the Palace of Westminster, a few years later, Barry was able to make a reluctant effort in this direction; here at New Court there is no attempt at all. The design essentially consists of a long but relatively shallow enclosure facing south, closed along its southern side by another Wilkins-inspired and cloister-like screen wall with central gateway. Behind this gateway, in the centre of the north range, is a somewhat pompous projection with a vast oriel rising through three storeys and polygonal angle turrets; it would be a gatehouse if only it led anywhere. There are more oriels – but of only two storeys this time – at the southern ends of the two side ranges. In the middle of the whole thing rises a refreshingly irresponsible glazed Gothic lantern, universally and understandably known as the Wedding Cake. New Court is not perhaps great architecture; but it is undeniably picturesque, it uses its ivy to great effect, and it adds much to the view from the Backs.

We may, I think, be forgiven for passing briefly over Scott's MASTER'S LODGE, some 100 yards north of the Library towards Bridge Street; nor need we be long detained by CHAPEL COURT, constructed behind the Chapel in 1938–9 by the architect of Guildford Cathedral, Sir Edward Maufe. That leaves us with only two more College buildings to describe, with an eight-century time lapse between them. The younger is the famous CRIPPS BUILDING, erected in the mid-sixties by Powell and Moya. It has received a good deal of praise over the past twenty years; one can only say that it deserves every bit of it. It consists of one immensely long range faced with Portland stone, four storeys high, zigzagging for perhaps 300 yards from the river bank behind New Court in a vaguely westerly direction. The bronze windows are broad, generous and occasionally bayed; the roof has regularly spaced penthouses; along the ground floor, a covered walkway stretches the entire length of the building. From about halfway along, a low single-storey Common Room block extends southward towards the back of the west range of New Court. Of all the post-war building at Oxford and Cambridge, this is among the most distinguished.

*The Senate House, Cambridge.*

Opposite the far end of the Cripps Building is the house known, for no good reason, as the SCHOOL OF PYTHAGORAS. It is not particularly beautiful; its sole claim to a mention here is its age, for it was almost certainly standing well before 1200. This makes it probably – but see Hemingford Grey – the oldest house in Cambridgeshire, and one of the oldest in the country. Inevitably, it has been altered over the years – most unforgivably of all by the addition of a most unworthy doorway and a disgraceful bay window (fortunately at the back) a few years ago – but it still looks venerable.

## St Mary the Great

*24; Market Hill*

This is the University Church – Cambridge's answer to St Mary the Virgin at Oxford. It is very large and grand, in the Perpendicular style of the great East Anglian wool churches like Lavenham or Long Melford, though its exterior is notably less fine than theirs. The tower, for example, despite its tall west window, has an oddly blind look, its four little polygonal turrets almost mingy. Inside, however, things improve at once. The tall, slender, many-shafted piers soar upward just a little higher than one would expect, giving the church a quite striking elegance; and the effect is further increased by the blank tracery in the spandrels and in the space between arcade and clerestory. The timbers in the roof are all original, provided by Henry VII in 1505, and there are some marvellous bosses over the nave. Only the galleries above the aisles are a pity – but they probably come in handy for University ceremonies.

## Senate House

*25; Senate House Passage*

The early eighteenth century saw two separate schemes for replanning the whole centre of Cambridge to make a magnificent architectural composition worthy of the grand Augustan age. The first and most ambitious was Nicholas Hawksmoor's; it came to nothing. The second, less than a decade later, was by James Gibbs, who in 1722 submitted plans for a mighty quadrangle open to the east, with a Senate House on the north, an identical south range for other University Offices, and a Royal Library to the west. Once again the plan failed to materialise; but it got further than Hawksmoor's, and the Senate House is the result.

It is a glorious building of Portland stone, its nine bays separated by giant Corinthian pilasters at the sides and by four fluted half columns at the slightly projecting centre, supporting the three-bay pediment. The ground-floor windows have alternating triangular and segmental pediments; Palladianism had arrived at last. The upper ones are round-headed, their keystones touching the entablature. The whole thing is surmounted by an emphatic balustrade, with urns at the three corners of the pediment.

The interior consists of a single tremendous room with a small ante-room. Galleries run round three sides, and on the south there is a high carved wooden 'reredos' of four Doric columns. The detailing, inside and out, is quite superb. How lucky, though, that Gibbs did not build its opposite number; the open space in front of it adds immeasurably to the effect.

## Sidney Sussex College

*26; Sidney Street*

Poor Sidney Sussex: founded at the close of the sixteenth century by Lady Frances Sidney, Countess of Sussex, it might have been as pleasing architecturally as any other building of its date in Cambridge. Indeed it probably was – until 1821, when it made the greatest mistake in its history. It decided on a facelift, and called in Sir Jeffrey Wyatville.

Now Wyatville was no bad architect when conditions were right for him – as they were, for example, at Windsor Castle; but at Sidney Sussex he was a disaster. He did not destroy HALL COURT, the nucleus of Lady Frances's College which Ralph Symonds had built for her over the ruins of a Franciscan friary in 1594; but he refaced it in a singularly unlovely cement, added crow-stepped gables and corbelled-out chimneystacks in an etiolated Tudor style, and generally tricked the plan out in his own personal vision of 'Elizabethan Gothic' – a particularly pointless exercise since the whole thing was Elizabethan anyway. In the northern end of the central block, the HALL mercifully escaped his attention, probably because it had been remodelled and classicised – and given a nice painted plaster ceiling below its hammer-beams – some seventy years before; so too did the CHAPEL in SECOND COURT immediately to the south, the rest of which Wyatville had treated in a similar way. This is by far the most interesting feature of the College, despite the fact that it is the third Chapel to be built on the site since the foundation. The first, of 1600, had been replaced by James Essex in 1776, but this second Chapel was in turn rebuilt – and considerably extended towards the east – by T.H. Lyon in 1912. Long, narrow and covered with a plain barrel vault, its style is a beautifully controlled Wrenian Baroque, with the walls divided halfway up by an elaborate cornice which intermittently breaks forward on pairs of fluted Tuscan columns. It does much to redeem Sidney Sussex from an architectural point of view.

The College's other principal consolation must be its gardens, spacious and beautifully tended. On your way to them you may admire – or not – the isolated range built by J.L. Pearson in 1891. Over a loggia of immensely broad depressed arches, its main interest comes from the segmental bay windows, grouped in fours, with shaped gables rising up between the groups.

## Trinity College

*27; Trinity Street*

Cambridge's answer to Christ Church at Oxford, Trinity has about it an air of spacious opulence that only the latter can match in either university; its Great Court covers an area even vaster than Tom Quad. True, its Chapel is not a cathedral in its own right; but where Christ Church was founded by Cardinal Wolsey, Trinity can claim to be the creation of Henry VIII himself.

Its history begins in 1546, when a small and exclusively clerical college known as Michaelhouse, which occupied what is now the south-west corner of Great Court, reverted to the Crown after the Dissolution of the Monasteries. Adjoining it to the north-east was King's Hall, established by Edward II in 1337; and Henry now seized the opportunity of amalgamating the two into a new foundation which would put that of his discredited cardinal in the shade. Dying in the following year, he was never able to judge the measure of his success. His daughter, Bloody Mary, in 1555 put in hand an ambitious building project which included the existing CHAPEL, a Master's Lodge and other ranges now demolished; but the man who gave GREAT COURT the appearance which in essence it still preserves today was Dr Thomas Nevile, who was elected Master in 1539. Four years later, largely at his own expense, he began the work; it was to continue for another nineteen.

The clearance of this immense central space involved not only the removal of the fifteenth-century south and west ranges of the old court of King's Hall and those built by Queen Mary, which had survived barely half a century; it also necessitated the resiting of one of its principal features, the early fifteenth-century King Edward's Tower, at the west end of the Chapel, some 70 feet to the north of its original position. All this, however, Nevile seems to have taken in his stride; and when his task was finished in 1612 he was able to contemplate what is probably the largest completely enclosed university court in the world.

Admittedly, it falls some way short of classical perfection. Despite his efforts, it remains irregular. The east and west ranges are not parallel, and the north range has an awkward kink in it. The various buildings of which it is composed are of different styles, periods and materials; there are no pretensions to symmetry. In fact, however, none of this seems to matter much; for, as in Tom Quad, the scale of these buildings is far too small for the space which they enclose. The quite splendid FOUNTAIN (1601–15, rebuilt 1715) does what it can – which is quite a lot – to remedy the situation by providing a focal point; but it remains impossible to see Great Court as anything approaching an architectural entity. It must therefore be taken step by step.

You enter by GREAT GATE, which was originally part of King's Hall and was built in fits and starts between 1490 and about 1530. Its east side is faced in stone; everywhere else it is of fine Tudor brick with stone dressings. I find it particularly satisfying: very broad and deep and four-square, with its four octagonal embattled corner towers. Henry VIII looks out eastward, towards Trinity Street; James I, his wife and son westward into the court. Pevsner describes these statues – which are all Jacobean – as 'wretched'; they are certainly not very good. The buildings flanking Great Gate, extending to the Chapel on the north and roughly the same distance to the south, were also part of King's Hall. They date from about 1490, with battlements of about 1600, and – as can be seen south of the Gate on the outside – are actually built of brick; the ashlar facing is an afterthought.

Following round anti-clockwise, we come to QUEEN MARY'S CHAPEL. Though one would scarcely expect it to rival that of King's, it remains a disappointment: somehow sad and lacking in lustre, like the Queen herself. (Angle turrets, as at King's, would have helped.)

*The Library, Trinity College, Cambridge.*

On the west it awkwardly abuts the repositioned King Edward's Tower; on the east, it is just as awkwardly cut into by the 1490 range, which it overshoots. The tall, identical Perpendicular windows have but a single transom and are devoid of tracery; those at the east and west ends, apart from having nine lights instead of four, are scarcely more interesting. Inside, things cheer up a bit. The ante-chapel, first of all, has a gorgeous painted ceiling and contains some fascinating statuary, including Roubiliac's superb study of Newton; it is separated from the Chapel proper by a most magnificent Baroque screen, which carries the organ and is echoed at the east end by an equally memorable reredos. The walls were until recently ablaze with Victorian wall paintings – all, alas, whitewashed over; what a pity.

And so to KING EDWARD'S TOWER, first erected between 1428 and 1432 and the oldest Gatehouse in Cambridge. Stone-built throughout, it is narrower and conceived on a scale a good deal more modest than that of Great Gate, though it too has octagonal turrets (one pair only, since it has only a single front). The statue is, predictably, of Edward III and is of 1601. The clock is unfortunate, since the tower is so obviously not designed for it; now that we all wear watches, could it not be removed? The wooden lantern is still more inappropriate, but so pretty that it deserves to remain.

At this point it is worth leaving Great Court for a moment and passing under the Tower where, immediately to your left, you can see a little more of the early King's Hall work, once the west range of a small subsidiary court. Back in Great Court, you come next to OLD LIBRARY RANGE, built by Nevile in 1600, and then – turning the north-west corner – to the MASTER'S LODGE. The northern half of this is also Nevile's, though somewhat altered by Salvin in the nineteenth century; the southern half (which nowadays includes the Fellows' Parlour and Combination Room) is in essence that built by Queen Mary, but all too little Tudor work is left. It directly abuts the HALL which, like so much else, was Nevile's gift to his College.

If Great Court were of normal size, the Hall would dominate the west side; it is sad that the court's vast dimensions prevent it from doing so. The tall pinnacled buttresses, the steeply sloping roof and the high, three-tiered lantern do their best; but they do not prepare one for the impact of the interior. Over 100 feet long and 50 high, it is easily the largest Hall in Cambridge, and by far the most beautiful. The tall four-light windows, supplemented by the two immense bays at the dais end, flood it with sunshine. The style, despite the date, is still basically Perpendicular; but the soaring hammer-beam roof looks forward to something new, for where we might have expected Gothic tracery in the woodwork we now find slender turned balusters, striking an unmistakably Jacobean note. There is fine contemporary panelling behind the dais, rising to a glorious Royal Arms amid a profusion of swirling strapwork.

Spare a look, before leaving, at the screens passage – marked on the east side by a floridly crested porch; it is considerably older than the Hall itself, having originally served the Hall of Michaelhouse before its dissolution. This, however, extended south from the passage rather than north as does its successor, and was subsequently converted into a COMBINATION ROOM. In 1774 it was remodelled, inside and out, by James Essex; hence the quietly distinguished Georgian building we see today.

The south range of Great Court along Trinity Lane – including the relatively modest QUEEN'S GATE, with its statue of Queen Elizabeth – and the southern half of the east range are entirely Nevile's work, still unashamedly Gothic. Being fairly uniform and devoid of subtle detail, they need no close inspection, so continue down the screens passage and into the College's second court, three sides of which were also built by Nevile and which consequently bears his name – NEVILE'S COURT. The north and south ranges are quite exceptionally elegant for their date (work finished in 1612) with their broad Italianate arcades – a far cry from the safe old Perpendicular of Great Court. They too have been touched up a little by Essex; his, for example, is the balustrade, which always seems to me to have been set too low above the second-floor windows. But the arcades, the key to the whole composition, are as they always were.

Except that they go on a bit further. In the first sixty-four years of its existence, Nevile's Court was only about 130 feet long, and was closed at its west end by a simple wall with a gate in the middle. Then, in 1674, Dr Isaac

Barrow, Master of Trinity, commissioned a new LIBRARY from his friend Sir Christopher Wren. Wren's first design, for a circular building strongly reminiscent of Palladio's Villa Rotonda at Vicenza, was abandoned; but two years later work began on the two-storey building which has, ever since, been the chief architectural glory of Trinity. Scale demanded that the Library should be set some way back; at the same time it was thought desirable that there should be direct access to it from the north and south ranges, which were accordingly extended to meet it – though in fact the direct access was never achieved. To the east, facing the court, there is an eleven-bay front – one further bay at each end is hidden by the side ranges – of two storeys; tall round-headed windows above, separated by attached Ionic columns, and at ground level an open arcade punctuated by tall Tuscan ones, supporting a deep Doric frieze. This arcade is considerably higher than those along the sides, but is carefully related to them: the heads of the arches are filled with solid lunettes and the bases of these – which together form a pronounced horizontal across the building – are the same height as the tops of the lateral arcades. The lunettes serve another purpose too: they brilliantly conceal the fact that the floor of the Library itself is in fact at their level, rather than at the level of the frieze above. By this means Wren gained another 6 or 7 feet of height where he needed it most, which in turn enabled him to place his bookcases below the windows and to ensure the greatest possible amount of light for the Library users.

Inside, the advantages of this ingenious arrangement become clearer still. Wren obviously took endless trouble over the furniture and fittings, planning his wooden bookcases so that they both ran along the walls and projected from them. Each of the thirty resultant stalls was given a writing table, book-rest and two stools, all of which he designed himself. The decoration is sparse compared to the Oxford libraries at Christ Church or Queen's, but there is some glorious wood carving by Grinling Gibbons, and fine busts against the ends of the bookcases by Roubiliac and Scheemakers. Thorwaldsen's life-size statue of Byron – rejected by Westminster Abbey – stands (or, more accurately, sits) at the south end, reflecting a solemnity which the poet seldom showed in his university days.

When the Library was completed, Wren seems to have felt that, despite all the trouble he had taken, his new building still threatened to overpower the rest of the court. Against the opposite range, therefore (that is, against the back of the Hall), he constructed a tribune. This takes the form of a modest classical composition – three arched niches separated by Tuscan columns supporting a pediment – standing on a raised terrace with three staircases, the centre one straight, the side ones quadrantal. It serves no utilitarian purpose; its function is merely to give more balance to the court, and in this it succeeds admirably.

After the Library, everything else we see at Trinity must be something of an anti-climax; it is, nonetheless, well worth while to take the short walk which begins at

*The Library and Nevile's Court, Trinity College, Cambridge.*

the College entrance in Trinity Lane, passes the so-called BISHOP'S HOSTEL of 1670 and a boring brick range of a century later by Sir Arthur Blomfield, and so enter NEW COURT, a Neo-Gothic creation of 1823–5 by William Wilkins. From the opposite side a short avenue of beech trees leads down to James Essex's three-arched bridge over the Cam, from which you can admire the other, austerer side of Wren's Library and enjoy a distant prospect of the New Court of St John's.

The other nineteenth- and early twentieth-century accretions to the College can safely be ignored.

## Trinity Hall

*28; Trinity Hall Lane*

Do not be misled: despite its name, Trinity Hall is just as much a Cambridge college as any other, and has no connection with its near-namesake to the north. Most colleges of medieval foundation began life as halls, adopting the name of college only in later centuries. Trinity Hall, however, was for obvious reasons unable to do so, and thus retains its old designation.

It is a good deal more ancient, in fact, than its grander and wealthier neighbour, having been founded by William Bateman, Bishop of Norwich, as early as 1350. Alas, it fell victim to the usual eighteenth-century tidying-up – Sir James Burrough, on this occasion, rather than the ubiquitous Essex – and there is precious little medieval work left. In PRINCIPAL COURT, one tiny two-light window has somehow survived in the extreme north-west corner, and there are a few more, rather larger, in the small court between the north range and Garret Hostel Lane; but they are not very exciting.

Principal Court thus presents a completely Georgian picture when viewed from the entrance – and, it must be said, an outstandingly pretty one. The ashlared ranges are all of two storeys (dormers come and go) with pediments in all the right places and a charming domed lantern above the centre of the west range. The southern end of this range contains the HALL, the interior of which was redesigned by Burrough in 1743–5: nothing really memorable perhaps, but quite distinguished in a restrained sort of way. It was extended to the south in 1892 when 'unfortunately and incomprehensibly' – the phrase is Pevsner's – the Georgian ceiling was taken down and a silly mock-Tudor one put in its place. Adjoining the Hall, but at right-angles to it along the south side of the court, is the CHAPEL. Licensed in 1352, it is the earliest chapel in Cambridge specifically intended for college use and, incidentally, the smallest. It has a pretty, heraldically painted ceiling. The tiny ante-chapel contains a fourteenth-century doorway that formerly led to the old Master's Lodge (now demolished) but the whole thing was remodelled in the early eighteenth century.

Leaving the court by the Hall passage, we emerge in another which is open to the west. To our left is Salvin's new MASTER'S LODGE of 1852 – though altered forty years later; to our right the most interesting building of Trinity Hall, its Elizabethan LIBRARY. Its ground floor is largely concealed in summertime by a wonderfully extravagant herbaceous border, from which the lovely old Tudor brick rises to a row of two-light windows and, somewhat surprisingly, a first-floor door: this originally led to a wall passage connecting Library to Lodge. The Library proper on the upper floor looks much as it did soon after it was built, with its books still chained to the bookcases – each of which has a steeply pitched book-rest above it and a finial like that of a church bench at the end.

Of nineteenth-century work, perhaps the most enjoyable is Waterhouse's east range of the minute NEW COURT which lies south of the Chapel. Waterhouse has much to answer for in Cambridge, but here he is relatively restrained – probably because of the lack of space in which to spread himself. (The pale stone is also a relief after his favourite dark red.) Apart from that, there are some unexceptional late Victorian and Edwardian buildings to the north-west of the Library towards the river, and a really admirable BRIDGE (Morgan & Partners, 1960), where for once the use of concrete rather than stone is entirely justified. The gardens are lovely: Henry James wrote: 'If I were called upon to mention the prettiest corner of the world I should draw a thoughtful sigh and point the way to the garden of Trinity Hall.'

## University Church

See St Mary the Great.

# Short List

## St Mary the Less

*29; Trumpington Street*

This church was originally known as St Peter-without-Trumpington Gate; the change of name can only be applauded. Although there are traces of earlier work – Norman and even Saxon – the whole church is to all intents and purposes a fourteenth-century one: Decorated throughout and very beautiful Decorated too, with a particularly lovely east window of six lights. (The north aisle windows are nineteenth-century replacements). The churchyard is a wonderful wild garden.

## St Mary Magdalene, Barnwell

*30; on Newmarket road (A45) in N of city, just beyond Barnwell Station*

This sad, forgotten-looking little church was formerly the chapel of the Leper Hospital at Stourbridge. Inside, however, is the best and purest Norman decoration in Cambridgeshire, especially fine around the doorways and the chancel arch. It was restored, alas, by Scott in 1867, who inserted the large west window.

## St Peter's

*31; Castle Street*

Standing on Castle Hill, over Magdalene Bridge, St Peter's is said to be on the site of an ancient Roman temple of Diana. Most of it was rebuilt in 1781, but it has mercifully retained its late Norman south doorway and a splendidly barbaric font with twin-tailed mermen.

## Stourbridge Chapel

See St Mary Magdalene, Barnwell.

## Castor

*32; 2½ miles W of Peterborough on A47*

Few saints can be more obscure than ST KYNEBURGHA, but her only church possesses perhaps the finest Norman tower in the country – two stages of two-light windows and bell openings, richly ornate yet with no loss of strength or masculinity, clearly confident of surviving the next 850 years as effortlessly as the last. The fourteenth-century lucarned spire we could have done without; but if we have to have one, we could hardly have hoped for anything more appropriate – short and squat, with no Salisburian airs and graces, and showing a sympathy for Romanesque proportions rare for its period. The whole effect is heightened by the setting of tower and crossing just halfway down the east–west axis; nave and chancel are the same length.

The interior is satisfying, though jumbled. Here again the eye is drawn to the crossing – four stalwart Norman arches with vigorously carved capitals; elsewhere, Gothic predominates. The nave dates, interestingly, from that moment at the very end of the thirteenth century when Early English (south arcade) was giving way to Decorated (north arcade); but the great east window that floods the whole church with light is uncompromisingly Perpendicular, dating from 1450 or thereabouts. The painted Casa Pupo angels in the roof are a disgrace.

St Kyneburgha's has some interesting curiosities. A nice crude inscription over a door in the south wall of the chancel (outside) records the dedication in 1124 and, over the south door, there is a Norman – possibly even Saxon – version of Christ Pantocrator. The door itself is a splendid piece of fourteenth-century workmanship, inscribed 'RICHARDUS BEBY RECTOR ECCLESIAE DE CASTRE FECIT'. Strangely, there is no Richard Beby recorded among the rectors of Castor – though there was one at Whittlesey not far away. He may, however, be the same as the 'Richard de Leycester' who was rector in 1372. Within the church are three fourteenth-century wall paintings of St Catherine in the north aisle, and a tiny Saxon sculptured stone (ninth-century?) in the chancel.

*St Kyneburgha's Church, Castor.*

## Cherry Hinton

*33; 1½ miles SE of Cambridge off A604*

ST ANDREW'S CHURCH is not, from the outside, particularly exciting. It is unusually long, of rubble with stone dressings and ashlar facing, with a low west tower. The most immediately noticeable feature is the chancel, which has no fewer than eight narrow lancets along each side, arranged in pairs with buttresses in between. What the east window would have been like we can only guess: three stepped lancets perhaps, or quite possibly five. Alas, it was replaced around 1500 with a five-light Perpendicular job – a great pity.

The interior gives a wonderful feeling of spaciousness, thanks to the breadth of the nave which, like the chancel, is outstandingly fine Early English work – five bays, the piers quatrefoil in section with nook shafts. The aisles, by contrast, are narrower and Perpendicular, though the windows have pretty little quatrefoils at the heads of the arches. Then, beyond a lovely screen, comes the chancel, which is obviously the showpiece of the whole church, as broad as the nave. The windows that we noticed on the outside now prove to be framed in deep splays by very slender ringed shafts rising almost to the roof, where they join together in deeply cusped arches in three parallel mouldings. Another continuous moulding runs the length of the wall, following the lines of the windows and of the blanks between the pairs. Equally ornate (and mercifully well preserved) is the double piscina, with dogtooth, and the sedilia: all very deeply recessed, with free-standing columns – threefold between the two piscinas, double on each side. The timber roof, with tie-beams, is of about 1500 like the east window, but is much restored; so too is the sacristy, the building of which unfortunately led to the blocking-up of the two easternmost lancets on the north side.

Returning down the nave, one vaguely longs for a few more benches – though the chairs that have been brought in instead are a good deal better than most of their kind. Then, probably for the first time, one notices the jambs of the tower arch. The arch itself is good safe Perpendicular, but are not those jambs, so square and solid, earlier than anything else we have seen in the church – Norman in fact? They are indeed: the only indication left to us of the massive church that stood on the site before the present one was built. How odd, one feels, that the early Tudor mason should have left them as they stood. Was it the stirrings of some deep-rooted sense of history that made him do so? If so, he must have been a most unusual man for his time. Or was it pure laziness? In either event, we have good cause to be grateful to him.

## Conington

*Two separate villages with the same name*
*34; 6 miles SE of Huntingdon off A604*
*35; 10 miles NW of Huntingdon off A1*

One of the many idiotic consequences of the redrawing of county boundaries in 1974 following the 1972 Local Government Act has been to give Cambridgeshire two Coningtons. The one in which we are primarily interested, which was formerly part of Huntingdonshire, lies between Huntingdon and Cambridge, just south of the A604.

ALL SAINTS' CHURCH stands in the grounds of the now demolished Conington Castle, the principal home of the Cotton family, and it still has a very private air about it. This is not to say that it is in any way modest – on the contrary it is large and quite outstandingly handsome, with a really spectacular three-stage west tower, crowned with four tall, crocketed pinnacles. It was built, very much all of a piece, around 1500. The four-light aisle windows are all absolutely regular late Perpendicular, with the same rather complicated tracery; they are echoed in those of the clerestory (three lights) and surprisingly short chancel. The tower is of stone, the rest good local cobble.

Here, alas, ends my first-hand description, since I have twice failed to gain admittance. But Pevsner writes of most interesting early nineteenth-century vaulting, and the Cotton tombs are said to be superb. I can only hope that future visitors will have better luck.

The other Conington, off the A1 just north of Sawtry, is also Cotton country. ST MARY'S CHURCH there contains more tombs of the family, including the only monument still existing actually *signed* by Grinling Gibbons.

## Elm

*36; 1½ miles S of Wisbech on B1101*

Apart from the top stage of the tower and a few later windows in the aisles and chancel, ALL SAINTS' CHURCH is Early English through and through, and a remarkably fine example of it to boot. The tower itself – if you ignore the battlements and spire – is one of the best of its date in Cambridgeshire. It must have been started around 1200: the west door is still round-headed. Above that, however, the tall, slender, pointed arcades occasionally pierced with lancet windows are almost copy-book examples of the style. Inside, there is a noble six-bay arcade surmounted by a slightly later clerestory of ten bays and above that a magnificent double hammer-beam roof.

The whole church displays a distinct and rather alarming list towards the south – an effect particularly apparent to anyone looking west from the chancel.

## Ely★

*37; 14 miles NE of Cambridge on A10*

The Abbey of Ely was founded by St Etheldreda, Queen of Northumbria, in 673. She was its first abbess, ruling over a religious community which seems to have comprised both men and women. She was succeeded by her sister, the irresistibly named Sexburga, Queen of Kent, and then by the latter's daughter Ermenilda, Queen of Mercia; the three royal abbesses are commemorated in the three crowns which to this day adorn the frontal of the high altar.

Not surprisingly, nothing of Etheldreda's time now remains; the present glorious building that is ELY CATHEDRAL was begun by Abbot Simeon, who was appointed by William the Conqueror in 1081 and, with an energy scarcely believable for one of his years – he was eighty-six – immediately began a great new church, which, sixteen years later, was raised to the status of a cathedral. Work then proceeded from the east end towards the west without interruption (except for a brief period when William Rufus expropriated the revenues) and by the middle of the thirteenth century the building was complete, including two short additional transepts flanking the west tower. There was, however, no paying-off of the architects and masons, for by then it had been realised that the old apsed Norman chancel was nowhere near big enough to accommodate the number of pilgrims flocking to St Etheldreda's tomb. Down it came, and in its place rose up a new chancel, or presbytery, aisled throughout its length but without ambulatory or apse. In 1252 it was dedicated, and for seventy years the men of Ely rested from their labours, richly satisfied as well they might be.

Meanwhile, the pilgrims continued to flock and the money to roll in; and in 1321 it was decided to follow the current fashion and to build a Lady Chapel. (Its unusual location, off the north-east corner of the north transept, was perhaps a compensatory show of independence.) No sooner had the work begun, however, than disaster struck: on 22 February 1322 the Norman crossing-tower collapsed, largely destroying the remaining Norman bays at the west end of the chancel. Ely was fortunate, at this point, in having as its sacrist, and thus in charge of the fabric, one Alan of Walsingham; and it was he, together with a master mason whose name is lost and a master carpenter from London named William Hurley, who was primarily responsible for the new enlarged octagonal crossing which is the cathedral's greatest glory. By about 1340 it was finished, and the shattered part of the chancel had also been rebuilt in the Decorated style; only the Lady Chapel remained, and in 1353 that too was complete. Soon afterwards the spire surmounting the west tower was removed and replaced by another octagon with polygonal angle turrets. Before the end of the century Ely looked much as it does today. The only important additions were the two chantry chapels of Bishops Alcock and West, begun respectively in 1488 and 1525; the only subtraction, the north-west transept which collapsed some time in the fifteenth century and was not replaced – hence the oddly asymmetrical appearance of the west front.

That front, however, remains deeply impressive – and is rendered more so by the immense west porch, or galilee, projecting forward from the tower. This, too, is early thirteenth-century; notice in particular the two superimposed rows of interlocked blind arcading inside – a theme derived from the choir aisle at Lincoln and repeated, in a rather different form, two-thirds of the way up the outer wall of the south-west transept nearby.

Simple blind arcading is the principal motif for the whole of this west façade – and, thanks to the endless variety of nicely judged shapes and sizes, very effective it proves to be. The only false note is struck by the outer portal, of twin arches separated by a central trumeau, with 'Decorated' mouchette tracery above; but pay no heed – this little folly is the work of one Francis Bernasconi, and dates from the early nineteenth century. (Its inner counterpart, equally anachronistic, is by George Gilbert Scott, who should have known better.)

So come inside now and take in the full splendour of the Norman nave, its three tiers of arches untouched since they were built. Austere? Monotonous? Not to me. That relentless, unbroken march to the crossing; those seemingly endless ranks of shafts rising from floor to roof, marking off the bays in military precision; even the wooden roof itself – Ely never had a vault – with its oddly agreeable Victorian painting: all these things combine to make the Ely nave as satisfying a vista, to my eye at least, as can be provided by any cathedral in England. How lucky, too, that that vista is finally closed, not by a great Decorated or Perpendicular east window, but by Early English lancets – far more appropriate here, in their stark simplicity, than any display of later bravura.

Bravura, anyway, is close at hand. When you have absorbed all that the nave has to offer, walk slowly east; then, halfway along, turn your eyes upward while the crossing slowly reveals itself. As it does so, there simultaneously dawns in your own mind the realisation that you are coming face to face with one of the architectural wonders of the world. The whole mood changes: Norman majesty is gone; all is light and space and movement. The eye shoots back and forth, no longer confined to perpendiculars and horizontals, but in soaring, swooping diagonals. There is a new freedom in the air. The long vistas continue, naturally, along the cardinal points; but between them, on the alternate sides of the octagonal space, tall four-light traceried windows give unexpected oblique illumination to the general rejoicing. Flanking them, the eight angle shafts suddenly burst out, like fireworks, into a profusion of ribs, upon forty of which – five from each shaft – there rises the lantern itself, so light, so airy, that it seems ready to take off at the first breeze. One finds it hard to believe that the supporting timber structure of the octagon – most of it hidden from sight – supports 400 tons of wood and lead.

The transepts are part of Simeon's original church, and consequently the oldest surviving parts of the cathedral, the south being slightly older than the north. They are shorter than they were, each having lost its innermost bay to make room for the octagonal crossing; since they were always extremely wide, with aisles running along the east and west sides, their width now comfortably exceeds their length and they seem a little stumpy. Apart from this, however, they have all the Norman virtues – which are in no way spoilt by the hammer-beam roofs, with angel supporters, added in the fifteenth century. While you are in the south transept, incidentally, do not forget to have a look at the Monk's Door just around the corner in the south-east angle of the nave, leading into the little that remains of the Norman cloisters. Dating from the mid-twelfth century, it compares interestingly with the roughly contemporary Prior's Door, also leading to the cloisters a few bays down towards the west.

*The nave and octagonal crossing, Ely Cathedral.*

Back now to the crossing, and on eastward to the choir, which was built simultaneously with it in the second quarter of the fourteenth century. There are only three bays of this choir, and it must be admitted that they have none of the majesty of the nave and transepts, none of the breathless excitement of the crossing. How could they? But they are beautiful nonetheless, and the tracery of the gallery openings in particular shows the Decorated style at its exquisite best. A glorious lierne vault, generously bossed, sets these off to perfection.

But if anyone sees Decorated as a form of liberation from the austerity of Early English, let him only walk eastward a few more paces. He is now in the presbytery, renewed as we have seen in the mid-thirteenth century to make an adequate shrine for an immensely popular saint; and a more sumptuous setting could scarcely be conceived. Only the Angel Choir at Lincoln – which is a few years later and was probably the work of many of the same masons and craftsmen – can compare with it for sheer opulence. Look at the mouldings of the arches, the trefoils and quatrefoils in the spandrels, the loving care that has gone into the shaping of every cusp and crocket and corbel and capital; there is surely as much celebration here as anywhere in the cathedral. Only the language is different.

*The Lady Chapel, Ely Cathedral.*

Now to the Lady Chapel, whither the fourteenth-century workmen returned as soon as they had finished the choir. Once again, the name of the architect is unknown, but he has produced a masterpiece. Unlike the choir, where the lines of the old presbytery had to be maintained and there was relatively little scope for anything but the adornment of already defined areas of wall, the Lady Chapel was started from scratch and completed in less than twenty years; consequently there is a marvellous feeling of harmony about it. This harmony, based on style and proportion, is simple enough; the complexity comes – to keep the musical analogy – with the rhythm. There are no flat wall surfaces here; the walls are lined, at the lowest level, with rows of seats as if in a chapter house, and above each seat is a highly intricate nodding ogee arch – that is, an arch which leans forward over the head of the sitter. As if this were not enough, there are also, all along the north and south sides, pairs of equally elaborate ogival sub-arches *behind* the seats, while at intervals, between the traceried windows, are broader seats projecting further forward than the rest. Above these latter rise two tiers of tall niches, all with the same nodding ogees, and there are yet more of these, set diagonally, across the corners. Thus the whole wall space seems alive with a gentle, dancing motion that enchants the eye as it leads it forward. In the spandrels of all these arches are carvings depicting the life and miracles of the Virgin – all, alas, sadly knocked about at the Reformation. The whole thing is crowned by another of those lovely lierne vaults, splendidly bossed.

Mercifully on the whole, Ely escaped the Perpendicular style, except in the two chantry chapels at the extreme east end. Bishop Alcock's, on the left, is little less than a small forest of late Gothic canopies, topped by a fan vault with a delightful filigree pendant. Bishop West's, on the right, is less sensational but perhaps the more interesting of the two; since he died as late as 1534, there are intimations of the Renaissance, particularly in the panelled roof. Both these chapels, however, are only appendices; the cathedral is complete without them – one of the half-dozen greatest cathedrals of England.

Before you leave Ely, wander through the precinct. Immediately south-west of the cathedral stands the former BISHOP'S PALACE, an odd combination of lovely Tudor brickwork and late seventeenth-century Baroque; at the time of writing it is a school for handicapped children, but I understand that it may not be one for much longer. The interior has been altered beyond redemption, though Bishop Goodrich's Long Gallery still survives – just. Many of the other buildings, including the PRIOR'S HOUSE, are now part of the KING'S SCHOOL – established by Henry VIII on an earlier Benedictine foundation of which Edward the Confessor was one of the most distinguished Old Boys – but there is still much to admire. The HEADMASTER'S HOUSE, for example, is fundamentally that which was built for Queen Philippa of Hainault, wife of Edward III, when she stayed at Ely to watch the building of the octagon to which she had contributed; it has a magnificent rib-vaulted undercroft, a tremendous chimneypiece and several other fourteenth-century features. The SCHOOL DINING ROOM, too, is well worth a visit since it is built into a long barn of about 1380, once the cathedral granary. The original timber roof is still in position – a marvellous survival. Near it is ELY PORTA, the great south Gatehouse to the precinct, begun in 1397. Best of all, however, is PRIOR CRAUDEN'S CHAPEL, built by Alan of Walsingham *c.*1322–5. Reached up a narrow spiral staircase, it is a tiny jewel, the Lady Chapel in miniature – as exquisite a monument of the Decorated period as you may ever hope to see.

## Etton★

*38; 6 miles NW of Peterborough off B1443*

Pure, unaltered thirteenth-century churches are all too rare in England; to find one as complete as ST STEPHEN'S is therefore no small cause for celebration. It looks as if it has not been touched since it was built, apart from some rather nasty little coloured glass borders round the lancets. Here is Early English at its best – and early Early English at that, because the bell openings in the tower are contained within a still round arch. The interior tower arch is of course properly pointed; it is, however, oddly off-centre with the three bay arcades, whose round columns have strange circular abaci and nice little heads carved in the stops. The aisle windows are double lancets with little circles in the central spandrels, the south windows of the chancel (there are none to the north) are the same except that the circles are trefoiled, there are quatrefoils in the clerestory, and the east window consists of five steeply stepped lancets.

But none of this really matters. The point here is the ensemble, in which everything is lovely and right. Look on it and be grateful.

## Fenstanton

*39; 4½ miles SE of Huntingdon off A604*

ST PETER AND ST PAUL is not a particularly prepossessing church from the outside, despite a pretty lucarned spire. It does, however, boast one outstanding feature: a seven-light Decorated east window of quite astonishing opulence for a small village. Opulent too, when you enter the raised chancel, are the four sedilia with their ogival arches and another row of inner ones, heavily cusped. In both chancel and nave large, intricately carved corbels support the timber roofs; the roof of the north aisle, on the other hand, features remarkably large angels, their wings not outstretched as one might expect but folded round their waists. On the north wall of the chancel is the tomb of Capability Brown.

The village also possesses a charming LOCK-UP – a square building of brick, with a clock turret. A few more windows and it would make a delightful summer-house. The date is probably late seventeenth century.

## Fordham

*40; 14 miles NE of Cambridge on B1102*

ST PETER'S is a large and splendid rubble church with a very broad, high tower, standing at the corner of a busy crossroads. Architecturally speaking, its chief glory is its Lady Chapel, a two-storey building placed in the same relation to the church as is its counterpart at Ely Cathedral, immediately to the north of the north aisle. The ground floor of this building takes the form of a rib-vaulted undercroft; the Chapel proper is above – approached no longer by the external newel-stair but by a modern wooden one just inside the north door. It has been much altered but has preserved its lovely windows, traceried and transomed, four lights to the east, three to the north and west. The style is still the purest Decorated, so it must date from very soon after the Ely Lady Chapel: probably 1360 or thereabouts.

The rest of the church is a jumble of periods. There are Norman windows in the north-west corner, an Early English chancel, Decorated arcades of five bays, Perpendicular clerestory, aisle windows, south porch and tower. Perpendicular too is the timber roof of the chancel, with angels along the wall plates and three abreast on the collar-beams. Stylistic distinctions of this kind tend, however, to be blurred by the exuberance of the painted decoration. There is a lot of it in the tower arch, more on the spandrels of the arcades and the capitals of the octagonal piers. But there is most of all in the chancel, where the brilliantly polychrome carved angels on the roof are joined by more angels, supported by cherubim, seraphim and saints, around the walls. These chancel frescoes, according to a wall plaque, are 'dedicated to the dear memory of Laura Mabel Townshend and were painted by her sisters Edith and Minnie, 1905'.

## Great Paxton

*41; 5½ miles SW of Huntingdon on B1043*

The CHURCH OF THE HOLY TRINITY is obviously much loved by its parishioners. The grass in the churchyard is beautifully mown, the topiary work is immaculate, and there is a carefully tended path, fringed with rose bushes, leading from the gate to the south door. At first glance, however, the building itself does not seem particularly noteworthy: merely a church of brown cobble with stone dressings and a rather low west tower. Then, suddenly, your eye is caught by the clerestory; those small, round-arched windows do not fit the prevailing Perpendicular picture. Surely they cannot be Saxon?

But Saxon they are, and Saxon – essentially – is the church itself. And proud, majestic Saxon at that, built on a formidable scale, with aisles and a crossing – rare phenomena indeed in the early eleventh century. Look first at the nave arcades. They begin a bit messily, owing to the construction of a west tower at the end of the nave in around 1380; hence the pointed arch on the south side, springing from a Saxon respond which was obviously brought across from elsewhere in the church. After that, however, the arcades get as it were into their stride, and most astonishing they are. For one thing, they have properly carved compound piers, quatrefoil in section with nook shafts. This alone makes them unique in England, since the only other Anglo-Saxon churches in the country with nave arcades – Lydd and Brixworth – have piers of crude, unshaped masonry.

There is no longer a crossing-tower; it was probably pulled down in the mid-fourteenth century, which would account for the building of the west tower shortly afterwards. Nor are there any surviving transepts, though the foundations of the north one were excavated in 1971. But the crossing itself survives, in what is now the eastern bay of the nave. Of the four original crossing arches, only one remains *in situ*, to the north. Its responds are once again extraordinarily sophisticated for their date – four slender shafts side by side, with those familiar nook shafts between. From these the arch soars up to a height, Pevsner assures us, 'unparalleled in early English architecture'.

The chancel, after all this, is a disappointment: no Saxon work, since it was completely rebuilt in the late thirteenth century – the date of the window on the north side with intersecting tracery – and again around 1500. The remains of the chancel screen are now beneath the tower arch; it has been replaced by a beam with a modern (though traditional) rood arrangement above it.

As you leave, spare a moment to look at the south door, with ironwork of the early thirteenth century. The church as a whole, for all its exceptional architectural interest, is not strictly speaking beautiful; this door is.

## Hail Weston★

*42; 1½ miles NW of St Neots off A45*

The star is awarded for charm; but ST NICHOLAS'S CHURCH has more than that. It also boasts a most remarkable west tower, entirely shingled – the rest of the church is in cobble – with a pyramid roof that descends below the ridge of the nave roof and then projects a foot or so all round. It is buttressed by heavy crucks to north and south, has twin bell openings within the pyramid and – oddest of all – on the south side a little three-light Perpendicular window, heavily cusped, in wood. Inside there are tie-beams, wind-bracing and scissor-bracing – tremendous carpentry. Nobody seems too sure about the date, but the later fifteenth century seems the most likely possibility.

The interior of the church itself is also a delight. Its timber roof is steeply pitched, with a kingpost towards the east end. One of the tie-beams is beautifully carved; the others are plain – presumably replacements. Eight brave old benches at the back are decorated with rather crude poppy-heads. It's all very unassuming, yet quite irresistible.

## Hemingford Grey

*43; 3 miles E of Huntingdon off A604*

Here is an astonishing house indeed – not for its beauty, for it is not in the strict sense of the word at all beautiful, but for its age and its quite extraordinary atmosphere. It must be one of the oldest continuously lived-in houses in England, or even in Europe; for it is built around – and into – a twelfth-century Norman hall. Of this several windows, of one and two lights, still survive; so too does the original doorway, which must have been approached, then as now, by an outer wooden stairway. In the hall itself is an even rarer survival – a complete Norman fireplace, flanked by two columns with scalloped capitals.

The discovery of this fireplace, and the most sensitive restoration of the house as a whole – which has considerable Tudor and Georgian additions – is due to the energy and vision of the present owner, Mrs Lucy M. Boston, who has devoted the last forty years to the house and its garden. She has even written a book about it – *Memory in a House* (London, 1973).

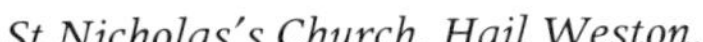

*St Nicholas's Church, Hail Weston.*

## Histon*

*44; 3½ miles N of Cambridge on B1049*

ST ANDREW'S CHURCH gains its star for one reason alone – its astonishing transepts. And even they do not announce themselves as especially remarkable from the outside, unless you spot the two triple lancets in the east wall of the south one. The church in fact looks distinctly unpromising at first sight, with a rather coarse west window by Bodley, who was also responsible for the row of circular windows in the clerestory.

Inside, the first impression is very little better. The nave, restored in 1857, and aisles are undistinguished, and the chancel is almost entirely the work of George Gilbert Scott, who lengthened it by 10 feet in 1874. Even the crossing is not what it should be, and is made quite unnecessarily narrow by the longitudinally running stalls. And so we come to those transepts. They date from the last quarter of the thirteenth century, and are unmistakably by the same hand that produced the very similar work in the Chapel of Jesus College, Cambridge (*q.v.*). Even they have been knocked about a bit: except for the two triple lancets mentioned above, all the Early English windows have been replaced by Perpendicular ones. It is the decoration of the inner walls that is extraordinary. Transepts by definition have three walls, the fourth side being open on to the crossing. At Histon, two of these three walls in each transept carry a continuous dado of blank arcading, all deeply and exquisitely moulded, with sunk trefoils or quatrefoils in the spandrels. Set into this, *both* transepts have a double piscina of exactly the same unorthodox form as in the Jesus Chapel: a broad semi-circular arch filling the available space but cut by two half arches springing from a central column. In the north transept only, the mouldings of the arcades also intersect; on the south not. One wonders which came first, and why the mason changed his mind.

The eastern walls of the transepts have no dado. Instead, they are filled by two tall arches, once again intricately moulded, framing the two groups of windows and supported on clusters of slender shafts, all individually ringed. In the spandrels are more of those sunken trefoils and quatrefoils, proportionately larger and of more complex design. On the north side, the right-hand arch is cut into by a deep niche, backless, through which the bottom of the window can be seen. On the south, the trumeau between the arches is interrupted almost at the top by a long, canopied niche. It is empty like the other, but has a delightful base consisting of two flying angels carrying off an apparently royal corpse.

Throughout, the impression is one of incredible sumptuousness which, because the workmanship matches the originality of conception, never appears fussy or overloaded. If only these superb artists had afterwards turned their attention to the rest of the church, what a glory it would have been!

## Ickleton*

*45; 8½ miles S of Cambridge on B1379*

ST MARY'S is another of those churches whose modest exterior belies the riches within. Built of flint and rubble, with a shortish crossing-tower and lead-sheathed broach spire – which has, rather surprisingly, a bell projecting to the south-west from the top of it – it is at the time of writing sadly (though one hopes only temporarily) disfigured by a painfully new-looking Decorated window at the end of the south transept, facing you as you approach. This is the consequence of one of the great tragedies of Ickleton's history: the deliberate act of vandalism by which, just before midnight on 24 August 1979, the church was set on fire by an arsonist. He was arrested the same night and the fire was soon brought under control, but not before the flames had spread to the roofs of the south aisle and transept, the crossing and the chancel, and the whole interior had been blackened by smoke. The stonework and windows also suffered severely; but the tower and bells, the fourteenth-century screen and most of the other furnishings were saved, as was the church's greatest glory, its nave. And, as the silver lining to a very black cloud, the subsequent cleaning revealed some hitherto unknown treasures – a remarkable cycle of twelfth-century wall paintings along the north wall of the nave and a fourteenth-century Doom painting over the chancel arch.

Few churches in the country have as perfectly preserved an early Norman nave and clerestory as Ickleton. More remarkable still, the four western columns, monoliths of Barnack stone, date unquestionably from Roman times. They have unusually flat cushion capitals, and the arches above are totally unmoulded. There are four bays, to which the tiny clerestory windows above do not correspond. These windows were soon to lose their *raison d'être*, anyway: in the early fourteenth century the south aisle was raised and broadened, the north soon afterwards following suit, and the new roof levels that were thus created came above the windows. This involved the building of a second clerestory, higher than its predecessor, and the scissor-braced roof that so miraculously escaped the fire in 1979.

For the rest, the south transept still stands, with its much-restored window; its northern companion had been already demolished, in 1791. The chancel, already a mess by the eighteenth century, was finally rebuilt altogether in 1882–3.

That leaves the wall paintings. The twelfth-century cycle in the nave is a considerable rarity; there are very few in all England of so early a date, and only one other in East Anglia – at Copford in Essex (*q.v.*). It is a true fresco – that is, painted directly on to the wet plaster – and dates from about 1170. On the upper level is the story of the Passion (which would probably have culminated in a Crucifixion on the east wall, lost when the wall was heightened and the Doom took its place), and below it three martyrdoms – of St Peter, St Andrew and St Lawrence respectively. The Doom, in its usual position over the chancel arch, has been much damaged in the lower parts; the upper section, however, is quite well preserved. It is iconographically orthodox except that, most exceptionally, the Virgin Mary appears topless.

## Kimbolton

*46; 7 miles NW of St Neots on A45*

'I thought 'twas absolutely best, to give it something of the Castle Air, tho' at the same time to make it regular . . . for to have built a Front with Pillasters, and what the Orders require cou'd never have been born with the Rest of the Castle: I'm sure this will make a very Noble and Masculine Shew.' So wrote John Vanbrugh in July 1707 to the 4th Earl of Manchester, at that time Ambassador in Venice, whose wife had called him in to advise on the rebuilding of the south front of KIMBOLTON CASTLE, which had collapsed some three months before. Twelve years later, all four fronts had been rebuilt to Vanbrugh's designs, and it is consequently to him that Kimbolton owes its present exterior appearance. Apart from the battlements, there is little about it to remind one of a castle; but it is none the worse for that.

The house – which was sold up by the 10th Duke of Manchester in 1960 and is now the home of Kimbolton School – has been little altered since Vanbrugh's time; its earlier history, however, is complicated and occasionally enigmatic. A castle is known to have existed on the site since the early thirteenth century; this was rebuilt, and doubtless made a good deal more comfortable, by Sir Richard Wingfield in the 1520s, and it was the Wingfield mansion in which the unfortunate Queen Catherine of Aragon spent the last twenty months of her life before she died in January 1536. But the Wingfields soon fell on evil days, and in 1615 the estate was sold to Sir Henry Montagu, later Earl of Manchester. He rebuilt in his turn, and it is the further remodelling of his work by his great-grandson, the 4th Earl, that we see today.

This 4th Earl,however, initiated two quite separate building programmes at different times. Around 1690, some seventeen years before Vanbrugh's arrival, we know that work was started on the interior courtyard and on the creation of a new Great Hall on the site of the earlier Hall in the east range. It was probably at this time too – though it may have been earlier – that the centre of the south range was extended some 15 feet into the courtyard to provide space for a new Grand Staircase.

Who was the architect for this work? No one knows for sure. The Clerk of the Works was one William Coleman, who is responsible for what written evidence we have. Coleman was to remain at Kimbolton through the time of Vanbrugh, from whom he was to win high praise ('If we had Such a Man at Blenheim, he'd save us a Thousand pounds a Year'); but he was almost illiterate, and would certainly have been incapable of such sophistication as we see in the courtyard. It is entered through a broad archway to the west, opposite the Hall range. This consists of four tall windows separated by Corinthian pilasters on tall plinths – at the level of which runs a row of small basement windows – and, in the centre, a doorway set at the level of the pilasters and approached by a broad staircase with a magnificent handrail of wrought iron. The door itself is framed by Ionic columns supporting a segmental pediment and has the Manchester arms above. The other three sides are simpler. Like the eastern one, they are of rubbed red brick (replaced in patches by a rather nasty, lighter

*The Queen's Room, Kimbolton Castle.*

variety) and they continue the row of basement windows and the wooden modillion cornice. (They also boast quite spectacular lead rainwater pipes.) All the principal windows, however, have scrolly acanthus crests above them, and it is these crests that give us our principal clue as to the architect; for almost precisely similar decorations are to be found on the Sessions House at Northampton and the Duke's Head Hotel at King's Lynn – the former probably and the latter certainly by Henry Bell. There is also a little festoon hanging from the volutes of the Ionic columns beside the door – just as can be seen at the Duke's Head and on Bell's Customs House at King's Lynn. The Customs House also has little grotesque heads similar to those in the acanthus crests on the north and south walls. Thus, although there is no documentary proof, the stylistic evidence points most convincingly to Bell.

It we are right, to Bell also belongs the beautifully panelled Great Hall. (There are more festoons on the oddly elongated pilasters framing the doorways.) The woodwork was originally painted white, but in 1938 was stripped according to the fashion of the time. Nowadays the room is sadly unfurnished, and is dominated by the delightful group portrait of the 4th Earl's six children – our first encounter with that other

great benefactor of Kimbolton, the Venetian Giovanni Antonio Pellegrini. But Pellegrini's full splendour is only seen when, passing through what was formerly the Red Drawing Room, we emerge in the Staircase Hall. He and Vanbrugh together – the latter adapting earlier work and probably re-using much of the wood decoration – have transformed a narrow, almost cramped, space into a dazzling Baroque fantasy. The three decorated arches (two above, one below) give a feeling of both light and lightness which is intensified by the length and gentle inclination of the staircase and its lovely wrought-iron balustrade. And the paintings are a joy. The main staircase panels portray a single triumphal procession, perhaps vaguely inspired by the Mantegnas at Hampton Court; higher up, the subjects become more light-hearted; among the monkeys, parrots and sumptuously dressed musicians there is one enchanting picture of cherubs tossing aside the inferior coronets of baron and viscount, and momentarily brandishing that of an earl before, one suspects, the ducal strawberry leaves descend from on high. (They very soon did.)

Pelligrini painted two other rooms at Kimbolton; the first is the Chapel. It is in the west wing, just south of the archway into the courtyard. The high west gallery (really south) on its three arches is almost certainly by Vanbrugh, though parts may date from the 1690 building programme. The paintings consist of a Transfiguration above the altar and the four Evangelists along the side walls; but the figure of St Luke, to the south-west, is a later replacement. These paintings are not really successful; Pellegrini just was not a religious painter. He is back at his ease again, however, in the tiny Queen's Boudoir, now used as an office by the headmaster's fortunate secretary, who confesses herself enchanted by the presence of Venus and Cupid canoodling above her head.

Next to this room is the Queen's Room, where poor Catherine lived and died, and next to that Vanbrugh's great Saloon, the most palatial room in the house, occupying the centre of the south front. I think that if I had been in his place I should have tried to lower the floor level at this point – as the room is raised over a high basement it should not have been too difficult – since it somehow seems too low for its length and breadth; this may be why Vanbrugh narrowed it at the two northern corners with free-standing Corinthian columns, a little as if he had intended a screen right across, and then thought better of it. In the centre is a splendid marble chimneypiece, crowned by a huge inverted scallop shell with garlands. It is thought to be by Alessandro Galilei, the young Florentine architect and designer who was working at Kimbolton in 1719.

Leaving the house by the Saloon door, we should now walk round it on the outside. That door, and the double stairway leading up to it, is the salient feature of the south front; the real *coup de théâtre* comes round the corner to the east – a tremendous Roman portico *in antis*, with giant Tuscan columns soaring up two storeys to the metope-and-triglyph frieze and two tiers of round-headed niches forming a closed bay on each side. A balustrade above makes it a little higher than the four ordinary bays on the wings. In front is a broad terrace with a flight of steps on each side, and from this terrace a third flight, even broader, climbs up to the portico, narrowing curvaceously as it does so. Since there are drawings by Vanbrugh for a totally different design of portico, and a drawing by Galilei of it much as it is today, it has been suggested that Galilei rather than Vanbrugh was responsible. In fact, however, Kimbolton was almost certainly finished by 1715, soon after the twenty-four-year-old Galilei had arrived in England; he seems to have designed the terrace and the stairs, but that is all.

Of the other fronts, the north has a five-bay loggia of depressed arches, their keystones meeting the sills of the windows above – a favourite Vanbrugh trick. Being on a slightly lower level, its basement windows appear as ground-floor ones, and an additional attic floor added in the nineteenth century over the five-bay centre makes the whole thing look distinctly uncomfortable. The entrance front, facing west towards the town, is also something less than satisfactory. It possesses, for one thing, an even number of bays – sixteen – which always makes for lack of focus. Admittedly the central doorway takes up two of them at ground-floor level, but even this does not entirely solve the problem.

This west front looks directly across the lawn to the main entrance and the Gatehouse designed by Robert Adam in about 1765. The rustication, and the heavy Gibbs surrounds to the windows on each side of the entrance arch, give it more gravity than we expect from Adam; it may be that he is deliberately seeking to reflect the Vanbrugian grandeur.

From the Gatehouse – though a little off-centre – the broad High Street of Kimbolton town runs off westward between rows of attractive if unpretentious houses, mostly Georgian, along each side. At the end, on the right, is ST ANDREW'S CHURCH. It has a fine west tower of *c.*1320 with a broach spire and three rows of lucarnes. Inside there is a nice high-pointed chancel arch, pale yellow rendered walls and a very high four-bay arcade. Good Manchester monuments abound, but the best thing is the ravishing painted screen to the south chapel, the figures of *c.*1500 in a remarkable state of preservation.

## Kirtling

*47; 16 miles E of Cambridge off B1085*

All that now remains of the vast mansion of the North family is the GATEHOUSE, an imposing Tudor affair of 1530 or so. It is of the predictable red brick, with blue brick diapering and uneven stone dressings on the corners of the tall polygonal flanking towers. There are four of these, embattled and with irregular fenestration – the days of symmetry were yet to come – the two front ones separated (though only just) by a tall, two-storeyed oriel. This is a beautiful feature in itself, having six arched lights with transom on each floor; but the effect is spoilt by the proximity of the flanking towers, which seem determined to squeeze it out of existence.

ALL SAINTS' CHURCH is nearby in the grounds, giving more the impression of a family chapel than of a parish church. It has a surprisingly ambitious Norman south doorway, with a figure of Christ in Majesty set into the tympanum rather than being carved directly in it. The interior is cool and uncluttered, but a mixture of dates: the north arcade, for example, is a good two centuries later than the south, the clerestory a century later still. The Perpendicular chancel has on its north side a most curious Renaissance window, dated in one of the spandrels 1564; it may well be connected with the memorial to Edward Myrfin, whose journey to the Levant a few years before that date is fascinatingly set out on a brass nearby. There are some good family tombs, too, in the misleadingly named North Chapel, just south of the chancel.

## Leighton Bromswold

*48; $7\frac{1}{2}$ miles NW of Huntingdon off A604*

ST MARY'S is a most beautiful church, and also a fascinating one both architecturally and historically. The sturdy west tower, faced in a cool, creamy ashlar, warns us from quite a distance that this is something unusual: it is a curious amalgam of the Gothic and the classical, erected in 1634. The west door, windows and bell openings are round-arched, with pilasters; on the other hand, it has diagonal clasping buttresses with set-offs and an embattled parapet. The buttresses are topped with pinnacles in the Gothic style, but those pinnacles take the form of classical obelisks.

Inside, Early English reigns. Nave and chancel are both of the late thirteenth century, despite three Perpendicular windows in the chancel, including (alas) the east one. In both the work is of the finest; note especially the double piscina – that curious motif of the deeply moulded arch intersected by two half arches as at Histon and at Cambridge, in Jesus College Chapel. But whereas at Histon the Early English transepts are nowadays the whole pride of the church, here the transepts seem to have been largely remodelled in the fourteenth century – see the Decorated east windows.

By the beginning of the seventeenth century the church was in ruins, the south aisle and original crossing-tower demolished, the nave without a roof. Then, in 1626, the Bishop of Lincoln offered the prebendal stall of Leighton Ecclesia to George Herbert, Fellow of Trinity College, Cambridge, the metaphysical poet. Herbert was still only a deacon – he was not to be ordained for another four years – but he immediately put in hand a major programme of restoration, with the help of his friend Nicholas Ferrar of Little Gidding (*q.v.*).

The church guide states, surprisingly, that despite his benefactions Herbert 'never set foot either in the church or the parish', an allegation which I find hard to believe. He never actually held the living – after his ordination he at once accepted that of Bemerton in Wiltshire – but to him are unquestionably due the fine timber roofs of the nave and transepts and much of the furniture. Of the latter the two most memorable items are the pulpit and the reading desk. They stand one each side of the chancel arch, and are identical – a reflection of Herbert's belief that prayer and preaching were 'equally useful' and consequently deserved equal precedence. They are magnificent pieces, with huge testers to serve as sounding boards. Identical too are the stalls and benches, and the low wooden screen is also in similar style. It is all very simple – Herbert was never a rich man – but it gives one an extraordinary feeling of what parish churches looked like and felt like in the early days of the Laudian reforms.

Just east of the church is a splendid Jacobean GATEHOUSE of 1616, of red brick with projecting corner towers. It was intended for a new mansion to be built on the site of Leighton Bromswold Castle; this, however, did not materialise.

## Leverington

*49; 1½ miles NW of Wisbech off B1166*

ST LEONARD'S CHURCH gets off to a fine start with one of the best towers in all Cambridgeshire, its lucarned spire clustered around with little octagonal turrets, military-looking yet devoid of menace. The whole building is of a nice warm grey limestone, and the standard is kept up by the south porch, with two storeys and a third, attic, one under the gable, and a pretty ogival arch repeated at first-floor level. Inside there is a broad late thirteenth-century chancel with a glorious Decorated east window, matched by another in the south chapel, just as beautiful but obviously a bit later since the tracery is far more free-flowing. The nave is later again – Perpendicular of about the middle of the fifteenth century – and has its original roof, tie-beamed and intricately carved. Alas, its effect is largely spoilt by a lower row of strainer arches unhappily (and unnecessarily?) inserted in 1901. Ignore them if you can, but the task is not easy.

The church possesses two other bonuses worthy of special mention: a memorable medieval font, centrally placed at the end of the nave – a siting which, when viewed from the east end, emphasises the slightly disturbing asymmetry of the plan – and a gorgeous Jesse window, much restored but still capable of giving a *frisson* of pleasure.

LEVERINGTON HALL, a noble manor house of the sixteenth and seventeenth centuries, stands hard by. At the time of writing, it is open to the public by prior appointment.

*The tie-beam ceiling of St Leonard's Church, Leverington.*

## Little Gidding

*50; 12 miles SW of Peterborough off B660*

The CHURCH OF ST JOHN THE EVANGELIST, Little Gidding, remains in a very real sense a memorial to Nicholas Ferrar, who founded a religious community in the village in 1625. Its numbers were small; they never exceeded about forty, nearly half of them members of the Ferrar family; but it possessed an influence out of all proportion to its size and was visited three times by Charles I – the last time in May 1646, on the run from the Parliamentarians. It was as a result of the shelter and concealment given him on this occasion that the church was sacked soon afterwards. The community survived only for a few more years; but Little Gidding is still a centre of pilgrimage, and has been further immortalised by T. S. Eliot in the *Four Quartets*.

The approach could hardly be more pastoral: through a farmyard, and then across a field in which sheep are safely grazing to the little rose-fringed path that leads past the tomb of Nicholas Ferrar – placed squarely in the middle of it – to the west door. The church itself is tiny: 60 feet long with a nave 17 feet across, brick-built but with a most idiosyncratic stone façade, dated (on the angle pinnacles) 1714. The doorway is straight-headed, with an enormous keystone and big corner brackets supporting a heavy moulded hood somewhat suggestive of Ancient Egypt. Above is a rusticated bell-cote, and above that a most curious perforated obelisk.

This 1714 restoration – necessitated because of the damage done by the Puritans – was undertaken by John Ferrar, Nicholas's nephew. He made the church still smaller – though it can never have been large – by removing the north aisle and several feet from the west end. Sadly, he also removed his uncle's pulpit – though the late fifteenth-century brass lectern, the brass tablets that form the reredos, the hourglass stand and the font all date from Nicholas's time. The inward-facing stalls are of 1714, though their panelled fronts may be earlier.

The floor – lozenges of black and white marble – is of 1920 and just as it should be. The stained glass windows of 1853, on the other hand – and especially the east window – are a disaster. Yet even they cannot altogether spoil the extraordinary quietness and peace of this little church. As Eliot wrote:

> *Here, the intersection of the timeless moment*
> *Is England and nowhere. Never and always.*

## Longthorpe

*51; 2 miles W of Peterborough on A47*

The massive square TOWER looms up a few yards from the main street. The late thirteenth-century hall house to which it is attached still stands, and despite heavy rebuilding in the early nineteenth century manages to retain a good deal of its medieval fabric, including its timber roof of about 1300. It is consequently considered by the experts to be one of the most important houses of

*The church of St John the Evangelist, Little Gidding.*

its date in the country. Now privately owned, it is not normally open to the public; nor is there any real reason why it should be, since the average visitor would find nothing much to interest him.

Our attention therefore is focused on the tower, which is astonishing; not so much architecturally – though by its sheer size it cannot fail to impress – as because it contains, in the first-floor Great Chamber, what is by far the most important series of medieval secular mural decoration in England. Even on the Continent there is little of a similar date that can match it. The tower itself is thought to have been added to the house in about 1300, and the wall paintings are of perhaps thirty years later. They are varied in their subject matter; we have a Nativity scene beneath a representation of the Seven Ages of Man, a Wheel of the Five Senses, the Morality of the Three Quick and the Three Dead, the Labours of the Months, plus any number of angels, saints and apostles, real and mythical beasts, and some brilliantly observed paintings of local birds. The whole extraordinary cycle was discovered only after the last war, when the tenant was cleaning up after the departure of the Home Guard. It is now in the care of the Dept of the Environment, and open to the public.

## March*

*52; 13 miles E of Peterborough on A141*

They started building ST WENDREDA'S CHURCH soon after 1300, and they finished it – with the rebuilding of the chancel by W. Smith of London – in 1872. Between those dates, the two principal building periods were around 1350 and 1500. The first of these saw the building of the chancel arch, the south arcade and the west tower, with a (later) lucarned spire above and a passage – presumably ensuring some time-honoured right of way – running through the bottom; the second saw the completion of the church as we see it today – a beautifully proportioned building of a warm honey-coloured rubble, with stone dressings, and generously embattled. The interior contains much to enjoy, including a wonderful west window in the tower, with three lights and swirling tracery; but all is overshadowed by the roof, which robs one of breath. Here is the finest double hammer-beam roof in all England, with serried regiments of angels – on the corbels, on the ends of both the upper and lower hammer-beams, along the ridge, even carved in relief (in two layers) along the wall plates – nearly 200 of them altogether. Above the corbel angels, for good measure, runs a row of standing saints under elaborately carved canopies. Such a profusion of splendour is rare indeed; only Woolpit in Suffolk – where the roof is of a remarkably similar design – can compare, but the effect there is somehow less overwhelming. Here it is tremendous, and on no account to be missed.

*The double hammerbeam roof, St Wendreda's Church, March.*

## Milton

*53; 3 miles W of Peterborough off A47*

When Sir William Fitzwilliam purchased the manor of Milton in 1502 – along with half a dozen others, including Castor, Etton and Northborough – it consisted of a village and a probably quite unassuming manor house. Both have disappeared. The village has left no trace, the manor house only a very slight one: in the great mansion that took its place, the Hall is set at an angle of some 15 degrees to the rest of the plan – a strong indication that it was built on the foundations of its predecessor.

As one approaches the house across the park, one's first impression is of tremendous length. The Tudor elevation alone is 235 feet long, and was to be extended a further 90 feet at the end of the century following. The precise dating of this Tudor building has presented a good many problems over the years. The two huge bay windows lighting the Hall and the Chapel at the far west end have depressed pointed lights that would suggest the middle of the sixteenth century; the other, square-headed, windows look more like 1600 or so. The most likely explanation is that the house took shape gradually from about 1550 onwards; this would also account for the other eccentricities of this north façade. There are no fewer than eight projections along its length, of which the porch – which has mullioned and transomed windows and battlements, but a round-arched entrance with orders on both floors – forms the third. West of this porch, however, the front is symmetrical, with the two aforementioned bays at the ends and three lesser ones between them, the central one projecting slightly further. There are two storeys only; the roof and dormers came later.

The Tudor house was thus complete by the beginning of the seventeenth century, and seems to have remained more or less unaltered until the arrival of William Talman in 1688. (Why Lord Fitzwilliam did not call in Sir Christopher Wren, who was his brother-in-law, remains a mystery.) Talman's initial reactions were not favourable; Fitzwilliam's steward wrote to his master: 'I could not find that he liked your house at all, but was rather for pulling it quite down. After some time ... we misspent ye rest of ye evening at the Talbot.' Talman's eventual suggestions for the remodelling of the house were never taken up; he did, however, build the beautiful stable range which continues the Tudor front to the east and then doubles round to make an open westward-facing quadrangle. It makes no attempt to continue the height lines of the older building; and yet, with its pedimented three-bay centre and lantern above it, makes a completely satisfying composition, most perfectly judged.

The Fitzwilliams continued to feel, however, that the house itself was in need of modernisation. In 1726 the 2nd Earl commissioned a series of drawings from James Gibbs, who apparently shared Talman's views: his *Book of Architecture* (1728) includes designs for a new Milton, reconceived as a Palladian palace. Perhaps because Fitzwilliam was not prepared to pull down his Tudor front or perhaps because – as Gibbs himself maintained – he died before anything could be done, these plans were fortunately never executed. The 3rd Earl, coming of age in 1744, returned to the quest. He first consulted Matthew Brettingham, then turned to Henry Flitcroft, the estimate for whose proposals (at £1,465) was a good deal cheaper; and it was Flitcroft's plans which, between 1745 and 1750, were finally put into effect. They had the great advantage (wrung most unwillingly from the architect) of preserving the entire north front, with all its internal partitions; to the south, however, they provided for a completely new range, back to back with the other, containing a series of elegant, sun-filled rooms. The style is Palladian (though the canted bays and Venetian windows within them are of somewhat dubious propriety), but Flitcroft has followed the design of the north front in that he has treated the western end – from the point opposite the old Hall – as a separate unit for purposes of symmetry. Within this, in an elevation of two and a half storeys, he gives us a nine-bay façade with projecting side wings and a one-bay pedimented centre containing a Venetian window on the *piano nobile*, a similarly shaped doorway below, and a small semi-circular 'thermal' window above. The roof is hipped, with rather tall chimneys. East of this composition there was a courtyard – replaced by the present broad bow-windowed Dining Room by Carr of York in *c.*1803 – beyond which Flitcroft provided a new service wing, now partially demolished.

But already before Carr's arrival another, greater, architect had made his contribution to Milton. This was Sir William Chambers, who was commissioned by the 4th Earl Fitzwilliam in 1770 to carry on where Flitcroft had left off. (The latter had died the year before, but work on the house had effectively stopped with the 3rd Earl's death in 1756.) Chambers was further instructed to reconstruct the roof on the Tudor north front, raising it sufficiently to allow for a series of servants' bedrooms to be lit by dormers. This he managed to do with remarkable success, using a canted roof (its vertical parts slate-hung) and larger, strongly pedimented dormers to carry on the emphasis of the projecting bays below. Behind this to the south, immediately above the pillared Hall that Flitcroft had provided as his ground-floor centre, Chambers designed the great Gallery that remains the single most spectacular feature of Milton.

Any tour of the house must, however, start at the beginning, in the North Hall. Like all the principal rooms, it owes its decoration to one or another of the eighteenth-century architects mentioned above; if you are looking for Tudor interiors, you had better leave at once. Three things only reveal its former identity: its immense height, its relation to the entrance – one still has a feeling of a screens passage, even though the screen itself has gone – and the soaring bay window with eight lights, three transoms and heraldic glass. Flitcroft it was who removed the old timber roof and replaced it with the deeply coved plaster ceiling; his also is the splendid chimneypiece in which is set a wind-dial placed over a map of Europe. The colour of the walls, too – a marvellous orange-pink – has remained unchanged since his day. Of the three rooms leading off to the west, the Smoking Room and the Ante-Room have lovely ceilings, then comes the Gothicky Flower Room. The extreme west end of the house, containing the former Chapel in the final bay, is no longer used.

If you follow what used to be the screens passage and leave the North Hall opposite the entrance, you will come to a pretty little lobby by S. Satchell (*The Buildings of England* miscalls him Tatchell) with a tiny colonnade above, lit by an oval lantern. It leads through to Carr's small Breakfast Room. The door at the dais end brings you to the main staircase, with its beautiful, partly gilded handrail and glorious plasterwork. It too has a lantern above. Then into Flitcroft's Pillared Hall, occupying the entire five-bay centre of his symmetrical south front. It is a wonderful room, divided into three by two pairs of stone Tuscan columns, their pale creaminess echoed in the colour of the walls and the stone-flagged floor. Passing back through the Staircase Hall, you then come to the Study, and beyond it Carr's Breakfast Room again and his bow-fronted Dining Room beyond, all with lovely views across the park to the half-hidden lake.

On the first floor, the decoration is due almost entirely to Chambers. Along the north front there extends a suite of marvellously elegant reception rooms, including what used to be known as the Peterborough Dining Room, a so-called Tea Room, and the former Green Drawing Room, now the Library; and parallel with these to the south is the great Gallery. Whether the general shape of this tremendous room was already planned by Flitcroft – it is tripartite, like his Pillared Hall below – or whether the form, as well as the decoration, is entirely due to Chambers is uncertain; the result, in any event, is stunning. The two end sections have depressed segmental vaults, the centre the shallowest of domes, supported on pendentives bearing ornamental medallions. The general style is Palladian, but with a light, imaginative touch to it that seems to derive partly from Adam and partly from the France of Louis XV.

Humphry Repton produced a Red Book for Milton in 1791; by this time, much of the park had already been landscaped, though we do not know when or by whom. It contains several small buildings of considerable charm, including a Gothick lodge by Repton himself – though Nash may have helped him with the details – and a small Corinthian temple by Chambers, no longer in its original position. Chambers is thought by Christopher Hussey (*Country Life*, 1 June 1961) to have also designed the little classical Orangery; and he may well have been responsible for the enchantingly fanciful Kennels, designed as a ruined castle.

## Over

*54; 9 miles NW of Cambridge off B1050*

ST MARY'S is most palatial-looking for an ordinary parish church. (Its early connection with Ramsey Abbey may have something to do with it.) The lower part of the tower looks thirteenth-century, but the whole thing was largely rebuilt around 1325, which must be the date of the deep, twin-turreted south porch with its two Decorated windows on each side. Above runs a frieze of very pretty ball-flower, its tendrils extending all along the south aisle. There are some fearsome gargoyles above, and then battlements. Parts of the church seem to have been recently re-rendered in a rather lighter colour, giving it a faintly piebald appearance; but it doesn't really matter.

You enter through a south door of tremendous proportions. The interior has the same palatial quality, but without the exuberance that is such a feature of the outside. The six-bay arcade looks about 1380 – during the fourteenth century the church was clearly never pressed for cash – and the polygonal shafts of the piers have most interesting carved and castellated capitals. There are also some lovely corbels, carved with heads and, higher up, figures – some of which are unfinished. They support a good timber roof with kingposts. The church is broad and well lit, thanks to the three-light Decorated windows to north and south, and the four-light ones with reticulated tracery at the east ends of the aisles. There is a tall, most delicate chancel screen of 1400 or so, which on the east side has even managed to preserve its ribbed coving.

And so to the chancel, which is Perpendicular, but only just; the curious tracery of the five-light east window and the three-light side windows – three to the south, two to the north – seems to mark the exact moment when Decorated was dying and the new style was still feeling its way tentatively forward. The pretty running wall plate of angels with outstretched wings presumably dates from the remodelling of the chancel in 1840. There are six stalls along the south side, probably from Ramsey Abbey, with nice arm-rests and entertaining misericords, and, just beyond the chancel arch, a splendid Jacobean wineglass pulpit with a heavy ogival tester. A stone bench runs around most of the church, where, in the old days, 'the weakest went to the wall'.

## Peterborough*

*55; 18 miles N of Huntingdon on A15*

In essence, the CATHEDRAL is a magnificent Norman abbey – begun in 1118, it only became a cathedral after the Reformation, in 1541 – with later additions at both ends. The west front (*c.*1215), with its three giant recesses, is surely one of the most dramatic in England. Being an afterthought, and one whose design was changed at the last moment from seven bays to five, it bears little relation to the building behind it; it is considerably broader for one thing, and purists may be offended that the doorways in the flanking recesses are out of alignment, and that the central recess is narrower than its fellows, rather than wider and higher, as at Lincoln or Norwich. But the effect is undeniably grand, and marred only by two features: one is the late fourteenth-century porch which has been stuck for no apparent reason into the central arch; the other, more disastrous still, is the north-west tower, which was conceived before the west front was thought of and now peeps up ridiculously behind and inward from the corresponding corner of the façade, looking much too low and ruining both the skyline and – since its south-west counterpart was never finished – the symmetry.

Inside the cathedral, the first bay is really a short western transept, Early English of *c.*1180, an agreeable early Gothic introduction to the superb mid-twelfth-century Norman nave, mercifully unbroken by organ or choir screen, marching confidently up to the east apse. The dominant effects here are those of light – most of the stained glass was destroyed in Cromwell's day, and the Norman aisle and gallery windows were subsequently enlarged – and of a marvellous broad-shouldered sturdiness created, more than anything else, by the depth and strength of the tribune gallery, as broad as the aisles above which it runs. These aisles are in themselves noteworthy, first for the lovely intersecting arcading along the walls, and secondly for their rib vaulting – among the earliest examples in Europe, though Durham beats it by a year or two.

With such assured stonemasons as this, and with so rich a supply of warm Barnack limestone readily available, it is odd that the nave of Peterborough, like that of Ely, should have remained unvaulted. Odd, but fortunate; for its painted wooden roof is one of the cathedral's glories. Inevitably it has been retouched over the years, but it still retains its original design and colouring from the early thirteenth century, with kings and queens, saints and bishops, musicians and monsters, like figures from some gigantic illuminated missal.

The crossing boasts pointed fourteenth-century arches to east and west with, high above, a lierne vault of painted wood – all right, but not a patch on Ely's miraculous lantern. To each side the robust transepts, with their alternating round and octagonal piers crowned with massively scalloped capitals and their ground-level blind arcades no longer intersecting, are largely ruined by appalling Victorian glass that makes one long for an hour of Cromwell. And so to the chancel. The effect is curious – a semi-circular Norman apse, with Norman arches framing early fourteenth-century

Decorated windows at the upper levels, an intricate fifteenth-century painted wooden ceiling above and, below, two highly ornate openings into the retrochoir of about 1500 flanking a huge *baldacchino* of Derbyshire alabaster ill-advisedly erected by J. L. Pearson in 1894. One can only say that it looks better than it sounds.

To pass from the east end of the Norman north aisle (where, under a plain grey stone without any inscription, lie the remains of Catherine of Aragon) into the early sixteenth-century retrochoir, built almost exactly 400 years later, is to span virtually the whole of English medieval architecture at a single step. Suddenly we are standing on the threshold of the Renaissance, under a triumph of virtuoso fan vaulting worthy to rank with that of King's College, Cambridge, and almost certainly by the same architect, John Wastell.

The cathedral has its curiosities: on the base of the trumeau (middle post) just inside the central porch is a curious carving of a figure said to be Simon Magus, upside-down, tormented by demons. Within, the west door is flanked by two portraits and an epitaph to the Elizabethan sexton and gravedigger Robert Scarlett, who buried two queens, Catherine of Aragon and Mary Queen of Scots – the latter subsequently transferred by her son, James I, to Westminster. In the apse lies the so-called Hedda Stone, Anglo-Saxon, carved with figures of the Apostles, *c*.800.

*The retrochoir, Peterborough Cathedral.*

Little remains of the old abbey buildings. Remnants of the arcaded walls of the INFIRMARY still stand opposite the end of the south transept, with two little Georgian houses built inside them. Best preserved are the OUTER GATE (Norman, with early fourteenth-century work superimposed) and, just inside on the right, the ABBOT'S GATE, early thirteenth-century with surprisingly good statues on both sides.

## Ramsey

*56; 9½ miles NE of Huntingdon on B1040*
*Includes Ramsey Abbey Gatehouse (NT)*

Founded in 969, Ramsey Abbey was one of the most important monasteries in England during the Middle Ages, but it has been rebuilt so often since the Dissolution that the present building gives little pleasure. It includes part of the thirteenth-century Lady Chapel, incorporated into the house that the Cromwell family erected on the site around 1600, but this in turn was added to and altered, first by Soane and then by Blore, and the result is, not surprisingly, a pretty good jumble. There remains only the GATEHOUSE, now in the care of the National Trust. Part of it has been removed to Hinchingbrooke (*q.v.*) but the truncated remainder has preserved some fine detail, notably the panelled buttresses and the friezes in fleuron and quatrefoil.

The pride of Ramsey nowadays is consequently not the abbey at all but the CHURCH OF ST THOMAS À BECKET. It seems to have been originally built as a guest-house or a hospital in *c*.1180; only in the thirteenth century was it converted into the parish church, in which capacity it still serves. There is a splendid west door of three orders, the capitals ranging from traditional Norman types through water-leaf (Transitional) to stiff-leaf (Early English), and a great broad nave which makes a tremendous impact. It is of seven bays – formerly eight – and the piers, both in their cross-section and their capitals, show the same wide variety as the west doorway. The arches of the arcades are already stepped, chamfered and pointed, that to the chancel taller but otherwise similar; the chancel itself, however, is completely Norman (building always began at the east end) with three round-headed east windows deeply splayed and an almond-shaped one above them, in the middle. It is vaulted in stone, with two great diagonal ribs. All the aisle windows are Perpendicular, but of no very special interest.

Traces of wall paintings can be discerned above the north arcade, but it is all very dim. The best of the stained glass, by Morris & Co. (not to be confused with the Morris and Sons' work in the south aisle), is a good deal more rewarding.

## St Ives

*57; 6 miles E of Huntingdon off A1123*

Apart from Wisbech and of course Cambridge itself, I know of no town or village in the county that uses its river as well as St Ives. It is spanned by a superb BRIDGE built *c*.1415 – about the time of Agincourt – with a tiny

*The fifteenth-century bridge and chapel, St Ives.*

CHAPEL halfway along it. (There are only two other chapels like this in all England – at Wakefield and Rotherham, both in Yorkshire.) After the bridge, the best bit of architecture is ALL SAINTS' CHURCH, beautifully situated at the very end of the main street by the Ouse. Its date is late fifteenth-century, and it has a really glorious spire, tall and slender as a lance. The interior is said to be equally fine; but the church is always kept locked, and although I have hammered at the door of the vicarage on three separate occasions I have never received any reply. Why cannot vicars put a notice in the porch saying where the key is to be found?

## St Neots

*58; 8 miles SW of Huntingdon off A1*

The soaring stone tower of ST MARY'S CHURCH with its four high pinnacles is visible from afar and constitutes an important landmark in this region of what used to be Huntingdonshire. The rest of the church is mainly rubble with occasional stone blocks and stone dressings – large, uniform, impressive, and generously embattled; but the 130-foot tower dominates all. Its stages are separated by bands of quatrefoil design and the buttresses, which reach halfway up the belfry stage, have their own free-standing pinnacles.

The two porches, to north and south, differ only in that the former is a nineteenth-century rebuilding (using, however, much original material) while the latter is of *c.*1490, the same date as the tower. Both are of two storeys, with two windows let into each side and a three-light window above the door – presumably once a schoolroom or priest's lodging. The interior is slightly spoilt to my eye by the too white clunch of the arcades, which are of five bays; but there is a glorious timber roof with angels and confronted animals along the wall plates. Aisles and chapels are also timbered, with crested cornices and more carved menageries. The short chancel has a ceilure of gold stars and bosses.

After such wealth, the church furniture proves a little disappointing, but the screens are good – especially that leading into the north chapel – and there is a stunning late Victorian monument to a Mr and Mrs Rowley by Thomas Earp, her effigy almost invisible through the ironwork of the gates.

Immediately to the west of the church stands BROOK HOUSE. Built about 1700, with seven bays, a hipped roof and dormers, it is as elegant a Queen Anne house of its kind as you could ever hope to see.

## Soham

*59; 5 miles SE of Ely on A142*

ST ANDREW'S CHURCH is not what it seems. The visitor might be forgiven, on first approach, for thinking it a fifteenth-century foundation, so noble is the Perpendicular west tower, so lavish the flushwork, which extends even to the stepped battlements and pinnacles – not only on the tower, but on the north porch as well. The interior, however, tells a very different story; suddenly, we find ourselves in a Transitional church of the late twelfth century, with – yet another surprise – a central crossing whose four mighty arches obviously supported the original tower. They are pointed, but the dogtooth and other forms of Norman decoration that cover the side of the western arch facing the nave show that the Early English, though heralded, has not yet taken a firm hold.

The chancel in its present form must have been built some 150 years after the crossing; it has a lovely east window with five lights and a swirl of tracery. Then after another century and a half comes the Perpendicular contribution – the tower, clerestory and the magnificent roof. Here, as at Isleham, there is an alternation of tie-beams and hammer-beams, the former carrying ten queenposts each, the latter small carved figures which, in the absence of wings, I take to be saints rather than angels.

## Somersham

*60; 5 miles NE of St Ives on B1089*

ST JOHN'S CHURCH seems to have been built in the early thirteenth century and to have received its west tower some seventy years later; nave, aisles and chancel are thus all of a uniform Early English, and a very high quality of Early English at that. The aisle windows were renewed in Perpendicular days, which is a pity, and some fifteenth-century stonemason was allowed to tinker with the capitals and bases of the arcade piers; but for all that the building looks, architecturally, much as it must have looked in the days of Henry III – and there are all too few churches in England of which that can be said. The chancel sets the tone beautifully, with its three unstepped lancets at the east end and four more running along each side (though the westernmost one on the south wall has been given over to the organ).

Nave and aisles are broad and spacious, and covered with a splendid timber roof, its tie-beams supported on arched braces and in turn supporting huge, heavy kingposts. The corbels below are exuberantly carved with angels, men and monsters, and the ridge above is generously bossed. Proportions are lovely throughout.

## Sutton-in-the-Isle

*61; 5½ miles W of Ely on A142*

ST ANDREW'S is a princely church indeed, superbly sited on an elevation above the village, largely faced with ashlar of Barnack stone and possessed of what must be the most unusual medieval tower in Cambridgeshire. Begun in about 1370, it was probably finished thirty years later and – apart from a relatively harmless restoration in 1869 – has not been altered since. It thus keeps its own feeling of unity, despite the fact that the thirty years in question saw the end of the transitional period between the Decorated and the Perpendicular styles. The church, however, remains overwhelmingly Decorated, and even when newly built must have appeared a little old-fashioned.

Work began, as such work normally did, at the east end, where the chancel boasts a fine five-light east window – Decorated, though is there not a slight hint of Perpendicular creeping in? (The windows to north and south seem somehow purer.) The chancel also has seats ranged along each side, with tall blank arcading running behind them, and big carved corbels supporting the roof. These corbels continue equally impressively in the nave, which leads straight out of the chancel on the same level – there are no steps. The aisle windows, like the side windows of the chancel, are still uncompromisingly Decorated, and a very fine display they make too.

Finally we reach the west end and that extraordinary tower, clearly designed to be the showpiece of the whole church. Even inside, it leaves one in no doubt of its importance, with a tierceron vault pierced with a wide octagonal hole for the bell ropes; but it is the exterior where it really makes its presence felt. There is a noble west doorway with a quatrefoil frieze above and below and, two stages higher, a most peculiar design of bell opening: three lancets on each of the four sides with carved roundels immediately above them. At this point the four sides are neatly converted into eight. The next stage is rather stubby – there is just room for the clock – and is immediately succeeded by another, smaller, octagonal stage above it. These two top stages are both embattled, and the top one is pinnacled as well. Pevsner points out that the whole idea is inspired by the Ely octagon; he is obviously right, though the treatment is, it must be admitted, nowhere near so successful. Nonetheless, it imposes itself on the mind and on the memory long after many more beautiful and more orthodox towers are forgotten.

## Thorney

*62; 7½ miles NE of Peterborough on A47*

Though now only a poor truncated remnant of an immense abbey church nearly 100 yards long, the CHURCH OF ST MARY AND ST BOTOLPH remains impressive. The west front with its angle turrets is still essentially Norman, and as such was complete by 1108; it was, however, extensively remodelled in 1638 when what survived of the long-ruined abbey was converted into the parish church. From this time we can date the ogival blank arcades, the frieze that runs above them and, very probably, the Perpendicular west window which has now been partly blocked. Then, too, the aisles were demolished, so that the side arcades now provide the lines for the outer walls. The piers have thick, chunky capitals, very crudely scalloped. The east end with its single broad lancet – its glass copied from Canterbury – is by Edward Blore, doing his Norman bit in 1840–1. Inside, the Norman triforium does not break the line of the principal shafting, which runs straight through it from floor to roof, with splendid effect. What a marvellous building, one feels, it must have been.

The present THORNEY ABBEY is not the abbey at all but a house – or, to be strictly accurate, two houses. The first, providing the main front, is an Elizabethan manor house with gables and mullioned windows; from this, a short link runs off to the rear to connect with a small Charles II house, built for the 5th Earl of Bedford by a local architect, John Lovin of Peterborough. Whether Lovin actually designed it is uncertain; the style is so like that of Peter Mills, whose Thorpe Hall (*q.v.*) is only a few miles away, that he may simply have been carrying out Mills's plans. Like Thorpe, it is rigidly symmetrical in its doors and windows, and has a hipped roof with dormers; but the scale is smaller, since Thorney has only two storeys to Thorpe's two and a half, and a single central chimneystack in ashlar, serving eight fireplaces.

Inside, several rooms have retained their original panelling – featuring the broad volutes and eared panels that are 'Artisan Mannerist' trademarks (compare not only Thorpe but also Tyttenhanger and Balls Park). During recent decoration much of this panelling was found to have been painted in rather charming *trompe-l'oeil*, though little of it remains today. There is also a magnificent staircase, carved along its whole length, right up to the attic.

Opposite Thorney Abbey stand two very fine village houses. One, the VICARAGE, dates from *c.* 1680; the other, with projecting wings, looks a little later.

*The superb roof of St Mary and All Saints, Willingham.*

## Thorpe Hall

*63; just W of Peterborough on A47*

Standing within the former Soke of Peterborough, Thorpe Hall is the *magnum opus* of that astonishing City of London bricklayer and leader of the 'Artisan Mannerist' school, Peter Mills, who was almost certainly responsible for the now-demolished Wisbech Castle and may well have built Tyttenhanger in Hertfordshire (*q.v.*). For many years a hospital, it is still sadly institutionalised; it is, however, a minor milestone of English architecture, and is well worth seeking out.

It was built between 1653 and 1656 for Chief Justice Oliver St John, and – apart from the east front, which was extensively and ill-advisedly remodelled in the 1850s – looks much as it did then. It is almost square and, on the outside, firmly symmetrical, the north and south sides being identical: two and a half storeys, seven bays, long and short quoins, and a hipped roof with dormers, their pediments by turns triangular and segmental. A similar alternation occurs on the first-floor *piano nobile*: the windows in the second and sixth bays have triangular pediments and the central one in the fourth a segmental one above a broad eared frame with volutes.

The essential symmetry continues within, the rooms being grouped on each side of axial passageways running right through the house. In the western half these rooms are sub-divided; in the east they tend to remain their full size – there is still a Hall in its traditional place – but the central east–west passageway here contains the principal staircase, its balustrade consisting of lavishly carved panels of openwork foliage. Most of the main rooms have preserved their panelling, rich in those same motifs that we saw in the central window and that occur again at Thorney Abbey (*q.v.*) and elsewhere; only here the decoration is distinctly more opulent, and extends to a number of rather heavy plaster ceilings. There are stables to the west in the same style.

## Willingham*

*64; 8 miles NW of Cambridge on B1050*

The first thing that strikes you as you approach ST MARY AND ALL SAINTS across the Fens is its spire, broached and with three stages of lucarnes, apparently tethered to the corner pinnacles of the tower below by flying buttresses. This tower, and indeed most of the church, is fine Decorated work dating from the early fourteenth century. A plethora of carved stones, however, many of which are preserved in the spacious south porch, attests to the existence of a stone-built church on the same site well before the Norman Conquest; note in particular the rough Saxon column shaft, with capital, on the east side of the porch – and, while you are at it, on no account overlook the two extraordinary carved label stops between the windows to east and west: to the west a blindfolded man whose cheeks appear to be sprouting wings, and to the east a man with a beard, making up his eyebrows.

The nave is composed of six bays, above which the walls show traces of paintings – although these are now sadly rubbed, they still provide a most interesting texture. Then comes a Perpendicular clerestory, and finally one of the really great Cambridgeshire roofs – a double hammer-beam with, at the east end, angels at three levels: they have mostly been renewed, but they are wonderful all the same. Some bear the symbols of the Passion, others musical instruments, and yet others the signs of the Evangelists and the Apostles. The east end of the nave is distinguished by a Doom painting which must have been magnificent; how sad that the figure of Christ was lost when the window was opened up above the chancel arch.

Approaching the chancel, we discover another of the glories of this church: its screens. Of the rood-screen itself only the painted dado survives, but the parclose screens to north and south are beautifully preserved. That to the south, surrounding the Brune Chantry, is fifteenth-century, with its tracery culminating in carved heads, those on the west side half-hidden in foliage. The northern screen, which encloses the Ely Chapel, is a good deal older; indeed, dating from *c.*1320, it is probably the oldest in Cambridgeshire. On the west and south in particular, much of the original colour remains to give life to the four green popinjays disporting themselves on a red floral ground.

The chancel was largely rebuilt in the 1890s, but in a most scholarly fashion; thus the east window, which replaces a Perpendicular one, is based on the original fourteenth-century fragments found *in situ*. It has a fine, flat roof of ancient date, which provides an impressive contrast with the splendour of that over the nave. A doorway in the north wall leads through to Willingham's last surprise: a separate sacristy, built entirely of stone. No one seems to know why it was built or what purpose it served; it may have been a separate robing room for the use of the Bishop of Ely on his way to Cambridge – the main road passed through Willingham until 1754. Its stone roof is carried on three slender arches, the interstices filled with delicate stone tracery. No parish church that I have seen contains anything remotely like it.

*The Yellow Drawing Room, Wimpole Hall.*

## Wimpole Hall*

*NT; 65; 8 miles SW of Cambridge off A603*

'Bird,' murmured Rudyard Kipling to his daughter Mrs George Bambridge, on first visiting the house of which she had just acquired the lease, 'Bird, I hope you have not bitten off more than you can chew.' It was an understandable reaction: Wimpole, which is still the largest house in Cambridgeshire, was then almost twice the size it is today, almost empty of furniture, and in an advanced state of disrepair. Barely a year after the Bambridges bought the property outright, the Second World War began; but as soon as it was over Mrs Bambridge, by then a widow, resumed the task of bringing the once great house to life again. Its present splendour is due largely to her – and to the National Trust, to which she left it, with a princely if ultimately insufficient endowment, on her death in 1976.

The first house on the site was begun in about 1641 by its owner, Sir Thomas Chicheley, who almost certainly designed it himself. The work was interrupted by the Civil War and Commonwealth – during which Chicheley, a staunch Royalist, was obliged to lie low – but was probably complete by about 1670. Seven bays across, with two principal storeys plus basement and attic, it corresponded precisely to the central block of the present house; half a century later, however, Edward, Lord Harley – to whom it had passed by marriage – commissioned James Gibbs to build on side wings: that on the east to contain a Chapel, that on the west a series of rooms to house Harley's collections of coins, manuscripts and antique sculpture, culminating in a splendid Library worthy of the greatest book collector this country has ever known. Gibbs had originally intended also to remodel the central block, but never did so; this task was left to Henry Flitcroft, who – Wimpole having by then passed to the Earls of Hardwicke – between 1742 and 1745 subtly transformed its style from Caroline to Palladian, removing Chicheley's lantern and Dutch gable and substituting on the entrance front a three-bay pediment, Venetian window, Diocletian window (semi-circular with two mullions) and boldly rusticated front door. The materials remained unchanged – a lovely warm red brick, and dressings of Portland stone.

For the next fifty years the main focus of attention moves from the house to the park, with Capability Brown continuing the work begun by Charles Bridgeman in the 1720s, extending and reshaping the prospect to the north, building the Gothick Tower designed by Sanderson Miller in 1750, and converting two square fishponds into three irregular lakes. Then, in 1791, there appears the ever-fascinating figure of the young John Soane, who was responsible for two major *tours de force* – the Book Room and the domed Yellow Drawing Room – together with other, more modest, work in the first-floor bedrooms. Ideally, the architectural history of Wimpole should have ended with him; alas, the house was still not grand enough for the 4th Earl of Hardwicke, who in the 1840s employed H.E. Kendall to add a new service wing to the east, reface the west wing to match it, and adorn each with a pointless and somewhat flatulent Italianate tower. Kendall also ruined the entrance front with a heavy Victorian porch and provided new stables to the south-east. Mercifully, towers and porch alike were demolished after the war by Mrs Bambridge; only the stables remain – in a parlous state at the time of writing. With the costs of demolition almost as high as those of reconstruction, their future is uncertain.

The house, as you approach it from the south, looks almost exactly as Flitcroft left it. The only notable alterations are at roof level, where Kendall has extended Gibbs's wing balustrading to the central block, adding terracotta urns and a tall central chimneystack. He may or may not have been responsible for the sculptured group above the pediment. It represents Charity, and is the work of J.H. Foley, whose best-known work is the statue of Prince Albert in Kensington Gardens.

When you are ready to enter the house, prepare for a shock. The Hall, with its floor of screaming encaustic tiles in complicated patterns which include the word 'SALVE!' – the first time I have ever seen a tiled exclamation mark – is enough to repel all but the hardiest visitor. Together with the two screens of Ionic columns it is, need one say, the work of Kendall. (Compare Soane's neo-classical columns in the Inner Hall just behind.) Fortunately, this mood does not continue; the two rooms that follow to the left of the Hall, the Ante-Room and South Drawing Room, are far more agreeable, the only Victorian contribution being the plasterwork of the ceiling and cornice which, if it fails to match the eighteenth-century elegance of the carvings on door-cases and chimneypieces, is basically harmless enough. What one does see in these rooms, as all over the house, is Mrs Bambridge's quirkish and delightful taste in pictures; I know few houses containing so many small and relatively unassuming ones that I should love to own.

The Gallery was created by Flitcroft from the three 'cabinets' built by Gibbs for Lord Harley's collections – the lost partition walls now being marked by the two columnar screens. It is a fine room, but offers little preparation for what follows. This is the so-called Book Room, designed to cope with the overflow of books from the Library; and one glance is enough to recognise it as the work of Soane. Here are his characteristic shallow, segmental arches, springing this time from bookcases that project out into the room from the side walls, the barrel-vaulted ceilings between them cut back along the outer wall into more shallow arches to give maximum illumination. It is a marvellous room – light, well-proportioned and utterly individual: no one but Soane could have achieved it.

Marvellous too is Gibbs's Library beyond, once the home of the best of Lord Harley's 50,000 books. The decoration on the coved ceiling is the work of Isaac Mansfield, the best plasterer of his time. The general appearance of the room, however, is very different from what was originally intended: in 1754 the 1st Earl of Hardwicke (who was Lord Chancellor for nearly thirty years) blocked up three of the five windows along the east wall to accommodate his own massive law library, opening out the bay window at the end to restore some of the lost light and moving the marble chimneypiece to the west wall – in which Soane was later to open up two more windows.

Retracing your steps through the end of the Gallery and the unremarkable Red Room, you emerge in Soane's ultimate show-stopper, the Yellow Drawing Room, designed to meet the need for a bigger, grander reception room suitable for balls, concerts and even amateur theatricals. The concept was nothing if not ambitious: by knocking together a number of small rooms on two floors and doing away with a subsidiary staircase, Soane managed somehow to create an ample T-shaped space rising through the whole height of the house. The base of the T, to the north, was square in plan and lit by two windows; the cross-bar was rounded off with a deep apse at each end and drew its light from above, through a dome with a glass lantern, carried on typically Soanian segmental arches. All these architectural motifs are further emphasised in the decoration – whether in paint, wood carving or stucco. (The two rather horrid painted lunettes were added in 1845; would that Mrs Bambridge had removed them as she did the gold and silver 'lincrusta' paper that formerly disfigured the walls.)

Through Flitcroft's Saloon – once the most formal room in the house but now utterly overshadowed by its staggering neighbour – and Soane's Inner Hall, you come to the foot of the Grand Staircase. The domed skylight is also by Soane; it was necessitated after he had blocked up the inner courtyard to the east to make a new service staircase in place of that which he had sacrificed for the Yellow Drawing Room. There is lovely eighteenth-century plasterwork to admire as you go up to the first floor, and much that is of interest in the upstairs bedrooms; but we must now press on to the last of the great glories of Wimpole – the Chapel. Not only a glory; also a surprise. Suddenly, without warning, we are in the world of High Baroque. Gibbs's was the overall concept; indeed, he had originally intended that his Chapel should be fully architectural, vaulted and arcaded. Then, deciding perhaps that the space was too narrow, he decided that the whole thing would be more effectively done in *trompe-l'oeil*, by his friend Sir James Thornhill, Sergeant Painter to the King. Thornhill has pulled it off magnificently. On the flat walls, gilded statues of the four Doctors of the Church occupy deep and shadowy niches, flanked by Corinthian columns; on the flat (though coved) ceiling, the light from the windows makes a *chiaroscuro* of the sunken coffers. Above the altar, behind a triumphal arch, the Virgin and Child receive the homage of the Magi – and can be seen doing so, when the doors are open, all the way from the Entrance Hall.

One of the most puzzling things about this splendid Chapel is why it exists at all, for the house has, almost within shouting distance, its own CHURCH. And one of the most puzzling things about the church is why the 1st Lord Hardwicke decided to rebuild it in 1749, since his

*The River Nene and North Brink, Wisbech.*

own magnificent Chapel was barely a quarter of a century old. But rebuild it he did, to the designs of Flitcroft, and it must have looked quite pretty with its pedimented and bell-turreted west front and its Venetian east window, until it was transformed into that nastiest of all styles, Victorian Decorated, in 1887. It is still worth visiting, however, for the sake of the north chapel, which has somehow survived largely intact from the fourteenth century and now contains an outstanding collection of family tombs.

There remains the PARK. Worked on at various times by Bridgeman, Brown and Repton, with buildings by Sanderson Miller, 'Athenian' Stuart and John Soane, it is obviously an important element in the history of English landscape. Alas, like all too many of its fellows, it is no longer what it was. The remains of Bridgeman's tremendous scheme of great axial avenues, which replaced the formal gardens of the late seventeenth century, are still visible; but the grandest of all those avenues, that which leads directly from the centre of the south front of the house for almost exactly 2 miles to the Octagon beyond the River Rhee, has been devastated by Dutch elm disease. Though partly replanted with limes and oaks, it will be many years before it regains its former splendour, and in any case not all the land concerned belongs to the National Trust. Much work, in the park as in the Hall, remains to be done, and will be as money becomes available; but Wimpole is already, outside Cambridge itself, one of the grandest sights in the county and one which should on no account be missed.

## Wisbech*

*66; 20 miles NE of Peterborough on A47*
*Includes Peckover House (NT)*

Few people arriving in Wisbech for the first time have any idea of the treat that lies in store, for Wisbech is a rare gem, and one of the most attractive towns in all East Anglia, if not in all England. Approach it, if you can, along the A47 from Peterborough or March. The road runs for some miles along the River Nene, leaves it briefly, and then returns just in time to provide the best possible introductory view of the town – a long row of Georgian houses lining the opposite bank, known as the NORTH BRINK. They are in no sense a terrace; each is an individual building. Heights, floor levels, fenestration and the pitch of the roofs all vary. Some are of stone, some of brick, some of stucco. A few are not even very distinguished and, seen by themselves, would scarcely merit a second glance. But the ensemble, seen from a distance over the water, is not easily forgotten. So perfect, indeed, is the sight that it is some time before one realises that the row of houses next to which one is standing constitutes, from the opposite side, just such another. The SOUTH BRINK, though a little more restrained, radiates the same quiet serenity. Together, the two form a broad, watery street; and I know of no Georgian street in the country that gives more pleasure.

Of all these houses, the most beautiful stands halfway along the North Brink. It is known as PECKOVER HOUSE (NT) after the family that occupied it for 150 years, and it has been the property of the National Trust since 1948. From the outside it looks simple enough: three storeys, five bays, built in a surprisingly attractive yellowish brick, with red-brick dressings. The windows are very slightly curved at the top; otherwise, the only obvious decoration is around the doorway, which is heavily rusticated and set between Tuscan half columns, with a segmental pediment – placed, perhaps, a little too high – above it. Inside, the decoration is rather more showy, but of immense sophistication and elegance. The rooms are all panelled, the doorcases, chimneypieces and overmantels all elaborately carved or stuccoed. The floors, where not carpeted, have kept their original scrubbed boards, the doors their original brass fitments. Furniture and pictures, not too plentiful, are exactly right. The house was built in 1722, and I know few others, even in Bath, that so effortlessly recapture the atmosphere of rich, cultivated, provincial life in the first half of the eighteenth century.

Good taste reigns everywhere; but good taste can get

just a wee bit dull and, seemingly to prevent such an eventuality, the Drawing Room suddenly bursts out into a single piece of unbridled Rococo as exhilarating as it is unexpected. It is an overmantel of carved wood, in which an eagle breaks away from the wall and seems on the point of flying free, bursting out of its surroundings of scrolls, garlands and festoons. It seems to be of about 1760; how it got there remains a mystery.

Peckover has a surprisingly large and beautifully tended garden of an agreeably old-fashioned kind. The garden front, less austere than that giving on to the street, boasts a Venetian window and a Diocletian one above it, with another rusticated doorcase – topped, this time, with a triangular pediment. These Palladian accretions are not, to my eye, entirely successful. No matter; the rest of the house makes up for everything.

## Wittering

*67; 10 miles NW of Peterborough off A1*

ALL SAINTS' CHURCH may not be beautiful, but it is unquestionably sensational – it contains the crudest, most barbaric chancel arch in all England. In essence it consists of three huge semi-circular mouldings and an outer one of rectangular section, coming up from the floor on each side and broken only by – what? They are not abaci, they are certainly not capitals; they consist of two huge blocks, one on each side, of roughly squared stone, about 18 inches high and tapering outwards towards the top so that they follow – again very roughly – the line of the arch. The single arcade is to the north and must date from around 1150. It has only two bays, separated by a fat, circular pier with a many-scalloped capital and a flat square abacus above it, the arches differently patterned – one with dogtooth and outward-facing zigzag and the other with a sort of reticulated double zigzag. At the west end, the tower arch is pointed; the roof is supported on long, tapering, conical corbels ending with a little bunch of foliage. Another pointed arch, between chancel and chancel aisle, has delightfully carved stops – on the left a leering head with protruding tongue, on the right a lady whose wimple goes straight across her mouth like a Tokyo traffic policeman. The chancel itself is late thirteenth-century; the east window takes the form of a double lancet with cusped heads, the spandrel being filled with an irregular quatrefoil.

The exterior is of rubble apart from the tower, which is of dressed Barnack stone and supports a short stubby spire. Nothing even hints at the savagery within.

## Yaxley

*68; 5 miles S of Peterborough off A15*

There was a Saxon church at Yaxley, and a Norman one too; but the ST PETER'S that we know today was begun only in about 1250. Work went on in fits and starts till towards the end of the fourteenth century, by which time the villagers already had a building to be proud of; but with increasing prosperity after the Wars of the Roses they began a programme of extensive improvements, so that it was not until 1540 or so that the church took on its present appearance with the glorious west tower and lucarned spire. Thus, stylistically speaking, it is even more of a hotch-potch than most medieval churches; but it has enough personality to weld all its styles into a quite remarkably satisfying whole.

Particularly interesting – almost an object lesson in architectural church history – are the moments at which the Early English style gives way to the Decorated from about 1290. That is what is happening in the end window of the north transept where the stepped lancets have trefoils in the tracery, an early premonition of the exuberance already visible in its opposite number in the south transept, which dates from only a generation or so later. The same phenomenon can be seen in the two eastern windows of the north aisle and in the south chapel – which, however, also boasts a far more liberated east window of fine cursive tracery. This, with the magnificent – if somewhat restored – five-lighter of the chancel, marks the mid-fourteenth-century apogee of Decorated, here shown to dazzling effect.

The Perpendicular work, which began in the late fifteenth century, had as its principal object the heightening of the church. It was now that the clerestories were added, to chancel as well as nave – which was given new four-bay arcades to support the additional weight. Another addition was the fine south porch with its niches and its proud beasts rampant on the gable. Most of the aisle windows were Perpendicularised and the whole building was given the timber roof we still see today. The interior walls were painted – the Resurrection in the north chapel, a Doom in its usual place above the chancel arch, what appears to be a rather naïve *memento mori* on the west wall – but the remains are too faint to give any real pleasure.

The most interesting monument is the curious pointed-arch panel in the north transept, with its carving of two upraised arms holding a heart. The latter almost certainly represents that of William of Yaxley, Abbot of Thorney, who died in 1293. The heart itself was found concealed behind the panel, in a specially made cylindrical box.

---

# Short List

## Anglesey Abbey

*NT; 69; 6 miles NE of Cambridge on B1102*

An Augustinian priory founded in 1135, it was much rebuilt by the 1st Lord Fairhaven in the late 1920s. Little of the original building remains except the Chapter House and the vaulted Canons' Parlour. The chief interest of the house now lies in its sumptuous furnishings and Lord Fairhaven's remarkable collection of works of art – together with the famous gardens, spacious and superb.

## Bluntisham

*70; 4½ miles NE of St Ives on A1123*

Polygonal apses are rare indeed in English medieval churches, and the early fourteenth-century apse of ST MARY'S is alone enough to qualify it for a place in this book. It is actually constructed on three planes, in each of which there is a two-light window with Decorated mouchette tracery – which would look even better if it were not painted. In both nave and chancel there are fine stone corbels, deeply and beautifully carved.

## Buckden

*71; 4 miles SW of Huntingdon on A1*

The first impression is the best: the stone tower of ST MARY'S CHURCH against the rich dark brick of the PALACE OF THE BISHOPS OF LINCOLN immediately behind it. But the church is a little sad; apart from a nice timber roof with angel supporters there is nothing much to remember. As for the palace, there remain principally the Great Tower and the outer and inner Gatehouses, and even here much of the fifteenth-century brickwork has been heavily restored over the past twenty years by its present owners, the Claretian Missionaries.

## Duxford

*72; 7½ miles S of Cambridge on B1379*

The early thirteenth-century CHAPEL of a Hospital of St John stands in a curious little village with several timber-framed houses, just behind Whittlesford railway station. The once-traceried east window is now bricked up, but those along the south side survive, with curious cusping rather like rabbits' ears.

## Godmanchester

*73; 1 mile S of Huntingdon off A604*

ST MARY'S CHURCH is very noble, with a tower of 1623 pretending to be Perpendicular, a good Early English chancel and stalls with misericords from Ramsey Abbey. ISLAND HALL in Post Street is of about 1750 and open to the public, but I arrived too late to see inside.

## Hinchingbrooke House

*74; 1 mile W of Huntingdon on A604*

Sir Richard Cromwell, great-grandfather of Oliver, began Hinchingbrooke House on the site of a dissolved nunnery, traces of which still remain. Continued by his descendants, it was sold in 1621 to the Montagus, shortly to become Earls of Sandwich. It is now a school. There are pretty Tudor bay windows and a splendid broad semicircular one to the south, dated 1602. Alas, the house was largely gutted by fire in 1830 and the rebuilding was entrusted to Edward Blore, whose heavy hand is all too apparent.

## Isleham

*75; 10 miles SE of Ely on B1104*

ST ANDREW'S CHURCH is not much to look at on the outside, and the west tower by Street is a disgrace. Inside, however, there is a fine fourteenth-century arcade with fifteenth-century decorations in the spandrels and a splendid roof supported by alternating tie-beams (each with sixteen queenposts) and hammerbeams with angels. There are good tombs, too, particularly in the south transept. ISLEHAM PRIORY, or what is left of it in the form of a small Norman chapel, unaltered and unadorned, stands 100 yards or so down the road.

## Keyston

*76; 12 miles NW of Huntingdon on B663*

The CHURCH OF ST JOHN BAPTIST is wonderful on the outside – grey stone, set on a hill above the village, with a lovely five-light Decorated east window and a fine tower and spire (the latter actually a rebuilding of 1882). The inside is disappointing, heavily scraped; but the chancel of *c.*1280 gives pleasure – despite the alarming outward slope of its walls – and the nave has a beautiful timber roof with open fretwork in the braces of the tie-beams.

## Madingley Hall

*77; 4 miles NW of Cambridge off A45*

Originally a magnificent Tudor mansion of about 1545, Madingley Hall is now used by Cambridge University for extra-mural studies, and it is too institutionalised to be of any great interest to the general visitor; but the eighteenth-century Saloon, a remodelling of the upper half of the original Hall, remains a splendid room with a fine plaster ceiling and superb doorcases. The huge ogee arch just to the left of the house is also worth noticing. It was originally the entrance to the old University Schools, and was brought here in the eighteenth century.

## Northborough

*78; 6½ miles NW of Peterborough on A15*

Here is a most remarkable survival – a MANOR HOUSE of the early fourteenth century. It was much altered some 300 years later, but has kept the huge windows with reticulated tracery and the west gable of the Hall range. It is now a restaurant and can be visited by appointment.

## Stow Longa

*79; 8 miles W of Huntingdon off A604*

ST BOTOLPH'S CHURCH gets in here entirely for the Norman tympanum over the priest's doorway on the south side. It consists of a wonderfully crude mermaid with her hair looking like a gable, flanked by two even cruder quadrupeds of indeterminate species. There is heavy zigzag in the round arch above, which is supported on two slender colonnettes with knot designs faintly reminiscent of Kilpeck. The interior, with its modest hammer-beam roof, is of no special interest.

## Swaffham Prior

*80; 9 miles NE of Cambridge on B1102*

Two churches with but a single churchyard stand high on a hill above the village. One, ST CYRIAC'S, has a good Perpendicular tower but the remainder, of the early nineteenth century, is being left to decay. The other, ST MARY'S, is what merits inclusion here, for it possesses one of the most interesting towers in the county. Both its bottom, square, stage and its second, octagonal, one are Norman; could it have been partly the inspiration for the Ely octagon, which it predates by over 150 years? Higher still, there are two more stages of sixteen sides, Early English. Struck by lightning in 1767, it is now romantically open to the sky.

# Cornwall

The most mysterious of all English counties, Cornwall is also, both culturally and geographically, the most remote. Of its 200-mile perimeter, only about 6 miles are actually in physical surface contact with the rest of the country; everywhere else, its border is formed either by the sea or by the swiftly flowing River Tamar. Sometimes, indeed, it hardly seems to be part of England at all. The Cornish language, admittedly, died out in the eighteenth century; but Celtic traditions are still strong, and reminders of Cornwall's distinguished Early Christian past still plentiful. Time and again one feels, standing on those tremendous cliffs and looking down on the grey Atlantic, that the spirit of Tristan, and even of King Arthur, are not far away; while any amateur of village churches large or small will find himself obliged to wrestle with a completely new and unfamiliar hagiography, peopled with figures like Saints Petroc and Carantoc, Nectan and Morwenna, Melorus and Melina, Gulval and Gunwalloe and countless others.

Geologically, too, Cornwall is unlike anywhere else in the country. Composed almost entirely of rock – fortunately, for a region whose constant exposure to the salt sea winds has resulted in a permanent shortage of timber – it has never lacked good building stone; but whereas elsewhere this would normally mean limestone or sandstone, here it means above all one of the toughest and most intractable of materials – granite. Now granite is immensely strong and virtually indestructible; there is no better stone for lighthouses, or heroic monuments, or prisons. But it is too hard to allow of delicate workmanship or fine carving, and – except when the clouds suddenly roll away after a thunderstorm and a myriad tiny scales of mica sparkle joyfully in the sun – it is usually a somewhat lifeless and depressing grey in colour. This gives a certain sombreness to many Cornish houses and churches, especially in winter or when the weather is overcast.

Almost equally prevalent is slate. When it is employed as a building stone it presents much the same problems for intricate modelling or moulding as does granite, though its colours are warmer and more varied; more often, however, we find it used for roofs – in which capacity, both practically and aesthetically, it is a good deal more successful – or for wall covering. Cornwall is the county *par excellence* for slate-hung walls. St Columb Major probably has a greater proportion of them than any other Cornish town, but they can also be seen to great advantage at Launceston.

Brick, for some reason, was never particularly popular in these regions. Before 1700, indeed, it seems to have been virtually unknown; the only important exception is at Ince Castle, which must date from around 1635; but that is at the extreme eastern end of the county, only a mile or two from Devon.

This basically unsatisfactory nature of the principal Cornish materials has had an inevitable effect on the architecture. Cornwall is not, we have to admit, a county of outstandingly beautiful buildings, though many Cornish churches have considerable charm. Though a few predate the fifteenth century – the Norman west portal at St Germans is unforgettable, and there is some fine Early English and Decorated work at Lostwithiel and Fowey – the majority of them are Perpendicular and of fairly regular (and characteristic) design. The archetypal Cornish church has a west tower of only two or three stages, without a spire, but probably embattled and pinnacled; from it there extends to the east what may seem a disproportionately long nave, tunnel-vaulted, with two aisles as broad and as high as itself and projecting as far as the east end of the chancel. This means that there is no clerestory, and no indication on the outside by a change in roof levels of where the nave stops and the chancel begins. The body of the church tends thus to be reduced to a sort of rectangular box, with only the porches to provide a touch of irregularity. Even inside the building, in the absence of a chancel arch, the only separation of nave from chancel is the screen, which normally runs the full breadth of the church, from wall to wall. Alas, a good many of these screens have disappeared altogether, or have been replaced by Victorian ones of varying quality; where they remain, however, they are always the most rewarding of all the furnishings, though carved bench ends and fonts (often of granite) can also give a good deal of pleasure.

Of post-Reformation religious buildings I have listed only that of King Charles the Martyr at Falmouth and, of course, Pearson's cathedral at Truro. Even as a piece of

Victorian Gothic it has its detractors, for reasons which I have tried to explain; it certainly falls far short of George Gilbert Scott's breathtaking achievement at Liverpool. Yet it remains a work of high quality which, even if slightly deficient in poetry and imagination, could have been created only by a master hand. Rising from the centre of the town in the French manner, with none of the usual English *cordon sanitaire* of close and precincts, it dominates without being crushing; architecturally as well as spiritually, Truro's gain has been immense.

Of Cornish military architecture – as the best examples of which I have chosen, from a fairly extensive field, Restormel, Trematon and Launceston from the thirteenth century, St Mawes and Pendennis from the sixteenth – there is little to add to their respective entries; we can therefore pass straight on to houses. Of the earlier period, the greatest and by far the best is Cotehele – one of the most magical of its date in the whole country, and one of the most beautifully sited. Then, in chronological order, comes Trerice – built, like Cotehele, around a medieval shell, but with its later elements dating from the later sixteenth century rather than the earlier. Another fundamentally Tudor building is Godolphin; but what we see of it today breathes more of the seventeenth century than of the sixteenth. Ince Castle, on the other hand, is clearly of Caroline origin, as is Lanhydrock.

There is only one Georgian house in Cornwall which might be called – just – a stately home. That house is Antony. There are however other, smaller, houses of equal elegance – Trewithen for a start, or the enchanting little Bonython. Then, when we come to the Victorians, we find ourselves back at Lanhydrock again – or at least in that part of it which was rebuilt after the fire of 1881, which is in its way as evocative of the late nineteenth century as is its Long Gallery of the mid-seventeenth.

I have left till last the one house which defies any form of categorisation. Monastery, church, castle, private house; medieval, Stuart, Georgian, Victorian; St Michael's Mount is all of them, and none of them. It stands, like Cornwall, almost encircled by the Western Ocean and remains, like Cornwall, a law unto itself.

---

## Altarnun*

*1; 7½ miles SW of Launceston off A30*

The name of the village means quite simply the Altar of St Nonna, or Nunna, who was the mother of St David of Wales; and ST NONNA'S CHURCH is to me one of the loveliest in all Cornwall. You approach it by a medieval pack-horse bridge over a swiftly running stream – a little gaunt on the outside, perhaps, with an unusually high pinnacled tower of granite brought straight down off the moor. Nothing but the Celtic cross in the churchyard dates from St Nonna's time – the sixth century – and there is only one major remnant of the Norman building that preceded the present Perpendicular one: the hauntingly barbaric font, with its four great bearded faces gazing out into space from each corner. For the rest, what we have is a broad and beautifully proportioned Cornish church, begun early in the fifteenth century and finished well before it was over, with two aisles and two porches, all with their original wagon roofs. Look closely at the arcade piers, and you will see another unique feature of the construction: each of them – base, shaft and capital – is carved from a single piece of moorstone, the name given to those blocks of granite which were (and still occasionally are) found lying about on the surface of the moors and consequently needed no quarrying. A fine wooden screen runs the full breadth of the building – though there is some modern work at each end – and a Jacobean altar rail with two splendid paintings of the same date completes the decoration.

*The font, St Nonna's Church, Altarnun.*

Or almost: there remain the bench ends, seventy-nine of them, and they are the glory of Altarnun. Some, but by no means all, are religious. Others are abstract designs with a distinctly Renaissance feeling about them – extraordinary that the Renaissance should have penetrated, even to such a degree as this, to so remote an area by the 1520s, when they were carved – while yet others depict what the church guide (by the Rev. Kneebone) calls 'Parish Worthies and Common Sights': sheep grazing, pipers piping and the villagers at their daily round – Merrie England at its multifarious best.

## Antony House

*NT; 2; 5 miles W of Plymouth off A374 (via Torpoint car ferry)*

About a mile east of Antony village, Antony House lies in a beautiful park running down to the River Lynher and probably laid out by Repton. Its architect is

*Antony House.*

unknown, which is surprising in view of the fact that it is beyond all doubt the most distinguished early eighteenth-century house in Cornwall and that – although it is now the property of the National Trust – it is still occupied by the family for which it was built. (A 150-year-old tradition has ascribed it to James Gibbs, one of whose designs may well have inspired the forecourt and the pretty arcaded wings in rich red brick; but the main block, in contrasting silvery grey stone, is not his style at all.) The design is austere and deceptively simple – just nine bays and two storeys, with the three central bays marked by a small and unassertive pediment, and a hipped roof with dormers. The simplicity of the lines is marred on the entrance side by a heavy early Victorian *porte-cochère*; the garden front, with its three diverging vistas down to the river, is far more rewarding.

Inside, the Queen Anne atmosphere embraces you like a warm, dark cloak. Furniture, fireplaces, above all the Dutch oak panelling – ubiquitous except in the Library, where it gives way to pickled deal – all combine to create an extraordinary unity, rare indeed in a house that has been continuously lived in for so long. Even the bubble lights on the angles of the staircase are original. It is all very grand and noble and might, one feels, become a little overpowering; certainly it is not the sort of house that tells many jokes. Cold winter evenings would suit it a good deal better than long summer afternoons. But the beauty is beyond question, the setting superb.

## Blisland

*3; 7½ miles NE of Bodmin off A30*

The fascination of Blisland lies in the contrast between the village and its church. The village is beautiful but austere: grey granite houses, mostly seventeenth- and eighteenth-century, all grouped round a spacious green with ash trees, with the slightly larger gabled manor house at the north-east corner. The CHURCH OF ST PROTUS AND ST HYACINTH is to the south, where the ground falls away quite steeply. Even from the outside it gives warning of a certain eccentricity; not many parish churches have a massive fifteenth-century tower soaring up from the extreme end of the north transept. But the real surprise awaits within. There is nothing austere here. One expects a quiet, restrained Norman interior with later accretions; what one gets is a riot of Victorian colour. Beneath the pretty celured wagon roof a dazzlingly rich and elaborate rood-screen and loft, the work of F.C. Eden shortly before the turn of the century, runs right across the church. Above and to the sides, statues of the Virgin and saints abound, coloured and gilded in the highest of High Anglican taste. (Suddenly the church's name seems less inappropriate.) The impact is overwhelming, and Blisland is often described as one of the pearls of Cornwall.

So it would be, if the whole church were Victorian; the trouble is that both Eden and Sir Ninian Comper – who was responsible for the 'Renaissance' altar – seem to have totally ignored the quiet, sombre atmosphere of the building. Red and white and green and gold simply don't go with grey granite. Moreover, Eden and Comper have succeeded in completely cutting off the chancel, rendering it not only almost invisible but inaccessible too. When I was there the doors in the screen were locked; I was told this was the usual state of affairs. It was all a very brave effort, that has clearly given many people much pleasure; but I wish it had never been made.

*Cotehele.*

## Caerhays Castle

*4; 9 miles S of St Austell off B3287*

Built by John Nash in 1808, Caerhays is his only Gothick castle that still survives. It is set in a marvellous position in the middle of a huge garden, ablaze (in the right season) with azaleas and rhododendrons, and with an additional profusion of peacocks. Although the property overlooks a bay, Nash just managed to squeeze in a lake between his castle and the edge of the cliff, so the fortunate owners can enjoy that rarest of views, a lake in the foreground and the sea behind. The castle itself is built within a wide outer rampart with corner towers. It is heavily battlemented, with a big round tower at one end and a square one (but with a higher circular stair turret) at the other. The basic material is Cornish granite, with a paler stone for the battlements.

The windows are curious, and very Nashish. They are nearly all of two lights, but with different forms of glazing; and they all have smaller lights running in a little row across the top. One can only assume that Nash was trying to give the effect of tracery at minimum cost; if so, he was not entirely successful. With the building as a whole, however, he succeeded admirably; it makes a splendid show with its woods climbing up behind and its garden in front.

I have not, unfortunately, seen the inside. Pevsner says that 'it is in keeping with the exterior' and refers darkly to 'a vaulted staircase at the end of a long gallery'.

## Cotehele*

*NT; 5; 8 miles SW of Tavistock off A390*

Here is the West Country's answer to Haddon Hall in Derbyshire. Here too is a medieval fortified manor house, added to in early Tudor times, set high above a rushing river's curve, with its terraced lawns and gardens above the valley. The scale may be a little smaller, the atmosphere a little more intimate and domestic; but both houses breathe the same magic.

Both, too, have benefited from similar strokes of good fortune. Like Haddon, Cotehele soon became merely the secondary seat of its owners. In the seventeenth century the Edgcumbes moved permanently to their newer, grander, more commodious house at Mount Edgcumbe (destroyed in the Second World War, though now restored). The old manor was never completely abandoned; the family continued to cherish it and even to live in it briefly, from time to time. But from 1627 – the date of the north-west tower – to 1862, when the east front was remodelled with a sensitivity and restraint remarkable for the time, Cotehele escaped all restorations and 'improvements'. To this day it remains a Sleeping Beauty house, much of the outside and virtually all the interior having survived untouched and unchanged for two, possibly even three, centuries. In the Great Hall, built by Sir Piers Edgcumbe in the first years of Henry VIII's reign, the trophies and banners, the arquebuses and pikes, the antlers and antelope horns and the magnificent oak furniture are still in the same places they occupied when William Gilpin described them in the eighteenth century. The barrel-vaulted Chapel also contains most of its original furnishings – including a weight-driven clock dating from the 1480s, the earliest in England still unaltered and in its original position. It is still in working order, though not in regular use. But then there is little use for it: at Cotehele, time stands still.

## Cury

*6; 5 miles S of Helston off A3083*

BONYTHON MANOR is a quite exceptionally elegant house of five bays, with two storeys over a high basement. It was built by an unknown architect (possibly William Wood of Truro) in the 1780s, and faced with silver-grey granite. Much of the distinction of the entrance front comes from the immensely broad door surround, which embraces not only the door itself but also two narrow lights flanking it. It too is of granite, so there is no contrast of materials; the form is roughly that of a Gibbs surround, with alternating long and short blocks, rising to a depressed arch over a shallow fan-light. Being several feet above ground level, it is reached by a graceful flight of eight steps of diminishing length. Above it is a similarly depressed Venetian window, and above that a pediment with a semi-circular central light.

Inside, perhaps the most memorable feature of the house is the staircase, which rises in a semi-circle at the far end of the Entrance Hall, from which it is screened by two fluted columns with feathered capitals. The principal rooms have all been most beautifully restored in the past thirty years to a similar standard of elegance.

## Falmouth

*7; 11 miles S of Truro on A39*

The CHURCH OF KING CHARLES THE MARTYR was begun in 1662, at a time when Falmouth was still a village of only 200 houses. From the outside it does not look particularly exciting, with its three parallel pitched roofs and slightly oblong tower; inside, however, it proves to be a building of considerable splendour and – something for which the Gothic exterior does nothing to prepare us – entirely classical in style. The barrel vault of the nave rests on a deep entablature which is in turn supported by marble columns with flattened Composite capitals. There is no transverse separation of the chancel from the nave, merely a delicate wrought-iron screen, beyond which the two easternmost columns on each side are of red Devonshire marble – making a notable contrast with the creamy white marble of those further west. The broad aisles are also tunnel-vaulted; they extend to each side of the chancel, from which they are divided by two more wrought-iron parclose screens of similar workmanship to the first. The Venetian east window and much of the east end dates from 1896, when it was largely remodelled by E.H. Sedding. It is to his credit that the church does not feel Victorian; one doubts whether, had it been Gothic, it would have escaped so lightly.

Of the furnishings, the most interesting is the pulpit, which is made up of sixteenth- and seventeenth-century carved pieces, both English and German. The hexagonal font, with its wooden pedestal and cover, is of about 1760. The glass is nearly all modern, but there are some interesting mid-eighteenth-century continental pieces in the lower part of the Lady Chapel window.

In the town, the important thing to remember is that it is a port first and a seaside resort very much second. There is thus no real sea-front promenade: the shops in the main street have back windows looking directly on to the harbour, with nothing in between.

## Godolphin House★

*8; 5 miles NW of Helston off A394*

The first vision of Godolphin House is unforgettable. It stands at the end of its drive, a long, low building of eleven bays and only two storeys, with a seven-bay, slightly recessed centre of which the ground floor consists of an open loggia, supported on fat, stocky Tuscan columns. This faces north, and proves to be the north range of an inner quadrangle, the south side of which is merely an embattled wall pierced with windows, all that now remains of another building which formerly stood beyond. The date is uncertain. Parts of the house – including a very pretty room in the east range with patterned ceiling beams and a wealth of linenfold panelling – are clearly of the early sixteenth century, but the north front is a good deal later: the cross windows and the way the hood-moulds are drawn in a continuous string-course suggests somewhere around 1660. The west range seems to be Jacobean.

Charles II is known to have visited Godolphin while he was Prince of Wales – the Godolphin family were ardent Royalists and distinguished themselves greatly during the Civil War – and the magnificent King's Room is named in his honour. Notice in particular the ornately carved wooden door surround; this had been sold by a previous owner of Godolphin and was subsequently found, quite by chance, by the present owner some years after he acquired the house in 1936.

This little story illustrates the hard times on which the house fell after the Godolphin family died out in the eighteenth century. Much of it was demolished in 1805 to make it more suitable for a farmhouse, and it was then occupied by a succession of tenant farmers until the 1930s. The excellent state of the house today is a tribute to the present owners, who have worked hard for nearly half a century to restore it to something of its former splendour.

*Bonython Manor, Cury.*

## Ince Castle*

*9; 4½ miles W of Plymouth*

Though Ince Castle is not really a castle at all, its setting – high on a headland, with stunning views over the River Lynher which flows round it on three sides – would do one full justice. Architecturally, the house's claim to the title rests on nothing more than its castellations and the four corner towers, slate-hung and pyramidally capped, which give it its character and its quite spectacular charm. This is further enhanced by its colour – the palest salmon-pink brick that soaks up the golden evening sunlight like a sponge. The entrance front proclaims itself with a broad external flight of granite steps rising straight up to the *piano nobile* – which is just as well, since there was no main staircase inside until the present owners inserted one some years ago, only narrow spirals leading up into the towers. A building as individual as this one is not easy to date accurately; the year 1540 inscribed in a cartouche over the entrance is almost certainly spurious, but if one were to put it at 90 or 100 years later one would not, I suspect, be very far wrong.

The interior is much remodelled; there is some fine modern plasterwork in the Drawing Room, but little to intrigue the architectural historian. In any case, Ince is not great architecture and does not pretend to be. But with Trematon (*q.v.*), its close neighbour, it must be one of the most appealingly picturesque houses in the county. It is not open to the public, though the lovely garden is accessible from time to time.

## Kilkhampton

*10; 6 miles NE of Bude on A39*

Two features above all qualify the CHURCH OF ST JAMES, Kilkhampton, for a place in this book. The first is its magnificent Norman south doorway of four concentric arches, sumptuously decorated and not surprisingly described as *Porta Celi* – the Gate of Heaven – by the sixteenth-century rector who built the porch. The second is the magnificent collection of carved bench ends – over 150 of them, twice as many as at Altarnun, though of much the same type. The wagon roofs are good, too – that of the chancel carved and bossed, with gilding, those of the nave and side aisles also carved along the principal rafters and purlins, but more modestly.

The rest of the church unfortunately falls below these high standards. It is tall and spacious, but the fifteenth-century arcades are not particularly distinguished, and the Victorian glass and floor tiles hardly help.

## Lanhydrock

*NT; 11; 2½ miles SE of Bodmin off B3268*

If Lanhydrock had not been gutted by fire in 1881 it would have been a real show-stopper. In a way it still is, since the north wing and, thank heavens, the tunnel-vaulted Long Gallery which is the glory of the house somehow escaped the flames. The Gallery quite literally takes one's breath away: 116 feet long, it boasts a plaster ceiling of astonishing luxuriance and complexity, with pendants, bosses, birds and beasts, scenes from the Old Testament and just about everything else that the seventeenth-century plasterer could think of. The overmantels are equally exuberant. Fortunately the Gallery comes almost at the end of the recommended tour of the house. Anything that follows it can only be an anti-climax.

Unless, that is, you are a devotee of Victorian country houses; for although the exterior of the south and east wings (except the entrance porch, which also survived the inferno) were rebuilt more or less as they had always been, the interior – in its furnishings, decoration and atmosphere – is Victorian-Edwardian through and through. William Morris wallpapers, heavy silk lamp-shades, engravings of Gentlemen and Players' cricket matches at Lords with outline keys underneath, stuffed animals on mantelpieces, viewers for stereoscopic photographs on the piano – all contribute to the general effect until one is left with an extraordinarily clear picture of what life must have been like for a well-off family of landed gentry in 1900 or so. And very agreeable it must have been.

Yet the infrastructure necessary to keep even a relatively modest country house going at that period was immense. The kitchen quarters at Lanhydrock are an education in themselves and actually require a separate itinerary. Apart from the great kitchen itself – a magnificent hall with a high trussed roof and the most impressive ventilation system to remove the smells from the roasting spits – there are larders, sculleries, a bakehouse and, finally, a lovely dairy where the central marble slab is surrounded by a little channel along which water flows from a spring in the hillside to keep the cheeses cool.

On your way out, stop for a few minutes at the charming little two-storeyed Gatehouse at the end of the drive. It is built entirely of Cornish granite and was begun in 1636. The Civil War intervened, however, before it was finished and its completion was delayed till 1651. Still basically Gothic but with many a little Renaissance flourish, it is crowned by a veritable forest of obelisks. From the middle of these, when it was first built, there once emerged a rather endearing little cupola – but this disappeared, alas, long ago.

## Launcells*

*12; 2 miles E of Bude off A3072*

ST SWITHIN'S, Launcells, is the loveliest church in Cornwall and the most unspoilt. Looked at from the purely architectural point of view, it is not in any way remarkable: the traditional fifteenth-century Cornish formula, with the two aisles the same dimensions as the nave, making it to all intents and purposes a three-naved church, and panelled wagon roofs. Its beauty lies in its perfect proportions, in the gentle contrast between its two arcades – the north in granite, the south in the rarer, and even more specifically Cornish, polyphant stone – and above all in the fact that it has entirely escaped the attentions of Victorian restorers. The old clear glass in the windows floods it with light, allowing one to see the beauty and fun of the early Tudor bench ends without any of the difficulty one experiences at Kilkhampton or even Altarnun; but the bench ends here are only the beginning. There are lovely old box pews in the north aisle, fascinating fifteenth-century encaustic tiles on the chancel floor, a Norman font, a Gothick pulpit (the most recent addition to the furniture) and – almost best of all – a simply splendid Royal Arms (Charles I) on the north wall, a good 6 feet high, in richly carved plaster with heavy strapwork ornamentation. It is all very domestic and unassuming – and it makes the spirit sing.

## Launceston

*13; 22 miles NE of Bodmin on A30*

I sometimes think that the entry into Cornwall across the Tamar is more like crossing a national frontier than a county border; if so Launceston, rising dark against its steep green hill beneath the jagged silhouette of its Norman castle, is very much a frontier town. It was also, until 1835, the Cornish capital – a somewhat inflated word, you may think, for a county town; but not, I would reply, when the county is Cornwall and the town is Launceston.

Its chief pride is its church, dedicated – and what a relief it is in Cornwall when one comes across a church dedicated to someone we know – to ST MARY MAGDALENE. It is relatively late in date, simply because this part of the town was in the Middle Ages only an unimportant suburb called Dunheved, Launceston itself being the quarter we now know as St Stephen, up the hill to the north. As such, it formed part of St Stephen's parish. (The church still stands, but is hideously scraped and Victorianised.) It was, however, allowed a chapel, to which the present fourteenth-century tower once belonged. It is a typically Cornish piece with its buttresses set back from the corners and stood until quite recently independent of the church, connected to it only by a small shop.

The church itself was built in granite by Sir Henry Trecarrel between 1511 and 1524. Granite, as I have mentioned earlier, is one of the most intractable kinds of building stone and almost impossible to carve. This astounding edifice, however, is inlaid with what Pevsner describes as 'barbarous profuseness': quatrefoil plinths, coats of arms galore, fleurs-de-lis, long Latin inscriptions, roses, thistles, pomegranates, angels (some playing musical instruments) and innumerable small figures. In a niche below the east window the Magdalen herself crouches, almost prone and apparently overwhelmed by her surroundings, as well she might be. The quality of all these carvings is not particularly fine; given the nature of the medium, however, it is a miracle that they were achieved at all.

The interior of the church does not really match up to the outside. It is of enormous length – eight bays of nave and chancel together – so the lavishness is still evident; the curious widening of the fifth bay from the west (necessitating a depressed four-centred arch) suggests that Trecarrel may have at first intended to build transepts; but there is no work of outstanding quality or particular exuberance of decoration. The arcade piers are cut, as at Altarnun, from single blocks of granite. The best item by far is the pulpit, a pre-Reformation piece in sumptuously carved wood which has recently been painstakingly restored and repainted. The bench ends are also well worthy of study. The wagon roofs, which are said to contain nearly a mile of carved timber and 162 saints and angels, have been much renewed but cannot fail to impress.

## Lostwithiel

*14; 12 miles SW of Liskeard on A390*

The glories of Lostwithiel are three. First there is its name – surely one of the most romantic in Cornwall, which is to say in all England. Then there is its church, ST BARTHOLOMEW'S, whose early fourteenth-century granite spire is quite unlike any other in the country, springing as it does from an octagonal screen of double lights, transomed, traceried and gabled. Every other light has a dormer window above it, also gabled. It is a brave and beautiful design, obviously Breton in origin, which stands out strangely in the Cornish countryside. The interior of the church is impressive more than exciting, with a huge Decorated east window of five lights and a memorable font. The third glory is the BRIDGE, also fourteenth-century, over the River Fowey.

Older than church or bridge is the Norman RESTORMEL CASTLE, on a high hill a mile or so away to the north-west. The simple circular keep is in a remarkable state of preservation, to the point where it is still possible to walk the complete circuit behind the battlements. The Great Hall and the rest of the two-storeyed residence built for himself by Edmund, Earl of Cornwall, around 1300 – and in which, sixty years later, the Black Prince kept Christmas – were ruined in the Civil War; but Restormel is nonetheless a grand and noble ruin, and the view over the valley of the Fowey is superb.

*Restormel Castle, Lostwithiel.*

*The church of St Morwenna, Morwenstow.*

## Morwenstow

*15; 6 miles N of Bude off A39*

Like Lostwithiel, Morwenstow is memorable for three reasons: in this instance its site, its famous rector and its architecture. The site is superb – lonely, swept by the Atlantic gales, standing only a few hundred yards from a sheer cliff top which is the highest in England after Beachy Head. Here the Rev. R.S. Hawker, the poet-priest who was rector of the parish from 1834 to 1875, built himself a hut from which he would go forth to salvage the bodies of sailors shipwrecked on the rocks beneath, more than forty of whom he buried by the upper churchyard wall. Hawker was an extraordinary figure. A drug addict, he was an increasingly High Churchman who became a Roman Catholic on his deathbed; he introduced the Harvest Festival into the Anglican liturgy; he married two wives, the first twenty years older than himself, the second forty years younger; and he designed the RECTORY with chimneystacks in the form of tiny church towers, all different and thought to be inspired by the various churches with which he had been earlier connected.

But it is with the architecture of the CHURCH OF ST MORWENNA – Pevsner mistakenly dedicates it to St John the Baptist – with which we are principally concerned. It possesses something rare in Cornwall, a largely Norman north arcade, and a very fine one too, the second arch in particular being richly carved with what we should call zigzag but which Hawker believed to represent ripples on the Sea of Galilee. The south aisle – and therefore the south arcade with it – is a sixteenth-century addition; but, with a degree of enlightenment unusual in those days, the old Norman south door was preserved and re-erected in its new position – with, however, one of its arches on the outer front of the porch. Otherwise the best things in the church are the carved bench ends – late sixteenth-century and good, but not so good as those at Altarnun or Launcells – and a nice crude Saxon font. The Early English chancel is unusually dark – so dark, indeed, that you might quite easily miss the beautiful wagon roof.

## Padstow

See Prideaux Place.

## Pencarrow House

*16; 4 miles NW of Bodmin off A389*

The house – which is not to be confused with Pencarrow Head, a good 25 miles away on the south coast – lies at the end of a beautiful private woodland drive near the little village of Washaway. It was built between 1765 and 1775, apparently by one Robert Allanson of York – though his name is not mentioned by Pevsner; nor, more surprisingly still, does Howard Colvin refer to him. The outside is pleasant, if unremarkable, Palladian on the east (entrance) front, with seven bays and two and a half storeys and a three-bay pedimented central projection with its own quoins; on the south side, however, Pencarrow contrives to look a good deal more vernacular and – thanks to the long hipped roof and deep eaves – somehow gives the impression of being rather older too.

The inside of the house is mostly contemporary, and surprisingly grand. There is fine plasterwork in the Music Room – which also contains a rather curious tripartite alcove, added in the 1840s – and beautiful panelling there and in the Entrance-Hall-cum-Library, brought, it seems, from Tetcott in Devon. Excellent furniture and pictures can be seen everywhere, especially the Molesworth family portraits by Reynolds in the Dining Room, and an enchanting Devis in the Ante-Room of the four St Aubyn girls looking across at St Michael's Mount.

## Penfound Manor

*17; 5 miles S of Bude off A39*

It is impossible to say just how old are the oldest parts of Penfound Manor. It was recorded in the Domesday Book, and the skeleton of the Great Hall may well date from not very much later. Obviously, there have been subsequent alterations and additions – a huge fireplace, for one thing, in a dark inner recess of which a well-directed torch will reveal a bottle of Jordan water, immensely old, placed there many centuries ago by some returning pilgrim and not to be touched without the unleashing of frightful curses. At some stage too – probably in the fifteenth century – a small bower was added at the south-west end, with a solar above it. At the other end, however, though the screen itself has long since disappeared, the screens passage has kept its black and white pebble mosaic floor, enabling the horses to be led through the house to the well at the back. Beyond this a small stream still runs an inch or two beneath the buttery threshold, next to which rises a wonderful Elizabethan dog-leg staircase said to have been built out of the timbers of a Spanish galleon from the Armada, salvaged in 1589.

In fact, Penfound probably contains fabric dating from every century between the eleventh and the seventeenth; but all has now merged into a wonderfully mellow, unified whole. Nothing spoils – nothing, one feels, *can* spoil – the atmosphere of deep calm, and silence, and ancient peace. It is not large; it gives itself no airs or graces; but the memory of it endures long after that of many a grander and more glorious mansion has passed away.

## Prideaux Place*

*18; just E of Padstow off B3276*

This glorious house stands on the edge of the oldest deer park in Britain, first recorded in the year 435. The animals are kept at a respectful distance by a narrow road and a charming stone wall, low and embattled, with little square gate-towers like chessmen in the centre. Behind this, the house extends its long, low front to the east. It was built on the Elizabethan E-plan, but its three projecting bays have lost the gables that once crowned them; these were replaced in the 1730s by continuations of the battlements that formerly ran only above the intervening spaces. The house has also gained an additional bay – of precisely the same style – at its northern end. In every other respect, however, it looks from this side just as it did when it was built by Nicholas Prideaux in 1592: seven bays, two storeys, the windows all mullioned with two, four or six lights. It is built entirely of the local grey stone, which looks marvellous against the trees behind.

The south front comes as something of a surprise, having been enchantingly Gothicised, partly in 1760, partly in 1810. Both the Library Tower to the left and the big swelling bow in the centre have been lowered, the latter as recently as 1961 – probably, one suspects, to its advantage. The former is embellished with a huge four-light window with Decorated tracery and a pretty quatrefoil above it. (There are similar quatrefoils running at first-floor level all the way along the stable block behind.)

The interior of the house is a delight. It has kept only one spectacular Elizabethan feature – the superb barrel-vaulted plaster ceiling of the original Great Chamber, very much in the same style as that at Lanhydrock (*q.v.*) though said to be somewhat older. Downstairs, the main reception rooms are all exuberant Georgian Gothick except for the Reading Room, whose simply glorious Restoration woodwork is said to have been brought from Stow, a house near Kilkhampton which was demolished in the eighteenth century. For the rest, there are marvellous Gothick ceilings, particularly in the Drawing Room and in the rib-vaulted Library in the Tower. Best of all, however, is the Staircase Hall, which is nothing short of sensational. A short initial flight divides at a low landing, part of it leading straight on into the Library Tower while the main continuation rises on up the west wall and beneath another huge traceried window, making another two right-angled turns before reaching the first-floor landing. Staircase and landing are all cantilevered out from the walls in an astonishing display of bravura; there are busts of Pitt and Fox on the landings surmounted by exuberantly crocketed Gothick canopies, and the whole composition is finished off by a tremendous coved plaster ceiling decorated with quatrefoils.

The Prideaux family – who adopted the additional surname of Brune in 1799 – are still living, after nearly 400 years, in the house built by their ancestor. For the last five generations it has passed in direct succession from father to son. May it continue to do so for many generations to come.

## Probus

*19; $4\frac{1}{2}$ miles NE of Truro on A390*

The CHURCH OF ST PROBUS AND ST GRACE – the church guide strongly disapproves of the second dedication, which it dismisses as an 'entirely medieval invention' – possesses a superb Somerset tower which seems to have found its way to Cornwall by mistake. Even in Somerset it would be among the most outstanding; here it is a prodigy, at 125 feet the highest, as well as the most beautiful, in the county. The Cornish granite has taken on a mass of green lichen, which gives it an almost underwater effect.

Inside, the beauty of the church resides principally in the loftiness of its seven-bay arcades and in the breadth of its aisles, which equals that of the nave. If only the splendour of its proportions could have been matched by the quality of its decoration: alas, it was restored with a disastrously heavy hand by G.E. Street in 1851. His influence was not entirely baleful: he has given it a very pretty screen, incorporating some old bench ends, and a most elegant font, centrally placed. But the prevailing atmosphere is now, thanks to him, overwhelmingly Victorian.

*The church of St Probus and St Grace, Probus.*

About a mile away to the east of the church stands TREWITHEN, a surpassingly elegant early and mid-Georgian house set in its own park with a small lake. The entrance front to the north is of rendered brick, with prominent granite keystones to the windows. It has two storeys and nine bays, the two-bay wings slightly projecting. There are in addition separate pavilions, one on each side, set at right-angles to the main block to form three sides of an open court. They have hipped roofs and very pretty little openwork cupolas. All this is of about 1730, or even a little earlier, and the same can probably be said of the east front, facing down a natural slope. It is of reddish brown ashlar and has in the centre a big canted bay marking the Drawing Room. The south front, on the other hand, looks distinctly later – an impression that is confirmed on going inside. The material is different again: this time it is the lovely silvery grey stone from Pentewan, given a faint rosy glow by the smooth lichen that covers it. Here it is the centre that projects, with an important-looking doorcase and all the windows framed. The impression is one of neatness and compactness, and perfect proportions.

The front door gives into a small vestibule, with a Library on the left; this in turn leads to the central Staircase Hall, top-lit through a glazed dome. A door in the left-hand wall leads through to the Drawing Room, which occupies the centre of the east front – a room of discreet distinction with a fine Palladian chimneypiece and pedimented doorcases, one with fluted Ionic columns. Beyond this room to the east is the Oak Room. Here the atmosphere – though not the period – changes entirely. The room is panelled in wood to its full height, with fluted Ionic pilasters and a broken pediment over the door. The dark walnut furniture suits it perfectly, and seems to make it everything a small early Georgian parlour should be.

And so we come to the showpiece of the house, the Dining Room. It occupies the five central bays of the south front, and is the work of Sir Robert Taylor, who was engaged at Trewithen in 1763–4. At each end is a two-column Ionic screen, behind which is a single groin-vaulted bay; the columns themselves are shorter than one might expect, the necessary height being made up by deep and extremely complex entablatures. Both columns and entablatures are echoed by pilasters on the back walls. The chimneypiece is of the lightest French Rococo, a style which is carried on in stucco over the walls and framing the pictures.

Upstairs, as might be expected, the rooms are simpler, though one bedroom has a similar screen to the one in the Dining Room, this time of fluted Tuscan columns, at its north end. There is also an immense Jacobean four-poster bed, most elaborately and fantastically carved. Between the first and second floors the main staircase is doubled to the west by a smaller one, with a pretty Chinese Chippendale balustrade.

Throughout the house one is conscious, again and again, of fine workmanship and meticulous attention to detail. Moreover, the various building dates, though all within the same half-century, give a welcome touch of variety without affecting the underlying unity of the building. Few houses provide a better object lesson in the development of architectural and decorative taste in the middle years of the eighteenth century.

## Restormel Castle

See Lostwithiel.

## St Buryan

*20; 5½ miles SW of Penzance on B3283*

The huge, proud, granite CHURCH OF ST BURYAN totally dominates the small, inconsequential, granite village. The fourteenth-century tower rises to a height of 92 feet. It has set-back corner buttresses, a polygonal stair turret, three-light traceried bell openings in the topmost of its four stages, battlements and pinnacles, but otherwise no decoration at all. Starkness and austerity are the rule, and the granite emphasises them still further. The body of the church is surprisingly long: six broad bays, with three-light round-headed windows under straight hood-moulds. There is no clerestory. A staircase to the rood-loft projects from the south wall.

Inside, the church becomes a little more welcoming. The feeling of strength is still there, but there is much beauty too in the three long tunnel vaults – all of equal height and length – of nave and aisles, and in the elegant four-shafted arcade piers. Why, one wonders, does so small a village boast so grand and spacious a church? Because it was a rich collegiate church, refounded by Bishop Brewer of Exeter in 1238 on the site of an earlier building traditionally established by St Athelstan in 930 as a thank-offering for his success in evicting the Danes from the Scilly Isles. (By the same token, it is a 'Royal Peculiar, Sinecure and Donative', and the priest and choir wear scarlet cassocks.) The church has in fact been largely rebuilt since Brewer's day, and the present structure must date from around 1500. Since then there have been several restorations, including one by Butterfield in 1872, but St Buryan escaped relatively lightly from them all.

Of the furniture, by far the most spectacular piece is the screen, which extends from one side of the church to the other. Much of it is said to have been renewed (by E.H. Sedding), but on the west side in particular it looks mostly original. Below a superb length of cresting runs a fantastic band of animals, birds and even fish, peeping out of rambling, clambering vegetation. The lower parts have long, narrow panels with a design of foliage, all painted, and there is a splendid kneeling desk made out of two old bench ends. All the real benches, and the floor, are new and boring.

## St Columb Major

*21; 8½ miles SW of Wadebridge on A39*

The CHURCH OF ST COLUMBA stands proudly above the little hill town, many of whose houses are slate-hung in typical Cornish fashion. The west tower is of four stages – in itself a rarity for this county – of which the bottom three are rather unattractively rendered; the good grey stone is visible only on the top stage, and at the bottom where broad pointed arches to north and south allow a processional way to pass underneath. The south porch is distinctly military-looking like a two-storeyed castle. It has one tiny trefoiled window above the door, and a two-light one to the east. (To the west there is only a drainpipe, ill-advisedly painted white.)

*The church of St Buryan.*

The interior is conceived on the grand scale, with nave, aisles, transepts, chancel and chancel aisles. The date is early fourteenth-century, though most of the windows are now Perpendicular and even the Decorated ones (in the south transept and chancel aisle) are renewed. There is a fine tunnel vault of wood, with square panels, large bosses and angels and a most magnificent rood-screen (with a complete loft and rood, to say nothing of St John and the Virgin) which is Victorian but perhaps in this case none the worse for that. The Victorians (I wonder who) also inserted an elaborate ceilure over the chancel, in which each of the square panels of the tunnel roof is sub-divided with diagonals and, over the altar, painted with stars. Notice also the unusually pretty fourteenth-century stone piscina.

The final treat is the bench ends; nothing unusual in style, but a very fine set with the Instruments of the Passion, monkeys playing musical instruments, and initials.

## St Germans

*22; 10 miles W of Plymouth off A38*

The CHURCH OF ST GERMANS stands on the site of the old Saxon cathedral of Cornwall. Sixteen years before the Conquest, however, it was shorn of its status and merged with the new diocese of Exeter, and by the time the present building was begun towards the end of the twelfth century the old foundation had become an Augustinian priory. Much of this late Norman work has, alas, been destroyed; but the west front remains untouched up to the level of the nave roof and is, to me, one of the most impressive Romanesque façades in the country. It is worth a long, hard look, this façade – and from some distance away, so that it can be appreciated in proper perspective. Then, too, you will see why I used that word 'Romanesque' rather than 'Norman'; St Germans is one of the very few examples of English architecture of the period that seem to have a distinctly European flavour. You would not be a bit surprised to come across it in Northern France, or parts of Germany, or even Southern Italy. Even the upper, octagonal, stage of the north tower – a thirteenth-century addition – seems to keep up the pretence.

*The great west portal of the church of St Germans.*

Two main features only give the game away: first, the south tower, whose corresponding upper stage is straightforward English Perpendicular, like a thousand others up and down the country, and looks distinctly uncomfortable in such alien surroundings. Second, and far more important, is the great west portal. There is no whiff of the Continent here – only pure Anglo-Norman, and at its breathtaking best. Considerably broader than it is high, it is composed of no fewer than seven orders, decorated with the usual motifs, richly but not excessively. It is one of the great Norman doorways of England, and the glory of St Germans. Go up close and enjoy it to the full; nothing inside the church can rival it.

There are several reasons for the disappointing quality of the interior. The proportions are wrong, for a start. The south aisle was broadened in the fourteenth century at its eastern end to make a reliquary chapel, and in the fifteenth century this broadening was continued to the west. Although the work was well done in itself, the result was to make the aisle slightly broader than the nave; and this unhappy state of affairs was compounded in the sixteenth century when the nave was shorn of the chancel – fortunately, the great east window was preserved and reset in its new position – and again in 1802 when the north aisle was demolished to make an Eliot family pew. What we now have, therefore, is essentially a double-naved church, sorely scraped and with much Victorian restoration, with only its two western bays testifying to its venerable Norman origins. Even the later Middle Ages have not left us very much to admire, except the Decorated east end of the aisle and the great east window – which, incidentally, contains glass by Burne-Jones, executed by Morris & Co. (There is more of this in the south window of the Lady Chapel.)

Next to the church stands PORT ELIOT, the house of the Earls of St Germans. It still conceals part of the thirteenth-century undercroft of the old priory, but most of what we see today is the work of Sir John Soane. This includes a magnificent circular Drawing Room, one wall of which is, at the time of writing, being covered with a mural painting of remarkable energy and power. The house is not open to the public.

## St Ives

*23; 7½ miles NE of Penzance on A3074*

A formidable-looking church from the outside, ST IA'S has a four-stage west tower – as I have noted before, these are exceptional in Cornwall – and a nave of seven bays, the whole thing seemingly hewn out of granite. The surprising thing is that this fine and spacious building was until 1826 merely a chapel of ease, the parish church being at Lelant.

The church is generally considered, nonetheless, to be one of the finest in Cornwall, with a particularly lovely memorial chapel to the south of the south aisle erected around 1500 by the Trenwith family. It also possesses a remarkable early fifteenth-century granite font, which looks marvellous in photographs, and a Madonna and Child by St Ives's distinguished resident, Barbara Hepworth. Alas, I have seen neither; I have tried twice to gain admittance to St Ia's, and failed both times.

St Mawes Castle.

## St Mawes Castle

*24; 8 miles S of Truro on A3078*

Together with its neighbour Pendennis (*q.v.*) across the Carrick Roads, St Mawes belongs to that chain of fortresses built by Henry VIII from 1538 onwards to protect the south coast from possible invasion by Francis I of France with Papal support. The two castles seem to have been designed with somewhat different purposes in mind; as Carew puts it in his *Survey of Cornwall*, 'St Mawes lieth lower and better to annoy shipping, but Pendennis standeth higher and stronger to defend itself.' As things turned out, the French invasion never took place; it was not till the Civil War that Henry's defences were seriously tested and Carew was proved right. Pendennis held out valiantly for five months against Cromwell's troops; St Mawes surrendered without firing a shot.

The fact remains that, of the two, St Mawes with its clover-leaf pattern of intersecting circles is by far the more visually interesting, a variant of the design that reaches its ultimate point of sophistication at Deal (*q.v.*). It represents only a brief transitional period in the development of military architecture, when the high keeps and gatehouses of the past that had served so well against the bow and arrow had been found ineffectual in the age of gunpowder and firearms, and before the introduction of the latest Italian ideas – with their spiky angle bastions of the kind seen in the later Elizabethan work at Pendennis. The plan is that of a low circular tower in the centre, with three low semi-circular lunettes, all of the local shale but with occasional pieces of granite and freestone added.

You enter from the north-east, passing through a hexagonal guardhouse and then over a two-arched stone bridge spanning a deep ditch. (At this point there was originally a drawbridge, which could be well covered by musketry fire from the cross slits to each side of the gate.) You now find yourself on the first floor of the keep, from which narrow stone staircases lead to the upper and lower floors and to the outlying bastions. In the basement is a kitchen, paved in stone and provided with a fireplace and bread oven; many of the roof beams are original. Above, on the second floor, is an octagonal gun room, a gun port (now glazed) in each of its eight recesses; while above this again is the garrison mess room with its granite fireplace.

Out on the bastions there are big casemates for cannon and small embrasures fitted with sockets for light guns as well as for the bolts that fastened the protective shutters. Bastions and keep are all surprisingly rich in decorative detail, with coats of arms, figure carvings and even Latin inscriptions in profusion. This is an unexpected pleasure in a working fortress, as are the gardens of flowering shrubs with which it is surrounded.

## St Michael Caerhays

See Caerhays Castle.

## St Michael's Mount*

*NT; 25; 3 miles E of Penzance on A394, then ½ mile off coast at Marazion*

If you are lucky enough to see St Michael's Mount for the first time, as I did, on a sparkling summer afternoon, the sight will take your breath away. No house in England can boast so spectacular a site, crowning as it does the crest of a great crag projecting several hundred yards out into the sea itself, by which it is totally cut off from the mainland for some twenty hours a day. But the Mount has a good deal more to offer than the purely picturesque. Its history goes back at least to the end of the fifth century, when the Archangel Michael is said to have appeared to some fishermen (just as he did at his two other, more famous, shrines: Mont St-Michel in Normandy and Monte Sant'Angelo in Apulia); well before that, it was almost certainly the island of Ictis, mentioned by Diodorus Siculus as having been an important centre for the export of Cornish tin. (Ancient legend even makes it the home of the giant Cormoran, slain by Jack the Giant-Killer.)

After the appearance of the Archangel, the Mount's sanctity was assured and it became a regular place of pilgrimage. There was a Celtic monastery there from the eighth century to the eleventh; then, some time before 1050, it was granted by Edward the Confessor to the Abbey of Mont St-Michel for the establishment of a cell of Benedictine monks. The first community seems to have simply occupied the old monastic buildings, but in 1135 building began in earnest and the church was consecrated in 1144. The link with Normandy continued until the reign of Henry V when, after his declaration of war with France, the Mount was declared alien property and transferred to his new foundation, the Brigittine Abbey of Syon (*q.v.*), with whom it remained till the Dissolution. For the next 100 years it was the property of the Crown and, during the Civil War, was stoutly – if ultimately unsuccessfully – defended by the Royalists. Finally, in 1647, the victorious Parliament nominated, as military governor there, Colonel John St Aubyn. Twelve years later he bought the property, and the St Aubyns have been there ever since.

It has not always been their principal home. Life on the Mount is not without its inconveniences – particularly during winter gales, when its inhabitants can be stranded there for a week at a time – and there have been extended periods when the family preferred to live on the mainland. And yet, for the past three centuries, the St Aubyns have continually added to the buildings and made them more comfortable so that now, while everywhere there are reminders of the Mount's past history both as a monastery and as a castle, the prevailing impression is that of a most agreeable country house – and one that is not only enchanting but exciting as well.

Whether you arrive by boat or across the causeway, you first find yourself at the little harbour and village. In the 1870s there were still some 300 permanent residents, with three schools, a customs house, a Wesleyan Chapel and three pubs; several of the houses go back to the seventeenth and eighteenth centuries. Access to the house is either by a stiff but exhilarating climb – during which one is rewarded by marvellous views – or by a lift, ingeniously concealed in the rock. If you choose the former, you will find the path winding round the Mount and almost encircling it, so that you eventually enter from the west – through a fifteenth-century four-centred archway.

The inner geography is inevitably complex. The house, as one might expect, is built on innumerable different levels, as well as having grown organically over the centuries. The last major additions were made by the then owner's cousin, the architect Piers St Aubyn, between 1873 and 1878; with his sheer walls and high balconies, perched dizzily above the sea, he has contrived to make the castle, if anything, even more sensational in appearance than it was before. Any tour should, however, start with the church. Though it is the oldest part of the castle buildings still standing, it dates only from the early fourteenth century, its predecessor having been destroyed in an earthquake, and is much restored. It remains, however, a building of much beauty and charm, with its exquisite little rose window at the east end and a pair of pretty Perpendicular two-lighters below.

There was formerly also a Lady Chapel, separate from the church, but by the eighteenth century this was in ruins and was accordingly converted in the 1740s into

St Michael's Mount.

the Blue Drawing Rooms, perhaps the most completely delightful in the whole house. The style is early Gothick Rococo, with a coved stucco ceiling, ogee niches and doorways and an overmantel with inward-curving pediment which looks almost like a piece of early *chinoiserie*. Since the Lady Chapel was free-standing, high on the north terrace, the exterior of these rooms was also important; it has been carefully restored in correct Gothic, with Y-traceried windows, crocketed ogee hood-moulds and high pierced parapet.

The other most memorable room in the castle is known as the Chevy Chase Room, so called for the plaster frieze of hunting scenes which runs round just below the springing of the timber arches of the roof. The frieze must date from the middle of the seventeenth century, but the room itself was originally the refectory of the old monastery and the masonry of the walls may well be of the twelfth century. The dado and doors are Gothic, but of the same date as the Blue Drawing Rooms. There is also a fine Jacobean oak table, but this is quite a recent arrival.

The castle is surprisingly large, and it is impossible to describe all the other rooms in detail. But in the remainder it is less their architectural quality that sticks in the mind than the fact of their very existence – warm, sunlit and comfortable on their extraordinary sea-girt crag, with the coast of Cornwall stretching away into the distance, far below.

## St Neot

*26; 5 miles NW of Liskeard off A38*

The church sets out, unashamedly, to impress. The approach to ST NEOT'S is up a narrow valley from the south, and the fifteenth-century south façade, pinnacled and embattled, with a similarly embellished two-storey porch, looks magnificent from a distance, against the dark hillside. Neither does it disappoint at close quarters: the south porch boasts a memorable tunnel vault, ribbed and bravely bossed, and there is further curious vaulting beneath the tower. But the true splendour of this church lies in its stained glass. Much of it was restored and renewed in 1829 by John Hedgeland, but in twelve of the fifteen windows about half the glass dates from early Tudor times, and very fine it is. Earliest and best is the Creation window at the east end of the south aisle; diagonally opposite in the western corner of the north aisle, the two windows telling the stories of St Neot and St George are also full of imagination and humour. But all the windows repay study – including Hedgeland's. How fortunate the church was to get him; one shudders to think what would have happened if the restoration had been delayed another thirty years.

## Tintagel

*27; 11 miles NE of Wadebridge on B2363*
*Includes the Old Post Office (NT)*

What would King Arthur say? This rocky cove on the north Cornish coast, which is associated more than anywhere else in England with his legend and which still bears one of the most musically evocative place-names in the kingdom, has sold its soul to the tripper traffic. In the village itself one building alone still stands out among the welter of car parks, coach parks, ice cream parlours and hamburger stalls. Known affectionately as the OLD POST OFFICE – by virtue of forty-eight years' service in that capacity from 1844 to 1892 – it is in fact a tiny manor house of the fourteenth century, almost miraculously preserved. Crouching low to the ground as if afraid of being blown away by the winter gales, its grey slate roof rising and falling like a swelling sea, it looks neither big nor grand enough to boast a real medieval Hall; yet the Hall is there all right, minute but unmistakable, its rafters blackened by smoke as all such rafters should be, with a screens passage on one side and, from the further corner, a spiral stair leading up to a small bedchamber. Beyond the Hall another small room has been restored as the Victorian village post office it used to be.

But for all the charm of this lovely old building, it is a relief to escape from the village and to walk ten minutes to the high headland and the remains of the medieval CASTLE. For the average visitor unversed in military archaeology these remains are too sparse to be of more than passing interest; but their setting – with that of the island beyond, on which traces remain of a sixth-century Celtic monastery – is the stuff of which poetry is made. With a little imagination, even the monstrous bulk of the late Victorian King Arthur's Castle Hotel on the cliff opposite can be incorporated in a Tennysonian vision of the way Tintagel ought to be – and even, up to a point, was.

## Trelowarren

*28; 6 miles SE of Helston off B3293*

The old house of the Vyvyans was begun some time about the middle of the fifteenth century. It has been much altered and enlarged since then, but the central block that faces you as you approach down the drive is still essentially of that time. It is a low, two-storey building, embattled and with a central bay, and it has windows of four, five and six lights, some round-headed and some straight. This block forms the eastern range of the three which enclose the entrance court. The Chapel block to the south has also retained some fifteenth-century work on its inner side, though the rest dates only from the seventeenth century and later. Of the seventeenth century too (1698) are the very pretty stables west of the house with their lantern and cupola. The north range of the house itself is Victorian, as are most of the interiors.

The principal exception is the Chapel, an enchanting piece of Rococo Gothick. Its precise date seems uncertain: Pevsner suggests *c.*1750, which I should have thought a little early, while the local guide-book – which is singularly uninformative about the house, being more of a potted family history – attributes it to Sir Viyell Vyvyan, who succeeded only in 1814. My own guess, for what it is worth, would be the 1760s. The Chapel is small and tunnel-vaulted, the ribs forming four-centred arches. Along the walls are set pairs of stalls with immensely elaborate pinnacled canopies, between three-light windows with quatrefoiled plate tracery. The doors, too, are most elaborately crested, with similar canopies or crocketed ogee arches.

The main part of the house is now leased to the Trelowarren Fellowship, an ecumenical charity. There are weekly concerts during the season, as well as Sunday services in the Chapel.

*Trelowarren House.*

## Trematon Castle★

*29; 3½ miles W of Plymouth off A38*

In a county as large as Cornwall, it is surprising that the two most desirable houses I know should lie within a couple of miles of each other. One of them, Ince Castle, has already been described; the other, Trematon Castle, is even more dramatically situated, commanding the Tamar on the left, the Lynher on the right with the grounds of Antony beyond, and, to the front, a tremendous prospect straight down the Hamoaze to Plymouth – not, heaven knows, a beautiful town but with distance lending, as usual, enchantment to the view.

Whereas Ince is, as I have said, not really a castle at all, Trematon most emphatically is – one of the grandest and best preserved in Cornwall, with a majestic oval keep (built by Robert of Mortain, William the Conqueror's half brother) towering like the prow of a great ship above the walls of the inner bailey and the thirteenth-century Gatehouse. Within the curtain walls lies a lovely, mysterious sunken garden and, in the middle of it all, an enchanting pink-washed battlemented house of 1808.

The property is not normally open to the public, but access to the keep and Gatehouse can usually be obtained by anyone making a written appointment.

*Trematon Castle.*

## Trerice

*NT; 30; 3 miles SE of Newquay off A3058*

Few sixteenth-century houses in Cornwall have been preserved so unspoilt as Trerice, the old home of the Arundells, hidden away in its secret valley some 3 or 4 miles to the south-east of Newquay. Built between 1570 and 1573 around the core of an earlier medieval manor house, it faces east across its little walled garden, a traditional Elizabethan E-shaped front of the local silver-grey limestone liberally dappled with lichen. It is of two main floors, with attic windows in the gables; these, like all the others on the east front, are mullioned with straight heads – that of the Great Hall, immediately to the left of the porch, having two transoms and no fewer than twenty-four lights, in three rows of eight. The only other touch of extravagance is provided by the fantastic ornamental gables, swooping and soaring in joyful arabesques across the pitch of the grey slate roof behind.

These gables, in fact, present us with something of a puzzle. Where can the idea have come from? Shaped Dutch gables do not appear elsewhere in England until the 1620s – and then, not unnaturally, in East Anglia. To find them in Cornwall some half a century earlier is almost inexplicable: one can only assume that Sir John Arundell, the builder of the house, saw some gables of a similar kind when serving in his youth as a soldier in the Low Countries, was struck by them and determined to copy them when he got home. But even this explanation seems improbable enough.

Inside, however, Trerice is built on the orthodox plan, with a screens passage leading directly off the porch, the Hall to the left and the service area to the right. As was plain from the window, the Hall rises through both principal floors. Its pride is its exuberant plaster ceiling, with narrow moulded ribs forming intricate geometrical designs containing scrolls, oak leaves, initials and pendants. The high chimneypiece is surmounted by an overmantel flanked by caryatids and bearing the date 1572. The one sad fact is the disappearance of the screen. In its absence a wall has been built across the north end of the Hall, with a single door in the middle. Above this wall, however, a tiny arcade reveals the existence of a minstrels' gallery above the passage.

Beyond the Hall a door leads into the Library, which is of relatively little interest since it was divided at the beginning of the nineteenth century into two small sitting rooms and restored to its original form by the National Trust only in 1969. Above it at the top of the staircase is Sir John Arundell's Great Chamber, now the Drawing Room. Wishing for more height than would otherwise have been available, Sir John merged the medieval solar with the attics above and, in the space thus obtained, built the extraordinary barrel-vaulted ceiling which is the glory of Trerice. Its design is even more elaborate than that of the Hall, and it has an exquisite frieze running below. Above this frieze and immediately underneath the vault at the west end are the arms of the 24th Earl of Arundel, who married Sir John's daughter Mary. Once again there is a tremendous overmantel with caryatids and the date 1573.

From this glorious room you can walk along the long west corridor (largely reconstructed by the National Trust), looking into the Musicians' Gallery on the way, to the rooms in the north wing. These too, however, are for the most part restorations – the north wing had become ruinous by the end of the last century – and are of relatively little architectural interest. No matter. The house itself remains a rare gem, and does enormous credit to the National Trust, whose achievement in restoring it to its former beauty is beyond praise.

## Truro

*31; 13½ miles SW of St Austell on A390*

The CATHEDRAL at Truro was the first to be built in England since St Paul's. Its architect was John Loughborough Pearson, and this – his *magnum opus* – demonstrates perhaps better than any other building his weaknesses and his strengths. He was, to begin with, curiously insensitive to local character: just as he could build a very French church in the middle of the Yorkshire moors (at Appleton) or a tough Midland church in Surrey (at Weybridge), so he could build in Cornwall – where there are virtually no spires and the churches are quite remarkably long and low – an edifice of soaring verticals, with no fewer than three Normandy Gothic spires. He was quite uninterested in surface decoration or detail, believing that any great religious building must be a unified structure, with every individual element justifiable only insofar as it contributed to the overall conception; at Truro you may wander as long as you like, but you will find no quirkish little surprises or syncopations of rhythm. Colour, too, and the individual texture of different materials, meant little to him; much as you may admire the undoubted splendour of his achievement, there will be moments when you find yourself longing for a little touch of Butterfield, or William Burges, or even Gilbert Scott.

*Truro Cathedral.*

But there are compensations. Pearson built his cathedral in Early English (except for those spires), and no one of his time understood the style better than he. Truro may not show much creative originality, but as a monument to his architectural scholarship it is impressive indeed; when Pevsner described its interior as 'in many ways a *beau idéal* of the Early English style' he was not speaking lightly. Secondly and more important, Pearson was a master of two particular arts, one technical, one conceptual: vaulting and the enclosure of space. This cathedral is stone-vaulted throughout – sexpartite in the nave, quadripartite elsewhere – and gains immeasurably thereby. Moreover, to walk round the building is to treat oneself to an endless succession of changing vistas and unexpected diagonals. (Walk directly eastward from the baptistery and you will see what I mean.) Even the nave has been placed at a slight angle to the choir – though this may in part be due to the limitations of the highly inconvenient and constricted site.

Less fortunate than Wren, Pearson did not live to see his cathedral finished. He died suddenly in 1897, leaving his son to see the work through to completion. This, as things turned out, was delayed until 1910, with the capping of the two west towers. Fortunately he had left a full set of drawings, so the designs are entirely his. The only exception is the south aisle, which he preserved from the late Perpendicular parish church of St Mary which formerly occupied the site. A typically Cornish conception, with a plaster tunnel vault divided into squares by narrow wooden ribs, it has nothing whatever in common with the surrounding Early English, the five-light traceried east window and broad four-centred arches striking a jarring note – another indication, perhaps, of the insensitivity mentioned above.

Others, I can well understand, might welcome this bold juxtaposition as a bonus – even as that very touch of oddness and eccentricity which is otherwise so noticeably lacking. And they may well be right. What I cannot imagine anyone liking is the modern Chapter House that has recently been added on the north side, together with a Memorial Hall. The heavy horizontality of those concrete and granite slabs displays a total lack of sympathy with the cathedral itself and with everything that Pearson was trying to achieve. Even blind medievalism would have been preferable to this.

# Short List

## Carnanton

*32; 4½ miles NE of Newquay off A3059*

A large and somewhat austere Georgian house, it is beautifully situated in the Vale of Lanherne. The main block is of seven bays on two and a half storeys, with a one-storey addition to the north added in 1810. The main rooms are said to have outstandingly fine plasterwork which took a team of sixteen Italian stuccadores two years to complete. Unfortunately I was not allowed in.

## Fowey

*33; 7½ miles E of St Austell on A3082*

A picturesque little town – once a prosperous port – Fowey has narrow streets from which, one day, all motor traffic will be banned. ST FIMBARRUS'S CHURCH stands in a charming square, watched over by a delightful little vicarage. A noble building of the mid-fourteenth century, it has a four-stage tower with decorative friezes at each stage. It is overlooked by the huge turreted bulk of PLACE HOUSE, the Walter Scott romantic mansion of the Treffreys family, which replaced their late medieval castle early in the nineteenth century.

## Mullion

*34; 5 miles S of Helston off A3083*

The CHURCH OF ST MELINUS (or Melina, nobody seems to be quite sure which) is of the late fifteenth century, carefully and lovingly restored by F.C. Eden, who achieved such a dramatic transformation at Blisland (*q.v.*). Its chief claim to fame, however, is not so much its architecture as its bench ends, among the finest and most complete in Cornwall. Although the subject matter is much what one might expect (Instruments of the Passion, and so on) there are occasional Renaissance motifs, such as cavorting *amorini*, which could not be earlier than 1535 or so.

## Penzance

*35; 13½ miles NW of Helston on A394*

Possibly the most unexpected – and certainly the dottiest – house in Cornwall is to be found in Chapel Street, and represents one of the rarest of architectural styles, that of the Ancient Egyptian Revival. Pevsner describes the EGYPTIAN HOUSE as 'consistent if not correct', but he may not have noticed the Royal Arms of England above the central window, which even boasts what might be considered Ancient Egyptian glazing bars. Two possible architects have been suggested: P.F. Robinson, who designed the Egyptian Hall in Piccadilly in 1812 and who was also responsible for Trelissick (*q.v.*), or John Foulston, who achieved something similar at the Public Library at Devonport, which was virtually destroyed during the last war. This splendid edifice is now the property of the Landmark Trust and is consequently available for rent.

## Pendennis Castle

*36; just SE of Falmouth off A39*

Facing St Mawes (*q.v.*), Pendennis Castle stares across the entrance to the Carrick Roads east of Falmouth. Unlike St Mawes, however, it is set on the highest point of its promontory, and was consequently able to defy the Parliamentarians for five months during the Civil War. When it was completed in 1546 it consisted only of its circular keep with the buildings attached to it on the north-west and the sixteen-sided curtain wall – the former of granite ashlar, the latter mainly of shale. The outer *enceinte* with its angular bastions – representing all the latest Italian thinking in military architecture – dates from 1583–98, while the Italianate outer gateway is almost certainly Jacobean.

## St Winnow

*37; 2½ miles S of Lostwithiel on B3269*

The old ST WINNOW'S CHURCH stands beside the Fowey, on the river's curve: a ravishing situation amid woods and green meadows. It is no great shakes architecturally, but has wonderful late fifteenth-century glass in the east window of the south aisle and a good Crucifixion – most unworthily set – in that of the chancel. The bench ends are good too, and there is a rare Cornish-style rood-screen, much (but extremely well) restored by E.H. Sedding.

## Trelissick

*NT; 38; 5 miles S of Truro on B3289*

P.F. Robinson prided himself on being able to build in any style – a fact which he had gone some way towards proving when he built the Egyptian Hall in London in 1812. (He may also have been responsible for the Egyptian House in Penzance (*q.v.*).) Here at Trelissick he produced an austere mansion in the Grecian taste, with a hexastyle Ionic portico copied from that of the Erechtheum in Athens. The park and gardens, with glorious views down to the Carrick Roads, are the property of the National Trust and open to visitors; the house is not.

# Devon

Cider and clotted cream, Old Uncle Tom Cobleigh and Sir Francis Drake – the Devon legend is a powerful one, and of all the counties of England, Devon to me has the most beautiful name – a name that conjures up now vistas of rolling green hills, with mellow lichened churches and thatched cottages nestling in the combes, now a rocky coastline of peaceful inlets and deserted coves. Even the thought of the dank autumn mists curling around Dartmoor evokes an agreeable *frisson*.

Nor is the impression altogether false – though the coaches and caravans of tourists, clattering and swaying bumper to bumper through the combes or parked on vast acreages of custom-laid concrete behind the coves, do much to mar the joys of Devon in high summer. At such times it is better to avoid the coast. Explore, rather, the heartland of this huge and heterogeneous county – only Yorkshire and Lincolnshire are larger – where, in any case, nearly all the best of its architecture is found.

The two most characteristic building stones of Devon are the grey granite of Dartmoor and the new red sandstone, beloved of the early railway posters, which dominates the south-east part of the county as far as a line running roughly from Crediton to Torquay. In the extreme north-east there is a belt of old red sandstone, its colours less violent and more varied than those of its younger neighbour; but most of the remainder is given over to a dark, slaty sandstone known as culm, an unlovely material whose chief quality is its attractiveness to lichens. There is also, at Beer, a very pale chalky limestone which takes carving well and can be seen in quantity – and to considerable effect – in Exeter Cathedral. In the villages, however, stone has always been reserved for the churches, public buildings, and the houses of the comparatively well-to-do. The typical Devon cottage is of mud, mixed with enough lime to allow it to set and strengthened with chopped straw and gravel; the local word is cob. Given a good thick thatch to keep the rain off, a well-built cob cottage will endure for centuries; given a regular coat of whitewash, it will also look quite ridiculously picturesque. All over the county there are villages of white cob cottages clustered round a red stone church that seem to have come straight out of a travel agent's window.

Architecturally, it must be admitted that Devon is not particularly distinguished. Its greatest building, beyond any doubt, is Exeter Cathedral, at least in the interior. Of the parish churches, nearly all were rebuilt or remodelled in the fifteenth century, and the relentless ubiquity of the Perpendicular ultimately becomes monotonous. There are some good towers, like that of Chittlehampton, but few indeed are of the Somerset class. Where Devon excels is in church furnishings – screens above all, traceried, fan-vaulted, carved with grapes and vine tendrils and painted with angels and saints; but also pulpits, carved bench ends and, rather surprisingly, south doors – of which that of St Saviour's, Dartmouth, is the best. Certain of the former cloth towns – Totnes and Tiverton, Crediton and Cullompton and Ottery St Mary – have churches of considerable size and magnificence; but the majority are small and unassuming. Only eight have towers over the crossing; even clerestories are rare.

The two most important cities of Devon, Exeter and Plymouth, were badly bombed in the Second World War. Much of the modern rebuilding has been nothing short of a disgrace, and – Exeter Cathedral excepted – they now have little indeed to detain us. The smaller towns have fared, however, a good deal better; once again, Totnes and Tiverton deserve a special mention, as do the Georgian seaside towns; of these Sidmouth is outstanding, but Dawlish, Teignmouth and Torquay (or parts of it) are not far behind.

Among country houses, the selection has been difficult indeed, for they range from fourteenth-century Littlehempston to twentieth-century Castle Drogo – not the most beautiful, but in many ways the most remarkable of all. Saltram is included for its interior, Sharpham for its situation, Powderham for its history, Ugbrooke for its park, Cadhay for its courtyard. The houses here described, however, are only a small sample of what Devon has to offer; the more you seek, the more you will find. Your search, admittedly, will not reveal any buildings of the very first importance; but it will open up as wide and as fascinating a variety of country house architecture as is to be found in any county of England.

## Arlington Court*

*NT; 1; 8 miles NE of Barnstaple off A39*

Not one of the great houses of England, or even of Devon, Arlington Court is the work of a local architect, Thomas Lee of Barnstaple. In essence it is merely a plain rectangular block of two storeys (a capacious basement for the staff is visible from the west side), five bays by three, with only its pairs of giant Tuscan pilasters at the corners and its agreeable little semi-circular Doric porch to stamp it as neo-classical – the style still more or less *de rigueur* for a West Country gentleman's residence in 1820. The effect is quite pretty, but somehow one cannot help finding it a little inadequate as a nucleus for the superb 3,500-acre park surrounding it.

On entering, however, one immediately sees that it is bigger and more grandiose than it looks from the outside. Much of the grandiosity admittedly stems from later in the century, when Sir Bruce Chichester enlarged the main Hall, inserting a huge stone staircase and a gallery, with round-headed windows and heraldic shields in coloured glass, along the landing. (He also added the stables, and a remarkably dreary north wing, of which the less said the better.) Such High Victorian accretions have done much to spoil Arlington's quiet Regency character, though there remains the fine succession of three rooms along the south front linked by scagliola columns and distinguished by very shallow arches – as a young man, Lee worked briefly as an assistant to Sir John Soane. These rooms can in fact be considered as one long saloon, occupying virtually the whole of the south side; they are, however, provided with sliding screens so that they can be closed off as necessary.

But the charm of Arlington, considerable as it is, does not lie in its architecture. It stems directly from the single personality dominating it – that of Miss Rosalie Chichester, daughter of Sir Bruce, who was born in the house in 1865 and lived in it almost uninterruptedly until her death in 1949. She bequeathed it to the National Trust, who have kept it exactly as it was in her day, and there is not a room in which her presence cannot be felt. Here are her albums, her collections of shells and snuffboxes, porcelain and pewter and bric-à-brac of every kind, and, everywhere, the model ships that she loved – including the 'Little Ships' which rescued the British Army from Dunkirk in 1940. (A posthumous addition to this last collection is a silver model of *Gipsy Moth IV*, in which Miss Chichester's step-nephew, Sir Francis, sailed single-handed round the world. She would have liked that.)

The park and woodlands are open to the public. There is a heronry by the lake, and a nature trail, and Shetland ponies and Jacob's sheep, and a carriage collection in the stables. I know of few more pleasant places in Devon in which to spend a sunny summer afternoon.

## Ashton*

*2; 10 miles N of Newton Abbot off B3193*

Perched on the side of a rocky hill overlooking a remarkably pretty village, the CHURCH OF ST JOHN THE BAPTIST (wrongly ascribed by Pevsner to St Michael) is one of the most perfect Devon churches you could hope to find. It is all Perpendicular, the nave and chancel dating from around the 1420s and the north aisle added considerably later, perhaps the beginning of the sixteenth century. It has scarcely been touched since.

Its great showpiece is the screen – or more accurately screens, since the parclose screen dividing the chancel from the Lady Chapel is if anything yet more remarkable than the rood-screen itself. The latter runs the whole width of the church – eight arches, with Perpendicular tracery and an enchanting frieze of birds, pecking away at bunches of grapes. The lower panels are all painted, with figures of saints, angels, evangelists, martyrs, an Annunciation and a Visitation. On the parclose screen the paintings are larger and more interesting still – Old Testament prophets of an uncompromisingly fifteenth-century kind, with great inscribed scrolls streaming behind them. This series of screen paintings is by far the best in the West Country, and one of the best in England; and as if that were not enough there is another medieval painting, this time on the north wall of the Lady Chapel. It represents Christ, with the Instruments of the Passion; this painting is now rather faded, inevitably, but it is still easily distinguishable.

For the rest, there are fragments of excellent medieval glass, particularly in the east end of the north aisle and the Lady Chapel, and a fine Jacobean box pulpit with a square tester. On your way out don't miss the bullet marks in the oak door of the south porch. They date from 1646, when the beautiful fourteenth-century house close by, PLACE BARTON, fell to the Parliamentarians.

*The church of St John the Baptist, Ashton.*

## Bradley Manor

*NT; 3; just SW of Newton Abbot on A381*

This small and astonishingly unspoilt fifteenth-century manor house lies hidden in the steep valley of the River Lemon, only just outside Newton Abbot but feeling wonderfully remote in its dense woodland surroundings. In its earliest form it was complete by 1427, when the tiny Chapel was added on the east front; then, towards the end of the century, an outer wall was built to connect the projecting porch with this Chapel, forming a corridor – actually divided into two rooms – running along the east side of the Great Hall. This wall, with its southward extension, now forms the entrance front of the house. Faced with roughcast, it has four big gables; in each, there is a pretty Gothic oriel, traceried and transomed and somewhat exaggeratedly embattled. Smaller windows, which do not project though two of them are similarly ornate (the others have been subsequently altered), run along the ground floor. At the north end is the Chapel with its three-light Perpendicular window. The western elevation is a good deal simpler, with the steeply pitched roof of the Great Hall running almost the entire length, the dormer window marking the solar at the far north end. (The central bay window is Victorian.) The south front proves, in a way, the most interesting of all – here we can see the outline of an even earlier house, built in the thirteenth century, whose Hall occupied the middle of this elevation. To the west, forming a right-angle with this old Hall block, stands a late seventeenth-century coach house.

The Chapel has a barrel roof with carved bosses where the ribs intersect; in the central boss is a bearded head which undoubtedly represents God the Father. The rood-screen has gone, apart from a single post, recently discovered in the house and restored. There is also a charming fragment of the fifteenth-century alabaster reredos which makes one bitterly regret the disappearance of the rest. From here you pass via a sixteenth-century Parlour into the Hall, which still has its timber roof with collar-beams and arched braces. It contains a good rough fireplace made up of three big pieces of moorstone – those huge slabs of stone found lying on the moors. Painted on the north wall are the Royal Arms of Elizabeth I. The only tragedy is the addition of the Victorian bow (seen from the outside when looking at the west front); this involved the destruction of all the other windows on the west side. The screen, too, is not original; it is a replacement made up of seventeenth-century panelling brought from the Mermaid Inn at Ashburton. On the other hand there is another very pretty screen set into the east wall, whose combination of linenfold panelling and, above it, various panels of Renaissance design must date it to around 1530. Further carvings on the other side of the screen can be seen from the Antechapel. From the south end of the Hall you cross the screens passage to get to the buttery and, beyond it, the fifteenth-century kitchen.

The interest of the upstairs rooms – apart from the old solar at the north end, which looks westward through the dormer noted from outside – is the line of decorative windows that are the principal decorative feature of the east front. In the little Priest's Room the window seems to take over completely, and the same is true to only a slightly lesser degree in the Oriel Room adjoining it to the south – from which, incidentally, a small squint gives on to the Hall. More interesting than either is the so-called Coat of Arms Room over the buttery, with its coved ceiling and carved oak overmantel.

Now turn right into the wing which contained the original thirteenth-century Hall. Here are two small rooms of enormous charm. One is a little William and Mary panelled Parlour, with a delightful plaster cornice of foliage, flowers and fruit, cherubs and jacks-in-the-green. Next to it is a room which has miraculously kept its late fifteenth-century wall decoration of stencilled black fleurs-de-lis, together with a sacred monogram of the letters IHS with the Emblems of the Passion. The theory has been advanced that this was painted as a replacement for a crucifix, which would have had to be removed during the troubles of Edward VI's reign. In the south-west corner are some fragments of the sixteenth-century Banqueting Room, of which this formed a part. These are described in the local guide-book as 'the as yet completely undigested classical bric-à-brac of the Italian Renaissance' – which says it all.

## Branscombe

*4; 5 miles NE of Sidmouth off A3052*

At first approach, ST WINIFRED'S CHURCH looks a little grim; with its sturdy square Norman tower and the round stair turret on the north side, the effect is almost as much that of a fortress as of a church. It is made odder still by the fact that this tower, though ostensibly a crossing-tower, does not in fact quite mark the crossing, since the transepts are set a little further to the west – an untidy sort of arrangement. (Perhaps it was to save the turret; though there must have been an easier way.) But the setting, in a gentle valley with a pretty if somewhat disorderly village straggling along the combe, softens the impression; and the interior is a joy.

It is also an education, for it includes work from every century from the eleventh (Saxon herringbone work at the base of the tower) to the present one. The nave – or most of it – is, like the tower, twelfth-century Norman; a century or so later it was lengthened, and given those curiously placed transepts, of which that to the north still retains its original lancet window. The fourteenth century contributed the Decorated chancel, the fifteenth the five-light east window and that at the end of the south transept. The sixteenth started badly: that disastrous wave of fanatical Protestantism that marked the unhappy reign of Edward VI took a terrible toll of wood and stone carvings, to say nothing of the medieval glass. But before Elizabeth was dead, the Wadhams of neighbouring Edge Barton had given the church one of its greatest glories – the superb gallery of carved oak across the west end, with its own separate staircase running up the outer wall.

From the seventeenth century on, the accent was, not surprisingly, on furnishings. The barley-sugar altar rails, which enclose the altar on all four sides, look to be of about 1680, and there is a simply beautiful late

*St Winifred's Church, Branscombe.*

eighteenth-century three-decker pulpit, with a golden torch of learning blazing above it – one of the very few in the county. Of the work of the last two centuries, which is neither intrusive nor important, nothing need be said.

There are plenty of other features too that should be mentioned: the splendid old roofs of chancel and transepts; the wall painting of a devil transfixing an over-amorous couple; Joan Wadham's tomb, with her two husbands kneeling opposite her; and much else besides. But what is wonderful about Branscombe is the way all these beautiful things harmonise with each other, telescoping the centuries to give the ensemble a curious unity of its own.

## Buckland Abbey

*NT; 5; 6 miles S of Tavistock off A386*

Historically, the great interest of Buckland Abbey is that it was the home of two of England's most famous admirals: Sir Richard Grenville of *Revenge* fame and, from 1581 onwards, Sir Francis Drake. Architecturally, it deserves its place here as a Cistercian abbey founded in 1278 and converted after the Dissolution, with remarkable economy of means, into an Elizabethan mansion.

Although the abbey was acquired by Sir Richard's grandfather as early as 1541, it was only when he himself came into his inheritance some thirty years later that its transformation took place. Surprisingly, perhaps, for the time, he made no effort to conceal its former function, retaining both the nave and the chancel, merely removing the end wall of the south transept to bring light to the principal rooms and building two floors through the length of the building. Thus the lineaments of the old abbey remain everywhere visible, inside and out. The house is still dominated by the massive crossing-tower, with the high arch into the south transept still in place and the traces of the former pitched roof above it. Grenville retained the former east wall of the transept, extended it further to the rising ground and built his new kitchens immediately behind it; the west wall he also retained for his staircase.

After the beauty of the exterior, and the pleasure afforded by the contrast of the rambling old grey stone building with the lush green of its secluded valley – the Cistercians always chose the remotest and most tranquil sites for their abbeys – the interior of Buckland cannot but be something of a disappointment. Although technically the property of the National Trust, it is administered by its leaseholders, Plymouth Corporation, as a naval and Devon folk museum. It is in consequence utterly devoid of atmosphere. The most interesting room is the single-storey Great Hall, which occupies the former crossing. Of Grenville's time are the plaster ceiling with pendants, the oak-panelled walls with their delicately carved pilasters, a plaster frieze over the fireplace adorned with figures of the Virtues and bearing the date 1576, when Grenville completed his work, and – best of all – a particularly fine plaster frieze on the west wall showing a knight reclining under a spreading vine, his shield hanging from its branches and his armour piled nearby. His horse, too, lies contentedly on the grass. In a glass case stands Drake's famous drum.

Compared with Grenville – from whom he acquired the house by distinctly devious means, knowing that his old rival would never surrender it to him willingly – Drake seems to have made relatively few alterations. His principal contribution to Buckland seems to have been the lovely little panelled Drawing Room on the first floor which contains his portrait by Gheeraerts – though a picture of a third sea-dog, Sir John Hawkins by Custodis, being larger, has pride of place over the mantel. In the Tower Room at the end of the first-floor gallery the Drake arms appear above the fireplace; we can also see the upper parts of the transept arches in the north and south walls and, to the east, a small window of fine granite tracery which formerly looked down on to the sanctuary.

An unexpected and somehow inappropriate feature of the house is the Georgian staircase of 1772, rising the whole height of the building with carved tread ends and three balusters to the tread. From a strategic point on it there is a fine view of the old chancel arch.

Finally, visitors should on no account miss the superb TITHE BARN of *c.*1300, over 150 feet long and 60 feet high to the roof ridge.

## Cadhay

*6; 12 miles E of Exeter off A30*

This fine manor house was built, probably between 1545 and 1550, by John Haydon, a prosperous lawyer who was legal adviser to the City of Exeter; he seems to have used the stone from the College of Priests at Ottery St Mary, demolished as a result of Henry VIII's Dissolution of the Monasteries a few years before. As he originally conceived it, it formed three sides of a square, with an open prospect to the south; the east front, with its mullioned windows, symmetrically projecting bays and central polygonal stair tower, is unchanged to this day, and gives us an excellent idea of how the whole house must have looked. It makes an interesting contrast with the north, entrance, front, which now has a late seventeenth-century aspect with stepped gables, sash windows and a pedimented front door with Gibbs surround.

What is perhaps the most delightful single feature of Cadhay, however, is due not to John Haydon but to his great-nephew Robert, who inherited in 1587. He it was who added the fourth side to the south, making no departures from the original style. His purpose seems to have been to provide the house with a Long Gallery – a man felt such a fool without a Long Gallery in the 1590s – but he incidentally provided it also with a small enclosed courtyard. All too often such courtyards can be rather grey, dismal affairs, but Robert soon resolved to make his something special. First he patterned the walls, not very expertly, with irregular chequering of stone and flint; then, over the four central doors, he inserted deep niches with heavy Renaissance surrounds, in

*The enclosed courtyard, Cadhay.*

which he placed statues of Henry VIII, Edward VI, Mary and Elizabeth. The result was what is now called the Court of the Sovereigns. Its precise charm is hard to define: it lies, I suspect, in the contrast between the monumental formality of the concept and the refreshingly unsophisticated manner of its execution. The scale alone precludes any grandiose effects; moreover the statues themselves, the work of a sculptor whose identity is unknown but whose provenance was decidedly local, have about them an endearing naïvety which is further emphasised by the wealth of the Renaissance motifs around them. I can think of no enclosed open space of similar size in any English house that has given me more pleasure.

But Cadhay has, alas, suffered many subsequent alterations less happy in their effect. It was a sad day, for example, when an eighteenth-century owner divided John Haydon's Great Hall horizontally to make two rooms, one above the other. (The lower of these rooms, now the Dining Room, lost at that time, but has now regained, its huge Tudor fireplace. The upper, known as the Roof Chamber, has preserved much of its original timbering; though its arched braces and hammer-beams are gone, it is still a magnificent sight.) In 1911, however, Cadhay underwent a far-reaching and sensitive restoration. While it remains, inevitably, a mixture of styles, it is a house of immense interest, character and charm.

## Castle Drogo

*NT; 7; 4 miles NE of Chagford off A382*

Here is a phenomenon indeed – a gigantic baronial stronghold of silver-grey Cornish granite, built by Sir Edwin Lutyens between 1911 and 1930 for Julius Drewe, founder of the Home and Colonial Stores, on land once owned by Drewe's putative forebear Drogo, a companion-in-arms of William the Conqueror. It stands magnificent on a great bluff, nearly 1,000 feet above sea level, at the entrance to the precipitous gorge of the River Teign and, to the south-west, the vale of Chagford. Whether it can be called beautiful is a matter of opinion; but Drewe was out to impress rather than to seduce and in this, with Lutyens's help, he triumphantly succeeded. The house in its final form – the designs were changed again and again – is, believe it or not, considerably smaller than was originally planned; it consists of two wings, each some 50 yards long, and set at an angle of 160 degrees to each other to obtain the maximum effect of the site. Seen from the north or north-west, it looks formidably stark and cheerless, with the small mullioned windows – which Lutyens uses exclusively, all over the house, in groups of anything between two and thirty-six – few and far between. At the south-east corner things improve, and the fenestration becomes a good deal more generous; but even here the aspect is hardly beguiling.

From inside, the views are naturally superb; but again and again one's eye is drawn away from the windows by the brilliance and almost uncanny ingenuity of Lutyens's imagination. Though the inner walls are almost all of the same uncompromising granite as the outside and seldom relieved by anything more than untreated timber, the atmosphere is less austere than one might think; at the same time one is always conscious of the raw, windswept location and the unevenness of the site. Levels constantly change; new perspectives suddenly open up when one is least ready for them; a dark passage is suddenly flooded with light; every corner conceals its own surprise.

*Castle Drogo.*

The size and scope of the domestic offices, also, leave one gasping. It could be argued that Lutyens was harking back rather too enthusiastically to the Middle Ages when he separated the Dining Room from the kitchen by 50 yards of granite corridor, or when he deprived the kitchen of all windows by running a curtain wall outside, lighting it only from a lantern in the roof. The scullery is even darker, lit by lunettes and supported on huge granite columns, vaguely Norman in feeling insofar as they can be seen at all.

Perhaps the most curious feature of all is the Chapel, built into the foundations of the Great Hall which formed part of the original plan but never materialised. A polygonal apse, lit by three round-headed windows, projects between the buttresses from an almost pitch-dark 'nave' like a dungeon. With considerable relief one emerges into the sunshine and finds one's way to the garden – which, significantly, Mr Drewe placed out of sight of the house; nothing so domestic, he insisted, could be allowed to spoil the rugged grandeur of the castle's surroundings. In a way, perhaps, he was right.

## Castle Hill

*8; 3½ miles NW of South Molton on A361*

Few great houses, with the possible exceptions of Audley End and Compton Wynyates, look more splendid from a distance than does Castle Hill. You see it on your right when driving from South Molton to Barnstaple – a long, low Palladian front with occasional cupolas, set halfway up a gentle rise; behind it rise thick woods, among which the sham eighteenth-century 'castle' from which the house got its name still stands, crumbling and forgotten; in front of it a lovely expanse of park descends to a tributary of the River Bray – altogether as fine a piece of artificial landscaping as can be seen anywhere in the county.

It is not, alas, quite what it appears. In March 1934 the whole central part of the house, including virtually all the principal rooms, was destroyed by fire; what we see is largely a rebuilding by the 5th Earl Fortescue of the house built for his ancestor by Roger Morris (with some assistance from Lord Burlington and Lord Herbert, which, one suspects, he could have done without) between 1729 and 1740. The work could not have been better done, and Castle Hill is still well worth a visit; but much, inevitably, has been lost – furniture, pictures and, most important of all perhaps, the patina of age.

## Compton Castle

*NT; 9; 4 miles W of Torquay off A3022*

At first sight it seems almost too good to be true, that tremendous north front rearing up like a great cliff at the end of the long, straight drive, with its battlements and buttresses, its oriels and machicolations, and the flag of the Gilberts fluttering so proudly above it all. For a moment you may ask yourself whether the whole thing is not just a little too symmetrical, a little too pat, somehow, for a medieval fortress; but you quickly dismiss the thought as unworthy. And so it is – up to a point. Compton is not in any sense bogus; on the contrary, it dates from the early fourteenth century and has been the home of the same family, with a single break, since before the battle of Crécy – nearly 650 years. That single break was, however, from 1800 to 1930; and already for a century before that the old building had been in a state of sad decay. The Great Hall had collapsed in 1750, at which time the Gilberts had been obliged to move out; and the castle continued to crumble until, by the time Commander Walter Raleigh Gilbert bought it back into his family in 1930, it was little more than a picturesque ruin.

What we see today, therefore, is genuine but heavily restored. Only the Great Hall is less a restoration than a

*Castle Hill.*

reconstruction – although probably a fairly accurate one, based as it is on first-hand historical and architectural evidence. Other parts of the castle have stood up rather more successfully to the passage of time. And there is something else, too, for which we can be grateful: the fact that, although much of Compton has indubitably been lost, not since the early sixteenth century has it been added to or altered. It thus remains to this day one of the very few medieval fortified houses to look, at least on the outside, almost exactly as it did in the reign of King Henry VIII.

The beginnings of Compton date, it is believed, from the time of Joan de Compton who married Geoffrey Gilbert before 1329. It was built on the usual medieval plan, with the Hall to the right of the screens passage, the pantry and buttery to the left, and the solar approached up a spiral stairway at the south corner of the dais end. The first series of improvements was made around 1450–75 and involved the creation of a Withdrawing Room beneath the solar, in the place of the old cellar, where the ceiling was raised by 2 feet; at the same time a tower was erected just to the west of the new room, and the Chapel was built or remodelled. (There is still some doubt whether the earliest building contained a chapel or not.) It lies immediately to the north of the Withdrawing Room, and one of its four-light windows with Perpendicular tracery can be seen on the entrance front, to the right of the central porch.

Then, about the year 1520, the Gilberts got to work again. They rebuilt and enlarged the service end of the Hall, making a steward's room (on the east side of the forecourt, opposite the Chapel), larder and great kitchen, with guest chambers and other more modest bedrooms above. They also decided to ring the whole building with the most impressive fortifications. The fourteenth-century house must itself have had defences – in those days one could never tell when they might be necessary – but these had probably been lost, or covered by the enlargements. They would in any case have been nothing in comparison to what now appeared. No fewer than four new towers were built, three on the east side and one more on the west, all heavily machicolated and four storeys high. At this time too the great curtain wall – forming most of the present entrance front – was erected to join the two wings. It was provided with two principal gateways, each with a portcullis, descending from a corbelled-out projection above.

Why, one wonders, was all this done? The Wars of the Roses had been over for half a century and England was, for the first time in history, a relatively peaceful country to live in. It has been suggested that the decision was prompted by recent French raids on Teignmouth, Plymouth and Fowey, but Compton looks as if it was designed to keep out an army rather than a small raiding party and there is certainly no indication that it ever experienced an attack of any kind at all, at least until the Civil War. We are left with the conclusion either that the Gilberts were being quite unnecessarily alarmist or that the whole thing was a piece of sheer swagger on their part – which seems by far the more likely explanation.

But the interest of Compton is not wholly architectural. The castle is also part of the fabric of that remarkable period of English history when the sea captains of Queen Elizabeth I – the great majority of whom were Devon men – were simultaneously keeping the King of Spain in his place and opening up the New World. Sir John Gilbert, Vice-Admiral of Devon, who led 1,000 men to Torbay when the Spanish Armada appeared off the Scillies in 1588, was a half brother of Sir Walter Raleigh, who spent much of his childhood at Compton, and a full brother of Sir Humphrey Gilbert, who in 1583 founded the colony of Newfoundland. Of Sir Humphrey's two sons, John (who inherited Compton) accompanied Sir Walter Raleigh to Guiana and was knighted by the Earl of Essex at Cadiz while Raleigh, the younger, was one of the eight holders of James I's Patent for the Colonisation of America (under which Jamestown was founded) and himself the founder of the Sagadahoc Colony of the State of Maine. It was, by any standards, a remarkable family; and it was a great moment for that family, and for the old castle, when in 1930 they were reunited. Although they transferred the ownership to the National Trust in 1951, the Comptons still live there; let us hope that they will long continue to do so.

## Cullompton★

*10; 12½ miles NE of Exeter on A373*

The west tower alone is enough to tell you that ST ANDREW'S CHURCH is something special. There are decorations everywhere: between the battlements at the top, at various irregular and unexpected points on the way down (these in the form of extremely worn carvings), even on the set-offs of the buttresses, alive with gargoyles and mythical monsters. Unfortunately the stone is so soft and friable that many of the figures can hardly be distinguished now, but nothing can destroy the extraordinary impression of wealth and sumptuousness. The body of the church, like the tower, is built of the local red sandstone, with dressings of Beer and Ham Hill. Before entering, do not miss the inscription running all the way along the outside of the outer south aisle. St Andrew's was endowed by John Lane and his wife Thomasin in 1526, and they were clearly determined that no one should be allowed to forget it. Note, too, the decoration on the buttresses between the windows – merchant ships and sheep shears: no need to ask where the Lane money came from.

The inside of the church makes a sharp contrast to the exterior. Whereas the latter looks worn and somewhat decayed, within everything is white, bright, spick and span. It is long (six bays) and broad – one aisle on the north, two on the south. Its lightness is largely due to one of those rare Devon clerestories, which allows a splendid view of the boarded wagon roof over the nave – again of breathtaking magnificence, with angels, bosses, and a great rood-beam above the screen, all intricately carved to the point at which one wonders how much strength it still possesses. The Royal Arms above are equally intricate – though one could wish them just a little bigger. The roofs of the north and the inner south aisles are flat, and are not gilded as is that over the nave; otherwise they yield little to it in splendour.

*St Andrew's Church, Cullompton.*

The screen, too, is an instantaneous eye-catcher. Brightly coloured, apparently freshly painted (at least when I saw it), its forest of tracery branches out into a deep cove on both sides. As so often in Devon – the greatest county of all for screens, not excepting those of East Anglia – it stretches right the way across the two original aisles, as does the Jacobean west gallery, supported by five fluted Ionic columns, with caryatids separating the carved panels above.

None of this opulence, however, ultimately holds a candle to the Lane Aisle, for which Cullompton is justly famous. Technically, it is not an aisle so much as a memorial chapel, divided from the south aisle proper by oddly shaped piers with carved figures of saints on three sides. It has both east and west windows of its own (the latter with six lights) and five four-light windows along the south, and is completely fan-vaulted, to sensational effect – greater, even, than that produced by the Dorset Aisle at Ottery St Mary, which is a few years earlier and its obvious inspiration. The short pendants down the centre between the fans bear more sheep shears and the Emblems of the Passion. Here is sumptuousness indeed; John and Thomasin had good reason to be proud.

## Dartington

*11; 2 miles NW of Totnes off A384*

Pevsner has described DARTINGTON HALL as the most spectacular medieval mansion of Devon, and so it is; but a few words of caution are necessary if the visitor seeking it out for purely architectural reasons is not to be disappointed. The Great Hall itself now looks, inside and out, much as it must have looked when it was built by Richard II's half brother, John Holland, Duke of Exeter, at the end of the fourteenth century; later, however, it was to fall on evil days, and by the time Leonard and Dorothy Elmhirst bought it in 1925 it was an empty and roofless shell; the present impressive hammer-beams – and the windows – are all modern replacements, though they could hardly have been better done. (The best genuine medieval roof at Dartington is that of the great fourteenth-century BARN a little to the north-east.)

The Hall forms the western end of a big open quadrangle. Opposite it is the still earlier MANOR HOUSE, while along the north side runs a long range which presumably accommodated members of the ducal retinue. Some parts are well preserved and the rest is beautifully restored, so the general effect is admirable.

The entire property, which comprises some 4,000 acres, is now owned by the Dartington Hall Trust, founded in 1931 by Mr and Mrs Elmhirst to further their great ideal – that of an educational, artistic and agricultural community with its own school, farm, studios and workshops, deriving its support from the land around it and its inspiration from the traditional arts, crafts and customs of the neighbourhood. The experiment is a fascinating one, and though the modern buildings beyond the courtyard seem to lack any real architectural distinction, they blend well enough – despite the variety of their styles – with the general ensemble.

*Dartington Hall.*

## Dartmouth

*12; 10½ miles S of Torquay on A379*

A delightful little town, Dartmouth is marvellously situated where the River Dart runs clear, between high banks, to the sea. Once it was one of England's chief ports, from which ships sailed to both the Second and Third Crusades and, later, to France for the Hundred Years' War. By this time, too, it had acquired a special importance and prosperity through the wine trade with Bordeaux. Nowadays its principal claim to fame is the ROYAL NAVAL COLLEGE, the huge and sprawling buildings of which reflect absolutely no credit on their architect, Sir Aston Webb, but are fortunately sited just far enough away from the town not to spoil it.

Among the secular buildings, the most memorable is the seventeenth-century BUTTERWALK, magnificently half-timbered and projecting over the pavement, from which it is supported by a granite colonnade. There is also an admirable pub, the CHERUB, on Higher Street, which has survived from Chaucer's day. But all the streets in the old town are a joy to walk through; as in all the best towns, it is the ensemble that counts rather than the individual buildings.

ST SAVIOUR'S CHURCH is of just about the same date as the Cherub, having been consecrated in 1372. It started life as a chapel of ease, the parish church at that time being St Clement's, Townstall, a long and exhausting climb up the hill. One of its greatest pleasures is the first thing you see on entering – a simply tremendous door in the south porch, with two leopards apparently guarding the Tree of Life, all executed in fourteenth-century ironwork with immense *brio* and dash. Then there is a fine Devon screen with loft (fifteenth-century, very ornate), an altar – formerly a communion table – made in Armada year, supported on carved and painted figures of the Evangelists that look like the work of some local maker of ships' figureheads, and a most remarkable pulpit, an octagonal wineglass of painted stone dating apparently from about the time of the Wars of the Roses.

Elsewhere, owing to the absence of an adequate guildhall, the church has a strong municipal flavour. Underneath the west gallery at the back there is a wooden archway through which Mayor and Corporation made their formal processions, subsequently taking their seats on the inward-facing pews immediately to the west of the screen; along the front of the gallery are the coats of arms of the mayors and other citizens of note.

Dartmouth's other best-known church, ST PETROX, though traditionally the site of a cell founded by the saint himself in AD 594, is basically a seventeenth-century building (despite a Norman font) and is of little architectural interest. It forms, however, a pretty, picturesque group with the CASTLE, a mile or so out of the town on the right bank of the river towards the sea. The castle itself is of the late fifteenth century, and remarkably well-preserved – a good deal better in this respect than its much restored counterpart at Kingswear, immediately opposite across the river. A huge chain stretched between the two castles used to close off the harbour to enemy ships in time of war; today, few places could be more peaceful – a perfect destination for a stroll on a summer evening.

*The west front, Exeter Cathedral.*

## Exeter*

*13; 16½ miles SW of Honiton on A30*

THE CATHEDRAL AND IMMEDIATE ENVIRONS

Of the thirteen English cathedrals which belong, architecturally speaking, to the first division, Exeter is perhaps the least appealing from the outside; seen from within, however, it is one of the best. It also boasts a curious idiosyncrasy which makes it – at least since the disappearance of Old Sarum – unique among the cathedrals of England: its twin towers, which are relics of the earlier Norman building on the same site and thus a good century and a half older than the rest of the structure, are set not at all where one would expect them, giving height and majesty to the west front as at Canterbury or York, Durham, Lincoln or Wells. Instead, they have been relegated to a position halfway down the nave, where the bases constitute two rather stubby transepts. Why this was done is a mystery; such an arrangement is found hardly anywhere else in England (but see Ottery St Mary) or in Normandy, and seldom even in the rest of continental Europe. If we look at Exeter, we can see why it is so rare: it doesn't work.

When the decision was taken in about 1275 to replace the old cathedral with a larger and more opulent version, and to incorporate the old towers in it, the most sensible course might have been to make them the principal features of the new west front, or alternatively to forget that they were there at all, and build two more where they were most needed – as was being done at about the same time at Lichfield. In the event, Bishop Branscombe and his architects maintained the Norman towers in their old position and – feeling presumably that two were enough – forebore to build any new ones to the west. The consequences were doubly unfortunate. First, the old towers imposed their own scale on the new building, keeping it disproportionately low; second, the all-important west front looks earthbound and triangular, crying out for that soaring verticality that has been refused. This feeling of squatness is further increased by the fact that the whole façade is arranged in three separate planes, like gigantic steps, receding as they go higher. The bottom step takes the form of a broad screen of statues in two tiers, interrupted only by the three distinctly inadequate entrances. As a screen it is fine enough, though sadly worn; but it has the unhappy effect of cutting off the base of the great west window from anyone looking at it from ground level. Unfortunately the wall in which this window is set itself cuts off, in precisely similar fashion, the gable window above the vault which marks the third and highest step. These windows are full of superb Decorated tracery, which makes it all the more frustrating that there is no way of seeing them properly from the ground.

But now step inside; and all is forgiven. Virtually the whole nave west of the crossing is the achievement of Bishop Grandison between 1327 and 1369 – Decorated Gothic at its spectacular best. One's first gasp is occasioned by the enormous length of the building, the central ridge of the vault running without interruption some 300 feet from one end to the other – the longest unbroken Gothic vault in the world. One's second gasp is prompted by the vault itself – a veritable forest of shafts, eleven to each bay, springing from just above triforium level to the ridge or to the transverse ribs running between the tops of the clerestory windows. Outsize bosses mark the points of contact all the way along, while below no fewer than sixteen further shafts are clustered in each of the great piers of the nave arcade.

Halfway down the enormous length of the nave it is cut by the pulpitum, or choir screen, a luxuriantly decorated loggia of about 1320 arcaded in two tiers: at floor level three depressed ogival arches, heavily cusped, with a profusion of tangled foliage in the spandrels; above it a row of eleven smaller arches, cusped again and crocketed as well, forming a sort of parapet. Above this rises a monumental seventeenth-century organ, so huge that one shudders for the safety of the screen which apparently has to support it, so prominent that it becomes a major architectural feature in its own right. Many harsh things have been said about this organ: Sir Darrell Bates, in his *Companion Guide*, compares it none too kindly to a performing elephant. Perhaps perversely, I find myself rather fond of it. Besides, it serves a vital aesthetic purpose apart from its obvious musical one. Whereas in other churches and cathedrals one may resent the breaking of the long vista from west to east, in Exeter some interruption is essential. The building is so long, especially in proportion to its height, that without something to arrest the eye the effect would be that of an interminable and distinctly monotonous tunnel. The placing of the organ where it is not only breaks the monotony; it also emphasises the grandeur of the building by introducing an element of mystery. The east end now becomes invisible: one sees only the seemingly endless line of the vault, stretching out towards infinity.

West of the screen and organ, the symmetry and regularity are broken by only one object of note. This is the little minstrels' gallery set into the north wall, at the level of the shallow triforium, the fifth bay up from the west. Here, under opulently decorated canopies considerably taller than themselves, fourteen angels (twelve facing the nave and one round the corner at each end) puff, pluck and saw away at their various instruments – adding (architecturally speaking) a welcome touch of syncopation to what might otherwise be slightly too relentless a rhythm.

The choir, which begins immediately beyond the screen, is for the most part a disappointment, the early fourteenth-century stalls having been replaced in the 1870s by new ones designed by Gilbert Scott. Mercifully, the misericords under the seats were allowed to remain; dated between 1230 and 1270, they are the oldest in England. More important still was the preservation of the bishop's throne. Completed in 1316 by Thomas of Winton and rising in a riot of oaken filigree 60 feet into the air, it is a work of breathtaking virtuosity, comparable in the Gothic idiom to what Grinling Gibbons was to achieve in the Baroque three and a half centuries later. Above the sedilia, too, are more wooden canopies contemporary with the throne, and of similarly haunting beauty. This eastern part of the cathedral is effectively closed by the great east window of nine lights. It was glazed in 1390, by which time the Decorated style was very nearly a thing of the past, and is the only major element in the whole cathedral which can be categorised as Perpendicular. Below and behind it, however, is the ravishing Lady Chapel, with its own magnificent tierceron vault and a seven-light window in which Decorated still reigns, and very majestically too.

Here and in the choir aisles, as well as off the north and south transepts, are to be found most of the tombs and chantry chapels that constitute another of the glories of Exeter. Of the latter, the best are the Speke and Oldham Chantries, at the east ends of the north and south chancel aisles respectively. Both were built in the early years of the sixteenth century. The former is ornamented within an inch of its life; the latter is rather plainer, but with a remarkable reredos.

It would be a mistake to leave the cathedral without a visit to the Chapter House, just beyond the end of the south transept. It is, rather disappointingly, rectangular – so many others are circular or polygonal – and a curious mixture of Early English and Perpendicular: the lower half is older than any of the cathedral proper except the towers, having been built during the second quarter of the thirteenth century, but the upper was completely remodelled in the early fifteenth and crowned in Edward IV's reign with a wooden roof of splendid quality, decorated with a curious design of fan vaulting in two dimensions.

### THE CITY

Apart from the cathedral, virtually all medieval Exeter vanished during the air raids of the last war, and the centre of the city is modern and strangely devoid of character. The only other important survival is the GUILDHALL in the High Street. The guide-books tell us that parts of it go back to 1330, which makes it one of the oldest municipal buildings in the country; but essentially it now consists of a fifteenth-century hall with a timber roof and a simply extraordinary Elizabethan façade giving on to the street and projecting over it on granite columns. Between these and the Renaissance upper storey – transomed and mullioned windows separated by pairs of columns on ornamented plinths – there runs a wildly eccentric series of brackets, obviously born of a sudden discovery by the architect that he had some 6 feet of spare space to fill and absolutely no idea of how to fill it. The result has a slightly Indian look about it – not beautiful, but impossible to forget.

Fortunately, the best of Georgian Exeter lies outside the walls and was to some extent spared the German bombs. The best is the elongated square to the east of the city known, rather perversely, as SOUTHERNHAY, in the centre of which is a most agreeable public garden.

## Exmouth★

*14; 9 miles SE of Exeter on A376*

In Summer Lane, just off the Exeter road to the north of the town, stand two extraordinary *cottages ornés*, built in 1798 by Miss Jane Parminter. Miss Parminter occupies a distinguished place in the long list of eccentric English maiden ladies. The first of the cottages, in which she lived with her young cousin till her death in 1811, she modelled – very loosely, it must be said – on the church of S. Vitale in Ravenna and called A LA RONDE. It is in fact not circular, but a regular polygon of sixteen sides, with windows, square and lozenge-shaped, set not in the flat walls but at the corners, and eight dormers in the roof, at the top of which is an octagonal lantern. Octagonal too is the central Hall, from which the rooms radiate. These rooms are even odder than the architecture, being packed with curious objects collected, or in many instances manufactured, by Miss Parminter from shells, seaweed, paper, feathers and several other media equally unexpected. The Living Room actually has a frieze of feathers; while the gallery running round the top of the Hall is decorated with further designs of feathers and shells, 'intended', the guide-book informs us, 'to echo the famous mosaics of S. Vitale'.

Equally dotty, in a somewhat austerer way, is the tiny CHAPEL a little further up the road, which was dedicated to the dominant objective of Miss Parminter's life, the Conversion of the Jews. This is presumably the significance of the somewhat enigmatic name she chose for the building, Point in View. In it, by the terms of a special trust, six poor Jewish girls were to receive instruction in the Christian faith. It has a stubby lead spire, four outsize chimneys and odd little windows with diagonal frames – an idiosyncrasy they share with A la Ronde. It is still used as a chapel, and non-denominational services are held there regularly during the summer months.

## Hartland

*15; 13 miles W of Bideford on B3248*

The CHURCH OF ST NECTAN occupies a marvellous position some 2 miles outside the village towards Hartland Quay: scarcely convenient for its parishioners, but a good deal more so for those in peril on the sea, for whom its 128-foot tower, the second highest in Devon, served as a landmark. It is fine fifteenth-century work, in four stages, embattled and pinnacled, with gargoyles below the battlements. In the east wall is a statue of St Nectan himself, the body contemporary with the church, the head apparently a later replacement.

On entering, the first thing that strikes one is the wagon roof of the nave – its central section is ceilured and painted with huge stars, red and blue on white alternating with red and yellow on blue. (Don't miss, either, the carved and painted roof of the Lady Chapel north of the chancel – this time a more elaborate polychrome design.)

The screen is tremendous, a real showpiece, running right the way across the nave and the two side aisles. The loft is adorned with incredibly delicate filigree carving along both the east and west sides – note the lovely twirling vine tendrils to the east – and has an iron crest. Five hundred years old, the whole thing is in a near-miraculous state of preservation; it has never been restored. The parclose screens are Victorian, and something of a come-down.

The so-called Pope's Chamber, up a tiny staircase in the north aisle, was where the priest or sexton lived in pre-Reformation times. It is now a little museum.

## Holcombe Rogus

*16; 8½ miles NE of Tiverton off A38*

Built around 1525–30 by the Bluett family, HOLCOMBE COURT looks very handsome indeed from the outside with its great four-storey Gatehouse; the usual twin towers are missing, but the massive polygonal stair turret and the three-storey oriel above the entrance ensure that it loses nothing in general effect. Immediately to the right of the tower, the Hall is marked by a transomed six-light window. There is nothing particularly original or sophisticated about the ensemble, but it somehow looks exactly the sort of mansion one would expect a well-to-do Devon squire to build for himself in Henry VIII's day.

Inside, it is a bit of a disappointment. In 1858 the Bluetts had to sell the house to pay off gambling debts, and a radical rebuilding followed. The results are nowhere near as disastrous as they might have been; the ceiling of the Hall, for example, captures the Tudor spirit admirably. But much, inevitably, has been lost. Perhaps the best surviving feature is the Elizabethan Long Gallery which was added in 1591 and runs the length of the front at second-floor level.

ALL SAINTS' CHURCH dates in its essentials from the fourteenth century. As you enter through a beautiful south porch of 1343 with a miniature fan vault your eye is caught by the Bluett family pew – a magnificent piece of Jacobean woodwork (and a considerable rarity), topped with medallions in relief depicting scenes from Genesis and Exodus. The Bluetts commissioned some fine tombs too; what a pity they had to leave.

## Kenton

*17; 7 miles SE of Exeter on A379*

A wonderful church, inside and out, utterly dominating the unassuming little village from which it rises, ALL SAINTS is a positive blaze of deep red sandstone with dressings of white Beer limestone standing out in almost too dazzling contrast. There is a tall (100 feet) pinnacled west tower in four stages, with three-light transomed bell openings in the top one, and an ornate two-storey south porch surmounted by figures thought to be Henry IV and his second wife, Joan of Navarre. These, being finishing touches, would fit in well with the date of the church, which is very slightly earlier – towards the end of the fourteenth century.

The interior is opulent, with an agreeable air of spaciousness, its breadth being very nearly a third of its length. It has seven bays, with comfortable side aisles which extend along the sides of the chancel. Another of those stunning Devon screens runs across the entire church, exquisitely carved with fan coving (partly restored, but with much care and sensitivity), St Michael and four angels in niches along the top, and forty saints

*All Saints' Church, Kenton.*

and prophets painted – rather more crudely – along the bottom. There are more painted panels set, under nodding ogee canopies, into the fifteenth-century pulpit, but these are obviously modern. The whole pulpit is, indeed, a bit of a hotch-potch, but the best elements of it are very fine indeed. It was saved thanks to the energy of the Rev. S. Baring-Gould, who wisely entrusted the restoration work – and also that of the screen – to Herbert Read. Kenton owes them much.

To the architect and builders responsible for the new roof of 1865, however, its debt is considerably less: the additional weight led to a serious subsidence of the arcade piers – a misfortune which resulted, according to the local guide-book, in 'some unnecessary alarm at the time, the Methodist cause at Kenton gaining many fresh adherents'. Some of the piers are indeed disturbingly out of true; one can only hope that alarm is as unnecessary now as it was then.

## Kings Nympton

*18; 13 miles SE of Barnstaple off B3226*

The CHURCH OF ST JAMES is not at all prepossessing from the outside with its very nasty, modern, rather French-looking spire covered with copper fish-scales. Inside it is a good deal better, with an agreeable lightness and freshness that it owes to the large, clear, Perpendicular windows in the south aisle and the plain whitewashed walls. There is no north aisle, but there is a north transept, which gives the building a rather curious ground plan. Another unusual feature – and a happier one – is the way the nave rises in three long shallow steps towards the west, which must make services a lot more agreeable for people sitting at the back. The box pews are eighteenth-century, with very pretty hinges, and there is as usual a lovely screen.

The chancel, on the other hand, is something of a disaster area, its wagon roof plastered over in Victorian times – obscuring the charming panelled ceilure which still exists over the rood-screen – and covered with a horrid painted decoration, which appears upside-down to those in the congregation unfortunate enough to be able to see it. After such an assault on the sensibilities the delightful Royal Arms painted above the south door and dated 1742 affords welcome relief.

Nearby, KINGS NYMPTON PARK is a Palladian villa built about 1750 by Francis Cartwright and loosely based on Marble Hill House at Twickenham. It is not, at the time of writing, open to the public.

## Knightshayes Court

*NT; 19; 2 miles N of Tiverton off A396*

Either you like it or you don't. If you don't, you will wonder why it could ever have been included in a book purporting to describe the best in English architecture. If you do, you will find at Knightshayes yet another proof that William Burges was the most consistently inventive, imaginative and entertaining of all the High Victorian architects. He built this house in the early 1870s for John Heathcoat-Amory, MP. In the century that followed it continued to be lived in by the Heathcoat-Amory family, and much of the original decorative scheme – by Burges himself and, after 1874, by J. D. Crace – was inevitably changed. Since 1973, however, when the property was bequeathed to the National Trust, this has been carefully restored wherever possible, and it is hard to find another house so thoroughly steeped in the atmosphere of Gladstonian England.

The approach through the grounds is a little forbidding as the great red sandstone house, enthroned on a vast terrace, looms larger and larger in the view. The south front is vaguely Elizabethan, with two projecting gabled wings, each with a canted bay projecting further still and taking in all three floors. The ground-floor windows of these bays have plate tracery in quatrefoil between their heads, giving a distinctly Venetian flavour. All the windows are mullioned and transomed. Gargoyles and fleurons abound. A close look at the central section reveals that it is almost symmetrical, but not quite; this game of 'approximate symmetry' was very popular with the architects of the time – enabling them, as they thought, to show a measure of wilful independence within a basically restricting discipline. (On the other façades, Burges dispenses with symmetry altogether.)

But although the exterior of Knightshayes looks much as Burges intended, the interior is only the palest reflection of what he originally planned. According to his usual custom, he had assumed responsibility for every aspect of the house: the stone carving and wood carving (always important elements for him), the stained glass, the painting, the furniture, the carpets and the curtains. But in 1875, when the house, stonework and woodwork were more or less complete but little of the other interior decoration had been even begun, he was dismissed. It has been suggested that his patron had suffered badly from the agricultural slump and simply could not afford Burges's extravagance. In fact, however, serious recession did not come for another five years; a more likely explanation is that Heathcoat-Amory was horrified as much by the exuberance and dazzling coloration of the schemes his architect had prepared for him as by its estimated cost. At all events Burges was sent packing, and was supplanted by J. D. Crace, whose family firm of architectural decorators could already boast five generations in the business. Crace, who had just completed his work on Longleat, was the most fashionable decorator of his day; he had none of Burges's rollicking fantasy, but – perhaps because he thought in two dimensions instead of three – he was a good deal cheaper.

Fortunately, Burges prepared a magnificent collection of drawings and watercolours to illustrate his proposals. This he had presented to the Heathcoat-Amorys in 1873; it remains in the house and has been of immense value during the meticulous restoration by the National Trust over the past decade. Thus, though nobody would pretend that Knightshayes could ever look as its creator originally intended, it probably comes closer to his vision now than it has done at any time in the past half-century.

Entering the house, you find yourself immediately in the Great Hall. The huge wooden screen, with minstrels' gallery above, was removed in 1914; but the pulpitum, a massive stone balcony supported by four columns of black Devon marble from which the squire could address his tenants and domestic staff assembled below, remains *in situ* – as does the timber roof with its typically Burgesian carved corbels. Beyond the pulpitum at the time of writing stands an immense wooden bookcase, designed by Burges for his own London house and on loan from the Ashmolean Museum. It gives us some idea of what Knightshayes would have been like if he had been allowed to continue as he had begun.

For the other rooms, which are for the most part more redolent of Crace than of Burges, I can only refer you to the Trust's admirable guide-book – a model of what such publications should be. The most interesting room of all is the Drawing Room. Alas, Burges was not permitted to complete his scheme of representing, over the north wall, 'The Assault on the Castle of Love'; but in 1980, during the restoration of the room, workmen accidentally discovered behind the plaster ceiling a brilliantly coloured design with gilded 'jellymould' concavities which is unquestionably his original work. This has now been carefully restored, and looks absolutely marvellous. If only his patrons had kept their nerve!

## Littlehempston

*20; 1½ miles N of Totnes off A381*

The OLD MANOR, sometimes inaccurately known as the Rectory, is a medieval gem. It dates from about the middle of the fourteenth century and, impervious to time, is essentially the same today – possibly because it became a nunnery about 100 years after its construction and remained church property until 1921. The Hall, with its braced timber roof, naturally dominates the house, and still preserves on the wall above the dais a fifteenth-century fresco of the Resurrected Christ. A circular stone staircase ascends to the solar, with a squint through which the lady of the house could peep down to see what was going on in the Hall. There are two enchanting little courtyards; the roofs are partly tiled and partly thatched; the windows are of two lights, occasionally transomed, some wood-framed. Most surviving houses of this age are dark and poky, and nowhere near as agreeable to live in as one might think; at Littlehempston, however, one can imagine being very happy.

The house is not open to the public, but serious students of the period can always write and ask permission to visit.

## Luscombe Castle*

*21; 1½ miles W of Dawlish off B3192*

Here is John Nash at his most carefree. Embattled his castle may be, but it could be stormed by a sparrow. Set in a gentle valley running down to Dawlish and the sea, in grounds laid out by Humphry Repton, it is almost a text-book illustration of the picturesque as conceived by Richard Payne Knight, Uvedale Price and their disciples. It was built in 1800 for Charles Hoare, the banker, and has suffered little change since. Gothick in its lack of symmetry, its playful pinnacles and the mock-Perpendicular tracery of its ground-floor windows, it is nevertheless almost as far from Udolpho and Strawberry Hill as it is from the neo-classical elegance of Nash's Regent's Park or Carlton House Terraces. The ground-floor windows all come down to floor level, as if determined to let in as much of the sunshine as they can. This enchanting little house is a joy to behold, and must surely be a delight to dwell in.

The owner does not open her house to the public. Nor, if it were mine, would I.

## Mamhead

*22; 7½ miles S of Exeter on B3381*

Anthony Salvin's first major country house was built on a splendidly picturesque site overlooking the estuary of the Exe. Salvin had been a pupil of Nash – or at least had worked in Nash's office – but the atmosphere of Mamhead is very different from that of Luscombe Castle close by. Its architect had many qualities: imagination, scholarship, much vitality and formidable technical skill. But he utterly lacked the light-heartedness of his former master and his solemnity shows through. Not that Mamhead is gloomy; the light Bath stone that provides the ashlar facing and the generous fenestration give it quite a welcoming appearance. But by 1828, when work began, the Regency spirit was dead, George IV had one palsied foot already in the grave, and the shades of Victorian pomposity were beginning to gather.

The style is not immediately easy to categorise. It is Tudor, I suppose, more than anything else. The plan is symmetrical, the roofs are steeply pitched and the gables have high, pinnacle-like finials which contrast a little oddly with the tall clustering Tudor chimneys. Salvin, one feels, is perfectly prepared to nod politely in the direction of the picturesque, but not at the cost of compromising his stern architectural principles. These principles, however, did not prevent him from curious stylistic juxtapositions: the Billiard Room, which first greets the visitor on entering through the front door, has a big oak screen and a Jacobean ceiling, but immediately behind it the Lower Gallery is unabashed fifteenth-century Gothic and the adjoining Staircase Hall actually has fan vaulting in the corners. Gothic, too, of a complicated curvilinear kind, is the ceiling of the Library.

On the slope to the north-west of the house is what is known as the 'Castle', an ornamental laundry and brewhouse built by Salvin in the local red sandstone and clearly inspired by the castle of Belsay in Northumberland, near his childhood home.

One of the virtues of Mamhead is its almost pristine condition. Until the 1950s it was completely unaltered; it did not even have electricity until 1953. Now that it has been institutionalised some superficial changes have inevitably had to be made, but the interior decoration is still basically unchanged since Salvin's day, with brilliantly painted ceilings and chimneypieces, and coloured glass in the larger and more important windows. It may not be a house in which one would choose to live; but as a historical document it has much to tell us.

## Molland*

*23; 7 miles NE of South Molton off A361*

From the outside, the CHURCH OF ST MARY is wonderfully unexciting. Don't, however, be put off; it possesses one of the most perfect and unspoilt eighteenth-century interiors to be seen in Devon. The nave is separated from the north aisle by a late fourteenth-century arcade of three bays – leaning outward at an alarming angle, but mercifully braced by modern cross-beams – and both nave and aisle have wagon roofs above and box pews below, the latter slightly raised towards the back for the musicians and the choir. In the aisle, surprisingly, is the pulpit, a splendid, richly panelled three-decker, towering above the already high pews and surmounted by an outsize tester with a trumpeting angel on top.

There is no chancel arch. Instead, a huge semi-circular tympanum descends from the roof to a point only a little higher than the capitals of the arcade piers. Like the walls and roof, it is whitewashed; but the space is largely occupied by a particularly fine version of the Royal Arms, flanked by the Ten Commandments. The little screen below is modest by any standards, let alone those of Devon; but, despite the splendour of the pulpit, modesty is the keynote of the whole church. It makes no pretensions to fine architecture; but it has a quiet country serenity that inspires affection.

## Ottery St Mary

*24; 12 miles E of Exeter on B3174*

The CHURCH OF ST MARY vies with that of the Holy Cross at Crediton for the honour of being the most important parish church in Devon. Aesthetically, however, although it is a considerable improvement on its rival, it falls some way short of perfection. Like Exeter Cathedral, it was built on the site of an earlier foundation, whose twin towers were retained to serve as transepts for the new building – an idea that proved no more successful here than with the cathedral itself. The effect of a lowish nave squeezed between two towers set halfway along its length is not a happy one; at Ottery, as at Exeter, the height seems somehow inadequate for the mass; and the stumpy, heavily ribbed lead spire that has been added to the north tower does not really help at all, serving only to throw the whole composition out of balance.

The similarity to Exeter is not altogether surprising, since Ottery was a collegiate church founded by Bishop Grandison soon after his enthronement as seventeenth bishop of Exeter in 1328. Before that time the manor had been the property of the Cathedral of Rouen, but the

*The church of St Mary, Ottery St Mary.*

existing church was nowhere near large enough or splendid enough for the bishop's purposes. A virtually complete rebuilding was called for, and as Grandison had recently begun work on the Exeter nave he had his model – to say nothing of an army of expert stonemasons – ready to hand. In 1337 a royal licence was granted by Edward III; five years later, the church was finished.

The result, if not exactly beautiful, is undeniably grand, particularly when seen in the context of what is, after all, a very small town. St Mary's boasts a generous clerestory (a rarity in Devon), two choir chapels to north and south which give the impression of eastern transepts, a Lady Chapel beyond the chancel, the famous Dorset Aisle (looking almost like a separate Perpendicular chapel) on the north side, and two porches of similarly later date, that on the north being two-storeyed. There are carved corbels and gargoyles and generous embattling; the only major disappointment where exterior adornment is concerned is in the tracery, which is – except in the unadventurous six-light west window of the Dorset Aisle – of the simplest possible, and sometimes actually non-existent. There is none, for example, in the eight-light east window of the Lady Chapel, which should be the show window of the entire church.

Inside, the general impression of grandeur continues – not only because of the proportions but even more, perhaps, because of the wonderful vaulting. It makes an extraordinary contrast to the meagreness of the tracery, particularly in the chancel, where the lines of the vault are almost tracery themselves, cusped and sinuously curving in a manner common in the Gothic churches of Spain but almost unknown in England. All this, it should be noted, is purely decorative; the ribs are performing no structural purpose, being merely applied on to a perfectly ordinary barrel vault. Elsewhere – in the nave, transepts and Lady Chapel – the curves are gone, but the lierne designs are still intricate and the decorative element is still to the fore. Why, one wonders, should there be so much lavishness in one department and such austerity in another?

The other pride of the church is the Dorset Aisle. Dating from the first quarter of the sixteenth century, it is contemporary with, and inescapably reminiscent of, the Lane Aisle at Cullompton. Both are fan-vaulted; but whereas the Cullompton pendants are carved with the Instruments of the Passion, those at Ottery are of the most curious openwork filigree, the centre one descending in a very unexpected spiral. There are also some enjoyable carvings on corbels and capitals, including one of an unusually lifelike elephant. After all this Perpendicular sumptuousness, Butterfield's polychrome font of 1850 comes as a nasty shock; but since Butterfield worked for over a year at the church, I suppose we must be grateful that he did not impose himself still more disastrously.

## Plymouth

*25; 22 miles SW of Totnes on A38*

A historic and venerable city, before the Second World War Plymouth would have warranted several pages to itself. Alas, in the spring of 1941 it was devastated by eleven nights of savage bombing, during which forty-three churches were destroyed and some 70,000 people rendered homeless. A few Elizabethan houses have survived around the Barbican (one of them, NO. 32 NEW STREET, is open to the public) and the Hoe itself has retained some of its old magic; but architecturally speaking the rebuilt city has little enough to offer. The best of what remains is the CITADEL, constructed by Charles II between 1666 and 1670. He said that it was intended as a defence against the French, but the people of Plymouth soon noticed that there were as many gun ports facing inland as there were looking out across the sea; having been staunchly Parliamentarian during the Civil War, they drew their own conclusions. The work was, moreover, entrusted to a French military engineer, Bernard de Gomme. From the outset it failed to impress English experts. 'De Gomme hath builded very sillily,' lamented Samuel Pepys.

Within the Citadel are several seventeenth-century buildings, mostly along the sides of the parade ground. None is particularly interesting. The pride of the Citadel is its entrance: a most august Baroque portal of two storeys, paired Ionic pilasters below, single Corinthian columns above, the whole surmounted by an outsize semi-circular pediment containing the Royal Arms. Trophies and lions' heads fill in the gaps. The design, Pevsner informs us, is attributed to Sir Thomas Fitz, or Fitch; but there is no documentary evidence and Howard Colvin is sceptical.

## Plympton

*26; 4 miles E of Plymouth off A38*

Now little more than a suburb of Plymouth, 500 years ago Plympton was a rich and prosperous town, thanks to an important Augustinian priory and a Norman castle, both of which still survive in vestigial form. Later, almost unbelievably, it saw the birth of no fewer than four major English painters: Northcote, Eastlake, Haydon and Sir Joshua Reynolds himself, who studied at the local GRAMMAR SCHOOL where his father was master – a long rectangular schoolroom supported on a rough stone colonnade. At the time of writing its future is in doubt, but I cannot believe that the authorities would be so pig-headed as to demolish it.

Nowadays, the point of Plympton is the great country house known as Saltram, described separately.

## Powderham Castle

*27; 8 miles SE of Exeter off A379*

Although there has been a castle at Powderham since the Norman Conquest and probably even earlier, the oldest part of the present building goes back no further than about 1400 when Sir Philip Courtenay, who had been knighted after the battle of Poitiers, began to build a large fortified manor house. Six towers of that house can still be identified on the outside; inside, however, the house has been altered and remodelled beyond recognition. No matter: it is more, rather than less, worth visiting on that account.

Leaving aside a few relatively unimportant Elizabethan additions, the first important changes were made in the middle of the eighteenth century, when the medieval Great Hall was divided into two (or, more precisely, into three, since the screens end was also split horizontally into two rooms, one above the other). The dais end then became the Staircase Hall, perhaps the greatest showpiece of the whole house. Forty years later, between 1794 and 1796, James Wyatt was called in to add a Music Room on to the north-east wing. The third bout of rebuilding came in 1840, when William Courtenay, 10th Earl of Devon, having made a tidy sum by selling his land along the estuary of the Exe to the new railway, spent it by turning his house the other way round, moving the main entrance from the east to the west side and constructing an impressively embattled Gatehouse, forecourt and Banqueting Hall. He then suggested that his architect, Charles Fowler, should re-Gothicise the whole exterior – a task which Fowler performed with much sensitivity and skill.

The Banqueting Hall, with its fine wooden panelling, its minstrels' gallery and its blaze of heraldry around the walls (reaching its climax over the fireplace) makes an awe-inspiring introduction to the house; it is the only principal room, however, apart from the Marble Hall – the lower part of the divided Great Hall, preserving the three original doorways to the screens passage – that continues to remind the visitor of Powderham's medieval origins. The general spirit of the house is overwhelmingly Georgian, and very beautiful Georgian at that. There are exquisitely stuccoed ceilings, noble marble chimneypieces and any number of fascinating pictures, my own particular favourite being the family group by Peters of the 2nd Lord Courtenay, his wife, son and eleven daughters; if only the artist had waited another year or two the total of daughters would have risen to thirteen. Loveliest of all the rooms is Wyatt's Music Room, with its bow window, coffered dome, scagliola pilasters and enchanting chimneypiece by Westmacott in Carrara marble.

And yet, when you first enter the Staircase Hall, even the Music Room is forgotten. Here, against a brilliant blue background, is a riot of Rococo plasterwork that takes your breath away – birds and animals, flowers and fruit, gardening tools and musical instruments tumbling over each other in lavish, if disciplined, profusion. Even the sloping undersides of the upper flights carry their load of garlanded vegetation. The extraordinary thing is that the craftsman responsible, one John Jenkins, is virtually unknown. And the staircase itself, probably by James Garrett of Exeter, with its beautifully turned corkscrew balusters and ornamented strings – that too is a major work of art.

Finally, there is the Chapel – the converted grange of the medieval castle, with some lovely old bench ends and an arched and braced timber roof still intact: once again a whiff, if only a faint one, of the fifteenth century when it all began.

*Powderham Castle.*

## Saltram ★

*NT; 28; 3½ miles E of Plymouth city centre between A38 and A379*

The great house stands in its splendid park of meadow and woodland near the River Plym. Saltram began its life in Tudor times as the home of the Bagg family but was purchased in 1712 by George Parker, sometime Member for Plymouth. By that time the old Tudor house had acquired a new west front in a restrained William and Mary style, and the new owner saw no need for further improvements; but on his death in 1743 his son John – and, more important by far, John's wife Lady Catherine – set to work to double the size of the building, giving it new south and east wings and adding considerably to that on the west. The result of their work is, in essence, what we see today; the name of the architect is unknown. The Parkers, who subsequently became Earls of Morley, continued to live in the house till 1957, when it was transferred to the National Trust; but they made few alterations after the eighteenth century, apart from the Doric balustraded porch on the south and the tripartite windows above it, added in 1818 by John Foulston of Plymouth.

Seen from the outside, Saltram is imposing rather than impressive, dignified rather than elegant; despite the pale stucco, there is something austere and heavy-handed about it. But inside it is a different story: here is a suite of rooms by Robert Adam as fine as any he ever produced – the only perfect and utterly unspoilt example of his work in the south-west – and, as a bonus, an outstanding collection of Reynolds portraits – Sir Joshua being a close friend of John Parker II and a regular visitor to Saltram. But neither Adam nor Reynolds greets the visitor at the door; the Entrance Hall is George II through and through, a wealth of exquisite workmanship in wood and plaster, the latter certainly Italian and most probably the work of Vassali. Next to it is the Morning Room, with its five Reynolds portraits; the interest here, however, is not so much the pictures themselves as the way they are hung – just as they were in the mid-eighteenth century, covering almost every square foot from dado to cornice.

In the Velvet Drawing Room Adam is not yet with us, but we can hear him coming. A screen of two fluted Corinthian columns at the north end suggests that something important is about to happen; the beautiful mirrors, with gilt-wood tables below them, flanking the door beyond, indisputably announce that that something is neo-classical. Through the door you go – and suddenly you are standing in one of the most beautiful rooms in England. The walls are hung with pale blue damask; the deeply coved ceiling is a riot of plasterwork – much use being made of sphinxes – by Joseph Rose, with painted roundels by Antonio Zucchi, in a design which is echoed, but deliberately not quite reflected, by the Axminster carpet which Adam designed for the room, as he did the furniture. The whole room is a single work of art; and it is a masterpiece.

The Saloon is a state room in the grandest sense of the word; the adjoining Dining Room shows us an Adam no longer striving, however brilliantly, for effect but providing a perfect, graceful, domestic atmosphere for everyday life. It is not as he originally planned it, since this room was intended as the Library; but when John Parker exchanged the positions of the two rooms in 1780 he summoned Adam back to Saltram, and all the redesigning necessary after the removal of the bookcases to the new Library was once again entrusted to the master. Adam did not, however, turn his attention to the new Library itself – even his bookcases were replaced with larger, sunken ones in 1796 – and the contrast is striking indeed. Gone are the colour, the lightness, the elegance. To many people the Library now seems frowsty – and so, in a way, it is. The National Trust, however, assiduously turns aside all suggestions to 'do it up'. It is in style not an eighteenth-century room at all, but an early nineteenth-century one; its frowstiness has been there for nearly 200 years and belongs to it just as much as the colour and exuberance belong to the Saloon. 'Let it stay as it is', they say; and, as nearly always, they are right.

Saltram is a big house, and takes time to see properly; but an hour or so should be left for the park, laid out by a certain Mr Richmond – of whom we know nothing but his name – in the style of Capability Brown, and dotted about with temples and pavilions. Of these, the Castle – really a little octagonal summer-house – may be partly Adam's work. There are also a very pretty little Orangery, a classical garden pavilion much used by Fanny Burney during George III's visit to Saltram and ever afterwards known as Fanny's Bower, and some magnificent stables.

*The staircase, Sharpham.*

*The church of St James, Swimbridge.*

## Sharpham*

*29; 2 miles SE of Totnes off A381*

High on a great spur surveying a hairpin bend of the Dart, Sharpham was built in about 1770 for Captain Philomen Pownall, RN, who had won nearly £100,000 in prize money for a Spanish galleon captured outside Cadiz. The architect was Sir Robert Taylor, whose curious genius is shown here at its brilliant best. In order to take the fullest possible advantage of his site, he placed all his principal rooms on three sides only – north, east and south – so that each should command a breathtaking view down to the river below. The fourth side is largely taken up by the magnificent staircase, rising in a sweeping oval through three floors and cantilevered out so that neither it nor the landings have any visible means of support. In front of it is an octagonal Entrance Hall with a circular peristyle of columns, more neo-classical than Palladian in feeling; on the upper floor Taylor's beloved oval is once again dominant, with two oval bedrooms and two oval vestibules running transversely – an extraordinary composition for which I know of no precedent in England.

Sharpham is, in short, as fascinating architecturally as it is beautiful in its setting; a wonderful house. It is not, however, at the time of writing, open to the public.

## Sidmouth

*30; 9 miles S of Honiton off A375*

Everything an English seaside resort ought to be, Sidmouth offers street upon street of charming white-painted Regency villas with bow fronts, verandahs and delicate wrought-iron balconies. The town is still essentially all of a piece, built around 1820, and as it is limited to the Sid valley between Peak Hill on one side and Salcombe Hill on the other it has been spared most of the horrors of later development; recent building, such as it is, has been forced into the upper valley behind the town and does not obtrude. There are no individual buildings to be listed, but the ensemble is a delight.

## Swimbridge

*31; 4½ miles SE of Barnstaple on A361*

The CHURCH OF ST JAMES at Swimbridge – or, as the parish guide prefers it, Swymbridge – is a memorable joy. It has an early fourteenth-century tower with a broach spire added as an afterthought; the nave and aisles, chancel and chancel chapels are, however, a good deal later, built around 1460 and in the half-century following. There is much to admire: the wagon roof, with panelling (that is, a celure) over the rood-screen; the early Tudor pulpit, carved with figures of saints under ornate canopies; and, best of all, the screen itself, a real breathtaker. It has admittedly been slightly restored (by Pearson), but the points of restoration are obvious and there are remarkably few of them. Even Devon, county of screens *par excellence*, has few to equal this.

For forty-eight years, from 1832 to 1880, the parish was in the care of the Rev. Jack Russell, whose name lives on in the breed of lively little terriers that he established.

## Sydenham

*32; 8 miles NW of Tavistock off A384*

A brave Jacobean house, it is basically unchanged on the outside except for the curious quasi-Venetian windows with small panes set into larger square ones. Inside there is a superb staircase of the same date as the house, with caryatids on the newel-posts. Half the ceiling retains its original Jacobean plasterwork and half has late eighteenth-century stucco – an interesting contrast.

The main Hall boasts a simply tremendous fireplace, dated 1656, rising the full height of the room so that the topmost figures are almost squashed under the ceiling. Oddly, another smaller fireplace stands nearby, at right-angles to it and sharing the same flue. Almost all the principal rooms have fine panelling, that of the Dining Room being inlaid in a delicate design of arabesques. The Master's Room conceals a secret staircase leading to the Dining Room below and another room – presumably the maid's – above.

*St Peter's Church, Tawstock.*

## Tawstock*

*33; 2 miles SW of Barnstaple off A39*

Here is a wonderful church indeed, agreeably placed on the banks of the Taw in rolling parkland just beyond the front lawn of TAWSTOCK COURT. This house of 1787, now a school, stands on the site of the huge Elizabethan mansion of the Earls of Bath, of which unfortunately only the fine Gatehouse survived a fire in Queen Anne's reign.

However, as the 86-foot crossing-tower makes abundantly clear, ST PETER'S is a good deal more than a dependency of a great house; such central towers are rare in Devon. Moreover, according to Pevsner, there are good technical reasons for supposing that the building, though ostensibly fourteenth-century, has its origins a good 200 years before that and that the nave is still essentially Norman.

At first sight, the body of the church looks deceptively plain, but it contains many items of curious interest quite apart from the extraordinary collection of monuments for which it is famous. Look, for example, at the wonderfully carved little sixteenth-century gallery, once part of the big house and now placed, with sublime disregard for tradition, high on the wall of the transept. Below it, the squire's pew is even odder: it must be early fifteenth-century, with a pretty little canopy all painted and carved with rosettes. Still in the transepts, look too at the plaster decoration of vines and tendrils, deeply undercut for *chiaroscuro* effect. In the chancel, resisting for a further moment the temptation of the tombs, pause to consider the beauty of the east window with its octofoil – and think how much lovelier still it would have been without that horrible Victorian glass; and on no account miss, in a niche in the north wall, the wooden effigy of an unknown fourteenth-century lady.

This brings us to the sixteenth- and seventeenth-century monuments, principally in the chancel and the chapel immediately to the south of it. They are jumbled together in wonderfully higgledy-piggledy fashion, but there is not one that does not prove, on close inspection, to be a considerable work of art, full of imagination and fantasy. Take your time over them: they are worth it.

## Tiverton

*34; 12½ miles N of Exeter on A396*

The inclusion of ST PETER'S CHURCH in this book is on account of one man only – John Greenway, the rich merchant and shipowner who, in 1517, added a south porch and south chapel, much as John Lane was to do at Cullompton a few years later. The porch has a beautiful stone vault with reliefs of animals, birds and fishes in panels; over the inner doorway the Virgin is borne up to heaven while Mr and Mrs Greenway, kneeling, look on. The same degree of unbridled ostentation continues for the length of the south chapel. It has only two bays, but they carry enough decoration for six: beneath a row of double-stepped battlements, pierced in a delicate filigree, runs a frieze of sailing ships; elsewhere, sacks of wool, staple marks and various other symbols of Greenway's trade and prosperity, together with copious repetitions of his initials, cover virtually every inch of the upper walls. The inside of the church is nothing special, and much restored; even the Greenways seem to have taken less trouble over the interior of their chapel, though they gave it a nice panelled roof with pendants.

Just to the north of the church stands what is left of the CASTLE, begun in 1106 but largely dismantled during the Civil War. Most of what remains, including the impressive Gatehouse, is fourteenth-century work; some of it has been built into a later Tudor building with Georgian additions, periodically open to the public.

## Totnes

*35; 8½ miles SW of Newton Abbot on A381*

According to local legend, Totnes was founded by Brutus, grandson of Aeneas, who sailed up the Dart and simultaneously founded Totnes and the British race. Totnes may just possibly not be quite as old as that, but it was already walled in the twelfth century – quite a bit of the wall survives – and the splendidly placed CASTLE goes back to 1086. After that there is a gap till the fifteenth century, which produced several fine town houses still standing, notably NICHOLAS BALL'S HOUSE in the High Street near the East Gate. For me, however, the charm of Totnes lies in the seventeenth- and eighteenth-century houses which make up most of the old town. Nearly all are slate-hung. Slate hanging, whereby house walls are covered with overlapping slates like fishes' scales, is very much a speciality of South Devon and Cornwall, and at Totnes it can be seen at its best.

ST MARY'S CHURCH dominates the town from the top of the hill, with a noble west tower of red sandstone rising a further 120 feet to the top of its huge pinnacles. It was built all of a piece, between 1430 and 1460, next to an earlier priory church of which next to nothing now remains. In those days, however, it had no north aisle; this was added only in 1542, after the Dissolution of the Monasteries had made the land available. (Nearly 300 years later still, in 1824, it was joined by an outer north aisle, originally scarcely larger than a side chapel but extended at each end in 1869.) The best things in the church beyond any doubt are the stone screen and the two parclose screens that run off it to separate the north and south chancel chapels. Devon is rightly famous for its wooden screens, but stone ones of this type are rare indeed; apart from that of Exeter Cathedral, there are only some half dozen in the whole county, and this is the best. The wooden rood-loft was removed by Gilbert Scott in 1862 – an act for which heaven may or may not forgive him. The winding stair that gave access to it survives, but is unaccountably situated halfway along the north side of the chancel, whence a wooden gallery led back along the top of the parclose – an extraordinary arrangement that leaves the experts baffled.

## Ugbrooke

*36; 9 miles SW of Exeter off A38*

The first house to stand in this pleasant valley on the banks of the little River Ug belonged to the Precentor of the diocese of Exeter; and the estate remained in church hands till it was seized by the odious Protector Somerset after the defeat of the Western Rebellion in 1549. By that time, however, the old house had been replaced by a large E-shaped mansion built, probably, in Henry VII's day. This passed by marriage into the Clifford family towards the end of the sixteenth century and remained in their hands, virtually unaltered, for the next 200 years.

Then, in 1763, the 4th Lord Clifford of Chudleigh called in Robert Adam to remodel the house, a task which was to occupy him until 1771. Adam decided on a 'castle' house – his first effort in this style – and demolished one wing, using the stone to link the remaining two. He then added the battlemented corner towers and designed all the principal rooms inside, including the Chapel, which also serves as a Roman Catholic parish church. (The Cliffords have been Catholics since 1673.)

The house, which is not of stone, but rendered in stucco, is only two storeys high except for the corner towers, which have three. Somewhat surprisingly, the principal elevations have an even number of bays – ten, including the two in each of the corner towers – which always gives a building a slightly unfocused look. One could also wish, perhaps, that the rounded window frames in cement had not been added in 1874. But, for all that, the house looks well – beautifully set in the superb park designed for it by Capability Brown, with its three lakes formed by ingenious damming of the Ug.

Visitors normally see the Chapel first – one of Adam's best ecclesiastical designs with its pairs of pilasters marching round the apse at gallery level. The galleries themselves, above the north and south aisles, have particularly charming openwork balconies. In the house itself, virtually all the decoration dates from the late 1950s and early 1960s; the 11th Lord Clifford abandoned it shortly before the Second World War, during which it was transformed into a school and later into a hostel for disabled former members of the Free Polish Army. After that, the principal ground-floor rooms were used as a grain store. The restoration has been beautifully done, but inevitably much has been lost.

*Totnes Castle.*

## Short List

### Bicton House

*37; 3 miles N of Budleigh Salterton on A376*

The house, now a college of agriculture, is of little interest, but the gardens are lovely and conceal, in their south-west corner, a mausoleum to the Rolle family by Pugin, which is well worth a visit.

### Bradninch

*38; 8 miles NE of Exeter off A396*

The CHURCH OF ST DISEN – the only one in the British Isles – has another of those splendid Devon rood-screens, painted with saints in 1528. It is not up to Ashton standards, but well worth a visit if you are in the neighbourhood.

### Chittlehampton

*39; 5 miles W of South Molton on B3227*

ST HIERATHA'S CHURCH must be included for its tower – fully up to Somerset standards, and you can't say more than that. It is early sixteenth-century, pinnacled at all four stages, and mellowed by marvellous orange lichen. The inside has some good features – carved capitals on the arcade piers, a wooden roof above the south porch, a wagon roof in the chancel – but it has been much restored and is, after the tower, a disappointment.

### Coldridge

*40; 10 miles NW of Crediton off A377*

ST MARY'S CHURCH is small, stubby and unassuming on the outside; the point, as so often in Devon churches, is the rood-screen, and a fine filigree pulpit. The parclose screen is also interesting: it is in a very different style, with strong European influences.

### Collacombe Barton Manor

*41; 3 miles NW of Tavistock off A384*

The house looks marvellous from the front: the central block of 1574 is in grey Devonian slate stone, beautifully set off by the Renaissance garden gateway. The Great Hall contains much fine plasterwork, including a vaulted ceiling with pendants. The rest is much altered.

### Crediton

*42; 7½ miles NW of Exeter on A377*

The CHURCH OF THE HOLY CROSS was the seat of the Devon bishopric until 1050, when it was replaced by Exeter; but the building, of blood-red sandstone, is a bit of a disappointment. The problem is the crossing, where the four arches are far too low and narrow and spoil the eastward vista to the high altar. These arches are good Transitional work of the twelfth century. Most of the rest is early fifteenth-century Perpendicular.

### Culmstock

*43; 13 miles E of Tiverton on B3391*

A mile and a half west of the town, at Spicelands, the little QUAKER MEETING HOUSE is an unexpected joy. It is pure and simple as one would expect, but perfectly proportioned and with an un-selfconscious beauty that is almost touching. There is a Burne-Jones window in the nearby ALL SAINTS' CHURCH, where a yew tree sprouts from the top of the tower.

### Flete

*44; 11 miles SE of Plymouth off A379*

Apart from an Elizabethan fragment in the south-east corner, the whole of this enormous house is the work of Norman Shaw and was built in 1878 of pale pink stone with granite dressings. A fine timber staircase rises from the middle of the Entrance Hall; the main reception rooms, each the size of a small house, have pseudo-Jacobean plaster ceilings and immense chimneypieces. One of these is set beside a columnar screen supporting marble panels carved with grotesques and has four small Burne-Jones windows to one side. The Dining Room is approached down a broad staircase which Mistinguett would have been proud to descend! The house has an enormous park and delightful gardens, admirably maintained by the Mutual Households Association.

### Great Fulford

*45; 9 miles W of Exeter off A30*

The Fulfords have lived here since the twelfth century, but the existing courtyard house was built in the days of Henry VIII: the date 1534 appears in the Great Hall, with its wonderfully exuberant carvings – three full-length near life-size figures, plus reliefs of Abraham and Isaac, Samson and the Philistine, and Adam and Eve adorning the overmantel. There is a fine carved William and Mary staircase in the immensely high Hall. The Chapel is of similar date, though first consecrated in 1402. The house was rather unimaginatively Gothicised in the 1780s. It stands in a magnificent park and has a perfectly lovely garden.

### Harberton

*46; 3 miles SW of Totnes off A381*

ST ANDREW'S is a fine fourteenth-century church with a particularly good tower – slender arrow slits rise all the way up the polygonal central turret. The splendid screen has been overpainted with saints and angels, said to have been inspired by members of the Victorian congregation. Best of all are the fifteenth-century wineglass pulpit and the Norman font.

### Lapford

*47; 10 miles NW of Crediton off A377*

One of the best screens in Devon – which is saying a lot – can be seen in the CHURCH OF ST THOMAS OF CANTERBURY. There is a fine rood above it, and above that a panelled wagon roof gloriously painted with sunbursts and stars. There are good bench ends, too. If the rest of the church measured up, what a treasure it would be; alas, it has been ruined by horribly scraped walls with artificial pointing, and simply dreadful windows like a public lavatory.

## Luppitt

*48; 4 miles N of Honiton off A30*

The pride of ST MARY'S CHURCH, which dates from about 1400, is the roofs of the nave and transepts and, in particular, the crossing between them, where huge diagonal arches intersect at an immense central boss (a modern replacement) representing a jack-in-the-green. There is a splendid font, too – Norman, with warriors clubbing each other, a centaur, and corner heads looking almost Aztec in their ferocity.

## Puslinch

*49; 7 miles SE of Plymouth off A379*

This sadly dilapidated but still beautiful Queen Anne manor house (though actually built around 1720) is of brick with dressings of pale grey stone. Inside are a good staircase, much fine panelling and several family portraits of quality.

## Shute Barton

*NT; 50; 3 miles SW of Axminster off A35*

Here is an important late fourteenth-century house, to which Lady Jane Grey's great-grandmother added an early Tudor wing, most of it now demolished; what remains (the tower and a single bay to the right of it) can be easily distinguished from the medieval building when seen from the east front. From the central courtyard you can enter the original kitchen, which has what must be the largest hearth in England. Two floors above – the intervening storey is an obvious later insertion – you can almost touch a magnificent old timber roof with wind-braces. The rest of the interior is largely remodelled and of relatively little interest. The Gatehouse – built on the axis of the demolished wing – is Elizabethan and can be rented by the week from the Landmark Trust.

## Tavistock

*51; 13 miles SE of Launceston on A384*

The fifteenth-century CHURCH OF ST EUSTACE (one of the only three in England so dedicated) is broad and spacious, with an air of considerable affluence. The outer south aisle of *c.*1440 has fine woodwork.

## Torbryan

*52; 5 miles NE of Totnes off A381*

Despite its drearily rendered exterior, HOLY TRINITY is a lovely church inside, washed in pale yellow. There are carved capitals on the arcade piers, a painted pulpit, Queen Anne box pews and another glorious screen. The south porch is fan-vaulted.

## Weare Giffard Hall

*53; 4 miles SE of Bideford off A386*

This late fifteenth-century manor house has a Gatehouse, on the first floor of which are two small windows depicting Henry VIII and Catherine of Aragon. The house itself is H-shaped, with the Hall forming the cross-bar, looking south across the valley. The original entrance must have been here, the east and west porches being later additions – the latter almost certainly appropriated from the church a few yards away. Apart from this, the exterior is astonishingly well preserved, as is the Hall with its superb hammer-beam roof, arched braces richly cusped, pendants and wind-braces. There is fine panelling too, with the Royal Arms of Henry VII and Queen Elizabeth. Elsewhere – especially fronting the minstrels' gallery – is much good sixteenth- and seventeenth-century woodwork, but all brought in from outside *c.*1830. The interior decoration is little changed from the days when the house was a rather second-class hotel.

## Youlston Park

*54; 4½ miles NE of Barnstaple off A39*

This early Georgian house must be one of the most enigmatic in Devon. The entrance front has been much altered – the Entrance Hall, at right-angles to the main block, is surely a later addition – and is not particularly prepossessing. The west wing, however, dating from the 1660s, contains a spectacular staircase with ornate plasterwork, leading eventually to the attics, its grandeur undiminished till you reach a point where you can no longer stand upright. There are also several superb plaster ceilings of the same date. Another room has floor-to-ceiling eighteenth-century Chinese wallpaper of breathtaking quality. At present the house is in a sad state of disrepair, but the owner is struggling manfully to restore it to its former glory.

# Dorset

Thomas Hardy's county has changed little since his day. Dorset remains, in the late twentieth century, quite astonishingly rural. But this does not make it monotonous: far from it. Few other counties can boast so rich a diversity of scenery, ranging from the dramatic – those high and windswept uplands with gigantic earthworks raised by primitive man, or the spectacular cliffscape off Portland – to the snugly domestic, that other Dorset of rolling hills and deep combes and sheep safely grazing. Such centres of population as there are tend to be small market towns – the only important exception being Bournemouth, which used to be part of Hampshire and in spirit remains so – and innumerable secluded villages with some of the best place-names in England, usually double-barrelled: Purse Caundle, Cerne Abbas, Winterborne Came, and my own favourite, Toller Porcorum. There are no big cities, no cathedrals, few heavy industries. On the other hand there are still any number of people who talk the way William Barnes wrote, and almost unbelievable quantities of livestock. To some extent this is due to the most fortunate fact that throughout its history Dorset has been a county of extensive estates, and has thus largely escaped the piecemeal development of the countryside and the appalling bungaloid sprawl that so disfigures its neighbour Devon.

Another blessing of equal magnitude is the splendour and profusion of available building materials. The two most celebrated products of the Dorset quarries are Purbeck marble and Portland stone. The former is not really a marble at all, but a hard shelly limestone that shares with marble its ability to take a high polish. I have personally always felt its beauty to be over-rated; when used – as it so often is – for wall shafting, its dark grey metallic sheen can often be unpleasantly reminiscent of drainpipes. There is no denying, however, that the contrast it provides with almost all other building stones made it enormously popular among the church and cathedral masons of the thirteenth and fourteenth centuries – during, that is to say, the Early English and Decorated periods – and led to its widespread use across the country. Later its popularity declined, only to be revived again by the Victorians.

Portland stone is of far greater importance. This aristocrat of limestones was already being worked in Norman days; it did not, however, receive recognition on a national scale until the time of Sir Christopher Wren, who preferred it to all others and used it not only for St Paul's but for virtually all his fifty-two other London churches. Wonderfully white in its original state, and contriving to look equally distinguished even when coated with London soot, it has the additional advantages of being even in texture and close of grain – a joy to work with, for architects and masons alike.

But Purbeck and Portland are not the only repositories of Dorset's geological wealth. Other fine limestones come – or came, for most of the quarries are no longer worked – from Portesham in the south-west, from Sherborne in the north-west and from near Sturminster Newton in the north. The far western corner of the county, near Bridport, produced the fine blue lias which is such a feature of Lyme Regis; then there is greensand from around Shaftesbury, and any amount of chalk (with its inseparable neighbour, flint) in that great belt of downland that sweeps across the county in a huge V, from Cranborne Chase to near Beaminster, whence it doubles back towards Dorchester, reaching the sea between Lulworth and Poole harbour.

So much for the stone; but the chalk belt also offers a humbler yet still most characteristic building material – that chalky mud which, when mixed with straw, provided what is known as Dorset cob. There are any number of small houses and cottages in this unexpectedly durable material still surviving – notably in the village of Milton Abbas, where it is almost universal. Meanwhile the clay country of the north-west has for centuries produced excellent brick. Most of the best brick buildings are Georgian, and tend to be concentrated in the towns – of which Blandford Forum is the most spectacular example. But it appears, too, in some of the earlier country houses, often banded with flints or with other brick of a different colour as at Anderson Manor.

With such natural advantages as these, Dorset should be a paradise for all lovers of architecture. And so, in a way, it is: and yet, again and again, the emotions aroused are those of enjoyment or affection rather than astonishment or wonder. Dorset buildings, both religious and secular, tend to be modest. The two great abbeys of Sherborne and Milton and the minster church of Wimborne are splendid structures indeed, but hardly in the league of the great cathedrals. As for country houses, one thinks immediately of Kingston Lacy and St Giles, of Crichel and Milton and of the largely demolished Eastbury; but there are no Chatsworths or Castle Howards, Longleats or Wiltons. It is only when one adjusts one's sights to the Dorset scale that the full richness of the county becomes apparent: above all, in that most English of all forms of domestic architecture, the medieval, Tudor or Jacobean manor house. King of them all is Cranborne, to me one of the most magical houses in the whole country; but there are countless others worth travelling a long way to see – Athelhampton, Purse Caundle, Bingham's Melcombe, Bettiscombe, Sandford Orcas, Mapperton. . . the list is almost endless, and the houses described in the following pages represent only a small fraction of it.

Of the period beginning immediately after the Civil War, Sir Roger Pratt's Kingston Lacy is by far the most important – though one must be careful not to forget the remodelling of Forde Abbey by Edmund Prideaux in the 1650s. And so we come to the Baroque: Vanbrugh at Eastbury – what is left of it – and Archer, that most individual of architects, at Chettle and (perhaps) Kingston Maurward. Of the Georgians, the greatest achievement is indisputably the Bastards' Blandford Forum – one of those towns which on each visit proves to be just a little better than one had remembered; towards the end of the century, the successive contributions to Milton Abbey by Chambers and Wyatt are also noteworthy – not least for the interest afforded by making a comparison of the two.

The Victorian contribution to Dorset architecture was, in the main, undistinguished. Of Canford Manor one can only say that it deserved to be turned into a school; Edward Blore was a boring architect at the best of times, and Barry's enlargement of 1847 produced only a sort of Palace of Westminster Mark II. Here at least, however, there was nothing much for him to spoil; how different, and how infinitely more tragic, his intervention at Kingston Lacy, where he rode roughshod over the work of a far greater architect than he could ever hope to be. His formal Italianate marble staircase is ingenious enough, but it has no possible place in a classical mid-seventeenth-century English house, and Barry should have known it. A far worthier monument to the century is George Devey's admirable addition to Melbury, or – best of all, perhaps – Norman Shaw's Bryanston. Of the twentieth century, as so often, I have nothing to say.

Finally, the churches. Dorset always gives an impression of great age – one has only to think of those tremendous prehistoric earthworks at Maiden Castle, Hambledon Hill and elsewhere, which fortunately fall outside the scope of this survey – so it is hardly surprising that the Saxon period should be well represented. Indeed, at Sherborne we have the remains of the largest Saxon church known anywhere in England. There is more Saxon work in the two churches, St Mary and St Martin, at Wareham. The Normans left their mark copiously, not only at monastic Sherborne and collegiate Wimborne, but in innumerable smaller churches throughout the county – of which those at Studland and Worth Matravers linger longest in the memory. The best Early English is to be found at Whitchurch Canonicorum, Yetminster and the Lady Chapel at Sherborne; the best Decorated – though there is all too little of it in Dorset – in the south transept of Milton and perhaps the spire at Trent. As for Perpendicular, there is quite simply an *embarras de richesse*; but no list would be complete without a mention of the tower at Beaminster and, above all, the fan vaulting in the Sherborne choir – the earliest in England. Two Georgian gems – Moreton and East Lulworth – and two Victorian *tours de force* – by Scott at Cattistock and by Street at Kingston – close the list.

One small item I have deliberately left to the end: St Andrew's, Winterborne Tomson. It seems to me to sum up, better than any other, everything that a little Dorset village church should be. Enormously old, yet at the same time modest and unassuming, rural and secluded, it has all the qualities of the county itself, and the same power of enchantment.

---

## Abbotsbury

*1; 8 miles NW of Weymouth on B3157*

The original *raison d'être* of Abbotsbury was the Benedictine abbey which was established there in the eleventh century. Little of it now remains; the only surviving building worthy of serious attention is the huge BARN – one of the largest in England – which dates, probably, from about 1400. It is of stone, copiously buttressed and with two porches – one of which, however, has almost disappeared – and is very nearly 100 yards long. About half is still roofed with thatch, and still in use.

The best view of the barn is to be had from ST CATHERINE'S CHAPEL, which stands on the top of quite a high hill just outside the town. You can reach it only on foot; before you set off, check with the post office whether it is open and, if necessary, ask them to lend you the key. It is an extraordinary little building, roughly contemporary with the barn, and since it was first consecrated has always been a place of pilgrimage – primarily, since St Catherine is the patron saint of spinsters, by ladies in search of a husband. The traditional prayer, we are told, was:

*A husband, St Catherine,*
*A handsome one, St Catherine,*
*A rich one, St Catherine,*
*A good one, St Catherine,*
*And soon, St Catherine.*

The walls are immensely thick for a building only 45 feet long, and divided into four bays by stout buttresses; all this strength and solidity being required to support the most surprising feature of all – a stone tunnel vault, slightly pointed and supported on eight transverse ribs, between each pair of which are three panels in two tiers. Incredible as it may seem, it is the only roof of its kind in England; you have to go to Scotland to find anything even remotely similar. There is little other decoration in the chapel. Of the four windows, one in each wall, only that to the east has any tracery remaining, and even that is very broken. There are, however, porches on each side, each being separately and similarly vaulted in stone.

Back in the town again, you should certainly spare a moment for the CHURCH OF ST NICHOLAS. Begun in the fourteenth century (north porch and aisle), it was continued in the fifteenth (tower and arcades), the sixteenth (clerestory) and the seventeenth (the south chapel doorway and probably much of the south wall). By far the most interesting peculiarity, however, is the plaster barrel vault over the chancel, erected by Sir John Strangways in 1638. It includes coats of arms within strapwork frames, six-winged seraphim, and angels holding above their heads inscribed banners looking for all the world like skipping ropes.

And now you can go and look at the swannery – six centuries old and the town's principal attraction – but somewhat outside the scope of this book.

*The church of St Nicholas, Abbotsbury.*

## Athelhampton Hall

*3; 5 miles NE of Dorchester on A35*

When Sir William Martyn became Lord Mayor of London in 1493, the manor house that he had ordered for himself just outside Puddletown must have been on the point of completion; and as we look at Athelhampton Hall today from the south (it is in fact nearer the south-west, but descriptions are much simpler if we stick to the cardinal points of the compass) we can see that house in front of us, largely unchanged. It is a low, battlemented building with a big projecting porch, the ground floor of which is completely taken up by its broad, deeply moulded two-centred entrance arch, the upper containing a little two-light window with a heavy square hood-mould. To the left, the Hall itself has two pairs of arched lights set surprisingly high up and separated by a buttress, and then a four-sided bay window which, since it stops slightly short of the main roof line, has its own separate battlements. (This window is generally referred to as an oriel, but oriels are strictly speaking projections from upper floors, whereas this shares a plinth and low string-course with the rest of Sir William's building.) To the right, the service end is nicely rounded off by a polygonal turret at the east corner. What Sir William would not recognise, however, is the tall triangular gable between that turret and the porch – an addition dating from the reorganisation of the domestic arrangements in the early sixteenth century.

He might also wonder what had happened to his solar, beyond the Hall bay window. This has disappeared, the few remaining traces of it having been incorporated in the new parlour wing which was built out towards the south in the 1530s or thereabouts. It is essentially of two storeys, but its two big gabled dormers – whose fronts break the line of the eaves to make a continuation of the outside wall – provide a second-floor attic; there is a further attic window in the end gable. All the windows in this range are, as one might expect, considerably bigger than those of Sir William's original range: four arched lights mostly, but with six and even eight (in two sets of four) at the southern end, between the angle buttresses – which, incidentally, support corkscrew finials on which are seated stone apes, the Martyn crest. An equally agreeable touch of decoration is provided by the diamond-shaped panels below the gables, with bunches of leaves at the corners. They are identical with those at Sandford Orcas (*q.v.*).

The other façades of Athelhampton are of less interest, the back parts having been mostly added towards the end of the last century. We can therefore go directly inside, to the splendid Hall. The timber roof, to begin with, is unforgettable because of the outsize cusps on the arched braces of the principal trusses – an astonishing conceit which I have seen, so far as I can remember, nowhere else. At right-angles to these – that is, following the plane of the roof itself – are big wind-braces, also cusped. (The stone corbels are seventeenth- or eighteenth-century additions; they seem to speak an entirely different language.) The second pride of the Hall is the bay window – vaulted, with deeply moulded shafts and cusped ribs to the roof. Each of its faces

*Athelhampton Hall.*

contains a tall, two-light window with double transom, rudimentary tracery and the original excellent heraldic glass. On the west side, the doorway that used to lead into the old solar now gives access to the Tudor wing. The fifteenth-century screen is a fine piece, but not the original one.

Of the other rooms in the house, the most interesting are those of the Tudor wing, though even these are largely nineteenth-century reconstructions. There is also a fine State Bedroom east of the Hall, with its original stone chimneypiece and a vast Jacobean four-poster from Montacute (*q.v.*) which, the guide-book notes darkly, 'has associations with Elinor Glyn'.

Until 1862 Athelhampton had an enclosed courtyard, with a magnificent early sixteenth-century Gatehouse running eastwards from the south end of the Tudor wing. Pictures show it as having been in very much the same style as the latter, with which it was contemporary, and with a splendid oriel – a true one this time – above the entrance archway on the inner face. Its demolition was a sad loss, though it probably made the house brighter and a good deal more agreeable to live in.

## Beaminster

*3; 5½ miles N of Bridport on A3066*

ST MARY'S CHURCH seems to soar above the charming little town, standing as it does on a high hill which is believed to have been a pre-Christian sacred site. Its glory is its magnificent tower, with statues set in niches within the buttresses, more statuary and elaborate carving in the middle stage and a host of little pinnacles climbing up all round. Alas, the general effect is largely ruined by the huge and hideous mid-Victorian window, utterly out of scale and style; how could anyone, even in the 1860s, have been quite so insensitive? Still, and despite the window, if the rest of the building maintained the standard set by the tower, we should have a prodigy church indeed. Unfortunately it does not.

PARNHAM HOUSE, just off the A3066 to the south, appears to have been built late in Henry VIII's reign. It is a typical E-shaped mansion of the date, faced in the glowing honey-coloured stone of the region. Within the E, there is no attempt at symmetry: on the east (entrance) front, the south projection extends much further than that to the north and has a generously proportioned staircase tower filling its inner angle; the porch with its fine two-storeyed oriel is nowhere near central; and the fenestration, too, is utterly haphazard. The north wing is clearly a seventeenth-century remodelling. None of this, however, matters a rap. Parnham remains, when seen from the east, a very beautiful house indeed.

From the south and west it is beautiful too, but very different; for between 1807 and 1811 the house was much enlarged and again remodelled, this time by John Nash. He fortunately left the entrance front alone, apart from the battlements and finials which one scarcely notices; elsewhere, however, he was a good deal less respectful. His windows too are mullioned, with bonnet-like hood-moulds; but now symmetry rules – in the fenestration, the buttressing and the regularly spaced finials with their candle-snuffer tops.

Inside, none of the Tudor work remains. The Hall, originally rising only a single storey (look at the windows on the east front) was doubled in height early this century; neither the screen nor the made-up fireplace belongs to the house. Nor indeed does the extremely good linenfold panelling in the Oak Room, with the painted frieze of early Renaissance heraldic devices above it; both were imported from another house in the West Country in the years immediately preceding the First World War – a period which also saw the laying out of the terraces and gardens. There is, however, a Drawing Room of about 1680 with a splendid overmantel and, in an upper room, an endearingly naïve Jacobean chimneypiece with a relief of Joseph and Potiphar's wife.

## Bere Regis

*4; 11 miles NE of Dorchester on A35*

From the outside the CHURCH OF ST JOHN THE BAPTIST looks just as one would expect a Dorset village church to look: warm, greyish, lichen-covered stone with Ham Hill dressings, and a particularly lovely west tower, built towards the end of the fifteenth century at the expense, in all probability, of Cardinal Morton (of Fork fame). It is chequered in stone and flint, and its set-back buttresses turn rather charmingly into crocketed pinnacles when they reach the height of the bell openings. These have double transoms and look more like windows – even though they are blank at the bottom. There are more pinnacles at the corners on the top, and battlements.

Apart from one or two slight vestiges of what may be Saxon work, the earliest visible parts of the church date from the years immediately following the Norman Conquest; it is mentioned in the Domesday survey of 1085. The font is of this date, and you can still see the corbel stone, above the arch of the Morton Chapel, which supported part of the old Norman nave. The first major alterations seem to have been made about 1140, the date of the south arcade – or rather of its three easternmost bays. The big round piers have scalloped capitals, carved with rather charming heads. The north aisle followed a little later, and both aisles were extended westwards around 1300. Soon after this the local Turberville family (Hardy's d'Urbervilles), the lords of the manor, built their funerary chapel at the eastern end of the south aisle, giving it the beautiful reticulated-tracery east window which contrasts so favourably with the round-arched Perpendicular one next to it. The late Perpendicular of Cardinal Morton's Chapel opposite – to the north of the chancel – is a good deal more successful.

But the pride of Bere Regis, unquestionably, is its roof – the most spectacular in Dorset. This too was a gift of Morton's; his coat of arms is carved on the underside of one of the four huge bosses in the centre of the tie-beams. The latter are supported on arched braces, most elegantly cusped, which are broken about two-thirds of the way towards the side walls by what look like hammer-beams (though in fact they serve no structural purpose) in the form of horizontal figures of – it is generally believed – the twelve Apostles, exuberantly painted. The braces have struts in their spandrels, but the tie-beams have more delicate cusping above them between the crownposts and the queenposts.

The church was rather thoroughly restored by Street in 1875, the date of the Hardman glass in many of the windows. The results, it must be admitted, might have been worse.

## Bettiscombe

*5; $6\frac{1}{2}$ miles SW of Beaminster on B3165*

The MANOR HOUSE at Bettiscombe is, to me, one of the most desirable small houses in England. It was built during the reign of Queen Anne, by one Nathaniel Pinney whose descendants lived there until 1984 – a simple building if ever there was one, with nothing at all pretentious about it, and yet with a few light classical touches which give it enormous charm. The material is a warm red brick, with vitrified headers to provide variety and quoins of Ham Hill stone not only

*The Manor House, Bettiscombe.*

on the angles of the house but also on the chimneystacks. It has two floors only, and only four bays strictly speaking – five if you count the front door, which is squashed in a little uncomfortably between the second and third windows but has no upper window above it. It has a delightful hood, however, with a triangular pediment and even a frieze of triglyphs below, supported (though, judging by the two iron stanchions, not entirely adequately) on scrolly brackets. The hood over the back door, which is still self-supporting, is conch-shaped and adorned with a huge scallop shell, from the bottom of which emerges the head of a rather solemn-looking *putto*.

From this side the house is revealed to be a little larger than it appears from the front: there are in fact two ranges, to east and west, ending in big gables. In the former we find an outstandingly pretty staircase, contemporary with the house, its newel-posts in the form of fluted Doric columns and with three turned balusters to each tread. Another feature that imprints the house in one's memory is the beautiful triple-arched screen in the Hall. Yet another – though less strictly architectural – is a screaming skull, whose removal from the house is invariably followed by the death of a member of the family. But if I lived at Bettiscombe, this would seem to me a small price to pay.

Later in the century the Pinneys built another house, RACEDOWN, a mile or so away. It is agreeable enough in its safe Georgian way but possesses none of the character of Bettiscombe. It is, however, something of a literary shrine, the Wordsworths having occupied it between 1795 and 1797, when they were visited there by Coleridge.

## Bingham's Melcombe*

*6; 9 miles SW of Blandford Forum off A354*

This is one of the loveliest of early Tudor Dorset manor houses – and, apart from its one memorable touch of swagger – one of the most enchantingly informal. Built higgledy-piggledy around its terraced courtyard, it seems the very essence of irregularity; nothing is opposite anything else, and there is hardly a right-angle anywhere. Its building history starts with the Gatehouse in the south-east corner: not remotely imposing or grand, and indeed looking – with its pitched roof, gable-end chimneys and sash windows – more like a two-storey Georgian cottage than anything else. Then you look again: at that great central archway, pointed, its two sides bearing only the faintest suggestion of a curve, and its two flanking buttresses. There is nothing Georgian about those – nor about the narrow spiral staircase just to the left of the entrance, leading to the upstairs rooms. The building in fact dates from the fifteenth century at the latest, and may be even earlier.

Passing through the Gatehouse, you emerge into the courtyard; opposite you is the Hall range, at the left-hand end of which is the great oriel for which Bingham's Melcombe is famous. The first thing to be said about it is that it is not really an oriel at all, but a two-storey extension of the Hall to the south, its façade developed into a splendid heraldic frontispiece. What strikes one first, if the sun is shining, is the contrast between the silver-grey limestone of the wall and the honey-coloured Ham Hill stone of the decorative parts. Reading from bottom to top, we start with a five-light mullioned window, the centre light being twice as broad as the others, above which is a magnificent carved coat of arms in a rectangular frame, supported on each side by beefy-looking *putti* – the Renaissance had arrived – with scrolls and acanthus leaves all round. Side shafts, beginning at the bottom corners of the frame, rise up to enclose another window – four-light this time, the same width as the carved panel below it – and continue to the line of the gable above, whence they emerge as finials halfway up each of the diagonal sides. Parallel to them on the outside of the oriel, two angle shafts – interrupted by a string-course above the lower window and by intricately carved capitals twice repeated above – provide further finials at the corners, surmounted by stone eagles. The design is almost identical to that which once adorned the entrance front of Clifton Maybank and is now at Montacute (*qq.v.*), and is clearly the work of the same craftsman. The stained glass in the lower window refers to Philip of Spain and Mary Tudor, and must therefore date from between their marriage in 1554 and Mary's death four years later.

Immediately to the right of the Hall is another, lower, gabled projection which marks the main entrance to the house. In former days, no doubt, there would have been a screens passage, with the usual offices on the right. This whole corner was, however, remodelled early in the eighteenth century. It is banded with stone and flint, and has Georgian sash windows like the Gatehouse. Left of the Hall oriel is another gable (taller, with a big chimney on top); this is broken into by the west range, a much simpler affair of three more modest gables with four-light windows rising just above the eaves, below which runs a passage with a lean-to roof. Within this passage, which is a later addition, can be seen a late fifteenth-century doorway; but the gables above, and the bedrooms within them, look Jacobean. The south (service) range also seems to date from the seventeenth century, though it is probably a little later.

The inside of the house, it must be admitted, has not survived as unchanged as its exterior. The Hall has been divided horizontally and is now the same height as the other ground-floor rooms; it has also, alas, lost its original panelling. Its most interesting feature now is the broad four-centred archway leading into the oriel, the capitals of its responds carved with foliage, deeply undercut. Within the oriel itself there are two doorways on the right, leading respectively into the corridor (and thence to the courtyard) and to the spiral staircase that leads to the small room above. Within the Hall itself, another door in the same wall leads into a lovely Drawing Room with a fine Jacobean overmantel and plaster ceiling of roughly the same date. The rest of the house is much altered, but somehow manages to retain its sixteenth- and seventeenth-century character.

There are wonderful gardens to the north and west, including one of the most magnificent yew hedges I have ever seen, three or four centuries old, the inside of it like a cathedral.

## Blandford Forum

*7; 16½ miles NE of Dorchester on A354*

'In grateful Acknowledgement of the Divine Mercy, that has raised this Town, like the PHAENIX [*sic*] from it's ashes, to it's present beautiful and flourishing State.' So runs the inscription on the Fire Monument in the Market Place, providing the explanation for the quite outstanding Georgian elegance of the town centre. Blandford – it used to be called Chipping Blandford, but the Latin translation was thought to accord better with civic dignity – suffered a calamitous fire in 1731, after which it was rebuilt by Act of Parliament and public subscription; and it was its great good fortune to have at that moment, living and working in the town, its two most distinguished native sons – John and William Bastard. These two brothers (whose father, Thomas Bastard, had founded the family firm of architect-surveyors towards the end of the seventeenth century) were put in sole charge of the rebuilding, and there can be no doubt that they did a superb job.

They began the CHURCH OF ST PETER AND ST PAUL in 1733 and completed it six years later. Unusually for a Georgian church of such importance, it is not placed axially; the limitations of the old site made this impossible. But it is conceived on a grand – almost palatial – scale nonetheless, and provides a noble focus for the Market Place. The tall square tower, elegantly quoined and balustraded with urns set at the corners, rises up immediately behind the west portal, with Doric pilasters and a big broken pediment; there are also pedimented porticoes halfway down the north and south sides. Two features only are not by the Bastards: the cupola on the tower (they had intended an ornate stone spire) and the chancel, ingeniously interpolated by Charles Hunt in 1896, the apse having first been moved eastwards on rollers to make room for it.

The interior is equally distinguished, with rows of unfluted Ionic columns supporting a straight entablature and quadripartite groin vaulting above. The groins are decorated, their arches slightly depressed. A charming west gallery with a gently swelling front and supported on small and slender wooden columns – Ionic again, but now fluted – was added in 1794. Massive side galleries followed in 1837 and can be seen in most of the old photographs; but they have now been removed – and quite rightly since, in the words of the local guide leaflet, 'they cut cruelly into the handsome Ionic columns and greatly impeded the light'. There are box pews throughout, and a handsome pulpit from Wren's London church of St Antholin.

The next most important building in the Market Place is the TOWN HALL of 1734: its ground floor an open arcade of three bays, then a deep entablature, and then three windows with alternating pediments, the whole thing crowned by a big triangular pediment with urns and acroteria. Most of the other buildings are of three storeys (though their roof line is lower than that of the Town Hall) and built of a dark red vitrified brick, many of them with white keystones above the windows. On the opposite side, don't miss the distinctly Baroque façades of the building at the point where East Street begins and of the RED LION INN two doors down. Each has a central carriage entrance, with giant pilasters above it carrying a pediment and framing two windows, one above the other. The former, whose windows have oddly heavy Gibbs surrounds, was John Bastard's own house. At the other end of the Market Place the NATIONAL WESTMINSTER BANK – formerly the Greyhound Inn – is even more ornate. All these designs are quite extraordinarily assured for a local firm of builders in an English country town; the most likely explanation is that the Bastards were in close contact with Thomas Archer, who lived only 20 miles away and with whom they had probably worked as joiners at Chettle House (*q.v.*) nearby.

There are plenty of other fine buildings in the streets around the Market Place, especially in East Street and West Street and in Church Lane, where COUPAR HOUSE makes a good claim to be the grandest domestic building in the town. Its only serious rival is the OLD HOUSE, a little further to the east in what is inexplicably known as The Plocks. One of the few buildings to survive the fire, it dates from about 1660 – a quite astonishing display of sculptured brickwork under a hipped roof far too big for it. The only other important survivor is the 1682 GERONTOCOMIUM – Blandfordese for almshouses – in Salisbury Street, which the fire never reached.

## Bridport

*8; 10 miles E of Lyme Regis on A35*

Another lovely town – it lacks, perhaps, the architectural unity of Blandford Forum, but has a breadth and spaciousness about it that is as satisfying as it is refreshing. ST MARY'S CHURCH is pleasant but unremarkable: basically Perpendicular, but with Early English transepts and a surprisingly good Victorian east end. I prefer William Tyler's TOWN HALL of 1785, its clock and cupola added at the beginning of the nineteenth century. But the beauty of Bridport resides more in the ensemble than in any individual buildings; in the distant prospects of rolling hills; and in the wide, wide streets testifying to the town's medieval prosperity as a centre of the cordage industry – which still continues. There are only three principal ones, all well worth strolling down. In South Street, just beyond the church, you will find a curious little medieval stone CHANTRY, probably dating from the fourteenth century, and at the top end, near the Town Hall, another stone building a good deal grander and of about 1520. Known as the CASTLE, it now houses the town's museum and art gallery.

East and West Streets together form the cross-bar of the T. In the latter, the late eighteenth-century ROPE AND NET FACTORY is still there, looking fully aware of its importance. The former starts off strongly with BEACH & CO.'s enchanting late Georgian shop front, and boasts plenty of fine houses on the way to the LITERARY AND SCIENTIFIC INSTITUTE, 1830s' neo-classical. There are particularly nice fronts, too, on Nos 74 and 115. But the most distinguished house of all, DOWNE HALL, is in none of these streets; it stands a little above the town in a tiny park of its own. Urban Palladian of 1789, it has a pedimented and pilastered front of Portland stone – the epitome of West Country elegance.

*Bryanston.*

## Bryanston

*9; 1 mile W of Blandford Forum off A350*

Now a famous public school, Bryanston House was originally built in the 1890s by Norman Shaw for the 2nd Viscount Portman, replacing an earlier house by James Wyatt. All that remains of Wyatt's work is the imposing Doric gateway which stands, flanked by two lodges, at the end of the mile-long drive; but Shaw's house, when one reaches it at last, comes as anything but an anti-climax. Its style can best be described as neo-Wren: red brick with stone dressings in abundance, hipped roof with dormers, tall chimneys above. They are handled, however, in a way which is very much Shaw's own.

The central block, seen from the entrance side, is of two principal storeys and seven bays, the two side bays (which have extremely tall windows, since they contain staircases) being enclosed between pilasters horizontally striped in brick and stone and slightly projecting. The front door is heavily rusticated with immense keystones breaking into a segmental pediment and is flanked by two windows with equally heavy Gibbs surrounds. The upper windows are simpler, but keep the same keystones and have in addition outer sills supported on brackets. Above, the chimneys are coupled together with arches *à la* Vanbrugh, with prominent stone quoins which repeat the stripy effect of the pilasters. To the sides, two-bay links lead to the spacious service wings that come forward at right-angles to form a courtyard. The garden front is plainer, since there are no pilasters and the seven bays march uninterruptedly across the house to the striped quoins at the ends. But even here Shaw could not resist a few characteristic flourishes: the lower windows have heavy architraves supported on huge scrolls. The wings, too, are brought forward in line with the centre, producing an elevation of enormous length.

The interior is, quite simply, tremendous. The focus is a vast central Hall, from which a broad straight corridor runs off in each direction to the far ends of the house. This Hall rises to the roof, the light coming down through a central dome, while giant Ionic columns support gracefully curving upper balconies. The principal rooms leading off Hall and corridors are inevitably smaller, but every bit as grand, all of them with magnificent plaster ceilings. Pevsner likens the cavernous Ballroom to the Baths of Diocletian – as well he might.

## Cattistock

*10; 8½ miles NW of Dorchester off A356*

Incomparably the best of all the Victorian churches in Dorset, ST PETER AND ST PAUL is in all its essentials the work of the George Gilbert Scotts, father and son. Sir Gilbert (the father) was responsible for the south aisle and the polygonal apse – an unusual feature, but the consequence of his professed discovery of a medieval apse on the site; all this is in his favourite 'Middle Pointed' style of 1300 or so, the moment when Early English is giving way to Decorated. One might therefore reasonably have expected his son – taking over seventeen years later, in 1874 – to have continued in the same idiom: but no. George Jun. was a devotee of Perpendicular. His north arcade and aisle echo the fifteenth century, or even the early sixteenth; certainly the brand-new tower which he built to the north-west (in place of the old north one, which he demolished) looks more Tudor than anything else. It is of pale grey stone, lofty and slender, and with exceedingly tall bell openings arranged in two pairs, separated only by a narrow shaft which continues up to form a small roof pinnacle. The sheer size of these windows, which are straight-headed, gives the tower a slightly blind look in certain lights; but with its four major corner pinnacles and its openwork stepped parapet it remains a spectacular piece of work and the *chef d'oeuvre* of its architect.

Within the tower, and separated from the west end of the nave by a stone screen, is the baptistery, one of the main features of the church. Apart from a font with an abnormally high cover, it is adorned with a huge mural of St George and the dragon and panels depicting saints, heraldic signs, and stencilled floral decorations. There is even an odd little two-light window. The nave itself strikes one as rather too short; it does, however, have nice carvings on the stops – presumably portraits. The chancel, beautifully framed by a very high arch, has five lancets round the apse and then pairs of lancets next to the arch itself. The copiously ribbed timber roof, shaped like the hull of a ship, is supported on carved stone corbels, and there is some more fine carving – the Evangelists this time – on the pulpit. But best of all is the westernmost window of the south aisle – a really superb William Morris creation of 1882.

## Cerne Abbas

*11; 7 miles N of Dorchester on A352*

The village is celebrated above all for its Giant, probably a Romano-British version of Hercules dating from the time of the Emperor Commodus at the end of the second century, and indisputably in a state of considerable excitement. The property of the National Trust, it has recently been restored by Messrs Heineken, whose product is known for reaching those parts that other beers cannot reach. Architecturally, however, the town boasts a beautiful church, the remains of an ancient abbey, and several remarkably pretty houses.

ST MARY'S effortlessly dominates the village. It is banded in alternate layers of flint and stone, with a fine Perpendicular west tower of stone only, graced by a niched statue of the Virgin and Child of about 1550 and a four-light window below it. Inside, the feeling is of spaciousness and light. There is a good eighteenth-century tower screen, but this is firmly upstaged by the stone screen of 1450 or so which until 1870 filled the entire space enclosed by the chancel arch, the Royal Arms being painted on one side and the Ten Commandments on the other. (See the fascinating photograph at the west end.) The chancel, despite its Perpendicular east window of six lights, is a good deal earlier than the body of the church, which is of the fifteenth and early sixteenth centuries; those trefoiled lancets must be of 1280 or thereabouts, though the wall paintings look the best part of a century later.

Of the monastic foundation, which already existed here in the ninth century, what little that remains can be seen in and around the garden of ABBEY FARM. But beware: there is much reconstruction and re-use of old pieces in new positions. Admire the opulent porch to the old Abbot's Hall with its two-storey oriel and forget the rest.

## Charborough Park

*12; 6 miles W of Wimborne on A31*

Built around 1660, Charborough Park is in the hipped-roof style of Coleshill or Kingston Lacy. At that time it had seven bays; but another four were added on to the east in 1741 to provide suitable accommodation for 'poor Fred' – Frederick, Prince of Wales – when he came to stay. Further enlargement took place in 1810 at the hands of John Nash; it was he who gave the house its present rendering and its central five-bay pediment on Ionic pilasters.

Inside, the principal feature is the great Staircase Hall painted by Thornhill from 1718; I must, however, confess to not having seen it, since I was not allowed in.

In the extensive grounds is an octagonal tower in the Gothic style, dating from 1790 but the top rebuilt and heightened after being struck by lightning in 1838. There are also three magnificent gates, erected in 1841 on the Wimborne–Dorchester road to celebrate the owner's success in getting the road re-routed so that the park could be enlarged.

## Charminster

*13; 1½ miles N of Dorchester on A352*

A pretty little village, Charminster is nowadays too close to Dorchester for safety. ST MARY'S CHURCH crouches in a valley, broad but low, with an early sixteenth-century west tower in proportion. It was built at the expense of Sir Thomas Trenchard of Wolveton and bears his signature in the form of the letter T, stylised into a cypher monogram. The pinnacles in triplets at the corners are a nice touch. At first glance all is Perpendicular, and late Perpendicular at that; but then look again at the clerestory and you will see, amid the fifteenth-century windows, four small Norman ones, which were uncovered only in 1896.

Were it not for those windows, the interior would come as a considerable surprise. Both north and south arcades are Norman, four bays long with heavy circular piers and roughly scalloped capitals, while a continuous nailhead ornament runs round the arches. These, however, are already pointed, so their date cannot be much before 1200. The round chancel arch must be a little earlier; but all churches were built from east to west, so this is only what one might expect. Beyond the chancel arch, alas, lies disappointment. The Norman chancel was pulled down in the seventeenth century, and replaced some 200 years later, around 1838, by the present boring little piece – the work being done so inexpertly that the seventeenth-century east window (which had formerly occupied the blocked-up chancel arch) was reset in its new position back to front.

The west end of the south aisle, unusually narrow, shows us the width of the original Norman church; the eastern half, on the other hand, is almost twice as broad – having been enlarged around 1480 to form the Trenchard Chapel. The north aisle is Victorian, the same date as the chancel. Again the earlier windows were re-used; but this time they are Perpendicular, and the right way round.

WOLVETON HOUSE – it is sometimes spelt Wolfeton – stands some half a mile to the south of the village. Its story begins with Thomas Trenchard (he of the church tower) who inherited the manor in 1495 at the age of

*St Mary's Church, Charminster.*

sixteen. His is the great twin-towered Gatehouse, its towers fitted out inside as dovecotes; behind them are to the north a chapel and to the south the old guardroom, now divided into guest rooms. Of the house he built, however, the greater part was tragically demolished in the late eighteenth and early nineteenth centuries; all that remains is the south-west corner. It is best seen from the south front and comprises the part extending from the polygonal garderobe turret between the third and fourth bays and the tall embattled stair turret to its right. And even this is not unaltered; the most uncomfortably cramped windows between these two projections – originally designed to light the Great Hall – could not possibly have been planned the way they are now. (Notice, however, the carving on the hood-moulds – a faint premonitory whiff of the Renaissance.) The rest of the south front, to the left of the garderobe, is a good deal more classical, and must date from the last two decades of the century. The windows in the centre bay on both floors were originally bowed and were reset in 1798 – hence their slightly lopsided appearance.

Entrance to the house is – and always has been – from the north, where a porch leads into a stone-vaulted Entrance Hall. The main staircase, also of stone, leads off to the right, the first straight, broad flight ending at a half landing, the second doubling back to the first floor. The arrangement seems simple enough nowadays, but in Tudor houses the staircases almost invariably rise round a square or circular well. The Wolveton design is found in only one other sixteenth-century house – Hardwick Hall in Derbyshire – though there was a third at Longleat (*q.v.*) until it was remodelled early in the last century. Beyond the staircase the Entrance Hall becomes a passage leading to the south front, with fine linenfold panelling, a Jacobean plaster ceiling and simply splendid carved doorways into the Hall and Parlour. The Hall, which was repanelled in 1862, is now of little interest; but the Parlour is magnificent with its carved Jacobean chimneypiece and overmantel (enriched with yet more sixteenth- and seventeenth-century woodwork in Victorian times) and an equally ebullient plaster ceiling. The Dining Room beyond is of the same date and much the same style; here however the overmantel, which represents in its central cartouche the Judgement of Paris, is of plaster rather than wood.

Upstairs, the Long Gallery has been sub-divided. The most important room which originally formed a part of it is now known as the Great Chamber – known also as the Eating Chamber, a name which is given additional weight by recent discoveries of innumerable walnut shells and bones beneath the floorboards. The barrel-vaulted plaster ceiling has gone, but the immense stone fireplace remains. It stands the full height of the room and contains figures not only of Faith and Hope but also of Red Indians with feathers in their hair.

Finally we come to the Riding House. Some 125 yards north of the house and not normally open to the public, it seems to be of about 1610 and is the earliest surviving riding school in England.

## Chettle House

*14; 6½ miles NE of Blandford Forum off A354*

Here is English Baroque at its virtuoso best, the only country house by that most endlessly fascinating of architects, Thomas Archer, to survive virtually intact. It seems to have been begun in 1710 – though Pevsner suggests a slightly later date – and to have been some twenty-five years in the building, during which time Archer had settled at Hale in Hampshire (*q.v.*), only 15 miles or so away.

Chettle House is built of a rich red brick, with dressings of Chilmark stone – except at the rounded north and south ends, where Ham stone was used when the upper floor was added in 1912. These ends are of five bays each, while the main body of the house has seven, the three central ones rising to an additional third storey above the high, vaulted basement. Archer's idiosyncratic hand is visible everywhere: in his treatment of the centre on the garden front, with its two rows of tall round-headed windows with big keystones and alternating bands of stone and brick between them; in the quirkish capitals to the pilasters which are such a feature of the house – capitals which are fluted and taper (rather than swell) as they rise; and above all in his predilection for curving corners, which occur not only at the two ends but also on the projecting centre of the entrance front. On both fronts, the two floors are surmounted by a deep cornice with brackets, above which stone balustrades run all the way round the building. Originally these balustrades excluded the curved ends – one of the several indications that these ends were originally of a single storey before being raised and then lowered again in the nineteenth century.

Archer's bravura is shown to equal advantage in the Entrance Hall – now on the garden side. His glorious staircase rises in two parallel flights along the north and south walls and then turns inward, the two flights meeting to form a balcony. Thence another short flight continues towards the centre of the house, passing along a tunnel-vaulted corridor until it forks again, the two new flights returning to form more balconies running all the way along the sides of the Hall. There are three turned balusters per tread, fluted Doric columns as newel-posts, and an extremely pretty carved panel of vaguely heraldic design on the central balcony. The doorways both here and in the bowed West Hall – now the entrance – have lunettes by Alfred Stevens, whose father was a local craftsman and decorator at Blandford. The rounded ends of the house were originally designed to contain two rooms each, and that to the north still does so; the south end, however, has had the two knocked together to form a Saloon, now rather unsuccessfully decorated in the style that the late Sir John Betjeman used to call '*Louis Singe*'.

Chettle House has now been divided into flats – a sad misfortune.

*Chettle House.*

## Christchurch

*15; 5 miles E of Bournemouth off A35*

The PRIORY CHURCH is the longest parish church in England – longer, and indeed larger, than several cathedrals. It was begun in 1094 by Ranulph Flambard, who later became Bishop of Durham and was principally responsible for the building of Durham Cathedral; had he remained at Christchurch it might well have become, like Durham, one of the great glories of European Romanesque. In the event, however, the building lost its original impetus; under the Augustinians, who took it over as a priory, work was to continue on it at intervals throughout the Middle Ages. It therefore emerges as something of a hotch-potch – though an utterly magnificent one.

Apart from the fine Perpendicular west tower, the first feature of the church that catches your attention as you approach is the tremendous north porch. But wait; continue past it until you are just beyond the north transept – for this is the showpiece of the exterior. All around the bottom, at ground level, runs a line of intersecting blank arcading (partly restored at the base) with fish-scale decoration in the spandrels. Above this, around the circular stair turret and a little beyond it, is another, simple, arcade with twin columns; higher still, around the turret, a big, bold, criss-cross design like an open trellis; and a third tier of arcading to finish the whole thing off at the top.

Now walk on, all the way round the church. The two principal periods of building activity now become obvious. Basically, everything east of the crossing is fifteenth-century – early around the east end and the Lady Chapel, later around the choir and towards the transepts. The time lag between the two is one of several pieces of evidence that the church formerly had a central tower over the crossing, which fell in the early fifteenth century, destroying much of the choir. (Another is the carving of a church, with just such a tower and a spire, above the entrance to the Draper Chantry Chapel at the end of the south choir aisle.)

West of the crossing, including much of the transepts themselves, the work is almost entirely Norman – though there has been a certain amount of restoration in Victorian times, especially round the windows. The only important exceptions are the tower and the splendid thirteenth-century north porch, two-storeyed (it is much higher than the nearby aisle) and vaulted in two bays. Here again, the vaulting is of the Victorian restoration, and so, it seems, is the inner doorway; but there is no reason to believe that the restorer (Benjamin Ferrey, in 1862) did anything but copy the original work.

The nave is Norman, and monumentally impressive, though we can only sigh at the disappearance of the original clerestory and at its thirteenth-century Early English replacement. There are nice scalloped capitals on the sides of the piers, and a scaly decoration in the spandrels. Agreeable, too, is the apparently haphazard way in which, at gallery level, some of the central columns supporting the twin arches are decorated, and others not. The vault is a replacement of 1819.

*The ornate reredos in the Priory Church, Christchurch.*

Beyond the screen, however, the vaulting over the chancel – a lovely pattern with liernes forming stars – dates from the early sixteenth century, when the interior was completely remodelled. Very slightly later, say 1530 or thereabouts, are the choir stalls with their marvellous misericords, several of which are a good deal older than the stalls themselves. But the *pièce de résistance* here is the reredos, described by Pevsner as 'one of the most monumental survivals of Decorated sculpture in England'. At its base, just above the altar, there is an irresistible representation of a recumbent Jesse; at the level above that, the Magi present their gifts to a standing Christ child, the ox and the ass gazing benevolently on.

Beyond the reredos to the east is the Lady Chapel – Perpendicular too, though a little earlier than the present chancel. Thanks to three enormous windows – five lights to the east, four to north and south – the east end of it is brilliantly illuminated, the west somewhat gloomy, despite the ebulliently ornate stone canopies along the walls. Oddly and not entirely happily, there is a 'domestic' storey above; its purpose is unknown.

## Church Knowle*

*16; 2 miles W of Corfe Castle off A351*

ST PETER'S CHURCH gets its star not for any particular architectural distinction but for its charm alone. It is quite small and unassuming, with a stubby little pyramid-capped west tower which was rebuilt, probably in much the same form as the original, in 1741. Apart from this and the nineteenth-century north aisle, the entire church dates from the end of the thirteenth century – the moment when Early English was just giving way to Decorated; note the bar tracery in the chancel and transepts. The building was perfectly cruciform until 1833, when the north wall of the nave was rebuilt in line with the end of the north transept, the archway leading into the south transept was made higher and the two lancets between the tower and porch elongated. At this time, too, the squints on either side of the chancel arch were opened further to form smaller entrances into the chancel. All three of these entrances, together with the east window, are now framed with pretty painted decoration of leaves and twining tendrils, presumably Victorian. The north aisle has no arcade as such, only the wooden posts that support a wooden gallery that runs all along its length, turning at the end to form a west gallery in front of the tower.

BARNSTON MANOR, which stands some three-quarters of a mile away to the west, is probably the oldest still inhabited house in Dorset, going back as it does to the 1280s or thereabouts. It is thus just about the same age as the church, and indeed possesses one double lancet window with a pierced quatrefoil above in almost exactly the same style as the bar-traceried ones there. (A second, now bricked-up, can be seen in the north wall of the west wing.) The three shallow buttresses with set-offs are further indications of this date. The entire east end is occupied by the Hall, which was divided horizontally in the sixteenth century and given its ceiling on heavy moulded beams and the big stone fireplace in the south wall. It has now been further partitioned. At its west end, a gabled cross-range contained the Parlour, with the solar above. It is here that we see the double lancet window from the inside, where it proves to have a window seat, a rebate for shutters, and even a vertical stone rib running between the lancets with shots for the shutter bolts. The sixteenth century also saw the addition of mullioned bays, which, although they are pretty enough in themselves, unfortunately make the house look a good deal less medieval than it otherwise would; but despite this, it remains a remarkable survival.

*The Manor House, Cranborne.*

## Corfe Castle

*NT; 17; 5 miles NW of Swanage on A351*

'*Unum omnium Anglorum castellum tutissimum*' is what they called Corfe Castle in 1139; but by that time there had already been for the best part of two centuries a castle defending the only major cleft in the Purbeck Hills. It was here, on 18 March 978, that King Edward the Martyr was murdered by his stepmother to make her own son king; and here, soon after his accession, that William the Conqueror built a new and stronger fortress – of which there remain a fragment of the Hall and much of the stone wall enclosing the inner ward. A keep followed, under William Rufus, and a century later the castle was greatly enlarged by King John – Corfe was one of his favourite residences. He built the so-called Gloriette – it was of Corfe that the word was first used to denote a relatively luxurious or elegant corner of a castle – of which the ruins can still be seen to the east of the keep, and also, with more serious intent, the great ditch between the inner ward and the outer bailey. The outer stages were all complete by the end of the thirteenth century.

The great testing time for the castle occurred, however, not in the Middle Ages but during the Civil War, when it suffered two tremendous sieges. On the first, in 1643, its commander, Sir John Bankes, was away; it was Lady Bankes who defended the castle in her husband's absence, repelling the besiegers with such vigour that they lost one-fifth of their number before they eventually withdrew. On the second occasion, three years later, the Parliamentarians wisely chose a moment when Lady Bankes was herself away in London; even then the castle put up a stout resistance and was finally taken by treachery rather than by force of arms. But the conquerors took their vengeance, reducing the building to the sad but unutterably romantic ruin that it is today.

## Cranborne*

*18; 18 miles N of Bournemouth on B3078*

The MANOR HOUSE is surely the most magical house in Dorset. It dates back to King John, who rebuilt the old royal hunting lodge in Cranborne Chase in 1207–8; and it is this which forms the nucleus of the present building. It consists essentially of a tall rectangular block with a square tower projecting southward from the south-west corner, four buttresses rising the full height of the building on the north side and two on the south, battlemented and with arrow slits in some of the merlons. Had it remained in its original form it would have been an interesting survival but little more; what makes it so uniquely beautiful is the remodelling undertaken between 1608 and 1620 by Robert Cecil, 1st Earl of Salisbury, to render it fit to serve once again as a royal hunting lodge, this time for his own sovereign, James I.

First, Cecil gutted the old building, which had long lain derelict, giving it its mullioned and transomed (and, on the ground floor, some double-transomed) windows – two storeys to the south, three to the north. Next, he heightened the south-west tower, finishing it off with a pyramidal cap, and echoed it with a similar one to the south-east. Thirdly, he added short side wings to the east and west; of these, the former has disappeared, while the latter was remodelled in 1647. Finally, and most important of all where the charm of the building is concerned, he added delightful three-bay Renaissance loggias to the centres of the two main fronts. That to the south is of two storeys: on the ground floor we have an open, three-bay arcade on Doric columns, their lower parts rusticated, carrying slightly depressed arches; above, a three-light window flanked by shell-headed niches. The cornice consists of four semi-circular merlons, of which the two central ones are filled with roundels carved with the signs of Libra and Virgo. A third roundel must once have occupied the circular frame just below the window, and nine similar frames scattered elsewhere across the south front presumably contained the rest of the zodiac; but these are all now empty.

The northern loggia is, if anything, prettier still. It is of one storey only, but raised on a high platform at the top of a flight of steps. Again there is a three-bay arcade, but this time the columns (which are thicker and have a pronounced *entasis*) support semi-circular arches with gaping lion-head gargoyles in the spandrels. The first and third arches are closed along the bottom by stone screens ornamented with strapwork. To each side of the arcade the usual shell niches, set rather low, are surmounted by carved relief heads in extravagant frames. Above the architrave is a deep frieze with more designs in strapwork, and the whole thing is crowned with an imposing heraldic crest. The master mason for the two loggias, as indeed in all probability for the rest of the work, was William Arnold, who was also largely responsible for the building of Wadham College, Oxford (*q.v.*). To him we can almost certainly ascribe the classicising of the buttresses on the north front by enriching them with pilasters, paired and fluted, in three different orders superimposed in tiers, and the two groups of three immensely tall chimneys, diagonally set, that impart to the front its final flourish.

Inside the house, much of the decoration is of the nineteenth century. There is, however, a most splendid panelled Hall with a broad four-centred fireplace, its upper walls covered with superb tapestries; and a lovely Drawing Room occupying the seventeenth-century western extension. This extension – it is really too small to qualify as a wing – is a curious combination of Gothic (the mullioned and transomed windows) and classical (the hipped roof and alternating long and short quoins). It is the work of Richard Rider, or Ryder, its Jacobean predecessor having been seriously damaged by the Royalist army who were quartered there during the Civil War. To Rider, too, we owe the fine classical gate piers at the end of the broad garden path to the north – through which the building appears, quite stunningly, as the fairytale house it is.

While in Cranborne, you should take the opportunity of a quick look – from the outside – at CRANBORNE LODGE, a most remarkable red-brick house of about 1740. It has a pretty pedimented porch on Ionic capitals, and the first-floor windows have stone surrounds and keystones of such exaggerated size as to give them an almost Mayan appearance.

## Crichel House

*19; 6 miles N of Wimborne off B3078*

There is a painting at Crichel of a charming Elizabethan house of four gables, with little busts in niches over the door and between the mullioned windows. It seems to have been painted in the late seventeenth century, and it is the only evidence we have of what the old manor house looked like; for in 1742 the entire building was burnt to the ground. Rebuilding, however, began at once, so quickly indeed that Sir William Napier, the owner, was able to inscribe the date 1743 on his new south front. Like its predecessor, it was relatively modest: five bays by seven, the material brick with stone dressings, two storeys only. This house, in the form that Sir William intended for it, lasted just twenty-two years; then, in 1765, it passed to his nephew, one Humphry Sturt, for whom it was nowhere near grand enough. In the next few years it was transformed from being the house of an ordinary country squire to something very like a palace. Sturt first added two blocks at the north-west and south-west corners, each projecting in both directions; next he built a completely new range the whole length of the east front, consisting of a Drawing Room, Hall and Dining Room; finally, at the south end, he filled the gap between his new Library to the west and his new Drawing Room to the east with a splendid recessed portico of five bays, and ran a continuous line of upper rooms around the south and east fronts. The east front as we see it today, with its imposing Venetian doorway, the Venetian window above it and the triangular pediment above that, is all Sturt's; the north front has been completely refaced in the last quarter-century, after the demolition of a Victorian service wing. Only on the west, in the recessed centre between Sturt's additions, can we get an unrestricted view of Sir William Napier's earlier house – though it can be spied again on the south side, both the ground and the first floors, behind the columns of the portico.

Sturt's architect is unknown. On both the two main fronts there is a disproportion between the immense height of the ground floor – made even more grandiose by two more Venetian windows flanking the portico – and the floor above, where not even the moulded architraves or (on the south side) the six pilasters delimiting and separating the windows of the five-bay centre can make these windows – eleven of them – look anything other than uncomfortably constricted.

The moment we enter the house, however, all this ineptitude disappears; Crichel possesses the most spectacular series of state rooms in all Dorset. In the older core of the house – Sir William's – the only major alteration made by Sturt was to move the staircase from what is now the vestibule, just inside the western entrance, to the centre. In doing so he considerably enlarged it and made a most magnificent Staircase Hall, lit through a lantern above; but the staircase itself is still of the early Georgian type with three variated balusters per tread and may well incorporate parts of its predecessor. The four principal rooms of the old house still untouched have retained, in all its essentials, their original decoration.

The new rooms are far more opulent. Sturt seems, however, to have used two different decorators, one rather more old-fashioned than the other. The former was still working in the style of William Kent with its heavy chimneypieces and monumental pedimented doorcases; it can be seen to best advantage in the Library and again in the Hall on the east side, where only the ceiling painting – probably an afterthought – seems to look forward to things to come.

There is no more perfect object lesson in the difference between early Georgian and late Georgian taste than that which is to be had simply by passing from this room to either of its neighbours. These, the Drawing Room to the south and the Dining Room to the north, are clearly the work of a very different hand – in all probability that of James Wyatt, whom we know to have been working in Dorset, at both Milton Abbey and Bryanston, in the 1770s. The Drawing Room, which ends in one of the great Venetian windows on the south front, has a marvellous ceiling in the form of a shallow barrel vault, painted in the style of Angelica Kauffmann, below which runs a shallow frieze supported on Corinthian pilasters. The Dining Room is, arguably, finer still; it has a marvellous ceiling again, but this time deeply coved, fluted in the corners, with *trompe-l'oeil* medallions within the coving. On the walls below are more medallions, larger now, but painted in the same style with classical scenes. Both painting and plasterwork are of the utmost delicacy, the general effect superb.

## Eastbury

*20; 5½ miles NE of Blandford Forum off A354*

In about 1717 one George Dodington, a Lord of Admiralty, commissioned a great country house from Sir John Vanbrugh. Dying only two years later, he never saw it finished but left it, together with £30,000 for its completion, to his nephew George Bubb, the son of a Weymouth apothecary. By 1738, when it was completed – by Roger Morris – it is said to have cost £140,000 and, of all Vanbrugh's houses, was exceeded in size only by Castle Howard and Blenheim. Here Bubb – who took the additional name of Dodington – lived in luxury and ostentation on a scale that made him famous throughout the country. 'His bulk and corpulency', wrote a contemporary, 'gave full display to a vast expanse and profusion of brocade and embroidery, and this, when set off with an enormous tye-periwig and deep laced ruffles, gave the picture of an ancient courtier in his gala habit or Quin in his stage dress.' On his death he left his friend Sir Francis Dashwood a considerable sum to erect a mausoleum on the hill at West Wycombe (*q.v.*). This still stands, and is now his principal memorial; for Eastbury passed to his nephew, Earl Temple, who after trying in vain to sell it and even offering £200 a year to anyone who would live in it, finally demolished all but the west pavilion, the entrance arch into the great kitchen courtyard that lay behind it, and the piers of the entrance gate.

This west pavilion constitutes the present house. Its centre is a square block of three bays and three storeys, the first-floor windows being at least twice the height of those above, with semi-circular heads. To each side there runs off a three-bay wing, with small round windows on the first floor, their ground floor being hidden by the nine-bay arcade that runs the length of the building.

The entrance arch into the courtyard is, if anything, even more memorable than the pavilion itself, owing largely to the two trees which have been allowed to grow from its top like something out of Piranesi. It remains a splendidly Vanbrugian piece, massively square and monumental, with a corbel table striding across the top and a vast volute at either side. Looking at these superb fragments, one cannot but feel a stab of sorrow for the great house that is no more – though fortunately there survives an old painting showing the central block as having an eleven-bay front of two storeys on a high basement with corner towers not unlike those of Blenheim and a vast five-bay centre with pedimented portico. On the garden side, according to *Vitruvius britannicus*, the centre had a big square attic instead of the pediment, the two lower floors being heavily rusticated and the columns of the portico ringed. But knowledge of what it looked like cannot make up for the loss of what was unquestionably one of the great houses of England. If only there had been a National Trust . . . .

## Encombe House

*21; 4 miles SW of Corfe Castle off B3069*

Few houses in England are more idyllically situated. The house lies – the verb seems the only one appropriate for a building so long and low – in a gentle valley between the Purbeck Hills and the sea, beside a lake which at first one almost thinks must be part of the sea itself, but which is in fact fed by a freshwater spring – though a little stream does run from the far end the few hundred yards down to the beach. Its style is harder to describe: Palladian of a sort, though more the staccato Palladianism of Lord Burlington and William Kent than the more strictly classical variety of Campbell or Paine. The inspiration, that is to say, comes more from Holkham than from Mereworth. But there are other influences too, the most noticeable one being that of Vanbrugh – in the way, for example, that the round-headed windows are linked by moulded string-courses, or the shallow projections at the centre and on the side wings are carried up beyond the roof line to form pedimented dormers.

Vanbrugh, however, would have been unable to resist a touch of drama; what is remarkable about Encombe is that, despite the strength and individuality of the design, drama has been deliberately avoided. How easy it would have been to give it a classical portico; instead, the lowness of the house has been stressed by the continued emphasis on horizontals in the strings and cornices. It is as if the architect were consciously playing down his creation, preferring it to merge into the surrounding country than to make any forceful statement of its own. This is not normally easy for an architect to do – but is perhaps rather easier when he is designing for himself. The manor of Encombe passed in 1734 to one John Pitt, a cousin of William Pitt the Elder, who seems to have been already quite well known as an amateur architect and who began designing his house at once. In doing so, however, he allowed for the existence of the earlier house on the site, demolishing most of it but re-using the foundations and at least one inner wall – that of the former Hall, which occupied the eastern end of the present Drawing Room in the centre of the south front. If, as seems likely, he retained other walls as well (though naturally recasing them with the fine Purbeck ashlar which is a feature of the whole house) this might account for the surprising lowness of the ground-floor rooms – which he has tried to disguise on the exterior by giving the windows tall, round heads, rising well above the inside ceiling level.

However that may be, Pitt produced a perfectly symmetrical south front of two storeys. In essence it consists of a three-bay central block, the middle bay having a relatively simple Tuscan doorcase rising, as we have seen, to a pedimented attic dormer. Next there comes, on each side, first a two-bay continuation, recessed but with a Tuscan colonnade on the ground floor on roughly the same plane as the central façade, and then a projection which comes forward two bays, presents one bay to the south and then turns outward again to connect with a three-bay wing with a separate hipped roof. These three-bay wings also have pedimented centres. The net result is that, of the fifteen bays, only once on each side do we find two adjoining bays receiving exactly the same treatment. However much one tries to analyse it, one remains ultimately mystified that so sprawling a composition holds together so well.

The north side of the house is less unchanged, having been remodelled – together with much of the interior – by Anthony Salvin in 1871–4. At that time, as happened to so many country houses, the entrance was moved from the garden front to the other side, the central ground-floor window being converted into a front door; Salvin also much improved the elevation by adding pedimented dormers similar to those on the garden front (though not here broken forward) and ball finials. His final, Vanbrugian touch was the addition of the arched central chimneystack. The present porch, on the other hand, is not his work; it is in fact an addition of 1959, having previously served as a garden temple.

Indoors, the turning round of the house necessitated a new Entrance Hall, with a pretty Georgian-looking (though in reality of course High Victorian) staircase leading up from the western end and a pair of columns marking off the eastern. From it you pass through to the Drawing Room in the centre of the garden front (formerly two small rooms, knocked by Salvin into one) from which two doors lead off respectively into the Morning Room, with its three eastward-facing windows, and into the eastern colonnade – now, with its fellow, glass-fronted – at the far end of which is the oak-panelled Library. West of the Drawing Room is the Dining Room, with a lovely view out on to the lake. Among the details are several superb neo-classical chimneypieces and, in the Morning Room, a fine plaster ceiling – though whether it is contemporary with the house or a convincing Salvin pastiche nobody seems sure.

Such, then, are the facts. The rare charm of the house is harder to capture. Though Encombe is not one of the great houses of England, there are few to me more desirable.

Forde Abbey.

## Forde Abbey*

*22; 4 miles SE of Chard off B3167*

Here is a wonderful house indeed. The story of Forde Abbey goes back to 1141, when thirteen Cistercian monks were settled just outside Thorncombe, on the borders of Dorset and Somerset. At the time of the Dissolution of the Monasteries in the 1530s the abbey passed to one Henry Pollard, but not before the last abbot, Thomas Chard, had built himself a new lodging on a scale that can only be described as princely. Such was its magnificence that Pollard apparently found any further building work unnecessary, and the abbey suffered no further major alterations until the time of the Commonwealth. In 1649 it was bought by Cromwell's attorney general, Edmund Prideaux, who over the next decade added to the house and embellished it in a most unpuritanical way; and it still stands substantially as Prideaux left it.

The abbey church, however, has gone – together with most of the cloister. It stood, so far as we can judge, immediately south of the surviving buildings, the west end of the nave roughly opposite the single-storey terrace and loggia added in the eighteenth century to the south front, its chancel more or less in line with the east end of the chapel (the former chapter house). This latter is the oldest part of the house as we see it today; the round arches with zigzag ornament and scallop capitals are enough to show that it must be contemporary with the foundation itself. Only the east window – five lights under a four-centred arch – is an obvious Perpendicular addition by Chard, whose abbreviated signature, indeed, appears in the spandrels.

Northward from the chapel runs the monks' dormitory, 168 feet long, carried on a vaulted undercroft of eleven bays divided longitudinally by a line of octagonal piers. The west side reveals the thirteen original lancets, unaltered. This building must consequently be a century or so later than the chapter house/chapel; so too is the refectory, immediately opposite it to the west, projecting north from what remains of Abbot Chard's cloister. On the upper floor, in the present Library, you can still see the recess from which the readings were given during meals, together with the splendid timber roof.

And so we come to Chard's contribution. The great porch of his new dwelling – completed, according to an inscription, in 1528 – sets the tone of what lies within. (Looking at it, one understands why King Henry finally decided that the monasteries had gone too far.) A basket arch leads into a fan-vaulted lobby and is surmounted by a tremendous oriel, rising two storeys to a broad carved frieze and battlemented parapet. On each of the two storeys the windows are identical: six lights divided by a transom – though below the transom Prideaux has removed the Perpendicular tracery and converted the six narrow lights into three broad ones with round heads. Below each window is another carved frieze, and yet another runs westward from this vast frontispiece along the top of Chard's Great Hall. (This last is of particular interest, since in it Renaissance motifs appear for the first time.)

The Hall – which may or may not have been used as a new refectory – is equally spectacular, even though Prideaux has reduced it from seven bays to five, using the two western ones to make smaller rooms for himself. Each bay is of four huge lights, round-headed and cusped, above and below the central transom; those in the north wall have now been blocked up to permit further building behind, but the Hall is still flooded with light – the more so since the windows rise virtually to the roof coving. The roof itself is a masterpiece on its own, divided as it is by intricately moulded timbers into square and triangular panels, each one painted, gilded and ornamented with stars.

It was presumably only after his Hall was finished that Chard started work on a new cloister. He got no further than the north range, and even this was left uncompleted; but enough work was done to allow us to imagine how magnificent the whole thing would have been. The bays have, once again, four-light windows with a transom; but here the central mullion in each bay forks into a Y, the three spaces so formed in the window head being filled with Perpendicular tracery. The motif repeats blank on the inner wall, except where the Early English arcading of the old lavatorium has been exposed.

And so to Prideaux. On the outside, his work can be seen immediately east of the great porch, in the three embattled bays of which the ground floor is hidden by the Georgian loggia: a large central round-headed window is flanked by two smaller straight-headed ones, above each of which is an *oeil-de-boeuf*, horizontally placed. These windows mark the Saloon, the grandest of Prideaux's rooms, gloriously rich – as are his Drawing Room and Dining Room, and his main staircase – in woodwork and plasterwork of surpassing quality. Much of the panelling is concealed by tapestries; but it can still be seen to superb advantage around the marble chimneypiece, with its fluted Corinthian pilaster to each side and exquisite overmantel. The stucco ceiling, of similar standard, bears in its centre the arms of Edmund Prideaux the Younger and his wife.

The Drawing Room and Dining Room, beyond the Great Hall to the west, appear to be somewhat earlier than the Saloon – which, as the arms on the ceiling show, was not completed until after the elder Prideaux's death. The plasterwork is of a slightly less sophisticated style, and the woodwork too shows traces of that somewhat irresponsible attitude to accepted architectural grammar that one associates with the 'Artisan Mannerism' school of Balls Park or Thorpe Hall (*qq.v.*). They remain, however, rooms of immense distinction. The staircase, too, is memorable, with its openwork panels of carved foliage in place of balusters, similar to those at Thorpe Hall, Ham House or – a little later – Sudbury Hall in Derbyshire. The carved bowls, piled high with fruit, standing on the newel-posts provide an additional touch of opulence; and on the inner wall the pattern of the carving is echoed in a painted dado.

This lovely house is made lovelier still by its setting amid green lawns, immense trees and the old monkish fishponds at the edge of the peaceable River Axe.

## Horton

*23; 5 miles NE of Wimborne off B3078*

ST WOLFRIDA'S CHURCH is L-shaped, which is unusual enough; and what makes it odder still is its tiny tower, which is tucked into the angle. It was almost entirely rebuilt in 1722 by a local mason named John Chapman, who shows every sign of having been influenced by Vanbrugh; he may indeed have been employed by him at Eastbury (*q.v.*). His north tower, small as it is, is unforgettable: it is surmounted by a curious structure more like a pyramid than a spire, out of which peep pedimented lucarnes. The north range of the church – in reality a sort of transept – was added in 1755 and actually clasps the tower.

So far we have been talking about the tower of Horton church; this, however, is not to be confused with HORTON TOWER, a spectacular brick folly standing on a hill immediately south of the village. It is of six storeys and built on a hexagonal plan, with domed circular towers rising up for the first four floors and the unadorned hexagon continuing for the last two. It was originally surmounted by an ogival cupola with an open lantern, but this collapsed in a thunderstorm early in the present century. The windows are all pointed, with lancets in the corner towers. The builder was none other than that Humphry Sturt who transformed Crichel (*q.v.*); it has been suggested that the architect was Thomas Archer, whom we know to have been fascinated by triangles and the interplay between flat and curved planes; I cannot but feel, however, that Archer would have produced something more imaginative; the present building seems to me to be somewhat lacking in *brio*.

## Kingston

*24; 4 miles W of Swanage on B3069*

The undistinguished village owes its immense CHURCH OF ST JAMES to the public spirit – to which was added, perhaps, a touch of megalomania – of the 3rd Earl of Eldon, who commissioned it in 1873 from G.E. Street at a cost of £70,000. Street did him proud – with the grandest church he ever built in England. Its focus is the tall square crossing-tower, high enough not to need a spire, with its long triple-lancet bell openings on each side. From the crossing run off an apsed east end, two surprisingly stubby transepts, and a nave with low aisles ending in a big rose window at the west end and a low arcaded narthex with lean-to roof by which one enters.

*The church of St James, Kingston.*

The interior is Early English, unadulterated: lancets everywhere (arranged in pairs, but not two-light), arcades on clustered piers of Purbeck marble with stiff-leaf capitals, broad pointed arches with many mouldings and a suggestion of dog-tooth. The windows in the aisles and clerestory are similarly shafted in Purbeck, as are the wonderfully high crossing and chancel arches. In the crossing itself, additional columns rise from corbels to create an impression of great richness; this is still further enhanced by the rib vaulting, which extends also to transepts and chancel. In the nave, the roof is of timber, with ornamental wind-braces.

The church is built of grey limestone, but the ubiquitous red lichen has warmed this to a rich pink. It looks particularly marvellous when it is bathed in the light of the setting sun.

## Kingston Lacy

*NT; 25; 2 miles NW of Wimborne off B3082*

Since the tragic destruction of Coleshill in 1952, only two buildings remain by that most archetypal of mid-seventeenth-century architects, Sir Roger Pratt. One of them is his own house at Ryston, Norfolk (*q.v.*), and the other, built between 1663 and 1665, is Kingston Lacy. Both, alas, have been much altered: Ryston by Soane, Kingston Lacy by Sir Charles Barry. But whereas the exterior of the former is now virtually unrecognisable from Pratt's original designs, the latter is still – from the outside at any rate – essentially a Pratt house. What we see from the architect's surviving drawing of the northern elevation is a nine-bay house of two storeys on a high basement, having a projecting three-bay centre with its own quoins and triangular pediment with coat of arms, above which is a hipped roof with dormers rising to a central balustraded flat with two chimney-stacks and a central cupola.

Barry, working between 1835 and 1846, faced the original brick with Caen ashlar, replacing Pratt's Chilmark stone dressings with new ones of Portland, and lowered the land in front so that the basement became a proper ground floor. To the seven-bay east front he gave a rusticated loggia in the Italian style, and towards the garden added false quoins to emphasise the three-bay centre, topping it with a similarly Italianate balustraded triple dormer. His finishing touch was to put tall square chimneys at the four corners.

These modifications sound fairly disastrous, and so, in a way, they were. And yet, in spite of all, Kingston Lacy remains an English seventeenth-century house rather than an Italian nineteenth-century one; and its setting in a glorious park (populated by a charming breed of red long-haired cattle) adds still further to its Englishness.

The ground floor is nearly all Barry's work. A stone vestibule leads to a stairwell, up which there rises a staircase of Carrara marble which manages a quite astonishing degree of grandeur considering the exiguity of the space available. At the half landing, in three shell niches, are life-size statues by Baron Marochetti of Charles I, Sir John Bankes – father of the original builder of the house – and Lady Bankes who, in 1643, successfully held out in Corfe Castle (*q.v.*) against a six-week siege by the Parliamentarians. On the first floor, the staircase ends with a triple-arched screen with saucer domes behind. There is a fine stucco ceiling in Barry's best seventeenth-century style.

The state rooms on this floor are, by any standards, magnificent – above all the Saloon in the centre of the north front, which takes up two full storeys and has a barrel-vaulted ceiling, painted with grotesques in the Adam style. They have, however, all been designed to show off to full advantage one of the best private picture collections in the country.

Kingston Lacy was bequeathed to the National Trust, together with the Corfe Castle estate, under the will of Mr H.J.R. Bankes in 1982. At the time of writing it is being restored, and should be open to the public in the summer of 1985.

## Lulworth

*26; 5 miles SW of Wareham on B3070*

When the exiled King Charles X of France was lent LULWORTH CASTLE for six months on his first arrival in England, he is said to have exclaimed as he caught his first sight of it: '*Voilà la Bastille!*' One can see his point: in a distant prospect, Lulworth looks everything a castle should be – a four-square, embattled cube with massive cylindrical corner towers. It is only when you approach closer that you notice that the windows are too large, too numerous and too symmetrical, and that the entire building is now nothing but a hollow shell, open to the sky. The former phenomenon is explained by the fact that the house was never really a castle at all but a vast Jacobean folly built around 1608 by Thomas Howard, 3rd Viscount Bindon; the latter by the fire that gutted it in 1929. Now, overgrown by creepers and with green trees pushing through the windows, it looks more romantic than ever before.

The castle – for so we must continue to call it – has three principal floors, with a fourth on the corner towers, and stands on a high basement to which, in the eighteenth century, a balustraded terrace was added. The windows are immensely tall, round-headed, and of two lights, divided by a slender mullion. A string-course runs along the top of each head, going all round the building except of course in the tops of the towers, which are similarly encircled. Three identical fronts (except that the west doorway has been given a Gibbs surround) are in coursed rubble, but the east, entrance, front is distinguished by a facing of Purbeck ashlar. Here the main doorway was embellished around 1700 with a curious arrangement not unlike a triumphal arch, with statues in shell niches to either side, each of them flanked by Ionic columns supporting an entablature on which stand life-size representations of Roman Emperors. Between them is a sort of rose window, consisting of six circular lights surrounding a seventh; but this can hardly be earlier than the nineteenth century.

In the grounds, only 100 yards or so away, stands the Roman Catholic CHURCH OF ST MARY, built in 1786–7 by John Tasker, a little-known but quite excellent Catholic architect who had been responsible for the Adam-style

*Mapperton Manor.*

interiors of the castle which perished in the fire. George III is said to have given permission for its building only on condition that it should not look like a church; and indeed it looks much more like an outsize garden temple. The basic plan is a quatrefoil, but the apsed east end has been slightly extended and squared off to provide for a sacristy and vestry. This gives the impression of being the main entrance – though it does not of course lead directly into the church. It has a Tuscan porch surmounted by an urn and set in a shallow round-arched recess; to each side is a round-headed niche containing a big stone urn, stonily aflame. All the windows are good, square, sashed Georgian. The west door is much simpler – a Tuscan porch again, but set directly against the rounded wall of the apse. The interior is a delight, with apses on all four sides and galleries on Tuscan columns to north, south and west. The dome is painted like the sky, with scudding clouds around a high lantern.

## Mapperton*

*27; 2 miles SE of Beaminster off B3163*

Dorset is quite amazingly rich in sixteenth- and seventeenth-century manor houses; few of them, however, are as lovely – or as unspoilt – as Mapperton. The approach suits the house perfectly: you drive straight up a long, tree-lined avenue, then pass between two tall gate piers. Only then is the enchanting little group of buildings revealed – on the left, the gates to the house itself, surmounted by two stone eagles on the point of taking flight and leading into a grassy court, enclosed by the house on two sides and the church on the third. Meanwhile to your right the lines of the two side ranges are continued by two twin stable blocks with big pedimented windows. The ensemble is perfect, both in the siting of the different blocks and in their relation to each other – as pretty a small architectural complex as you could ever hope to see.

The oldest part is the house's projecting north wing. It was built by one Robert Morgan in about 1550, and the front which faces the court remains unchanged. The style is identical with that of the contemporary parlour range at Athelhampton – three- or four-light windows with arched lights and hood-moulds, and a tall gabled dormer with barley-sugar shafts up the side. More of these shafts on the corners are heraldically topped with the gryphon of the Morgans. The north-facing back of this wing has been rather superficially Georgianised, but this – thank goodness – cannot be seen from the court.

The eastern range of the house, facing the gates, is fundamentally of the same date as the northern, but was remodelled some 100 years after it was first built. Of this time, clearly, are the mullion-and-transom cross windows, the projecting two-storey porch, the dormers and the stone balustrade running round the top. Within the porch is crudely cut the date 1661, which presumably refers to this remodelling, together with the initials R.B. for Richard Brodrepp, whose forebear acquired Mapperton in 1618. The Brodrepp coat of arms with its four swans is carved above the entrance; the four-centred inner door, on the other hand, still has the gryphons in the spandrels and must therefore be part of the original house. It must have been Brodrepp, too, who built the two stable ranges, the southern of which bears the date 1670.

Inside the house, the front entrance leads predictably into the screens passage, with the Hall immediately to the left. It is dominated by the immense Jacobean overmantel at its northern end, bearing the arms of James I in the centre of a broad strapwork frame on which are perched two sturdy *putti* with eagles on their upraised hands. This, together with the slightly more restrained one of similar date in the Morning Room, was brought early in the present century from Melplash Court nearby, which was then a dower house of Mapperton. Apart from the Hall itself, the most interesting rooms are all in the north wing. There are four of them altogether – two up and two down, divided by a central (and very pretty Georgian) staircase. The eastern pair both have very fine Tudor ceilings, especially the upper room, where the narrow moulded ribs sweep down into pendants. Here too is a fine Renaissance frieze, with heads in roundels supported by fish-tailed *putti*.

The gardens of Mapperton are as beautiful as the house. I cannot say more.

## Melbury Sampford

*28; 11 miles NW of Dorchester off A37*

Set on an eminence – a rare thing in itself for a sixteenth-century house – Melbury stands in a superb deer park overlooking the Blackmore Vale. It is not, in the final analysis, beautiful, for the original sixteenth-century work has been largely overlaid by modifications and additions of the seventeenth, eighteenth and nineteenth centuries; it is, however, unfailingly interesting and fascinatingly enigmatic; and it possesses one feature of considerable architectural importance.

Building seems to have started soon after 1500 with a single square block around a central courtyard, with gables at the corners of the north and south fronts. The builder was Sir Giles Strangeways, of whom we find John Leland writing round about 1540: 'Mr Strangeguayse hath now a late much buildid at Mulbyri quadrato, avauncing the inner part of the house with a loftie and fresch tower.' That tower still stands, providing a focal point for the huge and rambling house, on the west range of the original square; a short, stubby wing projects, however, still further to the west, so that architecturally it becomes a sort of crossing-tower. The only things that prevent it from looking frankly ecclesiastical are, first, its hexagonal shape – though it in fact rises on squinches from a square base – and second, the six-light transomed windows that occupy the entire breadth of five of its six sides, giving light to a small room with marvellous views over the surrounding countryside. (The sixth side contains a small fireplace and has a still taller staircase-tower attached.) These generous windows suggest that the room must have been intended from the first as a sort of belvedere – in which case it must be one of the earliest ever erected in England.

*Melbury Sampford.*

The first major changes to Sir Giles's work occurred during the 1690s, the architect being most unusually commemorated in a portrait which still hangs in the house, inscribed 'Mr Watson, architect to Thomas Strangways Senr Esq who enlarged & adorned the house 1692'. Howard Colvin suggests that this may be the John Watson who is known to have worked on alterations at Wroxton Abbey, Oxfordshire, some ten years before. He was not, it must be admitted, very good. On the north and south fronts, where he provided five bays separated by two tiers of superimposed pilasters surmounted with a segmental pediment and a balustrade with dormers above, the results were moderately successful; but with his completely new entrance front Mr Watson met his Waterloo. Of the eleven bays with which he had to deal, he separated the three end ones on each side with quoins, making a five-bay centre; his double row of half columns (used in the same way as the pilasters on the north and south fronts) extends however only across the central three bays, and his ungainly triangular pediment does not quite cover even these. (Being also slightly too steep, it somehow gives the impression that its two sides have been pushed towards each other.) The result is that one is left in some doubt as to where the centre begins and ends – an oddly unsettling experience.

It seems hard to believe that anyone could have found Melbury too small; such, however, were the sentiments of the 5th Earl of Ilchester, who in 1872 commissioned a two-storey Hall – to be used as a Library – from Anthony Salvin. This battlemented block of two canted bays, its double-transomed windows filling all the available space, was added to the west, to be followed twelve years later by a whole new west range beyond it, ending in a massive south tower with oriels on three storeys. The architect for this last campaign – Salvin having died in 1881 – was George Devey, and a very fine job he did.

The interior of the house contains many rooms of considerable splendour, but relatively little of the sixteenth and seventeenth centuries. There are, however, two fine staircases, confusingly close to each other, one of them – a magnificent William and Mary construction presumably inserted at the time of Mr Watson's remodelling – in a hall painted by Lanscroon in 1701 in a style described by Pevsner as puddingy.

## Milton Abbas

*29; 6 miles SW of Blandford off A354*

The old Benedictine abbey and Sir William Chambers's great house stand cheek by jowl in a beautiful natural amphitheatre of wooded hills, while the Georgian model village remains discreetly tucked away three-quarters of a mile or so to the south-east, looking down on to Capability Brown's artificial lake. The overall effect is spectacular, only slightly marred by the immense bricked-up arch on the abbey's west front – where the nave should have been – and the absence of any real architectural relationship between the two main buildings.

The ABBEY was founded in 932 by King Athelstan as a College of Canons, and converted into a monastery some decades later by his nephew Edgar. The great twelfth-century abbey church was burnt to the ground in 1309; rebuilding, however, must have started almost at once, since apart from the north transept and the crossing-tower virtually everything we see today is Decorated, and early Decorated at that – 1330, say, at the latest. It consists of a seven-bay choir, a crossing and two transepts, and is alas truncated not only to the west – where the nave was never built – but also to the east, where there was once a long Lady Chapel, two smaller chapels on each side of it, and an ambulatory or retrochoir. The loss of these accounts for the most unsatisfactory east end, where a disproportionately squat seven-light east window surmounts a five-bay blank arcade, along which the springing of what was formerly a rib vault can still be seen.

The north and south sides of the choir are a good deal better, with a regular system of three-light windows in both aisles and clerestory and rows of traceried flying buttresses, each with two heavily crocketed pinnacles. Then come the transepts, that to the south a full bay longer than its fellow and finished off by a superb south window of seven lights with reticulated tracery. The stubby north transept caps this – I am sure deliberately – with an eight-lighter, but the Perpendicular tracery is nowhere near as effective.

This north transept is the work of Abbot Middleton, who ruled the abbey from 1481 to 1525; he was also responsible for the lierne vaulting in both transepts and for the crossing-tower. The later is a noble piece (though one might perhaps have wished it just a little higher) with twin bell openings, each of two lights, on all four sides and a parapet of pierced quatrefoils. Pinnacles rise at the centre of each side as well as the corners. And so to the sad west front. Apart from the tower, the best part is the fenestration of the south transept, where there are more traceried windows of great delicacy. But the unequal length of the transepts means a lack of symmetry which is the more disturbing for being relatively slight, and that vast blocked arch is, to me at any rate, a genuine eyesore – and not helped by Gilbert Scott's ridiculous little west porch. Close inspection reveals more springers of a nave vault and the beginnings of both aisles and clerestory, both Perpendicular. Then everything suddenly stopped, probably with Middleton's death in 1525 – and the Dissolution saw to it that the work was never resumed.

Inside as out, one is struck by the continuing contrast between the grey of the Portland stone and the orange of the Ham Hill. There is flint, too. The huge windows flood the building with light, but wherever one looks one feels the restorer's hand, first of James Wyatt in 1789 and then again of Scott in 1865. In the absence of a nave one enters directly at the crossing, supported on four piers of clustered shafts and sumptuously fan-vaulted. The east end is largely blocked by an enormous stone reredos – three rows of canopied stone niches, all empty of statues and equally devoid of any imagination or fantasy. Wyatt restored it, carefully eradicating all traces of the damage wrought by Cromwell's soldiers; it might, one feels, have been more interesting if he had left it alone. There is no upper cresting, just a sudden harsh horizontal which

*The Benedictine abbey, Milton Abbas.*

appears to cut cruelly into the east window – although, as we saw from the outside, this anyway stops too soon. Of the remaining furniture, little – apart from the tall wooden pyx cover – survives from the Middle Ages; there are, however, a few good monuments, especially that in the north transept which was erected to Lady Milton in 1775 by her husband, later to become the Earl of Dorchester, the builder of the house. The design is by Robert Adam, the carving by Agostino Carlini. In the great south transept window, the Hardman glass was designed by Pugin.

Now for the house itself. Since 1954 it has been MILTON ABBEY SCHOOL. One's first reaction is to ask why it should have been built so uncomfortably close to the abbey church; but the answer is soon revealed. Lord Dorchester was determined that the only surviving piece of the monastic buildings, Abbot Middleton's Great Hall, should be incorporated in his house, forming an integral part of it. Chambers accordingly designed the mansion round a big square court, with the Abbot's Hall occupying the centre of its southern side. The front entrance, leading into the old screens passage, is inside the court. With its two-storeyed porch, carved with shields bearing the arms of England, the abbey and its founder, and with the monogram and rebus of Abbot Middleton in the spandrels of the arch, it is impressive enough; but it gives no indication of the magnificence of the Hall itself. Even Abbot Chard's Great Hall at Forde, for all its exterior splendour, cannot match its contemporary here. Its grandeur is focused, above all, on its quite breathtaking timber roof, a veritable forest of virtuoso woodwork. The date, which appears on a string-course of the west wall and again on the screen, is 1498. The design is basically hammer-beam, but with unusually short hammers, the principal ones resting on long stone wall shafts which end at the bottom with shield-bearing angels. The intermediate ones, set a little higher up on the wall plate, are carved with grotesque figures playing musical instruments; the arched braces which spring from them have pendants shortly before their apex, while those rising from the principals support collar-beams with panelled tracery in the space above them. Against the rafters on each side are four rows of heavily cusped wind-braces. It is, all in all, as complicated a design as could possibly be imagined, and there is not an inch visible anywhere that is not carved or moulded; yet the ensemble radiates a calm assurance that compels not only admiration but astonishment.

The Hall's carved wooden screen, making a perfect foil to the roof, is also memorable, again richly moulded and panelled. Its two arches are the slenderest of ogees, many-cusped and many-pinnacled, giving it a light, soaring quality as against the massiveness above. Pevsner is unconvinced by it, and suspects eighteenth-century tamperings; but it looks all right to me.

I wish I could say the same of the rest of the house. Chambers, try as he might, was never at home in Gothic. (How much more convincingly Wyatt would have done it!) It is simply not enough to give a pointed arch to some of the windows, to run a row of quatrefoil windows along the attic storey and pierced parapets – instead of balustrades – along the roof line. Chambers's classicism shows through everywhere: above all in the rigid symmetry of his composition. A seven-bay, three-storey centre, attached by two-bay, two-storey links to three-bay, three-storey corner pavilions – the analysis of the south front sounds more Palladian than Gothic. On his entrance front, to the north, there is a Tudorish Gatehouse only one degree more convincing, with a three-sided bay to left and right.

Inside the courtyard the Gothic is more tentative still, and the moment he enters the house Chambers – to his evident relief – gives it up altogether. The ground-floor state rooms along the west front are all his, two of them having ceilings inspired by Wood's *Palmyra*. When this suite was completed, however, Chambers resigned; his place was taken by James Wyatt, who was responsible for all the principal rooms on the first floor. But there is no Gothic here either; Wyatt stuck firmly to his Adam style, as usual to admirable effect – especially in the barrel-vaulted Saloon which forms the centre of the west front, where walls and ceiling are rich in delicate plasterwork.

Leaving the house we turn immediately east – where, high on the hill above the abbey church, up a flight of some 200 steps, stands the little CHAPEL OF ST CATHERINE. In medieval days it was a favourite shrine for pilgrims, particularly unmarried ladies, who would pray (as at Abbotsbury, *q.v.*):

*St Catherine, St Catherine,*
*O lend me thine aid,*
*And grant that I never*
*May die an old maid.*

Even if their prayer was not granted, the pilgrimage alone earned them – according to an inscription of *c.*1200 on the south doorway – 120 days' indulgence. This chapel is the oldest part of the entire abbey complex. It is Norman, flint-built, consisting only of a tiny nave and chancel. The chancel arch that divides them has triple responds with scallop capitals, and to the west a hood-mould with beak-heads.

Finally, the MODEL VILLAGE. This was begun only *c.*1780 at Lord Dorchester's expense – an act not, however, as philanthropic as might at first appear, since he had already for the past ten years been systematically demolishing the little market town of Milton Abbas which had grown up around the abbey. Of this, by 1790 not one stone was left on another, its admittedly meagre population being resettled at the new location, safely out of sight of the mansion. There is, so far as I know, no record of any serious protests – it was not after all either the first time or the last that communities had been similarly swept away on the whim of local landowners – and the model village is, it must be admitted, almost absurdly pretty – a long main street winding up the hill, with thatched cottages evenly spaced along it but distanced from it by broad grass verges. Halfway up on the right is Wyatt's CHURCH, looking just as it should from the outside, but alas ruined within after a misguided remodelling (and enlargement) by W.J. Fletcher in 1888–9. Opposite is a charming row of ALMSHOUSES, originally built in 1674 in the old town and re-erected here in 1779 – an act of unusual sensitivity in Georgian times. There is some doubt as to how much of the village was designed by Chambers, and how much by Capability Brown, to whom Lord Dorchester is known to have paid £105 for plans in 1773. Brown's, almost certainly, was the general scheme, siting and layout – including the beautiful artificial lake below the village. Chambers probably designed the cottages themselves; but since he left Milton some six years before work on the village actually began, there may well have been alterations in the interim.

## Moreton*

*30; 8 miles SE of Dorchester off B3390*

ST NICHOLAS'S CHURCH is a joy – as pretty an example of Georgian Gothick as you could ever hope to see. It was built, on the site of its medieval predecessor, by James Frampton, the local squire, in 1776. Its two principal features are the tower and the apse. The tower, halfway along the south side, has on that side a big three-light bell opening and above it a roundel with scalloped surround. The tracery of the bell opening is identical with that of the windows of the side chapels flanking the south door and of the five windows of the apse: all of three lights, the tracery cusped and intersecting to form a design of trefoils and quatrefoils. The whole thing is wonderfully airy and light-hearted; and the miracle is that this quality was preserved when the church was enlarged – with a north aisle and a west porch – in the 1840s. A century later, on 8 October 1940, the north wall was blown in by a German bomb, all the glass destroyed and the interior decoration of the whole building practically obliterated; the restoration was, however, exemplary, and is now almost undetectable.

The bomb disaster had, moreover, one extremely fortunate result; it enabled the windows to be filled with glass which is not coloured but *engraved* – by the most brilliant of living glass engravers, Laurence Whistler. There is no space here to describe them in detail, but no one who is familiar with his work will need me to say just how exquisite these windows are. They have a lightness and delicacy which accord quite perfectly with the rest of the church, and are worth driving a long way to see.

T.E. Lawrence – of Arabia – is buried in the cemetery across the road, his headstone lettered by his friend Eric Kennington.

## Purse Caundle

*31; 4½ miles E of Sherborne off A30*

Edward IV was on the throne of England when the MANOR HOUSE was built, in 1470 or thereabouts, and though it has been added to once or twice there have been scarcely any major changes since Jacobean times. The original nucleus seems to have been L-shaped, consisting of a Hall range running north and south, from the southern end of which, beyond the screens passage, an east–west range projected eastward to the present road, ending with the charming little canted oriel – four narrow lights surmounting a frieze of shields and a stocky buttress – under a tall gable. To this in the mid-sixteenth century there was added, in the angle of the L, a new block about 30 feet long, masking the Hall from the east but providing it with a large and commodious corner bay similar to that at Bingham's Melcombe, 10 miles or so away. This block was probably given its two-gabled ashlared front in James I's reign – a period when the Dorset masons seem to have been perversely fond of sticking tall square chimneys on top of gables, even when there were windows almost immediately below.

The fact that there are no fewer than three of these chimneys on the E-shaped south front suggests that all three of the projections on which they appear must also belong to this period, together with the whole range to the west of the centre projection – that to the east being of course (apart from its own projection) part of the original building. The right-hand end, indeed, contains the Great Chamber – after the Hall itself the grandest room in the house. This is something of an anomaly: in most houses of the date, the Great Chamber (or solar) was placed above the dais end of the Hall and not at the service end with all the noise – and smells – that went with it. Why this arrangement should have been decided upon at Purse Caundle remains a mystery.

The main entry into the house is by the left-hand doorway in the east front, which leads via a small vestibule into the screens passage. (This doorway has clearly been reset; why?) There on our left are the two doorways which originally gave access to the buttery and pantry; on our right, the Hall. It has kept its fifteenth-century timber roof with tie-beams, crown-posts flanked by curving queenposts and supporting collar-beams above, and two rows of wind-braces along the sides. A pretty – though restored – decorative wall plate of quatrefoils runs below the wind-braces. Above the collars the principal rafters disappear, somewhat disconcertingly, into the plaster. At the far end of the Hall is, as we have seen, the slightly later bay; adjoining it to the south is another curious little room of the same date, which formerly contained a well and newel-stair; these, however, were removed in 1873 owing to a troublesome fairy who frightened the occupants every evening when they went to bed. Opposite the Hall bay an original doorway with a four-centred arch leads into the north-west wing, where a late seventeenth-century oak staircase rises to two bedrooms above, in one of which the original moulded timbers of the ceiling are exposed. North of the Hall is a delightful panelled Parlour, Jacobean but not aggressively so.

Of the south wing there is little to be said, since it contains only two rooms of importance. The Great Chamber on the first floor is memorable for its strikingly deep barrel vault, divided into square panels by moulded beams. It is lit at the far end by the oriel window mentioned above, while a small door immediately to the right opens into a little bedroom with a plain barrel ceiling which may formerly have been used as an oratory. It has a two-light window in the east wall, rebated on the inside to allow for shutters.

The importunate fairy is not the only evidence of the supernatural at Purse Caundle. The *Shell Guide to Dorset* reports that many people have heard the mysterious chanting of plainsong, and at midsummer the sounds of a hunt in full cry. Haunted or not, it remains full of atmosphere: a house in which time, if it has not actually stopped, at least has very little meaning.

## Sandford Orcas*

*32; 3 miles N of Sherborne off B3148*

A village of immense charm, Sandford Orcas is set in a narrow fold in the hills on the borders of Somerset – to which it belonged before a boundary change in 1896. The MANOR HOUSE is one of the loveliest and most unspoilt in either county, built probably in the 1530s of golden Ham Hill stone with a marvellous patina of

*Sandford Orcas Manor.*

lichen. It stands at the far end of the village, up against the church, yet somehow contrives to remain at the same time curiously hidden, facing as it does away from the street and towards the country beyond.

You approach the manor through its Gatehouse, which is attached rather unusually to its north side – the principal entrance front being to the east. This is a most impressive piece in its own right, and provides a splendid introduction to what is to come. The main carriage arch is broad, four-centred and extremely tall, flanked by buttresses of similar height with foliage on their capitals and surmounted by a big lozenge-shaped empty frame of stone, with bunches of leaves at the four corners. This is exactly the same motif as one sees on the parlour wing at Athelhampton, and makes it almost certain that it was built by the same hand. The topmost of these leafy bosses actually breaks the line of the three-light window frame of an upper room – now a bedroom – beyond which a tiny projection may have been originally intended as a garderobe but was probably used as a chapel by the house's recusant occupants. It has a charming little four-light window, its mouchette tracery forming a Catherine wheel.

Once through the Gatehouse, a right turn brings you to the east front. It is early enough to have made no attempt at symmetry: the two-storey gabled porch is not in the centre, and its window is not even at the same level as the corresponding window in the gabled bay to the right of it. Even the symmetry of the two principal gables is more apparent than real, since the left-hand one is an addition of 1873. But none of this matters, nor detracts in any way from the beauty of the ensemble. The Hall, which was always of a single storey, goes off to the left from the screens passage, and possesses, as well as a fine Jacobean screen, two magnificent canted bays to each side of the south-eastern angle, so close as to be almost continuous, and numbering eighteen lights altogether. The same system is continued in the Great Chamber immediately above. The grandeur of this room is in marked contrast to the modesty of the south-facing solar beyond the newel-staircase – a small, low room built over a basement that was probably intended as a cellar.

In the centre of the porch, above the four-centred doorway, is another lozenge panel identical with that of the Gatehouse except that it contains a shield with heraldry: the arms of the Knoyles impaling those of the Frys. (Oddly enough, no record of such a marriage has ever been traced.) To each side of the porch there rises an octagonal angle shaft, whose tops have a curious scroll motif, once again reminiscent of Athelhampton.

The interior perfectly maintains its character and atmosphere; most of the furnishings – including a lot of good Jacobean panelling – are, however, relatively recent imports, so have little to tell us about the house's history. The most spectacular item is a highly exuberant overmantel featuring the arms of James I, brought from Joiners' Hall, Salisbury. But Sandford Orcas does not go in for spectacle – it has no need to.

## Sherborne*

*33; 19 miles N of Dorchester on A30*

The focal point of this beautiful little country town is the ABBEY. There are many instances in England of early medieval abbeys subsequently becoming cathedrals; Sherborne, however, contrary to the general rule, began as a cathedral – of the see of Wessex, in AD 705 – and only went monastic in 998. So it remained until the Dissolution, for the best part of the next four centuries providing in its nave (as abbeys so frequently did) a parish church for the local townspeople; but such arrangements were never popular with monks – who tended to resent secular invasions – and some time in the later fourteenth century a new parish church was built immediately to the west of the abbey. If next to nothing of this now remains, it is because when the abbey was dissolved in 1539 its church was bought by the town and ALL HALLOWS, prematurely redundant, was demolished. The only traces of it still remaining are the lower half of the north wall and, attached to the abbey west wall, the responds of the aisle arcades and side chapels.

The abbey church itself rests on Saxon foundations; Saxon, too, is the rubble-built west wall, up to clerestory level, where the rubble gives place to the more general Ham Hill stone. In Saxon days this was in fact an interior wall, abutting a massive 'westwork' which consisted of a central west tower and west transepts projecting beyond the north and south walls on either side. A few vestiges of this still survive, notably the plinth of the north transept beyond the boundary wall at the corner of the School Library; but the demolition must have taken place before the building of All Hallows, and it was only after this too was pulled down that the present west front assumed the shape that we see today. Oddly enough, however, it tells the architectural story of the building better than anywhere else, incorporating as it does material from all three periods of its history: the Saxon cathedral, the Norman abbey, and the Perpendicular parish church. The indications of the two latter periods scarcely need pointing out; neither, however, is completely unaltered. The low Norman doorway to the right of the central one in fact has a narrower, Perpendicular one within it – an additional restriction on freedom of movement between the abbey and All Hallows which so infuriated the parishioners in 1437 that they actually set fire to the abbey church – permanently discolouring the walls of the choir. The door was blocked up completely in the eighteenth century. Of the big nine-light west window, only the upper part is original; the two lower tiers of lights were added in 1847 by R.C. Carpenter – who, incidentally, discovered in the process a two-tier Saxon arcade, formerly an opening from the Saxon west tower into the nave. The present main entrance to the church, below the west window, is almost certainly the re-used west doorway of All Hallows.

Turning to the south front, we begin with the two-storey south-west porch. This too is Carpenter's work. On the ground floor he was content to make a faithful copy of the Norman original of *c.*1170 with its rib vault and plethora of zigzag; on the upper floor, somewhat less successfully, he replaced an innocent if inappropriate fifteenth-century structure with a Norman pastiche. The rest of the front is all Perpendicular, although the walls of the south transept are Norman and there is a blocked Norman window high on its east wall. For the rest, one notices that the clerestory windows, of five lights, are considerably larger than those of the aisle, which have only three. The two small chapels flanking the transept are of the same style and date as the aisles themselves, and have the same continuous quatrefoil frieze above them. The south window of the transept is a big eight-lighter, its two principal mullions rising up to the main arch – a characteristic of all the clerestory windows, including the west one. Behind the transept rises the crossing-tower, each of its four sides having a pair of two-light windows, transomed and traceried, divided by a slender buttress; there is a similar buttress at each end, so that they are doubled at the corners. The pinnacles that crown them, however, are Carpenter's again, copied from Milton (*q.v.*).

Beyond the transept comes the choir. It is slightly longer than the nave, and its importance is further stressed with pinnacles and flying buttresses. The windows are larger, too – those of the chancel aisle having four lights, those of the clerestory six. Then, at the east end, comes a surprise – and not an altogether happy one. Although the basic structure remains Perpendicular, the south-east chapel (of St Mary-le-Bow) and all that lies behind it – the west half of the Lady Chapel and the vestry beyond – were in the sixteenth century the house of the headmaster of Sherborne School. What we see from the south is thus a rather grandiose, utterly secular-looking bay with two tiers of four-light, straight-headed mullion windows separated by heraldic shields and topped by the arms of Edward VI between barley-sugar colonnettes. (Work, however, obviously continued after the King's death in 1553, since the date 1560 is recorded round the corner to the east.)

The Tudor style is continued on the east bay of the Lady Chapel, but here we are once again in the world of pastiche: it was built as recently as 1921, as a war memorial, by W.D. Caröe. And so finally we come to the north front – or, more probably, we don't, since it can be seen only from the court of the School. It is anyway, in most of its essentials, a mere repetition of the south. The only exceptions are the Chapel of Bishop Roger, east of the transept, whose east window of three stepped lancets gives us the one touch of Early English to be seen on the exterior, and the windows of the north aisle, which are Victorian Decorated.

We enter by the south-west porch – and there is the Sherborne nave in all its glory. The Perpendicular piers of all five bays are ornamented with tall, narrow panels, cusped at the top, curving inward where the line of the arch requires them to do so. Immediately above them runs a string-course, with stone angels set regularly along its length; then come those huge clerestory windows, and finally the glorious fan-vaulted roof – which extends, with various changes in design, through most of the building. In the nave, the fans do not touch at the central ridge as they do, for example, at King's

College Chapel in Cambridge; they leave a space down the middle, which is filled by an intricate system of liernes. Such, nonetheless, is the impact of the ensemble that one hardly notices the curious fact that the whole nave is very slightly irregular: the piers on the north side stand over a foot to the west of their opposite numbers to the south, and the arches are all of subtly different widths. The probable explanation is that Abbot Ramsam, who was responsible for the fifteenth-century rebuilding of the nave, could not afford to start completely from scratch and was accordingly obliged to retain the original Saxon piers, which he simply encased in Perpendicular panelling. (This would also account for the retention of the Saxon west wall.) He did, however, rebuild his new clerestory on an absolutely regular plan, regardless of the fact that the two storeys of each bay would not precisely correspond.

The nave ends towards the east with the great Norman crossing arch – which shows signs of a subsequent settlement of the foundations – above which we can still see the outline of an old doorway from the lantern walk, now blocked up. Behind the arch the crossing itself seems predominantly Norman, though the piers with their extraordinary cross-sections are almost certainly of Saxon origin. The east tower arch, towards the choir, was removed when the choir was rebuilt in the first half of the fifteenth century and reset above the new fan vaulting, which was then extended westward over the crossing – as had been done a little earlier at Gloucester; thus the crossing, for all its Norman elements, now seems to be incorporated in the choir.

The fan vaulting is continued in the north transept, which is however in most other respects Norman – see the arch to the aisle on its western side and the single shaft and capital still exposed on the wall opposite. The Wykeham Chapel immediately to the east is Norman too, despite the fan vault and fifteenth-century window; it contains a marvellous tomb, commemorating Sir John Horsey and his son who died within four years of each other in the 1560s. Looking west down the lierne-vaulted aisle, you can see at the end the principal Saxon feature still surviving inside the church: a tall, narrow doorway with a high semi-circular arch, which once led into the now-vanished transept of the westwork.

The south transept also has a Norman arch to the aisle. It is not, however, fan-vaulted, having instead a seventeenth-century timber roof with bosses, possibly the gift of the 3rd Earl of Bristol, whose splendidly Augustan tomb by John Nost stands against the west wall. It is flanked by two side chapels, that of the Holy Sepulchre to the east and that of St Katherine to the west. The former has a nice fifteenth-century wood carving of St James, but little else; the latter another marvellous tomb in which John and Joan Leweston lie beneath a high classical canopy with fantastic cresting. It is thought to be by Allen Maynard, who was responsible for much of the decoration at Longleat. This chapel was used as a family pew by Sir Walter and Lady Raleigh when they lived at Sherborne, but they did not have the benefit of the glass in the glorious south window, which was designed by Pugin and inserted in 1851.

*Sherborne Abbey.*

And so we come to the choir itself. Again, the eye turns automatically upward to the fan vault, which is similar to that of the nave but further enriched with heraldic painting in the panels. (It can be seen to best advantage by dropping a coin in the box against the south-east crossing pier, thereby switching on the floodlighting; would that more churches and cathedrals would follow the example.) The many-shafted piers run uninterruptedly up from the floor, parting only at the springing of the clerestory arches, where the central shafts burst out into the vault while those to the side – which enclose a narrow splay of painted panels – go on to form a continuous frame around the windows themselves. A single row of similar painted panels, broader now and with trefoiled cusping, runs between the top of the arcade and the bottom of the windows, and yet more of the same frame the Victorian reredos (by Carpenter again). The stalls, with their slender wooden canopies, are also Victorian, but have fine fifteenth-century elbow-rests and misericords.

The north choir aisle gives access to Bishop Roger's Chapel, with the Early English window mentioned above. Equally interesting is the two-tiered Norman arcading on the south wall, which originally extended all round the choir aisles and quite possibly the transepts as well. The vaulting of this aisle and its southern counterpart is continued round the ambulatory behind the high altar, with pendants to carry it across the opening to the Lady Chapel. Here, at last, we come to the only other thirteenth-century part of the church. Entrance is through a most elegant archway with detached shafts carrying capitals in stiff-leaf in three orders. The chapel was originally three bays long, but the two eastern ones were destroyed at the time of the Dissolution; the third bay was added, as we have seen, by Caröe in 1921. It contains an exquisite reredos in engraved glass by Laurence Whistler. The Chapel of St Mary-le-Bow to the south was also of three bays, its present east wall having been added in 1560 to form the Headmaster's House. This domestic transformation also accounts for the fireplace – but not, of course, for the fan vaulting, which was there already.

The monastic buildings are all now part of SHERBORNE SCHOOL. Of the cloister, which was built in the late fourteenth century against the north aisle, the wall shafts of the south and west ranges (the latter against the Library) can still be identified, together with the springing of the vaults. In the south-west corner are the few remaining traces of the westwork of the Saxon cathedral. The south cloister range was two-storeyed, the upper floor containing the former Guesten Hall with a fine timber roof, firmly wind-braced. Long derelict, it was restored by Carpenter in the 1850s. The old Abbot's Hall now forms part of the School Chapel. It stands on a Norman undercroft and has another fifteenth-century roof with wind-braces, but virtually all else is Victorian. The Abbot's Lodging to the north-east is, by contrast, nearly all of the fifteenth century. Its huge chimney has the signs of the Evangelists, still just recognisable, carved on its north face.

The rest of the School is principally the work of Carpenter and his partner Slater, and more recently – during the first quarter of the present century – of Sir Reginald Blomfield. There remains only one historic building that should be mentioned – the DINING HALL OF SCHOOL HOUSE, built in Jacobean days as the Schoolroom. It too carries the arms of Edward VI, who refounded it in 1550 – the original school went back to the eighth century and boasted King Alfred as an Old Boy – but is much restored.

Across the street from the abbey to the south-west stands the ALMSHOUSE OF ST JOHN THE BAPTIST AND ST JOHN THE EVANGELIST which, apart from a big extension to the north by Slater, still looks much as it did on its completion in 1448. The original range is that to the south: a long, two-storeyed Hall with a lower, single-bay Chapel at its eastern end. The refectory at the western end is recognisable from the outside only by its larger windows of two and four lights respectively, the other windows on both floors having only one. All these windows have deep hood-moulds, those on the ground floor being continuous and thus giving a crenellated effect. There are four tall octagonal chimneystacks at the roof's edge. The door, at the east end just before the chapel, is flanked by ogee-headed niches; the chapel itself has big three-light windows to south and east, with normal Perpendicular tracery. In former times the ground floor was used as a dormitory for twelve poor men, while four poor women slept upstairs; since Slater's enlargement, however – a most successful operation by which the building gained an arcaded cloister and a further block to the north with an elaborate oriel – the occupants nowadays all have rooms of their own. The Chapel contains a superb late fifteenth-century Flemish triptych which should not be missed.

Sherborne possesses two castles. The first, now in ruins and known as the OLD CASTLE, was built by Bishop Roger of Salisbury between 1107 and 1135. In 1592 it seems still to have been in moderately good condition – good enough at least to take the fancy of Sir Walter Raleigh, who leased it in that year from Queen Elizabeth and began trying to convert it into a modern house. He soon gave up the attempt, however, deciding instead to build himself a brand-new mansion some quarter of a mile to the south; half a century later the castle, having been a Royalist stronghold, was incapacitated and largely gutted by the Parliamentarians under Fairfax. It is now only a shell, looked after by the Dept of the Environment, worth visiting above all for the great four-storey Gatehouse, sadly battered but still noble, and for its magnificent ashlared masonry: as Pevsner rightly emphasised, it is not so much a fortress as a very strongly defended palace.

The title of SHERBORNE CASTLE passed to Raleigh's mansion, and this building, in 1600, seems to have consisted only of the rectangular centre of what we see today. To this Sir Walter now added the four polygonal inner turrets, one at each corner. He placed his Hall to the south, where it occupied the western two-thirds of the front, the eastern third – together with the entire east front behind it, including the north-east and south-east turrets – being given over to the Parlour. The turrets, all identical, are of four storeys, the fronts between them of three, but rising to a fourth in the centre thanks to a huge shaped gable on each of the four sides. Between the north and south gables runs a high balustraded platform amid a forest of tall square chimneystacks. The turrets have similar chimneystacks, interspersed with heraldic beasts.

All too soon poor Raleigh fell from favour and, after a long imprisonment followed by his ill-fated Orinoco expedition, met his death on the scaffold in 1618. Already in the previous year Sherborne had been granted to Sir John Digby, the English Ambassador to Spain; and it was Digby who in about 1625 added the four long projections running north and south from Raleigh's corner turrets and ending in further polygonal turrets of their own. The effect was to form narrow – rather too narrow – courtyards to north and south, closed with elaborate stone gateways. Where Digby succeeded was with his proportions: by giving his new ranges only two storeys instead of three, and his new

*St Nicholas's Church, Studland.*

turrets only three storeys instead of four, he ensured that the central block should remain the focal point of the building. He was, moreover, scrupulously careful to continue in Raleigh's style, to the point where it would be almost impossible, from architectural evidence alone, to tell that the house was of different dates.

Although much of the interior was redone in the middle of the last century by Philip Hardwick, Sherborne Castle can still boast several memorable rooms. One of the most attractive is the Library, in Strawberry Hill Gothick of *c*.1760, with bookshelves that rise to ogee heads in a faintly Indian fashion. Busts in circular niches fill the spandrels. This occupies the south-east wing; in the north-east, beyond the totally Victorian Solarium (Raleigh's Parlour) with its monumental pseudo-Jacobean chimneypiece, is the Red Drawing Room. This has retained its original plaster ceiling – a glorious affair with roses, fleurs-de-lis, griffins and all the fun of the heraldic fair including a wonderfully tentative ostrich, the Digby emblem. Upstairs, the Green Drawing Room has no fewer than three magnificent chimneypieces, the largest having in its overmantel a simply gigantic strapwork coat of arms. Finally, in the north-west wing is the panelled Oak Room, virtually unchanged since the 1620s, with two internal porches, extravagantly carved.

The castle stands in a park laid out by Capability Brown in 1756, enlarged and improved by him in 1776–9, but now largely given over to agriculture. His magnificent lake lies immediately north of the house. On its shore is a charming Gothick DAIRY with a Roman mosaic pavement reset in its floor, opposite a most distinguished neo-classical ORANGERY of 1779.

## Studland*

*34; 4½ miles E of Corfe Castle on B3351*

ST NICHOLAS'S CHURCH almost certainly goes back to Saxon times, and there is little indeed in the building we see today that can be much later than *c*.1100. The exterior is not beautiful in any real sense, with the big, square, stubby tower between nave and chancel; but it is full of character, and apart from the south porch – added in the eighteenth century – and some of the windows, it stands much as it has stood for nearly nine centuries. The tower was never completed, its builders probably having lost their nerve when they realised just how much weight – the walls are up to 6 feet thick – they were piling on the slenderest foundations; hence the stunted bell-stage and the saddle roof. Its position is that of a crossing-tower; but there is no sign of anything resembling a transept. Instead the tower is supported by heavy buttresses, two thick and one thin, on the north and south sides. On both these sides, too, running westward from the tower, are memorable corbel tables.

But the real impact of St Nicholas's comes when you go inside. Crossing arch – if it can be called a crossing – and chancel arch have round, deeply moulded heads; their triple responds have scalloped capitals with naïve but charming carved decoration. The arches to north and south – what *did* happen to those transepts? – are higher, but simpler. The only false note is the chancel east window, which must be of the early thirteenth century: a triple lancet, very faintly stepped, the centre light cusped. Both the space beneath the tower and the chancel itself are rib-vaulted – a considerable extravagance for a little village church.

## Trent

*35; 3 miles NW of Sherborne off B3148*

ST ANDREW'S is a vastly rewarding church. On the outside, its beauty is above all due to the local stone with which it is built and to the lovely Decorated south tower. It has a most unusual window on the ground floor, then two more stages of windows with Y-tracery, then a little corbel table with carved heads, then a parapet carved with quatrefoils and ornamented with pinnacles, and finally a tall octagonal spire – and spires in Dorset are rarities indeed. Nave and north chapel are earlier than the tower – see, in the latter, the blocked Early English lancet – the chancel later, obviously a Perpendicular rebuilding. The nave was lengthened in 1840 or so and given its polygonal baptistery (now the vestry) at its west end. Inside, the Victorian additions are seen to include the plaster rib vaults in nave and chancel, the Minton tiles, and the extremely unpleasant glass in the north and south windows.

*St Andrew's Church, Trent.*

But the real point of St Andrew's is the furnishings. First, the fifteenth-century screen, said to have come from Glastonbury. Its rib-vaulted coving is still in place, with the rich bands of foliage above. Some time in the eighteenth century the loft above was enlarged to make a singers' gallery. Next, the bench ends: these are of *c.*1500, and are carved with Symbols of the Passion and other devices. During the Puritan desecrations they are said to have been hidden by the parishioners for safety. Those which are carved with letters form the beginning of the 'Hail Mary' when grouped in the right order, but when they were replaced it was still thought safer to mix them up so that the prayer was illegible; they have never been rearranged. Finally, the pulpit: 1650, Netherlandish, carved with religious scenes and some rather daring nudes. There are also some good tombs, and some fine pieces of medieval glass jumbled in the east window. But the oddest feature of all, perhaps, is the monument to Ann Gerard, who died in 1633. It is set somewhat uncomfortably in the east respond of the arch leading into the north chapel, where two small angels support her coat of arms; meanwhile, around the inside of the arch there runs the legend 'ALL FLESH IS GRASS, THE GLORY OF IT IS AS THE FLOWER OF THE FIELD' in looking-glass writing. Thus, if the young ladies in the manor pew were admiring themselves in their mirrors instead of listening to the sermon, they would read these words and be reminded of their vanity.

There is a fascinating group of stone buildings clustered round the church. Of these the best is the CHANTRY, presumably built for the local priest in about 1480. DAIRY FARM, opposite, is of similar date, as is much of the interior of CHURCH FARM nearby.

## Warmwell House

*36; 7 miles NE of Weymouth on B3390*

Standing on the site of a medieval predecessor, Warmwell House was built soon after Sir John Trenchard inherited the property in 1618. This was an age that loved to experiment with unusual designs, and Warmwell was planned as a southward-facing suntrap, with side wings projecting diagonally forward from a three-bay centre; both centre and wings have two storeys and a second-floor attic set in a huge shaped gable. On the ground floor is a central recessed loggia of just two bays, within which the front door is flanked by those shell-headed niches so characteristic of the county.

The Hall is immediately to the right of the entrance, single-storey as it has always been and now serving as the Dining Room. Its principal feature is the huge Jacobean chimneypiece and overmantel. Behind, the great staircase of stone rises two short flights and then makes a long diagonal dog-leg; unlike the Trenchards' other great house at Wolveton, however, it does not double back on itself. From the first-floor landing the Long Gallery – not very long, but a delightful room for all that – runs backward to the right, while above the Hall is the Drawing Room, once the Great Chamber. Then it boasted a barrel vault; nowadays the ceiling is deeply coved with stucco around the frieze and a most curiously canted window alcove, similar to one below, its plan forming a scalene triangle. That is one of the great charms of Warmwell – the way the rooms shoot off at such surprising angles and assume such unexpected shapes. In several of these rooms the original Jacobean panelling and carved woodwork has survived.

The house stands in its small park, at the end of an avenue of chestnut trees, the copse of beeches behind it setting off its silver-grey limestone to perfection.

## Weymouth

*37; 8 miles S of Dorchester on A354*

The best of Weymouth is everything that a Georgian seaside resort should be; indeed the English seaside was virtually invented here, on the day in 1789 when George III first lowered himself gingerly down from a bathing machine while a band played the National Anthem. The ESPLANADE is a magnificent creation, over half a mile of continuous terraces overlooking the briny, and it extends northward to ROYAL TERRACE and, best of all, GLOUCESTER ROW. This brings us to the wonderfully dotty CLOCK TOWER, erected to celebrate Queen Victoria's Golden Jubilee in 1887.

That is for a start; but there are any number of other terraces of which any holiday town might be proud; and plenty of good buildings too, among them the ROYAL DORSET YACHT CLUB and of course STATUE HOUSE and its opposite number at the entrance to ST MARY STREET – obviously designed to set off George III's statue, which is not at all the grandiloquent equestrian affair one might have expected but an exceedingly jolly little effigy of His Majesty in his coronation robes, painted in primary, almost fairground, colours – just the thing, once again, for the seaside.

At Weymouth, however, as in other Georgian and Regency resorts, it is the ensemble that counts, rather than any individual buildings. You do not need to bother much with any interiors, except perhaps that of ST MARY'S CHURCH, built by a local man, James Hamilton, in 1815–17. There you will see, above the reredos, a huge representation of the Last Supper, painted in 1721 by Sir James Thornhill, who was born in Weymouth and was for some time its Member of Parliament.

## Whitchurch (or Whitechurch) Canonicorum

*38; 4½ miles NW of Bridport off A35*

The church after which the village is named is, so far as I know, unique in England in that it preserves the bones of its patroness, St Candida – or, more properly, St Wite – in an early thirteenth-century shrine beneath the north window of the north transept. ST CANDIDA'S or ST WITE'S CHURCH, however, is a good deal older than the shrine: it has a Norman south doorway leading to a Norman south aisle – round-arched, with circular arcade piers, their capitals carved with scallops and a primitive kind of water-leaf. The briefest examination of these piers shows that from the outset the Norman builders – who never bothered much with foundations – had serious subsidence problems: there is indeed reason to suspect that the north aisle may soon have collapsed altogether. In any event, a major new building programme seems to have started in the closing years of the twelfth century, beginning with this north aisle, which was given four full bays, making it longer than its southern counterpart and considerably more elaborate. The arches are pointed, with intricate mouldings – one is additionally carved, rather oddly, with a bold zigzag – the piers of complicated section with foliated capitals in several variations (including most striking trumpet scallops), all most finely wrought.

These delicate capitals continue in the two transepts, which are also characterised – especially on the north side – with a profusion of wall shafts, giving as always an impression of great opulence. There is more of this shafting round the stepped triple lancets of the chancel east window; this too makes a fine prospect from the west end, framed in the magnificently broad chancel arch. Though heavily restored, it remains the most successful window in the church, since the ends of the transepts were given Perpendicular ones some time in the fifteenth century, while those of the aisles and clerestory are all Victorian. The most important Perpendicular feature, however, is the west tower, rising through five stages to its embattled top, its eight angle buttresses ending in crocketed pinnacles which reach up just above the battlements, where they are joined by four more, halfway along each side.

The shrine of St Wite – about whom we have no definite information of any kind, even his or her sex being to some degree in doubt – consists essentially of a plain stone sarcophagus with a Purbeck marble top and three almond-shaped openings below through which diseased limbs, bandages and the like could be thrust in the hopes that they would somehow benefit through even greater propinquity to the saintly remains. For the rest, there is a Norman font – recovered from a field a mile away in 1848 – with a design of intersecting arches, and some carving on the choir stalls which appears to be French or Burgundian, sixteenth- or seventeenth-century. The best of the tombs is that of Sir John Jeffrey (who died in 1611) in the north wall of the chancel. He lies beneath a recumbent effigy and amid a positive labyrinth of Jacobean strapwork.

## Wimborne

*39; 9 miles SE of Blandford Forum on B3082*

The exterior prospect of WIMBORNE MINSTER is, it must be admitted, something of a disappointment. The oddly indiscriminate way in which the builders have used brown and grey stone gives it an unpleasantly skewbald look, and it has another problem with its towers. Ideally, if a church is not satisfied with its crossing-tower and wants something at the west end as well, it should have not one west tower, but two; this is, after all, the pattern of the majority of English cathedrals. A single west tower makes the building look straggly and somehow unstable, and when both towers are roughly the same size and shape the effect is more unfortunate still. Such is the situation at Wimborne. Neither of its towers dominates. It lacks focus.

All this is the more regrettable since the Minster is, in other respects, a building of great importance and distinction. Its story begins with the foundation of a Benedictine nunnery on the site as early as AD 713, and a century and a half later it was chosen by Alfred the Great as the burial place of his brother. Then in 1043 Edward the Confessor endowed a College of secular Canons, and in 1318 Edward II declared it a Royal Peculiar, thereby exempting it from diocesan jurisdiction. Of the collegiate buildings, virtually nothing remains; fortunately, however, the church itself survived the Dissolution of the Monasteries intact, and apart from two nineteenth-century restorations – T.H. Wyatt's in 1857 and J.L. Pearson's in 1891 – has been little altered since that time. The principal exception – and a serious one at that – is the Norman crossing-tower, whose fifteenth-century stone spire collapsed in 1600. Its ungainly top, corbelled out and crowned with ungainly obelisks that have nothing whatever to do with the lovely Norman work below them, is Jacobean and has already lasted three and a half centuries too long.

Its effect is even more unwelcome in that the two lower stages of the tower are virtually the only Norman features still surviving on the outside of the Minster, unless we count the unadorned west wall of the south transept. The rest of the building shows, roughly speaking, a gradual progression from the Early English of the east end to the Perpendicular of the west. In the east window of the chancel, the three stepped lancets with the pretty plate tracery above them are of *c.*1250; in the transepts, the four-light north window with geometrical tracery must be very little later – some twenty years perhaps – while the south window of five stepped lancets under a single arch is also probably of 1270–80. When we reach the nave aisles, the development from bar tracery to cusped Y-tracery is apparent as we continue westward, while above them the clerestory gives us our first taste of Perpendicular in preparation for the west tower – a fairly run-of-the-mill example of the style dating from 1448–64, although the west door and window are both Victorian. The only later additions which spoil the tidiness of this admittedly somewhat simplistic east–west scheme are the fourteenth-century choir aisles (beware – there are more Victorian windows here) and, on the south side, the Decorated choir vestry with a library above, just to the east of the transept. The eastward extensions from here, containing sacristy and clergy vestry, are modern and can be ignored.

Only when you go inside Wimborne Minster do you realise to what extent it still remains a Norman church. The nave was extended two bays to the west in the fourteenth century, but its four eastern bays are splendid late twelfth-century work: round piers, scalloped capitals and arches which, though already slightly pointed, are still copiously decorated with zigzag. They have charmingly carved heads at the points. The crossing is more impressive still, its tower standing on four massive Norman arches. Above them runs a narrow wall passage, screened by arcades of Purbeck columns supporting small round arches. Below, there is fortunately no screen; you can therefore enjoy an uninterrupted view eastward through choir and presbytery to the high altar and the triple lancet, which

we have already seen from the outside but which is here much enriched by wall shafts and ornate mouldings. These start by following the curve of the lancets but then break outwards again to embrace the plate tracery above. All this can be enjoyed from a distance; only when you yourself enter the choir, however, will you see the fineness of the detail – in particular the carved stops on the hood-moulds (they look late Norman, so have presumably been re-used), the opulence of the mouldings and the sheer panache of the piscina and sedilia.

Before leaving, it is worth making a quick visit to the rib-vaulted sacristy and the lovely fourteenth-century crypt, now used as a Lady Chapel. This too is vaulted, and the arches running across the centre are gently cusped – a most unusual motif in this context. The famous chained library is of interest to bibliophiles, but not to simple lovers of architecture.

Elsewhere in the little town, the PRIEST'S HOUSE in the High Street – now a museum – is worth a quick visit; it is the only secular medieval building in Wimborne. The Square – the name by which the market place is generally known – is of little interest, but WEST BOROUGH, which runs northward from its north-west corner, is a fine Georgian street. The best Georgian house of all is, however, not there but at the end of a little lane running out of King Street, immediately to the south of the Minster. This is DEAN'S COURT, a seven-bay house of brick with stone dressings, dating from 1725.

## Wimborne St Giles

*40; 7½ miles N of Wimborne off B3078*

Anthony Ashley Cooper, afterwards 1st Earl of Shaftesbury, laid the first stone of the present ST GILES'S HOUSE on 19 March 1650 – incidentally introducing to Dorset the new classical style of English architecture, pioneered

Came House, Winterborne Came.

by Inigo Jones and made famous by Sir Roger Pratt. (Captain Rider had acted as a sort of John the Baptist some three years before with the west wing at Cranborne (*q.v.*), but had kept the windows mullioned and transomed.) This mid-seventeenth-century house survives, though much remodelled, in the present seven-bay east front, and was much enlarged within the following half-century by the addition of two long wings running westward from each end. There followed in the 1740s, a massive Georgianisation by Henry Flitcroft, which included a vaguely Palladian entrance to the north surmounted by a pedimented window. Soon afterwards – it is hard to say exactly when – battlements appeared, though some have since been removed, and the house was given the rather unattractive rendering that has robbed it of much of its charm. The long north and south wings were made even longer by Philip Hardwick in 1854; he also raised two rather Italianate towers about halfway along them. At the time of writing there are plans to demolish some of the Victorian additions – and quite right too.

The principal point of the interior is the continuous suite of exceedingly grand state rooms by Flitcroft; but when I visited the house it was deserted and tragically dilapidated and I could see little in the gathering gloom.

The neighbouring ST GILES'S CHURCH is of 1732, and largely what one might expect. The surprise is its most extraordinary north aisle, added by Sir Ninian Comper after a fire in 1908. He was also responsible for a good many of the furnishings – which, though not quite as spectacular as, for example, at Wellingborough (*q.v.*), are predictably colourful and idiosyncratic. Finally, there are some marvellous Ashley tombs. Just outside the church to the north – they are indeed attached to the tower – is a pleasant row of ALMSHOUSES, built by Sir Anthony Ashley in 1624, featuring a big central gable.

## Winterborne Came

*41; 1½ miles SE of Dorchester off A352*

Not many houses are depicted on the funerary monuments of their architects, but there is an elevation of CAME HOUSE – on a partially unrolled scroll, together with a measure, a pair of dividers and a T-square – at the foot of the wall tablet to Francis Cartwright in the church of Blandford St Mary. Clearly, it was considered the masterpiece of this little-known local man, whose Palladian villa at Kings Nympton, Devon, and south front at Creech Grange (*q.v.*) are his only other claims to fame. The north front of Came is dated 1754: Palladian again, seven bays on two storeys with a three-bay centre of attached Corinthian columns supporting a big triangular pediment containing a coat of arms and garlands. The south front – formerly the entrance – is rather more exuberant: only five bays, with the central bay tripartite and featuring a Venetian window above an elaborate Ionic doorcase. The whole house is faced in grey Portland stone.

The interior, wonderfully unchanged after more than two centuries, relies principally for its effect on a series of magnificent Rococo plaster ceilings. That of the Dining Room has frolicsome *putti*, that of the Hall a *rocaille* centrepiece and frieze of shells. Most memorable of all, however, is the Drawing Room, where the mouldings are entwined with garlands and the centrepiece consists, somewhat alarmingly, of a gilded eagle with radiating thunderbolts.

The OLD RECTORY, half a mile away to the north-east, is a charming Gothic *cottage orné* in which William Barnes, the poet, lived during his period as rector.

## Winterborne Tomson*

*42; 8 miles SW of Wimborne off A31*

ST ANDREW'S must be everybody's favourite church. It is built of coursed rubble, with a semi-circular apse at the east end, and its south front – if that is not too grand a name – has one little Norman window at the west and three fifteenth-century mullions, round-headed two-lighters with hood-moulds. The weatherboarded bell-turret could hardly be smaller.

The inside is even more enchanting. All the early seventeenth-century pine box pews are still there, together with the two-decker pulpit (with tester), communion rail and the simplest of timber screens. Walls and ceiling are plastered, the latter being divided by thin timber strips with bosses at their intersections, radiating downward around the apse. The pretty west gallery is approached by unworthy modern stairs – the only false note. Can nobody do something about them? Thomas Hardy would have; he loved the church, which was exquisitely restored in 1936 in his memory.

## Woodsford Castle

*43; 4 miles E of Dorchester off A352*

With its seemingly endless thatched roof, the disappearance of four of its five towers and the addition of several sixteenth- and nineteenth-century windows, Woodsford Castle no longer looks particularly forbidding; but it is in fact the only fortified fourteenth-century manor house in Dorset to be still inhabited and there are still enough arrow slits, loopholes and other defensive features to indicate its early history. Licence to crenellate was granted by Edward III as early as 1335. The result was a long, narrow building, running north and south and probably forming the east side of a closed court. On its own east side there were three towers, two at the ends and one more or less central; of these the north-east one still stands. Two more towers occupied the corners on the west, courtyard, side.

In the eighteenth century Woodsford was converted into a farmhouse; at that time an extra storey was inserted under the roof, and a big square wing added at the north-west angle. Inevitably, there were other important internal alterations as well; but the principal rooms can still be traced on the first floor, including the Hall at the northern end (lit by windows to the north and east), the Chapel adjoining it (still retaining its Decorated piscina) and then four more rooms, the last of which – at the south end – seems to have been another big Hall room. There thus appear to be two separate suites; Woodsford must have been a substantial house indeed.

*Woodsford Castle.*

*St Andrew's Church, Winterborne Tomson.*

## Worth Matravers

*44; 3 miles SW of Swanage off B3069*

This delightful small village has a fine Norman church dedicated to ST NICHOLAS, the most unaltered of any in the county except for Studland (*q.v.*). It consists of a west tower – whose pyramidal top is one of the few alterations, dating from 1867 – a nave and a slightly lower chancel. All are built of the local rubble with stone dressings, and all were *in situ* well before the end of the twelfth century.

Look first at the splendid corbel table, running along both nave and chancel on each side of the building; you will then be free to turn your attention to the south porch. This was in fact made up in the eighteenth century from materials taken from a demolished chapel, of 1170 or thereabouts, which formerly stood against the south wall of the nave. It is rich – some might say over-rich – in deeply carved zigzag, but the most fascinating part of it is the tympanum above the doorway. Despite the damage it suffered at the hands of the Parliamentarians in 1645, its subject is still easily identifiable as the Coronation of the Virgin – still a most unusual subject for the late twelfth century and probably the earliest carved representation of it in England.

Inside, it is the chancel arch that immediately captures the eye. Three orders of columns with scalloped capitals support three concentric semi-circular arches replete with still more zigzag, fairly crude in execution but none the less impressive for that. The Royal Commission on Historic Monuments has claimed that this arch, which must date from 1130 or so, was introduced from elsewhere, citing as evidence for this assertion the fact that the jambs on the west side show traces of side altars, which must originally have existed on either side. They may well be right, though the case does not seem to me to be entirely proven. Whatever its origin, the arch now frames the other principal alteration in the Norman work – the three-light Decorated east window with reticulated tracery. The contrast between the barbaric quality of the one and the refined delicacy of the other proves, rather to my surprise, to be a delight in itself.

Some 2 miles to the south-west of the village is the promontory known as ST ALDHELM'S HEAD – where, on the very edge of the cliff, stands a tiny Norman chapel. Low and square, and firmly buttressed against the winter storms, it must have been built some time in the second half of the twelfth century. There is a plainish Norman doorway in the west wall which leads into a single space some 25 feet square, with four rib vaults springing from a central pier. Strangely enough, there is no sign of an altar or piscina ever having been here. The whole building could scarcely be more simple and unadorned, but it has a marvellous atmosphere of loneliness and desolation.

# Short List

## Bothenhampton

*45; ½ mile E of Bridport off A35*

The CHURCH OF THE HOLY TRINITY was built between 1887 and 1889 by E.S. Prior, in high Arts and Crafts tradition. The outside is scarcely promising, but the interior is immensely impressive with three great sweeping transverse arches across the nave pre-echoing the sort of thing Nervi was to do nearly a century later. The bare stone of the inner walls, so unsightly in scraped medieval churches, here looks strong, clean and totally successful. Plenty of imaginative touches, too: note how the pulpit has been corbelled out and the side of the chancel arch hewn away to provide a platform for the preacher.

## Bradford Abbas

*46; 3 miles SW of Sherborne off A30*

ST MARY'S CHURCH has a wonderfully broad, square tower with no fewer than eleven canopied niches on its west front, above and around a most elaborately cusped outer arch with an ogee gable. Inside, too, it has much to recommend it, including a fifteenth-century stone screen and fine roofs to the nave and aisles. In 1800 it would probably have deserved a star; alas, during the last century it has lost its rood loft, box pews and west gallery; worst of all, in 1890, it was scraped so mercilessly as to make any real enjoyment impossible. A tragedy, nothing less.

## Brownsea Island

*NT; 47; in Poole harbour*

This lovely wooded island, much of it a nature reserve, contains only two buildings of any interest, neither of them great architecture. The CASTLE, which began as one of Henry VIII's forts, was enlarged and remodelled by the notorious William Benson, who bought it in 1721 – three years after he had displaced the octogenarian Wren as Surveyor of the Works. It was made even grander by Col. W.P. Waugh, who had bought the island in 1852 in the belief that it contained deposits of china clay worth a million pounds, and invested well over a quarter of that sum in borrowed money. Four years later, however, he discovered that the clay was of so low a grade as to be practically useless, went bankrupt, and fled the country. He it was who built ST MARY'S CHURCH. It never had an incumbent, and now serves as a little museum.

## Canford Magna

*48; 1½ miles SE of Wimborne on A341*

The CHURCH – dedication unknown – has a chancel that started life as a Saxon nave, a Norman nave built on to it, and a Norman north tower. With so remarkable an architectural history, it is a pity that it is not more pleasing to the eye. It remains, however, a good deal prettier than CANFORD MANOR – now Canford School – which, despite the combined efforts of Blore and Barry, is very hideous indeed and is made still worse by the grey and lifeless brick of which it is built. Barry's Great Hall has a certain monstrous grandeur, though. The vast fifteenth-century kitchen, wrongly attributed to John of Gaunt, looks quite interesting from the outside with its rare louvred chimney; alas, I could not get in.

## Chalbury

*49; 4 miles N of Wimborne off B3078*

The unassuming little whitewashed church of ALL SAINTS stands on the top of a hill, with wonderful views on every side. It goes back to the thirteenth century, but its point is its perfectly preserved eighteenth-century interior: box pews, west gallery, and a lovely deep screen shaped like a depressed Venetian window with a tiny pew built into its thickness.

## Chantmarle

*50; 5½ miles E of Beaminster off A356*

This fine old Jacobean house is now a police training college. Originally E-plan, it is now, alas, bereft of its two main wings. In the centre is a three-storey gabled porch with a semi-circular first-floor oriel; the doorway below is round-headed in a square frame and flanked by two shell niches – the only Renaissance touches in a house which, built as it was between 1612 and 1623, must have seemed old-fashioned even then. An earlier, Tudor, wing has been preserved behind the house to the west.

## Clifton Maybank

*51; 3½ miles SW of Sherborne off A37*

Sir John Horsey's splendid mansion of *c.*1550 was largely demolished in 1786. All that remains *in situ* is part of the west wing, much remodelled and enlarged early this century. The south front retains its original windows in the two unequal gables and its three octagonal buttress shafts, rising in four stages to a parapet pierced with quatrefoils. The Tudor oriel on the west front has been resited – far too high. The best surviving feature of the house is the centre of the entrance front, but this is now incorporated in that of Montacute (*q.v.*).

## Creech Grange

*52; 3 miles SW of Wareham off A351*

The house is originally Tudor, but was given a quite distinguished classical south front by Francis Cartwright of Blandford in 1738–41. Then, in the 1840s, the east (entrance) front was also refaced, once again in Portland stone ashlar, in the same early Elizabethan style as its predecessor presumably was. Things get a bit tricky at the south-east corner, where the two façades meet.

## Dewlish

*53; 8 miles NE of Dorchester off A354*

A beautifully proportioned house, Dewlish was built in 1702 at the end of a long, shallow valley, a little to the south of the village. The entrance front, to the north, is ashlared in Portland stone, has a fine doorcase and pretty shaped gable at the centre; the garden front is of brick, originally red but now nearly grey with lichen. At the east end it is stone again, but orange Ham Hill. The principal fronts have eleven bays, on two storeys plus dormers. Inside, the best feature is the staircase, some half-century later than the house, lovingly moulded to the sides and underneath. The other rooms, despite two fine chimneypieces, are relatively modest.

## Folke

*54; 2 miles SE of Sherborne off A3030*

ST LAWRENCE'S CHURCH earns its place here not so much by its valiant (though not entirely successful) early seventeenth-century attempt at the Perpendicular style, as by the immense Jacobean screens with outsize strapwork. That across the chancel, for example, has two immense Ss – rather like those on a violin – each about 5 feet long, forming a crest above the central doorway. Another arch, scarcely less exuberant, stands in the central bay of the north arcade and presumably once led to a family pew, now alas dismantled.

## Hanford House

*55; 3 miles NW of Blandford Forum off A350*

Built in 1623, Hanford House remains externally almost unaltered, although the central court has now been roofed in to form a big central Saloon in which the inner doorway to the house now stands under the glazed roof, to somewhat curious effect. An upper room in the north-east corner has a fine ceiling with pendants bearing strapwork, caryatids, knights in armour and all the fun of the Jacobean fair. Pevsner thought it 'a piece of great vulgarity and ugliness'; I found it rather fun. A pretty eighteenth-century CHAPEL stands some 50 yards away, low-lying in a quiet dell.

## Iwerne Courtney (or Shroton)

*56; 4 miles NW of Blandford Forum off A350*

RANSTON HOUSE, a quarter of a mile south-east of the village, was built in 1753, almost certainly by one of the Bastards of Blandford Forum. The five-bay west front remains, but the house has recently been cut down and remodelled and the other fronts are by Louis Osman, who designed the Prince of Wales's crown. Inside, the main feature is the staircase, which has a beautiful wrought-iron balustrade, restrained Rococo plaster-work and pairs of columns – those on the first floor having the curious inward-curving volutes that are a Bastard trade mark. The wall and ceiling paintings are by Andrea Casali, and contemporary with the house.

## Iwerne Stepleton (or Stepleton Iwerne)

*57; 3 miles NW of Blandford Forum on A350*

STEPLETON HOUSE stands beside a lake, produced by the damming of the little River Iwerne. It is a fine manor house of the second quarter of the seventeenth century, but radically remodelled some fifty years later, when it received its hipped roof and sashed windows. In 1758 the elegant Georgian side pavilions were added, together with the pretty three-bay centre to the south (entrance) front. These were probably the work of John Bastard. Inside, the principal focus, as at Ranston, is the staircase – the stucco less restrained this time. There is a most elegant arcade on the upper landing, with carved masks on the keystones.

## Kingston Maurward

*58; 3 miles E of Dorchester off A35*

The old MANOR HOUSE of *c.*1590 is, on the outside, the perfect Elizabethan E-plan house with five straight gables but otherwise virtually no decoration. It was saved in the nick of time from destruction by the local council a year or two ago, but the interior has been remodelled, if not actually rebuilt. KINGSTON MAURWARD HOUSE dates from 1717–20 and was originally of brick; it was cased in ashlar in 1794 as the result of a visit by George III who, on being shown round by the owner, Morton Pitt, said nothing but 'Brick, Mr Pitt, brick' over and over again. By his next visit, the work was done. Pevsner suggests an attribution to Thomas Archer, but there is no evidence. It is now an agricultural college.

## Kingston Russell

*59; 4½ miles N of Abbotsbury off A35*

This is a house of considerable distinction, of which the garden front to the east cannot be much later than the mid-seventeenth century (the windows are mullioned and double-transomed) while the copybook Palladian west front was added in the 1730s. The outer bays to north and south are of 1913, by Philip Tilden, and should be ignored – if only such a thing were possible. More or less derelict before its purchase in 1913, the house had lost nearly all its interiors apart from a good early Georgian staircase. Nelson's friend Captain Hardy was born in the house, and J.L. (*The Rise of the Dutch Republic*) Motley died here.

## Lyme Regis

*60; 5 miles SW of Bridport on A3070*

A late Georgian seaside resort of immense charm and modest architectural distinction, Lyme Regis possesses no single building of really outstanding quality. BROAD STREET, climbing up from the town centre on the sea front, is the most rewarding thoroughfare; it leads, after a fork in the road, to POUND STREET, which possesses what is certainly the most memorable of Lyme's buildings. It is known as BELMONT, and its exuberant decoration, all in Coade stone, was done for Mrs Eleanor Coade herself in 1784. ST MICHAEL'S CHURCH is another oddity: a Norman church at its west end, with a later Perpendicular one tacked on to the east. THE COBB, really a long and massive breakwater, is enormously old; it goes back at least to the reign of Edward I, who died in 1307.

## Puddletown

*61; 5 miles NE of Dorchester on A35*

The Weatherbury of *Far from the Madding Crowd*, Puddletown boasts a lovely broad church, ST MARY'S, with a noble north aisle and good timber roof, with ribbed panels, to the nave. The deep west gallery, with organ, is dated 1635. The church has box pews throughout, and extraordinary painted inscriptions, including a very Germanic-looking one with texts inscribed on a book, held at top and bottom by two hands. The south chapel has some remarkable early tombs. WATERSTON MANOR, one and a half miles west of the town, is an enchanting little seventeenth-century house full of surprises – its south front with as many classical motifs as a pattern book, used quite ungrammatically but with considerable charm, its east bearing a magnificent Elizabethan frontispiece obviously imported from somewhere else.

## Shroton

See Iwerne Courtney.

## Smedmore

*62; 3 miles SW of Corfe Castle off A351*

Only a few hundred yards from the sea, Smedmore was built in the early seventeenth century by Sir William Clavell – though the manor has changed hands by inheritance only, and never by sale, since the days of Henry IV. The house has kept its Jacobean core, but relatively little of this is visible from the outside: in *c.*1700 Edward Clavell gave it a new south-west front and installed the oak panelling in what is endearingly known as the Cedar Room, and in 1761 his son turned the whole house round ninety degrees, giving it a new entrance front to the north-west with two portly bows and a Hall between them. (Bows in the 1760s were an innovation indeed.) Inside, there is extremely pretty plasterwork in the Dining Room, good marble chimneypieces – a particularly splendid Rococo one upstairs – and a noble oak staircase of the early eighteenth century.

## Stepleton Iwerne

See Iwerne Stepleton.

## Toller Fratrum

*63; 9 miles NW of Dorchester off A356*

The 'Fratrum' refers to the Knights Hospitallers who were here, associated with Forde Abbey. ST BASIL'S CHURCH is, architecturally speaking, hardly worth a glance; but it contains two things which anyone would be sorry to miss. The first is a fragment of an eleventh-century relief of St Mary Magdalene washing the feet of Christ, inset over the altar; the second is the twelfth-century font, which I shall not attempt to describe. LITTLE TOLLER FARM close by dates from *c.*1540, a long, narrow, ashlared block (originally part of a larger complex) with pretty carved gables including a monkey with a mirror. The thatched outbuilding is detailed with similar fantasy.

## Wareham

*64; 10 miles NW of Swanage on A351*

ST MARY'S CHURCH has a lovely Decorated chancel with fine windows to east and north; for the rest, it was more or less ruined by an 1840s' restoration. More rewarding is ST MARTIN'S, where much Anglo-Saxon work remains: note the typical long-and-short work at the corners of the east end and the north-east angle of the nave; also the north window of the chancel. In the north aisle stands Eric Kennington's monument to T.E. Lawrence, looking oddly out of place.

## Winterborne Anderson

*65; 8 miles SW of Wimborne Minster off A31*

ANDERSON MANOR looks a wonderful house from the outside – a three-storeyed, E-shaped building of plum-coloured brick, the bluish horizontal bands being achieved by the laying of every third course in vitrified headers. There are copious dressings of white stone, the centre is a canted bow rising through all three storeys, and the windows are mullioned and mostly transomed. Three equal gables have tall brick chimneys rising in groups of four behind. The date is 1622 and the exterior is virtually unchanged; inside the house, however, there is unfortunately little or nothing of the seventeenth century left.

## Winterborne Clenston

*66; 4 miles SW of Blandford Forum off A354*

The MANOR HOUSE, probably of *c.*1540, built of flint and greensand in alternating bands and Ham Hill dressings, is symmetrical (the northern extension is a seventeenth-century afterthought) in a way most surprising for its date. The most striking feature, however, is the central projection, five sides of an octagon, culminating in a huge blank gable quite alarmingly corbelled out on each side: hardly beautiful, but impossible to forget. Nearby is a magnificent BARN with seven immense hammer-beams, opulently moulded. They have obviously been re-used, and were most probably taken from Milton Abbey (*q.v.*) after its dissolution.

## Winterborne Herringston

*67; 2 miles S of Dorchester off A354*

The house, originally Jacobean, was largely remodelled by Thomas Leverton from 1803 in the Gothick taste and externally has little distinction. What earns it its place here is the utterly spectacular Great Chamber, its barrel-vaulted plaster ceiling adorned with a profusion of birds, beasts and monsters, and in one place the feathers of Charles, Prince of Wales, which enable us to date it as between 1612 and 1625. Five huge pendants include three in the form of openwork globes; inside the central one a little boy is climbing a tree, while his friends sit round its base. Can fantasy go further? Yes, it can – in the wildly exuberant carved panelling at one end. No restraint, no discipline; but goodness, what fun they must have had.

## Yetminster

*68; 5 miles SW of Sherborne off A37*

ST ANDREW'S CHURCH has a long, low, Early English chancel with three stepped lancets at the east end. Nave, aisles and west tower are all Perpendicular of *c.*1450. The three-bay arcades are high, with small carved capitals, while the timber roofs have bosses and original painting, especially in the north aisle. The square tower has a stark rectangular stair turret, which from the north looks distinctly menacing, but it has some splendid gargoyles and a particularly cheerful golden weathercock. The village street is full of charm, and still mercifully unspoilt.

# Essex

'A fair county, bearing the full proportion and five and thirty miles square, affording all things necessary to man's subsistence, save that the eastern part is not very healthful in the air thereof.' So wrote Thomas Fuller – who, as perpetual curate of Waltham Abbey, knew what he was talking about. Even if he was wrong about the air, the legend died hard, surviving well into Jane Austen's day: Mr Woodhouse was horrified to hear that Emma had risked her health on a visit to Southend. In all other respects, however, Fuller was absolutely right – righter, perhaps, than many people today readily believe, for in the late twentieth century the generally held view of Essex is usually something less than ecstatic. Dormitory towns, ribbon development, flat, bleak marshes – such, when the county is mentioned, are all too often the pictures conjured up in the mind.

The reaction is understandable, but unfair. Essex does indeed possess these things in plenty, and many other phenomena equally unlovely; but there is much beauty too, and it comes as an unfailing surprise to the uninitiated to find that a great deal of the county is still quite remarkably unspoilt. Even Brentwood – outer suburbia *par excellence* – is almost surrounded by open country except along the line of the A12; a mile or two to the south you can find yourself among leafy country lanes with a distant prospect of gentle hills – you might almost be in Shropshire. And the further you go to the north and east, the more rural becomes the landscape, the more self-contained the towns and villages. For the industrial revolution passed Essex by, together with the rest of East Anglia; and of much of the county it can still be said that there is nowhere so close to the capital geographically that is so remote from it in spirit.

Though Essex once boasted the capital of England, it is nowadays a modest sort of place, undramatic and domesticated. It has no great cities, no large towns even – the biggest, Southend, has a population of well under 200,000 – and no real cathedrals; that of Chelmsford has been dignified by the name only since 1913 and remains essentially the parish church it always was. Urban public building has kept to a similarly modest scale; though nearly every town boasts a generous quota of fine buildings from every century from the sixteenth on – and some go back a good way further – most of them are, or were, private houses and are notable more for the contribution they make to their surroundings than as works of art in themselves. In the country and villages too it is the private buildings, rather than the churches, that excel – though this rule has plenty of exceptions, as we shall see. They also make considerably more of a splash.

Architecturally, Essex has always laboured under a handicap: the virtual absence of any building stone worthy of the name. Kentish ragstone could be brought in from across the Thames estuary; but it is coarse, brittle and almost impossible to work and often seemed, except in the south-east corner, hardly worth the trouble. That curious yellow concretion known as septaria and the aptly named conglomerate puddingstone were still worse – even nastier than they sound. So Essex builders continued down the ages to fall back for the most part on their traditional local materials: timber, flint and brick. Where the first of these is concerned, the county's most venerable monument is the little church at Greensted, whose walls of vertical oak logs have stood since the middle of the ninth century. Equally remarkable, though a good deal more recent, is that extraordinary series of late medieval timber towers, of which Blackmore and Margaretting are the best, with Navestock running a worthy third. The big disappointment is the wooden roofs of the churches; though many are fine, none really bears comparison with the great *tours de force* of Norfolk and Suffolk.

Flint, considered simply as a building material, can be most effective when used well – the porch at Fingringhoe is an obvious example – but it really appears to its best advantage in flushwork, of which Essex possesses two notable showpieces: St John's Abbey at Colchester and

St Osyth's Priory. It is with brick that the local builders produced their best work. In the early fifteenth century there was a sudden proliferation of splendid brick mansions. Faulkbourne, Horham Hall, Leez Priory, the superb, shameless exhibitionism of Layer Marney – these are only the beginning; and as many a fine Georgian house bears witness, later generations did not lose their skill.

What is the most memorable building in Essex? Layer Marney would certainly be a contender; so would the much amputated but still magnificent Audley End. Many people, I suspect, would vote for Hedingham Castle, everything a Norman tower keep should be and much more besides. Others might prefer the quiet majesty of Waltham Abbey nave. My own favourite, however, is none of these; it is a building so simple as hardly, you might think, to merit the description of architecture. But when I am old and grey and immobilised, and all those other glorious piles are fading or merging in my darkening brain, I believe I shall still remember the sight of the tiny chapel of St Peter-at-the-Wall out beyond Bradwell, standing as it has stood for thirteen centuries, lonely and remote across the fields, at the edge of England.

## Audley End

*1; 1 mile W of Saffron Walden off B184*

John Evelyn described Audley End in 1654 as 'a mixt fabrick, twixt antiq and modern'. His words were true then, but are still more so today. Though not begun until the first decade of the seventeenth century, this tremendous house – like its near contemporary, Hatfield – was built on a medieval plan with Great Hall, screen and gallery, and was thus born old-fashioned; and since that time there has been so much demolition, restoration and rebuilding that little of the original structure now remains. All the subsequent work has, however, been so carefully and sensitively done that, from the outside at any rate, Audley End still appears almost wholly Jacobean. Much of the interior, too, gives the same impression at first glance; it is only when you look closer at the decorative detail that the truth begins to dawn.

No house in England – with the possible exception of Compton Wynyates – is more spectacular from the road; the sudden sight of Audley End by an unsuspecting motorist on the A11 is enough to provoke a nasty accident. Looking down on to it from that elevation, across the Cam and the great green lawn, one finds it hard to believe that the original house was well over twice the size: that a huge outer courtyard, of which the present west front formed the east range, extended towards the river, and that the three ranges existing today were formerly closed by a fourth, forming a second, inner, courtyard beyond. James I is said to have acidulously remarked that the building was too large for a King, though it might possibly suit a Lord Treasurer – a point which was doubtless appreciated by its builder, the Earl of Suffolk; he was at that time Lord High Treasurer of England, but was disgraced soon afterwards.

Of this original house – built in pale grey Ketton limestone by the half-Dutch mason and surveyor Bernard Janssen (or Johnson) – the two porches have been preserved, and part of the Great Hall with its particularly splendid screen at the north end. Opposite the screen to the south, however, instead of the low dais and closing wall that might have been expected, there rises another screen in the form of a two-tier stone arcade, from the lower side arches of which two parallel flights of stairs rise magnificently to the Saloon. The effect is not only surprising but intensely dramatic; and it comes as no surprise to learn that it is the work of Sir John Vanbrugh. So – a good deal more unexpectedly – is the ceiling above, of pseudo-Jacobean strapwork; only the acute eye will notice the way its design reflects that of the obviously eighteenth-century gilded iron balustrades beneath it.

It was Vanbrugh too who, in about 1711, advised the demolition of the great outer courtyard; and less than thirty years later the new owner, Lady Portsmouth, pulled down the extreme eastern range – leaving the house more or less the size we see today. On her death it was passed to her nephew, the 1st Lord Braybrooke. He it was who built the present galleries running east of the Hall and who commissioned Robert Adam to redecorate the suite of rooms on the ground floor of the south range. These rooms, vandalised by the 3rd Lord Braybrooke who considered the neo-classical style decadent and debased, have recently been beautifully restored by the Dept of the Environment (whose work, it must be said here, has been quite outstanding throughout the house). In the Great Drawing Room an interesting subtlety can be observed: the patterned silk wall hangings are continued, with the details of the design carrying on exactly, into the upholstery of the precisely placed furniture below. There is also a lovely plaster ceiling, the western part of which is entirely modern (though you would never know it). Unfortunately the room is villainously low; but Adam has done his best with it, dropping the dado to give the walls as much height as he can, and providing an impressive object lesson in what a great artist can do with intractable material. Next door, the Painted Drawing Room (or Alcove Room) is, however, a little gem – neo-classical through and through, with Pompeian designs by Biagio Rebecca on the walls and a delightful *trompe-l'oeil* frieze above.

The other show-stopper of the house is the Chapel – an irresistible confection in Strawberry Hill Gothick, completed in 1786. Halfway along the (liturgical) south side there is a wonderful wooden throne raised up on three polished steps, while the gallery for the family along the back – endearingly, if unconvincingly, fan-vaulted – is provided, very sensibly, with a fireplace. (Rebecca's stained-glass window is, perhaps, a less successful touch.) Behind the Chapel, along the north range, are two further suites of rooms which have recently been returned, as nearly as possible, to the way they looked in the 1830s under the 3rd Lord Braybrooke. Matching them in date are the corresponding first-floor rooms in the south range, the best of which is the agreeably

Audley End.

opulent Library with pilasters, frieze and another elaborate plaster ceiling. The series culminates in the Saloon. Here is the best ceiling in the house: its subject is the sea, and among the pendants and the strapwork are represented all the denizens of the deep. So sophisticated is the modelling, so superb the condition, that one is tempted to dismiss it as yet another inspired eighteenth- or nineteenth-century pastiche. Far from it. The ceiling, together with the towering chimneypiece, are both from the original Jacobean house. The frieze, however, dates from the 1760s – it is by Adam's best plasterer, Joseph Rose – and the wall decoration from much the same period; notice in particular the clustered columns and capitals flanking the pictures – another little whisper of Strawberry Hill Gothick where least expected. The portraits themselves, representing the predecessors of the 1st Lord Braybrooke, include no fewer than six by Rebecca; an inscription in the north-west corner panel records the completion of the decoration in 1785 by Braybrooke, 'to commemorate those through whom with gratitude he holds these possessions'.

A word must also be said about the gardens, which are essentially the creation of the 1st Lord Braybrooke and Capability Brown. Beginning work in 1763, Brown redesigned the grounds between the house and the road, altering the course of the Cam, building a ha-ha and adding clumps of trees at strategic points. For the buildings necessary to complete his conception, he turned to Robert Adam who, over the next thirty years, provided the two bridges – the northern, 'Tea House' bridge, constituting a tiny Ionic temple in its own right – two more temples, commemorating the end of the Seven Years' War in 1763 and George III's recovery from his first fit of insanity, a column in memory of Lady Portsmouth and several minor ornaments.

In view of all the alterations and additions Audley End cannot, despite its exterior appearance, be viewed as a Jacobean house; but all this subsequent work is so imaginative and stylish that the interest is greater rather than less. It is a hotch-potch, but a remarkably fascinating and rewarding one.

## Beeleigh Abbey

*2; 1 mile NW of Maldon off A414*

The approach to Beeleigh does not immediately suggest anything remotely ecclesiastical. The surprisingly tall, timber-framed house with its steeply pitched tiled roof looks more like an Elizabethan manor – at least from the entrance side. It is only when one walks round to the east front that the three-light fifteenth-century windows with their low transoms and Perpendicular tracery give the game away; one is then less surprised to learn that this was an abbey of Premonstratensian canons, which was founded in the 1180s and continued in being until its dissolution in 1536. It consists, in its present form, essentially of the old chapter house, the first-floor dormitory with its undercroft, and a three-storey sixteenth-century extension to the south which links these to the rather sparse remains of the buildings originally forming the south range of the cloister court.

The chapter house is vaulted, with two ranges of four bays each, divided by a row of three free-standing octagonal columns of stone. The two double-light windows at the east end are not original; the single lancet

*The church of St Peter-on-the-Wall, Bradwell-Juxta-Mare.*

window, however, remains unaltered. To the south, separated from the chapter house by a single smallish room, is the dormitory undercroft. It too is divided by a row of columns, this time running laterally from north to south and of Purbeck marble, and is vaulted according to the same system; the ribs, however, are chamfered rather than moulded. In the west wall is a huge fireplace with a frieze, probably taken from one of the abbey tombs, of angels playing musical instruments. Here, then, must have been the warming house.

The dormitory above, now housing the superb library of Mr W.G. Foyle, has as its principal architectural feature a wagon roof of collar-beams and arched braces of chestnut, presumably of the fifteenth century. Forty-six feet long, it would be a marvellous room in any circumstances, even without its contents.

The building has been most sensitively adapted to serve as a country house, without losing its character or atmosphere.

## Blackmore

*3; 7½ miles SW of Chelmsford off A414*

The total absence of any good building stone in Essex – or even high-quality rubble – led to the development of one of its chief architectural glories: timber churches. Most have long since lost their original naves and chancels, but in well over a dozen cases the wooden tower has been preserved; and the best of all these towers is that of the PRIORY CHURCH OF ST LAURENCE, Blackmore. Its three diminishing stages, each crowned with a lean-to roof, are all treated differently – the bottom timber-framed, the second with vertical and the top with horizontal weatherboards. The whole would have an almost pagoda-like appearance were it not for the shingled spire. The date of this remarkable structure is probably around the middle of the fifteenth century. It contrives to be both sturdy and graceful at the same time, but the outside view is only half the story; it must also be seen from within, where the massive beams and braces are an equally impressive work of art.

The tower arch leading from here into the nave is an imposing Norman affair with three orders of columns: undecorated, but grand enough to show that it must originally have been the main west door of the Norman church, built two centuries before the tower as an Augustinian priory. (This is confirmed by the two arched windows above and the small circular one higher still.)

Nearly all the Norman church has gone – though plenty of fragments survive embedded in the north wall – and has been replaced by later building (fourteenth-century on the north, sixteenth- on the south) where wood has given place to brick. The dormers along both sides of the roof provide a pleasant touch of informality.

## Boreham

*4; 3 miles NE of Chelmsford off A12*

BOREHAM HOUSE, now locally known as FORD HOUSE after its present owners, is unquestionably the world's most beautiful tractor and equipment training centre. The imposing brick façade, set back from the A12 and separated from it by a long, rectangular, reflecting pool, was designed *c.*1727 for Benjamin Hoare, the banker, almost certainly by Henry Flitcroft – not Gibbs, as is sometimes suggested. The wings were enlarged and altered by Thomas Hopper in 1812. The house is not, unfortunately, open to the public, but a polite telephone call will almost certainly arrange admission to see the two most opulent rooms – the Entrance Hall and Saloon. If I were Ford's I would get rid of the Victorian *porte-cochère* – there's no need to keep rain off *tractors*.

## Bradwell-Juxta-Mare*

*5; 8½ miles N of Burnham-on-Crouch off B1021*

It is some twenty minutes' walk from the end of the motor road to the CHURCH OF ST PETER-ON-THE-WALL, but worth it a hundred times over. Architecturally, it must be admitted, there is nothing particularly remarkable about this little church, built on the edge of the Roman fort of Othona (of which only a few stones remain) gazing out over the grey North Sea; but the importance of St Peter's lies not in how it looks but in what it is: in all probability, the oldest church in England of which so much of the original fabric has been preserved, having been built by St Cedd on the very spot where he landed from Lindisfarne in 653 on his mission to evangelise the East Saxon invaders.

The semi-circular apse, the western porch and the two little *porticus* to the north and south have disappeared, but the nave still rises, virtually unrestored, to its full height of some 24 feet. Original too are the west doorway and the high square windows, set in walls 2½ feet thick, made principally of re-used Roman material from the fort. In only two places does a large area of masonry betray signs of rebuilding: halfway along the two side walls, where, after the church had been turned into a barn some time in the seventeenth century, the local farmer cut doorways for his carts. The roof and floor are modern, but none of that seems to matter. This grand old building, standing solitary and desolate where the long low flats slope down to the sea, retains a numinous quality which I for one find deeply moving.

## Castle Hedingham*

*6; 8½ miles NE of Braintree on B1058*

It seems almost unfair that such a ravishingly pretty village should also boast the best-preserved Norman tower keep – and one of the most impressive – in the country and an unspoilt late Norman parish church of rare beauty. Both were built by the de Veres, later Earls of Oxford, to whom Hedingham fell at the time of the Conquest. The CASTLE is the earlier; high on a mound, rising nearly 100 feet above the surrounding trees, it is approached along a path leading past a brave pedimented house of 1719 and then over a footbridge spanning the moat. There are four floors, of which the principal ones were the first and second. The Hall occupied the second floor: a magnificent room some 30 feet high, surrounded by a gallery halfway up the wall and dominated by a huge Norman arch soaring across it. There and in the room below are tremendous fireplaces like church portals, each with its own arch decorated with zigzag. Further zigzags outline the windows. The keep could never have been comfortable, but it was certainly grand.

Descending the mount on to the main road, we walk through the whole length of the village – the best houses are in ST JAMES STREET and QUEEN STREET – to ST NICHOLAS'S CHURCH. There is nothing on the outside to suggest its true age; the huge, square, step-battlemented tower is obviously Tudor, and the embattled aisles and clerestory together with nearly all the windows point fairly obviously to the fifteenth century. Inside, however, the church is suddenly transformed. The noble six-bay arcades have exquisitely carved capitals; the chancel arch, pointed but with zigzag, must date from the very end of the twelfth century, since it marks the precise moment when Norman gave way to Gothic. Fascinating, too, is the fenestration in the chancel: blind and windowed arches alternating along the sides, and at the east end three shafted lancets beneath a large wheel window with eight columnar spokes – a rare motif in England, where only four others exist, though frequent enough on the Continent.

Finally two other, later, features must be mentioned: the screen, of about 1400, in which oak is turned into lace and tiny portrait heads are carved into the cusps of the arches; and the double hammer-beam roof added some ninety years afterwards, a worthy crown for a marvellous church.

*Castle Hedingham.*

*Paycocke's, Coggeshall.*

## Coggeshall

*7; 6 miles E of Braintree on A120*
*Includes Paycocke's (NT)*

PAYCOCKE'S (NT) in West Street is described by Pevsner as one of the most attractive half-timbered houses in England: a brave claim, and fully justified. It was built in about 1500 for Thomas Paycocke, the leading weaver and clothier of the town, and though the fine façade has been partly restored it still looks much as its first owner must have known it. This façade is worth a careful look, if only for the wealth and fantasy of its carving, beside the doors, in the spandrels and, best of all, along the frieze.

The interior confirms the impression of wealth. Though this is only a relatively modest town house, there is decoration and fine workmanship everywhere; look, for example, at the ceiling joists and the bressummers over the fireplace in the Hall and Dining Room.

Paycocke's has a pretty little garden from which one gets a good view of the south-west wing. The south end of it is obviously considerably older than the street frontage, and may well go back to the thirteenth century. If so, it is a remarkable survival; Tom Paycocke would have had little use for anything so pokily old-fashioned.

The CHURCH OF ST PETER-AD-VINCULA received a direct hit from a German bomb in 1940, losing its tower and much of the nave; but the south arcade and clerestory have survived and the whole church has been beautifully and unfussily restored. The south chapel contains a monument to a Mrs Honywood, who died in 1620 leaving 367 descendants.

## Colchester

*8; 14½ miles E of Braintree on A120 (A12)*
*Includes Bourne Mill (NT)*

Up to the Second World War, Colchester was wonderful. The earliest recorded town in England, it was actually the seat of government in Roman times (though later abandoned in favour of London) and is still prodigiously rich in Roman remains, including most of the walls and a good deal of the great gate to the west, now known as BALKERNE GATE. It also possessed the largest Norman castle keep in existence anywhere, built on the foundations of the Roman Temple of Claudius; the tremendous eleventh-century remains of the first Augustinian priory in England; seven medieval parish churches, and well over 200 houses built before the reign of Queen Anne.

And yet, despite all these undoubted treasures, Colchester is not a beautiful town today. The High Street, still marking the old Roman thoroughfare, has been given over to the most insensitive development imaginable, and the whole centre of the town is a mass of car parks, shopping piazzas and acres of faceless concrete. Such phenomena, in a town of Colchester's importance, are I suppose to some extent inevitable; but the situation did not need to be as bad as this. The hideous tower blocks of the University of Essex on the skyline – proven guarantors of student unrest – somehow seem to epitomise all that this once lovely town has been called upon to suffer in the past half-century.

Concentrate, then, on the individual buildings. We may as well begin with the CASTLE, which serves as a focal point for all Colchester. Formidable enough even now, it must have looked a lot grimmer in Norman days when it rose to four storeys and was faced with stone, tile and ashlar. It is thought to have been begun around 1085 and completed some fifteen years later. It sustained two great sieges: the first in 1216, when King John personally wrested it from the hands of Philip Augustus of France, and the second during the Civil War, when Royalist Colchester held out for twelve weeks against Cromwell. In 1683 it was bought by a building speculator who demolished the two top floors for their raw materials. It is now a museum.

Now to ST BOTOLPH'S PRIORY. Don't be deceived by the immense pseudo-Norman tower of 1838; the great ruin stands immediately to the north, and hugely impressive it is. All that remains after the 1648 bombardment is part of the west front – decorated with blind arcading in re-used Roman brick and containing what is left of the earliest circular window in England – and two storeys of the nave arcades, supported on massive circular piers nearly 6 feet across; but this is more than enough to suggest the majesty of the church. Majesty – not opulence: surface decoration seems to have been kept to the minimum. It was the proportions that counted; note the way the two west towers stand outside the line of the aisles – an innovation here, but one which was to be copied by the Early English architects of Wells 150 years later.

What other buildings of Colchester linger especially in the memory? The spirited flint flushwork of ST JOHN'S ABBEY GATEHOUSE, ostensibly almost untouched since the fifteenth century; HOLLYTREES, a superb Georgian house of 1716, standing opposite the castle and sharing its museum functions; SCHEREGATE, an ancient postern in the wall with a medieval timber-framed house built on top of it; plenty of nice old houses in NORTH AND EAST HILLS, and EAST AND WEST STOCKWELL STREETS; and, just outside the town, BOURNE MILL (NT), an enchanting little conceit built by Sir Thomas Lucas in 1591 as a fishing lodge. The outsize end gables, with their joyfully irresponsible finials and curlicues, suggest the hand of the Dutch Protestant refugees who had established a community in Colchester. It is open to the public and strongly recommended.

## Copford

*9; 3 miles SW of Colchester off B1022*

The CHURCH OF ST MICHAEL AND ALL ANGELS (formerly St Mary the Virgin) is pretty enough on the outside with its squat little broach spire and semi-circular eastern apse; but this scarcely prepares one for the interior, which is not only almost untouched twelfth-century Norman but also contains a series of contemporary wall paintings unrivalled in Essex. Unlike the church itself, certain of these have been restored by an unfeeling Victorian hand; but the worst of the restorations – notably in the apse and above the sanctuary arch – have at least the virtue of being immediately distinguishable from their unspoilt neighbours. The latter, which compared with most of their kind remain in a remarkable state of preservation, can give considerable pleasure, especially those along the north wall.

Architecturally, the unity of the interior is broken only by the later addition of the south aisle and – far sadder – the removal of the original tunnel-vaulted roof, unique in England except for the Tower Chapel in London. The springers remain, but the timber roof with kingposts of about 1400 is no substitute for the lost vault – which was almost certainly frescoed, too.

## Dedham*

*10; 6½ miles NE of Colchester on B1029*

One of the most perfect small towns in England, Dedham is a knockout. Each house is prettier than the next and the great tower of ST MARY THE VIRGIN – Constable's church – soars up over the town, the gentle valley of the Stour, and the surrounding water-meadows. Apart from the church, there is no point in singling out individual buildings; fine as many of them are, their importance is in the contribution they make to the ensemble. A short walk down the High Street will reveal the lot.

St Mary's was begun in 1492 – the year Columbus discovered America – at a time when the prosperity of the clothing towns of East Anglia was at its height. In style it really belongs less to Essex than to Suffolk just across the river, a member of that glorious Perpendicular group of which Long Melford and Lavenham are the prime examples. Like them, it has an extremely long nave and chancel and a high clerestory giving almost as much illumination as the windows of the aisles; the whole church is thus flooded with light. The grandest feature, however, remains the splendid tower of knapped flint with copious stone dressings – a landmark long before Constable's day. It is independent of the church in structure, and is pierced by a north–south passageway leading into the churchyard with a panelled vault of much heraldic elaboration.

A rather charming tablet inside the church laments a lady who died in 1748 'in consequence of having accidentally swallowed a Pin' – lodged, we are reliably informed, in a Christmas pudding.

## Faulkbourne Hall

*11; 2 miles NW of Witham on B1018*

A curious history is attached to Faulkbourne Hall. It started in the early fifteenth century as a relatively unpretentious timber-framed house. Then, in 1439, Sir John Montgomery received a licence to crenellate and began to turn it into a castle. In the days of the Wars of the Roses castles still served a most useful purpose; but gradually the danger receded and the house began to turn back into a mansion – though by now something on a far larger scale than the original house, and keeping the obvious outer accoutrements of the castle. Glimpsed through the trees from the road, it seems to have a mysterious, almost fairytale quality. The rich red brick momentarily reminds one of Tattershall or Herstmonceux, but its irregular plan endows it with a degree of informality that those two towering contemporaries could never possess. Even the huge square tower, as asymmetrically outsize as the single claw of certain crabs, with its overhanging *tourelles* in a vaguely French style, defies us to take it entirely seriously.

*Faulkbourne Hall.*

Inside and out, there have been plenty of additions, notably a broad timber staircase of the seventeenth century behind the one-storey Hall of the original house; there is other, nineteenth-century, work too – predictably less successful. But the essential late medieval flavour remains, and the house lingers in the memory with a strange persistency.

## Finchingfield

*12; 8½ miles NE of Great Dunmow on B1057*

This village would win my award as the prettiest in Essex; indeed, it must be one of the prettiest in the country. It has everything English villages ought to have: a bridge, a duckpond, a perfectly sited church with a Norman tower, and a triangular village green with the houses grouped picturesquely but quite unselfconsciously around it. There is even a windmill – on the hill overlooking it from the north.

ST JOHN THE BAPTIST is a mixture of styles: inside, the Norman tower arch has been preserved, the octagonal piers of the south arcade are Early English, and the windows nearly all Decorated except those in the clerestory of the nave which are Perpendicular; those of the chancel clerestory (an unusual feature in itself) are Decorated again. The screen to the south aisle is a fourteenth-century gem, the rood-screen itself a little later but very nearly as fine.

If you drive up the hill and past the windmill, you will come almost immediately to SPAINS HALL, lying some way back from the road on your right, its west front facing you across the lawn. It is late Elizabethan, built of red brick with rather sparse stone dressings, vaguely E-shaped but in fact conceived on a very irregular plan, with the projections unevenly spaced and of different widths and lengths. The chief decorative feature is the row of curly Dutch gables, but even these vary in size and shape though they all have funny little brick finials on the top. The positioning of the Hall is at once apparent from its huge nine-light window with a double transom. Another point of interest is the curious corbelling-out of the northernmost gable, in which the brickwork is of a slightly darker colour; but this whole bay was added in 1890 and can therefore be effectively ignored.

The history of Spains goes back to the fourteenth century, and possibly even earlier; there was certainly a timber-framed moated manor house on the present site, a fragment of which still survives in the north-west corner. It was, however, almost completely rebuilt around 1585 by one William Kempe, who some thirty-five years later was so stricken with remorse for having unjustly accused his wife of infidelity that he vowed himself to silence and spoke not a single word for seven years. The house today is still, in most of its essentials, that which he left to his nephew Robert; to Robert, however – who was later to be knighted in the Great Hall by Oliver Cromwell – must go the credit for several of the ornamental features that lend it distinction: the silver-leaded rainwater heads, for example, with their initials R.W. and their date 1637; the Dutch gables; the wainscoting in the Hall and the adjoining parlour, now the Drawing Room; and the staircase, with its acorn finials, leading up to the Great Chamber and the bedrooms above the Hall.

After Robert, Spains seems to have suffered little alteration for some 130 years. By this time it had passed to the Ruggles family; it was John Ruggles who in 1768 built the extremely sophisticated little Baroque cupola over the east wing and – a good deal more spectacular – the huge depressed Doric arch, rusticated and topped with a triglyph frieze, which dominates the Drawing Room and frames the canted bay which he added to its eastern end. He also inserted a straight staircase at the screens end of the Hall – rising to a Venetian window overlooking the moat – and, in the Hall itself, a charming Gothic Revival screen which was most unfortunately removed at the end of the last century. His Library, by contrast, remains virtually unchanged: panelled, with an Adam-style mantelpiece and a Flemish tiled fireplace, the bookcases forming concave curves in the corners. There is also a pretty neo-classical Dining Room. On the outside, the eighteenth-century work shows best when the house is seen from the lake to the south and there are only the tall pairs of Tudor chimneys to tell of its earlier origins.

In the gardens to the east, beyond the magnificent old spreading cedar tree planted in 1670 and now 186 feet across, stands a little brick building, square and embattled, of two storeys and with polygonal corner shafts and towers. It is known as the PRAYER HOUSE, but is more likely to have been used as a banqueting house in Elizabethan and Jacobean days.

Spains Hall may not be one of the great houses of England, but there are few ancient manor houses which have remained so unspoilt and so untouched by time.

## Fingringhoe★

*13; 4 miles SE of Colchester off B1025*

A disappointing village, it is, however, possessed of a magical church which redeems everything. ST ANDREW'S is beautifully set, near a little pond fringed with oak trees; it has a nice square-topped tower, horizontally striped with limestone and flint, and a pretty flushwork porch. It has no pretensions, and needs no improvement. Inside, there is an old wagon roof over the Norman nave, its bosses at present slightly over-painted (but they will weather down in time), and traces of medieval wall paintings, including a gigantic St Christopher. The fresh whitewashed walls give it a feeling of being near the sea, and the broad windows of plain glass let in the misty Essex light. There are plenty of features to notice: the original door, for example, with its simply magnificent old iron handle, or the feathery figure of St Michael, with dragon, in the spandrels above. But this is a church in which the atmosphere counts more than any excellencies of craftsmanship. Few Essex churches have made me feel so happy.

## Great Bardfield

*14; 7½ miles NE of Great Dunmow on B1057*

Another delightful Essex village with houses grouped around a triangular green; it too has a windmill, and another most interesting church. Unlike St John's at Finchingfield, however, ST MARY THE VIRGIN stands at some distance from the green, near the fine timber-framed GREAT BARDFIELD HALL on the Braintree road. It is of the fourteenth century throughout, except for the little recessed spire which must date from around 1720. The tower itself is broad, square and embattled, without buttresses. There is a fine south porch with a two-light window to the east flanked by pretty quatrefoils. The original carved oak door is still in position.

Inside, the *pièce de résistance* is the magnificent stone screen which completely fills the chancel arch. It is highly ornate, traceried with double cusps and crockets, with sculptured heads of Edward III and Queen Philippa on the label stops to north and south. (We could, I think, have done without the rood itself – the crucified Christ, the Virgin and St John – which is a late nineteenth-century replacement by Bodley and looks it.) There is more good carving on the label stops of the four-bay arcades, especially the last but one on the north side.

The windows are most unusual. Most have been renewed, but obviously to the original design, which is not at all what one would expect in a fourteenth-century church and does not in any sense conform with the Decorated style as we normally understand it. They are all (except the east window) straight-headed, and their tracery is more international Gothic than specifically English. Can they, I wonder, be the work of some continental craftsman?

*St Andrew's Church, Fingringhoe.*

## Great Bromley

*15; 7 miles NE of Colchester on B1029*

One might think that dark red ironstone and knapped flint with flushwork made a rather unhappy combination, but at ST GEORGE'S CHURCH they set each other off beautifully. The ironstone tower is the grandest feature on the outside, many-tiered, with elaborate corner buttresses which reach right up to the pinnacles of the step-battlemented summit. The south porch, fifteenth-century, is rich in flushwork and surrounds an ornate portal of three orders with the original door. Adam and Eve inhabit the spandrels above. The flushwork continues, unusually but with considerable effect, on the clerestory of the nave.

All churches, if they are architecturally worth visiting at all, are worth walking round on the outside, and this one repays the trouble even more than most. Standing superbly on gently rising ground, it looks glorious from any angle – everything, one feels, that an Essex village church should be. A circumambulation also ensures that you do not miss the west door – another fine piece of fifteenth-century carving.

While the impression given by the outside is entirely Perpendicular, the interior reveals at once that St George's is older than it looks. The south arcade in particular is early fourteenth-century work with pretty carved capitals – all, that is, except the westernmost which is distinctly macabre. The nave is tall and noble, the two-light clerestory windows providing an oddly broken rhythm – seven of them covering three interior bays. Between them are seated figures; above them the church's crowning glory, a double hammer-beam roof, carved and painted in the two easternmost bays.

Almost everything here is a joy to behold – not forgetting, high up on the inner wall of the tower, the row of bellringers' hats, the oldest dating from 1716.

## Great Waltham*

*16; 4½ miles N of Chelmsford on A130*

Samuel Tufnell bought the Jacobean manor house known as LANGLEYS in 1711, at the age of twenty-nine, and immediately began to transform it into the beautifully proportioned Georgian building that we see today. It is best appreciated from its own gardens (by Charles Bridgeman); two and a half storeys of warm red brick, the hipped roof partly concealed by a parapet, with projecting side wings and pedimented centre producing a rhythm of 2–3–3–3–2. No surprises so far; there is elegance in plenty, but nothing unusual. For Mr Tufnell, however, elegance was not enough. Inside his house, he threw restraint to the winds, providing himself with a two-storeyed Saloon of staggering opulence, magnificently gilded and adorned with heavily fluted Corinthian pilasters. He was, so far as we know, his own architect, though helped by his cousin William and possibly by another relative, Charles Tufnell, who is known to have worked at Westminster Abbey. The Saloon admittedly shows occasional signs of an inexperienced, if talented, hand. This does not matter in the least; if anything, it adds character to a room which, in virtually any other medium-sized house of its period, would be the *pièce de résistance*.

But not at Langleys, for Mr Tufnell had two more trump cards up his sleeve. Although there is nothing outside to suggest the fact, during his rebuilding he managed to preserve in the north wing two simply stupendous rooms from the earlier house, rooms boasting so exuberant a display of Jacobean plasterwork as to leave one gasping. The ceiling of the Library is vaulted, that of the old Dining Room (or Parlour) flat; both are a riot of intricately decorated strapwork, cartouches and coats of arms, all sumptuously gilded. The fireplaces, too, catch at the breath: caryatid-framed figures of Peace and Plenty in the parlour, a rather more flowingly Baroque representation of the five senses in the Library – where, as an additional *bonne-bouche*, a large angel dressed in red with dazzlingly golden wings and holding an elaborate escutcheon occupies the lunette formed by the barrel vault above the windows. Another pleasantly allegorical figure, this time of Doctrine, faces him (or her) from the other end.

It is impossible to give in words an adequate impression of the effect of these two rooms: one might as well try to describe a firework display. Suddenly stumbled upon amid their tranquil early Georgian setting, they are one of the greatest architectural surprises in Essex.

## Great Warley*

*17; 2 miles S of Brentwood on B186*

Here is a really special treat. In a little Essex village, surprisingly rural despite being only a mile or two outside Brentwood, virtually on the road but discreetly masked by trees, stands the richest, most complete and most dazzlingly virtuoso *art nouveau* church in England – ST MARY THE VIRGIN. The architect, Charles Harrison Townsend – designer of the Bishopsgate Institute, the Horniman Museum and the Whitechapel Art Gallery – was commissioned in 1901 by a local resident, Mr Evelyn Heseltine, to build a church in memory of his brother Arnold, father of Peter Warlock, the composer; and three years later he completed it, with the spirited assistance of the Detroit-born Mr (later Sir) William Reynolds-Stephens.

Seen from the outside, the church is not particularly promising: pebble-dash walls, a prominent rounded apse, far more heavy buttresses than would seem strictly necessary, a similarly fussy roofscape and a spire, at the summit of which looms (the word is chosen with care) an outsize and somewhat menacing dove. Inside, however, the *art nouveau* takes over. It is very much of the English style; you will look in vain for the flowing sinuosities of Guimard in Paris or Horta in Brussels. Apart from the shape and proportions of the building itself, virtually everything is the work of Reynolds-Stephens; and the ensemble is a triumph. The first thing to catch the eye is the screen – a row of stylised trees in bronze, their roots clasping the low wall of green marble in clawlike fashion, each containing an oxidised silver angel within its branches, above which it bursts into a profusion of mother-of-pearl flowers and pomegranates in crimson glass. More trees – roses this time – span the barrel-vaulted roof; the walls carry a sort of frieze of lilies in

*The church of St Mary the Virgin, Great Warley.*

aluminium leaf; the pendant electroliers are also vaguely floral in design; it comes as a bit of a shock to discover that the material selected for their framework is *galvanised* iron. The pulpit consists of a large cross of beaten copper, supported by trees with triple stems, a design vaguely echoed by the lectern opposite. The organ, with its series of repoussé panels illustrating the Benedicite, is also worth a special look. Everywhere, the standard of craftsmanship is extraordinary, and the overall impression is one of restrained emotion, deep intelligence and considerable wealth. Only the windows and the west wall – wholly inadequate replacements after bomb damage in the last war – detract from the general splendour, but not enough seriously to spoil one of the most fascinating church interiors anywhere.

## Greensted-Juxta-Ongar

*18; 1 mile W of Chipping Ongar off A113*

Approach ST ANDREW's with respect, for this is the oldest wooden church in the world and the only example of a Saxon log church to have survived anywhere. The walls of the nave are constructed of oak logs, split vertically down the middle and set vertically like a stockade, the rounded side outwards, grooved and tongued together to keep out the draughts. Pitch-black and hard as concrete, they have never been replaced, and dendrological tests have given a date of AD 845. Inevitably, the rest of the church has been rebuilt and remodelled more than once; there are three pretty Tudor dormers on the north side, but otherwise little of major interest.

## Havering-Atte-Bower

*19; 6 miles W of Brentwood on B175*

BOWER HOUSE, an elegant red-brick Palladian house of five bays looking south across the Thames valley, was built by Henry Flitcroft in 1729. It was not, as Pevsner suggests, his first house – that honour must now go to Boreham nearby; and indeed it may well have been his success at Boreham that brought him this new commission from a prosperous Serjeant-at-Law named John Baynes and with it an association with two already famous names – Charles Bridgeman and Sir James Thornhill. Bridgeman it was who laid out the extensive 'pleasure grounds'; Thornhill was responsible for the decoration of the stairwell, which he painted with mythological scenes in *grisaille*. Most of this painting was unaccountably covered over with wallpaper in 1959; and though the Ford Motor Company, to whom the house now belongs, hopes gradually to restore them to view, progress is slow.

Some time between 1797 and 1816, two small single-storey wings were added to the house, canted towards the south. Who built them remains a mystery, but one rather wishes that he hadn't; while not actively ugly, their tall round-headed windows accord ill with the simple classicism of the main block and detract from its beauty. Inside, the house contains much fine plasterwork and wood panelling. These are today enjoyed principally by the Ford dealers who come to Bower House for training, but the company takes great pride in its property and a visit can easily be arranged.

## Ingatestone

*20; 6 miles SW of Chelmsford on B1102*

Sir William Petre, Secretary of State under Henry VIII, Edward VI and Bloody Mary, built INGATESTONE HALL some time between 1540 and 1565 in pleasant Tudor brick around an irregular courtyard. In the eighteenth century, alas, the west range (which included the Hall) was demolished and the building divided up into apartments for Catholic families; it was only after the First World War that Lord Petre restored the house and returned to live in it himself. Much of what we see today is in fact his work, including nearly all the windows. Of these, however, a few original ones remain on the west side of the east range; the step gables and many of the chimneystacks are also old work, and very nice too.

The north wing and the Long Gallery in the east wing are leased to Essex County Council and open to the public. The Long Gallery in particular has some good furniture – not all of the period – and some excellent family portraits, including one of Arabella Fermor, a lock of whose hair was stolen by the 7th Lord Petre, also represented. The consequent family feud was neatly defused by Alexander Pope's 'Rape of the Lock'.

The CHURCH OF ST EDMUND AND ST MARY has a terrific tower of diapered red brick, erected some half a century before the house, and the tombs of the Petres – a memorable group.

## Kelvedon Hatch

*21; 4 miles NW of Brentwood on A128*

You approach KELVEDON HALL through a magnificent entrance, flanked by lodges with niches and urns – the work of Lord Gerald Wellesley, later 7th Duke of Wellington, who was called in to supervise the repairs and alterations when, after a brief and unhappy period as a Roman Catholic convent school, it returned to private hands in 1937. From here a short drive leads round to a small ornamental lake, and there on your left is the house: a very plain, red-brick, early Georgian mansion of seven bays and three storeys. The three-bay centre is slightly recessed but otherwise without any major emphasis: decorative features are confined to four corner urns and a quite modest pedimented doorcase, centrally placed below. To each side, linked to the main block by low and somewhat cringing quadrants and standing at right-angles to it so as to form a forecourt, are two pretty pavilions: three bays by two, with false *oeil-de-boeuf* windows and lanterns above.

The garden elevation, which looks down a gentle slope (this part of Essex is far more undulating than one somehow expects it to be) to a distant view of London, is almost as plain as the entrance front; here, however, the centre projects very slightly beneath a triangular pediment. Instead of a doorcase we have rather a deep porch supported on columns, and instead of the side pavilions there are two single-storey wings, each of three bays. Though these are in the same plane as the house, they abut it rather awkwardly, since none of their three horizontals – the roof line, the string-course or the point of springing of the round-headed window arches – coincides with those of the main block.

The name of the architect is not recorded; indeed, there may not even have been one. With the help of a few good models and pattern-books a house designed on such straightforward classical lines should not have been beyond the capabilities of any competent local builder. The real interest is inside. The front door leads directly into a broad Hall – in which it proves to be one of eight, each with its own richly moulded and pedimented doorcase. Another pediment crowns the chimneypiece and is itself surmounted by an elaborate picture frame, carved in similar style to form the overmantel. All this is in the noble idiom of William Kent and must date from 1740 or thereabouts – as must the main Staircase Hall. There, on the ground floor, are the same splendid doorcases – except that the principal one has been given a broad segmental pediment and fluted Corinthian pilasters – while the upper walls are exquisitely stuccoed with garlands and trophies, and the arabesques that swirl across the first-floor landing are echoed in the wrought-iron balustrade.

Surprisingly, however, the other main rooms do not share this style. Elsewhere – particularly in the Drawing Room, the Dining Room and the beautiful gently barrel-vaulted ground-floor bedroom which formerly served as the Chapel – the decoration is Adam rather than Kent, and must be a good thirty to forty years later in date. Only once more, in one of the upstairs bedrooms, do we find ourselves back in George II's day; otherwise, Adam reigns – even at the head of the exceedingly pretty back staircase, where there are three balusters per tread and the wealth of delicate ornament far exceeds what one would normally expect to find in the domestic quarters.

Two other features deserve special mention. The first is the little Study off the Hall, which boasts an enchanting painted ceiling in the Pompeian style, obviously brought back by the late eighteenth-century owner from the Grand Tour. The other is the equally delightful pavilion by the swimming pool. It is purest Austrian Baroque, and might have come straight from Salzburg – a surprising building indeed to find in the heart of rural Essex, but no less pleasurable for that.

## Lawford*

*22; 7 miles NE of Colchester off A137*

The outside of ST MARY'S CHURCH seems to be made of just about everything the builders could lay their hands on – flint, freestone, brick, septaria and that most unlovely of conglomerates, puddingstone. Inside, first impressions are not much more promising; the nave arcade, for example, dates from 1826, the chancel arch from 1853. But now enter the chancel – and you enter another world. To say that it is the best fourteenth-century chancel in Essex is not saying enough; it would be unforgettable anywhere. The east window, imposing as it is, has been renewed; but, of the eight huge three-light windows along the north and south walls, each attempts to outdo the next in the exuberance of its tracery. Never is a design repeated; several occur nowhere else. Owls and squirrels inhabit the carved stone foliage that climbs round their frames, and the easternmost window of the north side has chains of cavorting little men, all conceived with an irresistible lightness and humour. Sedilia and piscina keep up the standard, though here some of the little figures have had their heads knocked off. But who wants an ornate Victorian carved reredos in a church like this? If it is trying to outshine the medieval glory it fails miserably.

And so, if you like the Decorated style in its fullest possible bloom, don't miss Lawford. Pevsner primly describes it as 'unhealthy luxuriance'; I love it.

At LAWFORD HALL nearby, a timber-framed Elizabethan house of 1583 lurks behind a Georgian brick show front of 1756.

## Layer Marney*

*23; 6½ miles SW of Colchester off B1022*

Tall Tudor gatehouses are always eye-catchers; one has only to think of St James's Palace and Hampton Court – or, in East Anglia, of East Barsham or Oxburgh Hall, where the twin towers soar up seven storeys above the moat. But nowhere in all England is there a gatehouse that can hold a candle to Layer Marney. As you approach the house up the drive you may feel a little disappointed: that gigantic Tudor bastion looming before you is certainly formidable enough, but somehow it doesn't give the same impression as the photographs. Take heart: enter by the central door, buy your ticket and then walk straight through the house to the garden. For it is there, on the south side, that Henry, 1st Lord Marney, set out to startle the world.

And succeeded. On the two hexagonal towers, topped with little shell gables in Italian terracotta, no fewer than eight storeys go rocketing up to glory. Between them, on the first and second floors of the house, are two tall five-light windows – not, as you might assume at first glance, of the traditional Tudor kind, but terracotta again, the mullions and transoms all carved with appropriate Renaissance patterns, the ogival heads with an intricate scroll design. This use of terracotta is interesting. When Lord Marney was building his house, in the early 1520s, it was still a very recent innovation and virtually confined to the Court; but Marney was captain of Henry VIII's bodyguard and had accompanied his master to the Field of the Cloth of Gold in 1520, so had presumably acquired a degree of sophistication rare among his less privileged contemporaries.

Weather permitting, it is well worth climbing to the top; there is some wonderfully improbable nursery wallpaper on the stairs. (Be warned, however, that the view from the top is nowhere near as good as that from the bottom.) Then, when you have had your fill of the Gatehouse, turn your attention to the CHURCH OF ST MARY THE VIRGIN a few yards to the west, so close as to be practically in the garden. Built in red brick with blue diapering at about the same time as the house, it has some fine Marney tombs and, rather more surprisingly, a large painting of St Christopher on the north wall – 'curiously rustic', as Pevsner says, 'for a place so intimately connected with the taste of the court'.

Just to the south of the house there is another long range; formerly the stables, it was converted to a Gallery early in the present century, those responsible having the good sense to retain the splendid timber roof while adding the huge Tudor-style windows and the genuine Jacobean fireplace. All very fine, no doubt; but Layer Marney *is* its Gatehouse; it is for that that we came, and for that that we shall return.

## Little Dunmow

*24; 1½ miles E of Great Dunmow off A120*

The CHURCH OF ST MARY occupies what was once the south chancel chapel, or Lady Chapel, of a priory of Augustinian canons. Not altogether surprisingly, therefore, its exterior is unpromising – and is not helped by the ridiculous-looking turret tacked on in 1872. The interior, on the other hand, possesses features of great beauty, particularly the five-bay arcade of about 1200 which originally marked the south side of the priory chancel and in the present church runs just inside the north wall. Above it is a row of extremely narrow lancets, but the light comes in chiefly from the south, through four splendid windows of three and four lights alternately, and also through the five-light east window, recently renewed. All have lovely flowing Decorated tracery except one, which is purest Perpendicular – 'a concession', opines Pevsner, 'to coming fashion'. Beneath these windows is a blank arcade, with quite enchanting carvings of people and animals in the spandrels. There is a superb tomb chest with effigies of Walter Fitzwalter and his wife, and a rather touching small ledger slab in the floor of the nave commemorating the death of a nine-month-old baby during the Great Plague. The Dunmow Flitch Chair in the chancel is a botched-up mess, but an endearing one.

*Layer Marney Tower.*

*Moyns Park.*

## Little Leighs

*25; 3½ miles SW of Braintree off A131*

LEEZ PRIORY stands about 2 miles to the north-west of the village, another one of those great Tudor mansions in warm red brick with which Essex is so splendidly endowed. It began as an Augustinian priory, but was acquired after the Dissolution by Richard Rich – infamous for his betrayal of Sir Thomas More – who built his house on virtually the same ground plan: Great Hall over nave, courtyard over cloister. Much of this was pulled down in 1753, but the Outer and Inner Gatehouses remain, *inter alia*, and very magnificent they are too. The Outer Gatehouse, twin-turreted and embattled, with such decoration as it possesses carved directly into the brick, is impressive enough; but the Inner – set, rather surprisingly, on a different axis, south instead of west – is far higher and grander, with four-light windows on two storeys between the turrets, mullioned and transomed. In the spandrels above the doorway are a Tudor rose and a fleur-de-lis.

It is not, at the time of writing, open to the public.

## Maldon

*26; 9 miles E of Chelmsford on A414*

A town of considerable charm, Maldon is built on a hill above the neck of the Blackwater estuary. There are any number of good houses, particularly in the HIGH STREET and on MARKET HILL. ALL SAINTS' CHURCH has two principal claims to fame: its thirteenth-century *triangular* tower – the only one of this shape in England, and it was not really a very good idea – and the quite astonishingly (and inexplicably) opulent south aisle. This is like nothing so much as the Lady Chapel at Ely writ small, and must be of about the same date, 1340. The big Decorated windows (all but the easternmost nineteenth-century renewals) are framed within a continuous arcade, the alternate arches between the windows being blank. Below this runs a smaller arcade of ogival arches, intricately moulded and set on columns with decorative capitals. The label stops in the spandrels are carved with heads, but these too have obviously been renewed.

In the High Street, on the site of the former CHURCH OF ST PETER – of which only the west tower now stands – is the LIBRARY founded by Dr Plume, Archdeacon of Rochester, in 1704. It is a plain, typically Queen Anne building of two storeys, the lower of which now houses a branch of the Essex County Library. That so distinguished a man of the cloth should have given his native town a library rather than rebuild the ruined church is an interesting sign of the way times were changing as the eighteenth century began.

## Moyns Park

*27; 3½ miles SE of Haverhill off A604*

Standing well back in its own grounds, just outside Steeple Bumpstead and only a mile or two from the Suffolk border, Moyns Park presents an impressive face to the world. This north-west front, of rich red brick with stone dressings, is typically late Tudor of the 1580s

– two and a half storeys crowned by four gables with attic windows and brick finials, and clusters of tall chimneys towering up behind. (The left-hand group collapsed early in the present century and was unfortunately rebuilt somewhat differently; otherwise the symmetry is complete.) A two-storey canted bay rises in each of the three spaces between the gables. All the windows are mullioned and transomed. Nothing, it seems, could be more simple or straightforward.

But a walk round the house on the outside shows at once that this is not the whole story. Moyns is then revealed to be U-shaped, with quite long timber-framed wings projecting out behind it; clearly the show front was only part of a planned remodelling of an earlier house. Of the two wings, that to the north-east is much restored and of relatively little interest; the south-west wing, however, gabled and closely studded, with in-fills of brick nogging and projecting first-floor jetties, strikes a note of happy informality which makes a delightful contrast with the somewhat austere façade.

The interior, and particularly the principal rooms on the entrance front, has been modernised – though the Hall, despite having lost its screen, still retains its timber ceiling. (The decoration is by John Fowler.) Only the smaller rooms in the south-west wing have really kept their Elizabethan atmosphere.

The two venerable mulberry trees standing in the courtyard behind are said to have been ordered by Charles II to provide food for the silkworms with which he hoped to create a silk industry of the kind he had seen in France during his years of exile. Nowadays they provide welcome perching for the hundreds of budgerigars from the open aviaries that close the court to the south-east.

## Paycocke's

See Coggeshall.

## Saffron Walden

*28; 14 miles NW of Great Dunmow on A130*

Together with Dedham, Saffron Walden gets my vote as the handsomest small town in Essex. Seen from a distance on the London road, it looks more like a picture of a town than a town itself, being almost entirely free of suburban sprawl. It has the remains of a CASTLE KEEP – not very exciting, but better than nothing – any number of medieval cottages, and in CHURCH STREET, starting at the corner of MARKET HILL, a row of four magnificent town houses of the fourteenth and fifteenth centuries, with seventeenth-century pargetting as fine as you can see anywhere. There is much fine Georgian building in the HIGH STREET, a red-brick TOWN HALL of 1760 or so and an agreeably irresponsible Victorian CORN EXCHANGE in the Market Place.

There is also the parish CHURCH OF ST MARY. Like St Mary's at Dedham, it isn't really an Essex church at all, but while Dedham is a Suffolk church through and through, Saffron Walden looks further west, towards Cambridge. It sits superbly on a high hill at the north end of the town, looking more like a small cathedral, its unusual length (nearly 200 feet) emphasised by a beautiful traceried stone arcade running along the outside of the clerestory, dividing the windows into pairs. There is a gracefully soaring spire supported by flying buttresses, and opposite it at the other end of the nave there are two small turrets whose resemblance to those of King's College Chapel is not wholly coincidental: the same master mason, John Wastell, was responsible for both buildings.

The interior is similarly grand: a generously proportioned nave of seven bays, with the spandrels elaborately carved along the arcades, and side aisles just as broad, all combine to give an impression of great princeliness – an impression only slightly diminished by a curious change of building material at clerestory level, where the prevailing grey stone unexpectedly gives way to clunch. There is a most noble wooden roof too – a little overworked by recent restorers above the nave, but with an entirely satisfying and more muted coloration over the snow-white chancel.

## St Osyth

*29; 4 miles W of Clacton off B1027*

This saint was an Anglo-Saxon princess, beheaded by the Danes, who after her martyrdom picked up her severed head and walked off, like St Denis, carrying it under her arm. The pride of ST OSYTH'S PRIORY is the tremendous Gatehouse, surely one of the proudest entrances to any monastic building in the country. Right the way across it, covering both the polygonal side towers and the two connecting bays and broken only by the gateway itself and its flanking niches, run no fewer than eight courses of intricate flushwork, culminating in a splendid array of chequered battlements along the top. A little surprisingly, the towers do not project above the centre as they do in most other gatehouses of the period, including St Osyth's nearest equivalent, St John's Abbey at Colchester; but faced with a building of such impressive style and quality one hardly feels like carping.

Once through the Gatehouse – having been careful not to miss the spirited encounter between St George and the dragon in the spandrels and the sumptuously fan-vaulted interior – you cross the great court to what remains of the brick mansion built for himself in 1527 by one of its abbots, John Vintoner: essentially a triple gateway crowned by a tall six-light oriel window. Even the latter is largely a restoration, but it still retains along its head a few rather tentative decorations in Renaissance style – among the earliest to be found in Essex. A little to the east stands a fine turreted tower, chequered with flint and septaria and built some thirty years later, after the Dissolution, by Lord D'Arcy, KG, Vice-Chamberlain to Edward VI; nearby is the Chapel. Though not originally designed as such – it was in fact part of the old refectory passage – it is a fine example of late thirteenth-century vaulting and, apart from a few ruined fragments, one of the earliest surviving parts of the priory.

Before leaving St Osyth's, it is worth sparing a little more time and having a look at the parish CHURCH OF ST PETER AND ST PAUL, with its Tudor brick arcades and hammer-beam roof.

*The north porch, church of St John the Baptist, Thaxted.*

## Terling Place

*30; 7½ miles NE of Chelmsford off A12*

The house stands at the end of the remarkably pretty village of Terling. It was built in the 1770s, in pale greyish white brick, by John Johnson, for over thirty years County Surveyor of Essex and designer of the Shire Hall in Chelmsford. As so often with houses of this date, the entrance was originally on the garden front; in 1818, however, Thomas Hopper was called in to turn it round and enlarge it. He provided a new Tuscan porch to the north, gave the south front a new blank arcade where the front door had been, and added two wings, sloping off at angles to the main block and ending in little pedimented temple fronts. The western one contains, virtually untouched, the absolutely fascinating laboratories of the 3rd Lord Rayleigh, the famous physicist and Nobel Prizewinner, and of his son (and successor in the title), another eminent man of science. It was here that the gas argon was discovered.

The main feature of the interior is the neo-classical Hall, rising through the two main storeys of the house, designed by Hopper where the first staircase had been. (He built a new one in a short projecting block to the right of his new entrance.) Around this Hall at first-floor level runs a Gallery; it is of cast iron and of great elegance, and the Ionic columns which appear to be made of yellow marble or scagliola are in fact of cast iron as well. Two of them carry the chimney flues from the downstairs rooms. Just below the Gallery there runs a broad frieze, in imitation of the Elgin Marbles, by Westmacott. (In *The Buildings of England*, Pevsner mistakenly attributes it to J. Henning, Sen.) All the doorcases on both floors are of beautifully marbleised wood. Elsewhere in the house there is some good plasterwork and several excellent marble fireplaces; but a redecoration carried out in 1850 is very much to be regretted.

## Thaxted

*31; 6½ miles N of Great Dunmow on B184*

In the later Middle Ages Thaxted was a large and prosperous town; now it is a small and beautiful one. Apart from the church there are no buildings of outstanding merit – a fact, however, which doesn't matter in the least for at Thaxted it is the whole, and not the parts, that matters. And there are, in any case, plenty of pleasant things to look at: the old TOWER MILL, for example, one of the town's principal landmarks, and the GUILD HALL, three-storeyed with double overhang. (Norman Scarfe, in his excellent *Shell Guide*, fulminates against the 1910 restoration of this charming building; I can only say that it still looks jolly nice to me.)

But the pride of Thaxted is its church – ST JOHN THE BAPTIST – the proudest reminder of its medieval prosperity. Admittedly, there was no importation of stone; the whole thing is built of local rubble. In all other respects, however, the question of cost was clearly of little importance. Take the tower – a magnificent construction in itself, but supporting a tall and slender spire of the most elegant grace, adorned with three rows of lucarnes diminishing in size from three lights to one as they approach the top. (It is actually a replacement, the original having been struck by lightning in 1814, but the copy was exact.) Or take the north porch, its two storeys making it almost as high as the transept behind it, its vault richly ornate with its liernes and bosses, shields and fleurons, figure frieze and gargoyles.

Inside, there is no deterioration in quality. The mid-fourteenth-century arcades are richly moulded, the broad aisles (south about 1370, north 1445) give a feeling of expansiveness and generosity; the huge windows of the aisles and the clerestory flood the building with light. The wooden roof has carved corbels, that over the chancel has tie-beams with kingposts. Oddly, perhaps, there are no chancel steps, but the chancel has miraculously kept its old tiled floor. Then there is a fine seventeenth-century wineglass pulpit with tester, and hanging garlands between the panels. And though most f the windows – except Kempe's east one – are ıercifully clear, there are a few excellent pieces of fourεenth- to sixteenth-century stained glass distributed bout. It is a church not only of much beauty, but of onsiderable character as well.

Just a mile or two outside Thaxted and straddling he parish border with neighbouring Broxted stands ORHAM HALL, one of the finest of the early Tudor brick nansions of Essex. The approach is dominated by a huge ay window of forty lights on the east (show) front, a iece of swaggering bravura which somehow sets off the aphazard informality of the rest of the façade. This vindow, as one might expect, marks the Great Hall, set n the traditional way off a screens passage. This rises he full height of the house – a not very successful allery having been inserted in 1906 to facilitate ommunication across it – and has a coved and coffered eiling with a central louvre, not, obviously, to let out moke from a central hearth but simply to provide ccess to a most unexpected but charming little lantern n the roof. In the south wing, which was built around n earlier, timber-framed house of around 1470, there emains a splendid old solar with huge tie-beams and ingposts.

## Tilty*

*2; 4 miles NW of Great Dunmow off A130*

ong ago, the CHURCH OF ST MARY THE VIRGIN was a *appella ante portas* of a nearby Cistercian abbey, of vhich nothing now remains but a few fragments of a wall in the field behind and the quiet country setting upon which the Order always insisted. The nave, Early English of about 1220, is humble enough; walls rendered in yellow plaster, no aisles, lancet windows widely splayed with clear glass except the three-light west window. Then, however, comes the chancel, a different matter altogether. There is no chancel arch, only an arch-braced tie-beam in the wooden roof; but beyond it, the little church is transformed. The chancel is broader, higher and infinitely more opulent than the nave, and about a century later in date – added, presumably, by some rich benefactor. When rich benefactors appeared during the Decorated period, architectural fireworks could confidently be expected; and Tilty was no exception. The huge five-light east window explodes into great swirls of flowing tracery with an exceedingly complicated design of circles and mouchettes; and its two neighbours on the north and south walls, though slightly smaller, are scarcely less ambitious.

The strange thing is that despite the extraordinary contrast between the two parts of the church, the same quietly domestic atmosphere pervades the whole interior. This may be due to the rendering of coloured wash on the walls, and the gentle blue-grey paint on the pews and organ. The exuberance of the chancel in no way crushes the modest nave, nor does it look in itself affected or pompous: a peasant in his finery, not an overdressed dwarf. Tilty, in short, is a little gem; those who drive straight past have no idea what they are missing.

*The Guild Hall, Thaxted.*

### Waltham Abbey
*33; 5 miles S of Hoddesdon off A10*

Although originally founded by Tofig the Proud, standard-bearer to King Canute, Waltham Abbey is effectively the creation of King Harold of England. Here he stopped to pray on his hurried journey from Stamford Bridge to Hastings, and here, after the battle, his body and those of his two brothers were brought for burial. The glorious nave, Norman in style although dating from before the Conquest, remains much as Harold knew it, but his transepts and eastern apse were destroyed at the Dissolution. Destroyed, too, even more tragically, was every vestige of a huge new Early English abbey added towards the end of the twelfth century by Henry II, in expiation of his guilt for the murder of Thomas à Becket. Of this abbey church, Harold's formed only the west end; continuing to the east, there was a choir considerably longer than the nave, then two more transepts and finally a retrochoir. The abbey today thus represents only a tiny part of what has been lost, and even that has survived only because at the time of the Dissolution it had served for three centuries as the parish church and was consequently inviolate.

Nonetheless, it is a magnificent survival; the earliest Norman nave in England, with something of the grandeur – if not the scale – of Durham, which it predates by some forty years. Like Durham, it has a system of arcades alternating between Composite piers and circular ones with a heavily grooved decoration. Above these arcades strides a great gallery, floorless, which in turn supports the clerestory; here the windows are in groups of three, a large central window flanked by two smaller ones in the form that later became known as 'Venetian'.

The effect of this nave, despite all the vicissitudes the abbey has suffered, remains utterly superb – at least so far as the north and south sides are concerned. The trouble comes at the east and the west ends. The former, behind the glorious arch to the Norman crossing-tower that marks the end of the original fabric, is now taken up with an extraordinary confection by William Burges dated 1859–60. Three fat two-centre lancet windows flanked by stubby columns with shaft rings like motor tyres, support a quatrefoil frieze, on top of which is a coarse wheel window. The effect is, admittedly, vaguely Romanesque, and I suppose it could be argued that it breaks the harmony of the building less than does the outspoken Gothic east end at Durham; but the details are such a jumble of different styles (whoever heard of Norman quatrefoils?) that the argument would not really hold. Burges could be fun when he started from scratch and it didn't matter; here he is a disaster, and distracts the eye from the Burne-Jones glass, which is first-rate and deserves a more considerate frame.

Part of the west end, though fortunately not very much of it, suffers from a disastrous attempt to Gothicise the whole church in the early fourteenth century. The effects of this are evident in the westernmost bay; we can only be thankful that work was stopped when it was – though not before the whole structure had shown alarming signs of imminent collapse if it were continued.

On the outside, this west end is now largely obscured by the somewhat ungainly tower which was erected after the original crossing-tower had fallen in 1552. Many of the old stones were apparently re-used – a fact which may account for the hotch-potch of material which detracts still further from its effect. The east end, not surprisingly, is still messier; only the north and south walls are moderately satisfactory in their muted way, and even they give little enough indication of the great glory that lies within.

---

## Short List

### Bobbingworth
*34; 1½ miles NW of Chipping Ongar off A122*

BLAKE HALL is a fine Queen Anne house, set proudly on a hill above the village. Two wings were added in the 1840s by George Basevi, and there is a magnificent staircase believed to have been brought from Schomberg House in Pall Mall. Alas, it was taken over by Fighter Command in the Second World War, and one of the wings has been almost completely gutted. At the time of writing the owner has plans to restore it as a wartime operations room.

### Bradwell-Juxta-Coggeshall
*35; 3½ miles E of Braintree off A120*

HOLY TRINITY CHURCH is said to possess fourteenth-century wall paintings of the finest quality, though in a poor state of preservation. Alas, I failed to get in.

### Clavering
*36; 3 miles SW of Newport on B1038*

ST MARY AND ST CLEMENT'S is a large and splendid church, all-of-a-piece Perpendicular and all embattled, standing at the end of a long and straggling village. The high wooden roof has tie-beams and queenposts and there are carved wooden angels, now wingless, above the clerestory.

### Cressing
*37; 4 miles SE of Braintree on B1018*

Here is the earliest settlement of the Knights Templars in England. After their suppression it passed to the Hospitallers, from whose time dates the first of the two tremendous BARNS, built about 1450. The second is some eighty years later. There is also a third, of 1623. Admission is by appointment only, with Cressing Temple Farm.

### Gosfield Hall
*38; 2½ miles W of Halstead off A1017*

The west front of the Hall still bespeaks a fine Tudor mansion of *c.*1545, but the other fronts are all remodelled. A hotch-potch, but an interesting one, it is nevertheless now the property of the Mutual Households Association.

## Great Braxted

*39; 10 miles NE of Chelmsford off A12*

BRAXTED PARK is at first sight a most imposing Georgian house of brick – two projecting wings coming off a nine-bay centre with a single-storey stone porch. It has hipped roofs, and a canted bay facing left towards a large and splendid lake. The odd thing is that the house does not stand on its original site; it was carefully taken down and rebuilt on its present location. The principal decorative feature is the windows, all of which have octagonal panes, four top and four bottom, with little lozenges in the interstices.

## Great Leighs

*40; 4½ miles SW of Braintree on A131*

ST MARY'S CHURCH has a fine Norman round tower of flint, to which some dolt has added a hexagonal spire, shingled and lucarned, in 1882. It has good stone carving in the chancel, an early red-tiled floor and a pretty eighteenth-century west gallery.

## Hadleigh

*41; 1 mile W of Southend on A13*

Hadleigh is really a suburb of Southend – and this is probably why the little Norman CHURCH OF ST JAMES THE LESS is kept permanently locked nowadays. It has an apsed east end, and anywhere else might have seemed a jewel; it looks extremely inappropriate standing, as it does, in the middle of a traffic island at a busy crossroads.

## Hatfield Broad Oak

*42; 7 miles NE of Harlow on B183*

The CHURCH OF ST MARY THE VIRGIN comprises the west end of a twelfth-century Benedictine priory, from the west door to the crossing; but the style today is more Perpendicular than anything else. There are some particularly good carved label stops on the north and south arcades, and a simply splendid stone monument to Sir Robert de Vere in the centre of the chancel. For all the good things it contains, however, the church seems somehow lacking in charm.

## Little Coggeshall Abbey

*43; ¾ mile S of Coggeshall off B1024*

The present Little Coggeshall Abbey is in fact a pretty if somewhat tumbledown house set into the old Cistercian abbey ruins by the side of the River Pant. The cloister arcade is still partly visible, as is the undercroft behind it. There is also the outer shell of what may have been the lavatorium, with rows of deeply splayed lancets on both sides. Round columns and deeply moulded arches are all in brick – the columns are believed to be the oldest of their kind in England.

## Little Maplestead

*44; 2½ miles NE of Halstead off A131*

It is sad to have to relegate one of the only five circular churches in England to a short list, but the ministrations of Samuel Carpenter, who restored ST JOHN THE BAPTIST in 1850, leave one no choice. Originally a Hospitaller church and so built, as was the custom of Military Orders, on the model of the Church of the Holy Sepulchre at Jerusalem, it is now drained of spirit and atmosphere alike.

## Margaretting

*45; 4 miles SW of Chelmsford on B1102*

Another of those splendid Essex timber towers, on ten posts, adorns ST MARGARET'S CHURCH. It is relegated to the short list only because there is an even better one at Blackmore. The east window contains good fifteenth-century glass.

## Mistley

*46; 7 miles NE of Colchester on B1352*

The central part of this interesting village is largely of the first half of the eighteenth century. Two curious TOWERS added in 1776 by Robert Adam to the now demolished St Mary's church stand, somewhat ineptly, by the Stour estuary.

## Pentlow

*47; 3 miles W of Long Melford on B1064*

One of the six Essex churches with a round tower, ST GEORGE'S also boasts what is even more interesting – a semi-circular Norman apse, with its three original windows. Alas for the Victorian restoration: most of the windows were remodelled, the box pews and west gallery torn out. The pretty wagon roof was also renewed, but fortunately on the ancient model. The late sixteenth-century north chapel with its panelled tunnel vault contains the splendid tomb of the Kempe family. PENTLOW HALL, standing within its moat just behind the church, is a magnificent survival – a timber-framed manor house of about 1500 with a twelve-light oriel window.

## Tolleshunt D'Arcy Hall

*48; 10 miles SW of Colchester on B1026*

Most of the timbers (including kingposts) of the original Hall roof of about 1500 have been retained at the house, together with the vast chimney and the two doors leading from the screens passage into the buttery and pantry. It has also kept its moat on three sides – mud on the fourth – which is spanned by a stone and brick bridge dated 1585. There is a lovely ground-floor room with early sixteenth-century panelling – linenfold, portrait heads in relief, etc. – and sumptuously carved beams.

## Tolleshunt Major

*49; 11 miles SW of Colchester off B1026*

BECKINGHAM HALL is an early Tudor house of about 1540, brick and timber-framed. The chief interest, however, lies less in the house itself than in the curious brick Gatehouse, two storeys high, with long walls of diapered brick going off each side to a corner turret at one end and, at the other, to a large gate set between two more turrets of a slightly different shape. These latter turrets and two more on the Gatehouse have inward-sloping battlements – very odd.

# Gloucestershire

The triune county *par excellence*, Gloucestershire does not divide itself into Ridings as Yorkshire does (or did, until that Local Government Act of 1972), nor into separately named regions in the manner of Lincolnshire; geographically, however, its three parts differ from each other more widely than those of either of the other two counties. As we drive out from London, our introduction to Gloucestershire is the part that most people know best, the Cotswolds – a range of limestone hills, running more than 50 miles from north-east to south-west, providing almost limitless quantities of what is perhaps the most beautiful building stone in England and enfolding some of England's most beautiful villages. Cotswold soil is thin on the uplands, but perfect for the pasturage of sheep; hence the immense prosperity of the region during the great wool boom of the late fourteenth and fifteenth centuries and the magnificent 'wool churches', which are even more opulent than their contemporary counterparts in East Anglia (where flint was the only building stone readily available).

The Cotswolds rise gently towards the west, then stop suddenly with a dramatic escarpment, in some places almost 1,000 feet above sea level, below which lies the Severn Vale, green and pastoral, with Tewkesbury at one end – on the border with Hereford and Worcester – and Bristol (which used to have its own county status but is now part of the new county of Avon) on the other. Between the two lies Gloucester itself, unspeakably vandalised by the so-called planners of the 1950s but still dominated by one of the great cathedrals of England; and, a few miles to the south-west, salmon-pink in the sunset, the towers and ramparts of Berkeley Castle where Edward II met his untimely and unattractive end.

And so, by way of a multitude of wildfowl – which, in winter, easily outnumbers the human population of the Vale – we come to the Severn; and beyond it the third face of Gloucestershire, the Forest of Dean. In 1600 Michael Drayton dubbed it 'the Queen of Forests all', and even today we can see what he meant. In his time the vast expanses of oak had not yet been invaded by the sad conifers of the Forestry Commission; yet even now the forest remains a mysterious, magic place. Hidden deep within it are ancient mines for both iron and coal, some of which were worked within living memory; but all are now abandoned, and their overgrown remains add a further dimension to the strange enchantment. The forest ends on a note of high drama: the looping, turbulent Wye, snaking its way through the dark ravine of Symond's Yat.

Gloucestershire was an important area in Roman times; in the second century, Cirencester was second in size only to London itself, and a number of Roman villas have been unearthed in its neighbourhood – notably at Chedworth, where some of the mosaic floors have survived. From the strictly architectural viewpoint, however, we cannot in this book go back beyond the Saxons, who settled in considerable numbers both on the Wolds and in the Vale – where, at Deerhurst, we can see one of the two grandest Saxon churches left in England. Gloucestershire can boast about a dozen churches of Saxon origin; the Normans, however, left over 100, a number that few other counties can match, to say nothing of Gloucester Cathedral and that other cathedral in all but name, Tewkesbury Abbey. Of these I have listed (or shortlisted) only my own particular favourites, and if readers find that I have left out theirs (Avening, perhaps, or Hampnett, with their stone-vaulted chancels, or Ampney St Mary, Harnhill or Little Barrington with their tympana) I can only apologise.

The Early English style is comparatively rare in Gloucestershire, and such as there is exists only in the Cotswolds; troubles with the unruly Welsh made it a time unpropitious for church building any further to the west. The little church at Wyck Rissington, feeling its way uncertainly towards the idea of tracery, is for me the best of the lot. Among the parish churches, good examples of Decorated are still less frequent, though the south transept at Minchinhampton is unforgettable. (There is another at Longborough.) The scarcity is, once again, not surprising: in the early fourteenth century the great wool boom was still to come, and the only extensive building was in the rich monastic foundations of Gloucester and Tewkesbury, whose finances were largely independent of local economic forces.

Then, with the arrival of the Perpendicular – which was actually born at Gloucester Cathedral – the county comes back into its own. Cirencester, Northleach, Fairford, Chipping Campden: these are churches that it is worth crossing England – or the Atlantic, for that matter – to see. And, what is more, the towns or villages in which they stand have remained, for the most part, quite miraculously unspoilt. The industrial revolution left Gloucestershire almost untouched; even the mills, at Chalford, Nailsworth and other places in the valleys around Stroud, tend to be of the seventeenth or eighteenth centuries and possess real architectural distinction. In the fleecy Cotswolds, these golden villages – Bibury, Bourton-on-the-Water, Upper and Lower Slaughter, Snowshill – look much as they have looked for two centuries and more.

As for domestic architecture, although much has been lost to that monstrous upstart the county of Avon, Gloucestershire remains as rich and as varied as anywhere in the realm. Any list of great houses must begin with Berkeley Castle; it would then carry on through Stanway, Cirencester Park, Barnsley, Daylesford and Sezincote to its high Victorian culmination at Westonbirt – or, if you insist, to Teulon's appalling Tortworth, now very properly a prison. But for me the joy of Gloucestershire lies less in the stately homes than in the smaller manor houses. Their number is legion, the task of selection again hopelessly invidious. Owlpen and Daneway are perhaps the most romantic, Chavenage the most unspoilt, Nether Lypiatt the most beautiful. Several more are described in the following pages; but there are scores of others, seen and unseeen, that I have no doubt are equally worthy of inclusion. Here is architectural wealth indeed; and it is a particular pleasure to record that most of these manor houses, being of manageable size, are still lived in – often by the descendants of those who built them several centuries ago. Long may they continue so to be.

---

## Ashleworth

*1; 5 miles N of Gloucester off A417*

This tiny village beside the Severn has a pretty church, ST ANDREW AND ST BARTHOLOMEW'S, which is partly Norman – the herringbone work in the scraped north wall looks Saxon, but old traditions died hard in this part of England – and has been added to in most centuries since. Next to it is ASHLEWORTH COURT, built around 1460 and an extraordinary survival. There have been a few changes – the Great Hall, for example, has been divided both vertically and horizontally – but the basic structure remains and the original timbers can still be seen upstairs. A little further down the road, ASHLEWORTH MANOR is of roughly the same date, but is timber-framed. It is now E-shaped, but the left-hand bar of the E when you face the front door is a remarkably subtle Victorian pastiche – which was itself extended on the garden side around 1904. The timbers are charmingly carved: those of the Hall (which is also now divided) with long parallel grooves, and certain vertical ones upstairs like columns. The front door is still *in situ*, and is very fine.

## Barnsley*

*2; 4 miles NE of Cirencester on A433*

First let us look at the village. It has no great set pieces, but the unassuming architecture is nearly all of it a pleasure to behold. About half is of the seventeenth century, the rest largely of the early nineteenth. Telephone wires are invisible, all either buried underground or run discreetly behind the houses. Only the television aerials remain to remind one of the times in which we live – and, alas, the traffic. For all that, the local council deserves our thanks and our congratulations – and of how many villages can that be said?

The pride of Barnsley is BARNSLEY PARK, a most dramatically beautiful house of the early eighteenth century. (The dates 1720 and 1721 appear on the rainwater heads, but there is good reason to believe that building may have begun soon after the beginning of the century, only to be suspended for several years after the death of Brereton Bourchier in 1713.) The architect is unknown. Historical evidence suggests that it could have been a certain John Price, who is known to have been working in 1720–1 (though not earlier) for Bourchier's brother-in-law, the Duke of Chandos; but none of Price's existing work approaches Barnsley Park for quality. Francis Smith of Warwick, William Townesend, even Sir James Thornhill have also been

*St Andrew and St Bartholemew's Church, Ashleworth*

suggested; but the late Mr David Verey, who knew as much about Gloucestershire as anyone – and lived himself at Barnsley House in the village – favoured John James, architect of St George's, Hanover Square. He may well have been right, though the house is considerably more exuberant than any of James's other buildings (except, perhaps, the now ruined Appuldurcombe on the Isle of Wight, for which James may not have been wholly responsible).

The entrance front, to the west, immediately proclaims the house as being something out of the ordinary. The three bays at each end have, on the ground floor, very tall windows with keystones running into the string-course, on the first floor rather heavy triangular pediments and, on the attic storey, horizontal labels. The three-bay projecting centre, though of the same height, is a good deal more complicated. Its dominant feature consists of four giant Corinthian pilasters supporting a deep and elaborate cornice, above which four smaller pilasters at attic level carry the blank triangular pediment of the house. The central window on this attic floor has a surprisingly grandiloquent little cornice of its own. On the ground floor the three central windows continue the keystone motif, but have round heads instead of straight ones.

The south front projects at the ends rather than the middle. Here the giant pilasters run right the way across, marking each angle of the one-bay projections and dividing the windows of the five-bay centre. Above the cornice, the smaller pilasters also reappear; in fact this front, with its round-headed ground-floor windows, echoes the centre of the entrance front – only the pediment is missing. The east front has a quite unexpected bay. The whole building is of the most marvellous golden stone, from nearby Quarry Hill.

The Entrance Hall provides a real *coup de théâtre*. It is divided crosswise by a two-storey screen, of round arches divided by twin pilasters. Above is a plaster ceiling of great beauty, with a coffered coving; there are nice vaulting effects where this meets the screen. The walls are a riot of stucco, white on a yellow ground, framing on the left a tremendous chimneypiece surmounted by reclining classical figures and on the right a statue in a niche. This plasterwork was long thought to be by that curious Anglo-Danish figure, Charles Stanley; but it has now been established as Italian, probably the work of Artari and Bagutti. The Inner Hall (behind the screen) is equally sumptuous, as is the staircase to which it leads. Beyond, filling the east bay, is the Library, decorated in Empire style by John Nash in 1807. (Nash also built the Orangery, a miniature Madeleine on Ionic columns, and the octagonal Pepper-pot Lodge at the end of the drive towards Bibury.)

Upstairs there is a lovely narrow little vaulted corridor with small shallow cupolas, together with the bedrooms above the Library. Their curious shape, almost like a lyre, is necessitated by the formation of the bow on the east front; it gives them a strange and intriguing charm. The other memorable feature of this floor is the Oak Room, its gigantic stucco chimneypiece standing out in almost blinding contrast to the dark eighteenth-century panelling of the walls. Here again the attribution to Stanley has been discredited in favour of the Italians. Is the portrait on the central plaque that of Queen Anne?

In 1927 the entire library of Sir Isaac Newton was discovered in the house – an additional distinction which it hardly needed.

BARNSLEY HOUSE nearby was built by Bourchier a few years before he started on Barnsley Park; it is inscribed with the date 1697, rather late for its five mullioned and transomed windows. In the garden is a late eighteenth-century Gothick alcove, and a Tuscan temple of *c.*1787, brought here from Fairford Park after its tragic demolition in the 1950s.

## Berkeley Castle*

*3; 10 miles SW of Stroud on B4509*

At first sight, it does not seem a particularly suitable place for a stronghold. The castle occupies a slight elevation, but there is no great dominating hill; and it seems even too far from the Severn to command it properly. Berkeley makes no attempt to impose itself on its surroundings. It does not tower above them; rather it crouches, so that when seen from a distance in certain lights it looks more like a sudden outcrop of pinkish grey rock than a fortress built by man.

Yet there has been a castle on the site since the Norman Conquest – and quite possibly before, since we know that the manor belonged to Earl Godwin, the father of King Harold. The foundations of the present keep probably go back to the days of William FitzOsborn, Earl of Hereford, to whom the entire region was entrusted by William the Conqueror; but relatively little Norman work now survives. The most obvious from the outside is at the base of the keep, where the door at the top of the steps, though partially blocked, retains its original twelfth-century arch. In the little room immediately above, King Edward II was held a prisoner and eventually murdered in 1327. In deference to his royal blood, his body was not flung into the dungeon through the hole in the floor a few feet away, but was taken to the Chapel of St John in the east bastion and thence to its burial place in Gloucester Cathedral.

The castle as we know it today is essentially a fourteenth-century building, having been radically remodelled by Maurice, 9th Baron Berkeley, in 1340–50. This is the date of the Great Hall, which still looks much as he left it, its splendid timber roof adorned with no fewer than six tiers of cusped wind-braces. Below them, towards the courtyard, the four deep windows, though outwardly straight-headed, have rere-arches of the characteristic 'Berkeley arch' type – polygonal on the outside, curved and cusped within. (There are particularly fine examples at St Mary Redcliffe, Bristol.) The sixteenth-century screen is obviously not the original one; it comes from Caefn Mably in Pembrokeshire.

From the door at the dais end – with another magnificent Berkeley arch – a staircase leads up to the fourteenth-century State Lodgings. The first, and to me the most interesting, is the Morning Room, which was the Chapel of St Mary until as recently as 1923 – hence

*Berkeley Castle.*

the three-sided apse at the east end and the lines from a Norman-French version of the Book of Revelation on the very pretty (and original) painted wooden beams of the ceiling. The French fireplace and doorway were introduced into the castle – together with a good many other medieval bits and pieces of the same provenance – by the 8th (and last) Earl Berkeley in the 1920s. Adjoining the Morning Room is the Long Drawing Room, in which the eighteenth-century furniture, fine as it is, strikes to me a slightly jarring note, especially when seen against the great wooden gallery which originally stood in the Chapel, where it served as the royal pew. The projecting part is carved with the Arms of King Henry VII. Last in the series of state rooms open to the public is the Small Drawing Room, a little less formal, with a roof of ships' timbers. Those beyond, which are occupied by the Berkeley family – the present occupant being the twenty-fourth of his line to live in the castle – are of outstanding quality.

The nearby CHURCH OF ST MARY is built of the same pink-tinged stone as the castle. At first sight it too seems to crouch; then one realises that it has no tower – or, to be more accurate, that its tower is across the churchyard to the north. (This is an eighteenth-century replacement and, apart from its position, of little interest.) Though the church's earliest fabric is roughly contemporary with that of the castle, the prevailing feeling within is thirteenth-century – Early English. The tone is set by the west end, with its five tall and stepped round-headed lancets, and is echoed by the south clerestory windows and, above all, by the exquisite arcades – seven bays, the shafts filleted and carved with stiff-leaf, deeply undercut. There are human heads, carved with similar sensitivity and skill, on the label stops and the corbels of the timber roof. Below the dizzily high chancel arch, the screen keeps up the standard. It is of stone, of the fifteenth century, and takes the form of a single segmental arch sub-divided into three sub-arches, all cusped. The two side arches have a rail halfway up, supported on small arcades rather than the more usual blank panels. Then comes the chancel, with its original thirteenth-century windows on the north, but a huge Perpendicular one to the east. Its seven lights were increased to nine in 1843. The south wall has more Perpendicular windows, the single Early English one being almost certainly the work of Scott, who restored the church in 1865–6.

The Berkeley Chapel, built on the south side in the mid-fifteenth century, contains superb tombs, perhaps the best being that of Thomas, the 8th Baron, who was in charge of Edward II during his imprisonment. (Whether he was implicated in the murder is not known.) That of the 11th Lord Berkeley and his son is also well worth inspecting. The church is exceptionally rich in wall paintings, mostly of the late thirteenth century.

Between 1729 and 1755, the church's vicar was the Rev. Stephen Jenner. His son, Edward, was born in the vicarage and it was here that he invented vaccination. His first vaccinations are said to have been performed in the little thatched hut in the garden.

*Arlington Row, Bibury.*

## Bibury

*4; 6½ miles NE of Cirencester on A433*
*Includes Arlington Row (NT)*

William Morris thought Bibury the most beautiful village in England; and it certainly deserves a place on anyone's short list. It possesses only one serious drawback: the A433 that drives straight through the middle. How one longs for a bypass! On a quiet Sunday morning in summer, however, Bibury is still the quintessential Cotswold village, with its gentle river crossed by two bridges. That of the eighteenth century, which takes the traffic, is guarded by ARLINGTON MILL, a grand old building of about 1650 – though a mill on this site is already mentioned in the Domesday Book; that of the seventeenth, a couple of hundred yards downstream, leads you to ARLINGTON ROW (NT), a straggling but picturesque terrace of weavers' cottages under a gabled roof. Most of them also date from the early seventeenth century, but the middle ones may well be two centuries older.

ST MARY'S CHURCH was already.important in Saxon times, though there is little Saxon work immediately visible on the outside: a little round window near the south porch, a lesene or two, and a bit of string-course. The church was, in fact, largely rebuilt in the twelfth century, after which never a century seems to have passed without succeeding Abbots of Osney in Oxfordshire – who held it as a 'peculiar' – adding to it or tinkering with it in one way or another. The miracle is that it should have kept its character and beauty as well as it has. Late Norman are the north and south doorways, and very slightly later still the south porch; it combines a pointed arch with dogtooth. Inside, the overall impression is of about 1200 and the transition from Norman to Early English. In the north arcade particularly, those big chunky piers, some with scalloped capitals, look Norman through and through; but the arches are slightly pointed again, and a glance at the short arcade to the south immediately shows what a change has come about within a single generation. From the north aisle, incidentally, the wall above this south arcade is seen to be the original outside wall of the Saxon church, its pilaster strips still *in situ*. There is a little window, even, high up at the western end.

Saxon are the jambs and imposts of the chancel arch, though the arch itself was replaced in the thirteenth century. This replacement must have been part of a major remodelling, when the nave walls were heightened and given a clerestory, while the chancel was lengthened and provided with its three lovely stepped lancets. A hundred years or so later again, the fine three-light Decorated windows were added to the north aisle; in the fifteenth century came yet another clerestory, the big Perpendicular window at the west end of the nave, the carved timber roof and the exterior embattling.

It is not often in this book that a churchyard gets a special mention, but at Bibury it must. Splendidly furnished, meticulously mown, sensitively planted, it has been dubbed by Alec Clifton-Taylor (who knows them all) 'perhaps the most enchanting churchyard in England'. I can only agree with him.

## Bishop's Cleeve

*5; 4 miles N of Cheltenham on A435*

ST MICHAEL AND ALL ANGELS is a large and most magnificent church, essentially late Norman of around 1175; the trouble is that it does not really hang together. The west front is symptomatic of the whole building; a highly ornate Norman west doorway with quantities of zigzag is surmounted by a gigantic three-light Decorated window with reticulated tracery. There are flanking turrets to north and south with tall pyramidal caps; that to the north has, however, been provided in addition with a huge and hideous fifteenth-century buttress, running forward. Beyond it, a broad north aisle ends in a four-light Perpendicular window and is embattled; to the south, by way of balance, there is only a pathetic apology for a south aisle, embattled too but with a different rake and with the tall tiled south porch sticking out most insensitively behind it. Nobody expects medieval churches to be symmetrical, but this is ridiculous.

The porch, taken by itself, is admirable, as is so much of the detail at Bishop's Cleeve. Its inner walls are embellished with interlaced arcading, and it is vaulted in stone. Inside the church is another muddle; the Norman nave arcade was originally of six bays, but every other pier was removed in the seventeenth century and all the arches consequently date from then. The chancel arch is also of about the same time, though the side arches from aisles to transepts are Norman and show all too plainly how much has been lost.

The best things in the church, for me, are the mercifully unspoilt fourteenth-century chancel, the timber roof and the Jacobean west gallery; but there – it is the individual bits that one remembers, not the ensemble. Interest? Yes, in plenty. Beauty? Some, in parts. Lovability? Alas, no.

## Bisley

*6; 3 miles NE of Stroud off A419*

Set back from the road behind its exquisite wrought-iron gates, NETHER LYPIATT MANOR is famous for being one of the prettiest small houses in England. Its plan is a perfect square of only 46 feet a side, allowing it a mere five bays; but its four floors – two principal ones, a tall basement and attic within the hipped roof – give it a feeling of considerable height. It reminds one inevitably of Ashdown in Oxfordshire (*q.v.*), but in a somehow quieter, more domestic way. It is also some forty years later, having been built, as near as we can tell, in 1702–5. No architect is known – more likely than not, the house never had one – but the local master builder (or whoever was responsible for the design) was obviously much influenced by Sir Roger Pratt's Coleshill, as well as his Clarendon House in London.

The house has three low single-storey wings, two of them contemporary with it but the third (to the north-west) added in 1923, in order to give symmetry to the west front (the entrance), facing the road. On this front the front door is set, in typical Pratt style, up a tall flight of steps to allow plenty of light and space to the basement below. Its porch is a mid-eighteenth-century addition. The windows on this side are all sashed; though elsewhere some of them retain their orginal mullions, the sashes seem far more satisfactory for a Queen Anne house of this type.

Inside, despite having been sorely neglected during the many years that it served as an ordinary farmhouse, the Manor has preserved much of its original panelling and most of its pretty stone fireplaces. There is a magnificent staircase, rising from basement to attic, made grander by the imposing wooden arches which lead into the well on the two main floors. It is constructed from a combination of oak and elm, but the wainscot dado is of mahogany – an opulent touch.

The house was for long the property of the famous harpsichordist, Violet Gordon Woodhouse. At the time of writing it has recently been bought by Prince and Princess Michael of Kent.

## Bledington

*7; 4 miles SE of Stow-on-the-Wold on B4450*

This is an enchanting Cotswold village with an enormous village green. ST LEONARD'S CHURCH stands on the top of a hill to the south, very neat; the spire looks a little puny for the rest, even though the whole building is on quite a modest scale. The general impression at first sight seems to be very much all of a piece – Perpendicular throughout, the clerestory having four three-light windows with semi-circular cusped heads; lovely Cotswold stone and Cotswold tiles.

The moment you go in, however, you realise that the church is not what it seems. The nave arcade (south side only) with its squat round piers suggests a date *c.* 1200; the east window of three stepped lancets was added perhaps a generation or so later, when the chancel was extended; and the three-light west window with its reticulated tracery must be mid-fourteenth-century.

But the really exciting time for Bledington was the fifteenth century, when the church was largely remodelled. First, a tower was built inside the west end of the nave, a hole being made in the roof to let it through. Then the nave walls were heightened, refenestrated and given a clerestory on each side. (Oddly enough, however, the north side remained aisleless, with the result that the north wall has two rows of windows.) Finally, the south aisle windows were given flat heads and Perpendicular tracery to match those of the north.

Now this sort of remodelling was going on in literally hundreds of churches during the fifteenth century. What makes Bledington remarkable is the breathtaking quality of the workmanship. Look at the nodding ogee canopies over the image niches in the window reveals. Look at that curious little recess between the south aisle and the south-west corner of the chancel. Look, indeed, at the detail and finish of all the fifteenth-century work. These stonemasons were craftsmen of a very high order indeed. And so were their glazier contemporaries, much of whose work still survives. One window bears the date 1470; even at that time, Bledington must have been a very exceptional church. It is still more so today.

## Bouthrop

See Eastleach.

## Buckland

*8; 2 miles SW of Broadway off A46*

The RECTORY, writes Pevsner, is 'the oldest and most complete medieval parsonage house in the county still so used'. The oldest part cannot be later than the mid-fifteenth century. Though principally of stone, its north wall is timber-framed, the first floor slightly projecting; it was against this wall, originally external, that a new and magnificent Hall was built around 1480. It is of two bays with a central hammer-beam truss, carved with angels bearing shields, and two tiers of wind-bracing. One of the Hall windows shows the White Rose of Edward IV and the name of the contemporary rector, William Grafton. Back in the old house, the newel-stair turns anti-clockwise – apparently an ecclesiastical pecularity since the clergy did not carry swords and did not consequently need to keep their sword-arms free. It leads to an upper chamber, also with its original timber roof, and a garderobe. At the north end of the Hall a cross-range was added in the early seventeenth century, though most of its interior is Victorian. The entrance front to the east has been somewhat altered over the centuries, though the medieval oriel is still there; the west front is almost untouched. It is a most remarkable survival.

*Chavenage House.*

## Chavenage House

*9; 2 miles NW of Tetbury off A4135*

A rare and splendid survival, Chavenage was built by a certain Edward Stephens on the site of a modest medieval manor in 1576 (preserving a few features of the original fabric) and has scarcely been touched since – apart from the addition of a separate west wing in 1905 which does not really affect the body of the house. One's first sight of it, standing at the end of a short, straight drive – down which a phantom coach is said to convey the departing shade of every lord of Chavenage dying in the house – is deeply impressive in an austere way. It maintains the traditional Tudor E-type plan, but with one distinctive feature: the two bays to the left (south) of the entrance are each completely taken up by a nine-light window, double-transomed, reaching to the eaves. All the lights are round-headed. Predictably, they mark the two-storey Hall and contain a good selection of medieval and seventeenth-century glass. The screen – the upper part of which shows signs of alteration – carries a minstrels' gallery and an eighteenth-century organ which (I quote from the local guide-book) 'still makes a noise'. During the Civil War, it is said that Col. Nathaniel Stephens (Edward's grandson, who was a moderate Parliamentarian and connected to Oliver Cromwell by marriage) received a visit from Cromwell and the latter's son-in-law Henry Ireton, who pressed him to support their efforts for the King's impeachment, which he ultimately agreed to do. Cromwell and Ireton stayed the night, and the two tapestry bedrooms which they are believed to have occupied still bear their names.

## Cheltenham

*10; 8 miles NE of Gloucester on A40*

Though Cheltenham has existed since Saxon times, it was only in 1718 that it came into its own. In that year a spring was discovered, the water from which was found to possess remarkable purgative properties. One Henry Skillicorne, who was fortunate enough to have married the owner of the land, then built on it and instituted a pumping system – the spa was born. Early progress was slow, but in 1788 the Royal Family came for five weeks, and Cheltenham's golden age began.

By a fortunate fluke, the fashion of watering places in England coincided with the happiest period in our national town architecture; and the growth of Cheltenham occurred at the precise time that we were in the throes of the Greek Revival. The result was a series of new promenades, squares and parades, and any number of elegant terraced rows, enlived with wrought-iron (and, later, cast-iron) balconies, articulated and defined by pavilions and porticoes and pediments, built for the delectation of the late Georgian upper classes who flocked to the town sometimes for reasons of health but more often for the delights of polite society or, frankly, the gaming tables. After the Napoleonic wars, when foreign travel once again became relatively easy, many of them abandoned Cheltenham for more exotic continental resorts; but the town merely replaced its floating population with a settled one, largely composed of retired army officers and civil servants from India.

*The Promenade, Cheltenham.*

Cheltenham can be seen properly only on foot, and the best place to start is from the unworthy Edwardian Town Hall in Imperial Square, whence you enter the upper part of the PROMENADE with its marvellous triple avenue of trees. It is an extraordinary thoroughfare to find in an English country town, not least because of its deliberately false perspective: the carriageway at the upper end is exactly double its width at the lower. Thus if you look down its length it appears extremely long, while from the other end it seems, comparatively speaking, no distance at all. It was laid out in 1818 and includes the magnificent group of terraced houses which have now been converted into the MUNICIPAL OFFICES; they would do credit to Regent's Park – and indeed anywhere else. There too is what must be the most elegant POST OFFICE in the country, formerly the Imperial Hotel. The QUEEN'S HOTEL is grander still, facing across the public gardens like some colonial Government House. It was built in 1838 by the Jearrad brothers, who – with John Buonarotti Papworth, whom they unceremoniously ousted in 1830 – are to Cheltenham what the John Woods are to Bath or the Bastards to Blandford. From it you enter the area known as MONTPELLIER, which was laid out by Papworth, together with neighbouring Lansdown. It begins with MONTPELLIER WALK, where the houses (by W.H. Knight) have shopfronts supported on terracotta caryatids, and has as its centre Montpellier Spa (now LLOYDS BANK) which was designed by G.A. Underwood (who had worked with Soane) in 1817 but had its Rotunda and Pump Room added by Papworth eight years later. Hence via Montpellier Exchange you pass into LANSDOWN, with its PLACE, CRESCENT AND TERRACE, the last – which dates from after the Jearrads' takeover – a most curious affair with its little first-floor pediments and heavy second-floor entablatures.

Across Lansdown Road is R.W. Jearrad's LYPIATT TERRACE, with gables and Italianate corner towers; and so into Suffolk Square – from which, if so inclined, you could take Park Place down to the Park, laid out in 1833. Otherwise, sparing a quick glance at ST JAMES'S CHURCH (1825–30), take Suffolk Parade, Montpellier Terrace and Parade to Vittoria Walk where, on the right, stands VITTORIA HOUSE, formerly Hygeia House, erected as the first spa building in 1804. Parallel to Vittoria Walk on the west is TRAFALGAR STREET, at the south end of which is a little group of enchanting Regency cottages, built in 1806. ROCK COTTAGE is actually a *cottage orné*, built of vermiculated coloured rocks and shells; Nelson's Captain Hardy is said to have stayed there for a time. From here Oriel Road leads back to Imperial Square.

This walk should give one a fair idea of the splendours of Cheltenham; but it does not by any means include them all. If there is time you should also walk through BAYSHILL (not missing the magnificent FAUCONBERG HOUSE, built in 1847 by Samuel Onley, and the charming FAUCONBERG VILLAS) to ROYAL PARADE, my own favourite of all the Cheltenham terraces. Another fascinating district is PITTVILLE, the creation of one Joseph Pitt, whose career began by 'holding gentlemen's horses for a penny' and ended in Parliament with £20,000 a year. (His architect was John Forbes, who worked at Cheltenham from about 1825 until 1835, when he was convicted of forgery and sentenced to transportation for life.) Its climax is the PUMP ROOM, whose great Ionic colonnade is copied from Stuart and Revett's engravings of the Temple of Ilissus. The interior is still more impressive, with further colonnades supporting extremely depressed arches and a gallery, the whole thing surmounted by a deeply coffered dome set with paterae.

It would be pleasant to conclude with some laudatory reference to those two great temples of education, Cheltenham College and Cheltenham Ladies' College. Alas, I cannot do so. Why, in this of all towns, was Gothic chosen? And a heavy, flat-footed Gothic at that? Both colleges are unutterably depressing, though the Ladies', which dates from the 1870s or later, is worse.

Chipping Campden.

## Chipping Campden★

*11; 9 miles N of Stow-on-the-Wold on B4081*
*Includes Market Hall and Almshouses (NT)*

One of the most attractive small towns in the Cotswolds – if not in all England – Chipping Campden owes its great distinction to wool, and to four outstanding benefactors down the ages: William Grevel, whose late fourteenth-century house survives with its tall, gabled bay window; Sir Baptist Hicks (d. 1629), who gave the town its MARKET HALL and ALMSHOUSES (NT) and built himself the great mansion, destroyed in the Civil War, whose lodges and gateway still stand next to the churchyard; C.R. Ashbee, who established his Guild of Handicrafts here in 1902; and F.L. Griggs, who founded the Campden Trust in 1929. Thanks to this admirable organisation, the town has been magnificently preserved, with scarcely an eyesore anywhere. There are houses of every century from the fourteenth onwards. It is unnecessary to single any of them out; you can see them all in half an hour, on foot.

ST JAMES'S CHURCH, like St John the Baptist in Cirencester, is one of the great wool churches of Gloucestershire. Remodelled in the later fifteenth century, it still bears traces of earlier work – a Norman tomb recess in the chancel, an Early English south doorway, a Decorated south porch – but these are easily missed amid all the Perpendicular splendour. The tower, inevitably, strikes you first: three stages divided by strongly emphasised string-courses, diagonal buttresses rising to high pinnacles, each with its own weathervane; and, along each side of the parapet, two ogee arches terminating in smaller pinnacles of their own. Still more pinnacles adorn the embattled parapet of the nave and aisles. The windows are all Perpendicular, with two-centred arches; those of the clerestory and the great west window have quatrefoils within the Perpendicular tracery, which dates them as late as the early sixteenth century. There is also a magnificent window of nine lights in the east wall of the nave above the chancel arch, a special pecularity of the Cotswolds.

The nave arcades are immensely tall, on slender octagonal piers with slightly concave sides – almost identical to those seen at Northleach. The responds to the chancel and tower arches are of exactly the same design. It is all a little too pat and impersonal for my liking, but the impressiveness cannot be denied. Fine monuments abound, particularly that of Sir Baptist Hicks and his wife by Nicholas Stone and Joshua Marshall's extraordinary memorial to Edward Noel, Viscount Campden, and his wife Juliana.

## Cirencester

*12; 10½ miles NE of Tetbury on A433*

Just as Bibury is the perfect Cotswold village, so Cirencester is everything that a Cotswold market town should be. It is dominated, inevitably, by its parish church, ST JOHN THE BAPTIST, the largest in Gloucestershire, whose tremendous south porch of 1490, three storeys high and three bays across, proudly advances right into the Market Place. So magnificent is this porch, panelled, orielled, and crowned with its lovely openwork parapet, that it demands to be treated as a building in itself; and it comes as no surprise to learn that for over 200 years, from the seventeenth century until the 1890s, it actually served as the Town Hall.

But the rest of the church lives up to it. Every detail of the exterior seems to speak of wealth and prosperity, while that most graceful of fifteenth-century towers proclaims it the greatest and grandest of the fifteenth-century 'wool' churches of England. Inside it is the same story. The chancel, admittedly, has survived from earlier days; originally built in the early twelfth century, it has suffered little structural change since the east window was enlarged from three lights to five in about 1300. Nearly everything else, however, is assured, confident Perpendicular – the Trinity Chapel off the north aisle, the narrow fan-vaulted St Catherine's Chapel to the north of the chancel and – last and most impressive of all – the nave itself, rebuilt between 1516 and 1530 with its serried rows of clerestory windows culminating in the glorious seven-light *tour de force* in the east wall, directly over the chancel arch. (Windows in this position are very much a feature of the high-naved Cotswold churches, but only that of Northleach is comparable to this.) The arcades themselves are wonderfully tall and slender; between the arches, on both north and south sides of each pier, carved angels hold the coats of arms – or merchants' marks – of all the wealthy benefactors who contributed. They deserve it, and could have no more fitting memorial.

The gently curving crescent of the MARKET PLACE contains much noble architecture, mostly eighteenth-century, but spilling over into the seventeenth and nineteenth. All too many, as might be expected in the commercial centre of the town, are ruined by shop fascias (dreadful word, almost as bad as the horrid things it is so often used to describe). How much longer, one wonders, will local authorities allow shopkeepers to desecrate so unnecessarily the buildings they are privileged to inhabit? But old unspoilt Cirencester still exists, for those prepared to seek it out. DOLLAR STREET, CECILY HILL, THOMAS STREET and, best of all, COXWELL STREET – still looking very much as it must have done in the seventeenth century – these are the places in which to linger, in which, as in the great church itself, the Cotswold spirit still lives on.

Alternatively, you may walk down Silver Street and emerge in front of a vast classical gateway set into a massive wall. Here is the point of intersection of two great Roman roads, Ermine Street and Fosse Way; between them, and within that gateway, lies CIRENCESTER PARK. Few English country houses, and fewer still with immense parks extending behind them, are so intimately attached to their towns; only Petworth springs immediately to mind. But the early eighteenth-century mansion that we see today was built in 1714–18 by Allen, 1st Lord Bathurst, on the site of an earlier, Elizabethan, manor house – parts of which were, in all probability, actually incorporated into the new building. As a sort of inner *cordon sanitaire*, Bathurst cultivated within the wall an enormous yew hedge, enclosing the east front of his new house like an outsize horseshoe: a typical gesture on his part, since he was always far more interested in landscape gardening than in architecture.

These priorities are all too clear after any visit to Cirencester. The park is utterly magnificent; indeed, it has been described by David Verey (in *The Buildings of England*) as 'the finest surviving example in England of planting in the pre-landscape manner' – in other words before the new 'natural' style of Bridgeman, Kent and Capability Brown took the country by storm. The house, on the other hand, was not a success. Bathurst was still a young man – he was to live till 1775 – but by temperament and upbringing he was an old-fashioned Tory who mistrusted the new high-falutin' classical ideas, based on Palladio and his like, that contemporaries such as Richard Boyle and Lord Burlington were introducing from Europe. (As Alexander Pope, Bathurst's close friend and protégé, put it: 'Who then shall grace or who improve the soil/Who plants like Bathurst or who builds like Boyle.') He resolved to be his own architect, advised only by local craftsmen – and it shows. He himself admitted it. 'How comes it', he once asked Pope, 'to look so oddly bad?' One answer to the question is that, perhaps because it was based too closely on the earlier house, it is far too narrow. In 1830 Sir Robert Smirke, as well as adding a wing on the north, actually brought forward the whole ground floor on the

*The church of St John the Baptist, Cirencester.*

east side to give it more depth; yet even now the main Entrance Hall is only a few paces across. On the west side, which remains unchanged, the feeling of constriction is even more marked; one never loses the impression of being in a superficially Georgianised house of the sixteenth century.

Where Bathurst came into his own architecturally was in his designs for follies and pavilions within his beloved park. His most ambitious was for what is known as Alfred's Hall, which was built in 1721 and is consequently the first romantic castellated folly in England – antedating Sanderson Miller's tower on Edgehill by twenty years. Another little building in the same style, the Round Tower, was to be added some time later. Pope's Seat, the Hexagon, the Horse Guards, Ivy Lodge – Bathurst continued to build them until his death, some classical, some Gothic, but all meticulously sited and thought out in every detail. Although he always firmly held out against the new fashion in landscape (and in fact lived long enough to see Capability Brown largely discredited by Richard Payne Knight and others), his ideas for park buildings were thus well in advance of his time: how sad that in the field of domestic architecture the same cannot be said!

*St Mary's Church, Deerhurst.*

## Deerhurst*

*13; 2 miles SW of Tewkesbury off A38*

ST MARY'S CHURCH is one of the two finest Saxon churches in England. Only Brixworth in Northamptonshire (*q.v.*) can hold a candle to it. It was probably begun in the late eighth century, and there seem to have been no fewer than three separate stages of building *before* the ninth-century Viking invasions; afterwards, early in the century following – still well over 100 years before the Conquest – there followed a major restoration and enlargement, which included the building of the tower.

This tower is extremely high, and immediately reveals itself as Saxon by the irregular long and short quoins, the absence of string-courses, the occasional patches of herringbone masonry, and the windows. (Even the fourteenth-century bell openings have obviously been inserted into earlier Saxon ones.) The west door and a window further up the west face also have curious pieces of carved stone projecting just above them, looking rather like hungry sealions. More Saxon work is to be found at the east end, around the surviving bay of the polygonal apse and the two *porticus* to the north and south; for the rest, patches of herringbone are still visible between the clerestory windows, but the windows themselves and the two aisles below are of the fifteenth and sixteenth centuries.

So much for the exterior. You enter by the west porch, in fact a three-storey Saxon *porticus* (though the floors are now gone) immediately beneath the tower, divided transversely into two separate chambers, the second of which leads into the nave. Notice, first, the lovely eighth-century relief of the Virgin and Child in the porch; next for the best results, walk directly up the incredibly tall, narrow nave to the chancel arch; then, and only then, turn and look back whence you have come. Virtually the entire west wall – and the north and south walls too, between the arcades and the clerestory windows – are part of the original church, and have been standing here for some 1,200 years, perhaps more. Each wall has a curious little triangular window about half-way up; in addition there is in the west wall, a little to the right of the window, a blocked-up round-headed doorway which must have originally given access to a wooden gallery; and, in the centre of the wall at clerestory level, an utterly unique feature – a double triangular-headed window, its central pillar and two side pilasters both fluted and reeded. Pevsner considers this a Carolingian motif, comparing it to the eighth-century abbey gatehouse at Lorsch in the Rhineland – which is, however, infinitely more sophisticated. The author of the excellent church guide, on the other hand, Dr Edward Gilbert, is reminded of a window in the Ethiopian monastery of Debra Damo. (And what a field of speculation *that* opens up.) The blank stone above may be a mutilated dedication stone, but is more likely to have carried a carved rood, now defaced.

Turning eastward again, take a close look at the chancel arch, a tenth-century replacement of a smaller, simpler one. The pilasters on each side are highly developed for their date, and the details of the capitals have no parallel in England; but more interesting still is

*Odda's Chapel, Deerhurst.*

the hood-mould with carved animals' heads on the stops, which betrays strong Scandinavian influence. Note, too, the two pairs of *porticus*, one on each side of the nave. These little side chapels – they cannot be dignified by the name of transepts – are still closed off from the central space by walls, in which the upper and lower doorways indicate that they were of two storeys. There seem to have been others further west; but around 1200 these were knocked together to form side aisles and opened up to the nave by the very beautiful arcades.

These arcades are the latest strictly architectural features in the church which merit attention, the more recent medieval work being on the whole undistinguished. Deerhurst has, however, one remarkable point of liturgical interest: the seating in the choir, which follows the puritan tradition of a central altar, with pews arranged to the east of it as well as to the north and south.

Though the seven-sided apse has almost gone, enough remains to be worth a special visit. Leave the church, and follow the north wall round to the east end. The surviving bay shows that the apse must have been of very much the same style as at Brixworth and Wing in Buckinghamshire (*q.v.*) with triangular-headed arches and perhaps round ones as well. In the south corner, between the pilaster strips, is the famous Deerhurst Angel, a tenth-century sculpture now much worn but still powerful.

There remains one other piece of sculpture that must on no account be missed. This is the font, a cylindrical stone vessel dating from the ninth century, carved with a Celtic 'trumpet spiral' design and bordered at top and bottom with a narrower band of Northumbrian vine scroll. When it was discovered by Bishop 'Soapy Sam' Wilberforce in 1844 it was serving as a washtub in a local farm. Subsequently the stem was found at Apperley nearby, the two were brought together and the font was returned to Deerhurst, where it almost certainly originated.

The church at Deerhurst would alone be enough to make it one of the most important sites in Gloucestershire; but there is also a CHAPEL, some 200 yards away to the south-west. This too is Saxon; for centuries it had been incorporated in an old timber-framed house, and its identity was only revealed in 1885, when routine repairs uncovered a double-splayed round-headed window. Also brought to light was an inscribed altar slab, thanks to which we can even give the chapel a precise dating – the only pre-Conquest building for which this can be done. It was dedicated to the Holy Trinity by Earl Odda on 12 April 1056. As a building, it is simple enough – just a nave and chancel with a horseshoe-shaped chancel arch. In its very simplicity, however, lies its charm; and it provides a strangely pleasing contrast with the splendours of the great church nearby.

*The Orangery, Frampton Court.*

## Eastleach

*14; 4 miles NW of Lechlade off A361*

Two lovely medieval churches in one village is a rarity indeed, but the River Leach which separates the churches once formed the boundary between two feudal domains. ST ANDREW'S, in Eastleach Turville, is originally Norman, as is made clear by the south doorway with its carved tympanum. In the thirteenth century a north transept and north aisle were added; but the latter must have been removed some 400 years later, judging by the style of the curious windows inserted in the blocked-up arches. Inside, the pride of the church is the Early English chancel, with its triple-lancet east window under moulded arches, exquisitely carved with stiff-leaf.

Across the river at Eastleach Martin – more usually known as Bouthrop – stands the CHURCH OF ST MICHAEL AND ST MARTIN. It is even older, having been founded by one of the Conqueror's knights, Richard Fitzpons, but unlike St Andrew's it has Decorated and Perpendicular additions; the fortunate thing is that these additions are of such high quality. The west tower has a pretty hipped roof (as compared with St Andrew's saddleback), and though one could wish it without the huge three-light Perpendicular window on the west, one cannot but be glad of the three really lovely Decorated windows of the fourteenth-century north transept. The chancel, like that of its neighbour, has triple lancets of the very late thirteenth century; but its arch has somehow managed to keep its Norman piers. There are some fine medieval benches at the back of the nave. The church, still lit by oil lamps, breathes a wonderful atmosphere of rural peace.

## Elkstone*

*15; 6 miles S of Cheltenham off A435*

Of all the Norman churches in the Cotswolds – and there are quite a number of them – ST JOHN'S, Elkstone is the most spectacular. From the outside it may not look especially remarkable: its most salient feature, the sturdy west tower, is in any case a Perpendicular replacement of the original one, which stood at the crossing but was removed – or, more probably, simply collapsed – in the thirteenth century. But a short walk round the building soon reveals its original date. Look, for example, at the magnificent Christ in Majesty in the tympanum over the south door, and the splendid corbel tables to both south and north; these are far more accurate indications of the glory that awaits you within.

There, the first thing you notice is the crossing arch – massive and monumental, with rows of zigzag on two planes and a hood-mould with dragon-heads on the stops. The responds have big chunky scalloped capitals; this, one feels, is everything a Norman crossing arch ought to be. Beyond is the crossing itself, a fourteenth-century rib-vaulted ceiling marking the place from which the tower once rose; then comes the chancel arch, with more zigzag; and then finally the lovely little stone-vaulted chancel, its ribs meeting in a curious boss composed of four grotesque heads, its light entering by way of a tiny east window with a carved frame of zigzag and paterae considerably larger than itself. There is a thirteenth-century lancet to the south of the chancel which fits in beautifully; only the Perpendicular window on the north side (there are three more in the nave) is a matter for regret. The nave roof, fifteenth-century, has kingposts and three tiers of wind-bracing above pretty box pews. This is a church to remember.

## Elmore Court

*16; 3 miles SW of Gloucester off A38*

The iron entrance gates, by William Edney of Bristol, are the best in Gloucestershire – so good, indeed, that the first sight of the house comes as something of a disappointment. Its sixteenth-century origin is established by the big bay window, mullioned and transomed; but the rest of the entrance front has undergone so much not very sensitive remodelling in the seventeenth and eighteenth centuries that it emerges as a pretty good muddle. This goes particularly for the fenestration to the right of the porch.

Once inside the house, things begin to improve. The Great Hall obviously suffers from a rather heavy Victorian hand, but the Drawing Room beyond, with its stone chimneypiece and dark Jacobean panelling, is essentially unaltered; with the Oak Room upstairs, it is the finest room in the house. The Great Staircase, also, is magnificent – a marvel of Elizabethan joinery. It is of solid carved oak, spare in decoration but giving an impression of terrific strength: even the handrail is nearly a foot deep.

The Oak Room, formerly known as the Great Chamber, is immediately above the Hall. Apart from the massive State Bed of 1636 and two fine Flemish tapestries, its pride is the superb late sixteenth-century chimneypiece, carved with caryatids, dragons and unicorns, richly gilded and preserving its original colours.

The nearby CHURCH OF ST JOHN THE BAPTIST is not of outstanding architectural interest, despite some good thirteenth-century work. Within it, however, are some of the most beautiful carved table tombs to be found in this part of the country.

## English Bicknor

*17; 17 miles W of Gloucester on B4228*

You could drive straight past the CHURCH OF ST MARY THE VIRGIN without giving it a second glance. The big square embattled tower is unremarkable, and much of the exterior walls has been rebuilt or refaced. But anybody who ignores it on that account will be missing one of the most remarkable examples of Norman church architecture and decoration in all Gloucestershire. There is a magnificent double arcade, apparently untouched since the twelfth century, supporting a clerestory and a wagon roof, with beautifully sculptured capitals to the piers – especially on the south side, where the scallops are enriched with foliage and, on one of them, little human heads. On the north side they are plainer except for the northernmost arch at the east end, which was probably the old north door before the aisles were added. This has deeply carved chevron ornament projecting outwards, and seven different beak-heads.

The nave is the oldest part of the church. In the thirteenth century the chancel was rebuilt – see the Early English chancel arch – and, presumably at the same time, a new tower was added at the west end to replace the original central Norman one. Surprisingly, however, the aisles were continued halfway along the chancel, thus providing what is now a vestry and a memorial chapel. There is a Decorated east window; otherwise the chancel is of little interest. But that splendid nave implants itself ineradicably in the memory.

The church stands in the centre of what was once a twelfth-century motte and bailey castle, of which practically nothing but the earthworks survives.

## Fairford★

*18; 8 miles E of Cirencester on A417*

ST MARY'S CHURCH is justly renowned for its virtually complete set of late medieval stained glass. This was specially designed for the church, and commissioned from the workshop of Barnard Flower, the foremost glass painter in England in the years around 1500. Flower was also responsible for the glass of Henry VII's Chapel in Westminster Abbey, none of which, alas, survives. Some pieces of the Fairford set have in fact also been lost, notably from the west window, shattered in the great storm of 1703; and other parts are badly faded. It remains, however, a staggering collection.

But glass is not all that Fairford has to offer. The church itself is a beautiful example of late fifteenth-century Perpendicular, having been completely rebuilt – except for the base of the central tower – by a rich wool merchant, John Tame, and his son Edmund. The exterior is wonderfully rich in carvings: on the buttresses of the tower, on the parapet, even on the string-course of the south aisle, where a small boy is seen edging his way along – or perhaps preparing to jump.

A fan-vaulted south porch leads into the church. Apart from some of the masonry around the crossing (with, incidentally, the remains of medieval wall paintings) it has complete architectural unity. The nave is of four bays, with broad four-centred arches supported by slender multi-shafted piers; the proportions could hardly be better. The chancel and two side chapels have timber roofs (as do the nave and aisles) supported by corbels carved with stone angels. There are beautiful choir and parclose screens (rare in the county) and the stalls have particularly entertaining misericords.

## Frampton-on-Severn★

*19; 9 miles SW of Gloucester off B4071*

This is an unusually pretty village, but in a manner quite unlike those of the Cotswolds. A long, wide green leads up between Frampton Court on one side and the Manor Farmhouse on the other to a group of old buildings clustered round the church. There is not a single jarring note anywhere.

FRAMPTON COURT was built between 1731 and 1733, probably by John Strahan, an architect from Bristol. David Verey, writing in *The Buildings of England*, is, I think, a bit unkind about the composition, which he describes as being one of 'naïve disharmony', though it must be admitted that the square, featureless wings with their grotesquely large Vanbrugh-inspired arched chimneys scarcely help the ensemble. The five-bay centre, however, its two principal storeys articulated by four giant pilasters supporting a triangular pediment, its basement partly concealed by a broad sweep of stone steps, is immensely successful. The interior is even more impressive, thanks to the glorious woodwork. In the Hall, the Drawing Room and the Dining Room one stops again and again in one's tracks to admire the fluted pilasters, and the exquisite carving of the capitals, the doors and the wainscoting. A marvellous staircase, its wood of a rather darker colour, has an extraordinary design on the open string – little cherubs upside-down – and, at its foot, a charming dog-gate which folds back into the dado. More superb joinery is to be found in two of the upstairs bedrooms; one would love to know the name of the craftsman concerned.

The house is a joy – but the cup is not yet full. In the garden to the north-west, at the end of a long rectangular reflecting pool, stands an Orangery – an Orangery of such riotous, exuberant Gothick playfulness as to make one laugh out loud. It is in the form of two connected octagons, with a single octagon above, and a jolly little cupola on top of that. The windows all have hexagonal panes, and ogival heads. Were I the fortunate owner, I should be sorely tempted to spend my summers here, my winters in the house.

Do not leave the village without taking a quick look at the MANOR FARMHOUSE, almost opposite across the green. Dating from about 1450, it has a stone ground floor – at least on one side – and projecting timber-framed upper storeys. The neighbouring barn is very similar in style, and clearly contemporary.

*Gloucester Cathedral.*

## Gloucester

*20; 8 miles SW of Cheltenham on A40*

THE CITY

Architecturally, Gloucester is a disaster area. Of the medieval city, practically nothing is left. Nor is there the excuse of war, as for example at Coventry. The destruction of Gloucester, than which enemy bombing could hardly have been more thorough, was the work of the planners of the 1950s, the most calamitous decade in our architectural history. In Westgate Street alone, no fewer than twenty-five *listed* buildings were demolished; in St Mary's Square only one remains. Among the casualties was a whole group of fifteenth-century timber-framed cottages; another, similar, group in St Catherine Street was bulldozed in the name of slum clearance. A few fine old buildings somehow escaped: BISHOP HOOPER'S LODGING, timber-framed of about 1500, is one of the few in Westgate Street; the NEW INN in Northgate Street is perhaps half a century earlier. And of course there are some survivals from the seventeenth and eighteenth centuries, of which Smirke's SHIRE HALL is as distinguished as any; but even that has been truncated and enlarged with an eight-storey extension made almost entirely of glass.

Before leaving the city, however (I thought it only fair, in this instance, to dispose of the city first and make the cathedral the climax of my architectural tour of Gloucester), there are two churches which, though neither of them is outstanding, will both repay a brief visit. The first, standing in a soulless modern precinct just west of the abbey gate that leads to the cathedral, is the curiously named ST MARY DE LODE. It has a tremendous Norman crossing, with a somewhat spindly Early English chancel at one end and, at the other, a stuccoed Gothic nave of 1826 supported on cast-iron columns. The contrasts are extraordinary; the Norman part wins, hands down.

The other church is ST MARY DE CRYPT, in Southgate Street. It too began in Norman times, but it was largely rebuilt in the Perpendicular period; Perpendicular is certainly the prevailing style today. The reason for visiting it is the chancel, which is thought to have been built by Henry Dene, a Prior of Lanthony in the latter half of the fifteenth century. An odd single sedile and Easter sepulchre on the north side, and the more usual triple sedilia and piscina on the south, have carved ogee canopies of superb quality; there are beautiful stone screens separating the chancel from the side chapels, a splendid roof with bosses and musical angels, and a string-course which runs through the windows to form transoms – a playful touch I have never seen before.

THE CATHEDRAL AND IMMEDIATE ENVIRONS

Amid all the devastation, we turn gratefully to the CATHEDRAL. They couldn't demolish that, if only because it would have needed an Act of Parliament to do so. (Even then, they managed to turn much of the Close, known here as College Green, into a car park.) Of all the English cathedrals it is one of the most beautiful and, historically, one of the most important: not just because William the Conqueror gave orders for the Domesday Book in the Chapter House, or because Henry III was crowned there at the age of nine with his mother's bracelet, or because the murdered Edward II was buried there, or because Richard II held a parliament in the precincts, but for a much more significant reason than any of those. It was at Gloucester Cathedral that some stonemason of genius developed the Perpendicular style and so changed, to a very considerable degree, the course of English architecture.

Let us, however, begin at the beginning. There had been a monastery at Gloucester since the seventh century, but it had fallen on hard times and by 1072 it numbered only two monks and eight novices. Then, fortunately, it came to the notice of King William, who decided to revive it and entrusted the task to his friend and chaplain, Serlo of Mont St-Michel. Serlo's energy was prodigious: he reconstructed the monastic buildings and, in 1089, began a new abbey church which was consecrated in 1100 in the presence of sixty monks. When he died four years later their numbers had risen to a hundred.

Most of Serlo's building survives today – a good deal more, in fact, than appears at first sight. His are the choir, the two transepts – all three now disguised by a thin veneer of Perpendicular panelling – the crypt and the ambulatory around the east end. His too – though it was not completed until twenty years after his death – is the tremendous nave, with those massive cylindrical columns that look as if they could hold up the firmament itself. Thus, within the church, there was relatively little for his thirteenth-century successors to do; their principal achievements were the vaulting of the nave in stone, the building of a crossing-tower and the addition of a Lady Chapel at the east end. Of these, however, only the nave vault remains; tower and chapel were both replaced in the fifteenth century, though the latter's west screen has been preserved, and can now be seen in the north transept.

In 1318 came a crisis. Serious subsidence was discovered beneath the south aisle, which was threatening imminent collapse. A row of stout buttresses was quickly built against the outside wall – they are still there, ornamented with niches, some of which retain their original statues – and the opportunity was taken to replace the tiny Norman windows with big new ones in the then fashionable Decorated style, with swirling tracery. These windows, and those in the triforium of the choir, are the only important Decorated features in the whole fabric – not surprisingly, for the style lasted less long at Gloucester than anywhere else.

It was the murder of Edward II in 1327 and his burial here that brought new wealth and prosperity to the cathedral. The dead King's many shortcomings were forgotten; in the public mind, he rapidly acquired the mantle of a saint and martyr. Pilgrims arrived in their thousands, and by 1331 there was enough money to begin an ambitious remodelling programme. It began in the south transept, where the south window, completed probably in 1335, is the oldest existing window in the Perpendicular style. (I say 'existing', because there is an engraving by Wenceslaus Hollar of the Chapter House of Old St Paul's, London, which clearly shows the long vertical mullions in its great window rising uninterrupted until they meet the edge of the arch at the top. The best date we have for this work is 1332; so that if the Chapter House had not been destroyed in the Great Fire it might have stolen the palm from Gloucester. On the other hand, the style here is so different from the untransomed Court style of London that it may well have been a totally independent development. Certainly in the years to come it would be Gloucester that influenced work in London, rather than the reverse.)

As the remodelling of the south transept continued, it is plain that the condition of the old Early English tower was also causing anxiety. The situation was remedied by running a flying buttress right through the church – a measure which, if not exactly beautiful, has considerable dramatic effect. The important thing to remember, however, is that during the work on the transept the old Norman fabric was not destroyed, merely covered with a skin of Perpendicular panelling. Exactly the same technique was to be used in the north transept some thirty-five years later; before that, however, the monks had turned their attention to the choir and presbytery. Here again the old Norman arcade was masked by a Perpendicular screen, but that was not enough; other, more drastic, action was called for. The roof was removed, the screen walls heightened and the old apsidal east end demolished. In its place was erected one of the cathedral's most memorable features – the largest stained-glass window in England.

The Crécy window, as it is usually called – it actually dates from 1350, four years after the battle – measures 80 feet by 38 feet and occupies the entire east wall. Of its fourteen lights, the outer four on each side are canted inwards for greater strength; it still seems a miracle that the roof can be supported on so apparently frail a structure. And what a roof it is – a lierne vault of indescribable complexity like some heavenly fishing net, every intersection marked by a great golden boss, the stars and fronds and animals' heads giving place towards the east end to the figures of angels playing musical instruments, until finally, over the high altar, we see the figure of Christ in Glory.

So successful was this vault that it was decided to extend it over the crossing. Here, however, was a problem: to continue the intricate pattern of liernes, further points of support were needed between the crossing arches. The master mason's response was a virtuoso flourish in the highest Gloucester tradition. Across the wide space on each side he threw a slender, graceful, four-centred arch; then from its apex he extended a short vertical mullion, braced by two short ribs curving away from the arch, from which the seven ribs of the vault seem to spring effortlessly. Since the arches actually bear no weight, the whole thing is an optical illusion; but it is none the worse for that.

The remodelling of the north transept in the 1370s brought to an end the major fourteenth-century work inside the cathedral, and for fifty years or so it must have remained almost free of scaffolding. Then, around 1425, it was decided to start work on the nave. Work began with the west front – one of the least successful aspects of the building – and continued through the two westernmost bays, which were given Perpendicular arcades and a lierne-vaulted roof. Then, thank God, it stopped. This was also the period of the south porch, which has ever since been the principal entrance to the cathedral. It was, however, much restored by Scott in the nineteenth century, and all the statues along the front are Victorian replacements.

Next, in about 1450, came the new tower. Whether its predecessor was removed because it was becoming too unsafe, or whether it was simply thought to be insufficiently grand, we do not know; but its successor is by any standards a marvellous creation, light as lace, rising

225 feet to an openwork filigree of a parapet and four corner pinnacles so tall that they have their own corner pinnacles and are almost towers in their own right. Even now, however, the work was not quite done, and with the completion of the tower the workforce – and what a body of craftsmen that must have been – was directed to the far east end and the Early English Lady Chapel. This was demolished, and in its place rose the beautiful building we see today, that represents the final flowering of Gloucester's own Perpendicular style. It is approached through a doorway from Serlo's ambulatory, under a little bridge marking the site of his apse. One's first impression, apart from admiration, is mild surprise at how little the style seems to have changed in the 150 years since the rebuilding of the presbytery; there is the east window, a little smaller but of almost identical design; there is the lierne roof and the multitude of bosses. The principal difference is in the huge windows that fill the side bays and flood the chapel with light.

So much for the architecture proper. Now begin your tour, starting of course with the nave. There are lots of things wrong with it: the awkward juncture of the arches with the columns, the disproportionately small gallery, the not entirely happy juxtaposition of its Norman twin arches with the Early English clustered columns from which the vaulting springs. One could also do without that remarkably boring screen. No matter. It is the overall impression that counts, and the nave of Gloucester thrills me every time I enter it. Now walk up the nave, and thence into the south transept, architecturally the most interesting corner of the whole cathedral. From here a flight of steps leads down into Serlo's crypt, where his building began in 1089. Its plan is identical with his plan for the eastern end above. It is groin-vaulted, the arches being supported on columns with simple Norman volutes. Before long, however, it must have been realised that these would not be strong enough to support the load above; the most important columns were therefore sheathed with big rounded responds and the arches reinforced by sturdy ribs.

Returning to the surface, go straight into the choir. A greater contrast with the crypt can hardly be imagined. The stalls, of 1370, are superb with their carved nodding-ogee canopies; they also have particularly good misericords. Continue into the presbytery – and here, for all your admiration of the Crécy window and the roof, spare a moment or two for Robert Curthose, Duke of Normandy, the Conqueror's eldest son, who died in 1134 at Cardiff Castle and whose painted wooden effigy (made in Bristol a century or so after his death) lies in an enchantingly balletic pose in the centre of the floor. Having spent most of his life in active opposition to his father, he was passed over for the English throne; it went instead to his younger brother, William Rufus.

Now go out to your right into the south ambulatory and walk eastward round it towards the Lady Chapel. Here, in a flash, you are back in Serlo's cathedral; those squat round piers surrounded his original choir. The windows around the outside are of course later insertions, but the broad round arches, the outer responds with their scalloped capitals, the groined vault above supporting the gallery – all these are unchanged since the eleventh century.

On leaving the Lady Chapel, take the northern ambulatory – where, on your right, you will find what is perhaps the cathedral's greatest treasure: the tomb of King Edward II, whose body was brought here in 1327 after his murder in Berkeley Castle (*q.v.*). Under the most marvellous of canopies – two tiers of narrow, heavily cusped ogee arches, crowned with a veritable forest of soaring pinnacles, all carved in finest Cotswold limestone – lies his alabaster effigy, dating from within a year or two of his death. His face, framed by the stylised curls of his hair and beard, stares steadfastly – and, it seems, a little reproachfully – upwards with wide open eyes from a pillow held by two angels. It is a curious irony that one of our worst kings should have what is incomparably the loveliest royal tomb.

From the north transept – after a brief pause for the screen from the former Lady Chapel – you now pass out into the CLOISTER. It was unusual to build cloisters on the north, but the city was presumably already encroaching on the south side and the monks sensibly put convenience before tradition. The entrance is in the south-east corner; as you descend the steps, you find yourself facing the long vista of the east range – and the earliest fan vaulting anywhere. Its precise date is unfortunately not known. The best we can say is that it was done during the time of Abbot Horton – somewhere between 1351 and 1377. (There was fan vaulting in the Chapter House of Hereford Cathedral in 1364, but the building was demolished in 1769.) The effect is stunning, particularly when, pursuing your circuit, you discover that the fan vaulting was continued on the other three sides, a fact which makes the Gloucester Cloister not only the most sumptuous in England, but also the one that gives the greatest sense of architectural unity. And yet, within this prevailing harmony, none of the four sides proves to be quite the same. The north walk contains a separately fan-vaulted lavatorium, with a long trough in which the monks could wash their hands; the west walk has a stone bench running the length of the wall; the south has each of its ten bays divided into two small recesses designed for monkish study, each of these in its turn provided with a little two-light window.

There are three openings on the outer wall of the east walk. The first leads into the SLYPE, a broad, tunnel-vaulted passage, its walls arcaded along each side. As these arcades clearly show, it is originally Norman, probably of the early twelfth century; but it was almost doubled in length in the fourteenth, when the Library above it was enlarged. It is in essence simply a passageway leading to the monks' cemetery, but in the Middle Ages it also served as a parlour or locutorium in which the monks could talk to each other – the rule of silence being always preserved in the Cloister – and where a fire was provided in cold weather. The second opening gives access to a spiral staircase leading to the fourteenth-century LIBRARY with its fine timber roof; and the third brings you into the CHAPTER HOUSE. This too is basically Norman, though it was much altered in subsequent centuries – most obviously at the east end, where the original Norman semi-circular apse was replaced in about 1380 by a deep canted bay and a nine-light window.

On leaving the Chapter House, turn right and leave the Cloister by the rib-vaulted passage leading out of the north-east corner. It will take you out past the Little Cloister to the six early thirteenth-century arches which are all that survives of the monks' INFIRMARY. The path then turns west, passing more monastic remains as it approaches Millers Green, where the mill once stood. On the south side of this is a building, now sadly truncated, consisting of a fifteenth-century timber gallery built over a thirteenth-century stone base. This is thought to have been at one time the Abbot's Hall, and it was in the thirteenth-century building that Richard II held his Parliament in 1378. It is still known as the PARLIAMENT ROOM.

And so we return to College Green and the melancholy face of modern Gloucester – a shattering contrast that makes one wonder, very hard, about the meaning of progress.

## Kempley★

*21; 12 miles NW of Gloucester off B4215*

This little village on the border with Hereford and Worcester possesses two outstanding churches – with almost exactly 800 years between them. ST MARY's dates from about 1100, and is above all memorable for the almost complete cycle of frescoes, painted not more than a generation later, all over the barrel vault of the chancel. They owe their remarkable state of preservation to the fact that they were whitewashed over during the Reformation and remained hidden – and forgotten – until they were discovered by the vicar in 1872. A well-intentioned coat of shellac varnish almost did them in, but they have now been rescued once again and, at last, properly consolidated. Christ in Glory occupies the centre; around him are the Evangelists, angels and saints. The architecture itself is not especially noteworthy, but there is an interesting tympanum representing the Tree of Life over the south door. (The door itself is another magnificent survival.) The west tower is late thirteenth-century, and has no entrance from the outside; it might well have been needed as a refuge against wild marauding Welsh.

The second church is that of ST EDWARD THE CONFESSOR. It was built by Randall Wells (who had been assistant to Lethaby at nearby Brockhampton) when he was still in his twenties, using only local labour and materials. It is, in its way, a paradigm of the Arts and Crafts movement. Extremely low walls support a huge, steeply pitched roof; inside, that roof seems almost to reach the ground, while painted tie-beams traverse the almost triangular space – one of them bearing an enormous, highly coloured rood with the Virgin and St John. There is no east window; only two rather surprisingly barley-sugar columns supporting a tapestry *baldacchino*. Equally curious is the pulpit – half an old one, re-used. Why did they not design something new? All the light for the nave comes through a huge west window, the same shape as the section of the church and very little smaller, criss-crossed with a diagonal stone grid. The only other window is a relatively modest, two-light one in the south-east corner, which provides illumination for the chancel. On the outside is a large relief carving of the Crucifixion – occupying the place where the east window should have been.

On the north side there is a long vestry (which might at first glance be taken for a north aisle), a chapel and a tower with a saddleback roof, all in the reddish Forest of Dean sandstone. Whether or not it is a beautiful group I am far from certain; but it is full of boldness, and imagination, and conviction, and strength.

## Leonard Stanley

*22; 3 miles SW of Stroud off B4066*

ST SWITHIN'S CHURCH stands next to a fine five-bay Georgian MANOR HOUSE and is itself Norman, part of an Augustinian priory founded in the early twelfth century. Its rough grey stone suits its broad, low profile: it must have looked lower still before the massive crossing-tower was given its later top stage. The only other vertical emphasis is provided by the big stair turret at the north-west corner, considerably higher than the tower.

The interior is aisleless, which gives it an impression of great length; but it has hefty, broad-shouldered crossing arches supported on the four original piers with twin attached half columns. Most of these have scalloped capitals, but some appear never to have been finished. The windows make up a fairly representative selection: Norman on the south, fourteenth-century on the north, with a late Perpendicular one on the west. The south transept, sadly scraped, has a round-headed lancet; the north is Perpendicular again. The chancel is largely a restoration by G.F. Bodley; but the shafts which divide its two bays have fine, vigorous Norman carving on the capitals – the Nativity on the south, the woman wiping Christ's feet on the north. There is another nice little carving above the aumbry, representing Adam and Eve as animals.

## Nether Lypiatt Manor

See Bisley.

## Newland★

*23; 19 miles SW of Gloucester on B4231*

Beautifully set on the brow of a hill in gently undulating country at the edge of the Forest of Dean, ALL SAINTS' CHURCH is all too often described in guide-books – including its own – as 'the cathedral of the forest'. This is a pity, since any visitor expecting anything remotely like a cathedral will be disappointed. What he will find, however, is a remarkably lovely thirteenth-century church, with a wonderful tower that can be seen for miles.

We see this tower – particularly if we are coming from the south – for so long before we see anything else of the church that it seems only fair to take it first. Its lower stage was built at the time the rest of the building was completed, roughly between 1280 and 1300; that is the

*All Saints' Church, Newland.*

date of the four-light west window with its Y-tracery. Fortunately, though, the builders made their walls 6 feet thick; obviously a tower was intended, and though the upper stages were not added for almost 100 years the delay was wholly beneficial, for the tower as we see it today represents the last flowering of the Decorated period and is the crowning glory of the church. The tall, delicately fluted spires of the four corner pinnacles make a subtle contrast with the yet taller, unfluted one that marks the belfry stair. Between these corner pinnacles runs a parapet pierced with trefoils, while from the middle of each side rises a small, slightly concave gable with a crocketed finial: a lovely composition.

The first thing that strikes us about the interior is the width, the aisles being only 3 feet narrower than the nave and giving a wonderful feeling of spaciousness. The five-bay arcades have octagonal piers, but are otherwise remarkably plain. Of the windows, those in the north aisle, of three stepped lancets, are late thirteenth-century, and that at the east end of the south aisle (now part of the Gryndour Chantry Chapel) with its intersecting tracery can be only very little later. The central east window is a later remodelling.

The chapel to the north of the chancel is clearly somewhat later than its opposite number to the south; it is Perpendicular, and must be of around 1400. One might at first glance be tempted to assign the same date to the little chapel in the south aisle adjoining the south porch; but its Perpendicular window is in fact a subsequent insertion; the chapel itself was added by Edward I in 1309 as a 'Chantry Chapel of King Edward's Service'.

Newland has a splendid collection of tombs and effigies. The tomb of Sir John Joce and his lady (he died in 1349) in the south aisle is the best; for curiosity value, on the other hand, the effigy of 'the Forester of Fee' is warmly recommended as a rare indication of what the well-dressed huntsman was wearing in the 1450s. Oddest of all is the brass in the south chapel, representing a medieval iron miner of the Forest of Dean with a hod and a pick in his hands and a candlestick in his mouth. He is shown in relief, rather than being incised – a unique feature.

Old houses surround the church, giving the impression of a small cathedral close. The early seventeenth-century ALMSHOUSES along the south side are particularly attractive.

## North Cerney

*24; 3½ miles N of Cirencester on A435*

ALL SAINTS may not be the most beautiful village church in Gloucestershire from the outside, but it is certainly one of the most superbly furnished. It lies long and low, against a lovely backdrop of trees, attractive in a rambling sort of way but oddly disorganised. Its saddleback tower is somehow typical of it; such towers can have considerable charm, but they hardly lend architectural distinction.

The church dates from early in the twelfth century, to which period belong the tower as far as the bell-stage (which is of about 1200), the south wall of the nave – though not of course the windows – and the south door with its diapered tympanum. Most of the rest of what we see from the outside is of the late fifteenth century, the consequence of a disastrous fire in the 1460s; the principal exception is the chancel, which is largely eighteenth- and nineteenth-century and looks it.

It is only when we get inside that the church reveals its worth. Starting from the west end, the first thing to be noted is the west gallery of 1754, to which the only access is, rather surprisingly, by an outside staircase. Above it on the north wall is a fine sculptured stone corbel portraying Henry VI. Two other similar corbels towards the east, supporting the fine fifteenth-century timber roof, show a priest (probably the rector who rebuilt the church after the fire) and Edward Stafford, Duke of Buckingham, who was beheaded by Richard III. To the south, the transept forms the late fifteenth-century Lady Chapel. It is separated from the nave by an exquisite parclose screen, the work of the Arts and Crafts designer F. C. Eden, whose contribution to this church was immense; it bears a representation of the Annunciation, with a magnificent heraldic crest above. Feast your eyes, too, on the lovely east window of this chapel, which must predate 1485 since it features the Yorkist badge of the Sun in Splendour; and on the three wooden statues on the reredos, all of a very similar date – the Virgin is French, the two bishops South German.

Just to the north of the chancel arch is a remarkably fine stone pulpit, its entire bowl cut from a single block of stone – probably by a Burford mason in about 1480. And so we come to the arch itself, architecturally the most distinguished feature of the church. It has, alas, been heavily restored; but we can date it with some accuracy, since the delicate carving on the respond capitals can hardly be earlier than 1180, while the round Norman arch can hardly be later than 1200. Above it is a most distinguished rood loft, also by Eden, who was additionally responsible for the reredos in the chancel.

Much of the beauty of the church is due to Eden's friend and patron William Iveson Croome. All Saints was fortunate indeed to have such a generous benefactor; would that there were more like him.

## Northleach

*25; 10½ miles NE of Cirencester on A429*

Northleach's pride is another of the great Perpendicular wool churches of Gloucestershire, like those at Chipping Campden, Cirencester and Fairford. When you approach ST PETER AND ST PAUL'S through the churchyard from the east it looks like a great ship – the nave soaring high above the chancel, its height emphasised by its own nine-light east window over the chancel arch, and the tremendous tower beyond, higher still. The chancel is generously pinnacled, the tower embattled, the nave both. The absence of pinnacles on the tower is a little surprising, and has been tentatively explained by the theory that a spire was intended; but the Northleach tower is very different in character from its more exuberant neighbours. Pinnacles would not really suit it, and it may well be that the original builders simply decided that it would be better without.

This tower, of 1380–1400, was the first part of the present church to be built – the east face bears the marks of the steeper, lower, nave roof of the earlier building, which was demolished to make way for its more opulent successor. The new church was begun soon afterwards and continued till almost the end of the century, finishing for all practical purposes with the completion of the south-east chapel in 1489. We enter by the south porch – not quite up to Cirencester standards, perhaps, but still a noble and beautiful creation in its own right. The outer entrance is crowned by a tall ogival hood-mould, above which the original statue of the Virgin, seated beneath a projecting canopy, remains *in situ*. Above her we find the Trinity, lower down St John the Baptist and St Thomas of Canterbury, all fine medieval work. The porch itself is two-storeyed, with a stair turret surmounted by a tall crocketed *flèche*; the ground floor is

*All Saints' Church, North Cerney.*

*Daneway House, Sapperton.*

elaborately vaulted and has image brackets with carved corbels, one of which depicts a cat playing a fiddle to an enraptured audience of three mice. The upper chamber has a fireplace, with a candle bracket on each side. The flue is cunningly concealed in the western buttress; the pinnacle above it also serves as a chimney.

The nave arcades are identical, each of five bays and having the same octagonal concave-sided piers and capitals as we see at Chipping Campden. At the base of the south-east pier is carved the name 'HENRIE WINCHCOMBE' – presumably the master mason. (The inscription on the opposite side, 'EDMUNDE – GRANT US HIS GRACE' remains a mystery.) The windows are, as one might expect, all Perpendicular; the only odd thing about those of the aisles is that they do not correspond with the bays of the nave arcades. The south aisle windows are transomed, considerably more elaborate than those to the north and, one suspects, slightly later.

Now to the chancel; and the chancel is, frankly, a disappointment. The arch itself is little more than a hole in the wall – no responds, no capitals – and the roof at its western end actually cuts into that marvellous eastern clerestory window. The reason seems to be that whereas the nave was maintained by the parishioners – who, in those affluent days, were prepared to contribute lavishly to their church – the chancel was the responsibility of the Abbey of Gloucester which was much less generously disposed. Indeed, the fourteenth-century doorway in the north wall suggests that it did not even completely demolish the old chancel but simply contented itself by putting new Perpendicular windows in the old masonry. On the south wall, the sedilia give us another useful clue as to the dating, in the shape of the double Tudor Rose, symbolising the marriage of Henry VII and Elizabeth of York in 1486. Their portraits can be seen on the corbels in the Lady Chapel.

## Oddington*

*26; 3 miles E of Stow-on-the-Wold off A436*

ST NICHOLAS'S CHURCH is set quite a long way from the sprawling village, down a dirt road; it is indeed so inaccessible that another church was provided, more central and convenient, in the 1850s – to which happy occurrence St Nicholas's doubtless owes its unspoilt quality and its star in this book. When the church was founded in the twelfth century its nave was what is now the south aisle; then, in the thirteenth, a new nave and chancel were added to the north, and a tower was raised on the end of the original building over what had been the chancel (where the old piscina is still in place). It seems, therefore, that when Henry III used to come to Oddington in the 1260s – to stay with the Archbishop of York, who had a palace here – the church looked much as it does today. The structural additions since his time have been the south porch, added around 1340 together with the Decorated windows on the south side, and the top stage of the tower, whose Perpendicular windows and battlements indicate the fifteenth century.

As you enter the church, you are immediately confronted with a huge Doom painting on the wall opposite. It must date from the late fourteenth century, when the Black Death was not only still fresh in men's minds but still making spasmodic reappearances. After seventeenth-century whitewashing it was only rediscovered in 1913, and during the following half-century became extremely faded; but in 1970 it was admirably restored by the Pilgrim Trust. At the time of writing, it looks marvellous. Its position on the north wall is unusual; Dooms were nearly always given pride of place above the chancel arch.

The nave, which has a good fifteenth-century roof, is surprisingly long and most agreeably lopsided, showing a marked list to the north; halfway down it there is a pretty, and equally lopsided, carved Jacobean pulpit, with sounding board. It stands on a single chunky turned leg, as from a huge oak table. Over the broad thirteenth-century chancel arch, instead of the Doom, are the Royal Arms dated 1835 – nice crude country work, just right. The chancel is lovely: almost as broad as the nave, lit by three separate narrow lights with cinquefoil heads at the east end and two tall lancets on each side.

Virtually abandoned for the past 130 years, but obviously not forgotten – it is very well maintained – this is a really lovely little country church. If only, one feels, the Victorians had decided more often to start again, rather than to restore and 'improve'; the Redundant Churches Council might have had a lot more work to do, but the architectural gain would have been incalculable.

## Owlpen

*27; 5 miles SW of Stroud off B4066*

Set most romantically at the bottom of a long deep combe is OWLPEN MANOR, with the little church (largely Victorian, but could be worse) nestling behind it and a wooded hillside rising up in the distance. Originally of the fifteenth century, the house was much enlarged around 1540 by the addition of a Hall and a Great Chamber above it. The Hall is still there, but has lost its screens. A new west wing was built on in 1616, with an embattled bay reaching right up into the gable; then, in 1720, the medieval east wing was remodelled and tall sash windows inserted. (In the centre and to the west, the windows remain mullioned.)

The eighteenth-century remodelling is still more noticeable inside the house, where an elegant little arched doorway leads through into a pretty panelled Parlour. A fine newel-staircase leads up to the Great Chamber, where there is a Tudor fireplace (added to in 1720) and the most extraordinary wall hangings on painted cloth, depicting the story of Joseph. The technique is naïve, in places almost crude; but no other complete set of such painted hangings exists anywhere. It is thought to be Dutch, but nobody seems too sure.

A little way east of the house is a splendid fifteenth-century BARN with nearly all its original timbers and an enormous wooden cider press lurking in a far corner. There is also a pretty early eighteenth-century CORN MILL with a frivolous little cupola.

## Painswick

*28; 10 miles SW of Cheltenham on A46*

Painswick earns its place here not for any single building but for the combination of a nice country house, a remarkably pretty town and the most spectacular churchyard in England. The house is now known, somewhat unimaginatively, as PAINSWICK HOUSE; I wish it had stuck to its original name of Buenos Ayres. Standing in a wooded park just outside the town, it consists of an almost square five-bay central block, built around 1735 in the excellent local stone, and two lower wings added 100 years later by George Basevi. The architect of the centre is unknown: John Strahan and William Halfpenny have both been suggested, on what seems to be rather flimsy stylistic evidence. Basevi's east wing provides a fine Entrance Hall with a screen of Ionic columns, but the two most memorable rooms are the Drawing Room and the Library, both in the main block: the first is a perfect cube, with a coved ceiling and fine Chinese wallpaper dating from 1831; the second has another coved ceiling with elegant plasterwork and a huge Vanbrughesque chimneypiece. The bookcases are by Basevi.

In Painswick town the grandest house is unquestionably THE BEACON, which is thought to be by John Wood the Younger and is now occupied by a firm of estate agents. Its interior is a marvellous celebration in Rococo plasterwork, probably the work of William Stocking of Bristol. But a short walk through the town will lead you to literally dozens more houses of only slightly less distinction. When you have finished, go and rest, briefly, in that marvellous CHURCHYARD, among the ninety-nine clipped yew trees (planted in 1792) and the superb table tombs, carved by various members of the Bryan family. Avoid, if possible, entering the church itself; it was restored in the 1880s with an unusually heavy hand, even for then.

## Sapperton

*29; 4½ miles W of Cirencester off A419*

ST KENELM'S comes as a delightful surprise. In essence a pretty but in no sense exceptional village church of the fourteenth century, it was rebuilt in about 1700 when it was given its present round-headed windows – which, incidentally, have kept quite a lot of their original green-tinted glass. At the same time, however – or very shortly after – it also received the far more unexpected gift of late Elizabethan or Jacobean panelling and woodwork from the old Manor House, including a most enjoyable set of carved bench ends. It is this mixture of the Jacobean and the Queen Anne style that gives the church its individuality and its very considerable charm.

DANEWAY HOUSE lies half a mile or so to the west of the village, in the wooded valley of the River Frome. It owes its name to the passage of the Danes down the valley in the year 894, racing to rescue their ships which had been detained by King Alfred. The earliest part is the long rectangular Hall block, which almost certainly goes back to the late thirteenth century; an Oratory (replaced in the seventeenth century by a Library) was added on to it in 1339, its trefoil-arched entrance being still *in situ*, while two of its windows have been reset into the walls of the buttery wing at the back of the house. Then, in Elizabethan times, the Hall was sub-divided, vertically to form what are now the kitchen, Dining Room and part of the passageway through the house, and also horizontally; the roof timbers in the upper room – now a Chapel – still show traces of the smoke from the old central hearth.

In 1620 or thereabouts the house was much enlarged by the addition of a tall gabled wing of no fewer than five storeys, with a single room on each and a spiral staircase. Two of these rooms have charming Jacobean plaster ceilings, and one has a small internal wooden porch. The topmost room, lit by a window in each of the gables, is reached only through a trap-door. There have been no additions worth speaking of, and very few major alterations, since the seventeenth century, and the house – one of the oldest manor houses in Gloucestershire – radiates a marvellous atmosphere of timelessness and peace.

*Sezincote.*

## Sezincote★

*30; 1½ miles SW of Moreton-in-Marsh off A44*

Though Sezincote may not quite possess the Xanadu exoticism of the Royal Pavilion at Brighton, it still could not be anything other than what it is – an English country house built for an Indian nabob, deliberately oriental in style. The nabob concerned was Sir Charles Cockerell, who had made a fortune while in service with the East India Company; the architect was his brother, Samuel Pepys Cockerell, who had recently designed the house at Daylesford only a few miles away for Warren Hastings. Cockerell had never been to India – his experience of foreign travel was limited to a single journey to Ireland – and at Daylesford he had avoided any obvious orientalising, apart from giving a slightly Islamic touch to the dome. At Sezincote, on the other hand, he went a good deal further; but by then he could rely on the expert advice of Thomas Daniell, whose watercolours of India were already famous and who probably knew more about Indian architecture than anyone else in England.

The result was a triumphant success, a brilliant synthesis of the neo-classical and the Indian. The regularity of the nine-bay façade and the big sash windows (round-headed on the five-bay south front) are orthodox enough; India comes to the fore with the heavily hooded first-floor windows on the entrance front, with the deeply recessed central bay reminiscent of a Mogul *iwan*, with the little corner turrets and above all with the big bulbous copper dome, set on a high square platform above the hipped roof. It is this dome that gives height to the house, which has only two storeys and from the garden side looks almost like a large and luxurious bungalow. The pale green copper makes a brave contrast with the bright yellow stone, said to have been specially stained to give it a more characteristically Indian tint. Certain of the Indian features are Hindu, but the general impression is overwhelmingly Islamic.

At least from the outside. Inside, we are back in Gloucestershire. The downstairs rooms are, despite much fine detailing, conceived on a relatively modest scale, low-ceilinged and informal. From the centre,

however, there rises a most magnificent staircase, with two short flights of stairs meeting on a half landing and then joining to soar up through the middle of the Hall – where they are supported on pretty decorative cast-iron girders – to the *piano nobile*. Here the rooms, particularly those along the south front, are very opulent indeed, with a wealth of fine plasterwork.

From the main block of the house a long arcaded wing, part Gallery, part Conservatory, extends in a gentle curve towards the south, culminating in an enchanting octagonal pavilion which tries very hard to pass itself off as some pleasure kiosk in a Mogul garden but cannot quite conceal a playful Gothick spirit. A less obtrusive extension slips off to the north to a similar pavilion which once served as Sir Charles Cockerell's bedroom.

The Indian element is continued into the gardens, in which Repton is thought to have had a hand, although there is no Red Book. They are made more exotic still by a bridge designed by Daniell and adorned with Brahmin sacred bulls, and a Temple of Sourya, the Sun God, which he is said to have modelled on the carvings on the island of Elephanta, off Bombay.

## Sherborne

*31; 5 miles NW of Burford off A40*

Unfortunately SHERBORNE HOUSE cannot be recommended. Built in the 1550s, it seems to have been extensively remodelled on the outside 100 years later, and on the inside by Lewis Wyatt and Anthony Salvin in the nineteenth century. The entrance front is chiefly notable for a plethora of fluted columns, Ionic and Corinthian, separating the mullioned windows on all three floors – an interesting conception perhaps, but hardly a beautiful one. The general effect is not improved by the presence of the parish church, so close that it seems to be growing out of one side of the house. (It is in fact connected by a corridor.) The place is now being used as a school, and serve it right.

Infinitely more worth a visit is LODGE PARK, a couple of miles to the south-west. Coming from the House, you cross the A40 and follow a little narrow road that leads in a dead straight line; suddenly, there it is on your right – a ravishing little two-storey house of five close-set bays, almost square in plan, with a deep three-bay rusticated loggia projecting at the centre and supporting a first-floor terrace. A flat parapeted roof, set curiously high above the five first-floor pediments, gives a clue to the building's original purpose; it was designed not as a house at all, but as a sort of glorified grandstand from which to watch deer coursing. The date is about 1650; the architect probably John Webb, though there is no documentary evidence. It was designed to consist of two rooms only, one on each floor, but the interior was largely remodelled in 1898 by Emily, Lady Sherborne, who added new rooms at the back. Fortunately these do not affect the main front or even the side elevations, which were originally limited to a single bay. It is perhaps not great architecture, but a delightful curiosity.

## Slimbridge

*32; 16 miles SW of Gloucester off A38*

Few of the thousands of visitors to the Severn Wildfowl Trust give a thought to the CHURCH OF ST JOHN, despite the fact that its beautiful, slender spire is one of the most prominent landmarks in the region. Did they but know it, they are missing a lot; for here is to be found what is almost certainly the best Early English work in all Gloucestershire. Look first at the west face of the tower – a lovely composition with its five image niches on the bottom stage and the curious elongated quatrefoil (which may once have served as a frame for a painting) occupying the stage above. The three-light window over the door is clearly a somewhat later insertion dating from the very beginning of the Decorated period – say around 1300; but only purists would cavil at it.

The nave arcades, of around 1200, are exquisitely carved in stiff-leaf, scallops and trumpets. Above, the corbel heads are equally splendid. Another joy (though a little later again) is the Decorated east window of the north aisle, almost Burgundian in its flamboyance. The clerestory was rebuilt, with new cornice, parapet and windows, in 1845; the job could hardly have been done better.

*Stanway.*

## Stanway*

*33; 11 miles NE of Cheltenham on B4077*

Stanway is more than a house. It is a whole cluster of buildings, all in glorious, golden Cotswold stone, nestling together at the foot of a high wooded hill surmounted by an eighteenth-century pyramid. Apart from the mansion itself, there is a magnificent fourteenth-century TITHE BARN, cruck-framed with a double tier of wind-braces, a charming VICARAGE of about 1650 and – most remarkable of all – the GATEHOUSE. This was built about 1630, which was late for gatehouses; it must be one of the last important ones in the country. But it is also one of the finest, its three-storey elevation crowned on each side with three tall shaped gables which are in turn surmounted by finials bearing scallop shells – emblems of the Tracys, who owned the manor until 1817. The double pediment of the entrance gateway rises as far as the centre gable and is flanked by bows of the same height. The hoary old tradition that it is the work of Inigo Jones can safely be discounted; but whoever was responsible – it was probably a local master mason – his work could not possibly have been improved on.

The entrance front of the house extends behind the Gatehouse and at right-angles to it, facing west. When you first go in, it all seems traditional enough, with a screens passage leading off ahead of you and the Great Hall – lit by a memorably magnificent bay window at the far end – immediately on your right. Only after you pass through the Hall do you realise how unorthodox Stanway really is, for it then emerges that virtually all the other principal rooms of the house, instead of being grouped around the Hall, have been concentrated in a long, later, wing extending from its far end towards the east. This gives them a splendid south-facing aspect across the walled garden, and provides the house with a ravishing south front. It has only two storeys, with a full-height gabled bay at each end and another gable over the centre, beneath which the first-floor window is opulently decorated with a keystone and voluted frame and the door below it with pilasters and a big segmental pediment. This door, like the main entrance to the west, is an eighteenth-century addition; but the rest of the south front was probably completed around 1640.

The house was originally a good deal larger than it is today; a north-east wing, which had been much remodelled by Detmar Blow in 1913, was demolished after the last war, together with other accretions by William Burn – a loss which need occasion no regret. What remains is one of the loveliest houses in Gloucestershire – and one of the most desirable ones I know anywhere.

## Tetbury

*34; 10½ miles SW of Cirencester on A433*

The focal point of Tetbury is its MARKET HOUSE of 1655, supported on wonderfully fat Tuscan columns showing rather exaggerated *entasis*. It has a most enviable weathervane with two golden dolphins. Surprisingly, it is not in the Market Place, which lies a few hundred yards to the east (down a pretty street ruined by a perfectly disgraceful post office) and to which both the TALBOT HOTEL and CREW HOUSE adjoining lend much distinction. Tetbury indeed, possesses any amount of really fine buildings; it is a good town to wander in.

Of all these buildings, however, the most remarkable is ST MARY'S CHURCH. Georgian Gothick, by Francis Hiorne of Warwick, it was consecrated in 1781. This was at the very beginning of the second Iron Age, and the arcades are supported on unbelievably high and slender clustered columns of wood, with iron cores running down the middle. Above, the roof is rib-vaulted in plaster; below, there are serried rows of high box pews. Perhaps the most unexpected feature of all, however, is Hiorne's addition of two long, low passages running along the outside of the aisles, with doors at regular intervals leading directly into the pews. In these passages have been grouped many of the tombs taken from the original church, together with several wall tablets. One of the latter, of the early nineteenth century, admirably conveys its author's obvious feelings of lassitude – coupled, perhaps, with a certain defiant peevishness:

*In a vault underneath*
*lie several of the Saunderses,*
*late of this parish: particulars*
*the Last Day will disclose.*

UPTON HOUSE at Tetbury Upton, a mile or two outside the town to the north, is a mid-eighteenth-century manor house of rare elegance. Its architect is unknown; John Strahan and John Wood the Elder of Bath have both been suggested, but more recent opinion favours William Halfpenny. The south front, seen from the road, looks marvellous: basically Palladian, but with a touch of Baroque exuberance (in the emphatic keystones of the ground-floor windows and the *oeil-de-boeuf* windows above) that lifts it out of the normal run of safe mid-Georgian houses – it is dated 1752 – and gives it real distinction. Inside there is a quite spectacular Saloon rising up two floors and exuberantly stuccoed, and an equally memorable oak staircase behind.

## Tewkesbury*

*35; 10½ miles NE of Gloucester on A38*

If there were any justice in the world, TEWKESBURY ABBEY would be a cathedral. It is certainly big enough, but there is more to it than that. St Mary Redcliffe in Bristol, despite its size and its beauty, contrives still to look exactly what it is – the largest parish church in England; Tewkesbury, very slightly smaller, gives the impression of a cathedral through and through. It dominates the little town, effortlessly, as all cathedrals should; it is perfectly set, with a wide and not too cluttered churchyard to the north and west and a broad expanse of lawn around the east end; it is built almost entirely of Caen stone, specially imported from Normandy, despite the proximity of the Cotswold quarries; and, from whatever angle you look at it, it is quite breathtakingly beautiful.

Inevitably, the tower is what strikes you first – and here Tewkesbury can claim a record, for this is the most massive Norman tower in existence anywhere. Only the negligibly small battlements and the pinnacles are later additions; they are of 1660. All the rest was almost certainly completed before 1170. The lowest stage above the crossing is plain, apart from two round-headed windows on each face and traces of the original, higher-pitched roofs; but the three upper stages are all enriched with blind arcading, the first and third additionally punctuated by bell openings. Thanks to this perfectly judged decoration, the tower possesses both elegance and grace – two qualities not invariably associated with Norman architecture.

The tower was, as one might expect, the last part of the abbey to be completed; the building had in fact been consecrated in 1121, only two decades after that of Gloucester, which it must have closely resembled. Unlike Gloucester, however, Tewkesbury thenceforth remained virtually inviolate, with the result that it still retains – especially on the inside – its original Romanesque character. Only once again in all its history was there any important programme of rebuilding, and that was in the early fourteenth century at the expense of the local suzeraine, Eleanor de Clare, her husband Hugh Le Despencer and – after the latter had been hung, drawn and quartered on charges of wielding an evil influence over Edward II – their son, another Hugh. This is work

*Upton House, Tetbury Upton, near Tetbury.*

that we cannot regret; it coincided with the all-too-brief Gloucestershire flowering of the Decorated period, and made the choir and presbytery one of the miracles of English church building.

The normal approach to the abbey, from the north, affords us a fine opportunity to contemplate its perfect proportions, and at the same time to note two more changes made by the Despencers – the three-light windows inserted in the blind arcading of the Norman clerestory and the beautiful Decorated windows of the transept and aisle. We now walk round to the west end, where a considerable surprise awaits us. Apart from two unimportant windows at the ends of the aisles, virtually the entire west front is taken up with an immense Norman recessed arch, 65 feet high, with six – originally there were seven – orders of roll mouldings supported on shafts with scalloped capitals. (One could wish that the west window, which it frames, were a little more distinguished; it is in fact a late seventeenth-century replacement, the earlier one having been destroyed in a gale in 1661.) There is structural evidence that it was originally intended to build twin west towers, as at Southwell; but the two little turrets, despite their altered caps, seem to me to do very nicely; nothing more is needed.

The interest of the south side of the abbey lies principally in the traces of the monastic buildings, including the Cloister, which was rebuilt in imitation of Gloucester in the early fifteenth century; but little of this now remains, except the doorway into the church. Then, passing the transept, we reach the beginning of the chevet of Decorated chapels that surrounds the east end, above which rises the roof of the choir with its pierced and embattled parapet and flying buttresses. The east end itself comes as something of a disappointment: just two rather mingy windows, one above the other, within two similarly superimposed blind arches. This was the site of the Lady Chapel, which was pulled down in the early sixteenth century to make way for a new one; alas, the Dissolution of the Monasteries put paid to that, so the abbey was truncated in vain.

Enter now, by the north door, and go straight to the middle of the nave. The initial impact is much the same as at Gloucester: there are the same huge columns (their diameters in the two buildings are almost identical – 6 feet 6 inches) – and the same rather half-hearted narrow capitals. Then one begins to notice the differences. From the strictly architectural point of view, Gloucester is finer: the arches there are delicately moulded and adorned with chevron, while Tewkesbury has two orders only, as plain as can be. Tewkesbury's fourteenth-century lierne vault, on the other hand, is far superior to Gloucester's simple rib vaulting of 100 years before, and, as an additional bonus, carries a marvellous series of bosses depicting the Life of Christ; it is only sad that the masons made this vault spring directly from the capitals of the columns and not, as at Gloucester, from a few feet higher. The effect is to make the roof seem uncomfortably low, squeezing the triforium and clerestory almost out of existence. Where Tewkesbury wins hands down, however, is in the view to the east. At Gloucester this is blocked by the centrally placed organ and the heavy stone screen beneath it; here, the organ has been relegated to the side, and the screen of carved wood is low and, in effect, transparent. In consequence we can rejoice in an uninterrupted vista the entire length of the abbey to the three Decorated windows of that wonderful presbytery.

As you walk slowly up the nave, and pass beneath the crossing-tower – originally designed as a lantern, but now obscured by the fourteenth-century vaulting – the beauty of the presbytery is gradually revealed. Before settling down to enjoy it, however, pause to take a look at the somewhat stubby transepts. That to the south still retains the little apsidal chapel to the east with its radiating ribs; in its northern counterpart, a similar chapel was removed in the early thirteenth century and the transept was extended to the north and east. Of this the eastern section still stands in the Chapels of St James and St Nicholas – now the choir vestry – where you can find the only Early English work in the abbey, and very fine it is too.

And so to the presbytery, and to the ultimate glory of Tewkesbury. Only the old cylindrical Norman piers – truncated and furnished with new capitals – remain to attest its Romanesque origins; for the rest, the four- and five-light windows in the polygonal apse and the breathtaking lierne vaulting are Decorated work at its virtuoso best. The vaulting must date from almost immediately after the great battle of Tewkesbury of 4 May 1471, when the victorious Yorkists, led by King Edward IV in person and his two brothers Richard of Gloucester and George of Clarence, burst into the abbey where the beaten Lancastrians had sought refuge and shed so much blood that the building had to be closed for a month before it could be reconsecrated. The two great central bosses, featuring the Yorkist emblem of the Sun in Splendour, seem to blaze down in a great paean of victory – although, as we know, that victory was to be short-lived.

The abbey contains another curious relic of the battle: the door of the sacristy, which is actually the westernmost of the chevet chapels on the south side, is covered on its inner face with iron plates made from the armour worn by the soldiers who were killed on the field. And immediately behind the high altar, an iron grating in the floor marks the vault in which the Duke of Clarence was buried, after being drowned in a butt of malmsey wine.

The chevet chapels are connected by the ambulatory, rib-vaulted in the fourteenth century. What is interesting here is the way in which the original Norman piers, retained to support the new presbytery, were also used for this vaulting – which, however, springs from a half capital set at a lower level. All the radiating chevet chapels were remodelled in the Decorated style, and several contain interesting monuments, notably the fourteenth-century tomb of Guy de Brien, who had served as standard-bearer to Edward III at the battle of Crécy. The best, however, are the three chantry chapels set within the walls of the presbytery itself. All are essentially Perpendicular. The most ornate is that erected by Isabel Despencer, Countess of Warwick, in memory of her husband Richard Beauchamp; the most memorable, however, is unquestionably the so-called Trinity Chapel on the south side, built around 1375–80 for Edward Despencer. It is fan-vaulted on the inside – this fan vaulting *could* be as early as that in the Gloucester Cloisters, and hence among the earliest surviving in England – but what remains in the mind is the gilded figure of the knight himself, on his knees facing the high altar, beneath a separate canopy rising from the roof. Just to the north-west of the high altar there is another very beautiful tomb, this time in the Decorated style and not a chantry chapel, to the younger Hugh Despencer – who was responsible, with his parents, for the remodeling of the abbey – and his wife Elizabeth. Most of the glass is modern, but there is some fine fourteenth-century work in the Decorated windows of the presbytery and a few fragments in the sacristy.

The TOWN is a joy to walk in, for two reasons. The first is that nearly all the older houses are timber-framed, while most of the remainder have Georgian brick fronts; there was virtually no new building in the town between the 1850s and the 1930s. The second is the quantity of tiny cottages of the seventeenth and eighteenth centuries built behind the houses fronting the main streets; this is because of a steady increase of population during that period, which in turn was the result of the change away from the cloth industry, in which the work was done in a single centre, to the knitting industry which was carried on in individual homes. The presence of the two rivers and the abbey precincts made it impossible for the town to expand outwards, so it was forced to increase in density instead.

## Toddington

*36; 10 miles NE of Cheltenham on A46*

ST ANDREW'S CHURCH stands secluded in the park of TODDINGTON MANOR – the last place you would expect to find a magnificent *tour de force* by G. E. Street. But there it is, and it is one of his best. The outside is of a slightly alarming yellow-orange stone, but the inside is of white ashlar – quite dazzling on a summer morning with the early sun flooding through the tracery of the big five-light east window. (Street has adopted his favourite early fourteenth-century style.) The chancel is rib-vaulted with large and intricate bosses and has an arcade of cusped pointed arches running round three sides and incorporating piscina and sedilia. There are wooden parclose screens, good furniture everywhere and a huge north chapel, similarly rib-vaulted, with Hanbury-Tracy tombs. The nave is aisleless, but has a magnificent hammer-beam roof; it is closed one bay from the west by a majestic stone screen of three huge stepped arches, as impressive as it is unexpected.

Immediately west of the church are the ruins of the Jacobean manor GATEHOUSE; the old MANOR was however replaced between 1820 and 1835 by a new building, designed by its owner, Charles Hanbury-Tracy, later 1st Lord Sudeley. Hanbury-Tracy was an amateur architect of no mean ability – he was chairman of the judges' panel appointed in 1835 to select the winning design for the new Houses of Parliament – with a real understanding of Gothic. His plan was one of three rectangles connected diagonally in a single line, each with an open court in the centre and, in the north-western block, a turreted and pinnacled Great Tower (modelled on that of Magdalen College) which would serve, despite its eccentric positioning, to bind the whole composition together. The idea has proved remarkably successful; a walk around the outside provides an apparently endless series of differing perspectives, and there are no two angles from which the building looks even remotely the same. The two-storey main block is surrounded by vaulted cloisters set with late medieval stained glass; some was sold in 1911 but quite a lot remains. The main state rooms are light and airy; the Music Room, with its gilded Gothic Rococo, would be almost frivolous if it were not so tremendously grand.

*St Andrew's Church, Toddington.*

The Manor is now a college for foreign students, but can be visited by appointment. It is an extraordinary achievement – one of the outstanding monuments of the early Victorian Gothic Revival – and deserves to be better known.

*Toddington Manor.*

## Westonbirt House

*37; 2½ miles SW of Tetbury on A433*

Lewis Vulliamy built Westonbirt House between 1863 and 1870 for the millionaire R. S. Holford – for whom he had just completed Dorchester House in Park Lane. With the demolition of the latter in 1929 to make way for the Dorchester Hotel, Westonbirt is Vulliamy's most important secular building to survive. He designed it as an Elizabethan prodigy house, with Wollaton Hall as his principal inspiration; yet Westonbirt stands in its own right, a thoroughly nineteenth-century work which somehow manages to capture the sixteenth-century spirit without ever slipping into plagiarism or pastiche. It has three storeys, with a five-storey ogee-capped tower rising from the centre, surrounded by a multitude of chimneys, pinnacles, finials and obelisks. The detailing is marvellous, wherever you look – *paterae* set between triglyphs, busts in deep-set circular niches, superimposed classical orders, strapwork, the lot. The front lodges are like the house's children; one feels that they will look almost exactly like it when they grow up.

The house is now a girls' school and is not normally open to the public. Holford's very splendid arboretum opposite will, however, welcome you warmly. It is considered to be the best in the country.

## Winchcombe

*38; 6 miles NE of Cheltenham on A46*

ST PETER'S CHURCH is the result of a joint effort by the Abbot of Winchcombe Abbey, who built the chancel, and the townspeople who paid for the rest – though not without a good deal of help from Sir Ralph Boteler of Sudeley. They got it only just in time, for the church was almost certainly built between 1458 and 1468 – and in 1469 Sir Ralph, a prominent Lancastrian, was forced to surrender himself and his estates to Edward IV. By reason of its size and date, it should rank among the great wool churches of Gloucestershire, but it must be admitted that Winchcombe cannot really compete with Cirencester or Northleach, Fairford or Chipping Campden. It is less ornate than any of these and – a serious weakness in any medieval church interior – it lacks a chancel arch.

Nonetheless, it is well worth a visit. The exterior is noted for its series of some forty grotesque heads – they are not strictly speaking gargoyles since they have no channels for the rainwater – and has a fine two-storey south porch, stone-vaulted. The interior was much restored in 1872 by John Drayton Wyatt, a partner of Sir George Gilbert Scott. It is beautifully proportioned, broad and spacious, but somehow unexciting.

## Wyck Rissington

*39; 3 miles S of Stow-on-the-Wold off A429*

This pretty village has an enchanting church, especially on the outside which is irresistibly naïve but at the same time full of character. ST LAURENCE'S is of lovely lichen-covered stone and has a short, broad tower. The base is probably Norman – its walls are 9 feet thick – but the church is essentially Early English, of which there is all too little in Gloucestershire. Before you go in, walk around to the east end; it has two pairs of lancets, each surmounted by a lozenge-shaped light with concave sides. All around, and indeed continuing around three sides of the chancel, runs a distinctly playful string-course, zigzagging about as it follows the lines of the fenestration. Beyond it a third, straight-sided, lozenge light leans slightly askew. From such beginnings the whole art of stone tracery was to develop, and here at Wyck Rissington we see the first tentative steps that led to the splendours of the Decorated style.

The limewashed interior is perhaps rather less memorable. It has suffered, unfortunately, from quite a lot of Victorian restoration, and even the addition of a nineteenth-century north aisle. But there is a pretty, busy chancel with lovely fourteenth-century glass – note especially the Crucifixion in the south window – and an unexpectedly fine tower arch. The nave has retained a good deal of the original stone benching around the wall – whither, of course, the weakest went.

# Short List

## Adlestrop

*40; 3 miles NE of Stow-on-the-Wold off A436*

ADLESTROP PARK, originally a late seventeenth-century conversion of a barn, was largely rebuilt and entirely remodelled between 1750 and 1762 by Sanderson Miller in his own individual style of Gothick. The show front, to the south, has only three bays – each, however, being triple-windowed. The two outer ones project forward; all three have charming openwork quatrefoiled parapets and pinnacles. The gardens are by Repton. ADLESTROP HOUSE, formerly the rectory, was once inhabited by the uncle of Jane Austen, who visited him there regularly.

## Beverston Castle

*41; 2 miles NW of Tetbury on A4135*

The castle probably began as a strongly defended manor house of about 1225; of this period are the northern part of the Gatehouse and the undercroft of the Hall. In about 1350 the building was extensively remodelled by Lord Berkeley, who added a new south-west tower and east Gatehouse. The first-floor Chapel with Decorated window is particularly fine; it has a beautiful groined roof and delicately sculpted sedilia and piscina. Above the Chapel is Lord Berkeley's Chamber; it too has a piscina in the small oratory. A long two-storeyed seventeenth-century house adjoins the tower; inside is a fine oak staircase. The BARN to the east is fourteenth-century.

## Blockley

*42; 3 miles NW of Moreton-in-Marsh on B4479*

NORTHWICK PARK, at the time of writing, lies derelict – a tragedy, since it is of considerable importance, the east front being by Lord Burlington. It is rather less austere than his usual style. I failed to get in, but what I managed to see through the windows suggests that relatively little is left of the original decoration.

## Clearwell Castle

*43; 20 miles SW of Gloucester on B4231*

Built by Roger Morris in 1728, Clearwell Castle is probably the second oldest Gothic Revival house in the country – Vanbrugh's Castle at Greenwich predates it by a decade. Neither building actually has any Gothic architectural detail, but the spirit of the medieval castle is there, light years away from the cool Palladian classicism that was the current fashion. Clearwell suffered a disastrous fire in 1929, and further serious damage through depredation and neglect after the last war. It was rescued in 1953 by Frank Yeates (son of the gardener in happier days), who with his family devoted the rest of his life to its restoration. His widow, son and daughter-in-law continue the work on a do-it-yourself basis. The outer shell of the building, the Great Hall and several original fireplaces survive, but much of the rest is facsimile – some parts more successful than others. The castle is nevertheless worth a visit, both for its historical importance and as an object lesson of how much one family, without funds, specialised knowledge or much outside help, has been able to achieve.

## Coln Rogers

*44; 6½ miles NE of Cirencester off A429*

The nave and the western part of the chancel of the charming little ST ANDREW'S CHURCH are Anglo-Saxon. The round-headed chancel arch, the blocked doorway in the north wall of the nave (when seen from the inside) and the tiny north window in the chancel (the only one that has been left untouched) all suggest a date around 1025. It was probably about a century later that the chancel was extended – though the east window, like the west tower, is Perpendicular.

## Doughton

*45; 1½ miles SW of Tetbury on A433*

Built in 1623, DOUGHTON MANOR is remarkably unspoilt on the outside. Built on the old H-plan with a multitude of gables, the architecture is vaguely symmetrical and the fenestration anything but. I know of few better examples of the 'Old Country Manor House Untouched by Time'.

## Duntisbourne Rous

*46; 3 miles NW of Cirencester off A417*

A ravishing little Saxon church on the steep bank of a stream, ST MICHAEL'S has a triangular-headed south door and lots of herringbone. Owing to the falling ground, a small crypt has been inserted beneath the Norman chancel to hold it up. There are various Early English and Perpendicular additions, including a very nice set of choir stalls with misericords and a jolly little saddleback west tower; the late seventeenth century (I should guess) provided the box pews and panelling. Since then, nothing – thank God.

## Flaxley

*47; 11 miles SW of Gloucester off A48*

The remains of a twelfth-century Cistercian abbey have been incorporated in a seventeenth-century house which, after a serious fire, was enlarged by Anthony Keck in 1777–83. Of the monastic buildings there survive a fine rib-vaulted undercroft – probably the refectory – two tunnel-vaulted chambers of the reredorter and, above, the fourteenth-century guest hall of the abbot with a magnificent timber roof. The later building is generally unremarkable, but there is charming decoration by Oliver Messel in some of the rooms.

## Frocester

*48; 9 miles SW of Gloucester off A419*

Approached via a timber-framed Gatehouse, FROCESTER COURT goes back to the fourteenth century, though it is much remodelled. But the important thing is the tremendous BARN, built around 1300, one of the half dozen best in England and the most perfectly preserved.

## Gatcombe Park

*49; 4 miles SE of Stroud off A419*

No one knows who built Gatcombe Park, around 1770; but we do know that it was bought by David Ricardo, the political economist, in 1814 and that a few years later he employed his kinsman George Basevi to make alterations and additions. It has hardly been touched since. The pedimented centre features a large Venetian window above a Doric porch. The one-storey bowed wings may be by Basevi; he certainly designed the Library inside, and probably also the stables and conservatory. The house is now lived in by Princess Anne.

## Great Barrington

*50; 3 miles NW of Burford off A40*

BARRINGTON PARK is a fine Palladian mansion above the Windrush, built for Lord Chancellor Talbot in 1736–8. The architect may have been William Kent; but Howard Colvin suggests it was more probably Henry Joynes, who had worked with Vanbrugh and Hawksmoor, and had been responsible for Talbot's town house at what is now Nos 57–8 Lincoln's Inn Fields. It has nine bays on two storeys and is said to contain fine plasterwork; but I was refused admittance. Visitors asking to see the house do so at their peril.

## Highnam

*51; 1½ miles W of Gloucester off A40*

Built about 1660, HIGHNAM COURT is a fine brick 'Artisan Mannerist' house with stone dressings and one-storey side pavilions. The glory of the interior is the plasterwork, probably by William Stocking of Bristol; but there is also a fine cantilevered eighteenth-century staircase in addition to the original one. The house is now used as a centre for music and the arts.

The CHURCH OF THE HOLY INNOCENTS is by the flamboyant Victorian architect Henry Woodyer (who also designed the VICARAGE and SCHOOL nearby). It has a tremendous spire with lucarnes and two rows of crocketed pinnacles. The interior is a riot of polychromy in the tradition of Pugin's St Giles, Cheadle. The church was commissioned by Thomas Gambier-Parry, who did the wall paintings (and later the roof of Ely Cathedral).

## Lasborough Park

*52; 4 miles W of Tetbury off A4135*

One of James Wyatt's later works, in Tudor Gothic style, the house was built for Edmund Estcourt in 1794. It is rectangular, two-storeyed and castellated, with three-storeyed angle towers and a central three-sided bay window, also rising to three storeys on the main front. The inside is almost unaltered, preserving much delicate classical decoration.

## Lechlade

*53; 13 miles E of Cirencester on A417*

A pretty town, Lechlade contains many pretty eighteenth- and early nineteenth-century houses. ST LAWRENCE'S CHURCH looks lovely from a distance, whether seen from Faringdon or across the young Thames from Wiltshire, its tall spire slim and graceful with a golden weathercock. It was completely rebuilt in the late fifteenth century, taking its place as one of the great wool churches of Gloucestershire. The exterior is rich in sculptures, like Fairford, and has some splendid gargoyles. There are fascinating and most original carved and painted bosses in the chancel roof.

## Matson House

*54; 1½ miles SE of Gloucester off A417*

Built about 1575, Matson House has two deep gabled wings projecting from the main range, and a single gable over the entrance. A battlemented parapet crowns the inward-facing side of the wings. The roofs are of Cotswold stone. Most of the windows have been sashed and have pretty Gothick cusped tracery – the result, probably, of Horace Walpole's two visits here. Much of the original panelling survives, and there is a fine eighteenth-century Hall and staircase. It is now a school.

## Mickleton

*55; 2 miles N of Chipping Campden on B4081*

MEDFORD HOUSE, halfway down the main street, is a ravishing town house of 1694, described by Pevsner as 'the textbook example of the slow transition from the vernacular Tudor Cotswold style to Queen Anne classical'. Long and low, of honey-coloured ashlar, it has two storeys with dormers, a hipped roof of lovely mellow stone tiles, and windows that are still mullioned. A brick extension of 1912 is largely hidden by a wall and hardly seems to matter. The present owner has done an admirable job of restoration, adding roughly contemporary panelling and a Jacobean staircase.

## Minchinhampton

*56; 3 miles SE of Stroud off A419*

The CHURCH OF THE HOLY TRINITY is originally twelfth-century, but the two features which earn it a place here are both later. The central tower is fourteenth-century, but was truncated in 1563 and crowned with a stone coronet – very odd. The south transept is of the same date, its south wall almost filled with a huge Decorated window, the lower part restored but the upper rose of great beauty. The roof is of stone slabs, supported by transverse stone ribs, so heavy as to require a close-set row of buttresses outside. The chancel was altered by W. Burges in the 1860s – hence the most remarkable east window.

## Prinknash Abbey

*57; 5 miles NE of Stroud off A46*

Begun *c.*1300, Prinknash Abbey was much enlarged in the early sixteenth century and again in the nineteenth. Much Tudor work still remains, including a carved head of Henry VIII in youth. In *The Buildings of England*, David Verey quotes Horace Walpole: 'It stands on a glorious but impracticable hill, in the midst of a little forest of beech, and commanding Elysium. The chapel is low and small, but antique, and with painted glass, with many angels in their coronation robes. Under a window is a barbarous bas-relief of Harry Young.' All of which, adds Mr Verey, is still true.

## Quenington

*58; 7 miles E of Cirencester off A433*

ST SWITHIN'S CHURCH is disastrously Victorianised but must be listed here for the sake of its north and south doorways, both mid-twelfth-century Norman work of outstanding quality. That to the north depicts the

Harrowing of Hell in the tympanum, set in surroundings of almost indescribable richness; that to the south offers a representation of the Coronation of the Virgin and is, if anything, still finer. QUENINGTON COURT nearby is now largely nineteenth-century, but the thirteenth-century Gatehouse dates from the time when the former building on the site was a Commandery of the Knights of St John.

## St Briavels

*59; 21 miles SW of Gloucester on B4228*

One of the chain of strongholds built or strengthened by Edward I in his campaigns against the Welsh, ST BRIAVELS CASTLE has as its most important survival the tremendous Gatehouse, built in 1292–3 and strong enough to be defended independently from front or rear. ST MARY'S CHURCH has a Norman south arcade and an Early English north one, and fine Transitional crossing arches that no longer have a tower to support. (The present tower, over the south porch, is of 1830.)

## Snowshill Manor

*NT; 60; 7 miles W of Moreton-in-Marsh off A44*

The manor house is of the traditional Cotswold variety, dating from about 1500, although it was altered and added to a century later and again in *c.*1720, when the south front was rather endearingly classicised. The house now contains – though only just – the almost unbelievable magpie collection of Mr Charles Wade (Motto: *Nequid Pereat* – 'Let Nothing Perish') who left the whole lot to the National Trust shortly before he died in 1956.

## Southrop

*61; 11 miles E of Cirencester off A417*

ST PETER'S CHURCH, with its herringbone masonry in the nave walls, might well be taken for Saxon; it is in fact of *c.*1100, though the chancel was rebuilt in the thirteenth century and has an east window in which we can see, as at Wyck Rissington, the earliest fumblings towards plate tracery. But the pride of the church is the Norman font, in which ladies in armour are trampling on prostrate vices. It is thought to date from *c.*1150 – in which case the freedom and vigour of the style put it well in advance of its time.

## Sudeley Castle

*62; 6 miles NE of Cheltenham off A46*

The castle looks magnificent from a distance. It was begun in the 1440s, improved forty years later by Richard of Gloucester (later Richard III) and again in the sixteenth century – when it was briefly the home of Queen Katherine Parr after the death of Henry VIII. After the Civil War, however, it was occupied by local farmers and allowed to fall into ruin. Much of what we see today is in fact an unusually sensitive restoration by George Gilbert Scott, dating from the 1850s.

## Temple Guiting

*63; 7 miles NW of Stow-on-the-Wold off B4077*

ST MARY'S CHURCH is a disappointment. Originally Norman and a property of the Knights Templars, it was by turns Perpendicularised, Georgianised and Victorianised, with the results that might be expected. The sixteenth-century gabled MANOR FARM, on the other hand, is utterly unspoilt inside and out, and the best of its date in the Cotswolds. TEMPLE GUITING HOUSE, of about 1780, adds further distinction to a charming and romantically secluded village.

## Upleadon

*64; 8 miles NW of Gloucester off B4215*

ST MARY'S CHURCH has two special points of interest. The first is the Norman north door with its carved tympanum. Alas, the soft Herefordshire stone has suffered badly over the centuries, and an attempt to patch it with limestone has hardly helped matters. The second is the timber-framed tower at the western end: vertical studding, brick-filled on the outside; within, huge black crucks rising through the roof to the belfry.

## Upper Slaughter Manor

*65; 2½ miles SW of Stow-on-the-Wold off A429*

Another sixteenth-century Cotswold house, built of local stone, it is L-shaped, the west front having large sheer gables capped by stone finials and a fine early seventeenth-century two-storey porch which has Renaissance details. There are mullioned and transomed windows. Beneath the house is a fifteenth-century stone crypt with a groined roof.

## Upton St Leonards

See Prinknash Abbey.

## Westbury Court Garden

*NT; 66; 9 miles SW of Gloucester on A48*

This is not strictly architectural, perhaps, but worth including as one of the very few seventeenth-century formal water-gardens still surviving. It has an enchanting Queen Anne summer-house of 1704, standing on stilts at the end of one of the 'canals', and a pretty brick and stone gazebo of perhaps twenty years later.

## Winstone

*67; 6 miles NW of Cirencester off A417*

Here is another pretty little Saxon church, though the many Norman details on ST BARTHOLOMEW'S suggest that it probably dates from the brief overlap period soon after the Conquest. The little window in the north wall of the nave is purest Saxon (compare Coln Rogers), as is the north doorway, now blocked; but the latter's opposite number to the south has Norman decoration. The chancel arch is Saxon, as is the chancel itself, though all its original openings have been blocked. There is not even an east window.

## Wormington Grange

*68; 12 miles NE of Cheltenham off A46*

This Georgian house of *c.*1770 was doubled in size and transformed in character in 1826–7 by Henry Hakewill, better known for St Peter's, Eaton Square. He preferred Tudor Gothic as a style, but his neo-classical additions here are unusually fresh and original. The stables in particular are a really beautiful job.

# Hampshire

Here is a county of contrasts. In the far south-west lies the New Forest, a law unto itself and a sort of miracle. It seems scarcely believable that so much of it should be so unspoilt after the nine centuries that have passed since it became a royal hunting reserve; there are parts of it in which one can still almost hear that arrow thudding into the heart of William Rufus. In the north-east and south-east of the county, however, we find regions which have obviously spilled over from Surrey and Sussex – the former largely heathland or gloomily coniferous, dominated by Farnborough and Aldershot, the latter the lovely rolling hill country of hardwoods made famous by the Rev. Gilbert White of Selborne. Between them stretches the serene and smiling expanse of chalk downs, among which flow the great and small streams which bring in fishermen by their thousands – for, as Thomas Fuller wrote, 'most pure and piercing the air of this shire; and none in England hath more plenty of clear and fresh rivulets of troutful water'.

Apart from a narrow strip near the Sussex border, Hampshire possesses little good building stone and has had to rely for the most part on chalk, flint, brick and timber. Partly for this reason, the general standard of parish churches is disappointing; there are, however, three glorious religious buildings – two of them formerly monastic, the third a chapel for almshouses – which would be outstanding anywhere: Romsey, Pamber and St Cross at Winchester. There is also Winchester Cathedral: not, perhaps, the loveliest of English cathedrals from the outside but certainly one of the grandest and most venerable. Among the more modest churches, there is a surprising amount of Saxon work still in evidence – notably at Breamore, Boarhunt and Titchfield – and much fine Norman, not only in Romsey, Pamber and the cathedral transepts but also at East Meon and the lovely little church of St Mary within the Roman fortifications of Portchester. Hampshire, in fact, has proved a good preserver of early architecture; one only wishes that the county had been luckier with its Victorian restorers, most of whom applied a distinctly heavy hand.

Where country houses are concerned, the record is better: Hampshire's two outstanding Tudor houses, Bramshill and The Vyne, could hold their own with all but the very greatest of their contemporaries, and nowhere in England more perfectly epitomises eighteenth-century elegance than Broadlands or Cranbury Park. Mottisfont, apart from its historical interest, enjoys one of the loveliest settings of any house anywhere; Highclere tells you all you need to know about Victorian grandeur; and few heroes can boast a more splendidly atmospheric shrine than the Great Duke of Wellington at Stratfield Saye. Finally, to all lovers of architecture, there is no nobler or more tragic site than The Grange, its tremendous portico still standing – though only just – lonely and magnificent above its lake.

---

## Avington Park

*1; 4 miles NE of Winchester off B3047*

The entrance front of Avington, which was built around 1710, almost certainly by John James – although there is no documentary proof – is distinguished without being, to me at least, entirely satisfactory. The massive Tuscan portico of wood which occupies the entire space between the two side wings is not broken forward as one might expect; instead, it is recessed, with the result that it looks constricted and somehow diffident, like a lady who has been lent a very large tiara and hasn't quite the panache to carry it off. The three large goddesses surmounting the pediment seem to be urging it forward to assume its rightful place; but it refuses to budge. The brick wings are pleasant enough – four bays of segmental-headed windows, divided into pairs by three giant pilasters – but their high balustrades increase the crowding effect, and the poor cowering portico retreats further than ever.

The interior of the house seems more than a little sad nowadays, divided as it is into seven separate flats. The main state rooms are, however, occasionally open to the public and are well worth seeing, above all because they have retained their original painted decoration. In the Great Saloon – which boasts, in addition, a splendid ceiling of gilded plasterwork – the paintings of the Four Seasons with flanking Muses are believed to be by Verrio and certainly predate James's building by a generation; they must have been brought in from elsewhere. The remainder, including the doors and doorcases, are of about 1760. The murals of the Red Drawing Room constitute something of a mystery. The local guide-book maintains that they date from about 1810 and represent the founders of the Royal Houses of England; Pevsner takes them to be characters from Sir Walter Scott and consequently the work of the mid-nineteenth century. On stylistic grounds it is hard not to agree with him. There is a lovely staircase with an inlaid banister, its lead balustrades adorned with honeysuckle.

The other room of considerable interest is the Library, which is painted with a Pompeian design and has an outer wall very slightly bowed – to admirable effect. Beyond it lies the Orangery. Both these are clearly later additions – presumably of the late eighteenth or early nineteenth century, though the dates are uncertain.

Across the garden is the little late Georgian CHURCH, perfect of its kind. Virtually unrestored, it has box pews, a two-decker pulpit, a nice Decalogue and some quite interesting wall plaques – including ones to the Countess of Carnarvon (who had the church built) and to the brother of the poet Shelley.

## Beaulieu Abbey

*2; 5 miles SE of Lyndhurst on B3056*

It is perhaps a little ironical that the vast majority of the tourists who flock to Beaulieu should make a beeline for the Motor Museum and spare only a cursory glance at the remains of King John's great Cistercian abbey. In doing so they miss a lot; but their loss is our gain.

The abbey remains fall into three parts: the ruined church and cloister; the former refectory; and Palace House, originally the Gatehouse but much enlarged by Sir Arthur Blomfield in 1872. Of the thirteenth-century church the ground plan is still clear, but the only sections left standing are those that abut the cloister – the wall of the south aisle and part of the west wall of the south transept. The cloister itself has fared slightly better, though it remains little more than a skeleton. (On the west side, the Domus building where the lay brothers were lodged has survived to make the present-day restaurant.)

On the south side of the cloister the old refectory still stands in all its glory. Some 125 feet long, it was built around 1230, its Early Englishness revealed by the triple lancets in the north and south walls – though the central one at the south end, above the altar (not having been intended as a church, the building is not properly orientated), has been blocked by a massive exterior buttress. On the west side (liturgical south) the fenestration becomes suddenly irregular; on the inside at this point there is a massive pulpit, originally intended for religious readings during meals. It is approached by eighteen stone steps inserted into the thickness of the wall and is flanked by a pointed and moulded arcade which is in turn supported on pairs of Purbeck marble columns. The wagon roof has some interesting bosses.

The abbey Gatehouse which forms the nucleus of Palace House today is two storeys high and two bays deep, marked by the two windows with Y-tracery facing south. On the first floor there was a curious arrangement – two separate chapels side by side, each with its own piscina. These still survive, in the Private Dining Room and the Upper Drawing Room respectively. The vaulting of the rooms below, now the Lower Drawing Room and Dining Hall, is a puzzle. It does not look altogether convincing, and indeed the *Victoria County History* calls it 'a modern restoration'; yet it appears in early nineteenth-century drawings and the official guidebook considers it 'original, though restored'.

Though the two gables above the Gatehouse (which run transversely to the rooms beneath them) are Elizabethan, the rest of the house is essentially Blomfield's – comfortable and competent, but not of outstanding interest.

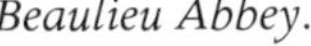

*Beaulieu Abbey.*

## Bramshill

*3; 3 miles N of Hartley Witney off B3011*

Since 1954, Bramshill has been the police staff college and is open to visitors only by special arrangement. You need, however, only approach it up its long drive – which runs north-east from the B3011 – to see that it is a Jacobean prodigy house of towering importance. The drive will bring you face to face with the south front (strictly speaking, the south-west), which is the glory of the house by reason of its great central frontispiece, rising three storeys – the whole height of the house. The ground floor is taken up by a three-bay loggia surmounted by an open strapwork parapet; this rises to a mighty semi-circular oriel, mullioned and double-transomed; above this, two round-headed windows are divided by a central pilaster which breaks out above it into another effusion of bolder, coarser strapwork thought to be a free-handed version of the Prince of Wales's feathers. At each side there rise three tiers of paired, tapering pilasters. Several features of this extraordinary design are said to have been brought back from Holland by the builder, Lord Zouche; there is certainly nothing else like it in this country. Behind the side arches of the loggia the brick façade is deeply recessed; the next bays to left and right break forward again to come level with the frontispiece; and the side wings, each of three bays, advance still further. The result of so many planes is to give the façade a degree of movement exceptional in a Jacobean house, almost Baroque in its effect. The three remaining sides are a good deal simpler, though still imposing. To the north, there is a shaped gable containing a statue of (presumably) Lord Zouche in a niche.

The one-storey Great Hall, panelled from floor to ceiling, has a contemporary stone screen, echoed by rusticated stone arches beyond the screens passage. Its only major alteration seems to have been a fine early eighteenth-century entrance door which gives, rather surprisingly, not into the passage but directly into the Hall itself. Emerging from the Hall, another surprise awaits us: the south-west, show, side of the house proves not to be the main one after all, so far as the internal arrangement of the rooms is concerned, for all the principal ones are ranged along the south-east front. Apart from the so-called Terrace Room – now the students' lounge and bar – most of these are on the first floor, up a Charles II staircase which was in fact only brought to Bramshill during the last century. Most sumptuous is the Great Drawing Room, with an impressive marble chimneypiece – one of three in the house – reaching to the pendant ceiling and a famous set of Rubens tapestries. There is also a most interesting Chapel, with a strapwork ceiling that bears the arms of Henry, Prince of Wales, who died in 1612. This ceiling, together with the stylised feathers atop the south-west front, has led to a theory that Lord Zouche originally built the house for the Prince; but there is no documentary evidence and the idea seems unlikely. The presence of the arms remains mysterious.

It must, of course, be admitted that the transformation of these magnificent rooms into classrooms, common rooms, lecture theatres and the like has radically altered their character. Particularly sad has been the fate of the Long Gallery, 128 feet long and one of the grandest in England, which now serves as the College Library; it suffers terribly from the work tables and bookcases which have been set transversely all the way down its length. But such changes are inevitable and we must not complain. The house is in capable and caring hands, and could even be restored, within weeks, to much of its former glory. Would that there were more like it.

## Breamore

*4; 3 miles N of Fordingbridge off A338*

The first thing to say about BREAMORE HOUSE is that it is nothing if not well-bred. In the last quarter-century of Queen Elizabeth's reign the fashion in architecture was growing ever more exuberantly ostentatious; the age of the prodigy house was at hand. The new style, however, clearly had no attractions for the wealthy London merchant, William Dodington, whose country seat near Fordingbridge, finished in 1583, was a model of dignified discretion: a traditional gabled E-shaped house in red brick with grey stone dressings and mullioned and transomed windows. Alas, for all its respectability it did not bring the family luck. Only seventeen years after its completion William Dodington, agonised over an impending law suit, flung himself from the tower of St Sepulchre's, Holborn; and in 1629 his daughter-in-law was murdered in the house by her own son, who was hanged in Winchester gaol shortly afterwards.

The exterior of the house looks much as it must have done when it was first built; certainly, it gives little sign of the serious fire by which it was very largely gutted in 1856 – a disaster which, incidentally, is not mentioned anywhere in the house guide-book. Even inside, the damage is well concealed, and the casual visitor might well be forgiven for thinking that the panelling and plaster ceilings were original. The illusion is made more complete by the furniture and pictures, most of which escaped the fire. Thanks as much to them as to the skill of the Victorian restorers, the atmosphere at Breamore is entirely that of the seventeenth and eighteenth centuries and the house remains well worth a visit.

Some 200 yards from the house in a corner of the park stands the Saxon CHURCH OF ST MARY, believed to have been built around 980. It is surprisingly large, and consists of an aisleless nave and chancel separated by a square central tower now covered with a pyramidal roof. There are no proper transepts – the cruciform design was unknown in Saxon times – but there is a side chapel, or *porticus*, narrower than the tower and projecting from it on the south side, which does duty as one. (A similar extension to the north has disappeared.) The church has been altered and enlarged, but much Saxon work survives: the *porticus* (apart from the Norman door on the east), the long-and-short work of the tower, the lesenes in the nave walls and seven small, high windows. Saxon too is the arch into the *porticus* from the crossing, with an inscription which, translated, reads 'HERE UNTO THEE THE COVENANT IS EXPLAINED'. A Saxon rood over the south door has been sorely mutilated. The rest of the church is largely fourteenth-century.

*Broadlands.*

## Broadlands

*5; 8 miles N of Southampton on A3057*

Standing little more than half a mile from the centre of Romsey, its lush green lawns sweeping down to the River Test, Broadlands looks – and arguably is – the perfect mid-Georgian country house. In fact it began as a small, unassuming Tudor manor, which it still essentially was in 1736 when the 1st Viscount Palmerston commissioned William Kent to deflect the course of the river and do away with the old formal parterres. Thirty years later, under the 2nd Viscount, Kent's work was completed by Capability Brown, who simultaneously began the infinitely more ambitious task of transforming the house into the elegant Palladian mansion that we see today. It was left, however, to Brown's son-in-law Henry Holland to fill in the open courtyard on the east side and to add the recessed loggia which occupies the three central bays of the east front.

It is through this loggia that you enter the house, passing directly through Holland's small octagonal Hall, lit by a central skylight, into the Sculpture Hall, decorated in the same cool neo-classical taste and containing various pieces of Greek and Roman statuary brought back by the 2nd Lord Palmerston from his Grand Tour. But these two rooms form only a preface to the house; and of the five principal rooms which follow on the ground floor, all are in their different ways magnificent, with lovely plasterwork on the ceilings, glorious pictures and furniture and that indefinable air of opulent serenity that pervades all the best eighteenth-century English interiors. The Wedgwood Room is exactly what it sounds like, its walls and ceiling exquisitely stuccoed in snow-white against a lavender ground; but the *pièce de résistance* is the Saloon, at the centre of the west front, in which walls and ceiling are once again treated in a single decorative scheme, this time in white and gold – a stunning performance for which Robert Adam and Angelica Kauffmann appear to have been jointly responsible. There are several bedrooms upstairs to which the public are admitted – beautifully decorated and furnished but without any particular architectural interest.

Inevitably, the house has now become something of a shrine to Lord Mountbatten, and many of the subsidiary rooms have been given over to a museum. In consequence Broadlands is a good deal more crowded than other houses of its kind. Try to visit it early in the morning and, if possible, on a weekday. And when you emerge, wander down to the river and look up at Capability Brown's west front with its giant Ionic portico, gently hipped roof and pedimented lower windows. This is the loveliest view of Broadlands; and yet, on any but the sunniest summer days, not one visitor in fifty takes the trouble to go and look at it.

## Cranbury Park*

*6; 6 miles SW of Winchester off B3043*

Your first sight of the house as you drive across the park reveals a long, low building of very red – almost scarlet – brick, curiously imposing despite its lack of height. The effect is achieved by various means: by the strongly emphasised giant pilasters which extend from ground level to roof line; by the Venetian windows on both storeys in both bays of the two side wings; and above all, perhaps, by the three-bay centre, of one storey only, in which the two windows flanking the *porte-cochère*, with their huge tympana and heavy Gibbs surrounds, reach up almost as high as the capitals of the pilasters.

Though there may have been minor alterations (the *porte-cochère*, for instance) since his day, the architect of Cranbury was the younger George Dance – whose brother, the painter Nathaniel Dance, married the widow of the house's owner, Thomas Dummer, soon after the latter's death in 1781. Dance was a convinced neo-classicist who had studied for six years in Italy in his youth; and here, surely, is his finest work. If the exterior is impressive, the interior is yet more so. Turning sharp right inside the front door, you at once find yourself in the Great Hall, a long room with an elaborate coffered tunnel vault. It possesses only one window – that immediately to the right of the door, whose pair of flanking Corinthian columns on the outside is reflected by another pair within. These are echoed in their turn by a third pair in scagliola at the far end of the Hall, forming a screen behind which is a semi-circular apse lit by a skylight. Halfway down the left-hand wall stands a marble fireplace of generous proportions by Dance's most gifted pupil, John Soane.

Most of the other principal rooms are reached through the Inner Hall, where a broad oak staircase, lit by a stained-glass fanlight, climbs to an upper gallery running the length of the Hall beneath another coved ceiling. These include the Drawing Room, the elegant but more austere Dining Room, and a ravishing little room with a tented ceiling and walls, copied around 1830 from one of the rooms of the Empress Josephine's house at Malmaison. At about the same date, John Buonarotti Papworth designed the Library, a lovely room divided halfway by a screen of Tuscan columns, its bookcases rising to the stuccoed ceiling, its decoration untouched for the past 150 years.

And so, finally, to the climax of the house – the Ball Room. This corresponds to the Great Hall on the other side of the front door but, unlike the Hall, is accessible only from the far end and possesses not only the apse and screen at that end but also semi-circular bays, without screens, on each side. The ceiling is in itself a *tour de force* of plasterwork, with graded coffering in the semi-domes; it has retained all its original colouring.

Architecturally this is one of the most fascinating country houses in Hampshire.

*Cranbury Park.*

## East Meon

*7; 12 miles N of Portsmouth off A3*

ALL SAINTS is a lovely village church set close up against a green hillside – so close that there is no room for a north aisle. Its pride is its Norman crossing-tower – firm and four-square, with triple round-headed bell openings richly decorated with zigzag on each of the sides, and similarly adorned circular openings above. The lead broach spire, anachronistic as it is, suits it to perfection. Coming down to ground level, there are good Norman doorways to west and south. It seems clear that, in its original form, the church must have been complete by 1150 at the latest. Inside, there is a good spacious crossing, with scalloped capitals on the responds to east and west.

The only important additions came in the first half of the thirteenth century, when a Lady Chapel was built out to the south of the chancel, from which it was separated by an Early English arcade. This was followed shortly afterwards by a south aisle, with another, simpler, arcade dividing it off from the nave. In the wall above this arcade, which was of course the outer wall before the aisle was added, the remains of an old Norman window are still visible.

Before leaving, don't forget to examine the font. Hewn from a single block of black Tournai marble, it is thought to have been a gift from Bishop Henry of Blois, William the Conqueror's grandson. The carvings, principally devoted to the story of Adam and Eve, are full of freshness and vigour – particularly that of Adam receiving from the Angel his first digging lesson.

A little to the south-east of the church there survives part of the COURT HOUSE of the Bishops of Winchester, built around 1400. The Hall has survived, and its original roof with kingposts – though the fireplace is later, about 1500. It can be seen by appointment.

## Farnborough

*8; halfway between Camberley and Aldershot on A325*

A huge and hideous house built in Swiss chalet style by H.E. Kendall Jun. in the early 1860s, FARNBOROUGH HILL was the home of the Empress Eugénie for nearly forty years from 1881 until just before her death in 1920. (She actually died, aged ninety-four, on a visit to her native Spain.) This house, despite its associations, would never alone have found a way into this book – though it's still good for a laugh. On the opposite hillside, however, across a shallow valley, stands something far more interesting: the Benedictine ABBEY built by Eugénie over the MAUSOLEUM in which her husband Napoleon III, her son Louis-Napoleon (killed in the Zulu War) and she herself are buried. The architect of both abbey and mausoleum was G.H. Destailleur, who had recently designed Waddesdon Manor. The three porphyry sarcophagi stand in the rib-vaulted crypt, that of Eugénie in the middle behind the altar. Above, the abbey church is in the French Flamboyant style, with much polychrome marble decoration. It is not open to the public, but can be seen by appointment – together with a small but interesting collection of Napoleoniana.

## The Grange

See Northington.

## Hartley Wintney

*9; 10 miles NE of Basingstoke on A30*

*Includes West Green House (NT)*

Built in warm red brick during the first quarter of the eighteenth century, and standing about a mile north of the village, WEST GREEN HOUSE (NT) must be one of the most totally desirable small Georgian houses in the country. Thanks to the high panelled Saloon, rising two storeys and occupying virtually all five bays of the west front, this front has one row of windows only, punctuated by a glazed door with a strongly emphasised Gibbs surround and the Rabelaisian motto 'FAY CE QUE VOULDRAS' inscribed above it. At what would be first-floor level, the expected windows are replaced by a row of five stone busts in circular niches – a delightful little conceit – above which comes a shallow wooden cornice and then the hipped roof, with urns at the corners and three pedimented dormers as a finishing flourish.

The house is planned around a fine staircase of about 1770 – the original oak one having been removed to another house nearby. The showpiece is the Saloon, with its coved ceiling and pedimented doors. But the other rooms, though less presuming, all share the same informal elegance that imbues the house itself. There is also a predictably delightful garden.

*The Hall, Highclere.*

## Highclere

*10; 6 miles SW of Newbury on A343*

When, in 1838, Charles Barry was commissioned by the 3rd Earl of Carnarvon to remodel his rather plain Georgian house, he little realised the scale of what his patron had in mind. Barry's first design, which increased the number of bays from nine to twelve, provided for twin turrets at the corners and included a separate, similarly turreted conservatory at one corner, was cast aside as being insufficiently grand; the second, considerably more opulent, was rejected on the same grounds; and it was only on his third attempt, when he submitted drawings for a vast mansion in a vaguely Elizabethan manner, surmounted by a high pinnacled tower, that he finally won His Lordship's approval. On 24 June 1842 the foundation stone was laid by Carnarvon's eleven-year-old son; and for the next seven years the peace of Capability Brown's famous park was shattered by the shouts of the workmen and the clatter of hundreds of carts, all loaded with building stone from the Bath quarries with which the old brick building was to be encased.

The result is the largest country house in Hampshire; and, if not the most beautiful, certainly the most impressive. Thanks to the angle turrets and the tower it is inescapably reminiscent of Wollaton in Nottinghamshire, but closer inspection reveals that the style is Elizabethan only at the most superficial level. The strapwork parapets and pinnacles, the obelisks and the carved panels under the windows may recall the late sixteenth century; but the windows themselves, in their regularity and uniformity, strike a distinctly Georgian note which even mullions and transoms cannot hide. (The effect is ultimately much the same as that of the same architect's Palace of Westminster, where the Gothic detail serves only to decorate an essentially eighteenth-century elevation.) Of the four fronts, that on the east is by far the most interesting, with the façade twice breaking forward, a square tower marking each point where it does so. Beneath these towers are deep round-headed niches instead of the windows that might have been expected; and these, together with the 1–3–1 pattern of the middle five bays, give a degree of articulation unmatched elsewhere.

Carnarvon died in 1849, when work on the interior had scarcely begun; and by the time his son decided to resume operations in 1861, Barry too was dead. The completion of the house was therefore entrusted to Thomas Allom, who had worked with Barry as an architectural draughtsman but possessed little of his master's talent. Neither seems to have been able to decide on any single style; but whereas Barry manages to synthesise the various influences into what Sir Ninian Comper was later to call 'unity by inclusion', Allom's less happy juxtapositions leave one somehow uneasy. First comes a Gothic Entrance Hall, tierceron-vaulted and formidably bossed, its polychrome floor gaudy with encaustic tiles designed by William Butterfield; there then follows a huge central Hall, lit by a skylight, Gothic in its superficial (stucco) decoration but almost Moorish in feeling. Beyond this there is a frankly seventeenth-century staircase, lit by Gothic windows. By far the best room in the house is the tremendous Library, separated only by a screen of fluted Ionic columns from the North Library beyond. Here the style is early eighteenth-century; the grand chimneypiece rises majestically between the bookcases until its broken segmental pediment meets the richly gilded coffered ceiling. And yet, as everywhere in the house, the Victorian atmosphere permeates all. Perhaps it is right that it should; since the Victorians never succeeded in evolving an original style of their own, their chief skill lay in the transmutation of other styles into their own image. Of this skill, Highclere is a superb – if not the supreme – example, and for this reason alone it is worth going a long way to see.

Some three-quarters of a mile away to the north-east, on the edge of Milford Lake, stands Barry's LAKE HOUSE, its yellow brick a good deal less presumptuous than the big house, but equally fanciful. Inside, it incorporates parts of the old Georgian Highclere, with features of interior decoration that may well be by William Kent.

## King's Somborne

*11; 10½ miles W of Winchester off A3057*

Sir Edwin Lutyens was only thirty-two when he designed MARSH COURT, just outside the village looking out over the Test. For his material he chose the local clunch – scarcely used since the seventeenth century – occasionally and quite haphazardly varying it with bits of flint, tile and dark red brick; for his style, a sort of modernised Elizabethan. Thus the entrance front to the north is E-shaped, with two quite long projecting wings and a one-bay gabled porch of a most extraordinary design: two concentric semi-circular arches connected only by three enormous elongated voussoirs common to both, leading into a tunnel vault of alternating squares of stone and tile. At least half this elevation is taken up by the tall, hipped roof, below which a line of small mullioned windows runs almost continuously between the sides of the porch and the angles of the wings. The windows at the ends of these wings are mostly transomed as well.

Owing to the slope of the ground, the south front is considerably higher than the north, and the Elizabethan influence proportionately stronger. There are three storeys instead of two, a big square bay with six-light windows (double-transomed on the first floor) and two smaller canted bays to the west of it. In further contrast to the north front, no attempt is made at symmetry. Several irregularly placed ranges of tall Elizabethan brick chimneys, of various designs including cork-screw, complete the effect.

Inside, the main rooms are heavily classical, with ceilings in rich, almost tongue-in-cheek, plasterwork. There is more clunch in the fireplaces, and what must be the only chalk billiard table in England. The Italianate garden, as might be expected, is lovely, with terraces, pools and a typically idiosyncratic pergola.

## Lyndhurst

*12; 9 miles SW of Southampton on A35*

The CHURCH OF ST MICHAEL AND ALL ANGELS rises on a steep bank above the High Street, a towering edifice of red brick with much polychrome decoration. It is the work of William White, the great-nephew of Gilbert White of Selborne and pupil of George Gilbert Scott, who built it between 1858 and 1870 on the site of its small and plain Georgian predecessor. In the days before Sir John Betjeman opened our eyes to Victorian architecture, most of us would have dismissed it as an appalling eyesore; many of us might still do so today, and indeed it must be admitted that, even to the enlightened, St Michael's is no great shakes from the outside.

The interior, however, is full of interest. There is a great feeling of space – the church seems even bigger than it did from the street – and much play is made with the multicoloured brickwork, in a style more reminiscent of Butterfield than of Scott. Even the nave arcades are of brick, though they are supported on Purbeck columns. The chancel is dominated by the reredos, a wonderfully vigorous fresco by Lord Leighton – the first to be painted in any English church since the Reformation – depicting the Wise and Foolish Virgins. Above it, the east window is given over to Sir Edward Burne-Jones's vision of the New Jerusalem; Burne-Jones was also responsible for the window in the south transept. Both these windows are from the Morris workshops. Note, too, the monument by Street, in the north wall of the chancel, to Mr and Mrs John Hargreaves. The Hargreaves family was prominent in Lyndhurst; Mrs Alice Hargreaves, née Liddell, who is buried in the family vault in the churchyard, was Lewis Carroll's inspiration for *Alice in Wonderland*.

## Micheldever

*13; 6 miles NE of Winchester off A33*

What makes ST MARY'S CHURCH memorable is the quite extraordinary central octagon with which 'an architect named Dance' – I quote the church guide-book – replaced the medieval nave in 1808–10. George Dance had done something of the kind already, in his rebuilding of St Bartholomew the Less in Smithfield twenty years before; there, however, he had designed a completely new church, retaining only the medieval tower. Here at Micheldever both the old west end and the chancel were preserved – though the latter was rebuilt in the 1880s.

The octagon is impressive rather than strictly beautiful. There is something stark about the uniform expanse of red brick, unbroken by any windows except small segmental ones very high up, where the clerestory might have been. At the lower level there are only arched niches, the deeper ones to north and south vaguely representing transepts, the shallower ones on the diagonals purely decorative. The plaster roof is vaulted in a pattern of stars.

Do not leave without looking at the group of three jolly monuments by Flaxman to members of the Baring family, illustrative of various verses of the Lord's Prayer.

## Minstead*

*14; 2 miles SW of Cadnam on A31*

You approach ALL SAINTS through the churchyard from the north. Were it not for the late eighteenth-century brick tower, you might almost think that you were coming up to an ordinary, rather messy cottage and not a parish church, so domestic are the windows, the gables, and the irregularly placed dormers in the steeply raked roof. It is only when you go inside that you realise what an extraordinary little church this is, the most quirkish and charming in all Hampshire. As can be seen from the north door, the building goes back to 1200 or so (and the Purbeck marble font looks even earlier) but the prevailing atmosphere is eighteenth-century rustic. Even by these standards it is by no means typical: how many such churches have *two* west galleries, one above the other? And a three-decker pulpit? And the original floor of old stone flags and red tiles? And two private pews on the north side, one furnished with remarkably comfortable seats and a fireplace?

And even this is not all. In 1790 such was the press of the congregation that it was decided to throw out a transept to the south. Part of the wall was accordingly removed, and the roof shored up by a magnificent column of cast iron, presumably one of the first of its kind. This additional space was in 1825 found to be still too small (despite the building of the upper west gallery seven years before) and the transept was further extended. It was these extensions that resulted in the little vernacular windows that give the church its cottagey appearance.

But at Minstead all is domestic, cosy, unassuming. And, wonder of wonders, the Victorians hardly touched it. Fall on your knees and be thankful.

*St Mary's Church, Micheldever.*

*Mottisfont Abbey.*

## Mottisfont Abbey*

*NT; 15; 4½ miles NW of Romsey off A3057*

This is a part of my youth; and of all the country houses of England it is, I think, the one I love the best. It could not be called classically beautiful – no building that began as a monastic foundation in the twelfth century and was subsequently converted, first into a Tudor mansion and later into a Georgian one, could aspire to be that – but even leaving aside its considerable architectural interest it radiates a quite extraordinary atmosphere of peace, and of mellow, timeless serenity. Many is the sunlit summer afternoon, with the tea table set out on the east lawn under one of those magnificent trees beside the swiftly flowing Test, on which I have reflected, helping myself to another cucumber sandwich, that here at Mottisfont I could happily live and die, and that earth, almost certainly, had not anything to show more fair.

To understand Mottisfont, it is a good idea to look first at the north front. Ignore, for the moment, the fenestration – Tudor below, Georgian above; apart from this, what you see is essentially the exterior of the twelfth- to thirteenth-century nave of the Augustinian priory. To your left is the crossing-tower: truncated now, but retaining the outline of the arch which formerly led into the north transept. It was shorn of its upper stages by William, 1st Lord Sandys of The Vyne (*q.v.*), Henry VIII's Lord Chamberlain, who acquired the priory after the Dissolution (in exchange for two inconsequential hamlets near London known as Paddington and Chelsea), and immediately set about transforming it into a residence appropriate to his rank and position. Down came the transepts and the chancel; down, too – and rather more surprisingly – came the cloister, dorter, frater and most of the residential areas. Up, by contrast, went two new wings running south from each end of the nave. The result was the traditional Tudor U-shaped house (there may even have been a central projecting porch to make it an E), with the old cloister garth as an open courtyard.

Little of Lord Sandys's house is visible today; some 200 years later, in the 1740s, the building was extensively remodelled by his descendant, Sir Richard Mill. On the north front, Sir Richard limited his work to the insertion of sash windows – including two 'Venetian' ones – in an agreeably haphazard way at first-floor level, and a row of dormers above. Why he left the Tudor windows on the ground floor remains a mystery, but we cannot be sorry that he did; a house like Mottisfont can take these little incongruities in its stride.

On the south front, however, he was a good deal more ambitious. Starting with the premise that the existing house, built on the plan of the old nave, was too narrow for those spacious Georgian days, he hit upon the idea of turning the north walk of the old cloister into a covered passage, above which he constructed a Long Gallery, for the first time giving separate access to the first-floor rooms, hitherto interconnecting. This now became the *piano nobile*, while the ground floor – which anyway disappears at the west end owing to the rise in the land – was set aside for the offices. Over the Long Gallery he built a second, bedroom, floor; finally he faced the whole thing in warm pinkish brick with grey stone dressings, crowning it with a modest triangular pediment.

Whom Sir Richard employed as his architect we do not know: a pity, for he did a remarkable job. His work cannot have been easy. Given a site sloping down towards a river, the obvious course is to build *along* the slope, so that the two principal façades can be symmetrical; at Mottisfont, the line of the old priory – and consequently that of Sir Richard's show front – ran *down* towards the river, an eighteenth-century architect's nightmare. He solved this problem brilliantly, by building out a terrace over the old cellarium in the south-west wing and relating it to a corresponding, though much smaller, terrace outside the Morning Room in the south-east. These two canted wings, though shorter than they were in Lord Sandys's day, still project considerably beyond the three central bays beneath the pediment; the recession is achieved in three gentle stages, decreasing in height as they proceed inwards, each stage with its own fenestration levels and individual hipped roof. The whole thing is immaculately judged, giving the south front of Mottisfont a degree of movement and a syncopated rhythm seldom met with in Georgian building.

Yet one is never allowed to forget that the eighteenth-century overlay is only skin deep. The south-west terrace is supported by the original rib-vaulted undercroft of the cellarium, bearing its load as stoutly and confidently as ever it did; in the south-east wing, a partly concealed mosaic angel by Boris Anrep marks the respond of one of the arches of the former chapter house, while round the corner on the east front there still survives a great thirteenth-century arch, which once led from the south-east chapel into the south transept. In one of the bedrooms along the north front, a corner of the wall has been cut away to reveal a section of one of the nave arcades.

The showpiece of the interior, however, is not medieval, Tudor nor Georgian, but firmly of the twentieth century. This is the Drawing Room, occupying the whole of the south-west wing, which was entrancingly painted by Rex Whistler in 1938–9, his last major work. (He was to be killed in action five years later, while still under forty.) The deeply coved ceiling, bearing at its centre the Sun in Splendour, is coffered in a design of intersecting tracery, executed in that virtuoso *trompe-l'oeil* of which Whistler was the acknowledged master; below the coving, slender *trompe-l'oeil* colonnettes frame trophied panels and, on the west wall, a niche from which a smouldering urn releases an ever fainter trail of smoke. High on the cornice, the artist has left a paintpot, brush and box of matches – except that he hasn't. All is two-dimensional, a fantasy and an illusion. Looking at the curtains of green velvet trimmed with ermine around the high windows, one is not even sure where, on the pelmets, the real ones stop and the painted ones begin.

For the rest, the interior may be thought something of a disappointment. It has no glorious furniture or pictures; it is not even particularly grand. Few rooms, apart from the Whistler Room, are open to the public, for the very good reason that there is little else to see. But if you are interested in tracing the history of a building down the centuries; if it gives you joy to see a fine old house harmonising to perfection with its natural setting; or, finally, if you can share the overflowing exhilaration of a young artist of prodigious talent at the very height of his powers, then it is to Mottisfont that you should come.

## Northington

*16; 7 miles NE of Winchester off B3046*

'Nothing', exclaimed the architect C.R. Cockerell on seeing THE GRANGE for the first time, 'can be finer, more classical, or like the finest Poussins. There is nothing like it this side of Arcadia.' When I first saw it, The Grange was a tragic, desolate ruin, barely visible through a forest of scaffolding which had been erected less as a prelude to its restoration than as a support against its total collapse; yet even then one could see what he meant. The young William Wilkins had been back in England only a few months from a four-year tour of Greece and Asia Minor when, in 1804, he was asked to remodel the seventeenth-century house (by William Samwell) then belonging to Henry Drummond; the result was, to all intents and purposes, a Greek temple – the purest, the grandest and the most impressive monument to the Greek Revival of any English country house.

Its inspiration was not the Parthenon, nor even the temples at Paestum that had so entranced the young John Soane a generation before. Rather surprisingly, it was the Theseum at Athens, still today the best preserved of the Greek classical monuments though also one of the dullest. There is, however, nothing dull about The Grange. Having encased Samwell's building in a suitably classical shell, Wilkins added to the east front a tremendous portico of giant Doric columns, six wide and two deep. In its austere solemnity it strikes one as somewhat overpowering for the simple residence of an English country gentleman; a diarist noted in 1823 that the transformation had served only 'to turn a good family house into a very bad one'. But its impact is undeniable. There is not – nor was there ever – anything fashionable about it. It makes no concessions. It is, rather, the expression of an ideal – of that primitive purity, born of simplicity, logic and truth, to which William Wilkins, Robert Smirke and their fellow architects of the Revival devoted their professional lives.

The sides, of nine bays, with a central three-bay projection breaking forward to the south, maintain the same high-mindedness. The two long wings carrying the building yet further towards the west are, however, something of an anti-climax. They, like the rather more distinguished Orangery behind, are the work of Cockerell and Robert Smirke.

*The Grange, Northington.*

The façade of The Grange has now been well restored and is under the care of the Dept of the Environment. Visitors are thus once again able to see the house, in its landscape, in the same way that Cockerell did. Alas, virtually nothing remains of the interior.

## Nursling

*17; 4½ miles NW of Southampton off M27*

About half a mile to the north-east of the village, at the head of a lovely avenue of limes and looking down on to the valley of the Test, stands GROVE PLACE. Its early history is obscure. It was probably built around 1560; certainly it was standing by 1565, since that date appears scribbled on one of the walls in the west wing. According to an old-established tradition, the house was built by Sir Francis Knollys, 'an exile for his religion in Queen Mary's days and a shining light in Queen Elizabeth's', for the entertainment of his sovereign; the Knollys family were certainly in possession by the early seventeenth century. The fact that the property had been occupied some years before then by James Paget, a London merchant – who decorated the Dining Room with the coats of arms of his own family and its connections – seems to contradict this theory, but Paget may have been merely a tenant. We shall probably never know.

The house is of rich red Tudor brick, with battlemented towers, copious gables and tall, diagonally set chimneystacks: the archetypal early Elizabethan manor house. It is built, in two storeys with an attic third, round three sides of an entrance courtyard, from the inner corners of which rise high octagonal stair turrets. The view of the house from this courtyard is completely symmetrical – perhaps unusually so for the date – except for the two first-floor windows on each side of the central coat of arms, one of which has four lights and the other only two; oddly enough, these are the only windows apart from those at the very tops of the towers that have retained their original stone mullions.

Fortunately, Grove Place never suffered any Georgian or Victorian transformations; it remained Elizabethan through and through. For most of the last century, however, it was used as an ordinary farmhouse, with the usual results: rooms were partitioned, fireplaces bricked up, panelling removed and ceilings allowed to decay. This probably accounts, at least in part, for the paucity of decoration inside the house. The oak-panelled Dining Room is the best preserved, with its frieze of mermaids and the Paget coats of arms ranged below them. It has an intricately patterned ceiling and an elegant – though far from showy – stone fireplace, features which can be found in several of the other rooms as well. There is also a tunnel-vaulted Long Gallery running across the top of the house, but such magnificence as it may once have possessed has long since passed away.

The two staircases in the corner turrets are as interesting as anything in the house. They differ surprisingly in design. The principal one, in the east tower, is of massive oak, winding up in a long, steep spiral around an open centre. There are no frills or furbelows – even the newels are quite roughly carved; the impression is one of solidity and strength. The western staircase, by contrast, has a square centre, timber-framed, through which a service lift – probably the oldest in England – runs right up to the Long Gallery.

Grove Place is now a school – a frequent metamorphosis these days, but one that is not calculated to show a beautiful house to its best advantage. It is, however, appreciated and well cared for, and has managed to retain much of its old character.

## Pamber Priory

*18; 4½ miles N of Basingstoke off A340*

Founded for the Benedictines in the early twelfth century, Pamber Priory had a shorter life than might have been expected, since it was dissolved by Henry V in 1414 – presumably on the grounds that, being a dependency of Cerisy-la-Forêt, it was a potential centre of subversion. The monastic buildings are all gone; gone too are the nave and transept of the original church. We are left with the crossing-tower (possibly truncated, but this is by no means certain) and the chancel, itself the size of a small parish church. The tower is supported on four very plain Norman arches, three of which are naturally blocked up in whole or in part; only that to the east remains as it was, giving access to the chancel.

This is perfectly preserved, and of rare beauty. Immediately beyond the arch, to north and south, are low arches which formerly led to chapels, surmounted by two quite small circular windows on each side. These too are now blocked up – a pity. All this is Norman work; beyond, Early English takes over, with four lancets along each wall, leading to the east window of three stepped lancets, so widely spaced as to occupy the whole of the east end. There is a tunnel roof of wood with nicely curving rafters and, on the south side, a very fine wooden effigy of a knight who looks as if he had fought under Edward III.

The building material is largely flint, but there is a good deal of Roman brick intermingled, probably from Silchester.

## Portchester Castle

*19; 4 miles NW of Portsmouth off A27*

Of all the great forts that the Romans built along what they called the 'Saxon Shore', between the Wash and Southampton Water, Portchester is the best preserved. Indeed, it is the only Roman stronghold in Northern Europe whose enclosing wall is still complete and of its full height. Archaeological evidence suggests that it was built around AD 280 and finally vacated by the Romans some ninety years later; but that was by no means the end of its story. In the twelfth century Henry I was to transform it into one of the three greatest royal castles on the south coast, and it was from here that he habitually sailed to Normandy. So did Richard Coeur-de-Lion, after the one fleeting visit he found time to make to his English kingdom during his ten-year reign. A hundred years later still, when the French were making calamitous raids in the south-east, Richard II put in hand the complete rebuilding of the palace under the direction of his famous master mason Henry Yevele (who was responsible for Westminster Hall as we know it today); it was thus a comfortable modern palace in which Henry V stayed on his way to Agincourt.

The outer wall forms an almost perfect square, and still retains fourteen of the twenty original round bastions and the double ditch that provided further protection on the landward side. On the east side and part of the south it extends to within a few yards of the water's edge. You go in by the land gate, to the west – originally Roman, but drastically narrowed by the Normans. Both the outer and inner gates, however, were much altered in the fourteenth century; a dripstone head on the former is thought to be a portrait of Queen Isabella, wife of Edward II – 'the She-Wolf of France'. It is a two-storey building; above the entrance is a small room used as a punishment cell for French prisoners of war in the eighteenth century.

Once within the enclosure, you see the keep and the Palace of Richard II immediately on your left, in the north-west corner of the fort. Before it runs a curving moat, with the inner Gatehouse immediately beyond. This gets older as you go further in: the first, rather shoddy, construction – it includes a small sentry box and fittings for the drawbridge – is of the seventeenth century, and of little interest; just beyond, however, the pretty little vaulted porch and two-order segmental arch are fourteenth-century again, and further still, the inner arch remains sturdy round-headed Norman. Now you are in the inner bailey, with the palace to your left, the keep in the further left-hand corner.

Richard II built his palace between 1396 and 1399, when he was deposed. It must have looked quite austere on the outside; apart from the two lions on the inner cornice, there is little exterior decoration. In essence it consists of a series of interconnecting rooms on the first floor. Only the first in the series, the kitchen which adjoins the Gatehouse, occupied the ground floor as well. Next to it was the Great Hall, approached by a flight of steps beneath a projecting porch. Around the corner, stretching along most of the western range, runs the Great Chamber, a good deal more splendid than the Hall, lit by four transomed two-light windows to the east. At the south-west corner of this magnificent room is the King's Inner Chamber – presumably his bedroom – which is small and distinctly poky; at the northern end is a tiny Exchequer Chamber and then the keep.

The keep is tall and commanding – particularly its two outer walls, with their fine trios of stepped buttresses. But it is only a shell. Inside, there are modern wooden floors and a wooden staircase to take you on to the roof – highly recommended in summer, for the view is magnificent – but otherwise little of interest except prisoners' graffiti and a rather advanced garderobe, or latrine, in the north-west corner of the first floor. The somewhat complex forebuilding on the east side of the keep provided the usual first-floor access and concealed a small chapel in its undercroft; but of this little now remains.

When you have finished with the north-west corner of the enclosure, cross it diagonally to the south-east, where stands the ancient CHURCH OF ST MARY. This is the only remnant of an Augustinian priory founded by Henry I in 1133; it is itself incomplete – the south transept has gone, the chancel shortened and the north chapel replaced – but it remains a beautiful and deeply satisfying building. One is struck first of all by its lowness; the crossing-tower, excluding its pyramidal cap, rises only to the roof line of nave and transept. But then one remembers that one is in a fortress, and all becomes clear: the church, by projecting far above the curtain walls, would be an obvious target for an

*Romsey Abbey.*

opposing army and would furthermore obstruct the view of the lookouts. The west front boasts a fine Norman door of three orders, above which is a west window of similar shape, flanked by two blind arches rather shorter and narrower, and decorated with inscribed quatrefoils.

The interior of the church is remarkably plain, aisleless, with a long five-bay nave leading to a most impressive crossing – four great round-headed arches, the capitals varying in quality but some of them interestingly carved. There is some fine Norman work in the transept, too – when you can see it for the vestry furniture. The real disappointment comes with the chancel. Truncated around 1600 and further ruined by a particularly nasty modern window, it has virtually nothing but the vestiges of ancient blind arcading along the side walls to remind us of what it must once have been. And yet, somehow, the general atmosphere of the church remains untouched, the Romanesque spirit as strong as ever.

On leaving, have a good look at the font – an intricate Norman affair of more blind arcading, interlinked this time, with twining tendrils above, within which are small carvings thought to represent the Garden of Eden.

## Romsey Abbey*

*20; 9 miles SW of Winchester on A31*

At the time of the Dissolution of the Monasteries the people of Romsey purchased the abbey church for £100, and it is lucky for posterity that they did: England without Romsey Abbey would be a diminished place indeed. The exterior, of whitish grey Chilmark limestone, is perhaps only moderately distinguished; one longs for a little more height on the tower instead of that faintly ridiculous seventeenth-century bell-cage. The inside, however, is nothing short of a revelation. As one stands at the west end, staring up towards the crossing, one's first reaction is of breathless admiration at the ensemble: at that combination of gracefulness and mass that the Romanesque, at its best, can exemplify better than any other architectural style. Then, as one looks longer and one's eye begins to move from the general to the particular, the impression changes. This tremendous nave, apparently the epitome of everything we think of as Norman, is in fact in a state of transition. At clerestory level, suggestions of Early English are visible in the very first bay west of the crossing. In the triforium, they appear in the third bay; on the ground, in the fifth. The last three bays to the west are thus entirely Gothic, and the step effect merely reflects the building methods of the time; builders worked from east to west, and the upper storeys were always slightly behind the lower ones.

If we now walk slowly up the nave, we notice another curious feature. Suddenly, one bay before the crossing, the rhythm changes. Instead of the compound piers to which we have been accustomed, we find ourselves faced, for no apparent reason, with a pair of giant columns, one on the north side and one on the south, rising up to the point of springing for the triforium arches. Was this, one wonders, originally intended for every bay of the nave? And if so, why did the master mason change his mind? We can, I think, be thankful that he did; uninterrupted rows of giant columns, as at Gloucester or Tewkesbury, can make a grand effect; but when they rise more than a single storey there is bound to be trouble, for no one has yet come upon a satisfactory way of running a horizontal course into the side of a column. At Romsey it is done, perhaps, as well as it could ever be; but the result is still unhappy, and we can only suppose that those responsible realised it and altered the plans before going any further.

Beyond the crossing the only surprise – but it cannot really be a surprise, since we must have noticed it from the beginning – is the east end. Romsey is something of a rarity in that instead of having a single east window it has two, side by side; and these, instead of being Norman as one might have expected, are Decorated, of the late thirteenth century. Below and behind them – set back a further bay towards the east – are two more windows of the same date and much the same design: three lights with three circles over, arranged in the form of a triangle. Seen from the west end, these two lower windows, perfectly framed as they are by two uncompromisingly Norman arches, suggest a strange telescoping of time. What seems to have happened is this. The original Norman Lady Chapel, which continued well beyond the present east end, was demolished around 1275 and replaced by a new one, to which the two chapels that make up the existing retrochoir formed an approach. At the same time the chancel was given its two big east windows. Later – the date is uncertain – this Decorated Lady Chapel was demolished in its turn, and its windows set back into the new east wall.

The chancel proper is of three bays, supported on a set of massive Norman arches springing from clustered piers and richly decorated with zigzag. Above these, the gallery is, it must be admitted, a little peculiar. It maintains the same basic system as that of the nave – twin openings, a super-arch embracing the two sub-arches – but whereas in the nave the space between super and subs is, as one might expect, filled in, in the chancel it is left open, while a small colonnette rises rather precariously from the point where the sub-arches meet to the centre of the underside of the super-arch, as if pretending to hold it up. At floor level most of the capitals are scalloped in the usual way; note, however, two splendidly carved ones, symmetrically placed to north and south, one of which portrays, *inter alia*, a seated man proudly brandishing a scroll bearing the words 'ROBERTUS ME FECIT'.

That leaves us with the transepts. Both are magnificently Norman, except for the regrettable Perpendicular window in the west wall of the northern one. The original Norman window was knocked out at the beginning of the fifteenth century when the townspeople, who had previously had to content themselves with the use of the north aisle for their devotions, were suddenly given the north transept as well, from which they built a further extension, four bays to the west, for their parish church. This necessitated opening the west wall of the transept, and the loss of the window. When the new church was demolished – presumably after the Dissolution – one of its windows was salvaged and used as a replacement.

Re-reading the above, I seem to have devoted all my time to picking out the inconsistencies and imperfections of Romsey Abbey rather than extolling its beauties. If so, I am sorry, for I should hate to give the impression that it is anything short of a masterpiece. Where I have been over-critical it is only because the general standard is so high that there is not really much to say about it; and though there are a few features which one could wish a little different, not one of them is an out-and-out eyesore. The building remains one of the noblest examples of Romanesque in all Europe; and if I had my way I would put up a memorial to those sixteenth-century citizens who saved it for us.

## Stratfield Saye

*21; 6½ miles NE of Basingstoke off A33*

In 1817, two years after Waterloo, a grateful nation offered the Duke of Wellington £600,000 for the purchase of a country house and estate. He considered several possibilities, including Bramshill and Uppark (which he rejected on the grounds that the steep approach would put too much strain on his carriage horses), and eventually settled on Stratfield Saye. It was a relatively modest mansion – too modest, in the opinion of most of his friends and admirers; it certainly could not compare with Blenheim, which the Duke of Marlborough had acquired in somewhat similar circumstances a century before. But it had a fine park, excellent farms and a splendid position overlooking the Loddon; besides, the Duke had every intention of building himself another, far grander, house across the river, for which Benjamin Dean Wyatt and C.R. Cockerell both submitted plans.

As time went on, however, he gave up these grandiose ideas. The charm of the old house was obviously beginning to grow on him, and no wonder. It was built in about 1640 by Sir William Pitt, formerly Controller of the Household to James I – a long, low (two-storey) building of brick, with projecting two-bay wings each crowned by a big Dutch gable. In the eighteenth century George Pitt, 1st Lord Rivers, added two more outer wings, longer but in identical style, inserted sash windows throughout and covered the brick with stucco; but the character of the house remained unchanged, and does so to this day. It possesses one or two quite lovable eccentricities, notably a row of short pilasters between the *upper* windows only (was there a similar row at the lower level, and if so, why was it removed?) and a curious quirk of the fenestration whereby the third and fourth ground-floor windows from the centre have only a single, centrally placed window above them, flanked by round-headed niches. Apart from Benjamin Wyatt's regrettable porch of 1838 and the charming little white cupola added by the 7th Duke – a talented professional architect – in 1964, there have been no subsequent additions to the entrance front. On the garden front, to the east, Rivers added a canted bay at the north end and Wyatt a conservatory at the south. Otherwise, apart from a pediment covering five bays – as opposed to the shrinking little one-bay affairs on the other side – the style is much the same.

Inside, the entire house is dominated by the spirit of the Iron Duke. The Entrance Hall, which rises through both floors and contains a Gallery running the length of the back wall supported on Ionic columns (made ostensibly of marble but in fact of wood), contains banners, flags, busts of Wellington and Napoleon, paintings of the Peninsular War, thank-offerings from the crowned heads of Europe and relics of the great man's funeral. The Library, almost unchanged since his day, preserves all its mid-eighteenth-century decoration (possibly by William Kent) and a large number of books from Napoleon's own library. The Music Room, despite its name, is given over to the memory of the Duke's favourite charger, Copenhagen, who carried him all day at Waterloo.

Apart from the Wellingtoniana, Stratfield Saye provides surely the best example in England of the eighteenth-century fashion for print rooms, in which the principal decoration consisted of prints stuck to the walls, usually in symmetrical patterns. Several houses described in this book possess a print room, often in a state of some dilapidation. Only here, so far as I know, can we find not one room but several, all in immaculate condition. Most impressive of all is the Gallery – a glorious room by any standards, and the pride of the house. At each end is a four-column Ionic screen; along the inner wall, under a noble cornice, a superb collection of bronze busts, partially gilded and standing on opulent Boulle plinths or cabinets; and, on the wall itself, the prints, largely devoted to scenes from Shakespeare, edged with gilt beading and collectively surmounted by a frieze taken from the Trajan and Antonine columns in Rome. A final touch of sumptuousness is provided by the actual wall: such parts of it as are left exposed are covered with burnished gold leaf. Thus, particularly at night, the whole Gallery seems to glow with a dark, almost Byzantine lustre.

The two other principal rooms of the house are the Drawing Room and the Dining Room. The former seems a little oppressive, thanks in large measure to the somewhat strident French wallpaper, ill-advisedly chosen by the Great Duke in 1838. The Dining Room, added by Lord Rivers in *c.*1775, is a good deal more successful. Here the showpiece is the magnificent ceiling taken from Wood's *Ruins of Palmyra* – though even this can hardly overshadow Hoppner's famous portrait of Sir Arthur Wellesley in India, his huge white horse rearing up behind him.

Even in the grounds it is not easy to escape from under the Duke's shadow; a majestic group of Wellingtonias ensures that he is not forgotten. But it is a particular pleasure to come upon the grave of Copenhagen, who survived till 1836, when he was twenty-eight. His epitaph reads:

*God's humbler instrument, though meaner clay*
*Should share the glory of that glorious day.*

*Stratfield Saye.*

## The Vyne*

*NT; 22; 4 miles N of Basingstoke off A340*

When, around the year 1515, William Sandys – soon to be ennobled by Henry VIII and made his Lord Chamberlain – demolished an old medieval manor house 4 miles north of Basingstoke and set about building himself a more up-to-date mansion, there was no question about what it was to be called. Whether or not The Vyne originally took its name from a Roman villa or inn known as Vindomis – 'The House of Wine' – we shall probably never know; but that name was certainly in current use by the thirteenth century, and is thus by far the oldest feature of the house.

The Vyne was finished by 1527, a basically two-storey building of wonderful rich red Tudor brick, with blue headers to form a diapering pattern and stone quoins. Not particularly original, you may think – but it was. Sandys was an innovator, and his house was many years ahead of its time. He dispensed with the usual moat; he adopted a symmetrical design, with symmetrical fenestration; he faced the building outwards, instead of on to an inner courtyard; and he gave it a Long Gallery. Half a century later, such things were commonplace; but in the first quarter of the sixteenth century they were rare indeed, and Sandys's Long Gallery was the first in England.

In 1535 the Lord Chamberlain entertained the King for the second, if not the third, time at The Vyne, together with the new Queen, Anne Boleyn. Soon afterwards, he seems to have lost interest in the house, neglecting it in favour of his new property at Mottisfont (*q.v.*); but his descendants continued to live there – Queen Elizabeth was received in considerable state in 1569 – until the time of the Commonwealth, when the impoverished 6th Lord Sandys sold the house to one of the most distinguished barristers of his day and future Speaker of the House of Commons, one Chaloner Chute. Chute, it seems, was just as ahead of his time in matters of architectural taste as Sandys had been; for it was he who commissioned Inigo Jones's son-in-law (or nephew) John Webb to add a classical portico to the north front. This portico – two Corinthian columns and two square angle pillars of rendered brick supporting a triangular pediment with prominent dentils – is the earliest on any English country house.

The third important building period at The Vyne began in 1754, when the property passed to Chaloner Chute's great-grandson, John. It was an extraordinary piece of good fortune that it did so, since John was the youngest of his father's ten children; he was also a dilettante in the best sense of the word, sophisticated and cosmopolitan – he had already lived over thirty years in Italy – an amateur architect of prodigious talent, and one of the closest friends of Horace Walpole, who described him as 'my counsel in my affairs, my oracle in taste, the standard to whom I submitted my trifles, and the genius who presided over poor Strawberry'. The Vyne, as well as Strawberry Hill, owes him much.

As you approach up the drive from the south, the house you see before you is smaller than in Lord

*The Vyne.*

Sandys's day; a front courtyard with a number of outbuildings, including probably a noble Gatehouse, have been swept away. There are other changes too: the windows have been remodelled twice – in Webb's time, when they were given their receding stone surrounds, and on some unknown later date when they were sashed. Webb was also responsible for the present design of the central porch and for the two doors facing each other across the terrace, all with broken pediments. The stone eagles, on the other hand, were placed there by John Chute, having been the gift of Horace Walpole. Apart from these, Chute's contribution to this front seems to have been limited to the canted bays at the ends of the wings; the rather similar treatment of the centre bay on the first floor above the porch is, however, Victorian. On the north front, facing the lake, the side wings have three full storeys, and there is an extrusion on the east consisting of the Ante-Chapel and Chapel. The latter was, until the mid-nineteenth century, concealed by trees; its two large blind windows are consequently Victorian, though they precisely follow the three original ones in the eastern apse. At the same time it was apparently thought desirable to remodel the Ante-Chapel windows.

One further feature should be noticed before we go inside. This is the Garden House, one of a pair of red-brick pavilions built by Chaloner Chute. It is in the form of a Greek cross with a central dome, and may well have been designed by Webb, although there is no documentary evidence.

Visitors normally enter The Vyne by way of the Stone Gallery, originally designed as a servants' dormitory but now housing pieces of sculpture and old maps acquired at various times by members of the Chute family. (The monumental wall tablets were another present from Horace Walpole.) This gives direct access to the series of reception rooms ranged along the north front, ending

with what is, for me, the pleasantest room in the house – the Chapel Parlour. Purists may cavil at the way a Tudor room is crowned with a Rococo plaster ceiling; curiously, however, the union is not unhappy, and Lord Sandys's linenfold panelling is a joy both to see and to touch. The Ante-Chapel next door, on the other hand, is a disappointment. Designed jointly by Chute and Walpole – and, quite possibly, other members of the Strawberry Hill 'Committee of Taste' – it seems somehow unimaginative and heavy-handed. Probably only the ribbed ceiling is original early sixteenth-century work.

No one could be disappointed, however, in the Chapel itself; it is superb, the perfect example of a rich man's private oratory of the 1520s. The windows, which are original, were made by a team of Flemish craftsmen – surprisingly enough in Basingstoke; the encaustic tiles before the altar platform and around the stalls are the work of another émigré, one Guido di Savino, who left his native Urbino and settled in Antwerp in 1512. (One tile bears the unmistakable likeness of Urbino's broken-nosed Duke, Federigo di Montefeltro, known to all through Piero della Francesca's famous portrait in Florence.) The stalls themselves are also considerable works of art: still Gothic, but with various motifs on the frontal cornice (boys blowing horns and shooting deer) which clearly show that the Renaissance is not far away. Look carefully, too, at the poppy-head finials. In two instances only did John Chute make alterations. First, he covered the upper walls with canvases depicting fan tracery in *trompe-l'oeil* (since regrettably moved to the Gallery); second, he erected on the south side a Gothick Tomb Chamber to the memory of his ancestor, the Speaker. The tomb itself – or, more accurately, the cenotaph, since Chaloner Chute was buried at St Nicholas's, Chiswick – is by contrast purely classical, the work of Thomas Carter the Younger. In all England, there is no piece of eighteenth-century sculpture finer or nobler than this.

On the south front there are two small rooms – the Strawberry Parlour, which was always reserved for Walpole when he came to The Vyne, and a not very distinguished Print Room. We then come to the Staircase Hall, John Chute's grandest *tour de force*. Tudor and Gothick are alike forgotten. Here all is coolly classical: the staircase, beginning with a single flight, forks at right-angles and then turns back on itself into a delicate upper gallery of Corinthian columns supporting an ornate entablature and a richly coved ceiling above. All this is achieved in a remarkably narrow space – 18 feet – without the least feeling of constraint. Horace Walpole described it as 'theatric', which indeed it is. John Chute's architectural talents need no further testimonial.

The Library (largely Victorian but with a chimneypiece by Webb) and the Tapestry Room with its delightful Soho *chinoiseries* bring us at last to Lord Sandys's Oak Gallery, running above the Stone Gallery, the entire length of the west wing. Here is the prototype of all the Long Galleries of England. Its particular glory is the linenfold panelling, four rows of it, of the highest possible quality, carved at top and bottom with intricate devices relating to Sandys, his family and his friends. Above one of the doors, the Royal Arms are upheld by two winged *putti* – a delightfully irreverent Renaissance conceit. One thing only mars the splendour: the decision, by some early nineteenth-century barbarian, to cover the whole thing with a layer of reddish brown paint. How one longs to scrape it off – but the National Trust, to whom The Vyne belongs, has reluctantly decided after careful study that to do so would not only cost a small fortune but would almost certainly damage the panels as well. So there is nothing to be done, and we must grin and bear it, seeking our consolation where we can. Luckily, at The Vyne, we do not need to look far.

## West Green House

See Hartley Wintney.

*Winchester Cathedral.*

## Winchester

*23; 18 miles SW of Basingstoke on A33 and A31*

THE CATHEDRAL AND IMMEDIATE ENVIRONS

Winchester Cathedral, 556 feet from east to west, is the longest cathedral in all Europe. In England, it is the second oldest; St Albans beats it by a year or two. But St Albans, as I lament elsewhere in this book, is a disappointment; Winchester is not. Admittedly, it has been much rebuilt; only in the transepts has the original Norman work been preserved. It cannot therefore produce the overall Romanesque impact of nearby Romsey Abbey – let alone that of Durham, the grandest Norman cathedral of them all. Still, the best of Winchester is as good as the best of Durham, and let it never be forgotten that Durham was begun in the year that Norman Winchester was completed – 1093.

It is sad that so magnificent and venerable a monument should be so unimpressive from the outside. The west front of Winchester is hardly a west front at all – it is little more than a cross-section of nave and aisles, as if it had been sawn off by some gigantic meat slicer. One looks in vain for west towers, or even an appropriate entrance, in place of those three oddly inept arches. Above them, a huge porch; almost half the elevation is taken up by a Perpendicular west window of nine lights, flanked by a pair of rather undistinguished pinnacles, and topped by a tall panelled gable supporting a canopied niche as tall as itself, in which stands a statue thought to be of St Swithun. To each side, the aisles are marked by two more windows, both of them far too broad for the space available. Winchester demonstrates, better than any other cathedral, the drawbacks of those outsize windows that became such a fashion in the fourteenth and fifteenth centuries; true, they flooded the interior with light, which was usually – though not invariably – a good thing; but they tended to give the exterior a curiously blind look. The final misfortune is the two broad stepped buttresses extending from the corners to north and south. Thanks to them, the elevation does not even have vertical sides and consequently appears somehow splayed, as if its back were broken.

But enough of this carping. It is time to go inside – and immediately the majesty of Winchester is apparent. From the west end, there is no trace visible of the cathedral's Norman origins. Twelve bays long and splendidly lit – at last those windows come into their own – the nave is a wonderfully homogeneous work by two successive bishops, William Edington and William of Wykeham, who together spanned the entire second half of the fourteenth century. (The lion's share is actually Wykeham's, built mostly between 1394 and his death ten years later.) It is not particularly high by cathedral standards – only 78 feet – but it is made to look higher by the many-shafted main arcade, which rises more than halfway to the vault, and by the narrowness of the bays – between which the central shaft of each pier rises uninterrupted to the point of springing. Here, in fact, is all the vertical emphasis so sadly lacking outside; and here, with exactly the same dimensions, the proportions are perfect. The sense of verticality has been further increased, in this late fourteenth-century remodelling, by the total elimination of the triforium and its replacement by a little low balcony. Above this, the clerestory begins at once – three-light windows, all by Wykeham, with blank arcading below and to each side. The tops of these windows seem almost to disappear into the lierne-vaulted roof.

Up now to the crossing and the transepts. The great thing to remember about the crossing is that the tower collapsed in 1107 – only seven years after William Rufus had been buried underneath it. (One can imagine the pious cluckings of the canons, attributing it to the wrath of God at the interment of so godless a monarch in so holy a place.) This accounts for the enormous size of the crossing piers – they were taking no chances this time – and for the obviously superior craftsmanship to be seen in the masonry immediately to the north and south of the crossing, at the entrance to the transepts.

These transepts are the glory of Winchester, virtually untouched since their building nine centuries ago. Above the main arcades runs a triforium of twin arches within a single super-arch, and above that a clerestory, with curiously irregular openings. In so majestic a context, however, irregularity hardly seems to matter. What matters is the alliance of simplicity and strength, light and shadow, straight line and curve. The material is lovely, too – the very pale Quarr Abbey limestone from the Isle of Wight that we also see at Romsey.

Passing into the choir and the chancel, we move on about 250 years. The big broad arches, with their marvellously rich mouldings and a profusion of carved heads and animals on the stops, are supported on eightfold clusters of columns of Purbeck marble. Somehow they give an even more sumptuous impression than the vast stone reredos – which is of the early sixteenth century, though all the statues are late Victorian replacements. The vault here is of wood, in a complicated lierne pattern generously bossed; it dates from the time of Bishop Fox in the first part of the reign of Henry VIII.

Behind the reredos is the retrochoir, which leads us back, with a wholly agreeable jolt, into the early thirteenth century. It is quite difficult to see it as an architectural whole, owing to the number of chapels and chantries. What anyone can appreciate is the fineness of detail: the shaft rings and the stiff-leaf on the capitals, the blank arcading along the aisles, the lovely doorway in the south-west corner, the entrances to the three chapels to the east. Of these, the central one is the Lady Chapel. Originally built by Bishop de Lucy at the same time as the retrochoir – though on the site of an earlier Norman chapel – it was greatly enlarged under Henry VII to mark the baptism and confirmation of his eldest son, Arthur, Prince of Wales. From this enlargement date the huge seven-light windows to north, east and south. (The discovery that the altar is dedicated to Charlotte M. Yonge comes as something of an anti-climax.) The ceiling is lierne-vaulted, its ribs cusped towards the centre, to make a decoration of quatrefoils. Below stands the chair in which Mary Tudor sat for her wedding, in this same cathedral, to Philip II of Spain; against the north wall is a fascinating though sadly faded series of early sixteenth-century wall paintings depicting the Miracles of the Virgin.

These are not, however, the only wall paintings in Winchester Cathedral, nor even the best. The adjoining chapel to the north, known as the Guardian Angels' Chapel, has a vault painted in about 1240 with portraits of angels in roundels. Better still – and more interesting in subject matter – are the paintings in the Holy Sepulchre Chapel, under the crossing arch to the north transept. These probably predate the Guardian Angels by about a decade. The Deposition and Entombment behind the altar are particularly fine. England has no better wall paintings of this date anywhere.

Then there are the tombs, often in little chantry chapels. The most opulent is that of William of Wykeham, halfway down the nave on the south side, but Fox, Gardner, Waynflete and Cardinal Beaufort are also splendidly commemorated. Beaufort, the younger brother of King Henry IV, was largely responsible for the condemnation of Joan of Arc; a modern statue of her has been placed opposite his tomb, so that she may confront him for all eternity. Other memorials are to Bishop Wilberforce (Soapy Sam) – a huge canopied affair by Gilbert Scott, occupying much of the floor space in the south transept – and, close by, in Prior Silkstede's Chapel, a modern memorial window to Izaak Walton, just above his grave. There is also a ledger slab marking the burial place of Jane Austen (north aisle, third bay from the west) with an epitaph which fails to mention her writings – though a nearby wall plate and window make good this defect. Grandest of all, and most impressive in its simplicity, is the tomb of William Rufus in the centre of the choir, the secret of his mysterious death buried with him.

South of the cathedral lies the Close, which contains much of interest. Of the Cloister proper, there is all too little left; but just beyond the end of the transept a mighty Norman arcade still marks the entrance to the Chapter House. Further south still is the DEANERY, formerly the Prior's Lodging, with a fifteenth-century Hall and a porch – really more of a loggia – having three pointed arches of much the same date. Behind it runs a very pretty Long Gallery of about 1670 in brick, projecting some way to the east. The other principal building in the Close is WOLVESEY PALACE, the Bishop's Residence since Norman times. The twelfth-century Great Hall is largely ruined, but there is a fine William and Mary house of *c.*1684, with a fifteenth-century CHAPEL (on Norman foundations) at the north end. South-east of the Deanery is the PILGRIMS' SCHOOL (late seventeenth-century) and, next to it, the PILGRIMS' HALL, which possesses the earliest known hammer-beam roof, probably dating from the reign of Edward III. Nearby, DOME ALLEY contains just four long, narrow houses, each of four gables. Izaak Walton died in one of them – No. 7, The Close.

After the cathedral, the most distinguished religious building in Winchester is the CHURCH AND HOSPITAL OF ST CROSS. It was originally founded in 1136 by Henry of Blois, the Conqueror's grandson who was also Bishop of Winchester, for the benefit of 'thirteen poor men, feeble and so reduced in strength that they can hardly or with difficulty support themselves without another's aid'. To this, in 1445, Cardinal Beaufort added his 'Almshouse of Noble Poverty', for 'those who once had everything handsome about them, but had suffered losses'. The two foundations are still in existence; the Brothers of the Blois foundation wear black gowns, while those of the Beaufort wear red.

The church was begun around 1160–70, the work continuing for about 130 years and covering the transition from Norman to Early English. It is the size of a large parish church, and is unusually high, with a massive square tower at the crossing. On entering the broad, stubby nave, perhaps the first thing one notices is the thickness of the piers, each some 5 feet in diameter. They support a rather nondescript tribune above which, rather surprisingly, is a Decorated clerestory of the 1330s. Decorated too is the five-light west window. The crossing – four tall arches, their points just perceptible, on clustered shafts – is fine indeed at the lower level. Higher up, however, the effect is disappointing, owing to a major restoration by Butterfield in 1864–5. This restoration presents us with a good many problems. The chancel arcades, for example: can they always have been pointed, or was this a conceit of Butterfield's? His, surely, is the wildly exaggerated dogtooth and zigzag; and we can only be grateful that his polychrome mural decorations, which by all accounts were wilder still, have been done away with. Zigzag is also a major feature of the transepts, where it continues even on the ribs of the vault; but this is not, I think, to be laid at Butterfield's door. Beyond the south transept is a small sacristy which dates from the time of Henry of Blois.

Emerging from the church, retrace your steps across the quadrangle to the BRETHREN'S HALL, just to the west of the Gatehouse. You reach it through a lierne-vaulted porch. It is basically the work of Cardinal Beaufort, whose arms and cardinal's hat appear in the windows; but the timber roof is about fifty years later. Beyond the Hall to the west is the MASTER'S HOUSE; the building then turns south for the long fifteenth-century range lined with tall octagonal chimneys, each serving four separate lodgings of three rooms each – living room, bedroom and kitchen. The accommodation is far from princely, but the beauty and peace of the surroundings would make up for a lot. There are many worse places in which to pass the evening of one's life.

The morning of it, on the other hand, could be more profitably spent at WINCHESTER COLLEGE, founded by William of Wykeham in 1382. His ideas were a good deal more ambitious than those of the founders of St Cross; he planned to accommodate no fewer than ninety-six boys and a further nineteen masters. The building was entrusted to the master mason William de Wynford, who was also responsible for the nave of the cathedral, the western towers at Wells, and Wykeham's other foundation, New College, Oxford. Most of his work here still stands, and constitutes the principal buildings of the College as we know it today.

You enter from College Street through Outer Gate, beneath a particularly memorable fourteenth-century statue of the Virgin with a smiling Child. It is a two-storeyed Gatehouse with a fine star vault, leading directly into the first of the College's two principal courtyards, known as Outer Court. To your left are the Warden's Lodgings, formerly the domestic offices, refronted in the 1830s by G.S. Repton (Humphry's youngest son); immediately to your left, in the same range as Outer Gate, is the Old Brewhouse, in 1932–4 converted into the Moberly Library by Sir Herbert Baker. The range opposite, to the south of the court, centres on Middle Gate, which is higher than its predecessor – three storeys instead of two – with three niches at the upper level, two of which contain statues of the Virgin and William of Wykeham. The third statue, an angel, has been taken down to preserve it. On the inner side of the Gate, which is of similar design, all three corresponding statues are still in place.

We are now in Chamber Court, the focus of College life. Around it are the lodgings of the scholars and members of the staff – don't miss the stops on the hood-moulds around the doors and windows – and, on the south side, the Chapel and the Hall. The Chapel, which is approached through an ante-chapel to the west, is six bays long; the most interesting feature of it is the wooden vault, the work of Hugh Herland, Richard II's master carpenter who was soon afterwards to construct, in Westminster Hall, the greatest hammer-beam roof in England. Here he has adopted a design of cusped liernes – a notable stage in the development of the fan vault, which was soon to become one of the glories of later Perpendicular architecture. (Another stage can be seen in the south-east chapel – Bishop Langton's – of the cathedral.) For the rest, this building strikes me as a little disappointing. Nearly all the original glass has gone (that in the Jesse window at the east end is of 1821–8) and the late fifteenth-century stone reredos has been heavily, if conscientiously, restored by Butterfield. The stalls, however, are original and have some good misericords; and the magnificent altar rail is by no less an artist than Edward Pierce. Opening off the nave to the south is the chantry chapel of Warden Thurbern, who died in 1450. It too needed some restoration after the tower above it had had to be completely rebuilt, by Butterfield, in 1862–3; but the lierne star vaults in the two bays are both original, and the windows contain much lovely medieval glass, including (in the western one) some of the original glazing from the Jesse window.

Immediately to the west of the Chapel, and in the same alignment, is College Hall, reached by the stairs in the south-west corner of Chamber Court. It boasts a fine timber roof, but this is in fact an early nineteenth-century replacement of the original, keeping the same design. Below the Hall is the College's first schoolroom, known as Seventh Chamber.

The Cloisters, behind the Chapel to the south, are oddly out of axis with it. Odder still, they enclose another chantry chapel, free-standing in the centre. This – the only chapel in England to be so placed – was built for the repose of the soul of John Fromond, a College steward who died in 1420. It has two bays, two storeys and a fine east window of about 1500. The chapel proper, on the lower floor, is in regular use by the junior boys; the upper room is a small library.

Turning sharp left out of the Cloisters, you at once come to the building known, quite simply, as School. This was built in 1683–7 to accommodate the increasing number of pupils. The popular attribution to Wren seems to be largely based on the theory that he was in Winchester at the time, working on Wolvesey Palace opposite; unfortunately, his connection with Wolvesey is supported only on the assumption that he was working in the College. The truth is that, so far as is known, Wren never worked in Winchester at all. But whoever its architect may have been, School remains a noble William and Mary building of red brick with copious stone dressings, a hipped roof and arched windows surmounted by garlands. The Headmaster's 'Throne' is in the south-west corner, the Second Master's opposite it: several classes would have been going on simultaneously under the same roof. Nowadays it is used as a reading room, and on the west wall there still hangs the grim warning whose Latin might be loosely translated as 'Learn, leave or be licked.'

Finally we come to War Cloister, built by Baker in 1922–4 as a memorial to the 500 Wykehamists killed in the First World War. It is one of the best things he ever did, the arches carried by coupled Tuscan columns, the walls covered with tablets, shields, plaques and a long inscription in flushwork. With this our visit to Winchester College ends. There are plenty of other buildings within its precincts, of varying quality; but it is time to return to the city.

THE CITY

Winchester has suffered much in the past century, but it still preserves traces of its splendid history. The thirteenth-century walls can still be seen along College Street and elsewhere, with two early gates, the thirteenth-century WESTGATE and the fourteenth-century KINGSGATE, which has the tiny CHURCH OF ST SWITHUN above it. The old Norman CASTLE can hardly be discerned from the outside, thanks to the various nineteenth- and twentieth-century County Offices and the Magistrates' Court; within it, however, Henry III's GREAT HALL – a double cube, built between 1222 and 1236 – survives in its entirety, the finest medieval hall in England after that of Westminster. On the west wall hangs a huge circular table top, thought to be of fourteenth-century origin but painted, for Henry VIII's visit in 1522, with the Tudor Rose, a picture of King Arthur, and his knights' names in black letter all round the edge. It looks more like a gigantic dartboard than anything else.

Although there are no really memorable streets in Winchester from the architectural point of view, several are well worth exploring on foot. North of the High Street, ST PETER'S STREET (AVEBURY HOUSE, 1690, is a gem), EASTGATE STREET and CHESIL STREET are about the best; south of it, look at GREAT MINSTER STREET and SYMONDS STREET, then turn right into ST SWITHUN STREET and right again into SOUTHGATE STREET, the grandest residential street in Winchester. Best of all here is SERLE'S HOUSE, now the Museum of the Royal Hampshire Regiment, a splendidly Baroque red-brick house of the early eighteenth century. KINGSGATE STREET and COLLEGE STREET have many lovely seventeenth- and eighteenth-century houses in excellent repair – probably because most of them are the property of Winchester College.

## Short List

### Boarhunt

*24; 3 miles NE of Fareham off M27*

The village has a small Saxon church, ST NICHOLAS'S, built a few years before the Conquest. Apart from the windows – mostly thirteenth-century lancets – it is structurally almost complete.

### Bramley

*25; 6 miles N of Basingstoke off A33*

The hotch-potch ST JAMES'S CHURCH has a bit of everything – Norman windows, Perpendicular screen, eighteenth-century west gallery on Ionic columns, thirteenth-century wall painting of the murder of Becket and a fifteenth-century one of St Christopher, medieval and sixteenth-century glass and a south transeptal chapel by Soane. What more can you ask?

### Burghclere

*26; 3 miles S of Newbury off A34*

The SANDHAM MEMORIAL CHAPEL, by Lionel Pearson, is noteworthy for the nineteen paintings by Stanley Spencer, executed between 1927 and 1932. All illustrate the Gallipoli campaign in the First World War, but there are no heroics – just the dreary, sordid, day-to-day chores that occupy so much of the private soldier's life.

### Eaglehurst

*27; 2 miles SE of Fawley on B3053*

LUTTRELL'S TOWER is an enchanting eighteenth-century folly built on the shore of the Solent by Temple Simon Luttrell and possibly designed by James Wyatt. It has three storeys of unequal height, the top one being the tallest and most important, all with Gothick windows. Both the main tower and the circular stair turret on the west side (which rises a further three storeys) are castellated. There is a semi-circular bay on the east side, and a single room on each floor, the top one with fine plaster and shell work. From the cellar a passageway leads directly to the beach, ideal for smuggling. This utterly irresistible building is now the property of the Landmark Trust.

### Easton

*28; 3 miles NE of Winchester off B3047*

ST MARY'S is an entirely Norman church (though the top of the west tower was altered by Woodyer in the 1860s). The excitement of the church lies in its chancel, with its finely moulded rib-vaulted square bay and rib-vaulted apse separated by an elegant arch with four orders of slender shafts. The arch into the chancel is also decorated with much finesse.

## Eversley

*29; 7½ miles SE of Reading on A327*

The plain brick ST MARY'S CHURCH is almost certainly by John James, who lived at – and also built – Warbrook House close by. Only the chancel is some two centuries older. The pretty painted screen has lilies said to have been designed by Charles Kingsley, who was rector here and of whom there is a rather alarming bas-relief in the north aisle, added in his memory in 1876. WARBROOK HOUSE is now a conference centre; any beauty it may have had is lost.

## Fordingbridge

*30; 6 miles N of Ringwood on A338*

The pride of ST MARY'S, a basically thirteenth-century church, is its north chapel, which has a fine fifteenth-century hammer-beam roof with tie-beams and queen-posts, carved angels zooming from the hammers and cusped arches below. There are big bosses carved into human heads and vegetable motifs, and a glorious Royal Arms of George I.

## Hale Park

*31; 4 miles NE of Fordingbridge off B3080*

Thomas Archer bought Hale Park in 1715 and two years later began remodelling the early seventeenth-century ST MARY'S CHURCH nearby, giving it transepts for the first time with the most curious (though distinctly Archerish) north and south doors. The pink-washed house with its giant Ionic portico may also retain some of Archer's work, but it was largely rebuilt by Holland in the 1770s.

## Hartley Wespall

*32; 6 miles NE of Basingstoke off A33*

The outside west wall of ST MARY'S CHURCH is stunning – timber-framed in a uniquely quirkish pattern, each of the timbers roughly cusped like gigantic dethorned rose stalks. The nave roof, with tie-beams and kingposts, is of the same date – about 1330. The rest is nearly all George Gilbert Scott and need not long detain us.

## Highcliffe Castle

*33; 6 miles W of Lymington on A337*

A tremendous Gothic pile, remodelled by William Donthorn in the 1830s and incorporating magnificent chunks of French Late Gothic and Early Renaissance from the Grande Maison des Andelys, Highcliffe Castle must have been splendid indeed to look upon in its day. Now, alas, much of the roof has gone and the fragments of hammer-beam glimpsed through the broken tracery give a feeling of sad – though undeniably romantic – desolation.

## Milford-on-Sea

*34; 3 miles SW of Lymington on B3058*

ALL SAINTS is inland and should be visited by all lovers of Early English architecture. It is almost completely of the late thirteenth century, its style derived from Christchurch Priory, Dorset. Only the south arcade and the end walls of the transept remain from the preceding late Norman church. With a roughcast exterior, it has wide aisles, windows of two or three or stepped three lights, a contemporary south porch and barrel- and rib-vaulted roofs.

## Odiham

*35; 7½ miles E of Basingstoke on A287*

*Includes King Henry's Hunting Lodge (NT)*

This charming town has plenty of good buildings in the High Street – notably the PRIORY, an interesting mixture of the fifteenth, sixteenth and eighteenth centuries. Just outside, a mile or so to the north-west, the remains of the early thirteenth-century NORTH WARNBOROUGH CASTLE comprise one of the only two octagonal keeps in England (the other is at Chilham, in Kent). But the palm, for my money, must go to KING HENRY'S HUNTING LODGE (or, as some have it, King John's), a Georgian eye-catcher in the woods to the east with three immense shaped gables almost as big as the house itself.

## Portsmouth

*36; 19 miles SW of Petersfield on A3*

There is much to see, but the visits are somehow unsatisfying. The CATHEDRAL goes back to 1180, but has been altered, restored, and more recently extended till it has lost all its atmosphere. The ROYAL GARRISON CHURCH is almost as old, but it too has suffered – not least by a very thorough restoration by Street in 1866. HM DOCKYARD is well worth a visit, but security regulations are endlessly frustrating. For an off-beat bonus, however, you might enjoy a quick look at Sir Ninian Comper's CHURCH OF ST PHILIP, Hawthorn Crescent, in the suburb of Cosham. It has white-painted vaulting on simplified Corinthian columns and an ornate *baldacchino* painted with angels and stars – a bit hygienic, but not without a certain quirkish splendour.

## Titchfield

*37; 8½ miles SE of Southampton off A27*

ST PETER'S CHURCH is noteworthy for the lower part of its tower, which is Anglo-Saxon and may go back as far as the eighth century. It was originally built as a west porch, in which capacity it still serves. Half a mile to the north of the village stood TITCHFIELD ABBEY, which soon after the Dissolution was converted into a mansion by Thomas Wriothesley, Earl of Southampton. Of this mansion the Gatehouse still stands, with parts of its two flanking wings – a shell, but a magnificent one.

## Wolverton

*38; 6 miles NW of Basingstoke off A339*

ST CATHERINE'S was built in 1717, and it is the best early Georgian church in Hampshire. The material is red brick with dressings of a darker brick, almost purple, but the proportions follow those of an earlier church whose medieval wooden roof is still in position. Inside, curious crooked screens separate transepts from crossing. It is an oddity, but an attractive and an intriguing one.

# Hertfordshire

If Hertfordshire were 100 miles from London instead of on its doorstep, what a delightful county it would be. Nothing very exciting, of course – it could never be that; but green and undulating, quietly unassuming and somehow restful. In the days of Thomas Fuller it was commonly said that 'such who buy a house in Hertfordshire pay two years' purchase for the air thereof'; but those days are over. The south and west of the county, linked to the capital through Baker Street Station and the Metropolitan Railway, have been known by the uninspiring appellation of Metroland for the best part of a century; and with every year, Green Belt or no Green Belt, suburbia creeps further.

This very proximity to the Great Wen, however, confers on Hertfordshire two appreciable blessings. The first is the absence of any major industrial town: the three largest, Watford, Stevenage and Hemel Hempstead, all have under 80,000 inhabitants at the time of writing, while the population of Hertford, the county town, numbers less than 20,000. This is not to say that you will ever find vast expanses of unspoilt countryside – the M1 and the A1 and their countless capillaries have put paid to that – but it does mean that much of the population still lives in small towns and villages, and that the concrete jungle is consequently a good deal less dense than you might expect. Even along its southern rim, there are few places in the county more than ten minutes' drive from a good place for a picnic.

The second blessing is the number of fine country houses built between the sixteenth and nineteenth centuries. One of them, Hatfield, is among the great show places of England; if only Theobalds, for which James I exchanged the Old Palace of Hatfield and in which he died, had also been allowed to survive! Alas, it was torn down in 1651, less than a century after its construction – according to Fuller, 'for the better partage of the soldiery'. Thus, he continues, 'from the seat of a monarch, [it] has now become a little commonwealth; so many entire tenements, like splinters, have flown out of the materials thereof'. Nor is Theobalds the only casualty; and the official vandalism of the past thirty years has cut a further terrible swathe through the fine buildings of Hertfordshire. Panshanger, for example, was demolished as recently as 1953; and those merciless fifties also saw the disappearance of two wonderful old inns that I remember with much affection – the Bell at Berkhamsted and the Swan at Rickmansworth. But much remains, nonetheless: no county that can boast such places as Ashridge, Gorhambury, Brocket Hall, Moor Park, Knebworth, Wrotham Park and that stunning confidence trick, Beechwood, need feel underprivileged.

Except in one respect . . . for Hertfordshire possesses no real cathedral. St Albans, though from the earliest times one of the most influential monasteries in the country, only achieved cathedral status in 1877; architecturally, in any case, it is a mess. But there are plenty of beautiful, if unsensational, parish churches, from early Norman at Bengeo – perhaps the most surprising survival in the county – to late Lutyens (completed by Sir Albert Richardson) at St Martin's, Knebworth. My own personal favourite is the irresistible piece of eighteenth-century high jinks at St Paul's Walden; the contrast between the two neighbouring churches of Ayot St Lawrence and Ayot St Peter is another pleasure not to be missed.

Churches, even more than secular buildings, suffer in Hertfordshire from one of the county's chief drawbacks where architecture is concerned: the lack of any good stone. Chalk clunch there is in quantity – though much of it actually comes from Totternhoe, a mile or two over the Bedfordshire border – but it is soft, friable, and tragically vulnerable to atmospheric pollution. The principal local materials are consequently flint and, above all, brick – occasionally 'white' (actually a sort of pale khaki) but usually a good rich red that looks as if it had been storing up sunshine for generations. The best of it can often be seen in the seventeenth- and eighteenth-century houses in the towns and villages; more than anything else, it gives the county its character. And that character is still strong – stronger by far than most people think as they hurtle through on rail or motorway. Hertfordshire may be Metroland; but it is much else besides.

## Anstey

*1; 7 miles SE of Royston off B1368*

ST GEORGE'S CHURCH is set high above the village, over which it exudes an air of considerable authority with its late Norman crossing-tower, the effect of which is not appreciably lessened by its 'Hertfordshire spike', a local idiosyncrasy which can all too easily look ridiculous. The tower and transepts are of knapped flints, the nave and chancel rendered, and the south transept has a little round stair turret and nice thirteenth-century lancets, which compare interestingly with the slightly later two-light windows on the south side of the chancel.

The south porch, though a relatively recent addition – 1475 or so – must have been lovely; it is now sadly worn, but don't miss those curious grotesque label stops. Inside, we find ourselves in a slightly crude, rustic church of much charm. The eye is immediately caught by the Norman crossing – four narrow round-headed arches forming a square – which Pevsner dates at about 1200; if he is right, the church must have been rather old-fashioned at the outset, since by this date the Early English style was in full swing. The chancel and transept are, by contrast, nearly a century later, and the chancel in particular is full of interest; note another pair of label stops on the north doorway, and some splendid misericords – still a little clumsy perhaps, being among the earliest in the country, but none the worse for that.

The nave shows regrettable signs of Butterfield's restoration in 1869–72, a visitation from which the rest of the church seems to have escaped surprisingly lightly; but it too boasts a rare treasure, compared to which even the misericords look sophisticated: a wonderfully barbaric Norman font with fork-tailed mermen.

*Ashridge.*

## Ashridge

*2; 3½ miles N of Berkhamsted off A41*

Most spectacularly set – as its name implies – on a high ridge of the Chilterns just outside the village of Little Gaddesden, Ashridge is surrounded by National Trust woodland and heathland and further embellished by glorious gardens which were originally laid out by Capability Brown and then remodelled by Repton early in the last century. The house itself is, in its way, equally spectacular: Gothic baronial at its most unbridled. It was built, on the site of a former monastery that had been converted to a mansion in Tudor times, between 1808 and 1814 to the design of James Wyatt on the instructions of the 7th Earl of Bridgewater; when Wyatt was killed in a carriage accident in 1813 his nephew Jeffrey (later Sir Jeffrey Wyatville) took over and continued the work with signal success.

The building, of the local Totternhoe chalk stone, is enormously long and straggling, with interior courtyards. The two salient features are the squat, square tower built over the main staircase and, further to the west, the stepped-back tower of the Chapel, topped by a tall dark spire. Between and beyond, all is calculated romantic confusion – but confusion on the grand scale. To see just how grand, all you have to do is to enter the main Hall, from which a monumental double staircase, with cast-iron railings of vaguely Perpendicular design, sweeps up across three sides to form a full-length gallery along the fourth. (From here there is an impressive view down on to the entrance lobby, which has a hammer-beam roof.) At this level, on all four sides, run arcades of four-centred arches with heavily and ornately canopied statues by Westmacott at the corners. There follows a fan-vaulted ceiling, and a lantern above that. The whole thing is conceived on the grandest possible scale and comes off sensationally well.

Since the house is now a management college many of the rooms have inevitably suffered. There are, however, several first-floor rooms which remain well worth a visit. Easily the most grandiose – though not the most beautiful – is the Drawing Room, now the Conference Room. This was remodelled in 1860 by Sir Matthew Digby Wyatt, who gave it a copy of Guido Reni's *Aurora* ceiling and simply tremendous doorcases of free-standing marble columns and broken segmental pediments. Far prettier is the Ante-Room, with its huge Gothic windows reaching to the ground and the wood carving in the style of Gibbons. There is also an imposing Library, again by Sir Matthew. But perhaps the most memorable of all is the Chapel, tall, apsed and fan-vaulted, with an ante-chapel opening up into the tower. Fonthill, one feels, could hardly have been better.

Although architecture more unsuitable for the study of advanced business techniques could hardly be imagined, Ashridge is perhaps the most superb example of romantic Gothic Revival in the country. It should not be missed.

*New St Lawrence's Church, Ayot St Lawrence.*

## Ashwell

*3; 4 miles N of Baldock off A505*

ST MARY'S merits inclusion here entirely on account of its west tower, the grandest of any parish church in the county. It has four stages, diminishing slightly in size, and is crowned by a tall octagonal lantern with a spike. It was built in the first half of the fourteenth century, shortly before the Black Death; and the graffiti on the inside walls still send a shiver down the spine: '*MCter X penta miseranda ferox violenta . . . superest plebs pessima testis*' – '1350, wretched, wild, violent . . . the dregs of the people live to tell the tale.'

Unusually, the church seems to have been started at the west end, with the building continuing towards the east until its completion in 1381. It is long and spacious, with an extended chancel, the whole thing very light, airy and generous-looking, yet at the same time austere and faintly lacking in character.

## Ayot St Lawrence*

*4; 3 miles NW of Welwyn Garden City off A6129*
*Includes Shaw's Corner (NT)*

For most people, Ayot St Lawrence means Bernard Shaw; but over SHAW'S CORNER (NT), where he lived for forty-four years and which now has the distinction of being the National Trust's most hideous property, it is kinder to draw a veil. Nor is there very much to be said about the OLD CHURCH OF ST LAWRENCE, which has been in ruins since Sir Lyonel Lyde, lord of the manor in the 1770s, found that it obstructed the view from his house and decided to pull it down. He had already removed the roof when the bishop ordered the demolition work to be stopped; but the damage was never repaired, and Sir Lyonel, his plans thwarted, could at least console himself with a picturesque Gothick ruin which was fortunately the height of fashion.

Meanwhile, he commissioned Nicholas Revett, recently returned from Athens and Asia Minor, to build a NEW ST LAWRENCE'S both as a replacement of the old one and as an eye-catcher. The result is a little neo-classical gem, with side colonnades and little aedicules at the ends, Sir Lyonel's urn tomb in one and his wife's in the other – after years of marital discord he directed that, since the Church had united them in life, it should make amends by separating them in death. The interior is quite plain, with transepts so short as to be scarcely worthy of the name and a nice semi-circular apse with deep alcoves suggesting an ambulatory, though on closer inspection they prove not to be connected. The floor is of black and white marble in a lozenge pattern, the ceilings of nave and apse coffered.

Notice, as you come out, the way the columns are fluted for 2–3 inches at top and bottom. This curious feature, which Revett copied from the Temple of Apollo at Delos, also appears in the porch that he built for Standlynch – now Trafalgar (*q.v.*) – in Wiltshire.

(If the church is locked, the key is to be found in the little white house opposite.)

*St Peter's Church, Ayot St Peter.*

## Ayot St Peter

*5; 2 miles NW of Welwyn Garden City off A6129*

A most remarkable Victorian church of 1874–5 by J.P. Seddon, ST PETER'S IS wilfully eccentric on the outside, with a diaper and cross pattern in red, white and blue brick, a tower whose shape defies description, and a clock whose blue and white mosaic face must be one of the oddest anywhere. So far, it is hard indeed to take the church seriously. Inside, however, the mood is very different: the decoration and furnishings are all of a piece, combining to produce a perfect example of how the Arts and Crafts movement influenced church interiors around 1880. Notice in particular the ceramic chancel arch (by the Martin brothers), the trefoil-shaped painted roof, the tilework in the chancel, and the curved communion rail which forms a complete circle with the apse.

## Balls Park

*6; 1 mile SE of Hertford off A414*

Lying in extensive grounds, Balls Park now forms part of the Hertfordshire College of Education. The general atmosphere is distinctly institutional, but the exterior presents much the same appearance as it did when it was built in the early 1640s. The architect is uncertain; Peter Mills is a strong possibility, Nicholas Stone another; there are obvious links with Tyttenhanger and with Mills's Thorpe Hall in Cambridgeshire (*qq.v.*).

It is an extraordinary house in many ways; and nothing, perhaps, is more extraordinary than the main entrance to the north. Whereas virtually all the rest of the house is of brick in the full 'Artisan Mannerist' tradition this entrance is of stone, but the Tuscan pilasters are partly superimposed on Ionic pilasters of brick. As these latter are also a little higher, the result is Tuscan capitals running directly into Ionic ones immediately above but a little to one side, which in turn give way to a pair of outsize corbels supporting a one-bay balcony to the floor above. The door itself has an arch which reaches only to the bottom of the Tuscan capitals, and the space between it and the underside of the balcony has been rather dottily filled by a vertical panel with another squat little pilaster carved on it in relief.

Despite this and other similar eccentricities, the two-storey house is nicely proportioned, confident and comfortable-looking, with a hipped roof, characteristically deep eaves and small one-bay central pediments. Inside there is a spacious central Hall (probably once an open court), a Long Gallery running the length of the east side and some rather good plasterwork. A funny, wayward house; one could grow very fond of it.

## Bengeo*

*7; 1 mile N of Hertford*

ST LEONARD'S CHURCH is one of those breathtaking surprises of which the Home Counties are still so blessedly full. The curiously named village has now been engulfed by Hertford; who would have thought to find, bang in the middle, a little Norman church of flint and rubble, practically unspoilt, of the early twelfth century? There have been one or two changes, none very serious: the later windows on the south side, for example, the south porch – beneath which, however, there is a door which probably goes back to Saxon times – and the Victorian bell-cote; but the church remains in essence what is always was, an aisleless nave leading to a deeply apsed chancel.

Inside, the chancel arch with its oddly matched capitals – a scroll on one side, a man's face on the other – also looks suspiciously like Saxon work and, together with the north and south doors, leads one to believe that a still earlier church must have stood on the same site. Just to the north of it, on the east wall of the nave, is a thirteenth-century wall painting of the Deposition. It is not quite complete, but what remains is in remarkably good condition. But then the whole church is an extraordinary survival, well worth the effort of finding it and even the hunt round the neighbouring houses for the key.

## Brocket Hall

*8; 1½ miles NW of Welwyn Garden City off A6129*

Few country houses in England provide such dramatic contrast between outside and inside. Brocket Hall is superlatively sited on an eminence above the River Lea, which broadens out beneath it into a lake, yet the house itself – which was built by James Paine in the 1760s – is quite exceptionally restrained. This is not to say that it is unimpressive; but it makes its effect by its position, by the long approach through a fine and spacious park and by its considerable size, rather than by any extravagance in its exterior decoration. What we see is, essentially, just a large square block of red brick, without a portico, without stone quoins or more than a minimum of stone dressings anywhere. The original design was for two and a half storeys, but a smaller additional storey was added in such a way as to cover the three central bays of the entrance front and the five central bays of the show front to the west. These five bays are also marked by five tall arched windows which denote the Saloon; beyond them at each end are the canted bay windows which were one of Paine's specialities. Even these, however, are almost aggressively plain and unadorned.

To go inside is suddenly to enter another world. Here are opulence and splendour on every side. There is a lovely Staircase Hall, with double stairs running up to a colonnaded gallery, lit by an elliptical glass dome; a ravishing little Library; and a Saloon that is distinctly palatial, with a coved ceiling painted and gilded. Most of the other ceilings in the state rooms are of the slightly later style we associate with Robert Adam, picked out in plasterwork of the greatest possible delicacy and finesse.

Paine also provided a bridge at the south end of the lake – not Palladian, but undeniably elegant.

## Gorhambury

*9; 2 miles W of St Albans off A414*

This imposing Palladian mansion, built between 1777 and 1784 by Sir Robert Taylor at the behest of the 3rd Viscount Grimston, has been completely refaced in the past quarter of a century. Where for the first 180 years of its life it wore a dress of the local Totternhoe clunch, it has now been reclad in Portland stone, and very splendid it looks. Clearly determined to make the greatest impact he could in the flat Hertfordshire countryside, Taylor gave Gorhambury a tremendous Corinthian portico, raised on a high plinth for still greater effect, leading directly into a huge square Hall – the black and white floor of which, together with the superb sixteenth-century glass that occupies much of the left-hand wall, came from the Tudor house built nearby in the 1560s and 1570s by Sir Nicholas Bacon, elder brother of the famous Sir Francis.

The garden front, looking out across the fields to the ruins of Sir Nicholas's house, is rather more restrained: here the portico is of attached Corinthian columns covering the three central bays, from which a double flight of steps curves down past the rusticated lower floor to the ground. Originally, the house had side wings in the approved Palladian style, connected to the centre by low linking buildings; these were, however, demolished early in the last century, when a two-storey extension was built at the north end. The symmetry suffers, but life has been made much easier for the present Lord Verulam and his family, who live in it, as a result.

The principal state rooms are perhaps more notable for their furniture and pictures than for their architecture. They include two superb fireplaces by Piranesi, in the Yellow Drawing Room and the Library respectively.

*The Staircase Hall, Brocket Hall.*

## Hatfield House*

*10; 21 miles N of London off A1*

Hatfield is the Cecils; the Cecils are Hatfield. No great country house has seen more of our history in the making; no family has done more to direct that history. Between 1558 and 1903, for almost one year in five, England had a Cecil at the helm; and throughout the present century, as two more heads of this remarkable family have risen to high ministerial office, Hatfield has maintained its pre-eminence – a house in which every room has served at one time or another as a council chamber, and every passage as a corridor of power.

It was begun in 1607 by Robert Cecil, who had succeeded his father, the great Lord Burghley, as chief minister to Queen Elizabeth I and was now serving – just as conscientiously but with considerably less enthusiasm – James I in the same capacity. Barely five years later it was finished, its date of completion, 1611, triumphantly proclaimed in stone above the south porch. But the historical importance of Hatfield was already established long before this. The Old Palace – one wing of which, containing the Banqueting Hall, still stands 100 yards away to the north-west, perhaps the finest example of medieval brickwork remaining in the country – had been expropriated by Henry VIII from the Bishops of Ely and used by him as a country home for his children. It was here that Edward VI, Mary and Elizabeth all grew up; here, too, under an oak tree whose sad remains are preserved in the park, that Elizabeth was told of her accession to the throne.

When Cecil received the Old Palace from James I in exchange for his father's property at Theobalds, it proved nowhere near grand enough for the most powerful, and probably one of the richest, of the King's subjects. The same could not be said of its successor. Here was a mansion in which a fine nobleman – Cecil had recently been created Earl of Salisbury – could receive his sovereign in a style befitting them both. In its essentials, Hatfield still looks much as it did in his day, the great Jacobean mansion *par excellence*, embellished and enriched by immense marble fireplaces – one of which is crowned by a near life-size statue of King James – and superb woodwork, seen at its best in the Hall screens and, above all, in the Grand Staircase, the virtuoso showpiece of the house. Admittedly, it possesses one or two features that might have been thought a little old-fashioned: the Long Gallery, for example, would have an Elizabethan air even without the Queen's straw hat and stockings exhibited there, while the Marble Hall – complete with minstrels' gallery – harks back to the Middle Ages, albeit seen through Renaissance eyes. With the south front, however, the Renaissance is upon us in earnest. The two massive wings of traditional brick are joined by an Italianate arcaded range of pale stone, in the centre of which rises a three-storey portico of Doric, Ionic and Corinthian columns superimposed. This is in turn echoed by the white timber clock tower above and behind it.

As originally designed, the arcade was an open loggia; it was closed in, however, in 1846 and became the Armoury. In consequence, just as the Marble Hall is

Jacobean–medieval, so the Armoury is Victorian–Jacobean – its atmosphere heightened by the child's rocking horse which during my last visit occupied a prominent position at one end, from which it could contemplate the 3rd Marquess who is monumentally enthroned at the other.

It was this 3rd Marquess who followed the example of his earlier forebears by becoming Prime Minister of England in 1885 and continuing, with two short interruptions, until he retired in 1902. His interests were scientific as well as political; thanks to him, Hatfield was one of the first houses to boast an internal telephone system and electric light. His grandson, Lord David Cecil, writes in his fascinating family history (*The Cecils of Hatfield House*) of how he enjoyed testing his telephones: 'Unsuspecting visitors . . . would be alarmed to hear, emerging from a mysterious instrument on a neighbouring table, the spectral voice of the Prime Minister intoning "Hey diddle diddle, the cat and the fiddle. . . ."' The electric light was still more alarming: 'The naked uninsulated wires stretched on the ceiling of the Long Gallery would suddenly burst into flames. My grandfather, conversing below, or his sons would nonchalantly toss up a cushion to put the flames out and then resume their conversation.' Hatfield was lucky to survive; we are even luckier that it has.

*Bishop's Palace, Hatfield House.*

## Hemel Hempstead

*11; 5 miles W of St Albans on A414*

A fortunate town, Hemel Hempstead – in that although its population has increased by some 400 per cent since the last war, all this planned expansion took place in a new development area to the south. The old town thus remains largely unspoilt, its HIGH STREET running along the side of quite a steep hill – which is why ST MARY'S CHURCH, though only a few yards away from the street, also stands considerably below it. There are plenty of good houses along its length, both medieval timber-framed and Georgian brick; but the treasure of the town is, as it should be, the church. So tall and slender is the ribbed fourteenth-century spire – rising to nearly 200 feet, it must be twice the height of the tower on which it stands – that one might be forgiven, at first glance, for not realising that the tower, and indeed the whole church, is Norman through and through: the largest Norman parish church in the county. Take a special look at the tower before you go in. Like the rest of the building it is flint with dressings of local clunch; but the top stage in particular is splendidly articulated with its twin shafted bell openings and little circular windows oddly decorated with bold Norman zigzag. There is a round staircase turret on the south-east corner. Look, too, at the splendid west door – first-rate Norman work on both the inside and the out.

The nave is also Norman, of about 1175: six bays, circular piers, scalloped capitals, the first and last arches on each side boldly decorated with more zigzag, and – a great rarity – a contemporary clerestory above. The Norman crossing has survived, the western crossing arch being noticeably horseshoe-shaped – that is, forming slightly more than a semi-circle and looking faintly oriental in consequence. The chancel beyond is of about 1150 – the oldest part of the church – and is rib-vaulted, another rarity for this date. It has, however, been so far altered in succeeding centuries that apart from two broad arches on the north side there is little Norman feeling left. The nineteenth-century 'Perpendicular' east window is a case in point. One feels distinctly sorry for Elizabeth, Lady Cooper, whose memorial it is. She surely deserved better.

Talking of windows, the fourteenth-century windows in the south wall would also be a pity, even if their tracery were genuine, which it isn't. But these are relatively small blemishes. St Mary's remains a magnificent Norman survival, of which its fortunate parishioners must feel proud – and for which the rest of us should be thankful.

## Hitchin

*12; 4½ miles NW of Stevenage on A602*

The CHURCH OF ST MARY is nothing if not grand – powerful testimony to the fourteenth-century prosperity of the town. You only have to look as far as the south porch to see the ambitiousness of the general plan: two storeys, the lower one lierne-vaulted, with a three-light window above the outer door and four niches for statues, two on each side; its own staircase turret; two more three-light traceried windows in the side walls; and an inner door on six orders of colonnettes with a scheme of shafting which merges in directly with the vault above. The rest of the church, heavily embattled, with its low west tower, another staircase turret and the characteristic Hertfordshire spike, keeps up the standard. The interior is similarly generous and comfortable, but it has undergone many tribulations over the centuries. The Puritans did their worst in the seventeenth century and much more fine medieval work disappeared in the eighteenth and nineteenth; the result has been to rob the church of much of its charm. The best things now are the roofs – especially those of the north and south aisles and the Chapel of St Andrew, just to the south of the chancel – and the screens separating this chapel and the corresponding one to the north from their respective aisles. The southern screen in particular, with its frieze of angels, is a joy to behold.

Of the many good secular buildings in the town, the most distinguished is the PRIORY. The original religious foundation was destroyed at the Dissolution, though remnants of the cloister can still be seen in the courtyard to the north; the site is now occupied by a most distinguished small mansion, its south front by Robert Adam. The five-bay central block has a single-bay wing on each side in the Palladian manner; these wings are characterised by broad Venetian windows giving on to the garden, while the centre has a pretty semi-circular porch, supported by two columns and two more half columns. Equally attractive is the way in which the little River Hiz has been turned into an ornamental watercourse and given a most endearing little bridge. Was this also Adam's idea, I wonder?

## Knebworth

*13; 1 mile S of Stevenage off A1*

With one's first view of Knebworth one is faced with such a riot of Gothic romanticism that one tends to overlook the fact that the house began as an early Tudor mansion of about 1490, built around a central quadrangle. Such, in essence, it remained until 1811, when Mrs Elizabeth Bulwer (née Warburton-Lytton) demolished all but one wing – now the west side, through which the visitors enter for their tour; but even this has now been altered almost beyond recognition. Mrs Bulwer's architect was Biagio Rebecca, who worked on the house – or what was left of it – for the next five years, covering the Tudor brick with the more fashionable stucco, Gothicising the windows, and adding towers and battlements with happy abandon.

That, one might have thought, was enough to be getting on with; but when Edward Bulwer-Lytton, the novelist, inherited the house in 1843 he immediately set to work again and with the help of H.E. Kendall Jun. transformed the house yet again to something resembling its present almost unbelievable appearance, enabling it to take its place among the most ebullient monuments of Victorian fantasy like Harlaxton, Bear Wood, or its nearer neighbour, Ashridge.

Only in its interior does the house reveal its early origins, and even then not at once, since the Entrance Hall is largely the creation of Sir Edwin Lutyens, the 1st Earl of Lytton's son-in-law. From here, however, you pass to the Banqueting Hall, and at once the secret is out, for this was clearly the Great Hall of the 1490 house. It is now a mixture of styles: the carved oak screen with its caryatids and the coved plaster ceiling criss-crossed with wooden beams are Jacobean; the superb panelling with its Corinthian columns and pilasters in wood and elaborate pediments – that at the dais end enclosing a tall round-headed arch – are of about 1700 and attributed to Talman; while with other less distinguished features, including the Dining Room chairs and the slightly dotty poem by Edward Bulwer-Lytton inscribed around the cornice, we are firmly back in Victorian England.

The High Victorian taste continues (after we have passed through the White Drawing Room and Library, in which the hand of Lutyens is once again apparent) in the tremendous pseudo-Jacobean staircase, designed by John Crace for Bulwer-Lytton, the newel-posts surmounted by Nubian slaves at the foot and, at the upper levels, by lions bearing armorial shields. Off the landing is the little room used by the poet as his Study, after which we are ready for what is, after the Banqueting Hall, Knebworth's greatest pride: the State Drawing Room. Here is Crace at his most exuberant and inventive: the armorially painted ceiling and frieze, the stained-glass window of King Henry VII, the intricate chimneypiece rising the whole height of the wall, the specially designed furniture and the chandelier all combine to produce a vision of Gothic splendour which may or may not appeal but which can scarcely fail to impress. Virtually unaltered since the day it was created, it is also a historical monument in itself – one of the most extraordinary survivals in the country of the fashionable interior decoration of the 1840s.

Of the remaining rooms the most interesting is the room named after Queen Elizabeth I, with its plaster ceiling, ornate panelling and simply terrific Great Bed. If the Queen did not sleep here – the tradition is unsubstantiated – she certainly should have.

## Moor Park*

*14; 3 miles SW of Watford off A4145*

It was in 1720 that Benjamin Styles, a London merchant who had made a colossal fortune out of the South Sea Bubble, bought Moor Park, a large seventeenth-century mansion of brick, surrounded by one of the most celebrated gardens in England, that had formerly belonged to the Duke of Monmouth. It was not, however, grand enough for Styles, who forthwith engaged Sir James Thornhill to remodel it completely. Thornhill was in some ways a curious choice, since

*Knebworth.*

although he was widely recognised as the finest painter in England – and had indeed just been appointed Sergeant Painter to the King – he had only recently begun to take an active interest in architecture and had never yet designed a major building. The transformed house, for all that, is nothing if not confident. Perhaps because it sits low in a dell – the great park is now a golf course – Thornhill has sought to emphasise its height by giving it a tremendous portico on the entrance front, with four giant Corinthian columns soaring up the full two and a half storeys to a richly decorated pediment. The effect of this vertical emphasis would, it is true, have been to some extent mitigated by the two Palladian side pavilions, linked by long curving colonnades, which formed part of his original design; but these were demolished at the end of the eighteenth century and the house looks faintly disproportionate as a result. On the garden side, where the portico is engaged, the effect is happier. The whole building, from the rusticated ground floor to the parapet around the roof, is encased in Portland stone.

The front door leads directly into the main Hall, a 40-foot cube rising the whole height of the house, reminding one of Clandon or Houghton, although it is infinitely more ornate than either of them. A gallery, supported on heavy voluted brackets, runs round all four sides; four large canvases by Amigoni, depicting the story of Juno and the peacock, are surrounded by garlands held by dancing *putti*; the magnificent doorcases have almost life-size figures reclining upon their pediments; scarcely an inch is left undecorated. The ceiling, too, is something of a *tour de force*: the central roundel presents, in *trompe-l'oeil*, an imaginary view up into a lantern with a circular gallery around it and figures looking down over the edge.

Behind the Hall, the Saloon is the one room of the house which was kept largely unaltered from the Duke of Monmouth's day; it includes another painted ceiling, of Apollo this time, thought to be by Verrio, and two tremendous chimneypieces with giant caryatids. The staircase, too, is painted all the way up, but is yet more remarkable for its curious shape, running as it does round all four walls of the well and ending on a long landing covering the whole of one wall and half of another. Once on the upper floor one can go out on to the Hall Gallery, adorned with mythological figures set in *grisaille trompe-l'oeil* niches; everything is as ornate as downstairs, though much is invisible therefrom.

These upper paintings are by Sleter, and the question inevitably arises: why did Thornhill, the greatest mural painter of his day, leave all the painting of his only major house to other, lesser, artists? The answer seems to be that Thornhill did in fact provide paintings for Hall and Gallery, but that after an acrimonious lawsuit with Styles in 1728 he refused to release them. Thenceforth the work on the house and its decoration may have been supervised by Giacomo Leoni, to whom the whole mansion was for long attributed, despite the fact that the relevant plates in Vol. V of *Vitruvius Britannicus* (1771) clearly bear Thornhill's name.

The last showpiece of the house is the Ballroom, which seems to have been decorated by Robert Adam (whom we know to have been responsible for the gateway and tea pavilion in the park). Its compartmented ceiling with Pompeian decorations is the work of Cipriani, and very nice too.

## Much Hadham

*15; 4 miles SW of Bishop's Stortford on B1004*

Much loved, much admired and much visited – especially by pilgrims to the shrine of Henry Moore – Much Hadham is architecturally the most interesting village in Hertfordshire. Walking down the long and rather straggly main street, one is brought up short time and time again by houses of real distinction: by THE LORDSHIP, for example, built in the 1740s with its own stable block, or by NORTH LEYS (Georgian too, of chequered brick) or by sixteenth- and seventeenth-century buildings ranging from quite grand residences like WOODHAM HOUSE to cottages of no pretension at all, timber-framed and weather-boarded. Just about halfway down stands MUCH HADHAM HALL with its hipped roof and big Venetian window, built in 1726–9, possibly by John James. To the south, towards the war memorial, THE WHITE HOUSE is a delightful essay in early nineteenth-century Gothic which conceals in an upper room, surprisingly enough, a wall painting of 1600.

Just west of the war memorial is the entrance to MOOR PLACE; though it was originally no bigger than several buildings in the village, its position in its small park immediately makes it a country house – and a very beautiful one too. According to the date over the front door it was completed in 1779, the architect being a certain Robert Mitchell – a Scotsman who, on the evidence of Moor Place, should be a good deal better known than he is. The house as he built it – and as it still stands, although it has been considerably enlarged since his day – is almost exactly square, with an elevation of just five bays on two main storeys plus a basement and an attic, the dormers of which are barely visible behind a balustraded parapet. It is of a lovely pale pinkish brick, with stone dressings; but this stone is used very sparingly, particularly on the entrance front, where the most striking feature is the row of five tall round-headed blank arches within which are set the lower windows and front door. On the east (garden) front, stone is used as a frame for the windows on both main floors. There are no quoins. Both doors, to east and west, have beautiful fanlights – particularly that on the garden side where the open fan shape is continued through 360 degrees to form an elliptical spider's web of exquisite elegance and delicacy.

The Entrance Hall with its frieze of rams' heads leads directly through into the Staircase Hall. It is here above all that Mitchell is determined to show us what he can do – and very impressive it is. The stairs with their lovely ironwork balustrade rise up on three sides, to a landing beneath a shallow coffered arch. On the inside of this is a screen of fluted Ionic columns, behind which a passage leads to two of the main bedrooms. Similar screens and galleries occupy the other three sides, and the light floods down from a circular lantern above. The walls have recently been painted a rich reddish orange which sets off the white stucco to perfection.

From this Hall lead off all the principal rooms of Mitchell's house. These are, on the ground floor, the Drawing Room on the garden front, with french windows and that marvellous fanlight; the Dining Room, with its ravishing chimneypiece adorned with urns and sphinxes; and the west-facing Library with an early nineteenth-century bookcase which was clearly made for it. The fourth room, which was originally designed as a Library, has now been converted into cloakrooms.

The only other major changes since Mitchell's day have been the extensions to north and south. Of these, the latter is by far the most important – a long L-shaped wing in almost identical style added in 1907 by Sir Ernest Newton for nurseries and kitchen. The northern extension is a tiny little single-storey office, hardly more imposing than a brick-built garden shed; it comes as a considerable surprise to learn that it actually had an architect, and that that architect was Norman Shaw; one wonders why he was hired – and, indeed, why he agreed to take on the job.

The beautiful stable block to the south with its weight-driven clock and pretty white lantern dates from the early eighteenth century and is consequently a good deal earlier than the house. It was in fact built for the previous Moor Place, which lay a little to the east of the present building and was replaced by it.

Before we leave Much Hadham, a word should be said about ST ANDREW'S CHURCH. It is a bit of a hotch-potch, with work easily recognisable from the thirteenth, fourteenth and fifteenth centuries. Despite a nice timber roof, finely carved stone corbels supporting the wall posts and two small patches of early wall painting above the north arcade, it somehow seems to lack character. Do not, however, miss the two big label stops on the west door of the tower – a gift to the church from Henry Moore in 1953.

## North Mymms House

*16; 1½ miles SW of Hatfield off A1*

Although much enlarged by Edward Blore and others during the last century, North Mymms House remains a remarkably fine late Tudor mansion in a lovely mellow diapered brick. The south front suffers somewhat from the later additions, which include the central bay window, and the corridors to the north and east wings which have turned the courtyard into a narrow, measly sort of affair; but the north is unchanged, with its double-transomed windows of four and five lights and pure round-headed entrance porch, the whole rigidly symmetrical. There are stone dressings, a low parapet, and pinnacled gables looking out over an unspoilt park. Alas, at the time of my visit the house had just come into new ownership and I was unable to see inside.

## Queen Hoo Hall*

*17; 3½ miles NW of Hertford off B1000*

Don't be misled by the star. You will find nothing spectacular at Queen Hoo Hall – which, at the time of writing, is anyway not open to the public. What earns this relatively modest Elizabethan manor house its distinction is the fact that it has survived virtually unchanged for the past 420-odd years. The show front, insofar as it has one, looks out on to the garden: two gently projecting wings with corbelled-out gables, each adorned with three honeycomb finials, but nothing at the centre to form the more usual E-plan. Everything is symmetrical except the windows. The material is brick throughout, including the mullions: a rich, darkish red except for the blue diapering along the upper half. The entrance front has three big chimneybreasts, each carrying a pair of tallish brick chimneys, square but diagonally set in the Tudor fashion.

The interior is as unspoilt as the outside. Even the original doors are still on their hinges, many with pretty carved linenfold decoration; the original staircase too, built round four posts, the old treads wonderfully scratched and scored by nine or ten generations of feet; also, if I am not much mistaken, an original bed. One of the first-floor bedrooms even has some contemporary wall paintings: a pretty frieze going all the way round, with some warriors on horses in one corner and King Solomon worshipping false gods over the chimneypiece.

From the upper rooms, and even from the garden, there is a breathtaking view over Hertfordshire – miles and miles with scarcely a single house in view, a sight almost as astonishing as the house itself.

*Queen Hoo Hall.*

## St Albans

*18; 5 miles E of Hemel Hempstead on A6 (take A414 off M1)*

The site of the first martyrdom to take place on British soil is marked by ST ALBANS CATHEDRAL; but alas, among all the medieval cathedrals of England it is perhaps the least inspiring. Even distance lends no real enchantment: it immediately strikes one as being disproportionately long for its height, crying out in vain for west towers, or a spire, or something apart from that broad, squat tower to give it a little verticality. As you approach, you notice too that the materials are equally unsatisfactory. Basically the building is of flint, strengthened by small Roman bricks from the nearby ruins of Verulamium. The ratio of brick to flint increases rapidly towards the crossing, and the tower is almost exclusively of brick. The overall effect is therefore somewhat messy, and the detailing distinctly coarse. Nor is this all; on top of its other misfortunes, the cathedral has also had to suffer the ministrations of that most disastrous of amateur architects, Edmund Beckett Denison, 1st Baron Grimthorpe.

To be fair to Grimthorpe, it must be admitted that he saved the structure; appearing at a time when it was on the verge of collapse and there were no funds to save it, he immediately stepped into the breach and, in return for complete control over the work, spent over a quarter of a million pounds of his own money on its restoration. But St Albans paid dearly for its rescue, particularly at its extremities: five gigantic lancets to close off the south transept, a so-called 'banker's window' in the north, in which the small circular openings were designed to correspond with the sizes of the various coins current at the time – yes, honestly – and a new west front of an ineptitude and ugliness bordering on the grotesque. Within, too, the lethal hand of Lord G. shows itself on every side. He is visually commemorated in his own west porch, peeping out of a spandrel in the unlikely guise of St Matthew; it is hard to know whether to wreathe him in garlands or pelt him with tomatoes.

The first church was erected in the early fourth century, within a few years of Alban's death, but the oldest work now remaining is of the late eleventh, when Paul of Caen, nephew of the great Archbishop Lanfranc, assumed charge of the abbey and began at once to rebuild it on a considerably larger scale. By 1088 it was finished. Today, the surviving Norman sections, notably the crossing arches and the first nine bays to the west on the north side of the nave, show that Paul and his men did a pretty crude job. There is none of the grandeur or nobility here that one finds, for example, at Waltham, 20-odd miles away. It was not their fault; with irregular flints and second-hand Roman bricks they could hardly hope to do much better. But the eye finds little consolation along those rough plaster walls, and the heart is sad.

Just over a century later, however, in the 1190s, things took a turn for the better. By this time the shrine of St Alban was attracting pilgrims from all over England and the abbey could afford to import good-quality stone. Surprisingly, Abbot John de Cella started his rebuilding at the west end; indeed, he started beyond it, adding three additional western bays and then working steadily eastward in the Early English style then current. He made no effort to harmonise with the Norman work; the new Gothic arcades were taller than their predecessors, so that both the triforium and the clerestory were pitched at higher levels. There was nothing wrong with that – he intended that by the time he had finished there should be nothing Norman left.

The trouble was that he never did finish. After five bays had been completed on one side and four on the other, the work ground to a halt. The result, particularly on the north side, is disastrous, as if two completely different churches had been stuck together by mistake. To the south, the situation is a good deal better, thanks to the five untouched Norman bays having collapsed of their own accord in 1323. By then, of course, the Early English style had given way to the Decorated; but the new bays that were built – by a still richer abbey – in the mid-fourteenth century accord pleasantly enough with their neighbours, constituting, with the Lady Chapel, by far the most distinguished part of the building as it stands today. Nonetheless the nave remains, as a whole, fairly muddled, and is not helped by a dull, flat, nineteenth-century wooden roof. Even some excellent medieval wall paintings on certain columns and piers cannot altogether redeem it, and it is with something like relief that one passes through the endearingly off-centre fourteenth-century stone screen to the choir. This at least is all of a piece, even though that piece dates from about 1900, with much polychrome decoration.

Just beyond the crossing to the east is the presbytery, and beyond that the shrine of St Alban himself – or what remains of it. It was vandalistically destroyed at the Dissolution in 1539, but some 2,000 small pieces of it were rediscovered in 1872 and as many as possible of these have been reassembled to give at least some idea of what it was like. Near it to the north is the Watching Chamber: a sort of wooden screen, with loft, of about 1400, from which a hidden monk kept an eye on the pilgrims. Along the beam is carved a pretty little series representing the labours of the months, to keep him amused when the traffic was slack.

And so to the easternmost extremity of the cathedral, the Lady Chapel. This was built as part of a major remodelling of the east end, which was begun in 1257 and continued over the next half-century, the Lady Chapel itself coming last – say about 1310. Its chief glory is the design of the windows, opulently adorned with tiny figures in elaborate niches, sinuously twining ball-flower and lovely flowing tracery; crocketry too, in profusion. These features are all – or almost all – original. Much of the blank arcading, however, and the stone-vaulted roof, is Grimthorpe's; before him the roof was vaulted in wood, like the presbytery. Two of the windows, to the north-west and south-west, are by Kempe.

Poor St Albans – it seems always to have been out of luck. None of the building operations ever quite worked out as intended, and the general impression is of botching up and making do. In the prevailing confusion there are moments when the eye lights on something of real quality, but even then, all too often, the setting lets it down. And when at last a saviour appeared, it turned out to be Lord Grimthorpe. With a friend like him, one is tempted to ask as one regains the sunshine, who needs enemies?

*St Albans Cathedral.*

## St Pauls Walden*

*19; 5 miles S of Hitchin on B651*

Although there has been a church here since at least the twelfth century, most of what we see today in ALL SAINTS dates from the early fourteenth. None of this work is, however, particularly distinguished; what makes the building such a triumph is the chancel – a piece of playful and worldly Baroque remodelled by one Edward Gilbert in 1727. It possesses its own screen, a most exuberant affair of columns, round-headed arches and bits and pieces of entablature, the whole surmounted by a golden sunburst. Beyond, the chancel itself is vaulted and charmingly decorated in stucco. The present colours, predominantly green and white, were chosen by the late Raymond Erith, FRIBA, and they suit the whole light-hearted, irresponsible little conceit to perfection.

*All Saints' Church, St Pauls Walden.*

## Salisbury Hall

*20; 3 miles SE of St Albans off A6*

This lovely old moated manor house lies in the flat Hertfordshire countryside, near enough to the A6 to be seen from it. It was built, on the site of an earlier house that had once belonged to Warwick the Kingmaker, by Sir John Cutte, Treasurer to King Henry VII, but was extensively remodelled by a London banker, Jeremy Snow, in the 1670s. All the entrance front is Snow's work, as is most of the interior; the atmosphere of the house is entirely of the seventeenth century – including the one-storey Hall, which remains however where it always was, in its traditional position just to the right of the porch.

This Hall, with its black and white stone floor and fine panelling, is the most interesting room in the house, and made more interesting still by the remarkable series of six large stone medallions, each a yard across, with profile heads of Roman emperors, Cleopatra and Zenobia. They are said to have been made for Sopwell Priory near St Albans, and were almost certainly bought by Snow; the panelling has obviously been deliberately lowered to accommodate them. From the Hall you pass through into the Dining Room, a good deal smaller, with a pretty and most unusual chimneypiece of painted wood and stone. There is another of these, but a reproduction this time, in the 'haunted' bedroom upstairs.

The ghost, or one of them, is said to be that of Nell Gwynne, who according to a long though unsubstantiated tradition lived here for some time with the Snows, discreetly receiving the King at the Caroline equivalent of weekends. More authenticated tenants were Mrs Jennie Cornwallis-West, formerly Lady Randolph Churchill, who lived here between 1905 and 1910, enjoying frequent visits from her son Winston; and, during the Second World War, the De Havilland Aircraft Co. The original prototype Mosquito, designed and assembled here, now stands behind the house.

## Tyttenhanger

*21; 2½ miles SE of St Albans off B6426*

An agreeable and most eccentric house of red brick, it was built by the author and traveller Sir Henry Blount in the 1650s. The architect is unknown, but Howard Colvin has convincingly suggested Peter Mills, who was certainly the architect of Thorpe Hall in Cambridgeshire and may have been that of Balls Park (*qq.v.*) – two houses which have obvious links with this one. Beneath a hipped roof, with dormers and a stocky little cupola, there are two and a half storeys, the first-floor windows in particular having elaborate brick window surrounds and outsize pediments, alternating triangular and segmental, which give them a distinctly top-heavy look. Everything speaks of the 'Artisan Mannerist' style, not least the brick quoins and the unabashed asymmetry of the north-west side, where, on both the principal floors, the fourth bay of five is stressed to a degree that seems almost ridiculous; the first-floor window, for example, cowers beneath a segmental pediment half as big again as the corresponding one over the second bay – so big, in fact, that it can hardly squeeze in between its neighbours.

The pride of the interior is the staircase, with a noble balustrade of pierced carving in a vaguely acanthus design similar to those at Ham, Forde Abbey and Sudbury; but the eccentricity is again evident on the first floor, where all the doorcases are differently carved in such outlandishly Baroque designs as to make one suspect the sanity of the carpenter or fear for one's own. Further up still, on the attic floor, there is a small Chapel completely walled in linenfold panelling, with two rows of vaguely Jacobean pews (but obviously much restored), a double-decker pulpit, good seventeenth-century glass in the windows and a Decalogue over the fireplace. More linenfold is to be found in the slightly anachronistic Long Gallery which runs the length of the house behind the dormers.

Tyttenhanger is now occupied by a firm of architects, who were kind enough to allow me admission. It is a house of much character and charm.

## Wheathampstead

*22; 4 miles NW of Hatfield on A6129*

ST HELEN'S is a lovely big church of local flint with stone dressings. Having a chancel as long as the nave and transepts of comparable dimensions, its plan is roughly that of a Greek cross, from the centre of which there rises a low tower, topped by a curious Victorian ribbed lead spire which adds much to its character. The chancel seems to be the oldest part – unless we accept the suggested pre-Conquest dating for parts of the south transept – and is Early English of about 1230; the three lovely narrow lancets at the east end are obviously of this period, though the windows in the north and south walls are equally clearly of the following century. The tower, with its heavy supporting piers and soaring arches, is of about 1290. (I like the way the bell ropes all hang down and then are gathered up again in a sort of central festoon above the crossing.)

The Decorated period of the fourteenth century produced wonderful things at Wheathampstead. Look, in particular, at the beautiful reticulated tracery of the windows at the extremities of the transepts, and at the carved detail of the other windows along the east and south walls – inside and out. Hertfordshire possesses no other Decorated work comparable to this, except in the Lady Chapel of St Albans Cathedral itself.

## Woodhall Park

*23; 4½ miles NW of Hertford off B1001*

Leased since 1956 to Heath Mount School, Woodhall Park was built in 1777 by Thomas Leverton, an admirable architect who would be better known if most of his work had not been demolished during the last century. This late Palladian house of whitish brick is probably his best surviving building, despite the fact that it has undergone considerable alterations since his day. Thus, only seventeen years after its completion, it was virtually turned round the other way, the principal entrance being transferred from the south (show) front round to the north, the former Saloon converted into an Entrance Hall, and a portico of coupled Ionic columns added in order to leave no doubt what had been done. Another storey was added to the wings at the same time.

Though to be taken over by a school is clearly not the most desirable fate for an elegant late Georgian mansion, the architecture and interior decoration are much prized by Heath Mount and are looked after as well as is humanly possible. It is still a positive pleasure to walk in through the main door and to find oneself in a pleasant room (originally the Saloon) decorated in the Etruscan taste and still looking in essence much as it must have looked in Leverton's day. The ornate Staircase Hall is another delight – and something of a masterpiece in the way that the architect has managed to insert his graceful continuous staircase (there are no landings) into an extremely narrow space without its ever looking crushed or crowded. The walls are decorated with painted panels of the Seasons in *grisaille*, with the Continents in colour above. On the upper floor there is also a delightful little Gothic Revival room – now divided into two – with two shallow cupolas in the low ceiling. It must have been the Chapel in Leverton's original scheme.

Then, finally, comes the Print Room, more or less contemporary with the house itself, having been designed in 1782. This, too, is a joy; the prints – mostly, but by no means all, Italian, by Piranesi, Bassano, Piazzetta and others – are mounted on thin canvas and stuck to the wall not only in a remarkably pretty arrangement, but each is enclosed within its own printed *trompe-l'œil* frame, complete with hooks, cords, ribbons and every other form of attachment. There are several similar rooms in other English houses – The Vyne, Stratfield Saye, Heveningham and Ston Easton, to name but four – but this one, to me, exceeds them all in the sheer ingenuity of design, and gives more pleasure than any.

## Wrotham Park

*24; 1½ miles S of Potters Bar off A1000*

Built by Isaac Ware in 1754 for Admiral Byng, Wrotham Park is still occupied by his descendants. Though it remains a Palladian building of great beauty, it has in fact been considerably altered; the original elevation allowed only one and a half storeys for the side pavilions and links, but in the middle of the last century an extra storey was added to these and, to preserve at least some of the proportions, Ware's three-bay hexagonal cupola above the pediment (based, possibly, on Lord Burlington's villa at Chiswick) was extended to form an attic stretching right the way across the central block. Even earlier, probably around 1800, the red brick of which the house was chiefly built was faced with a cement stucco, incised with lines to suggest ashlar.

In 1883 the house was completely gutted by fire. Thanks to the energy and devotion of the staff, who were able to move virtually the entire contents out on to the lawn within four hours, the furniture and paintings today remain intact. Unfortunately, however, the house was rebuilt as it had been immediately before the conflagration, except that bays were added at each end – they now accord rather oddly with the octagonal side pavilions – and the beautiful Staircase Hall was slightly spoilt by the addition of a flat ceiling, where there had been formerly a view straight up into the lantern.

Despite all this, Wrotham remains one of the finest houses in Hertfordshire, set in the middle of its superb park laid out by Samuel Lapidge, chief gardener at Hampton Court, with advice from Capability Brown, whose assistant he had formerly been.

# Short List

## Baldock

*25; 5 miles N of Stevenage on A505*

The name Baldock is said to be a corruption of Baghdad, given it by the Knights Templars in the thirteenth century – a fact (if it is one) which has nothing to do with architecture but which I find it impossible not to report. The big rubble CHURCH OF ST MARY looks, from the outside, worthy without being distinguished; the interior is nearly all fourteenth-century, with admirable carved stops on the arcades and as corbels supporting the timber roof. The screens go all the way across – though only that across the south aisle has a proper loft – and would look a lot better without the horrid Victorian varnish.

## Beechwood

*26; 2 miles N of Flamstead off A5*

If the house lived up to the promise of its east front it would be a treasure indeed. Alas, this glorious show-piece was added to an otherwise undistinguished building in 1702; and though Roger Morris, Capability Brown and Sir W. Chambers all worked on the house subsequently, the rest is a disappointment. But that marvellous façade of brickwork in Flemish bond, with red stretchers and blue headers, the hipped roof with dormers and the perfectly judged three-bay pediment – William and Mary at their tip-top best – cannot possibly be forgotten.

## Haileybury

*27; 2½ miles SE of Hertford off B1197*

The original design for a training school for the East India Company was by William Wilkins, architect of the National Gallery – which this building superficially resembles, especially in its unfocused look, straggling on with an occasional accent but nothing to pull the whole thing properly together. The huge dome of Sir Arthur Blomfield's Chapel, added in 1876, helps in this respect; but it hardly suits the neo-classicism of the rest.

## Little Hormead

*28; 3 miles E of Buntingford off B1038*

ST MARY'S, a tiny Norman church of flint, stands alone on a little hill above the village, hardly touched since the thirteenth century when they rejigged the chancel. Unassuming and uncluttered, it might have been included on charm alone; it has, however, one astonishing feature utterly at variance with the prevailing simplicity – a north door contemporary with the church (*c*.1140), of wood but overlaid with a wildly exuberant display of ironwork: birds, flowers and dragons incorporated in savage arabesques. The Vikings themselves, one feels, are not far away.

## Marden Hill

*29; 2 miles NW of Hertford off B1000*

This originally undistinguished yellow brick Georgian house by the little-known Francis Carter was imaginatively altered by Soane in 1819. Soane's are the Ionic porch and staircase and a curious L-shaped room above the Entrance Hall. It is not open to the public.

## Stanstead Abbots

*30; 5 miles E of Hertford on A414*

ST JAMES'S lies about a mile outside the village to the south-east: no wonder it is now the responsibility of the Redundant Churches Fund. It is virtually all fifteenth-century, including the timber south porch, with the addition of a north chancel chapel of 1577. Go inside (if you can get in) and you are back in the mid-eighteenth century: all plastered, simplicity itself, barrel vault, tie-beams with kingposts, a modest three-decker pulpit, box pews, plenty of improving inscriptions. Pity they couldn't swop it for Waterhouse's ST ANDREW'S, central but boring.

## Theobalds

*31; ¾ mile E of Waltham Cross off A10*

Of the Old Palace built by Lord Burghley and given by his son to James I in exchange for the Old Palace of Hatfield, virtually nothing now remains. The nearby THEOBALDS PARK COLLEGE, however, though itself undistinguished architecturally, boasts as its main gate Sir Christopher Wren's TEMPLE BAR, erected in Fleet Street in 1672 to mark the entrance to the City and moved here in 1888.

## Wormleybury

*32; 5 miles S of Hertford off A10*

Built in 1767–9 by the Scottish architect–engineer Robert Mylne, this is a not especially distinguished building of yellow brick with a slightly later giant portico. The main interest lies in the three rooms decorated by Robert Adam, with wall and ceiling paintings by Angelica Kauffmann. At the time of writing the house is not open to the public.

# Isle of Wight

The Isle of Wight has many qualities; architectural distinction, however, is not one of them. Ten old churches are actually mentioned in the Domesday Book; nowadays, alas, none of them is of the very first quality. For me at least, there is more pleasure to be derived from such Victorian splendours as Scott's All Saints at Ryde or – best of all – the hugely enjoyable St Mildred's, Whippingham, than from any of the medieval survivors. Best of all is Quarr Abbey, erected in the years immediately preceding the First World War by a French Benedictine of genius, Dom Paul Bellot, and one of the most astonishing buildings of the twentieth century to be found anywhere in the country; but Quarr is an exception to every rule, a case apart.

Domestic architecture, too, is disappointing. There are some charming manor houses of the sixteenth and seventeenth centuries – though a good many of them have been rather spoilt inside; but of the eighteenth, when one might have expected several rather grand Palladian houses of the kind so plentiful in neighbouring counties on the mainland, there is only one – Appuldurcombe – and that is now only a broken husk. It is not till we reach the last year of that century that we are brought up short by James Wyatt's Norris Castle, as far from the Palladian as anything that could be imagined – a wild pseudo-Romanesque conceit, formidably embattled, exploiting the romantic aspect of the island in a way that no other building has done before or since.

Osborne, by contrast, seems almost discreet – and certainly a good deal better bred. It may be no great shakes architecturally (though it looks fine enough from the garden front) but its Victorian – and even more its Albertian – associations and the miraculous fact that it has been preserved virtually unchanged for well over a century make it, for the average sightseer, the most rewarding building on the island.

The only other English monarch to have any close link with the Isle of Wight was the unfortunate King Charles I, who was imprisoned briefly after the Civil War in Carisbrooke Castle. Alas, much of this now looks almost as Victorian as Osborne, and with less excuse; the exterior, however – above all the Gatehouse and parts of the curtain wall – remains undeniably impressive.

In the past twenty years or so, the uncontrolled growth of the tourist trade has spoilt all too much of the Isle of Wight, but, mercifully, there are still a few places where traces of the old Victorian seaside architecture survive. Of these, Ryde and above all Ventnor are the best. Even there, however, one has that feeling of constriction and confinement which pervades so much of the island – that feeling that there is simply not enough of it to go round. Too many people, too many houses. For those who go there to sail, such considerations matter little; the sea gives them all the elbow-room they need. But for us landlubbers, claustrophobia soon sets in.

---

## Appuldurcombe House

*1; 2 miles NW of Ventnor off B3327*

Once the most magnificent building on the Isle of Wight, Appuldurcombe House has remained unoccupied – except by troops in the two world wars – since 1909, and has crumbled away until it is now only an empty shell under the care of the Historic Buildings and Monuments Commission. The shell, however, is virtually complete, and since the architecture is both curious and distinguished it merits a place here.

When Sir Robert Worsley returned from his Grand Tour in 1690 he demolished the old Tudor house in which his forebear had entertained Henry VIII, leaving, in his own words, 'not one stone standing'. In its place he erected, between 1701 and about 1712, a great house in the grand manner – so grand that Colen Campbell was to include it a few years later in his *Vitruvius Britannicus*. The architect was almost certainly John James, whose name is mentioned several times in the contemporary correspondence about the building; if the elaborate decoration of Appuldurcombe seems at variance with the rather more severe style that we usually associate with him, this can probably be explained by the relatively early date; he designed the house before he was thirty, and lived to be seventy-four.

The basic plan is one of a square centre of two and a half storeys, with rectangular angle pavilions projecting from each corner of the north and south fronts. These are of two storeys only, that is, lower than the centre, but are topped with massive triangular pediments which give them far more prominence – an effect that is further emphasised by the tall chimneys, connected by an arch *à la* Vanbrugh, which rise up immediately behind them. The other principal decorative features are the giant Corinthian pilasters between the bays and, on the inward-facing sides of the pavilions, tall niches in frames identical to those of the windows, with triple keystones set into the square heads. In addition the entrance front – to the east – has a central doorway topped by a large circular window with swags of drapery to each side, the whole composition framed by giant columns, also Corinthian, originally supporting a broken pediment with escutcheon. (These, together with the urns and statuettes which surmounted the attic, were subsequently removed.) On the south front the space between the pavilions was filled, during the first half of the last century, with a Doric colonnade and cast-iron gallery above. The *porte-cochère* to the west dates from the same time.

The general effect is thus distinctly Baroque rather than Palladian, more reminiscent of William Talman's south front at Chatsworth, or even Vanbrugh and Castle Howard, than of Campbell or William Kent. There is nothing else remotely like it in the Isle of Wight, and its shameful fate, caused by apathy and neglect, has resulted in a tragic loss for the island. We can only be grateful to the Dept of the Environment for having preserved what was left; with a house of such quality, even a partial rescue is well worth while.

## Arreton Manor

*2; 3½ miles SE of Newport on A3056*

A roughcast stone house built on the E-plan probably in the first quarter of the seventeenth century, Arreton Manor was almost certainly complete by 1639, the date engraved on the porch; and apart from the building of an inoffensive one-bay extension to the west in 1812 it has changed remarkably little. All three projections of the E are gabled, and the house's two floors are increased to three beneath the gables – where, however, the attic windows are as tall as those below. They are mullioned like all the rest, have three lights and their own hood-moulds. On the two principal floors the hood-moulds form part of continuous string-courses running the length of the façade. The ground-floor windows, of five lights in the outer projections, have been reset, and the porch has been extended forward, unforgivably, in brick; but the general impression of the entrance front is a pleasant one, and the groups of tall, diagonally set chimneys add still further to the overall effect.

The interior – though the occasional olde-worlde touches, presumably introduced to please the tourists, are much to be deplored – preserves much the same atmosphere. The Hall and Dining Parlour, which together occupy the site of a medieval hall house owned by the monks of Quarr, each have broad, four-centred stone fireplaces and fine panelling to the ceiling. The upper rooms, which include a Long Room and a pretty Jacobean bedroom, are worth a quick look but are not lastingly memorable.

*Appuldurcombe House.*

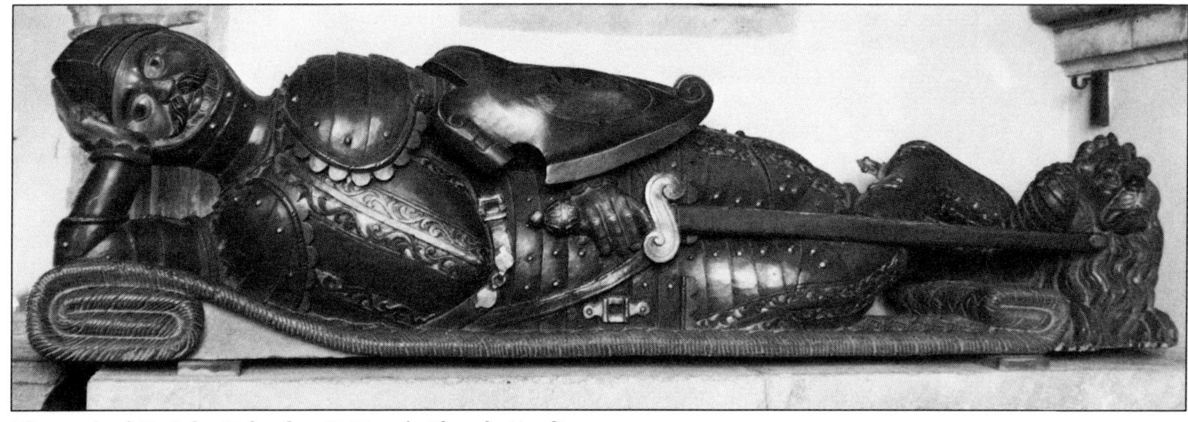

*The tomb of Sir John Oglander, St Mary's Church, Brading.*

## Brading

*3; 4½ miles S of Ryde on A3055*

ST MARY'S CHURCH has a west tower, with a processional way running straight through it from north to south. It has a stubby little recessed spire, and cannot therefore be earlier than the end of the thirteenth century. Nave and aisles are, however, appreciably older, for there is a south door of about 1200 and Transitional north and south arcades which must be of much the same date. It is they, more than anything else, that strike you the moment you enter the church: five bays long, they have capitals scalloped in the Norman manner, but fine, properly pointed arches above them. The chancel is a little later, but not much. Very pretty in an unassuming sort of way, it has three stepped lancets, a Victorian reredos which looks like Clayton and Bell, and – like the rest of the church – a nice timber roof. It also boasts a splended fifteenth-century tomb – but this is only a beginning, because the church is full of them. Best of all are those in the memorial chapel of the Oglanders, immediately to the south of the chancel, where you should note in particular the tomb of Sir John Oglander. He reclines on his right side on a partially rolled-up mat, his head resting on his elbow; he carries a heavy sword and shield, and one leg is crossed over the other. So, you may say, do countless other effigies of the later crusaders. But – wait for it – Sir John died not in 1300, but in 1655. Here is a piece of genuine historical romanticism of the kind which never became really popular till the days of Sir Walter Scott. Sir John wasn't old-fashioned; he was 200 years before his time.

South-west of the village are the remains of a ROMAN VILLA of the third century. One wing is preserved under cover to protect a number of rather good mosaics depicting figures from classical mythology. NUNWELL MANOR, about three-quarters of a mile to the west, is also worth a visit, although it is not open to the public. From the front it looks a fairly straightforward house of the mid-eighteenth century: seven bays, the three centre ones swelling out in a gentle canted bow, with low wings on each side. Closer inspection, however, reveals traces of an earlier house, probably of Henry VIII's time. Charles I is said to have stayed here at some time during his imprisonment at Carisbrooke nearby.

## Carisbrooke Castle

*4; 1¼ miles W of Newport on B3401*

The oldest and grandest castle on the Isle of Wight, Carisbrooke has been a stronghold since Roman times. The earliest part of the surviving fabric, however, goes back only to the twelfth century – probably soon after Henry I granted the land to Richard de Redvers in 1100. In subsequent centuries it was to prove its usefulness on several occasions by successfully defending the island against French raids, but achieved a degree of fame only in 1647–8, when Charles I was imprisoned there; he tried to escape, but failed at the critical moment to squeeze himself between the bars of his window. After this, the castle lapsed once more into relative obscurity. The former governor's residence is now open to the public as the Isle of Wight Museum.

You enter from the west, through an Elizabethan gateway bearing the date 1598; a stone bridge across the moat then leads you to the Gatehouse, and a most formidable affair it is: two round battlemented towers flanking a broad four-centred arch with no fewer than three grooves for portcullises. Above is a small, two-light window and above that – just below the tops of the towers – four deep machicolations. The basic date is about 1335, though the tops of the towers and the machicolations are perhaps a century or so later. You are now within the Norman curtain wall; to your right is the sixteenth-century custodian's office, and behind it the modern Chapel on the site of its medieval predecessor.

In front of you to the east stand the principal domestic buildings of the castle. Alas, they are much restored – and with a heavy Victorian hand; but the lower parts of the Hall do in fact go back to the twelfth century, when they probably formed part of a chamber with an undercroft. They were then lengthened and transformed into a Hall in the 1270s by Countess Isabel de Fortibus, who also added a tiny Chapel (now housing a staircase but still recognisable), a Great Chamber and various offices. Just south of the Chapel, another three-storey block was added around 1390; here, the most interesting room is the solar, which has retained its original fireplace. North of the Hall is another series of buildings, now in ruins. It was from one of these that the King made his ill-fated escape attempt.

If you follow the north curtain wall to the east, you come to a flight of steps leading up to the huge earthwork on which stands what is left of the keep. Like the wall, it dates from the second quarter of the twelfth century. An irregular polygon in plan, it must once have stood considerably higher than it does now, but it still gives a formidable impression of impregnability. The remaining buildings within the curtain walls – those opposite the gap halfway along the east side – need not detain you. You may, however, be interested to see, over the well at the south-east corner of the courtyard, the enormous late sixteenth-century treadmill, still functioning and operated – according to strict union rules – by a most contented-looking donkey.

## Cowes

See Norris Castle; Osborne House.

## Godshill

*5; 6 miles SE of Newport on A3020*

The hill on which ST LAWRENCE'S CHURCH now stands has been a place of worship since pagan times; this is the fourth church to have been built on the site. It dates, for the most part, from the early fourteenth century – there are some lovely Decorated windows, especially those of the chancel and the south chapel; but the most curious thing about it is its plan, for this is a double-naved church, with transepts but no aisles, and no structural division between nave and chancel. The two naves are separated by a rather coarse six-bay Perpendicular arcade; but this must have replaced an earlier one, since the transepts would not otherwise be placed as they are. There has also been some even later remodelling: the four-light west window of the south nave is seventeenth-century work, and the north transept was classicised in 1741 when it became a memorial chapel to the Worsleys of Appuldurcombe.

The church is wonderfully rich in monuments. The best by far is that of Sir John Leigh, who died in 1529, and of his wife Agnes. It stands between the chancel and the south chapel. Sir John's feet rest on a pig, on which two tiny bearded monks are crouching, telling their beads. The worst is the simply awful sarcophagus of Sir Richard Worsley, partly concealed (thank God) by the organ. But more beautiful – at least to me – than any monument is the wall painting in the wagon-roofed south transept: Christ crucified on a 'Lily Cross', a triple-branched flowering lily symbolising purity. It dates from around 1450; it alone would be worth coming to the church to see.

## Norris Castle

*6; on coast at East Cowes*

To those approaching the Isle of Wight from the north-east across the Solent, Norris Castle makes an unforgettable impact: a fairytale castle, silhouetted against the sky, its lawns sweeping down almost to the water's edge. It was built in 1799 by James Wyatt in what might loosely be described as the Norman style – though any twelfth-century architect would be astonished at the description. (No Norman castle would have so many windows, round-headed or not, ranged in orderly rows.) Norris is dominated by a tall, round tower of three and a half storeys – the attic half storey marked by a row of tiny circular windows – at the extreme eastern end, with a slender stair turret rising higher still; it then continues in a deliberately asymmetrical, haphazard form towards the west. Every inch of the skyline is embattled. Here, one feels, is a house conceived almost entirely for its dramatic effect: an invaluable preliminary exercise for what Wyatt was to do, on a far more ambitious scale, at Belvoir two years later.

Not surprisingly in the circumstances, the interior comes as something of a disappointment. Here the most memorable feature is the Library, with the original Wyatt bookshelves still *in situ*; and, of course, the breathtaking views across the Solent.

*The thirteenth-century Chapel, Carisbrooke Castle.*

*Osborne House.*

## Osborne House★

*7; 1 mile SE of East Cowes on A3021*

Few people, one would imagine, looking out across the Solent from Cowes to the coast of Hampshire, would be inescapably reminded of the Bay of Naples. Such, however, was the reaction of Prince Albert when Queen Victoria brought him on his first visit to the Isle of Wight. For some time the royal couple had been looking for what Her Majesty described as 'a place of one's own, quiet and retired'; and in the thousand-acre Osborne estate they found exactly what they wanted. From the first, the Prince was resolved to design the new house himself, and the result – faithful to his first impressions – was the outsize Italianate villa, complete with *campanile*, which began to rise (with some assistance from Thomas Cubitt) in the summer of 1845.

The original plan was a rather irregular L-shape, with a roughly square Pavilion Wing containing the principal state rooms and the private apartments above them and facing north-east across the straits, to which was attached a long Household Wing running from a point some 30 feet from its southern corner to the south-west. In 1890, however, the so-called Durbar Wing was added opposite the Household Wing to form a great entrance courtyard, by which visitors still arrive at the house. This courtyard is dominated by the five-storey Flag Tower, topped by a three-arch loggia and a square roof with deep eaves in the Tuscan manner. It is linked to the Household Wing by a single two-storey bay with a broad Venetian window, which in turn sets the pattern for the whole eleven-bay front of that wing, clearly inspired by Palladio's Basilica at Vicenza.

Behind this Palladian front the Household Wing continues to the south-east in a rather disorganised and higgledy-piggledy way, with another courtyard behind the entrance one and a number of further extensions and outbuildings. These make architectural sense only on the garden front, from which terrace gardens – still, in the Italian manner, adorned with statues, fountains and loggias – sweep gently down towards the sea. On this side the Pavilion Wing is characterised by a generous three-bay bow rising the full height of the building. To the right, a short link leads to the end of the Durbar Wing and is of little interest; to the left, however, the Venetian-windowed link which we saw from the courtyard side carries us on to the garden front of the Household Wing: eleven bays again, the centre three grouped closely together and treated as a single unit, though differently on each of the three storeys. On the ground floor they, together with the other four bays on each side, have heavy rusticated surrounds which add still further to the Italianate flavour of the whole thing. There follows another two-bay link, and then the Clock Tower. This is in the same style as the Flag Tower but – although it is slightly lower – has six stages instead of five.

The fascination of the interior lies in the fact that after the Prince Consort's death in 1861 the Queen gave orders that the house should remain exactly as he had left it, as a tribute to his memory. It was here, surrounded by countless reminders of him, that she died forty years later, and since no subsequent sovereigns have ever wished to live there it remains just as she – and indeed he – left it. The one alteration was the addition of the Durbar Room, which was designed in the most exotic Indian style – the work of one Bhai Ram Singh, assisted by Rudyard Kipling's father, John Lockwood Kipling. Walls and ceiling are a riot of intricately carved plasterwork, there are some charming oriels at first-floor level and a gallery, and the room boasts a vast fireplace surmounted by a plaster peacock. The woodwork is of teak throughout.

From the Durbar Room we go on to the Pavilion Wing through the Grand Corridor, which runs uninterruptedly round the three sides of the entrance courtyard. We are now back in the days of Prince Albert, and each room brings us new treats. In one room everything seems to be made of deer antlers; elsewhere is a billiard table designed by the Prince, with painted decoration, wonderfully fussy; and, in the Drawing Room, a piano set with porcelain representations of famous Italian pictures and life-size statues of the royal children in allegorical guise. Upstairs, in the Queen's Private Suite, we find a distinctly macabre collection of the limbs of royal infants, modelled in marble; and, in the Queen's Sitting Room, the twin desks at which she and her husband worked side by side: curiously touching. Next to it is her dressing room, her bath and loo, and finally the bedroom with the heavily canopied bed in which she died, complete with an immense memorial tablet in bronze (to Albert, above his side of the bed), most ill-advisedly inserted by their sorrowing children.

In the grounds, yet further delights await us. Among them is a genuine Swiss chalet, imported in sections and re-erected in 1853–4, in the enchanting kitchen of which the royal children are said to have learnt to cook. There is also another, bogus, Swiss chalet built to house their diminutive gardening tools and their collections of curiosities. A toy fort, with earthworks and a wooden cannon, was built by Prince Arthur of Connaught at the age of ten. Finally – and best of all – there is the Queen's bathing machine from which, for the first time in her life, on 30 July 1874 at the age of fifty-five, she cautiously descended into the sea.

## Quarr Abbey★

*8; 2 miles W of Ryde on A3054*

It may not be to everyone's taste, but to me there is no question: Quarr Abbey is far and away the most exciting – and indeed astonishing – building in the Isle of Wight. It was built by a community of French Benedictines who left France in 1901 as a result of anti-clerical legislation. They first settled at Appuldurcombe (*q.v.*) but abandoned it in 1907 for Quarr, where they pulled down the existing Victorian house and immediately began work on the new abbey. The architect was one of their number, a certain Dom Paul Bellot, who before taking his monastic vows had studied at the Ecole des Beaux-Arts in Paris. His style can best be described as twentieth-century expressionist, but his genius is all his own. His medium is brick, almost exclusively; but he uses it with such imagination, such consummate virtuosity, that it seems inevitable, and absolutely right. Monotony is avoided by various means: by the use of subtly different colours for the headers and the stretchers, and even in the pointing; by laying in formal patterns; and above all by the endlessly varied relief decoration – friezes, niches, stepped recesses, ornamental corbelling, all somehow forming an integral part of the architecture itself, beautifully balanced, perfectly judged.

The abbey church begins with a low, rather short nave, its west front consisting of a stepped gable flanked by two small square turrets with pyramid tops. This is followed by a vast choir, almost twice as high and announced on the outside by a tall south tower constructed in its upper stage on a circle of brick columns supporting first a cylindrical drum and then a conical cap in a way oddly reminiscent of a Turkish *türbe*. At the east end of the choir there rises a broad square tower, once again with corner turrets.

The interior, flooded with a warm yellow light that filters through the tall, orange-stained lancets of the east end, is more impressive still; again and again one is left gasping by the sheer *brio*, and the inexhaustible wealth of imaginative detail. Best of all are the soaring arches beneath the east tower, their spandrels pierced with double rows of lancets. Only a master – a superb artist and a consummate craftsman – could have created such a majestic vision as this.

It is not often, in England at any rate, that one comes upon a masterpiece on this scale by an architect of whom one has never heard. Although he died as recently as 1943, the name of Paul Bellot remains virtually unknown here – just as it does in France, Belgium and the Netherlands where his work can also be seen. Had he not renounced the world for a monastic life, however, his influence would certainly have been immense: we should be hailing him today as one of the great men of our time, for the whole course of western architecture in the twentieth century might well have been changed.

*Quarr Abbey.*

## Shalfleet

*9; 4½ miles E of Yarmouth on A3054*

The great west tower of the CHURCH OF ST MICHAEL THE ARCHANGEL looks at first glance more like a castle keep. Its appearance may have been somewhat more ecclesiastical before the removal of its spire in 1912, but those vast dimensions can never have been anything but forbidding. It is Norman, and must date from very soon after the Conquest – certainly well before 1100. Norman too is the north doorway, with its two orders of columns with scalloped capitals and its extraordinary carved tympanum representing a bearded man apparently scratching the heads of two affronted lions, whose tails turn unexpectedly into exuberant foliage.

The interior has a graceful thirteenth-century south aisle on slender round columns, and a chancel of the same date with bar tracery above the triple-lancet east window. There are box pews, and a fine timber roof to both nave and chancel. The west window has been reset higher up – presumably to make room for the west gallery which was added at the very end of the eighteenth century but has now unfortunately been removed again. Still more unfortunately, the church has been scraped and restored with a somewhat heavy hand. Beautiful as it is, it strikes one nowadays as being a bit short on atmosphere.

## Whippingham

*10; 3 miles SE of Cowes on A3021*

ST MILDRED'S, Whippingham: the very name sounds improbable enough, but the church's actual appearance is even more so. It is the parish church of the Osborne estate, and was built between 1854 and 1862 by Albert Jenkins Humbert, the architect of Sandringham – with a good deal of help, it need hardly be said, from the Prince Consort himself. The crossing-tower, in particular, is quite unlike any other in England. Large and square, with a row of six lancets set into blank arcading along each side, it continues in a low pyramid with tall, pointed *tourelles* at the corners to an octagonal lantern supporting a slender spire. The style is Early English more than anything else – the transepts have rose windows – but the aisleless nave is Norman. The furnishings are more interesting for their royal associations than for any intrinsic merit, but there is a splendid *art nouveau* grille by the ever-fascinating Alfred Gilbert, and a bronze plaque to the memory of Sir Henry Ponsonby by Countess Feodora Gleichen, best known for the verse inscribed by Queen Alexandra on her funeral wreath:

*To dear Feo Gleichen*
*Who was always so near our heart;*
*Oh how we shall miss her*
*Nor her wonderful works of art.*

---

# Short List

## Farringford

See Freshwater.

## Freshwater

*11; 2 miles SW of Yarmouth off A3054*

A mile or so to the south-west of the town stands FARRINGFORD, now a hotel. It was here that the poet Tennyson lived from 1853 until his death in 1892. (He later bought a house in Surrey, but Farringford remained his principal home.) The house has inevitably been much altered, but the yellow-brick front with its vaguely Gothic flavour remains much as it always has. The architect is – not altogether surprisingly – unknown.

## Newtown

*12; halfway between Newport and Yarmouth off A3054*
*Includes Town Hall (NT)*

This is the most ancient borough in the Isle of Wight, in the loveliest, most unspoilt area. The TOWN HALL (NT) stands on a little hill just outside the town. A charming building of 1699, when it was put up by public subscription,' it is small and unpresumptuous, with its little portico tacked on askew. Though still used for council meetings, it is occasionally open to the public.

## Ryde

*13; on N coast 8 miles NE of Newport on A3054*

A pretty seaside town, Ryde must once have possessed considerable elegance though now it seems to have run sadly to seed. Its former prosperity is well illustrated by ALL SAINTS' CHURCH – a fine essay in his favourite Middle Pointed style by Sir George Gilbert Scott with remarkably opulent furniture of carved marble, especially the font, pulpit and reredos. It is set high, and the tall spire makes a splendid landmark for miles.

## Shorwell

*14; 5 miles SW of Newport on B3323*

A charming village, beautifully set beneath the downs, it offers a church – ST PETER'S – which, though not of the highest quality, is nevertheless well worth a visit. Though it was probably begun around 1200, the general impression is Perpendicular; of this date are the most enjoyable wall paintings of St Christopher over the north door. The south chapel contains, *inter alia*, a most endearing sixteenth-century painting of the Last Supper which comes from the church of Thingvellir, Iceland.

## Swainston House

*15; 5 miles W of Newport on B3401*

In 1982 Swainston House was being advertised as a hotel; but I found it deserted and boarded up. It is a curious amalgam: a medieval wing to the east, with an upper Hall and thirteenth-century window, and to the west a quite elegant late Georgian residence of nine bays with a central portico *in antis*. It deserves a better fate: I can only hope it finds one.

# Kent

The fact that it is the principal highway between London and the Continent has given Kent cause, over the past 2,000 years, for both rejoicing and regret. On the positive side, it has always been the first to receive the new ideas coming from across the Channel – including even Christianity itself which, although not entirely unknown in England before the arrival of St Augustine, received from him new impetus and direction. Had Kent not been so placed, it is most unlikely that Augustine would ever have chosen it for what is still today the mother church of all England and the brightest jewel in the Kentish crown – Canterbury Cathedral. This constant traffic between the capital and the coast – to say nothing of the unceasing stream of pilgrims who for over three and a half centuries came flocking from all over Europe to the shrine of the martyred Archbishop – brought Kent the prosperity it has always enjoyed. For most of its history its roads have been better, its trade more buoyant and – outside the great primeval forest of the Weald – its population more dense than any other rural region of similar size; and when, besides these advantages, we remember the richness of its farmlands, the mildness of its climate, and the beauty and variety of its landscape, Kent appears a fortunate county indeed.

And so it is. Kent could even be said to have profited from its greatest theoretical drawback – its vulnerability to attack from continental Europe. As long ago as the third century AD the Romans were protecting this dangerously exposed stretch of the 'Saxon Shore' with forts at Reculver, Richborough, Dover and Lympne. The Normans, as usual, built castles by the score – at Dover again, and Canterbury and Rochester, to name but three. The Hundred Years' War produced much fine defensive building (Scotney, Penshurst, Leeds) and the 1540 invasion scare gave rise to Henry VIII's castles at Deal, Walmer and Sandown. The miracle is that – perhaps because of all these precautions – Kent was never invaded. Even William the Conqueror preferred the coast of Sussex when the moment came. And the architectural heritage of Kent has been immeasurably enriched.

Another problem that Kent has somehow managed to turn to good advantage is its shortage of good building stone. Of this it is not totally bereft; East Anglia, for example, fares far worse. In the west of the county, the Wealden sandstones can look very fine indeed; one has only to think of Tunbridge Wells. But the county's only limestone, the coarse and ever-intractable Kentish rag, is seldom capable of giving much pleasure (Boughton Monchelsea is an exception) and most of the churches in the east of the county – and a good many domestic buildings too – have very wisely fallen back on flint, which not only looks a good deal better if well set but also stoically resists the salt sea winds. For their more important work, Kentish builders have taken advantage of their favoured geographical position and have quite simply imported Caen limestone from Normandy. Otherwise, where this was too expensive, they have used brick – and for five centuries Kent has produced the best bricks in England. Tiles are another speciality, both for roofing and – especially in the Weald – for outside walls. Tile-hanging was seldom thought appropriate for great houses; it is essentially a modest style and looks better in a village street than anywhere else – where it can produce quite startling effects of *chiaroscuro* on a sunny summer day. Timber-framed and weather-boarded houses are also to be found in abundance. Thus the deficiency of good stone, which in other regions has had a lamentable effect on the local architecture, in Kent seems if anything to have had the opposite effect, giving Kentish vernacular styles more range and variety, perhaps, than can be seen in any other single county.

Ecclesiastical building is inevitably dominated by Canterbury; it seems almost unfair that Kent should be one of the only two counties in England to possess a second medieval cathedral. Rochester is not and never will be in the top league, but it is second in age only to Canterbury itself and has far more to offer the visitor than most people imagine. These two cathedrals possess all the best Norman building in Kent, though Barfreston, St Margaret's at Cliffe and New Romney should also be on anyone's list. For Early English, the two most extraordinary surprises are Brookland (above all for that astonishing belfry) and Stone; Hythe and Minster-in-Thanet are also not easily forgotten.

To the Decorated style Kent made its own most individual contribution – the so-called Kentish tracery in which the cusps are split and curled back like a partially peeled banana. This can be seen to curious effect at Chartham, and in St Anselm's Chapel in Canterbury Cathedral. The cathedral is also the best place to study Kentish Perpendicular – in Henry Yevele's nave and John Wastell's Bell Harry tower.

The story of secular domestic architecture – once we have got the medieval castles out of the way – effectively begins in Kent with Old Soar, Plaxtol; it is of about 1290, though there is not enough of it left to earn it more than a place on the short list. Ightham Mote, on the other hand, built less than half a century later, is a moated manor house of breathtaking beauty, unique for its date in England. In 1341 Sir John de Pulteney obtained his licence to crenellate Penshurst, though its medieval character has been largely lost under later accretions; and well before 1400 the exterior of Hever was looking much the same in its essentials as it does today. And so we come to the fifteenth century and, halfway through its course, the building of Knole. True, we tend to think of this, the most magical of all the great houses of England, as predominantly Jacobean; but we are wrong to do so. Knole was standing, in all its rambling majesty, long before the House of Tudor had ever been heard of in the Weald. On the other hand, part of its magic is its extraordinary atmosphere of timelessness; to enquire too deeply into its age seems almost like impertinence.

The sixteenth century in Kent was very largely a period of vernacular building – more usually, at this date, timber-framed than in brick. Among country houses, one thinks not so much of Lullingstone (where only the Gatehouse gives the show away) as of stone-built Boughton Monchelsea and of the wondrous brick tower that is almost all that remains of Sissinghurst, where Vita Sackville-West's sublime garden does much to console us for the loss of one of the county's great Elizabethan houses. Then, towards the end of the century, comes Cobham Hall – like the great Queen herself, long on grandeur but perhaps a little short on charm.

True Jacobean houses of importance are rare in this corner of England. Somerhill and Chilham Castle, the two principal ones, are both too much altered to merit more than a place in my short list. The same, you may argue, could be said of Lees Court, which *is* included; but here, one suspects, the exterior was always the most remarkable feature of the house, and since that has survived intact it did not seem possible to omit it. Lees Court and its near contemporary, Chevening, have both been attributed to Inigo Jones, almost certainly wrongly in both cases. Both are however memorable in their different ways, though Chevening was largely transformed, inside and out, in the eighteenth century and belongs more properly to the later period than the earlier one. The two houses that speak most clearly of their time are Broome Park, the principal Kentish example of cut and moulded brickwork, and – my own particular favourite – Groombridge Place, where the clock stopped in 1660 and has not moved since.

Pausing for a moment to admire the Queen Anne transformation of Lullingstone, we pass on to the Palladian Age, where Kent boasts one house of national – indeed, international – importance. Colen Campbell's Mereworth Castle (the description is manifestly ridiculous) is a direct copy of Palladio's Villa Rotonda, the only real differences having been dictated by the climate. Godmersham Park, built a decade later, is quieter and more restrained, but in a far lovelier setting.

When we look for later Georgian houses of the first rank, we find rather surprisingly that Kent has relatively little to declare; Adam's Mersham le Hatch is an early work and well below his usual standard, while Broome Place, though distinguished enough on the outside, has lost most of its interior decoration. In religious architecture at this period, however, no list would be complete without mention of the church at Mereworth, a curious cross between St Paul's, Covent Garden, and St Martin-in-the-Fields. The nineteenth century yields two more churches that linger in the memory, both in Ramsgate – Henry Hemsley's St George's, and St Augustine's by A.W.N. Pugin. The latter was completed in 1850; and only ten years later Philip Webb was putting the finishing touches to the Red House for William Morris at Bexleyheath – which still belongs morally to Kent even though for administrative purposes it has now been engulfed in Greater London.

The selection that follows is, I know, hopelessly inadequate for one of the richest and most architecturally varied counties in all England. It is offered merely as a sample, and as a pointer to what lies beyond.

---

## Barfreston*

*1; 6 miles NW of Dover off A256*

An absolute stunner of a church, ST NICHOLAS'S was built around 1180; although it is tiny – just a nave and a chancel, together measuring less than 50 feet from east to west – it boasts a wealth of sculptural decoration as rich as that of any church of its date in England. The walls are divided almost exactly halfway up by a double string-course; below it they are of flint, above of Caen stone ashlar. The show side is to the south, and is dominated by the doorway, flanked with columns whose capitals are carved with animals fighting and charging knights. Above is a magnificent broad arch of three orders, the first of a leaf design, the second with more animals (many of them playing musical instruments) and the broad outer band largely given over to the signs of the zodiac and the labours of the months. The tympanum shows Christ in a mandorla, surrounded not by the beasts of the Evangelists nor by the blessed and the damned, but by a jumble of human heads and monsters. Above the door, the scheme of fenestration – basically that of tall round-headed windows, the larger ones blocked up, the smaller ones glazed – has been thrown sadly off-balance by the arch, which rises above the string-course and gets in the way; the mason's attempt to overcome this problem is endearingly inept.

The east end, facing the road, features a magnificent wheel window in the gable, its spokes in the form of colonnettes, its rim adorned with more parading animals. Three of the four Evangelists' beasts, missing

*St Nicholas's Church, Barfreston.*

from the south tympanum, turn up rather surprisingly here, together with a rather mutilated knight on a horse. There is a fine carved corbel table, and an upper string-course that follows the line of the windows.

The interior of the church, though somewhat plainer, is every bit as satisfying as the outside. The chancel arch, tall and narrow, carries once again three orders of beautifully preserved Norman decoration, and is flanked by blank arches which presumably once contained altars. There is obviously any amount of French influence here – reaching Barfreston, in all probability, via Canterbury Cathedral. But though the ideas are French, the workmanship of the shallow relief carving seems quintessentially English. So, at least, I thought at the time. I long to go back and see it again.

## Belmont

*2; $4\frac{1}{2}$ miles S of Faversham off A251*

Standing on rising ground in the middle of a beautiful park some half a mile to the north-west of the village of Throwley, Belmont was built by Samuel Wyatt for the 1st Lord Harris, victor of Seringapatam in India and conqueror of Tippoo Sahib – whose sword, buckler and magnificent swansdown hat are kept on display within the house. According to a Coade stone plaque, Wyatt completed it in 1792 – fifteen years after he had finished Herstmonceux Place in East Sussex (*q.v.*), one of whose elevations is almost identical with the east front of Belmont. Unlike Herstmonceux, however, Belmont is not all of a piece: when Harris bought the estate in 1780, there was already a house on the site – and a fairly new one at that, since it had been standing for only eleven years. This house was large and relatively commodious, built round an extensive stable court; but it failed to please its new owner. He did not demolish it; such a course would have been expensive and, in the circumstances, ridiculous. Instead, he instructed Wyatt to encase the south-east corner. The result is that, though less than a quarter of a century separates the old building from the new, Belmont presents to the visitor two very different faces. If you approach it through the stable court, all the buildings you see are a fairly undistinguished mid-Georgian; if, however, you go straight to the front entrance, you find an elegant neo-classical house, faced with pale yellow mathematical tiles, of considerable urbanity and sophistication – an impression strengthened when you walk around to the principal front, commanding the splendid view across the park to the east.

This east front is of two storeys and nine bays, the three outer ones on each side being set in deep segmental bows rising to the roof and crowned with shallow domes and low, circular belvederes above them. Below the upper windows are large plaques of Coade stone, some square and some round, carved with swags, *putti* and, in the centre, a composition of most curious charm: a female figure reclines, somewhat precariously, on the edge of a brick bastion bristling with cannons, her elbow resting on an acanthus capital, while she indicates a plan of Belmont. In the background, beneath some exotic palm trees, rises the house itself, seen from the all-important south-east corner.

Those palm trees are one reminder of Harris's Indian life; another, perhaps, is provided by the two deep verandahs on the south and north sides. That to the south, featuring an Ionic colonnade of three bays, emphasises the middle bay by doubling the columns on each side; it is all the more surprising to find that the entrance door is not in this bay but in the left-hand one, the other two sets of what are apparently french windows being in fact dummies. This suggests that the original plan was for a five-bay south front, and that Harris suddenly changed his mind too late for the design to be altered. As it is, the building breaks off rather suddenly at this point, where it is joined by a long, lower Orangery – still presumably Wyatt's, however, since it carries another plaque with the date 1790. The northern verandah contrives – through narrower spaces between the columns and no doubling – to squeeze in four bays instead of three; surprisingly enough, however, it is a little shorter, since the corridor which runs straight through that part of the house from the front door passes behind its western end to culminate just beyond it in another deep bow.

As the south front makes clear, all Wyatt's principal rooms lie to the right of this corridor, except the small Entrance Hall and the Staircase Hall which share the same axis. The latter is particularly successful, and reveals for the first time that the central part of the house is a good deal higher than it looks from the outside, and that a whole extra storey is concealed beneath the roof. Lit from a central glazed lantern, it rises up by easy flights to the first floor; one is then surprised to see a higher gallery above, to which the only access is by the back stairs.

The Staircase Hall gives directly on to the central room on the east front, which is the prettily panelled Dining Room. It is flanked by two rooms of almost identical size and shape – the Drawing Room and the Library. They occupy respectively the southern and the northern bows of the front, and Wyatt has preserved their symmetry by bowing them at the other end as well, making them into straight-sided ellipses. The Drawing Room has an austerely beautiful chimneypiece of white marble and marvellous ebonised eagles, hovering within gilded scrolls, above the doors; the Library has preserved all its original inset bookcases and grained walnut panelling, with a series of painted plaques below the frieze – unchanged since Harris's time.

There are some delightful family portraits, of which my favourite represents the 2nd Lord Harris, aged about ten, pole-vaulting over the gates of Richmond churchyard.

## Bexleyheath

See London section.

## Boughton Monchelsea Place

*3; 5 miles S of Maidstone off A229*

It was unusual in Tudor times to build your house on the top of a hill; but that was what Robert Rudston did in the 1560s, using the site of an ancient fortified manor house which commanded, as it still commands today, one of the most spectacular views in all Kent. To stand at the south-east corner of the house on a clear morning and to gaze down at the fallow deer in the park – they have been there for at least three centuries – and then beyond to the huge expanse of the seemingly uninhabited Weald is to experience a real lift to the spirits; and when you turn to look more closely at the building behind you there is no sense of anti-climax. There it stands, low and four-square, its creamy grey walls of Kentish ragstone flecked with yellow lichen, battlemented above the second storey but with gabled dormers marking an attic – four flat-topped ones projecting to the crenellations themselves on the east front; five more, simpler and more retiring, to the south. This present roof line is largely the result of alterations made between 1790 and 1820, as are the gently Gothicised windows and the clustered Gothic columns of the shallow-vaulted front hall; but these changes have been effected with the lightest of touches and they seem to add, if anything, to the house's charm.

The inside is smaller than one might imagine, since the north and west ranges were in fact demolished around 1740 and replaced by single-storey brick extensions. The best feature is the fine broad staircase of William and Mary's time, which makes an interesting contrast with the upper flights of the original Elizabethan stairs remaining at the further end of the house.

There is plenty of good furniture, including a particularly splendid Jacobean four-poster bed and, opposite it in the same room, a superb carved wooden chest of the fifteenth century; but Boughton Monchelsea is no stately home. It is simply a lovely old Kentish manor house, remarkably unspoilt, with an agreeably Edwardian style of interior decoration which the present owner (1979) inherited and has seen no reason to change. There is also a lovely peaceful walled garden, from which the high brick chimneystacks can be seen rising above the verdure in picturesque and disorganised abundance.

*St Augustine's Church, Brookland.*

## Brasted Place

*4; 3 miles E of Sevenoaks off A25*

The house was built in 1784–5 by Robert Adam for Dr John Turton, who was physician to George III and whose ornate neo-classical tomb may be seen in the village church. The five-bay entrance front is fine and noble as you might expect, but contains no surprises; far more original, however, is Adam's treatment of the garden front, where the bays have been reduced to three and the deep and shady portico is supported on twin pairs of giant Ionic columns. These are reflected at the corners with angle pilasters of the same size. Two rather high dormers project like ears on either side of the pediment.

The house was greatly enlarged during the nineteenth century – not, alas, to its advantage. Scarcely any of the Adam interior has been preserved, and though I have not been inside I gather that I have not missed much. There remains, however, a certain historical interest, for the future Napoleon III lived here in 1840, before his first, unsuccessful, attempt to seize the French throne.

## Brook

*5; 4 miles E of Ashford off A20*

The very first sight of ST MARY'S CHURCH is enough to show that here is a church which, if not strictly beautiful, is nonetheless something to be reckoned with. The huge, square Norman tower at the west end is as wide as the nave (and almost as long) and could almost be considered a higher projection of it. It is in three clearly defined stages; and when you go inside and climb, in the south-west corner, the spiral staircase which has survived intact since the middle of the eleventh century at the latest, you find that the second stage is occupied by a separate chapel – a rare phenomenon indeed in English church architecture, though relatively common in France and Germany. In its east wall are set three round arches under a containing arch, the two outer ones looking down into the short, stubby nave. In the centre there are the remains of a wall painting of the seated Christ in the act of blessing; but 800 years of sunsets (there is a west window immediately opposite) have faded it badly.

Other paintings of perhaps a century later, and a good deal better preserved, decorate the nave and chancel. In the chancel they alternate, black-on-white and white-on-black, a curiously sophisticated and surprisingly successful device; in the nave there is a similar alternation, only here red takes the place of black. The two are separated by a round chancel arch of splendid proportions – though smaller than the tower arch, now filled in by a wood and glass screen. Much of the fenestration has, alas, been altered – the three lancets in the chancel at the cost of several of the paintings; and the Decorated window in the north wall of the nave, though fine enough in itself, is sadly inappropriate here. But the ground plan of the church remains precisely as it was before the Domesday Book, as do its general appearance, its massive walls of unknapped flints, and above all that extraordinary tower. It is altogether a remarkable survival.

*St Mary's Church, Brook.*

## Brookland*

*6; 6 miles NE of Rye on A259*

Let us take the belfry first, for this is what brings most people to ST AUGUSTINE'S CHURCH, Brookland. It is constructed entirely of timber and stands detached, a few yards from the north aisle. Its shape is that of three hollow octagonal pyramids, of diminishing size, placed one on top of the other. The largest and lowest stands on a vertical base only just high enough to accommodate the doorway; the smallest and highest carries a weather-cock. Inside, within the octagonal ambulatory, is a square core formed by four immense vertical wooden posts supported by scissor struts and arched braces. The date is about 1250 – which makes it contemporary with the church – but the upper section dates from the replacement of the bell cage some two centuries later.

You enter the church through a curious fourteenth-century timber porch with a double opening like a horsebox, to the left of which is, first, a battlemented stair turret leading to the roof, and then, in the north-west corner, a funny little excrescence, formerly a schoolroom, with a wide, rectangular, diamond-paned window. The interior is typical of the marshland, very light thanks to its clear glass, its long, broad aisles extending almost (though not quite) its whole length. The arcades are oddly asymmetrical – six bays on one side, seven on the other – and lean out alarmingly: not, as many people believe, a deliberate reminiscence of the shape of the Ark, but the effect of severe subsidence, which has necessitated the building of numerous buttresses, flying and otherwise.

Much of the church's considerable charm is due to the fact that it escaped the Victorian restorers – all of it, at least, except the chancel, and even that might be worse. It is, predictably, the oldest part of the church, mid-thirteenth-century, with nice big lancets to north and south and shafted rere-arches. The original triple lancet in the east end was replaced in the sixteenth century by the present three-light job. The aisle windows are of 1790 – square-headed, of two lights, and unremarkable, except for a big Decorated one to the north which has a few fragments of contemporary glass. (More, and better, will be found in the north aisle east window.) There is a big Perpendicular window in the chapel at the east end of the south aisle – to which, rather unexpectedly, one descends a step; just to the right, by the piscina, a late thirteenth-century wall painting depicts the murder of Thomas à Becket.

Before leaving, take a long and careful look at the font, which is the church's greatest single treasure. It is made of lead, one of only thirty remaining in the whole country, and is Norman or possibly Flemish work of about 1200. The design is principally composed of two tiers of arcading. Around the upper tier are the signs of the zodiac; around the lower, the labours of the months. After the font, the rest of the furniture comes as a bit of an anti-climax; but there is a delightful graveside shelter, designed to keep the minister dry during funerals. Everybody else, presumably, just got wet.

*Broome Park.*

## Broome Park

*7; 7½ miles N of Folkestone off B2065*

The second quarter of the seventeenth century was an exciting period in English architecture. Inigo Jones had already broken away from the Jacobean style; but the general taste, not yet ready for his cool Palladian classicism, turned instead to the Dutch and Flemish fashion, with a new and unprecedented emphasis on the gable – shaped, voluted and crowned with multiple pediments. This 'Artisan Mannerism' favoured the use of brick rather than stone and, as its name implies, was normally created not by professional architects but by the craftsmen themselves – the masons, joiners and bricklayers. Perhaps the best-known example is the Dutch House at Kew; but the most exuberant is unquestionably Broome Park, once the residence of Lord Kitchener of Khartoum.

It was built in 1635–8 in rich red brick, on an H-plan that was perfectly symmetrical along both axes. (The porch on the north and the bow on the south front are both later additions.) A deep projecting cornice runs all round above the first-floor windows, giving it a horizontal thrust to balance the verticality of the strip pilasters that are another salient feature of the design; thus the entire second floor becomes an attic storey – though the rooms are still of considerable height – and its windows form an integral part of the extraordinary gables which make the house so unforgettable. These can best be examined from the entrance front. Of the five recessed bays that form its centre, the four flanking gables are the most restrained; each consists of a lozenge-shaped window above the main one, above which a free-standing section rises on scrolls and is topped by a triangular pediment. The central gable is a good deal more ornate, but itself only points the way to those on the two single-bay projections (that form, as it were, the base of the H). Each of these incorporates a mullioned and transomed window of six lights which is flanked, at the bottom level by blank rectangular niches, then by double volutes in the form of an S. Next, above the windows, rise two superimposed broken pediments, the first triangular, the second segmental, framing a round-headed niche whose outsize keystone appears to support the missing moulding from the upper pediment. If this sounds complicated, I can only protest that it is a wild over-simplification.

The interior has been much changed – largely by Kitchener himself. It does, however, contain a superb Saloon by James Wyatt, with plasterwork in the Adam manner. The heavy Jacobean Hall, with its two gigantic chimneypieces copied from those in the Gallery at Hatfield, is – as one might expect – Kitchener's own.

The house has recently been converted into flats, and is therefore relatively easy of access, at least as far as the exterior is concerned.

*Canterbury Cathedral from the north-east.*

## Canterbury*

*8; 58 miles SE of London on A2*

THE CATHEDRAL AND IMMEDIATE ENVIRONS

The heart, the mind and perhaps even the soul of English Christianity are encapsulated in the Cathedral Church of Christ, Canterbury. Just as its Archbishop bears the title of Primate of All England (as opposed to the Archbishop of York, who is merely Primate of England – a nice distinction) so, of all the cathedrals in the country, that of Canterbury stands supreme. Though it may lack the immensity of York, the drama of Durham, the opulence of Lincoln, it yet possesses a presence, an air of quiet, serene authority, that no other English religious building can equal; nor is this surprising, for the history of Canterbury goes back very nearly fourteen centuries – to the year 597, when St Augustine arrived with strict orders from Rome to reconvert us. For nine of those centuries, moreover, the cathedral has been indissolubly linked with the most popular of all medieval martyrs, St Thomas à Becket, who was murdered within its walls in 1170 and whose shrine was, after Rome and Jerusalem, more visited than any other in Christendom. It is also quite breathtakingly beautiful.

None of the existing fabric, it must be admitted, can be traced back to Augustine's day, nor even to the Saxon cathedral that occupied the site until four years after the Norman Conquest. This was demolished in 1070 by Lanfranc, William the Conqueror's Archbishop, who replaced it with a much larger one – of almost exactly the same dimensions indeed, and probably much the same design, as the Abbey of St Étienne at Caen. I say 'probably', because Lanfranc's cathedral has vanished almost as completely as its predecessor: the very next Archbishop, Anselm, pulled down the choir and built another still larger (thereby almost doubling the size of the cathedral) which he lavishly decorated with stained glass, frescoes and marble pavement. This magnificent edifice was consecrated in 1130; alas, in 1174 it was gutted by fire and left an empty shell. The way was thus made clear for the two men to whom the eastern half of the Canterbury interior is principally due: William of Sens and, after his fall from the scaffolding early in 1179, his successor William the Englishman. The former rebuilt the choir and the east transepts; the latter then extended it further eastward to accommodate the shrine of St Thomas, to whom, less than a decade after his death, miraculous cures were already being credited. Thus it is William the Englishman that we have to thank for the marvellous Trinity Chapel that so dramatically closes the east end of Canterbury Cathedral, and the lovely little corona beyond.

At this time the nave and the west transepts were still Lanfranc's; but as more and more pilgrims flocked to Canterbury 'the holie blissfull martyre for to seeke' and the cathedral coffers grew steadily heavier, so the pressure mounted for the old Norman fabric to be replaced by something more up-to-date. Work began in 1378 and continued on and off for well over a century: John Wastell's superb central tower, Bell Harry, was not completed until 1503. By then only one important part of Lanfranc's old cathedral remained – the north-west tower. Doubtless there were plans to replace it; its south-western neighbour had been finished as early as 1434. We can only assume that after the building of Bell Harry it took the authorities some time to amass sufficient funds to carry on, and that by the time they had done so the Dissolution of the Monasteries put paid to the whole idea. Lanfranc's tower thus managed to survive until 1832, when the present replica of the south-west tower was erected in its place. Was this a tragedy? Certainly, for the architectural historian. For the rest of us, I'm not so sure. I prefer Romanesque to Perpendicular any day; but those three towers, despite the widely separated dates at which they were built, give the cathedral, when seen from the west, a stylistic unity and grace that it could otherwise never have had, and which I for one cannot find it in my heart to regret.

*Bell Harry, Canterbury Cathedral's great central tower.*

Viewed from the east, the whole picture changes. Apart from a glimpse of Bell Harry towering up behind, almost everything we see is either Romanesque or the very earliest Gothic. Anselm's work remains in the two eastern transepts with their enchanting little staircase towers, and in the two side chapels – that to the south is named after him, the other being dedicated to St Andrew – whose oblique setting shows that they had once flanked the apse before the lengthening of the east end. His also are the windows in the three bays of the choir aisles, amazingly large for the early twelfth century. The rest is the work of the two Williams, French and English, all completed within the ten years 1174–84. William of Sens heightened the choir walls and provided them with a clerestory. To support them, he also added the flying buttresses; low and inconspicuous, they barely clear the aisle roofs – but mark them well, for they are the earliest exposed flying buttresses in England. The Trinity Chapel and corona were built from scratch by the English William. The former is marked by a series of deep buttresses, the spaces between them filled with huge windows; the latter has, from the outside, a strangely castle-like appearance; much of it, however, dates only from the middle of the eighteenth century.

We enter by the south-west porch, a two-storeyed structure of considerable opulence, with statues in niches beneath a forest of crocketed canopies. Its outside was almost entirely renewed in 1862, but the lierne-vaulted interior is the original early fifteenth-century work. We pass through the inner door and find ourselves in one of the greatest Perpendicular naves in the country. It is the work of Henry Yevele, builder of Westminster Hall, and his partner Stephen Lote. So soaring are the clustered shafts, so brilliant the light, that it is hard to remember that all the horizontal dimensions, including the breadth of the bays, were dictated by Lanfranc's ground plan, and that the piers we see today are really his old Norman ones in an outer Gothic casing. Only the height was increased; Yevele heightened his roof to the level of the English William's east end. Since, however, the latter is raised on a crypt and the nave is not, the proportions of the two could hardly be more different, and the feeling of height is further increased by the fact that the vaulting shafts, three to each pier, go rocketing straight up to the capitals, at clerestory level, from which the vault springs. The clerestory windows are quite modest in size; the splendour of the natural lighting is due not so much to them as to the huge aisle windows, which rise to the same height as the arcade and are as broad as the buttressing will allow.

The view to the east is broken, first by a strainer across the western crossing arch with a delicate design of punched quatrefoils (inserted by Wastell to strengthen the supports of Bell Harry) and second, at the top of a flight of steps on the eastern side of the crossing, by a tremendous stone screen – or, more accurately, a pulpitum – of stunning magnificence. On each side of the great central doorway into the choir are the statues of three kings, in niches under tall crocketed canopies. The two nearest the doorway are known to be Ethelbert and Edward the Confessor; the others are generally identified as Richard II and the three Henrys who succeeded him, but since the screen is known to have been erected by Prior Chillenden – who died in 1411, before Henry V's accession and Henry VI's birth – and since all six seem to be by the same highly skilled hand, we cannot be sure. In any event, the identification is less important than the quality and rarity; for, monuments apart, there are no finer examples of early fifteenth-century sculpture surviving anywhere in the country.

Now walk up the aisle, under Wastell's strainer arch, up a few steps to the centre of the crossing; and look up. There, dizzyingly high above you, is the brightly coloured and brilliantly fan-vaulted base of Bell Harry. Another fan vault adorns the roof of the Lady Chapel, built off the east wall of the north transept. Its opposite number on the south side, the Chapel of St Michael, is a little earlier, and vaulted rather more simply with liernes. All Saints' Chapel, immediately above it, is simpler still, going no further than tiercerons.

From these west transepts, stairs lead down into the crypt. Suddenly, we are back in the early twelfth century, in the days of Anselm. But Anselm's crypt was quite unlike any that had been built in England before. It is high, and well above ground; it has windows, and is full of light. Moreover, since it escaped the 1174 fire it is in a quite remarkable state of preservation. It possesses two outstanding glories: the carved capitals of its supporting columns and the wall paintings in St Gabriel's Chapel, on the south side; but whereas, in the whole canon of English Romanesque, the former are merely as good as anything of their kind, the latter are unique. Walled up for nearly 700 years, they have kept the freshness of their execution and the brilliance of their colouring; but the really remarkable thing about them is their unEnglishness. There is a spiritual, hieratic quality about them which speaks compellingly of Byzantium. Now early twelfth-century England had only one cultural link with Constantinople: Sicily, where the Norman King Roger II, crowned in the very year that Anselm was consecrated, commissioned from Byzantine painters and mosaicists works as fine as any to be found in the imperial capital. Thus the paintings in St Gabriel's Chapel are, in their way, the counterpart of the mosaic portrait of St Thomas of Canterbury which can still be seen in the apse of the Cathedral of Monreale, placed there as a gesture of contrition by Henry II's own daughter, Queen Joanna of Sicily.

Of less interest than this chapel, but of considerable beauty nevertheless, is the Chapel of Our Lady Undercroft at the eastern end of the crypt. It was here, we are told, that the Black Prince expressed a wish to be buried; its present decoration, however, dates from after his time, when a certain Lady Mohun founded a chantry chapel here in 1396. Near it, under the south transept, is the erstwhile Black Prince's Chantry, now used as a church for the few Huguenot families who came to Canterbury during the French wars of religion and have remained here, as honoured residents, ever since.

Emerging from the crypt, we now enter the choir. Although it had been considerably enlarged by Anselm, who had given it a pair of eastern transepts and two small chapels beyond them, the murder of Becket in 1170 and the resulting flood of pilgrims meant that even Anselm's extensions were hopelessly inadequate; and the fire of 1174 provided a perfect opportunity for its rebuilding on an even more ambitious scale. The problem for the two Williams who took on the job was those two chapels, St Andrew's and St Anselm's. They could not be demolished, and in order to incorporate them in his new design without lessening the breadth of the choir aisles – which were vital for processional purposes – William of Sens narrowed the three eastern bays of his choir. At the same time, by adding a clerestory, he greatly increased its height, replacing the earlier flat roof with a sexpartite rib vault, and introduced a new element of colour contrast by the use, for certain carefully chosen vertical shafts, of dark Purbeck marble. The result of all this is, at least to my eye, not wholly satisfactory; despite the ingenuity of William's design the choir, as it were, somehow fails to sing. But as an example of the way in which a master mason of exceptional ability tackled the problems of the transition from Romanesque to Gothic, its importance can hardly be overstressed.

Working from the west, William had reached the sixth bay of the choir when he met with his accident; it was at this point, in 1179, that his namesake William the Englishman took over. The pilgrim boom meant that there was no shortage of funds, and the Englishman's work was completed in all its essentials within the next five years. His scheme was for a progression of rising levels: choir, presbytery, Trinity Chapel, each was to be set higher than its neighbour to the west. This seems to have been his own idea rather than his predecessor's, for the sixteen steps leading up to the Trinity Chapel cut across the last piers of the choir; but it was certainly a highly theatrical one, worthy of the shrine of the saint, which was moved to its new position before the high altar in 1220. Equally impressive was the backdrop, a semi-circular apse of five bays, with gallery and clerestory separated by radiating ribs and supported on coupled columns, one behind the other, of Purbeck marble. Behind this screen of columns, and barely perceptible in the half-light, are other groups of clustered piers forming the beautiful circular corona – 'Becket's Crown' – now known as the Chapel of Saints and Martyrs of Our Own Time. It is tiny, only 26 feet in diameter: but its huge windows contain some of the best stained glass in the cathedral – which is to say in England. Until a few years ago it was empty save for St Augustine's chair, a splendid thirteenth-century throne of Purbeck marble in which every Archbishop of Canterbury is installed. This has now been moved forward into the Trinity Chapel, with great loss of dramatic effect.

Becket's shrine has gone – destroyed on the orders of Henry VIII, who for good measure had the murdered Archbishop condemned as a traitor and a rebel. All that remains to mark the place is the mosaic floor – a fine piece of early thirteenth-century *opus Alexandrinum*. For sumptuous tombs, however, we do not need to look very far; for only a few feet away, on the south side of the Trinity Chapel, is that of Edward, the Black Prince.

*The nave, Canterbury Cathedral.*

There he lies in gilded copper, armed *cap-a-pie*, on a high tomb chest with painted shields and beneath a painted wooden canopy. High above hang replicas of his funeral achievements – shield, helm, gauntlets and tabard. (The originals, or what is left of them, can be seen in the south choir aisle.) Opposite, on the north side of the chapel, stands the tomb of Henry IV and his Queen, Joan of Navarre. Whereas the Black Prince was represented hieratically, these two effigies are obviously portraits. Solicitous angels adjust their pillows and crowns.

There are many other tombs of comparable magnificence, mostly of past archbishops; but I doubt very much that I am alone in finding more moving than any of them a simple inscription in the north-west transept, just by the entrance of the passage that leads into the Cloister. This transept was, as we know, rebuilt in the fifteenth century, but in deference to the particular holiness of the spot, the original floor was left untouched. On the wall above we read the words: 'THOMAS BECKET/ARCHBISHOP*SAINT*MARTYR/DIED HERE/TUESDAY 29TH DECEMBER/1170.'

We now leave the cathedral proper, and pass through the CLOISTER. Originally built by Lanfranc, it was remodelled by Prior Chillenden (1390–1411) with lierne vaults and painted heraldic shields for bosses. The big four-light windows which look out on to the central garth come as a bit of a surprise, since – despite the short vertical bars rising from the points of the arches – their tracery is completely Decorated in feeling, a style which at that date was distinctly *passé*. These windows were surmounted on the outside by tall ogival gables, copiously crocketed, but none of the existing ones is original. The only survivor of the earlier Cloister retained by Chillenden was the north wall, which dates from the building of the refectory immediately beyond it in 1226–36. This is distinguished by a low stone seat running all the way along, above which rises a very pretty free-standing arcade with trefoil arches. Part of the lavatorium can still be seen, where the monks washed before going in to their meals.

If you walk clockwise round the Cloister, you will almost complete the circuit before you come, halfway along the east side, to the entrance into the CHAPTER HOUSE. This is one vast, single room – there is no antechamber or vestibule – nearly 100 feet long, of immense height, and, to me at least, profoundly impressive. Rebuilt in 1304, when Decorated was in full flower, its lower half is surprisingly austere, almost bereft of adornment apart from the arcading which surrounds the central space; and even this abandons its restraint only for a moment, when it breaks slightly forward under a canopy to mark the seat of the Prior. Thus the contrast is all the greater when, just above the windows, the bare white walls give way to a wooden roof of memorable splendour – the largest in England after Westminster Hall, which it predates. The near-tunnel vault is formed by seven separate cants, all intricately ribbed in a pattern of stars. Beneath it, the windows are Chillenden's, and Perpendicular: he was more up to date here than in the Cloister.

Returning to the Cloister, turn right and then right again along the passage, mysteriously known as the Dark Entry, which runs along the north wall of the Chapter House. Immediately to your left is the new (1953) Library by J.L. Denman; *The Buildings of England* describes it as 'neo-Norman-cum-Tudoresque', which just about sums it up. It occupies the southern third of Lanfranc's old DORMITORY, built in 1090 or thereabouts to accommodate no fewer than 150 monks; if, on emerging from the Dark Entry into the Infirmary Cloister, you turn left and walk past the end of the Library wall to where the remaining two-thirds of the ruins still lie open to the sky, you realise just how enormous it was. Little survives but the broken shafts of the columns of the undercroft; but it is fascinating to see how they have been carved in the big bold zigzags and spirals that are so much a feature of the cathedral crypt and – more famous still – the nave at Durham. These columns are earlier than either.

The Infirmary Cloister is a true cloister only on the south and east. The Norman east arcade is now doomed to support the Wolfson Library (1964–6), vaguely

Tudor, in a violent red brick – a superimposition which does it no good at all. The south range, of 1100 or so, is interrupted halfway along by a most enjoyable LAVATORY TOWER, from which a passage runs south to join the north-east transept of the cathedral. It is octagonal, and its first-floor mullioned and transomed windows give it a fifteenth-century air; but the arches below and the vaulting – supported by a core of four inner piers – reveal the true date as being around 1150. The upper part was originally a huge cistern, from which water was channelled to the neighbouring buildings; alas, none of the early plumbing arrangements has survived.

The INFIRMARY proper ran eastward in a long line from the south-east corner of the Infirmary Cloister, with its own Chapel in the same axis beyond it. Oddly enough, it seems to have been even bigger than the main dormitory – a long, seven-bay Hall with aisles to north and south. Of both Hall and Chapel, only the south arcades have survived, and then only in part. Both are of the same date, the very early twelfth century; but one was built for men and the other for God, and the architecture shows it. The Hall arcade could hardly be simpler, with its big round piers and sturdy arches, unadorned except for two plain square orders. The Chapel, by contrast, has compound piers of considerable complication, and capitals obviously carved by the same masons whose work we have seen in the crypt. The square-ended chancel is a fourteenth-century addition.

Between the west end of the Infirmary Hall and the north-east transept of the cathedral stands a square building raised, like the Lavatory Tower, over an open arcade. This was formerly the Treasury, and now serves as a vestry for the cathedral, from which it must be entered. See it if you possibly can: the octopartite rib vault that forms its roof is unique in England.

Back now to the Infirmary Cloister, whence a door in the east side takes you through the Green Court. On your right is the long, low DEANERY; the flint buildings facing you to the north are the old BREWHOUSE and BAKERY (early fourteenth-century, but much restored after bombing in the Second World War), separated from the GRANARY by a big Perpendicular gateway, with postern, known as the FORRENS GATE. To your left you will see Prior Chillenden's PENTISE, which runs from the Kitchen Court just north of the refectory for some 100 yards as far as the COURT GATE – a covered way, roofed with tie-beams and scissor-braces, along which the pilgrims would return to their lodgings after making their devotions at the shrine.

At the Court Gate we are really in the precincts of the KING'S SCHOOL, which has a good claim to being the oldest school in the country; although refounded as a grammar school in 1541 – the 'King' is Henry VIII – it has origins going back to a monastic foundation of the seventh century, and can boast among its alumni Christopher Marlowe, William Harvey and Somerset Maugham. Both the Gate and part of the southern end of NORTH HALL which adjoins it date from the 1150s; the latter includes three bays of the splendid Norman arcade, and a simply marvellous outside staircase, emerging at right-angles to the building under a later gabled roof.

### THE CITY

So much for the cathedral and its monastic appurtenances. They are by no means all that Canterbury has to offer; although the city suffered severely during the war – among the casualties was St George's church, where Marlowe was baptised in 1564, and the house in which he was born – there are still a number of fine buildings from the fifteenth century on to reward the stroller. Space allows me to mention only a few of the best.

Most venerable of all is ST MARTIN'S CHURCH, probably the earliest place of Christian worship surviving in England. It is here that St Augustine came to pray on his arrival in Canterbury in 597, and here that he baptised the Saxon King Ethelbert. (The King was a willing convert, having been softened up by his wife Bertha – daughter of the Frankish King Clovis – who had already adopted Christianity. Thanks in large measure to her, Augustine found many Christians waiting to welcome him and, in St Martin's, at least one church.) The west tower is Perpendicular, but the nave and tiny chancel – it is only 15 feet across – are principally of stone, with occasional courses of Roman brick; parts of the chancel are of this brick exclusively. It is impossible to date it with any accuracy; all we can say is that it is not later than the seventh century, and could be earlier. The church may well have been enlarged after Augustine's mission, and the earliest fabric may date only from then; alternatively, it may be the very same building to which – according to Bede – Bertha came to pray before his arrival. The only part which can be said with any certainty to be pre-Augustinian is the square-headed block doorway at the west end of the south wall of the chancel.

The EASTBRIDGE HOSPITAL OF ST THOMAS THE MARTYR (St Peter's Street) was built as a hospice around 1190 on a bridge across the Stour. The flint-faced building seen from the street is obviously two centuries or so later, though the Norman round arch is still in position over the later pointed one. Inside, the most interesting part is the Norman undercroft; but in the Chapel upstairs there is a remarkably beautiful contemporary wall painting of Christ in Majesty, with the symbols of the Evangelists around him. Opposite, the OLD WEAVERS' HOUSE is a fine building, gabled and timber-framed, of 1561.

Another river-straddler, even more picturesque, is GREYFRIARS, off Stour Street. The Greyfriars were Franciscans – they changed the colour of their robes later – the first of whom arrived in Canterbury in 1224, while St Francis was still alive. This building, which probably served as the warden's lodging, dates from about half a century later. With its two arches spanning the river – here hardly more than a stream – and narrow lancet above, it is characteristically unassuming; but on a sunny morning it looks quite ravishingly pretty.

Now to ST AUGUSTINE'S ABBEY. This was his first foundation, dating from 598. (That which subsequently developed into the cathedral was founded only on his second visit, in 602.) Here too he was buried – outside the walls, according to the tradition of the early Christians in Rome. Within its precincts there stood, in the seventh century, no fewer than three churches; but all three were levelled in 1070 to make room for a splendid new church: anything, it seemed, that Lanfranc could do, the Abbot of St Augustine's could do better. Alas, this great church was levelled in its turn at the time of the Dissolution, to be incorporated in a new palace built for Henry VIII; and in the first quarter of the present century the three seventh-century churches were excavated. Not much of them can be seen, but the surviving ruins have their fascinations for anyone of an archaeological turn of mind.

This book, however, does not concern itself with archaeology, and St Augustine's would not have found a place in it were it not for the great gateway, which was retained as the principal entrance to Henry VIII's palace. It dates from 1300–9, by which time, thanks to the popularity of St Thomas and the wealth of his shrine, the abbey could no longer hope to rival the cathedral in splendour; but it never gave up the struggle, and FYNDON GATE, as it is called, exploits the potential of the Decorated style on a far grander scale than anything the cathedral has to offer. Within, to the north and west of the abbey remains, there rise in place of the palace the buildings of ST AUGUSTINE'S COLLEGE, the first important work by William Butterfield. The College was founded in 1844 by A.J.B. Beresford-Hope (who was later to finance Butterfield's masterpiece, All Saints, Margaret Street) for the training of missionaries, and was deliberately designed on monastic lines. Though much of Butterfield's original decoration has gone, the Chapel and the Library in particular are still well worth a visit.

Finally, the WALLS: they enclose almost exactly half the medieval city, to the south and east; the north-west never needed a wall, being adequately defended by the Stour, so relatively little of the fortification has been lost. Most of what we see today dates from the fourteenth and fifteenth centuries, though a section to the south-east was abominably restored in 1958. It is of flint, with projecting bastions at fairly regular intervals along its entire length.

The CASTLE, just inside the walls at their south-western extremity, is Norman but of no particular interest. Far more impressive for my money is WESTGATE, built between 1375 and 1381. With its two terrific round towers it still looks much as it always has, a marvellous survival.

## Charing

*9; 6 miles NW of Ashford on A20*

The CHURCH OF ST PETER AND ST PAUL stands proudly next to the ruins of the Archbishop's Palace – formerly the medieval manor house – where Henry VIII was entertained in 1520 on his way to the Field of the Cloth of Gold. Not surprisingly in the circumstances, it is conceived on the grand scale, with the most ambitious tower in the county. Nothing ornate, mind you; Kent never went in for the sort of fancy work beloved of Somerset or Northamptonshire. But it is tall and noble, with much fine detail; look at the moulding of the battlements, the labels over the windows and bell openings, and the brave west door of about 1540, some seventy years after the rest of the tower. Look too, once inside the church, at the glorious tower arch giving out on to the nave.

On Tuesday 4 August 1590, disaster struck. The whole church – though not the tower – was gutted by fire, 'chanced', according to a contemporary account, 'by means of a birding-piece discharged by one Mr Dios, which fired in the shingels, the day being extreme hot and the same shingels very dry'. The present roof-beams, dating from two years later, are painted in the Spanish manner – presumably Mr Dios's attempt to atone for his deplorable marksmanship. Especially when seen to their best advantage, from the east end looking west, they appear to be carved – a possibly unintentional piece of *trompe-l'oeil*, but no less remarkable for that.

Most of the rest of the interior dates from the early seventeenth century, though the shell of the original, aisleless building (with a particularly fine Decorated north transept) still remains. There is a simply magnificent Royal Arms, proudly painted and dated 1716, its effect in no way diminished by somewhat unorthodox punctuation in the motto.

Don't leave Charing without a quick stroll down the exceedingly pretty VILLAGE STREET – a lovely collection of vernacular architecture, with buildings of every century from the thirteenth (part of the stone building just to the left of Pierce House) to the twentieth.

## Chartham ★

*10; 4 miles SW of Canterbury off A28*

ST MARY'S, built in the last decade of the thirteenth century, is a church of many treasures; one only is visible from the outside. This is the tracery, the outstanding example of the form known as Kentish, with internally cusped quatrefoils, the cusps themselves peeled back, as it were, like the two sides of a fleur-de-lis. The design is to be found not only in the four-light east window but also in the eight two-lighters to the north and south of the chancel; the latter are less easy to see, being set between deep buttresses. The rest of the exterior is unremarkable, apart from the continuous hood-mould which looks vaguely Victorian but is in fact the same age as the church. There are knapped flints throughout, with dressings of pale grey stone; a good tiled roof; and a big square tower.

Going in, one immediately notices that the church is a good deal grander than it looks from the outside. There are the windows again, looking more sumptuous than ever; but now they have competition – in the wooden roof. The nave, chancel and transepts (there are no aisles) are all of wagon form, with six cants. The chancel has been given a rather boring ceilure, with wooden ribs forming a simple grid pattern; everywhere else are deep, close-set rafters giving a feeling of mystery and depth. Best of all is the crossing, where two great timber arches spring diagonally from the corners of the transepts, meeting in the middle with a huge carved wooden boss.

The brass, along the east wall of the north transept, is the fourth earliest in the country and the most impressive I know. It is of Sir Robert de Septvans, who died in 1306. His shield, ailettes and surcoat all bear his emblem, the winnowing fan; and his hair is a dream.

## Chevening

*11; 3 miles NW of Sevenoaks off A21*

Bequeathed some years ago by the Stanhope family to HM Government, Chevening was briefly occupied by Prince Charles. Its change of ownership necessitated a major programme of restoration, and since this in turn resulted in the removal of the yellowish grey 'mathematical tiles' which had disfigured the house ever since the 3rd Earl Stanhope – father of Lady Hester – slapped them on in the 1780s, it now looks better than it has done for the past 200 years.

In *Vitruvius Britannicus* (Vol. II, 1717) Colen Campbell noted that Chevening was 'said to have been built by Inigo Jones'. There is no evidence for this and on stylistic grounds it seems unlikely; on the other hand, there is a long family tradition that the house was built for the 13th Lord Dacre, who died in 1630. This theory, if true, would mean that it was quite remarkably in advance of its time; since the type of house that it represents, which found its ultimate exemplar in Sir Roger Pratt's Coleshill, only crystallised into a style some twenty years later. Sceptics, however, were considerably shaken some years ago by the discovery that St Clere (*q.v.*) – a house only a few miles away at Kemsing which, until both were remodelled, was very similar to Chevening – was completed not later than 1633. It therefore looks as though the old tradition may be right, in which case Chevening emerges as a pioneer house of immense importance – one of the first country houses built on the double-pile plan (with the principal rooms going off to each side of a central corridor) as introduced by Jones, and one of the first examples of the Coleshill style which became the *beau idéal* of English domestic architecture in the later seventeenth century.

Unfortunately it is almost impossible to see it in this light today, since the 'improvements' by Thomas Fort early in the eighteenth century and – far more radical – by James Wyatt, working for the 3rd Earl, towards the end of it, have altered it beyond recognition. What one now sees is a handsome three-and-a-half-storey house, newly but most skilfully refaced in red brick, with Ionic pilasters and stone dressings. On the north, entrance, front two quadrant links lead to two-storeyed red-brick service blocks, presumably by Fort. The place is noble in its way, but not exceptional.

Inside, however, the house boasts, together with much fine panelling and some splendid chimneypieces, one spectacular *tour de force*. This is the circular staircase inserted in 1721 by Nicholas Dubois, running straight up from the weapon-encrusted Hall two full storeys, one complete gyration per storey. This in itself would be remarkable; what makes it almost miraculous is the fact that it is attached to the wall at two points only, one immediately above the other. So breathtaking a feat of technical legerdemain imparts a springiness which might unnerve some; but the visual impact is unforgettable.

## Cobham

*12; 4 miles W of Rochester on B2009*
*Includes Owletts (NT)*

'Really,' said Mr Pickwick, 'for a misanthrope's choice this is one of the prettiest and most desirable residences I have ever met with.' I'm not sure that 'pretty' – or even 'desirable' – is quite the word for the grandest sixteenth- to seventeenth-century mansion in Kent, but Mr Pickwick was a man of peculiar tastes; and Dickens, who knew the area intimately and later lived just across the park at Gads Hill, may have been prejudiced.

*St Mary's Church, Chartham.*

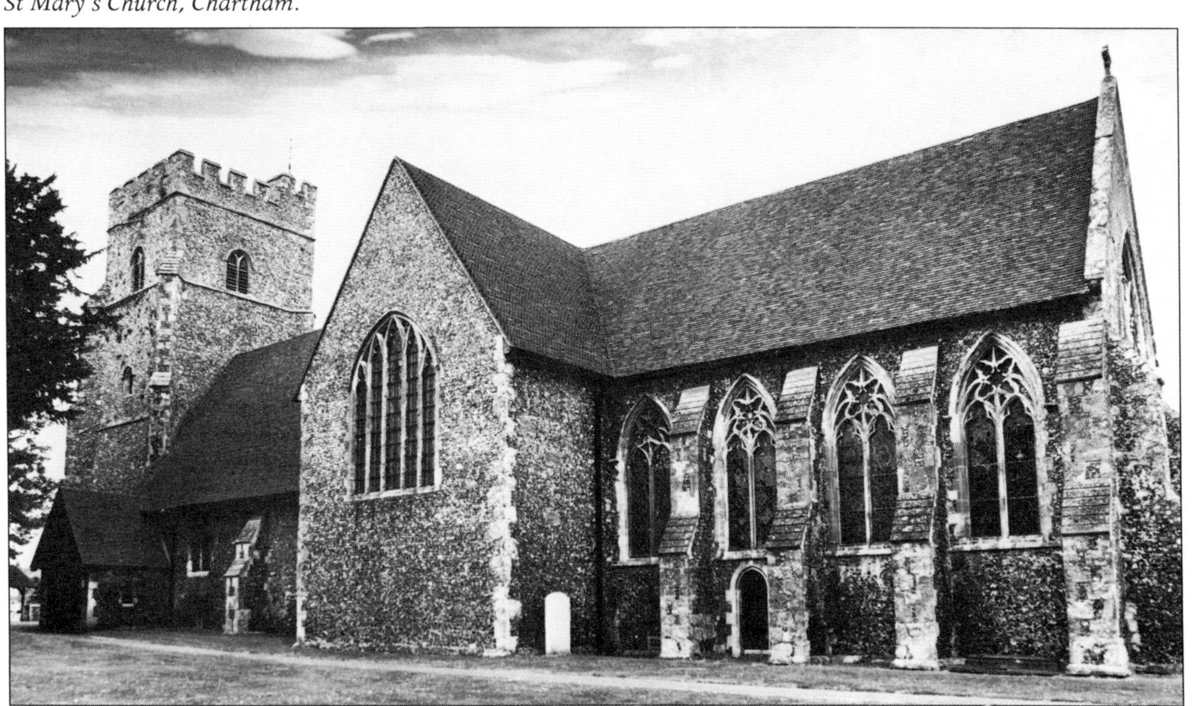

COBHAM HALL started as a medieval manor house, on to which, between 1580 and 1602, the 10th Lord Cobham added two immense wings, projecting from each end towards the west, with four-storeyed towers at each end. These wings are of a beautiful salmon-pink brick, with stone dressings. The southern one looks particularly noble when seen from the outside across the park; its fifteen bays, only two storeys high apart from the towers, could easily have been monotonous, but the gentle breaking forward of the fourth, eighth and twelfth gives it just the degree of articulation it needs, while the tall brick chimneys, arranged in pairs at perfectly judged intervals, redress the balance between vertical and horizontal. The northern wing is less satisfying as a whole – the main entrance was moved there early in the last century – but it boasts, on its inner side, one of the two great showpieces of the house: a three-staged stone porch in high Renaissance style marking the way into the Chapel, extraordinarily exuberant and assured for the early 1590s.

Meanwhile the central block remained medieval – perhaps because Cobham's son and successor was involved in the plot to put Lady Arabella Stuart on the throne and sent to the Tower – the house being forfeited to the Crown, from which it passed to the Dukes of Lennox. Then, in the 1660s, the 6th Duke of Lennox and Richmond replaced it with a new block featuring four Corinthian pilasters and entablature. Long thought to be by Webb, it is now known to have been the work of Peter Mills, a successful (though nowadays largely forgotten) architect of the time. The original design was of two storeys only, with hipped roof and dormers; the attic floor was added by Sir William Chambers in 1768–70, and Tudorised half a century later by Humphry Repton – who also landscaped the park – and his sons John and George.

*Cobham Hall.*

Cobham Hall is now a school; the interior, in consequence, does not look its best. A surprisingly strong influence here is that of James Wyatt, who left virtually no mark at all on the outside but who did an immense amount of interior work between 1785 and 1810. Indeed, much of the fascination of the house lies in the seemingly continual change of styles, as Elizabethan, Baroque, neo-classical and Gothick succeed each other with bewildering speed. Three rooms deserve special mention: the Reptons' Library; Wyatt's enchanting little Vestibule with its Ionic screen and apsed recess; and, wonder of wonders, the great Gilt Hall itself – one of the most glorious rooms in the entire county. It too is a bit of a hybrid. Its location in the seventeenth-century central block means that there is no Elizabethan work; but the tremendous gilded plaster ceiling of 1672 might, one feels, easily crush Wyatt's delicate neo-classicism at floor level. That it does not do so is probably due to Chambers, who seems to have designed the upper walls when the Hall was converted into a Music Room in 1779 and provided with galleries and an organ. (Howard Colvin, however, finds no evidence for Chambers working at Cobham after 1770, so we cannot be sure.) These additions provide a gentle transition between the two styles and remove any feeling of top-heaviness.

After a tour of the house, visitors in a determined frame of mind may like to seek out Wyatt's extraordinary MAUSOLEUM, a mile or so away in the woods to the south-east. Built in 1783 for the Earls of Darnley (who, through a rather complicated succession, now owned the estate) it was never used; and with its Doric columns, symbolic sarcophagi and stone pyramidal roof it now stands derelict, forgotten and utterly magnificent. It will not stand much longer, so see it while you can.

Now to the CHURCH OF ST MARY MAGDALENE, which houses the most memorable collection of brasses in the kingdom. They have been relaid and twice restored, but with no loss of authenticity. Superb as they are, however, they should not blind one to the church itself, which has a real architectural distinction of its own. The chancel in particular, built on a collegiate scale, five bays long and broad in proportion, is grandly impressive Early English of about 1220 and was endowed 150 years later with a piscina and sedilia of sumptuous splendour.

Just to the south of the church is the COLLEGE, built and endowed by Sir John de Cobham in 1362–70 around two quadrangles. Its original purpose was to house five collegiate priests, but the foundation was dissolved by Henry VIII and in 1596 the buildings were converted into twenty-one almshouses. So they remain today, the medieval hall now doing duty as a common room, a pleasant and peaceful setting in which I for one should be only too happy to live out my declining years.

OWLETTS (NT), once the home of the architect Sir Herbert Baker, who left it to the National Trust, is a relatively unassuming brick house of 1683 at the north-western edge of the town, on the B2009. One feature only makes it exceptional: the staircase, which occupies three whole bays and boasts a spectacular plaster ceiling dated 1684, luxuriant with leaves, fruit and flowers. The house is open to the public, but only at the stated times.

*Dover Castle.*

## Dover

*13; on coast 74 miles SE of London on A2*

From almost every angle, and whether viewed from land, sea or air, DOVER CASTLE looks magnificent. This most strategic position in all England was already fortified in the Iron Age; later it was added to by the Romans who built a lighthouse, by the Saxons who built a church, and by the Normans who built the keep and inner curtain wall towards the end of the twelfth century. More work was done as a protection against Napoleon in the nineteenth and Hitler in the twentieth, and the castle remained garrisoned until 1958.

As in most working castles, the interior contains more of interest than of beauty. For this reason, and because its very size precludes any full description here, serious visitors should provide themselves with the first-rate guide-book published by HMSO and follow the itinerary it recommends. If, however, their time is short, my advice is that they should hurry straight to the keep – a fascinating building, part castle, part palace, which still preserves much of the character given it by Henry II in the 1180s in spite of having been modernised and generally made more comfortable in the fifteenth century. Its *pièces de résistance* are the two chapels, one situated above the other – glorious Norman work, both of them, and with a richness of decoration which comes like a benison amid such austere surroundings. The arches (all of them round, though at nearby Canterbury pointed arches had already begun to appear by this time) are elaborately moulded, zigzagged and dogtoothed, and the proportions, for all the smallness of scale, are perfect. The upper chapel, which is rather larger than the lower, is generously rib-vaulted – which makes it look richer still.

Outside the keep, the Roman lighthouse – rather preciously known as the PHAROS – is well worth a visit. It is externally an octagon, enclosing a square central chamber, and was originally cut back in steps like a telescope, though these are now almost gone. Of the five original storeys the top one is medieval. For centuries this grand old building served as a ready-made bell-tower for the Saxon CHURCH OF ST MARY IN CASTRO that nestles, seemingly for protection, up against it; and one could only wish that this too had been allowed to keep its character. Alas, Sir George Gilbert Scott was let loose on it in 1860 and, as if that were not enough, Butterfield in 1888 plastered it with mosaics of quite shattering awfulness. He might as well have blown the whole thing up.

*Godinton Park.*

## Godinton Park

*14; 2 miles W of Ashford off A20*

A little to the west of Ashford, Godinton provides a welcome contrast to the unlovely suburban sprawl which reaches to its gates. There is quite a long drive, among towering and venerable trees, before you reach the house, set back on a low terrace behind a clipped yew hedge. It is of warm red brick, two-storeyed, but with big shaped gables – each containing an attic window – that give it its character and enable us to date it to around 1630. In this we are, on the whole, perfectly right: most of the house was indeed built early in the reign of Charles I by Captain Nicholas Toke, and the rainwater heads bear the date 1628. Captain Toke did not, however, start from scratch. The house he inherited was probably built in the late fourteenth century, and parts of it still remain, most obviously in the little central courtyard where bits of old timber framing speak for themselves. In the Hall, too, the tie-beam and kingpost are ancient survivals – as are the smoke-blackened rafters in the roof, now concealed behind the Captain's panelled ceiling.

The principal fronts are symmetrical, the original entrance being to the east, where the two outer gables crown modestly projecting wings while the two inner ones have canted bay windows beneath them, mullioned and with a double transom on the upper storey. The south front is similar but a good deal simpler, without projections or bays. The present entrance front to the north is an early nineteenth-century pastiche of the prevailing seventeenth-century style – and rather more successful than one might expect. The Hall, by contrast, looks more recent than it is. Originally medieval as we have seen, it is now almost exaggeratedly Jacobean thanks to large quantities of panelling inserted piecemeal early in the last century. Much of this is extremely fine – particularly the carving around the fireplace and in the overmantel.

Having inspected the Georgian Dining Room and the Priest's Room (which, incidentally, provides the background for R.B. Martineau's *The Last Day in the Old Home*, now in the Tate Gallery) we emerge at the foot of Captain Toke's magnificent staircase. The fact that he gave it a special bay to itself, projecting into the courtyard, is an indication of the importance he attached to it; and it is unquestionably, after Knole, the most memorable seventeenth-century staircase in the county. It brings us to the outstanding room of the house, the Great Chamber. Here the walls are richly panelled, every inch of them, right up to the coving of the ceiling, to which pretty little strapwork finials point upward at intervals. At one end, the great chimneypiece bears the Toke arms, together with carvings of Adam and Eve, St Hubert's stag, and little figures hunting, bear-baiting and – as far as one can make out – pig-sticking. Along the walls to north and west runs a frieze even more extraordinary, illustrating the various techniques of musket and pike drill – subjects presumably of special interest to the Captain, who fought bravely for his King during the Civil War. For the sake of this room alone, a visit to Godinton Park is amply repaid.

## Goudhurst

*15; 10 miles E of Tunbridge Wells on A262*

This charming village climbs up a steepish hill to the church on the top. The houses vary much in their vernacular styles – timber-framed, weather-boarded, tile-hung – but nearly all make a valid contribution to the overall effect.

The most interesting house of them all stands back a little from the road in its own garden on the outskirts of the village near the foot of the hill. This is PATTYNDENNE (or PATTENDEN) MANOR, a restored, yet at the same time astonishingly well-preserved, Wealden hall house built around 1470 – the typical house, one might say, of a well-to-do yeoman farmer in the days of Edward IV. The exterior looks, perhaps, a little too tidy; the remarkably close studs are, however, the original timbers, which probably owe their survival in a large degree to the stone foundation wall in which they are set. Notable too are the projecting jetties, which continue right round the house – a rare feature indeed. They are supported at the corners by four trunks of oak, inverted so that the natural outward curve of the wood could be put to best advantage. Entrance is by the original oak door and through the original screens passage, with the Hall immediately to the left. In the later sixteenth century, after the introduction of the huge stone and brick chimney, it was divided horizontally to make an additional bedchamber above – where the tie-beam and kingpost of the Hall are still in position and the rafters remain soot-blackened from the open fire below. Behind the Hall, the Parlour retains some of its original fifteenth-century panelling and diagonal 'dragon' beams to support the joists of the jetties. To the back there are two extensions: a small Elizabethan cross wing which was used as a kitchen, and a Victorian corridor (including a staircase) running behind the lower half of the Hall and the Parlour beyond. These do not, however, in any way spoil the house, which preserves an extraordinary atmosphere – thanks in large measure to the love and care lavished on it by its most sympathetic owners.

A little further from the centre of the village – it lies in fact about $1\frac{1}{2}$ miles to the south-west – is FINCHCOCKS, a brave Baroque house built in 1725 by an unknown and probably local architect – the theory that the entrance front elevation was designed by Thomas Archer is surely untenable – in no fewer than three different shades of red brick: bright red for the window dressings, dark red for the very tall chimneys and parapets, and a paler, pinkish red for everything else. The basic plan is that of a seven-bay central block of three storeys (plus a dormered attic almost hidden behind a high parapet) flanked by two-storey wings projecting forward one bay, the connecting wall curving round in a convex quadrant.

The central block strikes one at first sight as distinctly odd: unusually tall for its length and breadth, it has a three-bay centre, broken slightly forward, rising the whole height up to and including the parapet, with a triangular pediment set over the first-floor windows. This has no supporting columns or pilasters, but from its ends there runs a continuous cornice (like the pediment, painted white) for another two bays on each side to the angles of the block, where Tuscan pilasters rise up to meet them. Ingeniously, however, these pilasters stop short, at a point level with the cornice of the side wings; the interstices are filled with tall pieces of white triglyph entablature. The wings have similar, shorter, pilasters but the same-sized entablature blocks, bringing the capitals beneath them somewhat awkwardly to a point halfway up the first-floor windows. These windows, like nearly all the main windows of the house, have only faintly curved segmental heads; only those in the quadrants and those below the pediment are properly round-headed. Two of the latter frame, above the porch, a rather battered statue of Queen Anne formerly in the Royal Exchange, set in a deep niche. She too is painted white, as are the porch and the bases, capitals and entablature blocks of the pilasters. The west-facing garden front is much the same, but without pilasters or pediment. The brickwork is of outstanding quality.

Finchcocks now describes itself as 'a living museum of music'. It houses a remarkable collection of early keyboard instruments, all restored to full playing condition, and organises regular seminars and concerts. Not surprisingly, therefore, the interior is somewhat bereft of other furniture. Architecturally, its most memorable feature is the large Hall on the ground floor which runs the whole depth of the house. On each side are fine panelled rooms – unusually high for their floor area, in order to match the Hall – and, in the north-west corner, a splendid staircase, leading to a spacious upstairs landing which has a fireplace of its own. The roof, when you eventually reach it after a long, steep climb, commands superb views over the Weald.

## Graveney*

*16; 3 miles NE of Faversham off B2040*

ALL SAINTS is a ravishing little church, unassuming and unrestored. The exterior is pretty enough: knapped flints with rubble stone dressing, a nice tiled roof and a low chunky tower with a circular stair turret. The rendered south porch, topped with an electric fitting of unusual hideousness, spoils the effect a little; but the latter at least may have gone before this book is published. The prevailing style is Decorated, probably of the early fourteenth century – though the two lancets in the north wall of the chancel indicate that the church is older than it looks. There is beautiful tracery in all the windows of the south aisle – best of all at its east end – and on the south side of the chancel. It is hard to understand why the main east window should have been replaced by a narrower Perpendicular one within a century of its construction; how can anyone have thought it an improvement? We can only be thankful that all the others were not changed at the same time.

Inside, the Norman chancel arch shows that the church is older even than was suggested by those lancets; but the arcades make it clear that the whole nave was rebuilt and enlarged in the fourteenth century. Chronology, however, is not what matters here. The beauty of the church depends on other things: on the broad aisles; on the quantities of clear glass in the windows, through which everything is flooded with light; on the lovely screen, which surely dates from Henry VIII's time; on the pale box pews; and on the wooden roof, which is unlike any other I know. And there are marvellous brasses, particularly that of John Martyn and his wife. Here is a church for which to be very, very grateful.

## Groombridge *

*17; 3 miles SW of Tunbridge Wells off B2188*

If you drive north from Sussex along the B2188, you meet the Kent border at Groombridge; and when you cross the little tributary of the Medway that marks the actual boundary, GROOMBRIDGE PLACE is virtually the first building that you see. No county could have a more enchanting introduction. There it stands, the perfect Restoration manor house of warm red brick – which is also used for the strongly emphasised quoins – its hipped roof and dormers calmly reflected in a moat of quite unusual breadth forming a huge square around it. Except for the early eighteenth-century sash windows, it still looks almost exactly as it did when Philip Packer built it in 1660. Obviously he chose the site of an earlier house – no one in Charles II's day would have dreamt of constructing even a token moat, let alone one on such a scale – and quite possibly its ground plan as well, for by then H-shaped houses were also long out of fashion; but the choice seems to have been dictated by convenience rather than by any desire to make a point. No house, certainly, could be less grandiloquent. Even the little Ionic portico extending between the wings – the only decorative flourish to be seen anywhere – seems deliberately understated. The inside is as perfect and as unspoilt as the exterior, its oak-panelled rooms marvellously light thanks to the large and plentiful windows, the furniture and pictures, too, exactly right. It is a warm, mellow, welcoming house – the moat has three broad bridges over which to cross it – in which it must, I feel, be a joy to live.

*Hadlow Tower.*

The little CHURCH OF ST JOHN THE EVANGELIST, beside a footpath leading through the park, was built by John Packer in 1625 to celebrate – according to an inscription on the porch – 'the most happy return of Prince Charles from Spain': most happy, in Packer's view, because Charles had returned *not* having married the Infanta, which had been the purpose of his visit. It is still Gothic, though a few little classical details have slipped in when nobody was looking. The best thing inside is the monument to Philip Packer, who is represented sitting half-naked, with his head lolling oddly over on one side. *The Buildings of England* interprets this as an attempt to suggest the moment of his death; the *Shell Guide to Kent*, however, has a more macabre explanation: that the sculptor has shown him 'with a broken neck, just as he was found in a nearby lake in 1686'.

## Hadlow Tower

*18; 4½ miles NE of Tonbridge on A26*

George Ledwell Taylor had three claims to fame, none of which seems to have actually won him any. First, he discovered the Lion of Chaeroneia, the memorial that still stands on the battlefield where Philip of Macedon smashed the Theban and Athenian armies in 338 BC; secondly, he persuaded William IV to call the new open space at the northern end of Whitehall 'Trafalgar Square' instead of 'William IV Square' as had previously been proposed; thirdly, he built Hadlow Tower. This extraordinary monument is the only memorable result of an architectural career that lasted a good half-century, but it makes up for a lot. It was erected in 1838–40 as an appendage to Hadlow Court Castle, which a wealthy eccentric, Walter Barton May, had designed and built for himself a few years before, and is obviously modelled on Beckford's tower at Fonthill – with the addition of a slim pinnacled octagon at the top. Indeed, it was probably in order to prevent a recurrence of the Fonthill catastrophe (Beckford's tower had collapsed in 1825) that Taylor was hired in the first place. If so, he earned his fee; for the tower still soars up 170 feet above the surrounding countryside, as bravely as it ever did, while the castle lies in ruins at its foot. It is one of the great follies of England, and deserves – as Taylor does – to be better known.

*Hever Castle.*

## Hever Castle

*19; 2 miles E of Edenbridge off B2026*

Although the interior of Hever Castle is little more than a superb Edwardian pastiche by William Waldorf Astor – later the 1st Lord Astor of Hever – and his architect Frank L. Pearson (son of J.L.), the exterior has been remarkably little changed. What we see today remains in its essentials the moated manor house erected by Sir John de Cobham in 1384, and such alterations as have been made date mostly from the sixteenth century. Despite its name, it is not and never was a proper castle, but a semi-fortified house of the kind considered suitable in the late Middle Ages for a local squire, but not in any sense for a great feudal lord.

When Sir Geoffrey Bullen, who had been Lord Mayor of London in 1459, bought Hever three years later, a new chapter began in the house's history; for it was there, in all probability, that his great-granddaughter Anne was born in 1507 and there (though this distinction is also claimed by Sutton Place in Surrey (*q.v.*)) that she was courted – and won – by Henry VIII. Anne Boleyn – the change of spelling somehow made the name more distinguished – became Henry's second Queen in 1533; but her triumph was short. Less than three years later she was arrested at a tournament in Greenwich on charges of adultery with no fewer than four men, including her own brother – charges which were tantamount, in the circumstances, to high treason. On 19 May 1536 she was executed on Tower Green. (In deference to her rank a sword was used rather than an axe, and a special executioner had to be brought over from France for the purpose. ) Even then, however, Hever retained its royal connection: the house was occupied by Henry's fourth wife, Anne of Cleves, after their divorce in 1540 and for the next seventeen years until her death.

Apart from the moat, Hever's only serious attempt at fortification is on the south side, which is dominated by a huge machicolated Gatehouse, complete with drawbridge and three portcullises – two of which have survived, and one of which is the last genuine medieval one in England still in working order. To each side rises an embattled angle turret, with arrow slits but no windows. The other three sides are unaggressive – just quiet, mellow, sixteenth-century elevations, cheerfully asymmetrical, with tall brick chimneystacks rising in pairs at odd intervals.

Astor's and Pearson's reconstruction of the interior is something of a *tour de force*; the prevailing style is that of Henry VIII's time, and though the whole thing is a pastiche, it is a pastiche of a very high order. The principal problem was one of space: the house was nowhere near big enough to support the Astor way of life. Being moated, it could not be extended laterally; to add another storey would have been out of the question. Their final solution was as ingenious as it was successful. On the north side of the house, and connected to it by a covered bridge across the moat, Pearson designed what appeared to be a medieval village: a cluster of stone and timber-framed cottages, grouped haphazardly around a system of courtyards, which in fact contained guest rooms, offices, servants' quarters and kitchens, all interconnected by corridors – perhaps a hundred rooms in all. It was a brilliant idea, and beautifully carried out.

The formal gardens to the east of the house are alone worth the journey to Hever. The Italian Garden, with its grottoes, pergola and Roman bath, was laid out as a setting for the new owner's remarkable collection of classical sculpture – a far cry from the world of Tudor England. Beyond it is an artificial lake extending over 45 acres: the Astors did nothing by halves.

## Hildenborough

*20; 5 miles SE of Sevenoaks on B245*

Thanks to apparently uncontrolled post-war sprawl Hildenborough is not an attractive village, and it is now little more than a suburb of Tonbridge. ST JOHN'S CHURCH, however, is well worth a visit, being the very first church to be built, in 1843–4, by Ewan Christian – a revolutionary with a touch of genius. Anyone who thinks of Victorian ecclesiastical architecture solely in terms of Scott, Street and Butterfield and their followers would do well to take a long, close look at this extraordinary building. The exterior, to be sure, does not give very much away, though the tapering tower, shingled even down to its lucarnes, is hardly orthodox; but the inside comes as a sort of revelation. The first thing that strikes one is the immense breadth of everything – the aisleless nave, the shortish transepts and even the apsidal chancel: a light and airy spaciousness made possible by the huge wooden pointed arches, deeply moulded, springing from corbels set only a foot or two above bench level and dominating all that lies beneath them. Despite the pointing of these arches, despite the lancet windows and even the triple stepped lancet at the east end, the feeling is something far more akin to modern Scandinavian design than to medieval Gothic; a church conceived according to a whole new open-plan philosophy, astonishing for the 1840s.

## Hythe

*21; 4 miles W of Folkestone on A259*

The town was one of the original Cinque Ports, and ST LEONARD'S CHURCH, proudly perched on the hill above the town, seems to proclaim the fact. Its Norman origins seem to have been modest enough – though little remains of the earliest fabric except the two small clerestory windows, now blocked up, on the north wall of the nave. Then, shortly before 1200, the first enlargement was begun: St Leonard's was given aisles and transepts. From this period dates the fine Norman doorway in the west wall of the north transept which gave directly on to the churchyard outside before the choir vestry was built in 1959.

Meanwhile, Hythe was growing steadily more prosperous, and some time during the second quarter of the thirteenth century the decision was taken to replace the chancel with something of real distinction. The proposed new elevation could hardly have been more ambitious, providing as it did for three full stages – arcade, gallery and clerestory, with a stone vault not only above the central space but over the chancel aisles as well. So ambitious was it, indeed, that the money ran out before it could be finished; the vaults and the upper section of the north wall were completed only in 1886, by J.L. Pearson. It also meant that – particularly when seen from below – the chancel looks quite out of proportion to the rest of the church. A further problem was that the extension to the east came right up to the edge of the churchyard; thus, to enable processions to make the tour of the new building without leaving consecrated ground, an arched and vaulted passage was constructed through the thickness of the buttresses. For some five centuries this has been the repository for a macabre collection of neatly stacked skulls and bones – yet another reason for the church's considerable popularity among summer visitors.

Seen from the nave, the chancel makes a tremendous impression, its immense height still further increased by the raised platform on which it is built – nine steps up from the crossing. (The altar is three steps higher still.) There are two bays on each side, with tall, intricately moulded arches supported on quatrefoil piers surrounded by eight detached shafts of Purbeck marble – a most sumptuous design. At gallery level, the bays are divided again, each having two pairs of pointed arches, each pair under an embracing round arch. The clerestory has trefoiled windows and a wall passage. Looking up, one finds it hard to believe that this is the chancel of an ordinary parish church. Only one thing spoils the effect – indeed, very nearly ruins it – and that is the east window, inserted soon after the Second World War. The sooner it is removed, the better.

## Ightham Mote*

*22; 6 miles E of Sevenoaks off A25*

The approach alone is unforgettable: a steep descent, twisting down one of those narrow, leafy Wealden lanes, gives no suggestion of what lies ahead. Then, suddenly, there it is – almost too good to be true, so perfectly preserved, so complete and self-contained in its seclusion as to make you wonder if you have not yourself slipped back into the Middle Ages: the fourteenth-century manor house of everyone's dreams, part timber-framed, part good vernacular Kentish ragstone, its walls dropping sheer, on all four sides, into the calm, almost miraculously clear waters of its moat.

The first thing to do is to walk all the way round it on the outside – preferably leaving till last the north front (the one to the left of the entrance, parallel with the road) which, though in other respects the loveliest of all, contains what is, for me, Ightham's only blemish – an eighteenth-century Venetian window at the right-hand end. This must simply be ignored – or forgiven, on the excellent grounds that the house has grown organically over the centuries. The entrance tower is itself a later addition, of 1500 or so; the wooden doors, with their linenfold design, are perhaps a quarter of a century later. Facing you across the court, however, is the nucleus of the early fourteenth-century house, the Great Hall. Much of it is still as it was when Sir Thomas Cawne built it in the reign of Edward III, in particular that splendid roof of stone and timber, and the little caryatid figures from which the great supporting arches spring. Original too is the two-light transomed window in the eastern wall. (The five-light one giving on to the courtyard is a later, fifteenth-century, refinement, dating from that time after the Wars of the Roses when house owners were beginning to demand new standards of physical comfort undreamt of in earlier days. The fireplace probably followed soon afterwards.) The only modern touch is the panelling by Norman Shaw.

The Hall is, as it should be, the showpiece of the house. Contemporary with it is the old Chapel, to which there is

*Ightham Mote.*

a squint from the solar – a fascinating room, not least for its extraordinary roof, in which the tie-beams run in both directions, with a kingpost rising from the point of intersection. But Ightham has two chapels, and it is the more recent one, built by Sir Richard Clement around 1520, that haunts the memory. One remembers it for its barrel-vaulted ceiling, painted with the Tudor Rose and the pomegranate of Aragon, the delicacy of its screen and the lovely filigree tester over its pulpit; but above all, perhaps, for its simple unity, the Gothic having nearly – though not quite – gone and the Renaissance being as yet barely foreshadowed.

Every room at Ightham, though, has its own character and its own beauty. Even the seventeenth- to eighteenth-century Drawing Room (that window again), out of keeping as it may seem with the rest of the house, boasts a splendidly Caroline overmantel and quite ravishing hand-painted oriental wallpaper. The faint exoticism breathed by this last conceit, strangely enough, does not hurt a bit, setting off the intrinsically English character of everything else as easily and naturally as pepper on a beefsteak.

Englishness is the other point to bear in mind as one wanders about this glorious place. It could of course be argued that, with very few exceptions like Mereworth or Waddesdon, no major house in the land could conceivably be imagined in any setting beyond the Channel. This is true; but it is also true that with every succeeding century – even the nineteenth – our cultural links with Europe grew greater and our borrowings more numerous – even if we did translate them, on adoption, into our own idiom. It follows that only in the oldest houses is the quintessential English quality to be found; and few, if any, houses in the kingdom have existed so long, and remained so pure, as this.

## Ivychurch

*23; 3½ miles NW of New Romney on B2070*

Broad and low, hugging the earth, seemingly crouching against the icy winds that sweep across Romney Marsh, ST GEORGE'S CHURCH conveys a feeling of quiet, self-confident strength. Its style is Decorated, but its rough, heavily lichened walls of dressed Kentish ragstone give it masculinity. There is a stocky, battlemented and much buttressed west tower with an octagonal stair turret; another stair turret fills the north-west angle of the two-storey south porch; yet another, circular and somehow unexpected, rises at the north-west corner of the north aisle. The main east window is five-light, early Perpendicular; that of the north aisle is also a five-lighter, but later and more complex in design. It is now blocked up. Most of the remainder are Decorated, and several – note particularly the west window of the north aisle – are very pretty indeed.

Inside, the seven-bay arcades run the whole length of the church, uninterrupted by a chancel arch or anything else. As the aisles are broad and the nave empty of pews, there is a wonderful feeling of space, and the clear glass fills the building with light. If the quatrefoiled clerestory windows had not been blocked up, it would have been lighter still. A stone bench along the south side shows where the weakest of the congregation went to the wall. The wooden roofs have kingposts and queenposts, and the north aisle its original stone-flagged floor.

## Knole*

*NT; 24; at Tonbridge end of Sevenoaks off A225*

It is not Knole House, or Knole Hall, or even Knole Palace; it is, simply, Knole; and when you look at it from a distance – particularly across the park from the north – you understand why. That great forest of towers and chimneys, of gables and battlements, of pinnacles and turrets and finials, looks less like an English country house than a small medieval town, or perhaps half a dozen of the oldest and mellowest of Oxford colleges clustered together. When you see it from the air, this collegiate impression becomes stronger still; for then Knole is revealed as being built around a series of quadrangles, some paved, some enclosing lawns of startling greenness, separated – or perhaps linked – by cross-ranges endlessly varying in style and splendour: the grandest being indeed on a palatial scale, but others more reminiscent of a row of cottages in some forgotten village of the Weald.

And yet, despite its size, Knole is a home, in which the Sackvilles have lived for over 400 years and in which they still live today – a fact which, as you gradually penetrate into its heart, becomes easier and easier to understand. There is nothing, anywhere, in any of its alleged 365 rooms ('one for each day of the year' as the guides love to say, though according to Nigel Nicolson, who should know, nobody has really counted) that is remotely cold or alarming – like Blenheim for example, or perhaps Holkham. Even the grandest of the state rooms seem to smile a welcome, while the very rambling quality of the huge old house gives it a strange intimacy of its own. To have known it as a child, as Mr Nicolson did, must have been very heaven. His mother, Vita Sackville-West, was actually born within its walls; she knew it, loved it and understood it better than anyone, wrote its history and, in her superb novel *The Edwardians*, evoked its atmosphere more brilliantly even than her friend Virginia Woolf did in *Orlando*. It has, she wrote, 'the deep inward gaiety of some very old woman who has always been beautiful, who has had many lovers and seen many generations come and go, smiled wisely over their sorrows and their joys and learnt an imperishable secret of tolerance and humour'.

For anyone who falls under the strange spell of Knole (and few visitors fail to do so) these two books are required reading. All I can hope to do here is to trace the briefest of historical outlines which may help in the understanding of its architecture, entering a simultaneous caveat that, seen from the narrow architectural point of view, the house is not – and has never claimed to be – particularly distinguished. The history begins, so far as we can tell, with the purchase of the manor by Thomas Bourchier, Archbishop of Canterbury, in 1456. For the next eighty years it served as one of the many archiepiscopal palaces, during which time it was improved and mightily enlarged by five successive primates until Henry VIII seized it from Cranmer in 1538. Henry, almost certainly, was responsible for the Green Court, the first from which the house is entered, and by his death seven years later Knole had essentially assumed the formidable ground plan that it covers today. In 1566 Queen Elizabeth presented it to her cousin Thomas Sackville, soon to be made 1st Earl of Dorset. Since, however, it was both let and sub-let, he was unable to take possession of his property until the Queen's death in 1603. He was by then sixty-seven, with only five years left to live, and he made few external changes except to the roofs, especially those of the south front – where the nine-light windows that mark his new range of state rooms are topped by a row of big shaped gables, the Sackville leopard standing proudly above them – and the west front, where these gables are continued on a slightly smaller scale on each side of Henry VIII's Gatehouse. The inside, however, he transformed, giving it the essentially Jacobean character that we see today.

This character is made manifest the moment we enter the house, through the door at the far side of the Stone Court which leads via the screens passage into the Great Hall; for there, rearing up before us, looms one of the grandest and most outlandishly ornamented oak screens in the country, crowned by the grand achievement of the Sackville arms almost scraping the plasterwork from the ceiling. Apart from the sheer vitality and exuberance of this screen the Hall itself is not especially remarkable; far more important architecturally is the Great Staircase to which it leads. Here, for the first time in England, was an attempt to make the staircase not just a connection between two floors but a major architectural feature of a

*Knole.*

country house, by giving it a broad spaciousness, brilliantly lit and sumptuously decorated, which both impressed as a work of art and served to heighten the anticipation of further splendours to come. The example was to be followed at Hatfield (which was begun in 1607) and at Blickling; but in neither house with the extraordinary impact of that at Knole, where the effect is further enhanced by the profusion of wall painting and *grisaille* decoration – to say nothing of the life-size nude figure of Giannetta Baccelli, mistress of the 3rd Duke of Dorset, reclining languorously at its foot.

The Staircase leads to the Brown Gallery, the first of the five that Knole possesses and the three that are included in the normal tour of the house. Here and in the Leicester Gallery, which opens off it, is the best of that extraordinary collection of seventeenth-century royal furniture amassed by the 6th Earl – who, as William III's Lord Chamberlain, enjoyed the enviable right to take for himself any of the palace furnishings which were considered worn or out-of-date. Here too one first encounters that other strange manifestation of the Knole magic: the power to preserve furniture and its coverings – velvet, silk or brocade – almost uncorrupted by time. Off the Leicester Gallery is the so-called Venetian Ambassador's Bedroom, so dominated by the vast state bed of 1688 that one scarcely notices that the room itself is early eighteenth-century – the indirect result, perhaps, of the fire that destroyed much of this corner of the house in 1623. It is with a good deal of relief, therefore, that one crosses the Gallery (past the seventeenth-century billiard table) to find that in the next grand bedroom, called the Spangle Room, and its attendant dressing room, we are back in the Jacobean world again, with marvellous panelling, a particularly fine overmantel, and an oak-ribbed ceiling of the same style as we have already seen in the Brown Gallery.

There follows an enchanting couple of small seventeenth-century rooms that still bear the name of Lady Betty Germain, an elderly widow who had served at the Court of Queen Anne and who practically lived at Knole between 1720 and 1750. Already in her day these rooms must have seemed very old-fashioned; but if she were to return now – and one sometimes wonders whether she has ever left – she would recognise them at once: not a stick of furniture has been changed since her occupancy. After the restraint of these rooms, the sight of the Ballroom comes as a considerable contrast; for this room, originally Archbishop Bourchier's solar, was panelled and decorated by the 1st Earl in about 1605 with sumptuous magnificence. The white-painted panelling has caused many a raised eyebrow, but is believed to have been this colour ever since it was first

*Leeds Castle.*

installed; the focal point of the room, however, is the tremendous chimneypiece and overmantel, a *tour de force* of Renaissance marble carving as good as anything of its kind in England. There is another, no less fine and probably by the same hand, in the Reynolds Room.

The tour ends, as it began, with a climax – a walk through the third of Knole's great galleries, the Cartoon Gallery, hung with copies of Raphael cartoons from which it takes its name, to the King's Room, the grandest of all the state bedrooms. The reference is to James I, who may well have slept in it – though not in the great bed which at present occupies it and was almost certainly made for his grandson, James II. Vita Sackville-West confessed that she never liked this room; she thought it vulgar, which it unquestionably is. Silver is all very well in its place, but it is not a suitable material for furniture, and though the workmanship – purely English – is beyond reproach, the general effect is deplorable: a salutary reminder of that dangerous moment in seventeenth-century taste, soon after the Restoration, when empty ornamentation threatened to overwhelm everything else, in a ham-fisted groping towards Rococo, but without the lightness of touch which is Rococo's saving grace.

I have written in greater detail about Knole than about most of the houses listed in this book simply because Knole is like no other house. Just why this is so is harder to analyse; it has something to do with its size, and its age, and its strange domesticity – that unique combination of informality and grandeur which can be felt so much more easily than it can be described. None of these qualities is carried to excess; there are a few larger houses in England, several older ones, a good many more homely and any number more grand. Nor, as I mentioned before, can it be particularly recommended for the beauty of its architecture. Nowhere in the world, however, will you find such an atmosphere, such a serene, self-confident dignity of age and wisdom. In a land full of wonderful houses, Knole is king of them all.

## Leeds Castle*

*25; 4 miles E of Maidstone on A20*

The first sight of Leeds Castle on a hot summer afternoon takes one's breath away. Set in the middle of its tranquil lake, surrounded by rolling parkland of the lushest green, it strikes one as being almost too beautiful, a medieval castle straight out of a fairytale – and every bit as unreal.

The extraordinary thing is that much of it, in essence, is absolutely genuine. It has been added to, of course, and restored – radically, in both the nineteenth and the twentieth centuries, and at enormous cost; but it remains at heart the same castle that Edward I made over to his Queen, Eleanor of Castile, 700 years ago and which he and she cherished above all others. It was Edward who built the present Gatehouse and ringed the whole complex with an outer bailey and curtain wall – for Leeds was a working castle with a job to do; his also, probably, is the ground floor of the so-called 'Gloriette' – that part of the building which projects furthest into the lake, beyond the two-storeyed bridge.

These are, so far as we can tell, the only medieval sections still remaining. The next royal improver was Henry VIII. He added an upper storey, with canted bay windows, to the Gloriette, and also the Maidens' Tower, the separate square edifice to the south-east, for his maids of honour. It was only in the 1820s, however, that there rose up the main block of the castle we now know. There was, doubtless, an earlier building on the site, but nothing is left of it except the long cellar, with its pointed tunnel vault, by which today's visitors enter the castle.

Almost exactly a century later, in 1926, Leeds was bought by Olive, Lady Baillie, who set about a complete restoration outside and in. The work was done with sensitivity and skill and, although some of the interior decoration inevitably smacks of the inter-war years, it is hard to see how Leeds could have been transformed into the warm and comfortable country house it is today at less cost to its atmosphere and character.

## Lees Court

*26; 3 miles S of Faversham off A251*

A marvel and a riddle – first the marvel, for the south front of this extraordinary house is unlike any other in England. Thirteen bays and two storeys are unusual proportions for a start; and the windows – absolutely plain and unframed, scarcely more than regular, rectangular holes in the rendered wall – are actually less important to the overall design than are what separates them: fourteen identical pilasters, so broad that they fill almost all the space available for them, set on gigantic blocks and with bold Ionic capitals from which hang swags so heavy and fat that they loll limply on the necking. Over all this, a shallow hipped roof spreads its deep eaves, supported on voluted brackets.

The riddle concerns the identity of the architect. The house was finished shortly before 1655, when its builder, Sir George Sondes, complained bitterly of what it had cost him. There is a long tradition that it is the work of Inigo Jones, whose influence is indeed plain to the most inexpert eye; but so dedicated a Palladian would never have permitted those outlandish proportions; there are, besides, a number of features – the lack of any emphasis on the centre except a barely perceptible increase in height of the five central ground-floor windows, and a doorcase too big for the space between the columns – which are awkward in the extreme. The house seems to have been a free, but remarkably courageous, adaptation of a Jones design on the part of an imaginative local builder who ultimately bit off a little more than he could chew. Still, he has produced something quite unforgettable.

Lees Court suffered a serious fire just before the First World War, and its sumptuous interiors were completely destroyed. We can now admire their splendours only in photographs. The red-brick stables to the north-east of the house are by Soane.

## Lullingstone*

*27; ½ mile SW of Eynsford off A225*

The ROMAN VILLA falls outside the scope of this book; having been burnt down in the fifth century, it now ranks as archaeology. The excavations are, however, well worth a visit, not only for the surviving mosaic floors (Bellerophon on Pegasus killing the Chimaera, and Europa with her Bull) and the traces of a unique fourth-century Christian Chapel, but also for their lovely riverside setting. From here a pleasant twenty-minute walk through the park takes you to LULLINGSTONE CASTLE.

It is not really a castle, and never was – even though the early eighteenth-century front largely conceals its true age. The most accurate indication of its building date is obligingly provided by the pretty turreted GATEHOUSE through which you approach it. This is of *c.*1497, which makes it one of the earliest brick gatehouses in England. Its builder, who was also responsible for the house itself, was Sir John Peche, companion and adviser to the young Henry VIII, whom he accompanied in 1520 to the Field of the Cloth of Gold. The setting is ravishing, with house, church and Gatehouse standing on three sides of an immense lawn while a series of lakes – artificially formed by damming the Darent – stretches away to the south.

The entrance front, to the west, gives no sign of the house's Tudor origins except its general shape, which would have been unthinkable in Queen Anne's day. It consists in essence of two symmetrical five-bay blocks of three storeys, their three inner bays projecting forwards, linked by a three-bay, two-storey centre with a pedimented porch. The south front gives away even less. On the two non-show fronts, however, Tudor canted bays and chimneybreasts have survived. Inside, the eighteenth century prevails once more, with a splendid Queen Anne Hall which completely occupies the two-storey centre of the west front. It contains a magnificent series of full-length portraits of the Hart family (descended from Sir John Peche's nephew) and the Dyke family, into which Anne Hart married in 1738. The Hart Dykes still occupy the house today.

In the beautiful panelled Dining Room you can still see the jousting helmet worn by Sir John when he won the royal tournament held by Henry VII at Westminster in 1494. Pass on then to the fine wooden staircase – constructed, we are told, for Queen Anne herself, with especially shallow treads to assist her in heaving up her elephantine bulk – which leads up to the State Drawing Room. This dates from the time of Queen Elizabeth and, like the Hall, occupies two floors in the north wing. It is covered by a contemporary plaster barrel-vaulted ceiling, with pendants and panels containing pattern-book portraits of various mythical or historical Romans all of whom, except for Nero, appear to have had exactly the same face. The wall panelling is Queen Anne again, and among the objects on display is one of the dolls with which she played as a child. Her State Bedroom adjoins; to see her bathroom, however, you must leave the house and follow the river southward to a little ruined bath house, with apsidal ends, built over a medicinal spring. It too was built especially for her benefit – though it does not seem to have done her much good.

Just across the lawn from the house stands the little flint CHURCH OF ST BOTOLPH. Originally Norman, it was completely rebuilt in the fourteenth century and then given a north chapel by Sir John Peche in 1500 or thereabouts. There is a marvellous rood-screen, also the gift of Sir John, bearing the pomegranate of Catherine of Aragon united with the rose of England and the Peche rebus, an E on a peach; marvellous glass, too, some of it going back to the fourteenth century. The porch, bell turret and pretty plaster ceiling were added by Percyvall Hart, who died in 1738. Finally, the monuments: they start with a brass to the memory of Sir John's father, Sir William; following it is Sir John himself, reclining beneath a canopy, his head on a beautifully carved helmet, his feet on a lion. Occupying the whole west wall of the north chapel is a glorious explosion of early eighteenth-century Gothick extolling the virtues of Percyvall Hart, friend of Queen Anne, transformer of the house, beautifier of the church and, after the Queen's death, staunch upholder of the Stuart cause. Lullingstone owes him much.

*Mereworth Castle.*

## Mereworth Castle

*28; 5 miles SW of Maidstone on A26*

It is sad indeed that at the time of writing Mereworth Castle is not open to the public, for it is not only by any standards a marvellously beautiful house; it is also an architectural milestone of the first importance. With the publication of the first volume of his *Vitruvius Britannicus* in 1715 Colen Campbell, Mereworth's architect, had been largely responsible for the launching of Palladianism in England, and by the time he began work on Mereworth in 1722 he was already an established architect who had completed the plans for Stourhead and Houghton, as well as those for the entrance front of Burlington House in London. Never before, however, had there been a deliberate adaptation by a British architect of a specifically identifiable Palladian villa; and what we see at Mereworth – even if we have to content ourselves with the view from the main gates on the A26 – is precisely this: Campbell's attempt at the wholesale transplantation of the Villa Capra, or Villa Rotonda as it is often called, from a hilltop near Vicenza to a damp and misty hollow in Kent.

In the circumstances, certain compromises had to be made. To begin with, there was the problem of chimneys, which Campbell solved without breaking his clear roof line by building a tall, hemispherical dome (in place of Palladio's flattish tiled cupola) and concealing his twenty-four separate flues within it, leading them up to a tall blind lantern at the top, whence the smoke finally escaped – often to the considerable alarm of passers by. Like the Villa Rotonda, Mereworth has a hexastyle Ionic portico on each of its four sides; but whereas Palladio prefaced each of his porticoes with a broad ascending flight of steps, Campbell has given this treatment only to those on the north and south; on the east and west they are merely look-out points, without direct access.

Inside the house, this neglect of Palladio's all-important theory of symmetry is carried still further. (The great circular Hall beneath the dome, which Campbell called the *salone*, is unexceptionable, and would have earned the master's full approval – though he might have thought the exuberant Italian plasterwork somewhat exaggerated.) However where the north front is taken up by a vestibule with two small rooms leading off it, the south is completely given over to a Long Gallery, a sumptuously dramatic room, ornamented to within an inch of its life with every device in the early eighteenth-century decorator's armoury, and crowned by a deeply coved ceiling by the Venetian Francesco Sleter which alone would make the journey to the house worthwhile.

The two side pavilions are a puzzle. In Vol. III of *Vitruvius Britannicus* (1725), which treats of the house in detail, they are not mentioned, and the probability is that they were built ten or fifteen years later. But by whom? In their placing, their proportions, and the way in which they reflect on a more modest level the style of the house itself, they could hardly be better done; yet it is unlikely that they are by Campbell, who died in 1729. Howard Colvin suggests Roger Morris, who he thinks may also have been responsible for ST LAWRENCE'S CHURCH close by, an extraordinary building whose exterior bears more than a passing resemblance to St Martin-in-the-Fields – the steeple is almost identical – but with deep eaves at each end reminiscent of St Paul's, Covent Garden. You enter it through an elliptical vestibule (actually the base of the tower) which, although very small, contains two completely separate staircases, one leading up to the west gallery and the other, on the opposite side of the ellipse, to a higher level in the roof. The inside is surprisingly plain, with a tunnel-vaulted roof supported on tightly set Doric columns and decorated with *trompe-l'œil* coffering. There is no chancel, and the pure Palladianism of the design and proportions accords oddly with the distinctly Baroque feeling of the exterior. A strange and intriguing church, it keeps asking questions and yet answers none of them.

## Minster-in-Thanet

*29; 5½ miles W of Ramsgate on B2048*

ST MARY'S is an enormous church for what is nowadays little more than a large and rather ugly village. Long ago, however, Minster was the focal point for the whole Isle (as it literally was) of Thanet, and the seat – as the name implies – of one of the earliest English abbeys, founded in AD 669. Early in the eleventh century the abbey was deserted and passed into the hands of St Augustine's, Canterbury, at whose instigation the present church was begun in 1027; little more than 100 years later, however, for reasons which are not entirely clear, it was found to be too small. In consequence, between *c*.1150 and *c*.1230, it was completely rebuilt.

The great empty nave, its five-bay arcades supported on sturdy round piers, conveys that impression of rock-like strength and solidity that is characteristic of all the best Norman work. So, even more forcibly, does the massive tower arch at the west end. The wooden roof, with kingposts, sets the whole thing off splendidly. Then, from the crossing eastward, we find ourselves in a later phase of the building. Here the style is Early English, and by this time there seems to have been more money available, since the entire four-bay chancel is vaulted in stone. (So are the transepts, but although the springing for their vaults is medieval, the vaults themselves were added only in the 1860s, by Ewan Christian.) It is unusually broad as thirteenth-century chancels go, and its breadth is further emphasised by the multiplicity of shafting round the triple-lancet east window, the flattened curve of the roof and the absence of a longitudinal ridge rib. The result is deeply impressive. In contrast to the bareness of the nave and aisles, the chancel has a magnificent set of stalls with particularly enjoyable misericords.

MINSTER ABBEY nearby is somewhat confusing since, although the buildings are Norman and are inhabited by Benedictine nuns, they were never part of the original abbey and have in fact been a convent for only the past half-century. They were actually a grange, from which St Augustine's, Canterbury, administered its vast holdings in Thanet. The ground plan was that of a square, open on the east, with a church – now demolished – to the south, a residential and administrative range to the west and a hall or refectory to the north. The date is early-to-middle twelfth century; although most of the windows were renewed in the early fifteenth century, a few of the original ones have managed to survive.

## New Romney*

*30; 9 miles SW of Hythe on A259*

Until the end of the thirteenth century, ST NICHOLAS'S CHURCH stood by the sea; ships could anchor beyond the churchyard wall. Then, after a series of terrible storms, the River Rother changed course and the sea receded. The great church now stands high and dry above the town. It has lost nothing of its old magnificence.

It remains, however, a baffling building – at least until its history is understood. First came an already rather grand Norman church, built during Henry II's reign – say around 1160. It had an ornate west front, with much blind arcading, lavishly decorated with zigzag; but almost as soon as it was completed the decision was taken to add a west tower of five stages, with a staircase turret. (If you stand under the tower today, you can look up and see part of the old front.) At some point, a spire was intended; its stump is still there. The oddest thing about the tower, however, is the fact that it was flanked to north and south by narrow aisles; it thus possesses three tower arches, instead of the usual one. Inside, the Norman arcades extend eastward for four bays, the round-headed clerestory windows being set rather awkwardly immediately above them.

The next important development occurred around 1330, when a splendid new chancel was added, with aisles equalling it in breadth. These broad aisles were then taken westward, along two bays of the old Norman nave. To the east, they extend as far as the chancel itself, so that the east end of the church – seen with particular advantage from the outside – now consists of three gabled bays, separated only by narrow buttresses, each with a superb Decorated window (five lights in the centre, three at the sides) with cusped reticulated tracery.

The last crisis in the history of St Nicholas's occurred in 1880, when John Oldrid Scott – second son of Sir G.G. – began to dismantle the Norman north aisle. Providentially, the Society for the Protection of Ancient Buildings had been founded only two years before, and its secretary, William Morris, lodged an immediate protest. The subsequent publicity was enough to prevent Scott from continuing, and the SPAB chalked up its first major victory. It was, however, a close shave.

## Old Romney*

*31; 2 miles W of New Romney off A259*

An unspoilt, unpretentious little country church some way from the village, ST CLEMENT'S has a charm all its own. The exterior sets the tone nicely – the enormous yew tree in the churchyard, the gently eccentric south-west tower with its stubby shingled spire, and the quiet rustic setting amid the fields. Despite the Decorated windows – and the single Perpendicular one of the north chapel – it is fundamentally a thirteenth-century building; but its precise dating is of little importance. What counts is the simplicity: the plaster walls and ceiling, the timber roof with its kingpost, the pink-painted box pews and the lovely little west gallery.

## Owletts

See Cobham.

## Patrixbourne★

*32; 3 miles SE of Canterbury off A2*

After Barfreston, ST MARY'S, Patrixbourne, is the most remarkable Norman church in Kent. Splendidly sited amid rolling downland, it too has a magnificent wheel window at the east end; the spokes are not in the form of columns this time, but four of them are in the process of being eaten by fearsome monsters. Below it are three round-headed lancets, widely spaced. For the rest, the ground plan is somewhat unusual: the tower with its outsize shingled spire rises up halfway along the broad south aisle. At its foot is the principal doorway, almost certainly the work of the same masons and stone carvers as Barfreston. It is flanked by two shafts on each side, but the arch above is of five orders, all intricately carved, surrounding a tympanum in which Christ sits, surrounded by a mandorla and with angels on each side. Beneath him, on the lintel, there is a seated figure – I wonder who – and gryphons. The whole thing is enclosed within an acute-angled gable, in the apex of which is a niche in which an Agnus Dei is faintly discernible. The material is knapped flint, in which larger chunks of Caen stone are irregularly set.

The inside is something of a disappointment, both arcades having been rebuilt by Scott in the 1850s; but the situation is saved by the really fascinating collection of Swiss glass of the sixteenth and seventeenth centuries. Eight of the eighteen panels are set in the south window of the south aisle; they include a particularly delightful one of Pyramus and Thisbe, neither apparently aware of the fact that the former has been impaled on a sword. The remainder are in the three lancets of the chancel – in the southern one a portrayal of Samson precisely copied from a woodcut by Dürer.

*The main doorway, St Mary's Church, Patrixbourne.*

## Penshurst Place★

*33; 3 miles SW of Tonbridge on B2176*

It seems almost unfair that two great houses of the size and splendour of Knole and Penshurst should exist within 6 miles of each other. Of the two, the former is the larger and, ultimately, the more memorable; but Penshurst is also conceived on a palatial scale, and its central part was already well over a century old when Archbishop Bourchier began his building work at Knole. Moreover, as we have seen, Knole was thoroughly Jacobeanised by the 1st Earl of Dorset in the early years of the seventeenth century; the medieval core of Penshurst, by contrast, has remained virtually untouched. If you want to see the grandest and most perfectly preserved example of an unfortified manor house in all England, it is to Penshurst that you must come.

Note, however, those adjectives and avoid disappointment. Penshurst is magnificent to behold, but it has none of the picturesque qualities of Ightham Mote, its close contemporary. Although little has been lost, so much has been added to it in the fifteenth, sixteenth and nineteenth centuries that, when you stand facing the south front, it takes you a moment or two even to pick out the position of the Great Hall, about three-quarters of the way along to the right. But enter that Hall, and you will see at once what I mean. Not only is it many times larger than Ightham's; it remains, architecturally, looking precisely as it did when it was built by Sir John de Pulteney in about 1340, except that the louvre in the roof, through which the smoke escaped from the central hearth, has been removed. Nearly all medieval halls, large and small, were fitted with wall fireplaces in the fifteenth or sixteenth centuries; but such a thing never happened at Penshurst. The only addition to the Hall that need be noted here is the screen, which carries on its frieze the ragged staff of the Sidneys and which must therefore postdate the grant of Penshurst to them in 1552. Even the huge trestle tables are thought to be original; Edward IV certainly dined at them and so, probably, did Henry V, two of whose brothers lived in the house.

It was the elder of these two, John, Duke of Bedford, who between 1430 and 1435 made the first considerable additions to the Pulteney house which, apart from the Hall, had previously consisted only of the solar – now the State Dining Room – the undercroft supporting it, and, at the other end, the kitchen offices. These additions comprise the two-storey block immediately to the west of the Hall, with their most unEnglish deeply splayed window reveals. From the evidence of the exterior this seems to have been a second Hall, even larger than Pulteney's; inside, however, the Elizabethan remodelling has wiped away every trace of it. By this time also, as was all too understandable in those uncertain days, the house had been surrounded by a crenellated curtain wall set with eight square or rectangular towers at the corners and halfway along the sides.

With the arrival of the Sidneys building began again, especially under Sir Henry, father of Sir Philip, who was born at Penshurst and wrote much of his poetry here. He began work in 1573, and for the next twelve years the

*Penshurst Place.*

house grew rapidly. A Great Chamber and a Withdrawing Chamber appeared in the Bedford Range, from the far end of which a new wing stretched off to the south, containing the almost statutory Long Gallery with a Nether Gallery running beneath it and taking in the south-west tower so that the galleries are lit on three of their four sides. Sidney also formed a whole new court in the north-west corner, with a stubby little Tuscan colonnade – an early Renaissance touch, predating the vaguely similar ones at Knole and Hatfield by a quarter of a century – running its north range eastward to the King's Tower opposite the old Hall. This work along the north side is, however, of rather less interest to us, since a good deal of it disappeared under the last serious outbreak of rebuilding between 1818 and 1860, and those parts which have survived are not normally open to the public. The nineteenth-century additions, by Biagio Rebecca and, later, George Devey, include the stables and virtually everything west of the Pulteney group. Though sensitive enough, they are in no way remarkable.

This rather dry account of its building history does the house less than justice. It has plenty of atmosphere, fine pictures and excellent furniture; and there are corners, especially in the gardens, where the spirit of Sir Philip Sidney still seems very much alive. Before you leave, however, return for a few minutes to where you began, to Sir John de Pulteney's Hall, where those mighty arched braces, deeply moulded purlins and smoke-blackened kingposts of English chestnut have looked down on the inhabitants of Penshurst and their guests for six and a half centuries. This is the house's chief glory – for me, one of the grandest rooms in the world.

## Ramsgate

*34; on coast 15 miles NE of Canterbury on A253*

Of the three neighbouring coastal resorts of the Isle of Thanet, only Ramsgate has saved its soul. Margate has sold out to mammon, Broadstairs to the Charles Dickens industry; but Ramsgate, though inevitably much changed from the time of W.P. Frith – whose painting of *Ramsgate Sands* was the sensation of the 1854 Royal Academy show, where it was immediately snapped up by Queen Victoria – still keeps a flavour of those even earlier Regency days when the English invented first the seaside and then an architecture to fit it. That architecture survives on the two cliffs that rise up from the harbour: on the West Cliff NELSON CRESCENT, THE PARAGON, and the slightly later (1826) ROYAL CRESCENT; on the East Cliff ALBION PLACE and, best of all, WELLINGTON CRESCENT.

Perhaps surprisingly for a town largely devoted to pleasure, the three individual buildings that stand out at Ramsgate are all churches. The old parish church, ST LAURENCE'S, is Norman, having begun life as a chapel of ease to Minster Abbey. You would never guess its age from its unprepossessing exterior, but the moment you go in the atmosphere changes; the sturdy round Norman piers are still in place after eight centuries, their arches already pointing the way to Gothic. To see just whither that way ultimately led, you must go to Church Hill, upon which ST GEORGE'S CHURCH was built in 1824–7 to a design by Henry Hemsley, a brilliant young architect who would be a good deal better known today had he not died in 1825 at the age of thirty-three. This is his only known work; it was completed, with a few alterations, by H.E. Kendall. A large church, Perpendicular in style, it boasts a simply tremendous west tower, crowned by a tall, pinnacled octagon linked to the tower pinnacles by flying buttresses. It may not be as sensational as the Boston Stump, from which it obviously derives; but it remains undeniably spectacular. Nor does the interior let it down. In all England there are few Georgian Gothic churches more imaginative than this.

Yet even St George's must yield second place to the Roman Catholic CHURCH OF ST AUGUSTINE, built at his own expense, between 1845 and 1850, by Augustus Welby Pugin. He intended it as a parish church, but when he died only two years after its completion it became part of a Benedictine abbey – which it still remains today. Pugin considered it his best work, better even than St Giles, Cheadle. If, like most people, you see it only from the road, you will be unlikely to agree with him; to get a proper view you must walk through the church into the churchyard behind. Even so, you will probably be disappointed; there is nothing particularly exciting about the long barn-like structure with its steeply pitched roof – you are actually looking at the south aisle – and the tall gabled transept advancing towards you with its odd little lean-to porch. The window tracery is not particularly adventurous, the crossing-tower distinctly in need of the spire that Pugin planned for it but never built, and which would have made the church higher than it is long. Where the quality really shows is in the textures – the alternation of knapped flint and Whitby stone, the care with which the wide range of colours within that stone has been exploited, that extraordinary feeling for his materials that characterised Pugin all his life.

*The church of St Augustine, Ramsgate.*

Inside, the Whitby stone is used throughout, and the same superb standards of masonry prevail. The breadth of the nave and side aisle, together with their comparative shortness – the arcade has only two bays – make the church seem almost square, with the great central pier providing a central focus. The decoration, though restrained in comparison with that of St Giles, is lavish by any normal standards; the details are all more or less consistent with the early fourteenth-century Decorated style that Pugin had chosen. It is, however, the fittings above all that give the church its magnificence. Pugin, in keeping with his conviction that mystery was a vital factor in church architecture, makes great play with screens: there are no fewer than three of them, not counting the magnificent wrought-iron gate at the entrance to the Lady Chapel, the work of his son-in-law John Powell after his death – at the express wish, we are told, of the architects of England.

The high altar in the chancel is, to my eye, slightly spoilt by the outsize brass tabernacle which was shown at the Great Exhibition of 1851 and presented to the church in Pugin's memory. Indisputably splendid in itself, it detracts from the 16-feet-high 'throne for the exposition of the Blessed Sacrament' – a masterpiece in painted and gilded stone. The altar itself is plain beneath its gorgeous frontals, unlike the carved stone altar in the Lady Chapel. Then, at the west end of the south aisle, we come to the font, intricately carved at all stages, its cover of carved oak soaring up to the roof.

Another fine screen separates the Pugin Chantry from the rest of the south transept. Beneath the big four-light window (by John Hardman, as are all the windows in the church) depicting scenes from the life of St Augustine lies the stone effigy of the architect himself, dressed in a vaguely medieval robe, his feet on two 'temple-haunting martlets' – his family emblem, repeated on the Minton floor tiles – his children kneeling beneath. The painted stone altar came from his private chapel in The Grange next door (see below).

Two of Pugin's sons contributed to St Augustine's. The Chapel of St John the Evangelist, known as the Digby Chantry, is by his eldest son Edward, while the adjoining St Joseph's Chapel and the Sacred Heart Altar at the east end of the north cloister are both the work of another son, Peter Paul. The most remarkable Stations of the Cross in painted terracotta on the wall of the north cloister are not, however, the work of any of the Pugins but that of the de Beule brothers of Ghent.

Immediately to the west of the church stands THE GRANGE, the house which Pugin built for himself in 1844. It has an embattled tower from which, during storms, he would scan the sea for boats in trouble. I could not get inside; *The Buildings of England* refers to a spacious Staircase Hall with unexpected *chinoiserie* balustrading, but adds that most of the original fittings, apart from some more Hardman glass in the Oratory, have disappeared.

*Rochester Castle.*

## Rochester

*35; 6½ miles SE of Gravesend on A226 and A2*

We cannot pretend that ROCHESTER CATHEDRAL is one of the greatest in England; I can only say that it is very much more rewarding than might be expected at first glance. It suffers from two initial disadvantages: an undistinguished exterior (excepting only the west door) which has not been improved by a weak crossing-tower and faintly ridiculous, stocky little herringboned lead spire, both of 1904–5 though based on earlier prints; and the absence of a close, with all the greenness and tranquillity that closes afford. Do not, however, be put off. Rochester is, after Canterbury, the oldest diocese in England, dating from 604; the initiator of the present building in 1076, Bishop Gundulf – much of whose work is still visible – went on to design the White Tower in the Tower of London; and the cathedral contains much fine architecture, and architectural detail, from every style and period.

There is no need to spend much time on the exterior – though it is no bad thing, at the outset, to walk some 50 yards or so along the north side. There, just beyond the transept and near the High Street war memorial, stand the remains of a square Norman tower, used by Gundulf as a treasury and a works office – and, quite probably, as a defence in an emergency, for in those early years after the Conquest the Norman position in Kent was still by no means secure. Return now to the west front. It looks, and is, a bit of a jumble, with that huge Perpendicular window, and battlements above, uncomfortably slotted in between the two inner turrets and threatening to crush the lovely Norman portal below – a pity, since it spoils what must have been, before the fifteenth century, one of the best Norman façades in England. (In fact, of the four turrets that constitute the principal feature of this façade, only one – the second from the right – is original from top to bottom. The other three were all wholly or partly rebuilt by Pearson in the 1880s.) The portal itself is mid-twelfth-century work, though the sculpture on the tympanum – Christ in Majesty, with angels, symbols of the Evangelists, and the Apostles strung out in a line along the lintel – has suffered sadly over the centuries. So, even more, have the statues of Solomon and the Queen of Sheba in the jamb shafts below. The first figures of this type are those at St Denis in France, *c.* 1140. These must be only very little later; they are certainly the oldest in England.

Inside the nave there is a splendid march of fine Norman arcading on the two lower levels. (The clerestory can be ignored as a wholly unworthy Perpendicular addition, dating presumably from the same time as the west window.) We are lucky to have that nave; as is plain from the last two bays before the crossing, there was a movement around 1300 to rebuild the whole thing in the contemporary Decorated style. Fortunately the scheme was abandoned before too much harm was done. Thus Rochester was able to preserve another unique distinction, though one not easily spotted: around the triforium there once ran a narrow wall passage. This is tunnel-vaulted, but the arches between the small pairs of columns – clearly visible from across the nave – are *pointed*: probably the first pointed arches to appear anywhere in the country.

With the crossing, and after this brief flirtation with Decorated, we find ourselves, rather surprisingly, in the thirteenth-century world of Early English. This is the result of two disastrous fires, one in 1137, the second in 1179, which together destroyed virtually everything except the nave. Fortunately, money for the rebuilding was soon at hand; a pious Scottish baker, William of Perth, was murdered just outside the city on the first leg of his pilgrimage to the Holy Land, whereat the monks of Rochester carried him back to the cathedral, gave him a fine funeral and a magnificent shrine, probably engineered a few miracles and before long were enjoying a profitable pilgrim traffic of their own. As a result of this, a new choir could be inaugurated in 1227 – with solid walls on each side and thus completely cut off from the choir aisles – and about fifteen years later the lovely north transept, where for the first time the cathedral was given a proper clerestory, and a very beautiful one too. In 1270 or thereabouts the south transept followed. It must have been soon after this that plans were drawn up for the rebuilding of the nave, and work was begun on the two bays nearest the crossing; but William, having achieved sainthood in 1256, soon began to wane in popularity and funds fortunately dried up. All that now remains of his wonder-working shrine is a marble slab in the north choir transept.

The south choir transept, however, boasts a far greater treasure than this – the doorway to the chapter room. Here is a really marvellous example of Decorated stone carving of about 1350 – a doorway which almost rivals in quality the two doors (though they are a century earlier) admitting to the choir aisles at Lincoln. The two largest figures, one on each side, represent the Church of the New Testament and the Synagogue of the Old, the latter blindfolded and bearing a broken lance like the famous one at Strasbourg. The heads of these two figures are nineteenth-century replacements, but all the rest is original and beautifully preserved.

Finally, the presbytery. The high altar itself was designed by George Gilbert Scott, but its surroundings date from the earliest years of the rebuilding after the fires – about 1200. There are no aisles, which is unusual, and only two storeys, which is unique in English medieval cathedral building; but the presbytery is none the less satisfying for that, the contrast between the pale stone of the walls and the dark Purbeck marble of the shafts and string-courses working as well here as it is unsuccessful elsewhere – at Salisbury, for example. Moreover, the absence of aisles gives it a breadth and spaciousness which is further emphasised by the sexpartite rib vaulting and the double row of three broad and well-separated lancets at the east end, the upper one very slightly stepped. Beneath it lies a magnificent crypt, part Norman from Gundulf's day, part Early English, several of the piers bearing evocative thirteenth-century graffiti.

Of the secular buildings of Rochester, the grandest by far is its still formidable CASTLE, standing immense on its mound opposite the cathedral. The original castle was another of Gundulf's constructions, but what we actually see today is its keep, a slightly later building of 1130 or so, five storeys high, and with corner towers rising higher still, to 125 feet – making it the tallest of English castle keeps as well as one of the best preserved. It has an extraordinary well shaft running through the middle, with openings at each floor level up to the Banqueting Hall, which occupies the third and fourth storeys – and, from its battlements, marvellous views over the great curve of the Medway that it was designed to protect.

TEMPLE MANOR, at Strood across the Medway, is part of a thirteenth-century flint manor house of the Knights Templars, now standing incongruously in the middle of an industrial estate and under the care of the *Historic Buildings and Monuments Commission*. The older stone part, with undercroft and first-floor Hall, was built in about 1240; the Hall has a rich doorway reached by an outer staircase with Purbeck marble shafts. Inside are wall arcades, and two lancet windows. The brick additions at the west and east ends date from the seventeenth century.

## St Clere

*36; 4½ miles NE of Sevenoaks off A225*

The first sight of St Clere, from the Pilgrims' Way which runs along the hillside to the north above Kemsing, is impressive indeed. Standing there in its park, at the end of a long avenue of trees, the tall building of lightish red brick has a firm, straightforward, no-nonsense look about it; a little austere perhaps, but an entirely appropriate residence for a cultivated gentleman of the late eighteenth century and a most excellent monument to the Age of Reason.

Then one looks again. Are those not octagonal angle turrets framing the five-bay entrance front, with low pyramidal caps just visible behind the parapet? And that extraordinary crest of high, diagonally set chimneys – would any self-respecting eighteenth-century architect have dreamt of such a thing? Suddenly the truth dawns: this simple-seeming house is a good century and a half older than it looks at first sight. But that in turn begs the next question: to what does it owe this strange semblance of youth? And the answer is, oddly enough, that parapet. Remove that in your mind's eye and allow the hipped roof to descend uninterrupted to eaves and a cornice; then put, if you will, a balustrade around the flat part of the roof and perhaps a lantern above – and there to all intents and purposes is a quintessential seventeenth-century house of the style of Coleshill, of Ashdown or even of nearby Chevening before the Stanhopes transformed it. Moreover if, as seems likely, the entrance forecourt was deliberately raised in the eighteenth century, the basement windows must previously have been visible from the front and the resemblance, particularly to the last two, more striking still.

The special importance of St Clere lies in the fact that of all these Coleshill-type houses it is the oldest – by some twenty years – that can be accurately dated, for we know that Bishop Bancroft consecrated its chapel in 1633. (The only other house of about the same date is Chevening

St Clere.

(*q.v.*), which is traditionally believed to have been built for the 13th Lord Dacre, who died in 1630; but there is no documentary evidence for this.) It is in any case quite astonishingly ahead of its time. Only those angle towers point to the former, Jacobean, age. But to Sir John Sedley, who commissioned the house, it must have seemed quite revolutionary enough already; probably he could not quite bring himself to sever every link with the past.

Looking at the house in close-up, one notices other characteristic seventeenth-century details. The brickwork is English, rather than Flemish, bond, and it includes the long and short quoins and window surrounds (which, incidentally, are eared at top and bottom) although these have at some time been given a cement rendering. But there is evidence of later work as well, notably the agreeable little solecism of a semicircular verandah projecting from the Morning Room on the western side, which presumably dates from about 1800. The canted bay of the Drawing Room, immediately to the south of it, seems to me a less happy addition. It dates from the 1880s, when the house also gained its unsightly *porte-cochère* and a long eastward extension; but this is in the same style as the earlier work, and such a good copy that it is not easy to see where it begins.

Inside, virtually none of the interior dates from before the early eighteenth century when, after the death of Sir Charles Sedley, childless and feeble-minded to boot, the property – already much neglected and run-down – was sold to the Evelyns. They it was who wainscoted the principal rooms on the ground and first floors with the large fielded panels which are still in position, and who introduced the noble staircase that we see today, with its mahogany balusters (three to each step) and elegantly carved brackets below them. It rises to a spacious landing which is now a room in itself.

Most of the interior decoration, however, is of a later date and need not particularly concern us here. Architecturally, there is only one other point to be made, but that is an important one. It concerns the arrangement of the rooms, which is on the 'double pile' plan, whereby a central corridor runs through each floor from end to end, with rooms going off to either side. The idea, which has the advantage of providing a succession of fine rooms to each front, is such a simple one that one wonders why it was not adopted earlier. It seems, however, to have been introduced only by Inigo Jones; and in this respect St Clere is once again, with Chevening, one of the earliest examples in the country.

## St Margaret's at Cliffe*

*37; 4 miles NE of Dover on B2058*

A really magnificent Norman church, ST MARGARET'S is built of rough flint dressed with Caen stone (and, more recently, brick). It has a squat but sturdy tower hardly rising above the ridge of the nave roof, clerestory windows set in shafted arcading, a fine late Norman north doorway and a most spectacular west one. This latter doorway has four orders of round arches set in a huge triangular gable containing thirteen figures in arches – some full-length and seated, some just heads – which presumably represent Christ and the Apostles, though the carving is too crude for any certain identification to be attempted.

The interior is dominated by the huge, high chancel arch, rising almost to the roof and ornamented with zigzag, from which two brave four-bay Norman arcades march westward down the nave, also profusely ornamented and with small grotesque masks in the label stops. Both aisles are Norman too, and contemporary with the nave – a rarity at this date. The clerestory windows, sitting immediately on top of the arches, are quite plain – surprisingly so, considering what a fuss is made of them outside. The chancel is longer, broader and higher than most Norman chancels, with three widely spaced round-headed windows at the east end and four slightly larger ones around the north and south walls. The high double light above the eastern trio can be dismissed as a recent insertion. The aisles originally had windows only at the east and west ends; these survive on the south side, but on the north the east window has been replaced by an Early English triple lancet, and the west window was moved round to the side wall when the vestry was added as part of Ewan Christian's restoration of the 1860s.

That leaves us with the tower arch, which is the only indication we have that the tower may be later than the rest of the church. Surprisingly, it proves to be pointed – the only pointed arch in the medieval building – and there are details of the moulding which indicate a date not much earlier than 1200. Everywhere else, except for the few later alterations mentioned above, the evidence suggests that the work was finished by 1150 or so. But now comes a mystery: if the tower was, as it appears, an afterthought, how can we explain the external arcading at clerestory level which continues across it without a break? Was this subsequently extended? If so, it was done with a skill not unmixed with a degree of low cunning. Or is the tower arch simply a later alteration? It doesn't look like one, and what, anyway, would have been the point? One would love to know.

## St Mary in the Marsh★

*38; 3 miles N of New Romney off B2070*

Here is another joy among the marshland churches, partly for the lightness and brightness – virtually all the glass in ST MARY'S is plain – and partly because no one has been getting at it. The tower is Norman all the way up to the top; for the rest, we seem to be in the latter half of the thirteenth century. About the latest architectural feature is the very early Decorated east window, with geometrical tracery; this looks about 1300. There is no chancel arch, or even any steps until you get right up to the altar; thus the entrance to the chancel is defined only by the place where the aisles stop and by the positioning of the pulpit. It contains nice, rather crude, trefoiled sedilia, with even cruder heads on the label stops, and a double piscina which, like all of its kind, can be ascribed to the reign of King Edward I (1272–1307).

For the rest, there is a fine kingposted timber roof; a simply splendid Royal Arms, highly coloured, of 1775; a good Decalogue on the west wall; and a plaque in memory of E. (*The Railway Children*) Nesbit.

A final distinction: in contrast to the usual flint, St Mary's is of stone.

## Saltwood Castle

*39; 2 miles NW of Hythe off A20*

Kent is a county of castles; Saltwood, therefore, is up against stiff competition. It is less picturesque than Leeds, less forbidding than Dover, less authentic than Bodiam. To a considerable degree, nonetheless, it possesses all their qualities, and it combines them in a way peculiarly its own. Of them all, it is the one in which I should most like to live.

In 1026 the manor, which had existed since Saxon times, was bestowed by King Canute on 'the Church of Christ in Canterbury'; after the Conquest, Archbishop Lanfranc took it over as his personal property, as did his successors after him. Strategically, on the other hand, the place needed a proper garrison, and the early history of Saltwood is largely one of an uneasy dual occupation, sometimes by the Church, sometimes by noblemen and military commanders. At the time of Henry II's accession, the castle was the property of Henry of Essex, Lord Warden of the Cinque Ports, Royal Standard Bearer and Constable of England; part of the Gatehouse to the Inner Bailey and the roofless Great Hall (though not of course its windows, which are considerably later) are generally thought to have been added by him. Unfortunately, however, Essex disgraced himself a few years later by showing quite uncharacteristic cowardice in a border battle against the Welsh, and in 1163 the King confiscated all his estates. The Archbishop of Canterbury, Thomas à Becket, immediately sought the restitution of Saltwood, his *'manerium praedilectum'*; but Henry gave it instead to a ruffianly local baron named de Broc, and the ensuing quarrel was to develop into the great rift that culminated, seven years later, in the Archbishop's murder. The crime was planned in the castle; it was from here that the four knights set off for Canterbury on 29 December 1170 – with an escort provided by de Broc – and hither that they returned that same evening, the dreadful deed accomplished.

The castle consists in essence of an Outer Bailey, roughly triangular in shape, and an oval Inner Bailey jutting into its western side. The Outer Bailey is mostly in ruins; though the cyclopean masonry in the lower courses of its south tower may well be of Roman origin, most of what we see today is probably the work of Henry Yevele (who had previously given Westminster Hall its glorious hammer-beam roof) in the late fourteenth century. He too may have been responsible for the design of the tremendous Gatehouse erected by Archbishop William Courtenay at the same period. Much of it has been restored: the two storeys of Perpendicular windows between the towers, each of three lights with transom; the four *machicoulis* above; and the battlements. But the restorations have been accurate and conscientious and the Archbishop, if he could see it today, would find it unchanged.

Within the Gatehouse a central passageway leads due west. The first part of it is obviously part of Courtenay's addition, though the inner of his two rib-vaulted bays is a late nineteenth-century rebuilding. Then comes a short flight of steps, at the head of which are the arch, hinges and portcullis grooves of the old inner gateway,

*The Hall, Saltwood Castle.*

now blocked at the far end by a four-light window. This inner gateway is topped by a tower, obscured on the exterior by Courtenay's building but clearly visible from the garden within, one of five built along the curtain wall of the Inner Bailey – all of them, oddly enough, projecting inside the wall rather than outside it in the usual way. From this tower two lower wings, modern but in similar style, branch out to the sides. These buildings together form the principal residential block; behind them the bailey extends over a vast lawn, still completely enclosed by the old battlements so that it is possible to walk the entire circuit along the top.

In doing so, one passes another important cluster of buildings, partly ruined and partly restored, extending along the south side. The first of these – that nearest the Gatehouse – is the Great Hall, possibly built by Essex, though the cusped intersecting tracery cannot be much earlier than 1300. By then the castle clearly no longer served any defensive purpose; had it done so, such windows – especially those towards the outside – would have been unthinkable. A little further to the west of the Great Hall, and at right-angles to it, is a second Hall, believed to have been used by the Archbishop for giving audiences. It stands on a vast tunnel-vaulted undercroft, but the magnificent room that one sees today – formerly the Library of Lord Clark, a previous owner – is largely a reconstruction by Philip Tilden dating from the 1930s. The timber roof, carried on huge oak trusses with perforated panels which in turn rest on carved stone corbels, may not be historically accurate but is a considerable achievement in its own right; another, smaller roof, coffered this time, covers the adjoining Parlour. These two rooms, their walls covered with superb tapestries and works of art, are the most memorable in the house, but are open to the public only by prior appointment.

## Sandwich

*40; 12 miles E of Canterbury on A257*

One of the original Cinque Ports, Sandwich is still a fascinating medieval town – though it suffers terribly from summer traffic. The sea receded in the sixteenth century, and is now a good 2 miles distant; but the town still has a maritime feel about it, besides being rich in reminders of the Protestant weavers who sought refuge here from France and the Low Countries in the early years of Elizabeth I's reign, and have left their mark on the architecture.

Of the three medieval churches of Sandwich, one – ST MARY'S – is a hopeless wreck, patched up but pathetic; the second, ST PETER'S, is basically thirteenth-century, but it too has been altered almost beyond recognition. It is nowadays best noted for being the church from which the curfew is rung every night at eight o'clock, by one of thirty-one able-bodied citizens, each of whom has his own date of the month.

The third church, ST CLEMENT'S, is the only one of the three to have kept its original Norman tower, centrally placed and adorned with three tiers of arcading. Inside, it proves to be supported on four noble crossing arches which, however, no longer mark a crossing since the transepts have disappeared – absorbed in the aisles when these were widened in the fifteenth century. All that remains is a nave, those two broad aisles, and the Early English chancel which, curiously, boasts its own primitive amplification system of sounding holes set beneath the stalls and high in the walls of the sanctuary. The nave has an angel roof on the East Anglian model – a strange thing to find in these parts.

Sandwich still has any number of medieval and Tudor houses, though some of them need a good deal of seeking out. It has also retained stretches of the TOWN WALL and one of its five original gates – FISHERS GATE, the lower half dated 1384, the upper 1571. The KING'S ARMS, in Strand Street, is a fine timber-framed house of 1592, and MANWOOD COURT, a little further on, shows what Sandwich could do with brick at much the same date. The GUILDHALL is a reconstruction as far as the exterior is concerned, but contains within it a seventeenth-century court room which has remained virtually untouched – a precious survival indeed.

Finally, THE SALUTATION – built by Sir Edwin Lutyens for Henry Farrer just before the First World War. It stands at the top end of Upper Strand Street – Queen Anne with Tudorish chimneys. The elevations are all subtly different, however, and the interior reveals the house to be nowhere near as simple as it looks. There are black Baroque corkscrew columns in the hall, and a transverse staircase that leads up to a special landing designed as an overflow from the Library.

## Scotney Castle*

*NT; 41; 6 miles SE of Tunbridge Wells off A21*

There are few more delectable or romantic springtime views in all England than that from the new Scotney Castle towards the old; a view down a rich wooded ravine, ablaze with flowering trees and rhododendrons, to the remains of a fourteenth-century castle and a half-hidden seventeenth-century manor house standing on an island in a quiet lake far below. So at least it appears. In fact the manor house is the successor to a medieval building, of which little trace survives, and which was fortified by its owner, Roger Ashburnham, probably after the sack of Rye and Winchelsea (*qq.v.*) by the French in 1377; the castle is the south corner tower of these fortifications, its *machicoulis* now topped with a delightfully unwarlike conical roof and lantern; and the lake is the moat which made the fortifications complete. But even this is not the end of the story; for the view, as we see it today, is the very deliberate creation of Edward Hussey, ironmaster, and his friend William Sawrey Gilpin, nephew of the Rev. William Gilpin, that Hampshire clergyman who more than anyone else could be said to have invented the early nineteenth-century cult of the picturesque.

When in 1837 Hussey commissioned Anthony Salvin to build him a house in the Gothic manner, he and Gilpin deliberately chose this site for its picturesque potential. To improve it, however, they bravely resolved to quarry the stone from the hillside immediately below. This created the ravine, which was then carefully and knowledgeably planted to produce, eventually, the wooded Alpine garden that we see today. Turning to the lake and island, Hussey went on to demolish some of the manor house until the suitably ruinous part that was left stood in what he felt was perfect relation to the medieval defences. A little more judicious planting, and his work was done.

Successive generations of Husseys carried on the work, above all the late Christopher Hussey, whose name is well known to all lovers of English architecture and whose widow still lives at Scotney. Their labours have cumulatively produced the supreme triumph of landscape gardening of the nineteenth century, just as Stourhead is that of the eighteenth. Yet their object was not purely landscape. It was to provide a picturesque setting for architecture, and although that setting is nowadays more spectacular than the buildings it was designed to frame, it never overshadows them. Rather does it lead the eye even more beguilingly towards them, keeping them always the centre of the composition. Scotney is therefore about architecture every bit as much as it is about landscape, which is why it finds a place in this book.

## Sevenoaks

See Knole.

## Sissinghurst Castle*

*NT; 42; 4½ miles E of Goudhurst off A262*

There is a memorable moment, as you drive west from Tenterden along the A262, when you first catch sight of the tall red-brick tower of Sissinghurst Castle rising up amid the green meadows of the Weald, the flag of the Sackvilles fluttering proudly from its mast-head. That tower, however, is in fact only a remnant, though an impossibly romantic one; for here, on the land which now nurtures one of the loveliest gardens in all England, there once stood a noble Elizabethan mansion, where the Queen herself spent the nights of 15 and 16 August 1573.

Her host was one Richard Baker – he was to receive a knighthood a day or two later – whose forebears had bought the medieval manor almost a century before and had built the moated courtyard house of which the present western entrance range formed a part. It started off quite unpretentious; but then, around 1535, Sir John Baker – a man of immense ability and ambition who was already making a name for himself at Henry VIII's Court and was five years later to be appointed Chancellor of the Exchequer – decided to improve it with the imposing central archway and Gatehouse which we see today.

Through a long legal career, and by various methods into which it is better not to enquire too closely, Sir John made himself one of the richest men in the kingdom; and his son Richard, who succeeded in 1558, at once set to work on a completely new house, immediately to the east of the old one, of which he demolished all but the entrance range. This new building formed three sides of a large square courtyard, the fourth (western) side consisting of a simple brick wall with the tower in the centre. A surviving engraving shows it to have been conceived on a majestic scale; but its period of glory was to be short. The Baker estate was broken up in 1661 and the whole property went into decline. A century later it was being used as a prison camp for French sailors captured during the Seven Years' War; up to 3,000 of them were kept there at any one time and one of the officers of the garrison was, briefly, Edward Gibbon. In about 1800, by now in a sad state of decay, the great house was demolished except for the tower, the south-east corner of the courtyard and the back wall of the south wing. Mercifully, the old entrance wing of the fifteenth-century house was also spared, as was the Priest's House a few yards beyond the courtyard at its north-west corner.

*The Gatetower, Sissinghurst Castle.*

This was the property that was bought by Harold Nicolson and his wife Vita Sackville-West in 1930, slowly made fit once more for human habitation, and further transformed by that glorious garden. Sir Richard Baker's Gatetower remains its focal point. It is built entirely of brick, rendered where necessary to give the impression of stone dressings. Its octagonal side turrets, which rise up a little higher than the centre, originally had ogival cupolas; their conical caps are a nineteenth-century substitution. The first-floor room was Vita Sackville-West's sitting room and study; the room above contains fascinating photographs showing the restoration of the house and, in the centre, the original Hogarth Press, formerly the property of Leonard and Virginia Woolf.

## Stelling

*43; 8 miles N of Hythe off B2068*

ST MARY'S CHURCH stands on its own, about halfway between the villages of Stelling Minnis and Upper Hardres. Architecturallly, it goes back to the early thirteenth century, but with the addition of two beautiful broad Decorated east windows – one to the chancel, the other to the south aisle – through whose clear glass panes light streams into the church. The original timber roof has for the most part survived – two big tie-beams over the nave, with kingposts.

Now for the furnishings, which are dominated by a very large three-decker pulpit with tester. It is set halfway along the north wall, immediately facing the entrance – over which is a gallery, curiously placed in the south aisle from which no view of the chancel is possible. What we see here is in fact a perfect illustration of that change of emphasis characteristic of the seventeenth and eighteenth centuries, when the pulpit became more important than the altar and the whole axis of devotion was turned away from the east towards the centre. At Stelling this arrangement was taken so far that the pews on the north side east of the pulpit actually face westwards, their backs to the altar.

The church is utterly unspoilt, and looks as fresh as its pretty grey-green paint. It seems to preserve the whole spirit of the eighteenth century – more, perhaps, than any other church in Kent.

## Stone

*44; 2 miles E of Dartford off A226*

'Why on earth', you will ask, as you draw up outside the CHURCH OF ST MARY THE VIRGIN, 'has he brought me *here*?' You are standing on the brink of a quarry, a cement works is spewing out dust in all directions, and even the great sweep of the Thames estuary below you is seen through a dirty haze of industrialisation. Dickens would have described it wonderfully – in fact I suspect that somewhere or other he probably did. Even the church itself does not look very exciting at first glance; it must have been better when that villainously low tower still had its shingled spire, but there is always something awkward-looking about chancels rising higher than their naves. Then you notice the big broad chancel windows with their geometrical tracery; all, perhaps, is not lost.

Inside, despite much dire Victoriana, you can see at once that this is a building to be reckoned with. The nave is surprisingly narrow, which makes it look taller than in fact it is, and the late thirteenth-century arcades – their piers enriched with shafts of Purbeck marble – rise to the level of the roof. The aisle windows have plate tracery that looks stylistically a generation earlier than the geometrical tracery seen from outside. Since medieval churches were almost invariably built from east to west, this may seem odd; John Newman in *The Buildings of England* suggests that this is simply because 'the new-fangled bar tracery could not yet be manipulated in any but the largest windows'.

Now to the chancel. The stone-vaulted roof and – it must now be admitted – the traceried windows are in fact the work of G.E. Street, who restored the church in 1859–60; but the important point to remember is that he invented nothing. There is sure evidence that the chancel was originally vaulted, and remained so until Civil War times; as for the windows, their dimensions are unchanged and the tracery itself was based on that of the east window of the north aisle, which remained largely intact. The lower parts of the chancel are virtually all original work – and that includes the trefoiled blank arcading that runs all the way round the two eastern bays, together with the spectacularly fine relief carving within the spandrels. This carving is the glory of the church; its interest, however, lies not only in its virtuosity but also in its extraordinary similarity to that found in similar arcading in Westminster Abbey – to the

*St John's Jerusalem, Sutton-at-Hone.*

point where there can be no serious doubt that the same master masons were responsible. And if they did the chancel arcade, they will certainly have done the whole church.

But why choose Stone – and where did the money come from? Because the manor of Stone was the property of the See of Rochester, and Rochester was, in the mid-thirteenth century, riding on a great wave of affluence owing to the popularity of St William of Perth. Thus, for St Mary the Virgin, the best was scarcely good enough.

## Strood

See Rochester (Temple Manor).

## Sutton-at-Hone

*45; 3 miles S of Dartford off A225*
*Includes St John's Jerusalem (NT)*

Apart from some red-brick Elizabethan ALMSHOUSES dated 1597, the village has little of interest. Half a mile or so to the south-east, however, set in a lush green meadow beside the River Darent and framed between a vast cedar and a magnificent copper beech, stands the house still romantically known as ST JOHN'S JERUSALEM (NT). It was in 1199 that Robert de Basing bestowed his manor at Sutton on the Order of the Knights Hospitallers of St John, whose English *Langue* was already well-established and run from their priory at Clerkenwell; and a generation later, in 1234, we find King Henry III – who was, by all accounts, a frequent visitor – ordering five oak trees from the forest of Tunbridge to be delivered to the Sutton commandery for the re-roofing of their church.

That church now forms the east end of the delightful house – the rest of it is principally of the seventeenth and eighteenth centuries – that still bears the Order's name. It fell into ruin when the English *Langue* was dissolved by Henry VIII in 1540 and its lands confiscated; in the last century it was even divided horizontally to form a billiard room above and a scullery below – in which a rather crude double piscina can still be seen in the south wall. But its three eastern lancets still survive – the central one just failing to escape the unnecessarily low seventeenth-century hipped roof – as do three more on the north and two on the south, together with some of the original walling and a pair of stone and flint buttresses, one on each side.

After the Dissolution the building lay desolate and abandoned until 1660; it was then bought from the Crown by Abraham Hill, who had introduced cider to Kent from Devon and was one of the founders of the Royal Society. Having retained 20 feet of the east end of the church as a private chapel, he then converted the rest into a delightful house of brick, with hipped roof and dormers, blocking up the original entrance to the south and using instead an existing door in the north wall of the tower.

In 1755 the property was acquired by Kent's greatest historian, Edward Hasted. He largely rebuilt the house, incidentally bankrupting himself in the process. He lowered the roof, restored the main entrance to the south side (the pedimented front door with its Gibbs surround is his), added a new Drawing Room where Hill's porch had been and Georgianised the entire west end by giving it a stucco rendering. Finally he introduced (possibly from another house) a handsome new staircase of broad Palladian proportions, lit by a generous round-headed window – the effect of which, alas, has been somewhat spoilt by the clumsy addition of Victorian indoor sanitation in 1870.

St John's Jerusalem remains a modest house, and the vestiges of the old church of the Hospitallers are, it must be admitted, exiguous. But it is beautiful inside and out; it is possessed of a rare charm; its setting, among what are nowadays London's outer suburbs, is little short of miraculous; and it is outstandingly fortunate in its present occupant, who is an architect and has done much to preserve it. Being now the property of the National Trust, it is open to the public during the summer.

## Tunbridge Wells

*46; 36 miles SE of London on A21*

The centre of Tunbridge Wells is the PANTILES, which is as it should be, for here are the actual springs of chalybeate water that gave the town its name and, after the discovery of their therapeutic properties by Lord North in 1606, its fame. Faith in these properties may have largely dried up, but the springs themselves still run and the Pantiles – known before 1887 simply and more accurately as the Parade – have retained much of their seventeenth- and eighteenth-century charm; indeed they are everything that a quiet pedestrian precinct in a historic county town should be, with pollarded lime trees and a pretty covered colonnade. Most of the principal buildings are rather later – the Bath House of 1804 for example, or the Royal Victoria Hotel, which is a misnomer in more ways than one, being no longer a hotel and anyway a building comfortably antedating the Queen's accession; but they all contribute to the general atmosphere, and a seat in the Pantiles remains a pleasant place to relax on a spring morning.

Just to the north, across the road, is the CHURCH OF KING CHARLES THE MARTYR – an interesting dedication, caused by the quantity of Royalist visitors who were patronising the Wells in the 1670s and who were determined to counterbalance the Puritan influence of the previous generation, which had actually gone so far as to name the gentle slopes surrounding it Mount Pleasant, Mount Sion and Mount Ephraim. The plain brick exterior gives little indication of the riches within, and even the inside may seem puzzling until one realises that the church was originally orientated north and south; only in 1882 did Ewan Christian throw out a short chancel to the east and turn the church round through 90 degrees. The pride of the building, however, remains its lovely plaster ceilings, those in the eastern part (except a slightly later addition in the north-east corner) by John Wetherel in the 1670s, the remainder in the following decade by one of Wren's chief plasterers, Henry Doogood. It is not perhaps the most classically beautiful of churches – and it is certainly not helped by a disgraceful east window of 1901 – but it has considerable period charm and complements the Pantiles to perfection.

In the seventeenth century and even through the eighteenth, Tunbridge Wells was still little more than a village and this was its only church. Early in the nineteenth, however, it began to expand rapidly, and from 1828 onwards became the scene of the most ambitious residential building project yet attempted in the county – Decimus Burton's Calverley Estate. Burton's principal inspiration was Nash's work in Regent's Park, in which he himself had been marginally involved. The estate was conceived – leaving aside one or two individual houses – in two main parts. The first, CALVERLEY PARK CRESCENT, is a charming terrace of seventeen three-storey houses, with a covered promenade in front supported on a slender row of cast-iron columns. The centre five bays and the ones at each end are gently emphasised by cornices and larger windows, but otherwise the whole thing is agreeably underplayed – far more modest, certainly, than any-

*The church of King Charles the Martyr, Tunbridge Wells.*

thing Nash would have designed. The material is the local sandstone, unrendered.

Just beyond, a rather spindly arch marks the entrance to CALVERLEY PARK itself. This is rather harder to see, the nineteen villas of which it consists each being set back and partially obscured from the road by hedges and shrubberies; but they too form a crescent, and from their upper storeys enjoy a splendid view over the prettily landscaped slopes of Mount Pleasant. All are different, but unified by the same vaguely Italianate style which they all share.

In this idiom, or in the neo-classical, Burton was a fine and imaginative architect. Where he really came to grief was in his attempts at Gothic, as at HOLY TRINITY, Church Road. It is worth a quick visit, perhaps, just to see how totally blind he was to what the Gothic style was about, how illiterate to even its fundamental rules of grammar. 'That unspeakable Goth,' John Newman calls him in *The Buildings of England*; one look at the inside of Holy Trinity will explain why.

## Westerham

*47; 5½ miles W of Sevenoaks on A25*

*Includes Quebec House and Chartwell (both NT)*

Westerham has been largely ruined in the past thirty years through insensitive development. It does, however, provide the postal address for no fewer than three houses which are all open to the public and all, in their different ways, of interest. Unquestionably the most desirable of the three is SQUERRYES COURT, whose entrance is on the A25 as it enters the town from the west. A typical red-brick William and Mary manor house built in 1681, it has two storeys (plus a row of dormers in the hipped roof) and seven bays, of which the centre three project slightly under a pediment with an oculus window. Instead of the quoins that one might expect, there are pilaster strips of rubbed brick at the angles. The garden front is identical, and looks out on to the lovely grounds with their woodland walks, formal gardens, flowering shrubs and a small lake. Inside, the rooms are nicely proportioned and there are some good Dutch and Flemish pictures, but no fine interiors. There is also a small collection of objects associated with General Wolfe, who was a local man and a friend of the family.

Wolfe-worshippers, however, would be even better advised to visit QUEBEC HOUSE (NT), which stands in the middle of the town (and on summer weekends suffers almost intolerably from passing traffic). Here he spent the first eleven years of his life, and the whole house is now a museum in his memory. The date looks about 1630. In plan it is almost a perfect square, three storeys high and with three pointed gables to each side. All the windows, alas, have been altered, but those under the gables still have their flat brick hoods. Inside, some of the fireplaces are of the sixteenth century, in other words older than the house and re-used; the staircase, on the other hand, looks rather later. The best room is on the first floor; nothing special, but furnished as the sort of mid-eighteenth-century drawing room in which the general would have felt at home.

*St Mary's Church, Westwell.*

The most famous house, and by far the ugliest, of the three is CHARTWELL (NT), bought by Winston Churchill in 1922 and his country home for the rest of his life. It too is a shrine, beautifully preserved by the National Trust, despite the quarter of a million visitors who pass through it every year. It is not, however, great architecture; when, a few years ago, I had to write a *son et lumière* script for it, I soon discovered that the less light you put on it, the better it looked. It began as a Tudor manor house, but was heavily Victorianised and then virtually rebuilt for the Churchills by Philip Tilden in the 1920s. From the garden front with its tall crow-step gables there is, however, a breathtaking view across the Weald.

## Westwell

*48; 1½ miles SE of Charing on A20*

Like so many of the smaller churches of Kent, ST MARY'S, Westwell, doesn't look much from the outside. Inside, two things strike you right away. The first is the breadth of the church, all the way along its axis until a yard or two from the east end when the two side aisles, each as broad as the nave itself, are eventually cut short; the second is the high stone chancel screen, which strides across the church after only four bays from the west, in other words a good way west of the chancel steps. Two round piers, slimmer and almost half as high again as those of the arcades, stand on each side of the central passage roughly on a line with the inner bench ends, and these, with the arcade piers opposite them, form a transverse colonnade of three pointed-trefoiled arches, with big roundels in the two spandrels on the western side. These arches neatly reflect the east end itself, with its three lancets at arcade level and two within the enclosing arch above.

Only when you advance beyond the screen does the church play its final trump card, by revealing that the entire roof east of the screen is vaulted in stone – a rare luxury for a remote country village. Now, too, one sees why that screen was necessary; the arcades alone could never have supported the additional weight. There is evidence that vault and screen were not part of the original plan – the awkward way the arcade piers supporting the screen have had to be built up speaks for itself – yet they are not appreciably later than the rest of the building, which leads one to deduce that there must have been a sudden, unexpected benefaction soon after the work had begun.

This unity of style adds, as always, greatly to the beauty of the building. Apart from the windows of the south aisle and the piscina and sedilia which are obvious fourteenth-century insertions, the entire interior dates from about 1250. There is only one minor eyesore: the square Victorian organ which effectively blocks out all the light from the windows in the south-east corner. How much better to have settled for a harmonium . . . .

---

# Short List

## Alkham

*49; 4 miles NE of Folkestone on B2060*

ST ANTHONY THE MARTYR is a flint church of much interest and beauty which once belonged to the nearby abbey of St Radegund. Part of it is early thirteenth-century, spacious and discreet; later in the century came the grand north chapel, extending halfway down the nave. Wide and graceful, it is arcaded down its whole length on slender Bethersden marble shafts, the arches richly and deeply undercut.

## Allington Castle

*50; 1 mile N of Maidstone off A229*

This small but romantic castle, moated and battlemented, was built by Stephen de Penchester in 1281 (though the battlements were added by Sir Martin Conway who, in the early 1900s, restored the castle with W.D. Caröe as architect). The ragstone curtain wall has a modest Gatehouse; at the south-east corner is the impressive thirteenth-century Solomon's Tower. Inside are two ranges of early buildings, a fifteenth-century hall porch and a Great Hall by Caröe. There is also a sixteenth-century range built by Sir Henry Wyatt, father of Sir Thomas, the poet. The castle now belongs to the Order of Carmelites.

## Bishopsbourne

*51; 5 miles SE of Canterbury off A2*

BOURNE PARK can be seen to perfection from the road, across the lake. It is a lovely Queen Anne house of red brick with stone dressings, the five central bays broken slightly forward under a deep pediment, with huge sash windows of twenty-four lights each, a hipped roof and dormers. There is much fine plasterwork within, and a splendid staircase with fluted columns for balusters. When I saw it, all was in urgent need of redecoration, but I gather that this has now been done.

## Bonnington

*52; 8 miles NW of Hythe off B2067*

ST RUMWOLD'S vies with Ruckinge as being the oldest church on Romney Marsh. It is named after an infant Saxon prince who professed his Christianity on the day of his birth, preached a sermon on the next day and died the day after. His tiny church is set amid quiet pastures a good mile from the village. The chancel is Norman, the nave Decorated. Architecturally it is no great shakes, but it gets high marks for charm, setting and atmosphere.

## Bredgar

*53; 3 miles SW of Sittingbourne on B2163*

SWANTON FARMHOUSE is a building of irresistible eccentricity. Though a fundamentally modest house of 1719, it has a façade which provides a staggering display of virtuoso brickwork in two colours. Whoever built it may have been a bit short on subtlety and even on taste, but he had a mind of his own all right – and he certainly knew his trade.

## Chilham

*54; 6 miles SW of Canterbury on A252*

The highly impressive remains of Henry II's flint CASTLE, built in 1171–4, still stand. Apart from Odiham (*q.v.*) it has the only octagonal keep in England. One turret projects from the east, while there are vestiges of another on the south. Between the castle and the village is Sir Dudley Digges's 'JACOBEAN HOUSE', finished in 1616 – also polygonal, this time five sides of a hexagon. Though worth a look, it has been much altered in the past three centuries.

## Deal Castle

*55; 8 miles NE of Dover on A258*

The castles at Deal, Walmer and Sandown were all built by Henry VIII in 1539–40, to protect the coast against an anticipated invasion by the French and Spanish, who were being encouraged by the Pope to recover England for the Faith. Of these Deal is the largest, most elaborate and best preserved. Its plan is like one six-leaf clover enclosed within another, the whole surrounded by a moat. There were five tiers of guns. The seaward side, which contained the Governor's Lodgings, was badly bombed in the Second World War and is now largely a reconstruction.

## Godmersham Park

*56; 10 miles SW of Canterbury off A28*

This lovely Palladian house was built by an unknown architect in 1732 and is set in a finely landscaped park. It is of brick, comprising a seven-bay central block with links to two-storeyed side pavilions. There is a hipped roof with dormers and urns along the front and, above the three central bays, a nice play of *oeil-de-boeuf* windows. Only the window pediments on the outer bays and the Gibbs surrounds in the links seem a little heavy and detract, very slightly, from the general effect. Inside, the Hall and Drawing Room are splendidly decorated in the high style of the period. If the other rooms were as sumptuous, the house would not have been demoted to this short list.

## Kilndown

*57; 6 miles NW of Hawkhurst off A21*

CHRISTCHURCH was commissioned by Lord Beresford in 1839 from Anthony Salvin, but failed to satisfy his stepson Alexander Beresford Hope, one of the leaders of the Gothic Revival movement, who in 1840 took charge of the building. He transformed the interior; it was painted, gilded and enriched with glowing golds, reds and blues until in 1845 the *Ecclesiologist* could acclaim it as 'a *whole* of colour . . . such as is to be seen in no other English church'.

## Larkfield

*58; 6 miles NW of Maidstone off A20*

The splendour of BRADBOURNE PLACE owes much to the masterly use of gauged brickwork. Completed in 1715, the nine-bay west front with its slightly projecting pedimented three-bay centre has brick of a lighter tone for the four paired pilasters at the angles. The north and south fronts have a recessed centre with projecting wings: note again the subtle coloration and the textural variety of the brickwork. There is an exceptionally fine staircase, and the main living rooms have plaster ceilings of 1774, the date of the big centre bow of the south front. The house is now East Malling Research Station.

## Linton Park

*59; 3 miles S of Maidstone on A229*

In a magnificent situation overlooking the Weald, the house was originally built in 1730 but was remodelled *c.*1825, with the result that it now looks as though a chunk of Carlton House Terrace had been transported to Kent. The remodelling may have been by George Basevi, who had been Cubitt's architect for Belgrave Square; certainly the portico is very reminiscent of Basevi's Fitzwilliam Museum in Cambridge, and there is a marked Grecian element as would befit a pupil of Soane. The main bedroom corridor is also very Soanish. The Entrance Hall is of 1730, the Drawing Room ceiling from Basevi's time.

## Lympne

*60; 2 miles W of Hythe off B2067*

Originally the residence of the Archdeacons of Canterbury, LYMPNE CASTLE is really a fortified manor house dating principally from the fourteenth and fifteenth centuries. It was rescued from dereliction between 1906 and 1912 when it was radically restored and added to by Sir Robert Lorimer. It stands magnificently on the high escarpment overlooking Romney Marsh, and its attractions nowadays are as much picturesque as architectural. ST STEPHEN'S CHURCH nearby has a Norman central tower but is too heavily Victorianised to be of much interest.

## Maidstone

*61; 36 miles SE of London off A20 and M20*

ALL SAINTS is Kent's grandest Perpendicular church. It makes a fine group with the stone Elizabethan ARCHBISHOP'S PALACE, and the late fourteenth-century COLLEGE OF PRIESTS, whose tall Gatehouse faces it.

## Mersham le Hatch

*62; 3 miles SE of Ashford on A20*

This, the first completely new house to be designed by Robert Adam, was finished, for the Knatchbull family, in 1766. The plan and elevations are not particularly exciting – a pedimented seven-bay main block with a low hipped roof, linked by balustraded corridors to square pavilions, and a bowed north front – but the decoration of the rooms shows Adam's new ideas after his stay in Rome. The house is now occupied by the Caldecott Community. The CHURCH OF ST JOHN THE BAPTIST has an unforgettable north aisle west window, with a row of thirteen lights in the bottom half and extremely odd tracery at the top. West of the church is COURT LODGE, a Decorated stone house of about 1350.

## Newington next Sittingbourne

*63; 2 miles E of Sittingbourne on A2*

The Perpendicular west tower of ST MARY'S CHURCH, banded in alternate stripes of flint and ragstone, is one of the finest in Kent. The interior, with a Decorated nave, old red-tiled floors, crownpost roofs (note particularly the thirteenth-century one in the south chapel), faded wall paintings, and fifteenth- and sixteenth-century fittings, is a joy.

## Nonington

*64; 10 miles SE of Canterbury off A2*

ST ALBAN'S COURT was built between the 1860s and the 1880s by George Devey. Now a college of physical education, it has a fine panelled Hall of vaguely Jacobean flavour. What remains of the old sixteenth-century house can be seen by the stables, a little way down the hill to the west.

## Old Soar Manor

See Plaxtol.

## Otham

*65; 3 miles SE of Maidstone off A274*

*Includes Stoneacre (NT)*

An enchanting village, very Kentish, it boasts fine views over the North Downs and a splendid collection of timber-framed houses. Of these, WARDES, which stands in the High Street, is the most venerable; its north front was certainly built well before 1400. SYNYARDS, also in the High Street, is perhaps 150 years later, with a gable added in 1663. More interesting to the average visitor than either of these, however – and open to the public to boot – is STONEACRE (NT). Originally built around 1500, it has been much restored, and even contains parts of other houses of similar date, added by Mr and Mrs Aylmer Vallance after they bought the derelict building in 1920. It is thus more of a recreation than a restoration; but the work has been done with much sensitivity and skill. Its *pièce de résistance* is the Great Hall, with its original gigantic tie-beam supporting a rare and remarkable kingpost with four engaged shafts.

## Plaxtol

*66; 2 miles SE of Borough Green off A25*
*Includes Old Soar Manor (NT)*
OLD SOAR MANOR (NT), $1\frac{1}{4}$ miles east of the village, is the remarkably well-preserved solar end of a thirteenth-century house, once the property of the Culpepers. The original kingpost roof is still in place; there is a garderobe at one end and a Chapel at the other. A red-brick Georgian farmhouse stands where the Hall used to be.

## Ruckinge

*67; 6 miles S of Ashford on B2067*
Perhaps the oldest of the eleven marsh churches, ST MARY MAGDALENE has a massive Norman tower surviving as high as the string-course (the top is thirteenth-century) and two Norman doorways to south and west, of which the latter has a pointed arch set within it. The windows are mostly Decorated, and the church has a kingpost roof.

## St Nicholas at Wade

*68; $6\frac{1}{2}$ miles SW of Margate off A28*
The knapped flint tower of ST NICHOLAS'S is visible for miles – a fitting introduction to this fine church. It has a rich late Norman south arcade with two green man heads on the capitals, and other work of the thirteenth and fourteenth centuries.

## Smallhythe

*69; 2 miles S of Tenterden on B2082*
*Includes Smallhythe Place (NT)*
A tiny village of considerable charm, it contains a red-brick church with crow-stepped gables in the Flemish manner and two fine timber-framed houses next to it – in one of which, SMALLHYTHE PLACE (NT), Ellen Terry lived from 1899 until her death in 1928. It has been kept, with many of her possessions, much as she left it.

## Smarden

*70; 6 miles N of Tenterden on B2077*
ST MICHAEL'S CHURCH, of the mid-fourteenth century, has one unusual feature: its aisleless nave, 36 feet across. So tremendous a breadth was far too great for tie-beams and it is consequently spanned by a scissor-beam roof with intersecting timbers. The church is thus popularly known as 'the barn of Kent'.

## Somerhill

*71; $1\frac{1}{2}$ miles SE of Tonbridge on B2017*
The plan for this grand Jacobean mansion, built in 1611–13, was provided by John Thorpe. It is H-shaped, with the hall axially across the depth of the centre bar of the H (compare Charlton House at Greenwich, and Hardwick Hall), the design being based on Palladio's plan for the Villa Valmarana at Lisiera. The elevations, though symmetrical, are less advanced, with straight-sided gables and tall chimneystacks. The only classical features are the round-headed doorway between Doric pilasters and the triglyph frieze of the porch. Inside the house has been much altered.

## Stoneacre

See Otham.

## Sundridge

*72; 2 miles W of Sevenoaks off A25*
COMBE BANK was built by Roger Morris *c.*1725 and was partly inspired by Lord Burlington's Tottenham Park, Wiltshire. The house has been much altered, but retains its fine staircase and some splendid mid-eighteenth-century decoration. The Walter Crane Room, decorated by the artist in about 1880, is based on some early sixteenth-century Florentine paintings of *amorini*; he used these for the frieze, but added vast doorcases, a chimneypiece and window shutters of his own design, together with a ceiling with the sun, the seasons and the signs of the zodiac in bronze- and silver-painted gesso.

## Tenterden

*73; 10 miles SW of Ashford on A28*
A delightful, typically Kentish market town, it is dominated by the soaring tower of ST MILDRED'S CHURCH, the best in Kent (even though the interior is a bit of a disappointment). The HIGH STREET is full of good buildings, including a number of seaside-style Regency houses and tile-hung Victorian ones.

## West Farleigh Hall

*74; 3 miles SW of Maidstone off B2010*
A fine two-storey brick house, it bears the date 1719. The nine-bay front is unusually long for its height, but an engraving of the same year shows a third storey, perhaps never built. The Hall, which rises the full height of the house, features an immense fluted Corinthian pier breaking through – but secretly supporting – a long first-floor gallery, at the ends of which short flights of stairs lead up to the bedrooms. The size and importance of this Hall and the beautifully textured polychrome brickwork seem to relate this house to Bradbourne, Finchcocks and Westwell House in Tenterden.

## Woodchurch

*75; $4\frac{1}{2}$ miles E of Tenterden off B2067*
ALL SAINTS' CHURCH is nothing wonderful on the outside, but has a beautiful uncluttered Early English interior with a timber roof and three noble lancets at the east end. There is fine detailing everywhere, but it is the atmosphere that counts.

# London

It is impossible to do justice to our capital city in a book that is so wide-ranging – especially when at the time of writing we have to include, within the boundaries of Greater London, a number of buildings which formerly belonged to the now deceased Middlesex or to Surrey, Essex or Kent, and which (if there were any reason, justice or logic in these affairs) would continue to do so. On the other hand, it must be admitted that the beauty of London, considerable as it is, is not primarily architectural; it depends far more on such things as spaciousness, and variety, and – most of all, perhaps – on the prodigious amount of green that it contains in its parks, squares and commons: a luxury that few other cities in the world can match on such a scale. There are in consequence rather fewer buildings of the very first order than one might expect in so historic a city, the more so since the most historic part of all – the City of London itself – has been virtually gutted, not once but twice, in the past three centuries.

The first of these disasters struck on Sunday 2 September 1666, at about two o'clock in the morning, when an oven caught fire in Farriner's bakery in Pudding Lane. Fanned by a strong wind, the flames spread rapidly; by the morning of the fifth, nearly 400 acres had been burned within the City walls and another sixty-three beyond. The buildings destroyed included eighty-seven churches, forty-four livery halls and 13,200 houses. Almost incredibly, only nine people were killed; but the medieval capital was gone. Virtually the only important survivor was the Tower itself, which lay just far enough to the east to escape the holocaust.

The second disaster was the Blitz, which effectively began with the major air raid of 7 September 1940, continuing uninterruptedly for fifty-seven consecutive nights (and frequently in the daytime as well) and intermittently for eight months. By 11 May 1941 a total of 18,800 tons of high explosive had been dropped on the capital. The casualties, predictably, were on a scale infinitely larger than anything dreamt of in former centuries: 15,000 people killed, and literally hundreds of thousands of buildings damaged or destroyed – including many of the City churches rebuilt by Sir Christopher Wren after the Great Fire.

And yet, in spite of everything, all was not lost. By the greatest miracle of all, St Paul's escaped major damage – though a bomb did in fact fall in the north transept and another destroyed the Victorian high altar. And in west London, where the concentration of buildings was often lower and the buildings themselves of less strategic importance, the destruction was relatively slight. In these areas, however, much the same could often be said of their architectural value. The western expansion of London is, after all, a comparatively recent phenomenon. At the time of the Great Fire London scarcely extended west of Charing Cross; in 1800 Paddington, Kensington and Chelsea were still separate villages, and what is now Pimlico and Belgravia was largely covered with green fields. Thus it is impossible really to understand London's architecture without first understanding its building history – on which the best recent book, covering the whole period from the Romans to the present day, is Christopher Hibbert's *London*. The same author has also edited (with Ben Weinreb) *The London Encyclopedia*, which is invaluable on specific points.

The list of buildings which follows is inevitably highly selective – so much so that I have dispensed with both the star system and the short list. I have, however, done my best to include all those of really outstanding architectural merit, even when – as with many of the City churches – they are very largely restorations, together with all those which, even if they are not architecturally in the very highest league – like Buckingham Palace, for example – any ordinary reader might justifiably expect to find in a book of this kind. Moreover, as London still remains to a very considerable degree a Victorian city, I have included a fair number of nineteenth-century buildings which, if not always masterpieces, nevertheless continue to play an important part in the life of the capital and to enjoy the affection of its inhabitants. Where I shall undoubtedly be taken to task, in this section of the book more than in any other, is in the way I have largely ignored the buildings of the later twentieth century. To such criticisms I can only plead – as I have already pleaded in the general Introduction – that this book represents a personal choice, and that if a building evokes no emotional response in me I am very unlikely to be able to interest the reader in it either.

One more point already made at the beginning of this book is perhaps also worth repeating here: that London churches, if they are still used for parish purposes and no other, are even likelier to be found locked than those elsewhere. To avoid frustration and disappointment it is therefore a good plan – particularly for the smaller and less well-known ones – to make enquiries in advance about opening times.

## Albert Hall

See Royal Albert Hall.

## All Hallows, London Wall

*1; London EC2*

A ravishing church that deserves to be better known, All Hallows is the work of George Dance Jun., designed when he was just twenty-four. Standing at the narrowest point of London Wall, it has an unusually pretty west tower of Portland stone, the lower parts square but topped by a pretty pierced circular cupola with four urns at its base. That is about all that is of interest, where the exterior is concerned. The inside, however, is a joy. It is aisleless, with a deep semi-circular apse; the roof is a barrel vault with shallow coffering, each coffer filled with star or cross designs in white and gold; it is supported by fluted half columns, above which runs a frieze but – daringly – no cornice. Immediately above the level of the frieze come the bases of the big semicircular windows, three on each side, forming penetrations with the vault. The inside of the semi-dome of the apse is coffered too, in a marvellous swirling design of lozenges getting smaller and smaller as they reach the top.

The essence of this church is space. There is absolutely no clutter – even the basic furniture has been kept down to the minimum. (Dance's star pupil was John Soane; it is easy to see where he got his inspiration.) The west end, with its gallery and organ case, is almost devoid of ornament. The pulpit, which stands unusually far towards the west – about halfway down the church – is entered by stairs built within the north wall, which is in fact the old wall of the City.

All Hallows was somewhat damaged in the Blitz, but has been most beautifully and sensitively restored by David Nye.

## All Saints, Margaret Street

*2; London W1*

Nowadays All Saints lies almost hidden in a narrow and relatively obscure street behind Oxford Circus, dwarfed by the surrounding office blocks; it is not easy to picture the way the church must have looked in 1859 when, ten years after its foundation stone had been laid by Dr Pusey himself, it was eventually consecrated – a great red-brick beacon of Tractarianism, its 230-foot tower soaring above the slums below. William Butterfield was only just thirty when he began it, but for the rest of his life kept the working drawings for it behind his chair, feeling – rightly – that it would always be his masterpiece. Not everyone agreed with him; even when first opened it received its full share of criticism, and three-quarters of a century later, when appreciation of Victorian architecture was at its nadir, All Saints was considered by most people little more than a bad joke. Today the pendulum has swung, and Butterfield and his colleagues are once again seen as the fine artists they were; yet even now strong men can be seen to quail before the sheer exuberance of this astonishing building. Most churches are intended to induce feelings of serenity and peace; All Saints induces neither. Instead, it subjects the visitor to a bombardment of remorseless decoration and dazzling colour until the eye and the spirit alike cry out for rest. Do not go if you are tired, still less if you have a hangover; if, however, you are feeling well and strong, ready to accept everything that can be flung against you, then the rewards can be very great indeed.

Little advance warning is given of the approaching onslaught. The church, clergy house and choir school are all grouped round a minute courtyard which, despite Butterfield's beloved patterned brickwork, contrives to look almost dingy. The only strong accents are the buttress immediately in front of the gabled gateway, which soars up to a high pinnacle, and of course the tower itself, fairly simple at its lower levels but giving way to a tall and slender broach spire sheathed in slate, irregularly striped, and with a ring of tiny lucarnes impossibly near the top.

So awkward was the site that Butterfield was obliged to squeeze the entrance to the church into the corner below the tower, so tightly that the door surround had to be broken off. Going in, you find the baptistery on your left, the south aisle to your right, separated from the

*All Hallows, London Wall.*

All Saints, Margaret Street.

nave (like its northern counterpart) by a three-bay arcade with granite piers culminating in an explosion of luxuriant stiff-leaf in Derbyshire alabaster. Above is a clerestory of three windows for each arcade bay, with a blank window between, and then the painted timber roof. Painted too, or stencilled, is every single inch of wall space – in the aisles, in the arcade spandrels, in the huge space above the chancel arch. As C.L. Eastlake so succinctly yet so discreetly expressed it in his *History of the Gothic Revival*, 'There is evidence that the secret of knowing where to stop in decorative work had still to be acquired.'

And yet the nave and aisles are positively drab compared with the chancel, from which the huge reredos, depicting in three ascending tiers the Virgin and Child, the Crucifixion and Christ in Majesty, each tier surrounded by Apostles and saints, blazes down through the whole church. Originally by William Dyce, they were replaced by paintings on canvas by Ninian Comper in 1909. The altar, according to the precepts of the Oxford Movement, was raised high; even the floor is a riot of polychrome tiles in red, white, blue, brown and yellow.

Of the rest of the furniture, the pulpit is, predictably, of coloured marble, intricately inlaid; behind it is an elaborate crucifix, which is echoed to the south by a canopied statue of the Virgin and Child. The windowless north aisle has an extraordinary series of biblical scenes portrayed on painted tiles. The stained glass is by various hands, some of them rather more skilled than others.

So there it is: early Victorian Anglo-Catholicism at its most extravagant, High Churchmanship allied with high craftsmanship with a panache equalled nowhere in London, and seldom in England. You may like it or loathe it, but it should not be missed.

## All Souls, Langham Place

*3; London W1*

Here is the only complete church by John Nash still in existence and appearing – at least on the outside – just as it did in his day. That it no longer has the same impact is a tragedy for which the BBC must take the blame; it must have looked wonderful when there was nothing else to close the northern end of Regent Street and the church could be seen for what it is – a key point in Nash's great scheme that ran all the way from Piccadilly Circus to Regent's Park.

Not, even then, that it escaped criticism. There were plenty of Nash's detractors who publicly deplored his shameless mixture of styles: a Gothic spire above a classical colonnade. He himself, however, had probably never thought of it in that light: for him, the design was simply a *jeu d'esprit*, a supremely ingenious way of dealing with that awkward dog-leg where Regent Street gives way to Langham Place. The circular vestibule of All Souls is in fact an adaptation of one of Nash's favourite tricks, the introduction of a circus to cover any sudden change of direction. The colonnade is placed precisely on the Regent Street axis; the church itself, however, goes off tangentially to the north-east in a manner as unexpected as it is unorthodox. It is plain and rectangular – the less anyone noticed it, the better.

All Souls was built between 1822 and 1824, and despite considerable damage caused by a landmine in 1940 remained virtually unaltered until the 1970s. Since that time, however, a new basement hall has been excavated underneath and Nash's floor replaced some 18 inches higher. Mercifully, his essential scheme for the interior has been retained: a Corinthian hall, with galleries on all four sides except where the eastern one is interrupted for the sanctuary, beneath a deep coved ceiling divided into rectangular gilded panels. The furniture is mostly new and unexciting.

## Asgill House

*4; Old Palace Lane, Richmond, Surrey*

Only a few yards from the Thames stands one of the most delightful of small Palladian villas, built in 1757–8 by Sir Robert Taylor for his friend Sir Charles Asgill who was to become Lord Mayor of London four years later. On the show side, which is naturally towards the river, the central feature is a big canted bay of two and a half storeys, the ground floor rusticated, the centre with a vermiculated Gibbs surround in addition. It is round-headed, with a mask in the keystone. Above it is a blind balustrade, then a tall pedimented window, then a small square attic window and finally a hipped roof with deep overhang. The canted sides are similar, but without vermiculation, mask or pediment. To each side of this centre is a canted wing, once again of precisely the same basic scheme but here crowned with a half pediment to give the impression that the two halves are meeting behind the projecting centre – a motif probably derived from Palladio's church fronts (notably those of the Redentore and S. Giorgio Maggiore in Venice) where they are used above the side aisles. Being lower than the centre, these wings have no attic storey.

The projecting centre forms, in plan, three sides of an octagon, and Taylor has pursued this idea in his interior, where the central room on both the principal floors is fully octagonal; the two flanking rooms on the ground floor have apsed ends, projecting within the canted exterior; since, however, the latter exists on the ground floor only, the corresponding rooms on the floor above are simply rectangular. The two storeys are linked by an entrancing oval staircase on the north side, leading to a first-floor landing which, despite its minute size, boasts not one but two Venetian arches on Ionic columns. One leads to the groin-vaulted central corridor, the other to the continuation of the staircase. On the top, attic, floor the octagonal room is replaced by two oval ones, with a tiny central lobby enjoying marvellous views over the river; the oval rooms have coved ceilings. The house was beautifully restored in 1969–70.

## Banqueting House

*5; Whitehall, SW1*

The Banqueting House is important both historically and architecturally – historically, because it was from a window in a now-demolished annex that King Charles I walked to his death on 30 January 1649, and also because it is the only surviving part of the old Palace of Whitehall; architecturally, because it is, with the Queen's House at Greenwich (*q.v.*), the first house in London conceived in the purely Palladian tradition by the first and greatest of the English Palladians, Inigo Jones.

Commissioned by James I in 1619 after the destruction of its predecessor by fire, it is quite a modest building in size: two storeys only above the high basement, and a mere seven bays across. Few of the countless civil servants who walk past it every day even notice it, far less give it a second glance. Think for a moment, however, of what English architecture was like in the first quarter of the seventeenth century; think of the great Jacobean houses, magnificent as many of them are, with their turrets and battlements, their emblazoned mottoes and their strapwork – and the cool elegance, the quiet sophistication of this building suddenly reveals itself as nothing short of revolutionary.

The broad and generous bays are separated on both the principal levels by columns and pilasters – Ionic below, Corinthian above. The columns, which are attached, are used to emphasise the three-bay centre, the pilasters the two outer bays on each side. They are doubled at the ends. A frieze of garlands with masks connects the Corinthian capitals on the first floor, beneath a high entablature and balustraded parapet; the windows here are straight-headed, with heavy projecting lintels on brackets. On the ground floor there are no garlands, and the windows have alternating triangular and segmental pediments. Surprisingly, there is no provision for an entrance on the main front; the entrance was to be at the north end, and was never properly finished, since King James had planned further extensions which in the event came to nothing. The present rather poky little entrance and staircase were added by James Wyatt in 1798. They are inadequate by any standards, but the contrast – and the consequent impact – is all the greater when you climb the stairs and find yourself in the great Hall itself. There are no other rooms. The ground floor is merely a vaulted undercroft, while upstairs the Hall occupies all seven bays of the frontage.

*All Souls, Langham Place.*

Here, as at Wilton, Jones created a perfect double cube, 55 by 55 by 110 feet, dividing it horizontally by a deep gallery supported on scrolly brackets and, below them, Ionic columns. The walls above the gallery are articulated with Corinthian pilasters, so that we have basically the same sort of composition as we saw on the outside of the building. The ceiling, too, was a considerable innovation. Gone was the Jacobean complexity of small panels in the shape of stars or lozenges, with bosses and pendants. Jones simply divided his immense space into nine rectangles, inscribing an oval in those at the corners and in the centre and outlining them with deep square ribs. This, however, is once again something that one tends to overlook, since one's eye is immediately captured by the paintings within these panels. They are the work of Peter Paul Rubens and, having been recently cleaned, are quite dazzling. The central oval depicts the Apotheosis of James I, attended by Justice, Zeal, Religion, Honour and Victory. The others are similarly allegorical. All are mounted so that they should be properly seen from the south – that is, the dais – end. One is therefore well advised to walk the whole length of the Hall before raising one's eyes to them.

## Bexleyheath

*6; Kent*

Darkest suburbia Bexleyheath may be, but it contains two buildings of rare price. The first is DANSON PARK, where in 1760 Sir Robert Taylor raised, on a gentle elevation, an exquisite small villa for Alderman John Boyd. It possesses only one main floor, with five bays to each side, a half-storey attic and a rusticated basement; but with its broad, double flights of steps leading up to a brave Corinthian doorcase, its pediment with small central eye and its projecting canted bays to east and west, it breathes as much serene Palladian elegance as many a house four times its size. Alas, poor Danson – when I saw it in 1979 it was boarded up and ringed with wire fencing. Even Capability Brown's miniature park provided little more than a *cordon sanitaire* against the encroaching sprawl. I understand that it was to be sympathetically restored and leased as offices, but that financial problems arose. Let us hope that someone else may step in and save it from further decay.

The second jewel in Bexleyheath's otherwise tawdry crown provides an awesome contrast – THE RED HOUSE, build exactly 100 years later by Philip Webb for his friend William Morris. There is no classical grandeur here. The style is, I suppose, Gothic insofar as it can be categorised at all; Morris himself described it as thirteenth-century, but the feeling is more that of an informal farmhouse, with everywhere an almost wilful avoidance of consistency or symmetry. Roofs are on different levels, windows are of contrasting shapes and sizes – though a number of pointed-arched ones, all in brick but all differently treated, provide a sort of *leitmotiv*. A dormer window boasts an outsize gable, half-hipped; a staircase projection is given a pyramidal cap with a *flèche* above it. On the west side, next to a huge chimneystack, a memorable oriel steps out brick by brick from a narrow buttress with alarming virtuosity.

Inside the house, one's eye is immediately drawn to the staircase, broad and sturdy, with the rough-hewn, no-nonsense feel about it which, despite so much exuberance of detail, seems to inform the whole house. The painted vault above is all the work of Morris and his friends – weekend guests were expected to help with the interior decorating – in simple, abstract designs pricked on to the plaster. It somehow manages to look as if it had been darkened by centuries of wood smoke, curling up to a small louvre at its apex. Of the rooms themselves, the Drawing Room is obviously the showpiece, with a simply tremendous fireplace dominating one wall and, across another, the immense wooden settle designed by Morris himself, to which Webb actually added a loft to form a minstrels' gallery (for dwarf minstrels). The walls are painted – not, it must be said, very successfully – by Burne-Jones; here, too, is the oriel we saw from the outside, quite obviously designed for the Lady of Shalott. But there is interest everywhere, in every square foot of wall space, even in the passages. Every window frame, every doorcase and lintel – the latter always projecting beyond the former, with three notches at each end – shows a careful, individual touch. The window panes are also a constant joy – painted in very medieval brown and yellow by Webb himself; animals, flowers and (on the ground floor) a series of very jolly little birds. Here is a happy house which, like Webb's later creation at Standen in West Sussex (*q.v.*) has the additional good fortune to be lived in by people who love, cherish and understand it.

## Blackheath

See Greenwich (Ranger's House).

## Blewcoat School

*NT; 7; Caxton Street, SW1*

A remarkable survival in old Westminster, standing just opposite Caxton Hall, the Blewcoat (or Bluecoat) School was built in 1709 as a perfectly ordinary local schoolhouse. It continued to serve the purpose for which it was designed until the 1920s, then fell into progressive decay and disrepair. In 1954 – just in time – it was bought and carefully restored by the National Trust.

This surprisingly distinguished building (whose architect is unknown) is of red and yellow brick, with dressings of rubbed brick and stone. Despite its windows on two levels it consists essentially of a single tall, panelled room over a semi-basement. The north-facing entrance front is, like the other three elevations, of three bays, the central doorway being of painted wood with fluted Doric pilasters; the original panelled oak door is still in place. Above it, in a semi-circular niche, stands a painted statue of a Blewcoat boy, with an inscribed plaque below giving the date of the building; a mask stares down from the keystone above his head. Above the brick cornice – which is carried on Doric pilasters of the same material – rises a high attic whose width is only that of the doorcase, consisting of a square panel which once contained a clock and a broken segmental pediment flanked by voluted stone brackets. Of the windows to the sides, the tall lower ones and the square ones above

The Blewcoat School, Caxton Street.

all have tall white keystones; only the basement windows are unadorned.

The south side is much the same as the north, except that the top pediment is unbroken and is surmounted by an octagonal chimney. Below it, instead of the clock panel, is an inscription dating the foundation of the school (which was formerly housed in Duck Lane) to 1688. On this side, too, the statue is replaced by a rather third-rate drawing on plaster. The west front has another Doric doorway.

The entrance to the schoolroom within is marked by four Corinthian columns; inside, tall pilasters rise to a high and intricate entablature with a dentilled cornice. The ceiling above is coved, and penetrated by the upper windows. The fine chimneypiece opposite the entrance is no longer in its original state but still possesses considerable elegance with its flanking niches and its moulded imposts and panels. Until the 1920s the overmantel contained panels inscribed with the Ten Commandments. I am glad they have gone; they would have introduced a note of gloom, whereas the room without them is one of the sunniest and happiest in London.

## British Museum

*8; Great Russell Street, WC1*

The story of the British Museum begins in 1753 with the bequest to the nation – against payment of about a third of their value – of his various collections by Sir Hans Sloane. They were joined almost at once by the Harleian collection of manuscripts and the Cottonian Library, and over the next three-quarters of a century by any number of other acquisitions, including the Towneley collection of antique statuary, Sir William Hamilton's classical vases, the Royal Library (with immense and invaluable contributions from both George II and George III) and the Elgin Marbles. By now Montagu House in Bloomsbury, which had been acquired by the Government in 1755 to house these collections, was bursting at the seams; so in 1821 Robert Smirke was invited to submit designs for what was originally intended to be an extension – consisting of three new ranges enclosing a quadrangle – and up they went, between 1823 and 1838. Only after their completion was old Montagu House itself demolished to make way for the great south façade that we know today.

Smirke was the most enthusiastic exponent of Neo-Greek architecture in the country, and his work is immaculate of its kind: a little cold, perhaps, but perfect in its proportions and its detailing. The great central portico is of eight giant Ionic columns, fluted and supporting a triangular pediment in which is an ornamental sculptured group by Westmacott, partly gilded and representing *The Progress of Civilisation*. The columns are doubled, the back row continuing with two more columns on each side and then breaking forward into two unpedimented wings, perfectly square, with six columns in each direction.

This magnificent front courtyard was, as we have seen, echoed by another to the north. Smirke's great inner quadrangle, however, existed for only seven years, from 1847 to 1854; for in the latter year it was filled in to form the Museum's other breathtaking showpiece, the Reading Room. This was the work of Smirke's younger brother Sydney, though the idea of making it circular was not originally his: it stemmed first from Gibbs's Radcliffe Camera in Oxford (*q.v.*) and more directly from a railway engineer named Hosking who proposed a mammoth 'Masonic Pantheon' for the site in 1848. Four years later the Museum's greatest Librarian, Sir Anthony Panizzi, sketched out a rough drawing; this was professionally redrawn and submitted to the Trustees and finally, after many alterations, brought into being by Sydney Smirke. It was opened in May 1857 with a formal breakfast eaten off the catalogue desks, under that magical dome 140 feet in diameter – beating by a foot that of St Peter's in Rome. To me it has always been one of the most marvellous rooms in London. Purists complain – with truth – that Smirke failed to make his dome consistent with his brother's Neo-Grecianism; but since the Greeks had no domes – or even arches – it is not easy to see how he could have. The cast-iron ribs on which the dome is supported are stressed in the interior, which is surely as it should be; and if their junction with the side walls and galleries looks a little awkward, it should be remembered that the original intention was to place statues at this point all the way round. And none of this really matters anyway; it is the overall atmosphere of the Reading Room that enthrals, the feeling of light and space, and the complete absence of Victorian clutter.

Sadly it will not continue in its present function for very much longer. Already at the time of writing, work has begun to move the British Library to the Euston Road. There are doubtless excellent reasons from the administrative point of view; but for all those who love the Reading Room and use it, its loss will be a tragedy.

## Buckingham Palace

*9; London SW1*

It must be admitted at the outset that Buckingham Palace is not one of the great buildings of England. It is the London residence of the sovereign, it is superbly sited and indisputably grand, and it contains some of the finest pictures and furniture in the world; architecturally, however, it is no very great shakes. But there – it is more visited, more stared at, than virtually any other building in the country, and for that reason alone it deserves at least a brief description in this book.

The first thing to be said about it is that it is not, by English standards, particularly old; even the Duke of Buckingham's original house on the site was built as recently as 1705, and virtually nothing of that now remains. It was by William Winde, the 'learned and ingenious' architect of Ashdown House in Oxfordshire (*q.v.*), and consisted of a central block with outlying wings connected by quadrantal colonnades; it looks lovely in old prints. But although it seems to have been good enough for King George III and Queen Charlotte when they moved in early in 1762, their son George IV demanded something better and commissioned his favourite architect, John Nash, to provide it. At the King's desire, Nash retained part of the shell of the old house and much of its original plan, but the transformation was complete, even to the materials. Where Winde had built his house of brick, Nash settled for Bath stone – which, characteristically, he bought himself and sold at a considerable profit to his contractors.

Building began in 1826, but two years later expenditure on the Palace became a national scandal and Nash was arraigned before a Select Committee of the House of Commons. On that occasion he was exonerated, but the King's death in 1830 deprived him of royal protection and he was dismissed, his career virtually finished. By this time the exterior of the building was complete, as he had intended it: three ranges enclosing a spacious courtyard, open towards the east except for a triple-arched gateway. Most of the state rooms, too, were ready for use – enough, at least, for George's successor, William IV. But soon after the accession of Queen Victoria in 1837 the Palace was found once again to be too small and Edward Blore – who had already been called in to tidy up the loose ends left by Nash some years before – was brought back to add a fourth wing to the east. It is this wing, which in 1913 was entirely refaced in Portland stone by Sir Aston Webb, that now constitutes the entrance front – a distinguished enough essay in the Edwardian *Beaux-Arts* taste, of three storeys (the ground floor rusticated) with a three-bay pedimented centre and side pavilions, framed by pilasters and articulated by columns and half columns respectively, and connected by six-bay ranges, slightly recessed. The building of Blore's wing necessitated, of course, the removal of the triumphal gateway with which Nash had originally closed his courtyard. This was re-erected at the north-east corner of Hyde Park, where it is now better known as Marble Arch.

Parts of Nash's original work can be seen on the north and south ranges from Buckingham Palace Road and Constitution Hill; but only those privileged enough to be invited inside the Palace itself will have the chance of seeing his principal front, which looks westward over the magnificent garden and lake. (As Pevsner has pointed out, Buckingham Palace is 'surely the only royal palace in any urban capital which has its lawns and lake and faces a park and not an urban square'.) Even this, however is not Nash at his most inspired. The main accent is provided by a generous semi-circular bow of five bays; from this three more bays go off in each direction to another more important bay, framed by pairs of columns; then three more bays again, and then once more the same effect. One-storeyed conservatories project at each end, the right-hand one of which was converted in 1843 into a Chapel. The trouble is that the five principal accents are all essentially of the same height (though the bow is crowned by a low semi-dome of copper): there is consequently little variation of roof level – certainly nowhere near enough for such a long frontage.

The interior is of extreme magnificence, though in the decoration Nash shows little of his usual lightness of touch. Perhaps the most impressive feature of all is the great staircase, designed to run up in a single central flight, then to fork and to return in two. This it does, but, as a result of the new ballroom range which was added by Sir James Pennethorne in the 1850s, a third arm now runs further forward from the point of bifurcation. The staircase is of marble and has most opulent balustrading in gilded bronze. It leads to a succession of superb state rooms too numerous and too opulent for any full description in these pages. They include a ravishing Music Room occupying the upper floor of the central bow, the semi-dome supported on eighteen scagliola columns with gilded capitals; a vast Blue Drawing Room, with more columns arranged in pairs, rising to a deeply coved ceiling with gilded saucer domes; and, at the north-east angle of the east front, an exquisite Chinese Luncheon Room largely composed of various pieces taken from the Brighton Pavilion. The Throne Room itself is somewhat more restrained in decoration, though its ceiling too is deeply coved; the throne recess is framed by a flat-topped arch flanked by winged Victories bearing a garland.

Thus, whatever its faults of taste and impurities of style, Buckingham Palace remains of an overall opulence probably unrivalled anywhere in the world. One understands that it is impossible, in the very nature of things, to open it to the public; the fact remains that, in terms of sheer spectacle, the public is missing a lot.

## Charlton

See Greenwich (Charlton House).

## Chiswick House

*10; Burlington Lane, W4*

When Richard Boyle, 3rd Earl of Burlington, decided in 1725 to build himself a small villa in the garden of his Chiswick estate, there was no question which style he would choose. It was ten years since the publication of Colen Campbell's *Vitruvius Britannicus* had launched

Palladian architecture in England, ten years in which Burlington, already the country's foremost patron of the arts, had made himself the high priest of the new style and had commissioned Campbell to remodel his great house in Piccadilly – giving it, incidentally, the first Palladian façade on this side of the Channel. For his Chiswick villa, however, he was determined to draw up his own designs, entrusting the interior decoration to his brilliant protégé, William Kent.

The building that now took shape was a composite design, based loosely on Palladio's Villa Rotonda (via Campbell's Mereworth), only with a single portico instead of four. Inevitably, it caused something of a stir in London society, where opinions were not entirely favourable. Lord Hervey unkindly remarked that the villa was 'too small to live in and too large to hang to a watch', while Lord Chesterfield, who disapproved of noblemen practising architecture, actually broke into verse:

> *Possessed of one great house for state*
> *Without one room to sleep or eat,*
> *How well you build, let flatt'ry tell*
> *But all mankind, how ill you dwell.*

This latter jibe was not altogether fair. The villa was not intended to be lived in: Burlington had a perfectly good Jacobean house only a few yards away. His idea was for a 'pavilion of the spirit', in which he and his dilettanti friends could surround themselves with paintings and sculpture, all in a setting of immaculate Palladian proportions; and in this he succeeded admirably. True, there were one or two features that might not have satisfied Palladio's rigid canons; the double staircases leading up to the front door would have seemed to him complicated and fussy – though Rysbrack's distinctly Baroque statue of himself (together with one of Burlington's other idol, Inigo Jones) might have mollified him somewhat. Here, as elsewhere, one suspects the less reverential attitude of Kent. But the interior is nobly impressive, with Kent's decorations giving warmth to the cold perfection of Burlington's style without ever detracting from its dignity. The Domed Saloon which forms, as it were, the still centre of the building, remains a little chilly, despite the pictures, classical busts and Kent's beautiful design of diminishing octagons inside the dome itself; but elsewhere there is plenty of life and movement, nowhere more so than in the Gallery where Burlington has brought off a real *tour de force* by dividing it into three. The central section is a broad rectangle giving out on to the garden, with an open apse at each end. One of these apses leads through to a small circular ante-room – which, though only some 15 feet across, somehow manages to contain six doorways, a window and an ornate fireplace without looking cluttered – and the other into an octagonal one. From either end the Gallery consequently offers a long vista, seen through two arches, which gives an extraordinary impression of space and distance, though its total length is less than 70 feet.

The garden, too, is by Kent – as important in gardening history as the house is in architectural, for it was Kent who, as Horace Walpole put it, 'leaped the fence, and saw all nature was a garden'. Here at Chiswick he put his ideas into practice for the first time, creating a free (though controlled) landscape in place of the formal symmetry of the seventeenth century and dotting it about with pavilions and temples, bridges and obelisks, a canal and a cascade. House and garden should thus be seen together as two parts of a single conception, the one an embodiment of formal symmetry, the other a deliberate rejection of it, but both inspired by the Palladian precepts of that inner harmony, natural or mathematical, which governs our physical world – the perfect philosophy for the Age of Reason.

*Chiswick House.*

## Christ Church, Spitalfields

*11; London E1*

At the time of writing Christ Church presents a picture of appalling dilapidation and neglect; but rescue is on the way. Meanwhile no amount of damp, decay and crumbling plasterwork can obscure the fact that this tremendous building is Hawksmoor's ecclesiastical masterpiece. The west front, it must be said, is more impressive than beautiful. For all his love of classical antiquity Hawksmoor could never quite suppress a sneaking yen for Gothic – think of the towers of Westminster Abbey – and here he has topped an already somewhat alarming arrangement of three diminishing triumphal arches one on top of the other, all resolutely classical, with a soaringly medieval broach spire rising to a height of 225 feet. (When it was originally built this spire also boasted lucarnes and flame-like crockets running up the angles.)

Inside, the nave marches majestically forward between tall Composite columns, set on high plinths and supporting even higher imposts. Above these springs the arcade; above this is a generous clerestory; and only then the flat, coffered ceiling. Four more columns provide a screen, crowned with a free-standing, three-dimensional Royal Arms (looking rather insecure over the structurally weakest point of the entablature) beyond which a massive Venetian window closes the vista. When Christ Church is restored to the glory it deserves – as St George's, Bloomsbury and St Mary Woolnoth (*qq.v.*) have already been – it will be one of the grandest churches in London.

*Christ Church, Spitalfields.*

## Dulwich Picture Gallery

*12; College Road, SE21*

Sir John Soane can be seen here at his most austere. Stock brick, stone dressings: even the mausoleum attached to the west side is almost devoid of ornament. Soane's commission was to design a gallery for the collection of paintings amassed by the art dealer Noel Desenfans for Stanislaus, King of Poland, but never sold to him. Instead, Desenfans had left the collection to his friend Sir Francis Bourgeois, who in return required that the building that was to be erected to house them should also contain a mausoleum to Desenfans, flanked by a row of almshouses. Soane prepared a number of alternative schemes, all more or less ambitious; but money was tight and he was obliged to pare down his designs, relying for his effect on line and proportion alone. The result cost less than £10,000, and is hardly likely to have much appeal to the average sightseer (though the pictures themselves will). But to Sir John Summerson, 'the building as a whole reaches a level of emotional eloquence and technical performance rare in English, or indeed in European, architecture'.

The principal motif is round-arched windows (many of them blank) set within larger arches of the same shape. The mausoleum, which projects in the form of a Greek cross, has still higher arches in which the straight-headed stone portals use only the lower two-thirds; these have acroteria, and are thought to have been inspired by details of an Alexandrian catacomb published in 1809, two years before work on the building began. They do not quite touch the jambs of the brick arch; and as you look more closely at the building you notice that this curious characteristic of disjunctiveness, of not quite touching, reappears again and again. Thus the former almshouses, running off in a low range on each side of the mausoleum, appear – by means of narrow recessions at each end – somehow separate from it, as also from the projecting wings at the north and south angles. Even the frieze is recessed, so that the cornice seems to float above the walls instead of resting on them. Above this cornice, there rises from the centre of the mausoleum a big cubical lantern of stone, with a tripartite rectangular window on each side and urns at the corners. This in turn supports a smaller square block with segmental pediments to the sides and a fifth urn on top. The walls of the cube have Soane's usual incised decoration, as do the three sarcophagi on the arms of the cross, above the stone portals.

The building is not as Soane left it. For one thing, it is considerably larger. Not only were the almshouses converted into additional gallery space at the end of the last century, but between 1910 and 1915 those new rooms were repeated on the east front, apart from the north corner which was added by Goodhart-Rendel in 1936. As to the interior, it was redecorated according to Soane's original designs in 1980–1 and the gallery part has never been seen to better advantage. The mausoleum looks, I suspect, much as it always has: the entrance room consists of a circle of Doric columns, carrying a shallow dome; beyond it, in what might be called the 'chancel', slender arcades without capitals support the yellow glass lantern which bathes the chamber in a faintly eerie light.

Go, then, to Dulwich, for the architecture as well as the pictures – but do not expect to be seduced as you might be, for example, at Sir John Soane's Museum in Lincoln's Inn Fields, or at Pitshanger (*qq.v.*). Nonetheless, the more you look the more you will see; for, despite its apparent severity, this is one of the most individual works ever designed by a man who, it seems, could not lay one brick on another without somehow adding a signature that was uniquely his.

## Ealing

See Pitshanger Manor.

## Edgware

See St Lawrence Whitchurch.

## Eltham

*13; London SE9*

The PALACE OF ELTHAM has existed since the days of Edward I, when the manor was presented to his son, the future Edward II, in 1305. For the next two centuries it was a favourite palace of the Plantagenet kings; it was here, on Christmas Day 1400, that Henry IV gave a banquet in honour of Manuel II Palaeologus, the only Byzantine Emperor ever to visit England. The earliest and most important survival today, however, is the Great Hall, which was begun by Edward IV in 1475. Already by the late sixteenth century the Palace was falling out of use, serving only as a hunting lodge; during the Commonwealth most of its older buildings were destroyed, and so the decline went on until in the last century the Hall was being used as a barn and, in 1828, the Crown proposed to pull it down altogether. Fortunately there was a public outcry and the building was saved – though it was only in the present century, thanks largely to the generosity of Sir Stephen Courtauld in the 1930s, that its preservation was finally assured.

It lies within a moat, which is crossed by a stone bridge – also, probably, of Edward IV's day. On the outside there is little to see: the walls are of brick, roughly faced with ashlar and ragstone, the six windows on each side arranged in pairs, with cusped heads, and set rather high to allow for tapestries below. Inside, the great glory of the Hall is its hammer-beam roof. At 100 feet long, it is smaller than that of Westminster Hall or Hampton Court, but scarcely less impressive. The horizontal hammers seem to clutch the vertical posts like clenched fists, while across the middle the four-centred arches support collar-beams immediately above them, each collar in its turn supporting a series of mullion-like queenposts with traceried tops. Along the sides run two tiers of cusped wind-braces arranged in contrary directions, and in the centre is the frame for the hexagonal louvre through which the smoke escaped from the central hearth below. The small stone fan vaults within the oriels contain the falcon-and-fetterlock badge of Edward IV.

Nearby, and serving nowadays as the club house of the Royal Blackheath Golf Club, stands ELTHAM LODGE, built by Hugh May in 1664 for Sir John Shaw, a wealthy banker and close friend of Charles II. Shaw had leased the entire Palace site from the Crown in the previous year, but seems to have taken no interest in the existing medieval buildings, preferring to build himself a new house further to the east. Together with his alterations and additions to Cornbury Park, Oxfordshire (*q.v.*), this is May's first known work and the *beau idéal* of the small Restoration country house. Built of red brick with stone dressings, its two storeys stand on a low basement, while the hipped roof carries two attic dormers. There are seven bays, the three-bay centre being framed by four pilasters supporting a pediment containing a coat of arms and garlands. The proportions are spacious, the rhythm relaxed. The only outward alteration of which one is conscious is the sashing of the windows, which now have small eighteenth-century panes instead of their original crosses. (We can ignore the rather clumsy refacing and repointing of the three left-hand bays.)

*The Great Hall of the Palace of Eltham.*

Inside, the central Entrance Hall leads via a screen of columns – a later addition – to the central section of the house with its two staircases. All the principal ground-floor rooms have fine plaster ceilings, the stucco work being especially good in the Card Room, immediately on the left as you go in. There are some good chimneypieces, too. The staircase is magnificent, with carved wooden panels like those at Ham or Sudbury (*qq.v.*), carved bowls of fruit and flowers on the newels and a heavy plaster ceiling in the style of Inigo Jones. The whole house is, in short, a delight.

## Enfield

See Forty Hall.

## Forty Hall

*14; Enfield*

This is a remarkable house, and something of a puzzle. We know that Forty Hall was built between 1629 and 1636 by Sir Nicholas Raynton, a prosperous haberdasher who became Lord Mayor of London in 1632, and this date is roughly confirmed by the extraordinary plaster ceilings and overmantels, and by the most elaborate screen in the Hall (now known as the Dining Room). The difficulty comes when we try to relate this still essentially Jacobean interior with the outside of the house, which appears as an extremely pretty William and Mary building – a good half-century later than the caryatids and strapwork within would have us believe. With two and a half storeys under a steep hipped roof, the material a pleasant rosy brick with stone dressings, only its tall brick chimneys suggest an earlier date.

The explanation seems to be that the house was remodelled on the outside in about 1700, presumably by the Wolstenholmes who then owned it and whom we know to have made certain interior alterations. There are certainly signs of major surgery, above all perhaps in the fenestration. The first and attic floors are of six bays, an unclassical and unsatisfactory arrangement as it leaves the composition without an obvious centre; the two central windows on each floor are narrower than the rest (though of the same height) and set a little uncomfortably close together, particularly in view of the very heavy stone frames – possibly another legacy from the earlier front? – with which they are all surrounded. On the ground floor the two middle windows are replaced by the front door; but this, with its projecting porch on fluted Ionic columns (note their garlanded capitals) and heavy segmental pediment, could not be earlier than the 1690s. The same goes for the door on the south side: Tuscan, but with the window above framed in a Corinthian aedicule. Finally – but surely significantly – the upper surrounds of the attic windows are almost lost under the eaves.

To these two building periods we must now add a third (though slightly less important) one; for while some of the eighteenth-century features of the interior – notably the elegant Ionic screen which divides the Staircase Hall from the so-called Raynton Room – can be associated with the Wolstenholmes, there are others which were added after 1787, when the house was sold to one Edmund Armstrong. To this period belongs the charming stucco work of the Entrance Hall, where plaster panels on the walls contain trophies, swags and garlands with an occasional portrait medallion in a circular frame.

Now the property of the London Borough of Enfield, Forty Hall is well maintained but sadly institutionalised. How one longs for the hand of the National Trust!

## Greenwich

*15; London SE10*

There have been associations between Greenwich and the Crown at least since the days of Duke Humphrey of Gloucester, the brother of Henry V, who built a Palace there on the banks of the Thames in 1427. It was there that he kept his library – the first great library in England to be owned by a single individual – which he left after his death to the University of Oxford, where it became the nucleus of the Bodleian. Later the Palace was a favourite residence of Henry VIII and of Queen Elizabeth. James I never liked it much himself, but settled it on his Queen, Anne of Denmark – for whom Inigo Jones was to build what is still known as The Queen's House. During the Commonwealth the Palace fell into disrepair; it was stripped of its contents and turned into a factory for making ship's biscuit. By the time of the Restoration it was in such a sorry state that King Charles II decided to demolish it and start again. The project, which was entrusted to Jones's son-in-law John Webb, was for three imposing blocks round a central courtyard, but only the west range was built – the present King Charles's Block. In 1669 the King lost interest and the work stopped. James II seems not to have cared about it, while William and Mary preferred Kensington and Hampton Court. At last in 1692 Queen Mary decided that the unfinished building should be completed, not as a palace but as a Royal Naval Hospital for sick or disabled seamen. The commission was given to Wren and the hospital opened its doors in 1705. It closed in 1869, and four years later re-opened as the Royal Naval College.

So much for the historical outline: now for the buildings themselves. Let us take THE QUEEN'S HOUSE first. Glimpsed nowadays between the two tremendous blocks of Wren's Hospital, it looks small and unassuming; indeed, it never aspired to be anything more than an Italianate country villa in a quietly Palladian style. It did, however, possess one supremely eccentric feature: it was built, presumably at the Queen's request, *astride* the main Dover road, with a block on each side and a bridge at first-floor level spanning the road itself. Its shape was consequently that of an H; it was only later that Webb filled in the open ends, giving the house the appearance of an ordinary square block. Later still, a new Dover road was built along another route, and where it had formerly run open colonnades were added to link the building with the National Maritime Museum of which it now forms a part.

The Queen's House was begun in 1616, but Anne of Denmark died three years later when it was still unfinished, and work stopped till Charles I decided to complete it for his own Queen, Henrietta Maria. Even then it was not finished till 1637 – the date of the open loggia on the south front, which is almost its only striking architectural feature. Indeed, the keynote of the entire building is its simplicity, which Jones has carried almost to the point of dullness: anything less Jacobean could hardly be imagined. It relies – as all Palladian buildings do, and The Queen's House is the first truly Palladian building in England – on the pure classical

*The Queen's House, Greenwich – now the National Maritime Museum.*

virtues of symmetry, harmony and proportion. Alas, it was ahead of its time: English taste was not yet ready for such restraint. Jones had little success outside Court circles, Baroque became the fashion, and it was only at the beginning of the eighteenth century with Lord Burlington that Palladian principles were at last enthusiastically adopted.

Inside, the main feature is the Hall in the centre of the north block. It is a perfect cube, the sides and height being all of 40 feet, and is surrounded at first-floor level by a gallery giving access to the state rooms. Apart from its painted ceiling (which replaces the original by Artemisia Gentileschi, now at Marlborough House), the Hall continues the austerity of the exterior; the state rooms, however, are comparatively sumptuous, with fine painting and plasterwork – especially in the Queen's Bedroom to the west.

Immediately to the east of the Hall is the so-called Tulip Staircase – the name comes from the pattern of the wrought-iron balustrade – a graceful spiral with no inner supports, on the model of that which Palladio built at the Villa Rotonda near Vicenza.

Beyond the colonnades, the two blocks of what is now the National Maritime Museum were added in 1807–16 by Daniel Asher Alexander, architect of Maidstone Gaol. It was a school for children of naval men until 1933.

Of the old GREENWICH PALACE, nothing remains but the undercroft which was added by James I in order to strengthen the foundations; while Webb's work is limited to the eastern parts of King Charles's Block – the north-western one, on the far right as seen from the river. It is a rather solemn two-storeyed front of twenty-three bays, having a three-bay pedimented centre with giant columns and three-bay angle pavilions – to which a third storey is added – with giant pilasters. When work was resumed in 1692 on what is now the ROYAL NAVAL COLLEGE, Queen Mary specifically commanded that The Queen's House should remain visible from the waterfront; Wren – who was giving his services free – accordingly split his composition along a central axis to provide an uninterrupted view of it – though admittedly rather dwarfing it in scale. His idea was to provide a counterpart to Webb's block (which he and his successors were to finish) and to add two further blocks behind them but projecting rather further towards the centre, to be crowned by tall cupolas. Wren, already sixty when he began at Greenwich, did not live to see the work completed; even during his lifetime he left a good deal of it to his assistant Hawksmoor – who certainly seems to have been responsible for the most wilfully perverse section of the whole composition, the west range of King William's Block (the south-western one of the four). Both fronts of this range, especially that which faces inward towards the courtyard, seem to have been designed in a fit of wild experimentation unthinkable in Wren, and of which indeed only Hawksmoor would have been capable. It is the south range of this same block that contains the Great Hall, the painting of which was to occupy Sir James Thornhill from 1708 for the next nineteen years. The Chapel, in the corresponding range of Queen Mary's Block opposite, took longer still: its interior decoration was not completed until 1743, and

*The Old Royal Observatory, Greenwich.*

was largely destroyed by fire soon afterwards. What we see today is a remodelling by James ('Athenian') Stuart of 1779–89. Queen Anne's Block, between this and the river, is largely Hawksmoor again, now behaving himself rather better. Finally, on King Charles's Block, Webb's river frontage was completed by Wren, the corresponding range to the south being contributed by Stuart in 1769 and the long west range – originally Wren's, but also destroyed by fire – by John Yenn as recently as 1811–14.

Of the interiors, only the Painted Hall and Chapel are memorable. The former, however, is something more: it is unforgettable. It is divided most dramatically into three – vestibule, main hall and upper hall – the various parts being separated by steps, cross walls, giant columns and pilasters. Thornhill's work, too, is superb of its kind: a gloriously Baroque depiction of William and Mary, attended by the four cardinal Virtues, fills the central oval of the ceiling, while the upper hall (which was painted only after the accession of the Hanoverians, and in which Thornhill was assisted by André) presents us with the landings of William III and George I and the family of the latter. The Chapel, with its shallow segmental vault and galleries – including a particularly pretty swelling-out west gallery – is cool neo-classical work of immense distinction and elegance. The four large statues in the octagonal vestibule and the altar painting of *St Paul and the Viper* are by Benjamin West.

Greenwich Park, which climbs up the hill behind The Queen's House, was laid out with straight avenues by none other than Le Nôtre himself. At the summit of the hill is the OLD ROYAL OBSERVATORY, built by Wren (who had started his own life as an astronomer) in 1675–6 'for the observator's habitation and a little for pompe'. The small red-brick building is of considerable charm – what appear to be its stone dressings turn out to be of wood – with a three-bay front flanked by two rather higher square turrets. The principal room inside is the Octagon Room on the upper floor, which was given a specially high ceiling so that Thomas Tompion's pendulum clocks could be accommodated. The two projecting side pavilions are additions of 1772–3 and, if anything, improvements; the later buildings are less fortunate.

Forsaking the park, you should now go and take a look at the CHURCH OF ST ALPHEGE – though it will probably be shut – which is Greenwich's parish church. An early medieval foundation built to commemorate the martyrdom of this Archbishop of Canterbury by the Danes in 1012, it was completely rebuilt in 1711–14 to designs by Hawksmoor. It is curiously set: what appears to be the main front, facing the street with a giant Tuscan portico in which an arch breaks through the heavy pediment, is in fact the east end. The entrance is from the sides, the west door being surmounted by a steeple. This is in fact an afterthought of 1730 and is the work of John James, for by that time Hawksmoor had already used his original design for the steeple on his church of St George-in-the-East (*q.v.*).

The interior is magnificent, and well worth any trouble that may have to be taken to gain admission. The span of 65 feet by 90 feet is in itself remarkable, considering that there are no internal pillars or arcades. What we have is just a single vast space, with a shallow chancel recess which is made to look deeper than it is by some cunning false perspective painting in *trompe-l'oeil* by Thornhill. Capacious galleries of wood run along each side, supported on slender wooden columns. The capitals of these were originally the work of Grinling Gibbons; most of them, however, were destroyed in the Blitz. The present restoration is by Sir Albert Richardson.

If you now head up CROOM'S HILL and its continuation, CHESTERFIELD WALK, you will find plenty of the best domestic architecture that Greenwich has to offer – and very fine it is. At the top is RANGER'S HOUSE, an immensely distinguished house now refronted in red brick with a brave Ionic doorway and Venetian window above. The main part dates from the first quarter of the eighteenth century, though the gallery in the south wing is an addition of 1750 (probably by Isaac Ware) and the bow-windowed north wing of after 1893. The house now contains the Suffolk Collection of Tudor portraits and is open to the public.

Emerging from Ranger's House, turn left along Charlton Way and then left again down Maze Hill to where Westcombe Park Road goes off to your right. Here, on the corner, is a surprise indeed – though it is a good deal more interesting than beautiful. VANBRUGH'S CASTLE, an extraordinary brick edifice, turreted and in places embattled, was built by Sir John Vanbrugh in 1718–26 for his own use – one of the earliest essays in medievalist nostalgia, a sort of Gothic Revival half a century before its time. As originally designed it was a straightforward symmetrical block; the eastern extension dates from after Vanbrugh's marriage in 1719 and was later twice extended to the south.

*Charlton House, Greenwich.*

Had you remained in Charlton Way and followed it eastward, and had you then continued down Charlton Road, you would shortly have reached CHARLTON HOUSE, the only major Jacobean mansion still surviving in London. It is of red brick with stone dressings and is E-shaped on both its main fronts, with four symmetrical bay windows at the ends of the wings and ogee-capped towers at their centres. In the centre of the entrance front, however, there is a tremendous stone frontispiece which rises through all three floors of the house. I am not sure that I would entirely agree with Pevsner that it is 'the most exuberant and undisciplined ornament in all England', but it is certainly worth a long and careful look. Inside there is a magnificent Hall of two storeys – running, most unusually, straight through the centre of the house from front to back; above it on the top floor is a Saloon with its original plaster ceiling and pendants, and a Long Gallery with another good ceiling and some heraldic glass. There are some good chimneypieces too. The house was built by Sir Adam Newton, tutor to Henry, Prince of Wales, and dates from 1607–21. It is open by appointment.

## Ham House

*NT; 16; Ham, Richmond, Surrey*

'Whenever my house becomes a public spectacle, His Majesty shall certainly have the first view.' So snapped the 5th Earl of Dysart, when George III suggested coming over from Windsor. But Ham *is* now a public spectacle, the property of the National Trust, and there is no house in Greater London more rewarding to visit. At first sight it may seem a little forbidding: the brick is not so much red as damson-coloured and the polygonal bays projecting towards the north have an almost Victorian look about them – though they date in fact from the first building of the house in 1610. At that time the appearance of the north front was rather different, with two Jacobean towers just inside these bays and a central projecting bay to roof level. The alterations were made in 1673–5 by Ham's most famous and formidable owner, Elizabeth Murray, Countess of Dysart and, by her second marriage in 1672, Duchess of Lauderdale; at the same time she added the oval niches and busts, and filled in the recess of the south front – the house had been originally built on the usual Elizabethan H-plan – thus providing an additional suite of rooms on each floor.

The interior is a good deal more cheerful. You find yourself at once in the Great Hall, placed asymmetrically along the eastern half of the cross-bar of the H, as was normal in the early seventeenth century. In those days, however, it occupied only the ground floor and must have seemed distinctly low; the pretty gallery above, in the shape of an elongated octagon, was an eighteenth-century improvement – and a very successful one too, even at the sacrifice of a first-rate plaster ceiling and the main dining room on the first floor. Immediately to the east of the Hall is one of the glories of Ham – the spectacular wooden staircase, rising up two floors around a broad open well; instead of balusters it has openwork panels carved with military trophies, with baskets of fruit on the newel-posts. It dates from 1637–8, which makes it one of the earliest, as well as the best, of its kind. The only two others I know that can compare with it are at Eltham Lodge (*q.v.*) and Sudbury; but they are of the 1660s and 1670s respectively.

All the state rooms are wonderfully rich, and have kept a good deal of the superb furniture installed by the Lauderdales, much of it still in astonishingly fine condition. It is this furniture, and a large number of equally good pictures, that provides the principal interest of the rooms, though the plaster ceilings are all worth looking at (note the extraordinary contrast between those of the 1630s and those of the 1670s), as is much of the distinctly Mannerist woodwork. The best of this is to be found in the Long Gallery, with its beautiful fluted Ionic pilasters; Thomas Carter, the joiner responsible for them, charged ten guineas for the lot.

The better to conserve the furniture and fabrics, much of Ham is kept, quite rightly, in semi-darkness. The low-key electric lighting is however so beautifully thought out that one's enjoyment is actually enhanced; particularly on winter afternoons, the house seems to glow gently from within, enclosing one in the elegant, opulent world of Van Dyck and Lely, a world from which one tears oneself away with reluctance and regret. No house, alas, can be a real time machine; but Ham comes as near to being one as any I know.

## Hampstead

See Kenwood.

## Hampton Court Palace

*17; Hampton Court*

On 3 July 1529 Thomas Wolsey left Hampton Court for the last time. His career had been one of the most extraordinary success stories in English history: the son of an Ipswich butcher, by the age of forty-four he had become Archbishop of York, Lord Chancellor of England, and a cardinal. He had built himself two country seats besides this one, and a town house which later became the Palace of Whitehall. Hampton Court alone possessed 1,000 rooms, scarcely too many for his household of 429; in addition, 280 silken beds were always kept ready for visitors. 'To reach his audience chamber,' reported a Venetian ambassador, 'one must pass through eight rooms; all are hung with tapestry, which is changed once a week.'

Now, however, his downfall was near. In an attempt to stave it off, he had already presented this most splendid of his palaces to his master, King Henry VIII; but Henry, furious and frustrated in his struggle to divorce Catherine of Aragon, needed a victim. In October, all the Cardinal's lands were declared forfeit to the King; thirteen months later, he was dead.

Wolsey had bought the manor of Hampton from the Knights Hospitallers in 1514, having consulted an international panel of doctors to select the healthiest spot within 20 miles of London. He had a passion – rare indeed in the sixteenth century – for hygiene; his new Palace had fresh water piped under the Thames from springs 3 miles away, and huge brick sewers leading back to the Thames, both systems so well-made as to last until the 1870s. But his passion for display was even

*Ham House, Richmond.*

greater. The immense west front of Hampton Court is, as Pevsner reminds us, 'the grandest of its date in Britain' – and this despite the eighteenth-century removal of the two upper storeys of the central Gatehouse. The arms above the entrance, be it noted, are not Wolsey's but those of King Henry, who moved in at once and began an ambitious programme of improvements. He even defaced the Cardinal's own armorial plaque, which can still be seen, successfully restored, on the inside of the Gatehouse, looking down on to the Base Court. Apart from Wolsey's motto, running round the lovely little room known as his 'closet', it is one of the few traces of his occupancy still remaining.

Indeed, if the builder of the Palace could return there today, there is little enough that he would even recognise. The Base Court is much the same, apart from the truncated Gatehouse, as is the eastern side of the inner Clock Court. For the rest, he would remember the Haunted Gallery, the three little rooms off the King's Guard Room – and not much else. The Chapel Royal is where he planned it, but its early eighteenth-century fittings would leave him baffled, and even the exuberant ceiling, vaulted and spangled with stars, dates from King Henry's tenancy.

Henry himself, though his surviving contributions to the Palace are even less extensive than Wolsey's, has left a far more identifiable mark, as have at least two of his wives. Anne Boleyn, whom he married in 1533 while his building programme was at its height, actually gave her name to the inner gateway leading into the Clock Court, whose fan-vaulted ceiling bears Henry's falcon badge and the intertwined initials H and A. Similar motifs can be seen in his Great Hall, splendidly – if, by 1535, rather anachronistically – hammer-beamed but otherwise sadly sterilised through over-restoration, and equipped with a polished wooden floor that makes it look more like a ballroom. Elsewhere we find the King's arms impaling those of his third wife, Jane Seymour, who gave birth to a son – later Edward VI – in the Palace, saw him christened in the Chapel Royal and died a fortnight later of puerperal fever.

Wife number five, Katherine Howard, has left a grimmer reminder of her presence at Hampton Court. After her arrest and before she left for her execution, she is said to have escaped from her gaolers to make a last appeal to the King, who was at mass. He refused to see her and she was dragged away; but the Palace still echoes on occasion with her screams, and more than one witness has testified to the vision of a ghostly figure, running in terror along the gallery that leads to the entrance to the royal pew.

After Henry's death Hampton Court continued as a royal palace, but there were no extensive alterations or additions until the accession of William and Mary in 1688. They found it ugly and uncomfortable and decided on a complete rebuilding, commissioning an entirely new set of plans from Sir Christopher Wren. We can only be thankful that this first idea, which would have involved the destruction of everything except the Great Hall, was never realised; it was eventually decided to demolish only the innermost courtyard, together with the state rooms and private apartments of the sovereign which surrounded it – a serious enough loss, all the same. In their place we now have two long, rather uninteresting elevations, preserving an absolutely flat skyline broken only by the chimneys, and, in the angle where they meet, the Fountain Court: all very dignified in a domestic sort of way, but sadly devoid of inspiration – so much so that one wonders whether Wren was really trying.

*Hampton Court.*

The Palace has one other architectural curiosity, all too often overlooked. It is to be found on the east side of the Clock Court, where the Gatehouse was rebuilt in the Gothic style by William Kent. This has nothing to do with the heavy, humourless Gothic of Wren and Hawksmoor; there is a new, completely different feeling about – lighthearted, almost tongue-in-cheek. Gothic Revival, in other words, is making here, of all places, its very first appearance.

Holy Trinity, Marylebone.

## Holy Trinity, Marylebone

*18; Marylebone Road, NW1*

One of the only three churches ever built by Sir John Soane, Holy Trinity was a 'Waterloo' church, belonging as it did to that group paid for out of the one-million-pound Thanksgiving Fund that was voted by Parliament in 1821 as a result of our safe deliverance from the Napoleonic Wars. Since it is orientated with its altar towards the north, what should properly be its west front in fact faces south. It features an imposing portico of four giant Ionic columns supporting an entablature with a characteristically Soanian key-pattern frieze, three inner doorways – the centre one being considerably higher – and three blank square recesses above them. To each side is a round-headed window, set high up; below the right-hand one is another recess, below the other an open-air pulpit added at the end of the last century. An intermittently balustraded parapet runs the length of the front, above which the tower rises at the centre. It has a square lower stage with detached Corinthian columns projecting at each end of the four sides – eight in all – each with its own projecting entablature and individual urn above. Then comes a tall colonnaded rotunda, topped by a circular stone cupola. Ionic half columns articulate the side walls.

The church has now been taken over by the Society for Promoting Christian Knowledge, and part of the interior has been converted accordingly. The apsed chancel is still used for services, but is no longer as Soane designed it – it was remodelled by Somers Clarke, with mosaic decoration, in about 1880.

## Houses of Parliament

See Palace of Westminster.

## Isleworth

See Syon House.

## Kensington Palace

*19; London W8*

A misnomer, one feels, looking at it across Kensington Gardens; there is nothing palatial about this straggling building of dark red brick. Only the right-hand end of it has any real form, while the rest, long and low, just seems to ramble off haphazardly in every direction. The formal-looking part is admittedly distinguished enough – though one would hardly call it beautiful – in a well-bred, late seventeenth-century way; with its eleven bays and two and a half storeys, the three-bay centre articulated by tall pilaster strips of slightly paler rubbed brick rising above the eaves to a windowless attic with four stone urns, it could well be taken for a gentleman's country house of medium size and little pretension. But nothing more.

And as such indeed it began. Before 1689 Nottingham House was a compact and relatively modest mansion with a good garden, the property of Heneage Finch, Earl of Nottingham. In that year, however, it was bought by King William III and Queen Mary who within a few months of their proclamation had acquired a deep dislike of the old Palace of Whitehall, where Mary complained that she could 'see nothing but water or wall'. The country air was better for the King's asthma; besides, like all Dutchmen he was an enthusiastic gardener, and saw possibilities here which would have been unthinkable in Westminster. Only the building itself was not altogether adequate; and Sir Christopher Wren was called in to make the necessary enlargements.

The problem was that neither William nor Mary knew quite what they wanted; moreover, they were desperately impatient to settle into their new home. In consequence, the work was done piecemeal and in a tearing hurry; part of it even fell down. There was never an overall plan, and the building remains confused – and confusing – both inside and out. Wren's additions and alterations – several of which may in fact be principally due to Hawksmoor, his Clerk of the Works – were complete by 1696, but even then the Palace was by no means finished; on the east side, all but the three left-hand bays (which formed part of the Wren–Hawksmoor building) were remodelled and refaced by the unspeakable William Benson and his friend Colen Campbell between 1718 and 1726, while other architects – notably Thomas Ripley – were working on less important sections further to the west.

The State Apartments, the only rooms in Kensington Palace regularly open to the public, occupy the whole south-east corner and this remodelled range, which runs the entire length of the east front. They fall into three groups, which can be conveniently designated by their centuries. The seventeenth-century group consists of those which have remained essentially as they were in William and Mary's day; the eighteenth-century rooms are those which were redesigned, painted and decorated by William Kent, who was working here from 1723 to 1727; while those of the nineteenth century together comprise a carefully restored monument to the period when Queen Victoria lived in the Palace with her mother before her accession. The first group begins with the

Queen's Staircase at the extreme north-east corner, where visitors start their tour. Like all Wren's (and Hawksmoor's) work at Kensington, it is simple, modest and restrained. It leads directly to the Queen's Gallery, with its tunnel-vaulted roof and mellow oak panelling, and thence to the exquisite little Queen's Dining Room – also panelled, though hardly more than an alcove – the Drawing Room with its high coved ceiling, and the blue-hung Bedchamber in which Mary II died.

Emerging from these last two small rooms, you enter a different world. Gone is Augustan good taste; here is the extrovert Italianate exuberance of William Kent. Although Kent started his career as a painter, painting was of all his skills the one at which he least excelled; and the actual execution of his work at Kensington does him little credit. Where he impresses is in his richness of imagination, his wealth of ideas, and his sheer animal energy. The ceiling of the Privy Chamber, a tremendous golden explosion of masks and *putti*, garlands and military trophies and lovely swirling arabesques, demands as a centrepiece something more exciting than Kent's pallid Minerva, reclining on a cloud of cotton wool; one feels much the same way about his immensely long ceiling to the King's Gallery, all nine bays of it – the overall conception is superb, the grand design strong enough to hold the whole composition together without effort; but the paintings themselves, scenes from the life of Ulysses in alternating round and octagonal frames, are weak and oddly lack-lustre. More complete successes, to my mind, are the Presence Chamber at the head of the King's Staircase – to which Kent has given the earliest Pompeian ceiling in England – and the breathtaking Cupola Room. In both these last he has eschewed classical figure painting altogether but, whereas in the former he has confined his attention to the ceiling, in the latter he has designed a glorious extravaganza of Ionic pilasters flanking gilded statues in niches and classical busts above them, trophies and garlands in all available interstices, huge marble chimneypiece and doorcases, and, crowning everything, a rich coffered ceiling, its height immensely exaggerated by *trompe-l'oeil*, rising up to a great central Garter star.

I have left the King's Staircase itself to the last, conscious that it slightly contradicts my argument. Apart from all the decorative themes already listed (plus a good many more) Kent has here actually covered the whole of his principal wall and some of his ceiling with figure painting – and yet brings the whole thing off triumphantly. The reason, I suspect, is that he is now depicting not mythological figures but ladies and gentlemen of the Hanoverian Court; there is not a trace of the inhibition that always seems to overtake him with classical subjects, and though his execution is still second-rate it is redeemed by the vivacity and exuberance and enjoyment that is evident in every stroke. Here, at last, he is having fun.

Of the three or four nineteenth-century rooms little need be said, since there is nothing architectural about them. They are delightful rooms, marvellously evocative of the 1830s, but the decoration is only in a few instances original. Their value, apart from the creation of atmosphere, is above all to emphasise what William Kent has temporarily allowed us to forget – that Kensington Palace is an essentially modest, unassuming sort of place. These rooms are of the kind that might be found on the second, bedroom, floor of many an English country house; one of them is actually known as the Nursery and indeed looks extremely like one. It is somehow comforting to reflect that the King of England was building Kensington Palace at the very moment that the Emperor Leopold of Austria was building Schönbrunn and Louis XIV was at work on Versailles.

## Kenwood

*20; Hampstead Lane, NW3*

The history of Kenwood goes back to Jacobean times, when the first house on the site was built by John Bill, the King's Printer; but the house that we see today is in all its essentials the work of Robert Adam. Although it had been largely rebuilt as recently as *c.*1700, it was still inadequate for the needs of William Murray, 1st Earl of Mansfield and Lord Chief Justice of England, who in 1764 commissioned his fellow Scotsman to undertake a complete remodelling – just as he had recently done for two other great houses near London, Osterley and Syon (*qq.v.*). Lord Mansfield, wrote Adam, 'gave full scope to my ideas'; and, though Kenwood was never as magnificent as the other two houses, it remains the only one of the three in which Adam was able to stamp his personality as unmistakably on the outside as he was on the interior.

The centre of the north (entrance) front remains much as Adam left it: three bays, deeply recessed under an Ionic tetrastyle portico of giant columns carrying a triangular pediment with a central medallion, with three flanking bays to each side which, while remaining of the same overall height, are of two and a half storeys instead of just two. Only Adam's angle pilasters have disappeared – or almost; they are concealed behind the two projecting wings of white brick which were added, at the request of the 2nd Earl, by George Saunders in 1793–6. There could be no more instructive example of the change in architectural taste which took place in the closing years of the eighteenth century: for the younger generation, Adam was far too flowery and ornate. Austerity and simplicity were now the rule – the only touch of decoration Saunders allows himself is in the door- and windowcases at the north ends of his wings.

The garden front, to the south, is much less altered. Here is a composition of which no one but Adam would have been capable. He heightened the whole front by half a storey, rusticated the ground floor, and above, over a heavily emphasised string-course, articulated his seven bays (two are lost on this side of the house) with a series of pilasters whose placing and spacing are equally curious. The order – if it can so be called – to which they belong is also one of his own devising. Originally they were decorated in stucco over their entire height, in the Renaissance manner; further bands of decoration extended horizontally in the form of a string-course below the attic windows and, in somewhat broader individual panels, above those of the first floor. The recesses where these decorations used to be can still be seen; the panels themselves have gone, however, as has the equally ornate decoration within the pediment. It appears that the material which Adam had selected for this work caused endless trouble from the start; Lord Mansfield used to complain that it would have been cheaper if he had had the whole thing done in Parian marble. Eventually – probably in the course of Saunders's work on the house – all the enrichments were removed.

The general aspect of this south front gains immeasurably from the two single-storey side pavilions. That to the left, the Orangery, was already in existence in Adam's day; he remodelled it and built the Library on the other side to match, linking the two to the centre with single-storey blocks of a tripartite design reminiscent of a Venetian window.

The interior of Kenwood includes one of Adam's most sumptuously spectacular *tours de force*: the great Library that occupies the eastern pavilion. Its shape is essentially rectangular, but both ends are apsed, the apses being separated from the centre of the room by screens consisting of pairs of fluted Corinthian columns carrying a deep entablature. It is spanned by a barrel-vaulted ceiling of great splendour, with plasterwork by Joseph Rose and painted panels by Antonio Zucchi. Though several of the other rooms have fine friezes and chimneypieces, none is of a standard remotely approaching this. Perhaps because of the absence of carpets – the house is permanently open to the public, so admittedly they would not last long – and the comparative scarcity of furniture elsewhere than in the Library, most of the rooms at Kenwood strike one as being rather cold and cheerless. There is, however, much consolation in the stunning collection of pictures left, together with the house, to the nation by the 1st Earl of Iveagh.

The glorious park surrounding the house is every bit as much a creation of the eighteenth century as is the building itself. The initial landscaping seems to have been the work of the Lord Chief Justice; his, certainly, is the delightful little imitation bridge that spans the lakes at their eastern end and provides additional interest and charm to the view from the house. Later, at the end of the century, the 2nd Earl is thought to have called in Humphry Repton for further improvements. The park adjoins Hampstead Heath, and one can nowadays walk freely in the hours of daylight between one and the other. Where else but in London is it possible to take in Rembrandts and Reynoldses, Gainsboroughs and even a Vermeer, in the middle of a country walk?

## Kew Gardens

*21; Surrey*

Architecturally speaking, the two heroes of Kew Gardens are Sir William Chambers and Decimus Burton. In 1756 Augusta, Princess of Wales – widow of George II's son Frederick – employed Chambers to give her son, the future George III, lessons in architectural draughtsmanship; and even though his efforts in this direction do not seem to have been outstandingly successful she commissioned him shortly afterwards to design a series of buildings for the pleasure garden at Kew, which her husband had instituted and which he was continuing to improve at the time of his death. Of these there survive the ORANGERY of 1757, seven bays of stuccoed brick, the first and last pedimented; three classical TEMPLES – of Aeolus, Arethusa and Bellona, dated 1760–3; a 'RUINED ARCH' of 1759–60, built partly of stone but partly, as Horace Walpole acidly pointed out, 'of Act-of-Parliament brick'; and Chambers's most famous and best-loved creation, the PAGODA of 1761.

*Kenwood House, Hampstead.*

Chambers was particularly well qualified to produce this last *pièce de résistance* of English *chinoiserie*, since he was one of the few Englishmen who had actually been to China, not once but twice, in his early youth as an employee of the Swedish East India Company; in 1757 he actually published a book entitled *Designs of Chinese Buildings, Furniture, Dresses, etc.* His ten-storey pagoda rises 163 feet, has a spiral staircase inside, and originally had no fewer than eighty enamelled dragons on the roofs. On close examination it now looks surprisingly un-Chinese, but it adds a pleasant touch of exoticism to the gardens and we can only regret the disappearance of Chambers's other buildings, which included a Turkish Mosque, a Moorish Alhambra and a House of Confucius, as well as a Palladian Bridge, a Gallery of Antiques, a Theatre of Augusta, a Menagerie, and about eight more classical temples.

The Gardens were handed over to the nation in 1841, and four years later Decimus Burton was called in to provide suitable entrance gates and various other buildings which had by then become necessary. Of these by far the most spectacular is the PALM HOUSE, which was completed in 1848. Burton had previously worked with Paxton at Chatsworth, so he had already had experience in this rather specialised field; and his Palm House with its great soaring lines is a far more exciting building than the Crystal Palace could ever have been. With its immense 360-foot length and its height of 62 feet at the centre, it is built exclusively of glass and iron, the latter being not cast but wrought. Burton was a fine architect, to whom we owe, *inter alia*, the Ionic screen at Hyde Park Corner and the archway at the top of Constitution Hill; but this grandest of all greenhouses must surely be his finest work. It certainly outshines his other buildings at Kew: the Museum of Economic Botany – now more prosaically known as MUSEUM NO. 1 – and the TEMPERATE HOUSE are both uninspired, though the vaguely Italianate CAMPANILE (built to serve as a chimney for the furnaces under the Palm House) has a certain restrained charm.

Some quarter of a mile west of the Pagoda is the QUEEN'S COTTAGE. Dating from 1772, it is an absolutely enchanting *cottage orné*, timber-framed and thatched. The main downstairs room is papered with Hogarth prints, while the corresponding upstairs room is charmingly painted all over with flowers, almost certainly by George III's third daughter, the Princess Elizabeth.

Within the Gardens stands KEW PALACE – if anything even more of a misnomer than Kensington Palace. The old red-brick house, built for the prosperous London merchant Samuel Fortrey in 1631, was taken by Queen Caroline on a ninety-nine-year lease in 1728 'for the rent of £100 and a fat Doe', and was thereafter in regular use by the Royal Family, including George III himself for a brief period after the demolition in 1802 of his former residence, the White House, opposite. His wife, Queen Charlotte, actually died there in 1818. But it is a palace in name only. Unfortunately its alternative description, the Dutch House, suits it very little better: Fortrey was indeed of Dutch extraction and there are features of the building which obviously derive from the Low

*The Pagoda, Kew Gardens.*

Countries, but its architectural style – that which Sir John Summerson has dubbed 'Artisan Mannerism' – is quintessentially English and exists nowhere outside England.

One of the principal characteristics of this style is virtuoso brickwork, and of this Kew Palace provides a superb example – surpassed only, perhaps, by Broome Park in Kent (*q.v.*). On its entrance front all the windows – not only in the three principal floors but even in the gables above them – have elaborate rusticated surrounds, except only those in the fourth (central) bay immediately above the door, which are singled out for even more individual treatment. These are round-headed – all the rest are square – and are flanked, on the first floor by pilasters and on the second by columns, all of brick. The door itself has pilasters too, broader and again rusticated. Heavy string-courses between the floors provide a useful horizontal emphasis – the house is tall for its width – and above the top one rise three Dutch gables with double-curved (S-shaped) sides and – a considerable innovation for 1631 – alternating pediments. Behind them, above the steeply pitched tiled roof, tall square brick chimneys, diagonally set, increase the verticality still more.

The house is open to the public in summer, and contains memorabilia of George III. Most of the interior detailing is in fact of his time, including a remarkably pretty staircase with three turned balusters per tread. One of the rooms on the first floor, however, known as the Queen's Boudoir, has its original plaster ceiling, still

*Kew Palace.*

entirely in the Jacobean tradition; it comes as quite a shock to realise that when it was inserted Inigo Jones had already been working at the Court for nearly twenty years. At first glance the overdoors of the King's Dining Room below could be thought to be more of the same; they are actually an eighteenth-century imitation, quite possibly by William Kent who is known to have been working at the White House in about 1730.

The lovely formal garden between the Palace and the river is another pastiche, still more successful. It dates from 1975 and could not possibly be bettered.

## Kew Palace

See Kew Gardens.

## Lambeth Palace

*22; Lambeth Palace Road, SE1*

The London residence of the Archbishops of Canterbury for nearly 800 years, Lambeth Palace was acquired by Archbishop Hubert Walter – who ruled England for the best part of a decade during the interminable absences abroad of Richard Coeur-de-Lion – in 1197. The monks of Canterbury, however, horrified at what they saw as a dangerous threat to their influence, appealed to the Pope, who ordered that the Lambeth buildings should be razed to the ground. Although there is no direct evidence, it seems that this order was obeyed; there is in any case no trace of any twelfth-century work remaining today.

What we have instead is a collection of buildings which vary wildly in their dates and styles. A visit to Lambeth starts off promisingly enough with one's entrance into the Palace through the great brick Gatehouse alongside the tower of St Mary's church (which has, however, nothing to do with it at all). This was the work of Cardinal Morton – more famous for his 'Fork' – in *c.*1495 and is a perfect example of an early Tudor gatehouse: red brick with pronounced diapering, a stone vault under the archway and flanking five-storey towers. It is at present used for storing archives and is consequently not open to the public, which is a pity – especially as Sir Thomas More is said to have inhabited the third floor of the northern tower and several of the rooms have very fine ceilings.

Once inside the gateway, you find the Great Hall (now the Library) immediately on your left. This is a very odd building indeed – the most astonishing combination of Gothic and classical that I know anywhere in London. Begun around 1200, it was remodelled and improved by Archbishop Chichele in the fifteenth century but then reduced to 'a heap of ruins' during the Commonwealth. The building we now see is thus the reconstruction, at his own expense, by William Juxon, the first Primate after the Restoration. Juxon retained the fundamental Gothic structure, with tall, transomed three-light windows and fourteenth-century-style tracery, divided by buttresses with big set-offs; these buttresses, however, end (on the north side) not in the pinnacles one might expect but in stone balls of purely classical inspiration. Odder still, the projecting ends, though they have windows of the same design (only taller and with an extra transom) are crowned with pediments. A modillion cornice runs the whole length of the building and the long and short quoins which appear at every available opportunity – including on the buttresses themselves – could hardly look more seventeenth-century if they tried. Finally the whole building is finished off with an exceedingly pretty lantern of two stages, first hexagonal and then circular, with pilasters ending in volutes. The interior is equally hybrid: here the windows contrast with a frieze of garlands, a completely Baroque doorway with pilasters and an open segmental pediment, and, above the fireplaces at each end, overmantels with coats of arms and curly acanthus cresting above. Over everything there extends a huge and heavy hammer-beam roof.

Another remarkable (if somewhat less spectacular) roof covers the Guard Room. It owes its preservation to Edward Blore, who largely transformed the Palace in the years following 1829 and who had it propped up while he completely rebuilt the room below. The room itself is now of little interest apart from the excellent collection of archiepiscopal portraits it contains.

Blore's principal contribution to the Palace is, however, the great Gothic pseudo-castle which dominates the inner courtyard, with its high central tower turreted at the angles and lower embattled wings to each side. Typically, he rejected the idea of brick, the prevailing material elsewhere, and opted – at vast expense – for Bath stone. Sadly, too, he was less respectful of the existing buildings than he had been of the Guard Room roof: the medieval cloisters which formerly occupied the site were completely swept away.

Immediately to the north of Blore's new building is the only truly medieval part of the Palace still surviving, the range which contains the Chapel. The latter was gutted in the Second World War and has preserved only its outer walls, its fine round-arched Early English doorway (two openings with pointed trefoil heads separated by a triple-shafted trumeau) and Archbishop Laud's splendid carved screen, which has now been moved to the Post Room adjoining. Virtually everything else is a reconstruction by Seely (Lord Mottistone) and Paget. A good deal more inspiring is the undercroft, rib-vaulted in three bays to each side of a central row of squat Purbeck columns. This probably goes back to the days of Archbishop Stephen Langton, who played a crucial part in the signing of Magna Carta in 1215. Its windows are simple lancets, which have blind trefoil arch-heads on the outside.

Architecturally, the two most interesting features of Lambeth Palace today are the Hall (particularly its exterior) and the undercroft. I cannot forbear to mention, however, two other items which linger long in the memory. The first is a pair of gloves, now kept in the Great Hall, given by Charles I on the scaffold to Juxon, then Bishop of London, who was with him at his execution. The second, preserved in a glass case in the gallery over the old cloister, is a somewhat dilapidated tortoise, which was introduced into the Palace garden by Archbishop Laud in 1633. There it lived happily for 120 years, until in 1753 it was accidentally killed by a gardener's fork.

## Law Courts

*23; Strand, WC2*

In 1865 a large site which had hitherto been occupied by particularly insalubrious slums was purchased by the Crown for nearly one and a half million pounds, the object being to accommodate all the superior non-criminal Courts of Justice. A competition was held in the following year and in 1868 G.E. Street was announced to be the winner. Work began in 1874, and the vast building was finally opened by Queen Victoria in December 1882. Street had died in the previous year of a stroke – said by many to have been induced by the innumerable delays and other problems which had beset the enterprise from the start – and the completion was directed by his son, working jointly with Arthur Blomfield.

For all those who do not actually hate Victorian Gothic, the Law Courts constitute one of the chief architectural pleasures of the Strand. No other building in central London, surely, breathes such an air of medieval romance; the towers and turrets, the spires and pinnacles – especially when the sun is reflecting off the white stone – can look almost like something out of a fairytale. Towards the western end, two of the largest turrets flank a huge pointed arch, above which runs a curious arcaded bridge. This, the main entrance, leads into a lobby, immediately to the right of which there opens out one of the most impressive Gothic spaces in London, the Great Hall. Any fantasy, even frivolity, that we might have discerned on the exterior has been completely swept away. Here we find ourselves in what seems to be a vast Early English cathedral, 230 feet long and over 80 feet high, with an east window of three stepped lancets, blank arcading and, crowning all, a sexpartite rib vault.

And it is almost completely empty. The courts themselves, and the myriad offices where the actual business of justice is done, are hidden away up little spiral staircases in the walls. This huge and echoing enclosure serves no practical purpose but to inspire wonderment and awe – which it certainly does.

## Little Stanmore

See St Lawrence Whitchurch.

## Mansion House

*24; Bank, EC2*

Although London had had a Lord Mayor since the twelfth century, it was only in 1734 that the City settled down seriously to the business of providing him with a special residence for use during his year of office. The following year, despite the entry into the competition of such architects as Gibbs, James, Leoni and Ware, the task was given to George Dance Sen. – presumably for no other reason than his position as Clerk of the City Works, since he had at that time only two fairly undistinguished buildings to his credit. Building began in 1739 and the first Lord Mayor to live there, Sir Crisp Gascoyne, moved in at the end of 1752.

Considering how awkward and constricted the site was, Dance did a creditable job. His exterior is purely Palladian, with a Corinthian hexastyle on giant columns projecting from a nine-bay front; there are two main floors, over a high rusticated basement. The relief in the pediment represents London trampling on Envy and introducing Plenty, and is by the young Robert Taylor, who started life as a sculptor. The two sides are also straightforwardly Palladian with alternating pediments to the windows, except that the second bay in from each end is treated somewhat spectacularly, with a big Venetian window below and, above it, a huge arched window so tall that it cuts into the attic. This attic runs all round the building. Dance had originally raised it higher still, with two pedimented blocks of considerable height set on the roof and running latitudinally across, above the spectacular bays. Their purpose was to give additional height to his Dancing Gallery and Egyptian Hall, but in old engravings they look utterly ridiculous; they were familiarly known as 'Noah's Ark' and 'The Mayor's Nest'. The former was removed by George Dance Jun. when making alterations to his father's work, including the roofing in of the central courtyard, in 1794–5; the latter followed in 1842.

Inside, there are most sumptuously decorated suites of rooms on both the principal floors, some in the tradition of William Kent, others in more light-hearted Italian Rococo.

## Marble Hill House

*25; Richmond Road, Twickenham*

'Every thing as yet promises more happiness for the latter part of my life than I have yet had a prospect of,' wrote Henrietta, Countess of Suffolk, to John Gay in 1731; 'I shall now often visit Marble Hill.' The poor Countess had indeed suffered her fair share of ill fortune: her marriage to a nightmare of a husband had ended, after several years of misery, in separation, and the position of *maîtresse en titre* to George II – of whom she never seems to have been particularly fond – can also have been anything but a sinecure. But if any house could provide consolation for a battered spirit, that house was Marble Hill. In those days, when Twickenham was simply an elegant little riverside village, there could have been no more perfect setting for a small Palladian villa, its lawns sweeping gently down to the Thames. Here Henrietta lived for the next thirty-six years, eleven of them – until his death – with her second husband, George Berkeley, on whom she doted; and here she entertained her countless friends, including Gay, her neighbour Alexander Pope and, after 1747, another equally rewarding neighbour, Horace Walpole, who had just acquired Strawberry Hill (*q.v.*).

The basic design of Marble Hill was the work of another of her admirers, Lord Herbert, a dilettante and amateur architect in the Palladian manner; the actual labour was entrusted to that most businesslike of professionals Roger Morris, thanks to whose industry the house was complete by the beginning of 1725. It has considerable elegance, without being in any way out of the ordinary Palladian run. The north front is grander than the south, but still makes no attempt to conceal the relative modesty of the building: this is a villa, not a mansion. Of the three storeys, only one has any pretensions to the status of *piano nobile*: the ground floor is, as usual, little more than a glorified basement, the attic just an attic. Of the five bays, three project slightly on a rusticated base, to form a pedimented centre with Ionic pilasters. The central window on the main floor also carries a well-bred pediment, and that is all. The south side is plainer, having no rustication or pilasters, but is otherwise much the same.

The entire house was most conscientiously restored in 1966 by the Greater London Council; though still at the time of writing somewhat lacking in furniture, it has some fine pictures and is well worth a visit. The centre of the house is the so-called Great Room, a cube of 24 feet unquestionably modelled on the Single Cube at Wilton, Lord Herbert's family house. There is a good mahogany staircase and most of the rooms have fine decorative detail. But Marble Hill is not a showpiece, and should not be approached as such.

## Natural History Museum

*26; Cromwell Road, SW7*

The winner of the competition held in 1864 for the design of the Natural History Museum – nowadays known officially as the British Museum (Natural History) – to be built at the southern end of the museums complex in Kensington was Captain Francis Fowke, the first architect of the Royal Albert Hall (*q.v.*). On Fowke's death a year later, however, the commission was given to the thirty-five-year-old Alfred Waterhouse of Manchester. As his two other best-known buildings in London – the Prudential Assurance Building in Holborn and University College Hospital – amply testify, Waterhouse was a Gothicist; here in Kensington, however, he decided from the very first on the Romanesque. His reason was curious, yet sympathetic: the prime mover of the project, Sir Richard Owen, wanted plenty of zoological decoration on the façade, a feature for which Romanesque was far better suited than either Gothic or Renaissance.

*The Natural History Museum.*

The building that eventually resulted, and was finished in 1880, is inspired above all by South German models. It is rigidly symmetrical for the whole of its 225-yard frontage, and its constant *leitmotiv* is the coupled round arch, which appears in one form or another in almost all the windows except those of the basement – where they are still coupled but have straight heads. The great central archway is flanked by twin towers 192 feet high, topped with tall octagons and spires; at the corners are broader, squatter angle towers with immensely high Germanic roofs. The whole building is faced with Waterhouse's beloved terracotta, buff and bluish grey. Only on careful inspection does one notice that it is indeed crawling with sculptured animals, living on the left, extinct on the right. On the centre gable, at the suggestion of Prof. T.H. Huxley, there was formerly a carving portraying 'Man: the Greatest Beast of All' – as triumphant a proclamation of Darwinism as could be imagined. Alas, it is no longer there.

Entering the Museum, you find yourself immediately in a vast open hall with a glass roof carried on steel arches and a monumental staircase rising up at the back. It takes you to the first floor only; should you want to go on up to the second, you return to a high bridge at the entrance end from which a further stairway flies upward again without any intermediate support. Long galleries on three floors disappear into the distance to the left and right of the entrance hall while, on the north–south axis, the central hall is flanked by three more, rather narrower, to each side. Once again, terracotta is everywhere, carved and patterned. On occasion it even screens the steel frame of the building, though elsewhere Waterhouse makes no secret of it and indeed exhibits it with pride.

Despite its enormous size, the Museum was found to be too small for its purpose in the 1960s, when a new wing was designed by a team of architects from the Dept of the Environment, led by James Ellis. It was completed, at the corner of Exhibition Road, in 1977. Inevitably, it has little to do with Waterhouse, who would have loathed it; personally, I find it a good deal more successful than I had expected.

## The Octagon, Orleans House

*27; Riverside, Twickenham*

Orleans House was built by John James in 1710. Between 1815 and 1817 it was leased by Louis-Philippe, Duke of Orleans – who was later to become King of the French – from whom it took its name. In 1926–7 it was demolished. And that is all that needs to be said about it.

One small annex to that house, however, escaped destruction; and that was the Octagon, a tiny pavilion consisting of a single room which was designed in 1720 by James Gibbs, allegedly for the reception of Caroline of Anspach, Princess of Wales – the wife of the future George II. It is one of his most enchanting *jeux d'esprit*. Built of yellow brick, with red-brick pilasters at the angles and generous dressings of Portland stone, it has on its three southward-facing sides tall arched windows whose sills descend to the plinth, with those long-and-short rusticated surrounds to which Gibbs gave his name and circular *oeil-de-boeuf* windows above them. Higher still are a cornice and quite deep entablature; and the whole building is crowned with a brick parapet. (In Gibbs's day it had urns on it; could not the Borough of Richmond, who were left the building in 1962, possibly run to a new set?)

The interior is domed, and most splendidly decorated in Roman Baroque fashion by those two princes of stucco, Artari and Bagutti. There are busts in the lunettes and medallions on the walls – King George and Queen Caroline are each represented twice – and an elaborately pedimented chimneypiece. The whole thing is little more than a folly, but it shows Gibbs and his two associates – they also collaborated with him on the Senate House, Cambridge, and at St Martin-in-the-Fields (*qq.v.*) – at the top of their form.

Of the low wings to each side, which also survived the demolition, one is now a small art gallery, displaying for the most part topographical paintings and watercolours left to the Borough together with the Octagon. There are also temporary exhibitions.

## Osterley Park

*NT; 28; Osterley*

Sir Thomas Gresham's 'faire and stately building of bricke', which he completed in about 1577, still lies at the core of the great house which was remodelled by Robert Adam between 1761 and 1780 and transformed into one of the supreme monuments of late eighteenth-century classical taste. It had been bought in 1711 by Sir Francis Childe, one of the earliest pioneers of British banking; he it was, in all probability, who refaced Gresham's four corner towers. But it was under his two grandsons – first Francis, and then after Francis's death in 1763 his younger brother Robert – that the great metamorphosis took place. It actually began some time before Adam's arrival on the scene: the long Gallery on the west side was already finished in 1759, and there is a tradition – unsupported, however, by any documentary evidence so far discovered – that it is the work of Sir William Chambers, who may also have designed some chimneypieces and furniture. But Adam's plans, when he submitted his final drawings in 1763, were far more ambitious – beginning with what was perhaps his most extraordinary idea of all: the portico.

Seen from a distance and at an oblique angle, this portico looks at first glance perfectly normal – just six tall Ionic columns carrying a triangular pediment in orthodox Palladian fashion. It is only on approaching it from the front that one realises there is no wall behind it, merely another identical portico facing inwards into the court. The distance between the two, however, corres-

*The Octagon, Orleans House, Twickenham.*

Osterley Park.

ponds to the thickness of the entire east front, and the roof of what amounts to an open colonnade is filled with a bold stucco design, white against a pale grey ground. This concept of a 'transparent portico' was not entirely new: William Talman had intended something of the sort for Witham Park in Somerset – though he never actually built it – and his idea had subsequently been borrowed by James Gibbs and published in *Vitruvius Britannicus*. But Adam was the first man to realise the concept in practice – and to do so with immense virtuosity and panache.

The entrance door faces the portico across the courtyard, whose inner walls are of the same rather hot red brick as the exterior; it is something of a relief to enter the house and to find oneself in a cool Entrance Hall with a floor of white stone. Adam had strong ideas about halls. They should be large, he wrote, apsed and decorated in stucco – and he designed the one at Osterley accordingly. It is impossible not to be struck by its similarity to its counterpart at Syon, a mile or two away; here again are the coffered apses, the antique sculpture in niches and free-standing, and even the plaster trophies on the walls. At each end, set within the apse, is an exquisite chimneypiece, surmounted by *grisaille* paintings superbly executed in *trompe-l'oeil* by Giovanni Battista Cipriani and containing fire grates of surpassing elegance, also designed by Adam – an instance of that unremitting attention to detail which one notices all over the house.

The Hall leads directly into the Gallery beyond – in which we are inevitably tempted to discern the hand of Chambers, especially in the furniture facing the windows and the two fireplaces. The inner walls are lined with pictures, hung frequently two deep and looking as if no one has touched them for 200 years. It comes as quite a surprise to learn that they are all recent loans from the Victoria and Albert Museum. There follows an Eating Room with a beautiful plaster ceiling entwined with garlands (but no tables, which were in those days normally kept outside and brought in only when required) and then just beyond it the Staircase Hall, with paired columns in two orders above and below the upper landing and sublimely delicate stucco decorations on the walls. The cantilevered staircase rises along one side to a half landing and then returns along the other. The wrought-iron balustrade (painted its original colour, a rather unpleasant shade of livid blue) is of course Adam's own design, as are the three lamps hanging below the lower columns.

These original colours, so carefully restored by the National Trust which owns Osterley, and the V. and A. which looks after it, are a constant source of surprise as one wanders through the house. Again and again they seem brighter, sometimes even harsher, than we expect. This is true of the ceiling of the Library, the next room we reach, and even more so of that of the Breakfast Room next door. The latter is known to have been completed before Adam's arrival; but could Chambers, one wonders, possibly have been responsible for that startling blue and yellow on ceiling and walls? The answer is that he was not: a somewhat red-faced V. and A. generously admits a mistake which will soon be rectified.

The north wing completed, we return to the Gallery and start on the south. It begins with the Drawing Room, which Horace Walpole, seeing it for the first time in 1773, pronounced to be 'worthy of Eve before the Fall'. The ceiling is of almost unbelievable opulence, its cofferings a riot of pink and green and gold, loosely inspired by a design in Wood's *Ruins of Palmyra* of 1753. Its design is echoed – but deliberately not precisely reflected – in the carpet below. Next comes a ravishing Tapestry Room, glowing rose-pink in its carefully controlled half light, the walls hung with mythological scenes depicting the loves of the Gods, designed by Boucher and woven by special order in the Gobelins factory. This leads through to the State Bedroom, in which the domed four-poster is an astonishing *tour de force*. Never in his life did Adam produce a more sumptuously elaborate piece of furniture. The slender columns supporting the canopy are set diagonally; from their entablatures hang heavy swags of silk and velvet, with gilded tassels at intervals, while at each corner, above, a small gilded sphinx rears up protectively. At the head is a design of nymphs, garlands and boys on dolphins, while crowning the whole thing is the ornamental dome, adorned with artificial flowers. It was too much for Walpole: what would Vitruvius think, he asked, of a dome decorated by a milliner?

He was equally critical about the last of Osterley's memorable rooms, the Etruscan Dressing Room. 'It is painted all over like Wedgwood's ware, with black and yellow small grotesques.... It would be a pretty waiting-room in a garden. I never saw such a profound tumble into the Bathos.' What Walpole was in fact seeing was the first of those Etruscan Rooms which were to be so fashionable in the next quarter-century. Adam himself was to design five of them; but this is one of the only two that remain. Once again, one is a little concerned about the colours of the ceiling; but the walls are treated with the most subtle delicacy and lightness of touch.

The splendour of Osterley resides, however, not only in the spectacular quality of its interior decoration but also in the fact that it is one of the very few late eighteenth-century buildings of the very first rank that have come down to us virtually unaltered. All the furniture that was designed for it is still there, most if not all in its original position. This gives the house an interest – and a value – even greater than that which it would anyway warrant as one of the showpieces of the most talented decorator of his time. London is indeed fortunate to have such a house on its very doorstep – open nearly every day too, and all the year round!

## Palace of Westminster

*29; London SW1*

The best vantage-point from which to contemplate the Palace of Westminster is the one from which Monet loved to paint it – Westminster Bridge. If the turgid river flowing beneath its walls is to be described (and it always is, whether we like it or not) as 'liquid history', this tremendous pile might be said to echo the same message in stone. To the innocent tourist it seems ageless, its sturdy Gothic epitomising and providing the perfect backdrop to the whole pageant of England's past. Did Queen Elizabeth sleep here? Is this where King Charles lost his head? Is that the tower in which the little princes were murdered? It comes as a shock, as well as a disappointment, to discover that the place is little more than 100 years old.

But look more closely, and it gives itself away. Beneath all the Perpendicular decoration, the finials and the crockets, lies a rigid symmetry utterly alien to the medieval spirit. And small wonder: for the architect, Sir Charles Barry, was a classicist far more at his ease with Italianate designs like those of the Travellers' or Reform Clubs in Pall Mall. His choice on this occasion had been forced on him by the terms of the open competition announced in 1835 for a new Parliament building – the earlier one having been burnt down the previous year – which specified that the style should be 'either Gothic or Elizabethan'; and his success in that competition was largely due to a set of 'exquisite and minute drawings' by his twenty-three-year-old assistant, Augustus Welby Pugin.

We have it on no less authority than that of Cardinal Newman that Pugin was 'a man of genius'. But, as Newman went on to say, 'the canons of Gothic architecture are to him points of faith, and everyone is a heretic who would venture to question them'. From the start he was out of sympathy with Barry's design, which he stigmatised as 'All Grecian–Tudor details on a classic body'; he may, however, have drawn consolation from the two great towers with which Barry broke the symmetry – the Victoria Tower and Big Ben. (The name, as pedants love to point out, is inaccurate, being properly applied only to the great bell; to call it the 'Clock Tower', on the other hand, would be distinctly unimaginative and pompous to boot.) At all events, the opportunity was too good to miss; and Pugin was given responsibility for the detail and decoration, inside and out, of the entire building.

No two men could have been more different in tastes or character; yet their collaboration produced what is arguably the greatest English building of the nineteenth century. To the stolid, methodical Barry the Palace owes

*The Palace of Westminster.*

the surprising simplicity of its basic design, consisting in essence of a single spine, starting with the House of Commons at the north and running southward through the three major lobbies, the House of Lords, the Princes' Chamber and the Royal Gallery, to the Robing Room and the Victoria Tower. To Pugin, brilliant, mercurial, dashing off literally thousands of drawings with never-flagging imagination and almost unbelievable speed, it owes its superb, picturesque flamboyance. 'I strive', he wrote, 'to revive, not invent'; but when invention was called for, he invented – effortlessly. No one, even in the Middle Ages, 'thought Gothic' as instinctively as he did; witness, over and over again, his extraordinary skill in adapting the medieval style to contemporary needs – Gothic clocks and umbrella stands, lamp brackets and coat hooks.

The only major failures in the building are in those features for which the responsibility lay with neither Barry nor Pugin but, surprisingly, with the Prince Consort. With his unshakeable belief in the power of art to uplift the soul, he arranged for a select committee to hold competitions among the leading mural painters of the day; the result was the series of gigantic frescoes by such notables as G.F. Watts, William Dyce and Daniel Maclise. Even the best are oddly lacking in distinction; most of them look as if they had been designed for jigsaw puzzles, for which purpose they should have been kept.

Of the present House of Commons, rebuilt by Sir Giles Gilbert Scott after its predecessor received a direct hit in 1941, the less said the better. The true splendour lies south of the great octagonal Central Lobby and, above all, in Pugin's masterpiece, the House of Lords. Ideally it should be seen on a dank November afternoon, when the light is fast fading behind the stained-glass windows. Then this terrific chamber emerges in all its richness of scarlet and gold, reaching its climax with the throne itself, the world's most unanswerable visual argument for monarchy. How fortunate, one feels, that it was given to the nineteenth century to provide a home for the Mother of Parliaments; what a mess the exquisite eighteenth would have made of it! Only the Victorians had precisely the qualities that were needed – and they did her proud.

## Petersham

See Sudbrook Park.

## Pitshanger Manor

*30; The Green, W5*

The house built by Sir John Soane for himself in 1801–2 stands at the corner of Walpole Park and now serves as Ealing Public Library. The house had originally been designed by his old teacher, George Dance, but of this Soane kept only two rooms in the south corner, presumably because of their remarkably pretty stucco decoration. The rest of the building he demolished, erecting in its stead a magnificent structure which, though unquestionably classical in style, could not possibly have been designed by anyone but himself. The first things that strikes one about it is its grandeur: this was, after all, a small country villa, its main entrance front of only three bays, and built of brick. To this Soane has attached a front that would do credit to a Temple of Jupiter, with four giant Ionic columns of Portland stone, detached and carrying a strongly projecting entablature on which stand four statues in terracotta in front of a high attic storey. This attic has no windows, only a carved roundel to each side and a square relief panel in the centre. Thus the only windows to the whole front are the two tall round-headed ones flanking the door. The middle bay of the attic is raised still higher and is crowned, like its neighbours, with an intermittently balustraded parapet.

Its present function does not exactly show the house off to its best advantage; nevertheless, the Entrance Hall and two ground-floor rooms have their own Soanian fascination. The Hall, minute as it is, is barrel-vaulted, the vault interrupted by a raised lantern. In the former Front Parlour is a shallow domed ceiling of much the same kind as that in the Breakfast Parlour at 13 Lincoln's Inn Fields (see Sir John Soane's Museum), supported on four columns with statues, while in the room behind is a splayed cross vault identical with that of the Breakfast Room of No. 12; Soane even had it painted in much the same trellis design.

## Richmond

See Asgill House; Ham House.

*Pitshanger Manor.*

The Royal Albert Hall.

## Royal Albert Hall

*31; Kensington Gore, SW7*

It may not be everybody's idea of great architecture, but it is a remarkable building by any standards, held in great affection by large numbers of people (including me), and unquestionably one of the sights of London. It had always been Prince Albert's idea that the profits of the Great Exhibition should be used to create a great centre for the arts and sciences, and in 1853 he commissioned drawings for a vast concert, lecture and conference hall from Gottfried Semper, architect of the Dresden Opera House. Semper produced some drawings but they were never used, and it was only after the Prince's death that the idea was revived by Sir Henry Cole, Chairman of the Society of Arts. Mistrusting professional architects as he always did, Cole commissioned plans from a captain in the Royal Engineers, Francis Fowke, financing the whole operation by selling long leases of the individual seats and boxes. Unfortunately in December 1863 Fowke died, aged only forty-two, and his place was taken by a brother officer, Lt.-Col. H.Y. Darracott Scott, RE: but, as neither Fowke nor Scott had any real architectural training, much of the detail was designed by others, above all Thomas Verity (who was largely responsible for the interior), Sir Matthew Digby Wyatt and R.M. Ordish, who had been involved with W.H. Barlow in the construction of the huge train shed at St Pancras Station and was therefore uniquely qualified to design and construct the immense glazed oval of the dome, 219 feet long, 185 feet across, and 135 feet high.

The result of all this is a domed cylinder of dark red brick, nearly 250 yards in circumference, with four porches of two storeys, and a single broad bay projecting. The main building is also of two storeys over a high basement, after which comes a parapet followed by the only major decorative flourish – a frieze of terracotta and mosaic running all round. Designed in sections by six different artists (including Poynter, Yeames and Stacy Marks), it was executed – with help from Minton's – by the South Kensington Ladies' Mosaic Class.

Inside, perhaps the most memorable feature of this enormous space is the deep 'promenade' which circles the entire building above the top row of seats. Another sensation at the time was the huge organ, by Henry Willis, which for many years was the largest in existence. The only problem was that every note played in the building was heard twice. That notorious echo – which prompted Sir Thomas Beecham to remark that the Albert Hall was the only place in the world where every piece of music played could be sure of an encore – was eliminated only in 1968–9.

Do not fail to glance at the ROYAL COLLEGE OF ORGANISTS, immediately opposite on the west, built (as the National Training School for Music) by that extraordinary architect-developer and patron of the arts, Sir Charles Freake, entirely at his own expense. Its architect was yet another officer of the Royal Engineers, Lieut. H.H. Cole. Anything less military, however, could hardly be imagined, since almost every available square inch is covered with *sgraffito* decoration. It sets off its gigantic neighbour surprisingly well.

## Royal Hospital, Chelsea

*32; Royal Hospital Road, SW3*

Early in 1681, Charles II commissioned Sir Christopher Wren to design a great hospital for invalid soldiers and retired veterans, much on the lines of that which Louis XIV had recently established with the Hôtel des Invalides in Paris. Until this time Wren had been almost exclusively concerned with churches, and this was his first large-scale secular work. The foundation stone was laid on 17 February 1682, on the site of an old theological college dating from Jacobean days; seven years later, 476 non-commissioned officers and men moved into the newly finished building, though the Chapel was not to be consecrated till 1691. The Hospital is still used for its original purpose, and – apart from minor alterations by Robert Adam in 1765–82 and the addition of the stables by Soane in 1814 – has been preserved almost intact since Wren's day.

According to John Evelyn, the inmates of the Hospital were to live 'as in a college or monastery', and Wren's design is, for him, unusually austere. His basic material is brick, and he uses the Doric order throughout. His original plan was of the simplest: three long ranges enclosing a central courtyard, the central one containing a Great Hall and Chapel and providing the focus of community life, the other two being given over to living accommodation. Later, in James II's reign, the central range was extended further outwards on each side and other wings were built parallel to these extensions at the far ends of the lateral ranges, forming two more courts and much improving the overall effect.

The main block is of twenty-seven bays. To both north and south, the three-bay centre is marked by a portico of giant columns (which Wren employs here for the first time) with a triglyph frieze and triangular pediment, attached on the north side, but on the south – that is, facing into the courtyard – projecting quite considerably and with a single-storey loggia on small coupled columns running off to the corners on each side. Architecturally, it must be admitted, this is something less than a complete success: there is not only an awkward join where the loggia roof meets the giant columns not quite halfway up, but also an unhappy contrast of scale between the two sets of columns. Above the loggia to each side is a row of tall round-headed windows, and above them – rather too close for comfort – a corresponding row of rectangular brick recesses. There follows a cornice, which continues round the portico and along the lateral ranges, then the steeply pitched roof and, in the centre, a tall lantern of Portland stone. This is characteristic of Wren and of the countless steeples that he was later to design for his London churches, with its detached columns projecting diagonally at the corners; here, however, it seems distinctly too small for the job. There is reason to believe that Wren suspected as much, since he is known to have sought permission to re-use one of the west turrets that Inigo Jones had designed for old St Paul's and that, having been saved from the Great Fire, was being carefully kept in store; it was 40 feet higher than the present lantern and would have made a far more satisfactory centrepiece. But the cathedral authorities were unwilling to allow the turret to be used for secular purposes, so the idea came to nothing.

The east and west ranges could hardly be simpler, with their three storeys of identical windows, rectangular and utterly unadorned, and uniform row of dormers above. The only break in the monotony occurs halfway along each range, where Wren has introduced a rather curious subsidiary portico with pilasters instead of columns. His problem here has been to allow the pensioners' lodgings behind to continue uninterruptedly; the unnecessarily deep frieze cuts most unhappily across two of the second-floor windows, breaking only in the centre to admit the middle one.

The main entrance leads directly into a tall octagonal vestibule with bent angle-pilasters, dark and a little bleak. To the left is the Chapel, to the right the Hall. In the Chapel we find, for the first time, an element of grandeur, though of a fairly restrained kind. Apsed and tunnel-vaulted, it is dominated by a splendid reredos with coupled Corinthian columns and Wren's favourite (for this purpose) segmental pediment, above which Sebastiano Ricci's painting of the Resurrection provides a welcome touch of panache after so much austerity. The Hall opposite is much plainer again, with a flat ceiling. It is in essence a refectory, and looks it. Verrio's huge painting of Charles II on horseback is an uninspired piece and does little to cheer things up.

Of the side ranges, of which each floor is divided into four immensely long wards which are in turn subdivided by thick oak panelling into cubicles, there is little to be said. The only small room capable of giving real pleasure is the Council Chamber at the southern end of the east block, a lovely oak-panelled room with an overmantel by William Emmett of which Gibbons himself would not have been ashamed. Formerly part of the Governor's House, it strikes a note of exuberance delightfully unexpected in such ascetic surroundings.

## St Anne's, Limehouse

*33; Commercial Road, E14*

Hawksmoor seems to have conceived of St Anne's as a companion church to St George-in-the-East; they stand within a few hundred yards of each other and he worked on them concurrently between 1714 and 1730. Of the two, St Anne's is the more successful: the tower, thanks to the free-standing buttresses on the second stage, has a lightness not given to its neighbour, and there is an unusual little apsidal porch at the west end that is as charming as it is unexpected. Both churches suffered in the Blitz but St Anne's was restored according (more or less) to the original designs, a Greek cross within a rectangle, culminating in a huge rounded east window flanked by columns – a frame that deserves a better occupant than Clutterbuck's gaudy Crucifixion.

Though still an active parish church and showing nowhere near the decay and neglect of Christ Church, Spitalfields, St Anne's is also, as I write, desperately in need of restoration. That two of the country's finest eighteenth-century churches should ever have been allowed to fall into such a state is a national disgrace.

## St Augustine's, Kilburn

*34; Kilburn Park Road, NW6*

Here is another *tour de force* of Tractarianism, but as unlike All Saints, Margaret Street, as any two High Victorian churches can be. The time difference is a mere twenty years – St Augustine's was begun in 1871 and finished in 1880 – but whereas William Butterfield achieved his effects with colour and surface texture, John Loughborough Pearson put his faith in space itself. His church affords a quite extraordinary repertoire of distant vistas, not only on the horizontal plane but on the vertical too, thanks to his upper galleries, his double aisles and – always and everywhere – his supreme technical mastery of his art.

It is not immediately appealing on the outside; few churches of that date are. It has, however, the advantage of a clear open site which allows it to be seen from a reasonable distance: high walls of a rather forbidding dark red brick, punctuated by tall and slender lancets (the 'Middle Pointed' or Decorated style was no longer *de rigueur* and Pearson always preferred the thirteenth century) and topped by one of the loftiest spires in London – over 250 feet – whose grey-white stone makes an abrupt contrast with the sombreness below. This stone is also used for the corner pinnacles which cluster at its base, as well as for the high pyramidal caps to the turrets which flank both the east and west ends. Between these turrets to the east, the lancets are doubled so as to form two tiers of three, the upper tier stepped; to the west, a row of five small ones is surmounted by an immense rose window with radiating spokes, the whole composition recessed within a single embracing arch.

We enter through a porch under the tower at the north-west end, and immediately find ourselves in a building whose architectural arrangement is like no other in England. The nave is, properly speaking, of five bays, its principal arcades being comparatively low – so low indeed that the broad arches can scarcely afford a point to them. Behind these arches runs another row, forming an inner and outer aisle; and along the top of the inner one Pearson has set his remarkable gallery. It extends virtually all the way around the church, turning into a bridge where it crosses the transepts and the nave, passing over the latter by means of the stone chancel screen. At the division of each bay of the nave, a transverse wall rises to the aisle roof; these walls are in fact the principal load-bearing buttresses, which Pearson has put inside the church rather than outside it, on the famous model of Albi Cathedral. Each is pierced by a small archway, to allow the gallery uninterrupted passage. All roofs are vaulted – that of the nave in brick with stone ribs, those of the aisles in stone throughout. Those walls which are not painted are mostly of brick, with stone dressings.

Deliberately, Pearson has underplayed his basic cruciform plan. The bays continue without a break over the transepts (the gallery giving still further continuity) and onward into the chancel, while the transepts themselves extend only a yard or two beyond the outer aisles. The south transept is continued eastwards to form a small apsed chapel dedicated to St Michael, with a radiating vault; the corresponding position to the north is occupied by a square-ended Lady Chapel.

*St Augustine's, Kilburn.*

The decorative scheme has been conceived as a coherent whole. It begins with a representation of Genesis in the western rose window (like all the glass, by Clayton and Bell) and continuing, in window and wall painting alike, to the Passion, Crucifixion and Resurrection in the chancel. Nowhere, however, is it over-insistent or aggressive; never is one subjected to the visual battering of All Saints, Margaret Street. Decoration here is simply an element, though an important one, in an overall concept in which everything has its own precisely calculated place. That is what makes St Augustine's one of the greatest of all nineteenth-century churches, and one of the greatest parish churches, of any date, in the country.

## St Bartholomew's Hospital

*35; West Smithfield, EC1*

A few yards south-west of the church of St Bartholomew the Great (*q.v.*) stands St Bartholomew's Hospital, founded in 1123, like the church, by Rahere (a worldly courtier of Henry I who underwent a religious crisis and became a prebendary of St Paul's), and the oldest hospital in London still on its original site. The kernel of the present building dates from 1730–59, and is the work of James Gibbs. It is built around three sides of a court like a Cambridge college of the date. (It was a pity that the fourth side had to be closed in by what is known as the George V Building in the 1930s.) Of the three ranges, the principal one is that to the north-west. Here a most opulent staircase of brown and gold, adorned with two huge religious paintings by Hogarth, leads up to an imposing Hall of eight bays, lavishly panelled and with a deeply coffered ceiling. Also within the hospital is the little CHURCH OF ST BARTHOLOMEW THE LESS; tower and vestry are both fifteenth-century, but the rest was built on a pretty octagonal plan by Thomas Hardwick in 1823, and later somewhat altered by his son Philip. (They were actually basing themselves on an earlier octagonal plan by George Dance, who did much the same sort of thing at Micheldever in Hampshire (*q.v.*).)

## St Bartholomew the Great

*36; West Smithfield, EC1*

With the single exception of St John's Chapel in the Tower of London (*q.v.*), the church of St Bartholomew the Great in West Smithfield is the oldest religious building in London. It was founded in 1123 by Rahere (see above), who originally intended it as an Augustinian priory, and the present building consists of the chancel, crossing and transepts of that priory church – the nave having been almost completely demolished shortly after the Dissolution. The only part of it still remaining is the thirteenth-century south entrance, now built into the timber-framed gateway to the churchyard; from this, a pathway leads to the present porch, added by Sir Aston Webb in 1893. Behind it is a brick tower which dates from 1628; to the right, the entrance to the heavily restored cloister.

None of this is particularly impressive; St Bartholomew's delays its impact until you are safely inside. Here is a very different story. Two parallel rows of massive circular piers with many-scalloped capitals march away eastward down the long chancel, then curve in on each other to form a rounded apse. As they do so, the individual piers huddle more closely together, with the result that the arches above them, which began semi-circular, now become elongated and narrower in order to maintain their former height. This same phenomenon, which produces an oddly Byzantine effect, occurs at the level of the gallery above; here, however, the apse arches – which are sub-divided into two – are nearly all of the nineteenth century. To the sides, the gallery consists of four arched openings per bay within a single huge semi-circular relieving arch. Above this is a Perpendicular clerestory of the late fourteenth century which comes as something of an anti-climax. Later still – early sixteenth-century, in fact – is the delightful little oriel at gallery level on the south side, the work of the Prior of the time who wanted a small oratory directly accessible from his lodgings.

*St Bartholomew the Great, West Smithfield.*

Originally, the apse had three radiating chapels in the French manner; all three, however, have disappeared, except for the lower wall of the southernmost. In their place is a Lady Chapel of *c.*1330, but this too bears the heavy imprint of Sir Aston Webb, as do the transepts. Yet we must not be too hard on Sir Aston; on the whole he seems to have done a conscientious and competent job, and the preservation of one of the loveliest buildings in London is largely due to him.

There is a fine, if retrospective, monument to Rahere just to the north of the sanctuary. Dating from about 1500, it consists of a tomb chest under a canopy; at the foot of the effigy, two little kneeling monks carry books inscribed with verses from Isaiah. The church's other, more recent, historical association is with Benjamin Franklin, who in 1725 worked in the Lady Chapel, then being used as a printing office.

## St Benet, Paul's Wharf

*37; Upper Thames Street, EC4*

This church always provides a moment of pleasure as one passes it, driving along Queen Victoria Street. There has been a church on the site since 1111 or earlier, but the present building is by Wren and dates from 1677–83. It is chequered in red and blue brick, and stands small and square and Dutch-looking under its hipped tile roof, its well-spaced stone quoins giving a jolly, stripy effect at the corners. The three tall round-headed windows to north and south have stone garlands above them – another playful touch – while the tower, set far back at the north-west corner, carries above its square base first a lead dome with roundels between the ribs, and then a lantern topped with a short lead spire.

The interior is wonderfully unspoilt. The north and west galleries remain, bowls of fruit lusciously carved on their fronts. The north aisle – there is no south one – is separated from the nave, and the north gallery supported, by tall Corinthian columns standing on high panelled bases. The furniture (apart from a rather heavy Victorian organ case in the north-east corner) is all just as it should be – especially the reredos with its Decalogue, Creed and Lord's Prayer all grouped beneath a high segmental pediment with four big urns on top. Best of all, to me, are the tremendous Royal Arms of Charles II over the doorcase beneath the tower.

The church is now used by Welsh-speaking members of the Church in Wales.

## St Botolph, Aldersgate

*38; London EC1*

There are three surviving London churches dedicated to the same fairly obscure Saxon abbot, of which this – rebuilt by Nathaniel Wright in 1788–91 – is certainly the finest. As so often in the City, the exterior is unpromising, just red brick with arched windows and a not very successful classicising east end of 1831 with a Venetian window between coupled Ionic columns. (Clocks within pediments are always a bad idea.) The best feature is the eighteenth-century west tower with its pretty wooden turret surmounted by a gilded weathervane. The inside, by contrast, is a real treat, obviously inspired by – if not actually modelled on – All Hallows, London Wall (*q.v.*). There are coffered apses at each end and deep galleries to north and south supported on square, panelled piers which at gallery level turn into Corinthian columns with gilded capitals. There is also a west gallery curving elegantly forward to contain an organ case of 1788. The columns support a deep entablature, above which the big semi-circular windows familiar from All Hallows cut into the barrel-vaulted roof. This is of a lovely pale Wedgwood blue and has exuberant stucco decoration.

In the centre of the eastern apse is an eighteenth-century transparency – the only one in the City – of the Agony in the Garden, framed by gathered-back curtains in purple plaster. It is by James Pearson, and dates from 1788. The modern glass in the other windows is a disgrace. Plain glass is always better in a Georgian church. But this is one of the few serious blemishes to a really lovely eighteenth-century interior.

## St Bride's, Fleet Street

*39; London EC4*

First of all, of course, one thinks of St Bride's celebrated steeple; whether one compares it to a carillon of bells or, more prosaically, to a wedding cake, it remains the best known – and incidentally, at 226 feet, the highest – of all the Wren steeples. It was added as something of an afterthought, in 1701–3; the church itself was one of the first Wren tackled after the Great Fire, and dates from between 1670 and 1675. As steeples go, it is not the subtlest of his designs, being basically just a series of four diminishing octagons surmounted by a spire; but there are plenty of indications, to anyone examining it carefully, that it was anything but a rough job. Take, for example, the interplay of column and pilaster on the pedimented lower stage; the placing of the urns above them; or the fact that the openings in the topmost octagon are square-headed, while all the rest are arched. Moreover, despite its apparent airiness, it is a remarkably strong and stable structure: it survived the Blitz, while the rest of the church was completely gutted.

It follows that the whole interior is a post-war reconstruction. That reconstruction has, however, been so beautifully carried out that I have no hesitation in including St Bride's in this book. The architect concerned, Godfrey Allen, has remained faithful to Wren where the structure is concerned: here are the coupled Tuscan columns with their outsize entablatures, supporting the arcades; here the tunnel vault, with penetrations for the circular windows of the clerestory; here the cross-vaulted aisles, now however somewhat obscured by the wooden stalls. For it is in the furnishings that the present interior differs from that of half a century ago. The seats have been arranged in collegiate fashion, facing inwards, and a new, distinctly Wrennish reredos featuring a broken segmental pediment (in which a large vesica of stained glass has been rather ill-advisedly inserted) dominates from the east end. Fortunately, all the remaining glass is clear.

## St Clement Danes

*40; Strand, WC2*

Apart from St Paul's itself, St Clement Danes is Wren's only apsed church; it is also the only one he reconstructed outside the City of London. (St James's, Piccadilly, was a brand-new building on which he started from scratch.) The reason why the old church was replaced was nothing to do with the Great Fire, which never spread so far to the west; rather was it the fact that by 1679 the structure was declared unsafe. Wren kept the tower, refacing it in Portland stone, but for the body of the church he produced a completely new design, the realisation of which he entrusted to the greatest of all his masons, Edward Pearce. The work as he intended it was finished in 1687, and the parishioners were so pleased with the result that they sent him one third of a hogshead of wine; but the building as we see it today was not completed till 1719, when the tower and steeple above the clock stage were added by James Gibbs. This must have made all the difference, for the tower in Wren's day was a sadly undistinguished affair; even the body of the church was unusually plain, with five identical bays and a small colonnaded porch on the south side.

St Clement Danes was gutted by bombs in 1941; the interior is consequently new, although the architect in charge of the restoration, W.A.S. Lloyd, has remained as faithful as possible to Wren's designs. From deep wooden galleries on three sides, white Corinthian columns rise up to carry a magnificent tunnel-vaulted roof, richly stuccoed and displaying a tremendous representation of the Royal Arms above the sanctuary. The bays above the galleries are all cross-vaulted. A small ambulatory runs around the apse, behind the altar.

In 1942 an ancient crypt was discovered below the east end. It has now been converted into a chapel, and is by far the most atmospheric part of the church, which is now the official place of worship for the Royal Air Force.

## St George-in-the-East

*41; Cannon Street Road, E1*

Hawksmoor's three great Stepney churches – Christ Church, Spitalfields, St Anne's, Limehouse and St George-in-the-East – were all begun in 1714. The other two remain, dilapidation apart, more or less as he intended them; but St George-in-the-East was gutted by incendiary bombs in May 1941 and its interior has been entirely remodelled. Only the outside, with its west tower that seems to explode upwards through a broken pediment, its heavily buttressed octagonal lantern and its four pepper-pot turrets, survives as Hawksmoor's work. Particularly when seen from the south-west, it still possesses all its monumental grandeur, towering like a great grey ship over the drab and depressing buildings all around.

*St George-in-the-East, Stepney.*

## St George's, Bloomsbury

*42; Bloomsbury Way, WC1*

The most extraordinary feature of St George's – the only one of Hawksmoor's six London churches to be built west of the City – is its steeple. Hawksmoor had a passion for classical antiquity, and here he took his example from one of the Seven Wonders of the Ancient World, the Mausoleum of Halicarnassus, improbably topping it with a statue of George I. The main portico, on the other hand, with its six giant Corinthian columns on a high podium, probably derives from Baalbek. Its massive assurance gives little hint of the difficulties the architect had to face. His main problem was that the narrow site had a pronounced north–south axis, so much so that Vanbrugh had actually submitted a design with the altar at the north end; but Hawksmoor insisted on liturgical correctness, with the result that the parishioners found themselves entering under a side gallery – an arrangement which, while perfectly acceptable in Gothic churches, seemed most reprehensible in the classical idiom. By 1781 they could bear it no longer, and moved the altar to the north where it is today – leaving, however, the lovely plasterwork by Isaac Mansfield in the eastern apse.

The general impact of the interior, with more Corinthian columns – this time arranged in pairs – supporting Hawksmoor's favourite depressed arches, is distinctly dramatic; and we can only feel grateful that when G.E. Street was called in to reorganise it in the 1840s he resisted all temptations to Gothicise. The old box pews were the principal casualty then; but several of the other original fittings remain, including the pedimented reredos and the pulpit. This latter used to be mounted on a slender central stalk and, we are told, would sway backwards and forwards 'like an enormous tulip' when the preacher ascended the fourteen steps to reach it or, presumably, if he accompanied his sermon with too much extravagance of gesture. The present more secure attachment must surely be regretted.

## St George's, Hanover Square

*43; St George Street, W1*

This church is the work of John James, who had been Assistant Surveyor to Wren at St Paul's. With Gibbs's St Martin-in-the-Fields and Hawksmoor's St George's, Bloomsbury (*qq.v.*), it was the first church to be built in London with a pedimented portico of free-standing giant columns; the date of the design is 1720 and the building was finished four years later. At one time it was intended to place a life-size statue of George I above the pediment – an idea that was fortunately not pursued. On the north side, facing Maddox Street, the giant order of the front is reflected by the heavy bands of rustication which embrace both tiers of windows, making of them a single composition. The west bay is differentiated from the rest by a separate set of quoins and a shallow pediment above, emphasising that it is here, and not with the portico, that the body of the church really begins. In the centre and immediately behind the portico rises a tower which features pairs of colonnettes projecting diagonally, a motif which the architect presumably

St Georges's, Hanover Square.

borrowed from St James's, Garlickhythe (*q.v.*). It is topped by a rather silly-looking little dome and weather-vane.

The interior is another borrowing from Wren – this time from St James's, Piccadilly (*q.v.*). Here is the same gallery on three sides, the same square piers supporting it, the same Corinthian columns rising from it to support a similar – though admittedly rather more depressed – barrel-vaulted roof. As at St James's, too, we have a Venetian window at the east end – even if here it is treated somewhat differently, with coupled supports and at one level only.

The dark painting on the reredos has been attributed to Kent, but also to his arch-enemy Sir James Thornhill. For the rest, St George's is principally interesting for its historical associations. Handel worshipped here for thirty-four years, and here Emma Hamilton, Shelley, Disraeli and George Eliot were all successively married.

## St James's, Garlickhythe

*44; Garlick Hill, EC4*

The steeple of this church is one of Wren's loveliest – a variant on that of St Stephen Walbrook and St Michael Paternoster Royal next door. It was added to the tower in 1714–17, some thirty years after the completion of the rest of the church, and consists essentially of three square stages with projections at the diagonals. On the bottom stage, immediately above the pierced parapet with its corner urns, these projections take the form of coupled Ionic columns; on the second, of scrolly volutes. On the third, they are almost invisible from below but are marked by tall corner pinnacles. At the very top is an infinitesimal dome, crowned by a weathervane.

The interior is a restoration (by James Lockhart-Smith) after much war damage – which would have been a great deal worse than it was if the 500-pound bomb dropped in 1940 had not fortunately failed to explode. The structure, however, remains completely Wren's: unusually high (it is in fact the highest of all his interiors) with Ionic columns dividing the nave from the aisles and widening out in the middle – their entablature returning to the outer walls – to suggest transepts, though there is no real crossing and the outer plan remains rectangular. Round-headed clerestory windows form penetrations in the high coving of the roof. Surprisingly for Wren, the chancel is considerably narrower than the nave; it is barrel-vaulted.

St James's is quite exceptionally rich in fine ironwork and woodwork, much of the latter having been brought from St Michael's, Queenhythe, after its demolition in 1875. This is true of the quite spectacular pulpit and tester and of the back screens behind the stalls. When I first saw this church it was little more than an empty shell; it is now once again a work of art and reflects immense credit on all who have been concerned.

## St James's Palace

*45; London SW1*

Though it stands at the foot of the hill which is St James's Street, St James's Palace dominates the street as surely as if it stood at its top – a great, four-square Gatehouse of red brick with blue diapering, framed by high polygonal turrets and presenting to the world the most impressive Tudor façade in central London. It was built by Henry VIII on the site of an old hospital for leper girls, and after the fire at Whitehall in January 1698 became the principal residence of the Sovereign, remaining so until George III moved to Buckingham Palace in the 1760s.

Though this principal front to the north is essentially unchanged, there is little else about the Palace that King Henry would recognise today. It too has had its share of fire – one in 1809 destroyed most of Friary Court – and there have been innumerable rebuildings and alterations. Some of these, however, by such people as Sir Christopher Wren and William Kent, have been ambitious works in their own right and have added to the architectural interest of the place. This is certainly true of Wren's state rooms on Engine Court, facing south across the Park. Of the earlier rooms, the most important is the Chapel Royal, T-shaped, for all the world like an Oxford college. Most of its decoration – the wood panelling, the stalls and box pews running east–west, the pretty draped west gallery with its four-centred arches – dates from about 1836, when much of the Palace was remodelled by William IV; the ceiling, however, panelled in crosses and octagons, is original and bears the date 1540. It has been attributed to Holbein, though not very convincingly.

More surprising are the Armoury and Tapestry Room, not so much for their contents – though these are not without interest – as for their decoration, which is by William Morris and dates from as early as 1866–7. They have also preserved their original fireplaces. From them a staircase goes up to the state rooms, several of which have decoration by Kent. In one of them, the Throne Room, there are some wood carvings by Grinling Gibbons as fine as anything he ever did.

Originally part of the Palace, though since 1809 separated from it by Marlborough Gate, stands the QUEEN'S CHAPEL. The indisputable work of Inigo Jones, it is the first place of worship built in England on purely classical lines, with no suggestion of Gothic anywhere. It was begun in 1623, finished four years later and was, somewhat surprisingly, Roman Catholic from the beginning, being served by a Capuchin friary installed in the Palace which gave its name to Friary Court. The exterior is restrained towards the west – though its east end boasts the first Venetian window in England – but the inside is of stern and solemn beauty. The roof is an elliptical tunnel vault, deeply coffered and painted in white and gold. Below it, the furnishings are almost all of 1662–80: they include a beautiful eastern gallery – which is answered by another, royal, gallery in the west where the large chimneypiece dates from Jones's day – an organ gallery to the south and some fine stalls. The Chapel is open only for services – a pity, for it deserves to be better known.

## St James's, Piccadilly

*46; London W1*

'I think', wrote Sir Christopher Wren of his new church in Jermyn Street, 'it may be found beautiful and convenient.' And so it has been, ever since. It was the only one of his London churches to be built on a completely new site, necessitated by the recent development of the area formerly known as St James's Fields by Wren's friend Henry Jermyn, Earl of St Albans. The church was begun in 1676 and completed eight years later. In those days Piccadilly itself did not exist and the church had one major entrance only, to the south, through an elaborate Ionic porch which was unfortunately removed in 1856. For the rest, it looks much as it did in Wren's day, except for the spire. He had originally intended a small domed steeple, but what eventually went up was a spire designed by one of his carpenters, Edward Wilcox. This was destroyed, together with much of the interior of the church, during an air raid on 14 October 1940. The present spire is the work of Sir Albert Richardson, who was responsible for the post-war restoration.

The outside of the church, which was spared by the bombs, is relatively modest: it is of brick, with dressings of Portland stone. Both north and south sides have two tiers of windows, round-headed above, only faintly arched below, while to the east there is a large Venetian window placed high up and another, of exactly the same dimensions but without the arch, immediately underneath it. On the north side, facing the pretty little courtyard garden, is an open-air pulpit. It was installed as recently as 1902 – when the volume of traffic noise was, however, still low enough to make outdoor services a possibility. It certainly would not be today.

As always with Wren's churches, the interior is a good deal more magnificent. Spacious and airy, it has north and south aisles with galleries above supported on oak-panelled piers. These curve round at the west end as in a theatre; from them rise Corinthian columns carrying high entablatures and, above them, the tunnel-vaulted roof, which is penetrated by shorter tunnel vaults to the north and south windows. This main roof spans a full semi-circle. Well-defined transverse arches spring from the entablature of each column, the spaces between being coffered in delicate and restrained plasterwork. It becomes a little more elaborate over the window arches, where there are winged angels flanked by garlands.

All this is of course restoration, but of the finest possible kind and faithfully reproducing Wren's designs for the original. Fortunately some of the furniture escaped destruction. Thus we still have the reredos and font, both by Grinling Gibbons, who also

*St James's, Piccadilly.*

worked on the organ case. The font, in which William Pitt the Elder and William Blake were both baptised, is a particularly remarkable – and surprising — piece, representing as it does the Tree of Knowledge, with Adam and Eve and the Serpent below. There is only one blemish – the glass of 1954 in the east window. It is actually quite good, but it does not belong here.

## St John's, Clerkenwell

*47; St John's Square, EC1*

The Order of the Knights Hospitallers of St John of Jerusalem built their church at Clerkenwell in the twelfth century, and had it consecrated by Heraclius, Patriarch of Jerusalem, in 1185. (On the same visit he performed a similar service for the Hospitallers' chief rivals, the Templars, at their church of the Temple (*q.v.*).) But when the Order was suppressed in 1540 their priory – having, unlike the Temple, no lawyers to protect it – fell on evil days. For the next four centuries the buildings, including the church, went through one metamorphosis after another; and although what was left of them was transferred at various dates after 1831 to the Most Venerable Order of the Hospital of St John of Jerusalem – a Protestant Order established in that year to maintain the traditions of the medieval Hospitallers – their luck did not change: the church was badly bombed in 1941.

It was restored after the war by Lord Mottistone, and very splendid it now looks; architecturally, however, the great interest is the crypt – for here, having miraculously escaped all the vicissitudes of the intervening centuries, is the chancel of the twelfth-century church. Five bays survive, the three western ones being Norman work of 1140 or so, the two eastern ones – aisled, with flanking chapels – of perhaps 1180. The whole thing is rib-vaulted. One's only regret is that the nave – which was probably circular, like that of the Temple – has been lost. This crypt, incidentally, possesses one outstandingly beautiful tomb, a late sixteenth-century effigy of a Spanish Knight of the Order, his page sleeping by his side. In all England there is no funerary sculpture more moving than this.

The only other part of the medieval buildings still surviving is St John's Gate, actually the gatehouse of the old priory, dating from 1504. After the Dissolution it was for a time (in Queen Elizabeth's reign) occupied by the Master of the Revels, who was responsible for the censorship of plays. Some thirty of Shakespeare's were licensed here, and he himself must countless times have trod the steps to the first floor.

## St John's, Smith Square

*48; London SW1*

'A very hideous church with four towers at the corners, generally resembling some petrified monster, frightful and gigantic, on its back with its legs in the air.' Such was Charles Dickens's description of the great church built by Thomas Archer between 1714 and 1728. Nowadays we tend to judge it less harshly; there is, after all, no prouder example of English Baroque in the Roman manner – in other words the Baroque of Borromini rather than that of Wren – in all London. Its most memorable feature, inevitably, is that quartet of corner towers, which have earned it the nickname of 'Queen Anne's Footstool'; they are not altogether as Archer designed them, but they remain single-stage versions of Borromini's church of Sant' Agnese in the Piazza Navona, Rome, on which they were obviously modelled. Essentially, the plan is that of a Greek cross with small rusticated quadrants at the re-entrant angles; the entrances are to north and south, beneath great Tuscan porticoes whose pediments are broken with smaller ones inserted into the recesses. They have lobbies inside which occupy the transepts, so that the interior becomes a long rectangular hall. The east and west ends, by contrast, contain gigantic Venetian windows divided by pilasters; higher up, above a triglyph frieze, is an attic consisting of another Venetian window – blank this time – crowned by a triangular pediment.

*St John's, Smith Square.*

Badly damaged by wartime bombing, St John's remained for a long time a ruin before being converted into a concert hall by Marshall Sisson in the 1960s. The loss was less great than it might have been, however, since the building had already been gutted by fire as early as 1742 and James Horne, who restored it, removed the twelve giant Corinthian columns that had been an important element in Archer's original interior.

## St Katherine Cree

*49; Leadenhall Street, EC3*

The curious word 'Cree' is a corruption of 'Christ' and is here an abbreviation of 'Christchurch', the name sometimes given to the priory of Holy Trinity within Aldgate, in whose cemetery the church was built. It is an unusual building in many respects, above all for its date, 1628–31. Churches of this period are rare indeed in England. St Katherine's was under the patronage of Archbishop Laud, and was actually consecrated by him in January 1631. Miraculously, it escaped the bombs and has come down to us remarkably little changed in its essentials – although the boxing-in of the aisles to make offices and the almost constant noise of typewriters detracts somewhat from the atmosphere.

The oldest part of the church still standing is the south-west tower of 1504. It has odd little windows that look more Saxon than anything else, and a circular cupola that was added in 1776. The body of the building has straight-headed three-light windows at aisle and clerestory levels, the centre lights very slightly higher than the others; to the west is a single large window with pediment; to the east, a rose like a Catherine wheel inscribed in a square, above five blocked lights.

*St Katherine Cree, Leadenhall Street.*

So much for the exterior. Inside, the arcade columns – which have fortunately been left free-standing – are tall and slender and support the semi-circular arches directly on their Composite capitals, with no intervening entablature. The arches themselves have coffering in their soffits. All this is classical enough, as are the rather unexpected pilasters between the clerestory windows; it accords oddly with the Gothicism of the east end and that of the windows themselves, to say nothing of the lierne rib vaulting of the nave and aisles. The liernes of the nave surround immense carved and painted bosses bearing the arms of city livery companies.

The Father Schmidt organ case of 1686 is quite exquisitely carved, as are the capitals of the fluted oak columns that support it, attributed to Grinling Gibbons.

## St Lawrence Jewry

*50; Gresham Street, EC2*

The Guild Church of the Corporation of London, and situated next to the Guildhall in that part of the City which was occupied by the London Jews until their expulsion by Edward I in 1290, St Lawrence Jewry in its present form was built by Sir Christopher Wren between 1670 and 1687. Unusually for City churches – which tended to be hemmed in by existing buildings – its exposed position obliged Wren to give it two show fronts: to the south, five tall round-headed windows flanked by two elaborately framed doors with big circular windows above them, and to the east a quite spectacular composition of four attached Corinthian columns carrying a pediment, pilasters at the corners and three arched niches, with two of the same round-headed windows alternating in between. The west tower has tall obelisk pinnacles; the steeple above it – which is set at a different angle, facing Gresham Street – carries quite a simple polygonal spire, with St Lawrence's grid-iron on top as a weathervane.

The church was gutted during the Blitz; it has been lavishly restored as befits its high municipal purpose – though, alas, the exquisite carved and panelled vestry with its superb plaster ceiling painted by Thornhill, generally considered one of the most beautiful small rooms in Europe, has been lost for ever – very much as Wren originally conceived it, with Corinthian pilasters supporting a high coved ceiling and much dark woodwork. And yet, for all its splendour, there is something chilly and lifeless about it; it has never been a real favourite of mine.

## St Lawrence Whitchurch

*51; Little Stanmore, Edgware*

The only survival remaining *in situ* of Canons, that most magnificent house and estate belonging to James Brydges, Duke of Chandos, which was sold off piecemeal in 1747, this little church would be famous if it stood in a country village instead of being hidden away in a London suburb. Turning off High Street, Edgware (the continuation of Edgware Road), to the left down Whitchurch Lane, you soon see on your right the short early sixteenth-century tower of cemented brick; it gives, however, little hint of the church attached to it, since this was completely rebuilt by Chandos between 1715 and 1720 as if it were his own private chapel. It immediately betrays its date with its high arched windows and massive Tuscan angle pilasters, but its splendid patron – Chandos had made his fortune as Paymaster General of Marlborough's armies – was clearly not much interested in the exterior; nor need you be. Go in, then, by the door in the south-west corner and – doing your best not to steal a glance at the nave immediately to your right – go straight through the door facing you and up the broad oak staircase, under some huge family hatchments, to the west gallery and the ducal pew. Apart from its fireplace in the back wall which has now been blocked up, it is still much as the Duke left it – the semi-circular apse behind painted with a copy of Raphael's *Transfiguration* by A. Bellucci – as are the two small flanking boxes, that for the servants on the right, for the bodyguard (since Chandos had many enemies) on the left.

From this box you have the best possible view of the interior of the church itself, an astonishingly theatrical setting; it has no aisles, but at the east end of the rather long, barrel-vaulted nave there is a sort of retrochoir behind the altar, framed by what would have been a classical carved wooden reredos, but which is open in the centre to reveal, between coupled Corinthian columns and beneath a broken segmental pediment, a small stage, a pretty little organ upon which Handel (who was the Duke's *maestro di cappella*) regularly played, and a backdrop of *trompe-l'oeil* statues, dramatically lit by an unseen window to the right.

This style of painting is continued over every square inch of walls and vault. In the chancel it is thought to be by Bellucci, in the retrochoir each side of the organ by Verrio, and in the nave – where Evangelists and Virtues line the walls and the Miracles of Christ occupy the vault – by Laguerre. All the original box pews are still in use (for this is an active parish church) and there is a pretty marble font, brought back by the Duke in 1716. The splendidly carved columns of the 'reredos' are said to be by Grinling Gibbons, though personally – excellent though they are – I have my doubts. The only thing that lets down the standard is the weak little carved wooden altar. It looks Victorian or later; surely it would be possible to find something a little more suitable?

St Lawrence's has a good claim to be the most thoroughly Baroque parish church in England, and is worth coming a long way to see. But you have not seen everything yet. Against the north side is the Chandos Mausoleum, also painted all over, with columns, statues and dome all in *trompe-l'oeil*. It is dominated by a vast marble monument to the Duke and his first two wives, the sculptor of which is unknown. It is certainly not by Gibbons, and Pevsner's attribution to Andrew Carpenter is equally unlikely since Carpenter quarrelled with Chandos early in his career and was sent packing.

At the time of writing the church is being immaculately cleaned and restored by a German firm. They are expected to have finished the work by 1985. Meanwhile it is normally open on Saturday and Sunday afternoons, with a guide who is happy to show one round.

## St Magnus the Martyr

*52; Lower Thames Street, EC3*

Rebuilt by Wren between 1671 and 1687 on the site of a church with similar dedication which had been there since at least the eleventh century, St Magnus the Martyr stood at the north end of old London Bridge – the first City church to greet travellers arriving from the south. It was a superb position, but a dangerously vulnerable one: the widening of the bridge in 1759–60 led to the removal of the western bays of the aisles and the building of a passageway beneath the tower; and worse was to befall when in 1832 the whole bridge was demolished and a new one built further to the west. The church stands now almost hidden between huge and hideous blocks, its immensely elegant west tower, with its tall octagon of Portland stone supporting a cupola and slender spire, utterly dwarfed by what lies behind them.

But St Magnus enjoyed one immense stroke of good fortune: it escaped the bombs. As a result, it possesses one of the richest and most unspoilt interiors in London. Admittedly, this has not survived altogether unchanged: as early as 1782 the windows along the north side were reduced to small round openings, apparently to reduce the noise of the traffic outside, and in 1924 there was a major 'restoration' in Neo-Baroque style by Martin Travers, giving the church the high Anglo-Catholic flavour that no visitor can fail to notice. Wren's, of course, are the tall, fluted Ionic colonnades and the barrel-vaulted roof penetrated by the oval clerestory windows; his, too, is the body of the great wooden reredos, in which the pelican, symbol of sacrifice, spreads its wings above the Decalogue, while Moses and Aaron stand full-length at each side. The rood above, however, and the side altars are Travers's work. There is also a simply splendid seventeenth-century pulpit on a slender wineglass stem with an enormous curly-edged tester. The only real misfortune is that somebody decided to put in modern stained glass. It is not too bad of its kind, nor is it particularly intrusive; one just wishes it wasn't there.

## St Margaret's, Westminster

*53; Parliament Square, SW1*

The little church in the shadow of Westminster Abbey has existed since the early twelfth century; the present building, however, is essentially that which was begun in 1486. We are lucky to have it: in 1549, Protector Somerset made an attempt to dismantle it to provide building materials for his new mansion beside the Thames, and was only dissuaded from doing so after the parishioners had rallied with staves and pikestaffs to its defence. In 1614 it became the parish church of the House of Commons, which it has been ever since.

In view of its special status and its unusually exposed position, it is hardly surprising that no one has ever left St Margaret's alone. In the 1730s the tower was rebuilt by John James; thirty years later an eastern apse was added on in Gothic Revival style, but was later removed. The porches are by Pearson and the interior was heavily restored in 1877 by Scott. And yet, in spite of everything, the basic structure remains: the eight bays which continue uninterrupted from one end to the other – there is no chancel arch – the three-light aisle windows, the five-lighters at the east and west ends, all this and much more still belongs to the old building in which John Milton and Samuel Pepys were both married and in which Caxton, Skelton and Sir Walter Raleigh all lie interred.

There is superb glass in the east window, made for the marriage of Henry VII's eldest son, Prince Arthur, to Catherine of Aragon. Before the ceremony could take place Arthur died and Catherine married his younger brother Henry; the glass was hurriedly removed to Waltham Abbey, but was installed in the church in 1758. The west window, in sharp contrast, is by Clayton and Bell; it includes representations of Queen Elizabeth, Raleigh, Milton and others connected with the church and is enjoyable rather than beautiful. The south aisle wdows by John Piper are lovely – or would be in their place. But their place is not here.

## St Martin-in-the-Fields

*54; Trafalgar Square, WC2*

Superlatively sited, St Martin-in-the-Fields looks out over Trafalgar Square from the north-east corner. Admiring it from across the Square, one tends to forget that this advantage dates only from the 1830s, and that at the time when James Gibbs designed and built what is probably the best known of all London's parish churches – between 1722 and 1726 – it faced only the 'vile houses' opposite it across St Martin's Lane. The opening up of the Square, however, did it no more than justice, for this is surely the most satisfying west front in London. Perhaps because it has been so widely copied, especially in America, I have myself never been able to understand the criticism that the placing of the tower in the centre of the west end, immediately behind the portico, looks awkward; to me it seems to sit happily enough. In any case the steeple, as everybody agrees, is superb. It stands on a square tower of two stages – the lower with a circular window on each side, the upper with a tall, round-headed bell opening and Gibbs surround – surmounted by a clock; above this is an octagonal lantern, its sides recessed, with attached columns at the angles; finally, above the entablature, comes the spire in the form of a concave-sided octagonal obelisk with four tiers of circular openings. Seen on a sunny summer afternoon, the Portland stone dazzling white against a blue sky, it can lift the spirit as thrillingly as any building in London.

Back at ground level – or, more accurately, at the top of a majestic flight of steps, for the ground slopes quite steeply downward towards the south – rise the eight giant Corinthian columns that carry the huge portico. (St Martin's was not quite the first church to be so adorned: Hawksmoor's St George's, Bloomsbury, and James's St

*St Martin-in-the-Fields, Trafalgar Square.*

George's, Hanover Square (*qq.v.*) beat it by a short head.) To north and south – and these sides should not be missed by any lover of architecture – the two tiers of five windows all have the heavy surrounds that were Gibbs's trademark, while the whole composition is firmly held together at the ends by recessed coupled columns between giant pilasters. The east front – it can hardly be called a façade – consists principally of a large Venetian window.

The interior is wonderfully joyful, thanks largely to the glorious plasterwork of that most celebrated pair of Italian stuccoists, Artari and Bagutti. The broad nave has no clerestory, and is spanned by a segmental tunnel vault supported on giant columns. The aisles are neither groin- nor tunnel-vaulted as one might expect, but have shallow saucer domes at intervals. The galleries, not content with occupying three sides of the church, curve round theatrically at the east end to embrace the narrow chancel, at the entrance to which royal boxes to each side command views of both chancel and nave.

St Martin's has kept its box pews – though they were lowered in 1858 – and a fine pulpit introduced, together with the choir stalls, in 1799. There is also a good William and Mary font – thus a little older than the church. Apart from these items there is not much furniture to detain you; but on your way out pause for a moment in the vestry hall to salute the bust of James Gibbs. London owes him much.

*St Martin within Ludgate.*

## St Martin within Ludgate

*55; Ludgate Hill, EC4*

The south front of the church has a quietly distinguished Portland stone façade, with the tower occupying the centre of three bays. Above them, scrolly volutes lead the eye up to the belfry with arched bell openings, above which again smaller volutes stand at the four corners of the ogee dome, with its charming little balcony and lead spire. The effect is distinctly Scandinavian: more like Copenhagen than London. Wren built it between 1677 and 1684.

Entering in the middle of the south side, you immediately find youself faced by a three-bay arcade with carved doorcases and a gallery above, a sort of narthex to the church which is at the same time, structurally speaking, a south aisle. Beyond this screen, the body of the church proves, a little surprisingly, to be cruciform – in that the chancel, nave and transepts (which are all of the same length) are barrel-vaulted, meeting to form a quadripartite groin vault at the crossing. The four corners have flat ceilings, and are marked off from the rest by heavy L-shaped entablatures carried on tall, slender Corinthian columns on high panelled bases.

Like St Magnus the Martyr, St Martin's escaped the bombs. Most of the furnishings are consequently original, though there is nothing really spectacular. The best pieces are the double chair for churchwardens just to the south of the reredos – the only known example of its kind – and the doorcases on the south side, the easternmost of which is attributed to Grinling Gibbons. The greyish green glass in the windows spreads a deep gloom and should be removed at once.

## St Mary Aldermary

*56; Queen Victoria Street, EC4*

Wren's most adventurous essay in the Gothic style was built in 1682 on the site of an earlier church whose tower still stands; it had been completed only half a century before, in 1629. With its chunky polygonal buttresses, shafted at the angles and panelled in between, it looks far more aggressively Gothic than any other tower in the City; this, surely, was why Wren decided for once to abandon his usual classical style and not because – according to a quite baseless legend – the benefactor who gave money for the rebuilding insisted that the new church should be a replica of the old.

The interior seems at first fairly typical late Perpendicular – as long as you keep your eyes down to arcade level. There is nothing unorthodox here among the tall four-shafted piers, the four-centred arches and the cusped three-light windows of the aisles. But the moment you lift your gaze roofwards the whole atmosphere changes. What you see is – or appears to be – fan vaulting, but fan vaulting of a kind that had never been seen before in an English church. The fans, which spring from clustered shafts between the clerestory windows, are of plaster rather than stone and do not meet along the central ridge as one might expect; instead, they extend only a third of the way across the nave, leaving space in the middle for huge central rosettes of intricate plasterwork, slightly recessed in the manner of saucer domes. The effect of these is not remotely Gothic, nor is it even Gothic Revival, which was not to begin for the best part of another century; rather is it a unique hybrid, the fruit perhaps of one of Wren's more playful moods, which captivates even if it does not altogether convince.

The church was tragically Victorianised in 1876 – the money coming, ironically, from the demolition and sale of the site of one of Wren's most original creations: St Antholin's, Budge Row, whose ground plan was that of an elongated octagon. Most of Wren's original furnishings were removed and replaced by safe Victorian substitutes. Only the roof gives pleasure now.

## St Mary at Hill

*57; Lovat Lane, EC3*

The old church on the site partially survived the Great Fire; the tower and side walls were consequently incorporated into the new one which Wren began in 1672 and completed five years later. The exterior is now of no particular interest, having been remodelled more than once; the interior, however, is a treat. It is Wren's first cross-in-square design, and is based on the Byzantine quincunx plan, in which a domed centre descends by means of pendentives to four free-standing columns – in this particular instance fluted and of the Corinthian order, rather freely interpreted. As at St Martin within Ludgate (*q.v.*), the four arms of the cross – corresponding to chancel, nave and transepts – are barrel-vaulted; the four corners have low, flat ceilings.

This interior is one of the proudest and most elegant in the City, and one of the least spoiled. Its real *pièce de résistance* is the west end, where a superb high gallery of carved wood, incorporating long glass windows with octagonal panes, carries a most magnificent organ, rising almost to the roof. To the east, a fine tripartite reredos, wonderfully carved and gilded, with a high arched centre beneath a broken segmental pediment, directs our attention to the Ten Commandments, the Lord's Prayer and the Creed. A tremendous pulpit, with tester to match, is approached not just by a few steps but by a gracefully curving staircase that would do credit to a small country house. The church also contains the only complete set of box pews in the City – a feature which adds enormously to the prevailing atmosphere.

So opulent is all this furnishing, so absolutely of the date, that one finds it almost impossible to believe that much of it – including the pulpit, lectern, and probably organ case – is actually the work of the early Victorian wood carver William Gibbs Rogers. If only more Victorian restoration had been like this!

## St Mary-le-Bow

*58; Cheapside, EC2*

The church is celebrated above all for its bells, the range of whose peal came in the late Middle Ages to define the limits of the City of London: 'to have been born within the sound of Bow Bells' is still the essential qualification for calling oneself a Cockney. Those bells were, however, silenced on the fateful night of 10 May 1941 when, in the worst of all the raids on the City, they crashed to the ground and were shattered, the church around them being left as a hollow shell.

The building that we see today is consequently an almost total reconstruction – though the bells that we hear were in fact recast from the metal of their predecessors. Apart from the outer walls, only one part of Wren's church escaped destruction; but that, by a merciful stroke of good fortune, was the most important feature of all – the steeple. Incredibly, it had remained in place while much of the belfry below had been consumed by the flames; and although it subsequently had to be dismantled while the tower was rebuilt, the exquisite construction that now tops St Mary-le-Bow is still that which Wren designed and built in 1678–80 – the proudest and most beautiful of all his steeples. Beginning immediately above the pilastered bell stage and set within a balustraded parapet with openwork voluted pinnacles at the corners, it rises first to a rotunda of twelve free-standing columns and thence, by means of curved flying buttresses, to a stage the plan of which is a cross superimposed on a slightly smaller square. This too has twelve columns, considerably shorter and more slender than those below. Finally comes a polygonal obelisk spire, with an outsize dragon, nearly 9 feet long, as a weathervane.

*St Mary-le-Bow, Cheapside.*

After this *tour de force*, the rest of the church can only be an anti-climax. Superbly rebuilt by Laurence King between 1956 and 1964, it faithfully follows Wren's original design, the main building standing a few yards to the south of the tower. The latter has a tremendous west doorway sunk back in a high rusticated niche, with a lunette above in which two little angels with garlands flank an oval window. To the right, after a one-storey link broader than the north aisle behind it, comes Wren's west front, brick with stone dressings, consisting of three bays with a big triangular pediment and long and short quoins. The central doorway has a segmental pediment on carved brackets, cutting into the sill of the tall round-headed west window above it. Two smaller but similar windows at a slightly lower level, one on each side, have circular windows above them. The east front follows a similar pattern, without the central door; to the south there is a projecting centre with another doorway and more tall arched windows.

Inside, the three-bay arcades are divided by piers with attached Corinthian half columns supporting a barrel-vaulted ceiling, into which the round-headed clerestory windows penetrate. None of the original furniture survives; as before, however, there are two pulpits, one on each side, making possible the lunchtime dialogues which have become one of the specialities of the church in recent years. Stained glass – alas.

## St Mary-le-Strand

*59; Strand, WC2*

Like St Clement Danes, St Mary's stands on an island site in the middle of the Strand. There has been a church on the site since at least the twelfth century – one of its first rectors being no less a personage than St Thomas à Becket – but it was demolished by Protector Somerset in 1549 to make room for his new mansion. It was replaced, very slightly to the north of the original location, only at the beginning of the eighteenth century by the first of the churches to be erected under the Fifty Churches Act of 1711; the architect selected was James Gibbs.

The church, consecrated on 1 January 1723, is one of the loveliest in London, a remarkable achievement considering that when he designed it Gibbs was only just thirty and that it was his first public building. He had recently returned from Rome where he had worked for several years in the studio of Carlo Fontana, and Roman Baroque influences are clearly discernible, though Gibbs was never to adopt them with the enthusiasm of his contemporary Thomas Archer. His west front begins delightfully with a semi-circular entrance porch, clearly inspired by the transept fronts of St Paul's; above it is a tall central arch, surmounted by a pediment on coupled columns. On both storeys there is a single flanking bay to each side. Immediately above the pediment the tower begins. From a plain, square base with a pedimented clock it rises through two stages which, though diminishing in size, are of essentially the same pattern of a central arch flanked by pilasters and, outside them, by free-standing columns; finally comes a slender top stage, still square but with concave sides, with a tiny lantern and weathervane to finish it off. The north and south fronts are both of seven bays, the windows separated by two orders of columns – Ionic below, Corinthian above. The lower ones (which are blank) have alternating pediments, a motif repeated at the level of the top balustrade, but over the even-numbered bays only. The east end, like that of St Paul's, is apsed, with long garlands of vine leaves hanging down each side of the central window.

Inside, one is immediately conscious of the narrowness of the site at Gibbs's disposal. There are no aisles, no side galleries – just a west balcony carried by columns in pairs. The walls are panelled, with pilasters above. The greatest surprise proves to be the ceiling, which is coffered in a curious design of squares and lozenges – inspired, apparently, by Fontana's church of SS. Apostoli in Rome. The apse is as delightful inside as it is out, framed by coupled columns in two orders and endearingly decorated with *putti* and clouds. Only the blue windows spoil the effect. The splendid pulpit originally hung from the wall; its short, stubby foot is a later addition. The lovely carved decoration may well be by Grinling Gibbons, including as it does his well-known signature of an open peapod.

## St Mary's on Paddington Green

*60; London W2*

In the first church to be built on this site John Donne preached his first sermon; in the second William Hogarth was married. The present building is the third. It was built by John Plaw, a somewhat obscure architect whose only church it is, between 1788 and 1791 – a square church of yellow brick, designed on the Greek cross plan, with a square centre, short projections at the centre of each side, a hipped roof and a pretty white cupola. It gives itself no airs; even the main entrance façade on the south side (though one now enters more normally from the west) has only a plain, brick-filled pediment carried on Tuscan columns and angle pilasters.

Why, you may ask, does it find a place in this book? Because in recent years it has enjoyed a rare piece of good fortune. The construction in the early 1960s of the Edgware Road flyover, while utterly destroying its peace and seclusion, involved the compulsory acquisition of a small parcel of church land immediately to the south; and with the very considerable sum which was paid in compensation it was possible to commission a full restoration by the best of all architects then working in that particular field, Raymond Erith. The result is a triumphant work of art. The church already possessed an interior of unusual architectural elegance, with its deep three-sided gallery, shallow dome on graceful pendentives and segmental barrel vaults in the arms of the cross. To this Erith has added a decorative elegance to match – with a marble floor, a carefully considered colour scheme and subtly restrained gilding. The result is one of the most exquisite late eighteenth-century interiors in London.

In the churchyard – and even closer to the flyover – is a seated statue of Mrs Siddons by Chavalliaud, based on Reynolds's painting of her as *The Tragic Muse*. On a wall of the gallery inside is a memorial plaque to 'a Child of Exiguous Beauty of Form and . . . a Precocity of Intellect of a Character probably Unparallelled' – who died in 1817 aged nine months.

St Pancras Station and Hotel.

## St Mary Woolnoth

*61; Lombard Street and King William Street, EC4*

This, the smallest and most compact of Hawksmoor's churches, presents a curiously idiosyncratic face to the world: the base heavily rusticated (including even the flanking Tuscan columns), the upper stage composed of two square towers which have somehow joined themselves together, like Siamese twins. On the north outside wall the rustication continues in an adventurous motif of deep niches, each containing two diagonally set columns with concave entablatures – as Baroque an invention as can be found anywhere in the country. The south side is much plainer, since before the building of King William Street in the last century it was almost invisible. Within, all is brilliant, the daylight pouring down through four huge semi-circular fanlights into the central square, and that familiar depressed arch framing a splendid Decalogue flanked by barley-sugar columns, very un-Mosaic. Not much spirituality here perhaps, any more than at St George's, Bloomsbury; but architectually St Mary's packs an undoubted punch.

## St Pancras Station and Hotel

*62; Euston Road, NW1*

It was not till the mid-1860s that the Midland Railway acquired a terminal in London. Having finally done so, however, its Board of Governors determined to celebrate the event in suitable style – with a building or buildings that could not be ignored. The work was begun by William Barlow, an engineer who had advised Paxton on the Crystal Palace and who by 1865 was planning a gigantic railway shed with a four-centred tunnel vault of glass and iron 690 feet long and spanning no less than 243 feet – at that time the broadest span anywhere in the world. Adjoining this, the Governors proposed a vast and luxurious hotel – the competition for which was won by Sir George Gilbert Scott.

Nearly ten years before, Scott had submitted designs for a new Foreign Office, to be built in the Gothic style. Although he got the job, the designs themselves were rejected, Lord Palmerston insisting that the new building should be classical in its inspiration; ever since, the belief has been widely held that the original Foreign Office designs were used for St Pancras. The story is in fact untrue; on the other hand, there can be no doubt that with the commission for St Pancras all Scott's pent-up frustration, all his guilt at his betrayal of the Gothic cause in Whitehall, all his ideas for the great secular Gothic building of his dreams were suddenly given free release. And this, the most wholly enjoyable of all his works, is the result.

The building gains much from its curiously shaped site – a long, narrow triangle – and from the fact that the trains, which have had to cross over the Regent's Canal, arrive in the station some 20 feet above ground level. This enabled Scott to lead the traffic dramatically up a curving ramp to either of the two huge portals which give access to the platforms. These portals rise up through the first floor of the building, the first-floor corridors running through the top of their arches on pretty little cast-iron bridges. There are two more principal floors above these – the fenestration becoming slightly less elaborate as the rooms get higher and cheaper – until we come to the parapet and then the steeply pitched roof with its two rows of dormers, separated at intervals by tall projecting crow-step gables.

And then comes the skyline, another marvellous Gothic extravaganza, seen at its best advantage from the rising ground up Pentonville Road to the east – especially against a red autumn sunset. There are two tall towers, a higher one for a clock at the eastern end and a lower, turreted one which conceals a water tank, and another forest of pinnacles over the entrance at the south-west corner. Everywhere the materials are of the very best: stone from Ketton and Ancaster, red and grey granite from Peterhead, slate from Leicestershire and Gripper's patent bricks from Nottingham – whenever possible, places served by the Midland Railway. The detailing too is superb, wherever you look. (Do not, I beg you, miss the capitals of the booking office columns.)

The tragedy of St Pancras is that it is no longer a hotel but a collection of featureless offices. The only major element of Scott's that has been left as it was is the magnificent Grand Staircase, rising the whole height of the building in graceful imperial swirls of cast-iron treads, stone rib vaulting and painted and stencilled walls. It was supplemented, for the aged and infirm, by several 'ascending rooms' – among the first lifts to appear anywhere in the world, hydraulically operated. In all England there is no more triumphant affirmation of the power, vitality, self-confidence and sheer panache of the Victorian age.

## St Pancras, Upper Woburn Place

*63; London WC1*

By the beginning of the nineteenth century the population of the Borough of St Pancras had increased to the point where the old parish church in Pancras Road could no longer cope with the number of worshippers. A new church was accordingly authorised in 1816; and two years later a design was accepted. It was the work of a surveyor (and steward to Lord Colchester) by the name of William Inwood, and of his son Henry William. William does not seem, as an architect, to have been particularly inspiring; Henry William, on the other hand, was a precocious boy who at the age of fifteen was already exhibiting at the Royal Academy. He was still only twenty-four when he and his father submitted their drawings for the church – after which he departed at once for Greece, to study its antiquities (with which he must already have been thoroughly familiar from books) at first hand.

St Pancras new church was the most expensive to be erected in London since St Paul's Cathedral. It reveals Henry William's knowledge and enthusiasm in every stone and stands today as one of London's most astonishing monuments of the Greek Revival. (How the Gothic Revivalists must have loathed it!) The Inwoods have, quite simply, translated St Martin-in-the-Fields into Greek. They took their hexastyle portico of fluted Ionic columns from the Erechtheum – about which, in 1827, Henry William was to publish a book – and their tower, essentially composed of two similar octagonal stages of diminishing size, both with detached columns, from the Tower of the Winds. The most surprising touch of all, however, is to be enjoyed at the eastern end of the building, where they added, as two almost separate wings, two duplicate copies of the Porch of the Caryatids on the Erechtheum. (The statues themselves are of terracotta, modelled around stanchions of cast iron by Charles Rossi; it was unfortunate that he made them a

*St Pancras, Upper Woburn Place.*

little too tall, so that slices had to be removed from their middles before they could be made to fit.) Between these wings, the eastern end of the church is apsed, with Ionic half columns.

The interior consists of an aisleless hall, with galleries to north, south and west carried on columns with lotus-leaf capitals copied from the Elgin Marbles. The whole is covered by a flat, coffered ceiling, unsupported. Originally the church was designed without a chancel; in 1889, however, the floor was raised at the east end, and screen and stalls inserted – the screen being a most extravagant affair of Ionic (but now unfluted) columns in scagliola. The Inwoods' Greek simplicity has been lost, but the dramatic gain is undeniable.

## St Paul's Cathedral

*64; London EC4*

On 2 September 1666 the Great Fire started in Pudding Lane. Three days later the city was a charred and empty shell. John Evelyn wrote: 'I left it this afternoon burning, a resemblance of Sodome, or the last day . . . the ruines resembling the pictures of Troy . . . the stones of Paules flew like grenados, the lead melting down the streetes in a streame, and the very pavements of them glowing with fiery rednesse, so as nor horse nor man was able to tread on them.'

The old cathedral, it must be admitted, had become a fairly inglorious hotch-potch, with a Gothic choir and a Romanesque nave that had been recased by Inigo Jones in the 1630s with classical pilasters instead of buttresses, and finished at the west end by a gigantic Corinthian portico. For the past thirty years, too, the central tower had been hidden under scaffolding to prevent its collapse, and already four months before the fire Christopher Wren had submitted plans for its reconstruction. Now, however, something more radical still was required. In 1668 the Dean wrote to Wren: 'What we are to do next is the present deliberation, in which you are so absolutely and indispensably necessary to us, that we can do nothing, resolve on nothing, without you. . . .' From that moment Wren, a man of thirty-five with no formal architectural training and only three buildings to his credit, was responsible for the new St Paul's. Forty-two years later, in 1710, the last stone was laid and the old man could gaze up at his achievement – perhaps the greatest building ever created by a single architect in his own lifetime.

Of the three separate designs that Wren was to submit, the final, successful, one was a rather awkward compromise, necessitated by shortage of money and the conservative views of the clergy who mistrusted his new-fangled Italianate ideas. It possessed, however, one all-important virtue: it gave him the right to vary it as he went along. Of this right Wren was to make full, if not actually unscrupulous, use; his final, 'warrant', design bears little resemblance to the St Paul's we know. In particular, he dropped the curiously clumsy idea of a small dome surmounted by a steeple, and reverted to his original concept of a greatly enlarged crossing, achieved by eliminating the inner piers. This was to be covered by a huge but relatively simple dome which, as he put it, would be of 'incomparably more grace in the remote aspect than it is possible for the lean shaft of a steeple to afford'. It soon became clear, however, that what was graceful in the remote aspect seemed strangely disproportionate and unsettling to those standing in the crossing below; so another, shallower, dome was constructed, within the first. This, subsequently covered by Sir James Thornhill with paintings that Wren rightly detested, in fact reaches barely higher than the point where the leading of the outer dome begins.

*St Paul's Cathedral, from Wren's house.*

Fortunately, other members of Wren's team were in a different class from Thornhill. Foremost among them was Grinling Gibbons, whose choir stalls (with the wooden screens behind them facing the aisles), organ case and bishop's throne are as magnificent as anything he ever did – which is to say as magnificent as wood carving can ever be. His work in stone is rarer and, it must be admitted, often less successful; but the twenty-six panels below the great ground-floor round-headed windows on the outside are full of the energy and invention that never deserted him. Then there was Edward Pearce, carver of the great cornice in the choir; Francis Bird, who was responsible for the exterior statuary – including the marvellous but seldom noticed relief, in the pediment of the west front, of the conversion of St Paul; and the Huguenot Jean Tijou, one of the greatest iron workers of his day. Tijou's gilded gates towards the east end of the choir receive their full share of wonder and admiration – but few indeed are the visitors fortunate enough to catch a glimpse of his circular stair in the south-west tower. Carefully protected from prying eyes by a door kept eternally locked (though possessed of a particularly tantalising keyhole), it is perhaps the greatest of all the unsung glories of the cathedral.

Of the innumerable monuments, only one *must* be mentioned – the statue of John Donne in the south aisle, miraculously saved from the Great Fire. Izaak Walton describes how Donne posed in his winding sheet, 'with his eyes shut, and with so much of the sheet turned aside as might shew his lean, pale and death-like face'. Sir Henry Wotton, who knew Donne well, said of the statue, 'It seems to breathe faintly, and posterity shall look upon it as a kind of artificial miracle.'

The same could well be said of St Paul's itself.

## St Paul's, Covent Garden

*65; London WC2*

Inigo Jones began his church for the 4th Earl of Bedford's new development in 1631, and completed it two years later; it can thus claim to be not only the first classically inspired parish church to be built in England, but – with the two exceptions of the Queen's Chapel at St James's Palace and St Katherine Cree (*qq.v.*) – the first place of worship in any style to arise in London since the Reformation, a century before. Horace Walpole's anecdote is often repeated of how Bedford – a Low Churchman careful with his money – told Jones that he 'would not have it much better than a barn', and how Jones replied, 'Well then, you shall have the handsomest barn in England.' The story may well be true, for Jones's master, Palladio, always associated the Tuscan order with farm architecture and St Paul's is a Tuscan building *par excellence*.

Its most immediately memorable feature is the huge pitched roof, with an immense overhang all round (and even within the gable) supported on plain, stout wooden beams. Facing the piazza is an open portico, created by two square Tuscan pillars at the corners and two round columns between them, all swelling out in a slightly exaggerated *entasis*. This was intended by Jones to be the main entrance front, but Archbishop Laud insisted that the east end – which it is – should be occupied by the altar, so entrance is now at the sides, and the big east doorway exists merely for show. The Portland stone of the front dates from a major renovation by Thomas Hardwick in 1788. Hardwick also reconstructed the roof and virtually the whole interior except the south-east chapel after a disastrous fire in 1795.

The interior is aisleless, and – with dimensions of 100 feet by 50 feet – a perfect double cube. There is a west gallery on Roman Doric columns; originally there were other galleries too, but these were removed by Butterfield in 1872 at the same time as he raised the level of the chancel. On the west screen hangs an exquisite carved wreath of flowers by Grinling Gibbons, who is buried here. It was placed there as a memorial to him in 1965.

*St Paul's, Covent Garden.*

## St Paul's, Deptford

*66; High Street, SE8*

This church has been fortunate indeed. It was blessed first of all in its architect, Thomas Archer, who built it between 1712 and 1730 in what was in those days a medium-sized town just south of London; and its luck held during the nineteenth century, when the social decline of the neighbourhood was probably instrumental in saving it from Victorian 'restorers'. During the last war it escaped the bombs; finally, in the 1970s, it was the recipient of £50,000 from the local authority and the same amount again from private contributions – enough to finance a really first-class renovation which has left it looking better, probably, than at any time since its eighteenth-century heyday. Few churches in London afford greater pleasure.

Archer's west front is a particular joy to behold. He begins with a semi-circular portico on giant Tuscan columns, within which the base of his tower projects as a smaller semi-circle. Then, above the entablature and balustrade, rises the tower proper: first a shallow drum with round openings at the four cardinal points, then a tall Borrominiesque centre, also cylindrical, with pilasters at the diagonals, round-headed arches below and more circular openings above; and finally a tall, slender steeple derived from St Mary-le-Bow. If it were not for this magnificent façade one might be forgiven for thinking that the church was in fact orientated at right-angles to the way it is: for the north and south fronts, instead of stressing the longitudinal aspect of the building, have imposing three-bay centres, heavily rusticated and topped by high pediments which are connected by a pitched roof running right across the church from one to the other. Odder still, these fronts are provided with immensely elaborate (and virtually useless) double staircases of the kind that Lord Burlington gave to his entrance front at Chiswick. The east end is apsed, its Venetian window following the apse's curve.

*St Paul's, Deptford.*

The interior, as one might expect from the deliberate ambiguity of the orientation, is very nearly square, but canted at the corners to allow for spiral staircases at the west end and vestries at the east. The staircases lead to small projecting galleries like theatre boxes. Back at ground level, the short (three-bay) aisles are delimited by giant Corinthian columns with gilded capitals. The ceilings are flat, with recessed panels; there and everywhere, the plasterwork is of an outstanding quality. The apsed chancel is flanked by pilasters and Doric columns, but is not otherwise remarkable.

This is not only one of the supreme parish churches of London; it is also an object lesson in how, even in these godless days, a great building can be redeemed and restored – not just architecturally but also as a centre for community life. One can only hope that the great Hawksmoor churches in the East End of London will be as fortunate, before it is too late.

## St Stephen's, Walbrook

*67; London EC4*

Of all Wren's parish churches, St Stephen's, Walbrook provides the most spectacular and unanswerable demonstration of his genius. He built it between 1672 and 1679, and in it we see him trying out – with complete success – ideas that he was later to bring to their fullest development in St Paul's. Its green copper dome is not immediately visible from the outside, but can be seen quite easily if one scouts around a little; what at first occupies the attention is the steeple of the ragstone west tower. It is set rather far back behind the parapet, and is therefore best studied from a short distance away. The two principal stages are both square, with projecting square corners; in the lower stage these extrusions are emphasised by Ionic columns. Above the upper one rises a tall and extremely slender spire, also square and with more horizontal projections which give it a pagoda-like appearance. Pevsner describes it as 'playful'; perhaps it is.

Certainly there is nothing in the interior that could be so described. Here Wren gives us first drama, then majesty. The drama comes immediately on entry, when we pass under an arched doorway with an oval window above and are at once faced by a dark staircase. It is an unusual approach to a church, but greatly strengthens the impact of what is to follow. Once at the top, we find ourselves standing in what we suddenly realise to be another rarity, a western apse, gazing up at a building for which nothing so far has given us any preparation whatever. The plan – though at first it seems difficult to believe – is a plain rectangle; within this Wren has designed what is basically a longitudinal church – since it has an extra bay, besides the apse, at the west end – but which, with its vast, deeply coffered dome and high glazed lantern, contrives to give the impression of a cross-in-square. Now domed cross-in-square churches always present the architect with the same problem – how to make the transition between the circular dome above and the square space below. The most usual method, used first by the Byzantines but later widely adopted throughout Western Europe, was by the use of pendentives; Wren, however, has adopted a far more original solution. He already had four principal arches, leading off to the groin-vaulted chancel, nave and transepts; he now added four more at the diagonals, and since these arches obviously had to lead somewhere he cut right-angled recesses behind them. All eight arches he carried on Corinthian columns, with an additional column at the right-angle of each recess. This gives us a total of twelve columns which are directly or indirectly concerned with the dome, and another four dividing the two bays of the nave. The deep entablature above them follows the four principal arms of the cross and also the lines of the diagonal recesses, thereby enclosing L-shaped spaces at each corner, to which Wren has given flat coffered ceilings. The light comes from the central lantern, the circular and oval windows around the lower walls, the round-headed windows in the clerestory and the three east windows, also round-headed, which have been filled with horrible modern glass. One longs for Benjamin West's painting of the Stoning of St Stephen, now on the north wall, to be replaced over the east window where it belongs.

Most of the furniture and fittings, which were not designed by Wren but were contemporary gifts from the Grocers' Company, fortunately survived when the church was bombed during the last war. The best pieces are the reredos, font cover and pulpit, which has an outsize tester with dancing *amorini*. The principal loss has been the removal of the box pews in 1888, making the high plinths of the columns look disagreeably naked. The damage was compounded by the laying of a nasty mosaic floor where they had been.

Among the monuments is that to Vanbrugh, in the north aisle, with his famous epitaph, somewhat improbably attributed to Hawksmoor:

*Lie heavy on him, Earth! for he*
*Laid many heavy loads on thee.*

## Sir John Soane's Museum

*68; 13 Lincoln's Inn Fields, WC2*

Soane occupied 13 Lincoln's Inn Fields for the last twenty-four years of his life, from 1813 to 1837, having lived for the previous twenty next door at No. 12. This and No. 14 – as well as No. 13 itself – are all designed by him and make a balanced architectural composition, with No. 13 providing the quite spectacular centre. But that is only the beginning; for Soane designed his residence not only to live in but also to house his considerable collection of antiquities and works of art. Moreover, having quarrelled with his sons, he decided some five years before his death to establish the building as a permanent museum for 'amateurs and students' and to endow it with most of his fortune. This is the institution that survives today, much as he left it – the most fascinatingly idiosyncratic museum in London.

*Sir John Soane's Museum, Lincoln's Inn Fields.*

Let us consider the outside first. No. 13 – but only No. 13 – has a slightly projecting front of Portland stone extending across all three bays of the ground and first floors and the centre bay of the second floor. On the attic storey – which was added in 1825 – and on the outer bays of the floor below, the windows are flanked by panelled pilasters only, which are in turn carried up to a characteristically Soanian balustrade with acroteria. The ground floor is relatively simple, with the front door on the left and two round-headed windows of the same size as the door opening beside it. Between these three bays are placed – decidedly oddly – two Gothic corbels taken from the north front of Westminster Hall. Two more of these corbels occupy corresponding positions on the first floor, which is much more ornate. The three windows here are still round-headed, but slightly broader than those below. Their sills rest on blind balustrades, while to the sides and across the top are those incised decorations of which Soane was so fond. More of these surround the square centre window of the second floor, which has doubled pilaster strips to each side and acroteria along the top. On the level of this window, standing at the angles above the outer bays, are two statues in Coade stone – free versions of the caryatids on the Erechtheum at Athens.

On entering the building, one is rather surprised to see the Hall growing gradually wider as it approaches the staircase, its left-hand wall encroaching further and further into the space properly belonging to No. 12. Immediately to the right are the Dining Room and Library, effectively forming a single room since their only division consists of two projecting piers serving as bookcases, from which springs a sort of canopy of three segmental arches. The north window of the Dining Room looks out on to the Monument Court, a wonderful hotch-potch of architectural fragments, mostly from buildings demolished in Soane's time; the ceiling, as Soane himself wrote, 'is formed in compartments, showing the construction of the floor above and is enriched with pictures by Henry Howard, RA'. The pictures, furniture and *objets d'art* are, as everywhere in this extraordinary house, too numerous to mention individually and anyway fall outside the scope of this book; but what gives these rooms their fascination is above all the way in which Soane has succeeded in creating a sense of illusion and space which seems effortlessly to transcend the limitations of his house. This he has achieved by doubling, and thus giving depth to, elements such as the dividing canopy, which might easily have been two-dimensional, and also by a quite brilliant use of mirrors, especially in the recesses over the Library bookshelves.

From the corner of the Dining Room a short passage, divided so as to form a minute Study and Dressing Room, leads through into the museum proper at the back of the house. At the end of it you turn right into a corridor full of antique marbles and casts which in turn leads into the Picture Room. This was added by Soane in 1824 and designed to accommodate an elaborate system of hinged panels which swing back to reveal further pictures behind them – an arrangement which enables a relatively small room to accommodate as many pictures as would normally fill a gallery over three times its length. Apart from two important series by Hogarth, *The Election* and *The Rake's Progress*, they include a good many architectural drawings by Soane himself.

Just outside the Picture Room, a narrow staircase leads down to what Soane liked to call the Crypt, the eastern part of which he fitted out – in a rather late burst of Gothic romanticism – as a monastic dwelling. The Monk's Cell and Oratory is now used for storage, but the Monk's Parlour remains as Soane designed it, its southern end ascending into a narrow recess behind the folding panels of the Picture Room above. Beyond it, a window gives a view into the Monk's Yard, with the 'ruins of his once noble monastery' – in fact two arches built up of stones taken from the old Palace of Westminster – and the 'Monk's Tomb', which is composed of miscellaneous bits and pieces. The Parlour itself is still more eclectic; anything less like an anchorite's cell could hardly be imagined. It is, however, a remarkable illustration of the way the eighteenth century conceived of the Middle Ages – as mysterious, gloomy and grotesque.

Leaving the Monk's Parlour, you see in front of you the long passageway of the Crypt, with openings on the left and, directly in front, the Sepulchral Chamber containing the great stone sarcophagus of Pharaoh Seti I. At this point the roof of the Crypt opens up, and the sarcophagus is wonderfully lit from what Soane referred to as the Dome, although the central space above is in fact not a dome at all, but a conical skylight. The other rooms to the south – including one ghoulishly known as the Catacombs – are of interest more for their contents than for their architecture, and need not detain us here. We can therefore return to the ground floor and follow the route we have just taken, but this time at the higher level: along the Colonnade to the 'Dome' itself. In many ways this is the most amazing part of the whole museum, such is the plethora of statuary and reliefs, urns and vases, columns, capitals and corbels, fragments of frieze and architrave, mouldings and medallions. Many are precariously balanced – or at least appear to be so – on the very edge of the balustrade surrounding the open well, down which one can peer between the pottery to the huge sarcophagus below. At the centre of the eastern end of this balustrade is Chantrey's superb bust of Soane himself, completed in 1829, surveying with justifiable pride the treasures teeming around him.

Immediately to the south of the Dome (though normally approached via two other rooms) is the Breakfast Parlour. Here we are out of the museum and back in the house proper – indeed in the most quintessentially Soanian room anywhere in the building. It has a shallow dome on pendentives, but detached from the walls at either end in such a way as to give the effect of a canopy. There is a tiny lantern, but most of the light enters indirectly, reflected from the side walls. Convex mirrors set into the pendentives produce still more curious effects, and there is a memorable vista through the window to the statuary, from here most dramatically lit, in the Dome behind.

On the first floor visitors normally see only the North and South Drawing Rooms, in Soane's day used principally for entertaining. After half a century's service as an architectural library, the South Drawing Room was refurnished in 1971 with Soane's own furniture, and now looks very much as he knew it. It is apsed on its west side, to conceal the awkwardly sloping wall we noticed downstairs, and the ceiling – like that of the North Drawing Room next door – has panels of Soane's characteristic shallow vaulting, faintly reminiscent of the Breakfast Parlour below, though on a much smaller and more modest scale. Until 1834 the part of the house which projects to the south was an open loggia, decorated – as Soane tells us and as we are not altogether surprised to learn – 'with pillars, busts and statues of eminent persons'; in that year, however, the entire loggia was glazed and now forms a sort of gallery running the whole length of the room.

The rooms on the second and third floors are not normally open and are of little architectural interest. You should therefore now pass through a door in the South Drawing Room – in Soane's day it was a cupboard – which leads through the party wall into the next-door house, No. 12. Here on the first floor are two rooms, with double doors between them; the front room has another vaulted ceiling. But the prettiest thing by far in No. 12 is the Breakfast Room, immediately behind the Dining Room on the ground floor. Here is the earliest of Soane's splayed cross-vault ceilings, charmingly painted over with a design of honeysuckle and columbine trailing across a trellis. After years covered over with paint and whitewash, it was most beautifully and faithfully restored a few years ago with a grant from the Pilgrim Trust. It was in this house that the Soanes lived from 1792 to 1813.

Here, in short, is the most rewarding of all the lesser-known sights of the capital. I have long lost count of the number of foreign visitors I have taken to see it; none has ever returned disappointed.

## Somerset House

*69; Strand, WC2*

Old Somerset House, one of the most historic domestic buildings of London, was originally built in 1547–50 for Protector Somerset, who demolished four old inns and a church to obtain his site and pulled down the Priory Church of St John Clerkenwell and St Paul's Charnel House and Cloister to provide building stone; he would have done the same to St Margaret's, Westminster (*q.v.*) if the parishioners had not turned out in force to prevent him. It was frequently used by Queen Elizabeth and James I's Queen, Anne of Denmark, and later by Queen Henrietta Maria, for whom Charles I ordered a magnificent new chapel from Inigo Jones, and who actually died there in 1652. By this time it had become accepted as a sort of queenly perquisite, and no one was surprised when Catherine of Braganza moved in as of right after the Restoration. With her departure, however, the old house began to lose favour and in 1775 it was razed to the ground to make way for the first great purpose-designed Government office building in England.

After some hesitation, the commission for this immense work was given to Sir William Chambers, who immediately went off to Paris to look at recent French examples of the genre. The first stone of his new building was laid in 1776. It was to consist in its essentials of four great ranges enclosing a vast quadrangle. Of these he began with the show front to the Strand, and for his design decided on a style by Palladio out of Inigo Jones. It has nine bays and two and a half storeys: an arcaded and heavily rusticated ground floor, then a parapet with intermittent balustrading, then a row of attached giant Corinthian columns between which the pedimented *piano nobile* and the attic are grouped in a single composition, and finally another balustrade and a raised centre. Further enrichments are provided by the carved keystones of the ground-floor arcade – bearded heads representing Ocean and eight great rivers – and again by statues of various Virtues on the raised centre, topped in their turn by still larger ones symbolising Fame and the Genius of Britain.

The three central arches are open to form a triple gateway, its bays separated by coupled Tuscan columns from which spring parallel tunnel vaults. Passing through into the central courtyard and turning back to look at this same north range from the inside, one is at once struck by how much bigger it is, spreading out in each direction behind the narrower houses in the Strand. After six bays to each side of the centre it turns southward for three more and then outwards again for another three. It stands, however, separate from the other three courtyard ranges. These form an uninterrupted three-sided block, still of two and a half storeys but considerably plainer in style. All three floors are now rusticated, and halfway along each range there is a slightly projecting Corinthian centre pavilion and domed timber lantern above, the south side having in addition a rather feckless little pediment raised on an attic; otherwise the whole thing looks quite unassuming and domestic – more like a rather well-bred street in London or Bath than anything else.

There remained one important front to think about – perhaps the most important of all in the days when much of the London traffic continued to go by river. With his Thames frontage Chambers had another problem: that of standing comparison with the Adam brothers' Adelphi, completed only a few years before (and shamelessly pulled down in 1937). In addition he had to cope with the immense length – nearly 300 yards – and the difficulties imposed by the river, then immediately below, for the Thames Embankments were still almost a century away in the future. He first built up an immense terrace on high arcades, most noble in their own right but nowadays only visible from across the water. Above these, he divided his main front into three, separating the individual parts with, at ground level, huge horseshoe arches echoing in their form the central water entrance in the arcade below, surmounted by graceful pedimented colonnades. They amount, in effect, to Palladian bridges – a delightful idea. The only trouble is that they are too small, as if they do not have the courage of their own convictions: the columns look somehow spindly, and the pediments do not break the roof line. The same weakness shows up even more disastrously in the centre, where there is another colonnade but without either a pediment above or an arch below. A frontage of such length calls for Herculean accents; those here, however, are weak and tentative, and as a result their effect is lost.

In his defence it should be said that Chambers never saw his river front complete – nor indeed any other major section of Somerset House apart from the north block to the Strand. Born in 1723, he found himself in 1795 unable to continue his immense undertaking and begged the King to relieve him of his responsibilities. The following year he was dead. Perhaps, had he been a younger man, he would have been bolder, or would at least have had the energy to make any alterations that seemed necessary. As it was, his work was finished only after his death, by other – and lesser – hands. He himself had planned smaller courts opening off the central one to east and west; these were completed only in the middle of the nineteenth century with Smirke's King's College (of 1829–35) to the east and Sir James Pennethorne's major extension to the west, facing the end of Waterloo Bridge.

Somerset House was never designed for pageantry or parade; nonetheless it possesses a number of splendid rooms in its less utilitarian sections, particularly in the first floor of the Strand range where the Royal Academy, the Royal Society and the Society of Antiquaries all had their headquarters. Nowadays the building tends to be associated in most people's minds with the Registry of Births, Deaths and Marriages, though it was in fact moved out in 1973. At the time of writing this fine building occupies a kind of limbo, having lost its former *raison d'être* and not yet found a proper new one.

## Southwark Cathedral

*70; London SE1*

It was in 1106 that two Norman knights founded, on the site of a venerable Saxon church at the southern end of old London Bridge, a priory of Augustinian canons dedicated to St Mary and colloquially known as St Mary Overie – that is, 'over the water'. It flourished for a century, but was then largely destroyed by a great fire which raged through Southwark in 1212. Rebuilding began at once, and the result was the first great Gothic church to be built in or near London; it is thought to have been carefully studied by Henry III's masons before they started work at Westminster in 1245. Work proceeded until 1273, then – for reasons which remain unknown – ground to a halt. It began again around 1310, and by the middle of the century was probably more or less complete except for the crossing-tower, the lower stage of which has been attributed to Henry Yevele and seems to date from *c.*1380.

*Southwark Cathedral.*

All this suggests that Southwark Cathedral – it gained the status of cathedral only in 1905, having been simply the parish church of St Saviour since the dissolution of the priory in 1539 – might still today be a fine combination of the Early English and Decorated styles. Alas, it was largely transformed in the nineteenth century and is now only a shadow of what it once was. The outside strikes one as particularly unpromising, and the immediate surroundings do nothing to help it. Tower and transepts are of ashlar, though of poorish quality, but all else is of knapped flints with stone dressings, looking like the work of Victorian journeymen masons – which is more or less what it is. On the tower, the chequered parapet is an original feature, though entirely renewed; the four tall pinnacles are by George Gwilt Jun., who restored or rebuilt much of the east end in 1822–5.

Inside, the remaining traces of the Norman church are too few and too fragmentary to be of much interest. Of the Early English building, however, the choir and retrochoir remain, and it is they that earn Southwark Cathedral its place in this book. The choir extends five bays east of the crossing, the retrochoir – including the four single-bay chapels at its far eastern end – another three. (How one regrets the vast sixteenth-century stone reredos that separates them and precludes any view of one from the other, as at Wells or Salisbury.) In the choir, the deeply moulded arcades rest on piers of alternating circular and octagonal section, each having three attached shafts rising uninterruptedly (except for their shaft rings) to the point of springing of the vault – which, unusually, is precisely at sill level of the clerestory rather than a little way above or below it. Between arcade and clerestory comes a wall passage with four arches to every one of the nave arches below; then the clerestory itself, in a tripartite design of three stepped arches with a single lancet in the middle one. These, however, were redone in the nineteenth century by Gwilt, as were the vaults of the roof.

The real pride of Southwark is the retrochoir, and we are lucky to have it. The chapel to the east was pulled down in 1830 as part of a road-widening programme (even then) and the whole thing was threatened with demolition; only at the insistence of Gwilt was it reprieved; he restored it 'gratuitously' three years later, but it has not suffered appreciably. The six free-standing piers are of a slender elegance that perfectly matches the equally delicate rib vaulting and the single and triple-stepped lancets in the side walls and east end. And, as always, one gets ever-changing cross-vistas as one walks across the space, the bays and pillars constantly re-aligning themselves in new perspectives. The date of all this is uncertain; but the triple cusped lancets in the north and south walls, stepped and with uncusped circles in their spandrels, indicate that the Early English style is on the point of giving way to the Decorated. Perhaps, therefore, 1260 or thereabouts would not be too wide of the mark.

The actual difference between the two styles as exemplified at Southwark can best be seen by comparing the two transepts. That to the north is uncompromisingly Early English – the pointed arches on their Purbeck

*The Gallery, Strawberry Hill, Twickenham.*

shafts in the north and west walls (though these make curious frames indeed for the Baroque monuments within them), the one- and two-light windows of the clerestory (there is no intermediate stage) all speak of the thirteenth century. Only the high four-light window at the north end seems – like those of the retrochoir already mentioned – to herald new ideas; but this is in fact the work of Robert Wallace (who also rebuilt the vaults) in 1830. The south transept, on the other hand, is Decorated through and through. The Purbeck marble has gone – it was no longer in fashion – and the tall three-light windows are of intersecting cusped arcading with a small cusped hexagon above. The extremely pretty south window of five lights is by Sir Arthur Blomfield.

So, indeed, is the nave. Already in the 1830s the original had fallen into disrepair; the roof was removed in 1831 and seven years later the whole thing was demolished. A replacement – by Henry Rose – was in position by the end of the decade, but was soon found hopelessly inadequate; and when in 1890 it was decided that a new diocese should be created for South London and that St Saviour's should be its cathedral, Blomfield was commissioned to prepare what was left of the church for its new role. His work may not be thought particularly inspired, but it is good Victorian Early English and probably a fairly close approximation of what the medieval church was like.

Southwark, to sum up, is not one of the great cathedrals of England; never having been intended as a cathedral at all, there is no reason why it should be. But both architecturally and historically it is not without interest – and the South Bank is not so rich in distinguished buildings that we can afford to despise such rare medieval survivals as this, fragmentary though they may be.

## Strawberry Hill

*71; Twickenham*

'I am going to build a little Gothic castle,' wrote Horace Walpole to his friend Sir Horace Mann in 1749, later explaining that 'the Grecian is only proper for magnificent and public buildings. Columns, and all their beautiful ornaments, look ridiculous when crowded into a closet or cheese-cake house… . one has a satisfaction in imprinting the gloom of abbeys and cathedrals on one's house…. One's garden on the contrary is to be nothing but *riant* and the gaiety of nature.' He was right about the garden; Strawberry Hill must have been a delightful site indeed before London engulfed it, descending to the Thames 'through two or three little meadows, where I have some Turkish sheep and cows, all studied in their colours for becoming the view … barges as solemn as Barons of the Exchequer move under my window; Richmond Hill and Ham Walks bound my prospect; but, thank God! the Thames is between me and the Duchess of Queensberry. . . .'

Where Walpole failed – if he ever really tried – was in the implantation of gloom. His is gay Gothic; neither outside nor in does the house seem any more formidable or inclined to take itself seriously than was its owner. He obviously had a genuine admiration for the style; never otherwise could he have immersed himself in it so deeply and so long – from the age of thirty in 1747, when he bought his 'little plaything house', to his death in 1797, by which time he had increased it to ten times its original size. But it amused him as well, and anything more light-hearted than the Library, the Rococo Cabinet or the staircase with arcaded 'Armoury' on the first-floor landing could hardly be imagined. This has nothing to do with the heavy-handed Gothicism of Wren at Christ Church, of Hawksmoor at All Souls, or even of Kent at Esher or Hampton Court; still less has it any of the reverential solemnity of a Pugin, a Pearson or a Street; the nearest spiritual equivalent I can think of is the Rex Whistler Room at Mottisfont (*q.v.*). To be sure, Walpole prided himself on his fidelity to ancient models: 'All Gothic designs', he insisted, 'should be made to imitate something that was of that time, a part of a church, a castle, a convent or a mansion.' Thus the fireplace in the Round Room is inspired by the tomb of Edward the Confessor, 'improved by Mr Robert Adam', the Library bookcases are taken from the side doors to the choir in old St Paul's, and the 'Decorated' tracery of the Cabinet ceiling from the Chapter House at York; but the interpretations are free indeed, all applied to utterly different objects, and are seldom more authentic than Pugin's Gothic coat hooks in the Palace of Westminster.

'Poor Strawberry', as Walpole liked to call it, had no single architect. There were in fact at least ten, not counting the remarkable Frances, Lady Waldegrave, who gave new life to the house in the last century and in 1860–2 added a whole new wing of her own design. But the names to remember above all are those of the two men who formed, with Walpole himself, the 'Committee of Taste' which approved all ideas and suggestions before they were carried out, and who were together – though working separately – responsible for a large part of the building. They were Richard Bentley and John Chute (of The Vyne). The lightest of the Rococo is Bentley's; his, for example, are the staircase, the screen in the Holbein Chamber and several of the wilder fireplaces. Chute had none of Bentley's high fantasy, but was a far abler architect; to him we owe the west front and Great Cloister behind it, the Round Tower (to which Lady Waldegrave added the top storey), the Great Parlour and the Library, for which Bentley's original designs had failed to receive 'the Strawberry imprimatur'. The Gallery, with its sensational mock fan vaulting inspired by the Henry VII Chapel in Westminster Abbey, owes something to both, and a good deal more to Thomas Pitt, Lord Camelford, who was co-opted on to the Committee of Taste after Bentley's final fall from grace in 1762. To Robert Adam belongs the Round Room, the design for its ceiling lifted from that of the rose window in old St Paul's; but nothing else.

In 1923 Strawberry Hill was bought by the Catholic Education Council; it is now occupied by St Mary's College, a Vincentian community who cherish it well and are happy to show visitors round by appointment. Here is an opportunity not to be missed.

## Sudbrook Park

*72; Petersham, Surrey*

The magnificent house built by James Gibbs in 1726 for the Duke of Argyll now shelters the local golf club. Its two principal fronts are remarkably similar (if you ignore the later addition to the portico on the entrance side, which should never have been allowed). They show a house of nine bays, essentially of brick but with a three-bay stone centre consisting of a portico *in antis* – in fact it projects very slightly – and two giant Corinthian columns with angle pilasters, carrying a deep entablature and raised balustrade above. Within the loggia so formed, the first-floor windows are round-headed instead of being segmental as everywhere else. The house stands on a rather high basement, and on the garden side – which remains as it was first designed – the entrance door is reached by means of a high and somewhat disproportionately spreading staircase, beginning with two flights parallel to the façade which then join into one and turn inwards towards the house.

The two porticoes are connected by a single room – an immense cube rising the height of the house which effectively divides the house in two: a separate staircase is required on each side. The decoration of this room shows Gibbs at his most extravagantly Baroque. The ceiling is vaulted, the vaults springing from an intricately moulded entablature which is carried on coupled pilasters. Magnificently ornate doorcases and plaster trophies on the walls complete the effect. In all England there can be no grander nineteenth hole.

## Syon House

*73; Isleworth*

On the night before the battle of Agincourt, Shakespeare's Henry V sinks to his knees. 'Not today, O Lord,' he prays,

*O not today, think not upon the fault*
*My father made in compassing the Crown!*
*...................... I have built*
*Two chantries, where the sad and solemn priests*
*Still sing for Richard's soul.*

It is ironical that the monastery of Syon, one of these two funereal foundations built by King Henry to expiate his father's murder of Richard II, should have been the origin of one of the most exuberantly ornate houses in England, seat of the indirect descendants and namesakes of Henry's heroic young enemy whom he himself killed on the battlefield – Harry Percy, called Hotspur, son of the 1st Earl of Northumberland.

After the Dissolution of the Monasteries in 1539, Syon became Crown property (serving briefly as a prison for Katherine Howard, Henry VIII's fifth wife, before her execution) and was subsequently appropriated by the Duke of Somerset, 'Protector of the Realm', on the

*Syon House, Isleworth.*

accession of the nine-year-old Edward VI. It was Somerset who began the present building, probably following the lines of the old cloister; soon afterwards, however, he was accused of wishing to fortify it – looking at the distinctly grim façade, one can understand why – charged with felony, and himself executed. The house passed to the family of Lady Jane Grey; it was at Syon that she was offered the Crown, and from here that she was rowed to London to be proclaimed Queen. Alas, poor Jane – she reigned just nine days before going in her turn to the block.

In 1594 Queen Elizabeth granted the lease of the ill-fated house to Henry Percy, 9th Earl of Northumberland, but the curse remained unbroken; the Earl was falsely accused of complicity in the Gunpowder Plot, and for the next fifteen years was obliged to exchange the delights of his new estates for the austerer disciplines of the Tower. After the Civil War Syon served for the second time as a royal prison – for the children of Charles I – and before the seventeenth century was out it was inherited by the three-year-old Elizabeth Percy, whose fate is was to lose her first bridegroom at the age of twelve and her second – to a bunch of hired assassins – at fourteen. With her third, whom she married after only three months' widowhood, she was more successful; and it was her granddaughter's husband – inheriting the earldom by special Act of Parliament and subsequently becoming 1st Duke of Northumberland – who made Syon basically what it is today. His method was simple, if expensive. To redesign the grounds he engaged Capability Brown; to transform the house, Robert Adam.

Adam's original plans were considerably more ambitious than what he was finally allowed to achieve. His proposal to roof in the central courtyard and transform it into an immense domed ballroom was rejected, and even his scheme for the main floor was left unfinished; of its four sides he completed only two and a half, consisting of five principal rooms and two minute boudoirs. But what rooms they are!

The Entrance Hall first: here is cool, neo-classical perfection, as symbolised by the Apollo Belvedere – the ideal of any eighteenth-century dilettante – which dominates it from the northern end. A little chilly for the arriving guest? Yes, and deliberately so; the contrast is all the greater when that guest is led up a few steps into the Ante-Room. This is like entering a jewel – small, square, but aglow with warmth and colour from the polychrome scagliola floor, up past the twelve verd-antique columns – dredged up from the Tiber and brought here in 1765 – to the golden statues just beneath the ceiling.

The Dining Room and Red Drawing Room follow – the former restrained because those using it have other things to think about, the latter a further explosion of sumptuous colour, with a ceiling by Angelica Kauffmann and a carpet designed by Adam for the room. Then, finally, comes the greatest surprise of all: the Library, converted from the Tudor Long Gallery, running the whole length of the east side and finished, in Adam's own words, 'in a style to afford great variety and amusement'. He himself clearly revelled in the challenge of treating an essentially Elizabethan feature in the classical idiom; and though purists may frown (Pevsner considers the detail 'most objectionable') few people could fail to be beguiled by this enchanting *jeu d'esprit*, or by the two tiny Boudoirs, one round and one square, which occupy the turrets at each end.

This spectacular sequence of rooms is enough to earn its creator a lasting place in the Halls of Fame, and makes Syon one of the showplaces not just of London but of all England. Before you leave, however, one more *bonne-bouche* awaits you. Go out into the garden and take a long, joyful look at the Great Conservatory. This is no ordinary greenhouse; it is a neo-classical mansion over 100 yards long, created in Bath stone, cast iron and immense acreages of glass, with a domed and pedimented central block and two curved wings ending in pavilions. Within, the ironwork soars skyward with a traceried lightness made lighter by the clambering vegetation. Not, perhaps, as original as Decimus Burton's Palm House at Kew, but better than anything Paxton ever did. The architect was Charles Fowler, who went on immediately afterwards to design Covent Garden Market. His name too should be remembered.

## Temple Church

*74; off Fleet Street, EC4*

According to an inscription over the inside of the west door, the Temple Church of St Mary was consecrated on 10 February 1185 by Heraclius, Patriarch of Jerusalem, almost certainly in the presence of King Henry II. It was built by the Knights Templars, who had moved their headquarters from Holborn some quarter of a century before, in the round form that they used for all their churches in imitation of the Church of the Holy Sepulchre at Jerusalem – a form that can also be seen at Cambridge, Northampton and Little Maplestead in Essex (*qq.v.*), as well as at Ludlow. When their Order was suppressed in 1312, all their property passed to their chief rivals, the Knights Hospitallers; and when these in their turn were dissolved at the Reformation the Temple Church passed to the two societies of lawyers who were their tenants. These lawyers, the Benchers of the Inner and the Middle Temple, were granted the freehold by James I in 1608, one of the conditions being that they should maintain the building for ever. Thus it is not, and never has been, a parish church; rather is it a private chapel – technically speaking, a Royal Peculiar like Westminster Abbey.

It has been altered in some degree over the centuries, and – though it fortunately escaped the Great Fire – suffered severe damage during the disastrous air raid on 10 May 1941, when the nave roof collapsed in flames on to the effigies of the Knights below. It has, however, been beautifully and immaculately restored (by Walter Hindes Godfrey and his son Walter Emil Godfrey) and has retained much of its old fascination. Its exterior can best be seen from the small courtyard to the south, where its curious barometer shape is most clearly evident: the circular nave swelling out on the left, topped by its circular embattled belfry, and the three-gabled five-bay chancel with its stepped triple lancets and tall buttresses marching off to the right. (From the north, where the level of the ground rises and there is a little turret rising to the Penitential Cell, the walls are of coursed rubble rather than ashlar and the view is a good deal less satisfactory.) At the west end is a quite magnificent Norman doorway in three orders, with superb carving, now sadly worn and weathered. Above it is a circular window with wheel tracery; this is hard to see from the outside, however, owing to a deep, rib-vaulted Gothic porch, heavily buttressed and gabled on three sides, which abuts the church just below it.

The interior, however, is what counts. It has been refaced, and much of the Purbeck marble – used here as an architectural enrichment for the first time in England – renewed; but the main features have all been preserved and the ensemble probably looks much the same today as it always has. The period is what is generally known as Transitional – that moment when Norman was giving way to Gothic – but the two styles almost invariably remain separate and remarkably pure. The circular arcade is high and pointed, resting on four-shafted piers with capitals carved (or recarved) mostly in water-leaf; around it runs a rib-vaulted ambulatory, with blank pointed arcading along the wall and a stone bench below; in the spandrels is a series of grotesque heads, quite a few of them original. All this is of course Early English work; the windows of the ambulatory, however, are round-headed and still Norman.

Above is a triforium – the only place in the building where the two styles can be said to overlap. It consists of intersecting arches, a typical Norman motif; but the arches are Gothically pointed. There are six of them to each of the arcade bays below, the third and fourth in each bay being open, the rest blank. Higher still is a clerestory – with round-headed Norman windows again – and then a timber roof.

On the floor are the effigies of the Knights: lying not, as one might expect, on tomb chests but on flat stone slabs set directly on the pavement, like wounded men just brought in after a battle. They were badly damaged in the bombing and no longer occupy their original positions, but this hardly seems to matter. To me, at least, their effect is deeply moving.

And so to the chancel, which is superb. It is later than the nave, having been enlarged in the second quarter of the thirteenth century when it was also given aisles to north and south, the same height as the centre. The whole thing is carried on slender four-shafted piers of Purbeck, and is rib-vaulted throughout. The triple lancets that we saw from the outside have detached Purbeck shafts; those at the east end have additional enrichments in the shape of head stops and blank elongated quatrefoils above the lower lights.

The church has little furniture of interest; the best is the reredos which was designed by Wren and which, after more than a century in the Bowes Museum at Barnard Castle, has been restored to the place for which it was intended. No one could nowadays pretend that it suits its Gothic surroundings, and one understands why Sydney Smirke (who was restoring the church at the time) removed it; but it seems to have settled in rather better than one might expect. As to glass, all the original windows were destroyed in the war, but the modern replacements in the chancel – by Carl Edwards – seem to me exactly right.

## Tower of London

*75; Tower Hill, EC3*

Relatively few Londoners ever visit the Tower, which is a shame – for here, at the eastern limit of the City, on the edge of the river and actually straddling the remains of the old Roman wall, is the greatest military bastion in all England, and by far the most fascinating. Of course it has been restored, rebuilt and added to on countless occasions since William the Conqueror gave orders for the building of what we now know as the White Tower in 1077 or thereabouts; and yet, somehow, despite the throngs of tourists, it has contrived to preserve its atmosphere and its magic. Perhaps the pomp and circumstance with which it is imbued, the Beefeaters and the ravens and the nightly Ceremony of the Keys, all have something to do with it; above all, however, it is the simple fact that those 18 acres within its walls are more saturated in English history than any other similar area in the realm.

*The Tower of London.*

The fortifications themselves are of two main periods, that of the Conqueror in the eleventh century and that of Henry III and his son Edward I, who together spanned almost the whole of the thirteenth. Of the first of these periods, the WHITE TOWER is the only survivor; but it remains the focal point of the whole complex. William had ordered the construction of a wooden fort on this most strategic of sites as soon as he reached London after the battle of Hastings, and only decided on a permanent building in stone a decade later; he entrusted the design to Bishop Gundulf of Rochester, who seems to have been as good a military architect as he was an ecclesiastical one. Completed in 1097, the White Tower is a three-storeyed hall keep of Kentish ragstone with Caen stone dressings, the largest of its kind in England barring that of Colchester. It was quite clearly intended for habitation as well as for defence. William is unlikely ever to have slept there himself, having been dead ten years by the time it was ready for occupation; but his sons William Rufus and Henry I may well have done so and his grandson Stephen made it his official residence. Here then is a building in which Norman and Plantagenet kings actually lived, in which on the third floor you may see the rooms in which they slept, and on the second both the Great Hall in which they ate and – most evocative of all – the Chapel in which they worshipped. This Chapel, dedicated to St John the Evangelist, is one of the most perfect and unspoilt examples of early Norman architecture to be found anywhere. Rising through two floors of the Tower above a crypt and a sub-crypt, it has massive round-arched arcades on sturdy circular piers with crudely scalloped capitals, curving inwards at the east end to form an apse, around which the tunnel-vaulted aisles continue in the form of an ambulatory. Above these aisles runs a fully developed tribune gallery, a continuous passage following the line of the arcade below. The roof is also tunnel-vaulted – a great rarity this side of the Channel – which adds immeasurably to the impact of the building.

Defence, however, was just as important. Each of the White Tower's four outer walls – apart from the south-eastern projection formed by the apse of St John's Chapel, its ground plan is almost (though not quite) a perfect square – varies between 11 and 15 feet in thickness, and those to north and south are further buttressed by a dividing wall running through the middle of the whole construction. Even if a besieging force somehow succeeded in crossing the moat and outer defences and finding its way into the Tower itself, its problems would still not be over: of the four corner turrets, only one – the circular one to the north-east – contains a stair rising all the way to the top, and that, we may be sure, would be most determinedly defended. The other three stairways rise one storey only.

Although there is evidence to suggest that various additions and improvements continued to be made to the Tower throughout the twelfth century, it is only with Henry III that we see it being effectively transformed. Beginning in about 1230, Henry planned to encircle William's keep with an immense curtain wall, studded at regular intervals with bastion towers, and to surround this wall with a deep moat. South of the White Tower he also built himself a new palace, which, as the principal residence of the most enlightened and cultivated of all our medieval kings – and incidentally, the most extravagant – must have been glorious indeed. Its destruction during the Civil War was a national tragedy almost on a par with the war itself. Near it, halfway along the south side of his bastion, he set a large, circular tower, guarding a water-gate and a flight of steps leading up from the river. Known nowadays as the Wakefield Tower, it contains on its upper floor a most beautiful vaulted chamber which is believed to have been the royal oratory.

Before his death Henry also had the White Tower whitewashed inside and out, thus ensuring for it the name that it bears to this day. He did not, however, live to finish his plan of fortification, which was only to be completed by his son Edward. He it was who built the curtain wall on the west side, setting the formidable Beauchamp Tower halfway along its length, and then surrounded the whole thing with yet another peripheral bastion and the existing moat, which was fed with water from the Thames. (The moat was drained, alas, in 1843; might it perhaps one day be filled again?) The completion of this project around the south side involved the building of a retaining wall and wharf along the river bank and a new water entrance leading under the wharf to a gate at the base of ST THOMAS'S TOWER, now generally known as TRAITORS' GATE. The Tower itself, named after Thomas à Becket (who had been at one time Constable of the Tower of London), contains another rib-vaulted oratory, dedicated to him.

By the end of the thirteenth century most of the fortifications were complete, and the Tower looked in its essentials much as it does today. To continue the story chronologically would therefore be pointless; it seems more sensible to describe the other buildings of particular interest in the order in which they are usually visited. We start with the MIDDLE TOWER and the BYWARD TOWER near the entrance in the south-west corner, both important elements in Edward I's defensive system. The present stone bridge that connects them across the moat replaces, of course, the original drawbridge. The Byward Tower was added to in the reign of Richard II and later in that of Henry VIII, when it acquired the timber-framed part on its inward side. (It was, unfortunately, abominably restored in the eighteenth and nineteenth centuries, which accounts for the faintly ridiculous-looking top storey.) Just beyond it on the left you look up at the BELL TOWER, so called from the pretty but distinctly dotty little wooden belfry precariously perched on the top. The tower itself is the only polygonal one within the whole *enceinte* and dates from a time between the two main building periods – probably around 1190, in the reign of Richard I. Beside and behind it is the timber-framed QUEEN'S HOUSE of about 1530, in which the conspirators of the Gunpowder Plot were subsequently interrogated. It faces on to TOWER GREEN, which you enter by turning left at the BLOODY TOWER, traditionally the scene of the murder of the two little princes in 1483. This dates from the time of Richard II, though the gateway below it is a century earlier.

The centre of Tower Green is taken up with the site of the execution block where seven of the Tower's most distinguished victims met their deaths, among them Anne Boleyn, Katherine Howard, Lady Jane Grey and the Earl of Essex. To the north of it is the CHAPEL OF ST PETER AD VINCULA, built in the first quarter of the sixteenth century on the site of a much older chapel. It has five bays of big three-light windows under four-centred arches with hood-moulds, but apart from the tombs of all the above and several others it is of relatively little interest. The same, architecturally, goes for the Victorian WATERLOO BLOCK (probably the work of Salvin) which now houses, *inter alia*, the Crown Jewels.

The three buildings along the east side of the inner ward are, first, the MUSEUM (formerly the officers' quarters) devoted to the history of the Royal Fusiliers and built at the same time as the Waterloo Block; then the brick HOSPITAL BLOCK (mid-eighteenth-century); and finally the NEW ARMOURIES (formerly the Horse Armoury) of about 1689. Once again, the contents of these buildings tend to be rather more interesting than the buildings themselves. The tour completed, one walks back to the entrance along Tower Wharf.

## Twickenham

See Marble Hill House; The Octagon, Orleans House; Strawberry Hill.

## Westminster Abbey

*76; London SW1*

A very odd sort of article is Westminster Abbey. It is no longer an abbey, since it has no monks; nor, however, is it a cathedral, since it is not the seat of a bishop; nor is it a parish church. Surprisingly, too, for the most celebrated religious building in the country, situated in the heart of its capital city, we have no certain information about its origins. Some say that the original Benedictine monastery on the Island of Thorns was founded as early as the seventh century, others hold that its history goes back no further than the tenth; all we know for sure is that Edward the Confessor began an ambitious programme of rebuilding in 1050, consecrated his new church on 28 December 1065 and died a week later, on 5 January 1066. Of his church nothing whatever remains above ground, though parts of his monastic buildings have survived. The 'abbey' that we see today is essentially the one that was started almost 200 years later, when Henry III laid its foundation stone on 6 July 1245.

Henry's purpose in rebuilding the church was primarily to do honour to King Edward, who had been canonised in 1161 and whom he had adopted as his personal patron saint, and to provide him with a worthy shrine. He drained the Exchequer dry in his anxiety to drive ahead with the work, and by 1255 the chancel, crossing, transepts and first bay of the nave were complete, together with a separate Lady Chapel which he had built some years earlier. After that the work seems to have slowed down, but four more bays had been added to the nave by 13 October 1269, when the body of the royal saint was ceremonially brought to its new resting place.

The most interesting feature about this building is almost certainly due to the King himself. Henry had a French mother and a French wife, he had had a largely French upbringing, and throughout his life he preferred the company of Frenchmen to that of his own subjects. Taking as he did an intense personal interest in his new abbey, it was hardly surprising that he should have entrusted the job to a French master mason. This man's name is recorded as Henry of Reyns, and when we look at his work today it is hard to discount the theory that he came from Reims, for of all the Gothic churches of England Westminster Abbey is the most French in style. The polygonal apse, with its ambulatory and radiating chapels, is wholly French, and bears strong stylistic similarities to Reims Cathedral; French too is the bar tracery in the aisle and chapel windows – an innovation seen at Reims for the very first time in European architecture. Most telling of all, perhaps, is the sheer height of the building. French cathedral builders always stressed the soaring verticality of their work, while English masons preferred a broad, four-square appearance. Westminster, with an interior height of 103 feet, is higher than any English cathedral – though Reims, at 117 feet, is higher still.

Henry III died in 1272, and it was over a century before his nave was continued. Indeed, what was left of the old Norman nave remained standing till 1375. The master mason was now Henry Yevele, creator of the present Westminster Hall. Strangely enough, however, for a man of such outstanding genius, Yevele was content to continue the nave in precisely the same Early English style in which Henry had begun it – showing thereby a respect for the past unparalleled in the Middle Ages. He completed the nave to its full length, and gave the building its present west front, up to the base of the towers; but it was apparently left wholly or partly unroofed, since we read of both Henry V and Edward IV – the latter as late as 1468 – being shocked by its ruinous condition and contributing large sums for its restoration and eventual completion. It was only in 1500 that Abbot John Islip put an end to the work as King Henry had originally planned it. Even then the abbey still lacked what is to most people its crowning glory – the Chapel of Henry VII at the far east end.

This astonishing masterpiece was begun in 1503 by Henry VII, and was completed in 1512 by Henry VIII as a chantry chapel for his father. The designer was almost certainly Robert Vertue, succeeded after his death in 1506 by his younger brother William. This was the end of the pre-Reformation work. There remained only the west towers – and those had to wait nearly two and a half centuries. In 1698 Sir Christopher Wren was appointed Surveyor to the Fabric, and he continued to work spasmodically on the abbey till 1722, only a year before his death. While recommending the completion of the west towers, however, he never got round to the job himself; it was left to his successor, Nicholas Hawksmoor, to whose designs the towers were finally begun in 1734. But even Hawksmoor never saw them finished: he himself died two years later and the work was completed in 1745 by John James. Now one thing only was left – a crossing-tower. Wren had wanted a tall and narrow dome, with Gothic detail; a very odd sort of hybrid it would have been, and we can be thankful that it was never built. Hawksmoor and James had plumped for a slender needle spire, which would have been a good deal better, but this idea too came to nothing. As a result, the crossing remains to this day unmarked by anything more than the totally inadequate little pyramidal cap which looks – on the rare occasions when anybody notices it at all – like a stopgap and was indeed designed to be little more.

*The west front, Westminster Abbey.*

If we are to examine the exterior in detail – as we certainly should, despite the fact that the stone has almost all been replaced at one time or another – the best place to begin is before the west front. The bottom half, as we have seen, is Yevele's, the top Hawksmoor's. Despite its being the work of two of England's greatest architects, however, many people find it disappointing. It is surprisingly narrow, not particularly grand, and certainly nowhere near as impressive as almost any of the great medieval cathedrals. (One reason for this is that the ceremonial entrance was not here, but by the north transept.) As will soon become clear, the lower stages simply continue the design of the nave and aisles. There is only one entrance, in the centre, through a slightly

*Westminster Abbey.*

projecting porch, prettily vaulted and flanked by a pair of now-empty statue niches on each side. Ten more niches, equally vacant but with canopies, run along immediately above the doorway, and above these is the tall, seven-light Perpendicular window with four transoms – the top two of which are connected by a band of quatrefoils – which rises to its apex between the bases of the towers.

To each side of this centre, and separated from it by broad projecting buttresses which break twice into pinnacles, are the west ends of the two aisles. Here Yevele has divided his composition into three stages. The lowest, standing on a high plinth, is a window of two cusped lights with a quatrefoil in the spandrel; next, above another frieze of quatrefoils, is a broad pointed arch inscribed within a square and itself containing three circles, their cusps forming more quatrefoils; finally, at the third stage – which is marked by extensions of the central transom of the central window – comes a three-light Perpendicular window, blank below its transom, louvred and traceried above.

Hawksmoor's towers, which flank a rather silly little gable with a small window full of Perpendicular tracery, are curious affairs when you come to look at them closely. At first sight they seem Gothic enough; then you notice, immediately above the clock on the north tower and at the corresponding point on the south, a broken segmental pediment which is purest Baroque; it is quite a shock to find it carried, not on the classical columns that one would expect, but simply on the ribs of the Gothic panelling that covers all the otherwise plain surfaces of the entire façade. The three-light bell openings above, too, have what at first seem to be ogee heads; then one notices that the two curving sides do not in fact meet at all but end in a flat platform rather like a seventeenth-century Dutch gable. Even the angle buttresses have their horizontal divisions emphasised in a way unthinkable to any medieval mason; only the topmost stage of all – the parapets and pinnacles – appears thoroughly Gothic; and even then the detailing gives it away.

The aisle façades continue the pattern of the west front, with a minor difference in the narrow gallery stage, where we find single, larger, foiled circles instead of trios of smaller ones. Pinnacled flying buttresses support the clerestory. (Flying buttresses are very much a feature of the abbey; they appear everywhere, often in two or even three separate tiers.) We now arrive at the north transept, the north front of which constituted the original show front of the entire building. Unfortunately it is now almost all the work of Sir George Gilbert Scott and J.L. Pearson, who remodelled instead of being content just to restore. We can therefore go on to the east end, which is purely a restoration and consequently an accurate representation of Henry III's original idea. Insofar as the plan of apse and side chapels permit, the scheme remains the same as we saw further west – though this was, of course, the first part of the abbey to be built. It seems almost impossible to believe that more than a century separates the east end from the west: what an extraordinarily self-effacing man Henry Yevele must have been!

And so we come at last to Henry VII's Chapel. Though attached to the main body of the abbey, it could hardly be more different in style. It consists of four straight bays to north and south and then five radiating chapels at the east end, and its entire outer wall is closely – one might almost say minutely – panelled; it rises to a high, pierced parapet, above which the buttresses end in tall, polygonal towers with richly crocketed pepper-pots. From these, flying buttresses, which are themselves pierced in an openwork design, swoop gracefully up to a high clerestory with five-light windows, another parapet of quatrefoils, and slender pinnacles. All the way round between the buttresses the wall never ceases to undulate, giving a sense of constant movement and offering endless sparkling facets to the morning sun.

As you enter the abbey from the west, your first impression is one of soaring height. No other religious building in England makes this particular impact to the same degree – not even Canterbury. Your second impression is one of clutter. You are – and you cannot possibly forget the fact – standing in the country's greatest mausoleum, and the tombs and monuments to England's famous dead are crowded and clustered and sometimes almost wedged together like furniture piled in some vast repository. Such is the confusion that at ground level the eye is scarcely able to see the building as an architectural entity; it is only when you look upward, following those purplish green piers of Purbeck marble to where they change their material and their colour and branch outwards in white tiercerons to the vertiginous vault, that the beauty, the logic and the coherence of this great church is suddenly revealed. It is a design – thanks to Yevele's heroic restraint – of quite remarkable unity. Only with careful examination do the three different periods of the nave's building emerge. The earliest is the first bay west of the crossing, which necessarily had to be built at the same time as the crossing itself. (Among other differences of detail, the shaft rings on the piers are of marble rather than bronze.) This bay must date from before 1255. The next four bays seem to have been built in the 1260s; then, at the fifth bay from the crossing, comes the break: from the sixth, Yevele's work begins. Henceforth the lancet lights in aisles and clerestory are cusped and the tracery in the spandrels of a different design; but the interesting thing is that even these very minor innovations are compatible with the Early English style – it is as if Yevele wanted merely to mark the change-over as subtly as he could, without introducing any note of modernism.

Four huge Purbeck piers of clustered shafts mark the crossing, anti-climactically bereft of a proper tower; it is a deprivation of which one is even more conscious when inside the building. From it the aisle transepts extend for three bays to north and south; that to the north is also three bays wide, that to the south only two, since its western aisle has been taken over by the east walk of the cloister. A wall with two tiers of blank arcading now runs between the arches of the west arcade, which otherwise continues (as does its eastern counterpart) on the same pattern as in the nave. More interesting is the end wall of this south transept, sub-divided into four stages below the great rose window. The lowest has blank arches – some containing paintings – with rosette decoration; next comes a wall passage marked with a row of lancets, deeply cusped; next, six tall lancet windows, of similar design; and then the continuation of the triforium. But now look carefully, for in the spandrels of the triforium arches, here and nowhere else in the abbey, you will see four tall sculptured figures: St Edward and a pilgrim in the middle, and in the corners two censing angels. They are original work of about 1250 and are among the most exquisite medieval carvings in England – though a good pair of binoculars is needed to do them full justice. The rose window is a renewal of 1890, but is almost certainly a faithful copy of the original. In the north transept, which is in most respects similar to the south, there are more carvings: two standing figures in relief, at the height of the third stage on the east and west walls – who are often identified as St Edward and Henry III but who don't look very like them – and a whole choir of angels in the window soffits. They seem to be of much the same date as those to the south, but are clearly by a different hand and are slightly lacking in finesse. Both transepts, incidentally, have most magnificent carved bosses in their vaults: binoculars again, unless you can manage to make your way to the Muniment Room above the walled-off western aisle of the south transept, from which three of the best can be seen at close range.

Immediately to the west of the crossing is the choir. It extends for three bays into the nave, being closed at the western end by a most elaborate pulpitum or choir screen, originally built by Hawksmoor but completely refronted and Victorianised (the only word for it, though the work was actually done eight years before the Queen's accession) by Edward Blore. Inserted into its northern arch and looking distinctly out of place amid all the cusps and quatrefoils is William Kent's entirely classical tomb of Sir Isaac Newton, with sculpture by Rysbrack. He reclines on a pile of scientific books attended by a pair of *putti*, while a huge celestial globe (on which is seated the figure of Astronomy) hangs immediately above, for all the world like a gigantic apple about to fall on his head.

At the east end of the choir is the sanctuary with the high altar, before which all English kings and queens have been crowned since William the Conqueror (apart, of course, from Edward V and Edward VIII, who were never crowned at all). Behind it is the reredos, the west side of which is by Scott; the back, however, is of *c.*1430, and has a fascinating painted frieze depicting scenes from the life of Edward the Confessor. And, while we are still in the choir, we should also take a long, attentive look at the east end of Henry III's abbey, soaring up above and behind the reredos. There are three straight bays beyond the crossing, and then the curve of the apse begins. Sturdy, circular piers of Purbeck marble, each with four slender detached shafts at the cardinal points, carry tall, intricately moulded two-centred arches with the original diapering still in the spandrels. Above is the gallery – a full one, not just a wall passage or triforium, its twin-arched openings with encircled cinquefoils above being repeated on the inside, immediately behind – and then finally the clerestory, of the same basic design but twice the height, the moulded ribs of the vault springing from only a foot or two above the level of the sills.

Directly behind the high altar and reredos is the focal point of the entire abbey – the shrine of Edward the Confessor itself. It is raised a little above ground level, and is approached up a rather mean little flight of steps from the north ambulatory. In the centre of this hushed and numinous chamber the saint's body lies in what is left of his tomb. Its base, and the surrounding pavement, are the original thirteenth-century mosaic, of that particular South Italian style known as Cosmati work, which can also be seen in the sanctuary. It is signed 'Petrus Romanus' and dated 1270. It stands about 10 feet high, with a heavy entablature; to each side are three deep recesses with trefoil heads at which pilgrims could kneel. Alas, when the monastery was dissolved in 1540 the tomb was despoiled and the golden coffer set with precious stones carried off. Only the body was left, in its wooden inner coffin, and removed to some obscure corner of the abbey safely out of the reach of pilgrim superstition. It was returned to its rightful place by Mary I in 1557, when the two-storey wooden superstructure was added. Opposite, behind the high altar, stands the Coronation Chair, fashioned, carved and painted by a certain Master Walter to contain the sacred Stone of Scone, brought from Scotland in triumph by Edward I in 1297. Around about are other royal tombs: Henry III, his son Edward I and Queen Eleanor, his great-grandson Edward III and Queen Philippa, his great-great-great-grandson Richard II with his first wife, Anne of Bohemia, and Richard's cousin Henry V, lying at his own request beneath a high chantry chapel, his helmet, shield and saddle resting on a wooden bar above.

We leave by way of Henry's tomb, and suddenly find ourselves at the foot of a broad flight of steps. They lead us out of the Middle Ages and into a world which, though perhaps not quite of the Renaissance, yet knew its arrival to be imminent. For here is that most glorious adjunct to Westminster Abbey, so contrived as to be entirely hidden and unsuspected from anywhere else within the building: the CHAPEL OF KING HENRY VII. It was built, as we have seen, between 1503 and 1512, and it marks one of the great turning points in English history – the moment when on the field of Bosworth the Plantagenets ended their long, tragic degeneration and left the throne open to the most arrogantly self-confident dynasty ever to occupy it, the House of Tudor. Henry VII's Chapel is the first great monument of the Tudor age, heralding it like a fanfare of silver trumpets.

Henry's original purpose in building his Chapel was to provide a shrine for his by then fairly distant predecessor Henry VI who, he hoped, was shortly to be canonised. It takes the form of a nave with four-bay aisles and an apsed chancel with radiating chapels like the abbey itself. The walls seem to be composed of two things only: statues and glass. The statues, almost a hundred of them, are ranged in tier after tier, above the arcades, against the walls of the aisles and radiating chapels, even on the panelling of the chancel arch. And everywhere else there is a profusion of glass such as only late Perpendicular architects dared to contemplate. The clerestory windows are all of five lights and double-transomed, while the great window which occupies the entire upper west wall has no fewer than fifteen lights, with three highly elaborate transoms in its middle section and the most astonishing three-dimensional tracery at the sides. Even this window, however, pales before the splendour of the roof. The aisles and chapels are all fan-vaulted with pendants; the nave and chancel are generally believed to be fan-vaulted too, but in fact they are something else: what Pevsner describes – and there is no other description – as 'a superbly ingenious fantasy on the theme of fan-vaulting'. The basic design can be compared with that of a normal timber roof supported on arched braces, which here take the form of stone ribs, heavily cusped, springing at regular intervals from between the windows as if to form transverse arches. While still some distance from each other, however, they disappear into the roof (though the line of cusping seems to project through it) and, at the point of disappearance, huge fan-shaped pendants descend. Structurally, these are not part of the vaulting at all, and indeed they manage somehow to give a totally unreal impression of being suspended in mid-air. But the rest of the roof is panelled in such a way as to suggest a normal fan vault, and the overall effect is breathtaking.

In the chancel, behind a superb late Gothic screen, we can see – though with some difficulty – the tomb of Henry VII and his Queen, Elizabeth of York. It is by the Italian Pietro Torrigiani, that rowdy young man who, when they were both apprentices of Ghirlandaio, bashed Michelangelo's nose in – but to whom it was also given to fashion the first Renaissance monuments in England. Henry and Elizabeth lie side by side in gilded bronze on a black marble sarcophagus adorned with wreathed medallions in copper gilt and, at the end, winged *putti*. Four exquisite angels sit at the corners. This lovely tomb is, in fact, very slightly later than Torrigiani's other, even greater, masterpiece – the tomb of Henry's mother, Lady Margaret Beaufort, in the south aisle. The Gothic canopy and buttresses to each side of the tomb chest can be ignored as the work of other hands; but the pilasters, the shields in wreaths, and the fine Roman lettering of the inscription – all these are

Torrigiani's own, as is the effigy itself: grave, wise, compassionate, obviously a portrait, and surely the most beautiful effigy anywhere in the abbey. The towering edifice close by, ordered by James I for his mother, Mary Queen of Scots, looks vapid in comparison, though it is a good deal more ornate than the one he had run up for his predecessor (who had, after all, had Mary executed), Queen Elizabeth.

If this book were seriously concerned with church monuments, the entry on Westminster Abbey would take up several hundred pages; fortunately, however, it is not. We can therefore now leave the abbey proper by a door in the south aisle and emerge in the Cloister. The north walk and that part of the east walk which lies against the south transept both date from Henry III's day; the tracery in the latter comes straight from the Sainte Chapelle in Paris, which is only two or three years earlier. The rest – much of it heavily restored by Blore, Scott and others – is mid-fourteenth-century. From a door a little more than halfway along the east walk, a low passage with an immensely complex vault leads to a staircase and thence to the Chapter House. The contrast between the cool emptiness and simplicity of this lovely building and the chaotic profusion of monumental furniture in the abbey proper could hardly be more dramatic. It is a polygonal chamber in the style of Wells or Exeter, with a central compound pier bursting out like a fountain to form the ribs of the vault. Six of the eight sides have immense four-light windows which flood the whole room with light; one (which abuts St Faith's Chapel) has blank arcading; the other contains the entrance, a double doorway with central trumeau. (This, however, together with the large seated figure of Christ, is a nineteenth-century renewal, dating from Scott's restoration.) A stone bench runs round the wall, with blank trefoiled arcading behind it – round-headed, for the first and only time in the abbey. Within this arcading is what is left of a cycle of fourteenth-century wall paintings, but they are too faded (or too badly restored) to give much pleasure. What has survived quite remarkably is the original tiled floor, on which, among the kings, queens, archers, knights and rose windows there depicted, King Henry placed the inscription 'UT ROSA FLOS FLORUM SIC EST DOMUS ISTA DOMORUM.' How right he was.

## Westminster Cathedral

*77; Francis Street, SW1*

When in 1850 the Roman Catholic hierarchy was re-established in the United Kingdom it was clear that a metropolitan cathedral would have to be built. It was not, however, till 1867 that Cardinal Manning purchased the land formerly occupied by the Westminster Bridewell, and not till 1894 that Manning's successor, Cardinal Vaughan, called in the Catholic convert John Francis Bentley to produce designs. The original intention, predictably enough, had been for a Gothic building; but Vaughan favoured an earlier style which would be simpler – and therefore quicker – to build, and for which the decoration could follow later as money gradually became available. He was also anxious that the new cathedral should not have to compete architecturally with the splendour of Westminster Abbey, only a few hundred yards away. He therefore suggested that Bentley should adopt the Byzantine style. To prepare himself for the task, Bentley travelled to Venice, Torcello and Ravenna; one is surprised, however, to learn that he did not go as far as Constantinople, for the designs that he produced on his return are a good deal closer to St Sophia than they are to St Mark's.

The great west front – which can now be properly appreciated for the first time thanks to the recent creation of a piazza between the cathedral and Victoria Street – makes an immediate impact with its bold stripes of white stone across the red brick which is the basic building material. It is dominated by the immensely tall Italianate *campanile* which rises 284 feet from above the first bay of the north aisle, square for most of its height but then suddenly breaking into small pinnacles from which there emerges an octagonal lantern surmounted by a dome. Domed too are the twin polygonal towers that flank the central portal – the latter the work of J.A. Marshall, who took over the work after Bentley's sudden death in 1902, on the day before he was due to receive the RIBA Gold Medal. Its own inspiration seems more Renaissance than anything else; indeed, when viewed from the west at ground level the building shows the influence of Italy more strongly, if anything, than that of the Greek world. It is only when seen from a height that it shows the full importance of the Byzantine element: in the eastward march of the four broad, shallow domes marking the four bays of the east–west axis; in the small towers clustering round them; in the tripartite segmental windows below; and – most of all, perhaps – in the design of the easternmost dome over the sanctuary, set on its sloping drum pierced, St Sophia-style, by twelve round-headed windows.

But if the exterior is merely striking, the interior is magnificent. You first pass across a narrow narthex, Byzantine again, and only then find yourself in the nave – the highest and the broadest in the country. It is divided into three immense square bays, separated by massive round-headed arches, from which pendentives rise to form the circular bases of the domes above. Bentley's idea was to have every square inch of wall encrusted with marble revetment or mosaic, as at St Mark's, and at the lower levels this has indeed been done. Further up, however, this decoration gives out, and the bare, very dark brick rises up until it disappears dramatically into the blackness of the roof above.

To each side of the nave is a narrow aisle, and beyond this a succession of side chapels, the dividing walls of which also serve as buttresses to support the weight of the domes. There are two of these side chapels to each of the first two main bays; then, at the third, the line is broken by the transepts – which, like the buttresses, are built within the main structure and do not project beyond the line of the outside walls. Unusually and interestingly, these transepts are divided down the middle on a north–south axis, by means of an arched screen supporting a twin tunnel vault above. This feature may well have been borrowed from St Augustine's, Kilburn (*q.v.*), as may also the way in which the nave gallery extends across the transept on a bridge, providing an unbroken line to the high altar. This stands immediately beneath the easternmost dome (that is, the fourth bay), which as we have noted is pierced by twelve windows around the base, and is covered by a towering marble *baldacchino* supported on eight columns of Verona marble and richly inlaid with *opus Alexandrinum*. Of similar workmanship but even more directly based on the medieval South Italian *ambo* is the sumptuous pulpit, brought from Rome and presented by Cardinal Bourne in 1934.

The sanctuary is flanked by the Lady Chapel to the south and, to the north, the Chapel of the Blessed Sacrament. The former, more richly decorated than any other part of the cathedral, has mosaics by Gilbert Pownall, who was also responsible for the mosaics in the tympanum above the high altar. It includes what must be the only representation in this particular medium of the Tower of London and Tower Bridge. The mosaics in the Blessed Sacrament Chapel are the work of Boris Anrep and illustrate various aspects of the Eucharist. Of all the works of art in the cathedral, however, perhaps the most remarkable is the relief series of the Stations of the Cross by Eric Gill, made during the First World War.

Few people – surprisingly few – visit Westminster Cathedral for other than devotional purposes, which is a pity. Besides being one of the most moving religious buildings in all London, it is of outstanding artistic and architectural interest. It stands too as an extraordinary tribute to the qualities of plain English brick; there is no steel reinforcement anywhere.

## Westminster Hall

*78; Parliament Square, SW1*

It was some half a century before the Norman Conquest that the English kings transferred their capital from Winchester to London. They first made their residence in the City; it was Edward the Confessor who decided on the move to Westminster, beginning the royal palace there at the same time as he started work on his new abbey. Of King Edward's palace, as of the extension built by William the Conqueror, nothing now remains: what has come down to us is Westminster Hall, which in its original form was the contribution of the Conqueror's son, William Rufus. He had in fact intended a whole new palace, and made no secret of his disappointment when

*Westminster Cathedral.*

he saw the completed Hall for the first time: 'a mere bed-chamber', he is said to have called it.

All that remains of the eleventh-century Hall today is the east and west walls; but they are enough to show that it was the same size then as it is now – at 240 feet in length, by far the largest Norman Hall in England and probably in Europe. Its 70-foot breadth was originally sub-divided into a nave and aisles, separated by rows of wooden supports; still, it must have been impressive indeed in those days: William's dismissive remarks were doubtless just swagger – he was that sort of man. His Hall, however, was severely damaged by fire in 1291, and though it was restored by Edward II it never properly regained its former splendour till it was taken in hand by Richard II in 1394.

The moment could not have been more propitious. Richard had as his master mason one of the greatest of medieval architects, Henry Yevele, who had recently completed the nave of Westminster Abbey across the way; he also had a carpenter of genius, Hugh Herland. Together, these two men produced a new Hall which, though no longer or broader than William's, was 2 feet higher and infinitely more magnificent. Its chief glory is Herland's timber roof – the earliest large hammer-beam roof in England and the finest anywhere in the world. Indeed, it is the sheer massiveness of the construction that strikes one first – the hammer-posts themselves are over 3 feet thick, and the whole roof weighs 660 tons. In recent years it has had to be reinforced with steel, largely owing to the ravages of death-watch beetle, but it is still essentially as it was in King Richard's day. The hammer-beams are supported on arched braces which, together with the main arches, spring from stone corbels set along the frieze running the length of the east and west walls just below the level of the windows. All the spaces – between these arched braces and the hammers, between the hammers and the main arches, between the main arches and the two tiers of collar-beams above them, and indeed just about everywhere else – are filled with tracery, while shield-bearing angels, prone and with their wings outstretched, are carved against the hammer-beams. The total height is 92 feet, the 70-foot span the widest of any timber roof in the country.

The two-light Perpendicular windows along the walls to east and west are all renewed and of no interest; more impressive by far are the great nine-lighters to north and south. The south window, however, is not in its original position, having been set back by Sir Charles Barry as part of his plan to build a high, broad dais at this end, as part of St Stephen's entrance to his Palace of Westminster. The window now appears through a towering arch, to each side of which are ranged six tremendous statues of kings, carved for the Hall in King Richard's time.

Westminster Hall has seen almost as much of English history as the Abbey itself. It was here that Edward II abdicated in 1327, presenting his fourteen-year-old son, Edward III, as King; here that Richard II was deposed and Henry IV proclaimed in his place; here that Thomas More, Anne Boleyn and Guy Fawkes stood trial, to be followed soon after by Charles I and, rather later, by Warren Hastings; here, finally, that kings and queens of England lie in state after their deaths. It is almost always open and should on no account be missed.

### Westminster, Palace of

See Palace of Westminster.

# Norfolk

Scenically, it must be admitted that Norfolk is not the most exciting of counties. Though not invariably as flat as most people seem to think, its occasional undulations never really amount to very much. Its 90 miles of coastline possess none of that jagged grandeur that characterises our western shores and – though they can sometimes run to a good broad beach and even a rather half-hearted attempt at a cliff – are all too often blurred by tidal marshes and saltings and bleak expanses of reeds; inland, there are vast areas of open heath, where such trees as exist at all tend to be short and stunted by the bitter easterly gales which have come straight from the Urals, encountering not a single obstacle on their course. The wonder is that, despite these defects, Norfolk can have so much beauty and so much atmosphere. The beauty comes above all from the light, from the huge skies that allow it more sunshine than is enjoyed by any other county; the atmosphere is born of tranquillity and a spirit of quiet independence such as I have encountered nowhere else in England. For much of its history Norfolk has been virtually an island – until the draining of the fens Antwerp and Rotterdam were far more accessible than London – and its people have developed their own customs and traditions, while remaining somehow more conscious than the rest of their compatriots of the lands beyond the North Sea. It is no coincidence that the first wave of prosperity to wash over East Anglia came directly from the Low Countries, in the wake of those Flemish weavers brought to England by Edward III.

Architecturally, on the other hand, Norfolk has no rival. What other county can boast, as well as one of the loveliest of all cathedrals, over 650 pre-Victorian parish churches still standing, to say nothing of nearly 100 more in ruins? Or over fifty monastic houses in various stages of decay? Or, as at Norwich and Castle Rising, two of the grandest Norman castles surviving anywhere? As for its great country houses, Holkham, Houghton and Blickling would alone give it a claim to supremacy which I suspect only Derbyshire might dispute; but there are countless others very nearly as fine (East Barsham, Felbrigg, Raynham, Oxburgh and Melton Constable just for a start) which surely tip the scales once again in Norfolk's favour. Finally there is Norwich itself – for me the fairest provincial city in England, not excluding York – and King's Lynn, one of the most unspoilt, distinguished, and utterly enchanting small towns to be found anywhere. I rest my case.

This stunning performance, on the part of a county which today by population ranks only twenty-second among the counties of England, is still more remarkable when one remembers that Norfolk is chalk country and – except for the soft reddish brown carstone of the north-west corner – virtually without building stone. When this has been essential, it has had to be imported, more often than not by sea from Caen or, later, by river from Barnack near Stamford. Otherwise, the local builders have used brick – and no one has used it better – or that most characteristic of indigenous materials, flint. Flint has a marvellous texture when used well, but it is no good for quoins or firm corners, a fact which explains the frequency of round church towers in the Saxon and Norman periods. There are 179 such towers in all England; Norfolk possesses 119 of them. The proliferation of flint also led to the invention of flushwork, another *spécialité de la région* capable of splendid effects in the right hands.

Surrounded by such a plethora of architectural wealth, the task of selection in Norfolk has proved even harder than elsewhere. Among the churches there has been little difficulty in the earlier periods; the Norman Walsoken, the Early English West Walton, the Decorated Snettisham or Cley – all these stick out a mile. But with the prodigious Perpendicular wool churches one is immediately in trouble. It is obvious enough where to begin – with Walpole St Peter, Salle, Cawston and St Peter Mancroft; but where does one go from there? With country houses it is the same story, once the big three have been safely listed. What follows, therefore, is a representative selection, a mere sampler of the riches that this most wonderful of counties has to offer.

## Attleborough

*1; 6 miles SW of Wymondham on A11*

ST MARY'S CHURCH makes a magnificent centre to the little town, set back as it is in a big green churchyard. It has a Norman crossing-tower, which is now an east one – the Norman chancel having long since disappeared – with an Early English top stage, identifiable from its plate-traceried bell openings. The rest is a very graceful essay in Decorated, with a four-leaf clover design of tracery that reappears in window after window, including the three-light east window, where we see it four times, and the five-light west one where it is repeated another three. The nave and the two transepts have kept their original Norman crossing arches, and the eastern one is there too, although it no longer leads anywhere. The transepts are especially interesting: although the south one is almost a century earlier than the north, stylistically they are almost identical. The only original Perpendicular element – since the east window in the south transept has been reset – is the two-storeyed north porch; it was built by Sir John Ratcliffe, who died in 1441. It has little sculptured heads serving as capitals to the shafts beside the doorway, and a tierceron-star vault within.

But the glory of St Mary's is its screen. In the reigns of both Edward VI and Elizabeth I – in 1547 and 1561 – orders were issued to remove all lofts from screens, since these were associated with both roods and organs, two things abominated by the early Puritans. Somehow, the screen at Attleborough escaped on both occasions. Its loft is complete on the west side (though it has lost some of its coving to the east) and, rarer still, has retained its high parapet, painted with the coats of arms of the episcopal sees. It stretches across nave and aisles, embracing a pair of side altars as it goes. The central entrance has a cusped ogee arch of almost Rococo fantasy and lightness; to each side, some of the bays are open while others are blocked with painted panels of full-length figures. A surprising amount of the old, pale, original colour has survived. The overall impact is not easily forgotten.

It is further increased by the wall paintings immediately above the crossing arch. On each side of a large central cross there are figures in two tiers, crude but lively and anything but hieratic. St Christopher, meanwhile, looms tremendous on the south wall.

## Barnham Broom Hall

*2; 3 miles NW of Wymondham off B1108*

Though quite near to Wymondham, Barnham Broom Hall is remotely situated and correspondingly little known. It is, however, a house of some importance as well as much beauty and immense charm; and it is fortunate in having been recently bought by a young and enthusiastic family who are restoring it with imagination and sensitivity. Of red brick, it is of three main dates. The southern section, diapered and with a crow-stepped gable, dates from around 1520. Next comes the centre, which is some twenty years later; it has a fine porch with a deeply moulded four-centred entrance arch crowned by another stepped gable with three pinnacles. The original doors are still in place and very splendid they are: linenfold, with the rose of England and the fleur-de-lis of France in the spandrels. The Hall within is now of one storey only and its breadth has been diminished by a passage, but it has kept its broad chimney, whose great bressummer carries in its right-hand corner the same carving as the door and is thus almost certainly of the same date. Above the porch is a delightful little room probably used by the recusant Chamberlayne family as a chapel, and above that again, up a tiny spiral stair, what must have been the priest's bedroom.

The north wing – to the right of the entrance – is a Jacobean addition. It is distinguished on the outside by a tall circular brick chimney and three pedimented windows on the ground floor, mullioned and transomed. It is, however, the first floor of this wing that contains the most spectacular feature of the house: the quite magnificent plaster ceiling of the main Drawing Room, with a big central pendant and a frieze in which, halfway along the north wall, is represented a winged figure – emblem of the Chamberlaynes – carrying an open book (symbolising Justice?) and wearing what looks like a skirt made of wheatsheaves. Here too is the date: 1614. Another room, now sub-divided, immediately to the north has a similar frieze of the same period, somewhat less ornate. In the far north end of the attic, beneath the splendid timber roof with its arched braces and collar-beams, is something of a curiosity: a fireplace with a four-centred arch and deep mouldings, which probably also dates from the early seventeenth century. (There is a similar phenomenon at Great Cressingham Priory, *q.v.*)

## Barningham Winter

*3; 4½ miles S of Sheringham off A148*

On its porch BARNINGHAM HALL carries the date 1612, when it was built for a member of the junior branch of the Paston family. The west front, of red brick with stone dressings, is unchanged since that date, and very remarkable it is: only five bays across, but with eight windows of no fewer than ten lights on the two principal floors, a porch that continues upwards into a four-storey frontispiece with a crow-step gable at the top and – the most unusual feature of all – two-storey dormers. These five immensely tall interruptions to the roof line are all flanked by polygonal buttresses with pinnacles and have a third pinnacle at the apex. All the windows are mullioned and – except the very topmost – transomed. More surprisingly, they are all pedimented as well.

The south front was to a large extent remodelled by Humphry Repton and his son John Adey Repton in 1805; the plans (signed by Humphry) are still in the house. It was they who added the bays and replaced the Jacobean windows with Gothic ones – a curious aberration, since in every other detail they were careful to respect the original character of the building, even to the extent of using specially made bricks of the same size. Humphry also extended the house eastward with a new Drawing Room; it must have been extremely narrow along this axis before he did so.

You enter the house to find the main staircase facing you across the Hall. Clearly it too is a Repton addition, with its central flight to a half landing and then two parallel flights reversing back against opposite walls to the first floor; and indeed the original stair survives immediately to the north of it. (The staircase 'with simple cast-iron railing' mentioned by Pevsner does not exist, and never has; he is right, however, about the two Flemish statuettes of saints, carved in oak, on the newels. They are of the fifteenth century, and superb.)

The interior of the house is nearly all of the nineteenth century. The grandest room is the great Saloon, in its day almost a long gallery, occupying the centre of the first floor on the west front. This has now been sub-divided into three – an unfortunate development perhaps, but an inescapable one for the owner, faced with the necessity of bringing up a young family in servantless post-war England. But at Barningham Hall it is the exterior, above all, that counts; and that memorable west front is worth going a long way to see.

ST MARY'S CHURCH stands in the grounds, just to the left of the drive as you approach the house. Its Perpendicular west tower, now an ivy-clad ruin, lends it an almost ridiculously romantic air. The only surviving section is the chancel, which has some nice Decorated tracery and is still used as the parish church.

## Beeston-next-Mileham ⋆

*4; 6 miles NW of East Dereham off A47*

There are four Beestons in Norfolk; this one lies roughly halfway between East Dereham and Swaffham in a strangely remote and underpopulated area. ST MARY'S horizontally striped black and white spire, rebuilt in 1873, provides a distinguishing landmark but is hardly prepossessing; persevere, however, for the rewards are great.

Apart from the top stage of the tower and the clerestory, the church is almost entirely Decorated; originally, the clerestory was too, and you can still see the outlines of the big circular windows which existed before the heightening of the roof in about 1400. How fortunate it was that they did not change the aisle and chancel windows at the same time; these are all lovely, particularly the reticulated five-light east window of the chancel and the three-light ones at the east ends of the aisles. (The west ends embrace the tower on each side.) You enter by the north porch, which has a little chequer flushwork but is not otherwise especially remarkable, and once inside your first impression – at least on a sunny day – is one of light. It is not, however, simply that which comes streaming through the windows; it is also that which is reflected by the pale, almost bleached timbers of the roof and, indeed, almost all the other woodwork as well. It is a marvellous roof, single hammer-beam, the hammer-beams resting on unusually tall wall posts with carved figures; between them are short horizontal pieces with more figures, supporting the principal rafters. Alas, the figures are nearly all defaced, thanks to the attentions of Dowsing and his men during the Civil War; but the texture of the roof is somehow so beautiful that one scarcely notices.

Drop your eyes, now, to the screens and the benches. All three of the screens, the central rood-screen and the parcloses to each side, are unusually fine, with traces of the original painting; best of the three is, however, the parclose screen to the north, a really exquisite piece with rich cresting and filigree tracery of breathtaking delicacy. The benches, too, are a joy, particularly those on the south side, which are raised on a platform about a foot above the level of the nave and very widely spaced so that the wonderful old red-tiled floor – another feature which adds immeasurably to the beauty of the church – is visible between them. They have lovely carved poppy-heads and some of the backs are pierced with little quatrefoils.

There is, in this wonderful church, only one serious blemish – the really horrible coloured glass in the tracery of some of the windows. Fortunately, there is not much; could it not be removed – and quickly?

## Beeston St Laurence

*5; 4 miles NE of Wroxham on A1151*

It was in the 1770s that Jacob Preston, in a sudden surge of enthusiasm for Strawberry Hill Gothick, decided to give his old manor house at Beeston a monastic front, complete with Y-traceried lancets, battlements and angle buttresses. Within ten years, however, he realised that this was not enough; the old house was demolished and a new one was built in similar but more thorough-going style further up the hill. This house, essentially unchanged, is the BEESTON HALL of today, still lived in by the Preston family.

One's first surprise is occasioned by the fact that the entire house, though actually built of brick, is faced with flints, squared, knapped and coursed. On a sunny day the shimmering effect is almost startling; one sees this treatment often enough on churches in East Anglia, though even then usually combined with flushwork, but seldom indeed on a country house. Beeston Hall is not large, comprising just two storeys of seven bays, with battlements that continue up the end gables and polygonal buttresses at the corners, ending in crocketed pinnacles. Most striking is the three-bay centre, projecting ever so slightly forward, in which the two side windows on each floor curve up in graceful ogees to little fleurs-de-lis. One can only regret the ugly little Victorian porch – but the owners are grateful enough for it in the winter. The garden front is simpler; there is no centre, and the evenly spaced windows are pointed only gently, and on the ground floor. Upstairs they are straightforward, sashed, Georgian.

So the architect, whoever he was – and we shall come to that in a minute – was not so enamoured of the Gothick as to overdo it, or allow it to become a bore; and this fact becomes still clearer when we go inside. Only the Hall, which has the lightest of plaster pseudo-vaults and distinctly playful hood-moulds over the doors, has any pretensions to medievalism. For the rest, a simple neo-classicism rules, most of the windows that are pointed on the outside having been cut down to square within.

Who built it? We shall probably never know for sure, but the best bet is William Wilkins the Elder, father of

*Binham Priory.*

the architect of the National Gallery. He was a friend and Norfolk colleague of Humphry Repton, who is known to have made frequent visits to Beeston and almost certainly advised on the landscaping, and he was an enthusiastic admirer of flint – particularly when squared and coursed – as a result of his studies of the medieval buildings of Norwich. If he was indeed responsible for Beeston, it must rank with Donnington Hall in Leicestershire as his best work, and one of which he might be justly proud.

## Binham Priory

*6; 7½ miles NE of Fakenham on B1388*

Though Binham Priory is a ruin, it is a magical one. Built of local flint and Barnack limestone, it was founded as early as 1091, but building went on until the middle of the thirteenth century – when they completed that astonishing west front. Don't be put off by the bricked-up west window: a sad reflection on that generation in the early nineteenth century that allowed it to collapse, and also perhaps on our own for allowing the eyesore to remain. Look instead at those parts of the west front that do survive, not missing the fascinating interplay of trefoils, quatrefoils, cinquefoils and sexfoils at the base, all leading up to the lovely octofoil at the top of the great west window itself, which has miraculously remained *in situ*. Notice, too, the delicacy with which they are undercut and the superb craftsmanship everywhere, even in such details as the dogtooth decoration. Gradually you realise that you are face to face with one of the supreme Early English west fronts in the country, in terms both of its perfectly balanced design and of its immaculate execution. Yet even this is not all. The middle window, ruined as it is, unquestionably carries bar tracery; and if Matthew Paris is right when he tells us that the west front of Binham was built by Richard de Parco – a prior who died in 1244 – then this tracery, and indeed the whole façade, is the first example of its kind in England, slightly predating that of Westminster Abbey, begun only in 1245.

Inside, the remains are limited to seven of the original nine bays of the twelfth-century nave – which now constitute Binham parish church. But the impact of this truncated nave is terrific, the massive Norman arches rising one above the other – intricately carved at ground level, plain in the gallery and in the clerestory, turning to Early English as they proceed towards the west. On the north wall, incidentally, there hangs an eighteenth-century engraving of the priory with the west front still more or less complete.

To the east and south of the church lie the ruins of the chancel, crossing and transepts, together with what is left of the old priory buildings, full of sadness and beauty.

## Blakeney

*7; 9 miles E of Sheringham on A149*

A charming little town – scarcely more than a village – at the edge of the marsh, Blakeney is still a practicable port if your boat is sufficiently small and the tide sufficiently high. It is also something of a shrine for naturalists, since Blakeney Point is an important bird sanctuary owned and managed by the National Trust. Architecturally, it has little to offer except ST NICHOLAS'S CHURCH; but that is very fine indeed. The exterior does not seem particularly promising; the knapped flint with which it was refaced in the 1880s gives it a rather gloomy appearance, and the little stair and beacon turret at the north-east corner look distinctly silly opposite the noble fifteenth-century tower at the other end.

But go inside, and you will see why Blakeney has found a place in this book. The Early English chancel, built in the very last years of the thirteenth century – rather late for this sort of thing, but East Anglia always tends to lag behind a bit – with its rib-vaulted roof (the ribs continued on shafts right down to the ground), splendid bosses and wondrous seven-lancet window, is everything such a chancel should be. (The only other seven-lancet east window in England is at Ockham, Surrey (*q.v.*).) The chancel is unusually low, since there is another room above it, approached from the turret; but low chancels have a mystery and intimacy of their own. In contrast, the fifteenth-century nave is astonishingly high, with a fine hammer-beam roof and carved wooden angels set horizontally, as if in flight.

There are several highly rewarding tombstones in the churchyard.

## Blickling Hall*

*NT; 8; 1½ miles NW of Aylsham on B1354*

Like Audley End, Longleat and Compton Wynyates, Blickling belongs to that select company of English country houses which reveal themselves without warning to the unsuspecting traveller in a genuine *coup de théâtre*. The winding green lane from Aylsham seems to hold no particular promise; then, suddenly, you round a corner – and that tremendous Jacobean façade of the rosiest red brick socks you between the eyes and practically drives you into the ditch. In fact, the house will prove to be more tremendous even than it at first appears: the medieval moat that had encircled its predecessor, though already drained and dry, prevented the architect, Robert Lyminge, from spreading himself to the extent of more than seven bays on this south front and on the opposite one to the north. To east and west, where the fronts run to eleven bays each, the length is almost double.

Before he began work on Blickling in 1619, Lyminge had been chief contractor at Hatfield; thence, surely, come the square corner turrets with their ogee caps, the shaped gables, the ornate stone porch, the pierced balustrading and even the tall central clock tower – though this last is a nineteenth-century reconstruction (by John Adey Repton) and not, it must be admitted, an entirely successful one. Happier far was Lyminge's decision to make up for the narrowness of his site by building two side wings, projecting forward from his south front beyond the moat. The Dutch gables on these wings – in other words, wings which are shaped and topped with small pediments – are dated 1624; they are thus, together with those a few miles away at Raynham, among the earliest of their kind anywhere in the country.

The two other principal fronts, those to the north and west, are in their present form largely the work of the Norwich architect Thomas Ivory, his son William and his nephew John, who were employed between 1765 and 1785 by the 2nd Earl of Buckinghamshire. Contrary to what used to be thought, the north side was never

open to form a courtyard; the Ivorys did, however, transform an irregular front into the present symmetrical composition by removing the whole centre between the Jacobean corner towers and shaped gables – it seems to have contained elements of the former medieval manor house – and replacing it by the three bays that we see today, unexceptionable if uninspired, with their tall pedimented windows.

Where once was a drawbridge, the dry moat is now crossed by a charming two-arched bridge with a pierced parapet – clearly Lyminge's work. Crossing this, you enter by the great porch with its Tuscan columns, figures of Victory in the spandrels of the arch and intricate heraldry above. A heavy panelled oak doorway then leads you through to the outer courtyard. At this point, before the eighteenth-century alterations, you would have been facing the Great Hall – which, unusually in Jacobean houses, was placed centrally, with its entrance in the middle across the court. It was also recessed between the two inner corner towers. What the Ivorys did was to sweep away the Hall altogether, bring the courtyard wall forward some 10 feet, and in the resulting space insert the present magnificent double staircase – far more impressive than its predecessor (which would have been built round a central well as at Hatfield) but incorporating nearly all Lyminge's original woodwork, including two of the carved figures on the newel-posts. This same laudable wish to preserve as much as possible of the seventeenth-century character of the house led the Ivorys to retain in several of the main rooms the

*Blickling Hall.*

original chimneypieces, overmantels and – the pride of Blickling – the plaster ceilings by perhaps the most brilliant of all Jacobean plasterers, Edward Stanyan. His work appears to splendid effect in the South Drawing Room and the Upper Ante-Room; but neither of these prepares the visitor for the magnificence of the Long Gallery, whose thirty-one principal panels, all surrounded by a labyrinth of strapwork, contain heraldic achievements and delightful allegories of the virtues and the five senses.

Even without that tremendous ceiling, or the several thousand priceless books that line its walls, the Long Gallery at Blickling would be one of the grandest in England. It runs a full 120 feet from end to end – more than half the length of the east front – but its considerable breadth ensures for it the character of a room rather than a corridor. Voices have been raised against the High Victorian Gothic bookcases and the painted frieze above them. They are the work of John Hungerford Pollen, an artist who deserves to be better known. When he designed the Blickling Library in 1860 he was fresh from working with Rossetti, Morris and Burne-Jones on the Oxford Union, while a quarter of a century later he was one of the leaders of the Arts and Crafts movement. Old photographs suggest that the Library as he left it might well have been somewhat overpowering; but the relatively little of his original decoration that remains today is of such quality that I for one would not have it changed.

Of the other principal rooms, nearly all have some feature or another that impresses them on the memory. The Brown Drawing Room has lost most of Pollen's decoration, but still contains the mid-fifteenth-century stone chimneypiece that originally stood in Sir John Fastolf's Caister Castle (*q.v.*) and was later removed by the Paston family, to whom the castle passed after his death, to their other house, Oxnead Hall. It was only when Oxnead was demolished in 1731 that the chimneypiece was acquired by the 1st Earl of Buckinghamshire, who brought it to Blickling. In the Dining Room there is a fine overmantel by Lyminge and decoration by Pollen and both the Ivorys; in the South Drawing Room on the first floor – the original Great Chamber – another glorious Stanyan ceiling, with pendants this time; in the Upper Ante-Room yet another, with a simply enormous central one; in the two Chinese Rooms – Lyminge's Withdrawing Room, divided into two by the Ivorys – some wonderfully preserved eighteenth-century Chinese wallpaper: and, in the Drawing Room leading off the north end of the Long Gallery, a neo-classical setting of surpassing splendour (by William Ivory) for the superbly arrogant tapestry of Peter the Great, the gift of Catherine the Great – his granddaughter-in-law – to the 2nd Earl when he was Ambassador to St Petersburg in 1762. William's too is the white and gold State Bedroom on the site of the Jacobean Chapel, the bed itself set back – in what must have seemed a distinctly old-fashioned manner – behind a screen of fluted Ionic columns.

Strictly speaking, this book has no business with gardens; it is worth pointing out, however, that at Blickling it is possible to trace the development of the English garden from the first half of the eighteenth century to the middle of the twentieth. The Doric Temple at the end of the central vista is almost certainly the work of Matthew Brettingham, dating from about 1745; towards the end of the century we find Humphry Repton replanting the park, enlarging the lake and designing the Orangery (where Nicholas Stone's statue of Hercules is another import from Oxnead), while his son John Adey – not content with the clock tower – built the arcades that join the wings to the south front. In 1872 the gardens were massively Victorianised, parterres being laid out on the east front with walls, steps, terraces and balustrades, by Sir Matthew Digby Wyatt. The whole thing was much simplified in the 1930s, when the former regiment of gardeners was reduced to little more than a platoon; but both park and gardens are still admirably maintained by the National Trust, and add immeasurably to one's enjoyment of one of the loveliest of the great houses of England.

## Castle Acre*

*9; 4½ miles N of Swaffham off A1065*

A castle, a church, and – with Binham – the finest monastic remains in Norfolk are what this pretty little town has to offer. The CASTLE, extending over 15 acres and embracing the town within its outer bailey, goes back to the second half of the eleventh century, the date of its horseshoe-shaped motte and what is left of the circular keep. The best-preserved element is, however, the great gateway giving on to Bailey Street, with its two round towers; this must go back to about 1250.

West of the castle, standing proudly on the hill overlooking the priory ruins, is ST JAMES'S CHURCH. There was clearly a church on this site in Norman times – indeed, the little arched window, now blocked, above the priest's doorway may well be a vestige of it – but the building we see today is essentially of the fourteenth century, enlarged and substantially remodelled in the fifteenth. (The east window is Victorian, by Ewan Christian.) Its furniture is more interesting than its architecture: there is a magnificently tall font cover, and both screen and pulpit have retained most of their lovely paintings, which cannot be later than *c.*1400.

And so to the PRIORY, which was founded in the 1090s by William de Warenne, 2nd Earl of Surrey, for Cluniac monks. It stands in the loveliest of settings, in a broad green meadow on the banks of the Nar, which makes it all the more tragic that the local authorities should have allowed a particularly unattractive camping site to be established immediately to the north-west – partially, but inadequately, screened by some magnificent chestnut trees. But the ruins themselves are of most memorable beauty and strangeness. The beauty, apart from the natural surroundings, resides principally in the great west front of the church, a considerable portion of which – largely owing to the stone facing of the flint rubble walls – has remained standing. With its huge round central arch of four orders and the rows of blank arcading – much of it interlaced – around and above, it seems, for the most part, almost a copy-book example of a Norman show front. Above it the great west window has been lost; but this is if anything a blessing, since – as is clear from the surviving pointed arch and the jagged remains of the tracery within it, it was a Perpendicular insertion. Otherwise, the only surviving suggestion of Gothic is to be found in the two Early English windows high in the right-hand tower; but they are original, simply representing the Transitional period that had been reached by the time the building had progressed to this point, and are thus, unlike the central window, an organic part of the composition.

The strangeness strikes you only as you enter the ruined nave and transepts: here the walls and piers – having long since lost any superstructure to support – have decayed or been sculpted by wind and weather into tall, fantastic shapes like petrified giants, somehow more redolent of the prehistoric than of the Romanesque. The east end – originally three-apsed – has almost gone; beyond the south transept, however, the twelfth-century chapter house, dorter and – forming the cross-bar of a T at the far southern end – the rere-dorter are still recognisable.

Best preserved of all, having kept its roof, is the prior's lodging, south-west of the main front. Though it too dates originally from the twelfth century, what we see today is in all its essentials of the early sixteenth – perhaps only a decade or so before the Dissolution. On the west side it has a broad porch with a four-centred arch, an area of chequered flushwork above, then a four-light transomed window and half-timbering under the gable. To the left, underneath another gable with seventeenth-century crow-steps, is a big square oriel marking the prior's solar. Inside it has a broad Tudor fireplace, with ceiling beams moulded and painted with flowers, and a big bay of nine lights (post-Dissolution) to the north making another oriel, semi-circular this time, on the outside. Immediately to the east of this is the old Prior's Chapel.

North of the ruins stands the Gatehouse, which must also be of about 1500. It has two entrances, one for carriages and one for pedestrians, and a lovely room, surprisingly large, in the porter's lodge on the east side.

## Castle Rising

*10; 4 miles NE of King's Lynn off A149*

Here we have another romantic ruin. Of the twelfth-century CASTLE built around 1138 by William de Albini when he married Henry I's widow, little but the keep remains, and the huge earthwork surrounding it. This keep, one of the largest and most ornate in England, still looks magnificent. The best part is the entrance – a round, moulded arch, richly decorated, leading to a wonderfully broad stone stairway. This is broken a little less than halfway up by a second great portal, above which gapes a sinister *meurtrière*, then continues to a third, which gives access first to a small vestibule and thence through yet another splendidly ornamented arch to the Great Hall. The Dept of the Environment have worked out an admirable itinerary through the rest of the

*Castle Rising.*

building, which is as evocative, on its lonely windswept hill, as a ruined castle could hope to be.

The CHURCH OF ST LAWRENCE has a fine swaggering Norman west front and a beautiful Early English chancel with an east window of three lancets, stepped and shafted. But it is too heavily Victorianised to give much real pleasure. A better bet is the HOWARD HOSPITAL just to the east – almost unchanged, even to the Jacobean wooden furniture, since the day it was built in 1614 as an almshouse for ten poor spinsters. Only the Chapel disappoints, having been rebuilt in 1880.

## Cawston*

*11; 4½ miles SW of Aylsham on B1145*

A rather forbidding church from the outside – largely because of the strangely sawn-off look of the top of the tower – ST AGNES'S quickly reveals itself as being one of the grandest parish churches in Norfolk. Of flint and with a tower faced in freestone, it was built (apart from the chancel and south transept) and endowed by the Earl of Suffolk in the early fifteenth century. Its crowning glory is the hammer-beam roof, enriched as it is with a copiousness of decorative wood carving that catches the breath – whirling tracery, flowery bosses, six half-length angels in every bay along the cornice, and other full-length angels, seraphim, Virgins and saints standing on the hammer-beams themselves. Below it, and inevitably to some degree overshadowed, are some good poppy-head benches and the original fifteenth-century rood-screen, with central doors (unusual in this part of the country) and twenty painted saints, crude but endearing, among them an irresistible St Matthew with spectacles. The chancel and south transept are a century earlier than the nave – about 1300. They have kept their lovely Decorated windows, and the transept has an enjoyable piscina with a dragon and a wild man in the spandrels. (These same figures recur round the doorway on the west side of the tower.) But again and again one's eyes are drawn back to that roof; with such a *tour de force* to contend with, nothing else seems to stand a chance.

## Cley-next-the-Sea*

*12; 7½ miles W of Sheringham on A149*

The flint-built ST MARGARET'S CHURCH at Cley (pronounced so as to rhyme with sky) is a little outside the town and not immediately easy to find; but the effort is well repaid. Once arrived, walk some 50 yards away to the south. The first thing that strikes you as you look back is the astonishing clerestory: huge cusped cinquefoiled circles alternating with two-light windows, all so close together that their moulded surrounds are almost touching. This is clearly fourteenth-century work, as is the next claim to your attention: the south transept which, although it has been a ruin for some four centuries, still boasts a stunning south window with more cusped circles – quatrefoiled this time – and a spherical quadrangle above. These two features alone would make the church a memorable one, but it still has a third trump card to play. The south porch was built 100 years later – work seems to have stopped for about a

East Barsham.

century between 1350 and 1450, presumably on account of the Black Death – but is every bit as magnificent; a tremendous ashlar-faced doorway, flanked by niches, framed by shields, surmounted by a pair of three-light windows with stepped transoms, and crowned with battlements worked in an intricate filigree that strikes one as more Moorish than anything else. Inside, the porch is tierceron-vaulted. You are thus already in a suitably awed state of mind by the time you reach the still more sumptuous inner door to the church itself.

As you walk down the nave, it is the size that impresses, the sculpture that charms. In the spandrels above the arcade – we are now back in the fourteenth century – are tabernacles resting on brilliantly carved corbel brackets, especially on the south side: St George and the dragon, a lion with a bone, musical angels, even an ill-bred imp farting at the viewer. There are more carved figures on the benches. After all this, the chancel comes as a bit of a let-down; the five-light Perpendicular east window with its coloured glass is not, frankly, very nice. But the six-light west window (also Perpendicular) is fine enough – and anyway, with so much splendour around, who would feel like complaining?

## East Barsham

*13; 2½ miles N of Fakenham on B1105*

A real show-stopper when you suddenly round a bend in the Fakenham–Little Walsingham road, it gives you the same sort of thrill as that memorable first view of Compton Wynyates. Here is everybody's perfect picture of an early Tudor (*c.*1520–30) manor house – and, incidentally, a supreme example of the virtuosity of which sixteenth-century bricklayers were capable. The work on the Gatehouse, unrestored and still in excellent condition, is best of all, so I suggest you leave it till last. Look first at the house itself, standing there with such swaggering assurance. It must be admitted at once that much of the building to the left of the porch is restoration, some as recent as 1938 – though that tremendous cluster of ten chimneys, all differently decorated, is original, as is virtually everything from (and including) the porch to the right. But the modern work has been done with sensitivity and skill, and scarcely detracts at all from the general impression.

What are the principal elements in this impression? The redness, first of all, and the high pinnacles that give the house an almost Indian look, and then perhaps the two parallel lines of frieze that run above the windows on each floor. These are not brick, but terracotta of almost precisely the same colour, and perform two invaluable services by both lightening the composition and binding the individual elements together. The Royal Arms over the porch, however, is in carved brick, and the griffin and greyhound supporters date the house incontestably to before 1527, when the greyhound was replaced by a lion.

By the same token the Gatehouse, in whose version of the Arms the lion has already made its appearance, must be of 1527 or a little after. Here the turrets are more obtrusive (and more orientalising) than ever, the brick-work decoration still more exuberant; even the battlements are panelled.

East Barsham is not at the time of writing open to the public. A pity; but the distant prospect alone on a sunny afternoon is enough to lift the spirit and to send one rejoicing on one's way.

## East Harling

*14; 7½ miles NE of Thetford on B1111*

The eye-catcher of the CHURCH OF ST PETER AND ST PAUL, East Harling, is the top of the tower, with its short lead spire supported on eight miniature flying buttresses. (It was copied by Street in 1895 for St Peter Mancroft in Norwich.) This, with the intricate design of battlements and pinnacles surrounding it, is obviously of the fifteenth century, as are the clerestory and the south porch; for the rest – despite a few later windows – an earlier date seems likely: say 1300 or very soon after. Within, there is another of those marvellous Norfolk hammer-beam roofs, very steep, and a particularly fine fifteenth-century screen to the south chapel, complete with its ribbed coving. The tombs are good, too, particularly that of Sir Thomas Lovell and his wife. His feet rest on a bundle of peacock feathers, hers on a pair of arms emerging from what appears to be a cushion and holding a scalp – very curious. The chancel is broad and satisfying, with a five-light east window filled with excellent fifteenth-century glass.

## Felbrigg Hall

*NT; 15; 2 miles SW of Cromer off B1436*

The first thing to do on arrival at Felbrigg is to take up a position under the trees 100 yards or so to the south-west. What you see is not one house, but two, joined together but sharing not a single common feature except their floor and roof levels. The south-facing one is Jacobean, brick with stone dressings, with three big projections, mullioned and transomed bay windows and 'GLORIA DEO IN EXCELSIS' in huge pierced stone letters along the balustrading. To the west, by contrast, we have a piece of gentle, unassertive William and Mary, entirely of brick this time and very finely finished, with a hipped roof and six neat little dormer windows. And what a contrast: it is almost impossible to conceive of two styles more completely at odds with one another – and the shock is all the greater when one realises that the two are separated by barely fifty years. The Jacobean house was completed in 1624, and in August 1674 the first plans for the proposed new wing were drawn up by one William Samwell, a gentleman architect well thought of in his day though now almost forgotten. It was finished in 1687. I know of no house in England that shows quite so dramatically the revolution in domestic building that took place in the middle of the seventeenth century.

But, with the exception of splendid plaster ceilings in the Drawing Room, Cabinet and Rose Bedroom (probably by the same plasterer who worked at Melton Constable), there is little evidence of seventeenth-century work inside Felbrigg. In 1750 James Paine was called in to remodel the house, and for the next decade did so with a vengeance, removing the Grand Staircase to make the new Dining Room with elegant Rococo plasterwork by Thomas Rose, transforming most of the other principal rooms and creating the delightful Gothick Library. He also seems to have provided the new service range to the east. More work, distinctly less successful, was done in the 1830s, particularly in the Great Hall.

Most of the interior decoration at Felbrigg, apart from that of the Dining Room and Library, I find rather stuffy and oppressive; it is not a house in which I would choose to live. But it has much fine furniture and lovely pictures, and it does make a change from the Broads.

*Felbrigg Hall.*

## Fritton★

*16; 8 miles NE of Beccles on A143*

ST EDMUND'S CHURCH gets its star for sheer charm. Thatched, with a Norman round tower and a Norman apse, its nave is, rather surprisingly, Decorated – if such a term can be used to describe so modestly vernacular a building. The oddest thing about it – and why it could not possibly earn its star architecturally – is its quite flagrant lack of symmetry. What clearly happened was that the church was widened in the fourteenth century by extending it to the south; but that those responsible did not bother (or could not perhaps afford) to make a separate aisle. The result is that both tower and chancel are totally out of axis with the nave.

Fortunately, the chancel was untouched. It is very old, and must date from about the time of the Conquest, if not a little before – there are lesenes on the outer wall. It is tunnel-vaulted – most unusual in a chancel – possibly in order to carry a tower, though it was never obliged to do so. The apse is semi-circular and vaulted, with three narrow slit windows framed by small colonnettes.

The furnishings are surprisingly good. They include a fourteenth-century screen (its vertical shafts are modern replacements), a few simple choir stalls, a three-decker seventeenth-century pulpit and a charming little organ of 1774. Finally, take a look at the wall paintings. The earliest seem contemporary with the church itself – the red scroll pattern round the east window of the apse and the decoration on the south respond of the chancel arch; the St Christopher on the north wall of the nave and the St John the Baptist in the splay of its south-east window clearly date from the fourteenth-century widening.

## Great Cressingham

*17; 4½ miles SE of Swaffham off A1065*

Never in fact a priory at all, but a magnificent manor house of about 1545 belonging to the monastery of Norwich, GREAT CRESSINGHAM PRIORY is a building of the utmost fascination. It is L-shaped, with one range running east–west and another northward from the eastern end, but by far the most important front is that to the south. The main section is now entirely of brick (older photographs show the ground floor rendered) and has three polygonal turrets, one at each corner and one in the middle; the former two have their own little pyramidal roofs – though connected to the main hipped roof behind – while the latter ends in a tall chimneystack with two tall Tudor chimneys. The left-hand turret has a little diapering at the base and, immediately above, three odd little blank niches with four-centred arches; beyond it, still further to the left, is the former principal gateway to the house – four-centred again, with decoration in the spandrels. An embattled wall descends from here westward to the moat and the remains of another turret, now barely recognisable. But these, in a way, are all minor details; it is the upper half of the main section that from the very beginning holds our attention. Immediately above the big transomed window in the left-hand bay, forming a sort of string-course, there runs a most curious frieze of intersecting arches, *upside-down*; and above this, rising up to roof level, on wall and turrets alike, are four courses of brick panelling with what looks like reticulated tracery at the top of each course, and in each panel an emblem in terracotta – a hand holding a falcon (the crest of the Jenny family) alternating with a monogram of J and E, standing for John and Elizabeth Jenny, by whom the house was built. Several of these monograms have also been inserted upside-down.

Walking round the western end of the house we find ourselves within the arms of the L and can now see the reverse side of the range we have just been looking at from the front. Here is the original entrance, under a four-centred arch with heavy hood-mould, and the original wooden door still in position. Immediately to the left of it, the wall bears quite a few traces of decoration in the form of a black and white lozenge design. Below, about a foot from the ground, runs a band of quatrefoils; above, the frieze of intersecting arches continues – still upside-down – and, above that, another black and white pattern of trefoil-headed panels of the kind we so often see in the flushwork of East Anglian churches. The mouldings round both the door and the three surviving windows (two of which are transomed, with arches below the transom as well as above it) are of terracotta: it is probably the oldest terracotta door in the country.

To our left, the other wing runs northward to what was obviously once a big open courtyard; there are ruins of former buildings at the further corners, where the moat comes round to close it off. The surviving range is timber-framed but rendered all over, and rises to a pitched roof with small dormers. It comes to an abrupt end in a north gable that bears the date 1674; the paler-coloured brick and a straight joint a foot or so in from the end suggest that it was subsequently sealed off, perhaps after a fire. The south end appears to abut directly on to the east–west range; but now comes a surprise. The room that occupies this south end – it has rather a low ceiling, with massive beams, heavily moulded – has as its end wall the continuation of the quatrefoil frieze and the black and white lozenge that we saw outside. On approaching to investigate, we discover that this north–south range in fact stops a foot or two away from its neighbour – a curious fact that the present owner (who has done a superb restoration job on the house in the past fifteen years) has brilliantly highlighted by opening up a well in such a way that the entire north wall is now revealed up to the top.

But the mystery does not end here. The north–south wing, which would at first appear to be a later adjunct, looks stylistically a good deal older than the decorated wall. Why then, if it were there already when the manor house was built, did the builders bother to go to such trouble decorating a wall which would never be properly seen? Did they intend to demolish the old range? If so, why not do so before building the new one? And why was the new range given an outside door at first-floor level, opening into a void? With the old range in place, this makes no sense at all; were it demolished, the door might at least have an outside stair. It could, I suppose, be argued that the 'old' range was in fact a later addition

*St Peter's Church, Great Walsingham.*

after all, and looks older than it is owing to the re-use of earlier timbers; the beams and joists in the kitchen at the eastern corner have certainly been re-used, as is clear from the way that their fifteenth-century painted stencil pattern continues into the walls at each side. But the dating of this range is not a matter of beams alone; it is based on the way the whole building is constructed. The problem, in short, remains unsolved – as does the further enigma of why the long attic, to which access is by ladder from the west turret and which runs the whole length of the main range immediately under the roof, should boast a rather grand fireplace of brick, with a four-centred arch, at its eastern end. But that's the sort of house Great Cressingham is.

And so to ST MICHAEL'S CHURCH. It has a most impressive west tower, with a frieze of flushwork shields and crowned Ms (emblem of the Archangel Michael) in foiled circles above the main door. There are more of the same round the south porch. Inside, we find a wonderful old floor like a rough sea and another of those magnificent timber roofs, its hammer-beams alternating with arched braces, but with what appear to be priests rather than the more usual angels on the hammers and the corbels below the wall posts. Four of these figures, two at each level on the east wall of the nave, are facing west, their heads being turned so as not to be embedded in the wall. The chancel roof is of 1864 – a bit of a come-down but made up for by the windows which are early Decorated of *c.*1300, set within huge blank arches on attached shafts. The five-light east window is a real glory, with stepped-up and stepped-down transoms, their level changing with each light, cusped arches below each transom and cresting above.

The rest of the church is of rather less interest, but there are four good brasses, one commemorating Elizabeth Jenny of the manor house. (She was, incidentally, a Spryng, one of the family who built the wonderful Spryng Chantry at Lavenham (*q.v.*).) Some good fifteenth-century glass of the Norwich school can be seen in the tracery of the windows of the north aisle.

## Great Walsingham

*18; 5 miles N of Fakenham on B1388*

Set high on a hill outside the village, ST PETER'S looks everything a Norfolk village church ought to be. Or almost everything: the chancel is gone. What is surprising is how little this seems to matter; the plain flint tower and the nave and aisles (flint again with stone dressings), ravishing Decorated windows all around and a pretty quatrefoiled clerestory seem to give it all it needs. Much of the beauty, I suspect, lies in the fact that, as at Elsing, virtually everything is of the same period – the mid-fourteenth century. This goes also for much of the furnishings, especially the benches. These are the pride of the church, and so they should be. They have marvellous carved poppy-heads (the word, incidentally, has nothing to do with poppies, but comes from the French *poupée*, meaning a doll) with carvings everywhere – men and animals, angels, priests and apostles. The wooden roof is good without being sensational, the floor agreeably tiled. A warm, friendly church, its charm grows on you the longer you stay in it.

## Gunton

*19; 6 miles S of Cromer off A140*

Standing as it does only 100 yards or so from Gunton Hall, ST ANDREW'S CHURCH, of grey brick with a four-column Tuscan portico, looks more like a garden temple than anything else. It comes as quite a surprise to enter and find oneself in an exquisitely furnished church with longitudinally placed stalls and a lovely little west gallery supported on fluted Corinthian pilasters. It was built by Robert Adam in 1769, and is the only Adam church still standing as he left it.

The earlier part of GUNTON HALL, by Matthew Brettingham, was gutted by fire in the 1880s. Most of what remains, including the colonnade, conservatories, and the three-storey bow that seems to have come straight from Brighton, is the work of James Wyatt in 1770 or thereabouts.

## Hales*

*20; 11 miles SE of Norwich on A146*

ST MARGARET'S CHURCH stands some way outside the modern village, just off the Beccles road on the left. It is another of those enchanting little Norman churches, all flint with a round tower; the nave and polygonal apsed chancel are thatched. As if that were not enough, there is a really grand north doorway, vigorously and imaginatively carved with just about every motif in the pattern-book. The interior is as simple as the outside, and pretty as a picture. Even the touches of modernity, like the wooden roof or the altar of undressed brick, (which is surprisingly effective against the whitewashed wall) are in no way inharmonious. One must, I suppose, regret the thirteenth-century windows which, though well enough in themselves, slightly spoil the Norman atmosphere, especially round the apse; but after 700 years they too have surely earned their place.

*The north doorway, St Margaret's Church, Hales.*

## Heydon*

*21; 13½ miles NW of Norwich off B1149*

A beautiful trinity – of mansion, church and village – each of Heydon's treasures is in its way outstanding. There is hardly a false note anywhere. HEYDON HALL itself was built in the early 1580s for Henry Dynne, Auditor of the Exchequer. It is a splendid sight from the little private road which passes the south front, standing back behind an immaculate green lawn: five bays of mellow red brick, of which numbers 1, 3 and 5 rise three storeys to tall pointed gables flanked and topped by high pinnacles, numbers 2 and 4 being of two storeys only and slightly recessed. All the windows are mullioned and transomed and – except for the three on the second floor – pedimented. The porch has polygonal angle shafts and a four-centred doorway; while the steeply pitched roof, which rises above the gables in front of it, is further heightened by a row of five ornamental brick chimneys at each end. The house was considerably enlarged to east and west in the eighteenth and nineteenth centuries, but most of the later additions have mercifully been removed by the present owner; there now remains only a single two-storey bay to the west and a three-bay, single-storey range to the east leading to a small pavilion. The Hall, to the right of the entrance, has a big seventeenth-century stone fireplace, but the rest has been much Victorianised.

And so to the village, and the CHURCH OF ST PETER AND ST PAUL. It has a brave west tower, diagonally buttressed, embattled and pinnacled, but with an oddly placed stair turret to the south which has pushed the pretty three-light traceried window in the fourth stage slightly to one side. In the stage below are square sound holes, cusped and bearing the Heydon arms. As can be seen from that window, the tower is fourteenth-century, but the body of the church as we see it today has been made thoroughly Perpendicular; on the outside the only traces of Decorated work still visible are the west windows of the aisles and the quatrefoil windows of the clerestory, most of which have been blocked; only the two easternmost to north and south remain untouched.

Despite the fine two-storeyed south porch with its tierceron vault, the normal entrance seems nowadays to be by the west door – giving one a fine view past the big, tub-shaped, centrally placed font, along the arcades (also of the fourteenth century) to the lovely rood-screen, tall and slender, the single-light arches most delicately cusped, much of the original colour still remaining. An inscription across the middle rail tells us that it was thc gift of John Dynne in 1480. Beside it is a fine wineglass pulpit with a seventeenth-century sounding board and, let into the back, a Flemish relief carving of *c.*1640 representing the Last Supper. Finally, you should not miss the wall paintings and the fascinating fragments of fifteenth-century glass including, in the south-west window, a Christ of the Trades, surrounded by various instruments of humble toil.

The village speaks for itself. Nothing is really outstanding, but it is the ensemble that is important – the way one house or row of cottages sets off the rest; and the ensemble here could hardly be bettered.

*Holkham Hall.*

## Holkham Hall*

*22; 2 miles W of Wells off A149*

Built between 1731 and 1756, Holkham is one of the greatest and grandest Palladian houses of England; but it does not immediately attract the eye in the same way, for example, as does Houghton, or Kedleston, or Prior Park. One reason, perhaps, is the grey-green local brick of which it is built: an unhealthy liverish colour, nowhere near as satisfying as the noble ashlar of its contemporary neighbour, Houghton. The elevation too is undeniably stern, especially on the north side from which you approach. But persevere: go round to the south front and stand some distance away, beyond the great ornamental basin with the Perseus and Andromeda fountain, and then look again, thinking in terms of symmetry, of proportions, of the constantly changing rhythm of salients and re-entrants, the perfectly judged relationship of the side pavilions to the centre block and of the different parts of each of these elements to each other. The austerity is still there, as indeed it was meant to be; but gradually the subtleties reveal themselves.

The architect of Holkham was William Kent; but such a statement, though true, is a dangerous over-simplification. The original concept was that of Thomas Coke, later 1st Earl of Leicester, who returned in 1718 from the Grand Tour where he had already amassed a magnificent collection of pictures, sculpture and *objets d'art* and – no less important – had made the acquaintance of Kent, and of Kent's patron Lord Burlington. Thus it was no wonder, when a few years later he resolved to build himself a splendid mansion in which to show off his treasures to their best advantage, that he should have decided on the now fashionable Palladian style, of which Burlington had made himself the leading advocate and high priest. Kent, who was working on the interior of Houghton only a few miles away, received the commission; but this was almost certainly on Burlington's recommendation, and since it was his first major work of architecture – though he was now in his mid-forties – the influence of his noble mentor was obviously still very strong. The Burlington hallmarks are everywhere – in the three-light Venetian windows, for example, which are such a feature of Chiswick House (*q.v.*), and the still more characteristic *staccato* treatment of the whole elevation; as Sir John Summerson has pointed out, there are scarcely ever two adjacent openings in the same plane and of the same design. Typical, too, of Burlington is the ruthlessness with which all superfluous ornament has been eliminated. The easy-going Kent, one feels, a decorator *par excellence*, would never have shown such restraint if left to himself, without that grim aristocratic mentor at his elbow forever insisting that a gentleman's house must eschew vanity and reflect only the old stoic virtues of reason, moderation and sound common sense. But there were other influences also, notably that of Coke himself and of the elder Matthew Brettingham – who, as clerk of the works, had responsibility for the actual construction and, later, in 1761, the audacity to publish all the drawings under his own name.

The interior is Kent's and Kent's alone. No house in England presents so extravagant a contrast between outer severity and inner opulence. Lord Hervey described how in a great Palladian house the 'base or rustic storey was given over to hunters, hospitality,

*Houghton Hall.*

noise, dirt and business', while the *piano nobile* was dedicated to 'taste, expense, state and parade'. At Holkham the real *tour de force* is the transition between the two – the Marble Hall, in which a slowly narrowing flight of steps ascends through a gigantic apse to a semicircular screen of four columns of Derbyshire alabaster at first-floor level, and thence under a second, small, apse to the Saloon. The idea is purely Palladian; the decoration, from the marble floor to the supremely intricate coffering of the apses and the sumptuous plaster ceiling derived from an idea by Inigo Jones, is of a Kentian exuberance of which Palladio could never have dreamed.

So dramatic is this Hall that anything following it seems certain to be an anti-climax. The Saloon, miraculously, is not – there can be no higher praise – and the other state rooms – thirteen of them altogether on the *piano nobile*, grouped round two interior courtyards – keep up the same breathtaking standard. As if to make up for the sombre exterior, Kent now throws all restraint to the winds: here are colour, splendour and exuberance, ostentatious perhaps but without ever a hint of vulgarity, the work of a decorator of genius who knows exactly how far he can go – and goes there. Here too is quality: of pictures, tapestries, sculptures and furniture, of silk and velvet, mahogany and marble. It is hard to believe that only a mile away, beyond the gardens and the lake and Capability Brown's deer park, lie the windswept marshes and the wild North Sea.

## Houghton Hall*

*23; 13 miles NE of King's Lynn off A148*

Less than 20 miles from Holkham, Houghton Hall is the only other Palladian house in the country that can rival it for sheer grandeur. It does not look today quite as its architect, Colen Campbell, intended when he designed it in 1721 for Sir Robert Walpole, the first Prime Minister of England; Campbell had provided for simpler, pedimented corner towers on the lines of Inigo Jones's at Wilton or those which William Kent was soon to design for Holkham, but they were changed by James Gibbs to the present stone cupolas. This distinctly Baroque departure from Palladian purity was much deplored at the time – a contemporary report describes the cupolas as having been 'obstinately raised by the master in defiance of all the *virtuosi*' – but it certainly lends the house additional character; and there is no doubt that Houghton, impure or not, is a good deal more pleasing at first sight than its neighbour. There are several reasons for this. The design is more compact, without the restlessness of Holkham; the side wings, connected to the main block by Tuscan colonnades, know their place and do not compete with the main house; and Campbell has permitted himself rather more ornament than Burlington allowed Kent. Above all, perhaps, there is that glorious golden sandstone from Aislaby in Yorkshire (whence it was shipped via Whitby to King's Lynn) which has given Houghton the loveliest ashlar facing in Norfolk.

The interior decoration was entrusted to Kent. Not having been the architect, he could not provide the sort of initial dramatic *coup* he was to achieve at Holkham; but his Stone Hall is, in its own way, every bit as impressive – so monumental in scale that one can hardly believe that it is on the first floor rather than at ground level. It is, incidentally, a cube – 40 feet along each side, precisely the same dimensions as the Hall in Inigo Jones's Queen's House at Greenwich (1616–69), the first Palladian building in England, 100 years before its time. But how different is the decorative style; perhaps in a deliberate attempt to offset the monumentality, Kent has given this tremendous room a deep coving around which runs a frieze of cherubs swinging on garlands almost Rococo in their abandon, their legs occasionally even hanging down over the key-pattern frieze below them.

The other state rooms are equally grand. Ceilings (many of them painted by Kent, though painting was never his *forte*), chimneypieces and the surrounds of doors and windows are as fine as can be found anywhere. Look, too, at the details – the window shutters, the hinges, the handles and keyholes; everywhere, the workmanship is stunning. The Common Parlour has gilded wood carvings by Grinling Gibbons, obviously transferred from an earlier house; the Green Velvet Bedchamber possesses the most sumptuous state bed I have ever seen; the Saloon with its deeply coved ceiling is hung with its original Genoa velvet; room after room is filled with Kent's own furniture, specially designed for it; and there are marvellous pictures, even though all too many of them were sold to Catherine the Great to pay off the debts of Walpole's eccentric grandson (much to the fury of the latter's uncle, Horace) and are now the pride of the Hermitage in Leningrad.

Opened to the public for the first time in 1977, Houghton is still less well known than most of the other great houses of England. Yet there is none more glorious, and none that speaks to us more dramatically of the wealth, the power and the splendour of the English aristocracy in its heyday, 250 years ago.

## Hoveton

*24; 7½ miles NE of Norwich on A1151*

Although only a small village and now virtually a suburb of Wroxham, Hoveton – pronounced not as in 'Hove' but as in 'hover' – boasts two churches and no fewer than three distinguished houses. HOVETON HALL is a simple early nineteenth-century brick house with a central bay; the OLD HALL is a Queen Anne manor house of much charm; but the best of the lot – indeed, one of the most enchanting buildings of its date in Norfolk – is HOVETON HOUSE. It was built by one Thomas Blofeld in 1670 or thereabouts, and remains in his family to this day. The north front – which since 1908 has been the entrance front – is irregular and unremarkable; that to the south, however, is a joy to behold. Of red brick with stone dressings, it too is simple enough in its essentials: eleven bays, two storeys, with a pediment and four dormers in a hipped roof. But it is the detail that captivates, the odd mixture of naïvety and sophistication. Look, for example, at the tall and quite disproportionately thin unfluted giant Corinthian pilasters that mark off the three-bay centre and appear again at the corners; or at the central doorcase (now containing only a window, the door itself having been moved one bay to the right) with more pilasters, fluted this time and less attenuated, and what Pevsner describes as 'a fancy pediment with a lot of not very disciplined vegetable carving'. Consider too the windows, which are not content with keystones at the top but also have brick aprons below, the two flanking the first-floor centre being brought down until they meet the stone string-course. The centre window between them is adorned with its own pair of pilasters with garlands and an ornamental head. Above it, the oddly high pediment – it is almost an equilateral triangle – has more garlands running within the sloping sides and parallel to them, as if they were pretending to be bargeboards. In the middle there is a little oval window, inserted some time later as an afterthought.

Of the interior, it can only be said that it fully maintains the standard. One remembers in particular the Dining Room in the south-east corner with its lovely carved fireplace and overmantel and, in the south-west, the Library with its bookcases of about 1800. Next to it is the Drawing Room with its three windows not quite equally spaced – a defect brilliantly disguised by the pair of mirrors hanging between them, one of which is subtly narrower than the other. In the centre is the Staircase Hall, from which a lovely staircase of pale wood with twisted balusters winds up beneath a remarkably pretty ceiling. This, together with most of the other plasterwork, is of the eighteenth century; but there is a little square alcove off the principal bedroom in which the original seventeenth-century stucco still survives, and very delightful it is.

The grounds were laid out by Humphry Repton; but to the east of the entrance front there is a beautiful walled garden contemporary with the house.

## King's Lynn*

*25; 11 miles N of Downham Market on A10*
*Includes St George's Guildhall (NT)*

The town of King's Lynn has a character all its own, compounded of several different elements. First of all, it is a seaport – no longer the third in the kingdom as it was in the fourteenth century, but still busy and prosperous, with ships from Rotterdam and Antwerp, Hamburg and Kiel and Bremen, discharging their cargoes at the same quays to which they have been coming for close on a thousand years, overlooked by marvellous medieval warehouses, tall and timber-framed. Secondly, it has absorbed, perhaps more than any other town in East Anglia, something of the Hanseatic spirit. Walking through the narrow streets and lanes behind South Quay, one half expects to hear the clatter of clogs on the cobbles behind; looking up at the steep hipped roofs and shaped gables of the seventeenth- and eighteenth-century brick houses, one would not be altogether surprised to spot the nest of some wayward stork. Look at the Tuesday Market Place. In Northern Europe it would be accepted as perfectly normal; but what other

English town of comparable size can boast such a vast expanse? Even Lynn's best-known and best-loved building, Henry Bell's Customs House, has a distinctly Dutch flavour about it.

In other respects the town can seem quintessentially English – though with a Norfolk accent. ST MARGARET'S CHURCH on the Saturday Market Place was begun in the early twelfth century by Herbert de Losinga, the first Bishop of Norwich, who had consecrated the first stage of his new cathedral there only a few years before. From the start he conceived it as an ambitious building: twin towers are a rarity indeed for a town parish church. Alas, all too little of Losinga's work is visible today except at the base of the south-west tower; the church was almost entirely rebuilt of white limestone in the thirteenth century, while the north-west tower, having subsided dangerously, was replaced by a Perpendicular one – in both senses of the word – in 1453. Nor was this the last of its tribulations: on 8 September 1741 a great storm blew down the spire from the south-west tower, leaving the nave a pile of rubble. Reconstruction began at once under the direction of Matthew Brettingham, who took time off for the purpose from his work on the still unfinished Holkham Hall; but he was a Palladian, not a Gothicist, as a comparison of his nave with the largely undamaged thirteenth-century chancel and transepts makes all too clear.

More satisfactory is ST NICHOLAS'S, technically not a parish church at all but a chapel of ease to St Margaret's; 200 feet long, it is the largest such chapel in the country. Except for its Early English south-west tower – left over from an earlier church and unnecessarily topped with a lead spire by Scott in 1896 – it was built all of a piece at the beginning of the fifteenth century. It has a terrific two-storey lierne-vaulted south porch, splendid east and west windows, and a fine timber roof with angels.

*The Customs House, King's Lynn.*

The walk between St Nicholas's and St Margaret's, through the Tuesday Market Place and then down King Street and Queen Street, takes in most of the architectural glories of the town. In the Tuesday Market Place stands the DUKE'S HEAD HOTEL, built in 1683–9 almost certainly by Henry Bell, a cultivated and well-to-do merchant who, after a Grand Tour which took him to 'most of the politer parts of Europe', returned to his native town, served twice as its mayor, and embellished it with several first-rate buildings, public and private. In King Street is the ST GEORGE'S GUILDHALL (NT), a noble fifteenth-century edifice of brick and stone which, bereft of its original purpose, became first a theatre – in which Shakespeare is said to have acted – then a warehouse, and then a derelict and crumbling ruin before being rescued in the 1950s to become an arts centre and focal point of the annual Festival.

The next landmark, in a street full of lovely houses, is Bell's enchanting stone CUSTOMS HOUSE of 1683, beautifully set on the corner of Purfleet Quay, with its hipped roof, dormer windows and tall lantern. In a niche stands a statue of Charles II, neatly corresponding to one of Charles I on the BANK HOUSE at King Staithe Quay opposite, reminding us of Lynn's staunch support of the Royalist cause in the Civil War, when the rest of Norfolk was equally fiercely Cromwellian. By this time King Street has suffered a sex change, and so we continue down Queen Street (don't miss the barley-sugar portal of CLIFTON HOUSE on the right) to where it broadens and curves off to the left into the Saturday Market Place. This is the best corner in the town. On the inside of the curve we come to the TOWN HALL. The first section is of 1895, but its flint and stone chequer and unforced combination of Gothic and Renaissance make it a perfect introduction for the splendid crescendo that follows. The next part is joyfully elaborate Elizabethan, chequered again, with a Renaissance portico, Queen Elizabeth's Arms at second-floor level and James I's in a shaped gable above that. And so to the climax of the Hall proper, originally built for the Guild of Holy Trinity in 1421, a good third of its surface taken up by a seven-light Perpendicular window of massive proportions. Behind this building are the ASSEMBLY ROOMS of 1766; beyond it is the eighteenth-century GAOL; opposite, the mostly seventeenth-century THORESBY COLLEGE. This is the hub of King's Lynn, though there are more excellent buildings to be seen further still to the south.

One further oddity remains to be mentioned, some half a mile from the Saturday Market Place to the east. This is RED MOUNT CHAPEL. Go first to the Catholic presbytery in North Everard Street for the key; they will give directions. This wayside chapel on the pilgrim road to Walsingham was built in 1485 – an octagon of red brick concealing, at first-floor level, a tiny cruciform shrine fan-vaulted over the crossing. The two staircases that lead to it within the octagonal shell must have been essential to deal with the crowds of pilgrims; in 1509 the revenues here were four times those of St Margaret's, St Nicholas's and the now demolished St James's put together.

## Knapton*

*26; 3 miles NE of North Walsham on B1145*

No one looking at the CHURCH OF ST PETER AND ST PAUL from the outside would dream that it could ever be awarded a star. It is of the usual flint, with a rather nastily rendered chancel and a distinctly mingy north-west tower – even if the weathercock with its magnificent tail *was* designed by Cotman while he was giving a drawing lesson at Knapton House. It is a great mistake not to buttress towers, whether they need it or not, and this one moreover cuts awkwardly into the west wall of the nave and jostles uncomfortably close to the pretty traceried four-light window. For the rest, the nicest touch is the little trio of steeply stepped niches above the south porch, the most surprising feature the nave windows (there are no aisles) which have Decorated mouldings, Perpendicular tracery and semi-circular heads.

And now inside, to the things that really matter: the roof and the font. Though the author of the church guide is, I think, pushing it a bit when he describes the roof as 'probably the handsomest parish church roof in the country', it is unquestionably one of the best in Norfolk. It is a double hammer-beam, dated 1504, with brightly painted angels on the hammers, kingposts and wall plates – 138 of them in all. Some, inevitably, have been renewed; one is not entirely unconscious of the heavy hand of Scott, who restored the church in 1882–3. But the workmanship, which extends to the deeply moulded collar-beams and the traceried spandrels above the hammers, is everywhere superb. ''Tis a beautiful conception,' the guide concludes. 'Tis indeed.

The font dates from the thirteenth century, and is thus a good deal older than the present church. It is octagonal, of Purbeck marble, resting on eight slender shafts. The real interest, however, is the font cover, which is dated 1704. It has thin balusters of its own and a broad ogival top. The vaguely Byzantine impression is increased by the inscription: the Greek palindrome 'NIPSON ANOMIMATA MI MONAN OPSIN' ('Wash my sins, not my face only') said to have been composed by the Greek Emperor Leo VI and also inscribed on the font of St Sophia at Istanbul.

## Langley Park

*27; 9 miles NW of Beccles off A146*

Designed and built by Matthew Brettingham in the 1740s in the intervals when he was not supervising the continuing work on Holkham Hall (*q.v.*), Langley Park looks at first sight a rather austere sort of house. It is of red brick, with seven bays to the entrance front and nine to the garden, and four corner towers in the manner of Holkham – though with low pyramid roofs instead of pediments. The four-bay wings (which were altered by Salvin) are connected to the main block by ungainly little quadrant links. The house has three storeys – four in the corner towers – the wings two, the links one. On both sides, a heavy cornice divides the first and second floors, giving the latter an attic feeling; on both sides, too, the three central bays are topped by a slightly mingy triangular pediment. On the entrance side only, there are quoins of even length at every possible opportunity and a Doric entrance porch which was added in 1829–30.

That is a somewhat bald description; but then, Langley Park is a somewhat bald house – on the outside. The interior is anything but, owing to the bravura display of plasterwork in all the main rooms. The Entrance Hall, which has a coved circular centre with allegorical figures and portrait medallions, leads straight through, in orthodox Palladian fashion, to the Saloon, the most opulently decorated room in the house. The ceiling, though elaborate, is comparatively restrained in style; but the principal door has a pedimented case with outsize *putti* playing above it, and at each end are large stucco versions of paintings – the *Combat of Lapiths and Centaurs* over the fireplace, and Guido Reni's *Flight of Helen* opposite. Smaller relief panels surmount the four other doors; elsewhere around the room are trophies, swags and garlands galore.

The other major *tour de force* is the Library in the east wing, where the ceiling decoration is composed around a huge marble relief of Diana and Actaeon. It is the work of Charles Stanley, a Dane who came to England in 1727 and stayed here twenty years. (He may well have been responsible for the Saloon panels also.) There are smaller, rectangular panels, too, all interconnected by twining tendrils. A most delicate frieze runs below. Adjoining it in the same wing is the Ball Room, converted from a Drawing Room in the last century and an object lesson in Victorian insensitivity. Where the other rooms, however ornate, never lose their eighteenth-century elegance, here the room is almost crushed by the weight of its immense coved ceiling, thickly encrusted with decoration for decoration's sake, with about as much subtlety as the platefuls of spaghetti it so closely resembles.

There is more outstanding plasterwork on the upper part of the staircase, featuring large medallions with busts in profile. The carpentry is fine, too: there are three twisted balusters to each tread and carved tread ends.

Langley Park is now a school – not an ideal function in the circumstances. But the astounding decoration is clearly appreciated and well looked after.

## Mannington Hall

*28; 18 miles NW of Norwich off B1149*

From the west or from the south, seen across its completely surrounding moat, the great three-storey house of flint with its battlements, its tall clumps of chimneys and its magnificently haphazard fenestration looks romantic indeed. Mannington Hall was probably begun in the late 1450s, and one's first reaction – at least from the west (entrance) front – is that it has changed very little since then. Closer inspection does not altogether bear this out, however; to the right of the modest Perpendicular doorway you can still see the traces of a great Hall window, now partially blocked – presumably when the Hall itself was divided horizontally at some unknown date. Moreover, the uncusped lights in some of the windows have an early Tudor look about them; and Pevsner has gone so far as to question whether the entire second floor may not be a later addition. If – as I incline to think – it is part of the original construction, are not its terracotta windows among the earliest in England? On the south side, the alterations are more obvious – in particular the addition in 1864 of the block to the east of the smaller polygonal tower. This was the work of Horatio, 4th Earl of Orford (of the 2nd creation), a keen antiquarian and considerable eccentric who was responsible for the wildly misogynistic inscriptions in Gothic black-letter around the outside and for the virtual transformation of most of the interior. He also built a large conservatory – later transformed by his nephew into a billiard and smoking room – further still to the east; but this was wisely demolished in 1969 to make way for the present delightful little east lawn.

Turning immediately right inside the front door, you come into the lower part of the Hall, now covered in beautiful Jacobean panelling brought there a century ago from Irmingland Hall nearby. The old fireplace still stands in its original position with its huge bressummer. Upstairs, there are fine Tudor fireplaces in the Red Chamber in the north-west corner and the Grey Chamber above the Parlour which lies beyond the Hall; but the rest bears above all the imprint of the 4th Earl: Victorian Gothic *par excellence*.

## Melton Constable

*29; 9 miles NW of Aylsham on B1354*

'O Lord, Thou knowest how busy I must be this day; if I forget Thee, do not Thou forget me.' So prayed Sir Jacob Astley before the battle of Edgehill in 1642, and his prayer was granted; but when I visited MELTON HALL, the house which his son and namesake built – probably to his own designs – a quarter of a century later, it looked God-forsaken indeed, and almost derelict. It was a painful sight, because since the destruction of Coleshill in 1952 few more splendid examples of the hip-roofed, dormer-windowed, brick-with-stone-dressings house of that period remain in the country. Inside, there is superb contemporary plasterwork in the Drawing Room and Staircase Hall; how long will it last?

Melton provided the location for the film of L.P. Hartley's novel *The Go-Between* – a poignant demonstration of how beautiful it must have looked in its heyday.

## Norwich*

*30; 111 miles NE of London on A11*

Perhaps I should make one point clear straight away. Despite my name, I am not myself a Norwich man. Though my paternal grandfather came of a Norfolk family my father received the title only in 1952; when I inherited it two years later I had never set foot in the place. Thus I have no interest to declare, and when I say that in my view Norwich is the finest provincial city in England I say it from the heart.

Few people, I suspect, would disagree with me to the extent of not putting it in the top three or four. It has no distinguished Roman history like York, it was never a great capital like Winchester, it is neither intellectual like Oxford nor scenically spectacular like Durham or Lincoln. Yet its cathedral yields in splendour only to the last two, and besides that it can boast an awesome Norman castle on a high mound in the very heart of the city: a heart which has not been torn out by modern developers, as has occurred with such tragic results at Gloucester and Worcester, but which still keeps its labyrinthine medieval plan – including no fewer than thirty-two medieval churches, far more than any other city of its size. It possesses two rivers, a port, a dazzlingly colourful market, its own individual school of painting and six museums, including the only museum of *mustard* in the country.

### THE CATHEDRAL AND IMMEDIATE ENVIRONS

Despite the evidence of its lucarned and crocketed spire (at 315 feet the highest in England after Salisbury), it is essentially a Norman building, and a remarkably pure one. An earlier spire fell in 1362, doing serious damage to the presbytery, after which the eastern end was given a far higher clerestory than before, with tall four-light windows and flying buttresses; but apart from this, and the new spire of 1490 or thereabouts, the exterior fabric of Barnack and Caen stone is essentially as it was in the middle of the twelfth century. Note particularly the rich geometric decoration of the crossing-tower and the magnificent east end with its almost unaltered Norman chevet of apse, ambulatory, tribune and three radiating chapels. It is a lovely composition, every bit as satisfying at close quarters as it is from a distance. Only the west front, I always feel, lets it down a little, but that may be partially due to Salvin's restoration in the 1830s; even as it stands, it seems to me infinitely preferable to the chaos that prevails at Salisbury.

And at least the entrance door is at the west end – vitally important if we are to get the full impact of the tremendous nave. This is cut off three bays before the crossing by the pulpitum, above which the modern organ neatly blocks out the view of the chancel; there is no continuous vista as, for example, at Ely or Peterborough, where the Norman arcades are not unlike those of Norwich and where the eye is drawn along them uninterruptedly to the east window itself. Nor, with so long a nave, is there any consequent feeling of frustration: these eleven majestic bays provide spectacle enough, as well as possessing one supreme attribute that neither Ely nor Peterborough can boast – the fifteenth-century stone vaulting, with no fewer than fifteen ribs springing from each shaft, connected by purely decorative liernes to form intricate designs of triangles, lozenges and eight-pointed stars, and further embellished with gilded bosses illustrating, from east to west, scenes first from the Old Testament and then from the New. This is not fan vaulting, in which the radiating ribs are all the same length, creating circular patterns – that would have been one degree too delicate for the sturdy Norman arcading beneath; one of the greatest miracles of Norwich is the effortless ease with which the Romanesque and the Perpendicular styles fuse together – so smoothly that it seems hard to believe that over three centuries separate the one from the other.

This same miracle is re-enacted at the east end. Here, admittedly, the wonderful four-light windows at clerestory level – they date from about 1370, marking the precise moment when Decorated was moving into Perpendicular – complement the Norman arcading rather than fusing with it; yet even here the vault seems to form a bridge between the two, its slender fronds sweeping up to form ever more complex patterns as the apse curves round to its fulfilment, the bosses proliferating in a controlled explosion of golden stars.

This, surely, is the finest apse in England. All too often our cathedrals, in marked contrast to those of continental Europe, have a flat, almost sawn-off, east end. That of Norwich is rich and round and strong, and possesses in addition a broad Norman ambulatory unparalleled in the country, enabling processions to pass behind the high altar and, incidentally, the bishop's throne above and behind it. This is another unique survival in these islands. In early Christian times thrones of this kind, and in this position, were the rule; they can still be seen in Ravenna and Torcello and in that most numinous of ancient churches, St Irene in Istanbul. In England, however, they have all disappeared, giving place to the shrine of the local saint which over the years virtually every other cathedral managed to adopt – venerables like St Thomas at Canterbury, St Hugh at Lincoln and St Cuthbert at Durham. All, that is, except one. Norwich never produced a saint of suitable status, and the throne has remained *in situ*. (St William of Norwich, whose doubtful sanctity rests on the allegation that he was a victim of twelfth-century Jewish ritual murder, was rightly ignored; so, more regrettably, was Julian of Norwich, a female mystic whose *Revelations of Divine Love*, composed at the end of the fourteenth century, still has its readers today. I am proud to record that this work has on one occasion been attributed to myself – by the United Reformed Church, who wrote to me a few years ago requesting my permission to reproduce certain extracts.)

*Norwich Cathedral.*

And so to the Cloisters, the most spacious in any English cathedral and, with Salisbury and Gloucester, the finest. The Prior's Door through which they are entered is another one of Norwich's masterpieces; above the arch is a seated stone figure of Christ, flanked on each side first by an angel and then by two other figures, all standing out radially from the centre and surmounted by crocketed ogival gables. The style is early Decorated, which means that it must date from the beginning of the rebuilding period; the original Norman Cloisters had been destroyed during an anti-clerical riot in 1272, and the present ones were begun in 1297. Starting with the east range, the builders worked round clockwise, but work came to a standstill for some fifty years after the Black Death and the circuit was not finally completed until 1430. The change from Decorated tracery to Perpendicular, which marks the interruption, can be seen clearly in the north-west corner; the structural system of the Cloisters themselves, however, remained constant – two-storeyed, tierceron-vaulted, and once again, like the nave, extravagantly and exuberantly bossed.

The Cathedral Close has much fine building in it, mainly Georgian but including the EDWARD VI SCHOOL opposite the cathedral to the north. Despite its name it was in fact founded, as Carnary College, in 1316 – well over 200 years before King Edward's day. The fine original Chapel still survives. For the rest, perhaps the most distinguished features are the two entrance gates to the Close on the west side. The ETHELBERT GATE, towards the south, is the exact contemporary of the College but was much restored in the last century (especially the flushwork roundels at the top) by William Wilkins, the Norwich architect who designed the National Gallery. The ERPINGHAM GATE of 1420, immediately opposite the cathedral west door, holds greater, if less obvious, rewards in the shape of rich and beautiful carvings in the side buttresses, the jamb and the arch. In the niche above is a statue of Sir Thomas Erpingham, who fought as an old man with Henry V at Agincourt:

> *Good morrow, old Sir Thomas Erpingham:*
> *A good soft pillow for that good white head*
> *Were better than the churlish turf of France.*
>
> *Not so, my liege: this lodging likes me better,*
> *Since I may say, 'Now lie I like a king.'*

*The Market Place, Norwich.*

The path leading down from the Ethelbert Gate brings you after a few minutes to Pull's Ferry and the WATER GATE, which was built in the fifteenth century, when the river was still one of the principal thoroughfares of the city. It is a walk well worth taking, and provides in addition the famous south-east view of the cathedral, the loveliest of all.

THE CITY

Set on a partly artificial mound with the traffic roaring around it, the CASTLE is an impressive building but not an altogether satisfactory one. It is a hall keep, in other words broader than it is long, and at first glance it looks distinctly bogus. So up to a point it is – having been refaced from top to bottom in the 1830s by Salvin, in Bath stone instead of the original Caen and local carstone; but Pevsner assures us that the decorative motifs (principally blind arcading in various sizes and stages) 'were all there and can be trusted'. This means that Norwich Castle, which dates from around 1160, is by far the most ornate Norman castle of its kind in England or, for that matter, in France either – the nearest parallel I can think of for it is the Palazzo Reale in Palermo. A gaol in the eighteenth century, a museum and art gallery today, it has an interior altered, alas, beyond recognition.

Fifty yards from Castle Meadow to the north lies London Street, now mercifully pedestrianised. It contains two magnificent fronts of radically differing styles, but both the work of everybody's favourite Norwich architect, George Skipper, born in 1854. One is the LONDON AND PROVINCIAL BANK – a rather florid Baroque; the other, now a part of JARROLD'S, is a twin-gabled brick building in what Sir Osbert Lancaster has felicitously labelled Pont Street Dutch. Formerly Skipper's own office, it is made still more enjoyable by a terracotta frieze depicting the top-hatted, frock-coated architect himself, in one scene directing his builders, in the other surrounded by his family, including a child with a hoop and a dog, giving instructions to his gardeners. A Skipper tour is, I suspect, one of the most rewarding off-beat walks one can take in Norwich. There seems no end to his range, or his inventiveness. His masterpiece is the NORWICH UNION in Surrey Street, which he built in 1903–4. (Pevsner, never lavish in value judgements, describes it as 'smashing' – praise indeed.) It is essentially Palladian in style, but with Skipperisms breaking out everywhere, particularly in the two single-storey rusticated wings that advance to form a shallow courtyard, ending in niches with statues. The interior is better still, with a sensational main hall, cupolaed and colonnaded and everywhere encrusted with polychrome marble. A somewhat similar building, smaller but no less ornate, is TELEPHONE HOUSE in St Giles's Street (No. 43). But for sheer fun the biscuit must go to the ROYAL ARCADE, an *art nouveau*-cum-Arabian Nights extravaganza of 1899 executed by Skipper in glazed Doulton tiles, leading straight out of Castle Street into the Market Place.

Certainly it is one of the great market places of England, made memorable by the joyfully striped awnings of its stalls. Its success architecturally, however, depends entirely on whether one can accept the CITY HALL, which occupies the whole of the west side of the huge square and, thanks to the rising ground, totally dominates it. Erected in the 1930s and obviously inspired by its opposite number in Stockholm, it is described by Pevsner as 'the foremost English public building of between the wars'. This, if true, would be a sad indictment of the architecture of the period; but my real objection to this distressing pile is its arrogance, the way it rides roughshod over the architecture around it, and particularly the GUILDHALL with which it forms the north-west corner of the square. This lovely building was completed in 1413, though it was given a new council chamber a century later. It can thus be compared, in style and period, to the Holy Trinity Guildhall – now the Town Hall – at King's Lynn; but whereas in King's Lynn a genuine visual excitement is generated, in Norwich what ought to be one of the grandest features of the city passes almost unnoticed under the shadow of a red-brick Leviathan that cares for nothing but itself. It comes as no surprise to learn that at the beginning of this century there was a serious proposal in the city council to demolish the Guildhall altogether; it was saved only by the mayor's single casting vote.

The south side of the Market Place fares better; not even the City Hall can completely dwarf ST PETER MANCROFT, Norfolk's grandest parish church and almost a cathedral in itself. It was consecrated in 1455, at a time when Norwich was the third – possibly even the second – city in the kingdom, and shows all the signs of good, solid, bourgeois wealth. The outside never seems to me entirely successful; the north front – that facing the Market Place – is uninspiring and even the huge west tower, elaborate as it is, fails to convince. (Street's ridiculous little topknot does little to improve matters.) Things are very much better inside. Unusually, it is a hall church: the glorious wooden roof marches straight from the tower to the east end, uninterrupted by any sign of a chancel arch. It is actually hammer-beamed, but the hammer-beams are hidden by a ribbed wooden coving – a feature peculiar to East Anglia and rare enough even here.

But the city has thirty-one other medieval churches and, with them, a redundancy problem of fearsome proportions. The Norwich Historic Churches Trust, founded in 1972 with the council as trustee, wrestles with it manfully, and several have now been converted to other uses, including a museum, a library, a community centre, a boy scouts' meeting place and even a furniture repository. Architecturally the most interesting I know – I cannot pretend to have seen them all – are ST MARY COSLANY with its round Saxon tower, ST MICHAEL COSLANY with its explosion of flushwork like Perpendicular tracery, and the very splendid ST GILES. The Free Churches, too, are stunningly represented by the exquisite OCTAGON CHAPEL, built in the 1750s by Thomas Ivory, the Norwich man who was responsible for much of the best Georgian architecture in his city. Finally, we cannot possibly overlook the Catholic CHURCH OF ST JOHN THE BAPTIST, built to cathedral proportions between 1884 and 1910 by George Gilbert Scott and his brother John Oldrid Scott. Here is Victorian Early English at its apogee. Pearson's Truro Cathedral is its only rival, but whereas at Truro all is tenuous and slender, here at Norwich the accent is on mass – a bulwark rather than an aspiration.

For the rest, it is impossible to give any proper account here. I can only suggest you buy a good city guide-book – *not* the official one, which like all of its ilk contains little but the opening hours of the municipal swimming pool and the telephone number of the Marriage Guidance Council – and wander for yourself.

## Oxburgh Hall

*NT; 31; 7 miles SW of Swaffham off A134*

The end of the fifteenth century in England was a time of hope. The Hundred Years' War and the Wars of the Roses were over and the kingdom was entering on a period of greater internal tranquillity than it had ever known. The indications were that an Englishman's home need no longer be, literally, a castle – that he could henceforth think in terms of comfort rather than of defence. At the same time he could never be certain of what lay ahead; and besides, great houses had been strongholds for so long that it was difficult to conceive of them in completely different terms. For some years yet lip service would continue to be paid to military considerations, although the owners of these new houses never deceived themselves that they would be able to withstand any but the most desultory and half-hearted attack.

Oxburgh, begun in 1482 by one Edmund Bedingfeld, is just such a house. At first sight – and the first sight of Oxburgh is even more thrilling than that of Blickling – it looks quite tremendous, with that majestic twin-towered Gatehouse of mellow brick sweeping up seven storeys to its battlemented parapets. But the arrow slits in the towers, strategically placed to defend the bridge (originally a drawbridge), accord ill with the four-light window immediately above the entrance, and the machicolations, far from being seriously intended for the pouring of boiling oil or indeed anything else on to the heads of the attackers, have been reduced to little more than a decorative frieze and string-course. No matter; the Gatehouse, which is among the best surviving examples of brickwork of the period in the country, is the glory of Oxburgh, the more so as it is the only part of the house to have remained almost untouched since it was built. On the first floor – behind that four-light window – is the so-called King's Room, where Henry VII slept in 1487 and which now accommodates the famous bed hangings containing fifteen panels embroidered by Bess of Hardwick and another thirty by Mary Queen of Scots herself. This room, and the Queen's Room above it, are reached by a circular newel-staircase made of cut brick – a staggering demonstration of the bricklayer's art. Look at the precision of the bonding as stair meets newel, at the barrel-vaulted underside, and at the moulded banister. Only one other brick staircase in the country, that of Faulkbourne Hall in Essex, can hold a candle to it.

The rest of the house has been sadly altered over the centuries. In 1778 Sir Richard Bedingfeld demolished

*Oxburgh Hall.*

the whole range opposite the Gatehouse, and with it the Great Hall; in the quarter-century following 1835 his grandson, Sir Henry, remodelled much of the rest; his are most of the windows – including the oriels – the tall Tudor chimneys and the great tower at the south-east corner, all picturesque if not quite archaeologically correct. The interior is also now essentially Victorian, much of it in Gothic Revival style.

Though National Trust property since 1952, Oxburgh is still lived in by the Bedingfeld family. Their Chantry Chapel in the nearby parish church of Oxborough (*sic*), ST JOHN EVANGELIST, which miraculously escaped when the falling steeple effectively destroyed the rest of the church, well repays a visit. The key is at the Gardener's Lodge. Worth seeing too is the Catholic CHURCH OF OUR LADY AND ST MARGARET – the Bedingfelds ignored the Reformation and remained staunch Catholics throughout their history – near the Gatehouse. It is said to have been designed by Pugin for Sir Henry in the 1830s, though I can find no documentary evidence for the claim.

## Rainthorpe Hall

*32; 8 miles S of Norwich off A140*

The house stands just outside Tasburgh to the north, and is approached down a long avenue. The north (entrance) front is undeniably impressive, although it could hardly be described as tidy. Basically it is of brick, but there is timber-framing on the first floor. It is in essence an E-plan house, but there is an extra gabled projection to the left of the porch, which is considerably off-centre. The house is mainly of the 1580s; but the entrance is certainly a good half-century earlier and there are several other features that must have seemed extremely old-fashioned in Elizabethan days. The conclusion is that Thomas Baxter, whose arms or initials appear in several places inside and out, did not build himself a completely new house when he acquired the manor in 1579 but contented himself with an extensive remodelling of the earlier one of *c.*1500. The two projecting wings end in vast gables, topped with pairs of tall brick chimneys; as the flues are straight, this means that the rather small end windows have to be relegated to the sides, with not entirely satisfactory results. These gables are each of three storeys, as is the porch with its big mullioned and transomed windows and polygonal angle shafts. Elsewhere the house is of two storeys, though there is a small dormer to the porch projection. We find a lower porch on the east front, of two storeys only, and on the long south front overlooking the lovely garden a polygonal stair turret (opposite the front entrance) and a bay bearing the date 1615, to say nothing – which, after all, is probably best – of a long Victorian wing of 1885.

The Hall was originally to the left of the entrance, but since the walls on both sides of the screens passage have now gone the former pantry and buttery, as well as the passage itself, have been incorporated into the great central space which now extends the whole distance between the two wings. Above is the Great Chamber, which has retained its Elizabethan plaster ceiling with thin ribs. Throughout the house there are quantities of fine woodwork, in the form of panelling and chimneypieces – a particularly splendid one, with an enormous overmantel, can be seen in the Hall. One of the upper rooms is hung, moreover, with beautiful embossed Spanish leather. But all of this – both the woodwork and the leather – though roughly contemporary with the Baxter house, is not strictly speaking a part of it, having been brought in by the Hon. Frederick Walpole, who occupied Rainthorpe between 1852 and his death in 1876.

Despite its slightly forbidding exterior, it therefore emerges as a house of considerable beauty and marvellous atmosphere – well worthy of its place in this book.

## Raynham Hall*

*33; 3 miles SW of Fakenham off A1065*

In all England there are few more beautiful houses than Raynham – and none, perhaps, that so perfectly exemplifies all that is best in English domestic architecture in the first half of the seventeenth century. 'Domestic' is the operative word: Raynham is not palatial, as is, for example, its exact contemporary, Blickling; such monumentality as it possesses is the work of William Kent, working a good 100 years later. Despite its size, there is a comfortable, homely feeling about it; it is a house designed not only to be admired, but also to be loved.

But who was the designer? Was it William Edge, whom we know to have built it for Sir Roger Townshend in the 1620s and 1630s? Or was it, as some have suggested, Inigo Jones himself? There is no space here to go into any prolonged discussion, but consider one detail only: the way the big stone volutes on the side gables end, just below the pediments, with Ionic capitals. Would a classicist like Jones ever have permitted himself such an ungrammatical conceit? My own guess, for what it is worth, is that Townshend and Edge together had studied Jones's work – in 1621 he had just completed the Prince's Lodging at Newmarket – and perhaps even shown him their drawings, but that the real credit for Raynham must go to Edge. If so, the partial destruction by fire of his only other major work, Hunstanton Hall, some 20 miles away, is even more to be regretted.

The house is built of warm red brick, with stone dressings. It is of eleven bays by seven, the two outer bays on each side being part of the north and south wings, which project quite considerably on the entrance (west) front but hardly at all on the garden front to the east. On both fronts, these wings are topped with big pedimented Dutch gables with circular windows below their pediments. Where the two fronts principally differ is in the central portions. To the west, the first-floor windows here are deliberately stunted, to make room for a generous attic storey between the gables which is in turn crowned by a three-bay shaped pediment with segmental sides and a beautifully carved oval cartouche in the middle. The doorcase, apparently of *c.*1680, rises through much of the first floor. It has a scrolly open pediment supported on slender Corinthian columns.

The east front is considerably grander. Here, although the two bays on each side of the three-bay centre are of only two storeys with a stone balustrade above, the centre itself is entirely faced with stone. A flight of broad steps leads up to a rusticated ground floor, above which rises a classical portico – four Ionic attached columns on tall plinths supporting a big triangular pediment. In the centre bay rises a high round-headed window with a carved stone panel above, and to each side is a normal-sized window topped by a small, square one. (This scheme is, incidentally, almost identical with Jones's drawings for the Prince's Lodging; some connection between the two is virtually certain.) Such porticoes were still, at this time, an exciting innovation and were peculiar to Jones; we do not see a projecting domestic portico anywhere else in the country until 1654, when John Webb – his nephew or son-in-law – added one to The Vyne in Hampshire (*q.v.*).

To enter the house is to pass instantaneously from the seventeenth century into the eighteenth; William Kent had been working through most of the 1720s for Sir Robert Walpole at Houghton, only some 5 miles away, so it was hardly surprising that he should come on to Raynham in 1730 at the request of Walpole's Secretary of State, the 2nd Viscount ('Turnip') Townshend. His is the spectacular Entrance Hall, centrally placed on the west side, with entrances at both ends. It rises one and a half storeys, the upper and lower windows being reflected in blank stucco frames all round the walls, which are further articulated by Ionic pilasters. Above these runs a pretty frieze with masks and garlands. The ceiling is terrific: a gigantic Townshend coat of arms in the centre, with smaller panels of equally dazzling plasterwork arranged geometrically around. The other principal ground-floor rooms are smaller, but equally sumptuous: the mouldings of the Saloon, with its splendid doorcases and overmantel, comprise almost a pattern-book of Kentian motifs, and there is an unforgettable State Dining Room, its service alcove partially closed off by a three-arched screen based on the arch of Septimius Severus in Rome.

The first floor can be reached by either of the two staircases, one with slender wooden balusters, the other – where they are of wrought iron – painted by Kent with statues in *trompe-l'oeil* niches; and so one comes, astonished, to the largest and most opulent room in the house, named – after a portrait of the Emperor Justinian's great general which, alas, no longer survives in the house – the Belisarius Room. It too is of one and a half storeys, and occupies the centre of the east front on the upper level. Seen from the inside, the three central windows give the impression of a huge Venetian window filling the entire wall; but the *tour de force* is, once again, the plaster ceiling. The mouldings seem far too deep and heavy for Kent and probably date from some half a century before his arrival; but the four painted panels enclosing the central oval could be by no other hand. Kent was always at his weakest with paintings of this kind, and these panels do not, to my eye, accord entirely happily with the almost unbelievably rich plasterwork around them; the chimneypiece is, on the other hand, a consummate success, and the tomato-coloured walls and superb seventeenth-century furniture magnificently complete the ensemble.

The present Lord Townshend is at present engaged in a complete restoration of this glorious house, which already almost certainly looks better than at any time in the past century. It is not normally open to the public.

## Redenhall

*34; ½ mile E of Harleston on A143*

ST MARY'S CHURCH earns its place because of its tower – the grandest late Perpendicular flushwork tower in the county and a real eyecatcher on the Harleston–Bungay road. The village clearly took a lot of trouble over it – it was sixty years a-building from 1460 onwards – and their efforts have been spectacularly rewarded.

## Salle★

*35; 6 miles SW of Aylsham off B1145*

The name is pronounced so as to rhyme with ST PETER AND ST PAUL – to whom is jointly dedicated one of the most hauntingly poetic churches in all East Anglia. It is in many respects a sister church to Cawston, a mile or two to the east; but whereas Cawston is a large and prosperous village, Salle – which was once a rich weaving community supporting six separate guilds – has dwindled to little more than the church itself, now rising immense and solitary from the fields.

It was built, all of a piece, of Barnack stone in the first half of the fifteenth century – the Arms of Henry V can be seen among the shields over the west door (third along in the right-hand row). Only the top stage of the tall west tower, with its richly ornate battlements, is a later addition of around 1500. This crowning flourish adds much to the tower's distinction – would that some benefactor had done the same for Cawston – for, though proudly proportioned, it otherwise carries little decoration except the traceried bell openings and the various features above and around the west door, including in the spandrels an odd pair of angels in what appear to be feathered body stockings. Just beyond the tower to north and south there are almost identical two-storey porches, their vaulted roofs nobly bossed.

Inside, all is silence and space, with a marvellous vista culminating in the great seven-light east window. As so often in these Perpendicular East Anglian churches, most of the glass is clear, so the whole church is flooded with sunshine. There is a graceful arcade, tall and slender, leading up to a generous clerestory and a wooden roof with angels which, though not perhaps quite as immediately impressive as Cawston's, is still more ingeniously constructed. Where Cawston has hammer-beams, Salle has short arched braces whose wall posts stand on what appear to be corbels but which are in fact the ends of the principal rafters of the aisles, projecting through the wall. Contemporary with the building itself are the wonderful carved stalls with misericords, the sadly damaged font – its high wooden canopy operated by a still existent pulley – and the wineglass pulpit, to which the Jacobeans added a tester and forward extension, turning it into a three-decker.

This lovely, lonely church, though virtually without a parish, remains beautifully tended at the time of writing, and occasional services are still held there. We can only pray that it continues as fortunate, for it is one of the glories of Norfolk.

## Shelton★

*36; 9½ miles NE of Diss off A140*

ST MARY'S CHURCH is a stunner. When first seen from the south the three terrific late fifteenth-century windows, set in stone-dressed, diapered red brick and surmounted by nine more of almost equal height in the clerestory, give warning that something memorable is about to happen; but they do not tell you the half of it. Only when you get inside does the splendour of the building really hit you. The colour first; it is a marvellous pinkish apricot which – particularly on a summer afternoon when the sun is streaming through those windows – makes the whole church glow; then the intensity of commitment to the Perpendicular style, above all in the way in which the mullions in the clerestory ignore the bottom of the window frames and sweep right down until they meet the arches. These are four-centred, and their outer mouldings have no capitals, so that they too carry the eye uninterruptedly to the floor.

The only sad thing about Shelton is that the work was never finished. Sir Ralph Shelton, dying in 1487, left orders in his will for its completion, but his executors obviously decided to cut a few corners. The roof, for example, is lower than it should have been: Sir Ralph can never have intended it to touch the top of his east window. Equally surprising, there is no real chancel. One has been artificially created by the bottom part of a splendid old fifteenth-century screen of worm-eaten wood, and a step down followed by three steps up to the altar gives a certain dramatic impact; but the arcades of a church do not normally run unbrokenly up to the east end, and the whole thing looks curiously truncated in consequence. No matter: Shelton is not like other churches and its eccentricities are part of its character. Here is a building that really lifts the spirit; one cannot ask for more.

## Sheringham Hall

*37; 4½ miles W of Cromer on A149*

The distinction of being the only house to have been designed by Humphry Repton from its very beginning, including the choice of its site, belongs to Sheringham Hall. Repton is said to have stationed himself at the edge of the woods above the park and to have sent his carriage on ahead; he watched its progress carefully and when it reached what he considered the perfect location blew his hunting horn. The coach stopped, and the land was pegged out accordingly. In the Red Book which Repton prepared for Sheringham – a facsimile of which is kept in the house – he expressed the opinion that it possessed 'more of what my predecessors called Capabilities' than any other place he had seen in fifty years, and described it as 'such a specimen of my arts as I have never before had an opportunity of displaying. This', he concluded, 'may be considered my most favourite work.'

In view of all this, it seems difficult to sustain the theory sometimes put forward that the architecture of the house is more the work of John Adey Repton than of his father – though John Adey was certainly involved in the building, and indeed supervised the work after Humphry's death in 1818. The three bow windows may well be his, if they are not still later additions. But Sheringham was probably still incomplete when the Reptons' patron, Abbot Upcher, died in February 1819 at the age of thirty-four. His widow lost interest in the house, which then lay empty for the next twenty years. Much of the interior decoration and furnishing therefore dates from the years around 1840.

The house is quite small: two storeys and five principal bays on the main south front, although subsidiary extensions behind and to the sides make it in fact rather larger inside than it looks at first. The main front has two short projections of a single bay, with a bow window on the ground floor, while across the three-bay centre runs a charming deep loggia on four pairs of Tuscan columns. The material throughout is a whitish brick, not normally a happy choice but here surprisingly successful, largely perhaps for the contrast it provides to the high wooded hill which climbs up immediately behind the house to shelter it from the sea winds.

You enter by a Tuscan porch on the three-bay west front, to find yourself in a most elegant Hall with a black and white octagon and dot floor. To your left is the Dining Room, to your right the first of the three rooms occupying the south front, the Parlour. There follows the Music Room, behind the loggia – a room of much delicacy and elegance – and beyond it the large and splendid Library, which takes up the whole end of the house, having broad bow windows to both south and east.

Behind the Music Room, in the centre, a really lovely staircase with a thin iron balustrade ascends to a broad transverse landing on the first floor and the principal bedrooms, all with glorious views across the park.

## Shotesham Park

*38; 5½ miles S of Norwich on A140*

Built by Sir John Soane in about 1785, the house stands at the end of a longish drive in a dell, so that it is approached from above and reveals itself only at the last moment. Of fine apricot-coloured brick, it seems at first sight surprisingly small; but this is largely because Soane liked to spread himself with his bays. The principal front has only five of them – indeed, looking only at the ground floor one might almost say only three, for numbers 2 and 4 have been reduced to round-headed niches; numbers 1, 3 and 5 have broad, tripartite windows reaching to the ground, somewhat reminiscent of Venetian windows except that the side parts are the same height as the centre, which is also straight-headed, and the big semi-circular tympanum above is reflected in a smaller, concentric one formed by the inwardly curving prolongation of the two inner divisions. The bays are articulated by six Ionic pilasters, set at irregular intervals and supporting an unadorned flat entablature, above which rises a shallow-pedimented attic half storey; curiously, however, the outside pilasters are set not at the angles but several feet towards the centre; the effect is thus that of a most sophisticated composition set against a plain brick wall. It does not, I know, sound particularly attractive; I can only say that it actually works a good deal better than one might imagine.

At the time of my visit the house was empty and I could not get in. It has now been bought by a Danish family who, the local estate agents tell me, 'have achieved wonders'.

## South Creake*

*39; 5½ miles NW of Fakenham on B1355*

The big flint ST MARY'S CHURCH stands on an eminence a little way out of the village, beyond a pretty row of houses with, opposite them, an orchard and duckpond. It has a short, stocky west tower, all fourteenth-century, with two-light Decorated bell openings and a lovely four-light west window with cusped reticulated tracery. The aisles have Decorated windows at their eastern ends, but Perpendicular ones along the sides – though even these have pleasant little quatrefoils set into their heads. There is an impressive south porch, too, with a deeply moulded two-centred arch, two-light cusped windows to each side and a flushwork frieze with crowned Ms (for Mary). A tiny statuette of the Virgin set in a high central niche looks interesting; alas, I had left my binoculars behind.

But it is the interior of the church – broad, spacious and flooded with light – that earns it its star. There are plenty of fragments of good medieval glass, but fortunately not enough of it appreciably to darken the building, and the pale stone of the immensely tall arcades together with the plain, whitewashed walls gives it a wonderful atmosphere of serenity and peace. The old, uneven, red-tiled floor has been preserved, thank goodness, and there is an exquisite screen with delicate panelled tracery above intricately cusped ogee arches. The wood is pale, and there are remains of paint below the dado. A companion to it is the wineglass pulpit, also with traces of paintwork, now standing on a modern base. The fifteenth-century octagonal stone font, on two high steps, is beautiful too but sadly defaced. The hammer-beam roof, with its brightly painted angels, has been much renewed. The principal weakness is the chancel, the most interesting feature of which is its very marked nod towards the south; its roof is a modern makeshift, which presumably keeps out the rain but does little more for the church.

For the rest, the church contains several unusual items including a hand-pumped organ, a magnificent fourteenth-century iron chest and a seventeenth-century bier with folding legs. Liturgically speaking, St Mary's is extremely high, and much of the other furniture – Stations of the Cross, etc. – reflects this persuasion. But it in no way spoils the general effect, which is enhanced by the most beautiful flower arrangements I have ever seen in any parish church – not there for any special occasion but part of the regular maintenance. Only a particularly hideous square of cheap carpet protecting a good fourteenth-century brass mars the beauty – but if my on-the-spot representations have borne fruit it will have gone by the time this book appears.

## South Lopham

*40; 4½ miles W of Diss on A1066*

ST ANDREW'S CHURCH has a great, thundering, utterly uncompromising and absolutely marvellous Norman tower of 1100 or so, simply – almost crudely – decorated with blind arcading, otherwise relieved only by the usual Perpendicular battlemented top. But 1100 was neither the beginning nor the end: just to the west of the north doorway is a round, obviously Anglo-Saxon window which probably goes back the best part of another century, while the chancel is Decorated of 1360–80. Inside the church, the over-riding impression is that of the (restored) five-light east window tracery seen through the perspective of the two huge Norman arches supporting the tower. There is a nice hammer-beam roof with angels, too. The lovely choir stalls – one of which is carved with an elephant and castle, crest of the Beaumonts – presumably commemorate the John Beaumont who married the widowed Duchess of Norfolk, lady of the manor of Lopham, and died in 1460.

## Swaffham

*41; 15½ miles SE of King's Lynn on A47*

ST PETER AND ST PAUL – a very common dedication in these parts – is an outstandingly splendid Perpendicular church. Its ornate west tower with its huge three-light bell openings and crow-stepped battlements (stone angels stand halfway along each side) and, most distinctive of all, the slender steeple which is almost a *flèche*, is a landmark for miles. It stands in the centre of the town in a huge leafy churchyard which would be even lovelier if someone had not rearranged all the gravestones in regimented rows, like soldiers. Seen from here, the north side is magnificent indeed: seven-bay aisles with a thirteen-bay clerestory above, embattled in brick which contrasts oddly with the rubble of which the rest of the church is built; only the tower is of stone. There is also a pretty little Sanctus bell turret at the east end of the nave where it meets the chancel.

Sadly, the interior is largely spoilt by the glass – dirty green in both aisles, with second-rate Victorian stuff at the east end. The former at least should be removed at once; not only would the whole building be lightened, but we should also get a far better view of the glorious double hammer-beam roof and the company of angels on hammers and kingposts. I suspect, too, that the additional light would make the church seem a good deal more spacious; at present the comparative narrowness of nave and aisles, the thinness of the piers and the height of the walls all combine to make one feel a bit constricted.

## Terrington St Clement

*42; 4½ miles W of King's Lynn on A17*

Alec Clifton-Taylor has pointed out that the Norfolk Marshland – that is, the extreme western corner of the county between King's Lynn and Wisbech – 'contains memorable churches in greater numbers than any other part of England of comparable extent'. ST CLEMENT'S is one of the grandest. The first thing one notices, apart from the general splendour, is once again the ashlar-faced tower; but this time the builders, who obviously intended to place it centrally over the crossing, must have lost their nerve at the last moment. Instead it stands detached, *campanile*-style, from the body of the church, though curiously – even awkwardly – close to it. Tower, nave and aisles are all embattled, the battlements themselves fully ornamented; this is a Perpendicular church – though the window tracery in both aisles and clerestory have Decorated elements – and even if it is built on a thirteenth-century foundation it certainly takes no pride in the fact. The elaborate south porch carries a monumental sundial, enjoining us to Watch and Pray.

Once inside, we are brought up sharply against a late eighteenth-century entrance screen – a curious enough feature in itself, with its musicians' loft above; but even this must take second place to the really extraordinary font cover, Gothic on top, Renaissance–Jacobean below, which opens out to reveal rather endearing paintings of the Life of Christ, with particular stress very properly laid on His baptism. Pursue your way east, to the good-for-nothing crossing – now anti-climactically covered with a simple wooden roof instead of that splendid tower – and the short, stubby transepts which have also failed to fulfil their early promise, though the three–two–one window pyramid in the south wall remains long in the memory. And so, finally, pass through part of another screen – medieval, but mercifully undefaced by Cromwell's vandals – to the chancel, with its own brick clerestory and its big five-light window. This is a noble church indeed.

## Thompson★

*43; 10 miles NE of Thetford off A1075*

ST MARTIN'S is a really lovely church, which with a little trouble and expense could be made lovelier still. It was built during the first forty years of the fourteenth century – apart from the south chapel and the flushwork battlements of the tower, which must be about 100 years later – and the exterior has hardly been touched since; it is consequently one of the most complete, as well as one of the most beautiful, Decorated churches in all East Anglia. The material is, as usual, flint with stone dressings. The only pity is the rather strident orange of the tiled roof; before 1913 it was thatched, and must have looked a good deal better.

The tower has a flushwork base in a chequer pattern, a broad and deeply moulded west door and, set almost immediately above it (a little too low), a most sumptuous three-light window of doubly reticulated tracery: even the reticulations have reticulations. In the top stage there is a much simpler two-light bell opening, with Y-tracery, but what I find particularly endearing is the little circular window on the south side, to light the stair turret, which has Catherine wheel tracery rather like that in the Palazzo Contarini-Fasan ('Desdemona's Palace') in Venice.

You enter by the south porch, which has a pretty triple niche, heavily cusped, above the entrance and its original south door with a border of trailing flowers and a simply magnificent key over a foot long – and the interior proves everything you hoped it would be. It

*St Clement's Church, Terrington St Clement.*

looks as if it had scarcely been touched since the sixteenth century – which is indeed very nearly true, since the restorations of 1910–13 and 1974 were largely limited to essential repairs. The butter-coloured walls of the nave (there are no aisles), the old red tiled floor, the original poppy-head benches, the unstained, canted timber roof, simple yet stalwart, the absence of fuss or meretricious decoration – all these things combine to give the building an intimate, domestic character: it is a church to be admired, certainly, but to be loved even more. There is a fine old family box pew on the north side, and a slightly altered Jacobean three-decker pulpit with tester. The screen is a particular joy; of the same date as the church, it has slim circular shafts instead of mullions and more 'Desdemona' tracery, while the original painted decoration in black, white and red is still visible on the dado.

The chancel would be even more beautiful than the nave, but for a single tragic circumstance: the lovely tracery of the five-light east window and the two three-light south windows is all blocked in, while the particularly fine north window is blocked completely. Is there no chance of their being opened up again? We can only console ourselves with the sedilia and piscina, cusped, ogival, with fantastic carving in the spandrels including an excellent jack-in-the-green.

Finally, we must on no account miss the Royal Arms on the north wall of the nave. They appear to be Queen Anne, but are in fact an alteration of an original which almost certainly goes back to Charles I.

In sum, it is a marvellous church. If only something could be done about those windows. . . .

## Tilney All Saints

*44; 4 miles SW of King's Lynn off A47*

ALL SAINTS, Tilney, is one of the great churches of the Marshland. It is built, like most of the others in this most favoured region, of stone – Barnack rag from Northamptonshire (now partly rendered), transported along the Fenland rivers from quarries which belonged in the twelfth century to the Abbey of Peterborough. This fact is relevant because, despite outward appearances, All Saints remains in all its essentials a twelfth-century church. Only the tower is later, having been added around 1240–50 and remodelled perhaps a century after that, when it was given its pretty canopied doorway with flanking buttresses and its rather too short stone spire. As to the rest, it too has been much remodelled externally, to the point where not a single Norman window remains (though traces are visible here and there). But notice how the string-course for the upper chancel windows extends back along the nave: a sure sign that there was already a nave clerestory in Norman days, and another indication, apart from its size, that this was from its very beginnings a church of considerable importance.

Inside, its age becomes a good deal clearer. The two arcades, each of seven bays, have broad round arches and – with two interesting but not ultimately important exceptions – massive circular piers. They continue right up to the east end, providing the chancel with flanking chapels, of which the southern now serves as a sacristy; there is nothing remotely resembling a chancel arch, or indeed any structural division between nave and chancel. Only at the western end is this architectural unity broken, where a single Early English bay links nave to tower. The tower arch is immensely tall – tall enough for one to be able to see the triple lancet windows on the west side; from the east, it frames the octagonal font most beautifully.

After the thirteenth century the principal modifications were to the fenestration and the roof. The windows are something of a jumble: Decorated, Perpendicular (including the big five-light east window of the chancel) and sixteenth-century. The roof, however, is magnificent – a double hammer-beam with upright, forward-leaning angels and others, prone, below. Technically, the upper hammers are 'false', in that they are not load-bearing and exist purely for decorative reasons, but the effect is none the worse for that. The chancel roof is simpler, with a single hammer-beam only; the angels here carry shields with various emblems, while more figures, unwinged, hold books or shields at the base of the wall posts. Most of the furniture, alas, is Victorian, but there is a fine Jacobean rood-screen and fifteenth-century parclose screens to the side; a good Royal Arms, too, dated 1711, and a lovely floor of old lozenge-shaped tiles.

Outside the church, two distinctly incongruous chimneys sprout up from the west end of the nave on the south side, just behind the tower. Is it not time they came down?

## Trunch

*45; 3 miles NE of North Walsham off B1145*

If we are to speak strictly from the point of view of architecture, there is little to say about ST BOTOLPH'S CHURCH. It seems to have been almost entirely rebuilt in about 1380, and therefore presents an ensemble most satisfying in its unity: Perpendicular, but only just, with little echoes of Decorated in the tracery of the tower openings and in one or two of the aisle windows. As well as the pleasant if unassuming south porch in the usual place, there is a second and much more surprising one halfway along the chancel over the priest's door, from which – odder still – a buttress appears to sprout.

But architecture is not the point at Trunch. Here the important things are three: the roof, the screen and the font canopy. The roof is a single hammer-beam with angels and rich tracery above the hammers. Anywhere but in East Anglia it would be famous; but in this neighbourhood it is one of many – and besides, it is overshadowed by the screen and the canopy.

And so to the screen. It is of 1502, with two-light divisions and ogival arches, richly cusped. What makes it remarkable, however, is the extent to which its original painted panels have been preserved – twelve of them, representing the Apostles, except that St Paul has elbowed out St Matthias. A beautiful piece indeed – but once again it has been upstaged by the font canopy.

This is the pride of Trunch. There are only four of its kind in England: two earlier (St Mary's, Luton, and St Peter Mancroft, Norwich) and one later, in Durham Cathedral. It dates from *c.* 1500. The base, which surrounds the font itself, consists of six oak shafts, each intricately carved, arranged in the form of a hexagon, supporting a tiny fan vault with a central pendant. The upper stage, which is smaller, has six broad tripartite canopies, still more richly carved, with nodding ogees. Originally, these seem to have been connected to the shafts below by little flying buttresses, but these have all been broken off – perhaps by Dowsing and his gang, who also destroyed three of the six panels below the canopies. The whole thing is surmounted by an open-work crown, ogival again and heavily crocketed, ending in a sort of top-knot the shape of an outsize tomato.

A final point of interest is the tomb (in the chancel) of Horatia Ward, who was married to the son of a former rector. She was the daughter of Nelson and Lady Hamilton, and their only child.

## Upwell

*46; $7\frac{1}{2}$ miles W of Downham Market on A1101*

If you are driving to Norfolk from the south-west – as, for best results, you should – Upwell will probably be your first port of call; and a fine foretaste it provides for the Marshland splendours to come. The square Early English tower of ST ANDREW'S CHURCH turns, as it rises, to a Perpendicular octagon; the churchyard has wondrously lichened gravestones by some excellent local carver; the porch boasts its original fifteenth-century wooden door with swans all round it and two grotesque corbels for the hood-mould.

The interior keeps up the standard, with both the nave and the aisle roofs hammer-beamed, carrying angels with great spread wings. There are also the Regency wooden galleries to west and north, two grand sets of Royal Arms, and enough box pews to accommodate a regiment. The brasses are good, too – one early fourteenth-century one to a priest in the south-west corner of the chancel, nearly 4 feet high under a huge canopy, and another (my favourite) to Mr Sinulphus Bell and his family, including the admirable Mrs Bell who 'never delayde by deeds and good usage to give him content'.

## Walpole St Peter*

*47; 8 miles SW of King's Lynn off A47*

After a rather boring tower, ST PETER'S CHURCH gets better and better – the finest in the Marshland, if not in all Norfolk. Built between 1350 and 1400 and stone-faced, it marks the transition between Decorated (the west window) and Perpendicular (most of the remainder). Everywhere there is a marvellous attention to detail; look, for example, at the buttresses of the south porch with their almost *chinoiserie* cut-offs, and the wonderful bosses within the porch itself, including a blood-curdling Last Judgement and – a considerable rarity in England – a *Pietà* in the north-west corner. Even the battlements are adorned with panels and gargoyles. And if (as you always must) you walk round the outside of the church, you are in for a big surprise when you get to the east end – for here the path actually burrows *under* the chancel. The reason for this curious arrangement was presumably the lack of consecrated ground to the east on which to lay out a processional route, though it could have been the need to preserve an ancient right of way;

in any case the effect is to give the church a raised chancel of haunting beauty.

At first entry, this chancel is in some measure obscured by another of those west screens like that at Terrington – only seventeenth-century this time – with three triangular pediments over nave and aisles. Beyond it the high pointed arches, intricately moulded, lead the eye forward over the varied box pews, past the pretty Jacobean pulpit, through the painted dado of a second screen and up no fewer than nine steps to the miraculous chancel. And what a joy it is: along the north and south walls, the stalls have beautifully carved poppy-heads and blank arches as a backing. Above there is a charmingly dotty spider's-webby design which is obviously meant to suggest rib vaulting. On each side of the seven-light east window are long narrow niches with stone dogs on top. Thanks to the clear glass in nearly all the windows, the church is almost as light inside as out; on a day when the sunshine is streaming in, there is no more beautiful place in all East Anglia in which to be.

## Walsoken

*48; 12½ miles SW of King's Lynn on A47*

ALL SAINTS is a church that nearly got away; Norfolk caught it only a yard or two from Cambridgeshire, illogically in a way, since Walsoken is now frankly a suburb of Wisbech. First impressions are disappointing: the Early English tower fails somehow to seduce, and the rest of the building is much spoilt by being unaccountably rendered in white. Enter quickly: things are infinitely better inside, where the huge seven-bay Norman arcade cheers you up at once. It must be of 1180 or thereabouts, just at the moment when the styles were about to change, since the chancel arch – while continuing the zigzag of the round-headed Norman ones – has a distinct point to it. It is a pity that the view through this arch ends with a rather aggressively Perpendicular east window; Perpendicular, too, come to that, are the aisle windows. None of these is bad in itself, but here they all detract from the bluff Norman masculinity of the nave. The wooden roof is supported on wall posts with carved figures against them, and there are also two enjoyable if crude sculptures of David and Solomon over the chancel and tower arches respectively. The church has some good carved bench ends, too.

## West Walton

*49; 10½ miles SW of King's Lynn off A47*

It would be worth the journey to ST MARY'S CHURCH to see the tower alone. Like that of Terrington, it stands detached and is stone-faced in ashlar; unlike its neighbour, however, it rises a more seemly distance from the church it serves and is pierced at ground level on all four sides by broad pointed arches. Effectively, this means that it supports itself on four squat legs; the impression it gives is that it has been removed from its former position atop the church and brought down to ground level for our closer inspection. This is an opportunity of which full advantage should be taken, for there are few braver examples of Early English church towers anywhere in the county. Look at those corner buttresses,

*The church of All Saints, Walsoken.*

with their gabled niches at the lowest stage, then ascending through three more stages of blind arches, receding as they go; look at the flat walls between – what there is of them, since the open arches at first-floor level and the huge two-light windows above them (with early plate tracery in the embracing arch) imbue the whole building with an unexpected lightness. Don't, however, look too hard at those pinnacles; they are later additions, out of period and, incidentally, scale.

And so to the church proper – the purest Early English church in East Anglia, and one of the first half-dozen in the whole country. The only serious flaws are the later buttresses at the west end – originally they were polygonal like those of the tower – an east window replaced in 1807 and some later, broader, windows which improve the light but sadly detract from the unity of the architecture. It seems, however, ungrateful to carp: the whole building breathes a sort of quiet nobility, which is confirmed by the sumptuousness of the detail and the brilliance of the workmanship. The circular piers of the nave arcades, for example, have been given detached Purbeck shafts and stiff-leaf capitals more reminiscent of Southwell or even Lincoln than of rural Norfolk. And Pevsner's eagle eye has noted that the clerestory windows are framed inside and out by blank arcading in such a way that on the outside there is a window to every third arch, on the inside to every second one. These latter alternate with paintings of heraldic wall hangings in *trompe-l'ocil* which are of the same date as the church itself.

## Wolterton Hall

*50; 7 miles S of Sheringham off B1354*

Sir Robert Walpole's younger brother Horatio built Wolterton Hall between 1727 and 1741. The architect was Thomas Ripley, who had been responsible for the building of Colen Campbell's Houghton for Sir Robert; and since Houghton bears the date 1727 on its windvane, it seems likely that Ripley went straight from one house to the other. The two great mansions could be said to stand in the same relationship to each other as did their owners; both are magnificent, but Wolterton one degree less so. It too is essentially Palladian, with its *piano nobile* over a rusticated basement, its pediments with elaborate coats of arms and its big Venetian window to the west; but the pediments are unsupported by columns, the scale is smaller (seven bays by three as against Houghton's nine by five) and – perhaps most important – it is built of brick which, beautiful as it is, cannot hope to match the superb Aislaby stone of Houghton. Sir Robert, in short, built himself a palace, with its classical statues on the parapets, its corner towers and cupolas; Horatio settled for a very grand country house. Almost exactly a century after it was begun, in 1828, it was made grander still, with the addition (by G.S. Repton) of a tall rusticated arcade along the south front, with a balustrade and broad open staircase at each end, together with a rather less successful east wing; but it remains, architecturally, a younger brother.

Inside, the family relationship – which on the exterior shows principally in the identical treatment of many of the window frames – is considerably more apparent. The entrance, on the north front, is nowadays from the ground floor – the original front door on the *piano nobile* survives as a porticoed french window but has lost the flight of steps which originally led up to it – from which you ascend to the Marble Hall, the first of the six sumptuous state rooms in the house. They surround a fine central stairwell rising the whole height of the building and lit through a glazed dome. It has a delicate wrought-iron balustrade in a lyre pattern, the work of a local blacksmith; but its most memorable feature is the number of windows – in the same ornate eared frames as appear on the exterior – let into these inner walls. Some of these light inner corridors; others are blank.

The first-floor state rooms are all to Ripley's designs, and while differing in size and character share the same superb quality of plasterwork, doorcases, chimneypieces and overmantels that we see at Houghton. All, alas, were badly damaged – though largely by water – in a fire which destroyed the attic floor and roof in December 1952. Virtually all the pictures, furniture and works of art were, however, saved, and the present owners have succeeded in restoring the damage so perfectly that the ordinary visitor today would never know that the disaster had occurred. Only the servants' rooms in the attics – which originally had dormer windows – were not replaced; in these servantless days there is no longer any use for them.

The beautiful grounds were laid out by Charles Bridgeman, who also worked at Houghton; the house has a splendid view south over the park to the lake.

## Worstead

*51; 3 miles SE of North Walsham off A149*

'I shall make my doublet all Worsted', wrote William Paston in the early fifteenth century, 'for the glory of Norfolk.' Not many small English villages have given their name to the language; Worstead, however, was one of the chief centres for the Flemish weavers who were encouraged by Edward III to settle in England, and it was they who, before the end of his reign, had brought such wealth and prosperity to the village as to enable it to build in 1379 one of the grandest parish churches in the county.

The date of ST MARY'S is significant, being as it were just on the cusp between the Decorated style and the Perpendicular. Thus, although the main body of the church was built in a single burst of activity, it contains elements of both. The tower, for example – a tremendous edifice well over 100 feet high – has Perpendicular-looking flushwork around the base but Decorated battlements around the top, while the bell openings have Perpendicular tracery but ball-flower ornament – a characteristic of Decorated, and early Decorated at that – around their frames. (The pinnacles of 1861, mentioned by Pevsner and described in the church guide as 'ghastly', have now been removed.) The chancel, where building would have begun, is Decorated; the aisles Perpendicular. A special word should be said about the south porch, a really magnificent piece of two storeys with a turret to the south-west and a flushwork parapet, below which the entrance is surmounted by three niches with a frieze of shields. Like all really good porches it has side windows (in this case with Decorated tracery) and a vaulted roof, its five bosses depicting the Virgin and Evangelists. The north doorway has no porch, but is otherwise very nearly as fine. In the clerestory there are two tall bays to every one in the aisles below, in fine East Anglian style.

Inside, thanks to the virtual absence of coloured glass, all is airy lightness. Tall box pews march uninterruptedly on both sides all the way up to an unusually tall and slender screen, its upper fringe of cusped ogee arches silhouetted against the tall five-light east window with its reticulated tracery. Only when one approaches it can one see the inscription bearing the date – 1512 – and the sixteen saints painted on the dado. (As well as the Apostles, they include St William of Norwich and, more surprisingly, my favourite saint, St Uncumber – otherwise known as St Wilgeforte – a Portuguese princess who, rather than marry a heathen prince, prayed for uglification and woke up the next morning with a thick black bushy beard down to her ankles.) Two parclose screens, to north and south, are of similar quality and have also kept their original coving. A fourth screen, dated 1501, closes the tower arch, behind which is a west gallery supported on arched braces. The dado, however, is painted with reproductions from – of all things – the Reynolds window in New College Chapel, Oxford. In front of it is an extremely ornate fourteenth-century font, with a still more intricately carved font cover of the tall, traceried type, very much restored. Restored too is the roof, a single hammer-beam on high wall posts.

Architecturally, it must be admitted that the inside of St Mary's does not quite live up to the promise of its exterior. Were it not for the east window and the furnishings it might even be considered a bit dull. It remains, however, an outstanding church – even for Norfolk; and, to me at least, St Uncumber makes up for a lot.

## Wymondham ⋆

*52; 9 miles SW of Norwich on A11*

Pronounced 'Windam', Wymondham is a ravishing town and would be well worth a visit even without its tremendous abbey. Lovely houses abound, medieval timber-framed like the GREEN DRAGON, Queen Anne like the VICARAGE in Vicar Street, stately Georgian in MIDDLETON STREET, TOWN GREEN and COCK STREET. No one should miss, in addition, the building which now houses the COUNTY LIBRARY but was originally a Chapel dedicated to St Thomas à Becket, founded in 1174 (only two years after his death) but rebuilt around 1400.

The ABBEY stands isolated at the edge of the town. It began as a Benedictine priory; but when William de Albini, formerly chief butler to Henry I and father of the builder of Castle Rising, founded it in 1107 he made a serious error of judgement in stipulating that part of it should serve as a parish church. This sort of partition was never a good idea. The early medieval history of Norwich Cathedral is overshadowed – or some might say enlivened – by countless squabbles between monks and townspeople; it was the same story at Wymondham. For well over 300 years the two communities were at loggerheads. Intervention by the Pope in 1249 produced a ruling that the monks should have the east end, transepts and south aisle, the people the north aisle and nave; but still the bickering went on, with the monks erecting dividing walls between the two sections, the people attacking monastery servants and on one occasion imprisoning the Prior himself. In about 1390 the monks built themselves a new, octagonal bell tower a little to the west of its predecessor – probably encroaching on parish property as they did so – which exacerbated relations still further. Inevitably, the people wished to do likewise, but were only able to start their own tower around 1448, after an uneasy peace had at last been concluded. These two towers of flint and stone, both sadly in need of parapets or pinnacles, standing at each end of the present church – the eastern, monastic area having been largely demolished at the time of the Dissolution – thus symbolise the two factions as well as giving the surviving structure the curious shape that has made it so immediately recognisable a landmark.

In view of all these tribulations, it is hardly surprising that relatively little of the original Norman work is visible on the outside of the abbey as it is today. Within, however, nave and triforium are wholly twelfth-century, though many of the piers have been shorn of their shafting and rather crudely sheathed. Only the clerestory has been changed – in 1450 or thereabouts, when a higher, Perpendicular, one was erected and crowned with the superb hammer-beam roof with angels which is one of the glories of Wymondham. At about the same time came the north aisle, which covers a greater area than the nave itself and boasts a hammer-beam roof of its own, very nearly as fine. The south aisle, by contrast, is a poor, lack-lustre thing, cobbled together in a reach-me-down sort of way a few years after the original one, being monkish, had been demolished.

Finally we come to the reredos which, unlike most reredoses, deserves a paragraph to itself. The work of Sir Ninian Comper in the 1930s, it serves the office of the great east window which the present abbey inevitably lacks, filling the east end with a blaze of gold and brilliant colour. How lucky we are that it was done when a great designer was still willing – and able – to work in the Gothic idiom. Had the work been commissioned today we should have had something aggressively modern or semi-abstract which, however splendid in itself, would have made nonsense of its surroundings. As it is, the same tradition can be seen at work throughout the building and the result is, to my eye at any rate, a triumph.

*Wymondham Abbey.*

## Short List

### Breccles (or Breckles) Hall

*53; 4½ miles E of Attleborough off B1077*

A house of beautiful Elizabethan brick, Breccles Hall contains a panelled room on the first floor with the date 1583 on the chimneypiece. It was built for the Woodhouse family and has a genuine priest's hole, Mrs Woodhouse at that time being a 'popish seducinge recusant'. Upstairs, too, there are contemporary Tudor wall paintings. The house was much altered and added to by Lutyens early in the present century, and the west (entrance) front is largely reconstructed; the south front, however, is unchanged. There is a fine contemporary entrance arch of brick, with two rings on top, like spectacles.

### Caister Castle

*54; 2 miles N of Great Yarmouth off A1064*

Built by Sir John Fastolf – Shakespeare's Falstaff – in 1432–5, Caister Castle is the earliest brick-built castle in the country. Now on the fringe of the hideous holiday sprawl of Great Yarmouth, it has lost much of its magic – though the high west tower, reflected in a singularly unappetising moat, retains a certain romantic beauty and on a clear day is well worth climbing. Otherwise simply walk clockwise as far as you can along the moat; only thus will you see the castle in even relative tranquillity.

### Elsing

*55; 4½ miles NE of East Dereham off A47*

An agreeably plain pink-washed church, ST MARY'S is all of a piece of the 1330s, very broad – it has no aisles – and of much quiet distinction. Its one flamboyance is the memorial brass to Sir Hugh Hastings, who built the church and died in 1347. In all England there is none more richly elaborate.

### Emneth

*56; 12 miles NW of Downham Market on A1122*

Nothing special from the outside, ST EDMUND'S proves to be a fine and spacious Perpendicular church with a Transitional chancel flanked by two-bay aisles. Its pride is the nave roof, where some of the splendid prone angels appear to be carrying models of the church itself. Trios of smaller angels, their wings outstretched, parade along the tie-beams, while other figures support the arched braces. The triple-lancet east window has lovely slender shafts. There is a fifteenth-century coved screen and finely carved capitals can be seen on each side of the tower arch. The monument to the younger Sir Thomas Hewer is by Nicholas Stone, 1617.

### Great Snoring

*57; 2 miles NE of Fakenham off A148*

The so-called RECTORY – it is no longer the real one – is part of the magnificent manor house built by Sir Ralph Shelton in 1525. It has polygonal corner turrets decorated with blank panels, cusped and canopied, and most remarkable terracotta decoration: an upper frieze of portrait heads in profile, left-facing men alternating with right-facing women, and odd little columns with heads on top of them. There are marvellous chimneys, too.

### Haddiscoe

*58; 4½ miles N of Beccles on A143*

The round flint tower of ST MARY'S CHURCH dates from Saxon times, although its chequered top is a fifteenth-century addition. The south porch contains a huge and most spectacular Norman doorway, above which, in low relief, is a seated bishop, hands uplifted as if in blessing. The rest of the church is early fourteenth-century.

### Heckingham

*59; 10½ miles SE of Norwich off A146*

Another charming little Norman church, ST GREGORY'S is of flint with a round tower, the nave and apse thatched. It is very similar to St Margaret's at Hales, where the north doorway was obviously carved by the same imaginative and vigorous hand as the south one here.

### Holt

*60; 9½ miles SW of Cromer on A148*

HOME PLACE is just outside the town on the Cromer road, near the Kelling Sanatorium. Pevsner says of the main, garden, front that it 'defeats description', and if he cannot describe this extraordinary edifice by E.S. Prior, who built it as a private house in 1903–5, neither can I. It is now a convalescent home and closed to the public, but amateurs of Edwardian outlandishness will find the exterior alone well worth a detour.

### Kimberley Hall

*61; 1½ miles NW of Wymondham off B1135*

Built in pale pink brick by William Talman in 1712, Kimberley Hall bears a big grey pediment with two wild men – the Kimberley crest – in the middle. It has side pavilions with quadrantal links and four corner towers added *c.*1760 by Thomas Prowse. Inside it has been much altered – the huge central staircase was inserted as recently as 1950 – but there remain two exquisite rooms, both by John Sanderson, with glorious plasterwork, and a beautiful secondary staircase in a flying spiral, with wall niches and a coffered dome above.

### Narford Hall

*62; 4½ miles NW of Swaffham off A47*

There is a splendid view of the house from the road to the south. The original part, of 1700, is of brown stone, with a pedimented centre in creamy ashlar. The Victorian additions to the right, dominated by a tall domed tower, are by William Burn. The house is said to contain a magnificent painted Hall by Pellegrini, with several fine fireplaces and much good plasterwork; but I was firmly (though politely) denied admittance.

### Necton

*63; 4 miles E of Swaffham off A47*

The CHURCH OF ALL SAINTS has been much Victorianised and would have no place here were it not for its marvellous roof – a single hammer-beam alternating with arched braces, with outsize angels along the hammer-beams in the projecting prone position, their wings outstretched. More spread-winged angels appear along the wall plate in a double row. All have a beautiful colouring, soft and muted, mostly if not entirely original. There is a fine pulpit of 1636, but not much else.

## North Runcton

*64; 3 miles SE of King's Lynn off A47*

The old ALL SAINTS' CHURCH was destroyed when the tower collapsed on it in 1701; the present building is a replacement by Henry Bell, who contributed generously towards its cost, with the addition of a chancel and south chapel in 1894. The tower has a pretty white wooden spirelet; the south front is dominated by a big arched window with pediment above. Behind this is a square nave supported on four columns, with a square vault and diagonal decorated ribs. The west gallery has gone – a pity.

## Pulham St Mary

*65; 3½ miles NW of Harleston on B1134*

ST MARY'S is a big flint church with a really sensational south porch, wildly ambitious and wholly successful. It is traditionally connected with William of Wykeham, who held the living *in absentia* from 1357 to 1361; but the porch is clearly Perpendicular and, if the story were true, would be a good half-century ahead of its time.

## Ryston Hall

*66; 1½ miles SE of Downham Market off A10*

Ryston (pronounced Riston) Hall is one of the only two surviving houses by Sir Roger Pratt, the other being Kingston Lacy, Dorset (*q.v.*). He built it for himself in 1669–72, but there is little left of his original work, the house having been radically remodelled by Soane in the 1780s. He removed the original hipped roof with dormers and made a proper first floor, arched the windows and removed the high segmental pediment which crowned Pratt's original centre. There were subsequent alterations in 1889 and again in 1913.

## Saxlingham

*67; 6 miles S of Norwich off A140*

The charming little PARSONAGE is by Sir John Soane, built while he was working on Shotesham Park close by. The big bowed centre rises half a storey higher than the rest of the house.

## Snettisham

*68; 10 miles NE of King's Lynn off A149*

ST MARY'S is a magnificent church, all Decorated, with a crossing-tower and tall spire of stone – a great rarity in Norfolk – which was in fact rebuilt in 1895. It is now sadly bereft of its chancel, but its chief glory is fortunately at the west end – a six-light window of easy, swirling tracery in which the stone seems to have forgotten its own character and liquefied. Do not, however, overlook the beautiful clerestory – two-light windows alternating with circular ones.

## Wiggenhall St Germans

*69; 4½ miles S of King's Lynn off A10*

ST GERMAN'S CHURCH is beautifully situated on the banks of the Ouse, but not otherwise very impressive from the outside, the tower (Early English, with a Perpendicular top stage) looking small and a bit silly. The inside is marred by the Victorian east window and its plain glass, but there is a nice brick and stone floor, a good Caroline pulpit (to which is attached the original hourglass with the sand still in it) and, best of all, the carved benches which rank with those of Wiggenhall St Mary.

## Wiggenhall St Mary

*70; 4½ miles SW of King's Lynn off A10*

Again, not much can be seen from the outside. ST MARY'S CHURCH has a Perpendicular tower of rubble and brick, while the rest is in stone with peeling stucco. Inside you find a grim chancel with a horrible modern window; the nave roof has timber beams and kingposts, but above that it has recently been redone on the cheap. The church seems in poor repair, less lovingly cherished than the other Wiggenhall churches. The pluses are the floor and magnificent old south door, the painted dado of the screen and the benches – surely the best in Norfolk and a real joy, early sixteenth-century with pierced backs, worth a long drive to see.

## Wiggenhall St Mary Magdalene

*71; 6 miles S of King's Lynn off A10*

Much the best of the Wiggenhall churches on the outside, ST MARY MAGDALENE is long, warm and mellow, the peeling stucco revealing rich red brick and grey stone dressings. The massive tower has a Decorated top stage, and there is a two-storey south porch with side windows. The fourteenth-century east window is a bit of a mess. The inside (ask for the enormous key at the house opposite) has nothing sensational, but the ensemble is more satisfying than either of the two churches above: a big, broad nave with a brick floor, a timber roof with angels and queenposts, carved arcade capitals, a 'weeping' chancel slanting north, and good fifteenth-century glass in the north aisle.

## Wiggenhall St Peter

*72; 5 miles S of King's Lynn*

The saddest of the Wiggenhalls, and the most evocative, ST PETER'S CHURCH is a roofless ruin on the edge of the Ouse, but with the walls still standing and a good deal of delicate Decorated and Perpendicular tracery left in the windows. Note the lovely bell opening in the tower.

## Wilby

*73; 3½ miles S of Attleborough off A11*

ALL SAINTS' CHURCH was built in the fourteenth century but gutted by fire in 1633; since its refurnishing at that time it has scarcely been touched. The box pews, three-decker pulpit halfway down the nave (the 'preaching' position), pretty west gallery and huge Royal Arms of Charles I create a marvellous rustic seventeenth-century atmosphere. On the north wall is part of a St Christopher painting which somehow survived the conflagration.

# Northamptonshire

Generally speaking, Northamptonshire is not one of those counties the very mention of which quickens the pulse. To people who do not live in it, it tends to be the sort of county through which you pass, as opposed to one to which you actually go. It has no coastline, no major city, no cathedral, no spectacular scenery. It does not even possess any readily definable character as do, for example, Suffolk, or Devon, or Shropshire. But it is not to be despised on that account. Architecturally, it is a county of endless fascination, following as it does that magical bed of oolite limestone that swoops up in a great crescent from Portland Bill in Dorset through the Cotswolds to the Cleveland Hills. This stone may vary in colour from a lovely creamy white to an iron-impregnated dark orange, but it is nearly always a stonemason's dream. Moreover, because of its seemingly endless profusion, it has always been cheap. Hence the quantity of exquisite small towns like Oundle, or villages like Aldwincle, built throughout of the same material, often quarried on the spot.

Hence, too, the splendour of the Northamptonshire churches. They are, I suppose, famous above all for their spires – though these are (with the notable exception of the loveliest of all, at King's Sutton) mostly to be found in the eastern part of the county. Spires, however, are not everything: two of the most magnificent Saxon churches in England, at Brixworth and Earl's Barton, were built centuries before such things were even invented; the former admittedly has one now, but it was added when the church below was already some 700 years old. And even in the later Middle Ages the spire was by no means *de rigueur*: you have only to think of Titchmarsh, or Lowick, or Fotheringhay.

Following its Saxon prodigies, Northamptonshire can boast two Norman churches of equal splendour, both in Northampton itself; Holy Sepulchre is one of the half-dozen surviving round churches in England, while St Peter's is opulent enough to be the cathedral the county so sadly lacks. For Early English, the palm must go to the exterior of Warmington, the interior of Aldwincle's All Saints, Polebrook, and two-naved Hannington; for Decorated, Finedon, Higham Ferrers and Kings Sutton – but let it be remembered that Northamptonshire also possesses (at Geddington and Hardingstone, now part of Northampton) two of the only three surviving Eleanor Crosses (there were originally eleven) erected in the 1290s. As for the Perpendicular, Lowick and Fotheringhay win hands down with their marvellous octagon-crowned towers – though the latter is almost as much a monument to the vandalism of the sixteenth century as it is to the virtuosity of the fifteenth.

Northamptonshire is always said to be the county of spires and squires – unkind people sometimes add 'mires' as well – and it does indeed have more than its fair share of spectacular country houses. Drayton, Easton Neston, Boughton, Althorp and Castle Ashby – all these patently belong to the first league; so, probably, would Kirby Hall and Stoke Park if they had survived. But there are countless smaller houses that also give immense pleasure – houses like Eydon or Courteenhall, Cottesbrooke or Lamport, to say nothing of those curious mystical conceits with which Sir Thomas Tresham celebrated the Trinity (at Rushton) and the Passion (at Lyveden New Bield – a romantic ruin if ever there was one). And, talking of ruins, mention must be made of the two great archways which are all that is left of Sir Christopher Hatton's great house at Holdenby, where Charles I was arrested by the Parliamentarians in 1647. Not even archways remain on the great mound that was once the site of Fotheringhay Castle, where Mary Queen of Scots was beheaded; and the county's third important historical landmark, the Civil War battlefield of Naseby, is at the time of writing threatened by a new trunk road.

## Aldwincle

*1; 2 miles N of Thrapston off A605*

Since there are two churches in the small village, one of them had to be redundant. The parishioners seem to me to have lost by the final decision, however, since although the magnificently spired ST PETER'S – where worship continues – is a fine medieval church, ALL SAINTS – where it has ceased – is a real beauty. One's attention is first claimed by the tower: no spire, but tall crooked crocketed pinnacles, battlements, a frieze of quatrefoils and gargoyles of much splendour. Below them there are two-light bell openings in pairs along each side, transomed, and with tracery below the transom as well as above it. The string-courses separating the four stages are all delightfully carved with animals and tiny monsters. The west door, too, is a magnificent piece; it has quatrefoils in the spandrel, a crocketed ogee arch with flowery finial, and rich mouldings all the way round. The south door is a good deal simpler; beyond it to the east is a Perpendicular south chapel, its exterior spoilt by a nasty pink rendering, grooved to simulate stone. Further on still, the priest's door has a most curious angular hood-mould. The Decorated east window – a pretty composition of four lights, with two quatrefoils above and a big sexfoil at the top – has been carelessly and cheaply restored, and from the outside looks a mess: a pity, since so few people see the inside any more.

On going in, the great surprise is to find the church a good deal earlier than one would have thought from the exterior. Where the external features are all fourteenth- or fifteenth-century, the nave and arcades are Early English – 1280 at the latest. The absence of furniture here is a positive advantage, enabling one to enjoy the simple perfection of a truly lovely church, fashioned in that superb creamy limestone that seems to radiate a light of its own.

John Dryden was baptised in All Saints, and born in the parsonage opposite. St Peter's, on the other hand, can claim Thomas Fuller – author of *The Worthies of England* – whose father was rector there.

*St Peter's Church, Aldwincle.*

## Althorp

*2; 6 miles NW of Northampton off A428*

To many people coming upon it for the first time, Althorp – pronounced by the *cognoscenti* 'Oltrup' – is something of a disappointment. What appears to be the whitish grey brick (in fact partly the 'mathematical tiles' so unaccountably fashionable in the last years of the eighteenth century) may well have something to do with it. The elevations too are rather dull; though the entrance front to the south-east with its double-stepped forecourt, its three-bay pedimented centre and its projecting wings is distinguished enough in its way, it seems to lack sparkle, while the two garden fronts are unrelieved in their uniformity. The garden itself is equally uninspiring. At the time of writing, astronomical sums of money have been spent on the house's interior – and, it must be admitted, to most magnificent effect. If and when any more becomes available, my advice would be to remove the present drab grey facing, revealing once again the original red-brick exterior – but I doubt whether there is very much hope.

This heavy Palladian exterior actually conceals a house very much older than one would at first suspect. The official guide-book inspires little confidence when it refers to 'the original Elizabethan house built soon after 1508'; but it was indeed in the first decade of the sixteenth century that Sir John Spencer built the first moated manor house and only some sixty years later that this was enlarged, being given a central courtyard and two projecting wings. This house has never been demolished, although there was much remodelling in the years after 1666 – the date of the grand staircase – and a good deal more around 1730 by Roger Morris. It was, however, Henry Holland who gave Althorp its present appearance – changing its colour in the process – in 1787–91, after which it has suffered no further major alterations apart from the addition of a Dining Room and a certain amount of consequential work by MacVicar Anderson in the 1870s.

Architecturally, then, the glories of Althorp are all in the interior; and of these the best come first, with the majestic Entrance Hall. Pevsner describes it as 'the noblest Georgian room in the county' – which is saying a lot when that county is Northamptonshire; but it is impossible not to agree with him. This Hall rises the full height of the house to a magnificent stucco ceiling, designed by Colen Campbell, deeply coved and coffered, decorated with paterae no two of which are the same. In the corners great plaster eagles seem about to take wing; below them there runs a beautiful frieze featuring the goddess Diana with a retinue of *putti*. Opposite the entrance door is another of great magnificence, flanked with Corinthian columns and with a tall broken pediment, while the walls are hung with huge canvases by John Wootton of horses, hounds and hunting.

The next glory – not as immediately appealing, perhaps, but even more interesting from the architectural point of view – is the great staircase beyond the Entrance Hall, which occupies what was originally the open courtyard of the house. It is of oak, and it rises in a single long straight flight – broken only by a short landing – to the end wall, where it branches briefly to meet the two broad galleries which run the length of the sides. It is, I think, more impressive than beautiful; but that is not the point. What makes this staircase unique is the fact that it dates from the 1660s, a time when staircases were still being built around narrow wells and conceived very much as vertical features. Outside Althorp, no staircase as monumental as this was to appear in England for another half-century. Unfortunately the surroundings here do it less than justice, the general character of the Saloon being uncompromisingly Victorian, the work of MacVicar Anderson. In Holland's time the staircase was painted white; would that it could be so again.

The other state rooms of the house are immensely grand and magnificently decorated after recent refurbishment; the visitor should however be warned that unless he goes on 'Connoisseurs' Days' (Wednesdays, at the time of writing) he will not be allowed into any of them; the best he can hope for is to peer over a sort of fence across an open doorway – not much use at the best of times, and still less so when the rooms are interconnecting and have no direct access to an outside corridor. Nor will he be able to see any but a few (and by no means the best) of the pictures for which Althorp is famous, or the furniture. The most interesting rooms are perhaps the Picture Gallery – the old Long Gallery of Elizabethan times – and the magnificent Library with its two screens of Ionic columns and Adamesque ceiling, once the home of the famous Spencer collection which now forms the John Rylands Library of Manchester University.

Finally, the stables, built by Roger Morris in 1733. According once again to Pevsner, 'it might well be argued that [they] are the finest piece of architecture at Althorp'. If we are talking about exteriors, he is surely right. It was Horace Walpole who first pointed out their similarity to Inigo Jones's St Paul's, Covent Garden, which was obviously their inspiration; from Jones, too (this time at Wilton), come the four corner towers. The Tuscan colonnade is, as it were, continued inside, where the columns are used to support most elegant vaults. How fortunate, too, that these stables were spared the mathematical tiles; Northamptonshire ironstone looks far better.

## Apethorpe

*3; 6 miles N of Oundle off A43*

A ravishingly pretty village of stone cottages, thatched or roofed with lichened Collyweston tiles, grouped around a spacious green, Apethorpe possesses a lovely church and a huge rambling house of medieval origin which somehow looks more like an Oxford or Cambridge college than anything else. Apart from a few beams dated 1354, the oldest part of APETHORPE HALL goes back to Sir Guy Wolston, who owned it at the end of the fifteenth century. In 1550 it passed to Sir Walter Mildmay, Chancellor of the Exchequer and founder of Emmanuel College, Cambridge, and in 1617 to Sir Francis Fane, later 1st Earl of Westmorland. It was above all these three owners who gave the historic house its present external appearance, though there is some mid-eighteenth-century remodelling and some substantial additions made by the Brassey family shortly before the First World War. Subsequently Apethorpe became a Roman Catholic institution and an approved school. When I saw it in July 1983 it was empty, and being prepared as a film location; the ultimate intention, I was told, was to transform it into a sort of cramming establishment in which Middle Eastern students would be prepared for American universities.

As a result of these recent tribulations, there is relatively little of the interior to make a complete tour of the house worth while. Sir Guy Wolston's Great Hall survives with part of its timber roof intact and a seventeenth-century minstrels' gallery, but the nasty modern panelling robs it of any atmosphere it might have had. It occupies the northern part of the east range of the principal court – of which, indeed, the whole north-east corner as far as the gateway and stair turret adjoining is of *c.*1500. (Notice the door leading into what was originally the screens passage.) By far the most interesting survivals are to be found within the south range. This was classicised in 1740–50 and given a three-bay Doric centre with pediment; it conceals, however, up a prettily stuccoed Georgian staircase at the western end, a suite of four magnificent Jacobean rooms. Three of them have deep coved ceilings, exuberantly stuccoed in early seventeenth-century style, and all have glorious chimneypieces – mostly contemporary, but one dated 1562. Jacobean too is the Long Gallery, which occupies most of the east range. Here the chimneypiece includes a standing figure of King David with harp, almost life-size, with two allegorical figures reclining on the sides of an open pediment, the head of Goliath above one of them, the fateful slingshot above the other. Between these two ranges – that is, in the south-east corner – rises a fine carved Jacobean staircase, moved to its present position in 1922.

As far as the exterior is concerned, the two principal façades are those facing to the north and the east. The north side is immensely long – about 240 feet from end to end – covering as it does two adjoining courtyards. (The western court is all of the sixteenth century, apart from an eighteenth-century Orangery on the south side, but is of no great architectural interest.) It contains what was the main gateway, with a four-centred arch and a three-

*Aynhoe Park, Aynho.*

light window above it, dating from the Wolston period; but this has all become somewhat confused by the addition, first of a classico-Jacobean front of 1653 and then, to the left, of a plain Georgian Library of 1750 or so. Beyond this to the west are the seventeenth-century kitchens (three tall windows) and then the offices.

The best front of all is that to the east. Pevsner describes it as 'the most stately and coherent Jacobean piece in the county' – and so it is, if we exclude the Jonesian front of Castle Ashby. It has nine bays and two storeys, but with three big shaped gables above and two smaller semi-circular ones between them. There is a projecting Tuscan porch, to each side of which, in Sir Francis Fane's day, ran an open arcaded loggia. This has now been closed in to make a ground-floor gallery, in the centre of which stands King James I in stone, receiving visitors somewhat threateningly as they arrive.

ST LEONARD'S, nearby, is a beautiful old stone church with a modest tower, mostly of the fifteenth century but with its all-important Jacobean south chapel of 1621. You approach it through rather forbidding lines of gravestones, rearranged regimentally. The interior is wonderfully unspoilt, with the original timber roof still over the chancel (and the nave too, although this is mostly plaster), the wall posts resting on fine carved corbels. There are traces of a big Doom painting above the chancel arch, but no screen – only a single shallow step marking the division. South of the chancel is the Mildmay Chapel – and a tomb to take your breath away. Sir Anthony Mildmay, son of Sir Walter, lies with his wife beneath a huge circular canopy surmounted by a lantern, from which hang bunched-back curtains flanked by nearly life-size figures of the virtues. In the east window behind is some fascinating glass of the same date as the Chapel itself: Adam and Eve, the Crucifixion, the Resurrection and the Last Judgement – English work, but in the Flemish style.

## Aynho

*4; 6 miles SE of Banbury on A41*

AYNHOE PARK (with an e) stands in the middle of Aynho village (without one) – a delightful and beautifully kept little community with more than its fair share of fifteenth-century cottages and an agreeable habit of growing apricot trees against the house walls, as it has done ever since feudal days when rent to the lord of the manor was paid in apricots. The great courtyard opens straight off the main street, with fine pedimented buildings on three sides, and gives an initial appearance of remarkable architectural unity. This, however, almost immediately proves deceptive. The house occupied by Richard Cartwright, who purchased the property and moved there in 1616, began life as a typical E-shaped Jacobean manor house, but was badly damaged in the Civil War and later underwent three major rebuildings over about a century and a half before assuming its present form.

The three architects responsible for these rebuildings were Edward Marshall, master mason to the King from 1660 to 1673, Thomas Archer (unproved, but beyond all reasonable doubt) and Sir John Soane. Marshall's task was to make the house habitable again for Richard's son John Cartwright, bringing it up-to-date at the same time. This he did by filling in the spaces between the bars of the E, leaving the Jacobean wings much as they were but giving the central part five bays with a grand façade rather in the Jonesian manner. Quite a bit of his work is still visible on the south front, where – apart from the entrance door and the windows, now sashed instead of mullioned and transomed – the two lower floors are essentially as Marshall left them. All this happened in the 1660s; within less than half a century, however, the workmen were back in force, this time under the direction of Archer. He it was who added the second floor and big pediment to Marshall's south front, continued the columnar frame of the central window to ground-floor level and refaced the three-bay Jacobean wings, adding a further single-storey, seven-bay wing to each side. Turning his attention to the north, he made this the principal entrance front, which he further ennobled with detached pavilions for stables and offices, projecting at right-angles to form the present open court. These appear cool and restrained enough at first glance; but look at the central arches, with those extraordinary mouldings and concave entablatures: no one but Archer could have been responsible for them.

By this time Aynhoe was a very considerable house; but in 1800 William Ralph Cartwright felt the need of further additions and called in Soane. His are the upper storeys to Archer's wings and, on the north side, the two short links joining Archer's pavilions to the main block, which he crowned with its central pediment. Apart from the pediment, these innovations were not, it must be admitted, altogether successful. Soane's style was too individual to blend easily with the work of others, and one cannot help feeling that the outside of the house, both to south and to north, looked better before he got his hands on it. Whether this is also true of the inside is, I think, more arguable. For one thing, very little of Archer's work is left; principally the screen of coupled Doric columns in the Entrance Hall and the exceedingly pretty staircase behind it. (One has only to compare this with Soane's White Staircase on the other side to see just how far English architecture had progressed between 1700 and 1800.) Nearly all the rest is Soane's, and quite unmistakably so. Look, for example, at his Drawing Room with its shallow apses at each end, its even shallower wall arch over the fireplace, and the barely perceptible vaulting; or his Library with its interplay of arches and – a lovely Gothick touch – the minute fans that make up the cornice.

Aynhoe is full of little details like these, which make it a particularly rewarding house to visit. Now the property of the Mutual Housing Association, it is beautifully maintained and open to the public on certain days in summer. To the south is a spacious park, landscaped by Capability Brown.

## Boughton*

*5; 3 miles NE of Kettering off A43*

The story of Boughton as we know it today begins in 1528, when Sir Edward Montagu, Lord Chief Justice to Henry VIII, bought the estate – at that time monastic – from the Abbey of St Edmundsbury. It then consisted of a Hall range with two wings projecting to the south, on to which he built, in somewhat higgledy-piggledy fashion around a system of courtyards, a small and relatively modest manor house. Subsequent generations added a little here and there; but the house in its present form is above all due to his great-great-grandson Ralph, who was created 1st Duke of Montagu in 1705 by Queen Anne. Already in the late 1680s he had begun work on the house, giving it a new show front to the north together with new halls and state rooms and, a little way away to the east, a magnificent block of stables.

Earlier in his career, the Duke had twice served as Ambassador in Paris, where he had acquired a deep love of French architecture; and the north front of Boughton is French through and through. The mansard roof, the applied pilasters above the horizontally rusticated ground floor, and indeed the whole spirit of the building unmistakably indicate a French architect. But who was he? Pierre Pouget, or Puget, who is said to have rebuilt Montagu House in London in 1686? Or Daniel Marot, whom we know to have been working at about this time at Hampton Court and Kensington Palace? Whoever he was, it is tempting to identify him with the similarly

*Boughton.*

unknown architect of Petworth, the only other building of the date in England with an equally Gallic flavour.

This north front, which comprises a nine-bay centre of one and a half storeys over a ground-floor loggia with wings, three bays by four, projecting from each side, conceals the earlier front immediately behind it; the latter, however, continues cheerfully eastward – first for seven bays, and then for another eleven – after the Duke's façade stops: a mid-seventeenth-century composition with hipped roof, dormers and cross windows, as quintessentially English as the other is French. Beyond, in the north-east corner, we come to the stables – French again, with a broad central archway, tunnel-vaulted within and pedimented above, rising two full storeys to a low, four-sided dome.

The main entrance into the house from the centre of the loggia leads – through a door very slightly out of alignment – into the Great Hall. This is a survivor from monastic times and was the focus of Sir Edward's manor house; it suffered, however, a metamorphosis at the hands of Duke Ralph, who concealed the great medieval timber roof with a barrel-vaulted ceiling painted by the French artist whose work is so much a feature of Boughton, Louis Chéron. High on the west wall within the curve of the vault, the ducal arms look magnificently down on the room below, the coronet with its strawberry leaves picked out in gold; Montagu had waited a long time for his dukedom and was clearly determined to make the most of it. And to justify it, too: in the adjoining Little Hall, which also rises through two storeys to a Chéron ceiling, he installed a tremendous stone chimneypiece in which a vast genealogical tree traces his descent from William the Conqueror.

Immediately to the north of the Little Hall is the superb stone staircase which leads up to the Great Apartment. This Staircase Hall is Chéron's masterpiece – a *trompe-l'oeil* triumph in which, above painted rustication echoing that of the north front, he has created a splendid composition of pilasters framing huge reliefs of soldiers and captives, with busts over the doors and a full-length statue in a niche, all picked out with gold paint as if made of gilded bronze. The whole thing is crowned by another of his painted ceilings. After such magnificence, the Great Apartment might easily disappoint; in fact it does no such thing. This series of five rooms, all with Chéron ceilings and floors in *parquet de Versailles* – its first appearance in England – with their pictures, tapestries and superb furniture, constitutes one of the most staggering examples of Queen Anne decoration anywhere in England. Walking through these rooms, one cannot but regret that the similar set intended for the corresponding north-west wing was never completed; though it is a memorable, if faintly eerie, experience to walk through the empty shell of this wing, lying as it does virtually untouched since the work on it stopped with the Duke's death in 1709.

One more of his creations should be mentioned: the so-called Egyptian Hall, which lies immediately east of the Great Hall and which he used as his dining room. (Chéron's *Triumph of Bacchus* on the ceiling above is thus not inappropriate.) We can then pass to the rooms surrounding the southern end of the pretty grassed-in courtyard known – from the monastic fish tanks that it once contained – as Fish Court. Here, immediately, the atmosphere changes; the spirit of Baroque splendour and parade disappears, and we find ourselves instead in the relative informality of a lovely old English manor house. Beyond the Egyptian Hall is the Audit Room Gallery, formed in the 1740s out of a narrow passage and the old Steward's Hall. It now contains one of the three remaining chimneypieces dating from the time of Sir Edward Montagu – though clearly not in its original position. Opposite across the court are the principal living rooms – the Drawing Room (whose sixteenth-century chimneypiece was brought to the house early in the present century) with the barrel-vaulted Library above it, the Morning Room with its pre-Civil War tapestries of playing boys, the Rainbow Room and pretty panelled Boudoir. In the south-east corner of Fish Court, an enchanting Chinese Staircase of *c.*1740 leads up to various bedrooms.

And all this is only a beginning. With its labyrinthine plan, its seven courtyards and its countless hidden rooms and unsuspected galleries, Boughton is – like Knole – a world of its own in which there is always some forgotten corner to be explored. It is not only a beautiful house; it is also, for me, a magical one.

## Brixworth*

*6; 9 miles N of Northampton on A508*

Here, astonishingly, in a small Northamptonshire village, stands a building which has been described (by Sir Arthur Clapham) as 'perhaps the most imposing architectural memorial of the seventh century surviving north of the Alps'. ALL SAINTS' CHURCH is generally thought to date from about 675, and though it suffered minor alterations in the later Saxon period there is little apart from the Norman south door, the thirteenth-century Lady Chapel, the fourteenth-century top stage of tower and spire, and the chancel – rebuilt in the nineteenth century according to the ancient plan – that postdates the Conquest. Originally it was a monastery, and considerably larger. The nave, for example, had broad aisles to north and south, which were later subdivided into separate chambers or chapels called *porticus*; but these, probably in the tenth or eleventh century, were for some reason demolished; the arcades were filled in and given round-arched windows, and thus became the outer walls that we see today.

Seen as a whole, the building has an austere and massive dignity about it; there is none of that rather endearing naïvety that characterises the tower at Earl's Barton. When you look at it more closely, one of the first things you notice is the number of Roman tiles embedded in the masonry, particularly in the tower, the semi-circular stair turret and the arches, where their placing, if not quite higgledy-piggledy, is certainly a good deal less regular than one might expect. We know that there was a fairly important Roman settlement nearby – a VILLA was discovered in 1966, and has recently been excavated, only half a mile away to the north – and these tiles were doubtless picked up from

*All Saints' Church, Brixworth.*

some ruined building and re-used. There are more to be seen inside; indeed, for all the untidiness of their arrangement they constitute one of the principal decorative features of the church. But what really strikes one about the interior of Brixworth is the combination of grandeur and simplicity. The grandeur comes above all from the height, emphasised by the tall clerestory windows – part of the original fabric – which are set above the spandrels of the arches rather than above the arches themselves, so as to create a zigzag rhythm of openings along the walls. There is scarcely a break between nave and presbytery – a triple-arched screen, probably not unlike the one high up in the west wall, existed till about 1300, when it was replaced by the present soaring single arch – but the chancel, apsed, elevated higher than usual, and approached only through a relatively narrow opening, has an air of mystery and remoteness about it that cannot fail to impress. It also possesses another great rarity, not immediately apparent: a sunken outer ambulatory, or ring crypt, formerly barrel-vaulted. Such things belong far more to the ninth- and tenth-century churches of France and Germany than to England, and even in continental Europe there is none so early as Brixworth's. (The outside string-course of Roman tiles strongly suggests that it was part of the original design and not an afterthought.)

The church has been beautifully, lovingly and, by all appearances, expensively maintained and restored, and quite right too. Is there any other building in the country which has been uninterruptedly used for Christian worship for thirteen centuries?

## Canons Ashby

*NT; 7; 13 miles SW of Northampton on B4525*

The name derives from the priory of Augustinian canons, part of whose great CHURCH OF ST MARY still survives. Alas, it suffered cruelly after the Reformation; all that now remains is the two westernmost bays of the nave and the north aisle and the broad north-west tower. The main west door with its magnificently shafted portal and the line of blank richly moulded arcading with trefoil heads in the arches demonstrate beyond a shadow of doubt that this was a most prosperous foundation in the mid-thirteenth century, and it seems to have been still flourishing when the tower was raised 100 years later. Later still – it must have been quite shortly before the blow fell – the huge five-light Perpendicular window was knocked into the west wall above the entrance; the south and east windows are obviously post-Reformation, dating from the time when the old priory had become a simple parish church. The building has undergone major restoration by the National Trust, who acquired it, together with the rest of the Canons Ashby estate, in 1981, and have now opened it to the public. The furnishings include the funeral achievements of Sir Robert Dryden, who died in 1708, among them a banner, a crested helm, pennants, tabards, a sword, a shield, gauntlets and spurs. The medieval tradition died hard.

Similar and yet more far-reaching restoration work has been carried out on the house itself, which stands 100 yards or so along the road. It was built in around 1550 by one John Dryden, an ancestor of the poet, and remained in the Dryden family until it passed to the Trust. There can be no house in the county so romantic, or so astonishingly untouched. The last major alterations were completed in 1710; since then, two and a half centuries have passed it by. You enter it from the east, by what is known as the Pebble Court – although the original entrance, as we shall see, was from the west – and there before you is the central Hall range of John Dryden's H-shaped house, its two wings ending with the left-hand side of the tower to the south and the big buttress to the kitchen wall immediately opposite it to the north. (The eastward extensions to these two wings were added by John's son, Sir Erasmus, some forty years later.) It is built principally of the local brown ironstone, supplemented with brick and, on the tower, with stucco. The Hall windows with their original leaded panes are mullioned with high transoms, and there are small attic windows similarly unchanged, squeezed in between the string-course and the tiled roof; the machine-made blue tiles of the 1920s have been replaced by beautiful hand-made red ones, which will soon acquire the moss and lichen that add so much to the charm of the court. It will then look precisely the same as in the photograph taken in the 1860s which I have before me now – and indeed as it did 150 years before that.

The Hall, approached up a broad flight of stone steps which leads into the screens passage, is quite modest in size. Sadly, it has lost its original timber roof – Sir Erasmus gave it a flat ceiling in 1590 – and its present appearance is more that of 1710, when Edward Dryden filled it with arms and armour and heraldic cartouches in what he imagined to be the style of a medieval hall. By then it had long since ceased to serve as the family dining room; before the end of the sixteenth century the Drydens were almost certainly eating in what is now known as the Winter Parlour, an enchanting little room behind the kitchen in which, under many later layers of paint and varnish, the original painted decoration of the 1590s has recently been discovered on the panelling. These delightfully naïve arabesques, coats of arms and even masonic symbols have now been meticulously restored, and the Winter Parlour has a strong claim to be the prettiest room in the house.

By 1710, however, it too seems to have outlived its purpose; for at this point Edward Dryden provided himself with a new Dining Room, larger and considerably more imposing, with oak panelling, giant Corinthian pilasters at one end and a grandiloquent doorcase with a broken pediment at the other. Soon afterwards he started on a new family 'Withdrawing Room', the decoration of which he seems to have entrusted to his cousin, Mrs Elizabeth Creed. Mrs Creed is known for the two painted monuments to her brother, The Rev. Theophilus Pickering, and Mr and Mrs John Dryden, parents of the poet (her cousin) in St Mary's, Titchmarsh (*q.v.*); here at Canons Ashby she used much the same technique. There are curious cut-out pilasters and a *trompe-l'oeil* frieze, all painted with much *brio* and a quite startling use of colour. The last of the principal rooms on the ground floor is the Book Room, added by Sir Erasmus in his eastward extension of the south wing in 1590 and still preserving the original chimneypiece and panelling. In the overmantel are the remains of contemporary plasterwork; the later armorial panels which until recently concealed them have been put on hinges so that both can be seen.

A splendid oak staircase of the 1630s leads up to the first floor, and to the Great Chamber. The Winter Parlour may, as I have suggested, be the prettiest room at Canons Ashby; but the Great Chamber is unquestionably the most spectacular. The magnificent chimneypiece and overmantel are of the time of Sir Erasmus; but what makes the room so absolutely unforgettable is the immense domed plaster ceiling which was added by his son, Sir John, during the first years of Charles I. The scheme is one of strapwork panels with swirling designs of thistles and pomegranates, and heads of what appear to be exotic Indian princesses. Above the chimneypiece is an immense coat of arms, and from the centre descends an outsize pendant with four curving caryatids.

Beyond the Great Chamber is the Spenser Room, named after the poet – a first cousin of Sir Erasmus by marriage – who was a regular visitor to the house. As none of the early inventories calls the room by this name, it was long thought to be an invention of Sir Henry Dryden, a Victorian antiquary; recently, however, restoration work has revealed quite well-preserved mural paintings in *grisaille* behind the panelling, depicting scenes of medieval chivalry very much in the style of *The Faerie Queene*. The room has a curious ceiling of *papier mâché*, with profile heads of the Four Seasons.

Go down the staircase again, and out through the door at its foot into the garden, also now restored to its former splendour. The south front of the house is not, it must be admitted, an aesthetic treat. It is basically the creation of Edward Dryden in Queen Anne's day – the windows are all sashed and there is a fine Baroque doorcase. The problem for Edward was the tower, which rises asymmetrically and in a most un-eighteenth-century way, and is of rendered brick, whereas the rest is of ironstone. Though the new rendering is more sympathetic in colour than its predecessor, the south front will, I fear, always have more character than beauty. The west front – formerly the Green Court, since it was the original entrance to the house and was turfed over in the 1840s – is a good deal more satisfactory; and of more interest, too, since while maintaining an overall unity of appearance it clearly shows the three principal building periods of the house. Just to the left of the big central doorcase is John Dryden's original door to his screens passage; similarly of the 1550s are the flat-arch mullion windows in the first floor and gable of the south wing. The straight-headed ones to the north and in the centre, however, must date from Sir Erasmus's day, or possibly from his son Sir John's. Finally the central door and the ground-floor sashed windows, together with the roof-top cupola, are the obvious legacy of Edward, with whom the building history of Canons Ashby comes to an end.

Now that the National Trust has opened the house, gardens and church to the public, go as soon as you can. Such immaculate survivals are rare indeed.

## Castle Ashby*

*8; 6 miles E of Northampton off A428*

There has been a castle here since a few years after the Norman Conquest, when King William gave the manor to his niece Judith; but the old building gradually fell into ruin and by the middle of the sixteenth century there was scarcely one stone left on another. The present house was built by Henry, 1st Lord Compton, almost certainly on the same site. He began it in 1574, and it must have been complete before Queen Elizabeth's death in 1603 as she is known to have stayed here. In essence, it is a fairly traditional Elizabethan courtyard house, with three long ranges to north, east and west – the north, central, range containing the Hall, the two side ranges having high polygonal stair turrets towards the ends of their inner fronts.

The south side of the courtyard was originally open. Then, in the 1630s, it was closed by a low, two-storeyed front; and if anyone is looking for a really impressive example of the revolution that occurred in English architecture in the first thirty years of the seventeenth century, it is to Castle Ashby that he should come. Is this new, classical front the work of Inigo Jones? Colen Campbell's *Vitruvius Britannicus* of 1725 attributes it to him, and Pevsner is inclined to agree; but most other modern experts are doubtful. It is in any case a most elegant composition, articulated by rusticated Tuscan columns and pilasters on the ground floor and unfluted Ionic ones above, with a three-bay pedimented centre

*Castle Ashby.*

enclosing a big Venetian window. (This last was a considerable innovation: the first Venetian window in England was introduced by Jones into the Queen's Chapel in 1623.) Above is a balustrade with lettering – a fashion which we occasionally see in Elizabethan and Jacobean buildings (Hardwick, Felbrigg, Temple Newsam, and of course the sixteenth-century part of Castle Ashby itself) but which looks oddly old-fashioned in a classical context. To the outside it reads 'DOMINUS CUSTODIAT INTROITUM TUUM', on the inside . . . 'EXITUM TUUM'.

The three Elizabethan ranges carry similar inscriptions from Psalm 127 ('Except the Lord build the house . . .'). All three were at first recessed on their outward faces, but the recesses have all been filled in. On the east side – the original show front, and the only one to be ashlared – this took the form of an open loggia between the Chapel on the south (another Venetian window, but dating this time from the 1670s) and the huge polygonal bows marking the Elizabethan Great Chamber on the north. Its five bays, each surmounted by a pair of windows, were filled in *c.*1670. On the north side there is another Great Chamber bow, echoed at the far end by another, added for reasons of symmetry in *c.*1720. The west side is of no particular interest, and is further marred by a huge and hideous water tower built in 1865 by Sir Matthew Digby Wyatt, who should have known better.

Inside, nothing of the old Elizabethan fabric remains except the undercroft of the Hall and Great Chamber. Of these two, once the principal rooms of the house, the Hall was completely Victorianised in 1884, when it acquired its present furnishings of pseudo-Jacobean panelling and galleries and its organ. The only genuine antique is the chimneypiece of 1599, which came from the old Compton house in Canonbury. The Great Chamber has been more fortunate. Now known as the King William Room (William of Orange insisted on dining here, instead of in the Hall, when he visited Castle Ashby in 1695), it has retained its superb plaster ceiling of 1625–30, deeply coved, with allegorical figures in cartouches, strapwork, etc. It also has some fine wood panelling of King William's day. There is another tremendous chimneypiece from Canonbury dated 1601, and a set of charming needlework panels depicting English country life, worked in the later eighteenth century by two maiden sisters, Lady Penelope and Lady Margaret Compton.

Of all the Comptons of Castle Ashby, the one who left the deepest personal imprint on the house seems to have been the 3rd Earl of Northampton, who died in 1681. He was responsible for the suite of three fine Drawing Rooms along the east front – where the loggia had been before – and for the great East Staircase behind them with its carved wood panels reminiscent of those at Ham or Sudbury. His too are the sumptuous state rooms above, panelled and tapestried, the epitome of all that late seventeenth-century opulence should be.

There is comparatively little eighteenth-century work in the house, and mercifully little of the nineteenth century either until about 1880 when – apart from the work on the Hall – there was a major remodelling of the Chapel and the Long Gallery. The architect chosen was Sir Thomas Jackson, remembered principally nowadays for his endlessly inventive work at Oxford. His work on the Chapel seems rather cautious for him: leaving (naturally) the 1630 ceiling untouched, he covered the lower walls with good safe panelling and left it at that. The Gallery, however, he transformed into a delightful classical composition of white and gold, with screens of fluted Corinthian columns at intervals. Occupying as it does the first floor of the Jonesian south range, it has windows on both sides – as cheerful a Long Gallery as I know anywhere.

The garden terraces to the east and north, with yet more biblical inscriptions in their balustrades, are the work of Sir Matthew Digby Wyatt in 1868; but they form only a small part of the magnificent Italian gardens on these two sides, which also include Wyatt's Orangery, beyond the church to the south-east. The park itself, need one add, is by Capability Brown, and includes a temple, a dairy and a remarkably pretty bridge.

The CHURCH OF ST MARY MAGDALENE also forms an integral part of the whole ensemble. It has a highly ornate Norman north door, reset and fairly heavily restored, and a Decorated north aisle; but it suffered severely in 1870 from the attentions of G. E. Street, and apart from a few Compton family tombs of fairly mediocre quality has little to detain us.

## Cottesbrooke Hall*

*9; 9 miles NW of Northampton off A50*

There will be argument till the end of time as to whether or not Cottesbrooke Hall was Jane Austen's inspiration for Mansfield Park; but there can be no two opinions about its beauty. Work began on it in 1702, the year Queen Anne came to the throne, and continued until 1713, the year before she died; there is no documentary evidence about the architect, but we can ascribe it pretty confidently to Francis Smith of Warwick. Like so much of his work, it is of rich red brick with dressings of pale grey limestone – though close inspection reveals that both the main house and the pavilions on either side rest on basements of the orangey brown ironstone that is something of a *spécialité de la région* – with giant Corinthian pilasters rising the full height of the building (here two storeys only) to a crowning balustrade. These pilasters divide the seven-bay elevation in the rhythm 2–3–2, and the centre is further emphasised by the central doorways – which are, incidentally, meticulously aligned with the spire of Brixworth church some 3–4 miles away. That on the garden front (the original entrance) has an ornate scrolly open pediment supported on Corinthian columns; that on the present entrance front is a good deal simpler. The change of orientation was entrusted in the 1770s to Robert Mitchell (the architect of Moor Place, Much Hadham, *q.v.*) who redecorated the present Entrance Hall and the Drawing Room and Dining Room to either side of it, giving the two latter rooms deep bows at the ends. Seen from the outside, they do not detract from the beauty of the house – though Mitchell found it necessary to double the angle pilasters on the garden front. They have pretty stone panels with swags round the top.

Also on the garden front are two pavilions, linked to the main house by blank quadrant walls. They have only one main storey, but are raised on high basements and have an attic floor marked by dormers in the hipped roofs.

So much for the outside. The interior is, if anything, better still. Perhaps the most spectacular feature is the Staircase Hall, its walls and ceiling covered with a glorious profusion of Rococo decoration in what appears to be stucco but proves on examination to be *papier mâché*. True plasterwork appears in several of the other rooms, one of which has retained its original panelling while another has the Elizabethan oak panelling from Pytchley Hall, demolished in the 1820s. One of the side pavilions contains a ballroom in what was formerly a kitchen. It was designed by Gerald Wellesley, later 7th Duke of Wellington.

At the bottom of the drive is ALL SAINTS' CHURCH, built in about 1300 and very much all of a piece. Inside there is a wonderfully tall tower arch rising to within an inch or two of the nave roof, which is a very shallow barrel vault. The magnificent three-decker pulpit to the side of the nave ('preaching position') has a big hexagonal tester. Opposite it in the south transept – the north one has gone – is the Langham family pew, with fireplace. A flight of wooden stairs with turned balusters leads us up to the tomb of Sir John and Lady Langham; he died in 1671. Opposite, in the east wall, lies the effigy of John Rede, who died in 1604, with his ten children kneeling in a doleful crocodile below.

## Courteenhall*

*10; $4\frac{1}{2}$ miles S of Northampton off A508*

Here is a treasure indeed: an exquisite late eighteenth-century smallish country house, by an almost unknown young architect, lived in by the same family and scarcely altered since the day it was built. Samuel Saxon was a pupil of Chambers who, when he was commissioned in 1791 by Sir William Wake, was thirty-four years old with as yet no major building to his name. (He is only known to have built two others, the Northampton General Infirmary and the sadly demolished Buckminster Park in Leicestershire, before his early death.) What he produced at Courteenhall, on a site chosen by Humphry Repton who was simultaneously laying out the park, was a restrained neo-classical house with three fronts; that on the entrance side somewhat austere with its Tuscan-columned doorway, but the garden front lighter and more relaxed, with a beautifully proportioned three-bay pediment and the columns a gentler and more delicate Ionic. Inside, all is coolness and serenity. The style is classical throughout; both the Entrance Hall and the Dining Room have screens of columns, Doric and Corinthian respectively (Courteenhall is a splendid place for studying the orders), and there is a ravishing apsed Library with curved mahogany doors and columns with palm-frond capitals, as if deliberately to dispel any suggestion of pomposity elsewhere. But in fact no such suggestion is made; the scale is small enough to ensure that the atmosphere remains undemandingly domestic. The staircase, lit by an oval and domed skylight, has its original wall decoration of simulated marble, as good as any I know.

Courteenhall is occasionally open to the public but, as always, please check the opening arrangements in advance. Once there, don't leave without looking at the stables. Built around 1750, and thus some forty years older than the house, they are conceived on the grand Palladian scale and make a fascinating contrast with the house. There is also, in the grounds, the SCHOOL HOUSE of about 1680, containing its original furnishings; and the village CHURCH OF ST PETER AND ST PAUL has some memorable tombs.

*Deene Park.*

## Crick

*11; 14 miles NW of Northampton off A428*

This very fine Decorated church, ST MARGARET'S, has a three-stage tower of local pink stone, with bell openings on the second stage, decorated with Y-tracery and cusps. There are some superb Decorated windows, one or two of them renewed in the aisles, and two immense ones in the chancel bays. (The south aisle is leaning rather precariously outwards.) The rest of the church is a rich warm gold Northamptonshire stone, but the redone windows are in the local pink, not the happiest of contrasts. Inside, the original stone floor remains, though the church as a whole is very much restored. The beautiful broad pointed arcades have finely carved capitals over the piers, which are circular to the south and octagonal to the north. A simple timber roof is supported by tie-beams on wall posts, which in turn rest on carved stone corbels (when I was there some workmen seemed to be painting these – surely a great mistake). In the chancel excellent stone carving can be seen on the stops on each side of the ogival frames to the big north and south windows, which have lovely Decorated tracery. Even better, where the tracery is concerned, is the east window – five lights – but it is ruined by unusually nasty glass. The north door of the chancel has an ogival head, with leaf decoration up the side rather like St Mark's in Venice, and two very good heads on the stops; the same design is found on the piscina and sedilia.

## Deene Park

*12; 4 miles NE of Corby off A43*

When Sir Robert Brudenell bought Deene Park in 1514, his family had already been living in Northamptonshire for 250 years; Mr Edmund Brudenell, who now lives there, is his direct descendant, twelve generations later. The medieval house in which Sir Robert settled was centred on the present courtyard whose east side, with its big canted bay window, marks the site of the original two-storey Great Hall. (Traces of this can still be seen in what is now the Billiard Room.) But in 1571 his grandson, Sir Edmund, decided that something grander was required and began work on the present Hall along the south range of the courtyard, marked by a nobly Italianate porch in what would then have been the very latest style. It is a splendid room, with a fine contemporary fireplace and magnificent panelling at the eastern end; but its greatest glory is the hammer-beam roof, which has curved wind-braces swirling backwards and forwards along the rafters.

There is plenty of other Elizabethan, Jacobean and later seventeenth-century work around this courtyard, which remained the nucleus of the house till about 1800; but only the extraordinary centrepiece of the east front is of note – a two-storeyed bay window of eight transomed lights on each storey, and topped by a shaped gable of vaguely Dutch design. Since the whole thing now forms one enormous chimneybreast – that of the old Hall – all the lights are blind; they are framed by alternately fat and thin attached columns (the latter rising rather alarmingly out of nothing in particular), the Ionic capitals of which, instead of supporting the frieze, form an integral part of it. The whole thing is of about 1570 – clumsy, primitive and a bit dotty, such spurious grandeur being anyway set at naught by the fact that the top of the gable does not even reach as high as the roof line where the neighbouring gables begin, and is also dwarfed by the big chimneystack above it.

The rest of the architectural history of Deene takes the form of a gradual westward extension of the south front. The oldest part, to the east, is Elizabethan, with its sash windows added in the early eighteenth century. The next section was added, by an apparently unknown architect, in the same style between 1800 and 1810; this includes the present Bow Room, Drawing Room and Dining Room, together with the White Hall with its pretty staircase climbing around a broad open well. Until 1984, when it was mercifully demolished, there was also a west end comprising a Ball Room, erected by the appalling 7th Earl of Cardigan in 1865 to make sure that nobody should forget his heroism in leading the Charge of the Light Brigade. Architecturally a disaster, built of a different stone on a different scale, it flaunted a monumentally awful alabaster fireplace by John Crace and much hideous stained glass designed by the Countess, who wrote a scandalous volume of memoirs (*My Recollections*, still to be found in second-hand bookshops and highly recommended) and for half a century after her husband's death lived at Deene, growing more and more eccentric as the years went by, finally dying in 1915 at the age of ninety. According to the local guidebook, 'She wore thick make-up and a blonde wig, and was often seen wearing her husband's regimental uniform or bare-legged in a short kilt.'

## Drayton House*

*13; 2 miles NW of Thrapston off A604*

There has been a house at Drayton since about 1300; the last important decorative work was done in 1850. The glorious building that we see today thus incorporates the fabric of five and a half centuries, making it, architecturally, by far the most fascinating of all the great country houses of Northamptonshire. Perhaps because it developed organically, bit by bit, perhaps because of the marvellous stone that prevails throughout, perhaps because of the way the centuries seem to intermesh as one wanders from room to room, it manages to preserve – despite the variety of style and period – an extraordinary unity of character, an unmistakable personality of its own that impresses itself upon any visitor within the first five minutes. Of all the houses listed in this book, only Knole has quite the same effect; and, curiously enough, it is above all of Knole that we are reminded as we drive across the park from the south-east and suddenly come upon what seems more like a walled medieval village than anything else: a veritable forest of towers, pinnacles, cupolas and chimneys rising up from within a perimeter wall which is, on the entrance side, almost devoid of windows and of distinctly threatening aspect.

Before we reach this entrance front, however, there is a vast forecourt to be crossed; and this is closed off to the south by a wrought-iron screen with, at its centre, a pair of gates of transcendent beauty, framed by tall stone piers from the tops of which two mighty eagles are poised to take flight. Surmounting the overthrow of these gates is a ducal coronet; and so we meet one of the owners of Drayton who was to leave an imperishable mark on the house – Lady Mary Mordaunt, wife first to the 7th Duke of Norfolk and then, after a divorce in 1700, to a Dutch soldier of fortune, Sir John Germain. The gates are almost certainly the work of Jean Tijou, the French immigrant who became the greatest ironsmith of his day, working for Wren at St Paul's, Hampton Court and the Clarendon Building at Oxford as well as at Burghley nearby. His hand can be recognised time and again at Drayton – in the gateway into the garden, in the grilles flanking the front door steps in the inner courtyard, in the Stone Staircase balustrade, and in several similar screens elsewhere about the park.

And so to that forbidding wall of the south range, built unmistakably for defence. It was in 1328 that Edward III gave Sir Simon de Drayton a licence to crenellate his old house; in those days every gentleman's dwelling had to be able to withstand a siege. Of Sir Simon's castle, this wall is the only major part that has survived the centuries; its former blankness is now

*The courtyard of Drayton House seen from the Dining Room.*

partly relieved by the mullion windows at the ends – inserted by the 3rd Lord Mordaunt in Queen Elizabeth's day – and by the central Gatehouse, built by Henry, 2nd Earl of Peterborough (Lady Mary's father) in 1676 when he shifted the main entrance round from the north side. We can, I think, be grateful that it remains as stark as it does; had it been given a complete Elizabethan or Baroque treatment all the way along we should have been deprived of the memorable moment of drama that awaits us as we pass though into the courtyard.

When, in 1702, Lady Mary and her new husband decided to remodel the medieval Hall, simultaneously providing themselves with a new entrance front within this inner court, they called in the Comptroller of the Royal Works, William Talman; and the elevation which Talman then designed for them is a masterpiece of Baroque exuberance – far more ornate than his work at Dyrham, Chatsworth or Uppark. In the centre of the seven-bay front is the main doorway, flanked by fluted detached columns which are linked by swags to a carved keystone. Above is an elaborate stone trophy. To each side, tall windows – the outer four with alternating pediments, the inner two with scrolly decoration – descend almost to the ground; above each is a blank panel serving as a frame for a bust on a bracket. Then comes the entablature; and finally a balustrade with urns, rising in the centre into a broken pediment supported by caryatids, the Germain coat of arms resplendent within it. Doric colonnades close off the courtyard to east and west. They too are Talman's, though dating from a year or two later. Within the door was the old screens passage, with the Hall immediately to the right. The former Talman did away with; the latter, now slightly increased in size, he totally transformed. The old hammer-beam timber roof was retained, but hidden under a barrel-vaulted ceiling; the walls were furnished with panelling and fluted Ionic pilasters. The purpose of the ceiling was probably to accommodate a huge painting, as had been done recently at Boughton not far away, and there is reason to believe that Sir James Thornhill was actually approached; but the scheme came to nothing, and the present painted decoration, relying heavily on marbleising techniques, is the work of one Alexander Roos in *c.*1850.

*The entrance front, Drayton House.*

Opposite the Hall, and occupying the left-hand side of Talman's front, is the Dining Room. With it we enter yet another style and period; for this exquisite room was transformed between 1771 and 1774 by Lord George Sackville, who had inherited the house from his distant cousin Lady Betty Germain, Sir John's second wife. A riot of lovely and delicate plasterwork, it seems more than likely to be the work of Sir William Chambers, though the evidence is circumstantial and we shall never know for certain.

Just outside the Hall at its north-east corner we come upon the first of Drayton's two great staircases, known as the Stone Staircase. It forms part of Talman's work, has a superb wrought-iron balustrade – Tijou again – and is most extravagantly painted on both the walls and the ceiling. This, then, is what would have happened to the Hall if the original plan had materialised; only here the painting is not by Thornhill but by Gerard Lanscroon, commissioned by Sir John and Lady Betty in 1712. (She herself, in suitably Baroque disguise, looks down approvingly from the ceiling.) It is all very magnificent – particularly since the recent restoration has brought out all the old brilliance of colour – but few people, I suspect, would not prefer the Walnut Staircase, which rises up the tall Tudor tower dominating the east side of the house. Despite its name, only the turned balusters and handrail are of walnut; the treads themselves are of oak, cantilevered out from the wall entirely without supports. The nearest parallel is Wren's Geometrical Staircase at St Paul's, but the Drayton version, dating from 1705, is slightly earlier. It leads to another marvellous room, the King's Dining Room, which occupies the upper floor of the two low towers which were added at either end of the Hall range in about 1460. (The lower floor is taken up by the magnificent undercroft of 1330 or thereabouts, majestically rib-vaulted and nowadays approached through a door in the east arcade.) The name is a reminder of James I's visit to Drayton in 1605, but in its present form the room dates from the 1670s, when it was remodelled by that same Lord Peterborough who built the Gatehouse. There he stands above the chimneypiece as seen by William Dobson, surrounded by portraits of his wife and family;

the walls around them are of pine painted to look like chestnut, and there is a noble plaster ceiling, thought to be by Edward Goudge. Furniture of spectacular quality lines the walls.

The tower containing the Walnut Staircase marks the southern end of the range added to the house by the 3rd Lord Mordaunt in Queen Elizabeth's reign; it must have been completed in 1584, the date which appears on its western façade. The idea was almost certainly to build a corresponding wing on the north-west to make a grand entrance courtyard, but this was never done. Apart from its vaulted cellar and the beautiful Long Gallery – now a Library – running the length of the second floor, it retains none of its original decoration; but the rooms it contains are no less interesting on that account. First comes the Green Drawing Room, which is one of the two rooms – the other being the Dining Room – which was decorated in the 1770s by Lord George Sackville in the neo-classical taste. Romney's portrait of him (on inheriting the house from Lady Betty he changed his name to Germain) hangs above the fireplace; equally interesting is the lovely stucco ceiling derived from a plate in Wood's *Ruins of Palmyra* of 1753. Beyond this are the Blue Drawing Room and the State Bedroom, with which we dart back in time once again to Lord Peterborough's day – when, in 1653, he commissioned designs for them from John Webb. In the first of these two rooms nothing of Webb's remains except the doorcases; in the Bedroom, however, we also find his monumental overmantel, with scrolly broken pediment and swags of fruit and flowers. The bed itself is Lady Mary Germain's – a most sumptuous affair of green velvet. Beyond is a delightful closet, the walls of which are panelled with sections of an early seventeenth-century coromandel screen.

The final miracle of Drayton is the fact that since the death of Lord George Germain in 1785 there have been virtually no major alterations in structure or in decoration up to the present day – with the exception of the Great Hall in 1850 and a certain amount of necessary modernisation in the 1880s. For the rest, the reglazing of certain of the Elizabethan windows with plate glass and the insertion of a rather curious window at the end of the Long Gallery in the early 1900s represents the sum of the damage. The contents, too, are almost all intact; nothing, over the years, has been removed, and scarcely anything sold. The present owner loves it, understands it and maintains it superbly. It is a fortunate house indeed. But then, it deserves to be.

## Earl's Barton

*14; 6 miles E of Northampton on B573*

At the first mention of Saxon church architecture in England, most people think of Earl's Barton; after seeing the extraordinary tower of ALL SAINTS for oneself it is not difficult to understand why. First of all there are the lesenes – those always rather pointless-looking pilaster strips which most Saxon builders used in moderation only, but which constitute here the principal decoration, being used as quoins ('long-and-short work'), blank arches and, two-thirds of the way up the tower walls, in a double row of zigzag like the decorative stitching on some gigantic peasant smock. Perhaps the most charming feature is provided by the five-light bell openings around the top – just below the superbly incongruous fifteenth-century brick battlements. None of this could possibly be called beautiful, and it possesses nothing of the nobility of Brixworth only a dozen miles away; but it is indisputably memorable and on the whole can be said to deserve its fame.

After that tower, the twelfth-century Norman work in the body of the church often tends to be overlooked; but there is an interesting tower arch, a fine south doorway and, in the chancel, much ornate blind arcading and stepped sedilia. The three pretty Early English lancets at the east end have nice glass, and there are Decorated reticulated windows in the aisles. Finally, the rood-screen, medieval in its origin but much restored and endearingly repainted with saints and butterflies in 1935, may not be to everybody's taste, but it is to mine.

## Easton Neston★

*15; 1 mile NE of Towcester off A43*

There are hundreds of houses in England larger than Easton Neston, dozens more awe-inspiring, several more majestic; but there is none more noble. The two giant Corinthian columns framing its central bay, the four pilasters of similar proportions marching off to each side, the restrained elegance of the window frames, the high rusticated basement that calls forth the sweeping double staircase with its magnificent iron railing, the proud coat of arms crowning the whole composition – all these, together with the immaculately judged proportions, the quality of the workmanship and the superb Helmdon stone which provides the ashlar facing, combine in such a way as to rob the first-time beholder, quite literally, of his breath. And yet, surprisingly perhaps, there is nothing dramatic about it, none of the theatricality of a Vanbrugh, the exhibitionism of a Talman, the wilfulness of an Archer. Easton Neston has a monumental quality which stamps it, as unmistakably as would a signature, with the name of one man: Nicholas Hawksmoor.

The architectural history of the house is not, however, as straightforward as might at first appear. Hawksmoor, wrote his contemporary John Bridges, 'hath very much departed from the first design'; the house that he finished in 1702 – the date inscribed on the east front – was in fact a remodelling of an earlier brick building, designed and probably to a very large extent executed in the ten years from 1685, of which a most magnificent wooden model exists in the RIBA. In the 1680s, however, Hawksmoor was still a young man – he had been born in 1661 – serving as 'domestic clerk' in the office of Sir Christopher Wren, who is known to have been consulted on the house as early as 1682. This first building, which had no giant orders but which bore many resemblances to what we see today – particularly on the side elevations – may well, therefore, have been partly Wren's work; and the same can be said for the house's interior, which probably underwent little change during the exterior remodelling. There is actually documentary evidence to suggest that the staircase was

*Easton Neston.*

designed by Wren and Hawksmoor jointly and that Wren built the Hall. Yet none of this detracts from Hawksmoor's achievement in giving the house its present aspect. In a letter of 1721 he writes: 'I had the honour to be concerned in the body of the house . . . . One can hardly avoyed loving ones own children.' It was indeed his child, and he had good reason to be proud.

The two main fronts, the entrance front to the west and the garden front to the east, are virtually identical, the only important difference being that to the east the giant columns at the centre are replaced by pilasters and there is no coat of arms. The balustraded parapet, too, is without the urns and little lions that punctuate the entrance front. The side elevations, however, come as something of a surprise. To the south, all five bays have an attic storey just below the balustrade; to the north, on the other hand, there are seven bays, and while the two outer bays and the centre have two storeys only (with very tall and necessarily narrow windows) bays 2, 3, 5 and 6 have not only an attic but also an additional mezzanine inserted between the first and second floors. It is a complicated design and not, perhaps, an entirely successful one; but it enables the architect to provide a number of small, intimate rooms in a way which would otherwise have been impossible, and unquestionably makes the house a good deal more agreeable to live in.

Entering by the front door, you find yourself in a broad vestibule, with the Hall on your right. It is extraordinary how, even at the beginning of the eighteenth century, one still finds echoes of the old medieval plan; by this time, however, the screens passage and the offices leading off it had been done away with; at Easton Neston the Hall was designed as a tripartite composition, with the broad central part rising the entire height of the house and the two ends – separated from the centre by screens of columns – of one storey only. The northern end occupied the central bay, where the screens passage would have been. Unfortunately, however, this original arrangement has been altered. The Hall has been shorn of its two ends, that to the north having been amalgamated with the small living room adjoining it to form a broad vestibule, that to the south to provide domestic offices. We are left with the centre only, now divided horizontally, and consequently rising one storey instead of two.

The great staircase, by contrast, remains just as it always was – and most magnificent it appears, rising unsupported from the centre of the house to the north wall and then returning on itself to the first-floor pilastered gallery, with brief intermediate landings at

the halfway points. It is of stone, with iron balustrading possibly by Tijou, and – after Hampton Court and Kensington Palace – one of the first of its kind in England. The *grisaille* murals of scenes from the life of Cyrus the Great are by Thornhill and make a pleasant contrast with the statues in shell-topped niches; the exuberant plasterwork on the vaulted ceiling features the intertwined Ls which one normally associates with Versailles but which here identify the builder of the house, Sir William Fermor, who was created Lord Lempster in 1692. (They appear again in the horizontal panels of the balustrading.)

Of the rooms on the ground floor, perhaps the most wholly enjoyable is that which occupies the south-east corner. It has served in the past sometimes as a drawing room, sometimes as a dining room; what makes it spectacular, however, is the astonishing plasterwork on walls and ceiling. The ceiling has in its centre panel a free stucco adaptation of Titian's *Venus and Adonis*, which might not perhaps be memorable in isolation; but the walls are bedecked with immensely elaborate plaster frames, so fancifully extravagant that one scarcely notices the hunting pictures within them. More curious still, they seem to take no heed of the proportions of the room, nor of the space available; thus one of them can only just squeeze itself between the overmantel and the corner; another is wedged even more painfully between the cornice and the doorcase. All this sounds inordinately clumsy, and so indeed it is; but the overall effect is of a careless, joyful ebullience that I for one find impossible to resist.

Upstairs, the central feature is the long, broad gallery that runs across the middle of the house from the east front to the west, being lit only by the great round-headed central first-floor windows at each end. Off it is a series of magnificent bedrooms, several of them with deeply coved ceilings and hung with superb tapestries, but also – at the north and south ends – the more modest mezzanine rooms, interconnected by little narrow corridors and short flights of steps.

Finally, a word must be said about the brick building of nine bays which forms the north side of the entrance courtyard. It has a pedimented centre, a hipped roof with dormers, and now contains a real tennis court. The windows are unusually tall – almost as tall as those of the house itself – and have stone frames. This building – which, apart from the attic, is of a single storey – predates the remodelled house and is said by Bridges to be by Wren. An extant letter from Wren of 1682 does not quite bear this out, suggesting as it does that, although aware of the progress of the building, he was not himself familiar with the site; but the possibility remains.

## Eydon*

*16; 16 miles SW of Northampton off B4525*

An almost exact contemporary of Courteenhall – it was completed in 1791 – Eydon (pronounced Eden) is another irresistible house by an architect who, though less obscure than Samuel Saxon, deserves to be far better known than he is: James Lewis. (His other principal claim to fame was the Bethlehem Hospital for Lunatics in Southwark, now the Imperial War Museum.) Whereas Courteenhall is neo-classical, Eydon is still Palladian – but Lewis's Palladianism has come a long way from Burlington's or Kent's. It has a grace and elegance that he owes not a little, perhaps, to Robert Adam, coupled with a curious ingenuity that one does not normally associate with the style at all. Look, for example, at the way in which, by means of simple balustrades, he has contrived to make a four-storey house look like a two-storey one; and notice how, by using columns taller and a little more slender than Palladio himself would have approved, and by other devices like wrought-iron railings instead of stone balusters, he has given the house an airy lightness far removed from Holkham, Houghton or Wardour. There are surprises too – notably the quiet *insouciance* with which the portico, which one would have expected on the entrance front, has been transferred to the back.

The interior is rather more orthodox – though none the worse for that. There is a central Staircase Hall, generously proportioned and lit from above through an oval dome of glass, with all the main rooms opening off it. Everywhere, however, the extraordinary feeling of lightness persists. Here, one feels, is not just a ravishingly beautiful house, but a happy one too.

*Eydon Hall.*

## Finedon

*17; 3 miles NE of Wellingborough on A510*

ST MARY'S is a wonderful church with a colour scheme typical of this part of the country – rich brown ironstone with generous grey stone dressings. After the colour, the first thing you notice about it is the shape of its windows – Decorated, and slightly ogival. Most have beautiful reticulated tracery, but all are of the same period: the whole church must date from the middle of the fourteenth century. The tower is particularly distinguished, carrying on the ogee motif at several different levels and crowned with a slender, gently recessed spire with lucarnes – a really lovely job. The south porch is another. It has two storeys, the upper one given over to a damp and dusty library, whose massive leather tomes of formidable theological learning look as if they had remained undisturbed for a couple of centuries at least. The lower, entrance, floor is vaulted, with splendid gargoyles.

Once inside, the attention is immediately captured by a big strainer arch, curved top and bottom, the double spandrels of which are most intricately worked with a design of quatrefoils within circles, and with jolly little crenellations running along the top. The south pier whence it springs is marvellously carved with tangled foliage and two jacks-in-the-green. The north side is simpler, with a comely pair of angels. But there are innumerable carvings all over the place, particularly in the various label stops; the vicar told me he had been there six years and was still finding new ones. There is a lovely five-light east window with the usual reticulated tracery, though the Victorian glass is a bit disappointing. That strainer arch, incidentally, is almost precisely repeated at Rushden nearby, which accordingly deserves an Honourable Mention here but not, on balance, a separate entry.

Finedon village has a very good ironstone VICARAGE just opposite the church, and several distinctly odd buildings – including the BELL INN – reflecting the Gothic taste of a Victorian squire, Mr Mackworth-Dolben. It also boasts two memorable towers just outside it – the WELLINGTON TOWER, built to commemorate Waterloo, and on the A6 to the south a mad and marvellous WATER-TOWER of almost Butterfieldian polychromy.

## Fotheringhay

*18; 3½ miles NE of Oundle off A605*

Of the castle where Mary Queen of Scots was imprisoned, and where she went to her death on 8 February 1587, nothing now remains but a great grassy mound. The pride of Fotheringhay is its church, and even this is not what it used to be. ST MARY AND ALL SAINTS still looks marvellous, with its flying buttresses and its great west tower that begins square and then becomes octagonal, each of the eight sides being almost completely filled by tall, three-light, transomed bell openings. It is a high tower by parish church standards, and is made to look even higher by the body of the church, which seems unusually short by comparison.

And there lies the tragedy; for the rich college founded in 1411 by Edward, Duke of York, grandson of Edward III, lasted little over 100 years. Then came the Dissolution, some years after which the building came into the possession of the Duke of Northumberland. He pulled down the huge chancel – with seven bays, it was considerably longer than the surviving nave – and the two-bay Lady Chapel beyond it, together with cloister, dormitory, refectory and chapter house. Nor would he have stopped there, but for the fact that the west end was used as the parish church – as it still is.

You enter the church by the north porch beneath the tower, its four-light window oddly off-centre. Since the aisles extend on each side of the tower, and since moreover it has high arches to north and south as well as eastward towards the nave, the effect inside is one of an immense narthex, with a lovely fan vault above. (It is dated 1529, only a few years before the end.) The nave is exceptionally broad, the aisles equally so, with the result that one feels, even more than one felt outside, the painfulness of the amputation. There is no real east end; no chancel arch, even: only a poor ghost of one in the botched-up east wall, with its sad apology for an east window – five lights, cusped, within a four-centred arch – ridiculously high beneath the timber roof.

There is a nice octagonal font and an even nicer pulpit, the gift of Edward IV, with a fan-vaulted tester. It has recently been repainted in brilliant colours, not quite well enough. The twin monuments, of Edward, Duke of York, the founder of the college, and of his son Richard, were erected by order of Queen Elizabeth in 1573 after she had been shown their two original tombs mouldering away in the ruined choir, defenceless against wind and weather.

## Higham Ferrers

*19; 5½ miles E of Wellingborough on A45*

The crocketed spire of ST MARY'S CHURCH, with its openwork flying buttresses and three rows of lucarnes, dominates the landscape for miles and offers rich promise of wonders in store; nor is that promise disappointed. The town, with its church and castle, has been rich ever since 1266, when it became the property of the House of Lancaster, to which Royal Duchy it still belongs; and it enjoyed a further stroke of good fortune in 1414 when one of its native sons, Henry Chichele, became Archbishop of Canterbury and one of the most powerful men in the land.

First, the west tower: only the bottom half is original, the top stage and spire having collapsed in 1631; they were immediately rebuilt in their original form. But the west doorway alone is enough to stop us in our tracks. There are two doors, side by side beneath a single arch, their jambs and arches marvellously carved, and in the tympanum above them ten roundels – not all of them complete in shape owing to the line of the arch – containing scenes from the New Testament. All are the product of the second half of the thirteenth century. Why they were not defaced during Reformation or Commonwealth we shall never know; we can only be thankful.

Inside, the initial impression is again one of a double-naved church; but appearances are deceptive. This is not a Hannington writ large. In the thirteenth century, when building began, it was according to the normal design – a single nave (that which forms the continuation of west door and tower) with south aisle and chancel. It was only after 1325 that there was added a north aisle as broad as the nave itself, and continuing into a Lady Chapel the same length and breadth as the chancel. This aisle was then given a subsidiary one of its own, still further to the north. At the same time the opportunity was seized to modernise the older Early English fabric by remodelling it in the now fashionable Decorated style. This accounts for the lovely five-light reticulated east window in the chancel, as well as the one in the fourteenth-century Lady Chapel.

The furnishings are splendid. Twenty of the old collegiate stalls are still *in situ*, with admirable misericords including a portrait of Archbishop Chichele under the Master's stall; and among the brasses is one of the finest anywhere – that of Laurence St Maur, who died in 1337.

Just outside the church, at the west end, is Chichele's GRAMMAR SCHOOL – a little three-bay building as Perpendicular as could be, pinnacled and embattled. It was in use until 1907. In 1428 the Archbishop also founded a BEDE HOUSE, to the south across the churchyard, with living quarters for twelve indigent old men and a woman housekeeper and a raised Chapel at the end. It has a huge fireplace, probably from the now vanished castle, but it strikes me as a cheerless sort of building, and with its narrow alternating courses of brown ironstone and grey limestone could never have been particularly attractive. Even the Bedesmen left it in the eighteenth century, and I can't say I blame them.

*The west doorway, St Mary's Church, Higham Ferrers.*

## Hinwick House

*20; 6 miles SE of Wellingborough off B569*

Built for Mr Richard Orlebar between 1708 and 1710, Hinwick House cost £3,848 4*s* 9*d*. Although, thanks to the preservation of the building book, the whole story of the house is quite exceptionally well documented, the identity of its architect remains a mystery. The book shows, however, that workmen on the site were regular employees of Francis Smith who, if recent research is correct, was simultaneously engaged on neighbouring Cottesbrooke and was later to build, with his son, the two wings and the Rectory at Lamport; and there is much at Hinwick to suggest that Smith may at least have had a hand in it. The east front, by which you enter, is distinctly grand with its giant Corinthian pilasters rising up two full storeys to the cornice, and a high, balustraded attic storey above that; to the south, the inner pilasters are replaced by niches, two up, two down, above which is a huge and curiously steep triangular pediment carved, with more *brio* than delicacy, to represent Diana in her phaeton. It is contemporary with the house, but so different from it in style and so awkwardly inserted into the attic that one feels it cannot conceivably have been part of the original design. Round the corner again, the west front is in no sense a showpiece, but boasts two projecting wings and a most noble door, to say nothing of a superb rainwater head bearing the date 1710 – which is echoed on the central bell turret of the stables opposite.

Inside, there is an oak staircase of great beauty, very much a feature of the house and strongly reminiscent of Francis Smith's at Mawley and Chillington, though much less ornate; it leads up to a huge tapestried first-floor landing, a magnificent room in itself. Upstairs, one of the bedrooms has its original French chintz wallpaper of 1720 or thereabouts – a rarity indeed. Hinwick is not one of the great houses of England, nor does it claim to be; but it is the perfect example of the Queen Anne manor house at its best. It has already sheltered ten generations of Orlebars, and I gather that the succession is generously assured. Long may it continue.

## Horton*

*21; 6 miles SE of Northampton on B526*

Though Horton House was demolished in 1936, the memory of it lives on in the MENAGERIE, built in the park as an eye-catcher by Thomas Wright of Durham in the 1750s. Behind it was a circular, moated enclosure in which the 2nd Earl of Halifax kept his collection of animals – which, according to Horace Walpole, included a tiger, a bear, raccoons and a quantity of warthogs. It has only one main front, which is to the north towards the site of Horton House; and that front is of pure Palladian inspiration, with two superimposed classical pediments in the style of the churches of the Redentore and S. Giorgio Maggiore in Venice, rusticated windows and a big central bow covering three bays crowned by a half dome. At each end a single-bay pavilion is topped with a pointed cupola. The material is principally the local limestone, with a harder, whiter stone for the carved ornament, probably from Helmdon.

The whole central block of the house is occupied by the Saloon – a beautiful room by any standards in the complexity of its shape and the perfection of its proportions, but made above all memorable by the glorious riot of Rococo plasterwork that covers it. The design of this was almost certainly Wright's own, but the execution was the work of the great Thomas Roberts of Oxford, who was responsible for the decoration of the Upper Library of Christ Church. Its theme is the signs of the zodiac – appropriately enough for this particular architect, who was also an expert astronomer and, incidentally, the first to establish that the Milky Way was composed of stars.

So much for description; but there is one other point to emphasise. This is the fact that in 1975 the Menagerie was derelict and crumbling. What we see today – and we *can* see it, for the house is open to the public on written application – is partly restoration, of a quite exceptionally meticulous and scholarly kind, but also to a very considerable degree a work of inspired reconstruction; and there can be no greater tribute to the present owner – but for whom the building would no longer exist – than to say that to the cursory visitor it is virtually impossible to distinguish the recent from the original. This is true also of the plasterwork, at least half of which is entirely new, the work of Christopher Hobbs. In short, the Menagerie is a triumph, and a staggering achievement. Hats off!

## Kelmarsh

*22; 13 miles N of Northampton on A508*

At first glance, KELMARSH HALL looks a typical red-brick country house of George II's time, notable if anything for its restraint. It has seven bays, with a very slightly projecting three-bay pedimented centre; a brick parapet with short bursts of balustrading and a two-angled hipped roof behind; an imposing doorway with fluted Corinthian columns and a big segmental pediment – triangular and segmental pediments alternate above the door and windows of the ground floor – and two-storey side pavilions with quadrantal links. That seems to say it all. One is rather surprised, standing out there in the entrance courtyard, to learn that this is one of the relatively few surviving country houses built by no less an architect than James Gibbs.

In fact, Gibbs's *Book of Architecture* which he published in 1728 – the very year in which building at Kelmarsh began – shows a considerably more elaborate design for the house; he had originally intended three storeys instead of two, a recessed centre instead of a projecting one, rusticated jambs to the windows, quoins at the angles and urns on the parapet. (Pevsner's assertion that Kelmarsh was 'restored' in 1956 to 'the appearance it has in Gibbs's original drawings' is surely mistaken.) Why Gibbs gave up these ideas is unknown; in the interior, however, he has allowed himself much more latitude. The front door opens directly into the Hall, which is central and rises the full height of the house. It has nowhere near the size or opulence of the one which he designed for Ragley Hall in Warwickshire, but it remains a magnificent enclosure of space with fine delicate stucco on walls and ceiling. On the side walls the architectural aspects are emphasised with what appear to be blank windows in plaster at first-floor level, while on the back wall we have three real interior windows giving on to a passage from which one can look down into the Hall. Below these windows on the ground floor is a three-bay arcade with another passage behind them – Gibbs was one of the pioneers of passages and corridors, still rarities in his day when directly intercommunicating rooms remained the rule – which broadens out towards the south into the Staircase Hall. The stairs themselves are of stone and have lovely wrought-iron balustrades, which are prolonged at the top of the second (reverse) flight to form a short gallery.

At the foot of the stairs to the right – but also giving directly on to the Hall – is a small room covered with glorious eighteenth-century Chinese wallpaper; this, with so much else of the interior decoration, is to be attributed to the taste and knowledge of Mr and Mrs Ronald Tree, who on becoming tenants in 1927 swept out a mass of nasty nineteenth-century work and gave the interior much of the decorative elegance it still possesses. Opposite this room on the further side of the Hall, the very pretty Dining Room has a shell apse and more lovely plasterwork.

Walking through the Hall on the central axis of the house we find, across the passage, the Saloon – at the time of writing almost unfurnished but clearly redecorated towards the end of the eighteenth century in the Adam manner. The ceiling is plain, but there is a pretty frieze, together with roundels in stucco over the doorcases and the smaller of the shallow niches which are another feature of the room. To one side of this is the Library and to the other a diminutive Boudoir.

And now, if the weather is smiling, walk out from the Saloon down to the lake and look back at the west front. Apart from a modest little coat of arms in the pediment it seems to be almost identical with the other; only the most eagle-eyed will notice that the order of the alternating pediments above the windows has been reversed. But we are not looking for variety. Kelmarsh is not an adventurous house – it is a house of quiet serenity and well-bred discretion, and therein lies its beauty and its strength.

The CHURCH OF ST DIONYSIUS close by has – apart from some good tombs of the Hanburys – only one feature of outstanding interest: the east window of the north chapel, which boasts a rare example of that curious phenomenon, Caroline tracery. It takes the form of a lozenge at the top, then two roundels, then three more lozenges, the lower points of which just cut into the three round-headed arches below. Not beautiful perhaps, but unquestionably odd.

## Kings Sutton*

*23; 5 miles SE of Banbury off A41*

Northamptonshire has the loveliest spires in England; the CHURCH OF ST PETER AND ST PAUL at Kings Sutton has the loveliest spire in Northamptonshire. It is Decorated work of perhaps 1370 or thereabouts, and soars up from a cluster of pinnacles on two separate levels – very slender ones at the corners, which are connected by equally slim flying buttresses to four more, rather more substantial, rising from the base of the spire itself. These latter actually have tiny sub-pinnacles of their own, and their own minute flying buttresses connecting them with the spire at the lower of its two levels of lucarnes. The effect is that of the most intricate and delicate filigree, through which the daylight shines at all sorts of unexpected points, and yet of strength as well. It is 198 feet high, crocketed all the way up, and topped by a weathercock, obviously in full crow and quite right too. Inside the church as well as out, Decorated prevails in the proportions and the fenestration, rising to a considerable climax with the east window of the south aisle; one is all the more surprised to come upon a chancel which, despite its Decorated side windows and Perpendicular east one, turns out to be unmistakably Norman, with blank arcading along the walls. But look again at the piers of the south arcade; they are round, and one is even scalloped. They must be Norman too, saved from the earlier Norman nave and brought back into service when the church was rebuilt in the fourteenth century. Finally, don't miss the monument to Thomas Langton Freke – 'Death, thou shalt die' and no mistake.

*The church of St Peter and St Paul, Kings Sutton.*

*Kirby Hall.*

## Kirby Hall

*24; 4 miles NE of Corby off A427*

Here's fascination: Kirby Hall is one of that select group of noble secular ruins – Cowdray, South Wingfield and a few others – that are still, today, more rewarding to visit than many a complete stately home. It has also managed somehow to preserve a quality of romance that not even the clinical ministrations of the Dept of the Environment have altogether eliminated. There is a plan of the house in Sir John Soane's Museum by the London surveyor, John Thorpe, inscribed 'Kerby whereof I layd ye first stone AD 1570'; Thorpe was only about five at the time – foundation stones were quite often laid by small children in Elizabethan days, that of Parham in Sussex, for instance, by a toddler of two and a half – and we can probably infer that his father, the master mason Thomas Thorpe, was responsible for the building. Who it was that actually designed the great new mansion for Sir Humphrey Stafford we do not know, but he had almost certainly travelled in France, or at least had the opportunity of studying recent French books on the latest architectural fashions there: the giant buttress-pilasters in the courtyard, though relatively common around Paris at this date, are of a type to be found nowhere else in England.

Sir Humphrey died in 1575 and the mortar and plasterwork can have been scarcely dry when the house was bought by the Queen's favourite, Sir Christopher Hatton. It was a typical piece of Elizabethan extravagance; Hatton was already building an immense house at Holdenby, only a few miles away, for the express purpose of entertaining his sovereign. He himself hardly ever came to Kirby, but he seems to have immediately embarked on a scheme of alteration and enlargement; and this was continued still more ambitiously by his second successor in the property, another Sir Christopher, who inherited in 1619 and twenty years later is traditionally believed to have commissioned Inigo Jones to remodel the house. There is no evidence to confirm the story; but a lot of work in Jones's style was obviously done at this period, and much of the interest of the house as it stands today lies in the contrast between the work of the 1570s and that of the 1630s.

This contrast hits you the moment you enter the courtyard. The entrance front, its balustrade oddly enlivened by alternating pediments raised on pierced and voluted gables, has appeared from the outside to be of the seventeenth century; but the south range, running parallel to it along the far side of the court, is equally obviously the original Tudor work. There are those giant pilasters, all Frenchified and fluted; and then, in the middle, a tremendous frontispiece, growing more and more exuberant as it rises, and ending in a high attic and gable that couldn't be more English if they tried. Now turn your back on this glorious Elizabethan conceit and look north, to the back of the entrance front; here at once you see the link between the two. There are the same pilasters, the two centre ones unfluted but carved instead with ornaments copied, Sir John Summerson tells us, from the title page of John Shute's *The First and Chief Groundes of Architecture*, 1563; between them, the ground-floor loggia goes back to Sir Humphrey's time, but above, the alternating triangular and segmental pediments point equally clearly to the Jonesian remodelling.

Now turn south again, where the high roof to the right of the porch betokens the Great Hall, the second bay from the corner marking, in traditional fashion, the dais end. (Its corresponding one on the other side of the porch, and the two projecting corner bays, are similarly enlarged purely for reasons of symmetry and swagger; they serve no practical purpose.) This Hall, despite its sad condition, is still beautiful and to me even moving; it must have been yet more splendid before the two windows in the fireplace wall were blocked up, and when it still possessed its original screens passage instead of the seventeenth-century gallery. Nowadays the best feature is the original Elizabethan roof, canted with four faces so that it forms what is very nearly a barrel vault. All the principal timbers are carved with leafy decoration, and sinewy S-shaped wind-braces weave their way to and fro between the beams.

The rest of the interior, including what is left of the Long Gallery which runs the whole 150-foot length of the west range, presents a sorry spectacle. Much of it indeed is an empty, roofless shell. Neglected since the beginning of the nineteenth century and derelict for nearly as long, Kirby is long past repair or redemption; and it is only thanks to the blessed decision which, in December 1930, put it under governmental care that any of it remains to tell us of the splendour that is gone.

## Lamport

*25; 8 miles N of Northampton on B576*

The best way to understand the architecture of LAMPORT HALL is to turn right immediately before reaching the front door and to walk round to the lawn on the west – or, strictly speaking, the south-west – side. There you will see the core of the present house: the five-bay rusticated front built for Sir Justinian Isham during 1654 and 1655 by John Webb. It is a surprisingly small building, of only one and a half storeys; but at that time Sir Justinian was actually living in his Elizabethan manor house which stood on the site of the present entrance front, facing the church. All he required of Webb was an addition – a tiny *palazzo* in the Italian style, possessed of a 'High Roome' in which he could receive, as he put it, *'des personnes d'honeur'*. He must have been delighted with the result which, despite its modest scale, was indisputably grand with its alternating pediments above the first-floor windows, its raised quoins and crowning balustrade. The interior, of course, was grander still; but we shall come to that later.

The centre of this west front as we see it today is very much as Webb left it, except for the windows themselves, which have exchanged their original mullion-and-transom crosses for sashes, and for the rather awkward-looking nineteenth-century pediment which has replaced the small single-bay one added by Webb as an afterthought in 1657. If it no longer gives the impression of a tiny Italianate jewel, this is because it now stands no longer in isolation but as the centre of a thirteen-bay façade – the extensions having been added in the 1730s and 1740s by Francis Smith of Warwick and his son William. We may regret that these extensions ever proved necessary; but it must be admitted that the Smiths did an admirable job, both tactful and discreet, maintaining nearly all Webb's horizontals apart from slightly increasing the height of the upper windows. The design for both wings was by Francis Smith, but he died in 1738 when only the northern one was completed; the southern was added by William a few years later, less for any practical purpose than simply to finish off the façade and to keep it symmetrical.

This last point becomes immediately clear when we walk round to the south front. Here William Smith's wing is revealed to be only two bays thick, with two blank arches on the ground floor (opened up into an arcade in one of Smith's drawings) and two blank windows above. Behind it, in the angle between the Smith wing and the long east–west range, is a small quadrantal bay with a porch below. This brings us to the next architect to be concerned with Lamport, Henry Hakewill, best known for St Peter's, Eaton Square, and his work at Rugby School. Working between 1819 and 1829, Hakewill gave the west front its present pediment and then rebuilt the north one on the site of the old

*Lamport Hall.*

Elizabethan house – although, as we shall see, the latter was not to last for long. The eastern part of the south front, however, is not his; it is in fact a remodelling of the old Tudor work by the Leicester architect Henry Goddard, and dates from 1842.

The last of the major alterations to Lamport was to the north front, opposite the church. Hakewill's work there seems to have found no favour with the Ishams, for only forty years after its completion the 10th Baronet called in William Burn. What we see today on this side of the house, including the deep Tuscan porch and the rather squat Italianate tower, is his. Hardly inspiring, perhaps, but it might have been worse.

And now, at last, we can enter the house. Ideally, we should do so from the west front, thus stepping straight into Webb's Great Hall, now known as the Music Hall. In fact, however, we shall probably go in at the front door, pass through the Entrance Hall and vestibule and then turn right into the Library which occupies the major part of Francis Smith's northern extension. Only the fireplace at the far end and its flanking giant pilasters are of 1732; the rest of the room is a remodelling by Hakewill of 1819. Whatever its date, however, it is a lovely room – everything a library should be, with its row of busts above Hakewill's bookcases and some marvellous library furniture, to say nothing of Charles I's own Bible.

Leaving the Library, we find ourselves in John Webb's building of 1655: first the Oak Room – its panelling put in as recently as 1907; next the Staircase Hall (the staircase itself is by Francis Smith, but the beautifully carved wooden panels from Webb's original balustrade can still be seen around the first-floor landing) and a delightful small Drawing Room; and only then the Music Hall. Rising the full height of the house, it is well worth waiting for. Notice first that, for all his Palladianism, Webb could not quite shake off the old medieval tradition according to which the Hall was entered from one end. He could easily have placed it centrally, but he did not. The fireplace (of stone) and the overmantel (of wood) are essentially as Webb left them, with the Isham swans at each side and the oddly Baroque broken pediment – really two broken pediments, one inside the other – above, enclosing the Isham arms. The swan also appears repeatedly on the upper walls and high coved ceiling. The cornice takes the form of beautifully carved inscriptions, which include the Ishams' favourite pun: 'I SHAM NOT'; above that there is a deep attic with profile busts alternating with trophies of flowers, fruit and musical instruments topped with garlands, vases, swans and eagles; and, finally, a glorious ceiling with mermaids and cavorting *putti*. All this dates from 1738 and is the work of John Woolston, a Northampton alderman – one of the few examples known to history of the arts of stucco and of local government going hand in hand.

No visit to Lamport is complete without a look at ALL SAINTS' (or ALL HALLOWS') CHURCH. It stands immediately across the road, opposite the north front of the house, and has been intimately associated with the Ishams for over 400 years. The tower is medieval – the bottom stage late Norman – as are the nave arcades and aisles; the rest belongs to the seventeenth and eighteenth centuries. To the seventeenth we can ascribe the north chapel of 1672–3, which may be the work of John Webb; it was certainly influenced by him, since the east window with its segmental pediment follows the design of the two outer windows of Webb's west front, and indeed shows exactly how they must have looked before they were sashed. Among the Isham monuments within, that to the Sir Justinian who died in 1730 is by Francis Smith.

Smith also built the RECTORY, just to the east of the church; by the time the eighteenth-century work started on the church proper, however – in 1738 – he was dead, and the remodelling was therefore entrusted to William. William's are the outer walls of the aisles, and also the present chancel with its huge Venetian window at the east end. For the aisle windows, by contrast, he seems to have preferred Gothic, with simple Y-tracery – a style which accords oddly with his classically rusticated south porch. What gives the church its interior joyfulness, however, is above all the plasterwork, especially that of the chancel ceiling; and for this again we must thank Alderman Woolston.

Of the church's only structural addition since the seventeenth century, the south vestry of 1879, there is little to be said – except that G.F. Bodley, whose fault it is, should have known better.

## Lowick

*26; 1½ miles NW of Thrapston on A6116*

ST PETER'S CHURCH has one of those west towers, like Fotheringhay, which immediately marks it out as something special. Like Fotheringhay, too, it features a tall octagon, with outsize transomed bell openings; but whereas at the other church the octagon stands free, here at Lowick it is partly concealed behind the tall crocketed pinnacles which rise from the topmost stage of the tower proper and to which it is connected by short flying buttresses. Since it also boasts eight pinnacles of its own, the effect is one of a veritable forest: too fussy, perhaps, to be altogether successful, but certainly not easily forgotten.

The tower was not completed till about 1480 and is the newest part of the church. Most of the rest was built between 1370 and 1415 – with a break for a few years after 1399, when Sir Henry Greene of Drayton, who was financing the work, was executed by Henry IV on his accession. The predominant style is therefore early Perpendicular, and very magnificent it is with its huge aisle windows, their four-centred arches and traceried transoms. One might have looked for a little more variety when it came to the east window of the chancel and its northern neighbour, but it seems churlish to complain.

As you enter by the south door – and on no account miss its magnificent iron hinges – you immediately notice a fine painted Royal Arms over the chancel arch and then, in the four-light windows of the north aisle, some really outstanding medieval glass. They come from a Jesse window in some earlier church and cannot date from later than about 1320 – a near-miraculous survival, particularly when set at such a low level. That same north aisle also has a brave timber roof, with its principal rafters moulded and big carved heraldic bosses. It runs the full length of nave and chancel, ending in a north chapel which contains the tombs of two prominent occupants of Drayton House (*q.v.*), Lady Mary Mordaunt and Sir John Germain – the latter probably by Francis Bird. Between it and the chancel is something better still – the tomb of Sir Ralph Greene (who died in 1417) and his wife, the two alabaster effigies recumbent, her hand in his.

The south aisle, which goes no further than the chancel arch, leads to the chantry chapel of Henry Greene, founded in 1467. Here are more good monuments, including those of Henry Greene himself and of Charles Sackville, 5th Duke of Dorset, by Westmacott. Best of all, however, is that of Edward Stafford, Earl of Wiltshire, who died in 1499. His effigy is of stunning quality. Note how the letters of the inscription round the edge are tied together; could this, I wonder, be an allusion to the Stafford knot?

## Lyveden New Bield

*NT; 27; 3 miles SW of Oundle off A427*

It must have taken considerable courage for a promising young man of Queen Elizabeth's day who had already been knighted by his sovereign suddenly to embrace the Roman Catholic faith; and still more to advertise his conversion by two of the most extraordinary buildings of their time, secular in themselves yet both nothing more nor less than sermons in stone. One is the Triangular Lodge at Rushton (*q.v.*); the other is Lyveden New Bield.

The Old Bield – this curious word is a corruption of 'build' – where Sir Thomas Tresham actually lived still stands, but has been too much altered to be of any real architectural interest. In 1594, however, he decided to erect a large summer-house nearby to symbolise the Passion. The architect was a certain Robert Stickells; but the whole concept can only have been Tresham's own. The plan is that of a Greek cross with a canted bay window, rising the full height of the building at the end of each arm. The ground floor carries a metope frieze with emblems of the Passion (including the Chi-Rho and Judas's money bags), the first floor a long Latin inscription in honour of the Virgin.

Alas, Sir Thomas died in 1605 and his New Bield was never finished. Like Kirby, it now stands a hollow shell in the midst of the fields, and it is probably thanks only to its remoteness that one brick has been left on another. It is still hard to find – 4 miles south-west of Oundle by the A427, but bear left after a mile and a half – and the last few hundred yards can be covered only on foot.

## Middleton Cheney*

*28; 4 miles NE of Banbury off A422*

ALL SAINTS is a large and wonderfully proportioned church built in the early fourteenth century at the beginning of the Decorated period – much of it by William of Edyngton, who later became Bishop of Winchester, gave the cathedral its present west front and ordained William of Wykeham. Be that as it may, it would not have found a place in this book but for the Victorian glass which, both in its quantity and its quality, takes one's breath away. In the east window alone, the Twelve Tribes and the figures of David, Isaiah, Abraham and Moses are by Simeon Solomon; St Paul and St John by Ford Madox Brown; St Alban and the Adoration of the Lamb by Burne-Jones; the four beasts and twelve banners by Philip Webb; and St Peter, St Augustine, St Catherine, Eve, the Virgin, Mary Magdalene, St Agnes, the Seraph and the censing angels by William Morris. But this is only a beginning; a leaflet available in the church gives a fuller list, and even this is maddeningly incomplete.

There is a pretty painted roof, but against this sort of competition it doesn't stand a chance.

*Lyveden New Bield.*

*All Saints' Church, Northampton.*

## Northampton

*29; 10 miles SW of Wellingborough on A45*

The story of Northampton is tragic indeed. In 1968 it had a population of 130,000; then it was designated a New Town, and long before this book is published it expects to have one of 230,000. Many of the best of the old buildings round the MARKET SQUARE – formerly one of the best in the country, almost as good as King's Lynn – have already been swept away, including the lovely old Peacock Hotel of 1676; and though Grosvenor Estates have rebuilt the charming three-gabled WELSH HOUSE on the east side (making it one of the few listed buildings in the country of reinforced concrete) and the so-called BEETHOVEN HOUSE next door to it with a pretty Gothick oriel, they have utterly destroyed the effect – and the scale – by their huge and hideous office block behind.

What remains amid the desolation? Several good buildings have managed to survive in the Market Square, notably around the north-west corner; and there are three others of importance which together constitute the focal point of historic Northampton: ALL SAINTS' CHURCH, the SESSIONS HOUSE and the TOWN HALL. The first two are exact contemporaries, built in 1676–80 immediately after the great fire of 1675 which destroyed over 600 houses, forming the whole centre of the town – though All Saints managed to preserve a good deal of its fourteenth-century west tower. It is a lovely building, probably by Henry Bell – architect of the King's Lynn Customs House – who has quite brilliantly incorporated the tower into his classical design without sacrificing its essential medieval character, wrapping it round with a deep Ionic portico (actually added in 1701, but to Bell's earlier design) with a statue of Charles II on top. Inside, the plan is that of a cross-in-square, with a central dome supported by four huge, unfluted Ionic columns and four equal tunnel-vaulted arms. It is all very stately and monumental – one of the very best of its date outside London. To Bell also has been attributed the Sessions House, but somehow I have my doubts. Fine as it undoubtedly is, with its richly carved segmental pediments on coupled columns (there is a triangular one on pilasters round the corner) it has a rather French feeling about it, and an air of heaviness, that seems hard to reconcile with Bell as we know him. And so to the splendid Town Hall, designed in 1860 by the twenty-eight-year-old Edward Godwin – French thirteenth-century Gothic, with Italian overtones; Godwin confessed that he had been reading *The Stones of Venice* just before the composition. Here, surely, is one of the great Victorian town halls; not, perhaps, quite up to Waterhouse's at Manchester, but in the same league.

Before we leave Northampton, there are two more churches that can on no account be missed. The first is the CHURCH OF THE HOLY SEPULCHRE, in Sheep Street. It is that rarest of rarities, a Norman round church, built *c.* 1110 by the Earl of Northampton on his return from the First Crusade. Round churches were usually foundations of the Military Orders – the Templars or the Hospitallers – built as reminders of the rotunda within the Church of the Holy Sepulchre at Jerusalem; the

Temple in London is an obvious example. This one was a parish church from the word go, and is still a parish church today. In other respects, however, it has been altered a good deal. The eight circular piers with their scalloped capitals still stand as they always did, separating the circular central space from an outer ambulatory; but they were given pointed arches to support in the fourteenth century and a new roof in the nineteenth. Moreover the small rectangular chancel which was part of the original structure was subsequently enlarged to form a nave, and a new chancel with a semi-circular apse was added by the inevitable Gilbert Scott between 1860 and 1864; so that the original circular nave now does duty as a baptistery only. But it is still a haunted, numinous place, and remains for me the most exciting thing in Northampton.

Finally, ST PETER'S CHURCH: though it does not have the atmosphere of Holy Sepulchre, it is of much the same date and has preserved a good deal more of the original Norman fabric. The outside is not especially promising; the tower seems too short for the nave and chancel (which run into each other without a break) and was in fact rebuilt in the seventeenth century, though a certain amount of the thirteenth-century decoration was preserved. But inside is another matter. St Peter's is far grander than most parish churches of its date. First, it employs a system of alternating piers for its arcade in a way usually reserved for cathedrals, or at least abbeys. Round piers with heavy shaft rings contrast with much more massive ones, quatrefoil in section, in which the inward-facing shafts shoot straight up to the roof while those facing the aisles clearly once supported transverse arches – the remains of which suggest that the aisles were considerably broader than they are now. Secondly, the capitals are fascinatingly carved, several of them with strong Saxon influences; could they have been taken from some earlier building, or was the tradition still so very much alive in the mid-twelfth century?

## Passenham ★

*30; 1 mile SW of Stony Stratford off A422*

A most remarkable church is ST GUTHLAC'S, serving a hamlet so tiny that it can scarcely be said to exist at all. It must have been built in the thirteenth century, but the original date is relatively unimportant; what counts at Passenham is the work done by Sir Robert Banastre in the 1620s. 'Bobby' Banastre was James I's Comptroller of the Household and Charles I's Court Victualler, a worthy enough figure, one would have thought; but the admirable guide to the church – one of the best I have seen – hints darkly at 'his reputed villainy, as reflected in local ghost stories'.

In the church, he concentrated on the chancel, endowing it with a most magnificent series of carved stalls, with elaborate crouching figures at the corners and misericords which must be among the last to be made before the Victorian Gothic Revival and could only, by that date, have been a deliberate archaism. Simultaneously he embarked on a scheme of interior decoration which has been carefully restored in the past few years, and provides a rare insight into the taste of the time. Around the chancel walls are painted full-length representations of prophets, Evangelists and saints, standing in niches with pretty shell apses behind them. The church guide suggests that they may be the work of J. de Crity, Sergeant Painter to the King, or even of Inigo Jones himself; but they have an Italianate look about them and seem to me to be more probably by some lesser Venetian or North Italian painter. Apart from any other considerations, religious painting had virtually died out in England since the Reformation; work of this kind – in a distinctly Renaissance, not to say humanist, style – was totally foreign to the English contemporary tradition and would, moreover, have smacked dangerously of recusancy. The whole conception is crowned with a beautiful sky-blue barrel roof, apparently supported on painted pilasters, representing the vault of heaven and sprinkled with golden stars.

The pulpit, though made up of Jacobean panels, is probably an addition of the late eighteenth century, as are the box pews and the west gallery on its four Ionic columns. The splendid frieze of mermaids, monsters and other assorted grotesques is taken from Sir Robert's now vanished chancel screen and bears his arms, with those of his third wife, Margaret Hopton. His own tomb is set into the wall of the chancel he adorned – at the expense, however, of poor St Mark, whose portrait it completely obliterates.

## Polebrook

*31; 1½ miles SE of Oundle off A605*

ALL SAINTS' CHURCH is rather marvellous, but distinctly odd. It is a very curious shape, to begin with: it actually looks longer from north to south than from east to west, and if the south transept were anything like as long as the north one the discrepancy would be greater still. The tower, too, is most unusually placed – in the south-west corner. You approach from the north side, and the first thing that strikes you is the quite spectacular north porch; it has two orders of columns, their capitals almost worn away, and three bands of dogtooth. The arch was obviously meant to be round, though the settlement of the building has thrown it sadly out of kilter; if, as Pevsner opines, it belongs to the mid-thirteenth century, one would have expected it to be pointed.

You enter, not here, but by the south door, to find a nave with two very different arcades – both Norman and round-arched, but with the arches on the south side almost twice the height of those on the north; they must be a little later – 1200, perhaps, with the north arcade *c.*1175. Above is a good timber roof with the crossed keys of St Peter carved on one of the tie-beams, probably a reference to the Abbey (now the Cathedral) of Peterborough, to which the church was granted in 1232. In fact this roof appears to be a seventeenth-century restoration, since the date 1636 is inscribed on one of the rafters; but the chancel roof is thought to be the original thirteenth-century one, with crowned heads carved not as bosses but in the centre of the moulded tie-beams. Of the transepts, the south one is short and stubby, with a three-light Decorated window as its most distinguished feature. That on the north however is – as we saw from

*Rockingham Castle.*

the outside – of very considerable size and importance. It must date from the time of the north arcade – 1175 or so – and is distinguished by its most elaborate blind arcading, extending over the entire length of the west wall and a good deal of the north one. It is copiously adorned with rosettes and fleurs-de-lis; once, too, there must have been carved heads at the meeting points of the deeply moulded arches – now all but two have gone. In the chancel there is more fine carving, including an ornate piscina with dogtooth and a curly quatrefoil in the spandrel between the two sub-arches. This must be mid-thirteenth-century, as is the lovely east window of three stepped lancets, the centre one only very slightly higher than its fellows, with colonnettes and multiple mouldings. The insides are deeply splayed.

The other furnishings are modest enough, though the fifteenth-century screen still has the remains of paintings on the north side of the dado. There are nice rough benches, too, but alas, all the glass is Victorian.

## Potterspury

*32; 5 miles SE of Towcester off A5*

The village itself is not prepossessing, but a mile and a half away to the west, in a splendid park with a 40-acre lake, stands WAKEFIELD LODGE, built in 1748–50 for the 2nd Duke of Grafton by William Kent. (A pleasing distant prospect can be obtained from the road which runs from the village past Wakefield Farm.) It is undeniably austere; Kent was an extrovert and exuberant interior decorator, but in architecture he always seems to have felt Lord Burlington's chilly eye watching over him. The general impression has been further spoilt by the later addition of an attic floor, which diminishes the effect of the towers and gives the building a degree of heaviness it can ill afford. But like Holkham Hall – which, on a smaller scale, it much resembles in spirit – it has about it a confident serenity that commands the attention. Admiration comes later.

The interior is dominated by the huge Saloon, occupying both main floors and surrounded by a balcony – the whole thing clearly inspired by Inigo Jones's Queen's House at Greenwich, and Kent's own work at Houghton twenty years before.

## Raunds

*33; $3\frac{1}{2}$ miles NE of Higham Ferrers off A605*

The west front of the west tower and spire of ST MARY'S CHURCH, seen from the bottom of the churchyard, seems quite extraordinarily busy. Trefoils, quatrefoils, lancets, blank arches, broaches, lucarnes – every open space seems to have represented a challenge to put in a new bit of decoration. For all that, the style is uncompromisingly Early English – though the beautiful spire is a rebuilding of 1826. Only inside the church do we emerge into Decorated, with the great six-light east window of perhaps 1280–90 marking the precise moment of transition between the two. This is one of the glories of Raunds. The other is the wall paintings – all of the fifteenth century and in remarkably good condition. The best are those in the spandrels of the north arcade (Pride and her Six Children, St Christopher, the Three Quick and the Three Dead) and over the chancel arch.

## Rockingham Castle

*34; 2 miles NW of Corby off A6003*

Originally built by William the Conqueror, Rockingham Castle stands on a strategic site commanding the valley of the Welland which has probably been fortified since Roman times. It remained a royal castle for nearly 500 years, and was particularly favoured by King John who, on his last journey north in 1216, left the massive iron chest which still stands in the Great Hall. Little if any of the original structure now remains; but the two sturdy semi-circular Gatehouse towers (apart from their nineteenth-century battlements) go back to the major reconstruction by John's grandson Edward I, as do the two doorways into the Hall.

Soon afterwards the castle fell into disrepair; it was little more than a ruin when, in 1553, one Edward Watson took it over on a lease from the Crown. His descendants are still living there. Watson at once set about converting the old castle into a comfortable (by Tudor standards) private residence. He divided the Great Hall horizontally into two, adding a west range including a Long Gallery – which, however, was completed only in 1631; his son carried on the good work as did his grandson, the 1st Lord Rockingham, ennobled by Charles I despite a rather ambiguous record in the Civil War.

After this there was no further serious building work till the nineteenth century, when Anthony Salvin was called in – first in 1839 and then again in 1851. His are the polygonal Flag Tower on the west front and the other, square, one at the extreme southern end. The house thus emerges, it must be admitted, as a fairly good hotchpotch; but because the successive builders tended to add to it rather than to alter what was already there, it still contains much to hold the interest and even to capture the imagination. It certainly captured that of Charles Dickens, who stayed there often and used it as a model for Chesney Wold in *Bleak House*.

ST LEONARD'S CHURCH nearby possesses some good monuments.

*The triangular conceit, Rushton Hall.*

## Rushton*

*35; 4 miles NW of Kettering off A6003*

This village was the home of the Tresham family from the early fifteenth century, and RUSHTON HALL – now belonging to the Royal National School for the Blind – preserves, at least externally, much of its Elizabethan and Jacobean splendour. But it is not for this that the village finds its way into these pages. What makes Rushton unforgettable is the tiny triangular CONCEIT of Sir Thomas Tresham, that high-fantastical sixteenth-century recusant whom we have already come across at Lyveden New Bield; but whereas at Lyveden he was intent on symbolising the Passion, here he produced, between 1594 and 1597, a joyful celebration of the Trinity. The ground plan is an equilateral triangle, each side 33⅓ feet long. There are three storeys, and each storey has three windows along each side. Much of the exterior decoration is composed of triangles and trefoils, and the rest is given over to elaborate religious symbolism far too intricate and profound to be explained here. (The official guide-book, by Sir Gyles Isham, is predictably a model of its kind and explores this symbolism in fascinating detail.) To us it all seems agreeably dotty; but it would not have seemed so to the Elizabethans, to whom rebuses, acrostics and puns were not simply jokes or parlour games but, on occasion, a form of secret language which could be endowed with profound spiritual significance. As Pevsner has pointed out, this extraordinary building is Tresham's profession, in stone, of a faith for which he had already spent fifteen years in confinement. It deserves to be taken seriously; then, and only then, will its secrets be revealed.

## Stanford*

*36; 7 miles NE of Rugby off B5414*

ST NICHOLAS'S CHURCH is not only a treasure in itself; it is also a treasure house of almost unbelievable richness. Architecturally, there is little of before 1300 and little more – except the pinnacles of the tower, which are rather heavy and graceless – later than *c.*1350. What we essentially have, therefore, is a spacious Decorated church built of the local stone – or stones, since the pink limestone and the rich brown ironstone are used apparently indiscriminately – set on a mound at the village crossroads. Some of the tracery is intersecting, some reticulated; a few windows have been restored, not always with the sensitivity for which one might have hoped; but the general impression is a delightful one and is somehow enhanced by the curious grassy bank which rises at the east end as high as the bottom of the five-light chancel window.

Now enter. There is so much to wonder at that you hardly know where to begin. You could start at the west end, with the pretty gallery on its Tuscan columns and the superb organ case of about 1600 which is said to have come from the Royal Chapel at Whitehall; or you could go straight to the chancel and choir and find sixteenth-century linenfold panelling of the highest quality, stalls and a misericord. You could even begin at the top, with the timber roof; its tie-beams are surmounted with tracery of their own, and the wall posts rest on

*Stoke Park, Stoke Bruerne.*

beautifully carved brackets. Your eye would then travel down the walls, past the huge and sumptuous hatchments, to the glass – and what glass it is! A good deal of it goes back to the early fourteenth century, and is thus contemporary with the church itself. It occupies nearly all the windows to the north and east. The majority of the glass on the south side belongs to the earlier or later sixteenth century, but is certainly not to be despised on that account. Nowhere in Northamptonshire will you find medieval glass to compare with this, in quantity or quality; though it is only fair to add that when I saw it a good deal of it was sorely in need of a clean.

And then there are the tombs – at least fifteen of which are worthy of more than a passing glance. My own favourite is that of Sir Thomas Cave, who died in 1558, and his wife, which has a lot of the original colour still surviving. The soles of her feet are particularly charming, surrounded as they are by the folds of her dress in cross-section. Beneath, their fourteen children kneel in piety. Nor should you miss the tomb of a later Sir Thomas, who died in 1613. As well as the eight of his offspring below there is a separate monument to his eldest son Richard – who died while a student at Padua – kneeling to one side under an arched canopy with obelisks; the two are joined by a scrolly inscription – a device I have never before seen used in this way. You can hardly avoid Felix Joubert's memorial to Edmund Verney of 1896; there are not many English parish churches which contain, in the north aisle, a full-size, full-dress statue of a grieving hussar. The helmet and gloves of the deceased – also in stone – have been reverently laid on the steps to the right.

When I visited Stanford in the summer of 1983 this wondrous church was being carefully and lovingly restored; by the time that these pages see the light of day it should be worth travelling a long way to visit.

## Stoke Bruerne

*37; 7 miles S of Northampton off A508*

It is, above all, the lovers of England's canals that go to Stoke Bruerne today – and quite right too, since just outside the village the Grand Junction Canal is carried up through seven locks, set so close together that they seem to form a gigantic aqueous staircase, before it disappears into a tunnel nearly 2 miles long. Here too is one of Europe's few canal museums – a delight to any connoisseur of the off-beat.

For an architecture book, however, STOKE PARK is what counts; for the house as originally built by Sir Francis Crane in 1629–35 was the first Palladian mansion in England. Colen Campbell, in *Vitruvius Britannicus*, states categorically that 'the Wings, and Colonnades, and all the Foundations' were by Inigo Jones. He adds that 'the Front of the House was designed by another Architect, the Civil Wars having also intervened', but this latter point is now only of academic interest, since the house itself was burnt down in 1886 and – after the relatively recent demolition of its pseudo-Jacobean successor – it is only the side pavilions (one was a Library, the other a Chapel) and the quadrant colonnades (possibly the first appearance in England of this Palladian device, derived from Palladio's pupil Vincenzo Scamozzi whom Jones had known in Italy) that survive today. They make a noble effect, not least because of the contrast between the creamy limestone of the walls and the rich brown ironstone of the giant Ionic pilasters and window surrounds. Perhaps they seem a little tall for their horizontal dimensions, but they were intended as parts of a large composition which would doubtless have redressed the balance. Anyway, it seems churlish to cavil at buildings as lovely as these – particularly when one remembers the great tradition which they heralded, nearly 100 years before their time.

## Titchmarsh

*38; 1½ miles NE of Thrapston off A605*

Occasionally spelt without its second 't', Titchmarsh stands on a little rise half a mile or so to the east of the Oundle–Thrapston road. Even from that distance one can see that its church tower is something special. Approaching nearer, one quickly realises that it is more than that: ST MARY THE VIRGIN has been described as possessing the finest parish church tower in England outside Somerset, and that is exactly what it is – a tower to be mentioned in the same breath as those of Batcombe, Evercreech or Huish Episcopi, utterly different in style as well as in quality from even the most distinguished of the Northamptonshire towers, relying as they do on the grace of their spires for effect.

Titchmarsh church has no spire, but a forest of pinnacles, not only at the four corners but also halfway along each side (where they are set diagonally and slightly smaller); and, as if this were not enough, additional little crocketed ogival crests at the quarter and three-quarter points. Below this run two friezes of a lozenge design, one above the top string-course and one below it; next, the bell openings, transomed two-light windows set in pairs, two to a side. On the next stage down, after another frieze, there is a single similar window, blank this time, between canopied niches. Another frieze of quatrefoils separates this stage from the one below, which contains a big double-transomed three-lighter and two more flanking niches; then, finally, comes the bottom stage, with a most magnificent west door with more niches again and big quatrefoils in the spandrels. Three more friezes surround the base. Pevsner bewails the fact that we do not know who paid for this glorious tower or when it was built; there is, however, in existence the will of one Thomas Gryndall, bequeathing money for the purpose in 1474. The crown may be a decade later.

*The church of St Mary the Virgin, Titchmarsh.*

The interior contains a few surprises, notably – in a church whose exterior shows little sign of any work earlier than the late fourteenth century – a reset Norman door in the chancel. The north arcade is almost copybook Early English, the south Decorated with an outsize leaf motif on the two central piers. The tower arch soars skyward and has battlemented capitals to its responds. There is a timber roof with crenellated tie-beams on arched braces, and pretty foil decoration above the latter and also between the beams and the roof above. The chancel is ceiled, but predominantly Victorian, with wall paintings by a former rector's sister-in-law. In the north transept a bust of John Dryden surmounts a wall memorial to his parents.

## Wellingborough*

*39; 10 miles NE of Northampton on A45*

There is only one word to be spoken on entering ST MARY'S, Knox Road, for the first time: *WOW*! Sir Ninian Comper was working on it from 1908 intermittently until his death in 1960, and his son has continued it since; he was a great church architect, but he never did anything better than this. Here, in a rather dingy residential area and a street that could not be more inappropriately named if it tried, is one man's visionary synthesis of all that is brightest and most beautiful in all the churches he has ever seen, regardless of style or period. 'Unity through inclusion' he called it – and he was right. The roof is terrific – a jungle of plaster lierne vaulting, with bosses by the thousand exploding all over it and long slender pendants, like parachutes descending in the middle of a firework display. The painting and gilding is still unfinished – only three bays out of eight when I was there – but already one is dazzled by the sheer effulgence of blue and gold. The rood-screen in particular, in which the rood itself seems merely to point the way to a tremendous Christ in Majesty above, is one of the great triumphal visions of our century; even Coventry, despite its scale, cannot approach it. The same spirit blazes from the high altar, with its huge *baldacchino* and the banner-bearing figure of the Resurrected Christ. Nowhere, indeed, in the whole building will you find anything tentative. All is confidence and conviction, the work of a man who was not afraid to take one gigantic breath of all he knew about architecture and all he felt about God, and let it all out together in one great bellow of praise. Would that there were more like him.

## Whiston

*40; 6 miles E of Northampton off A428*

ST MARY'S CHURCH is set high on a hill, and is accessible only on foot. Its key, however, is kept in the village below, so make sure you get it first and take it up with you. After five minutes or so of steepish climb, your first reward is a close-up view of the immensely grand west tower, orange ironstone nicely played off against the pale grey ashlar, with a wealth of rich detailing and an obvious perfection of craftsmanship that suggests immediately that this is no ordinary village church. Look carefully, for example, at the gargoyles; and how often does one see battlements that are not just moulded round the edges but have traceried panels set into them?

The same feeling persists when you go inside. There you realise something else. This church was built all of a piece, in a single generation at the start of the sixteenth century, and has scarcely been touched since. It was raised, we now know, by one man – Sir Anthony Catesby – with his wife and son. (An eighteenth-century local historian, J. Bridges, records that there was once an inscription in the glass to this effect, giving the completion date of 1532 – a year also mentioned on the tomb of Sir Anthony's descendant, Thomas Catesby, on the wall of the sanctuary.) The carving that was so much a feature of the tower is continued splendidly within – in the spandrels of the arcades and the stops between the arches – and there are lovely angel corbels supporting the wooden roof which, incidentally, is of uniform height, nave and aisles. All the main beams are carved and moulded.

When I visited the church in January 1979 there appeared to be no electricity; the benches had high sconces with real candles, half-used, stuck in them. Evensong, in winter at any rate, is presumably held by candlelight, and very beautiful it must be.

## Wicken

*41; 3 miles SW of Stony Stratford off A422*

We may find it difficult to take the CHURCH OF ST JOHN THE EVANGELIST entirely seriously; but it is none the worse for that. The west tower is the relic of an earlier, Jacobean, structure; but everything else is the work of that highly enjoyable country squire and amateur architect Thomas Prowse, in gay Strawberry Hill Gothick. It was built between 1758 and 1767. Prowse was a close friend of Sanderson Miller (whom he helped with designs for Hagley Hall), but his exuberance went further than Miller's ever did. The chancel is a mad explosion of false fan vaulting in plaster, with pendants, the vaults springing straight up from corbels with no supporting shafts. Nave and aisles are tunnel- and groin-vaulted – the latter in quite a complicated way, the vaults here springing from half columns in pairs. Clearly Prowse was experimenting; equally clearly, particularly in the chancel, he was having fun. This is not great architecture, any more than Strawberry Hill; but how much poorer we should all be without it.

*St Mary's Church, Whiston.*

## Short List

### Cotterstock

*42; 1½ miles N of Oundle off A605*

ST ANDREW'S CHURCH would get a full listing were it not for the horrid scraping of its interior, which has largely destroyed its charm. This is a tragedy, since it has much to recommend it: the south porch, for example – embattled, with a gable crowned by monsters and splendid gargoyles to each side; or the vast Decorated chancel with its marvellous five-light east window. The church is beautifully situated, too, looking down over the water-meadows of the Nene. Of several fine houses in the village, the best is COTTERSTOCK HALL: basically Jacobean, but remodelled in 1658 and with a tall Victorian extension at the back containing what is now the principal staircase.

### Gayton

*43; 6 miles SW of Northampton off A43*

The MANOR HOUSE is a most remarkable building, *c.*1540, conceived on the plan of a Greek cross. It has three storeys, including the gables. The entrance gives directly on to the Hall, from which a short stair leads to a solar and small minstrels' gallery. There is one completely panelled room, with most of the panelling original. Upstairs, the staircase well and three other rooms radiate off an inner, windowless, room, formerly – on the evidence of two wooden columns now partly hidden by the later wall – part of the room opposite the stairs.

### Hannington

*44; 7½ miles NE of Northampton off A43*

ST PETER AND ST PAUL is that *rarissima avis*, a thirteenth-century church with two naves. In a small village church like this one, what it means in practice is that instead of having the two parallel arcades one would normally expect, it has one, marching straight down the middle. The effect is distinctly unsettling, rather like having a classical portico with an odd number of columns. It also presents the problem about what you actually do with the arcade when it reaches the chancel arch; at Hannington, about three-quarters of the way along the third bay, it simply disappears into the wall above. There follows a conspicuously narrower chancel, with windows of interesting tracery – early Decorated, perhaps 1280 or thereabouts. The pulpit, pretty if slightly battered, has openwork panels made, it appears, from a hollowed out tree-trunk; the screen over the west door seems to be a companion piece.

### Lilford Hall

*45; 5 miles NE of Thrapston off A605*

The house must have been spectacular in its day, and still makes a fine show when seen across the park. Alas, the owner lives abroad, and the place is now empty and semi-derelict. The nine-bay bow-windowed front is of 1635 or so, but the memorable row of thirteen chimneys connected by arches is a later addition of 1711. Inside there is said to be a fine Entrance Hall and staircase by Flitcroft, who also designed the stables; but I was unable to get in to see them. The village no longer exists, having been demolished in 1755 when the park was enlarged; subsequently the church was pulled down as well.

### Oundle

*46; 8 miles NE of Thrapston on A605*

One of the most delightful small towns in the county, it achieves its effect less because of the quality of any individual building than because of the extraordinary impression of unity it gives – largely because, like Bath, the same beautiful stone has been used throughout. In the centre on a little hill stands ST PETER'S CHURCH, its churchyard surrounding it, gravestones lurching in all directions in most agreeable disorder. It has a wonderfully tall and slender lucarned spire, but the interior is horribly scraped and generally disappointing. The SCHOOL does not intrude; its buildings are largely Victorian, by A.C. Blomfield.

### Rothwell

*47; 3 miles NW of Kettering on A6*

HOLY TRINITY CHURCH stands like a cathedral above the little town, approached by what seems almost like a processional way. It is built of the local tawny ironstone (the colour of the interior is quite marvellous on a sunny day) and is mostly of the thirteenth century, though the clerestory (which extends to the chancel where there is even an embryonic triforium) is of the fifteenth. There is a charnel house under the south aisle with a splendid array of skulls and bones. The MARKET HOUSE of 1578 was the gift to the town of Sir Thomas Tresham of Rushton and Lyveden (*qq.v.*), though it was not completed till 1895.

### Southwick Hall

*48; 3 miles NW of Oundle*

A pretty little limestone village, Southwick is dominated by the Hall, the south-west corner of which goes back to the early fourteenth century; most of it is, however, Elizabethan. It has been altered and added to in the sixteenth, eighteenth and, alas, the nineteenth centuries, though as all the remodelling has been done in the same local stone and with the same Collyweston slates the various periods blend harmoniously enough. There is a nice vaulted crypt, now the Entrance Hall, and a fine oak-panelled bedroom upstairs.

### Warmington

*49; 3 miles NE of Oundle off A605*

The exterior of ST MARY'S CHURCH is beautiful indeed apart from its broach spire, whose oddly projecting lucarnes make it look unpleasantly knobbly. For the rest, the Early English tower, nave and aisles could hardly be better. If only the interior had kept up the standard: alas, the dark, stained roof – vaulted, most unusually, in timber, though now largely Victorian – gives no pleasure, while the red-tiled floor is nastier still; it comes as a relief to find the old stones still *in situ* in the chancel. Screen and pulpit are both tragically over-restored, and the benches are as boring as can be. Gaze reverently at this church from a distance; don't go in.

# Oxfordshire

Essentially, Oxfordshire is a wide, flat plain, some 30 miles across, forming the bed of the Thames Valley. It is bounded on the east by the Chilterns, which are of chalk, and on the west by the Cotswolds, which are of stone. In the north-west, near Banbury, it meets the Midland ironstone belt; in the south, having acquired a large area of Berkshire as a result of the iniquitous redrawing of the county boundaries that took effect from 1974, it now extends as far as Wantage and the Berkshire Downs, where the chalk reappears. The heart of the county, being predominantly of clay, has scarcely any good building stone; here the houses have consequently tended to be of brick or silver-grey flint, or – until the eighteenth century – were timber-framed, except when there was enough money available (as for the building of the Oxford colleges) to bring the stone in from outside.

As a result of all this Oxfordshire is unusually varied in both its landscape and its architecture, and there is no characteristic building style for the county as a whole. All we can say by way of generalisation is that for the past 500 years at least it has been consistently prosperous. This prosperity began in the late Middle Ages with the growth of the wool industry, and accounts for the number of splendid Decorated and Perpendicular churches. In the seventeenth century, being easily reached by river from London, it became a favourite region for country house building and has remained so till modern times. There has also been the continued influence of the University, which for some twenty-five generations has attracted rich young men from every corner of the land, implanting in them a lifelong affection for the city and its surroundings, to the advantage of all concerned.

For all these reasons, the later medieval churches of Oxfordshire far outnumber the earlier. There is the Saxon work of Langford and North Leigh, and the quite magnificent Norman west front of Iffley; as for Early English, Witney is about the best, though it was much remodelled in the fourteenth century. From about 1300 on, however, things begin to look up: Dorchester Abbey alone would provide enough material for a whole book on the development of the Decorated, but there are plenty of other churches too – Adderbury, Bloxham and Ducklington for a start – to demonstrate the genius of the local masons at the moment when Oxfordshire architecture and stone carving reached its highest peak of virtuosity. Adderbury, with its stunning early fifteenth-century chancel, is also one of the most remarkable showpieces of the Perpendicular, as are the nave at Chipping Norton, the porch at Burford, and the chapels at North Leigh and Stanton Harcourt. But these, admittedly, are parts of churches rather than churches themselves; for a single, all-of-a-piece epitome of the later Middle Ages you must go to Ewelme – just as, if you want to feel yourself back in the seventeenth century, you must go and sit for an hour or so in Rycote.

As for country houses, there are so many to choose from that the final selection has been a nightmare. Blenheim is indubitably the grandest, Broughton surely the most beautiful, Chastleton and Beckley the most unspoilt – for as long as the proposed M40 extension can be held at bay. For the rest, one remembers the old, monastic, wing of Thame, the Palladian splendour of Nuneham, the mellow tranquillity of Greys Court, the sublime elegance of Ditchley. But that is only the barest beginning – we have scarcely touched on the Victorians or even on the many beautiful small towns and villages which have somehow managed to preserve their integrity, or most of it, through the age of the motor car. Still, the buildings described on the following pages should at least serve to whet the appetite; from then on, it will be up to you.

## Abingdon

*1; 6½ miles SW of Oxford off A415*

The pride of this pretty old town on the banks of the Thames is the COUNTY HALL, occupying the centre of the Market Place. In the seventeenth century Celia Fiennes called it the finest town hall in England, and there is no doubt that of all the free-standing town or county halls in the country built over open arcades, Abingdon's is the grandest and most distinguished. The builder is known to have been Christopher Kempster of Burford, one of Wren's most trusted master masons, who was to go on to build Tom Tower at Christ Church, Oxford, and later spent almost fifteen years working on the dome of St Paul's. Whether or not the design was actually his we do not know; it certainly shows strong Wren influence.

Abingdon's beginning was in the little cluster of houses that grew up at the gates of the great abbey on the Thames – a huge and venerable foundation, established in 675, which dominated the town for eight and a half centuries until the Dissolution. Little of it now remains, except for the late fifteenth-century gateway of three vaulted bays next to the church of St Nicholas (which was itself never part of the abbey) and a range of buildings along the river. At the west end, next to the Custodian's House, is the CHEQUER, a massive square building of the thirteenth century – though the two-light Decorated windows are obviously later – with an extraordinary tall chimney, unique in England, culminating in three tiny stepped lancets, under a gable, for the smoke to come out. The stone-canopied fireplace where the smoke began its journey is also remarkable, though sadly damaged. Beyond the Chequer runs a Long Gallery, *c.*1500; originally divided by partition walls into several small rooms, it is now a single unit magnificently roofed in timber with tie-beams and crownposts.

*The County Hall, Abingdon.*

Of Abingdon's two medieval churches, ST NICHOLAS'S has a curious and not entirely satisfactory west front. At ground level there is a late Norman doorway, flanked by two blind arches. Above this and slightly to the left is a single Early English lancet, the first of what was once a row of five. The frame of the second can be seen beginning, but at that point the line was broken and replaced in the fifteenth century with an enormous Perpendicular window. This is once again off-centre in relation to the Norman work below, but forms a new axis for the tower, which was built at about the same time. The north side of the church has retained rather more of its Norman character; on the south, everything is Perpendicular except for two Decorated windows which seem to have slipped in by mistake. The whole thing is, in fact, a bit of a mish-mash, nor is it particularly redeemed by the interior.

With ST HELEN'S, however, the situation improves. Here the oldest part is the Early English tower at the north-east corner – note the lovely triple doorway on the north side – supporting the fifteenth-century spire that is such a feature of the Abingdon skyline. This tower, and a section of the east wall, were the only parts of the original church that were left when, probably around 1380, the people of Abingdon decided to build themselves a new church, grander and more spacious. Work went on for the best part of a century and a half, until by 1539 – just about the time when the demolition gangs were moving into the old abbey – the job was done: the result was an enormously broad church, considerably broader indeed than it is long, with the central nave flanked by two aisles on each side. These unusual proportions do not enhance its beauty, and the heavy hands of Victorian restorers have not helped either; but St Helen's possesses one outstanding feature for which much must be forgiven: the superb painted roof of the inner north aisle. It takes the form of a huge Tree of Jesse, reaching its climax at the east end of the north side with the Crucifixion. The date is about 1390. A sensitive restoration in the 1930s did nothing but good.

Leaving St Helen's, make a point of visiting the churchyard, which is bounded by no fewer than three sets of ALMSHOUSES. Those to the left form a fine range of chequered brick, with pedimented gable, of 1718; in the centre are the CHRIST'S HOSPITAL ALMSHOUSES which date back to 1446, though the exterior has obviously been altered since. Finally, to the right, are the TWITTY ALMSHOUSES of 1707, again in brick, but this time with a hipped roof and a lantern.

There are plenty of good houses still standing in Abingdon, in all the streets that converge on the Market Place. If only something could be done about the traffic! If ever there was a case for pedestrianisation, this is it.

## Adderbury

*2; 3 miles SE of Banbury off A423*

ST MARY'S is a beautiful church crowning a beautiful village, both of dark golden ironstone. It was begun in the thirteenth century, as can be seen clearly enough from the blocked-up windows in the east walls of the transepts; but around 1300 it was remodelled and considerably enlarged, and most of what we see today is Decorated, apart from the Perpendicular chancel (best appreciated from the outside) which was added in 1408–19 by Richard Winchcombe, the master mason who was later partly responsible for the Divinity School at Oxford.

Apart from the splendour of its proportions and the variety of fine tracery in the aisle windows, the great joy of Adderbury is its sculptured decoration. The carving around the parapet of the west tower – which is almost, if not quite, as good as that of nearby Bloxham – is too high to be seen properly without binoculars; but that along the aisle cornices is within easy range and can consequently be enjoyed to the full. The south side has some amusing grotesques, but the north is even better – with musicians, monsters, archers, twin-tailed mermaids and a host of other conceits, all of the early fourteenth century. Fifty years or so later, all this exuberance was gone; by the time Perpendicular began towards the end of the century the stone carvers had become staid and sophisticated. Adderbury marks, as memorably as anywhere in the country, the final phase of that blessed period when they still had a sense of fun.

The interior is a disappointment. Three separate nineteenth-century restorations are more than any building should be allowed to undergo, and despite several fine details which have somehow survived – the carved capitals in the transverse arcades of the transepts, for example – most of what we see is the work of J.C. Buckler (1831–4) or, later in the century, George Gilbert Scott or his son John Oldrid. The timber roof is fourteenth-century, but the sad scraped walls supporting it tell their story all too clearly and create an atmosphere of gloom which only a return to that glorious exterior can properly dispel.

## Ashdown House*

*NT; 3; 3½ miles NW of Lambourn on B4000*

The distant prospect of Ashdown House, set in its little downland park just off the road between Ashbury and Lambourn, is one of the most delightful architectural surprises in Oxfordshire. Almost automatically, one stops the car for a longer, closer look. Here is the perfect Dutch doll's house, miraculously transported from the Netherlands to the rolling English countryside. Though its three storeys and five close-set bays make the centre of the building an almost perfect cube, its half-hidden basement and steeply hipped roof with three neat dormers and octagonal cupola give it a height considerably greater than its breadth; but this only adds to its charm, and the two flanking pavilions, each of a single storey – though with still steeper roofs and taller chimneys – provide a degree of horizontality without detracting from the quirkish character of the house itself.

Ashdown was completed in about 1665 for William, 1st Earl of Craven. He had intended it for the love of his life, Elizabeth, Queen of Bohemia, the sister of Charles I, who has gone down in history as the Winter Queen. Alas, she never lived to enjoy it; she died in 1662, in Lord Craven's London house. But her portrait and Craven's, both by Honthorst, hang (among many others of members of their two families) in the Hall.

*The aisle windows of St Mary's Church, Adderbury.*

This association with the exiled Queen gives us a clue to the architect of Ashdown. There can be no certainty, but the most likely candidate seems to be William Winde, whom we know to have served as Elizabeth's Gentleman Usher for the last year of her life. We know, too, that Winde did much other work for Craven, notably at Hamstead Marshall, only 17 miles away, where he took over the works on the death of Sir Balthazar Gerbier (this house was burnt to the ground in 1718), and twenty years later at Craven's other house, Combe Abbey in Warwickshire, which he was largely to remodel. The principal objection to this attribution is that Winde – though the precise date of his birth is unknown – could scarcely have been out of his twenties when Ashdown was built; but this seems hardly conclusive. On the other hand, the fact that he spent his formative years in Holland – with the colony of English Royalists in voluntary exile from the Commonwealth – could well explain the Dutch appearance of what would have been his first major work of architecture.

The interior is, it must be admitted, disappointing, and Ashdown earns its star for its exterior only. Most of the rooms have lost their seventeenth-century character and there is no original furniture. The most interesting feature is the massive staircase which occupies one complete quarter of the plan and rises magnificently the whole height of the house. For the rest, one can be content to look at Ashdown from the outside – a beautiful, melancholy monument to the Queen it never saw.

## Beckley Park*

*4; 5 miles NE of Oxford off B4027*

The Black Prince kept his horses in Beckley Park, and Richard, Duke of Cornwall – King John's son, who was the only Englishman ever to be elected Holy Roman Emperor – built a hunting lodge there, which he surrounded with a triple ring of moats. That lodge has gone (though the moats essentially survive) and was replaced, probably in the 1560s, by another – of diapered brick with stone dressings. Architecturally, its three-storey façade is handsome without being in any way exceptional; while the back, with its three tower-like gabled projections rising the whole height of the house – the central one containing a wooden newel staircase, the outer two simple garderobes – is more dramatic than beautiful. What puts Beckley in a class by itself is the extraordinary way in which the centuries have passed it by. Some of the original work has gone, notably a bay window over the porch, the original chimneys and perhaps some of the panelling; but virtually nothing has been added, at least since Jacobean times. The oak staircase remains as it was the day it was made; the original floorboards are still in place, together with all the stone fireplaces, all the windows (two with their original lead glazing and even some of the glass) and most of the doors.

But Beckley is not just an astonishing historical survival; it is a house of mystery and magic. Its atmosphere is overwhelming, and further strengthened by the loneliness of its setting, looking out over the low, flat, desolate fields of Otmoor. Alas, at the time of writing there are plans afoot for a new motorway which threatens to come within a few hundred yards of the house. If it is allowed to do so, it will destroy something unique and irreplaceable.

## Blenheim Palace*

*5; 8 miles NW of Oxford on A34*

In all English history, no single man ever received greater material reward for his services to the state than John Churchill, 1st Duke of Marlborough. Those services were indeed considerable: at the battle of Blenheim in August 1704 he had administered the first serious check to the grand schemes of Louis XIV for European supremacy, and he was to follow it with a whole series of splendid victories over the next six years, while his great palace was already beginning to take shape just outside the little town of Woodstock. The reward, however, was unparalleled; for the building upon which Queen Anne had resolved – with the consent of Parliament – and of which she personally approved the plans and a scale model in June 1705, was to be not simply a worthy residence for a triumphant general; it was to be a national monument to the glory of her own reign, a royal palace in everything but name, England's answer to Versailles. Fortunately for posterity, this decision was taken at the moment when the Baroque – of all architectural styles, the one most suited to the expression of worldly magnificence – had reached its apogee; fortunately, too, there was ready at hand the most inspired exponent of that same style, a successful playwright who, though already forty years old, had turned his mind seriously to architecture only five years before – John Vanbrugh.

The story of the building of Blenheim – of the Marlboroughs' fall from favour in 1710 and their self-imposed exile two years later, of the cutting-off of government funds, of the resumption of work at the Duke's own expense in 1716, of the worsening relations between Vanbrugh and the Duchess, leading to the architect's resignation in protest at his 'intolerable treatment' – is too long (and too painful) to be told in

*Beckley Park.*

*Blenheim Palace.*

detail here. Everyone was made miserable. Vanbrugh agonised over the soaring costs, wishing he had never left the theatre, and struggled to maintain his sanity while dealing with the most impossible woman in England: the Duchess, who by her own admission 'mortally hated all gardens and architecture', and would infinitely have preferred a medium-sized house by Wren. Most pathetic of all was Marlborough himself, who was largely incapacitated by a stroke in 1716 and spent the last six years of his life wandering disconsolately through his huge and still unfinished palace, occasionally stopping before his youthful portrait by Kneller and murmuring, 'This was once a man.' In the year of the Duke's death Nicholas Hawksmoor, who had been Vanbrugh's assistant and had resigned with him, returned to finish the work; but when Vanbrugh himself visited Blenheim with Lord Carlisle in 1725 he was refused admission.

In the circumstances, it seems little short of a miracle that Blenheim turned out as well as it did. The setting, first of all, is superb. What we see now is largely the work of Capability Brown, who in 1764–74 enlarged the little River Glyme into a great ornamental lake and replanted the surrounding parkland. He was in fact completing the work that Vanbrugh had begun; in doing so, however, he raised the water level by 15 feet, deliberately submerging the lower storey of the Grand Bridge, which his predecessor had designed not only to bring the formal approach road across the river, but also to serve as a banqueting house – it possessed several inner rooms – during the summer months. This submersion is not, on the whole, to be regretted; the bridge as designed was obviously far too ponderous for the modest little stream beneath, and had already attracted the none-too-gentle mockery of both Alexander Pope and Horace Walpole. Moreover the top half of the structure that remains above the water somehow harmonises remarkably well with the Claude-like surroundings; and few people seeing it for the first time would ever guess what had happened, or what lies beneath.

And so to the palace itself. From a distance, it looks more like a declaration of war, with that extraordinary roof line bristling with turrets and look-outs; and the impression is strengthened by the East Gate, which is flanked by bastions resting on cannonballs. One almost expects a drawbridge and portcullis. But pass on into the Great Court – and immediately the mood changes. The castle is a castle no longer. The turrets and look-outs are revealed for what they are – curious temple-like excrescences, arcaded on all four sides, which crown the four corner towers and are themselves surmounted with tall pinnacles like gigantic chessmen, capped with ducal coronets. Before you is the great central portico, its pediment barely able to contain the Marlborough coat of arms, the colonnade a subtle combination of round columns, square columns and angle pilasters. Above and behind it are the two corners of a broken pediment and, behind these again, what looks like yet another pediment but is in fact little more than the gable of the clerestoried Great Hall. The centre block extends for three bays on each side of the portico, two storeys above a basement as is normal throughout the palace; then come two concave quadrant arcades, leading the eye round to the front towers, from which straight arcades run back to the point where the two huge side courts lead off to left and right towards the kitchens and the stables respectively. The gates to these two side courts, beneath the clock towers, are crowned with carvings by Grinling Gibbons in which the Lion of England grasps, with obviously evil intent, the Cock of France between his claws. The whole composition is intensely dramatic: Vanbrugh's years in the theatre were not spent in vain.

The south elevation, looking towards the garden, is a good deal simpler: a portico similar to that on the north carries, instead of a pediment, a straight entablature, above which stands a colossal bust of Louis XIV, which Marlborough took from the city gate of Tournai and set above his house, as he put it, 'like a head on a stake'. There is a corresponding central block of nine bays, but the links to the corner towers are straight and not curved, since here there is no courtyard to enclose.

The principal state rooms of Blenheim are laid out in the form of a T, with the Great Hall, 67 feet high, running longitudinally away from the front door to join the Saloon at the centre of the south front; from this three sumptuous rooms extend on each side towards the towers. The Hall is awe-inspiring, not only for its height but for the immense proscenium arch which frames the entrance to the Saloon, crowned by the Arms of Queen Anne and supported by pairs of fluted Corinthian columns with side pilasters. A two-storeyed stone arcade runs along each side, and the ceiling is occupied by an immense painting by Sir James Thornhill, in which Marlborough shows Britannia a map of the battle of Blenheim – explaining to her, presumably, how he won it.

Vanbrugh had apparently intended Thornhill to paint the Saloon as well, but after his resignation the Duchess decided that Sir James was too expensive at 25 shillings a yard, and hired Louis Laguerre instead. He has completely covered the ceiling and walls, stopping only for Hawksmoor's great doorcases in white marble. (The double-headed eagles above the doors are those of the Holy Roman Empire, of which Marlborough was a Prince.) The general effect is superb – considerably better, one suspects, than Thornhill could have done.

The three rooms leading off to the east of the Saloon – the Green and Red Drawing Rooms and the Green Writing Room – have Hawksmoor ceilings and some glorious portraits. (Of the two contrasting groups in the Red Drawing Room, depicting the 4th and 9th Dukes and their families, by Reynolds and Sargent respectively, my own feeling is that Sargent wins hands down.) The Green Writing Room also has a stunning tapestry of the battle of Blenheim. The three corresponding rooms to the west, all with further fine tapestries, are decorated in the French style, with gilded *boiseries* brought over from Paris in the 1890s. The second and third have the original fireplaces in purple and white marble, carved by Grinling Gibbons; and very nasty they are too.

The last of these great rooms is the Long Library, which runs the full length of the west front, swelling out halfway down into a semi-circular bow. Vanbrugh intended it as a picture gallery and planned a ceiling by Thornhill; in fact, the room remained undecorated until after the 1st Duke's death in 1722, when the work was taken over by Hawksmoor. He engaged Isaac Mansfield to do the plasterwork, left the ceiling unpainted, and himself planned a staggeringly virtuoso treatment of the walls and ceilings that makes the room, with the Great Hall, the most architecturally interesting in the house. It is divided into five sections (each of three bays except the centre, which contains the bow and is of five) with walls in each section breaking forward or receding. The two outermost bays are set apart by Hawksmoor's characteristic flattened arches, coffered on the inside; each has a gallery, clerestory and dome, also coffered most elaborately. At one end there is an organ, installed in 1891 by the 8th Duke and his American wife – the first of three successive American Duchesses.

Finally we come to the Chapel, in the south-east corner of the Stable Court. This, once again, is a Hawksmoor creation, and with its great arches, pilasters and plasterwork speaks much the same language as the Library. Against the north wall (the Chapel is liturgically back to front) stands the tremendous tomb of the 1st Duke and his Duchess, designed by William Kent and carved by Rysbrack – life-size figures in white marble of the ducal pair with their two sons (both of whom died young) and, at a lower level, flanking the sarcophagus, History and Fame. Envy wriggles underneath, trapped by the weight of the sarcophagus. Pevsner finds it stodgy; I don't.

There are formal gardens, laid out early this century by the 9th Duke, on each side of the palace – a parterre on the east and, on the west, the Water Terrace Gardens on two levels, the lower one containing a small-scale copy of Bernini's famous fountain in the Piazza Navona in Rome. It was in the park here, in the Temple of Diana, that Mr Winston Churchill proposed to Miss Clementine Hozier. In its ensemble, Blenheim is unique: certainly the most palatial house in England. 'We' – that is, the Royal Family – 'have nothing to equal this,' said George III. He was right.

## Bletchingdon Park

*6; 7½ miles N of Oxford on B4027*

Although theoretically Bletchingdon Park was only remodelled by James Lewis in 1782, the result is so characteristic of both the period and the architect that we can consider it a complete rebuilding. Like Eydon in Northamptonshire (*q.v.*), it is a Palladian villa with neoclassical overtones, almost as near to Nash or S.P. Cockerell as to Lord Burlington. Part of the lightness, as at Eydon, comes from Lewis's use of delicate wrought-iron railings instead of stone balustrading; these (renewed) are particularly effective around the front portico, with its big semi-circular flight of steps. The basement floor has round-headed windows with Gibbs surrounds – orthodox enough, but perhaps a little exaggerated here? Another feature, odder but more successful, is the way in which important windows are set into arched recesses with flanking pilasters.

Now a school for English studies, the interior has lost some of its ancient elegance. Decoration is *à la* Adam – though not all of it is original – and there is some good plasterwork; also a particularly fine staircase, lit from above through a glass dome. Outside in the garden there stands the only Ionic dog kennel I know, with a pedimented portico.

## Bloxham ★

*7; 2½ miles SW of Banbury on A361*

Long before you reach Bloxham, the distant prospect of tower and spire tells you, more clearly than any words could do, that you are approaching a very special church indeed. ST MARY'S is set majestically on a hill above the pretty ironstone village, from which that most graceful of Oxfordshire spires soars another 200 feet into the sky, springing from a beautifully proportioned fourteenth-century tower with four clustering pinnacles and a little stone gallery of admirable workmanship (binoculars recommended).

Though most of the building is of the fourteenth and fifteenth centuries, it was built on the site of a twelfth-century church, of which various pieces remain and have been re-used. This can be clearly seen from the vaulted, two-storey south porch, where the old Norman doorway was remoulded in 1340 or so – producing that always curious phenomenon of a pointed arch with bands of zigzag, the use of two different stones giving it a polychrome effect. And there is also some thirteenth-century work – notably the nave arcades, very grand with their four bays of double-chamfered arches leading down a fine perspective to the high chancel arch and a wealth of carving behind.

Carving: once you have got used to the sheer scale of everything, this is the next thing that impresses, for there are carvings wherever you look – on the corbels, on the label stops, on the arcade piers (stiff-leaf on a column in the south, portrait heads on one in the north). And on the outside too: don't miss the corbel table along the north wall – where, incidentally, the windows have much fantastic Decorated tracery – nor the Last Judgement (of about 1350) over the west doorway.

The great west window actually manages to combine carved figures in its tracery; and on the south side of the church there was added, early in the fifteenth century, a noble chapel in the Perpendicular style with yet more elaborate fenestration, including one window of seven lights and two others of five. Within it are several monuments to the Thornycroft family, including a particularly enjoyable statue of Sir John, portrayed in all his youthful vigour although he died at sixty-six.

This noble building did not altogether escape Victorian restoration – by G.E. Street – but the damage done was far less than might have been expected. And the east window, by Burne-Jones, Morris and Philip Webb (who was responsible for the *art nouveau* sky), if not altogether appropriate in this particular setting, is in itself a considerable work of art.

St Mary's Church, Bloxham.

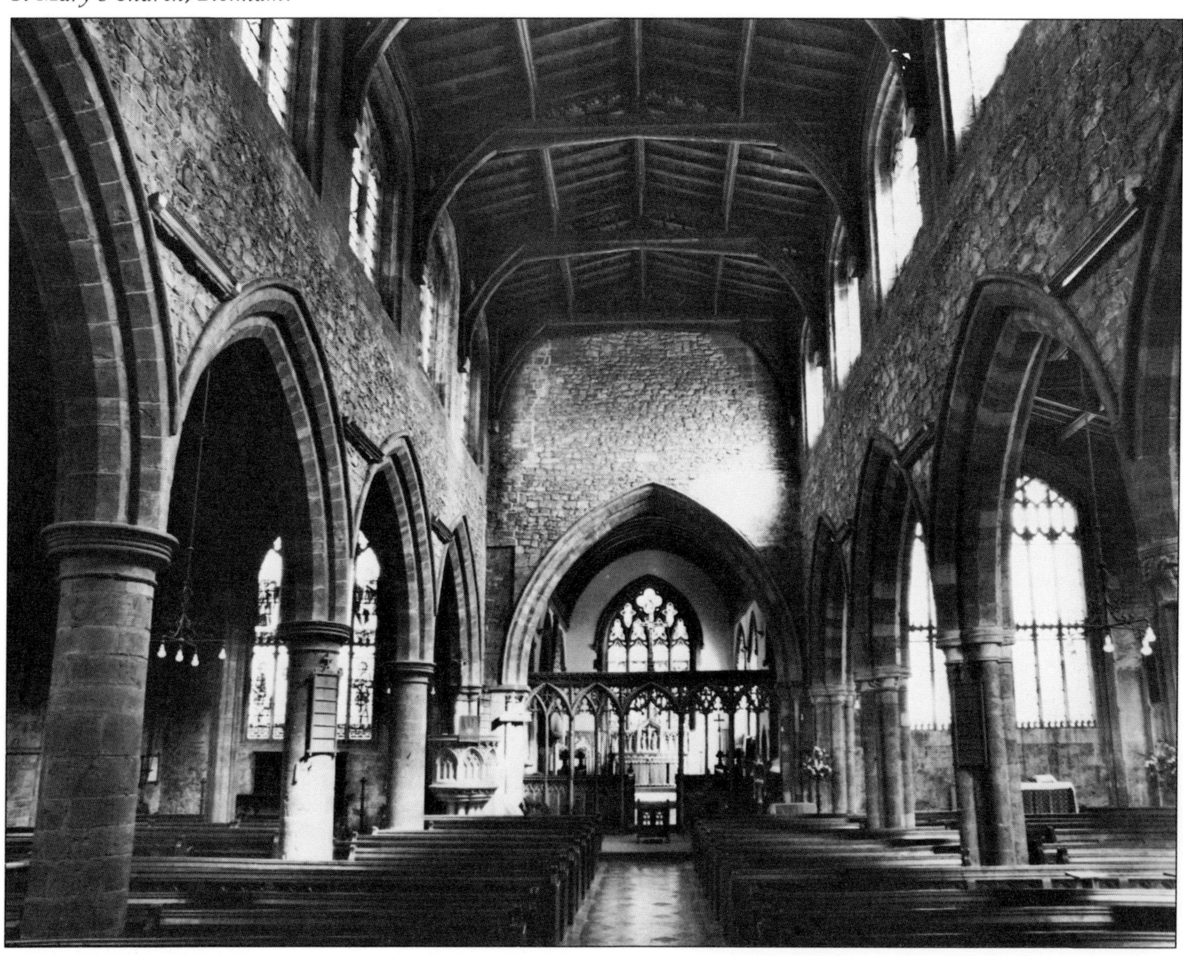

## Broughton*

*8; 2 miles SW of Banbury off B4035*

We pass the little CHURCH OF ST MARY THE VIRGIN in the park on the way to the castle, so let us examine it first. It is a lovely building, completed, probably, in a decade or two around 1300, just at the time that the Early English style was giving way to the Decorated. There is a nice, friendly, bucolic look about the west tower, with its octagonal broach spire and four little gabled lucarnes, and a fine Decorated west doorway; the south doorway, on the other hand, is still Early English – another illustration of the way medieval churches were always built from east to west. Most of the windows have beautiful Decorated tracery – that of the great east window renewed by the Gilbert Scotts, father and son, in the 1870s, but none the worse for that; the only important exception is the big Perpendicular one of five lights in the south aisle: fine enough in its way but here, frankly, a bit of an eyesore.

Going in, one notices that the nave and south aisle – there is no aisle on the north side – are almost the same width. This often suggests that the aisle was a later addition, but here everything seems roughly the same date; if there was an earlier church on the site of the present nave, it has been so completely rebuilt as to be effectively lost. The greatest treasure is the superb ogival stone screen leading into the chancel. It has a central arch, with three smaller openings to each side, all crocketed, supporting a cornice carved with a row of heads. More heads decorate the label stops of the arcade.

St Mary's has three splendid tombs, all along the south side. Beginning from the west, the first is that of Sir John de Broughton, who built the church and died in 1315; it is recessed and very elaborate, with an ogival canopy ending in a huge finial that breaks across the splay of the Perpendicular window above (which cannot have been built till the best part of a century later). Overlapping the left-hand side of this tomb, with an insensitivity that seems shocking today, is another – free-standing this time, tall, canopied, very white, and surmounted by four bears carrying shields. It is thought to have been intended for Edward Fiennes, who died in 1528, but was never completed and stands empty. Thirdly, in the chancel, is a double tomb carrying fine alabaster effigies of an armoured knight and a lady. They are identified in the church guide as Sir Thomas Wykeham and his wife, Lady Margaret; but, as Pevsner has pointed out, they do not belong together. The lady's clothes are half a century earlier than they should be, and her face is stylised and without individuality; that of Sir Thomas, on the other hand, is obviously exactly like him.

Finally there are wall paintings, of roughly the same date as the church. Scenes from the life of the Virgin run nearly the length of the chancel north wall, there is a Wheel of Fortune on the east, and a fine Crucifixion, against a blood-red ground, on a column behind the font.

And now to BROUGHTON CASTLE – though, strictly speaking, it is not really a castle at all but a fortified manor house set in a broad moat, built by Sir John de Broughton in about 1300. Since then it has only once been significantly altered: in the second half of the sixteenth century, when the roof of the Great Hall was lowered to accommodate two storeys above it, twin two-storey bays were added to the north front, with an oriel between them topped by a heraldic shield, and – in the interests of Renaissance symmetry – a broad rectangular bay was built on at the west end to counterbalance the Chapel at the east. At the same time the less important south front was given two gabled staircase towers at each end of the Great Hall. A substantial redecoration of the interior took place in the 1760s, probably (though there is no documentary evidence) at the hands of Sanderson Miller; but apart from one or two small windows with Gothick glazing in the east wing the outside was not affected.

What we see, then, as we cross the moat from the north over its only bridge – defended by a Gatehouse of 1406 – is essentially the Tudor façade. Only to our left does the medieval solar wing, buttressed and crenellated, with the two-light Decorated window of the Chapel, reveal the true age of the building. Once we go inside, however, it becomes plain that the Tudor façade is itself little more than a shell; behind it, Sir John's original manor house still survives.

The first of the principal rooms we enter is the Great Hall. Stylistically, it is a curious mixture, the rough fourteenth-century stone (laid bare by the Scotts) contrasting oddly with the huge Tudor bays, mullioned and transomed, and more oddly still with the exuberantly Gothick plaster ceiling and its outsize pendants. A further confusing element is the fact that during the sixteenth-century reconstruction the Hall was turned, as it were, back to front, the new state apartments being built in the added west wing, where the screens passage and service areas had originally been. But this arrangement, unusual as it was, had one great advantage: it meant that the old solar wing could be preserved at the east end of the house, where it is still in use today.

Access to this solar wing is through either of the two doors with pointed arches in the east wall of the Hall. These lead to a series of connected passageways, rib-vaulted, with splendidly carved corbels, leading in turn to the straight Chapel stairs and the spiral to the solar. Here too, in what was once the undercroft, is the Dining Room, similarly vaulted – furnished, presumably during the Tudor redecoration, with some lovely double-linenfold panelling and a fireplace.

Now comes the Chapel – two storeys high, fourteenth-century Decorated, and virtually untouched. In the tracery of the three-light east window are three cusped circles with shields, inscribed within a larger circle; below it is the original altar – not a block or table, but a stone slab resting on three sturdy brackets. Adjoining the Chapel, and connected to it by a squint, is what is known as Queen Anne's Room, named after the Queen of James I, Anne of Denmark, who slept here in 1604; more heavy stone corbels support the window sill, but the *pièce de résistance* is the fireplace – a magnificent mid-sixteenth-century affair reaching to the ceiling, its disarmingly squat Corinthian columns proclaiming the Renaissance but simultaneously revealing a still very imperfect comprehension of what it was all about.

The gallery, which runs above the Hall for most of the length of the house, is Sanderson Miller Gothick, with panelled doors and clustered colonnettes reaching up to the cornice. Leading off it at the eastern end is a wonderful room called the Star Chamber. The hand-painted Chinese wallpaper would alone make it memorable enough; but the pride of the Chamber is its fireplace – the most remarkable at Broughton, and probably in Oxfordshire. Where that of Queen Anne's Room is English through and through and still quite unsophisticated, this is French, and infinitely more assured. It too rises to the ceiling. The lower stage, consisting of the fireplace surrounds in which paired Tuscan pilasters support a triglyph frieze, is of stone; the upper is a riot of the lightest and most delicate stucco. Here the Tuscan order gives way to the Ionic, the paired pilasters are separated by mythical figures in relief, and two more figures, representing the winds and almost free-standing, support a central panel in which dryads dance around an oak tree. The same scene, by Rosso, is to be found in the Galerie François I at Fontainebleau, where the style is also very similar; we can only assume that the Broughton version is the work of the Italian craftsmen who were brought over by Henry VIII to work in his new palace of Nonsuch in 1538. It was certainly not executed *in situ*, and its exact provenance remains a mystery.

At the western end of the gallery, the Great Parlour – more usually called the White Room – has a tremendous plaster ceiling with huge pendants surmounted by tiny cherubs, all linked by an intricate design of the kind that was soon to be formalised into strapwork. Birds, heraldic animals and coats of arms fill up the larger space. But it is the room beneath this, on the ground floor, which must by any standards be considered the most beautiful in the house. It is known as the Oak Room. The date is late Elizabethan, but thanks to the tall mullioned windows it is much lighter and more cheerful than such rooms often are. The walls are covered with oak panelling from the floor to the plaster strapwork ceiling, with giant fluted pilasters rising to a deep cornice. The door is in the corner, and emphasised by an ornate internal porch capped with obelisks and a high strapwork cartouche, from which another obelisk soars to the ceiling. Beneath it runs the inscription 'QUOD OLIM FUIT MEMINISSE MINIME JUVAT' – 'There is little joy in the remembrance of the past': a most appropriate legend if, as seems likely, it was placed there soon after the Restoration of Charles II in 1660.

But in another sense, there is great pleasure to be had in wandering through Broughton, where the past seems close indeed. It is regularly open to the public during the summer months; the opportunity should not be missed.

*Broughton Castle.*

## Buckland House

*9; 4½ miles NE of Faringdon off A420*

Built for Sir Robert Throckmorton, Buckland House started life as an exquisite small Palladian villa designed by the younger John Wood of Bath. It was, perhaps, a little unorthodox: although the noble Corinthian portico was at first-floor level, standing on a rusticated base, the principal rooms were on the ground floor, with the result that that base rises almost halfway up the building. To each side an unusually long link leads to an octagonal angle pavilion; but though these pavilions, like the links, are of a single storey, their steeply sloping roofs topped with little cupolas give them the additional height they need and prevent the whole composition, about 260 feet long, from looking too extended.

Such, in essence, was the appearance of the house until about 1910 when, under the threat of a visit from King Edward VII, Romaine Walker was called in to increase the accommodation. He trebled it, adding an east and west block the same height as the centre – two and a half storeys – and attached to it, but projecting to the north to form a three-sided court. Inevitably, so drastic an enlargement changed the whole character of the house: a Rococo villa became a stately home. On the other hand, it must be said that Walker did the job as sensitively as it could possibly have been done, maintaining on his new blocks the window levels, the string-courses, the line of modillions and even the ravishing frieze of stone garlands from the original house.

Although Buckland is now a university college, it has retained a surprising amount of its original interior decoration. The central Saloon, for example, has a simply splendid coved ceiling, with Guido Reni's *Aurora*, in a distinctly Baroque stucco version, riding triumphantly across the centre. Remarkable too are the two pavilions; to the east the Library, to the west the Chapel. Octagonal on the outside, these buildings prove on entry to be basically cruciform, diagonal walls having been built across the re-entrant angles. The Library ceiling is as grand as that of the Saloon, given over as it is to a single huge painting by Cipriani, probably executed by himself and Biagio Rebecca. The Chapel may not have been a chapel at all: Pevsner has pointed out that, if it had been, the altar would have stood at the west end, which he considers unlikely – though there are in fact plenty of precedents for such an arrangement. It certainly has an ecclesiastical air about it, since the walls have all been left in the original stone. Here again is a beautiful stone frieze with garlands.

It is all immensely elegant – one cannot help wishing it was still as it was when Wood and Throckmorton knew it, before that fatal enlargement. And the irony is that, after all the fuss, Edward VII never came.

## Burford*

*10; 7 miles NW of Witney on A40*

A beautiful, if slightly self-conscious, little town, for anyone coming from London by car there could hardly be a more beguiling entrance to the Cotswolds than Burford. Essentially, it consists of one long High Street, running down between rows of pollarded lime trees to the River Windrush, with little alleys branching off to the sides and courtyards behind – the medieval plan, in fact, which has never changed since the town first became important soon after the Norman Conquest. For the next four centuries it grew increasingly rich, largely through sheep farming, until by 1500 it had become one of the principal wool towns in the Midlands. When the importance of wool declined, the coaching trade continued to bring in money; and in the twentieth century Burford has become quite a tourist attraction, both for its undoubted picturesqueness and for the excellent (if expensive) antique shops that line the street.

*The west doorway, St John the Baptist, Burford.*

There are so many good houses, dating from every century from the fourteenth to the eighteenth, that it seems almost invidious to single out individual buildings. Mention should be made, however, of LONDON HOUSE, on the east side, a remarkably well preserved merchant's house of the fifteenth century; and, on the west, the OLD VICARAGE of 1672, with its three Dutch gables. This is not to be confused with the OLD RECTORY in Priory Lane – a really lovely five-bay house of 1700, almost certainly the work of Christopher Kempster, builder of Abingdon Town Hall (*q.v.*), who was a Burford man and owned a quarry nearby. Of the same date – though with later accretions – is THE GREAT HOUSE in Witney Street; Pevsner ingeniously suggests that the castellation of the parapet and chimneys is a visual pun on the name of the builder, John Castle.

The most interesting building in Burford, however, remains the church, dedicated to ST JOHN THE BAPTIST. Its lovely slender spire – seen to great advantage from the Oxford road – suggests a Perpendicular building of the early fifteenth century, an impression that is strengthened by the broad traceried windows and the magnificent south porch with its high crocketed pinnacles. Before you enter the church, though, walk round to the west doorway. There you will find a magnificent Norman arch of three orders, with rich zigzag decoration and the remains of figurative carving, now alas almost worn away by the prevailing wind. The door itself is of the same date, as are those wonderful iron hinges, their long tendrils spreading like a creeper across the old timbers. Now step back a few paces and lift your eyes to the tower; the two lower stages are also the purest Norman work of the twelfth century.

A Norman church, then, with later additions; but it is only when you go inside that you realise just how varied, and how complicated, those additions were. At first sight the basic ground plan of the building is almost hidden by a plethora of aisles and chapels, of curious angles and even of differing floor levels. Apart from the west wall of the nave, the only Norman work visible here is in the four piers supporting the tower at the crossing; look especially at the south-west one, where a little round-headed doorway leads to the turret stairs. This doorway is earlier than anything we have yet seen – probably a remnant of the previous eleventh-century church on the site. And on the south wall of this same pier, high up, you will find something a good deal older still – a pre-Christian carving of about AD 100, which the builders of the present church were enlightened (or superstitious?) enough to incorporate into the fabric.

At the very end of the twelfth century, with Burford's wealth steadily increasing, it was decided to enlarge the church with an aisle and transept to the south; of this work, however, there remains only the broad pointed arch connecting the two elements, since the next half century saw a more ambitious rebuilding of this part of the church and the further addition of another transept to the north. (The two transepts originally had tower arches considerably higher and wider than the present ones – their outlines are plain to see – but by 1500 or so it was found that the tower was becoming unsafe and they were partly filled in.) Also around 1250 the old apsed chancel was replaced by a much larger rectangular one – the sedilia establish the date beyond any doubt – and a guild chapel was erected, as a completely separate building, a few feet to the south-west.

There was only one major contribution to the church in the fourteenth century – the square chapel which was added immediately to the west of the south transept and which was dedicated to St Thomas of Canterbury. Raised over a crypt, it is reached by a steep flight of steps leading up from the south aisle. Then, in the fifteenth, the whole building was remodelled and given the overwhelmingly Perpendicular complexion it bears today. The nave arcades were renewed, the walls above heightened to provide a clerestory; the hoods were given splendidly carved head stops, almost certainly portraits of individual benefactors; a north aisle was added to balance that on the south; the tower was heightened and given its spire; a curious little chapel was built at the east end of the north arcade and dedicated to St Peter (it owes its present Victorian aspect to G.E. Street, who restored it to within an inch of its life in the 1870s); further chapels appeared on each side of the chancel; and the guild chapel, somewhat reshaped, was incorporated into the main building. This last operation was not entirely successful, since the chapel had a different axis from that of the church; the result, to my eye at any rate, looks distinctly odd. Finally, there came the south porch and the remodelling of nearly all the windows.

There are several admirable tombs, including that of Edmund Harman, barber-surgeon, and his wife. He died in 1569, which makes the Red Indians playing around the inscription even more surprising than they would otherwise have been. The other outstanding monument is that of Sir Lawrence Tanfield and family, dated 1628. Lady Tanfield's inscription, complaining that her husband should have been buried somewhere more distinguished, may not be in the best of taste; but much can be forgiven her for her little poem on the north side.

We owe one last debt of gratitude to Burford church; for it was here that William Morris, horrified by Street's restorations, first decided on the action which led to the foundation, in the following year, of the Society for the Protection of Ancient Buildings. His first step was to complain to the vicar, whose reply, though unsympathetic, is worth recording: 'The church, Sir, is mine; and if I choose to I shall stand on my head in it.'

## Buscot

*11; 3 miles NW of Faringdon on A417*

*Includes Buscot Park and Buscot Old Parsonage (both NT)*

A bit of a fraud, though a beautiful one, BUSCOT PARK (NT) was first built around 1770 in a well-bred Adam style, probably by the amateur Edward Loveden Townsend for himself. In 1859, almost derelict, it was bought by an extraordinary Australian gold millionaire who planted acres of sugar beet from which he distilled potent liquors on nearby Brandy Island. Thirty years later, Sir Ernest George (architect of Claridge's Hotel) added a large wing and Victorianised the entire house.

By this time there was little that Townsend would have recognised, or even wished to. After the death of the Australian, however, the estate was bought by Sir Alexander Henderson, later the 1st Lord Faringdon. He it was who filled it with its present superb collection of pictures, not only Old Masters but also some splendid Pre-Raphaelites: the Saloon walls are largely occupied by the series by Burne-Jones known as *The Legend of the Briar Rose*, all in the thick gilded Renaissance frames designed by the artist.

It was left to the 2nd Lord Faringdon to reconstruct Buscot, slowly, carefully and at considerable expense, to something like its pristine appearance. Down came all the Victorian accretions; up went two detached classical pavilions which suit the house to perfection. The architect for all this was Geddes Hyslop. Only the neo-classical Entrance Hall is not, perhaps, entirely successful; the Grecian mural paintings by Elroy Haldall are not quite good enough. (His *chinoiserie* Dining Room is a lot better.)

Go, then, to Buscot for the pictures, and the furniture, and the *objets d'art*, all beautifully displayed in a lovely Georgian setting. They are jewels indeed; their setting is pretty, but paste. Far more beautiful – and more genuine – is the OLD PARSONAGE (NT), a ravishing stone house of about 1700 with two storeys of five bays beneath a hipped roof: unpretentious but, in its way, perfect.

## Cassington

*12; 5 miles NW of Oxford off A40*

ST PETER'S CHURCH has a nice, plain, chunky exterior with a tall fourteenth-century broach spire but enough Norman work on the tower below it, on the north and south doors and on certain of the windows, to show that the body of the church is a good two centuries earlier; it was in fact consecrated before 1123. Like so many churches in this part of the country, it has a fine corbel table which runs all the way round – the carved heads not quite up to the scale of Adderbury, perhaps, but well worth a long, close look.

The interior is another surprisingly agreeable combination of the Norman and the Decorated. Norman are the crossing arches, boldly zigzagged, the font and the vaulted chancel; Decorated are the east window (wherein the crossed keys indicate the dedication to St Peter), west window, two nave windows and the screen – though the upper part of this is much restored. There are also some fourteenth- and fifteenth-century wall paintings, including a great Doom over the nave arch; but they are too faded to be of much interest to non-specialists. I prefer the benches – wonderfully rough pre-Reformation jobs, as evocative as anything in the building.

## Chastleton House*

*13; 5 miles NW of Chipping Norton off A44*

Here is one of those magical Oxfordshire manor houses, like Beckley Park, that has somehow survived the passage of nearly four centuries virtually unaltered. It was built, and probably designed, by a rich wool merchant from Witney, Walter Jones, in the early years of the seventeenth century, and manages to be both austere and dramatic at the same time. The austerity shows itself in the quiet dark brick, sober stone dressings and the absence of any superfluous decoration – unless you count the crenellations and steps to the gables. The drama is provided by the quite remarkable entrance front: five narrow gables close together, the second and fourth breaking forward, the central one recessed but asserting its predominance with a flight of five steps projecting further forward still. There is only one bay per gable, but these five bays are effectively increased to seven by two massive staircase towers set halfway back on each side, adding even more movement to the façade. Oddly, at first sight, there seems to be no front door; this proves to be set in the side of the second gable – the only departure (even if an almost invisible one) from the strict symmetry of the rest.

The placing of the door means that the screens passage, instead of running directly back from the centre, takes a parallel course some 10 feet to the left – an arrangement that allows the Hall itself to assume the central position. It is quite low, occupying as it does only one of Chastleton's three storeys; formerly it had inner windows giving on to the court, but these have now been blocked. The walls are panelled; the plainness of the huge stone fireplace contrasts strikingly with the screen – a riot of carved satyrs, columns, strapwork cresting and scrolls of acanthus. There are two fine Parlours on the east side – the larger one at the back of the house boasting a fine plaster ceiling with fleurs-de-lis and a frieze of winged chimaeras; but the real showpiece is the Great Chamber on the first floor. Here Mr Jones pulled out all the stops – the walls not only panelled but

*The Hall at Chastleton House.*

carved and painted as well, the plaster ceiling heavy with pendants emerging from a forest of fruit, flowers and vine tendrils, the chimneypiece rising to the roof, proudly bearing the Jones arms. On the same floor are several other rooms only fractionally less grand; above, running the whole length of the north front, is the tunnel-vaulted Long Gallery, once again richly panelled and with more ornate plasterwork.

It is a romantic and wonderful house; but at the time of my visit its state of dilapidation was pitiful to behold. The owners – descendants of Walter Jones – were clearly unable to undertake the immense amount of restoration that their house now needs if it is to survive into the twenty-first century. Let us hope that by the time this book sees the light of day the situation will have improved; otherwise I can only urge the reader to betake himself to Chastleton at the earliest opportunity, while it is still there.

## Chipping Norton*

*14; 11 miles NE of Burford on A361*

The CHURCH OF ST MARY THE VIRGIN is magnificent, inside and out. Even from a distance you can see the outstanding quality of what is in fact its chief pride – the soaring late fifteenth-century nave, unequalled anywhere in the county outside Oxford itself. This shows itself in the remarkable clerestory that runs its whole length, broken only by three narrow buttresses, and in the huge seven-light east window rising above the much lower chancel. The west tower, rebuilt in 1825, is dignified without being especially remarkable; considerably more interesting is the hexagonal two-storeyed south porch, with its four massive buttresses (more than one would have thought strictly necessary) splendidly vaulted within and guarded by some excellent gargoyles.

Enter the church now, through the wonderfully carved south door. It is immensely broad, with two north aisles and one south one; but none of these can hold a candle to the nave itself, the clustered shafts of those exquisitely slender piers shooting straight up to the timber roof, only momentarily breaking the almost uninterrupted expanse of glass that forms the clerestory. Between them, the spandrels of the nave arcade are decorated with trefoils and quatrefoils, above which runs a row of blind cusped arches.

Of the three aisles, the southern one is the shortest; but it is also the most impressive, by reason of the tremendous six-light window which occupies the entire east wall and which is said to have been brought to St Mary the Virgin from nearby Bruern Abbey after its dissolution in 1535. Of the north aisles there is less to say, except that the arcade that separates them, being obviously earlier than those of the nave, must be the old north arcade re-used.

The chancel, with the adjoining north chapel, is the oldest part of the church – early thirteenth-century. (Its east window and the one next to it on the south side are obviously later interpolations.) From the chapel into the chancel runs a squint of a most unusual design, its three upper lights looking curiously oriental. Beneath it is a piscina; the sedilia, on the other hand, are of 1876, at which time the whole church was mercilessly scraped. But no amount of scraping could spoil the elegance and lightness and disciplined intricacy of this glorious building.

*The church of St Mary the Virgin, Chipping Norton.*

About half a mile out of the town on the Moreton-in-Marsh road stands the BLISS TWEED MILL, one of the most sensational of all Victorian factory buildings. Its architect, George Woodhouse, clearly intended it to suggest an opulent country house – and so it would, if its cupola did not suddenly sprout a huge factory chimney, giving it rather the look of a monstrous plumber's mate. Set amid the rolling Oxfordshire hills, it stands as a magnificent monument to late Victorian industrial prosperity.

## Compton Beauchamp*

*15; 7 miles S of Faringdon on B4507*

It is impossible to see COMPTON HOUSE for the first time without experiencing a lifting of the spirit. As you descend from the B4507 into the village, there it stands, to the left of the road, at the end of a short avenue of limes, beyond a splendid grille of wrought iron. This north front is of about 1710 – two and a half storeys, with four giant Doric pilasters standing on a rusticated base. Along the top runs a deep balustrade; at the sides, recessed two-bay wings, of two storeys but considerably lower than the centre.

It is only when you start walking along the sides of the house (beyond the moat, which protects it from the east, west and south) that you realise that it is a great deal older than it looks from the front. The two side wings, it now becomes clear, are basically of the sixteenth century: their Queen Anne façades have been erected to conceal the Tudor gable ends which are still in place behind them. Along these east and west sides, stone immediately gives way to brick, with sloping roofs above; the eighteenth century seems aeons away. There is only one eyesore: a hideous plate-glass extrusion halfway down the east side. How so screaming a monstrosity can have been conceived of, let alone actually built, passes all comprehension. (But do not blame the present young Swedish owner; it distresses him too.)

The south front – basically Tudor, though the windows have been sashed – is as informal as the sides: two towering chimneybreasts rise shamelessly up the middle, with a scalene gable at each end. The fenestration between these chimneybreasts and the outer corners is wildly irregular, though the two sections reflect each other symmetrically. What delights one here is the setting: the wide, clear moat, the banks of trees placed well back on each side, the long unbroken vista to the south.

The house is built round an inner courtyard, of which the walls are of stone. This is really the only part of the house where both the sixteenth- and the eighteenth-century work can be seen properly at the same time – a pedimented doorway on one side, mullioned and transomed windows on another.

Apart from the north front, Compton Beauchamp has no outstanding architectural distinction, but it is a house that it is difficult indeed not to love. Few houses so perfectly combine Georgian elegance with Tudor domesticity; few are so exquisitely placed, so satisfactorily moated. Just beyond the moat to the south-west is the delightful little fourteenth-century CHURCH OF ST SWITHUN with a lovely Decorated east window and, both there and in the north transept, some quite glorious medieval glass. In the south transept the head of Christ is said to have come from Justinian's church of St Sergius and St Bacchus in Istanbul. I wonder: fully three-dimensional religious sculpture was rare indeed among the Byzantines of the sixth century.

## Cornbury Park

*16; 5 miles N of Witney off B4022*

No one knows when the history of Cornbury Park really begins. It may go back to the twelfth century, and was certainly in existence as a royal hunting lodge in the Forest of Wychwood in the early fourteenth; but the oldest part of the present house is neither venerable nor even particularly interesting – a modest little gabled wing at the western end, built around 1500. Cornbury today is essentially a seventeenth-century building, and a very important one.

Its importance lies, first of all, in the fact that it possesses, on the south front, the earliest surviving classical façade of any country house in England. (Stoke Park (*q.v.*) was a little earlier, but only the pavilions stand today.) This was designed in 1631 for the Earl of Danby by Nicholas Stone, who had worked in Holland as a young man and had subsequently been closely

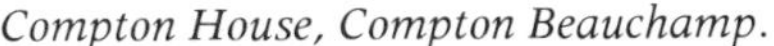

*Compton House, Compton Beauchamp.*

*The stables at Cornbury Park.*

connected with Inigo Jones. Stone's seven-bay wing lasted, in its original form, for only some thirty years before it was altered; but the central porch remains unchanged and, at the far west end, a tiny corner still shows how the fenestration was originally planned, with little *oeil-de-boeuf* windows at mezzanine level.

After the Civil War, Commonwealth and Restoration, Cornbury was granted by Charles II to Edward Hyde, soon to be created Earl of Clarendon; and he it was who in 1663 called in Hugh May to build him some new stables. These, so far as we know, constitute May's earliest surviving building and also the first classical stable block to be added to an English country house. With their fourteen bays, pedimented centre, carefully placed niches and two-storey side pavilions, they can be seen as a remarkable Palladian composition in their own right. The following year May came down to Cornbury to see the work in progress, bringing with him John Evelyn, the diarist, who was also a competent amateur architect; and the two of them together designed 'a handsome chapell that was yet wanting'. Whether this was the Chapel that was eventually built at Cornbury thirteen years later is not known, but it seems likely. The Chapel as it now stands is, in any case, a masterpiece. Private chapels of this date are rare indeed; and this one, with its deeply coved ceiling, its superb plasterwork and its glorious wooden fittings – particularly handsome at the east end behind the altar – would do honour to any Oxford college. It also reminds us, as Christopher Hussey has pointed out, 'how little Wren originated of the decorative style associated with his name'.

The last part of Cornbury to be designed – though not to be built – was May's east range, begun in 1666. Here his inspiration was not so much Palladio as the new style of houses he had seen in Holland during the Court's exile – such buildings as Jacob van Campen's Mauritshuis, built thirty years before. More directly, he was probably also influenced by his patron's London house which had just been completed by that other great amateur architect of his day, Sir Roger Pratt. The result, at any rate, was a long range of eleven bays, combining a central three-bay pediment with a hipped roof, running at right-angles to Stone's wing and thus facing east. Here, in essence, was the so-called 'Wren house' which was to dominate English domestic architecture until the end of the century and beyond.

Sadly, the interiors of Cornbury have now almost disappeared – Stone's destroyed by May, and May's by an unknown Victorian architect who, for good measure, added a tower and a hideously inappropriate portico to May's front. These later accretions were removed in 1901–6, and the house has recently been most beautifully restored by its present owner; but what has gone can never be replaced, and it is sad indeed that so much should have been lost of a house that has played so important a part in our architectural history.

## Ditchley Park*

*17; 5 miles NW of Woodstock off A34*

'It is not the Bulk of a Fabrick, the Richness and Quality of the Materials, the Multiplicity of Lines, nor the Gaudiness of the Finishing, that give Grace and Beauty and Grandeur to a Building; but the Proportion of the Parts to one another and to the whole, whether entirely plain, or enriched with a few Ornaments properly disposed.' So wrote James Gibbs in his *Book of Architecture,* published in 1728 when Ditchley Park was nearing completion. Ditchley is his most important country house; and certainly he never built anything that more perfectly illustrates the truth of his precept. The main block – which is connected by curved single-storey links to side pavilions with cupolas – could scarcely be plainer. The four outer bays of its eleven-bay south front are broken forward, as are the three central ones to a rather lesser degree; but apart from the somewhat assertive quoins, a prominent cornice above the second-floor windows, and a triangular pediment with Gibbs surround to the front door, it is virtually devoid of ornament. On the two principal floors even the windows are identical, with their keystones above and their brackets below. Ditchley makes its point by quiet elegance, nothing more. It is arguable that it would look even more elegant were the large rectangular chimney-stacks a little less obtrusive, particularly when seen from the equally restrained seven-bay west front; but such criticism seems almost impertinent when levelled at a house of such distinction. In any case, we know that Gibbs's original design was for a hipped roof as on the pavilions; we can only assume that the 2nd Earl of Lichfield, for whom it was built – or Francis Smith of Warwick, who actually did the building – had different ideas.

The interior of the house is more distinguished still – and so it should be, considering the fact that it is the work, at least so far as the main rooms are concerned, of Henry Flitcroft and William Kent. The quality is apparent – indeed it practically knocks one down – the moment one enters the front door, which leads directly into the Hall. In its conception this tremendous room is entirely due to Kent. Rising through two storeys, it is almost a perfect cube. The two principal doorways and the overmantel have figures of the arts and sciences reclining above the pediments – the Saloon door, topped by Geography and Astronomy, is particularly magnificent. Elsewhere around the room, on high brackets adorned with garlands, are various busts of literary worthies, two of which also surmount the two mythological paintings flanking the Saloon door. These also are by Kent, as is *The Assembly of the Gods* on the ceiling. (He started his career as a painter, but, curiously, it seems to have been the branch of the visual arts in which he was least at ease; no wonder he gave it up altogether as time went on.) The stucco work is by three of the best craftsmen of their day – Vassali, Artari and Serena; here, however, they were kept on a fairly tight rein. Kent was obviously determined – and rightly – that nothing should spoil the majesty and unity of his overall conception.

In the adjoining Saloon, on the other hand, the three stuccoists were given their heads. Within a basic framework provided by fluted pilasters they have produced lovely, light-hearted, flowing designs over walls and ceiling, with especially rich overdoors, decorated niches and almost life-size figures of Minerva and Diana. We know that this work dates from 1726, yet the date comes as a considerable surprise: the freedom

*The Hall at Ditchley Park.*

and unorthodoxy of the designs seem far indeed from the grandiloquence of Kent's Hall, something that one would not have expected for another generation, or even more.

Of the other principal rooms, the Velvet Room takes its name from the superb material with which the walls are hung. The design represents the Hindu god Shiva, and the velvet was actually bought in India in about 1730. The fireplace is by Henry Cheere. The White Drawing Room and Green Silk Room are both the work of Flitcroft. The Library, which was formed from two separate rooms in 1933, and the Dining Room are of rather less interest; their decoration has also suffered to some degree from their use for the regular conferences held by the Ditchley Foundation – though the whole house is an object lesson in how it is possible to run a flourishing institution without looking institutional.

Ditchley was the regular weekend retreat during the Second World War of Sir Winston Churchill – particularly on those weekends when the moon was up and Chequers was an easy target for the enemy bombers. It is still in essence a weekend centre – nowadays for Anglo-American discussions on questions of common interest.

*The Abbey of St Peter and St Paul, Dorchester.*

## Dorchester Abbey*

*18; 10 miles SE of Oxford on A423*

The Abbey of St Peter and St Paul marks the place where, in AD 634, King Cynegils of Wessex was baptised by St Birinus in the River Thame [*sic*] – an event which, in its turn, led to the establishment of Christianity in the south and west of England. Historically, therefore, it is a shrine of primary importance, which makes it all the sadder that there should have survived not a single trace of the Saxon church that once stood here. What we have is, in essence, a building of various periods from the twelfth to the fourteenth centuries, plus a sturdy if rather unexciting west tower which was completely reconstructed in the seventeenth. Of all these periods, the fourteenth century is by far the most important for Dorchester. The impression that one gets as one walks through the churchyard to the south porch is overwhelmingly of the Decorated style, but there is more to it than that; for it was in about 1340 that there appeared in this small village a sculptor-designer of quite stunning originality whose work here is unparallelled not only in England but in all Europe.

Most of the Norman work remaining is to be found along the north wall of the nave and the western arch; it will not detain us long. Of considerably more interest is what happened in the thirteenth century, when the north choir aisle was added. This was begun on a relatively modest scale, but around 1290, when the offer of papal indulgences to all contributors brought a sudden influx of funds, the plans were changed in favour of something a good deal more ambitious. By this time the Decorated style had arrived; hence the lovely windows with their rich geometrical tracery. The new aisle was separated from the old monastic choir by a wonderfully opulent three-bay arcade, rising from clustered piers, with stiff-leaf in the spandrels.

The obvious success of this splendid project and the continued generosity of the parishioners provided all the encouragement needed to keep up the good work. The next stage was accordingly the construction of a corresponding south choir aisle – a little plainer, perhaps, than its opposite number (the stiff-leaf has gone) but worthy enough nonetheless. Then came the climax. In about 1340 it was decided to extend the choir eastward – and this extension is the glory of Dorchester. The entire east wall is taken up with a truly memorable east window. It is essentially of six lights, but the figure is not immediately easy to compute owing to the fact that the tracery – a fascinating and unique variation on the reticulated – instead of confining itself to the head of the window extends right down to the bottom. A broad stone buttress divides most of the window vertically into two parts; but, just above the springing of the arch, it tapers away to give place to a wheel containing a star design – this last feature, it must be admitted, being the work of William Butterfield, who restored the church in 1846–53. Already from a distance the window is stunning in its splendour; as you approach closer, however, still more beauties are revealed. The tracery is not only cusped and crocketed, rising at one point to little pinnacles standing free; it also carries its own small sculptures, depicting scenes from the Passion and Resurrection.

Such a masterpiece alone would assure the church's fame; but Dorchester can boast another, almost equally remarkable and only a few inches away. This is the Jesse window on the north side; unlike other Jesse windows, however, it tells the story of the antecedence of Christ as much on the tracery itself as in the glass. Jesse, the patriarch, lies along the sill; the stone tree springs directly from his body, its trunk and branches carved with Old Testament figures. Some of the figures, including the Virgin and Child at the top and the figure of Christ, were destroyed by Cromwell's unspeakable soldiers; much of the original glass, too, has gone. But the window remains, like its neighbour, something utterly idiosyncratic and quite unique – something that it is worth travelling a long way to see. The south window opposite also has sculptured figures, this time depicting the funeral of St Birinus; and the piscina and sedilia are obviously the work of the same, quirkish, master hand. Behind the latter are four little windows of a curious flowing design, in which we can see the oldest glass in the abbey. Being of the thirteenth century, it must clearly have been taken from an earlier window, now destroyed – perhaps the east window of the Norman church.

At about the same time that the east end was being so miraculously transformed, more work was going on in the south-west of the church, where a new aisle was being built for day-to-day parish use. It contains three objects of interest: behind the altar a contemporary wall painting of the Crucifixion (suffering, alas, from over-enthusiastic Victorian restoration); the unusual – and, with visitors, deservedly popular – 'monks' corbel' on an arcade column, representing sleeping monks and intended, presumably, as a warning against sloth; and (my own favourite) a late eighteenth-century memorial slab to one Sarah Fletcher who died, we are informed, 'a martyr to excessive sensibility'. But it is, above all, that miraculous chancel for which we remember Dorchester – and for which, again and again, we return.

## Ducklington

*19; 10 miles W of Oxford off A415*

Standing at the far end of the little village, the CHURCH OF ST BARTHOLOMEW, though quite a modest building in itself, makes an immediate impact through the splendour of its Decorated windows. It consists of a short, square, embattled tower to the west and gabled ranges running off it – the whole thing built of the local grey stone (including the roof tiles) and heavily lichened. Within, the first impression is one of great breadth, owing to the spacious aisles to north and south. Here, more clearly than from the outside, one can see that the church is not originally Decorated at all but Transitional, of about 1200; look, for example, at the south arcade with its combination of sturdy round piers, supporting arches which are just beginning to point. But then look at its northern counterpart; here the piers have a quatrefoil section and there are ornate label stops, carved with heads of a king and queen in the aisle side, coiled snakes towards the nave. Obviously the old north aisle was replaced around 1340 by a new and far more sumptuous one, the arcade being remodelled as well as the windows – though, oddly enough, the broad, characteristically Early English window splays were retained and the Decorated tracery simply set into them. At the eastern end of this aisle is the double tomb of the founders, topped by glorious ogee canopies carved with heads, vines, oak leaves and, in the spandrel, a curious little somnolent figure reclining against the side of the arch.

The chancel is a bit of a hotch-potch – basically Early English with lancets, but including a slightly later window on the south with plate tracery and a full-blown Perpendicular one, looking distinctly inappropriate, in the all-important east. It is only partly redeemed by the little sculptures in the tracery depicting the Coronation of the Virgin – somewhat on the lines of the east window at Dorchester but with nowhere near the same exuberance. The ceilure over the altar is similarly lacking in bravura; I prefer the wooden roof of the nave, with its three pretty little clerestory windows, endearingly asymmetrical – two on one side, one on the other.

At the time of writing the church still has little or no electric light that I could find; candles in glass bells are fixed to the bench ends all the way down the nave. Winter evensong must be lovely.

## Edgcote House

*20; 7 miles NE of Banbury off A361*

The stables of Edgcote House were built in 1747 by William Smith, the eldest surviving son of Francis Smith of Warwick. Unfortunately he died in that same year, aged only forty-one, and though by the time of his death he may have completed designs for the house, it is equally possible that these may have been largely the work of its builder, William Jones. Whichever takes the credit, Edgcote remains one of those enviable medium-sized country houses in which this part of England is so rich. It is marvellously situated on a hill, commanding a delectable landscape of lake and woodland and park. Though built in the heyday of Palladianism, it remains untouched by it, harking back – like its near-contemporary, Trafalgar in Wiltshire – to the earlier Caroline days of Lamport, or the late lamented Coleshill. There is a hipped roof and a cornice with modillions. Much of its charm lies in the contrast between the rich brown local ironstone and the pale grey stone dressings of the three-bay pediment and lavish window surrounds.

Inside, the accent is on craftsmanship. The woodwork, by the London firm of Abraham Swan & Co., is outstanding, but the plasterwork (J. Whitehead) runs it close, and there are many splendid fireplaces.

## Ewelme*

*21; 4½ miles SE of Dorchester off B4009*

This pretty little village at the foot of the Chilterns boasts as perfect a late medieval architectural group as one could wish: a church, almshouses and a school, all founded by William de la Pole, later to be created 1st Duke of Suffolk, and his wife Alice, the granddaughter of the poet Chaucer. Alice's tomb alone is worth the journey.

Of the earlier church that stood on the site, the tower still stands, square and very plain, with outsize diagonal buttresses. It is built of a combination of flint rubble and limestone, as is the church, ST MARY'S, which de la Pole set up against it – a church which still looks, outside and in, very much as it did when the work was finished around 1450. It is long and relatively low – particularly towards the east end, as it is built on slightly rising ground – with regular fenestration at aisle and clerestory level. The chancel is the same height as the nave; when we go inside we shall find that there is not even a chancel arch to divide the two. The roofs are embattled at all levels – north and south porches, aisles, nave and tower.

It is, in fact, a fairly plain exterior, giving a strong impression of unity, but of little else; there is nothing remotely grand or gaudy about it. The interior is equally well-bred, but here there is rather more decoration, of the kind one would expect: restrained, but quietly expensive. The north arcade is a good example, with its richly moulded arches, their label stops in the form of angels holding shields except for the one nearest the font, where there is a representation of a king: crowned, generously bearded, and almost certainly Edward III. These same arches continue in the chancel, to both north and south; the south arcade of the nave, however, is noticeably less ornate. Why? Did Suffolk's money show signs of running out? (His dukedom, acquired in 1448, might have landed him with considerable expense.) There is a fine wooden roof, supported on stone corbels carved with grotesques of various kinds, which runs the length of the church. Over St John's Chapel, however, which was provided immediately to the south of the chancel for the use of the almshouses, the roof is flat, with carved angels and shields in abundance. This chapel is the same breadth as the chancel, and yields nothing to it in opulence except that its east window is of only four lights as opposed to the chancel's five. Between the two, in the second bay of the arcade, stands the first of Ewelme's two memorable tombs. It is that of Thomas Chaucer, the poet's son (and nephew by marriage of John of Gaunt) and of his wife Matilda; they died in 1434 and 1436 respectively. Brasses representing the couple are let into the top, while around the sides a host of heraldic shields traces their genealogical descent.

The second tomb, in the eastern bay of the same arcade, is a considerable work of art. It commemorates Thomas and Matilda's daughter Alice, Duchess of Suffolk. Her alabaster effigy lies in a tall frame of panelled stone, above which runs an elaborate cornice with three tiers of decoration, the lowest of which consists of a row of winged figures, alternately crowned and tonsured. This cornice is also divided vertically into three, by four stone columns on each side, supporting wooden figures – among the earliest examples of English figure wood carving in existence. Alice herself is dressed as a nun, but wears also a ducal coronet and, on her left fore-arm, the Order of the Garter. The admirable church guide informs us that this effigy was used by both Queen Victoria and, later, Queen Mary as evidence of where the Garter should properly be worn by ladies. There is another example of the practice at Stanton Harcourt (*q.v.*). Behind the Duchess's head is a splendid Gothic canopy, carved from a single piece of alabaster; four little angels hold her pillow. The tomb chest on which she lies bears another row of full-length carved figures with shields; and below that, at floor level, behind a row of traceried openings only a few inches high, there is a second effigy representing the Duchess's corpse, naked, shrunken and decayed – a really haunting *memento mori*. Above, the underside of the tomb chest is painted with frescoes, still amazingly brilliant since scarcely any light reaches them, and totally invisible unless you lie flat on the floor and look upwards.

The ALMSHOUSES just to the west of the church are interesting, first because they are among the earliest to be built around a central quadrangle, and secondly because, with Shirburn Castle and Stonor, they mark the earliest use of brick in this part of England. The thirteen dwellings share a continuous roof (now tiled, but originally thatched) which, after a break for the first-floor windows, continues in a projection from the walls supported on wooden posts to form a cloister. A pretty gabled entrance occupies the middle of each side. The almshouses are still in use, their occupants appointed by the lord of the manor, the Earl of Macclesfield.

Finally, the SCHOOL, which claims to be the earliest church school now incorporated in the state system and still using its original building. Its two storeys, similarly of brick, have little decoration except at the window heads; but there is a fine timber roof in the upper room.

## Faringdon

*22; 9 miles NW of Wantage on A417*

Whether or not, as the tradition goes, it was at Faringdon that King Alfred burnt the cakes, it is certainly one of the oldest Saxon towns in the south of England. One would have liked, therefore, to note at least some Saxon traces in ALL SAINTS' CHURCH; alas, splendid as it is, none of it appears to go back beyond the twelfth century. To this period belongs the noble nave, with its deeply moulded round arches supported on comparatively slim circular piers. There is, however, none of that squat stockiness that characterises most Norman work in this country; the proportions seem to be feeling their way towards Gothic, and this impression is borne out by the stiff-leaf carving on the capitals, which could hardly date from much before 1150. The same goes for the clerestory windows above. Then, some three-quarters of a century later, it was decided to enlarge the church with a new chancel, rather longer than one might expect, with a number of slender lancets including three – very slightly stepped – in the east wall. In the south wall is a double piscina and most elaborately carved triple sedilia, whose cinquefoil canopies suggest that they must be half a century or so later than the trefoiled piscina. The crossing is most impressive – four tremendous piers each carrying eleven orders, but all differently carved, with trumpet scallops and a lot more stiff-leaf. The arches are pointed and extremely tall, in sharp contrast to the remarkably stubby square tower which they support.

As for the transepts, they too offer a good deal of variety. The south one is Victorian, the north Early English but with a Decorated west chapel containing a beautiful four-light window with reticulated tracery.

Directly to the north of the church is FARINGDON HOUSE, former home of the composer–painter–writer–pianist–eccentric *par excellence* Lord Berners. It was built in the 1780s by Henry James Pye, who despite being – and I quote the *Dictionary of National Biography* – 'destitute alike of poetic feeling or power of expression' was appointed by Pitt to be Poet Laureate. (It was his first birthday ode to George III, with its endless references to 'feather'd choirs', that gave rise to the nursery rhyme verse 'When the Pye was opened/ The birds began to sing . . . .') The house – architect unknown – is modest in size: just five bays, with two storeys plus an attic and basement which, owing to the shelving ground, acquires the dignity of a ground floor on the north side. There is a lowish hipped roof, a balustrade which is interrupted for the dormers and an arrangement of tall chimneystacks rising from above the side walls. But what gives the south front its real distinction is the centre bay, which features a high pediment rising to the height of the roof ridge, its base broken by a huge, round-headed, shallow recess in which are contained both the central window of the first floor – almost twice the height of its neighbours – and a small, round-headed window above it. The front door is set beneath a deep Tuscan porch and flanked by deep rusticated niches containing statues. A lower balustrade at ground level echoes the upper one, and the composition is completed by the twin arches, with the same broken pediment and similar rustication, on each side of the house.

On entry one is immediately faced with the most memorable architectural feature of the house – the staircase. It is a double staircase, but one that does exactly the opposite of what you might expect: instead of starting with a central flight to the half landing and then breaking into two, ascending on opposite sides of the well, the Faringdon staircase starts with two parallel flights up the sides which then unite above the door to form a single flight leaping across the centre to the upper floor. The half landing is carried on a segmental arch, in its turn supported by columns and pilasters, the balustrade breaking, turning and curving most stylishly at the sides; while the main landing is carried on a round-headed three-bay screen, its two supporting columns identical with those opposite and marking the foot of the two parallel flights. It is, to say the least, an unusual arrangement, though of the greatest possible elegance.

Apart from a certain amount of delicate and restrained plasterwork, the house possesses little else that is architecturally memorable. But no account of Faringdon, however brief, can possibly omit a reference to what is surely the last full-size FOLLY tower to be built in England. Erected by Lord Berners in 1935 in the teeth of violent local opposition (it has now of course become a universally popular landmark), it is of brick, 140 feet high, with an arcaded observation room and a pinnacled and battlemented octagonal top. The architect was Lord Gerald Wellesley, later 7th Duke of Wellington.

## Great Coxwell Barn

*NT; 23; 1½ miles SW of Faringdon off A420*

'Noble as a cathedral' was William Morris's opinion of the Barn at Great Coxwell. Professor Walter Horn, an acknowledged expert on the subject, went further: it is, he writes, 'the finest of the surviving medieval barns in England, and one of the most impressive structures of its kind in the whole of Europe'. It was probably built soon after 1204, when King John granted the Manor of Faringdon to the Cistercian Abbey of Beaulieu in Hampshire (*q.v.*). The walls are of Cotswold stone, strengthened by numerous buttresses faced with ashlar, the roof of Cotswold stone tiles. On one side there is a deep transept, originally the principal entrance. There is another entrance in the wall immediately opposite it. Both these doors are original; those at the ends, however, date only from the eighteenth century, when they were probably widened to accommodate the larger carts which were then coming into use.

Inside, resting on tall stone bases, are two rows of surprisingly slender oaken posts, dividing the space into a nave and aisles. Thirty feet above the ground, they are joined together by tie-beams and longitudinal roof plates. All these tie-beams, like the posts themselves, are original, though six of them were reinforced in 1868. Original too are the struts and trusses; only the rafters have been renewed. In the upper part of the transept there are still traces of the loft in which the monk in charge would sleep; this seems to have been destroyed in the eighteenth century, when the whole porch was converted into a stable. On the opposite side, however, the original dovecot still survives.

*Great Coxwell Barn.*

*Greys Court.*

## Greys Court

*NT; 24; 3 miles W of Henley-on-Thames off B481*

Of the fortified medieval manor house built by Sir John de Grey in 1347, the big square 'keep' and two smaller, octagonal, towers still survive in good condition; a fourth tower is in ruins; and, in long hot summers, the outlines of the old courtyard walls and the two Gatehouses can still be seen in the turf. The house itself, however, which occupied the north-west corner of the courtyard, is essentially of the sixteenth and seventeenth centuries. It appeals immediately by its very texture – bands of red brick alternating with grey flint, the show front to the east consisting of four bays and two storeys, with attic windows in the three big gables which form the principal feature. All the windows are mullioned and transomed. There is a pretty seventeenth-century stone oriel on the south front, set over a gabled brick porch; the main entrance seems originally to have been on this side, and to have been moved round to the east only about 1750, when the Stapleton family, to whom the manor had passed some years earlier, made some important alterations and additions. Of these the most immediately obvious is the two-storey bow at the north-east corner, with its six tall arched windows. This marks one end of the grandest room in the house, the ground-floor Drawing Room, with its exuberant Rococo plasterwork and fine marble chimneypiece. Neither the architect nor the decorator is known for certain, but there seems little reason to doubt Christopher Hussey's attributions to Henry Keene of Oxford for the building and, for the decoration, to Thomas Roberts, also of Oxford. There is more elaborate stucco upstairs, where the frieze in one of the bedrooms is taken directly from Robert Wood's *Ruins of Palmyra*, published in 1753.

The various outbuildings to the south and east of the house are of about the same period or perhaps a little earlier – say the mid-sixteenth century. First there is the Dower House, formerly known as Bachelors' Hall from the seventeenth-century inscription over the door, 'MELIUS NIL COELIBE VITA' – 'Nothing is better than the celibate life.' Next, between Bachelors' Hall and the Keep, is a building known as the Cromwellian Stables, having been reputedly used as a mess room by the Parliamentarians during the Civil War. Finally we come to the Wheelhouse, where a well is surmounted by an immense treadwheel which was until 1914 operated by a luckless donkey, by whose efforts the water buckets were drawn up to the surface.

Greys Court is not one of the great houses of England; but there are few which have more quiet and peaceful charm. Since 1968 the whole complex, with nearly 300 acres of surrounding land, has been the property of the National Trust. The delightful garden includes a most unclaustrophobic maze, inspired in 1980 by the Archbishop of Canterbury.

## Iffley*

*25; 1½ miles SE of Oxford city centre*

No fewer than six churches were built in and around Oxford between 1130 and 1180; but of these only one has survived fundamentally unchanged. That is the CHURCH OF ST MARY, Iffley, and it has remained one of the most miraculously preserved twelfth-century village churches not only in Oxfordshire but in all England. A few alterations were inevitably made over the years, but three successive restorations in the nineteenth century – all far more careful and sensitive than one would have had any right to expect – have removed most of the damage. And the church is not only unspoilt: it is also sumptuous, with elaborate decoration inside and out.

The basic plan could hardly be simpler: a big square tower separating an aisleless nave on the one side from a two-bay chancel beyond. The tower, untouched but for its seventeenth-century battlements and two Perpendicular windows at its base, has three stages and two arched bell openings on each side, all being of three recessed orders and identical except that one (on the south side) is decorated and the others are plain – not the only evidence that the church was never entirely finished. Of the chancel, the only important point to be made about its exterior is that the easternmost bay with its three single lancets is an Early English remodelling – or perhaps an addition. That leaves us with the nave, and the nave is the glory of Iffley. The west front has three stages. (The little blind window at the top of the gable is Victorian and can be ignored.) At the bottom level we have a broad west doorway, distinctly forbidding with its six receding orders bereft of capitals, but rich in zigzag and beak-head and enclosed with a semi-circular hood-mould carved with the symbols of the Evangelists and signs of the zodiac. Above the door and forming the middle stage of the façade is a circular oculus with more zigzag; this is in fact a nineteenth-century creation by J.C. Buckler, but following the outline of the original Norman window which had been replaced by a Perpendicular one. Above this again, the three carved and recessed windows under the gable seem to echo the main doorway, except that they are flanked by columns with capitals.

*St Mary's Church, Iffley.*

The north doorway – these were used, in the Middle Ages, principally for funerals – is comparatively plain; but that to the south is carved with even more vitality and verve than its western counterpart. On the right capital are symbols of Good – a knight protects and encourages his companion, and Samson kills a lion – while on the left we are reminded of the powers of Evil: a centaur family illustrates the Fall of Man, a siren brandishes a sword, and the crowned head almost certainly represents Henry II, the murder of Thomas à Becket having occurred only a few years before.

The interior of the church keeps up the standard. The chancel, both its twelfth- and thirteenth-century bays, is vaulted, the tower arches deeply zigzagged and, on the west side, further ornamented with a stylised flower pattern. There is some good glass, too, though rather later than the rest of the church – late fifteenth-century.

Iffley is now a part of Oxford, and the church is by far the best thing of its date in the city. It should not be missed.

## Kidlington

*26; 6 miles N of Oxford off A423*

ST MARY'S CHURCH presents a rather stark and 1930s' appearance from a distance, with its plain, square tower and oddly featureless spire; it is, however, a good deal better than it looks. It was begun in the thirteenth century – see the lancets in the north transept – but was much remodelled in the fourteenth; and it is above all as a Decorated church that we must consider it – and admire it – today. There is a high nave (supporting a later clerestory), a generous south aisle (though no north one) and two lovely little chapels leading off the transepts to the east, with fine curvilinear tracery in their windows. Elsewhere the windows are mostly reticulated; only the east window, alas, lets the side down with a rather uninspired Perpendicular affair – the result, probably, of a decision to lengthen the chancel in the fifteenth century. Perpendicular too are the end windows of the transepts; there is no indication that these were lengthened, so why couldn't the fifteenth century leave well alone?

And come to that, why can't the twentieth be a little more sensitive? If a church has thirteenth-century stalls (with misericords) and two fifteenth-century benches to boot, is it really necessary to fill it up with chairs in pale blue imitation leather which would do little credit to a bingo hall? Must the good fifteenth-century parclose screens be spoilt by plate glass? Must the medieval niches be filled with modern statuary that looks as if it had been carved by Eskimos out of walrus tusks? Perhaps these abortions will have gone by the time this book appears. I hope so.

## Kingston Bagpuize

*27; 6 miles W of Abingdon on A415*

Standing in its own grounds at the edge of the village, KINGSTON HOUSE was probably built around 1715; the architect is unknown, but stylistic evidence suggests one of that brilliant group that trained under Wren in the Board of Works: John James, perhaps, or Christopher Kempster (who owned the quarry near Burford) or the Townesends of Oxford. The east front is almost copybook Baroque, yet with a distinct character of its own. It is of brick with creamy stone dressings, and has a three-bay pedimented centre slightly projecting from the two-bay wings. This centre is two and a half storeys, with an additional semi-circular attic window in the pediment; the wings are of two storeys only. All have separate quoining, and share a strongly emphasised string-course above the lower windows as well as a cornice above the upper. The windows have curious keystones which project further at the bottom than at the top, so that they catch the light, and bracket-like stones supporting their sills. Those of the ground floor have round heads, those of the first floor segmental ones. The porch is heavily rusticated, with bases and capitals of Tuscan pilasters oddly emerging; the frame of the central window above curves out towards the bottom to clasp it. There is no parapet, but the outer corners of centre and wings carry flaming urns, emblems of the Blandy family for whom the house was built. The west front is identical except for the porch; the four-bay sides have pediments formed by the shallow pitched roofs of the wings.

*The staircase, Kingstone Lisle House.*

Of the interior, the principal feature is the staircase, which rises up three sides of the vast Hall, flattening out into a landing above the front door, and continuing as a gallery along the fourth side. The underside is elegantly panelled, with a course of dentils around each panel. The main rooms, though not individually remarkable, are all fine examples of Queen Anne carpentry.

## Kingstone Lisle House

*28; 4 miles W of Wantage on B4507*

Here is an absolutely fascinating house. At an early stage KINGSTONE LISLE HOUSE got itself into a muddle; but so endearing is this muddle and so gloriously eccentric its solution that one can only feel grateful for it. Nobody at Kingstone Lisle ever played safe. Owing to a scarcity of documentary evidence its history is unusually obscure; on stylistic grounds, however, one would guess that the entrance front might be 1740 or so: seven bays with a three-bay pediment, a Gibbs surround to the former front door and prominent keystones over the round-headed windows – all nice, modest, unassuming mid-Georgian. The trouble may have begun when in 1812 the owner, a Mr Atkins, hired a respectable builder from Lechlade, Richard Pace, to add wings – in one of which a new and most individual entrance was constructed, including a long corridor with a coffered tunnel vault supported by quite tall statues above the frieze. Around then it was decided completely to remodel the garden front – so completely, indeed, that it is virtually impossible to relate the two façades in any way to each other. Bays, fenestration, even floor levels are different.

When the work was done, Mr Atkins and Mr Pace – or their successors – found (to their surprise, one would like to think, though they must have known what they were letting themselves in for) that they had got themselves a problem. The old staircase no longer served; somehow a new one had to be constructed, able to connect five different levels irregularly spaced, And so there resulted the great Kingstone Lisle *tour de force*. To call it a staircase is to do it less than justice: it is a wild force of nature, leaping from wall to wall like a flying fox, taking space and span in its stride, breaking out and recoiling again and all the while creating perspectives that would cause Piranesi himself to blink his eyes. What wayward genius was responsible? Not Pace, surely: he would have been horrified. George Basevi has been suggested, or C.R. Cockerell. But we should have known, had the architect been as famous as these; the date, after all, cannot be earlier than 1820 or thereabouts. The credit must probably go to some obscure amateur who was intrigued by the challenge and decided – with sufficient knowledge to give a fair hope of success, but not enough to cramp his style – to have a go. He achieved something that is unique, so far as I know, in English architecture.

At the end of the drive is the tiny CHURCH OF ST JOHN THE BAPTIST, with a Norman chancel – though its east window is Decorated – and a nave of about 1200. There are fourteenth-century paintings on the walls and a splendid north door that was probably already in place when Magna Carta was signed.

*St Matthew's Church, Langford.*

## Kirtlington Park

*29; 8 miles N of Oxford off A4095*

This fine Palladian house was built in the 1740s by William Smith, son of Francis Smith of Warwick; Smith had been Gibbs's master mason for the Radcliffe Camera in Oxford, and at Kirtlington he seems once again to have been guided by his old master, following – though not slavishly – designs submitted by Gibbs a year or two earlier. He died in 1747, and his work was completed by John Sanderson, who was also responsible for most of the interior decoration.

At first sight the house makes a considerable impression, conceived as it is in the grand manner, with a big pedimented centrepiece and side pavilions. There is no portico, but this lack is amply compensated for by the broad double staircase, running the length of the house, leading to the front door on the *piano nobile*, which is raised unusually high – or perhaps the staircase just makes it seem so – over a rusticated basement.

The interior is said to be very fine, and there is a famous room decorated with paintings by the Frenchman J.F. Clermont of monkeys dressed as huntsmen shooting rabbits from horseback, and other pretty Rococo conceits. More, however, I cannot say, since the owner would not allow me in.

## Langford

*30; 6 miles S of Burford off A361*

ST MATTHEW'S CHURCH stands at the end of a straggling village, built entirely of the local stone. From the outside the immediately striking feature is the tower, which is entirely Saxon – though it may have been built by Saxon craftsmen soon after the Conquest. It stands between nave and chancel like a crossing-tower – except that there are no transepts – and has arched bell openings twinned on each of its four sides. The two lower stages have pilaster strips and central pilasters – that to the south resting on a relief carving of two men apparently locked in combat. Two more reliefs have been reset above the south door and on the east wall of the porch – the former so clumsily that the Virgin and St John are facing away from the crucified Christ, not towards him.

The inside is curious in that the north and south arcades, which were added when the church was given aisles around 1200, while Early English in every other detail, yet remain purely Norman in the most obvious one – their round arches, so tall, so slender that they scarcely look English at all. Pevsner has compared them to those of an early Christian basilica; in a different context, they might almost be taken for Renaissance. Their columns, some 20 feet high, have elaborately carved capitals (mostly stiff-leaf) above which are abaci shaped like Maltese crosses.

The tower arches, too, are unusually high. They are also very narrow, and are linked by a tunnel vault some 12 feet long into which the organ has been most uncomfortably squeezed. The result of this awkward arrangement is that the chancel is effectively cut off from the body of the church and – since it is a good deal broader than the tunnel – only partially visible to the congregation. The altar has accordingly been placed to the west of the west tower arch, and very sensibly too.

The chancel is nowadays undistinguished. There is a theory that it has been shortened – the east window has obviously been chopped about – but if so the apparently original thirteenth-century buttress outside the north-east corner would seem hard to explain. The most unusual and to me the prettiest touch is to be seen in the little concave lozenge lights set in the spandrels of the paired lancets. There are more lancets of the same thirteenth-century date in the west wall; otherwise the windows are Decorated and Perpendicular.

*Milton Manor.*

## Mapledurham House

*31; 4 miles NW of Reading off A4074*

Ostensibly, Mapledurham is a fine Tudor manor house. It stands next to the church on the banks of the Thames – a picture-book example of village England. There is even a water mill, exactly where it should be. The whole place, one feels, is over-acting like mad.

But, if we are going to be purist about it, we shall have to admit that Mapledurham is not quite as good as it looks. The house is basically genuine enough, begun in about 1585 and still preserving some at least of its Jacobean plasterwork. The show front, to the east, of red brick with blue diapering, has however been twice remodelled – first in the late eighteenth century when three gabled dormers were removed and sash windows inserted, and then again about fifty years later, when mullions and transoms were restored and two-storey bays added on each side of the central door and on the two projecting wings. At this time, also, the house was given its distinctly inept battlemented stone porch and a rather silly little gable above it.

Inside, too, much has been altered. Fortunately, much also remains. The two oak staircases are still *in situ*, both with newel-posts in the form of Doric columns rising right up to the flight above. There is an admirable plaster ceiling with portrait heads, several other good ceilings in the north-west wing, and some particularly splendid work in the Saloon, where the portraits in the medallions are of Romulus and Remus and various Roman Emperors. The palm, however, must surely go to the Chapel – the house has always been Catholic. This is an enchanting creation in Strawberry Hill Gothick, and gives Mapledurham just that little extra zip which – thanks to all those alterations – it otherwise seems to lack.

## Milton Manor*

*32; 4 miles S of Abingdon off B4016*

Standing in its own grounds (which include a small ornamental lake) just outside the village, it seems the ideal English manor house – red-brick, its five bays separated by giant pilasters, with a broad string-course running between the lower two of its three storeys, and a tall hipped roof. This central part was completed in 1663, with all four elevations equal in size and the garden and entrance fronts identical; just over a century later, Stephen Wright – who in his youth had been the chief assistant to William Kent – added short side wings in the same style (one and a half bays, the half bay containing a niche), new sash windows and doorways, and stables behind. He also redecorated the interior, while leaving untouched the basic plan: three identically sized rooms on each floor, the fourth quarter being taken up by the magnificent Caroline staircase.

The inside of the house amply fulfils the promise of the exterior. The Drawing Room, for example, has a lovely panelled plaster ceiling with wreaths of oak and bay and a splendidly Baroque overmantel. The Dining Room, still painted in its original apricot, has another fine mantelpiece and is charmingly alcoved to boot. Upstairs, one of the bedrooms has preserved its eighteenth-century Chinese wallpaper. But the two most wholly enchanting set-pieces are the Chapel and the Library, both in the most light-hearted Gothick imaginable. They are the work of Stephen Wright, but John Chute of The Vyne, who was a friend of the house's owner, Bryant Barrett, probably advised him. The Library in particular, with its bookcases, fireplace, door and window frames all enchantingly Gothicised, is a gem. The house is open to the public.

## North Leigh★

*33; 4 miles NE of Witney off A4095*

A church of much fascination is ST MARY'S. Like its comparatively near neighbour at Langford, it has a Saxon tower which was designed to be central; here, however, the old nave was demolished in the late twelfth century and the chancel converted into a new one, the tower thus suddenly finding itself at the west end of what was in effect a new church. Apart from the tower, which with its twin-arched bell openings bears a marked resemblance to Langford, the outside of the building has little of interest; but the interior is a very different story. The two arcades, though of much the same date as Langford, have pointed arches, but springing from broad round Norman piers. They are of two bays; but when, probably around 1330 or so, the aisles were extended towards the west, new arches were cut – rather daringly – in the north and south walls of the tower. By then, at the other end of the church, a new chancel had been created, and at some early stage – precisely when we do not know, but certainly by the fifteenth century – this in turn had been lengthened westward, at the expense of the nave; the responds of an earlier chancel arch can still be seen, well to the east of the present one. Over this later arch (and the outsize stone screen ill-advisedly inserted by Street in 1864) can be seen the first of North Leigh's two principal glories: a formidably strong Doom painting, whose brilliant range of colour can by no means be attributed entirely to its restoration in 1967.

The other glory is the Wilcote Chapel, at the eastern end of the north aisle. It was built in about 1442 as a chantry chapel for Lady Elizabeth Blackett (who ordered it), her first husband, Sir William Wilcote, and their two sons, one of whom had been killed at Agincourt. Sumptuously fan-vaulted, it is thought to be the work of Richard Winchcombe, who worked on the Oxford Divinity School. In the north wall, which divides it from the chancel, set in an elaborate ogival arch is the tomb of Sir William and Lady Elizabeth; further east in the same wall is a tiny but ravishing piscina on a bracket. There is some interesting stained glass, too, including an extraordinary design featuring the letters of the alphabet.

Not in the same league as this, but still of considerable interest, is the curious secondary extension of the north aisle, added early in the eighteenth century as a burial chapel of one James Perrott. It is the work of Christopher Kempster of Burford, one of Wren's master masons who had worked with him on St Paul's, and is the only piece of ecclesiastical architecture of this date in the whole county outside the city of Oxford.

A more modest memorial, yet much more touching, is that to the Rev. James Musgrave and his wife ('they were near to each other and to all around them') and their two children, who died aged two months and seven years respectively ('circles tho' small are yet compleat').

*The Library, Milton Manor.*

## Nuneham Courtenay

*34; 7 miles SE of Oxford on A423*

'The cheapest pennyworth that was ever bought in Oxfordshire': thus did Sir Simon (later Viscount) Harcourt describe the manor of Nuneham when he bought it in 1712 for £17,000. It was not, however, until 1760 that his grandson, the 1st Earl, abandoned the ancestral seat of Stanton Harcourt (*q.v.*) and commissioned a Palladian villa, known today as NUNEHAM PARK, from the architect Stiff Leadbetter. At the same time he demolished the existing church and village and personally got to work – with a little help from his friend 'Athenian' Stuart – on plans for a new church which, though it might occasionally be used for Christian worship, would be designed as an ornamental classical temple and serve principally to enhance the view. A new village was built along the Oxford road, discreetly out of sight of the house.

Visually, at least, this venture into the picturesque proved a great success; the trouble came when the Earl realised that Leadbetter's villa was nowhere near big enough to allow himself and his family to live in the style to which they were accustomed. An ordinary English mansion could have almost limitless extensions at the back for its domestic offices; but in an Italianate villa all four fronts were equally important. Side wings were therefore built, projecting at right-angles from the east (and entrance) front, linked to the main block by quadrant arcades – over which, as another afterthought, two important rooms were added – a State Bedroom to the north, a Library to the south.

The 1st Earl died in 1777, drowned in an attempt to save his little dog, which had fallen down a well. His son, a young man of strongly republican – if not actually revolutionary – ideals, immediately began stripping the house of what he considered its Palladian pomposities, including the outside double staircase to the *piano nobile*. The ground floor was brought into general use, a new interior staircase opened up, and the side wings each given an additional storey. All this was the work of Capability Brown, who also re-landscaped the gardens and park – his last work before his death. Robert Adam was called in to advise on the interiors, together with Brown's partner and son-in-law Henry Holland.

In 1831 Nuneham passed to a cousin, Edward Vernon, Archbishop of York, who took the name of Harcourt. Finding the house, even after Brown's considerable enlargements, quite inadequate for 'modern notions of comfort', he instructed Sir Robert Smirke to build a whole new wing beyond the existing south extension. This wing, six bays long, three storeys high, with a pedimented garden front, preserved the original style of the house – insofar as this still existed after the addition of a rusticated extension the full length of the entrance front. The first-floor gallery and balustraded parapets, of 1904, have unfortunately obscured it still further.

That being said, the house – now leased by Messrs Rothman's – still makes a fine impression. Brown's staircase, with the ornate iron balusters which he himself designed, is rich in plasterwork, as is the elliptical lantern above. 'Athenian' Stuart's Red Drawing Room has a marvellous ceiling; the Octagonal Saloon, with its big Venetian window facing west towards the Thames, is finer still. The new tenants maintain it with loving care, and the gardens, though no longer possessing quite the picturesque impact of two centuries ago – William Mason's informal, wandering flower garden between the North Terrace and the church was the first in England and a milestone in gardening history – is still a pleasant place to stroll in on summer afternoons.

The 1st Earl's CHURCH, being primarily a garden ornament, stands atop the hill north of the house. Its principal feature is the broad Ionic hexastyle portico which occupies most of its (liturgical) north side; this is, however, a fraud, since the entrance into the church is through a much smaller semi-circular porch to the west. The nave leads under a central cupola, where it swells out slightly; then it narrows again and continues to another gentle swelling at the apsidal east end. There are no pews, just high upright stalls ranged along the walls in threes. It is a pretty eye-catcher, but very little more.

*Nuneham Park, Nuneham Courtenay.*

*Hawksmoor Quad, All Souls College, Oxford.*

## OXFORD

### All Saints

*35; High Street*

The church is said to have been designed by Henry Aldrich, Dean of Christ Church, though nobody seems too sure. (As we know for a fact that he designed Peckwater Quad in his own college, there is nothing improbable about the idea.) It was erected between 1701 and 1710; the steeple is of about ten years later and is said by Howard Colvin to 'represent a compromise between Aldrich's original proposal and an alternative one submitted by Nicholas Hawksmoor after the Dean's death'. It closes off the end of the Turl in an eminently satisfactory manner, with its arched bell openings surmounted by a columned rotunda which serves as the base for the spire – and almost, in terms of proportion, as part of it. The plain, rectangular, aisleless interior has been most sensitively and imaginatively converted into the Library of Lincoln College (*q.v.*).

### All Souls College

*36; High Street*

'The College of All Souls of the Faithful Departed' was founded in 1438 by Henry Chichele, Archbishop of Canterbury, in memory of those killed in the Hundred Years' War. Being the only Oxford college of medieval foundation which restricts its membership to graduates, it enjoys a somewhat special prestige in the University; and it is all the more surprising to find the High Street frontage so unassuming. Even the four-storey GATETOWER seems to be there not with any desire to impress, but simply because a gatetower was expected; its lierne vaulting appears only when one actually passes through to the FRONT QUAD.

This too is modest in scale. Some might even call it cramped, in a medieval sort of way, but herein lies its charm; for it remains virtually unaltered since its completion in 1441. Along the east range run the eight windows of the OLD LIBRARY, set very closely together and further bound to each other by a continuous hood-mould. (This is well worth a visit; it has a tunnel-vaulted Elizabethan plaster ceiling and Gothic Revival mural decoration of 1750 by Sanderson Miller.) The north range is taken up by the CHAPEL, approached along a narrow fan-vaulted passage. Like that of several Oxford colleges it is T-shaped, having a two-bay ante-chapel at the west end, with transept-like extensions to north and south; this is separated from the Chapel proper by a magnificent wooden screen in black and gold, with a broad arch surmounted by a high broken pediment. Originally of 1664, it was remodelled by Thornhill in 1716. Apart from this screen, the Chapel's supreme glory is its reredos, which entirely fills the east wall with statuary, each figure standing free in its high canopied niche. These figures in fact date only from 1872, the originals having been torn out and smashed by the Protestant Visitors in the reign of Edward VI; a century later, the whole glorious framework – it dates from 1447 – was plastered over; it was forgotten until 1870, when it was rediscovered, restored by Scott and, as it were, repopulated. At the same time, the original timber roof was also brought to life, and very splendid it is with its hammer-beams and carved angels.

Immediately east of the Chapel, another passage leads out of the Front Quad. Mark it well: the first bay is fan-vaulted, since it led to the original Hall, now demolished. Then, suddenly, the style changes. Gothic shafts give way to Ionic half columns, the fan-vault fronds to cool groin vaulting and a shallow saucer dome. We emerge into the NORTH QUAD, and into the world of Nicholas Hawksmoor. Hawksmoor was called in by the College in 1709. Drawings show that he first considered a classical design, but the obvious need to incorporate the Chapel in the south range seems to have decided him on Gothic. In a continuation of this range beyond the entrance passage he placed his new HALL – surprisingly restrained for him, with a shallow tunnel-vaulted ceiling – keeping the Chapel's fenestration, though without the tracery.

The show side of Hawksmoor Quad is that to the east, with its twin towers which, together, form one of the landmarks of Oxford. They must, I suppose, be described as Gothic, but it is a Gothic which Hawksmoor transmuted into something entirely individual, if not quirkish. The bottom four stages, below the unexpectedly fussy frieze, are rather plain, such decoration as there is being limited to the narrow square buttressing and the pronounced string-courses and hood-moulds. Only above the embattled parapet and the crocketed

*The Chapel, All Souls College, Oxford.*

corner pinnacles do we find in these towers an even superficial resemblance to any medieval style. But original they certainly are, and full of character; and no one, I suspect, would have them any different.

The chief architectural interest of the north range, which contains the vast CODRINGTON LIBRARY, is the contrast between its Gothic exterior and the cool classicism which reigns within. The windows echo those of Chapel and Hall to the south; the extraordinary three-light Gothic affair in the west wall, featuring Perpendicular tracery over a round-headed arch, proves when viewed from inside to be a Venetian window of Palladian purity. The interior of the Library is fearfully noble and a little austere; it is of immense length with a broad recess halfway along its north side where stands Cheere's statue of Sir Christopher Codrington, the rich sugar planter who left the College all his books and £6,000 with which to house them. The shelves cover all four sides; the dark grey-painted woodwork is Hawksmoor's own.

The west range of the Quad is simply an arcaded screen with a central domed octagonal Gatehouse. Splendid gates of wrought iron – also of Hawksmoor's design – face Catte Street and the Radcliffe Camera opposite.

## Ashmolean Museum and Taylorian Institution

*37; Beaumont Street*

It is perhaps a pity that when the architect Sir Robert Taylor died in 1788, leaving £65,000 for the teaching of modern languages at Oxford, he did not leave designs for the building that was later to bear his name. When the University received his bequest almost half a century afterwards, it was decided that the Taylorian Institution should be housed under the same roof as the old Ashmolean collection – which, having begun as the natural history and anthropological hoard amassed by the gardener John Tradescant, had by now swelled to include the fine arts and overflowed from its original home near the Bodleian. The result was an open competition, won in 1840 by C.R. Cockerell.

Cockerell's design is in essence H-shaped, the right-hand upright being given over to the Taylorian and fronting on St Giles, while the main Ashmolean façade – the cross-bar – faces Beaumont Street. This latter consists of a deep tetrastyle Greek portico on fluted Ionic columns and surmounted by a seated figure of Apollo, flanked on either side by windowless walls, articulated with pilasters and carved wreaths. The effect is curiously French, but not unsuccessful. The two wings, on the other hand, presented problems. First, they are higher than the centre – always a dangerous idea, though here, thanks to the length of the Beaumont Street front, Cockerell just manages to get away with it. Secondly, they are a good deal heavier in style, relying as they do on boldly projecting columns or half columns, crowned with statues and urns respectively and supporting a remarkably deep attic, which a series of small carved panels does all too little to lighten. Third, and most serious of all, these wings create total confusion in the corners where they join the centre, half columns and pilasters being squashed uncomfortably together to the point where it is hard to believe that they are parts of a single integrated design.

## Balliol College

*38; Broad Street*

It is one of Oxford's sad ironies that Balliol, which has a good claim to be the second oldest college in the University, should be architecturally one of the least distinguished. The foundation began when John Balliol set aside eightpence a day for the maintenance of sixteen poor scholars, as a penance for having in 1255 kidnapped the Bishop of Durham; but although the fabric of the new LIBRARY, formed by the west and part of the north sides of the FRONT QUAD, can be seen (even through James Wyatt's remodelling) to be fifteenth-century work, most of the rest is quite aggressively Victorian, and not even very good Victorian at that. It should be better: Salvin, Butterfield and Waterhouse were among the most resourceful and imaginative architects of their day. But at Balliol none of them was at his best.

Most of the Broad Street frontage – except for Henry Keene's eighteenth-century stretch at the west end – is by Waterhouse. This includes the entire south range of the Front Quad. Neither this nor the east range, coarser and monumentally insensitive in scale, gives any indication of his genius; and the feeling of gloom induced is not diminished by the pink-striped exterior of Butterfield's CHAPEL to the north – less unbridled, fortunately, than his later work at Keble, but informed here with an arrogance that enables him to ride roughshod over his surroundings. The inside, from which the surroundings are visible, might have been more satisfactory; alas, it was emasculated in 1937, the polychrome plastered over, the whole thing made colourless, safe and dull.

Beyond the Chapel is the beginning of the Library, the continuation of which extends all down the west side, replacing the medieval Hall. Wyatt completed the transformation in 1794. His are the tall two-light windows and the battlements on the west; those on the north are original. His too is the pretty plaster vaulting in both ranges, together with the bookcases and fittings.

The angle tower, joining the two ranges, is by Salvin, and it is at this point that one enters the GARDEN QUAD. Large, sprawling and L-shaped, it is much more a garden than a quad, and not very successful as either. The best bit is Keene's south-west corner, which we have already seen from outside; after that, the long west range is a hopeless muddle: first Keene, then a bit of Queen Anne work revamped by Basevi in the 1820s, then a classicising stretch by E.P. Warren of 1912, then a short burst by Salvin, and finally more Warren, this time doing his William and Mary bit. Round the corner, on the north side, is Waterhouse's new HALL, of 1876–7, with its broad outer staircase – once again strangely devoid of his normal *brio*, inside and out. All that can be said is that it is infinitely better than the two buildings of the 1960s which flank it. Will Balliol's architectural curse never be broken?

*The Bodleian Library, Oxford.*

## Bodleian Library

*39; Broad Street*

There have been three successive University Libraries at Oxford. The first was the gift of Bishop Cobham of Worcester in about 1320; the second that of Humphrey, Duke of Gloucester in 1489; and the third and last was the creation of Sir Thomas Bodley, a scholar of Merton (where he lectured in Greek and Hebrew) and later Queen Elizabeth's Ambassador to the Netherlands, who devoted his energies after his retirement in 1596 to giving the University the library it deserved. It opened in 1602 with 2,000 books; but Bodley's greatest *coup* was his agreement with the Stationers' Company in 1610, whereby the Company undertook to send the Library a copy of every book entered at Stationers' Hall. Nowadays all books published in the United Kingdom and a good many from abroad are represented by a statutory Bodleian copy, and the Library's 75 miles of shelving hold well over 4 million volumes – a figure which increases with nightmare rapidity year by year.

Duke Humphrey's ORIGINAL LIBRARY, now part of the Bodleian, remains *in situ* above the Divinity School, with its pretty painted tie-beams and countless panels carrying the University's shield; its stall bookcases are of *c.*1600. The main Library continues briefly in what is known as the SELDEN END, of 1634–7, above the Convocation House directly to the west; but its greater part will be found to the east, around the SCHOOLS QUAD, in an immense three-storey block of 1613–24 with Gothic transomed windows of four lights, dominated by a five-storey tower halfway along the east range. Three sides of this tower are unremarkable; the west side, however, facing into the quadrangle, is the grandest Jacobean architectural frontispiece in the whole of England. Its five storeys are an object lesson in the five architectural orders – reading from the ground, Tuscan, Doric, Ionic, Corinthian and Composite – the fourth storey containing a statue of James I offering his works to Fame on the one hand and to the University on the other.

Entrance to the Bodleian is by way of the PROSCHOLIUM. This curious building, which constitutes the west range of the Schools Quad, is slightly earlier than the rest, having been built separately as a sort of vestibule for the Divinity School behind. It is panelled all over, in four tiers of cusped blind arcading, the monotony being broken only by the central door with its high and most unorthodox gable, a broad seven-light window above it, and the two corner staircase towers which are similarly decorated. On its upper floor is the 'Arts End' of the Bodleian, its coffered and painted ceiling echoing that of Duke Humphrey's, its galleries supported on slender wooden colonnettes.

All these sections of the Library are open to the public and contain glass cases exhibiting some of its greatest treasures. They should not be missed.

A modern extension, the NEW BODLEIAN, stands a little way to the north, on the corner of Broad Street and Parks Road. It was built in Cotswold stone between 1937 and 1941 by Giles Gilbert Scott. Beyond these bare facts, the less said about it the better.

## Brasenose College

*40; Radcliffe Square*

The east front of Brasenose faces the Radcliffe Camera, which is something of a challenge. The College, however, takes it in its stride. The unpretentious but quietly distinguished GATEHOUSE of 1512, with its panelled front and high oriel, faces confidently out into the Square; beyond it to the south comes the seventeenth-century work, the Library and the east end of the Chapel; further still, opposite St Mary the Virgin, we reach the nineteenth century and the High Street frontage, of which more later.

The Gatehouse ushers us directly into the OLD QUAD, which dates from the College's foundation in 1509. It is not strictly beautiful, perhaps, with its endearingly irregular fenestration, the heavy hood-moulds to the ground-floor doors and windows, and the rows of close-set dormers added in the early seventeenth century; but it is rich in that peculiar Oxford charm shared by so many of the smaller colleges. On the north side is a huge sundial of 1719. To the south runs the HALL, with its wide canted bay window – a fine eighteenth-century room with a shallow plaster barrel vault within which, at the dais end, is a magnificent Royal Arms and, below, the original brass door-knocker (taken from a medieval building on the site) which gave the College its name.

A passage from the south-east corner of the Old Quad leads directly into the CHAPEL QUAD – and into the seventeenth century. To the left is the LIBRARY, above a shallow cloister (now filled in) of most curious design: a frieze of carved garlands runs along the top, divided into bays by attached pilasters, and in each bay is a pair of oval windows, set very close together. The effect is that of being stared at by a regiment of owls. The date is 1657–9; the style, of which Brasenose must be the unique exemplar, can only be described as Commonwealth Baroque. The CHAPEL, begun in 1656 and completed ten years later, is every bit as odd – not so much torn between Gothic and classical as cheerfully choosing what it likes best from each of them: Gothic tracery in the windows, classical urns on the parapet, columns and pediments vying with crockets and cusps. The interior has a roof unlike any other in the country – painted plaster fan vaulting with pendants, but applied over a fifteenth-century timber roof (itself removed from St Mary's College of the Augustinian Canons) whose hammer-beams project through the plaster. The effect is, surprisingly, delightful. Do not in your astonishment fail to notice Sir William Richard's memorial tablet to Walter Pater in the ante-chapel. Pater was the College's most distinguished fellow; all the same, appearing here in the company of Plato, Dante, Michelangelo and Leonardo da Vinci, must he not be feeling a little out of his league?

West of the Chapel is the NEW QUAD, in which all the other buildings (except the fifteenth-century KITCHEN which predates the College and has mercifully been preserved) are the work of T.G. (later Sir Thomas) Jackson. They were built in two bursts, the first in 1886–9, the second in 1907–9, and they include a long

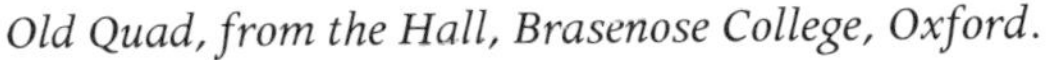

*Old Quad, from the Hall, Brasenose College, Oxford.*

frontage on the High, of seven bays, each with its oriel. Both here and within the Quad, it is hard to see how any architect of the date could have done better. There is a fine GATEHOUSE of four stages, broad and sturdy and supporting a magnificent Royal Arms; and the carving, here, above the oriels, and in the cusped tracery in the window heads, provides just the right degree of decoration to give lightness without diminishing the basic strength of the design.

Finally, tucked away in a corner behind the west range of New Quad, is an in-fill dating from 1959–61, when the College was desperate for more accommodation. It is by Powell and Moya, a model for what they were later to achieve at Christ Church, and is a small, hidden masterpiece.

## Castle

*41; off New Road*

Oxford Castle was founded by Robert d'Oilly, the city's first Norman sheriff, in 1071 – the usual motte and bailey affair. It was here that the ex-Empress Matilda, daughter of Henry I, withstood a three-month siege by King Stephen in the winter of 1142, before escaping by rope from a tower and fleeing over the snow – camouflaged, it is said, in a white robe – to Wallingford.

The mound is still much in evidence opposite Nuffield College, and has kept its well: but the original shell keep has vanished without trace. What remains is the CRYPT OF THE CHAPEL OF ST GEORGE, groin-vaulted and supported on chubby round piers with outsize capitals, crudely carved; and the early twelfth-century TOWER which also served as one of the wall towers for the castle's defence. Neither is easily visited, since both nowadays form part of Oxford Prison, a grisly institution if ever there was one.

## Cathedral

See Christ Church (Chapel).

## Christ Church

*42; St Aldate's Street*

The creation of Cardinal Wolsey, Christ Church certainly looks the part. Infinitely grander and more spacious than any other Oxford college, boasting the cathedral as its private chapel, it has about it that same air of refulgent superiority that characterised its begetter. Even the name by which it is familiarly known, 'The House' – and it is the only college to have such an alternative appellation – is less of a nickname than an honorific: 'The House of Christ' is its full title, *Aedes Christi*, carrying the clear enough implication that here alone is a foundation meet for the Saviour to dwell in.

Its Gatehouse, TOM TOWER, arguably Oxford's best-known landmark, is, in its corpulent self-assurance, itself almost a portrait in stone of the unspeakable cardinal, suggesting his pride and vaingloriousness far more successfully than Francis Bird's statue of him above the entrance. Apart from the sixteenth-century bottom stage, the tower was designed by Sir Christopher Wren, who adopted – not without some reluctance – the Gothic style 'to agree', as he put it, 'with the Founder's work'. Significantly, however, he did not adopt the twin-tower model that was usual for Tudor gatehouses and that Wolsey had certainly intended, reverting instead to the single, centrally placed tower which was by that time – 1681 – the accepted Oxford tradition. The result is a building which, although certainly more true to Gothic principles than, say, Hawksmoor's work at All Souls, is very much a creation of its time. The ribbed ogee cap – which crowns the whole edifice and is repeated beneath the four diagonal bell openings as well as on the small side towers to the west – is a favourite late Perpendicular feature which goes back to Wolsey's Hampton Court and beyond; its shape is echoed on the crocketed canopies above the openings, and in the outsize gables above the five-light windows to east and west on the second stage. But the expanses of unrelieved plain surface, the clear-cut austerity of the basic design – these things speak of the seventeenth century rather than the sixteenth, and quite right too. The tower takes its name from its 6-ton bell, Great Tom, which nightly rings the 101-stroke curfew at 9.05 p.m. – nine o'clock by the Oxford meridian.

After so imposing an entrance – you pass beneath an elegant piece of Wren's fan vaulting – TOM QUAD comes as something of an anti-climax. Not, heaven knows, by reason of its size: at nearly 90 yards square, it is easily the largest quadrangle in Oxford. But the surrounding buildings are neither high enough nor distinguished enough to enclose it convincingly, or to give it proper cohesion. Wolsey had obviously envisaged Cloisters, as at Magdalen; they would have provided architectural interest and a feeling of depth, which would have made all the difference. The two towers built at the north-east and south-east corners (by Bodley and Garner in the 1870s) might have held a more modest area together: here, they simply give up the struggle.

In the south-east corner of Tom Quad is the entrance to the huge, echoing staircase that leads up to the HALL. It was built in 1805 by James Wyatt, but the roof above is most opulently fan-vaulted – the work of an artificer named Smith and probably dating from just before the Civil War, which makes it a piece of remarkably early Gothic Revival. The Hall itself, approached through a broad ante-chamber, is of Wolsey's time and is conceived on a Wolseian scale. It boasts a tremendous hammer-beam roof, with gilded bosses and four-centred arches connecting the hammer-beams both latitudinally and longitudinally. The panelled walls are heavy with portraits; only the hundreds of plastic chairs are a disgrace; what would His Eminence have said?

And so, stopping briefly to admire Wolsey's cavernous great KITCHEN, we come to the CHAPEL. It opens off a rather poky little Cloister, strangely out of scale with the rest of Christ Church's enclosed spaces, which was originally part of the Anglo-Saxon convent of St Frideswide. So indeed was the original church on the site, though it apparently became an Augustinian priory in 1122. The core of the present building dates from rather later in the twelfth century; the upper stage of the crossing-tower and the squat, somewhat graceless spire – one of the earliest in England – were added some fifty

*The Cathedral, Christ Church, Oxford.*

years afterwards. This, essentially, is how the exterior remained until, at the time of the foundation of the College in 1525, Wolsey demolished the three western bays of the nave to make room for his quadrangle. He had no compunction about this, since he was already planning a far larger College Chapel; but he had got no further than the foundations when he fell from power in 1529. So his otherwise magnificent foundation had to make do with the truncated old church, and the new diocese of Oxford, established by Henry VIII in 1542, found itself with one of the smallest cathedrals in the country.

Fortunately, the new cathedral possessed one feature of such startling splendour as very largely to make up for its modest size and now unfortunate proportions. This was the roof of the choir, which had been re-vaulted around 1500 or a little before. The master mason was almost certainly William Orchard, who was buried in the cathedral (perhaps as a reward) and had been responsible for the glorious vaulting of the Divinity School in the 1480s. So beguiling to the eye is this roof, so intricate its patterns of tiny liernes, so delicate its rows of pendants, that one scarcely notices the fine Norman work below with its curious triforium, set within the main arcade rather than above it.

At the crossing, round arches lead to choir and nave, pointed ones to the two aisled transepts. (The south transept has an aisle on the east side only, the west one having been taken over by the Cloister.) All this is part of the original work, though much restored in 1870–6 by Scott – who added a west bay to the nave in an attempt to improve the proportions. Throughout, it maintains that curious sunken triforium, which leads to several awkward problems – not least the need to split the capitals of the main piers into halves, a lower half supporting a smaller arch and the roof of the aisle, an upper half for the main arch enclosing the triforium. The principal later additions are the two chapels immediately east of the north transept: the Lady Chapel and the Latin Chapel. The former, which actually includes part of the transept aisle, dates from soon after the completion of the church; it probably owes its position to the proximity of the city wall, which made it impossible to put it behind the choir. Between it and the choir aisle stands the much reconstituted tomb of St Frideswide. It was put together by Scott out of innumerable broken bits, and looks it. Opposite is an extraordinary wooden watching loft with a fan vault inside, from which pilgrim traffic could be supervised. There is something similar at St Albans, but as far as I know nowhere else. One bay of the chapel contains in its vaults a rather pretty fourteenth-century painting of angels with censers.

The Latin Chapel – so called because its services were held in Latin up till 1861 (with a brief interruption during the Commonwealth) – dates from about 1325: see the lovely flowing window tracery. The east window, incidentally, has early stained glass by Burne-Jones, depicting scenes from the life and death of St Frideswide – it is by far the best of his several windows here. Of all the glass in the cathedral, however, the prize must go to the glorious window in St Lucy's Chapel (part of the eastern aisle of the south transept), dating from 1340 and containing, among many other subjects in its ornate reticulated tracery, a splendid representation of the murder of Thomas à Becket. Of the other monastic buildings surviving in whole or in part, the most important is the CHAPTER HOUSE, whose Norman doorway is clearly older than the rest, which is beautiful, cool Early English work at its most assured. (Notice the carved stops and bosses and the painted vault at the east end.) To the east and south are other remains, less noteworthy; they include PRIORY HOUSE, the DORMITORY and REFECTORY. Then comes the range of MEADOW BUILDINGS, built by Deane of Dublin in the 1860s. There is much fine Victorian architecture in Oxford; but it is not here.

Turning back with a shudder, we retrace our steps through Tom Quad, leaving it by the north-east corner and finding ourselves almost at once in the second of Christ Church's two great quadrangles, PECKWATER QUAD. Designed by Henry Aldrich, who began it in 1705 while he was the College's Dean, it is smaller than its neighbour but a good deal more satisfying in the smooth classicism of its three connecting ranges. Perhaps the overall impression is a little cold; it certainly would have been if a south side had been added in the same idiom. But this Aldrich had deliberately left open for a free-standing block, residential like the others but not uniform with them. He himself died in 1710 before this could be built, leaving his tentative drawings for it to his friend – and another still more gifted amateur – Dr George Clarke of All Souls; and when in 1716 the College decided to fill the empty space with a new LIBRARY, it was to Clarke that the work was entrusted.

The result is the most distinguished building in all Christ Church: seven broad bays, separated by giant unfluted Corinthian columns (Aldrich's idea), their two storeys crowned by a deep cornice and balustrade. The lower floor between the columns – which Clarke had originally intended to leave as an open loggia – is of buff Clipsham stone, as are the capitals; all else is white Portland, and the contrast adds considerably to the building's impact. Chronic shortage of funds delayed completion for over half a century; in consequence the style of the interior is of around 1760. Here, arguably, is the most beautiful room in Oxford, running the length of the first floor, with exquisitely carved bookcases – pedimented on one side, galleried on the other – and stucco work of breathtaking quality by Thomas Roberts. The vista is closed at the end by a high Venetian window.

CANTERBURY QUAD, beyond Peckwater, is little more than a courtyard. It is the work of the young James Wyatt, who gave it a splendid Doric triumphal gateway; but it was no good trying for the monumental effect of Peckwater without having sufficient space to bring it off. In the south range the new PICTURE GALLERY, built by Powell and Moya in the sixties, is everything such a building ought to be. The same architects later went on to construct a further range north of Tom Quad running along Blue Boar Street. This 'BLUE BOAR QUAD' seems to me less successful, though it has been much praised.

*The staircase to the Hall, Christ Church, Oxford.*

## Clarendon Building

*43; Broad Street*

Named after Edward Hyde, 1st Earl of Clarendon, who was made Chancellor of the University by Charles II on his Restoration, the Clarendon Building was erected by Nicholas Hawksmoor in 1711–15 as a home for the University Press. A more solemnly impressive printing house could scarcely be imagined, with its four giant Tuscan columns supporting a deep entablature with triglyphs and a pediment. There are two floors over a high basement, a tiny attic and a row of statues – several of them replacements – to set the whole thing off. The press was moved elsewhere in 1830, and the building is now part of the Bodleian.

## Convocation House

*44; Broad Street*

Opening off the Divinity School and beneath the Selden End of the Bodleian, Convocation House essentially consists of a large room lined with carved wooden stalls and a throne at the end for the Vice-Chancellor. Grave and fearfully austere, it more than once housed the Parliament of England, driven from London by the Plague. Like the adjoining Vice-Chancellor's Court Room, it has rather crude and overpowering fan vaulting added in 1758 by William Townesend.

## Corpus Christi College

*45; Merton Street*

Corpus, as it is always known, was founded in 1517 by Bishop Fox, Lord Privy Seal under Henry VII and VIII. It is tiny, and possesses all the charm that its overblown neighbour Christ Church lacks. You enter it from Merton Street, passing under a stocky square Gatehouse, and find yourself in the unassuming little FRONT QUAD – just two storeys, with attics marked by dormers, surrounding the famous sundial of 1581 with the College's emblem, the pelican in her piety, standing on top. The HALL is there, on the left as you go in, but so modest that you can only tell it from the outside by its taller two-light windows. Inside, it proves to be grander than one expects, with an original hammer-beam roof – a little too elaborate, perhaps, for the modest space it covers – and much fine woodwork of *c.*1700 by Jonathan Mayne. Mayne was also responsible for the carving in the CHAPEL, which similarly dates from the time of the College's foundation. Like the Hall, it allows itself only one note of exuberance: an ill-judged east window of 1931. For the rest, it remains agreeably, restfully, subdued. Next to it is the LIBRARY, forming the south range of the quad. It was described in the eighteenth century as 'neither large nor unusual', but in fact contains stall bookcases of 1604, heightened a century later when they were also fitted with formidable locks and chains for protecting the books, and some good Jacobean plasterwork.

Passing through the south-east corner of Front Quad, between the Chapel and the Library, you come to what is optimistically known as FELLOWS' QUAD. Insofar as it ranks as a quad at all, it is the smallest in Oxford; in fact, it is little more than a yard, with a little Cloister running along its northern side and the back of FELLOWS' BUILDING along its southern one. The latter is unquestionably Corpus's grandest effort. Probably the work of Dean Henry Aldrich of Christ Church – the resemblance to Peckwater Quad is unmistakable – with or without the collaboration of William Townesend, it has a splendid pedimented south front of eleven bays looking over Christ Church Meadow. It was here that Ruskin lived when he returned to Oxford in 1870 as Slade Professor.

Directly east of Front Quad is EMILY THOMAS QUAD – she gave the College £100,000 in 1919 – with the fifteenth-century KITCHEN closing it to the north and the so-called GENTLEMEN COMMONERS' BUILDING of 1737 to the east. The later buildings are generally undistinguished. Do not, however, let pass any opportunity of seeing the gold and silver plate which Corpus, alone among Oxford colleges, somehow managed to avoid surrendering to Charles I in 1642. The founder's late fifteenth-century crozier is a miracle to behold.

*Front Quad, Corpus Christi College, Oxford.*

*The Divinity School, Oxford.*

## Divinity School

*46; Broad Street*

The oldest lecture room in Oxford, the Divinity School was begun in 1427, largely at the expense of Humphrey, Duke of Gloucester – which is why he was allowed to build his library on top of it (see Bodleian Library). Work on it continued, however, till the last decade of the century, and it was only in *c.*1480 that the decision was taken to give it a vault appropriate to its high purpose. The master mason was William Orchard – his initials appear on one of the bosses – and it is thanks to him that this long rectangular room is famous throughout the world as one of the triumphs of secular Gothic architecture. Its five bays are divided by four sweeping four-centred arches – there are two more framing the end walls – every one of which has a pair of deep pendants halfway up each side, from which the innumerable liernes fan out, with carved bosses at the points of crossing. The six-light windows in all the bays along each side ensure that there is no Gothic gloom; in the sunshine, the School looks more like a celebratory firework display than anything else.

That marvellous vault is obviously what everyone remembers about the Divinity School. I suspect, however, the presence of another, secret, ingredient of its peculiar magic: its proportions. The roof is only just high enough not to be oppressive, and those great four-centred arches give a marvellous feeling of spaciousness and breadth – the sort of feeling that belongs more to the sixteenth-century Italy of Palladio than to Plantagenet England.

## Examination Schools

*47; High Street*

Sir Thomas Jackson's first building in Oxford is as ebulliently adventurous as anything he ever did. The Schools were designed in 1876, and struck an instantaneous death blow to the Oxford Gothic Revival. Waterhouse, Scott and Butterfield went out of the window; in came the new eclectic style – basically English seventeenth-century *à la* Pratt and May and the 'Artisan Mannerists', but with a fair smattering of anything else that took Jackson's all-embracing fancy: Italian Renaissance, Tudor Renaissance, châteaux of the Loire, Palladio, Georgian. Here was 'unity through inclusion' long before the days of Comper.

The best-known front of the Examination Schools is that which faces the High Street. Already Jackson nails his colours to the mast with a front of five bays, of which the two on each side are occupied by immense eight-light windows, triple-transomed, but the central projecting porch is of a Venetian-window design, with a raised triangular pediment above. Additional height is provided by towering chimneystacks of Elizabethan proportions but Vanbrugian inspiration, a steeply pitched roof and a two-storey polygonal lantern with an ogee cap. The chimneystacks are actually set not on the roof but on the sides of the projecting wings, which are topped off by tall classical balustrades with high angle finials. The lobby, immediately inside the entrance, turns out to be a huge Hall with a hammer-beam roof.

All this is original enough; but now turn the corner into Merton Street, where the east side of the Schools forms the backdrop to a vast gated quad. Facing you is a towering frontispiece comparable in grandeur with that of the Schools Quadrangle but in the same stylistic *macédoine* as the High Street elevation. This time, too, William and Mary swags and garlands have been added to the mix. The side wings here are of seven bays each, ending spectacularly with a six-light window and a minute Venetian one in the gable above. Purists may disapprove of Jackson, and aesthetes may scoff; but there is a fertility of invention, an enviable self-confidence and – most important of all – a sheer panache about the man that takes one's breath away. Oxford needed him, and he was to spend the next forty years transforming it more than any other single architect. He deserves to be far better known than he is.

## Exeter College

*48; Turl Street*

Founded by its eponymous bishop in 1314, Exeter should be able to offer endless architectural interest. In fact it ought to be ashamed of itself: as a college it could never leave well alone. As a result, even the William and Mary front towards the Turl has been sheathed in an early Victorian Gothic skin, and the CHAPEL, built by Scott in 1854–60 to designs derived from the Sainte-Chapelle, is of unrelieved awfulness. Its great height totally overpowers the innocuous Front Quad, while its interior is an orgy of meretricious decoration that makes a sorry contrast with the cool restraint of its glorious exemplar. (It is in fact the third Chapel the College has possessed, replacing a mid-seventeenth century one with splendid Jacobean furniture; when, 200 years later, this became too small for its purpose, the Rector and Fellows simply blew it up.)

The grim record is partially redeemed by the HALL, which has somehow escaped destruction. Not even this is original, having been erected by Sir John Acland in 1618, in a rather self-consciously archaic style with broad three-light Perpendicular windows; but at Exeter one must be grateful for small mercies, and not the least of these are the splendid Jacobean crests of the screen, salvaged from the old Chapel.

## Green College

*49; Woodstock Road*

*Includes Radcliffe Observatory*★

For many years the University dreamed of founding a new college exclusively devoted to the study of medicine, to be built adjoining the Radcliffe Infirmary; but the project was endlessly delayed through lack of funds. Then the gift of a million pounds from Dr and Mrs Green of Dallas transformed the situation and Green College, as it is now to be called, is well on the way to completion. It will incorporate two of the buildings which Oxford owes to the munificence of Dr Radcliffe – the infirmary and the observatory. The RADCLIFFE INFIRMARY, originally designed by Stiff Leadbetter, can never have been particularly inspired; it is now ruined by nineteenth- and twentieth-century accretions and is not worth looking at. The RADCLIFFE OBSERVATORY★ is a very different matter. To say that it is the most beautiful observatory in the world is not to say much; to say that it is the most beautiful building in Oxford is to stick one's neck out, but I for one am happy to do so. It was begun by Henry Keene in 1772 but in 1773 the Radcliffe Trustees adopted a new design by James Wyatt. Keene died in 1776 and his son took charge of the building work under Wyatt's direction. It was not completed till 1794.

You would never know it was an observatory. (It has not actually been used as one for years.) In shape its elevation is a stepped triangle: the ground floor has fifteen bays, the first floor five, while the second is a 'Tower of the Winds' in the form of an octagon with alternating long and short sides. The long sides have tripartite windows with all-embracing pediments, the short ones two simple sash windows, one above the other. On the three southward sides, the angles of the walls are carried downwards to form broad canted bays on the first and the ground floor – where there is a projecting, pedimented porch on fluted columns. At all levels carved reliefs appear above the windows – the

*The Radcliffe Observatory, Green College, Oxford.*

ground floor has *paterae* and garlands, the *piano nobile* the signs of the zodiac in Coade stone, the tower carved animals by John Bacon, who was also responsible for Hercules and Atlas, supporting a globe on the roof. The north elevation is a surprise, for here the lower floors swirl out in a great semi-circle. Inside, there are just three rooms, one above the other, all enchanting, and now converted into Dining Hall and common rooms.

The surroundings have for years been a mess: all prefabs and parked cars belonging to the infirmary next door. But Green College, already living up to its name, has now given it a delightful garden from which this little masterpiece can be enjoyed as it deserves to be.

## Hertford College

*50; Catte Street*

The long and peculiar history of Hertford College has no place in this book. Suffice it to say that, having been founded (as Hart Hall) before 1301, it did not become a college until 1740 and remained one only for little over half a century, by which time its governing body was reduced to a single dotty old don. It was resurrected in 1874, but only after part of the building had collapsed in a cloud of dust; which explains why much of what we see today is the work of Sir Thomas Jackson.

Not all of it, however – for the sixteenth-century OLD HALL survives (though Jackson was to build a new one) at the eastern end of the north range of the quad, where it is recognisable by its three-light windows; there is pleasant seventeenth- and eighteenth-century work on the east side, opposite the entrance; and, to the south, the OLD CHAPEL of 1716 (now the Library) stands immediately west of Jackson's new one. And older than any of these is the little octagonal ST MARY'S CHAPEL, which only came into the possession of the College when in 1898 it bought the corner site immediately north of New College Lane. This dates from *c*.1520 but, apart from a pretty carved Annunciation above the south doorway, is too much restored to be of any real interest.

For the rest we have Jackson, working for the most part with his usual panache. His best-known feature is the 'BRIDGE OF SIGHS' spanning New College Lane, which dates from only just before the First World War; his most dashing, however, is unquestionably the staircase leading up to his HALL on the north side of the quad, embodied in a splendid TOWER whose mouldings and broad round-headed windows follow, in the manner of Blois, the sloping curve of the stair within. The huge strapwork crest above the entrance to this tower and the swooping Baroque parapet above show just how little Jackson cared about stylistic purity; yet his tower, like his bridge, constitutes a spectacular *tour de force* which it is impossible not to admire.

For the College's main façade, on Catte Street facing the Bodleian, Jackson chose the Palladian manner, with three Venetian windows separated by attached Corinthian columns over a pedimented, rusticated base. All this is flanked by two canted bays of three storeys – the centre bays have only two – to connect with the simple three-storey ranges to each side which date from the 1820s.

Finally, the CHAPEL. Jackson has given it a north-west tower, answering the Hall staircase tower across the quad, and a hint of a Cloister, just two bays long, against the north side. In the five-light east window, of which there is a fine view from New College Lane, he takes up the Venetian window motif once again, by making the centre light taller and round-headed. The other windows, with their columns, pilasters and curious low transoms, are very odd. Pevsner describes them as 'irresponsible'; but this was part of Jackson's charm. What a joy it is, particularly at this period, to find an architect of public buildings who never feels the need to play safe.

## Jesus College

*51; Turl Street*

Another small, intimate college, Jesus has strong Protestant and Welsh traditions, having been founded in 1571 by Queen Elizabeth I at the petition – and expense – of Dr Hugh Price, Treasurer of St David's Cathedral. It contains, however, little outwardly visible sixteenth-century work except for the south-east corner of the FRONT QUAD; and even that had an extra storey added in 1815. (Structurally, the whole entrance side of the quad is Elizabethan, but it was refaced inside and out in 1854 by J.C. Buckler, who also added the GATEHOUSE.) This front quad has a curious charm, due partly to its size and partly to its several small eccentricities: the flagged path that takes a curving course from Gatehouse to Hall passage, asymmetrically dividing the turf; the obvious muddle that was made of the entrance into the Chapel; the lovely shell hood over the doorway of the PRINCIPAL'S LODGINGS; the alarming lurch of the Hall range. The INNER QUAD, by contrast, is a far more ordered affair. Begun in 1639, it was not finished for some seventy-five years; but it has a strong feeling of unity owing to the somewhat relentless succession of ogival gables – and to the hood-moulds on all three storeys that take in both doors and windows and form a continuous frieze. One is grateful for the projecting bay, oriel, chimneybreast and clock on the east side for breaking the monotony.

The CHAPEL was consecrated in 1621, but lengthened to the east only fifteen years later – an afterthought which had disastrous architectural results in the south-east corner of the Front Quad. Inside, it suffers from a Street restoration of 1864, good in individual details but sadly damaging to its character and atmosphere. The HALL, built at the same time, has fared better, apart from the effective loss of its hammer-beam roof, ceiled over in 1741 with a shallow barrel vault to make an extra floor above. It has a fine Jacobean screen, featuring a number of rather lovable dragons. Finally, in the west range of the Inner Quad, we reach the LIBRARY, completed in 1679, though the bookcases and other Jacobean details come from its predecessor of 1626.

So much for the historic side of Jesus. The twentieth-century extensions to the north (along Ship Street) and to the west are less distinguished – though the OLD MEMBERS' BUILDING at the far western end, built by Mr Fryman of the Architects' Design Partnership in 1969–71, displays an antipathy to the right-angle that makes the Front Quad look positively Pythagorean.

## Keble College

*52; Parks Road*

Among Oxford's most famous graffiti are the words said to have been chalked on the walls of Keble: 'Think not of this as a college: more as a Fair Isle sweater.' The shaft strikes home; Keble is a late work (1868–82) of William Butterfield, in which he has given the fullest possible rein to his passion for polychrome brickwork. Over a background of deep red, his designs run riot in contrasting colours of buff, yellow, blue and black, sometimes diapered, sometimes chequered, in horizontal bands, dotted lines or zigzags. The style is at its most abandoned in the vast CHAPEL, which towers over the principal quad like a great proclamation of the Anglican Church Triumphant; indeed the whole College constitutes a sort of apotheosis of the Oxford Movement, translated into architectural terms.

For a century people have laughed at Keble; and it is important to remember that even in Butterfield's own day many people had their doubts. (Others had none at all: John Ruskin gave up his daily walk in the Parks to avoid having to look at it.) But just as it cannot be despised, so it cannot be ignored either. And even if you find it hard to agree with Goodhart-Rendel that the Chapel is 'possibly one of the three or four buildings in Oxford of most architectural importance', you may well agree with me that its interior, at least, is of striking and resonant beauty. It is immensely high, and with its height further emphasised by the level of its windows set a good halfway up the wall and by its broad, soaring quadripartite vault, it has an air of spaciousness altogether lacking in Butterfield's other great religious building, All Saints, Margaret Street, built some quarter of a century earlier. But there is the same delight in colour, and in the careful contrast of materials – which include dazzling mosaics by A. Gibbs, an old associate of Butterfield's, who was also responsible for the stained glass.

Vast as the Chapel appears to be, the HALL, which faces it across LIDDON QUAD, seems vaster still. It is longer than that of Christ Church. In the upper part much prominence is given, just as it is in the vaulting of the Chapel, to the carefully exposed brickwork – and the same feature appears yet again in the adjoining LIBRARY, to the east beyond the oriel. This range divides Liddon Quad from its neighbour, named after Dr Pusey. PUSEY QUAD is not really a quad at all, having no south side and only a very inadequate east one; but everywhere at Keble Butterfield seems to be trying to get away from the traditional system of closed quadrangles, opening up views beyond them in a way that would have been anathema to the medieval college builders. The same tendency can be seen in the way in which he arranges the students' rooms along corridors, instead of grouping them in the traditional manner around staircases.

Keble became a true self-governing college only in 1952; but by 1970, after a centenary appeal, it was able to commission a new range and quadrangle along the side of Blackhall Road, to the south-west, and part of Museum Road to the south. The BLACKHALL ROAD frontage, extending well over 100 yards, is grim indeed: a windowless expanse of almost unrelieved yellow brick – its very colour a seeming act of defiance against the rest of the College. Inside, however, the contrast could hardly be greater: four storeys of tinted glass, canted at the base to allow for a sunken passage. The architects are Messrs Ahrends, Burton and Koralek.

## Lincoln College

*53; Turl Street*

The College was founded in 1427 by Richard Fleming, Bishop of Lincoln, as a theological seminary for the training of young priests to combat the teachings of Wyclif. Though Fleming died four years later, having built little more than the GATEHOUSE, and Lincoln was to continue a hand-to-mouth existence for many years to come, the FRONT QUAD was finished by about 1480 and – having escaped the fate of other medieval quadrangles, which nearly all had an extra storey added to them sooner or later – still looks essentially the same as it did then. Not exactly the same, since the roof has been given dormers and all the windows other than those of the Hall have been sashed; but thanks to its smaller scale – the lack of height makes it look even smaller than its neighbour, Jesus – Lincoln has managed to preserve much of its unassertive medieval character. Like Corpus, it is a very pleasant place in which to be.

The HALL is on the east, opposite the entrance. It too is small; its three modest bays do not even take up the whole side of the quad. But it still has its fine original roof with wind-braces, and even the octagonal louvre that let out the smoke from the central hearth. There is nice William and Mary panelling, too, and a screen of the same date; Sir Thomas Jackson's Gothic fireplace of 1891 is regrettably less successful. Behind the Hall to the north-east, abutting Brasenose Lane, you will find the original KITCHEN, tall and square, with another good timber roof well preserved.

The passage through the south range leads to CHAPEL QUAD, built between 1608 and 1631. The ranges to east and west have kept their mullioned windows; that to the south is formed by the CHAPEL itself, begun in 1629 and consecrated two years later. Outside it strikes one as somewhat sombre and forbidding, with its four identical three-light Perpendicular windows looking about two centuries older than they actually are; but the interior is another story. There is a marvellous canted wooden roof of 1686–7, bearing in its panels the gilded arms of the College's principal benefactors; a beautiful cedarwood screen of the same date; and wooden stalls with misericords at the back and intriguing statuettes at the front. The glass is also worth a close look. It is by the Fleming Bernard van Linge and is dated 1629–30. That of the six-light east window is particularly rewarding – a comparison of parallel scenes from the Old and New Testaments.

Beyond the two quads, in the direction of Brasenose, the nineteenth-century buildings include the GROVE BUILDING by Sir Thomas Jackson. It shows little of the imaginativeness we see in the Examination Schools or at Hertford. Of recent work, by far the most successful – indeed, it is something of a triumph – is the conversion of All Saints' church (*q.v.*) into the College LIBRARY.

*Magdalen College, Oxford.*

## Magdalen College

*54; High Street*

It was the great good fortune of Magdalen (pronounced Mawdlin) to be built outside the city walls. Thus from the start it has always been able to spread itself and is today, with over 100 acres, by far the most spacious of the Oxford colleges. Its founder, William of Waynflete, to whom the land was granted by Henry VI in 1457, was not only Bishop of Winchester; he had also recently been appointed Chancellor of England and was by now, under a weak and frequently insane King, one of the most powerful men in the realm. Money presented no problem to him, and his buildings went up rapidly, occasionally incorporating parts of the old Hospital of St John which had previously occupied the site. The basic scheme was for a vast Cloister, to be the centre of College life – unlike that of New College, which had been designed as a burial ground – containing the kitchen, buttery and students' lodgings, with the Chapel and Hall forming its south range. Entrance was to be from the west, and it was here that Waynflete built his great Gatehouse, known as the FOUNDER'S TOWER. Now that one enters the College from the High Street, this has lost some of its impact; but it remains Oxford's grandest medieval gatehouse, four storeys high, with beautifully carved two-storey oriels on each side and a high polygonal stair turret crowned by a spirelet copiously crocketed. The Cloister itself is equally satisfying. It fortunately escaped the later third-storey additions which nearly all medieval Oxford quadrangles suffered sooner or later; and the broad three-light ground-floor windows, traceried at their tops – which have just the hint of an ogee – and separated by buttresses (some with supporters) are perfectly judged. More stone carvings run round the string-course above. The master mason here and for the Chapel was William Orchard, whose work we have seen at Christ Church and in the Divinity School; his eye seems to have been as flawless in his handling of large spaces as it was in the details of a vault.

From the north side of the Cloister there is a marvellous view of Magdalen's famous bell-tower (of which more anon), rising up from behind the three-light windows, battlements and pinnacles of the CHAPEL. For this sight alone it is worth making a circuit of the garth before entering the Chapel, which you do via the 'muniment tower' (not really a tower at all) at its west end. The interior, it must be admitted, is a bit of a disappointment, being largely a restoration by Lewis Cottingham in 1829–34 of James Wyatt's remodelling of 1790. It is T-shaped, with a transverse ante-chapel as at Merton and New College. Cottingham's are the excellent stone screen and reredos, and the rib-vaulted roof which he copied from Wyatt's. His too are the Chapel stalls, replacing the fine fifteenth-century ones with misericords, many of which are now in the ante-chapel.

The HALL is a continuation of the Chapel range towards the east; the division is obvious from the Cloister. It is on the first floor, approached by stairs in the south-east corner. Here too there has been much restoration (by Bodley and Garner in 1902), but the linenfold panelling is genuine – it is said to have been brought from Reading Abbey after the Dissolution – as is the Jacobean screen. Note too the curious early sixteenth-century panels set into the woodwork behind the high table. Then, on leaving the Hall, spare a glance for the KITCHENS immediately to the east, and particularly for the three blocked lancet windows on the north side. This vestige of Early English must date from the thirteenth century and thus have formed a part of the old Hospital buildings.

The time has now come to leave the precincts of the Cloister, and to head north towards the NEW BUILDING across the lawns. Oxford has few more enchanting prospects, with the grove and deer park to the left, the River Cherwell flowing gently through the meadows to the right; it was lovelier still before Dutch elm disease took its toll a few years ago. New Building ahead of you was almost certainly designed by that Dr George Clarke of All Souls who was responsible for Christ Church Library, and was built by William Townesend. It is enormously long – twenty-seven bays, the central five very slightly projecting under a deepish pediment – and has three floors, with an arcade running along the ground floor of the south front. It seems to have been intended as the first step towards another immense quadrangle; Wyatt and Repton, who much disliked it, had plans for Gothicising it and for building similar ranges to east and west that would link it with the Cloister. Fortunately these were scrapped before any harm was done.

Now continue westward, passing the Cloister on your left followed by the PRESIDENT'S LODGINGS – mostly Bodley and Garner, though they include the Founder's Tower. Turn left as soon as possible; on your left across an open quad is what remains of the old GRAMMAR HALL, originally built as a grammar school to prepare boys for the College. It dates from 1614, has a square bell-tower and is formidably buttressed – to particularly curious effect when seen from the west, where the tall gables and rows of mullioned windows give it a totally domestic appearance. Then, just south of the Grammar Hall, comes the beginning of the long zigzag range known as ST SWITHUN'S BUILDINGS. Bodley and Garner started them off with quite a bang – another tall tower with a two-storey oriel – and followed with a whole series of oriels along the south side towards the High. It is all good, strong, imaginative work – far superior, for example, to Waterhouse's Broad Street frontage at Balliol. After 70 yards or so it turns sharply north, after which we soon reach the end of the nineteenth-century work. The northern continuation, subsequently snaking west again to form LONGWALL QUAD, is a good deal later – Sir Giles Gilbert Scott playing safe between 1928 and 1930. The quad is closed off to the south by the LIBRARY, another nice little piece of Victorian Gothic, this time by J.C. Buckler, 1849–51.

I have left the best till last: the BELL-TOWER, Magdalen's most famous building, from the top of which the College choir sing a Latin hymn at 6 a.m. on May Day, and the first building of 'real' Oxford that you see as you come over the bridge on your way from London. It was begun in 1492, the year Columbus discovered America, and finished in 1509, when Henry VIII succeeded to the throne. The top stage is the same on all four sides, with twin three-light bell openings, then a frieze and tall parapet, partly pierced. Eight tall crocketed pinnacles complete the composition. More even than the deer park, it seems to symbolise Magdalen; and a lovelier introduction to Oxford could scarcely be imagined.

## Merton College

*55; Merton Street*

Despite occasional claims by University College and Balliol, to Merton must go the distinction of being the oldest of all the Oxford colleges. It was in 1262 that Walter de Merton, Chancellor of England and later Bishop of Rochester, obtained a licence to allot the revenues of two manors in Surrey for the support of 'clerks' studying at a university, and two years later he received royal sanction in a deed which still exists in the Merton Library. A further royal statute of 1274 specifically establishes the College at Oxford.

If, then, Merton seems a bit of a jumble, it must be excused on grounds of age, remembering that many of its buildings date from well before the development of the traditional collegiate plan. The Chapel, for example, does not form part of any quadrangle simply because when it was begun in 1289 quadrangles had not yet been invented. The Hall, too, almost certainly stood isolated for the first century or two of its existence, as did the roughly contemporary smaller Hall – probably the Warden's – parts of which may still be seen in the north-east corner of Front Quad.

FRONT QUAD is entered through the GATEHOUSE, which dates from 1418, when Henry V gave licence to crenellate. Beautifully vaulted and bearing a contemporary tympanum carved with the Agnus Dei and John the Baptist, it leads straight into an enclosure which was obviously never planned as a quad but simply grew up organically over the centuries. Directly facing you as you enter is the porch (of 1579) which gives access to the HALL. Here is Merton's first disappointment. Structurally it is the oldest building in the College, mentioned in a document of 1277; alas, between 1872 and 1874 Gilbert Scott restored it to within an inch of its life. The job was quite well done – if it had to be done at all – but it successfully transformed a medieval building into a Victorian one. Mercifully, Scott spared the door, with its marvellous arabesques of late thirteenth-century ironwork; for the rest, this grim pile offers little comfort.

Immediately to the west of the Hall, a narrow passage under an early Tudor archway takes you past the old sacristy and treasury and so, turning sharply to your right, into the oldest quadrangle in Oxford. MOB QUAD – the origin of its name remains a mystery – is entirely fourteenth-century, the north and east ranges having been completed by *c.*1335, the south and west by *c.*1380. The big four-light dormers were added in 1623 to improve the illumination in the LIBRARY, which occupies the two later ranges. Built in 1371–9, it has a good claim to be the oldest library in the country, but as we see it today it dates essentially from 1600–25; its atmosphere, with carved wood panelling and plasterwork, is Jacobean through and through. It remains a lovely, tranquil room beneath its canted wooden roof.

A passage in the north-west corner of Mob Quad now takes you to the CHAPEL, which you enter by the south transept. The first thing that strikes you about it is its size; and your surprise is all the greater when you realise that it is only a fraction of what Walter de Merton originally had in mind. What we see today is the choir, crossing and transepts; Merton also planned a nave, with two side aisles, which would have given it almost twice its present length. Why he envisaged such a leviathan of a building for a College of some forty Fellows and twenty-five undergraduates is far from clear; the most likely answer is that he was simply determined that his secular foundation – any Fellow taking Orders was required immediately to resign his Fellowship – should not appear inferior to the great monastic orders already established in the town.

At all events, this huge truncated Chapel provided the T-shaped model (the transepts having become a transverse ante-chapel) that New College and Magdalen and several other colleges were later to follow. It is – the fact must be faced – considerably more impressive than it is lovable. The choir, as we might expect, is the oldest part. It dates from the last decade of the thirteenth century – exactly the moment when Early English was giving way to Decorated – and no finer illustration of this process exists than the truly gigantic east window. The intersecting tracery clearly stems directly from the old lancet shape, while the roundel at the top derives from the geometrical tracery that came in around 1250; the designer, however, has not yet succeeded in linking the two styles together in such a way that one flows easily out of the other.

After the choir was finished there seems to have been a pause; the crossing – without the tower – was not built till the 1330s. There followed another thirty-year wait for the south transept and an even longer one for the north, which was completed only in 1424. Last of all

*The tympanum on the Gatehouse, Merton College, Oxford.*

*The Cloisters, New College, Oxford.*

came the rather squat tower, its top stage very like that of Magdalen, though half a century older. The general impression of the Chapel inside is fine enough, but oddly charmless. The best features are not, strictly speaking, architectural: the superb contemporary glass of the choir – though parts have been restored; the brass lectern of *c*.1500; the screen, part of a larger one designed for the choir (rather than the crossing) by Wren; and the green marble font given by Tsar Alexander I in 1816. There is a rather nasty organ of the 1960s and a most enjoyable *trompe-l'oeil* painting on the west wall suggesting what the Chapel would have been like if the nave had been built according to the original plan. It contrasts curiously with Butterfield's painted roof.

South of the Hall lies FELLOWS' QUAD, built in 1608–10, all of a piece and – as if to prove that Merton was still capable of blazing the trail – the earliest three-storey quadrangle in Oxford. Like Schools Quad in the Bodleian (which was built a few years later) it has a towering frontispiece to the south; but despite this laudable effort it just misses real distinction. In fact it looks considerably better from the outside, in Merton Fields, whence you get a rather charming view of alternating gables and chimneystacks, with the lavishly pinnacled tower rising up behind.

Of more recent work, Butterfield's GROVE BUILDING (beyond Mob Quad to the south-west) was sadly emasculated in the 1930s, while ST ALBANS QUAD, built in 1904–10 by Basil Champneys to the east of Front Quad, proves to be a surprisingly enjoyable excursion in Arts and Crafts Tudor. The garden buildings further east still are sorry affairs indeed.

## New College

*56; New College Lane*

In 1379, nearly eighty years before William of Waynflete founded Magdalen, another Bishop of Winchester who was also Lord High Chancellor of England established his own foundation, 'The St Mary College of Winchester in Oxford', which, to distinguish it from the other dedication to the Virgin which we now know as Oriel, has always been called New College (never just 'New'). This bishop was William of Wykeham, who three years later founded the great public school at Winchester to ensure that his students should have undergone proper preparation by the time they reached the University. Fortunately coming upon a splendid site just inside the north-east corner of the city walls – the relevant section of which he had to undertake to keep in good repair, which is why they still stand today – he started building in 1380; within six years the Great Quadrangle was completed, with Hall and Chapel ranged end to end along its north side and lodgings for fellows and students – another innovation, since till then students had always lived outside the colleges, in halls of residence – around the other three. By then the Cloister, too, was well under way; though this was never designed to be a centre of College life, on the pattern soon to be seen at Magdalen – rather was it intended as a place of burial for the dead and of calm retreat for the living. It still, after over six centuries, preserves a curious remoteness; many a modern undergraduate scarcely sets foot in it throughout his three years in the College.

The approach down New College Lane makes a right-angled turn around the corner of the Cloister, then passes between two featureless walls (on one of which I remember seeing chalked the two words 'READ BEDE', surely the most academic of all graffiti) to the GATE-TOWER, the oldest of its kind in Oxford. The statues on both sides – of the Virgin, the Angel Gabriel and the founder – are modern replacements, but William's original oak doors, from the late fourteenth century, are still in position. Through them we enter the GREAT QUAD, and very fine it is too, despite a good many alterations over the years. The range of Chapel and Hall, ending in the four-storey Muniment Tower at the north-east corner, is essentially intact, but the three other ranges – which were given a third storey and battlements towards the end of the seventeenth century and sashed windows at the beginning of the eighteenth – have completely lost their medieval character. (In 1949 Warden Alic Smith pressed for an overall replacement of mullions, and was unfortunately allowed to try out his ideas on the northernmost window of the Founder's Library, on the first floor of the east range. Mercifully, however, that one experiment was considered enough and his plan progressed no further.)

The interiors of Chapel and Hall are, it must be said, disappointing. The CHAPEL has suffered, together with so much else in Oxford, from the attentions of George Gilbert Scott; a pity, for it must have been magnificent. It is T-shaped, in the manner of Merton, with a two-bay transverse ante-chapel containing the famous 'Reynolds Window' – a Nativity scene with the seven virtues attendant beneath, designed by Sir Joshua in 1777 – but dominated by Epstein's *Lazarus*, as strong as the other is weak and (as Horace Walpole put it) washy. The Chapel itself has kept its four-light windows, transomed and with panel tracery; but most of the rest, including Pearson's reredos which completely fills the east end, the hammer-beam roof (replacing a plaster vault by Wyatt), most of the stalls, the sedilia and piscina, are Scott's and look it. There is little joy to be found except in the spectacularly good misericords beneath the stalls – the only original parts of them still remaining – in the founder's crozier (north wall of Chapel) and in El Greco's sublime *St James*, presented to the College in 1961 by Major A.E. Allnatt.

The HALL, too, was re-roofed by Scott; but he was fortunately prevented from doing such a thorough job there as in the Chapel. The principal feature is an immense quantity of linenfold panelling; but the effect is far better at night when we are spared the effect of the peculiarly nasty heraldic glass by Clayton and Bell.

A passage through the east range of the quad – which, incidentally, conceals Wykeham's original Library and another above it remodelled by Wyatt – brings us into GARDEN QUAD, not really a quadrangle but a symmetrical open space broadening out in three separate steps to the garden itself. First, the fifteenth-century 'CHEQUER' immediately to the left was refaced in 1682 and balanced with a similar one opposite; then, some thirty years later, new buildings were added, set progressively further apart from each other but keeping the same principal axis. Running across where an east range might have been is a superb screen of wrought iron, made by Thomas Robinson in 1711, with gates leading into the garden – an agreeable sunken lawn with an artificial mound at the far end and herbaceous borders running along the old city wall to the left.

North of the wall a broad grassy strip runs westward, virtually the length of the entire College, to an unworthy little free-standing LIBRARY building (Sir Hubert Worthington, 1939) which is almost on a level with the Cloister. It is lined along Holywell Street by a bleakly uninspired Victorian range – Scott again, but added to at the eastern end by Basil Champneys. All that can be said of them is that at least they are easier on the eye than David Roberts' SACHER BUILDING, which the College built along the Holywell frontage in 1961–2. Where formerly there ran a row of little seventeenth- and eighteenth-century lodging houses, unassuming, untidy and wholly delightful, we now have a long façade largely composed of grey slate: uniform, characterless and utterly devoid of humanity. Such is progress.

## Old Ashmolean

*57; Broad Street*

In 1677 Oxford University received as a gift from one Elias Ashmole a collection of natural, historical and anthropological curiosities, most of them inherited from the son of their original collector, John Tradescant; and in the following year work began on a building designed to house and exhibit them, while also providing space for lecturing and experimentation by the Professors of Natural Philosophy. That building was completed in 1683 and inaugurated by James, Duke of York – the future James II – whose cypher and crown can be seen on the north front. The architect has now been more or less definitely established as Thomas Wood, a local master mason.

The north front – that visible from the Broad – is distinguished but not particularly assertive. The important side, curiously enough, is that to the east, facing the Sheldonian, where a tremendous ceremonial doorway dominates the narrow façade. In a way this is a pity, since the Sheldonian overshadows it, giving it scarcely room to breathe, let alone to assert its very considerable presence. The boldly projecting porch consists of a pair of unfluted Corinthian columns on each side, supporting a massive segmental pediment, its base broken back to the wall behind and forming a sort of conch within it. The doorway itself has a big voluted pediment and richly carved entablature below. All around, and in broad vertical bands down each side of the cross window above, are superb carvings of fruit and garlands by William Bird.

As the Ashmolean collection increased it soon outgrew this building and was eventually transferred in the last century to its new home in Beaumont Street (see Ashmolean Museum and Taylorian Institution). Its old home was then used for a number of purposes – including the compilation of the Oxford English Dictionary, much of which was actually written within its walls. It now serves rather appropriately – since it contains the earliest chemistry laboratory in England – as a Museum of the History of Science.

*St Mary's Quad, Oriel College, Oxford.*

## Oriel College

*58; Oriel Street*

Although Oriel was founded in 1327, in theory by Edward II and in fact by his Almoner, Adam de Brome, it possesses no medieval work – having been demolished and rebuilt, virtually from scratch, between 1620 and 1650. You enter it from Oriel Square on the west, from which you already notice the cresting of little shaped gables that is something of a College trademark, passing under a still-Gothic GATETOWER with a big canted oriel window above. (This window, it should be pointed out, is not the origin of the College's name, which comes from a tenement called La Oriole that once stood on the site.) There is said to be a marvellous Jacobean room behind the oriel, with panelled chimneypiece and fine plaster ceiling; but I have not seen it.

The FRONT QUAD is very much of a set-piece, the north, south and west ranges all with almost identical elevations echoing the exterior façade: three storeys, a continuous hood-mould around the doors and two-light windows at all levels, and the same shaped gables running like a frieze along the top. The uniformity is broken only on the east side, which is something of a show-stopper. This totally symmetrical composition starts, in each corner, with a tall canted bay, transomed, having Jacobean cresting above and a rather under-sized doorway below; then, moving inwards, we have a single row of three great windows under broad pointed arches, each of three lights, transomed and with heavily cusped tracery; finally, in the middle, a projecting porch, so wide as to overlap the inner half of the two central windows, with more cresting in pierced strap-work which includes, in openwork lettering, the words 'REGNANTE CAROLO' – surely the most monumental ablative absolute anywhere. Above it, between the windows, are two near-identical and somewhat sheepish-looking statues of Edward II and Charles I; above them, the Virgin and Child; and, crowning all, a surprisingly classical composition of a segmental arch supported on tall pilasters, momentarily interrupting the shaped gables which otherwise continue along the range as if nothing had happened underneath them.

The porch leads up to the HALL, which occupies the left-hand side of this front. It is quite small, with good eighteenth-century panelling and a hammer-beam roof. The right-hand side, by contrast, is an anti-climax, as it becomes immediately obvious that the windows exist only for the sake of symmetry. In the corner is the ante-chapel, from which the CHAPEL itself marches off, slightly obliquely, to the east. (Entrance is via the little door beneath the bay window.) Although it is quite pretty, with a west gallery and a lovely cedarwood screen, it will not detain you long. Before leaving Front Quad, however, you should try to see the OLD LIBRARY, which extends along most of the first floor of the south range.

A passage through the north side takes you through to BACK QUAD, three of whose ranges carry on where its neighbour left off – though those to left and right are nearly a century later in date. The whole character of this quad is however changed by the Palladian LIBRARY which now faces you, framed by two perfectly placed trees. James Wyatt built it in 1788. Among all his work at Oxford, there is nothing – except the Radcliffe Observatory – more perfectly satisfying than this simple two-storey block, its seven bays rusticated on the lower floor, where the round-headed windows are set into deep arches, and articulated on the upper by a row of attached Ionic columns, with square-headed windows and sunken oblong panels above them.

Behind the Library is ST MARY'S QUAD. Historically, it is not part of the College at all, having been incorporated into it only in 1902. Before that it had been a separate hall of residence, dependent on Oriel but having its own identity. Thus it possesses its own seventeenth-century Hall and Chapel – the former below the latter in the south-east corner – though they are no longer used as such. The west range dates from 1826, a pleasant essay in undoctrinaire Gothic with two particularly irresponsible oriels slapped on for fun; the east, more surprising still, is a seven-bay timber-framed house of 1743 with dormers, its framing so square and regular as to make it look almost like a mathematical diagram. That leaves the northern end; and with it the building designed by Basil Champneys in 1908 as the result of a bequest by one of Oriel's most successful *alumni*, Cecil Rhodes. Its main façade faces on to the High, opposite St Mary the Virgin; even there it makes quite an impact. The front to the quad is essentially the same: a rusticated ground floor with broad round-headed windows, the rustication blocking a pair of columns on either side of the doorway and a single one between the windows. The first floor has niches for statues instead of columns, but the latter return again on the second, which is topped by a broken triangular pediment with, in the centre, another statue and a further segmental pediment over that. The usual shaped gables go off predictably to each side. The odd thing is how well it works. Every one of the four ranges of St Mary's Quad is of a different century; yet the ensemble gives, to me at any rate, real pleasure.

## Oxford Union Society

*59; St Michael's Street*

Venerable as the Union may be, no one could describe any of its red-brick buildings as an architectural treat. It finds a place here entirely because its first debating chamber, built by Benjamin Woodward in 1857, has wall paintings by Morris, Rossetti, Burne-Jones, Val Prinsep, Spencer Stanhope, Hungerford Pollen and Arthur Hughes. Today they are sadly faded; but Morris's ceiling, which he himself repainted in 1875, remains a joy to behold. This room is now the Old Library, a new and utterly undistinguished debating hall having been built in 1878 by Alfred Waterhouse. Why did Oxford always bring out the worst in him?

## Pembroke College

*60; St Aldate's Street*

Tucked modestly away behind St Aldate's, Pembroke is from the outside perhaps the least impressive of all the older Oxford colleges. It comes as no surprise to learn that it started life as a congeries of little medieval halls of residence, which only coalesced into a college in 1624 as a result of two munificent endowments, one from an Abingdon dyer and the other from a Shropshire parson. It was named after William, 3rd Earl of Pembroke, who was Chancellor of the University at the time. The GATEHOUSE is a mess, botched up in 1829–30 by a local builder in an unhappy attempt to inflate and Gothicise a perfectly respectable William and Mary affair. Done with panache, the result might have been interesting, even praiseworthy; alas, Mr Daniel Evans had neither the imagination nor the courage for the job.

It seems to have been Evans, too, who refaced the mid-seventeenth-century buildings of OLD QUAD, into which the Gatehouse leads. Here, however, his intervention has been a good deal less disastrous: the quad has been spared the addition of the third storey suffered by the vast majority of its fellows, the alternating square and pointed dormers are not intrusive, and there is a considerable bonus in the shape of the ubiquitous window boxes, which in the summer make it the most colourful quad in Oxford. From it a passage leads west into CHAPEL QUAD, at least four times its area and naturally conceived on a much grander scale. Facing you as you enter, beyond a luscious expanse of lawn, are the four tall Perpendicular windows of the HALL. This is the work of John Hayward, its date 1848. It is immense – far larger than the size of the College could ever have warranted – but it has all the verve and style so lacking in that wretched Gatehouse. It even possesses a staircase tower, projecting at the north end – a rare attribute indeed for an Oxford Hall. The inside keeps up the standard admirably, with the hammer-beam roof that was *de rigueur* at that date for any college with pretensions to importance.

The long north range of the quad is in two parts, both by Hayward; the east range is the back of Old Quad, except that at its northern end it broadens out to accommodate the Library. And so we come to the south range. Half of this – the western half – is simply a long embattled wall: the old city wall, as a matter of fact. The eastern half is occupied by the CHAPEL. On the outside it is an unremarkable classical building of five bays. It was built only in 1732; before then the College used the south aisle of St Aldate's. The interior however is – or should be – the pride of Pembroke. In 1884 it was 'enriched and beautified' by C.E. Kempe, whom we normally think of as a stained-glass man. He did the glass here too, in what Pevsner happily describes as 'a kind of Holbein–Swiss–Renaissance style'; but he also did just about everything else – the classical marble altarpiece with Ionic columns, topped by three winged heads of *putti* under a pediment that might have been less squat if the roof had been a bit higher; the polychrome saints on brackets between the windows, with elaborate, almost Siamese-style canopies above their heads; and the wildly exuberant ceiling, all flowers, inscriptions and twining tendrils. The general riot of colour aloft contrasts delightfully with the plain eighteenth-century stalls and screen at a lower level, and makes this one of my favourite Oxford chapels.

Since the last war, Pembroke has managed to make itself a whole new quad, the NORTH QUAD, between Chapel Quad and Pembroke Street, the principal architects being Worthington & Sons (1956) and C.P. Cleverly (1966–7). The new LIBRARY of 1974 is by Sir Leslie Martin.

## The Queen's College

*61; High Street*

In all Oxford there is no grander architectural statement than Queen's; but it was not always thus. Robert of Eglesfield, its founder, was a man of no great wealth; he was, however, chaplain to Queen Philippa of Hainault, wife of Edward III, and he had the admirable idea that by calling it after her but *not* mentioning her by name he might ensure, or at least encourage, the support of all future royal consorts. Over the next six and a half centuries – the foundation was in 1340 – this wheeze worked remarkably well: indeed, two successive benefactions from George II's Queen Caroline earned her a statue over the Gatehouse. Some of Eglesfield's other ideas, however – notably that the College's course in theology should last for eighteen years – have proved less practical. His statute requiring that the Provost and twelve Fellows, representing Christ and the Apostles, should sit nightly round three sides of the high table in imitation of the Last Supper, wearing scarlet gowns to remind them of the blood of the Saviour, is also – more regrettably – no longer observed. Still, all is not lost: the College is still summoned to dinner not by a bell or a gong, but by a trumpet.

Queen's as we know it today possesses none of its medieval buildings. They were all swept away in the ninety years between 1670 and 1760 – a fact which, when we look at the overwhelming classical splendour that replaced them, we cannot in all honesty regret. Oddly enough, however, there are few of these new buildings about which we can make any sure attributions – as will become all too clear in the paragraphs that follow. Logic, though not chronology, demands that we begin with the FRONT QUADRANGLE. (It seems almost blasphemous to call it a quad.) The south side of 1734, running along the High Street, is simply a screen of rusticated arcading, with a central Gatehouse above which stands Queen Caroline, protected from the elements by a cupola set on pairs of Tuscan columns, grouped radially. The arcading continues beneath the ends of the eastern and western ranges, which rise two further storeys to high pediments. Curiously, however, the faces between the windows are blank: where one expects columns or pilasters one finds nothing but a smooth expanse of ashlar. There is obviously no question here of insufficient funds, still less of inadequate architectural knowledge; it is a gesture of deliberate severity. The Queen's College is not to be trifled with.

We are reminded of this fact still more forcibly when we enter the quadrangle. The initial impression is very, very grand. The east and west ranges continue the motifs – or absence of them – that we saw from the High: thirteen bays of two storeys above an arcade, with a segmentally pedimented attic storey over the central three. Only facing us to the north do we find attached columns and pilasters; but this, as is clear from the single high row of round-headed windows – they seem to be standing on tall plinths – is the range containing the HALL and the CHAPEL. The two were built within four years of each other – Hall 1715, Chapel 1719 – and share much the same character. Both are articulated within by pilasters, but the Chapel gains monumentality by its deep apse, rising the full height of the edifice to a circular roundel painted by Sir James Thornhill. The rest of the ceiling has a profusion of exquisite plasterwork. The whole interior has recently been restored to its original colour scheme of peach-coloured walls and pale grey pilasters, and looks marvellous. There is also early seventeenth-century Flemish glass by Abraham van Linge, taken from the earlier Chapel, and a glorious screen, presumably designed for it.

The time has now come to talk attributions. Hawksmoor has frequently been suggested; he is known to have done a lot at All Souls next door, and he certainly made seven alternative sets of drawings for Queen's.

*The Library, the Queen's College, Oxford.*

*North Quad and the Library, the Queen's College, Oxford.*

Unfortunately none of these accords with the buildings as we see them today. Informed opinion now believes that only the south side of Front Quad, that is the screen and Gatehouse, can confidently be identified as Hawksmoor's and that even this was modified by William Townesend who did the building. As to the rest of the quad, it was probably a joint effort by Townesend and Dr George Clarke of All Souls. (Singly or together, these two had a hand in virtually every important architectural undertaking at Oxford between 1715 and 1740.) Hawksmoor may have been at hand with occasional advice, but nothing more.

Through now, between Hall and Chapel, to NORTH QUAD. It was here that the classical remodelling of Queen's began – with the east range, built at the expense of Sir Joseph Williamson in 1671–2. The architect, for once, is known: it was Wren. Unfortunately his work can nowadays be seen only from the outside, in Queen's Lane; around 1730 it was heightened, lengthened and also thickened at one end to conform to the same axis as Front Quad – Wren having followed the more oblique line of the Lane. What we now have is another severe, impersonal complex – all grandeur, no heart.

Except to the west. Here is the LIBRARY, built between 1692 and 1695, free-standing, its extremities disappearing behind the north and south ranges. It is in fact eleven bays long and of two storeys, both with tall arched windows. (The rusticated ground floor was originally an arcade, but was closed by C.R. Cockerell in 1843–5 to make more room for books.) It is a building of crisp distinction with its three-bay pediment on first-floor Corinthian pilasters, and it looks every bit as good from the Provost's garden on the other side; but nothing outside prepares you for the interior. The nearest equivalent among Oxford libraries is unquestionably that of Christ Church, and Dean Henry Aldrich, designer of Peckwater Quad there, may well also have been responsible for this astonishing building. But – and this is the point to remember – while the Library of Queen's is structurally only twenty-five years older than that of Christ Church, some seventy years separate the two interiors. Thus while the latter speaks with delicacy and elegance of the 1760s, the former is William and Mary through and through. The difference shows most strikingly of all in the plasterwork – Baroque in one, Rococo in the other. At Queen's, too, the bookshelves are still arranged in stall plan, projecting outward from the walls. They are gloriously carved.

Three twentieth-century additions must now be mentioned. First, the new PROVOST'S LODGINGS, by Raymond Erith, 1958–9: safe Neo-Georgian – which was doubtless what was asked for – and none the worse for that. Second, the so-called QUEEN'S LANE QUAD, across Queen's Lane on the opposite corner of the High. Here Marshall Sisson has ingeniously managed to preserve a series of seventeenth- and eighteenth-century shop fronts, adding new buildings, again Neo-Georgian, to north and east – a triumphant success that makes one wish that similar sensitivity had been shown elsewhere. Third and last, and not geographically attached to the College at all, is the FLOREY BUILDING, built in 1968–70 by James Stirling near the Cherwell beyond Magdalen Bridge: three huge five-storey ranges, raking back – they have to be shored up behind – around an irregular polygon. So much for the quad concept: there is scarcely a right-angle to be found anywhere.

## Radcliffe Camera

*62; Radcliffe Square*

Dr John Radcliffe's medical knowledge was sketchy, even by the standards of his day; but he possessed charm and wit in plenty, and rapidly rose to the top of his profession. Dying in 1714, a few months after Queen Anne – who detested him, and whom he refused to visit on her death-bed – he left £40,000 for a new library building at Oxford. It was another twenty years before the land on the selected site could be cleared. Hawksmoor submitted designs for a rotunda, and even produced a model (it survives in the Bodleian), but the contract was finally given to James Gibbs. Gibbs kept the idea of the rotunda, and the building which he began in 1737 and completed twelve years later consequently became the most famous – and, perhaps, with Magdalen Tower, the best-loved – in Oxford.

It has four stages: first, a rusticated ground floor of sixteen bays, pedimented archways and round-headed niches alternating. (All the archways were open until 1867, when they were closed and a single doorway inserted to the north.) Next comes a tall stage of paired Corinthian columns, with two tiers of windows and niches, similarly alternating, between them. Next, above a deep entablature and half-hidden by a decorative balustrade, is the drum, with more windows between its buttresses; and finally the dome, heavily ribbed, and with round openings like portholes. For those of us who are used to the proportions of St Paul's, this dome may seem a bit small for the building; it rises to a similarly modest lantern.

Inside, the lower floor with its shallow saucer vault is of comparatively little interest: the upper one, reached up an elliptical spiral staircase with wrought-iron handrail and a very pretty plaster vault, is superb. Eight huge piers, each with pairs of attached pilasters, carry tall arches with beautifully carved spandrels, below the tops of which runs a stuccoed gallery. The dome is coffered in diminishing hexagons; somehow it looks much bigger than it did from the outside.

The building is used as an additional reading room for the Bodleian, to which it is connected by an underground passage. Among much incidental sculpture is a statue of Radcliffe and a bust of Gibbs – and so there should be; Oxford owes them a lot.

## Radcliffe Observatory

See Green College.

## St Barnabas

*63; Cardigan Street*

> *Good Lord, as the Angelus floats down the road,*
> *Byzantine St Barnabas, be Thine Abode.*

Thus wrote Sir John Betjeman of this church. On the outside the effect is more Italian Romanesque than anything else; Thomas Combe, who endowed it, specified (though an Anglo-Catholic) that 'not a penny was to be thrown away on external appearances'; and his architect, Arthur Blomfield, confined himself to an occasional modest remark in brick as the only relief from the silence of the cement rendering with which the church is covered. Thus the design must speak for itself, which it certainly does: apses both east and west, round-arched arcades, and, originally, a free-standing *campanile*. (It was joined up in 1887, eighteen years after the church was built, to make room for the organ.)

It is, however, the interior that earns St Barnabas its place here. Here is surface decoration a-plenty: rich mosaics in the spandrels of the north arcade, long rows of saints and martyrs at clerestory level above, a Gothic *baldacchino* over the altar, and an east end that glistens with gold leaf and is crowned by a Christ Pantocrator in the conch of the apse, for all the world as if we were in Monreale or Cefalù.

## St Catherine's College

*64; Manor Road*

The only Oxford college to be the brain-child of a single man, St Catherine's is the work of the Danish architect Arne Jacobsen, who built it between 1960 and 1964. Mr Jacobsen was not a delegator; he designed not only the buildings themselves but the gardens and the furniture, the door handles and the teaspoons. And, let it be said here and now, he has done a marvellous job.

Of course it is not everybody's idea of an Oxford college. Indeed, it is not mine. My idea of a college is one that has grown up organically over five or six centuries – something wayward, and illogical, with little mysteries and secret places and not entirely predictable moods. St Catherine's is none of these things. It is cool,

*The Radcliffe Camera, Oxford.*

*The Hall, St Catherine's College, Oxford.*

clinical, rigidly symmetrical and uncompromisingly rectangular, for which the only designer's instrument required was the T-square – and, when it came to the lawn and the bicycle shed (for Mr Jacobsen was nothing if not thorough), a pair of compasses.

The present entrance is admittedly oblique; but this, we are assured, is only temporary. It takes us past the circular bicycle shed and the cubical warden's lodgings. We then cross a long strip of ornamental water and pass under a range of rooms to the CENTRAL COURT. You can hardly call it a quad, though that is technically what it is; its five principal buildings, grouped around a central circular lawn, make up a precise rectangle 200 yards long. Down the long sides stretch the residential ranges, in three storeys of which the upper two project, the identical bays having windows extending from floor to ceiling. The north end, to the left as you enter the court, is taken up by a T-shaped block, of which the cross-bar contains the JUNIOR AND SENIOR COMMON ROOMS (covering identical areas) and the upright, projecting southward towards the centre, is occupied by the HALL. Here, as elsewhere throughout the College, the specially made sand-coloured brick is exposed along the walls; in the Hall – the largest in either Oxford or Cambridge – there is an echo of the old beamed-roof tradition, though the beams are really deep, narrow slabs of some unidentifiable material. Supported on dark grey piers, the high table has spindly high-backed chairs of a strongly individual design; the undergraduates get plain benches.

Continuing down the court, beyond the circular lawn, we come to two very similar blocks, once again of identical size. First is the WOLFSON LIBRARY, then the BERNARD SUNLEY LECTURE ROOMS. Both have projecting upper floors. Between them rises the 70-foot BELL-TOWER – reduced, as one might expect, to its barest essentials, just two high slabs of concrete with two cross-pieces for solidity's sake and the bell platform on top.

All this sounds very soulless, and in a way it is. What gives St Catherine's its character and life – and, let's face it, its beauty – is the planting of its garden. Here, at last, logic and symmetry go by the board, though balance and composition are as important as ever. The placing of trees, bushes and flowering shrubs, the irregular alternation of lawn and flagstone, the little isolated screen walls and hedges that break up the spaces, the explosions of campus pampas and the sudden unexpected patches of heather – all these things break up the hard edges and soothe the spirit, turning cold mathematics into warm humanity. This garden is not an adjunct to the architecture; it is an integral part of it. Few of the old traditional colleges could say the same.

## St Edmund Hall

*65; Queen's Lane*

One of the oldest, and also one of the newest, of the Oxford colleges, St Edmund Hall was opened in the thirteenth century, which puts it, in terms of age, in the Merton–University–Balliol league. On the other hand, as its name implies, it continued for some seven centuries as a students' hall rather than as a college proper, and was indeed the last of these medieval halls to survive. It received college status only in 1957 – but, rightly, has not changed its name.

Although it stands only a few yards from Queen's, a greater contrast between the two could hardly be imagined. Queen's is Augustan, grandiloquent; 'Teddy Hall' is just what its universally used nickname implies: amiable, quirkish and cosy. The façade – if that is the word – that it presents to Queen's Lane sets the mood perfectly: no gatehouse, just a seventeenth-century doorway, and no attempt whatever to make an impression. And the FRONT QUAD into which it leads is even more of a jumble: few quads in all Oxford – and certainly no front quad – convey quite the same impression of slapdash informality. The only edifice in it with any architectural pretensions at all proves on closer inspection to be just as informal and unstuffy as the rest; and it is not even centred properly.

The building history of this wholly delightful hotchpotch begins with the north side, on your left as you go in; even then it is not all that ancient. The further half, or at least the two lower floors of it, dates from 1596, while the nearer half is a meticulous copy of 150 years later – an astonishing piece of deliberate archaism for the mid-eighteenth century. At some point the second-floor addition was made, with its dormers; but nobody seems to know exactly when. Going round the quad anti-clockwise, look now at the entrance range, to the west, built between 1635 and 1659. At the north end of it is the minute but otherwise unremarkable OLD HALL. The oriel marks the PRINCIPAL'S LODGING, which was considerably enlarged in 1826, both to the south and around the corner of the quad to where the ashlar facing stops. Then, further along the south range, comes the new LIBRARY of 1927 – now itself superseded by a yet newer one in the neighbouring church of St Peter-in-the-East (*q.v.*); finally, the so-called CANTERBURY BUILDING of 1934, which is really an extension of the pleasant old seventeenth-century house that occupies the right-hand side of the east range.

And so to the left-hand side of that same range. Here at last the place has made a determined effort to move with the times. Perhaps it was the burst of new building at Queen's in the 1670s that inspired it to follow suit as best it could, for the date seems to be *c.*1680. The architect is unknown – but it certainly was not Sir Christopher Wren. The salient feature of this rather touching attempt at a classical front is the pair of giant attached columns on each side of the entrance bay, supporting a tiny little pediment like a hat, with a bell let into the middle. The two windows (still mullioned) on either side of the door are pedimented too, triangularly. The door itself has an odd-looking segmental affair, flattening out at the sides; but its most endearing feature is that in order to keep this pediment at the same level as its fellows – for the door is considerably lower than the windows – it is supported on each side by a pile of carved books. This must be a playful reference to the OLD LIBRARY upstairs. Downstairs, this utterly secular front surprisingly conceals the ante-chapel, the CHAPEL itself projecting out behind it: seventeenth-century, with pleasant panelling and screen, glass in the east window by Morris, Burne-Jones and Philip Webb, and altarpiece (of Christ at Emmaus) by Ceri Richards.

Beyond the Chapel something very odd happens. We enter a new world – a late 1960s' world of concrete in which Gilbert Howes has contrived to insert a spacious quad and two surprisingly large buildings into a small area behind the High. In doing so he has scored full marks for ingenuity and almost as many for sensitivity, so far as the surroundings are concerned. (If only the western block had had four storeys instead of five!) Here, obviously, is the St Edmund Hall College of the future; but it is rambling, untidy old Teddy Hall, with its window boxes and wisteria, its petunias and wild, lurching robinia in the corner, that we remember and love.

## St John's College

*66; St Giles Street*

The only college in Oxford whose front quad predates the college itself – much of it by over a century – St John's began life in 1437, when Archbishop Henry Chichele founded – a year before All Souls – a Cistercian house which he named, appropriately enough, after St Bernard. With the Dissolution of the Monasteries a century later the land and the existing buildings were given to Christ Church; and it was from Christ Church that they were bought in 1555 by Sir Thomas White. A rich merchant tailor and former Lord Mayor of London, White was also a fervent Roman Catholic who had rejoiced at the restoration of the old religion by Mary Tudor two years before. His foundation of St John's (the patron saint of tailors) was thus partly a thank-offering and partly a sign of his determination 'to strengthen the orthodox faith, in so far as it is weakened by the damage of time and the malice of men'.

We go into FRONT QUAD through Chichele's GATE-TOWER, with his original statue of St Bernard still standing in the topmost niche. In the corresponding position facing into the quad is a statue of St John by Eric Gill – not one of his best. It is a pleasant quad. The idea of a circular lawn and radiating flagstones was a mistake, and one slightly regrets the eighteenth-century window sashing; but at least nobody added an extra floor, and the general impression remains agreeably unpresumptuous. The western (entrance) and southern ranges are the oldest; the eastern was completed only after the re-foundation; the northern, obviously enough, contains Hall and Chapel – their windows showing equally obviously which is which. They are both a little disappointing. The HALL, standing on the site of St Bernard's kitchen, dates from 1555, but was done over around 1730, when the present windows were inserted, the old timber roof covered with a plaster vault and a note of grandeur introduced in the shape of a massive marble fireplace by William Townesend. Behind it is the BUTTERY with a vaulted cellar below, hardly changed since Cistercian days; beyond that the SENIOR COMMON ROOM, its marvellous woodwork of 1676, its still more ravishing stucco ceiling (by Thomas Roberts) of 1742. The CHAPEL is an almost complete remodelling by Edward Blore of 1843. It has some good seventeenth- and eighteenth-century monuments, but very little else.

Standing at the entrance to Front Quad, with Hall and Chapel on your left, you see two doorways in the east range opposite. That to the left takes you into the PRESIDENT'S LODGINGS, that to the right into the College's greatest architectural pride, CANTERBURY QUAD. This we owe to William Laud, President of St John's from 1611 to 1621 and Archbishop of Canterbury from 1633 until his execution in 1645. One building, it is true, he found already there: the OLD LIBRARY of 1596–1601, occupying about half the south range. This he left, though he may have refaced it. The rest is all his own work and that of his architect – whom Pevsner suggests may have been Nicholas Stone, although there is no documentary evidence. It was built between 1631 and 1636. The east and west are the show sides: identical ranges, the upper floor of quite simple two-light arched windows – which, together with the crenellations, continue round all four sides – but the lower consisting of a broad, deep Renaissance arcade of eleven bays, supported on slender Tuscan columns with busts in the spandrels. It is all very opulent; more sumptuous still, however, are the twin frontispieces facing each other across the quad – only two stages, the lower an archway flanked by pairs of over-decorated Doric columns, the upper one a tremendous composition with pairs of Ionic columns on tall, elaborately carved plinths and supporting a huge segmental pediment topped by a free-standing crown. Between the columns a triangularly pedimented niche contains on the east range a statue of Charles I and on the west one of his Queen, Henrietta Maria, both by Lesueur.

Now walk through the east range, under Charles I and out into the garden beyond. On this side the range has gables at each end and a row of five oriels, the left-hand one a good deal larger than the rest and marking the east end of the Library, which Laud extended first to the south-east corner of his new quad and then round the corner along part of his garden front. (It is worth having a look at this Library if you can get in. It has kept all its original late Elizabethan bookcases and benches.) Round the corner again, the outside of Canterbury Quad's north range is more surprising still: it has a run of small shaped gables all along the top, on the lines of University College, or Jesus, or Oriel.

NORTH QUAD, which can be entered from Front Quad, from the garden or through a separate entrance on St Giles set in a boring building by George Gilbert Scott Jun., has two small seventeenth-century buildings at its south end and, much more interesting, a free-standing block on the east side built in 1958–60 by Michael Powers of the Architects' Co-Partnership. Compared with much subsequent Oxford building, these 'beehives' with their outsize hexagonal lanterns on top look nowadays a trifle staid. But they mark the University's first real departure from the cautious Cotswoldery of the thirties and the immediate post war years. As such they should be respected or reviled – but not ignored. If you are uncertain which way to react, you cannot do better than study the new SIR THOMAS WHITE BUILDING beyond, extending as far as Museum Road, by Arup Associates and dating from the mid-seventies – surely the most courageous architectural step taken by any Oxford college since the war. Here, lightness is all, the pre-cast concrete frame providing little more than a scaffolding into which the huge square windows are set. An L-shaped range embracing a split-level garden, it has all the unity, logic and strength of purpose that gives Canterbury Quad its distinction – and will one day be similarly admired.

## St Mary the Virgin

*67; High Street*

Here is a spectacular church by any standards – which makes it all the more surprising that so few visitors to Oxford ever seem to notice it. So start off by simply standing on the south side of the High at the corner of Oriel Street and looking across at it. The part nearest of all to you is one of St Mary's most memorable features: the south porch, which was added in 1637 by Nicholas Stone. It has bold barley-sugar columns – which Pevsner believes were inspired by one of the Raphael cartoons bought by Charles I in 1623 – with enormous volutes outside them and, set in a broken segmental pediment with scrolly ends, a separately pedimented niche with a statue of the Virgin. The fan-vaulted doorway is the oddest touch of all. For wild extravagance, this porch has few rivals in the whole of English Baroque.

Behind the porch is the south aisle, all good clean Perpendicular, with strong embattling and buttresses generously pinnacled; behind that the clerestory, in a similar style; and then St Mary's astonishing tower. It must have been begun around 1300, and finished perhaps a quarter of a century later. The bell openings have three lights with intersecting tracery; but one hardly notices them, such is the almost unbelievable proliferation of ornament of the stage above. Four tall lucarnes, each surmounted by a steep gable heavily ball-flowered, stand at the base of the spire; each of these is flanked by statues in canopied niches, forming the tops of the corner buttresses, while from behind the statues, on the higher level, spring four tall diagonal pinnacles with twin gables attached to each side, each gable with its own separate pinnacle. Even the pinnacles have pinnacles, and everything has ball-flower. Whether the effect of all this exuberance is aesthetically satisfying must be a matter of opinion; but it is not easily forgotten.

The interior, overwhelmingly Perpendicular, is noble but dull. St Mary's is, and always has been, a parish church; but it was also the focal point of academic life. The three-bay, rib-vaulted CONGREGATION HOUSE, standing just east of the tower (now a brass-rubbing centre), was originally built in 1320 and was the first building that actually belonged to the University; till then all academic business was conducted within the church and, even afterwards, St Mary's continued as the city's most important place of assembly. (It was here that Archbishop Thomas Cranmer was tried – and sentenced – in 1554.) Not till the inauguration of the Sheldonian in 1669 did it altogether lose its secular function. This explains the presence of such curiosities as the Chancellor's Throne in the Brome Chapel, where the Chancellor's Court met until 1643, and another, later, one under the West Gallery.

## St Michael

*68; corner of Cornmarket and Ship Street*

The rough rubble tower of this church is a familiar Oxford landmark. Having been built in the first half of the eleventh century, it is the oldest building in the city; its long and short quoins and two tiers of bell openings with their stocky little columns are copy-book examples of Saxon work, and it is a miracle that it should have survived for very nearly a millennium.

The interior has little of interest, owning to a radical restoration by Street in 1853, and a serious fire exactly a century later. There is, however, some really beautiful thirteenth-century glass in the east window, and a stone *sheila-na-gig* – a female figure of somewhat exhibitionistic character – which may be 'viewed on application'.

## St Peter-in-the-East

*69; Queen's Lane*

This fascinating old church, parts of which go back to the tenth century, has recently been converted into the Library of St Edmund Hall (*q.v.*) – in consequence of which only the crypt can normally be visited. It is a good crypt as crypts go: about 1135, with five bays, two aisles and a number of carved capitals. The church itself has a Transitional, pointed-arch nave and chancel (the east window is later), with Early English additions to the north, and a Norman tower with a Perpendicular top stage; but it is no good pretending that it gives much pleasure nowadays to any but the readers.

*The Sheldonian Theatre, Oxford.*

## Sheldonian Theatre

*70; Broad Street*

Soon after the Restoration, Oxford University decided that it could no longer continue to transact virtually all its important business in the church of St Mary the Virgin (*q.v.*). Gilbert Sheldon, a Warden of All Souls who became Archbishop of Canterbury in 1663, therefore gave in the same year £12,200 for the construction of a theatre in which the *Encaenia* – the annual presentation of honorary degrees – and other ceremonies could be held. As architect he chose his friend the Savilian Professor of Astronomy, Christopher Wren.

Wren was still only thirty-one, and the Sheldonian was his first work of architecture. He took as his model the Theatre of Marcellus in Rome, which he knew from the engravings of Serlio. Oddly, perhaps, he decided that it should face south, towards the Divinity School, which means that the most usual view – that from the Broad – is of its semi-circular back. This is in fact no bad thing. Although Wren's oval dormers are gone from the roof and his original lantern was replaced in 1838 by a larger one by Edward Blore, the back of the Sheldonian remains a good deal more interesting – even showy – than the front of most other buildings; and that great sweeping curve – echoed by the wall that separates it from the street, its piers topped by the celebrated (though recently renewed) Roman Emperors' heads – makes a more lasting impression on the casual passer by than the straight classical front would ever have done.

Besides, that classical front is not altogether a success. The seven-bay ground floor – its two outer bays having blank shell niches instead of windows – supports seven more bays above it, of which the central three are so strongly emphasised by four tall pilasters and a deep, heavy pediment that the outer ones (of which numbers 1 and 7 are again blank) look uncomfortably lost. Heavy half pediments go down on each side, but at an angle which causes them to meet the entablature of the first floor a little too far in. The result is an awkward flattening out of the half pediments at the ends – a line that would be perfectly acceptable on a Chinese pagoda but would have given Palladio a fit.

The interior has banked seating at two levels: a gallery runs all the way round, supported on marbleised wooden columns. Alas, Wren's original roof construction – of whose design he was so proud that he presented his drawings to the Royal Society – has been destroyed. (The span of 70 by 80 feet was far too great for any single wooden beam, and floor supports would have interfered with the ceremonies as well as spoiling the spectators' view; he accordingly designed an ingenious solution by which several timbers dovetailed together were supported by a triangulation system of trusses.) Despite the loss of the roof, somehow the ceiling painting was preserved, in which Religion, Art and Science are busy triumphing over Fury, Hatred and Malice. It is by Robert Streeter, who was Sergeant Painter to Charles II; but it is not very good.

## Trinity College

*71; Broad Street*

The College of the Holy and Undivided Trinity came into being in exactly the same way and in exactly the same year as did St John's; only this time it was Sir Thomas Pope who acquired the buildings of the medieval Durham College and established within them a new foundation that would staunchly uphold the ancient faith. In May of the following year, 1556, the first President was installed with twelve Fellows and eight scholars, with letters patent granted by Mary Tudor and her husband, Philip of Spain. In those days the College was set some considerable distance back from Broad Street, as indeed the heart of it still is today: the only ancient building of real consequence on the street frontage is the many-gabled KETTELL HALL at the extreme east end by Blackwell's bookshop, built by President Kettell as a private house in 1618–20. Thus, despite the fine eighteenth-century iron gates leading into the so-called FRONT QUAD – it is not really a quad at all, but a garden – the GATETOWER itself is still 100 yards away to the north. It is an intensely classical affair, having been built all of a piece with the adjoining Chapel in 1691–4; the architect is unknown. Its middle stage features an ornate arched window, lavishly carved and looking a little top-heavy, above which rises a square balustraded tower surmounted by allegorical statuary.

The CHAPEL continues the lines of the Gatetower down to the window arch; but the windows of its four bays, while of the same breadth and style, extend a good deal lower, the moulding that runs beneath them meeting the bottom stage of the Gatetower at a point rather above the springing of its arch – an awkward juncture that spoils the effect of the harmony prevailing higher up. Once inside, however, all is forgiven. Amid the stunning display of late seventeenth-century woodwork, the Age of Reason reigns supreme: one is hard put to find any sign of Christianity. But how can one cavil at such sublime workmanship? Is that tremendous reredos, with its tumbling profusion of foliage, flowers and fruit, its ornamental urns and reclining figures above, the work of Grinling Gibbons? There are no documents to say so, but few other hands, surely, would have been capable of such a combination of delicacy and assurance. In the coved plaster ceiling – in which one is almost surprised to find a representation of the Ascension – the virtuosity continues in another medium. The founder and his second wife, recumbent in alabaster, are preserved from all this exuberant secularity in a rather curious cupboard on the north side of the altar: a kind thought, since they would scarcely have approved.

After such opulence the HALL, just inside the Gatetower to the left, is something of a come-down. It was built in Kettell's day, its interior remodelled in the 1700s. The best thing in it is the sixteenth-century Swiss glass – which one longs to see transferred to the Chapel, where it could most advantageously replace the perfectly horrid Victorian stuff put in in 1885.

Chapel and Hall together make up two sides of DURHAM QUAD, the centre of the former College; a few of its original windows are preserved on the east range, which contains the OLD LIBRARY. The north range, which is shared with GARDEN QUAD beyond, is the work of the ubiquitous William Townesend. It was built as a deliberate echo of the north range of Garden Quad, which was originally erected by Sir Christopher Wren in 1668; but Wren's work has since suffered so many alterations – including the removal of its pediment and dormers and the addition of a third floor – as to be practically unrecognisable. The west range is another essay in the Wren style, this time of 1682.

Since the east side of Garden Quad is in fact open to the garden, you may as well take advantage of this fact; then, after 30 or 40 yards, turn right down the path that leads you back into Front Quad. The north side of this, east of the Chapel, is taken up with the PRESIDENT'S LODGINGS, a gloriously ebullient Neo-Jacobean work by Sir Thomas Jackson. Once again, as at Hertford, one realises how much Oxford owes to this splendid figure. Jackson's, too, is the long range to the east – behind which Trinity conceals, somewhat furtively, its twentieth-century buildings. There is a neo-classical library of 1925–7, but the rest are all of the 1960s, mostly grouped around CUMBERBATCH QUAD. The name seems oddly appropriate: the various elements, though all by the same firm of architects (Maguire and Murray) seem altogether to lack cohesion, each striving after its separate effect with no regard for the unity of the whole. A mini-quad to the south abuts Blackwell's, for whom the plans also included a vast underground showroom; one cannot help feeling that they had the best of the deal.

## University College

*72; High Street*

For over five centuries University College managed to convince the world that it was the first of the Oxford colleges, claiming King Alfred the Great as its founder. Although this fiction has now been exploded, it remains very old – indeed the oldest if you date its beginning to the year 1249, when one William of Durham left the University 310 marks to maintain a dozen advanced students of theology. Unfortunately, however, the earliest statutes were not issued till 1280, sixteen years later than those of Merton; so Univ., as it is almost invariably called, has had to be content with second place.

Architecturally, it must be admitted, it comes a good deal lower. Despite its age, it possesses virtually no medieval buildings and, as we see it today, goes back no further than 1634, when FRONT QUAD was begun. In style this is almost a carbon copy of the Inner Quad of Jesus – or more accurately vice versa, since the Jesus quad is very slightly later. There are the same two-light windows, the same continuous rising and falling head-moulds on the three storeys, even the same oddly shaped gables. This system is also carried on across the outer façade giving on to the High Street, where the monotony is broken by a three-stage GATEHOUSE carrying a statue of Queen Anne, replacing an earlier one of King Alfred. In the corresponding position on the inner face, James II in Roman costume stares out across the quad, to where, opposite him, a two-storey Gothic oriel of 1802 separates HALL from CHAPEL.

The façades of these two buildings are identical, each with three big traceried windows, and battlements above. Externally they are contemporary with the quad, but internally both have been remodelled – the Hall in 1802, the Chapel by Scott in 1862. (The two westernmost bays of the latter were added as recently as 1904.) Of the Hall, only the hammer-beam roof has survived from the seventeenth century; of the Chapel, only the stained glass (by Abraham van Linge) and the woodwork.

Even when it was built, Front Quad must have seemed a bit old-fashioned – which makes it all the more astonishing that RADCLIFFE QUAD, which rose immediately to the east of it the best part of a century later (1716–19) apes it in almost every detail. Statues of Dr Radcliffe – superbly portrayed by Francis Bird – and of Mary II replace James II and Queen Anne, and there is a simple wall with a blocked-up gateway to the south where the Front Quad has its Hall and Chapel. For the rest, the two have nothing to choose between them. How sad that Radcliffe, who gave Oxford two of its most glorious architectural masterpieces, should here have been posthumously responsible for one of its most boring quadrangles – and in his old College, too.

There are several outbuildings scattered haphazardly about to east, west and south; they include one (on High Street, towards Magpie Lane) by Barry, a LIBRARY by Scott and MASTER'S LODGINGS (on Logic Lane, a former thoroughfare now incorporated into the College) by Bodley. But, if the truth be told, in all Univ. there is only one thing that gives me any real pleasure. It stands in the north-west corner of Front Quad under a rather depressing dome by Basil Champneys, and is Onslow Ford's monument to the poet Shelley, accepted by the College (after it had been rejected by the Protestant Cemetery in Rome) as a sort of belated expiation for having expelled him after his publication of 'The Necessity of Atheism' in 1811. It represents him drowned on the Viareggio beach and is shamelessly sentimental – just as it should be.

## University Museum*

*73; South Parks Road*

Few visitors nowadays ever penetrate to the Museum – a pity, for it is one of the best things in Oxford. It is also of considerable historical significance, since it effectively marks the moment when the University first recognised that natural science was a fit subject for serious study. The original idea came from the Reader in Anatomy, Dr Henry Acland; but the drive and impetus, and the choice of both the architect and the style of the proposed building, came from Acland's close friend John Ruskin. The architect was the young Irishman Benjamin Woodward, who was to die in 1861, six years after the work was begun and well before it was completed; the style was a rather free version of Ruskin's beloved Italian Gothic. Or at least it was meant to be.

In fact, architecturally speaking, the museum is very much a law unto itself. Tall, square and symmetrical, built of contrasting buff and red stone, it presents a massive west front of six bays and two storeys, with a central tower and a steeply pitched roof with dormers, looking, to my eye at any rate, more Flemish than Italian – an impression strengthened by the geometrical tracery in the tower and upper windows. The interior, however, is a revelation. First of all, one realises that the really important building material is not the stone, or even the brick of the inner walls, but cast iron. This in itself was revolutionary. Iron and glass were considered 'railway materials'; England possessed only one major building in iron – the London Coal Exchange, built a few years before (and barbarously demolished in the 1960s). Moreover, Woodward used his materials frankly and without inhibition, making no attempt, for example, to hide the bolts and rivets in his tall, pointed arches. His plan was for three broad, parallel 'naves', separated by lower and narrower 'aisles', all carried on tall piers of four clustered shafts breaking into superb foliated capitals and, above them, wrought-iron spandrels of glorious exuberance.

The surrounding walls are divided horizontally into a tall ground-floor ambulatory supporting a somewhat lower arcaded gallery. Here the iron and glass give way to brick and stone (of virtually every variety to be found in these islands) but the virtuosity of the carving continues unabated. The best are those along the west side, which are the work of a brilliant family of Irishmen, the O'Sheas, who were brought over from Dublin expressly for the job. They started with foliage; then, warming to their task, they began to populate their leafy capitals with animals. It was only when they started on human beings, and in particular caricatures of prominent University figures, that their contract was

*The University Museum, Oxford.*

brought prematurely to a close. Perhaps it was because of this that the University suddenly tightened its purse-strings. Not till early this century was work on the capitals continued, and even now it is unfinished.

No matter. The museum reflects, as nowhere else in Oxford, the energy and high ideals of Victorian England at its best: its high-minded didacticism, professing as it did to assemble 'all the materials explanatory of the organic beings placed upon the globe'; and its steadfast faith, both in the architecture of the future and in what Ruskin hopefully described as 'the genius of the unassisted workman'.

## Wadham College

*74; Parks Road*

When, in the first decade of the seventeenth century, Nicholas Wadham of Merifield in Somerset and his wife Dorothy planned the College they had decided to endow, they chose a local West Country architect, William Arnold, who had remodelled the Manor House at Cranborne in Dorset and had almost certainly been responsible for Montacute. Arnold could thus scarcely have had better qualifications. And yet, the moment he was transported to Oxfordshire, his genius seems to have deserted him; the FRONT QUAD of Wadham is one of the least attractive in Oxford, at least among the old foundations. Its entrance front has the grace to be set back a little from Parks Road, but this only means that one sees it better; and there is something distinctly forbidding about the rigid symmetry and soulless uniformity that meets one's gaze. The impression is strengthened on entry into the quad itself. Once again, the symmetry is complete, except in the north-west corner where one does not at first notice it, and where the ever-admirable Thomas Jackson has fiddled around a bit to improve the WARDEN'S LODGINGS. For the rest, the north and south ranges mirror each other perfectly – three storeys; straight, strongly emphasised string-courses; square windows of one, two or three lights; and battlements – while to the east we are faced with the equally symmetrical range of CHAPEL and HALL, separated by a four-stage frontispiece featuring the three orders in the approved sequence and statues of Mr and Mrs Wadham, with James I predictably above them. In itself it is a nice enough piece of work, but the scale is too small to make any real impact: where majesty is required, we find only diffidence.

To the left of this frontispiece is the ante-chapel, to the right the Hall, each with four identical round-headed windows with Gothicising – but not strictly Gothic – tracery in their tops. The Hall has a louvre, marked by a little hexagonal lantern; symmetry demanded a corresponding one, so – quite unnecessarily – the ante-chapel has one too. This ante-chapel has, in the familiar Oxford style, the Chapel itself projecting at right-angles behind it; symmetry demanded a similar projection behind the Hall, despite the fact that neither is visible from the quad itself, so the kitchen wing was designed accordingly. As to the interiors, the Chapel is memorable principally for a really exquisite screen, carved with great sensitivity and finished off with a virtuoso piece of openwork cresting. Behind it are the pews for the College servants. Its five-light east window is by Bernard van Linge, signed and dated 1622. The Hall – third largest in Oxford after Christ Church and New College – has another fine screen and a most remarkable timber roof, all original. Technically, it is a hammer-beam, but it is unlike any other I know: an extraordinary filigree of ornamental braces and pendants, exuberant and quite shamelessly exhibitionist. Equally sumptuous but less grandiose is the SENIOR COMMON ROOM behind, panelled, garlanded and stuccoed in the best early eighteenth-century tradition.

The only other seventeenth-century building in Wadham – dating, however, from some eight years after the original foundation – is that which lies on the west side of BACK QUAD, between Front Quad and Holywell Street. It is of no particular interest; the best that can be said of it is that it is less boring than the long modern building opposite. This was actually put up in the 1950s, though it looks twenty years older. The memorable feature of Back Quad is what goes on to the south – a high raised terrace, approached by flights of steps at each end, backing the agreeable clutter of old houses and shops of Holywell. Only when one climbs the steps is it seen to conceal a little irregular courtyard – which only needs a roof, one would imagine, to provide an admirable fall-out shelter – known as FELLOWS' COURT. A little further along the terrace, a smaller well illuminates the basement of Blackwell's music shop, above which a three-tiered study block looks out across the quad. This adventurous and surprisingly successful addition to the amenities of Wadham is the work of Gillespie, Kidd and Coia and dates from 1971–2.

The same firm, five years later, followed up with a still more ambitious project: the construction of a new LIBRARY, built with the gift of £125,000 from the Iranian Imperial Foundation and named after the sister of the late Shah, Princess Ashraf. Part yellow concrete, part brown-tinted glass, it impressed me far more than I had expected from the photographs.

In the garden below is a statue – if it can so be called – of Wadham's most celebrated Warden in recent years, the late and much lamented Sir Maurice Bowra. He has been cut off most painfully at the midriff, as if sawn in two by a conjuror, and then placed on a chair like a particularly ghastly amputee. Thus, at Oxford, are the great rewarded.

## Worcester College★

*75; Worcester Street*

It is exceptionally lucky that Worcester exists at all, and luckier still that it exists in the form it does. Like St John's and Trinity, it began life as a monastic establishment – originally, in 1283, the property of Gloucester Abbey but fifteen years later granted to the Benedictine Order. After the Dissolution it became a Hall – retaining its old name of Gloucester – but only just; at various moments it narrowly escaped being taken over as the palace of the newly established Bishop of Oxford, as the site for St John's or later for Wadham, or as a college for Greek Orthodox clergy. Ultimately, in 1714, it was refounded as Worcester College, thanks to a £10,000 bequest by a rich Worcestershire landowner, Sir Thomas Cookes. An even more important benefactor, however, was Dr George Clarke of All Souls, designer of the Library of Christ Church, who, as well as founding fellowships and scholarships and bequeathing to the new college the bulk of his fortune together with all his books and manuscripts, was almost certainly responsible for planning the new buildings. In doing so he sought the help of his friend Nicholas Hawksmoor, and his drawings may have been further amended in detail by William Townesend, who did the actual work of construction; but the entrance front facing Beaumont Street and the north and east ranges of the main quad are due, in all their essentials, to him.

The ENTRANCE FRONT forms a little quad of its own, since the centre – in fact occupied by the Library – is set back some way from the street while the two wings, representing Hall and Chapel, project forward on each side. Each of these wings ends on the east in big Venetian windows with circular niches and garlands above. The impression is severe rather than welcoming; and the contrast strikes you so much the more forcibly when you pass through the gate into the MAIN QUAD. Clarke obviously planned a symmetrical Palladian group of buildings in the manner of Queen's, or of Peckwater Quad at Christ Church, and we can only be devoutly thankful that his vision was never realised; for what we have is one of the most enchanting architectural juxtapositions Oxford has to offer. To the right, on a high terrace above the central greensward, is his north range of nineteen bays and three storeys, with a pedimented three-bay centre slightly projecting, and round-headed ground floor doors and windows, beneath a strongly emphasised string-course. To the left, however, where we might have expected the same, we find what appears to be a little row of two-storey medieval cottages – in fact, the lodgings of the Benedictine monks sent to study at Gloucester College in the days before the Dissolution. Each cottage served a different monastery; four still have the monastic coats of arms above the doors (though not all these are in their original places). It is this wholly delightful antiphony between the two sides of the quad, separated by a good 300 years, that makes Worcester one of my favourite colleges.

The quad is open to the west, which gives on to the garden, another jewel in Worcester's crown since it actually boasts its own cricket ground and a lake replete with ducks. In the north-west corner, beyond Clarke's range, is the PROVOST'S LODGING, a noble building by Henry Keene; in the north-east another fifteenth-century range, almost hidden behind the Chapel, heads off towards Walton Street. And so we come to the east side. It is Clarke once again – similar in style and height to the north range, but with two storeys looking on to the quad instead of three, and with a similar treatment of the ground floor except that here the round-headed openings form a real arcade, with a sort of Cloister behind. It is from this Cloister that Chapel and Hall lead off. Let us take the CHAPEL first.

It is the work of James Wyatt, who took over from Keene on the latter's death in 1776, and it was completed

*The Main Quad, Worcester College, Oxford.*

in 1791. In 1864, however, it was remodelled by William Burges – in what was, even for him, a mood of high ebullience. In deference to the College's wish for a synthesis between the Gothic and the classical, he looked to Raphael – and in particular his work in the *loggie* of the Vatican – for his inspiration for the murals, and possibly even to Pompeii for the ante-chapel. But, as was inevitable with Burges, Gothic won. He added a heavy carved centre to the ceiling, statues to the niches, stained glass (by Henry Holiday, who also did the murals) to the windows, mosaic to the floors. The stalls, with the wild animals on the ends, are Burges's own; they could hardly be anyone else's. The words of the *Te Deum* run round the dado, those of the *Benedicite* round the cornice; and it is a delightfully wicked and characteristically Burgesian touch that the latter should have been so spaced that the word 'GOD' appears, golden and alone, immediately over the Provost's stall.

The HALL had, for the first century of its existence, much the same architectural history as the Chapel – completed by Wyatt in 1784, redone by Burges in 1877. But even before Burges was allowed to begin work the Fellows forced him to emasculate his designs, and the final result was but a pale reflection of what it should have been. Thus from the beginning the Hall fell between two stools; and, from the 1920s on, successive alterations gradually removed more and more of the Burges work until, in 1964, it re-emerged virtually as Wyatt had left it. It was a sad decision, and one which, I suspect, is already being regretted. But the damage is done.

South of the Quad – from which, incidentally, there is an enjoyably picturesque view of the medieval range – several new buildings have sprung up in the past half century, including a predictably boring NUFFIELD BLOCK of 1938 and an infinitely more distinguished NEW BUILDING of 1961, in brown brick with a mansard roof, by Sir Hugh Casson. Yet another building, by Peter Bosanquet, rose between them in 1971, and at the time of writing a further block, gift of the Sainsbury family, is rising behind the Provost's Lodgings to the north.

---

## Rotherfield Greys

See Greys Court.

## Rousham Park

*76; 12 miles N of Oxford off A423*

Exceptionally, we are going to take the garden first; for here is one of the most important gardens in England. It is the work of William Kent, whom – leaving aside his multifarious other talents – Horace Walpole described as 'the father of modern gardening'; and Rousham stands as the one surviving embodiment – still essentially unchanged – of his philosophy. There is no other word for it: for the gardening revolution of which Kent was the prophet was based on a completely new conception of nature and landscape. Gone were the days of formal planting in the French style – of abstract designs in privet and box, of knot gardens, quincunxes and topiary. Artificiality was out; henceforth landscapes must look natural, but – and this was the important part – natural in the way that nature *ought* to be, rather than as it actually was, so that the final effect should be similar to that of a painting by Poussin or Claude. Pope, himself a superb gardener, put it best:

*Consult the Genius of the Place in all,*
*That tells the waters or to rise, or fall,*
*Or helps th' ambitious Hill the heavens to scale,*
*Or scoops in circling Theatres the Vale,*
*Calls in the Country, catches opening glades,*
*Joins willing woods, and varies shades from shades,*
*Now breaks, or now directs, th' intending Lines,*
*Paints as you plant, and, as you work, designs.*

The Rousham garden was first laid out by Charles Bridgeman in 1721. Though he was already feeling his way towards what was called the 'education' of nature, his designs were still largely formal; little remains of them except the Bowling Green and the long *allée* leading to the statue of Apollo. All else is the creation of Kent, working 'without level or line', softening, curving, and moulding; using statuary, buildings, trees, water, even distant landmarks, to make a succession of sudden, unexpected vistas all combining to form the perfect eighteenth-century ideal of the picturesque.

The house was originally built around 1635, but was largely remodelled by Kent in 1738–40. On the entrance front, he replaced the mullion windows with pretty, octagonally framed sashes (not the hideous Victorian plate-glass affairs which have such a depressing effect on the visitor today), adding a straight embattled parapet and an ogival cupola in the centre. On the garden side to the north, he provided two low pavilion-like wings in the Palladian manner, with statues in Gothic niches – a curious though remarkably successful fusion of two contrasting styles. (He was not, however, responsible for the three projecting wings on that same side; these were the work of William St Aubyn, who enlarged the house still further in 1860.)

Though Kent made relatively few structural alterations – both the original oak staircases, for example, remain *in situ* – he left his mark on nearly all the rooms. (The only notable exception is the so-called Oak Chamber, which preserves all its Jacobean panelling.) The one-storey Hall, occupying the central five bays of the entrance front, is not of any special architectural interest; to the east of it, however, the so-called Painted Parlour – originally the kitchen – is ravishing: Kent at his most inspired. It is a small, lowish room, but he has not hesitated to give it the full treatment: painted ceiling, magnificent doorcases (even though three of the four doors are false), a splendid chimneypiece with exuberantly carved overmantel, scrolly brackets on the walls, their form echoed in the window frames, specially designed furniture, specially selected pictures – the lot.

The other memorable room is the former Library in Kent's west wing; since, however, its bookcases were removed when it was remodelled in 1764 by Thomas Roberts of Oxford, it is now known as the Great Parlour. Roberts preserved Kent's extraordinary deeply vaulted

*Rousham Park.*

ceiling, together with his chimneypiece and gilded overmantel, but surrounded the doorcases and portraits with the Rococo plasterwork that was his speciality. It is a superb room, and there are few which better illustrate the remarkable development in the direction of lightness and fantasy that took place in English interior decoration in the middle years of the eighteenth century.

## Rycote*

*77; 4 miles SW of Thame off A329*

The CHAPEL OF ST MICHAEL stands in the grounds of Rycote Park, a great house of the early sixteenth century which was burnt to ashes in 1745. It was consecrated in 1449 and the exterior has remained virtually untouched ever since; what makes it memorable, however, is the splendour of its interior fittings, which span the seventeenth century from 1610 to 1682.

One's first sight of the west tower already gives promise of the sumptuousness within. It has four stages: west door; three-light window with cusped arches; image niche with canopy (but no longer any image); and twin bell openings, the same shape as the window. All stages except the niche have strongly emphasised hood-moulds. These features are all on the west side; the other three sides are simpler, and there is a polygonal stair turret at the south-east corner. Of the chapel itself, the north and south sides are of five bays, divided by prominent buttresses; all the side windows are of two lights, in the same style that we have already seen on the tower, and with the same hood-moulds. The east window is similar, only with five lights, sub-divided into ten from just below the springing of the arch.

Now for the interior. The principal surviving fifteenth-century work is to be seen in the roof, which runs without interruption the whole length of the building – a long timbered tunnel with a central ridge beam, two parallel purlins on each side and regular rafters. About two centuries after its construction it was painted and decorated with little golden stars cut out of cardboard. Alas, too little of all this remains to give us much impression of what the general effect must have been; but a small section has been redone at the west end, and very charming it is. Other survivals are the benches in the nave and the stalls in the chancel – good, but not remarkable.

The seventeenth-century work starts with the west gallery, which has a balustrade across the front and is supported by tapering wooden columns with Ionic capitals; its underside is painted with stars. Standing below it and looking east up the nave your eye rests, fascinated, upon the outstanding features of Rycote – its two great pews, one to each side of the chancel steps. The lower part of the fifteenth-century rood-screen forms their eastern walls, with an open classical arcade about 3 feet high running above and supporting a semi-circular arch (surmounted by a splendid piece of three-dimensional ornamental strapwork) which gives access to the chancel. In the pew to the north – believed to have been built about 1610 as the tomb of the Norreys family, lords of Rycote since the 1540s – this arcade continues round the south and west sides; on the north, against the wall, is the little staircase that gives access to the carved wooden loft, presumably once a musicians' gallery. The panels of this loft are elaborately carved with an open, fretted design almost Arabian in feeling; a good many frets have had to be renewed, but without prejudice to the overall impression. There is more painting inside the pew, on the ceiling and also on the panelled wall just east of the loft stairs.

The southern pew is, if anything, more remarkable still, topped as it is by a ribbed, ogivally domed canopy which adds to the oddly oriental effect created by the fretwork loft opposite. This is supported by a row of columns, below which runs the same design of arcade as exists in its northern neighbour – providing an important unifying architectural feature. Despite this, however, the pew seems to be of a slightly later date, and was almost certainly constructed for the visit of Charles I to Rycote in 1635. Immediately to the west of it is a lovely square Jacobean pulpit, with canopy.

Just as the nave is dominated by the two great pews, so is the chancel by the magnificent carved wooden reredos of 1682. An old theory that it was the work of Grinling Gibbons has now been discounted, but he would certainly not have been ashamed of it. It compares interestingly with its predecessor of 1610, which has now been relegated to the north wall under the tower – damaged and relatively unsophisticated, but of much charm.

The Chapel at Rycote is one of the lesser-known treasures of Oxfordshire – one of those magnetic buildings which, once you know of their existence, it is difficult to pass by.

*The Chapel of St Michael, Rycote.*

## Sparsholt

*78; 3 miles W of Wantage off B4507*

A pretty rendered church at the foot of the North Downs, HOLY CROSS has a thirteenth-century west tower and shingled broach spire. One's interest is first caught by the north door, which was almost certainly in place before 1200. It is of oak, with marvellous old ironwork, and is flanked by columns bearing capitals carved with both stiff-leaf and water-leaf, the hood-mould resting on animals' heads. Inside, the Decorated style prevails, notably in the chancel (of Downs clunch) where the five-light east window has fine reticulated tracery, and also in the south transept – the north one was demolished about 1785 – where the end window is similar, but of four lights only. Also in the south transept are three very fine tomb recesses, ogival in shape and generously cusped, with wooden effigies representing Sir Robert Achard (who died in 1353) and his two wives. (Funerary sculpture in wood is a considerable rarity in Britain; there are fewer than a hundred examples, all told.) A fourth canopied tomb is to be found in the chancel, together with highly ornate sedilia, piscina and Easter sepulchre, all of the same fourteenth-century style and date. Yet even these are modernities compared with the font, which may well date from the eighth century.

## Stanton Harcourt*

*79; 9 miles W of Oxford on B4449*

The great medieval manor house of the Harcourts, STANTON HARCOURT MANOR, was pulled down in the middle of the eighteenth century, when the 1st Earl moved his seat to Nuneham Courtenay (*q.v.*); there survive just the Great Kitchen – saved only because it stood apart from the house – and the north-east tower, which owes its preservation to its position over the Chapel. The Kitchen alone is worth the journey. Built probably in the late fourteenth century and re-roofed in 1485, it is the grandest example of its kind in the country, Glastonbury not excepted: over 30 feet square, with an embattled parapet and an octagonal pyramid roof. It has no chimney: the smoke escaped through louvres in the roof, now replaced by windows. There are two open fireplaces against one wall, and three ovens opposite them. At the top of the stone walls the square is transformed by squinches into an octagon, from each angle of which an immense timber beam soars up to the apex, while concentric and diminishing octagons of arched wind-braces complete the spider's-web image. The locals, asserted Alexander Pope, 'believe the witches keep their sabbath here, and that once a year the Devil treats them with infernal venison, viz. a toasted tiger stuffed with tenpenny nails'.

Pope stayed at Stanton Harcourt in 1717–18 while he was translating the *Iliad*, and has given his name to that surviving north-east tower. It was built in the 1460s. On the ground floor is the Chapel, projecting to the west, with a fan-vaulted chancel and a three-light Perpendicular east window. Above it is a priest's room with Jacobean panelling. Pope's room is on the very top. It too has seventeenth-century panelling, but I confess that I have not seen it.

The other glory of this memorable village is the parish CHURCH OF ST MICHAEL. Tradition claims that it was built by Queen Adeliza, widow of Henry I; the surviving Norman features (north and south doorways and windows in the nave and tower) are certainly mid-twelfth century, though there is little of the sumptuousness one might have expected of a royal foundation. About 100 years after Adeliza's death, the church was altered and enlarged; the nave was left aisleless, but transepts were added and the chancel lengthened, and it is above all to this chancel that St Michael's owes its considerable distinction. The east window alone is enough to set it above all but a few of its Oxfordshire contemporaries, with three beautifully judged stepped lancets separated on the inside by clustered colonnettes and stiff-leaf capitals. There is another, similar, group on the north wall; that on the south had to be sacrificed when the Harcourt Chapel was built around 1470.

As you enter the chancel, pause and take a close look at the rood-screen. It too is of the thirteenth century – the oldest surviving wooden screen in England, with its hinges, locks and bolt all still intact. The painting at the south end on the nave side is thought to be St Audrey, the seventh-century Abbess of Ely who gave the word 'tawdry' to the English language. Note, too, the curious marble structure against the north wall of the chancel. It has quite recently been identified as part of the shrine of St Edburg, brought from Bicester to escape destruction during the Dissolution of the Monasteries. The exquisite carving is probably the work of Alexander of Abingdon, the greatest English stone carver of the early fourteenth century.

The Harcourt Chapel south of the chancel was the church's last significant addition. (The beautiful timber roof of the nave must have been completed a generation or two before.) The style is a simple Perpendicular, the builder probably William Orchard, who designed the vault of the Oxford Divinity School. Three bays long, it is crammed with the tombs of the Harcourts; that of Sir Robert Harcourt, who died in 1471, and his wife shows her wearing the Garter on her fore-arm, as does the Duchess of Suffolk at Ewelme (*q.v.*). Against the north wall lies their grandson, another Sir Robert, who was standard-bearer to the future Henry VII at the battle of Bosworth. The remains of his standard hang above him; I find them strangely moving.

## Stonor Park

*80; 5 miles N of Henley-on-Thames on B480*

You might well be forgiven, on seeing Stonor Park for the first time, for thinking that it had been built in the seventeenth century and remodelled in the eighteenth; but you would be wrong. That long brick south front, its central range of sixteen bays broken only by the slightly projecting centre with its porch and high gable, is in fact little more than a screen. Behind it there rambles an old medieval house, parts of which go back to the late thirteenth century. They were built by Sir Richard de Stonor, Knight, whose descendants still live there today; the house can thus boast the longest record of continuous ownership by a single family of any in England.

*Pope's Tower, Stanton Harcourt.*

One bay of Sir Richard's old Hall still survives at the eastern end of the house, running back towards the wooded hillside; but it was not long before it was hidden, and almost forgotten, in a welter of haphazard later building. (Its central arcade can still be seen, now bricked up and forming the side of an inner courtyard.) For two centuries after 1350, as the prosperity of the Stonors increased, the house grew and grew, wing being added to wing sometimes in the same line, sometimes at right-angles, like a game of dominoes; then, around 1545, Sir Walter Stonor decided to impose order and symmetry. He faced the whole house – which by now extended round three sides of an open court – with a brick front, giving it mullioned windows of various sizes and topping it with a regular zigzag of gables. In the centre (or nearly) he placed a relatively modest porch, and added the charming groups of statuary – Plato's four Cardinal Virtues (Prudence, Justice, Fortitude and Temperance) and Our Lady of Mercy – which still stand today under their strapwork canopies. There is at Stonor a picture of the house showing this remodelling; it was painted about 1690, and shows that the building had changed scarcely at all in the century and a half that had elapsed since the work was done. For this, however,

*The Hall, Stonor Park.*

there was a very good reason: the Stonors were recusants, and had had to lie low.

Only with the more liberal attitudes of the mid-eighteenth century were they able to raise their heads once again and return to work on their house. In the 1750s, under the architect John Aitkins, it was given another new front with sash windows. All the gables were swept away except the one over the porch, and the house was given the pretty hipped roof with dormers and the straight horizontal cornice that it has today. The interior, too, was largely remodelled, much of it in a very pretty Gothick – a hint of which is given to intending visitors by the two windows above the porch.

The screens passage, in which you find yourself the moment you enter the front door, is another pure Gothick fantasy – as unlike a true medieval screens passage as anything ever was or will be. So too is the Hall which opens off to the right – not Sir Richard's thirteenth-century original, but the northern half of a slightly later one of about 1350, cusped, crocketed and pinnacled until it would do credit to Strawberry Hill itself. (The southern half was converted into a Drawing Room in 1834, by which time the first wave of the Gothic Revival had passed – hence the Ionic columns.) Of the other rooms, perhaps the most interesting is the Library. Long and tunnel-vaulted, it was converted from the old solar during the 1545 remodelling and contains a remarkable collection of Catholic books of the seventeenth century, secretly printed or smuggled in from abroad. There is some ravishing French wallpaper of 1819 in the Dining Room and some sensationally awful nineteenth-century French furniture in 'Francis Stonor's Bedroom' upstairs.

Finally – although, standing as it does between the car park and the front door, we may have visited it first – we must consider the Chapel, claimed to be one of the only three in England in which mass was said regularly all though the sixteenth, seventeenth and eighteenth centuries. It was probably built by Sir Richard in 1280 or so; then it was extended west in the 1340s, and given its brick north tower – now topped with a Georgian wooden lantern – in 1416–17. Considering its distinguished history, our surprise is all the greater when we go in and find ourselves back once again at Strawberry Hill: this time, however, the Gothick is not that of Aitkins but of James Thorpe, working between 1796 and 1800. With its vermilion walls and Wedgwood blue and white vaulted wooden roof it is undeniably pretty, and without its painted glass windows (contemporary, by Francis Eginton) it would be prettier still; but such frivolity accords oddly with Stonor's noble record of persecution and recusancy. How much better if it had been allowed to grow old gracefully, rather than dressed up in fashionable new clothes that did not suit it.

## Thame Park

*81; 1 mile SE of Thame off B4012*

Architecturally speaking, Thame Park is two completely different houses; and therein lies its charm. Approaching it in the normal way, up the drive from the west, you take it as just another mid-Georgian house in good, safe, rather dull Palladian style, with a pediment surmounting the three slightly projecting central bays of a total of eleven; two and a half storeys, double staircase to the *piano nobile*, ashlar-faced, no surprises. Nor, indeed, do we expect any from William Smith of Warwick (Francis's competent but not particularly imaginative son) who built it for the 6th Lord Wenman in 1745.

To the right of the house as you look at it is a large cypress, next to which a path leads round to the south. Follow it, and look again. All is changed. Before you, leading off at right-angles from the Georgian front and facing south, is a long, rather rambling early sixteenth-century range, broken by two bays and a stair turret and culminating at the east end with a three-storey tower projecting forward. This is all – or nearly all – that remains of the Cistercian abbey which occupied the site from 1138 to the Dissolution in 1539; it served as the lodging of the last two abbots – the second of whom, Robert King, was responsible for the tower and the surviving interior decoration.

I say 'nearly all' because there are a few remains of thirteenth- to fourteenth-century work in the domestic range which runs parallel to and behind the south front. They consist chiefly of four buttresses with blocked-up arches between them and are of minimal interest. The Abbot's Lodgings, on the other hand, are lovely. The part west of the tower divides itself approximately down the middle, ending with the stair turret and the point where the roof changes pitch. This was built by Abbot Warren in about 1500; it consists of an upper and lower Hall, both lit by the bay. It seems, however, that the Abbot soon found it inadequate and decided to extend it eastwards, thus providing himself, *inter alia*, with another spacious five-bay Hall – timber-roofed, with kingposts and arched braces – on the first floor. Last came the tower, with its fine corbelled-out oriel window to the west, which Abbot King must have built soon after taking office in 1530.

Of the original interiors, not much remains except in the Abbot's Parlour, a ravishing little room on the first floor of the tower, which King caused to be decorated between 1530 and 1539 in the highly fashionable style of the Italian Renaissance. Linenfold panelling covers the lower part of the walls, above which there runs, right round the room and across the internal porch in one corner, an uninterrupted row of panels carved with portrait heads in medallions, mermaids, urns, arabesques and other Renaissance motifs. Some of the carving has disappeared (the decoration was carved separately and then glued to the background), and other parts – particularly the portraits – seem to have been deliberately defaced; but the general effect, of white on bluish green, remains a joy to behold. Above the panels there runs a narrow frieze of similar design with the initials R.K.; and the design even continues along the beams supporting the ceiling. There is one other room on which King has left his personal imprint: the Library, at the extreme western end of the first floor. This room, despite a pretty boarded ceiling, has none of the sumptuousness of the Parlour; but here, amid more Renaissance ornamentation on the frieze, the Abbot's full name is proudly inscribed: 'ROBERTUS KING'.

Returning to the 1745 house, we enter through the front door on the ground floor – not that at the top of the outer steps, as the architect had originally intended – pass through a columned lower hall, remodelled by the present owners, and so up an inner staircase to the Great Hall, the most magnificent room in the house. It is, at first glance, more than a little reminiscent of Ditchley with its fine stucco – almost certainly by Thomas Roberts of Oxford – elaborate carved doorcases and tremendous chimneypiece. From it we can pass directly to the so-called Pine Room, the only other on the *piano nobile* that retains all its original decor. The others are, rather surprisingly, a riot of French Rococo – 1830-style, all pink and gold – which strikes a distinctly jarring note amid such quintessentially English surroundings.

Until the early 1980s Thame Park could boast, in Abbot Warren's Upper Hall, one of the world's greatest collections of Japanese arms and armour. It provided a most unexpected touch of scholarly eccentricity, and its removal, when its owner sold the house, is very much to be regretted.

## Uffington

*82; 7 miles NW of Wantage off B4507*

Seen from the village street ST MARY'S CHURCH, with its octagonal crossing-tower and its triple-lancet east window, looks noble indeed. Despite the fact that the top storey of the tower is an eighteenth-century addition, the general impression is indubitably Early English and it comes as no surprise to discover that the church was built around 1250. What is considerably more of one is the south porch – quite disproportionately grand even for a church as important as this, the door itself clearly original and very fine. Inside, prepare for a slight initial disappointment: the nave has been much rebuilt (we know that the west wall with its curiously shaped lancets dates from 1677–9) and is of relatively little interest. But go up to the crossing; from here, to the north, south and east, everything is as a fine Early English church should be. Or nearly everything: a large Decorated window with reticulated tracery has been let into the south wall of the chancel. It is a splendid window of its kind, it admits much welcome light, and if only the church had been built a century later we should have been delighted to see it. But here it seems a pity, and it sits uneasily among the surrounding lancets – three, stepped, to the east, and rather more pointed ones in pairs along the north wall and flanking it on the south.

But the real eccentricity of the church is to be found in the windows in the three chapels along the east walls of the transepts. Each is of three stepped lights, but instead of having the pointed-arch tops of the normal lancet these are abruptly cut off at the top by a straight-sided gable (projecting on the outside) into which the mullions run. Pevsner is inclined, though hesitantly in the absence of any documentary evidence, to attribute this also to the seventeenth century, but it would have been surprising at any date before, let us say, Norman Shaw.

## Widford*

*83; 1 mile E of Burford off A40*

ST OSWALD'S CHURCH stands alone among the water-meadows beside the River Windrush. It must have looked much the same when it was built in the thirteenth century – on the site of a Roman villa, part of whose mosaic floor remains *in situ* in the chancel. True, the nave windows have been altered and the east window with its reticulated tracery is a replacement of fairly recent date; but none of this seems to matter. There are lovely box pews, a splendidly ramshackle pulpit botched up from a late medieval screen, and a brave timber roof that runs down the whole length of the church, ignoring the endearingly crude chancel arch that makes a half-hearted attempt to interrupt it. The chancel walls are painted on both north and south, though the mid-fourteenth-century work is now sadly faded, and there is also a somewhat later representation of St Christopher on the north wall of the nave.

The church is not, as you may have gathered, architecturally distinguished, but it has an unassuming rustic simplicity which I find irresistible; hence its star.

## Woodperry

*84; 6 miles NE of Oxford off B4027*

Standing just outside the village of Stanton St John, Woodperry reflects the grand style in miniature. You approach it along a broad avenue leading up to splendid iron gates; and there stands the house in front of you, across what is in effect an elliptical forecourt formed by quadrant arcades and flanking pavilions on one side and iron railings linking the pavilions to the gates on the other. It is a magnificent composition, in no way diminished by the smallness of the scale, which was due to the fact that the banker John Morse, who built it in 1728–31, was a bachelor of sixty without heirs. (He did not even own the land, which he had leased from New College, Oxford.) A five-bay Italianate villa was quite enough for his purposes; grandeur, in English at any rate, was nothing to do with size.

We cannot be too sure of his architect, but there are records of payments by him to the Oxford mason William King. Although, so far as we are aware, King never designed a house by himself, we know that he was an apprentice and later a colleague of William Townesend, who had been largely responsible for the front quadrangle of Queen's and had worked on at least a dozen other Oxford colleges. There is thus a strong possibility – to put it no higher – that at Woodperry King was following Townesend's designs. One thing is certain: it is a very Oxfordshire house. Palladian in its essentials, it is full of details of what might be called Oxford Baroque, deriving from Hawksmoor's work at the Clarendon, All Souls', Queen's and Worcester Colleges and, of course, at Blenheim. Look, for example, at those heavy, unmoulded, round-headed window frames and the keystoned arches of the linking arcades.

At first glance, the whole thing seems quite confident and assured; only when you look more closely do you note the weaknesses – the curiously formless side pavilions, for example, or the awkward way in which the links are joined to the centre. The pediment, too, looks somehow uneasy: not surprisingly, since it has no proper supports. The odd thing is how little any of this seems to matter; Woodperry remains a very beautiful house indeed.

This same lack of assurance becomes even more evident, however, when we go inside. The whole strength of a Palladian design is based on its symmetry, normally on a straight axis running through the centre of the house from the front door to the back. At Woodperry, this axis somehow gets lost, and the architect's ill-advised attempt to increase the size of the Hall and the Drawing Room lands him in terrible muddles elsewhere. At this point, fortunately, a new element comes to the rescue. So rich, so lavish, so imaginative is the interior decoration that architectural shortcomings are at once forgotten. The Hall, for example, is divided from the Staircase Hall by an arcaded screen, with fluted columns; opposite, two magnificent pedimented door-cases somehow manage to make the relatively small space look twice as big, and twice as important, as it really is. (One of these doors is false; and even the other seems to lead nowhere in particular.) The ceiling is sumptuously moulded – not, as one would expect, in plaster but in carved wood; and how many other houses do you know with egg and dart mouldings on the window frames? Do not, incidentally, leave the Hall without taking a long, close look at the picture of Westminster Abbey in the overmantel – the best evidence we have that there was once, though not for very long, a spire over the crossing.

The other pride of Woodperry is its staircase – like the Hall, the work of a joiner of genius named Thomas Fawsett. Each tread rests on its own carved bracket, and Fawsett seems to have given almost as much attention to the underside of the flights as to the top. The landing floors are exquisitely inlaid, the walls panelled and further enriched with a guilloche design.

It is in a way unfortunate that the house was almost doubled in size in 1879–80, when another Oxford architect named Codd added a three-bay pedimented wing to each end of the house on the garden side. On the other hand, it is hard to conceive how the work could have been better done. Once again, one feels that Woodperry enjoys some strange invulnerability; even when things go wrong and catastrophe stares it in the face, it somehow emerges unscathed. A blessing indeed – but no more than it deserves.

## Woodstock

See Blenheim Palace.

# Short List

## Ashbury

*85; 8 miles SW of Wantage on B4507*

Set a little to the south of the village and above it on the side of the Down, ST MARY'S CHURCH has a lovely broad uncluttered chancel of about 1300, a fine roof with kingposts and queenposts, and an atmosphere of spaciousness and calm. At the bottom of the village street there is a MANOR HOUSE dating back to the Wars of the Roses, made of the same combination of chalk and lichen-covered brown stone as the church.

## Bampton

*86; 5 miles SW of Witney on A4095*

ST MARY'S CHURCH is originally late Norman but much rebuilt in about 1300 and partly remodelled by Ewan Christian in the 1860s. The problem of constructing an octagonal spire on a square base is prettily solved by flying buttresses at each corner, surmounted by statues (one a Victorian replacement) on clustered columns. The interior is scraped, but with interesting features, notably the Norman arch enclosed within the thirteenth-century one supporting the east wall of the tower, and the cinquefoiled inner frames to the aisle windows.

## Banbury

*87; 25 miles N of Oxford on A423*

Essentially, ST MARY'S CHURCH is by S.P. Cockerell and dates from 1790, though it was in fact completed by the architect's son, C.R. Cockerell, some thirty years later. A curious mixture of the neo-classical and the Baroque, it faces the world with a semi-circular Tuscan portico topped with a flattened copper half dome, beyond and behind which rises a tall tower in three stages and a cupola. The idea is nothing if not original, and works surprisingly well. The interior has, I understand, been much altered; alas, on three recent visits I have found the church locked.

There is a very grand seventeenth-century house at 85–7 HIGH STREET; it can be visited by appointment.

## Blewbury

*88; 3 miles S of Didcot on A417*

ST MICHAEL'S CHURCH is a large, impressive, cruciform church in a picturesque village. It is of Norman origin, as can be seen from the water-leaf capitals of the crossing piers. The original crossing-tower has disappeared and has been replaced by a Perpendicular west one. The crossing and chancel were rib-vaulted in *c.*1190 and the nave is of about the same date, The south chancel chapel of *c.*1300 has a fine screen. Of the fourteenth century are the north arcade and the chancel windows.

## Childrey

*89; 1½ miles W of Wantage on B4001*

A large, basically thirteenth-century church, ST MARY'S has both Decorated and Perpendicular alterations. There are good benches and brasses in profusion, and fifteenth-century glass in the north transept. The oldest and perhaps the most interesting item is the font, made of lead, probably in Henry II's day.

## Chislehampton

*90; 7 miles NE of Abingdon on B480*

ST KATHERINE'S CHURCH was built in 1762 and has hardly changed since: nothing smart or sophisticated, but possessing considerable charm, especially the beautifully preserved Georgian interior. It may well have been built by Samuel Dowbiggin, who was certainly the architect of CHISLEHAMPTON HOUSE nearby – his only fully documented work.

## Great Haseley

*91; 8½ miles SE of Oxford off A329*

The west doorway of ST PETER'S CHURCH, together with the nave, betrays the church's late Norman origin. The chancel, however, built by an unknown benefactor, is early Decorated and very fine indeed, particularly the great east window.

## Hanwell

*92; 2½ miles NW of Banbury off A41*

ST PETER'S CHURCH has some good carvings round the outside wall of the chancel, probably by the same sculptor as those at Adderbury and Bloxham. The nave capitals are also carved with considerable panache. HANWELL CASTLE, just east of the church, is really a manor house built about 1498; it has a fine three-storey tower with two embattled octagonal turrets – for decoration, however, rather than defence.

## Heythrop House

*93; 4 miles E of Chipping Norton off A34*

Thomas Archer's most important country house is relegated to the short list only because it was completely gutted by fire in 1831. The Roman Baroque front, though restored by Waterhouse, is much as it always was, and shows the powerful influence of Bernini; the service wings, however, have been twice rebuilt and have nothing to do with Archer's original designs.

## Kelmscott Manor

*94; 2½ miles SE of Lechlade off A417*

The late Tudor grey stone manor house was the home of William Morris between 1871 and 1896. Although the north wing, which projects at right-angles to the main block, was added about 100 years after the original building, the house has a nice, integrated, all-of-a-piece feel about it; but for the Morris connection, however, it would probably not have found a place here. It can be visited by appointment only. Morris's tomb in the churchyard is by Philip Webb.

## Minster Lovell Manor

*95; 15 miles NW of Oxford off A40*

The ruins of the great manor house of the Lovell family are picturesquely set on the banks of the River Windrush. It was built in the 1430s by the grandfather of Richard III's famous crony, whose estates were confiscated after Bosworth. Of the original three ranges built round an open courtyard, only the central one has partly survived, including the Hall and some extensions to the west. The four-storey south-west tower is a slightly later addition. After nearly two centuries as farm buildings, the ruins are now in the sanitising care of the Dept of the Environment.

## Rotherfield Peppard

*96; 3 miles SW of Henley-on-Thames on B481*

WYFOLD COURT, built by Barry's pupil George Somers Clarke in the 1870s, is described by Pevsner as a 'Nightmare Abbey in spirit, French Flamboyant Gothic, with a touch of Scottish Baronial, in style', a perfect description, to which any additional comment is superfluous. It now houses Borocourt mental hospital – though I can think of few buildings less therapeutic. I have not been inside, but never mind – the exterior says all that needs to be said.

## Shirburn Castle

*97; 1 mile NE of Watlington on B4009*

A very real castle of the late fourteenth century, it stands in a moat complete with drawbridge, four-square, with round corner towers like its almost exact contemporary, Bodiam. Much of it is of brick, the earliest in Oxfordshire. Had the interior measured up to the outside, the castle would have been described at greater length; but it was remodelled as a gentleman's residence in the early eighteenth century and several more times in the nineteenth. There is a pleasant park with good formal gardens. It is never open to the public.

## Shotover Park

*98; 2½ miles W of Oxford on A40*

The house was probably built around 1715 by William Townesend, Hawksmoor's assistant at Queen's College, Oxford. The exterior is undistinguished – seven bays of three storeys, but with a rusticated loggia built beneath it on the garden side where the ground falls away. The wings are of 1855, by Joshua Sims, who also added the entrance porch. Inside, the best room is the exuberantly stuccoed Entrance Hall – green and white, with a screen of two columns and a short flight of steps to the Saloon, which is panelled in oak with Gibbonsish carving and boasts a sensational view down the ornamental water to a Gothick pavilion – probably also by Townesend but possibly by Gibbs. There is a good staircase too, cantilevered out round all four sides of the well.

## South Newington

*99; 4½ miles SW of Banbury on A361*

The CHURCH OF ST PETER AD VINCULA possesses Oxfordshire's finest medieval wall paintings. Particularly interesting are those in the north aisle, dated *c.*1330, executed in oil on plaster in a delicate courtly style comparable to that of contemporary miniatures. There are rather more primitive fifteenth-century paintings in the nave.

## Stanton St John

*100; 3½ miles NE of Oxford off B4027*

The CHURCH OF ST JOHN BAPTIST has a lovely chancel of *c.*1300, when Early English was just turning to Decorated. Note particularly the east window, whose design is probably unique. There are also fine fifteenth-century screens and elaborately carved sixteenth-century bench ends. (See also Woodperry.)

## Witney

*101; 13½ miles W of Oxford on A40*

ST MARY'S CHURCH looks fine indeed, dominating the south end of the little town from across the broad green. You approach it from the north – passing on the left a row of remarkably pretty ALMSHOUSES – and are almost stopped in your tracks by the breadth and splendour of the seven-light Decorated window facing you at the end of the north transept. The tower is noble too – if a little on the heavy side – with its octagonal spire, tall louvred lucarnes and massive corner pinnacles. Alas, the interior is a disappointment, apart from a good Early English chancel. The nave walls are rendered in drab-looking plaster, and Street's restoration in the 1860s was anything but helpful.

## Yarnton

*102; 5 miles NW of Oxford off A34*

ST BARTHOLOMEW'S is a mid-thirteenth-century church, enlarged in 1611 by Sir Thomas Spencer of Yarnton Manor. To this date belong the south porch and the Spencer Chapel, with its painted walls and roofs and grand seventeenth-century monuments. Particularly splendid is the Jacobean screen ornamented with zigzag, strapwork and bosses.

## Yelford Manor

*103; 3½ miles S of Witney off A415*

The house, moated and timber-framed, dates from the early fifteenth century; it was probably built soon after Agincourt, and shows little outward sign of alteration – though there was in fact some internal remodelling in Jacobean times. The house, and the tiny village surrounding it in what must be one of the remotest corners of Oxfordshire, together constitute a romantic and remarkable survival from the Middle Ages.

# Somerset

Now a truncated county, Somerset lost its northernmost part – including the city of Bath, its greatest architectural pearl – to Avon (in conjunction with which this section should be read) as a result of the 1974 local government reorganisation. It remains, however, a beautiful county – in some ways more beautiful than before, since many of the more unsightly industries and coal mines now find themselves the other side of the border. And it is quite remarkably varied, from the ruggedness of Exmoor in the extreme west to those faintly alarming Somerset Levels in the centre – a large part of which lies below sea level – and then rising again to the drama of the Mendips and the Cheddar Gorge before settling back to the peaceful rolling hills of the east and south.

Where it has been supremely fortunate is in the quality and variety of its building stone: the grey carboniferous limestone of the Mendips, the hard red sandstone of the Quantocks, the blue lias of the Polden Hills and the oolitic limestone of the eastern and south-eastern borders. These last are the most important and the most beautiful of all, including as they do the creamy Bath stone, the greyer Doulting stone from near Shepton Mallet of which Wells Cathedral is built, and – one of the most glorious of all building materials – the golden brown stone from Ham Hill near Montacute. Only on that low-lying central plain around Sedgemoor do we see brick coming into its own, and even then in a relatively modest way. There are no brick churches in the county, and no important brick house dating from before the end of the seventeenth century.

Architecturally, the supreme glory of Somerset is Wells. It has a strong claim to the title of the loveliest of all our cathedrals, and certainly neither of its two principal rivals, Durham and Lincoln, can equal the serene perfection of its setting. Wells, despite its splendid Cloister, was never a monastic foundation; for these we must look to Muchelney and Stogursey, Bruton and Stavordale, Witham and Cleeve, and of course Glastonbury, whose connection with Joseph of Arimathea and King Arthur has given it a reputation – one might almost call it an aura – unique in the entire country. It has always struck me as being surprisingly devoid of atmosphere, perhaps because of its slightly too antiseptic surroundings; but there can be no denying its architectural beauty or importance. Wells and Glastonbury, as we see them today, were begun in 1180 and 1184 respectively, and, as Pevsner has pointed out, 'with these two buildings Somerset suddenly leaps into the forefront of architectural events in England'. It is not insignificant that Wells was the first building in all England to make use exclusively of the pointed arch.

Among parish churches, the choice has been hard; but it will be noticed that the large majority of those described in the pages that follow are wholly or predominantly Perpendicular in style. The Saxon and Norman periods are poorly represented in Somerset, while Early English work is utterly outshone by Wells, and to a considerable degree by Glastonbury as well. The same goes for the Decorated, as far as Wells is concerned; but here it is no longer possible to ignore the proximity of Bristol (described under Avon), which, though it has not technically been part of Somerset since 1373, is geographically and architecturally inseparable from it. At Bristol and at Wells, between about 1290 and 1330, there took place a revolution in architecture, and particularly in the treatment of space within it, unparalleled anywhere else in Europe. The chancel aisles of Bristol, the retrochoir and – whatever one may think of them aesthetically – the three gargantuan strainer arches at Wells were the result. They were phenomena of a kind that no parish church could hope to match.

But with the arrival of Perpendicular, the parish churches come into their own. Their interiors can sometimes be disappointing, admittedly; again and again, the Victorian restorers appear at their ham-fisted worst. But the exteriors, and above all the west towers, are sublime. Somerset towers are in a class apart, unmatched by any other English county, and whole books have been written about them. Many different factors go to make a beautiful tower: the arrangement of the buttresses, the proportions between the stages, the increasing richness and intricacy of decoration as the tower rises, the arrangement of the bell openings (with or without the perforations known as Somerset tracery) and the elaboration of the pinnacled crown – all these things the Somerset architects of the fifteenth century understood better than anyone else in England. Fortunately, the region was going through a period of prosperity comparable with that being enjoyed, at much the same time, by East Anglia; and few parishes that could afford a magnificent tower begrudged the expense. Indeed there were several cases where the tower went up to the detriment of everything else: that of Leigh-on-Mendip, for example, is over 90 feet high, while its chancel has been understandably compared by Alec Clifton-Taylor to a potting shed.

Where domestic buildings are concerned, Somerset has lost to Avon the Norman manor house at Saltford, one of the oldest inhabited houses in England, but there is still a fair amount of thirteenth-century work in the Bishop's Palace at Wells (where, however, the Victorians have a good deal to answer for) and the extraordinary fourteenth-century survivals at Meare. Nunney Castle, too, is of this period, as is the castle at Farleigh Hungerford – of which, however, too little is left to earn it a separate entry in this book. For fourteenth-century manor houses, the best is surely Clevedon Court (now in Avon); from the century following, Cothay is a marvellously unspoilt survival. Then come the Tudors: Barrington Court, Brympton d'Evercy, Lytes Cary, Mells, Poundisford, Gaulden Manor – these are just the beginning, and for all those not mentioned in the following pages I can only apologise. The series comes to a glorious climax in Armada year, with the building of Montacute, one of the great houses of England.

After 1600 the pace seems to slacken. One thinks of William Arnold's work at Dunster Castle, of the great Jacobean ceiling at Nettlecombe and, oddly enough, of that remarkable collection of church furniture at Croscombe. The next milestone along the way is not till the reign of William and Mary, when we find ourselves faced with the unashamed grandiloquence of Halswell House. At this point mention should also be made of Dyrham, now in Avon, but a Somerset building in all but name. The same must be said for Vanbrugh's Kings Weston, with which the eighteenth century opens; and indeed for virtually the whole of the city of Bath, which was little more than a village when Queen Anne paid it a visit but was a social centre second only to London itself before the end of the century. It was through Bath, in the persons of John Wood the Elder and his followers, that Palladianism came to Somerset – though the county was already no stranger to the cool, classical sophistication that had immediately preceded it: in Bristol, Queen Square had been designed as early as 1699 in deliberate imitation of the squares of London, and was at that time bigger than any of them.

During the eighteenth century domestic architecture in Somerset acquired new *élan*; I have singled out Ven House at Milborne Port, Crowcombe, Ammerdown, Hatch Court and Widcombe Manor among others – and of course Ston Easton, whose Rococo plasterwork is surely among the most sumptuous in the West Country.

And there this survey ends. I know of no outstanding nineteenth-century architecture anywhere in Somerset, unless you include the delightful – and occasionally delicious – Neo-Grecian terraces of Clifton, which are strictly speaking once again outside our area. Nor, alas, have I been able to include anything of real quality from the twentieth. But Somerset is rich enough, even without them, to stand comparison with all but a very few English counties – and, for my own part, there are few parts of England that I am happier to revisit.

---

## Ammerdown House

*1; 3 miles SE of Radstock off B3139*

When James Wyatt built Ammerdown House for James Samuel Jolliffe in 1788, he had in mind a mansion which, though noble in its proportions, would be comparatively modest in scale. It was to have a tall, rusticated ground floor rising almost half the height of the building, then a bedroom floor, then an attic. To his principal front, on the east, he gave three broadly spaced bays featuring, on the ground floor, Venetian windows set back in arched recesses. The central window on the first floor was also tripartite, but pedimented, and on the two upper floors the bays were separated by coupled Tuscan pilasters. The south front extended two bays only, but here the Venetian windows on the ground floor were separated by blank niches; on the upper floors they were reflected by square niches at the ends and ordinary windows in the middle, thus providing full-sized intermediate bays.

Wyatt's plan was realised; but it did not last long. In 1857, the north and south fronts were extended westwards to provide a three-sided entrance courtyard, which was itself filled in in 1901. The result is that while Wyatt's original east front remains unchanged, the south front is now effectively seven bays long on the upper floors – the blank niches at the ends now containing statues – with three Venetian windows and four blank niches at ground level. The west front, also, looks more or less as Wyatt intended, though it is now several yards further forward and a new and rather more grandiloquent porch has been added further to the north.

Unfortunately I was not allowed to see the interior; but *Country Life* photographs show a long Dining Room with exquisite original plasterwork; an equally elegant Drawing Room, originally two separate rooms and thus with two fine fireplaces which are said to have come from Egremont House, Piccadilly; a Smoking Room with a massive columnar screen, the vaguely Corinthian columns being reflected with pilasters on the end wall; and a most fanciful staircase well in which the rectangular first-floor gallery is topped by an elliptical lantern, the transition being affected by means of pendentives panelled to suggest fan vaulting. The formal gardens were designed by Sir Edwin Lutyens in 1901.

## Axbridge

*2; 17½ miles SW of Bristol off A38*

*Includes King John's Hunting Lodge (NT)*

The church dominates the little town from a hill above the main square – a dangerously exposed position for any church that is not of the best. Fortunately ST JOHN THE BAPTIST meets the challenge. The style is Perpendicular throughout, with pierced quatrefoil parapets wherever a less distinguished church might have had battlements – around the aisle roofs, the south and west porches and the top of the tower. It is a magnificent tower by any standards except those of Somerset, rising high and slender above the crossing, with canopied statue niches to east and west on the lower stage and, on the upper, two-light bell openings flanked by blank windows of the same design. Pinnacles stand at the corners, and to the north-east there is a higher stair turret. The aisle windows are all big four-lighters.

Inside, the great excitement is the roof of the nave – a barrel vault, plastered all over in 1636 in a most exuberant style which can only be described as Jacobean Gothic – a network of slender ribs, all heavily cusped and yet occasionally descending in the form of pendants. It is the work of a local craftsman, George Drayton, who was paid 10 guineas for it. The inside of the crossing-tower, by contrast, is fan-vaulted. After these two displays of opulence, the chancel comes as something of a disappointment. It too once boasted a plaster ceiling, inserted in 1670, but the rain got in and ruined it. It was replaced in 1879 by the present undistinguished job.

The so-called KING JOHN'S HUNTING LODGE (NT) in the square below is nothing to do with King John or with hunting; it is, however, a fine timber-framed house of 1500 or so with gables and two jetties. Extensively restored in 1971, it is now a museum.

*The church of St John the Baptist, Axbridge.*

## Berkley

*3; 2 miles NE of Frome off A3098*

The CHURCH OF ST MARY THE VIRGIN is as enchanting as it is unexpected – plain and somewhat austere on the outside but full of lightness and frivolity within. It was built in 1751, almost certainly by Thomas Prowse, the country gentleman and gifted amateur architect who was living at the time in the Manor House opposite. The impression at first sight is that of a very plain square box surmounted by a tower; the feeling of squareness is even stronger when you go in and find four giant columns supporting another, central, square from which an octagonal dome rises to a lantern. The surprise is in the decoration of this dome – sumptuous Rococo arabesques of white stucco against a background of an unusually brilliant blue. More plasterwork of a similar kind adorns what passes for the chancel arch – although the church has no real chancel, only an apsed recess at the east end.

The MANOR HOUSE is Georgian too, though there are traces of earlier work on the side nearest the church. It has five bays, the three-bay centre emphasised by giant Ionic angle pilasters. This too was once thought to be by Prowse, but is now known to have been built in the early 1730s for his mother, Abigail Prowse, by Nathaniel Ireson. In the main Hall there is a good deal more plasterwork, clearly by the same hand as that in the church; the background here, however, is not blue but crimson.

## Bishop's Lydeard

*4; 5 miles NW of Taunton off A358*

They built ST MARY'S CHURCH of the local red sandstone, lightening the effect with dressings of Ham Hill. It dates essentially from the fifteenth century, and – as so often in this county – the *pièce de résistance* is the west tower of about 1470. Of its four stages, the bottom one possesses a tall four-light transomed window immediately above the entrance; the second and third boast a two-light window to each side, set back in a splayed surround and with so-called Somerset tracery; and the top has three-light traceried bell openings, two on each side. At the level of their tracery, the paired angle buttresses flower into crocketed pinnacles. Above is a parapet pierced with quatrefoils, battlemented, with perforated merlons; more pinnacles spring up from the corners and smaller, more slender, ones from halfway along each side. There is a taller stair turret rising from the north-east corner, bearing a proud golden weathercock. After all this bravura, the rest of the exterior cannot help but seem a little tame.

The best feature of the interior is the chancel, re-designed by Sir Ninian Comper in 1923 with his characteristic love of gilded opulence and colour; but the church has retained its original benches with their splendidly carved ends, and a most beautiful screen of the early sixteenth century with ribbed coving and the Apostles' Creed in Latin running the length of the frieze. The rood above it is by Comper again, and shows the same exuberance; it comes as quite a surprise to learn that it dates from as recently as 1948 – a whole quarter of a century later.

*Brympton d'Evercy.*

## Bruton

*5; 7½ miles SE of Shepton Mallet on B3081*

ST MARY'S is a fine old stone church in a pretty little town straddling the River Brue. The most immediately surprising thing about it is its north porch, really a tower in its own right. It rises three full stages – the stair turret is higher still – and must indeed have served as the church tower until the great west tower was built in the middle of the fifteenth century. This is one of the grandest towers of Somerset – over 100 feet high, its stepped angle buttresses rising to crocketed pinnacles at the level of the bell openings, which take the form of three two-light windows to each side. Taller pinnacles rise from the corners of the parapet, which is embattled and pierced with a design of quatrefoils, shields and roses. Lower down on the west front are five canopied niches and a big six-light west window.

The north aisle and north tower are, together with the crypt below the chancel, the earliest parts of the building. Even these, however, do not go back before the early fourteenth century. The south aisle follows soon after, and only then the nave, which was remodelled early in the fifteenth. Then comes the west tower and then, between 1506 and 1523, the clerestory – which must be contemporary with the timber roof, typically Somerset in its design, with kingposts and tracery above the tie-beams. Last of all we come to the chancel, rebuilt in 1743. It is the work of Nathaniel Ireson and retains almost all its original fittings. The shallow tunnel vault has ribs springing from pretty Rococo brackets. Instead of an east window there is a pediment containing the arms of the Berkeley family.

Of the rest of the church furniture, the best is Jacobean. It includes a particularly good screen, now kept beneath the tower.

## Brympton d'Evercy

*6; 2 miles W of Yeovil off A3088*

In all England, there are few more exquisite groupings of manor house, priest's house and church than at Brympton d'Evercy; and the warm and golden Ham Hill stone sets all three of them off to perfection. ST ANDREW'S CHURCH is the oldest, parts of it going back to *c.* 1300 although the chancel must be a century or so later. From its west end there rises a most extraordinary bell-cote, projecting from its base on all four sides, with two round-headed openings per side. It looks distinctly top-heavy, but none the worse for that. Inside, there are a stone screen, a few pieces of fine medieval glass and a simply beautiful effigy of a priest in the north transept. He is said to have continued his work fearlessly during the Black Death until he was himself stricken. Other good monuments can be found in the Perpendicular north chancel chapel.

Next in date is the PRIEST'S HOUSE, standing between the church and the manor. It is a very simple building of two storeys with a pitched roof, its only outstanding feature being a polygonal embattled stair turret towards the eastern end. It led up to the Hall, which seems to have been, somewhat unusually, on the first floor, and to the Great Chamber. Behind it rises a tall chimneystack. The windows are nearly all two-lighters, round-headed, cusped and transomed.

And so to the MANOR HOUSE. One might almost think it was two houses, so different are its two principal fronts. To the west, where it composes so beautifully with the other buildings, we see it for what it essentially is – a house built, for the most part, in the reign of Henry VIII but to some extent remodelled some half a century later under Queen Elizabeth. From her time are the big broad double-transomed windows which mark the almost centrally placed Hall on the ground floor, and the three cross windows above. The staircase turret and the window to the Great Chamber on the far left are, however, from Henry's time. The only post-Tudor feature visible on this side of the house is the pseudo-Gothic embattled porch, which was added in 1722. It fits in perfectly, so we need have no regrets.

The south range could hardly be more different. It was the work of the splendidly named Sir John Posthumous Sydenham, Bart, and was begun in 1678. How the name of Inigo Jones (who died in 1652) ever became associated with it remains a mystery; he would certainly not have taken it as a compliment. Despite its obvious pretensions and attempts at grandeur, it remains equally clearly the work of a provincial builder determined to follow the current fashion but without any real idea of the basic classical grammar that lay behind it. He has given his front, for example, an even number of bays – always a mistake, since it leaves a house without a central focus. (The only central feature here is a drainpipe.) This solecism is underlined by the system of alternating pediments above the windows of both floors, so that not even symmetry is possible. But, let me quickly add, none of this matters a bit. If anything, it merely adds to the house's character and charm.

Inside, perhaps the most memorable feature is the immensely extended staircase, which rises against the outside wall of the Staircase Hall past no fewer than four intermediate landings. There is an Elizabethan fireplace in the main Hall, and some good eighteenth-century panelling in the principal rooms. But it is the outside that one remembers best, and the lovely gardens, created in early Victorian days and still as beautiful as ever.

## Cothay

*7; 4 miles NW of Wellington off B3187*

Here is a rarity indeed: an almost perfectly preserved English manor house dating from the last quarter of the fifteenth century. The only other obvious example that springs to mind is Great Chalfield in Wiltshire (*q.v.*), but Cothay is incontestably the more impressive of the two. Entrance is through a detached Gatehouse – a good deal more restored than the house itself – consisting of a broad, squat tower, buttressed and embattled, at the southern end and a short wing of two storeys extending northwards. The entrance is through the bottom of the tower; above it is the coat of arms of the Bluett family, the builders of the house and its first occupants.

The house stands 100 yards or so to the west; its principal front faces east, towards the Gatehouse. Two big projecting wings with massive gables enclose, first, the porch (which projects just as far, but is narrower and has a smaller gable) and then, immediately to its right, the recessed east front of the Hall, its pair of two-light mullioned and transomed windows separated by a buttress. These, like all the other principal windows, have round heads above the buttress – the only exception being the four-light transomed window on the ground floor of the north end, which was obviously enlarged in Elizabethan times. The west front, too, looks much as it has looked for the past 500 years, the exception here being the projecting Dining Room which was built on to the end of the screens passage in the early seventeenth century. The north gable on this side is distinguished by a charming little oculus window, traceried with three mouchettes in the form of a wheel.

Cothay has a most magnificent Hall, rising the full height of the house and with a great timber roof of arched braces, plus three rows of wind-braces along the side walls. Another roof of similar pattern covers the solar, on the upper floor beyond the Hall's northern end. Of the two rooms below it, the Parlour – facing east – has another fine timber ceiling of richly moulded beams and good Jacobean wainscoting; the Library behind it has a later seventeenth-century decoration. Surprisingly, it lacks a fireplace, having apparently been first intended as a store room; indeed, the only elaborate chimneypiece in the house is that of the Jacobean Dining Room; it has an overmantel of four standing figures with heraldic crests between them.

Perhaps the most interesting survivals within the house are the wall paintings in two of the bedrooms in the south wing. In the Green Room there is a frieze of painted parchment scrolls on a crimson background; below it is a painting of the Immaculate Conception in which the Christ Child is transported towards His mother along a ray of light, emanating from the Hand of God. Further along the same wall there stands a lady in mauve. The south wall, beyond a door of the same age as the house, provides us with a beautifully drawn figure of a man, in tabard and cap. Next door, in the Gold Room, we find a still more remarkable work: a Madonna and Child in a landscape, the sun and moon behind them and a distant church on the horizon, framed within a decorated roundel of blue and white. These paintings can claim to be unique, in that there is no comparable series of domestic – as opposed to ecclesiastical – paintings anywhere in England. They, together with others in the Hall and Parlour (of which, however, only traces remain) all date from the late fifteenth century and are thus contemporary with the house.

All the above information comes from published sources and the photographs in the *Country Life* articles of 1927. I myself have not seen Cothay, permission for me to visit it having been refused.

## Crewkerne

*8; 9 miles SW of Yeovil on A30*

To say that ST BARTHOLOMEW'S CHURCH had ideas above its station would be uncharitable, but not altogether unjustified. Its west front alone is more reminiscent of some great abbey than an ordinary parish church of a modest market town. Here, between a pair of tall polygonal turrets, is a seven-light window with an embattled transom and most distinguished tracery; below this we find a broadly imposing doorway with a big ogee gable and quatrefoils in the spandrels, flanked by side niches containing statues and surmounted by busts. To each side the west windows of the aisles are conceived on a similarly massive scale; four lights and transoms, with tracery above and below. From the sides, the building makes its effect with the unusually tall clerestory of three-light windows in five bays; below it

St Mary's Church, Croscombe.

the aisles are of only three bays, but make up for it by the size of the windows, each of which has no fewer than six lights – generosity indeed. And then there is the crossing-tower, with bell openings so tall that they seem to occupy almost its entire height. The two-storey south porch is fan-vaulted, gargoyles abound, and the glorious Ham Hill stone seems to radiate a special warmth of its own.

Inside, the immense breadth and height of the church affords marvellous perspectives and unexpected diagonal vistas – especially to the north-east, where the seemingly endless transept has not one but two chancel chapels leading off it. The piers of the three-bay nave arcades emphasise their height by a wonderful slenderness, directing the eye up past the clerestory to the magnificent timber roof, its principals supported on huge full-length stone angels. Above the crossing, the base of the tower is fan-vaulted. With such lavish fenestration everywhere the church is flooded with light – the more so since many of the windows have clear glass in them; one could wish they all did, since what coloured glass there is proves to be lamentably undistinguished. At the west end of the aisles are two galleries added early in the last century, and very nice they are.

Such a sumptuous church deserves a really good guide. The existing one is a disgrace.

## Croscombe

*9; 2½ miles SE of Wells on A371*

Though ST MARY'S is a fine church of the fifteenth and sixteenth centuries, it earns its place here not for its architecture but for its quite astonishing collection of Jacobean church furniture. All the woodwork of the church, excepting only the wagon roofs of nave and chancel (the latter was remodelled in 1664) dates from 1616 – see the inscription on the pulpit. It is of black oak, and somewhat funereal in appearance; but the effect is mitigated by the sheer exuberance of the design. Best of all is the rood-screen; it has two tiers of openings, each of two lights (though they are separated by pendants only), then a deep panelled entablature, then elaborate strapwork cresting with a plethora of obelisks and, in the centre, an achievement towering almost to the roof with a coat of arms inserted. The pulpit and its majestic tester are, however, very nearly as spectacular, as are the readers' desks, the parclose screens, the chancel stalls and many of the box pews.

The tower has a spire, and though not precisely datable looks as though it is probably a little earlier than the body of the church; by the end of the fourteenth century, spires were going out of fashion. The oldest part of all however is, curiously enough, the outer doorway to the south porch, which is unquestionably Early

English. It does not look grand enough to have been brought from somewhere else; the only conclusion is that it alone was left when an earlier church on the site was demolished and that the new building was erected behind it – but why this should be remains a mystery.

## Crowcombe

*10; 4½ miles SE of Williton off A358*

On 6 July 1734 a contract was drawn up between Thomas Carew, MP, and Nathaniel Ireson, the Warwickshire architect who had settled at Wincanton eight years before. It provided for a house to be built by Ireson 'on foundations sometime since laid and carried up by Thomas Parker, Architect'. Of Parker, virtually nothing is known except that he was responsible for certain works in the neighbouring church; CROWCOMBE COURT as we know it today is essentially the work of Ireson, and is his masterpiece. Having recently built Stourhead to the designs of Colen Campbell, he might have been expected to adopt Campbell's somewhat rigid Palladianism; Crowcombe, however, remains faithful to the principles of robust provincial Baroque; his inspiration comes not from Burlington or Campbell but from the Bastards at Blandford Forum (*q.v.*) and, above all, from Thomas Archer. Particularly Archer-like is the seven-bay south front, where the three-bay centre is delineated by giant Corinthian pilasters rising two storeys to the deep entablature that encircles the house. Above this is a third, attic, storey in which a Venetian window breaks through a triangular pediment. A broad balustraded staircase rises to the central doorway, which is surmounted by an open, scrolly pediment supported on brackets; above it, the first-floor window is flanked by leafy volutes. Around the corner, the east front is of five bays, with angle pilasters whose capitals curl inwards *à la* Bastard and a central doorway with a heavy Gibbs surround. To the west is a vast stable court: a most forceful and self-confident design in which the ground floor of the house – here rising four floors because of the falling ground – is of rusticated arcading.

The interior is rich with stucco and has a noble staircase rising around a central well, with three spirally turned balusters per tread and Corinthian-column newels. There is an ornate plaster ceiling and a complete Jacobean panelled room, exuberantly carved, imported from the old manor house in the village.

When I visited Crowcombe in 1981 it was in a sad state of disrepair; it had however recently been acquired by a new owner, who told me that he was going to restore it to its former magnificence, partition it into flats, and ultimately open the main rooms to the public. It would, he thought, take five or six years. So we shall see.

The house is of brick, with Ham Hill dressings. The nearby CHURCH OF THE HOLY GHOST, by contrast, is of the local red sandstone. Its pride is the south aisle, early sixteenth-century and wonderfully opulent, with three-light transomed windows, richly traceried above and below the transom. Even the south porch, fan-vaulted on the inside, has a three-light window above the door. Inside there is a glorious collection of benches, carved in 1534 with infinite fantasy and imagination.

## Downside Abbey

*11; 4½ miles N of Shepton Mallet off A37*

It was in 1814 that the Benedictine Community of St Gregory the Great, which had first made its way to England from post-Revolutionary France some twenty years before, found its permanent home at Downside. In those days the only important building on the estate was the pretty Queen Anne house with a hipped roof which is now occupied by the headmaster of Downside School. This was extended westward in 1823 by H.E. Goodridge (the Bath architect who had built Lansdown Tower for William Beckford), first with a Chapel of vaguely Early English character, and then with a further wing for use as a school – a most curious affair with a projecting ground floor, so that it gives the impression of an aisle with a clerestory above. Thirty years later Charles Hansom – brother of the architect-cum-inventor of the hansom cab – added a further L-shaped range with dormers, a corner tower and an oriel at the end, which was unfortunately lost when, in 1911, Leonard Stokes blocked it with a big square tower, beyond which he placed another L-shaped block to form the school's principal quadrangle. This was completed by a short re-entrant block by Sir Giles Gilbert Scott in the 1930s, during which period he also built the beginnings of a science block behind Stokes's tower.

Already by the 1870s, however, the original Chapel had become far too small and a vast new church with a monastic building attached was begun a few hundred

*Downside Abbey.*

*Dunster Castle.*

yards away to the north-west. The original architects were Archibald Dunn and Charles Hansom's son Edward, but as the building was to continue for the next century they were followed by several others. Of the church we see today, Dunn and Hansom can take the credit for the crossing, the transepts and the first part of the tower – placed, most unusually, at the end of the south transept. Theirs too is the ambulatory at the east end, with its long projecting Lady Chapel and the smaller radiating chapels in the manner of the great French cathedrals. The choir and sanctuary are principally the work of Thomas Garner in the first years of this century, the nave and the rest of the tower by Scott. The church consequently possesses little stylistic unity; the fact that it hangs together so remarkably well is due, I suspect, to its immense height, the richness of its ornament (tempered only by a certain monastic austerity) and – perhaps most of all – the dazzling whiteness of the stone. The detail is superb throughout, and there are some splendid decorations by Comper, in his usual brilliant gold and polychrome. His too is a good deal of the glass. Added to all this, there are several outstanding paintings (including a wondrous Flemish triptych of the early sixteenth century) and pieces of late medieval sculpture.

The monastic range to the south-west of the church is less inspired. More interesting are some of the post-war buildings, including a six-storey hexagonal library by Francis Pollen.

## Dunster

*12; 1½ miles SE of Minehead off A396*

*Includes Dunster Castle (NT)*

First, ST GEORGE'S CHURCH: it began in the late twelfth century, as part of a Benedictine priory established around 1170 as a daughter house of Bath Abbey; of this early church, however, there remain only a column of the west doorway and the attached columns built into the west faces of the piers of the crossing. Apart from these vestiges, the oldest remaining part of the building is the thirteenth-century chancel, but this has been much restored (by Street in the 1870s); the three stepped lancets of the east end, for example, are entirely Victorian. For the rest, we are in the later fifteenth century and the beginning of the sixteenth; building seems to have continued on and off until the Dissolution.

The undeniable impact made by the church on all those who visit it is in large measure due to the tremendous screen which extends across the entire breadth of the nave and aisles five bays from the west end. Fifty-four feet in length – the longest in England – it was erected after a quarrel between priory and townsfolk in 1499 to separate the monks' choir from the parish church. Its ribbed and panelled coving supports a broad loft, still in a remarkable state of preservation. There follows one more bay to the east, before we come to the crossing. The south aisle then continues eastward beyond the transept, to an arch of most peculiar conformation. Originally part of the thirteenth-century building, it seems to have been broadened in early Tudor times to allow for a wider arch – not, one feels, a happy alteration. Across the middle of this arch is another fine screen with deeply undercut carvings of flowers and fruit; more screens of similar type stand on each side of the main altar, now placed beneath the crossing-tower. The remaining furniture is disappointing.

A small door in the north transept leads to what was the old Cloister – now a charming garden – and thence across the road to a large and splendid dovecot. The whole church is of red sandstone, very restrained in decoration. The tower in particular is quite exceptionally plain by Somerset standards.

And so to the CASTLE (NT). There has been one at Dunster since Saxon times, though the oldest surviving feature today is the thirteenth-century gateway to the lower ward, flanked to the left and right by semi-circular towers. The medieval castle was sold in 1376 to the Luttrell family, who owned it for the next six centuries; only in 1976 was it given, with its park, by Lt.-Col. Walter Luttrell to the National Trust. The present building is of three principal periods. The first is Jacobean, resulting from George Luttrell's commissioning of William Arnold (whose work we know from Wadham College, Oxford, and Cranborne Manor, Dorset, *qq.v.*) to build him a more convenient house in the lower ward. The second was towards the end of the same century, when Colonel Francis Luttrell remodelled the Dining Room (giving it one of the most superb plaster ceilings of its date in the country) and installed the glorious staircase. Finally there were the various transformations effected by Anthony Salvin between 1868 and 1872. His contribution to the house was to dramatise it, giving it once again the appearance of a castle, adding towers, turrets and battlements. He also added the short range that runs south-east from the Gatehouse, that is to say at right-angles to the entrance front.

You enter the castle to find yourself in the Outer Hall – Salvin's creation – from which you pass through one of two stone archways into the Inner Hall. This was the hub of the Jacobean house, and has preserved Arnold's plaster ceiling (with pendants) and a sixteenth-century overmantel. (There is also a fascinating allegorical portrait of Sir John Luttrell wading naked through a tempestuous sea.) It leads directly into the Dining Room, with its plaster ceiling of 1681 and beautiful panelling of oak veneered in walnut – the most distinguished room in the house. We do not know for certain the name of the plasterer responsible for the ceiling; the most likely candidate seems to be Edward Goudge, who did much magnificent work at Belton House in Lincolnshire.

Returning through the Inner Hall you come to Francis Luttrell's other *tour de force*, the Staircase Hall. Clearly the ceiling is by the same hand as that of the Dining Room; the staircase itself, which rises in three flights to the first floor round an open well, is in fact built into one of the medieval towers – a D-shaped projection in the castle's south-east corner. The balustrade, set between massive newel-posts supporting carved vases of fruit, is a masterpiece of wood carving in the style of Eltham, Ham (*qq.v.*) or Sudbury Hall, Derbyshire – carved panels of elm, 4 inches thick, in which animals and *putti* cavort amid fronds of acanthus. They seem, for the most part, to be hunting scenes; but there is also a military trophy in the centre of the upper landing and, in one of the panels, a heap of coins which include Charles II silver shillings of 1683–4, Irish halfpennies and a few Portuguese pieces, presumably in honour of Queen Catherine of Braganza.

Upstairs, the three most interesting rooms – and the only ones shown to the public – are the Morning Room, the Gallery and King Charles's Room. In the first, the principal points of interest are the pictures showing the castle in the early eighteenth century before Salvin's alterations; in the second, the extraordinary leather wall hangings – obviously of the seventeenth century and probably Dutch or Flemish – depicting the story of Antony and Cleopatra; in the third, the plaster overmantel dated 1620 and containing a charming if crude representation of the Judgement of Paris. This room is said by tradition to have been occupied by Charles II (when Prince of Wales) in 1645.

Visitors normally descend by the so-called Oak Staircase next to the Gallery – part Elizabethan, part Jacobean, part early eighteenth-century. The remaining ground-floor rooms to which it leads are all Salvin's work and are of relatively little interest.

Finally, the town. It is one of the prettiest small towns in Somerset, with the castle proud on its hill to the south and the little embattled FOLLY TOWER (of 1760–70) on another elevation to the north. In Market Square the two principal buildings are the octagonal YARN MARKET of 1589 and the LUTTRELL ARMS, which is of *c.*1500 though much altered in the 1620s. The NUNNERY in Church Street is in parts even older – fourteenth-century, with two timber-framed overhangs. The whole place is a delight.

## East Brent

*13; 8½ miles SW of Axbridge on B3140*

ST MARY'S is a pretty grey stone church with a nicely proportioned if unassuming tower supporting a tall polygonal spire of extreme elegance. It has a fine west front with a seated statue above the west window, and a south porch which has retained its original fifteenth-century door, carved with tracery. The wall paintings here, the work of a curate to the Archdeacon of Taunton in 1873, do not improve the general effect.

The point of the church, however, is not the spire, fine as it is, and still less the rest of the exterior. It is the roof of the nave with its plasterwork of the early Gothic Revival, obviously of the same date and by the same craftsman – George Drayton – as that of Axbridge (*q.v.*). Unlike Axbridge, however, the background is no longer painted: the design is now white on white. Big pendants hang from the central ridge. The pretty interior also features a west gallery extending halfway across the nave, supported on columns with carved tendrils climbing up them, a wooden eagle lectern of the fifteenth century – there are only twenty others in the country – and a splendid set of fifteenth-century benches with carved ends. The chancel is a rebuilding of the 1840s, but the remaining architecture is all Perpendicular.

## Evercreech

*14; 4 miles SE of Shepton Mallet on B3081*

ST PETER'S boasts one of the best of the church towers of Somerset – which is the same as saying of the church towers of England. Not as richly ornate as, say, North Petherton or Huish Episcopi (*qq.v.*), it is better proportioned than either and never seems to be weighed down by its decoration. Like Chewton Mendip or St Cuthbert's at Wells (*qq.v.*), it emphasises its height by extending the bell openings downwards in the form of blank panels – a device which gives it a soaring verticality which few of the other most celebrated Somerset towers possess. It is crowned with an embattled parapet of pierced quatrefoils and, at the four corners, forests of closely set pinnacles of which the highest springs from only just below the sills of the bell openings. Meanwhile intermediate pinnacles rise up the centre of each side from the sills of the blank panels. Behind, the rest of the church gives the appearance of being dwarfed; but it too is richly decorated with pierced quatrefoil parapets and pinnacles.

The surprise of the interior is the wooden gallery which runs along both of the nave arcades; it creates an atmosphere of quiet domesticity which is strangely at variance with the splendour outside. So too, though in a different way, is the fine wooden roof with angels on tie-beams and kingposts, all painted like a fairground. This, we are always being told by the experts who know about such things, is how roofs used to be painted in the Middle Ages; but did they really have such bright colours in those days?

## Glastonbury

*15; 5½ miles SW of Wells on A39*

There are two legends about Glastonbury which distinguish it from all other English shrines and give it a special mystique of its own. The first is that Joseph of Arimathea came here with the Holy Grail and built the first Christian church in England; the second is that it was the burial place of King Arthur. There is no foundation for the St Joseph tradition, which first appears in the thirteenth century; on the other hand, recent research suggests that the site of Arthur's tomb, now marked in the grass just east of the crossing of the abbey church – the tomb itself, in black marble, survived only until the Dissolution in 1539 – is the authentic resting place of the great British general of the early sixth century who for a generation checked the advance of the Saxon invaders across the country and later passed into legend.

What is indisputable is that there has been a monastery at Glastonbury since the seventh century. Originally a Celtic foundation – there is another tradition which associates it with St Patrick – it became Saxon under King Ina of Wessex *c.*708; in 943, King Edmund appointed St Dunstan as its Abbot. Alas, any buildings that may have survived from these early periods, together with the great Norman abbey which arose during the half-century following the Conquest, perished in the great fire that destroyed Glastonbury in 1184. The ruins that we see today are those of the new church which was begun immediately afterwards and on which work was to continue intermittently up to the Dissolution.

*Glastonbury Abbey.*

In fact, if we are to be strictly accurate, we should describe it as two churches, although they are contiguous and share the same east–west axis. To the east is the Abbey Church proper, to which we shall return presently; to the west the LADY CHAPEL (sometimes known as ST MARY'S CHAPEL), marking the site of the old wattle church of St Mary, the most venerable of all the shrines that have been destroyed. This Lady Chapel is now the best preserved of all the Glastonbury ruins. Curiously, since it was only five years in the building (it was consecrated in 1189), it is a mixture of styles – part Norman, part Early Gothic. In plan a simple rectangle of four bays with high angle turrets (only two of which have survived), its exterior decoration consists of intersecting blind arches ornamented with zigzag set at an angle of 45 degrees and surmounted by tall round-arched windows. At the west end three of these windows, here exceptionally adorned with the same oblique zigzag that we have seen below, are set closely together and stepped. All this is fairly orthodox late Norman; what comes as a surprise is the realisation that the interior – now open to the sky – was originally rib-vaulted with pointed arches. Moreover, although it continues the intersecting blind arcading, many of the enrichments are of stiff-leaf foliage of a purely Early English variety. One notices too that the mouldings of the upper windows continue unbroken all the way round; any builder working in the accepted Norman idiom would have interpolated capitals at the springing of the arches, turning the jambs into columns. Look, finally, at the north and south doorways. They too are round-arched; of their four orders, two have normal columns and capitals, two do not. The figurative carvings on the voussoirs seem Gothic too, but are probably later additions.

Of the ABBEY CHURCH itself only fragments remain, though some are of considerable size. The most complete survival is the early fourteenth-century Galilee Chapel at the west end, adjoining the Lady Chapel; apart from that, we have part of the west front and of the outer wall of the south aisle, part of the eastern crossing piers and of the east walls of the transepts, and sections of the walls of the choir aisles and retrochoir. But the ground plan is clearly laid out in the grass, and the surviving evidence is enough to tell us what the great building must have looked like in about 1400. First comes the Galilee, the same breadth as the Lady Chapel, to which it was virtually an extension; it too has blank arcading, but this time the arches have trefoiled heads and do not intersect. Beneath it was a crypt, which was subsequently extended below the Lady Chapel.

From the Galilee a broad pointed arch with four orders of shafts led to the west door of the nave – a depressed arch containing a trefoiled tympanum. The nave itself was slightly broader than the Galilee, the two aisles doubling its breadth again. It was nine bays long, with triforium as well as clerestory; the eastern half was, at least on the lowest stage, Early English of the mid-thirteenth century, but the triforium and clerestory, together with the west end of the nave arcades, seem to have been added in the early fourteenth. With the transepts – or what is left of them – we are back in the original late twelfth-century church; lower arcade and triforium are both framed in a single embracing wall arch with zigzag. The triforium arches, however, are trefoiled – a nice touch. For the clerestory, we have pointed arches with shafts.

The original twelfth-century chapel was of four bays only; in the fourteenth century, however, the removal of the choir from the eastern bays of the nave necessitated a short eastward extension forming a retrochoir, the surviving remains of which mark the easternmost limits of the ruins. Of the aisleless 'Edgar Chapel' – added *c.*1500 to house the monuments of the early Saxon kings whom the abbey claimed as founders – nothing is now left.

The same is unfortunately true of most of the monastic buildings, with the all-important exception of the ABBOT'S KITCHEN which is thought to be of *c.*1370 and is one of the best-preserved medieval kitchens anywhere. It is square in plan, but the fireplaces in all four corners give it an octagonal interior, and this octagonal shape is continued in the truncated pyramid roof and the two lanterns above it – a larger one topped by a smaller. It is now a museum. Another museum, devoted to Somerset rural life, includes the splendid ABBEY BARN of 1500; it has a fine collar-beam timber roof.

The connection between abbey and town is marked by the ABBEY GATEHOUSE, a fairly uninspiring building despite its generous central bay window, canted, mullioned, transomed and embattled. Far more rewarding is the thirteenth-century COURT HOUSE in the High Street, a two-storey building in stone with an eight-light window to the right of the doorway and a six-light canted oriel above. More sumptuous still, with its three stone-faced storeys and battlements above, is the GEORGE INN, built for pilgrims in the fifteenth century and still a hotel today. Two sets of ALMSHOUSES are also well worth a look: ST PATRICK'S (of 1517, but altered) off Magdalene Street and ST MARY'S next to the eighteenth-century PUMP ROOMS. These latter almshouses are a particular joy: they go back to the fourteenth century, the little chapel being a century older still.

And so to the two other Glastonbury churches worthy of a mention. Of ST BENIGNUS – commonly, but inaccurately, called St Benedict's – little need be said except that it was founded by Abbot Bere around 1520, obviously on the site of an earlier church, of which the chancel arch has been preserved. ST JOHN'S is a much more magnificent affair, with a wonderfully graceful tower, the second tallest among the parish churches of Somerset, surmounted by a huge and most exuberant crown. The chancel has an east window of seven lights, and the north transept a bronze cross and hair watch-chain that belonged to Dr Pusey.

A third church, ST MICHAEL'S, once stood on the summit of Glastonbury Tor. Only its truncated tower now remains, one of Somerset's best-known landmarks. Those who walk up to it will find it unexpectedly rewarding, not least for the two relief panels flanking the west door: St Michael holding his scales and a lady milking a cow.

## Halswell House

*16; 3½ miles SW of Bridgwater off A38*

Halswell House comes as a considerable surprise: a huge and rather heavy-looking three-storey house of buff-coloured stone, built for himself by Sir Halswell Tynte in 1689. Howard Colvin has convincingly attributed it to William Taylor, who had been responsible for certain alterations at Longleat a few years before. If he is right, such an attribution would, he points out, establish Taylor 'as a designer of some importance'; it would indeed, for Halswell is as sophisticated a house as any in the county. It is, perhaps, a shade fussy, particularly in the centre where the front door – set back into a round-headed concave niche – makes a single composition with the central first-floor window above it. Rusticated pilasters, quarter columns, carved trophies and ornamental keystones below vie with broken pediment, coat of arms, swathed garlands and more pilasters with voluted bases above. But the building has height, mass and presence enough to take all this in its stride. Sir Halswell was, one suspects, a proud man – to call your house by your own name is hardly a sign of modesty; if so, he must have been well pleased when he first saw his new residence complete.

Inside there is a fine staircase rising round a square open well and some quite distinguished plasterwork; good contemporary fireplaces too. On the whole, however, one is better off outside, where the grounds offer several further pleasures – an Ionic temple, a stepped pyramid 'in honour of a pure nymph' and even a monument to a horse that died while winning a wager for its owner.

*St Mary's Church, Huish Episcopi.*

## Huish Episcopi*

*17; 13½ miles E of Taunton on A372*

It is the west tower above all that brings people to Huish Episcopi; of all the celebrated Somerset towers, that of ST MARY'S CHURCH is one of the grandest. It rises 100 feet through three stages separated by friezes of quatrefoils to a broad battlemented crown of finest filigree, with tall corner pinnacles (each with a detached shaft on the outside ending in another pinnacle) and yet more pinnacles at the halfway points. Until 1845 all these pinnacles had spearheads rising up from the middle; what a pity they were taken down. Still more pinnacles rise up along and around the set-back buttresses, the three-light windows of the middle stage and the pairs of transomed two-light bell openings of the upper.

But there is a good deal more to this glorious church than its tower: the south doorway for a start, built of Ham Hill stone (discoloured by fire) towards the end of the twelfth century. Framed in all the zigzag is an early medieval oak door of startling beauty. Inside, we are in the fourteenth century: an aisleless nave, transepts and chancel. (No crossing-tower: it wouldn't have stood a chance.) The nave has a blue-washed wagon roof with Victorian stencilling – not what one might have asked for, perhaps, but the colour (though not the stencilling) is said to be authentic and the effect is unexpectedly successful. When we reach the crossing the surprise is the north window of the north transept – the only piece of *swirling* geometrical tracery I know. Another curiosity is the way the chancel arch, the arch that leads into the north transept and the two that open into the south chapel (a later westward extension of the transept) have sides which, having curved inwards to begin an ordinary pointed arch, then straighten out again long before the apex. This south chapel has a window by Burne-Jones.

## Ile Abbots*

*18; 8½ miles SE of Taunton off A378*

ST MARY THE VIRGIN boasts another of those marvellous Somerset towers. Less fussy, perhaps, than Huish Episcopi, it makes its effect first by the intricacy of its pinnacled corner buttressing, second by the perfect calculation of its windows and bell openings, and third by the statues, in their tall canopied niches, which enrich the lower and middle stages. It too culminates in a crown of pierced battlements, with high corner pinnacles. A stair turret rises higher still on the north-east. Of the statues, it is worth mentioning that they are all the original ones. Few medieval parish churches can say the same.

Having absorbed the perfection of the tower, walk round past the distinctly swagger north aisle (a pierced and pinnacled parapet again) to the chancel – another lovely piece of about 1300. The east window is of five beautifully stepped lancets, and there are more lancets, in groups of three, in the north and south walls where they are surmounted by quatrefoiled circles.

Now go in, by the south porch: once more, a fine bit of display. It is fan-vaulted, with a big pendant centre boss. Inside, there is a wonderful feeling of lightness and space. Everything seems surprisingly simple, even the

*The Minster, Ilminster.*

north aisle that looked so opulent from the outside. There is no south aisle, and the single arcade is undistinguished. More surprises, however, await in the chancel – not only its exquisite proportions (which can be properly appreciated only from the inside) but above all the piscina and sedilia, which are unlike any others I know. Yet in the end such details count for little: at Ile Abbots the beauty of the interior is a matter of atmosphere, of quiet architectural harmony rather than meretricious decoration. Those who arrive, gaze at the tower and then drive on are missing more than they know.

## Ilminster

*19; 9½ miles NW of Crewkerne on A303*

The MINSTER is magnificent indeed on the outside, though perhaps a little disappointing in its interior. Once again the tower dominates; but it is not really one of that class of ornate Somerset towers that we are beginning to know so well. For one thing it is a crossing-tower, so that it lacks a bottom stage; for another, being modelled on that of Wells Cathedral, it possesses a certain austerity and tends to avoid decorative flourishes. There are three two-light transomed bell openings on each side, with tracery, and these are continued blank all through the stage below – not just the piers between the windows but even the mullions between the individual lights. The piers also continue upwards, where they become roof pinnacles; because of the tripartite design there are consequently two intermediate pinnacles on each side rather than the more usual single one. The west front, having no tower, makes do with a five-light window, with embattled aisle fronts on each side. The aisles themselves have broad three-light windows. Then come the transepts, very narrow and in reality little more than chapels. The southern one has a five-light end window but is otherwise unremarkable; the northern, on the other hand, which constitutes the Wadham memorial chapel, is something of a show-piece, built soon after Sir William Wadham's death in 1452. The north window rises above the level of the parapet in its own gable, crocketed and pinnacled. Finally we come to the chancel, three bays long with a five-light east window also under a gable and looking out over a rather unfortunate little vestry which crouches beneath it.

Inside, the three-arched arcade dates from only 1825 – a great pity, since the arches correspond with neither the aisle bays nor the clerestory windows. Some comfort can however be found in the fan vaulting under the crossing, as at Axminster and Crewkerne. Spare a look too, at the roof of the nave: good Somerset tie-beam stuff, with kingposts and tracery. Apart from this, there is little of outstanding architectural interest; but nobody should miss Sir William Wadham's tomb chest or that of Nicholas Wadham, who died in 1618, and his wife. The brasses on the lid are among the best in England.

## Kingsbury Episcopi*

*20; 7½ miles NE of Ilminster off B3168*

It is difficult to go on writing about the great church towers of Somerset; superlatives become exhausted, and there is always another masterpiece to be described. Yet no list could possibly exclude that of ST MARTIN'S at Kingsbury, a fraternal – but not identical – twin to that of the neighbouring manor also in the hands of the Bishop of Bath and Wells, Huish Episcopi. The two are of the same date and the same height, though Kingsbury is if anything even more lavishly decorated. Not only, for example, does it have quatrefoil friezes separating its three stages and running below the parapet as at Huish: it also has one around the base. The west window on the central stage is richer too, in its tracery as well as in the number of its lights, which have risen to four. The two twin-light bell openings on the upper stage are more slender and elegant. Both towers are of the same glorious Ham Hill stone – though the churches behind them are principally of blue lias – and glow gold in the setting sun.

From the south the impression is equally fine: a two-storeyed south porch, a broad aisle with generous three-light windows, a five-lighter to the south chapel and a wonderful long chancel with more five-lighters to the north and south as well as the east. Once again, as at Crewkerne and Ilminster, there is a low vestry projecting below it – the only feature one would be happier without. Even the pretty quatrefoil frieze below the gable fails to make up for it entirely.

The tower is almost as grand inside as out. Its soaring arch – panelled, as so often in these parts – reveals a fan-vaulted roof; but this one might have expected. Far more surprising is the way the eastern tower buttresses appear inside the nave. One feels that this was done of necessity rather than deliberate design, but the architects turned it to splendid effect by giving the buttresses niches of their own and connecting them by another panelled arch. The other memorable feature is the chancel, flooded with light through those tremendous windows, seen through a lovely rood-screen embellished with delightful little angels. The nave itself, it must be admitted, possesses none of the fantasy of Huish and is even just a little bit dull; but with such splendour around it, who could complain?

## Kingston St Mary★

*21; 3 miles N of Taunton*

Another breathtaking tower, of red sandstone this time (apart from the dressings which are of Ham Hill), characterises the exterior of ST MARY'S CHURCH. There are the usual set-back buttresses, with applied pinnacles, a single two-light window flanked by canopied niches on the middle stage, and virtually the same window twinned for the bell openings. The climax is kept for the crown: first the little animals crawling up the corners of the parapet – 'hunky-punks' they are called in Somerset – and then the corner pinnacles themselves, each of which has no fewer than four subsidiary pinnacles on detached shafts. There are tall intermediate pinnacles too, without the shafts, but each with its own individual hunky-punk. The south porch is of one storey only, but it has a lovely broad four-centred arch and is fan-vaulted within – quite apart from the parapet of pierced quatrefoils which continues along the south aisle.

After all this profusion of late Perpendicular – the tower, like nearly all the great towers of Somerset, dates from about 1490 – the interior of St Mary's comes as a surprise. Architecturally, we are back in an aisled church of Henry III's time: the nave arcades have four bays of double-chamfered arches on circular piers with circular capitals above them. Only the big five-light east window breaks the spell; but this has the advantage of flooding the church with light and allowing a proper view of the other great pride of Kingston, its fifteenth- and sixteenth-century benches with their typical carved ends. Above the whole thing is a beautiful wagon roof, timber-ribbed, with gilded bosses at the intersections, the panels whitewashed.

The church has one other asset on which it can deservedly congratulate itself: the best church guide in Somerset. Would that others might follow its example!

## Leigh-on-Mendip

*22; 5 miles NE of Shepton Mallet off A367*

ST GILES'S is a small church, almost dwarfed by its tower. It is built not of the usual Ham Hill or blue lias or red sandstone, but of the local grey oolite; and is one of the loveliest in Somerset. The upper stage has three twin-light bell openings, transomed, and these are repeated blank on the stage below. Something of the kind also occurs at Ilminster, but there the heavy vertical piers between the windows almost negate the division of the stages; at Leigh, the horizontal division remains paramount. Once again, the tripartite pattern results in two intermediate pinnacles instead of one on each side of the topmost parapet.

Inside, the church is disappointing, having been mercilessly scraped by Victorian restorers. Its two best assets are an unusually complete set of medieval benches – carved, but not very imaginatively – and the remains of a splendid timber roof in both nave and chancel. (As the latter is quite villainously low, one gets a particularly good view of it. I know of few chancels into which one steps down instead of up.) There are small square panels with intricately moulded ribs, half angels and whole angels, kingposts, queenposts and marvellous carved tie-beams. When I last saw it, however, it looked to be in dire need of attention. Without expert treatment, it is unlikely to last much longer.

## Lytes Cary Manor

*NT; 23; 2½ miles NE of Ilchester off B3151*

This lovely medieval manor house stands among broad green meadows. When you arrive at the garden gate, however, and get your first view of Lytes Cary at the far end of a stone-flagged path leading through rows of clipped yews, do not hurry to approach it: the eastward-facing entrance front before you tells most of the building history of the house.

The earliest part is the Chapel, which projects towards you at the far left. When it was built, by Peter Lyte in 1343, it was free-standing; to this day there is no direct access to it from within. It is lit by a three-light east window, with two-light windows to north and south; the latter are, somewhat surprisingly, square-headed, but all have reticulated tracery characteristic of the period. Inside, the Chapel has preserved its original timber roof, with arched braces and collar-beams.

The next projection immediately to the right marks the eastward extension to the dais end of the Hall, which was added around 1530 – a fairly frequent phenomenon at the time, when squires and their families were beginning to seek relief from the hubbub of the Hall and a greater degree of privacy and comfort for themselves. There is an oriel above, on carefully moulded corbelling. Next, in the neighbouring recess, is the three-light window of the Hall itself, apparently substituted for an earlier one at about the same date. From this time too is the projecting porch, with a precisely similar oriel over a broad doorway set in a four-centred arch.

At one time there was probably a further projection beyond the porch, giving Lytes Cary the traditional E-shape; alas, by the end of the eighteenth century the Lytes – and their house – had fallen on evil times. The estate had been sold, and the purchaser had leased the north end of the house to a local farmer. In 1810 a neighbour wrote that the old buildings to the right of the porch had recently been demolished and a farmhouse built on the site. It is this farmhouse, with its steep pitched roof, that we see today at the north-east corner. It is far too high for the rest of the building and utterly ignores its fenestration.

But this is the only serious eyesore. With the south front we come to another huge bay window, marking the

*The Great Chamber, Lytes Cary Manor.*

Great Parlour and dated 1533. The windows are of the same design as those of the Hall, narrow and with four-centred heads, the bay having eight lights on each of the two floors and the flanking windows six. The former has a coat of arms between the two storeys and a tall embattled crown with a frieze of pierced quatrefoils below the merlons. The whole thing forms a symmetrical composition – most unusual for so early a date.

The Great Hall, immediately on the left when entering, is believed to have been rebuilt by Thomas Lyte, who succeeded to the manor in 1453. It has a splendid timber roof with arched braces, three tiers of cusped wind-braces, and an intricately carved cornice of pierced tracery with shield-holding angels at the foot of each principal rafter. The screen is not original, but the fifteenth-century fireplace is still *in situ* – a broad depressed arch with quatrefoils in the spandrels. The two big panelled arches at the dais end, leading respectively to the oriels and the staircase, both seem to be part of John Lyte's reconstruction of *c.*1530.

The next room of major importance is the Great Parlour in the south wing. When the house was bought in 1907 by Sir Walter Jenner (who on his death in 1948 left it to the National Trust) he found this room being used as a farm store. Fortunately the Jacobean panelling and chimneypiece had only been painted over and were otherwise more or less intact. The Little Parlour adjoining was in similar disrepair, being used as a carpenter's shop; it too was restored by Sir Walter.

Finally, the Great Chamber, immediately above the Great Parlour: this is the showpiece of the house, for it boasts a canted plaster ceiling of exceptional quality with the Arms of Henry VIII at the eastern end. The design of the rest – an intricate pattern of stars and kite-shaped panels formed by thin moulded ribs – is once again well in advance of its time. Most of the original wainscot has alas gone, but the inner porch at the top of the stairs has kept its old linenfold panelling.

The west wing of the house was added by Sir Walter Jenner and is of no architectural interest.

## Martock*

*24; 4½ miles SW of Ilchester off A303*

A large church and an extremely grand one, ALL SAINTS has not, like so many of its Somerset neighbours, made a showpiece of its tower. This is not undistinguished, but it has no important statements to make; far more impressive are the east end, with its five separate stepped lancets, broadly spaced, each under its own hood-mould; the lovely high, six-bay, four-light clerestory, added in 1513, with its parapet of pierced quatrefoils and battlements; and the two-storeyed south porch with its ribbed star vault on head corbels. All this makes the building history clear enough: a thirteenth-century Early English chancel which was left untouched when the rest of the church was rebuilt in the fifteenth century, and a further heightening of the nave when the parish became even wealthier early in the sixteenth. It was presumably during the first Perpendicular rebuilding that the west tower was substituted for an earlier one over the crossing and a new nave and aisles were built, together with the two side chapels flanking the chancel.

The moment we enter the church we see why the nave was heightened: to make room for one of the great timber roofs of Somerset, and indeed the whole of the West Country. The basic construction is the usual Somerset one of tie-beams, moulded, carved with four-petalled flowers on the sides, and surmounted by a filigree of intricate cresting. At the centre of each, and on each side, is an angel with outstretched wings bearing a shield. Between each pair of angels rises a kingpost, with a shorter queenpost on each side going up to the principal purlins, while between these posts runs a tracery screen of pierced quatrefoils. Between the tie-beams are high collar-beams, and these also have kingposts which continue downwards, through the collar, to form heavy carved pendants. Behind and above the beams, the roof is ceiled with 768 panels, filled with pierced patterns of six different designs.

The tie-beams are carried on wall posts, below which are stone angels; below there are exceedingly ornate canopied niches. If these ever had statues, they were destroyed by the Puritans in 1645, but their backs were later painted – by the look of them, not long after the Restoration – with figures of the Apostles. At the lower level we have six-bay arcades, with blank tracery in their spandrels – a purely East Anglian motif, which appears nowhere else in Somerset. Less surprisingly,

*The great timber roof of All Saints' Church, Martock.*

both tower arch and chancel arch are panelled. The chancel arch is not a noteworthy piece; it is, however, unusually broad, reflecting as it were the similarly shaped embracing arch round the five lancets of the east end. (There is a lovely perspective as you look eastwards from the tower.)

But then the whole of this church is a joy; even the restorations by Ferrey and Scott in 1860 and by Ewan Christian in 1883–4 have not seriously altered its atmosphere. Moreover, like Kingston St Mary, it has an absolutely first-class guide-book, some 9,000 of which have been sold to the considerable benefit of church funds. Other parishes please note – and copy.

Opposite the church stands the TREASURER'S HOUSE – so called because the Rector of Martock was Treasurer of Wells Cathedral. It is 700 years old, and still inhabited. There is a wing of *c.*1280 with a two-light solar window, and at right-angles a Hall range of *c.*1330, with a roof of arched braces and four rows of wind-braces. Behind is a fifteenth-century kitchen.

## Meare

*25; 4 miles NW of Glastonbury on B3151*

The key to an understanding of Meare is the fact that in the Middle Ages, as its name implies, it stood at the edge of a huge lake, said to have been 5 miles in circumference. Beside this lake stood – and still stands today, though the lake itself is long since drained and dry – a SUMMER PALACE to which the Abbots of Glastonbury used to come for fishing holidays. It has survived in its entirety and with remarkably few alterations for a building of *c.*1340, although the three big pointed windows have been blocked up. It is L-shaped, with the abbot's chamber and private apartments ranged along the first floor facing south, and the Great Hall, also on the first floor, in the north wing.

Nearby to the east is a humbler building, known as the FISH HOUSE. It is of much the same date and has survived in even greater completeness: only a garderobe tower has disappeared. It constitutes as fine an example as can be found anywhere of the perfect small – very small – house of the early fourteenth century: two storeys with a tiny Hall rising up through both of them, a parlour at one end and a pantry and buttery at the other, with living quarters over.

ST MARY'S CHURCH is of approximately the same date as these two buildings. At the east end the three lancet lights are stepped in reverse, with the middle one lower, and geometrical tracery in the space so formed. In the later fifteenth century there were Perpendicular additions by Abbot Selwood of Glastonbury; his, clearly, are the aisles and clerestory. (His initials are on the ornamental parapet at the east end of the south aisle.) Entering through the south door – not missing the wonderfully flamboyant ironwork on the door – you find a nave and aisles of no particular architectural interest: the best part of the interior is the chancel, not only for the way the tracery marks the perfect point of transition between the Early English and the Decorated styles, but also for its admirable timber roof with, of all things, cusped wind-braces – a rarity indeed in a church.

*The Manor House and St Andrew's Church, Mells.*

## Mells

*26; 4 miles NW of Frome off A362*

According to popular tradition, the nursery rhyme about Little Jack Horner refers to the Steward of the Abbot of Glastonbury at the time of the Dissolution of the Monasteries. On his way to deliver the title deeds of various local manors to Henry VIII in London, he is said to have extracted those of Mells (in some versions, from the inside of a pie in which they were being transported for safety) and kept this particular 'plum' for himself.

Whether we accept the story or not, the Horners and their descendants have lived at Mells since King Henry's day, and the manor was, and is, a considerable plum. The MANOR HOUSE itself still looks much as it must have looked in Tudor times – though it was thoroughly restored in about 1900 – with its tall gables and mullioned and transomed windows rising up behind the wall just west of the church. ST ANDREW'S, too, is a beauty. It is of local grey stone, mellow with lichen, and possesses another of those astonishing west towers: almost the twin of St Giles, Leigh-on-Mendip (*q.v.*).

For the rest, St Andrew's is – as so often in Somerset, where they struck it rich around 1400 – late Perpendicular. Its dates, so far as we can judge, seem to be between *c.*1450 and *c.*1520. On the south side there is a two-storeyed porch with a concave-sided gable over the entrance and a fan vault within; then, a little further to the east, comes a most curious polygonal chapel, also of two storeys, the gift of a London draper in 1485.

The interior of the church has been scraped by Victorian restorers and is on the whole disappointing, though the inside of the tower has another fan vault and there is a quite good (though not outstanding) timber roof – or is this also Victorian? The most interesting part is the Horner Chapel in the north-east corner, in which stands something most unusual in an English parish church: an equestrian monument. It commemorates Edward Horner, who was killed in the First World War, and is the work of Sir Alfred Munnings.

The little town offers much to delight the eye, especially NEW STREET, which runs down from the church to the High Street. It was laid out by Abbot Selwood in about 1470 as part of a plan to redesign Mells in the Roman manner, with four straight streets meeting at a central point. One is glad that he got as far as he did; relieved, perhaps, that he got no further.

## Milborne Port

*27; 3 miles NE of Sherborne on A30*

There is oddly little Saxon work to be found among the churches of Somerset, considering the proximity of Wiltshire and Gloucestershire where there is so much; and the CHURCH OF ST JOHN THE EVANGELIST at Milborne Port is thus of considerable importance. The odd thing about it is that the obvious Saxon characteristics are so inextricably intermingled with perfectly straightforward Norman features. The chancel has those curious pilaster strips, called lesenes, in its south wall, and a tier of pilastered arcading; but there are unmistakably Norman windows too, Norman columns and curious capitals of carved plaster that could not possibly be pre-Conquest. There is also a Norman crossing-tower and south doorway, though the latter is much reconstructed. (The tympanum, however, is original.) The rest of the church is of relatively little interest, having been largely remodelled by the Victorians.

About half a mile east of the town and clearly visible from the A30 is VEN HOUSE, a large and imposing Queen Anne mansion. The architect was Nathaniel Ireson, who was apprenticed to Francis Smith of Warwick before he came and settled at Wincanton, and Ven is much more a Midlands house than a West Country one: brick with stone dressings, two and a half storeys, with giant Corinthian pilasters rising to just below the attic, seven bays by five. The offices to the east and the conservatory to the west were added by Decimus Burton in the 1830s; he also remodelled much of the interior, removing the main staircase to make new living rooms.

*The Great Hall, Montacute House.*

## Montacute House*

*NT; 28; 4 miles W of Yeovil on A3088*

Loveliest of all the great Elizabethan mansions, Montacute stands at the foot of a great conical hill, the *mons acutus* – nowadays topped by an eighteenth-century folly tower – that is one of the landmarks of Somerset. Few houses in all England exert such a spell. The secret lies partly in the rich honey-coloured Ham Hill stone, so that the building appears bathed in a perpetual sunset; partly in the smooth green lawns and clipped yew hedges with which it is surrounded; and partly, too, in the pavilions and lodges, the turrets and obelisks and gazebos, that beguile the eye in every direction. But there is also the magic of the house itself: in its grandiloquence, its symmetry, its vast expanses of glass, and its effortless fusion of the Gothic with the Renaissance, everything that a late Tudor prodigy house should be.

It was built, almost certainly by William Arnold – who worked at Dunster and Cranborne as well as at Wadham College, Oxford – for Sir Edward Phelips, who was later to become Speaker of the House of Commons and Master of the Rolls under James I. The work was begun in 1588 – Armada year – and was probably completed in 1601, the date carved over the east doorway. This, in Sir Edward's day, was the principal entrance to the house; so it had better be described first. The front follows the traditional Tudor E-plan, with a projecting wing – very broad, but of only a single bay – under an elaborately shaped gable at each end and a smaller one under a semi-circular gable in the centre, containing the porch. There are three principal floors, with attics in the end gables: on the lower two the windows – of three to five lights – are double-transomed; the upper floor has one transom only. But what is particularly fascinating is the number of Renaissance touches. Thus the canted bays on the side wings have segmental pediments; the storeys are separated not by simple string-courses but by full-bodied classical entablatures; the chimneys are shaped like columns; and there are statues of the Nine Worthies between the second-floor windows and in the central gable, all in full Roman dress. The curious circular niches just below the windows of the first floor were presumably intended for busts, and the even odder shell-headed niches that stand in pairs along the plinth may well have had the same purpose.

To the north and south the façades are somewhat plainer, each of them dominated by a huge semi-circular oriel, corbelled out from the wall at first-floor level and then rising across three transoms through the whole of the second floor and up into the gable. These mark the ends of the Long Gallery, which runs the entire length of the house. And so we come to the west front, which is as interesting as the east, though for rather different reasons.

In 1786 Edward Phelips, the owner of Montacute, decided to change the entrance to the west front, connecting it by a straight drive to the main road, and at the same time to add to this front a two-storeyed range for corridors – conveniences which scarcely existed in Elizabethan times, when you frequently had to pass through several other people's bedrooms before reaching your own. Architecturally, this could have been a disaster; but Phelips was astute enough to use for his new front part of the main front of Clifton Maybank, Dorset (*q.v.*), which was being partly demolished at that moment. 'On the 2nd of May,' he writes in his diary, 'my wife and self attended the sale of materials of Clifton House, then pulling down. We bought the porch, arms and pillars, and all the ornamental stone of the Front to be transferred to the intended front at Montacute, besides which we purchased the chimney piece in the drawing room, some windows, wainscot, lead and marble, etc.'

Clifton Maybank was built around 1550 – some forty years before Montacute – but by West Country standards it was well in advance of its time and the additions were an unqualified success. Indeed the porch, which was a considerable work of art in its own right and now became the centre of the new west front, is one of the most fascinating features of the house. It too is a hybrid of Gothic and Renaissance: the broad frieze of quatrefoils and shields would not look out of place in any Perpendicular church, nor would the deeply moulded four-centred arch of the doorway, nor the polygonal angle buttresses, nor the pinnacles – were it not for their Ionic capitals; but the coat of arms in the lozenge above the door, though itself a replacement by Edward Phelips, still retains its original setting in which it is supported by a pair of *putti* of a purely Renaissance kind. Above them, the initials of John and Edith Horsey (née Phelips), the builders of Clifton Maybank, also remain inviolate.

The Great Hall is immediately to the north of the screens passage; to the south, where the buttery and pantry would originally have been, is a small Dining Room created by Lord Curzon, who threw the two rooms together in 1915 when he was living there. The Hall itself is a relatively modest affair for so large a house, and rises only a single storey; one must remember that by the later years of Queen Elizabeth's reign such halls had no longer the importance they had enjoyed in former days, most families preferring to eat in the Great Chamber. It possesses, nonetheless, a fine screen of Ham Hill stone with white stone dressings and most elaborate strapwork cresting. Halfway along the west wall is a large but austere stone fireplace, with Tuscan columns and a metope frieze; but the oddest feature of the room is a long relief in plasterwork stretching right across the dais end, illustrating the story of a henpecked husband who, having treated himself to a drink when he should have been minding the baby, is beaten by his wife with her shoe and is then carried round the village on a pole to be mocked at by his neighbours. Something quite so naïve and bucolic might seem to sit uneasily amid the relative severity of the rest of the Hall – but few country squires in Elizabeth's day would have thought so.

There is another plaster frieze in the Parlour, which occupies the north-east corner of the house beyond the Hall. It is, however, somewhat more dignified, owing to the Phelips coat of arms which is repeated at regular intervals against a background of particularly charming animals. The two-tiered stone chimneypiece is also of the same date as the house, but the wood panelling is not. Opposite the Parlour, in the north-west corner, is the Drawing Room; having been redecorated in the nineteenth century it has little to detain us apart from the chimneypiece, which was rescued from Coleshill when it was destroyed by fire in 1952.

The main staircase – of stone, as is its less important fellow, and one of the last to be built round a solid core – leads up to a number of splendid bedrooms, one of which, known as the Crimson Room, has another deep plaster frieze and some superb original wainscoting. The Hall Chamber adjoining, originally the master bedroom of the house, has a two-tier stone fireplace; of more interest to most people, however, are the two large needlework panels from Stoke Edith in Hereford and Worcester – enchanting illustrations of country house life in the early eighteenth century. In the north-west corner, the so-called Garden Chamber was used by Lord Curzon as his bedroom during his occupation of Montacute between 1915 and his death in 1925; his bath is discreetly concealed within a Jacobean cupboard. The most important room on this floor, however, is the Library, formerly the Great Chamber. It has a particularly elaborate internal porch culminating at the top in a forest of pinnacles, a vast chimneypiece with carved overmantel rising to the roof in Portland stone, and another of those deep plaster friezes which are a feature of the house. The bookcases and ceiling are Victorian, but the heraldic glass is original, as it is in the Hall below.

Finally, the Long Gallery, running 189 feet, the entire length of the second floor: it is of relatively little architectural or decorative interest, having lost all its Elizabethan panelling and plasterwork during the last century – when it received its curiously canted ceiling, punctuated with distinctly apologetic pendants. Today, however, it is hung with a superb collection of Tudor and Jacobean portraits – more than ninety of them – from the National Portrait Gallery.

## North Cadbury

*29; 5 miles W of Wincanton off A303*

Here we have another of those delightful Somerset compositions of church and house together, as at Brympton d'Evercy or Nettlecombe. This time the church – ST MICHAEL'S – is the more important of the two, though the rambling old Elizabethan manor house is unquestionably the more romantic.

Let us take the church first. It is of brownish grey stone, heavily lichened, and is set high on a hill above the village; from the west end, on a sunny day, the view looks like a travel advertisement for the West Country. The west tower, on the other hand, is anything but one of those typical Somerset showpieces; its only touch of fantasy is the little south-east stair turret which rises above the embattled parapet and is crowned by a little cap in the shape of a polygonal pyramid. This in turn is neatly echoed by just such another at the corresponding corners of the north and south porches, and it is here that the richness of the church first becomes apparent. The two porches are identical, two-storeyed, and have two tiers of cusped panelling running behind the doorways, above which rise tall, crocketed ogival gables. Inside, they are lierne-vaulted. Beyond them, the aisles run two more bays eastward with big three-light windows, panel-traceried. There follows a three-bay chancel, its windows similar to those of the aisles but set a good deal higher. A taller five-light window practically fills the east end. Porches, nave, aisles and chancel – and even the long, low vestry below the chancel on the north side – have tall, plain parapets. The consistency of the early Perpendicular style and the all-round symmetry (excepting only the vestry, which is slightly later) make it clear that the church was built all of a piece in the early fifteenth century – in fact, as we happen to know, by Lady Elizabeth Botreaux in about 1417.

The interior is tall and somewhat narrow – an impression increased by the verticality of the unusually high nave arcades – of five bays – with their multiplicity of clustered shafts, and also by the sixteenth-century benches, which project a little too far inwards. (They have, however, enchantingly carved ends, for which one forgives them much.) Above, between the regular three-light windows of the clerestory, short wall posts on angel corbels support a typically Somerset timber roof: panelled, with tie-beams and kingposts. Beyond the chancel arch this roof continues at the same height, but is here treated slightly differently, with queenposts. Beneath the high chancel windows the lower walls look rather blank; until 1850 they were covered by high canopied stalls – Lady Elizabeth having originally intended a collegiate foundation for her church – but these were then removed, and all that remains is a few misericords against the east wall of the south aisle. The east wall of the chancel below the window is taken up by a modern reredos; but the carved and canopied niches to each side are original and still bear traces of their original colouring. Original too, at the other end of the church, are the eight blue-robed saints in the west window.

NORTH CADBURY COURT dates mainly from the 1580s, and is built of the same stone as the church. Behind the symmetrical Elizabethan north front, however, there runs an earlier wing which dates probably from Henry VIII's time and in which the Hall roof still survives. The south front now dates in its essence from 1790, when the Tudor courtyard was filled in and the windows sashed.

## Poundisford

*30; 3½ miles S of Taunton off B3170*

A fine old house of roughcast over rubble with ashlar dressings, POUNDISFORD PARK was built late in the reign of Henry VIII, probably in the 1540s. The design is the usual H-plan and rigidly symmetrical – unusual for so early a date. On the entrance side, what would have been

*North Cadbury Court.*

the courtyard between the two projecting wings is almost filled in, by the porch on one side and the Hall oriel on the other, the two balancing each other exactly. On the garden side these inner projections are absent and the general impression is very much the same as that of Barrington Court (*q.v.*) – though the latter is a good deal larger and somewhat more sophisticated.

William Hill, who built the house, lived in it for another quarter-century, during which time he continued to work on the interior. He must have decided to redo the Hall in about 1570, giving it a plaster ceiling with pendants, the spidery ribs forming star and lozenge patterns and including both his initials and those of his wife. In style it much resembles that at Mapperton in Dorset (*q.v.*); they must be among the oldest of their kind in the West Country. The Hall screen, also reminiscent of Mapperton's, seems to have been remodelled at the same time and the gallery above walled in; a pretty little oriel now opens into the Hall. The upper floor was originally reached only by a spiral stairway leading up to this gallery; some of the rooms here, as well as the gallery itself, have plaster ceilings of a similar kind. The room to the north-west of the Hall, now the Library, was formerly the Justice Room; its ceiling is more interesting still, since it derives from the models introduced by Inigo Jones and the Proto-Palladians in the mid-seventeenth century. The nearest local example of this type of work is to be found among Edmund Prideaux's innovations at Forde Abbey, Dorset (*q.v.*), and it has been suggested that the ceiling at Poundisford may be attributed to one of the assistants engaged there. Finally, there are two rooms which date from the eighteenth century – a small Parlour and a long and elegant Dining Room with a screen of two Ionic columns. The date is *c.*1738. The house is complemented by a large and most agreeable garden with a pretty brick summer-house of 1680 or thereabouts.

POUNDISFORD LODGE nearby is of the same date as the Park and of much the same character. It too has some good plaster ceilings and two original fireplaces, but has suffered rather more drastic internal remodelling.

## Shepton Mallet

*31; 5 miles SE of Wells on A371*

The CHURCH OF ST PETER AND ST PAUL has elements of both glory and tragedy. Outside, the glory is the west tower dating from about 1380, making it the oldest of the great towers of Somerset, with corner shafts and pinnacles rising up parallel with the buttresses but separately, being connected to them by tiny flying buttresses; on the top stage, which is crowned by a parapet of pierced quatrefoils, the two-light bell openings are flanked by blank windows of the same design. Here the tragic elements are two: the minor one is that the spire was begun but never continued. The stump is covered by a rather silly little pyramid roof, big enough to intrude but too small to make any serious statement of its own. The major tragedy is the building that some barbarian has erected immediately in front of it – labelled 'The Centre', whatever that may mean. Insensitivity on this scale is almost beyond belief.

*The church of St Peter and St Paul, Shepton Mallet.*

Inside, the roof takes one's breath away. It is a wagon roof, hailed by Pevsner as 'the most glorious of all the wagon roofs of England', with 350 panels and over 300 bosses, every one of them different. Angels line the wall plates along each side, marking the points from which the principals spring. Here is glory indeed, and the church would have been given a star had not the rest of the interior been so heavily Victorianised and so devoid of character or charm. But in 1837, 1847 and again in 1861 the 'restorers' did their worst: the old Norman east end was only one of the casualties. And one wonders whether the long process of desecration has stopped even now: one of the few unusual and charming features that I remember when I first visited the church in the early 1960s was the pair of west galleries over the aisles. They were torn out in 1966.

## Stogursey

*32; 8 miles NW of Bridgwater off A39*

The curious and not particularly euphonious name is an English corruption of Stoke Courcy. ST ANDREW'S started as the church of a Benedictine priory, founded around 1100; and the Norman crossing is still in place, as sturdy and four-square as ever it was. Above the chancel arch is a Norman window, which nowadays looks into the chancel. The eight columns of the crossing arch have wonderfully carved capitals, worth examining carefully. The transepts both have apses on their eastern walls; the original Norman chancel had one too, but it was lengthened and largely remodelled towards the end of the twelfth century and simultaneously enriched with much zigzag. The extreme eastern end is, alas, Victorian.

The rest of the church is early fourteenth-century Perpendicular, and, though most attractive, of a good deal less interest. So are the chancel aisles from the outside, though not from within. Of the exterior, the best feature by far is the Norman crossing-tower; it must be very early indeed, since recent work has brought to light a quantity of herringbone masonry.

There is a nice crude Norman font, carved with four masks, and a set of mid-sixteenth-century bench ends.

## Ston Easton Park

*33; 15½ miles S of Bristol on A37*

The house is now a hotel, and there can be few hotels anywhere in the country of such architectural distinction. It seems to have been begun around 1740, but the architect is unknown; John Wood the Elder has been – not very convincingly – suggested, largely because we know that Wood the Younger redecorated the Saloon in 1769. The principal (south) front, of brownish grey stone, is at first sight a little austere. At the corners are two-storey towers with shallow pyramidal caps, which are linked by a single two-storey bay to the seven-bay centre. This in turn has two slightly projecting inner wings, and an attic half storey. Thus the eleven bays of the front are divided in a distinctly *staccato* rhythm: 1–1–2–3–2–1–1. On the ground floor the rather heavy portico is flanked by pairs of Tuscan columns; on the first floor the three central windows have alternating pediments; while on the attic floor the central bay is taken up with a coat of arms with garlands.

But it is the interior of Ston Easton that really impresses – above all by the sumptuousness of architectural detail. Already in the Entrance Hall, with its high coved ceiling, the plasterwork is remarkable enough to raise one's hopes for what lies beyond; it proves to be the Saloon, and those hopes are not disappointed. The central doorcase, in the style of William Kent, with its gloriously carved entablature supported on fluted Corinthian columns and crowned by a high triangular pediment, must be the most opulent of its kind in Somerset. To each side are *grisaille* paintings in *trompe-l'oeil* with ornate plasterwork frames. Above is a lovely frieze of shells and floral garlands and a panelled ceiling, in the oval centre of which the eagle of Jupiter is descending out of the sun, surrounded by attendant thunderbolts. Elsewhere are busts in high pedimented niches.

The Drawing Room and Dining Room to the east of the Saloon are of less monumental grandeur but equal quiet elegance, as is the Library in the south-west corner. Next to it is an enchanting little Print Room, the prints here being arranged around extremely pretty fitted cupboards with ornamental panels and broken pediments. In the west wing, two small panelled rooms are left over from the earlier sixteenth- to seventeenth-century house on the site.

The garden is the work of Humphry Repton, whose Red Book of 1792–3 still survives. He it was who transformed the 'dark, silent pool' to the north of the house into 'something so far more cheerful and interesting in the busy motion of a running stream, that there can be no doubt which ought to be preferred'.

## Tolland

*34; 9 miles NW of Taunton off B3188*

GAULDEN MANOR – sometimes known as GOLDEN MANOR – stands at the end of a long avenue of hazels about a mile to the east of the village. It is built of local red sandstone and seems to date principally from the sixteenth century, though parts may be older. There is no promise from the rough domestic exterior of anything out of the ordinary; but the moment one steps inside the house and enters the Great Hall one realises that Gaulden is something very different from a normal run-of-the-mill Somerset farmhouse.

That difference is due to the fact that Gaulden was long associated with the old West Country family of Turberville – Hardy's d'Urbervilles. It cannot be conclusively proved that it was the retreat of James Turberville, Bishop of Exeter, who was imprisoned in the Tower by Queen Elizabeth on his refusal to take the Oath of Supremacy in 1559 and is known to have settled in this neighbourhood after his release four years later; if so, he may well have been responsible for the deep plaster frieze which runs around the Hall and the adjoining 'Chapel', and which appears to illustrate the vicissitudes of his life: there, at any rate, are the Scales of Justice, a Tower, and a Virgin and Child Triumphant. On the overmantel, and presumably by the same hand, are the arms of the Turbervilles; while the decoration of the ceiling itself consists of three big roundels. Those at the ends carry reliefs of King David and his harp and of the Angel of Death, blowing his trumpet over a skeleton; from the central one descends a heavy ribbed pendant.

If on the other hand the Bishop never lived at Gaulden, this extraordinary decoration must have been commissioned by his great-nephew John Turberville, who bought the manor in 1639. This is certainly more likely to be the date of the oak screen which separates the Hall from the 'Chapel'. (The inverted commas are necessary because there is nothing nowadays remotely religious about this little parlour – if indeed there ever was.) This screen is elaborately panelled and features fluted pilasters; oddly enough, they have no capitals, only carved human heads in the frieze above them. Over the doorway are the initials I.T. Above the screen, but not touching it, a plaster arcade of pendants hangs from the ceiling, with winged angel heads in the spandrels. Above the Great Hall and forming part of what was originally the solar is a bedroom with another Turberville coat of arms in the overmantel, this time impaling the arms of Willoughby, the family into which John Turberville married.

The delightful garden is the work of the present owners and is occasionally alive with chihuahuas.

*Wells Cathedral.*

## Wells*

*35; 5½ miles NE of Glastonbury on A39*

THE CATHEDRAL AND IMMEDIATE ENVIRONS

For many people, Wells will always be their favourite English cathedral. It may lack the towering majesty of Durham, the dazzling sumptuousness of Lincoln; but there is a warmth and serenity about it which no other cathedral possesses in quite the same way. It offers many surprises and, indeed, one or two moments of high drama; but it inspires no awe. An intensely beautiful building, it is at the same time a supremely comfortable one: one of those few great monuments of world class in which one always feels at home.

There was a collegiate church at Wells in the eighth century, and there has been a bishop – apart from two brief periods in the Middle Ages when the see was disputed by Bath and Glastonbury – since 909; but the cathedral as we know it today was probably begun some time in the 1180s, the work being given new impetus after the election of Bishop Jocelin in 1206. To him above all belongs the credit for the glorious Early English work of Wells, including the nave, the transepts and the great west front. The cathedral was consecrated in 1239, and Jocelin died three years later; after his death came one of those troubled periods referred to above, and it was only towards the end of the century, around 1285–90, that work began again. By that time, however, the Early English style had given way to the Decorated; and for the next half-century there were employed at Wells several of the most inspired architects and stonemasons in the whole history of English cathedral building.

And that was it – or very nearly. Throughout the Perpendicular period – of such tremendous importance in Somerset – although there was much done in the precinct, the cathedral itself underwent only one major alteration: the addition of the two towers at the corners of the west front. Whether this step is to be applauded or regretted we shall now have to consider.

The first thing to be understood about the west front of Wells is that it was designed as a gigantic screen and intended above all for the display of statuary. There were originally no fewer than 340 individual statues, nearly half of them over life-size, each gazing out from its own canopied niche. Of these, some 160 are still in place, though mostly damaged or partly worn away; yet Wells remains even now the supreme repository of thirteenth-century statuary in the country. The original work is divided horizontally into three stages. First comes a deep plinth, bare of anything except a few simple mouldings and broken only by the three doorways – almost the only features, one feels, where inspiration was lacking. They are poor, mingy, tentative things, unworthy of the sublime building to which they give access. Surely they must belong to the earliest phase of the work, before the arrival of Bishop Jocelin on the scene? Above them runs a line of blank arcading: trefoiled arches in pairs, each with its own little pointed gable above, each pair connected by a pointed arch with a larger gable above that, and recessed quatrefoils in the spandrels. (Formerly every arch held a statue of its own; two only remain today.) Above the two side doors which mark the aisles and again beneath the centres of the towers, which project on each side like western transepts, windows were later inserted – in the fifteenth century, judging by their Perpendicular tracery.

Before describing the third stage, it would be as well to note the principal vertical lines of emphasis on this west front. It consists above all of buttresses, six of them, jutting boldly out a considerable distance from the wall and casting deep shadows in the noonday sun. On the lowest stage these buttresses continue the line of blank arcading on their sides as well as their fronts, the only surprising feature being the ruthlessness with which their corners bisect the recessed quatrefoils, creating an unnervingly jagged silhouette. On the third stage, however, they become considerably more important, since it is only within them – and between the three

*The west front, Wells Cathedral.*

slightly stepped lancets that mark the end of the nave – that the statues are contained. Here, out of reach of all but the most determined vandals, these statues are a good deal more plentiful; most of the niches are still occupied, two on the north and south sides of each buttress, one to the west, in two tiers. The wall space between the buttresses is once again given over to blank arcading, soaring up in pairs of arches past both tiers and even beyond, to where another blank arcade, as squat as the other was lofty, runs the whole length of the front.

At this point, before the construction of the south tower in the 1390s, everything stopped – except above the nave, where the present rather curious stepped gable was already in position. Set between the two central buttresses – which terminate, unlike their fellows, in little gabled aedicules – it consists of, first, a tier of cinquefoiled arches with statues; next, a taller tier of trefoiled arches with slightly later statues of the Apostles; and finally a cusped elliptical niche in which Christ once sat in Judgement (only his legs now remain) flanked by trefoiled arches and those same awkwardly bisected quatrefoils above them. The crowning pinnacle is almost certainly a fifteenth-century afterthought – and not a happy one.

And so to those towers. Though they are of the same basic design, the northern one is slightly later – about 1430 – and a little more elaborate, since it has niches with highly ornate canopies set into the buttresses. But the main characteristic of both is that well-known Somerset speciality in which the bell openings continue blind down the next stage of the tower. For the rest, they are not insensitive – the lines of the buttresses, for example, are faithfully retained and an obvious effort has been made to give a unity to the whole elevation – but they do strike one, nonetheless, as just a little bit dull. Part of the trouble is, I think, that they too look somehow truncated: there are no turrets or pinnacles, and the weak blank parapet, with the tiniest and most ridiculous crenellations I have ever seen, leaves the eye unsatisfied. It has been suggested that spires were intended; but spires were out of fashion by 1390 – let alone 1430 – and they would have had the effect of dwarfing the crossing-tower. The problem remains unsolved.

Now go round to the north side of the cathedral – and immediately another mystery is explained. The insignificance of the three west doors, unfortunate as it is, becomes easier to understand the moment we see the north porch; for here, clearly, was the ceremonial entrance to the building. The doorway is flanked by buttresses ending in tall pinnacles with high pyramid caps; it has no fewer than ten orders of columns, with shaft rings and wonderfully carved capitals; relief panels in the spandrels; and, in the gable, an extraordinarily intricate composition in which three small stepped lancet windows are set within a larger group of six stepped blind lancets. The interior of the porch is exquisite: two rib-vaulted bays, the walls with two tiers of deeply cut blank arcading, the outer mouldings of the upper arches criss-crossing with each other; there is marvellous carving in the spandrels of both tiers and on the sill of the upper one.

Continuing round the church, we see that although the aisle windows have been given Perpendicular tracery, they and the nave are all part of the Early English work, as is the clerestory above. There are corbel tables at both levels. The transepts too date from Jocelin's time. They are broad, with both east and west aisles, but project only two bays on each side. Then, on the north, we come to one of the glories of Wells: the Chapter House. Its full splendour is revealed only when we go inside; what we see from the exterior is a tall octagon with radiating buttresses rising to high pinnacles and, between them, broad four-light windows of Decorated tracery – still semi-geometrical rather than flowing, and probably of about 1306. From it a fifteenth-century bridge, known as the CHAIN GATE, consisting of a line of two- and three-light windows at first-floor level passing across the road, leads to the Vicars' Hall.

The placing of the Chapter House means that the east end of the cathedral can be seen more easily from the south side. Immediately to the east of the transepts is what remains of Bishop Jocelin's chancel – three bays of it, which continue after an obvious break (and the beginning of a row of flying buttresses) for three more bays of fourteenth-century work until we come to the east transepts and the retrochoir. These, and the single-storey apsed Lady Chapel beyond them, are also Decorated, and almost certainly date from the second decade of the century – the slightly more rigid tracery of the Lady Chapel windows suggesting that the latter is probably just the earlier of the two.

Of the same date, or very nearly, is the crossing-tower, though it was somewhat altered around 1440. It is a lovely composition, strong yet serene, and seems to me to sum up the whole spirit of Wells. It stands on a low base with slim blank arcading – the point reached by the early thirteenth-century builders; from there, between 1315 and 1322, rose a tall single stage of extremely thin and elongated lancets, three to each side; and this in turn was taken over some 120 years later, when the lancets were transomed and partly filled in so as to make bell openings above the transom and blind arches below, with tracery added to both. A forest of pinnacles rises at each corner, with two smaller pinnacles along each side marking the divisions between the openings below.

And so, finally, we enter the cathedral, not by the gorgeous north porch but from the west end; and there before us, at the far end of the nave, is the first great *coup de théâtre* of Wells. A broad crossing arch, thick-set and almost crudely moulded and beginning its spring only just above the ground, soars up to its apex at triforium level; then, astonishingly, the two sides cross and swoop on upwards in an S-shape, forming as it were another arch, upside-down, balanced on the head of the one below. These two intersecting Ss continue to a point halfway up the clerestory, when they turn inward once more to form the crossing arch proper. This effect would in itself be extraordinary enough; but it is made stranger still by the addition of two huge open roundels in the spandrels on each side of the point where the two arches cross. What we actually see is, inevitably, a huge monster, mouth agape, eyes staring, confronting us down the nave, for all the world like one of those Leviathans beloved of medieval wall painters, gobbling up the ungodly on the Day of Doom.

The contrast between this almost barbaric conception and one of the most exquisite Early English naves in the country is so harsh as to be almost shocking. Alec Clifton-Taylor, who knows more about English ecclesiastical architecture than any man alive, has condemned it as a 'grotesque intrusion', and so indeed it is. True, it was never part of the original plan and is in fact a strainer arch erected, together with its two identical companions to the north and south of the crossing, only in the 1320s, when the weight of the recently completed tower made emergency strengthening measures necessary. But there are many ways of shoring up towers, some of them perceptible only to the trained and alert eye; that the fourteenth-century architect should have chosen a method as dramatic as this can only mean that it was deliberate. Pevsner has suggested that he was brought in from Bristol, the only other place where, in the choir aisles of the cathedral, one sees the same originality of spatial imagination. It may well be; but there is a brashness here which is absent in Bristol. As purists, we must deplore it – and yet, and yet. . . .

It seemed right to deal first with the strainer arch because it so immediately captures the attention. Let us now look at the nave itself – preferably westward from the crossing, so that we shall not be further distracted. How much of the work is Jocelin's, how much that of his predecessors, we do not know; but the whole thing was certainly finished by 1240. The stress, one notices, is entirely horizontal; Wells was having no truck with the new French Gothic verticality such as we see, for example, in the eastern parts of Canterbury or, to a lesser degree, at Lincoln. The height from floor to roof is only 67 feet, while nave and aisles seem quite exceptionally broad. (On the outside, as we have seen, the two west towers extend the front still further.) The arcade piers are thick and many-shafted, and the profusion of stiff-leaf carving – as everywhere at Wells, of stunning quality – on capital after capital gives, when viewed in perspective, a horizontal emphasis almost as compelling as the unbroken string-course above or the equally uninterrupted line of the triforium arches above that. This continuous triforium is, it must be admitted, the one serious weakness in the overall design. In the transepts the arches are divided into pairs by the vaulting shafts; here, for some reason, the springing of these shafts is raised to only just below the sill of the clerestory, and a certain monotony is the inevitable result. When they do spring, it is in groups of three, meeting at equidistant points along the ridge of the roof – which proves, rather surprisingly in view of all this horizontality, to be without a central rib. (The ridge rib had not yet been invented, though at Lincoln it was only a few years away.)

If we examine the detail rather more carefully, we can see a very slight stylistic division after the six eastern bays of the arcade; in the clerestory, where work was always a little behind, it comes one bay further to the east. The most obvious change is the abandonment of the head stops between the arches; the stiff-leaf on the capitals, too, becomes much more lush and luxuriant. These eastern bays, together with the transepts and crossing (but not of course the strainer arches) constitute the oldest part of the cathedral today; and though it may appear old-fashioned in some respects, in others it proves a pioneer: it is, for example, the first medieval building in the country in which the pointed arch is used exclusively: there is not a single round arch anywhere.

Take your time in the transepts; for there, as in the eastern bays of the nave, there are wonderfully spirited carvings to be enjoyed, on the capitals and elsewhere – men and animals, monsters and grotesques, even little stories told in consecutive scenes. You should then, if possible, descend to the only other Early English part of the cathedral: the undercroft of the Chapter House. You reach it through a splendid doorway just to the right of the staircase which leads to the Chapter House itself. This opens on to a low but most ornate vaulted passage – with a ridge rib this time (so it must be a bit later than the nave) and big carved bosses into the bargain. At the end of it is the undercroft, octagonal like the Chapter House above it, and with a central pillar, also octagonal though the sides are slightly concave. Big circular piers march sturdily round the walls.

*The Chapter House staircase, Wells Cathedral.*

And now, to understand quite how dramatic was the revolution in English architecture that occurred at the end of the thirteenth century, make for the CHAPTER HOUSE itself. Chapter houses at an upper level are rare in English cathedrals, but at Wells the phenomenon is doubly fortunate: first because it permits the comparison with the earlier undercroft, and second because it provides us with the most exciting staircase in any cathedral anywhere. This uninterrupted flight of stone steps, broad, shallow, uneven and worn by the feet of nearly seven centuries, rises for about a third of its length and then, magically, forks. Half of it swings round in a wide arc to disappear into the Chapter House to the right; the rest continues forward through a four-centred archway with a former north window above it and leads eventually on to the Chain Gate which we saw from the outside. The splendour of the effect is due not only to the splitting of the staircase – which occurs without any suggestion of a landing – but also to the sheer length of the straight part, which seems almost to disappear into the distance. One does not at first realise that both these factors were the result of a lucky chance: the Chain Gate was not built until 1459, and the staircase originally led to the Chapter House only. One is all the more admiring of the fourteenth-century architect who decided that the Chapter House should be entered from the west rather than more directly from the north choir aisle. From there the stairs would admittedly have been a good deal steeper, but still not impossible. Anywhere else but at Wells, one would attribute the existing arrangement to a laudable consideration for the disabilities of the older members of the Chapter; at Wells in the early Decorated period, one cannot be sure.

That staircase is a difficult act to follow; but the Chapter House, suddenly revealed as the stairs wheel round to the entrance, is fully worthy of its approach. Indeed, it is the most beautiful of its kind in England. The entrance itself is a joy to behold: the basic design is of two arches, heavily cusped, springing from wall shafts at the sides and a slender central trumeau, and supporting in their common spandrel a large open triangle with convex sides, of similar dimensions and with similar cusping. The whole composition is contained within another broad embracing arch. In view of the great thickness of the walls, this design is repeated on the inside and the out, leaving a little vaulted space in the middle. Now enter the chamber itself. The walls are lined with stone seats, supported by slender shafts carrying canopies, with pinnacles between. Above are the big four-light windows already mentioned. But the beauty of this marvellous room lies, above all, in the vaulting. As in several other polygonal chapter houses, it springs from a central pier, from which a multiplication of tierceron ribs branches out as in a palm tree; but whereas that of Westminster Abbey was designed with sixteen ribs, that of Lincoln twenty and that of Exeter (if it had been continued all the way round) twenty-four, at Wells there are no fewer than thirty-two, spraying out like some tremendous fountain to an octagon of ridge ribs above. It is astonishing to think that, dating as it does from the first decade of the fourteenth century, this miraculous conception is separated by only some fifty years from the undercroft below. The Decorated style was to continue for another half-century, but it is arguable whether it ever produced anything more perfect than this.

Returning now to the cathedral proper, we come next to the choir. It is of six bays, the three to the west being part of the original Early English work of *c*.1200, the remaining three belonging to the 1330s and consequently – apart from the Perpendicular fan vaulting beneath the crossing-tower – the most recent part of the whole building. The fourteenth-century architects obviously did what they could to give a unity to all six bays, and up to a point succeeded – as they certainly did with the glorious lierne-vaulted roof, a reticulated design making much play with the cusped square and clearly inspired by the Bristol chancel. They were less successful, however, when they tried to continue their scheme of wall decoration towards the west; and as these western bays were further done over by Salvin in 1848–54, we had better – so far as we can – ignore them, and concentrate on the three eastern bays, which technically form the presbytery. They are closed off to the east by three slender pointed arches, through which one looks beyond to the retrochoir and Lady Chapel; but since these are both of a single storey, the great seven-light window above the three arches is in fact the east window of the cathedral.

The chief interest of the presbytery lies in what happens in the central section between the arcade and the east window – or, on the north and south sides, between arcade and clerestory. Here the entire wall space is covered by a filigree of tall, very deep niches, with pinnacled canopies above them. In the niches are full-length statues (renewed), on pedestals which vary in height according to the level of that point of the arch from which each rises – since both the pedestals and the paired slender shafts that separate the niches descend right into the arches below instead of stopping (as happens further west) at a horizontal ledge just clearing the top of the arcade. This cheerful acceptance of the idea of straight lines cutting obliquely into curves – it can be seen again in the east window, where two of the mullions rise straight up into the arch – is generally thought of as a hallmark of the Perpendicular; so indeed is the tendency to panel over all blank wall spaces. These are only two of the several indications perceptible at Wells of the shape of things to come.

The choir aisles – in which the sharp division between the two styles can once again be easily identified – lead round to the east transept, retrochoir and Lady Chapel. They are in fact slightly earlier than the presbytery, work having started on the Lady Chapel even before the Chapter House was complete. This was originally conceived as an elongated octagon, standing as a separate building independent of the cathedral – as a glance at the superb and completely self-contained star-within-a-star vaulting, one of the earliest lierne vaults in England, makes clear. While the Chapel was still being built, however, it was decided to link it after all to the main building; and the retrochoir, with the projecting east transept, was the result. The problem was how to retain the polygonal character of the Lady Chapel when part of it was engulfed in the rectangular retrochoir; it was solved by means of two free-standing, many-shafted piers marking the western end of the octagon, and then two more in similar positions one bay further to the west. Halfway between the two but further out towards the sides are two additional piers marking the west ends of the two side chapels. Thus there are six altogether, and from each there springs a forest of shafts; moreover, as the first two pairs occupy, both latitudinally and longitudinally, the centres of their respective bays rather than the corners, there is a fascinating display of diagonal cross-vistas, changing kaleidoscopically with every step one takes. Certain of the shafts on the piers are even picked out in dark (Purbeck?) marble – for almost the last time in medieval architecture – providing an additional counterpoint to this dazzling three-dimensional fugue.

Finally we come to the CLOISTER, opening off the south aisle of the nave. Since Wells was never a monastic foundation, this was built more as an ornamental luxury than as a necessity, and was used mainly for processional purposes. In consequence there is no walk on the north side – the one adjacent to the cathedral. The three walks as we see them today are almost entirely of the fifteenth century; the east walk of *c*.1425, the west of *c*.1465, and the south begun *c*.1466 and continuing till the end of the century. Despite these different dates, however, the general design of all three walks remains the same: six-light windows with transoms, lierne vaulting above. On the upper floor of the east walk we find the Library – a marvellous room originally 160 feet long, and the largest fifteenth-century library in England. It suffered a good deal under the Commonwealth, however, and the present bookcases and wall panelling are of 1685. Opposite, over the west walk, is the Singing School, with a fine timber roof.

Just to the south of the Cloister stands the BISHOP'S PALACE. How fortunate, one feels, is the Bishop of Bath and Wells to live in so magnificent a house, and in so exquisite a setting. You approach it from the Market Place through a Gatehouse known as the BISHOP'S EYE, built – like the Chain Gate, the West Cloister Walk and so much else in Wells – by Bishop Bekynton, who held office from 1443 until his death in 1465; you then find yourself in a lush green enclosure of lawns and whispering trees, bounded on your left by the walls of the Cloister and on your right by a broad moat into which juts another GATEHOUSE, fourteenth-century this time, with two polygonal towers and an Elizabethan oriel. Within this inner enclosure, you see the great palace away to your left: it is of varying styles and periods. The Chapel and the ruins of the Great Hall date back to the end of the thirteenth century, and very beautiful they are. The former has a high tierceron-vaulted roof with huge and intricate bosses, and a wonderful six-light east window with intersecting tracery and an octofoil circle in the top; the latter must have been one of the finest halls in England – 115 feet by 60 feet, with tall, two-light, transomed windows rising to the roof on both sides.

*The Bishop's Eye Gatehouse, Bishop's Palace, Wells.*

Alas, it was deliberately reduced to its present state in the last century to provide 'a picturesque ruin'. Can desecration go further? It is, incidentally, one of the earliest halls in England to have been given what was to become the standard arrangement of dais end, screens passage and offices beyond.

A short way away to the south-west stands a huge fifteenth-century BARN with a fine timber roof and wind-braces. Formerly the property of the Bishop, it has now passed to the city, who have turned it into a kind of sports centre; the outside, however, with its copious buttressing and transomed slit windows, is unspoilt.

The other important buildings of the precinct are all to the north of the cathedral. The most interesting of all are VICARS' HALL and VICARS' CLOSE behind it. They should of course ideally be entered from the Chapter House Stair and over Chain Gate. The Vicars, or more properly the Vicars Choral, were a body of deputies to the prebendary canons who were required to be present in the choir for all the main services. In the middle of the fourteenth century they were formally recognised as a college and given statutes of their own, together with individual cottages down a long, narrow quadrangle with a Hall at one end and a Chapel at the other. The Hall, at the southern end, is of 1348 or thereabouts. It was slightly remodelled in the fifteenth century but has scarcely been touched since. It has a pointed wagon roof with slender curving rafters, Decorated or Perpendicular windows on all four sides, linenfold panelling and a big stone fireplace with a reading desk tucked in behind it.

Vicars' Close stretches away to the north – not really a quadrangle at all, but a quiet cul-de-sac lined with cottages. It is that rarest of survivals, a planned street of the mid-fourteenth century, 150 yards long. Astonishingly too, for its date, it was given a deliberately exaggerated perspective, the two long ranges being 9 feet closer together at the north end than they are at the south. A natural rise in the ground increases the illusion still further. The cottages, which seem to date from around 1360 – work having been interrupted by the Black Death – originally consisted of one room up, one down, a spiral staircase, a small yard and a latrine; in early days the only heating would have been by a fire or brazier in the middle of the ground floor, the smoke rising through the upper room and passing out through the roof. The fireplaces and chimneys were added by the executors of Bishop Bekynton after his death in 1465. In more recent times most of the cottages – which are still occupied by the Vicars Choral and other members of the cathedral staff – have inevitably been altered or modernised in one way or another; but No. 22 has been restored to what – apart from the chimney – must be very like its original appearance. At the centre of the far (north) end is the CHAPEL. In the fourteenth century it consisted of the ground floor only of the present building; it was once again Bekynton who left money for the Vicars' Library above, the battlements and the bell-cote. The two-light windows to the south, it will be noted, are already Perpendicular. The Library has a timber roof with wind-braces. The Victorian building to the right is a disgrace to the Close and should be pulled down at once.

Emerging from Vicars' Close, turn to your right and walk westward along Cathedral Green. Once under Chain Gate you first pass on your right the present THEOLOGICAL COLLEGE LIBRARY, formerly the Archdeacon's House but now hopelessly Victorianised; then the Chancellor's House – now the MUSEUM – originally Tudor but again altered beyond recognition; next, the old DEANERY which is a good deal more interesting. It is a noble fifteenth-century courtyard house, refenestrated around 1700 but retaining its original battlements and corner turrets, now used as the Diocesan Offices. Entrance is from the courtyard to the east. The old Hall still exists inside, with a pretty little fan-vaulted oriel which once looked on to the inner court, now unfortunately filled in.

At this point, you may either continue in the same direction, emerging from Cathedral Green at BROWN'S GATE, another fifteenth-century Gatehouse, or, more interestingly, cut southward across the Green and enter the north-east corner of the Market Place through yet another, known as PENNYLESS PORCH and again a creation of Bekynton's. His also, though you would hardly guess it, is the row of shops with regular bay fronts along the north side of the Market Place. Known as Bekynton's *Nova Opera*, they date from about 1460.

THE CITY

Outside the Cathedral Precinct, the one building in Wells that towers above all others, both literally and in its architectural importance, is ST CUTHBERT'S CHURCH. It is the largest parish church in Somerset, and one of the most magnificent; yet such is the splendour of the cathedral that most visitors to the city pass it by without a second glance. Set well back from the High Street, in the middle of a spacious churchyard, it appears to be Perpendicular through and through, and – judging by the uniformity of the windows – built all of a piece. The west tower is huge (122 feet), but it needs to be; for the body of the church itself consists, besides the tower, of a six-bay nave with aisles, then a bay occupied to the south by a porch and to the north by a so-called Treasury, then an outer chapel of two bays, then a transept, then a three-bay chancel chapel, and finally a chancel projecting one bay further still. Nearly all the windows are of five lights, with notably unimaginative tracery; every roof is parapeted with blank arcading, and there are crocketed pinnacles to be seen above the nave.

The tower has the same uniformity and simplicity. To the west, there is a six-light window above the door, with three niches above; there follows, on all four sides, the immensely tall single stage such as we see in different forms on all three of the towers of the cathedral – the traceried bell openings in the top half, then an ornamental transom, then a blank extension below, longer than the openings themselves. Finally comes a high parapet, panelled and embattled, and beautiful high pinnacled turrets at the corners, seeming to develop effortlessly from the set-back buttresses lower down.

All this is copy-book Perpendicular: the interior, however, tells a different story, and an extremely odd one. A large church of the early thirteenth century stood on this site, but proved, one supposes, insufficiently grand for the more prosperous fifteenth; roof and clerestory were accordingly removed, leaving nothing but the piers, which were then heightened, on exactly the same cross-section, a further 11 feet. The arches were then replaced on top of them, together with their hood-moulds and head stops. That was a beginning: next, the Perpendicular masons added another bay to the west and finally the tower, at the same time rebuilding the chancel – lengthening it slightly as they did so – and adding a sacristy on the north side. Lastly they added the two chapels to the west of the transepts and refenestrated the whole thing. Subsequently, in a separate early sixteenth-century campaign, the nave was further heightened by the addition of the clerestory and the church was given its present magnificent timber roof. It is of the usual Somerset type, with tie-beams; they have tracery and queenposts above, angels with shields in the middle. More angels line the wall plates between them.

Particularly when compared to the immensely tall tower arch, the chancel arch seems oddly small, not even spanning the entire width of the nave. This is because the thirteenth-century church had a crossing-tower, and the huge piers flanking the arch were needed to support it. Curiously enough, this tower seems to have been left *in situ* during the Perpendicular rebuilding, for we know that it collapsed in 1561. For at least a century, therefore, the church must have had both a crossing-tower and a west tower – and very strange it must have looked.

Architecturally, the other most interesting features of the church are the Treasury, opposite the south porch, and the two chapels – St Catherine's Chapel and the Lady Chapel – which occupy the original north and south transepts respectively. The Treasury, part of the original Early English church, has somehow been allowed to retain its lancets. St Catherine's Chapel, the second of the two chapels to the east of it, has a sadly mutilated stone reredos on the east wall which also dates from the earlier building, with two rows of canopied niches. It was deliberately destroyed by the Reformers of Edward VI's reign and plastered over, to be discovered again only in 1848. The Lady Chapel immediately opposite across the church has another, even finer, reredos of 1470, illustrating the Tree of Jesse. It too was tragically vandalised, but a few pieces remain to tell us of its outstanding quality; the best of them can now be seen at the west end of the aisle. In the centre is another thirteenth-century window. Finally, do not miss the pulpit – a marvellous piece of wood carving dated 1636, with representations of Old Testament scenes in scrolly cartouches.

From St Cuthbert's you may either return directly to the Market Place via the High Street – looking in at both the KING CHARLES PARLOUR on the left with its splendid mid-seventeenth-century staircase, and the KING'S HEAD with its fifteenth-century roof – or, if you have time, walk across the churchyard to the ALMSHOUSES in Chamberlain Street, founded by a bequest from Bishop Bubwith in 1436. The Chapel has a good timber roof with four tiers of wind-braces. Further on to the north-east on the other side of Chamberlain Street are HARPER'S ALMSHOUSES, built in 1713 'for the perpetual use . . . of 5 poor men, old decayed Woollcombers of this City of Wells'.

At the end of Chamberlain Street fork left into NEW STREET with its fine Georgian houses and then right into THE LIBERTY, so called because it marks the boundary of the Liberty of St Andrew, an area of 52 acres with no parish affiliations, outside the jurisdiction of the Bishop and responsible directly to the Dean and Chapter. The best houses here are the ORGANIST'S HOUSE at No. 3 (*c.*1700 with vestiges of a fifteenth-century house here and there), ST ANDREW'S LODGE (the former Charity School) of 1713 with its pedimented front door and cross windows, and THE CEDARS (1758, by Thomas Paty of Bristol). Where North Liberty turns sharp right and becomes EAST LIBERTY there is, on the further side of the road, a fine hipped-roof house of 1699 (built by a Dr Claver Morris for £807 14*s* 6¾*d*). Of the three remaining houses in East Liberty, the first is of 1736, the second of 1819. The last, the DEAN'S LODGING, looks outwardly like a Jacobean manor house (though it is unfortunately difficult to see from the road); but it is built round an early fifteenth-century core, parts of which still exist within. Finally, turning right into St Andrew's Street, we come almost at once to TOWER HOUSE on our right, in the south gable of which there is a blocked two-light window of *c.*1320. Opposite to the left is a curious house, much altered, known as the PRINCIPAL'S HOUSE. Originally fourteenth-century, it had a most distinguished north porch added on in Bekynton's time – the tracery is identical with that of the Chain Gate – with a three-light window above. Chain Gate itself is only a few steps further on, and so our perambulation is ended.

## Westonzoyland

*36; 3 miles SE of Bridgwater on A372*

The first thing that strikes you as you stand by a pretty little row of thatched cottages and look up at the CHURCH OF ST MARY THE VIRGIN is the height and beauty of its tower. Over 100 feet high, it has four main stages above the west door: the first has a four-light west window, the next two have two-light windows flanked by canopied niches, and the top one has a central two-light bell opening with similar blank ones to each side and attached pinnacles around and between them. The set-back buttresses end in their own pinnacles just short of the parapet rather than linking up with the corner pinnacles at the summit, which is a pity; and the embattled crown has an intermediate pinnacle in the middle of each side, instead of the two which would have been more natural above a tripartite composition. But these are minor blemishes. The south is another show front, embattled on aisle, clerestory, two-storeyed porch and south chapel, the south window of which is further embellished by a niche on each side. Only the chancel lacks battlements; but it is lower and – as one can see from the Decorated windows – a good deal earlier than the rest.

The real glory of this church is revealed, however, only on the inside: it is the nave roof that takes your breath away. In all Somerset – perhaps in all the West Country – there is none better. The basic design is very much the local product: huge tie-beams with kingposts, the pitch relatively low, principals and purlins forming small square panels. What is unique is the degree of elaboration. There is, first of all, a multiplicity of angels – on the corbels holding the arched braces beneath the tie-beams, on the wall plates beneath the intermediate principals, and, biggest and best of all, in the centre of each tie-beam where, with wings outspread, they seem to be supporting the kingposts themselves. To each side of these kingposts, two tiers of tracery fill the space right up to the ridge. And even this is not all, since between each pair of tie-beams is a curving collar-beam at a higher level, having at its centre a massive pendant carved with thick foliage. There are also very beautiful bosses, with what appear to be leaves shooting out from the corners, at every available opportunity.

After a roof like this, everything else seems inevitably an anti-climax, though there is another excellent roof in the south transept chapel. Both transepts, incidentally, now show themselves to be later than the nave: to the south there is an obvious change in the stone and the

*The nave roof, St Mary the Virgin, Westonzoyland.*

appearance of a four-centred arch, while to the north we find one of the clerestory windows looking pointlessly into the transept.

Two other features seem worth mentioning: first, the fan vault under the tower; second, the screen. It dates only from the 1930s (though the lower half looks as though it had been re-used) but has a complete loft and a rood above it.

The battle of Sedgemoor – the last to be fought on English soil – took place nearby on 6 July 1685. Five hundred of Monmouth's defeated rebel soldiers were kept prisoner in the church, in which five died of their wounds. Later, a further twenty-two were hanged outside. A copy of the church register in the south-west corner tells of heavy expenditure on frankincense to purify the building afterwards.

## Short List

### Barrington Court

*NT; 37; 3 miles NE of Ilminster off B3168*

Much of the architectural interest of the house depends on whether it was built, as was formerly thought, by Henry, Lord Daubeney in the first quarter of the sixteenth century or, as is now suspected, by William Clifton *c.*1560. If the first, it is one of the most advanced houses in the country: almost symmetrical E-plan, with tall transomed windows and a veritable forest of spiral chimneys and crocketed finials. If the second, it is simply a large and impressive early Elizabethan house like many others. Derelict by 1900, it was given to the National Trust in 1907; thus most internal features (apart from two chimneypieces) are recent imports by the Lyle family, who have occupied it since 1920. They include good woodwork, especially in the Small Dining Room.

### Batcombe

*38; 9 miles SE of Shepton Mallet off B3081*

ST MARY'S CHURCH is a typically Somerset phenomenon, an intrinsically rather boring church with a perfectly magnificent tower. It is in the usual reddish grey local stone and unusually late – about 1540. The two upper stages are treated together, with immensely tall two-light windows grouped in threes on each side, attached pinnacles between. Below on the east stands a figure in a niche, surrounded by six angels on the wing in high relief.

### Bridgwater

*39; 15½ miles W of Glastonbury on A39*

ST MARY'S CHURCH in this pretty, late Georgian town has a tower of red sandstone with one of the few spires in Somerset and unusual Decorated tracery, especially on the transept fronts and round the doorways. The porches have interior balconies, and there is a splendid Jacobean screen in the south transept. The MARKET HALL, with its semi-circular portico, shallow dome and tall lantern, was built by an amateur, John Bowen, and is the best building in the town; THE LIONS, on West Quay, is the most enjoyable. If, as Pevsner says, the Bridgwater quays are a minor edition of Wisbech, here is the poor man's Peckover.

### Chewton Mendip

*40; 15 miles S of Bristol on A39*

At 126 feet, not counting the turrets, the church tower of ST MARY MAGDALEN is the tallest in Somerset, and one of the most beautiful. The traceried, transomed bell openings (two per side) are repeated blank in the stage below. The tower ends in a 'Gloucester crown' – an elaborate parapet with pierced battlements and very high corner turrets. It is fan vaulted on the inside; for the rest, the church is scraped and devoid of charm.

### Cleeve Abbey

*41; 3 miles SW of Watchet off B3190*

A Cistercian house was founded here in 1198. The church has gone, but some of the monastic buildings remain, of which by far the most interesting is the new REFECTORY, created by the last Abbot in the early sixteenth century. It has a marvellous wagon roof of timber, with angels supporting not only the principals but the sub-principals as well. A reader's desk is built into the thickness of the wall. The whole complex is in the care of the Dept of the Environment, who have recently completed a thorough restoration.

### Doulting

*42; 1½ miles E of Shepton Mallet on A361*

ST ALDHELM'S CHURCH qualifies for an entry here by reason of its quite astonishing south porch. It dates from about 1500, though with its curious concave-sided gable it could almost be a piece of Gothic Revival. The octagonal crossing-tower and spire are pretty too, from a distance, though closer inspection shows them to have been remodelled in Victorian times. The inside is a perfect example of Victorian restoration at its worst.

### East Lambrock

*43; 8 miles W of Yeovil off B3165*

The OLD MANOR dates from about 1470, though there is a plaque giving a date of 1584 just outside the Elizabethan-panelled Dining Room. A Parlour was added about 1602. The delightful garden is the work of Mrs Margery Fish, the writer on horticulture. ST JAMES'S CHURCH nearby dates from the late twelfth century (see the chancel arch), though the east window is of *c.*1300 and most of the others Perpendicular.

### East Quantoxhead

*44; 4½ miles NE of Williton off A39*

The COURT HOUSE has been the property of the Luttrells (of Dunster) for some seven centuries. It does not look particularly interesting from the outside, and I failed – through no fault of the present occupants – to get in; but there is said to be a fine old Hall with, surprisingly, a four-light window on the end wall behind the dais. There are also some superb Jacobean and Caroline fireplaces of wood and stucco with carved overmantels representing scenes from the New Testament.

## Hatch Beauchamp

*45; 5 miles NW of Ilminster off A358*

A noble Palladian house of Bath stone, HATCH COURT was built by Thomas Prowse of Axbridge, a gentleman architect who was MP for Somerset for over a quarter of a century. (He was even offered the Speakership in 1761, but declined on grounds of ill health.) Prowse was a friend of Sanderson Miller, with whom he is known to have worked on Hagley Hall; and the design of Hatch Court – which dates from precisely the same time – is strikingly similar to that of Hagley, though on a smaller scale. It has a pretty five-bay loggia on the south front, canted bays on the sides, and little towers at the corners. There is a fine Staircase Hall and good plasterwork, but little else in the house is original.

## High Ham

*46; 3 miles N of Langport off B3153*

ST ANDREW'S is not the sort of church one would expect to find in Somerset. It looks out on to a village green – itself a rarity in these parts – and has a tower that is short, squat and simple, giving the game away only by the tracery in its bell openings. Inside, things are a lot better. The tall clerestory windows allow plenty of light to the fine tie-beamed roof, excellently carved with angels. Screen, bench ends and font cover are all worth careful examination. The whole church was rebuilt in a single year, 1476, by Abbot Selwood of Glastonbury, of whom there is a portrait in the east window.

## Hinton St George

*47; 4 miles SE of Ilminster off A356*

Now turned into flats, HINTON HOUSE has a distinguished south front which seems to be Queen Anne, though parts of it go back to the 1630s. Later it was remodelled by Matthew Brettingham and later still by James Wyatt and Sir Jeffrey Wyatville. The Gatehouse and clock tower were brought from Clifton Maybank (*q.v.*).

## Muchelney

*48; 15½ miles E of Taunton off A378*
*Includes Priest's House (NT)*

Originally this was the oldest monastic foundation in Somerset after Glastonbury, going back to the seventh century. The church has vanished, apart from an exposed ground plan, but there remains part of the fan-vaulted SOUTH CLOISTER WALK and most of the ABBOT'S LODGINGS, in which the principal room has a most opulent fireplace with carved lions above it and a pair of two-light transomed windows with glass bearing the initials of Abbot Broke (1502–22). The neighbouring parish church of ST PETER AND ST PAUL has a fan vault inside the tower and wonderfully unsophisticated paintings on the wagon roof of the nave. The fourteenth- to fifteenth-century PRIEST'S HOUSE (NT) stands a little way to the north-east. It is thatched, and has a Hall rising two storeys, the whole height of the building.

## Nettlecombe

*49; 7 miles SW of Watchet on B3190*

ST MARY'S CHURCH and NETTLECOMBE COURT only a few yards away form a delightful group quite separate from the village, which was moved in the eighteenth century so as not to spoil the view. The church has the only seven-sacrament font in the West Country (said to have been presented by Chaucer's daughter-in-law, the Duchess of Suffolk) and two tremendous Raleigh tombs, set in recesses so deep that they project beyond the outer wall. The house, built by John Trevelyan in 1599, has retained its Elizabethan south front – though not, alas, all its windows – but the west front is Georgian except for its pinnacled central gable. In the Great Hall is a sumptuous plaster ceiling with pendants, and there is a most elegant Rococo staircase of 1733.

## North Petherton

*50; 3 miles SW of Bridgwater on A38*

It may seem churlish to relegate a church with one of the finest of all Somerset towers to a short list; but good towers are plentiful in these parts, while churches which are otherwise as boring as ST MARY'S are mercifully few. The top stage of the tower looks uniquely opulent by reason of the narrow band of panelling running between the bell openings and the parapet, each panel being filled with Somerset tracery. The inside is Victorianised; the rood-screen is in poor taste and the reredos appalling.

## Nunney

*51; 3 miles SW of Frome off A361*

Standing in what is virtually the middle of the village, NUNNEY CASTLE is completely surrounded by a deep-water moat, beside which there flows a pretty, rushing stream: the effect could hardly be more picturesque. It was begun in 1373, its plan that of a simple rectangle with round towers at each corner – there is no courtyard or keep. There were four storeys altogether, the Great Hall occupying the second. The castle is said to have been in regular use until the Civil War, though since it is extremely low-lying and does not seem to be protecting anything in particular one wonders whether it was of much strategic use. Next to it is the outstandingly handsome MANOR FARM HOUSE – early Georgian, with a slightly outward-curving hipped roof of red tiles.

## Selworthy

*NT; 52; 3 miles W of Minehead off A39*

An enchanting MODEL VILLAGE inspired by Blaise Hamlet (*q.v.*), Selworthy was built by Sir Thomas Dyke Acland in 1828 for his estate pensioners. The pretty thatched and whitewashed cottages were grouped around a village green and overlook one of the most beautiful valleys in all Somerset. Above, ALL SAINTS' CHURCH has a superbly lavish south aisle of 1538 with a marvellous wagon roof; there is also an enchanting Squire's Pew in the form of a tiny Gothic pavilion. All this is part of the Holnicôte Estate – 12,440 acres that are now the property of the National Trust.

## Stavordale Priory

*53; 5½ miles SE of Bruton off A303*

This is one of the rare examples in England of a medieval priory church completely converted into a private house

– the original conversion having been made early this century by T.E. Collcutt. The old aisleless nave is now a long kitchen–dining space; the chancel arch is still visible in the present hall; and the chancel – which now has Tudor windows set into the original arches – is a living room, from which the fan vaulting of the church's north chapel can be seen through a specially inserted glass window. The splendid timber roof of both nave and chancel, its tie-beams carrying huge bosses and supported on each side by carved corbels, runs through all the upper rooms.

## Tintinhull House

*NT; 54; 5 miles NW of Yeovil off A303*

The house began life as an unassuming Somerset manor of about 1600. Some 120 years later, however, one Andrew Napper added a beautiful west front of dressed Ham stone – keeping, however, the original mullioned and transomed cross windows. They look a little archaic, but give the house character as well as elegance. The triangular pediment, set in a hipped roof, flanked by tiny dormers and having an ornate *oeil-de-boeuf* window in its centre, contrasts pleasingly with its smaller segmental counterpart over the Tuscan porch. The interior is pleasant without being exceptional, but the garden is famous and a joy to behold.

## Witham Friary

*55; 4½ miles SW of Frome off A359*

The CHURCH OF ST MARY, ST JOHN THE BAPTIST AND ALL SAINTS is all that remains of the first Carthusian monastery to be established in England, founded in 1178. The builder was St Hugh of Lincoln, who was the third Prior before his translation. Only the three eastern bays are original, the westernmost (with its bell-cote) having been added in 1876. The east end is apsed. All this is more likely to have been the chapel of the lay brethren than the monastic church itself.

# Suffolk

Among all the counties of southern England, Suffolk shares with Essex one inestimable advantage: its perfectly awful communications with London. Still unblest – except in the extreme north-west corner – with anything resembling a motorway, and therefore separated from the capital by mile after mile of choked and choking suburbia or, for rail travellers, the formidable deterrent of Liverpool Street station, it has contrived to preserve its character and its strange, understated beauty in a way that not even its neighbour Norfolk can altogether match. Physically, that beauty consists almost as much in the light as in the land itself – a light that changes constantly, restless as the sea, under the hurrying clouds of that immense East Anglian sky; dappling the vast cornfields beneath, and occasionally throwing into unwonted and undeserved relief the great ditches that have been draining them for centuries and that account, incidentally, for one of the many Suffolk idiosyncrasies which can be endearing if you have time to spare and utterly maddening if you do not – roads that writhe and wriggle like an angry snake as they cross the dead-flat countryside. To the west, these flatlands give place to the chalk downs around Newmarket (which never seems able to decide whether it belongs to Suffolk or not) and the heathy Breckland north of Bury; to the east, their character is gradually changed by the advances of the great river estuaries of the Stour, the Orwell, the Deben and the Alde; they become ever saltier, reedier and more windswept until they reach the North Sea itself and provide, between Felixstowe and Southwold, the most magically mysterious stretches of coastline in all England.

Architecturally, Suffolk is a miracle. Indeed, it is two miracles. The first is the sheer splendour of its vernacular building, unrivalled – to my eyes at any rate – by that of any other county. The second is that it should have achieved this distinction despite the virtual absence of any building stone worthy of the name. Just occasionally, it is true, in the coastal region between Woodbridge and Aldeburgh, one comes upon houses – and, at Chillesford and Wantisden, church towers – built of the brownish grey coralline crag, easily recognised by the quantity of tiny shells and marine fossils embedded in it. Also in the south-east, between Orford and Felixstowe, there is a certain amount of septaria, a clayey limestone unattractive in appearance but hardy enough to have sustained Orford Castle for the past eight and a half centuries and the base of Little Wenham Hall for nearly as long. At the opposite corner of the county, the chalk downs provide a certain amount of clunch; but this is too soft to stand up to Suffolk winters. We are left with flint – grey, intractable, totally dependent on mortar to hold it in place and to provide the filling between its rough and rounded edges, but superbly enduring and, when well used, ruggedly beautiful.

And wood. One thinks of it first, perhaps, in connection with the timber-framed houses and cottages that are inseparable from one's memories of Suffolk – including those moated manor houses of the fifteenth and sixteenth centuries of which several hundred have survived, essentially unchanged, into the present day. But to see the real virtuosity of Suffolk woodwork you must go to the churches and raise your eyes upward – for the timber roofs of Suffolk churches are, quite literally, breathtaking. Earl Stonham – singled out by Pevsner as the most beautiful single hammer-beam roof in England – Framlingham, Kersey, Ufford ... the list could be continued almost indefinitely. The best for me, to which I have returned again and again, is Mildenhall; the most remarkable, unquestionably Needham Market, despite the Victorian restoration and the boringness of the church below.

Finally, brick. Historically, Suffolk brick is of enormous importance since it was here, so far as we can tell, that the art of brick and tile making – lost after the departure of the Romans – was rediscovered. The little church at Polstead has brick arches which, if original, can hardly be later than about 1200; even those at Little Wenham, though some three-quarters of a century later, are still among the earliest non-Roman bricks in England. It was, however, only with the Tudors that brickwork reached the point in its development when it could give real pleasure to the beholder; and there are few counties where Tudor brickwork can be seen to better advantage than in Suffolk. The collection starts with Hadleigh (where the Deanery Tower dates from 1495) and continues through West Stow Hall to Melford Hall, Kentwell and Helmingham. In many parts of the county, scarcely a village seems to lack its Tudor manor house with clusters of tall, decorated chimneystacks and occasionally a gatehouse, as at Erwarton Hall, that is more a light-hearted *jeu d'esprit* than anything else. Brick also shows to spectacular effect in the great curving ornamental gables that were introduced from the Low Countries early in the seventeenth century. Most of it is a good rich red; but in Suffolk you will also find a distinctive, if not ultimately very satisfying, white brick. It lasted from the thirteenth century (Little Wenham again) to the nineteenth, when the main centre of production was Woolpit. You can see it to best advantage at Hengrave Hall, and in many of the town houses of Ipswich and Bury. For some reason or another, however, it was hardly ever used in churches, except occasionally for porches or towers; some of the latter were actually refaced in brick in the eighteenth century. Grundisburgh is one of the best.

For churches, flint has ever been the rule; there are of course exceptions, but they are surprisingly few. One of the problems of flint building is always said to be the impossibility of producing clean right-angled corners; hence, one is always told, the tradition of the round tower in late Saxon and Norman times. (Why then, one wonders, did they not build round churches as well?) Suffolk has about forty of these round towers, a few of which may indeed be pre-Conquest. They are picturesque, but scarcely distinguished. By far the most important Norman monument in the county is the Gatetower of Bury, though the castles of Framlingham and Orford possess, in their relative solitude, a good deal more atmosphere.

You will search Suffolk in vain for any outstanding Early English work, and even good Decorated is relatively scarce; there is, however, an astonishing east window at Mildenhall, very early (*c*.1300) but with *seven* lights and oddly jagged tracery of a kind I have seen nowhere else. (Prior Crauden's Chapel at Ely comes nearest, perhaps, but is a quarter of a century later in date.) If you prefer your tracery flowing, Stowmarket will be your best bet. If, on the other hand, you are looking for oddities, you cannot do better than the immense stone trellis of Barsham. It is not particularly beautiful, and it may not even be thirteenth-century at all; but it is certainly unique.

And so, finally, to the Perpendicular, which is the glory of Suffolk. We think instinctively of Lavenham and Long Melford, Kedington and Clare and the other great churches of the south-west, in the rich wool country along the banks of the Stour; but there is another sumptuous seam to be struck in the east – at Blythburgh, Walberswick and Southwold. (Another once-great church is Covehithe, a mile or two up the coast, but it is one degree too ruinous to find a place in the pages that follow.) The fifteenth century was the golden age of flushwork – though it seems to have started as early as 1320, at Butley Priory – and in all these majestic buildings the virtuoso juxtaposition of knapped flints and freestone contributes mightily to their impact. It can also give an entirely justified impression of opulence, especially when it includes those huge Gothic letters and monograms: IHS for Jesus, M for the Virgin Mary, a crowned S for Sanctus. As to the interiors, I have already mentioned the timber roofs; the other all-important element, for me, is the light. Suffolk churches are mercifully free of Victorian glass, while much of the good medieval work (though not, thank God, at Long Melford) was destroyed by the Puritans under the unspeakable William Dowsing. In consequence, thanks to the plain glass which fills the immense Perpendicular windows in the aisles and clerestories, church after church is flooded with that all-pervading East Anglian light – an unfailing lift to the spirit on grey November mornings and an unadulterated joy on sunny summer afternoons.

For secular architecture, the list must start with Little Wenham; it then continues through those innumerable medieval hall houses – the palm going to the magnificently moated Helmingham and to Giffords Hall with its spectacular double hammer-beam roof – and to a few town houses of much the same date, the most memorable of which is Alston Court, Nayland. And so to the sixteenth century, which has left us not only several great mansions such as Hengrave, Melford Hall and Kentwell but many smaller houses of infinite charm: Thorpe Hall at Horham, for example, with its passion for pediments – obviously the *dernier cri* in 1560.

After Queen Elizabeth, however, the standard seems to drop; the seventeenth and early eighteenth centuries produced little of real importance. Even Hintlesham – one of the most desirable houses in the county – is really only a façade of 1720 concealing a Tudor building beneath it, although its plaster ceiling of the 1680s is one of the sights of Suffolk. But then, in 1778, comes Heveningham (alas, badly damaged by fire just before this book went to press) – and in a single bound the county retrieves its reputation, for here Sir Robert Taylor and James Wyatt, ably assisted by Capability Brown, together created one of the most exquisite houses in all England. The century closes with another bang: Ickworth may not, perhaps, be quite the nonpareil of neo-classicism its eccentric Earl-Bishop had intended, but it is certainly unforgettable; and there is even an odd nobility about it, if one is in the right mood.

There are several vast Victorian piles in Suffolk; nearly all, however, have been built round the nucleus of some earlier house. Neither Somerleyton, nor Shrubland, nor Elveden is a completely new creation; nor even was Flixton, a gigantic Jacobethan confection by Anthony Salvin, almost as fantastic as Harlaxton Manor, before it was tragically demolished in 1953.

Of the twentieth century, in Suffolk, the less said the better.

## Bacton

*1; 5 miles N of Stowmarket off B1113*

The fact that there is not very much to say about ST MARY'S CHURCH is no reflection on its quality. There is a really beautiful fourteenth-century west tower with some flowing tracery in the bell openings – a most unexpected place to find it. The rest is mostly Perpendicular, with a deep, generous clerestory whose doubled windows (which alternate with a series of different flushwork designs) flood the interior with light. The roof is a double hammer-beam, carved and painted to boot; if only the figures – presumably saints or angels – had not been sawn off, what a glory it would have been. A Doom painting can still be dimly discerned over the chancel arch.

## Beccles

*2; 7½ miles W of Lowestoft on A416*

ST MICHAEL'S CHURCH is marvellously sited above the River Waveney, and immediately strikes one because of its most curious tower, standing separate from the church – 'not safe to build the steepal on the cliffside' notes a contemporary document – and apparently unfinished. It is faced entirely in stone and was begun in 1500, but the little Tudor pepper-pot turret at the corner is no substitute for the parapet and pinnacles that it never had.

The church proper is originally of the late fourteenth century, and several Decorated windows remain on the north side. It was, however, largely remodelled in Perpendicular style, which now prevails almost everywhere else. The most spectacular element is the glorious south porch: it too is faced in stone, with polygonal angle buttresses ending in crocketed pinnacles above the exquisitely crested parapet. The interior is tierceron-vaulted, with bosses – another lavish touch.

And then there are the windows – broad, generous, copious, East Anglian through and through. The seven-light window of the chancel is just about as broad as it is high, and there is a four-light aisle window on each side of it; while the west end, unusually, is almost as generous. The aisle windows are of three or four lights, and the clerestory above provides an agreeable syncopation: thirteen windows above the eight bays of the nave.

The interior is a bit of a disappointment. On the Eve of St Andrew, 29 November 1586, the church was gutted by fire. The timber roof was completely destroyed, together with many of the furnishings. The present single hammer-beam, reinforced with tie-rods, is doubtless serviceable, but hardly inspired.

There were fires, too, in the town itself, which is why Beccles possesses few buildings predating the last serious outbreak, in 1680. The most interesting is ST PETER'S HOUSE, on the Old Market, with its surviving elements of the old St Peter's Chapel, regularly used until 1470 by the fishmongers of the market. It is now a stately brick house of the late eighteenth century, prim Georgian on the front, a rather lighter-hearted Gothick behind. Finally, out on the Bungay road, stands ROOS HALL. It was built in 1593, a rectangular brick box of two and a half storeys with a steeply pitched roof ending in many-stepped gables. Angle buttresses at the corners are extended to form round pinnacles of decorative brickwork, but these are dwarfed by the much taller chimneys of similar design rising from projecting chimneybreasts nearby. The ends of the house beneath the gables are of four storeys, the breadth of the windows diminishing with height – five lights, four, three and two. The windows, like all the rest, are mullioned and (except for the top two-lighter) transomed; but they have all, oddly enough, been given triangular pediments – clearly, the Renaissance is on the way.

## Bedingfield

*3; 4½ miles N of Debenham off B1077*

You approach FLEMINGS HALL through a pair of most remarkable iron gates with a motif of tangled vine leaves: vaguely *art nouveau* but with more than a touch of Arthur Rackham. They were bought in 1902 from the Duke of Westminster. The house itself, its long, straight front broken only by a projecting two-storey porch a little to the left of centre, stands across a narrow moat spanned by a brick bridge. The ground floor is of brick, except on the sides of the porch – the front of which, however, is of brick all the way up to its crow-stepped gable and three dunce's-cap pinnacles; the first floor is timber-framed, with close studding, as is the whole of the back of the house. A curious feature is the treatment of the two ends, which have a regular two-bay fenestration on two storeys and then sweep up into big shaped gables containing two little windows, side by side, in the shape of horse collars. At the base of these gables are tiny pinnacles, set diagonally; at the top, tall brick chimneystacks each with four clustered octagonal chimneys, one of them flueless and purely decorative.

All this makes the dating of the house a bit of a problem. The present owner believes the left-hand end to be of *c.*1380 and the rest – beyond an obvious joint – some two centuries later. Other authorities (including the Statutory List) attribute the entire building to *c.*1550. In any case, the gable ends are almost certainly subsequent additions of the early seventeenth century. The porch, too, with its triangular pediments over both the door and the upper window (and it must be said that they look very odd indeed in company with a four-centred arch and a crow-stepped gable) must be later, surely, than 1550 – though not, perhaps, more than a couple of decades. Inside it is a lovely timber door with similarly classical aspirations and thin, curiously rusticated pilasters.

This leads us, predictably enough, into the Hall, which has been divided horizontally – presumably during the late sixteenth-century alterations and additions – so that now its upper timbers constitute a prominent feature of an upstairs bedroom. (The topmost timbers of all appear in the second-floor attics.) This room, as indeed do all the rooms of the house, owes much of its immense charm to the fantasy and creative imagination of the owner, Mr Angus McBean. He has brought in panelling, wooden gilded pilasters for the book-cases, and various splendid bits of Jacobean woodwork which he has most ingeniously pieced together to make bedheads, overmantels and any number of other delightfully decorative conceits which are easier to admire than to describe. He has unearthed some magnificent wooden balusters – said to have come from the bridge of an Elizabethan ship – for the 1580 staircase which had lost its original ones, while preserving the treads and the majestically massive handrail. He has also inserted a long row of dormers in the roof – a brave step perhaps, but one which need occasion no raising of eyebrows: not only do they look absolutely right, but the truth is that nearly every window in the house has been altered at one time or another; only two can be said with certainty to be unchanged since Tudor times.

In short, the whole of Flemings Hall bears the stamp of an astonishingly inventive artistic personality, and I was sorry indeed when Mr McBean told me that he was putting it up for sale. It will never be the same again.

## Blythburgh*

*4; $5\frac{1}{2}$ miles NE of Yoxford on A12*

The first time I entered the church, it was to find Mstislav Rostropovich playing an unaccompanied Bach cello sonata all alone at the east end of the nave; but HOLY TRINITY, Blythburgh, needs no such help. It makes its own impression, inevitably, ineluctably. The process begins when you are still some way away, approaching across the flatlands to the south, and you suddenly see that marvellous silhouette against the vast Suffolk sky: more glass than wall, with a proud west tower four-square and embattled. As you come closer, you see that the long south aisle is topped by a diaper design in flushwork above which, instead of a normal parapet, runs a row of broad pierced quatrefoils with little ogee tops. It is entirely Perpendicular, built between *c.*1450 and 1480 of knapped flint and structurally unaltered since.

Inside, the impression is first of all of light and space, which is increased by the great height of the arcades on their narrow quatrefoil piers until nave and aisles seem to be almost one. Apart from a few fragments in the tracery heads of the aisle windows, the glass is everywhere clear and the light floods in from all around – particularly in the mornings, through the immense east windows, that in the chancel of five lights, those of the north and south aisles of four each. The aisle windows are of three lights only, but are supplemented by the eighteen closely set bays of the clerestory. Another joy is the roof: painted tie-beams on a white background, with huge angels, wings outspread, soaring each way, east and west, from the central bosses. The aisles have lean-to wooden roofs, supported on big arched braces pierced with the same design of quatrefoils inscribed in circles that we saw outside.

The church has mercifully kept its lovely old floor of red brick and tile, and the benches, also original, have wonderful carved ends representing the Deadly Sins, the trades and the seasons. The north and south doors are still pitted with the shot holes made by William Dowsing and his men when they forced an entrance in April 1644. Once inside, they destroyed several statues, tore out the brasses from the tombs and even peppered the angels in the roof with their blunderbusses, though failing – mercifully – to bring any of them down.

## Boxford

*5; 6 miles SW of Hadleigh on A1071*

This is a delightfully pretty village – apart from a rather nasty garage development at the north-eastern end – in which ST MARY'S CHURCH stands halfway up the hill that rises up from the banks of the little River Box. Of this church, the most remarkable feature is the north porch, built entirely of timber in the fourteenth century and, considering everything, quite well preserved. What is interesting is the way in which the wood was used as if it were stone, being carved with Decorated tracery in the approved style and with wooden ribs supporting a now largely non-existent vault. The south porch makes a striking contrast, far more opulent and built of stone – but, unfortunately, a stone of poor quality which has

*Holy Trinity Church, Blythburgh.*

had to be restored again and again. It is of the later fifteenth century, richly decorated with carved head stops, gargoyles, and so on; but everything seems to have got a little out of hand.

The inside is predominantly Perpendicular; there are four-bay arcades, which extend a further two bays to make chancel aisles. The tower is roofed at first-floor level in timber with arched braces, the tower arch being spanned by a tiny little west gallery. The other thing to notice while we are still at the west end is the font, which has a very jolly sixteenth-century ogee-shaped cover that opens like a cupboard to reveal biblical quotations within. Moving up to the chancel, we find a quite elaborate ceilure (the nave roof itself is of little interest) and some unusually nasty modern glass in the east window; like several other windows of the church, it has curious tracery – in fact Perpendicular, but looking like Decorated which somebody has tried to Perpendicularise.

Above the chancel arch there is a painting of Christ flanked by angels. Another, older and more interesting, representing a crowned king, can be seen just to the left of the south aisle east window. To the left of this again, two canopied niches, one above the other, also contain the remains of paintings. (The two opposite, south of the window, are simpler and have only vestigial traces of painted decoration.)

Looking back down the church from the east end you notice that the main tie-beams of the nave have carved heads on their east sides; there are more good carvings on the timber beams and bosses of the south chancel aisle.

The narrow strip of floor connecting the north and south doors is still the lovely old stone. Would that this had been allowed to remain elsewhere.

## Bury St Edmunds*

*6; 14 miles E of Newmarket on A45*

It was in AD 870 that Edmund, the young Christian King of the East Anglian Saxons, gave himself up to the Danish invaders in the hope that by so doing he would save his people. Since he also steadfastly refused to renounce his faith, his subsequent execution earned him a martyr's crown. Of the great Norman ABBEY that was raised, in the years immediately following the Conquest, over the saint's shrine, there survive today only the two tremendous gates giving into the precinct and, within, a few fragmentary remains. The destruction was deliberate. Had the abbey – instead of Norwich – been given cathedral status in the eleventh century, as it very nearly was; had Henry VIII made it the centre of a new see in the early sixteenth century, as he very nearly did; or had the citizens of Bury needed a new or bigger parish church at the time of the Dissolution of the Monasteries, the great building would have been saved. As things turned out, it was abandoned and despoiled, its stones re-used for other, lesser, purposes. And yet, mercifully, the ground on which it had stood was never built over. The vast precinct remains inviolate, covering some 35 acres. Walking through it, one is not surprised to learn that it was one of the half dozen richest and most important Benedictine foundations in the country.

The older of the two gates, the NORMAN GATE, built between 1120 and 1148 on the main axis of the abbey church some 70 yards to the west, was obviously designed to emphasise this fact still further. The broad entrance itself projects slightly between two little attached turrets with pyramid caps; it is of four orders, beneath a gable. Of the three upper stages, the first has two round arches, their upper halves blank, their lower containing pairs of smaller arches; the next has a similar basic design, only taller and more elaborate with three containing arches instead of two; and the top has a further three, but in the lower half three roundels instead of the paired smaller arches – reminiscent of Norwich Cathedral, which was under construction at precisely the same time. There are few Norman towers anywhere as impressive as this one.

The other gate, known as the GREAT GATE, is in fact considerably lower – 62 feet compared with the Norman Gate's 86 feet – though exceeding it slightly in length and breadth. Built in 1327 after an earlier one on the same site was destroyed in a riot, it provides a perfect example of the way the Decorated style could be adapted to a fundamentally secular purpose. Its canopied niches are now bereft of their statues, but this hardly seems to matter: the proportions are perfect, the details endlessly inventive, and the contrast with the Norman Gate just down the road to the south could scarcely be bettered.

Very much closer still to the Norman Gate – so close, indeed, that it uses it as a bell-tower – is the former parish church of St James, since 1914 ST EDMUNDSBURY CATHEDRAL. Basically its style is late Perpendicular – it was begun in 1510 and completed some forty years later after a gift of £200 from Edward VI – but it has been greatly transformed, first by Scott, who gave it a new chancel and roof in the 1860s, and more recently (and far more importantly) by the present Cathedral Extension Scheme which began in 1960 and is still in progress under the direction of Mr Stephen Dykes Bower. Of the original work – it is probably by John Wastell, who was responsible for the upper parts of King's College Chapel and was a Bury man – there remains the west front, with its huge central window, transomed with seven lights, and its two five-light companions marking the north and south aisles; the north and south walls with their three-light windows and clerestory above; and, inside, the nave with its soaring nine-bay arcades. The principal additions since 1960 have been the north-west porch with the cathedral Library above it, the still unfinished Cloister and a completely new choir with flanking chapels, replacing Scott's chancel. His hammer-beam roof remains over the nave.

The new choir is traditional in style and beautifully done. It is a pity that the elaborately moulded arches of the arcades should be allowed to die into the square piers as they do, and I could have wished that the triple east window with its pretty reticulated tracery could have been stepped and not inserted into a square, box-like frame; but these are relatively minor points, and the intricately painted timber roof anyway makes up for a lot. When the work is finally completed and the cathedral receives its new tower, its north transept and the rest of its Cloister, it should be a magnificent addition indeed.

But St James's is not the only great church of Bury. When the decision was taken to make it the centre of a new diocese, there were many who considered that cathedral status should be given instead to the CHURCH OF ST MARY, which is slightly longer than St James's and every bit as splendid. It is older too, with a fourteenth-century Decorated chancel (though the chancel aisles are 100 years or so later) and a late fourteenth-century tower. The nave was begun a little later, in 1424. The west front is in very much the same style as that of St James's; at St Mary's, however, set as it is on a street corner, we get a marvellous view of the south side with its fourteen bays (including the chancel) all of identical three-light transomed windows, plus the clerestory with its twenty windows, two to each of the bays of the nave. Tower, nave and aisles are all embattled, and there are two crocketed pinnacles at the east end of the clerestory. The north side is less distinguished, but it has a fine fifteenth-century porch panelled in the shape of a wheel with a big stone pendant carved with angels.

The interior of St Mary's is glorious. Its pride is the timber roof – what a contrast with Scott's in St James's – hammer-beamed with angels and wondrously carved arched braces. Look at it carefully, with binoculars if possible; and the longer you look, the more you will see. The chancel has a late Perpendicular four-light east window and another fine timber roof, panelled and painted, with lovely carved bosses (binoculars again).

There are so many other good buildings in Bury that it is difficult to know where to start. Robert Adam's OLD TOWN HALL of *c.*1780 is probably the most distinguished, with its rusticated ground floor and Venetian windows above. Soon after it was built it was adapted for use as a theatre, remaining one until 1819, when William Wilkins erected the THEATRE ROYAL, of which his father became the lessee. The main architectural centre of the town is, however, Angel Hill, dominated by the Norman Gate and St James's. Opposite these is the ANGEL HOTEL of 1779, pedimented and ivy-clad; to the south, the ATHENAEUM, at the back of which is Adam's elegant Ballroom, its shallow tunnel vault delicately stuccoed, with a sweeping double staircase at one end and, along the inner side, a deep segmental alcove with a columnar screen.

Any walk through the centre of Bury will yield its rewards. Buildings that stick in my memory are CUPOLA HOUSE in the Traverse, a splendid building of 1693 with a pitched roof and dormers and a playful Baroque cupola on top; ANGEL CORNER, Queen Anne, next to the hotel; and, in the Market Place, the late twelfth-century MOYSE'S HALL – restored admittedly, but one of the oldest domestic buildings in England. Finally, next door to it, BOOTS THE CHEMIST'S: the ultimate proof that Bury, for all its beauty and its antiquity, can still on occasions let its hair down.

## Butley

*7; 6 miles E of Woodbridge off B1084*

Once there was an Augustinian priory; now there is only a Gatehouse – but what a Gatehouse! The date is about 1325, and the flushwork decoration, not in any sense tentative but positively exuberant, is consequently the earliest anywhere that can be accurately dated. On the outside there are two gates, for carriages and pedestrians respectively, flanked by two projecting wings whose inner sides are canted towards the entrances. Above these entrances is a chequer pattern containing thirty-five heraldic shields – whence comes the accurate dating – and above this a two-light window with mouchette tracery, flanked by the ghosts of two similar windows, their outlines and tracery picked out in flushwork. At the top, within a tall gable, are three niches, the centre one with a deep and elaborate canopy. The projecting wings have on their inner, canted, sides more flushwork designs, and on the front two more ghost windows with intricate but different tracery. The general effect is more astonishing than beautiful; but once seen it is not easily forgotten. The inner façade, facing south, is differently organised but equally vivacious.

After two centuries of dereliction the building was converted into a dwelling house in 1737. The former carriageway is now an arched and vaulted Hall, carried out in stretcher-bonded fourteenth-century brickwork of a remarkably high quality.

## Clare

*8; 7 miles W of Long Melford on A1092*

If it were not for its atrocious wirescape, Clare would be an even prettier place than it is. ST PETER AND ST PAUL stands in its spacious churchyard on an eminence in the centre of the town – giving itself, one feels, almost a cathedral air. Its history starts with the west tower, which is Early English to clerestory level – although one of those vast Perpendicular windows has been punched through at the west end – and a top stage of perhaps 1400. It is embattled, but there are no turrets or pinnacles – a pity, since it is not quite tall enough for the length of the church behind it. In a building so exposed on all four sides, such errors of proportion tend to show up. The rest of the building is all late Perpendicular, begun in about 1460 and continuing past the turn of the century. The chancel underwent a major restoration in 1617. Only the south porch was preserved from the earlier church on the site, losing part of its inner bay to the broader aisle within. The nave and aisles are of six bays, marked at aisle level by three-light windows, closely set and unusually high; these are echoed in the clerestory – one for one, not doubled as so often in East Anglia – which continues the length of the chancel. At the meeting point with the nave there rise two short rood-stair turrets crowned with crocketed spirelets, not an altogether happy idea. The interior is as one would imagine: light, airy, spacious and a little bit dull. The odious Puritan Dowsing is at least partly to blame.

CLARE CASTLE is now reduced to a jagged fragment of the thirteenth-century shell keep. It was first built soon after the Conquest, and later acquired two baileys; the inner one was taken over, with singular insensitivity, for the railway station; in the outer one you may still see what remains of the Benedictine PRIORY founded by Gilbert de Clare in 1090.

*St Mary's Church, Dennington.*

Clare was, however, also the home of another priory of far greater importance, if of slightly less antiquity; for it was here, in 1248, that Richard de Clare founded the first Augustinian house in England. The CELLARIUM survives; it was converted into the Prior's Lodging shortly before the Dissolution and has been used as a residence ever since. It is now inhabited again by a Roman Catholic Order.

There are plenty of fine old buildings throughout the town. Among the most interesting are THE GROVE, a gabled house of the fifteenth century in Callis Street and, half a mile or so out on the Chilton road, a late twelfth-century CHAPEL with its original Norman doorway, now converted into a cottage.

## Dennington*

*9; 3 miles N of Framlingham on B1116*

You approach ST MARY'S CHURCH from the north. Reading from right to left, you see a square, somewhat stolid tower of flint and stone, with brick battlements and a polygonal stair turret rising up the north-east corner; a four-bay Perpendicular nave topped by a six-bay clerestory; finally, a four-bay aisle, Decorated, with reticulated tracery, the effect slightly marred by an insensitive north chapel which the church would be better without. It is nice, pleasantly proportioned, but nothing remarkable.

Now enter, by the north porch – niched above and to the sides, panelled in flushwork below. The nave arcades prove to be fourteenth-century rather than fifteenth – older, that is, than the aisle windows. But the pride of nave and aisles is the magnificent display of benches, the arms as well as the ends carved with a profusion of tracery, angels, animals, birds and monsters – including a sciapod, that fabulous creature which was believed to hop around the deserts of Africa on one enormous foot; when it got tired, it would lie on its back in the sand, its foot extended above it like a sunshade. Sciapods are often seen in old bestiaries, but this is thought to be the only carved representation of one in the country. The aisles have flat roofs, supported on arched braces painted with tracery patterns; they have obviously been redone, but presumably to the original designs.

And so we come up to the chancel arch and to the two really breathtaking parclose screens to north and south. They date from the early fifteenth century, but might have been put up yesterday, so immaculate is their state of preservation. The entire loft is still there, with its delicate filigree balustrading; and the screens themselves are heavily cusped, with pendants, and painted red, green and white. In the Bardolph Chapel to the south is the alabaster tomb chest of Lord and Lady Bardolph; he fought at Agincourt and is said to have organised Henry V's funeral at Westminster. The whole chapel is most sumptuously carved; it is only a pity that the effigies themselves are not more distinguished.

The chancel arch may indeed be, in Pevsner's words, 'painfully incorrect'; but it has beautifully carved stops on the responds – a king and queen, with intricate foliage above them. There are more carved heads on the hood-moulds of the north and south chancel windows – but then the entire chancel is a major work of art. It gets better and better the longer you look at it: the fineness of the workmanship on the colonnettes framing the windows, the unorthdox but wonderfully effective canopies over the piscina and sedilia, even the treatment of the little south door. A wooden pyx canopy, carved from a single piece of wood, hangs above the altar: a rarity indeed.

## Denston*

*10; 9 miles SW of Bury St Edmunds off A143*

ST NICHOLAS'S CHURCH is another knockout. The short, stubby west tower is the earliest part (about 1375) but the rest of the church dates from 100 years later; it was probably completed shortly before 1500. Looking up at it from the road to the south, one is struck first by the splendour of late Perpendicular at its best – those enormous three-light aisle windows, traceried and transomed – and second by the fact that there is apparently no chancel. The south porch is low, and in scale surprisingly modest; the tracery in the side windows makes one wonder whether part of it at least is not a survival from an earlier building. It has, however, a fan vault inside, with a shield as the central keystone, and a pretty little castellated holy water stoup on the exterior of the south-east corner.

The interior confirms one's earlier impression: the great nave arcade marches up a full seven bays to the east end, wonderfully untouched and unspoilt. There is no chancel arch; only the dado of the rood-screen to mark a division, and above it, most exceptionally, a moulded and embattled rood-beam. The fine timber roof has tie-beams, every other one of which is supported on arched braces which are also carved, and a lovely opulent wall plate with affronted animals. The benches are carved, like those at Dennington, with animals and monsters, but here there is a bonus: a set of splendid stalls with traceried fronts and, in four cases, misericords. There is some good glass, particularly in the east window, but it is all fragmented. Finally, be sure you do not miss the admirable sixteenth-century tomb to the north of the high altar. The couple commemorated – we have no idea who they are – are represented at the lower level, dead and lying in their shrouds, somewhat in the manner of John Donne in St Paul's.

## Earl Soham

*11; 4½ miles W of Framlingham on A1120*

ST MARY'S CHURCH beguiles us at once by being actually *signed*. Curious inscriptions on the tower buttresses – including what appears to be a verse – inform us that it was built by Thomas Edward and his assistant Ranulph Colnett, presumably around 1475. They were probably responsible for the nave, too; at any rate, they had good reason to be proud of both. To the tower they gave a wealth of ornament in flushwork, and a west doorway flanked with niches; to the nave a flushwork-chequered porch and a very pretty south doorway within it, and a magnificent double hammer-beam roof. It has no angels (were they chopped off?) but full-length figures standing on the wall posts and – though for this Messrs Edward and Colnett can obviously take no credit – a remarkably fine example of the Royal Arms of Charles II on the south wall. There is a good font too, but this has, predictably, been bashed about. (Fonts were easy game for Dowsing and his thugs, for whom the destruction of roof carvings often seemed too much like hard work.) Yet again, there is a memorable set of carved benches, with poppy-heads and carved animals looking both ways, east and west. In contrast to those at Dennington, where they stopped halfway down the nave to give place to box pews, those of Earl Soham continue the whole length of the nave.

The chancel is Decorated, and consequently the oldest part of the church. It has lost its original roof, but has kept its fine three-light east window.

## Earl Stonham

*12; 4 miles E of Stowmarket on A1120*

The CHURCH OF ST MARY THE VIRGIN is, on the outside, a bit of a mess; most of the lower part of the exterior has been rendered in a particularly unattractive cement, with disastrous results. What remains of beauty is the fifteenth-century tower, with its flushwork decoration on base, buttresses, parapet and battlements (though its diagonal buttresses have too many set-offs, giving it an unfortunate tapering look) and the clerestory, with more flushwork between the two-light windows. A mildly surprising feature is the presence of transepts, emerging as they do rather awkwardly from the east end of the nave, just before it gives way to the considerably shorter and lower chancel. Gradually the truth dawns, and is

*The roof of St Mary the Virgin, Earl Stonham.*

confirmed when you go inside: St Mary's is a cruciform church, without a crossing-tower. In former days it may well have had one; but some time in the early fifteenth century a new west tower was built, and the Decorated window which had formerly closed the west end was reset in the west wall of the tower. There are plenty of other Decorated windows, too, and – in the chancel – even a thirteenth-century lancet. The church is, in fact, a good deal older than it appears at first sight.

Inside, its supreme glory is the timber roof. Had it not been for the loathsome Dowsing and his men, it would probably have been the most sensational roof in all Suffolk, and even now it is worth travelling a long way to see. And fortunately one can see it extremely well, thanks to the generous clerestory – a rare thing indeed in an aisleless church. Unfortunately, however, it is marred by electric lights of such awfulness that much of the beauty is lost; they should be removed at once. It is a hammer-beam roof, with arched braces, pendants and kingposts; the spandrels are all carved, the wall posts figured, the collar-beams embattled, the rafters moulded. A glorious sight – although, even as one looks, one curses the Puritan vandals again and again.

There are good wall paintings, too – or were, for they seem to be fading fast. Best is the Doom over the chancel arch (which, incidentally, is not really a chancel arch at all, springing as it does directly from corbels which are set only a little lower than the wall posts, and having neither imposts nor responds). There are traces of others in the north and south transepts.

## East Bergholt

*13; 8 miles SW of Ipswich off B1070*

Constable's native town contains any number of houses – many of them early Tudor – which he would still recognise. THE GABLES, a few hundred yards north of the church, is a particularly good example. ST MARY'S CHURCH is early Tudor too, part flint (with flushwork) and part brick. The tower was begun most ambitiously in 1525, with a passage through it from north to south; unfortunately, yet somehow endearingly, it was never finished, which is why the bells are kept in the curious wooden bell house in the churchyard. There is a sumptuous north doorway and a still more opulent south porch; the interior to which they lead is however a disappointment – much vandalised by the Puritans and ham-fistedly restored. The best things are the tomb to Edward Lambe with its delightful epitaph and the Easter sepulchre with its wall painting of the Resurrection.

## Elveden

*14; 4 miles SW of Thetford on A11*

Set in the middle of a park, ELVEDEN HALL impresses as you approach it only by its colossal size; the vaguely Italianate twenty-five-bay front, of brick with stone dressings, gives no outward indication that it conceals an oriental palace unparalleled outside India – having been transformed in the 1860s by Maharaja Duleep Singh into something that made him feel at home. The *pièce de résistance* is the vast central Hall of white Carrara marble, all intricately carved by a specially imported regiment of Indian craftsmen, its cupola supported on ogee-shaped pendentives, its doors covered with plates of beaten copper: wonderfully unlike Suffolk. The house was then bought in 1899 by the 1st Lord Iveagh, who – incredibly – thought it not big enough and had it enlarged by William Young, the architect of the old War Office building in Whitehall. When I visited it, Elveden Hall was empty and locked up; but even peering through the windows was a treat in itself.

The originally Norman CHURCH OF ST ANDREW AND ST PATRICK was similarly transformed at the expense of Lord Iveagh – this time by W.D. Caröe. The style has been happily described by Pevsner as *art nouveau* Gothic – after which there is really nothing more to say.

## Euston

*15; 3 miles SE of Thetford on A1088*

The story of EUSTON HALL begins with the Tudor courtyard house in which Edward Rookwood entertained Queen Elizabeth on the night of 10 August 1578. In 1666, however, it was bought by Lord Arlington – the first 'A' of the Cabal, Charles II's advisers – who transformed it into a Frenchified château, giving it corner pavilions with mansard roofs and domes. Arlington seems to have kept much of the former fabric of the house, and it is hard to say whether it was his fault or Rookwood's that less than 100 years later the building was 'ready to fall, being so very slightly finished, and all the materials so very bad'; by then, however, salvation was at hand. Arlington's daughter Isabella had married Henry FitzRoy, the second of Charles II's sons by the Duchess of Cleveland, who at the age of twelve was created Duke of Grafton; and in 1750 their son, the 2nd Duke, called in Matthew Brettingham (who had succeeded William Kent at Holkham Hall) to undertake a further remodelling.

What we see of the house today is, in all its essentials, Brettingham's work. He was employed at Euston for six years, recasing the whole building in red brick with stone dressings, completely revising the fenestration, adding pediments and replacing Arlington's domes with low pyramidal roofs *à la* Holkham. He also added a façade to the north front – making it two rooms thick – and a porch with a rusticated doorway to serve as an alternative main entrance. Finally, he turned his attention to the stable block opposite, giving it another rusticated arch with pediment and a lantern above and turning the space between into the fine entrance courtyard we see today.

So Euston remained until the beginning of the present century, when a disastrous fire destroyed the south wing and nearly all the west, including the great painted ceilings by Verrio. (Mercifully, the famous collection of seventeenth-century portraits was got out in time.) Subsequently the two wings were rebuilt to Brettingham's old designs; but by 1952 the vast size of the house had made it unmanageable and it was once again reduced to that part which had escaped the conflagration – the north and a little of the west wing, the latter being retained to accommodate the Dining Room and some of the larger pictures.

The park was first taken in hand for Lord Arlington by John Evelyn, who planted the oldest avenues of trees. The 2nd Duke called in William Kent, who serpentined the stream and introduced his beloved little clumps of trees, adding a charming little domed temple as a banqueting house, a pedimented gateway to the west with flanking lodges and a nearby wash-house for their occupants. The work was completed by Capability Brown.

The only other building which needs special mention is the church. The outer walls and the fabric of the tower are medieval, but ST GENEVIEVE'S as we know it today essentially dates from 1676. The architect may have been William Samwell, who had designed the King's House at Newmarket and the west wing of Felbrigg (*q.v.*); but he died the same year, so would never have seen it finished. Another candidate – who may alternatively have taken on the work after Samwell's death – is Henry Bell of King's Lynn. The windows are mostly round-headed Wrenaissance, but there is an odd suggestion of simplified tracery in the south window of the south transept. The interior is delightful, with a vaulted plaster roof and depressed crossing arches with coffered soffits. The bay in the south aisle adjoining the transept has an elaborate stucco ceiling marking the Arlington family pew.

## Eye

*16; 4 miles SE of Diss on B1077*

A beautiful town, Eye has an absolutely stunning church – at least on the outside. The tower, in particular, is surely the best in Suffolk which, where towers are concerned, cannot usually hold a candle to such counties as Somerset or Northamptonshire. But the tower of ST PETER AND ST PAUL is an exception: tall (over 100 feet), of five stages, exquisitely proportioned and panelled in flushwork over its entire height. The west door is topped by a frieze of shields, above which comes a huge, segmental-headed four-light window with transom, and then two more windows, one above the other, before we reach the bell openings (also traceried) and the exceptionally high panelled parapet, step-battlemented and pinnacled. With each stage, the polygonal corner buttresses become more and more slender, yet somehow the tapering look is avoided. The ground floor is fan-vaulted, the floor above opens with a stone gallery on to the nave. What more could one ask?

You enter by the impressive south porch, of two stages and Perpendicular like the tower. The front is ashlar-faced, the sides panelled in flushwork; but here, curiously, the original flints have been replaced by brick. Some like the result, some don't. (I don't.) The doorway within comes as a surprise, being a good 200 years earlier; it must have survived from a previous Early English church on the site. There are no signs of anything else of this date within; but the arcades and several other minor features are unmistakably Decorated, so the fifteenth-century work seems to have been an enlargement, not a complete remodelling.

The church has a good but not outstanding timber roof, and the only screen in Suffolk with complete loft and rood – restored in 1929 by Sir Ninian Comper.

## Framlingham ★

*17; 6½ miles W of Saxmundham on B1119*

First, the church: ST MICHAEL'S is a magnificent building by any standards, dating from between about 1460 and 1520, but with its immense chancel added some thirty years later again. It possesses a good strong west tower, not spectacular in the manner of Eye but with flushwork on the base and just below the parapet and – a delightful touch – little lions instead of the usual pinnacles. The buttresses too have flushwork panels and the bell openings on all four sides take the form of mighty four-light Perpendicular windows. There is still more flushwork between the clerestory windows, which are topped by a long inscription with little lead angels (recent, but none the worse for that) at regular intervals along it. They conceal – not very successfully – tiny drainpipes. The huge chancel chapels are of four bays, with curiously transomed three-light windows.

The interior has a wonderfully openwork feel about it, a spaciousness due partly to the broad and extremely high chancel arch – late twelfth-century, and the sole survivor of an earlier church – and the equally wide aisles to each side of the slender arcade, but partly also to the fact that the chancel is actually a little wider than the nave. Thus the church seems to open out as it goes eastward, rather than narrowing in the usual way. The great splendour of the nave, however, is its timber roof, perhaps the best in Suffolk. Its hammer-beams are concealed by an exquisite ribbed coving like fan tracery or, more exactly, the top of a rood-screen, springing from corbels placed halfway up each side of the clerestory windows. At the foot of the latter there runs a string-course, from which half columns rise between the windows to the level of the corbels. Did they once support statues? But there are no niches. Or more coving? But there is hardly room. The collar-beams are castellated, and have arched braces.

At the west end of the church, the diminutive Ionic gallery supports a very ornate little organ. It is of considerable importance, its case (dating from 1630) being one of the only eight to have escaped the wholesale destruction of organs by Cromwell and its pipes (of 1674) being the only set of their date of which all are original and still playing. The gallery itself was designed as a foil for the classical wooden reredos at the east end.

And so we come to the chancel. It was ordered by Thomas Howard, 3rd Duke of Norfolk, to provide a mausoleum for his family, and in particular for the remains of his son-in-law Henry Fitzroy, Duke of Richmond, one of Henry VIII's bastards who died aged seventeen in 1536 and had, until the Dissolution, been buried at Thetford Priory. It now houses one of the most remarkable groups of early Renaissance monuments in England. Apart from the Fitzroy tomb – which also contains the body of his wife, who died nineteen years after her husband, and which is decorated with an enchanting little frieze carved with stories from the Book of Genesis – there is also that of Thomas Howard himself, who escaped execution only because Henry VIII died on the very night before he was due to go to the scaffold.

*Framlingham Castle.*

So much for the church: now for the CASTLE. It was begun by Roger Bigod, who received the land from Henry I at the beginning of the twelfth century. His defences were destroyed by order of Henry II in 1175–7, and apart from a few traces of the Hall and Chapel nothing of before this time remains; but another Roger, the 2nd Earl of Norfolk, began again in about 1190, and it is his basic structure, of a curtain wall with thirteen square towers, that we see today. Of this type of castle, which was brought back from the Crusades, Framlingham is one of the earliest examples. You enter over a bridge and under an entrance gateway (both of them built by Thomas Howard, 3rd Duke, whose tomb you will have seen in the church) and immediately find yourself in the inner court of the castle. Opposite you and a little to your right is what is left of the pre-1175 buildings, incorporated into the curtain wall; while on your left, occupying the site of the second Roger Bigod's Great Hall, is the Poor House, founded according to the terms of the will of Sir Robert Hitcham when he died in 1636, bequeathing the castle to Pembroke College, Cambridge. (His tomb, supported by kneeling angels, is also in the church.) Some of the Hall windows survive at the north end; Sir Robert's original building, now lived in by the custodian, is at the south end. The central part is of 1729.

By a spiral stairway in the eleventh tower – the third on your left from the entrance, just behind the south end of the Poor House – you can climb up to the wall walk. It originally ran the full circuit of the walls, and although it is now open only along the west side, the short walk still possible is well worth taking. Anybody anxious to know more about this splendid place is strongly advised to buy the excellent booklet by the Dept of the Environment, available on the spot.

## Fressingfield

*18; 8 miles W of Halesworth on B1116*

Seen from the north across the churchyard, ST PETER AND ST PAUL looks a good, typical, Perpendicular Suffolk church – modestly distinguished but not in any way outstanding. The Decorated chapel north of the chancel and the pretty Sanctus bell turret crowning the eastern gable of the nave are certainly bonus points, but nothing more. Only on going round to the south side does one find something really special – the sumptuous south porch built in about 1420 by Catherine de la Pole in memory of her husband, who died of dysentery at the siege of Harfleur, and of her son who was killed shortly afterwards at Agincourt. (The tomb which she shares with her husband can be seen at Wingfield (*q.v.*).) Amid a profusion of flushwork panelling, a broad two-centred arch carries an angel bearing the Wingfield arms and a hood-mould with carved label stops representing a king and queen – probably Henry V and Katherine of France. The carved spandrels are obviously a good deal later – seventeenth-century or even eighteenth. Above are carved two enormous roses, and above them, between empty canopied niches, is a small two-light Decorated window. (It must have seemed very old-fashioned by then, but we find the same phenomenon at Wingfield.) The porch is finished off with a cresting of stone quatrefoils, short pinnacles at the corners and a central statue; there are some gargoyles for good measure round the sides. Inside is a tierceron vault, resting on corbels carved with the signs of the four Evangelists.

Inside, the church plays its two remaining trump cards: the benches and the roof. The former date from *c.*1470, and though some have been mutilated by the Puritans, the collection as a whole remains the best in Suffolk. Nor is it only the bench ends that are carved;

most of the back rests are similarly adorned with flowers, shields, mouchettes and trefoils. Notice in particular the back benches on each side of the nave, which are also carved below the back rests – that to the north with emblems of the Passion, that to the south with those of the two dedicatory saints, Peter and Paul.

The hammer-beam roof of the nave has unfortunately lost most of its angels, but there is some lovely decoration on the wall plate in a design of twisting vine leaves. The north aisle roof is also well worth a look. That of the chancel, however, though still essentially medieval, has obviously been much renewed. The south aisle roof is modern, apart from a few corbel heads.

Outside in the churchyard, immediately to the east of the south porch, is the tomb of Archbishop Sancroft, who crowned James II and refused to sign the oath of allegiance to William III in 1688. The Archbishop actually lived from 1690 until his death at UFFORD HALL, a mile or two to the south-east. Here is another of those wonderful medieval survivals, in which Suffolk is so astonishingly rich. Timber-framed, but covered with a layer of pinkish ochre plaster, it stands within its moat (now partially blocked) presenting on its long south front an almost baffling array of windows, large and small, sixteenth-century mullions and seventeenth-century casements, spaced with a wild and wilful irregularity. Most extraordinary of all, below the gable at the right-hand end, is the group of four casements immediately beneath a row of no fewer than sixteen small Tudor mullion lights. The house clearly once possessed a high central Hall, but is now of two storeys throughout, with attics in the two end gables. This horizontal division of the Hall probably dates from around 1600, when the present Jacobean staircase must have been inserted. The South Parlour – which contains the sixteen-light window – would then have received its splendidly moulded cross-beams with leaf-stop chamfers. There is an extremely pretty little Back Parlour beyond and, most unusually, another small stair at the back leading to another room at mezzanine level. It is not great architecture, perhaps, but nevertheless a house of much beauty and, in its unspoilt timelessness, immense charm.

## Giffords Hall*

*19; $4\frac{1}{2}$ miles NE of Nayland off A134*

The Giffords came to the manor, whose great house still bears their name, in 1281; vestiges of their original house can still be seen in the north-east wall of the Gatehouse range. But the Gatehouse itself and indeed the major part of Giffords Hall as we know it today is the work of George Mannock, who was born about 1468 and probably started to build his new, up-to-date residence some fifty years later. It is by no means an architectural unity; additions and alterations have been made in every succeeding century including this one. But it has retained its atmosphere, its beauty and a curious, indefinable magic that is all its own. Tudor and Georgian, brick and timber-framing and flint, all live happily together in harmony and equilibrium. Not only is it a lovely house; it is also an object lesson in co-existence.

Mannock's proud Gatehouse makes a grand show across the green lawn that fills the forecourt. Its two

*Giffords Hall.*

The Hall, Giffords Hall.

ribbed polygonal towers are embattled, with diagonally set pinnacles, but the overall effect is anything but forbidding: the windows, with their four-centred arches, are plentiful – they are set, incidentally, in rendered brick that only pretends to be stone – and further lightness is suggested by the two friezes of cusped tracery and the additional tracery decoration in the spandrels of the richly moulded four-centred arch. This was quite clearly a peaceful country manor house; there was never any question of defence. To the left, a modest two-storey range runs westward; it is basically of the same period as the Gatehouse, but is of flint until it reaches the big corner gable, the first-floor level of which is timber-framed. To the right is the end of the Georgian range, which we see more clearly as we enter the courtyard.

This is oddly irregular in shape; only one of its corners forms a right-angle – a fact that further increases its charm. The Gatehouse on the inside is richly diapered, and crowned by three stepped gables with heavily crocketed pinnacles; rising half gables, similarly pinnacled, form the corners. (These pinnacles too are all diagonally set – a playful Suffolk touch seen also at Flemings Hall, Bedingfield (*q.v.*).) Opposite on the north side is the Hall range with its big brick porch and timber-framed upper storey. The latter it is quite possible to admire, but not to take too seriously: the oriel with its pretty bargeboarding is Victorian, although surprisingly successful in its context – a good deal more so, it seems to me, than the large Venetian window with which some ham-fisted eighteenth-century dilettante decided to modernise the Hall. Next to this there appears another curious eccentricity: a big broad chimneybreast with a two-light window set plumb in the middle. The smoke was in fact conducted to each side of it through separate curved flues; but the effect, at first sight, is oddly worrying.

Beyond the Hall to the west and all along the western side of the courtyard there are half-timbered ranges with exuberant brick nogging, again largely of the nineteenth century. (Would that all Victorian medievalising were as well done as it is here.) To the east, the range was almost entirely rebuilt in the eighteenth century, when the windows were all sashed. Unexpectedly, however, it has retained its splendid timber roof – something one would never guess as one walks through the elegant Georgian rooms beneath.

These rooms, light, airy and flooded with the morning sun, must add much to the already considerable delights of life at Giffords Hall. It is the great Hall itself, however, in all its Henrician splendour, that is the glory of the house. It is not large – only 34 feet by 24 feet; the timber roof, however, could hardly be more splendid – a double hammer-beam, with five great free-flying trusses and two more embedded in the end walls. In the spandrels of the arched braces are carvings of charm and freshness; apart from the usual motifs of musical instruments, crowns, thistles and pomegranates, there is a delightful if somewhat unappetising fish on a plate, and a mouse crawling into an upturned pitcher. Amid such lively evocations of the Middle Ages, the intrusion of the Venetian window somehow seems all the more unfortunate; one longs for the tall, many-transomed bay window which must have been removed to make room for it. But this is merely a passing regret – for a minor blemish in a house of much beauty and endless fascination.

## Gipping

*20; 4 miles N of Stowmarket off B1113*

The CHAPEL OF ST NICHOLAS is thought to have been built in 1483, by Sir James Tyrell – who, in that very same year, was almost certainly responsible for the murder of the Princes in the Tower on the order of Richard III. Could it, one wonders, be a token of penitence for the crime, an attempt at restitution? We shall never know. It remains a beautiful little building, chequered all over with flint and stone and occasional pieces of rather more formal flushwork. It is marred only by the perfectly hideous rendered west tower, which was erected in the last century and should be pulled down in this one. The flushwork is of an extremely high standard: the family emblem of the 'Tyrell knot' is much in evidence. Another favourite device is the outline of a traceried window. The real windows are enormous, filling up virtually all the space of the bays between the buttresses to the point where both the north and the south doorways have to be fitted into their frames. The east window, of five lights, is even bigger.

The interior is bare, and flooded with light. There is, however, a rather curious annex to the north, entered through a west door around the top of which runs the inscription: 'Pray for Sir Jamys Tirell and Dame Anne his wife'. If this injunction was ever heeded, it was certainly unsuccessful: on 6 May 1502, on a charge of treason, Tyrell was beheaded on Tower Hill.

## Great Saxham Hall

*21; 4 miles SW of Bury St Edmunds off A45*

The house was originally thought to have been by Robert Adam, but we now know that Adam's plans were scrapped and that the building is largely the conception of its first owner, Hutchison Mure. However Mure sold it before it was completed, and the side wings are by Joseph Patience Jun. It is a stately house and an elegant one, with a portico raised on four giant Ionic columns supporting a triangular pediment with palm fronds, and broad corner bays framed by pier-and-column pairs. It was, alas, altered in Victorian days: pediments were added to all the windows, bow windows added below and balustrades above – to say nothing of a nasty extension to the left which makes nonsense of the general symmetry.

Nor was that the full extent of the damage. The glory of the house was its octagonal music room, rising into a third storey – the rest of the house has only two – and enchantingly painted *à la* Angelica Kauffmann. This was divided horizontally and converted into bedrooms and cubicles for the lesser servants. The present owner of the house is, however, determined to restore it to its former splendour.

The grounds were laid out by Capability Brown, who was almost certainly responsible for the several pavilions – the 'Moorish Gothic' temple, the Tuscan tea house and the rusticated polygonal lodge.

## Grundisburgh

*22; 4½ miles NW of Woodbridge off B1079*

From the outside, ST MARY'S CHURCH looks like nothing on earth. The mid-eighteenth-century red-brick tower would be all right in its place, but when tacked on to the end of a Gothic church some three to four centuries older it looks distinctly odd. The flushwork between the clerestory windows is nice too, but its effect is spoilt by the nasty rendering of the aisle below.

But do not be discouraged; there is better to come. Above the nave is one of the loveliest hammer-beam roofs in all Suffolk, which is to say in the whole country. It is in fact a double hammer-beam, with angels along both rows and even on the kingposts, and a most opulently carved wall plate. The roof to the thirteenth-century chancel is very nearly as good, with branching kingposts and braces. There is a big, worn St Christopher on the north wall and an exceedingly pretty, delicate screen.

A little to the east of the church stands a remarkable timber-framed house from early in the reign of Henry VIII. It is called BAST'S, and was built by Thomas Walle, or Awall, a member of the Salters' Company – hence the salt cellars on the corbels to north-west and south-west.

## Hadleigh

*23; 10 miles W of Ipswich on A1071*

Here is a really beautiful market town, at least so far as its centre is concerned. All the streets around the High Street are rewarding in their various ways; but the climax is the ensemble of quite spectacular medieval buildings to the south and west of ST MARY'S CHURCH. The church quite properly dominates, if only by reason of its size and height – tower and big ribbed leaden spire together measure 135 feet. For the rest it is the usual Suffolk church of thc fourteenth and fifteenth centuries, rubble with stone dressings – distinguished enough but not, inside or out, particularly memorable. Far more impressive architecturally is the DEANERY TOWER, actually the surviving Gatehouse from a great palace built by Archdeacon Pykenham in 1495. It is of brick, and elaborately diapered; its two polygonal towers are of six stages, each stage being distinguished by panels crowned by pairs of trefoiled arches and the occasional window being inserted at random. There are tall step battlements on top. The middle part has two floors above a broad four-centred arch, each with a pair of windows and more trefoils above.

Opposite the church is the timber-framed GUILDHALL. The centre, which dates from around 1430, is of three storeys, each of the upper two having its separate jetty so that it in fact projects twice. Some forty years later it was given two-storey wings to east and west, and a long extension running off behind it to the south. Of these, the west wing has gone; but the east remains, with its fine old Long Room (with musicians' gallery) which was used as a town Assembly Room in the eighteenth century. So too does the southern extension, with magnificent timber roofs on both floors – the upper one with six collar-beams and kingposts.

## Helmingham Hall

*24; 9 miles N of Ipswich on B1077*

The house stands proudly in the middle of a broad, limpid moat; the drawbridge is still raised at nine o'clock every evening. Its form is that of a quadrangle, built round a central courtyard in the manner beloved of the early sixteenth century, and despite several major alterations it still preserves its Tudor character with its diapered brickwork, its stepped gables surmounted by tall finials, its generous mullioned bays and its clusters of decorative brick chimneys. It was begun in 1511, on the site of a medieval manor known as Creke Hall, by Lionel Tollemache – the Tollemache family still lives there – and seems at that time to have been largely timber-framed, with overhangs both outside and inside the courtyard. (Parts of this timber framing can still be seen on and around the main gateway.) The original Great Hall was on the north side, the entrance to the screens passage being opposite the gateway across the courtyard.

*Helmingham Hall.*

In the middle of the eighteenth century – apparently around 1760 – the Tudor timber framing was found to be no longer compatible with Georgian ideas of elegance and was deliberately concealed, on the lower floor with an outer covering of brick and on the upper with the then popular mathematical tiles. At the same time most of the gables were removed – apart from those at the corners – and the mullioned windows were sashed. But it was not to last for long. Only some forty years later Wilbraham Tollemache, 6th Earl of Dysart, called in John Nash and his assistant John Adey Repton to Gothicise. Back went the mullions, together with a completely new treatment of the entrance which was now given an oriel above the gateway and a new stepped gable above it. From this time, too, are the pretty bridges over the moat to south and east. So far, so good; but Nash then went on to cover the entire house with his favourite greyish stucco, running battlements round the top.

This too – thank God – proved transitory. In 1841 came a further remodelling, almost certainly by Anthony Salvin – although there is no documentary evidence for his involvement. He bricked in the courtyard overhang and remodelled much of the west range; to him also is due much of the interior, but not all of it. There is still an exquisite Georgian staircase and two or three other rooms – including a wonderful Library – of the same date.

The house, in short, can hardly be said to have come down to us unscathed; yet it remains, to my eye at least, one of the most completely satisfying buildings of Suffolk. The setting, in the middle of a rolling deer park, is a delight; the rich red brick glows in the afternoon sun; the wild forest of finials, pinnacles and chimneys shimmers back from the breeze-rippled water of the moat; and the whole house seems to breathe an extraordinary sense of unity and contentment. It is much loved and cherished – and deserves to be.

## Hengrave

*25; 3 miles NW of Bury St Edmunds on A1101*

Once one of the most spectacular – and architecturally one of the most important – of the great early Tudor houses of England, HENGRAVE HALL was built by Sir Thomas Kytson, a London merchant, between 1525 and 1538 – the date inscribed over the main doorway. It possesses strong stylistic affinities with Hampton Court (*q.v.*), and again with Thornbury Castle in Avon (*q.v.*), of which Kytson is thought to have seen a model. It is not, alas, what it was; the moat has gone – as it has at Hampton Court – and the great entrance front to the south, once

perfectly symmetrical, has been largely spoilt by extensive remodelling of its right-hand end: work which included the facing of the yellow brick with stone and the substitution of battlements for the original gables. But all is not lost, for the house still retains its quite sensational centrepiece, one of the most flamboyant and fascinating examples of early Renaissance stone carving anywhere in the country.

The word 'Renaissance' needs, perhaps, some qualification, for at first sight this extraordinary composition seems essentially Gothic. The four-centred arch over the door with foliage in the spandrels could be found in hundreds of late Perpendicular churches, as could the transomed windows above, with their arched lights; the two flanking towers are also as Gothic as could be, with their polygonal section, windows with hood-moulds, panelled upper stages and crocketed caps. But that astonishing tripartite oriel, though harking back to the Gothic trefoil, has about it a sort of secular opulence which seems to herald a whole new philosophy of life, and the naked *putti* supporting the shields and the coats of arms express it still more clearly, reminding one as they do of their little terracotta brothers frolicking across the entrance front of another of Hengrave's near-contemporaries, Sutton Place in Surrey (*q.v.*).

The promise of this tremendous entrance is not, alas, fulfilled, since the interior of the house was more or less ruined in a disastrous 1930s' remodelling. It leads into a square inner courtyard, dominated on the north side by a big canted bay window, rising double-transomed through both storeys of the old Hall. Oddly, however, there is no door immediately opposite the entrance giving access to the screens passage as one finds, for example, at Helmingham, and as one would expect. Instead there is a corridor running round three sides of the courtyard – an innovation which must have seemed distinctly avant-garde at the time it was built. The Hall itself, with its nineteenth-century hammer-beam roof, is a disappointment, apart from a nice bit of fan vaulting within the window bay; indeed, the only other feature of the whole interior worthy of note is the Chapel. Since the house is now occupied by an ecumenical religious community this is clearly a room of considerable importance, and it is therefore a pleasure to record the existence there of a superb set of contemporary stained glass, comprising twenty-one scenes from Genesis and the Gospels.

Hard by the house is the little CHURCH OF ST JOHN LATERAN. Its round tower is possibly pre-Conquest, its chancel of about 1300, the rest early fifteenth-century with a few Tudor additions. Two affectionate-looking lions guard the doorway in the flushwork-decorated south porch, and the north chapel of *c.*1540 has some splendid tombs.

## Hessett

*26; 5 miles SE of Bury St Edmunds off A45*

Essentially, ST ETHELBERT'S is a late Perpendicular church, which was added to and embellished – according to an inscription along the outside of the north aisle – by one John Hoo, who died in 1492. Only the three-light east window is earlier; its flowing tracery shows the chancel to be perhaps 150 years older than the rest. There is a lovely south porch in stone and knapped flints, with St George and the dragon in the spandrels; a fine parapet along the north aisle (added by Hoo) with shields and foliage between the arches, which have trefoil heads; a pinnacled clerestory, lit by big three-light windows; and a brave west tower, not particularly high but quietly distinguished nonetheless with a chequered base in flushwork and further decoration on the parapet and battlements.

The interior is broad and bright and retains most of its fifteenth-century characteristics – though the roof shows all too clearly the damage wrought by the Puritans in the 1640s. The font was the gift of another Hoo in 1500 or so; the benches too are original, simple and unadorned. The wall paintings are especially interesting: apart from St Christopher above the north door there is a fascinating representation of the Seven Deadly Sins, pictured as branches of a tree growing out of Hell, and below it Christ of the Trades, showing tools and – surprisingly – amusements, including the six of diamonds. Such glass as was saved from the Puritans has been preserved in the aisle windows, in one of which St Nicholas is shown blessing a boy with a golf club.

## Heveningham Hall

*27; 4 miles SW of Halesworth on B1117*

The aristocrat of Suffolk houses, Heveningham Hall stands in all its Palladian splendour in the park designed for it by Capability Brown. Its exterior is the work of Sir Robert Taylor in *c.*1778, and is surely his masterpiece. He began with the modest Queen Anne house belonging to Sir Gerard Vanneck which, remodelled, became the centrepiece of the new mansion: seven bays of two and a half storeys, separated by detached giant Corinthian columns over a rusticated and arcaded ground floor and crowned not, as one might expect, by a pediment but by a heavy attic decorated with garlands, urns, recumbent lions and a coat of arms. From this centre two-storey links, each of five bays, lead off to three-bay corner pavilions of the same basic design as the centre except that the giant columns are now attached and that they support not attics but pediments, each with a small central roundel. The whole effect is perfectly judged and – despite its 280-foot length – exquisitely proportioned; there is no eighteenth-century house anywhere else in the county of remotely comparable distinction.

Perhaps a little surprisingly after such a *tour de force*, Vanneck did not invite Taylor to design the interior. This task went to the young James Wyatt; and it has to be said that he kept up the standard superbly. For his Entrance Hall, working in the Adam manner, he provided a design of which Adam would have been proud – equalled only, perhaps, by the latter's great Ante-Room at Syon. It has a deep barrelvault, coolly neo-classical but with just a suggestion along the sides of fan vaulting – the subtlest of hints towards the Gothic of his later years; screens of scagliola columns at each end; and a floor of stone and marble reflecting the design of the ceiling.

In all the other principal rooms on the ground floor, Wyatt was assisted by the mural painter Biagio Rebecca. Several of them, unfortunately, suffered in some degree from a fire in 1949; and though they were quite respectably restored soon afterwards the Dining Room was repainted in a particularly violent shade of blue which detracts considerably from its overall effect. The Library, which is decorated with profile heads of English, French and classical authors, has a screen of columns towards the Dining Room and a generous Venetian window in its west wall. Behind these rooms to the north are the Drawing Room (which was never completed by Rebecca) and the Saloon, where the subdued *trompe-l'oeil* shows him at his restrained best. Here as elsewhere most of the furniture is by Wyatt, designed for the positions it continues to occupy. The Saloon leads into the charming little Etruscan Room – arguably the most refined of all those rooms which appeared in English country houses as a result of the excitement caused by the uncovering of Pompeii in 1748.

All these rooms are to the west of the Entrance Hall; to the east of it, the only two of any importance are the Morning Room – whose comparative plainness suggests that it may have been designed by Taylor before Wyatt's arrival – and the Print Room, another bow to a prevailing fashion but now looking somewhat dilapidated.

Dilapidation has indeed been all too evident throughout this wonderful house for the past few years, especially since its purchase by the government in 1970. When the above was written it had recently been sold to a wealthy Arab; alas, as this book goes to press there is news of another fire, which has seriously damaged a good third of the house, including several of its finest rooms. Its future is now more uncertain than ever.

## Hintlesham Hall

*28; 5 miles W of Ipswich on A1071*

The approach up the front drive to Hintlesham Hall presents you with what appears at first sight a fairly straightforward early Georgian stuccoed façade: a five-bay centre with two-bay wings projecting towards you, a porch on Ionic columns with ground-floor rustication and, above it on the first floor, a Venetian window with Corinthian pilasters dividing the bays on each side. This window is in turn crowned by a tiny pediment set against the high parapet. The deception is complete – until your eye travels higher still, above the hipped roof, to the tall Tudor chimneystacks.

For what you see is indeed a façade, and nothing more. Hintlesham Hall was built, by one Thomas Timperley, in the reign of Queen Elizabeth I; seen from the garden front, or either of the two sides, it unashamedly reveals the rich Tudor brickwork (though much has been rebuilt and remodelled, and sash windows are now general) and the immense chimneybreasts supporting the high ornamental brick chimneys that first gave the game away. Only on that entrance front did Richard Powys, who had acquired the house in 1720, apply the quoins and the string-courses, the pilasters and the pediments that so effectively transformed it. His, too, is the stucco – its earliest appearance on Suffolk domestic architecture, setting the fashion which was to continue for well over a century to come.

Once inside the house, however, you realise that Powys's transformation was after all rather more than skin deep; no sooner are you inside the front door than you find yourself in a long ground-floor gallery which, with its first-floor counterpart, he built on to the original Tudor front, thus reducing the length of the projecting wings from five bays to four. Only when you have passed through this gallery do you come to the Hall itself. Though still in its original position, it too has been heavily remodelled, with painted panelling and pedimented doorcases on the two end walls. It rises the height of the house to a deeply coved ceiling above a projecting cornice, leaving space for a row of clerestory windows along the garden front. Among a number of other fine rooms on the ground floor is one of only moderate size with a low canopied dais at one end; it was used in former days by judges on circuit.

There are two staircases, the older of which – no longer in its original position – is of walnut and must date from the very end of the seventeenth century, with high newel-posts carved with vases of flowers and fruit. A later, mid-eighteenth-century staircase is more elegantly restrained, with slim barley-sugar balusters and prettily carved tread ends. Whichever you take, you soon emerge in the first-floor Long Gallery. This, as we have seen, is a Georgian addition, the Elizabethan house never apparently having had one. It is broad enough to serve as a room in its own right, and is indeed treated as such. Leading out of it at its eastern end is the Drawing Room – the finest in the house, with one of the most spectacular late seventeenth-century plaster ceilings in all East Anglia, surpassing the work at Felbrigg or even, I believe, at Melton Constable. These tangled skeins of foliage and fruit are carved with a profusion of detail that defies description, and undercut to the point where they are completely separated from their ground so that you can see the daylight through the hole – *ajouré*, as the French call it.

To the west of the house there are several groups of outbuildings, some of which appear to go back to the fifteenth century and even before. Others have been transformed into the cookery school which has been run by Robert Carrier as an adjunct to his famous restaurant in the house itself. Alas, both of these closed down at the end of 1982, and the house has now been sold.

The gardens, in which flowers and vegetables grow charmingly side by side, contain ornamental *pièces d'eau* to both front and back. They were presents to the house from Mr Carrier on its 400th birthday a few years ago.

## Horham

*29; 4½ miles SE of Eye on B1117*

Few of the houses described in this book can be more remotely situated than THORPE HALL, standing as it does at the end of a farm track a good half mile from the road between Eye and Stradbroke. As an additional protection, it is also completely encircled by a moat. The plan is simple enough. If we ignore – as we safely can – the little low service wing which was probably added in the early nineteenth century, we find a rectangle with short axial projections to north and south. The body of the house is of two storeys only, but the projections, which rise to the level of the ridge of the roof, are of four. The windows, apart from those in each of the gables of these projections, are all transomed and of two, three or four lights; and all of them, without exception, carry nicely proportioned triangular pediments. These, like the rest of the house, are of brick; almost certainly, however, they would have been covered with plaster to simulate stone, just as the mullions and transoms of the windows themselves have been. At each end of the house, above the gable, rises a stack of four octagonal brick chimneys, below which, high in the gable, is a pair of tiny *oeil-de-boeuf* window openings. As a date, 1580 or thereabouts seems to be the best bet in the absence of any documentary evidence; and apart from the botching-up of the west side wall as a result of the building of the service wing, the exterior remains totally unchanged since that time.

As to the inside, the principal structural alteration seems to have been the moving of the staircase. This, one suspects, must originally have occupied the southern projection – a fact which would explain the absence of a door or window here at ground-floor level – but now rises up in a broad spiral almost in the centre of the house, just west of the central hall. Apart from this, the most interesting purely architectural feature of the interior is the set of tiny narrow rooms within the projections, and the diminutive timber staircase leading up to the attic floors. The main rooms are surprisingly broad, spacious and airy for a house of this date.

After some years of virtual dereliction, Thorpe Hall has been lovingly restored by its present owner; it must be a joy to live in.

## Icklingham

*30; 8 miles NW of Bury St Edmunds on A1101*

Once two separate parishes, Icklingham is now one: a fact which accounts for the way ALL SAINTS' CHURCH, long redundant, has escaped the hands of Victorian restorers. The two tiny blocked Norman windows in the north wall show that its fabric goes back to the eleventh century; but there was clearly a major remodelling some 300 years later, and the style is now predominantly Decorated, with some really glorious window tracery, particularly in the south aisle. The big south-west tower, however, does not look later than 1300.

The interior is all spaciousness and light and a wholly refreshing absence of clutter, from the scissor-braced timber roof to the pleasant old tiled floor. The benches are nearly all the original fifteenth-century ones, backless and for the most part very plain. Of the same date is the dado forming the base of the rood-screen. The church is, in fact, entirely unpretentious, just as its steep thatched roof promises that it will be. But as an unspoilt Suffolk interior, it is hard to beat, and the Redundant Churches Fund – who for the past ten years have assumed responsibility for it – deserve our congratulations and our thanks.

## Ickworth*

*NT; 31; 3 miles SW of Bury St Edmunds on A143*

It is an astonishing building by any standards – that vast, towering rotunda, 100 feet high, with its shallow dome and circular parapet around the top; then the two quadrantal arms, broken forward slightly halfway along to accommodate a small room, leading to nine-bay pedimented wings, each as big as a largish country house. No other English mansion looks remotely like it; like Hardwick or Castle Howard, to have seen it once is to recognise it for ever.

Though the final design is not the work of any one man – the work was supervised by an Irishman called Francis Sandys, probably working to sketches by an Italian architect, Mario Asprucci the Younger – the concept was unquestionably that of Frederick Augustus, Bishop of Derry and later 4th Earl of Bristol, that extraordinary collector, connoisseur and traveller who gave his name to countless Bristol Hotels all over Europe. All his life he seems to have had a passion for circular buildings: in 1787 he had commissioned Sandys and his brother Joseph (who was the Bishop's chaplain) to build him another rotunda house at Ballyscullion in Ireland, and a few years before that his friend John Soane had designed him a circular 'doghouse'. But Ickworth was far grander than anything he had previously attempted.

*Ickworth.*

Work began on the great house in 1795, and continued until 1803, when it was brought to an abrupt halt by the Bishop's death. By this time the rotunda was almost complete – though it had not yet acquired a permanent roof – but the wings had barely risen above ground level. Little more was done until 1824, when the 5th Earl – soon to become the 1st Marquess – was at last able to bring his father's work to something approaching completion. Even then, however, he left the west wing unfinished; it was in fact no longer necessary, since the Bishop's immense art collection – for part of which it had been intended – had fallen into the hands of Napoleon's army when it invaded Rome in 1798, and was subsequently confiscated.

The rotunda is of stuccoed brick, and rises two and a half storeys. The ground floor is articulated by unfluted Ionic columns, with round-headed windows between them; above the windows and just below the level of the capitals runs a frieze in terracotta and Coade stone, executed by the Carabelli brothers of Milan after Flaxman's illustrations of Homer. There follows a deep entablature, and then another row of columns, Corinthian this time, separating the twenty-two bays of the first and attic floors. Above these columns runs another, similar, frieze, then more entablature, and finally the segmental dome and parapet.

The Bishop's plan had been to live in the rotunda and to use the wings for his art collections; his son, however, decided to live in the east wing and to devote the rotunda to entertaining; it is here, in consequence, that we now find the principal state rooms. Coming in through a pedimented portico, we find ourselves immediately in the great Entrance Hall, lit by a shallow inner glass vault beneath the dome. Open screens run down each side – the staircase, after several ideas for a grander one had been rejected, was tucked away behind the left-hand arcade by Arthur Blomfield in 1909 – the centre being taken up with Flaxman's celebrated group, *The Fury of Athamas*.

From the Hall, the Drawing Room leads off to the left, the Dining Room to the right. Each has a slightly curving outside wall, and each is tremendously high – over 30 feet – in order, as the Bishop put it, that his 'lungs might play more freely'. They are fine rooms, both of them, with splendid mahogany doorcases and window fittings; even more spectacular, however, is the Library, which faces south beyond the Entrance Hall. Encompassing five bays, the curve of the outer wall is still more pronounced; but the room's segmental shape is cut by a screen of scagliola columns one bay from each end.

Finally, we come to the two rooms rather surprisingly placed halfway along the east and west corridors. To the east is the Smoking Room – a relic of the days when smoking was relegated to rooms as remote as possible from the centre of the house. To the west is the Pompeian Room. Ickworth, one might think, was a little late for such conceits, most Pompeian Rooms – or Etruscan Rooms, as they were also called – dating from the later eighteenth century; this, however, stems from a second wave of neo-classicism, being the work of J.D. Crace – he who wrought such havoc at Longleat – in 1879.

In all these rooms – except the last, where the overall scheme of decoration does not allow it – there is a wealth of superb furniture, pictures and *objets d'art*. Even without the Earl-Bishop's collections, Ickworth remains a very grand house indeed.

## Ipswich

*32; 18 miles NE of Colchester on A12*

Ipswich ought to be a lot prettier and more interesting than it is. A prosperous port for the best part of a thousand years; the seat of two important Augustinian priories; birthplace of Cardinal Wolsey whose projected college, if he had not fallen from grace, might well have compared with his other foundation of Christ Church, Oxford; possessor of more surviving medieval parish churches than any other town of its size in the kingdom, it promises – or *should* promise – a great deal. Alas, insensitive development and ham-fisted planning have ruined the ensemble; beautiful buildings remain in Ipswich, but they are individuals and they need seeking out.

Of the churches, by far the best is ST MARGARET'S. Opulently decorated in the East Anglian style with plenty of flushwork, it boasts a south transept with its own pair of polygonal flanking turrets. Inside there is a marvellous double hammer-beam roof, charmingly painted in the late seventeenth century. The vestry has a large set of Prince of Wales Feathers dated 1660, and one of the remaining angels round the font bears a scroll inscribed 'SAL ET SALIVA'.

Among secular buildings, pride of place must go to the gloriously ebullient SPARROWE'S HOUSE in Buttermarket. Ostensibly, it is of about 1670. The wooden posts of its ground floor, all richly carved, carry brackets which in their turn support an overhanging upper floor with five oriels. Here the walls are of plaster, and carry wildly extravagant pargetting and stucco reliefs; those beneath the windows represent the four continents that had been discovered by the seventeenth century. In fact, the house is a good deal older than it appears at first sight. One of the rooms inside has a fifteenth-century hammer-beam roof, and there is plenty of evidence of work around 1600. Thus the exterior is really only a remodelling; but no other house in England, surely, has been remodelled quite like this one.

Sparrowe's House is a difficult act to follow; but no visitor to Ipswich should leave without seeing CHRISTCHURCH MANSION and, if possible, its contents. The house itself, which stands on the site of the Priory of the Holy Trinity, was built in 1548–50 in rich red brick, copiously diapered. The ground floor is virtually all of this date. The upper floor was, however, rebuilt after a fire in about 1670; this was obviously when the house received its shaped gables and the rather curious design of its porch, flanked as it is by giant Ionic columns supporting a balcony. The interior is mostly of the seventeenth and eighteenth centuries, but now contains a fascinating museum of old Ipswich.

There are several other domestic buildings in the town which are well worth a look if you have the time – two, in particular, in NORTHGATE STREET: No. 7, at the corner of Oak Lane, which goes back to the fifteenth century, and the surviving gateway to the house of Archdeacon Pykenham (a little brother, as it were, to his magnificent edifice at Hadleigh (*q.v.*)). My final recommendation is, however, religious again: the UNITARIAN CHAPEL in Friars Street, built at the very end of the seventeenth century. With box pews, a beautiful tulip-base pulpit, fine galleries and a splendid brass chandelier, it is a delight.

## Kedington*

*33; 2 miles NE of Haverhill off A143*

A stunning church is ST PETER AND ST PAUL, though perhaps more for its furnishings and monuments than from the strictly architectural point of view. The style is late Early English: see how the tracery forks tentatively into a Y-shape, the first step towards the exuberance of the Decorated, and compare it with the fully-fledged Decorated of the west window of the north aisle – obviously a fourteenth-century addition. (The chancel east window is, equally obviously, a fifteenth-century one.)

Grateful as one is for bright interiors, one could have done without the Victorian skylights, cut with typical insensitivity through a false hammer-beam roof that must date from Tudor days. But there is little else to cavil at. A lovely uneven brick floor – it is strange how much difference these old floors make to the feel of a church, particularly in East Anglia – offers a pleasant contrast to the cobbles of the south porch; a west gallery of *c.*1810 projects forward in a sweeping semi-circle; to each side, children's pews climb up the west ends of the aisles, with a special seat opposite from which the schoolmaster can keep an eye on them; the pulpit is a splendid Jacobean three-decker with tester, hourglass and wig pole, while the rood-screen, of much the same date, is most unusually collapsible, like a folding door. Its predecessor seems to have been used to make up the Barnardiston pew, delightfully canopied and with separate compartments in which the sexes could be decently segregated. And then there are the Barnardiston tombs. I like Grissel's best; she died in 1609 and has a lovely epitaph – alas, too long to quote.

## Lakenheath

*34; 6 miles N of Mildenhall on B1112*

A church has stood on the site of ST MARY'S since the seventh century, but the oldest feature of the present building is probably the Norman chancel arch. On the outside, we can go back no further than the bottom two stages of the tower, which are of the late thirteenth century. It was finished off in the fourteenth and very pretty it is, with its crow-step battlements and tiny spire, but I wish they would remove the unsightly excrescence to the west of it: apart from being an eyesore, it conceals a most impressive west doorway. Seen from the normal southern approach, the rest of the church looks a jumble not only of styles but of materials too – ironstone, flint, clunch, red brick, Barnack limestone and (in the tower) a lighter-coloured sandstone from heaven knows where; the ensemble is attractive enough, but not particularly distinguished.

Inside, the chief glory is the roof, with traceried tie-beams and hammer-beams alternating and huge angels (smashed by Dowsing and his men, but renewed) against the hammers. For the rest, as at Kedington, it is the furniture rather than the architecture – largely fourteenth-century – that commands attention. The benches are particularly enjoyable, carved as they are with various monsters, a unicorn and a most accomplished contortionist. There are also good monuments, a magnificent Royal Arms of Charles II at the south door, and the best Early English font in Suffolk. Finally, on a pier to the north, there are some wall paintings of the fourteenth century including one of St Edmund, King and Martyr, clutching the three arrows with which the Danes killed him.

## Lavenham *

*35; 9 miles NW of Hadleigh on A1141*
*Includes Guildhall (NT)*

Of all the villages of Suffolk, Lavenham (pronounced with a short 'a', as in 'have') is the most enchanting. It is a monument to the great boom in the cloth industry which occurred between about 1380 and 1550, and seems to have changed amazingly little since. Here you will find not just individual timber-framed houses but whole streets of them, their overhanging jetties leaning and lurching like drunken platoons. CHURCH STREET, WATER STREET with its FLEMISH WEAVERS' COTTAGES, SHILLING STREET, BARN STREET – wander where you will, you will probably end up in the MARKET PLACE, on the south side of which stands the GUILDHALL (NT). It was built in the 1520s by the guild of Corpus Christi, one of the three founded to regulate the wool trade; later it became a prison, a workhouse, an almshouse, a wool store, a home for evacuees, a restaurant and a school, but it survived all these vicissitudes. Another guildhall, formerly that of the Blessed Virgin but now known simply as the WOOL HALL, dates from 1464. It stands on the corner of Lady Street and now forms part of the Swan Hotel.

And so to the great CHURCH OF ST PETER AND ST PAUL which dominates the village. In all Suffolk, there is only that of Long Melford to equal it. Though the chancel is Decorated – look at the lovely cusped tracery of the east window – the rest is late Perpendicular, most of it built at the expense of John de Vere, 13th Earl of Oxford, Henry VII's Captain-General at Bosworth and lord of the manor, and of three generations (all called Thomas) of the Spryng family, the most prosperous of the Lavenham merchant houses. The immense tower, of knapped flints with copious stone dressings, is 141 feet high – perhaps

*The Guildhall, Lavenham.*

a little too high and massive for the church, whose length is only 15 feet more; it would have been higher still if it had been given the battlements and pinnacles that were obviously intended for it. But the sight of it standing so bravely on its hill, and the simple splendour of its conception, stifle criticism. Not that it is lacking in fine detail; notice the way the buttresses are themselves buttressed, and on no account miss the flushwork plinth around the base, decorated with the starry shields of the de Veres, the merchant marks of the Spryngs, the crossed keys of St Peter and the crossed swords of St Paul.

The main body of the church seems to be composed almost entirely of windows: seven bays of four lights in the aisles, twelve of three lights in the clerestory, all of them transomed. Attached to the south aisle are a superbly ornate south porch and a three-bay south (Spryng) chapel at the east end; everything but the chancel itself (which, despite its great windows, is distinctly less exhibitionist) is crested with intricately decorated battlements, often to a design of trefoils set within panels.

You enter through the south porch, passing under a four-centred arch with the Oxford boar in its spandrels and a niche containing modern statues of the two dedicatory saints flanked by six de Vere shields above. The porch itself is fan-vaulted – a foretaste of what lies in store. The interior, indeed, does not disappoint. The six-bay arcades are exquisitely moulded, the area between them and the base of the clerestory windows most delicately carved. The timber roof is perhaps a little more restrained than one might have expected, being supported on arched braces with only small figures of angels – or are they humans – at their bases; the two eastern bays of the nave, however, have a special ceilure, picked out with gilded bosses to most excellent, and subtle, effect. The happiest feature of all, to me, is that wonderful five-light east window, lending as it does the unexpected touch of flowing Decorated to the prevailing Perpendicular. (It's a pity about the Victorian glass, but it might – just – be worse.)

The other pride of the chancel is its woodwork. By a rare stroke of fortune it has kept the original screen, of about 1330; few churches in England can boast screens of such an age and in such condition. Only the dado has been lost; the doors, which had also disappeared, were discovered in a local shop early in the present century. Original, too, are the choir stalls – the carved ends, alas, defaced but the misericords remaining intact. Yet the most virtuoso wood carving at Lavenham is not in the chancel, nor in its screen, nor in the fine parclose screens at each side; it is in the two aisle chantries, the Spryng Chantry to the north and the Oxford Chantry to the south. The former is perhaps the most spectacular; it was built to enclose the tomb of Thomas Spryng III, who died in 1523, and it is a miracle of filigree craftmanship. (Spare a special glance for the figure of St Blaise, the only Christian martyr to have been *combed* to death, and consequently the patron saint of wool carders.) The Oxford Chantry, however, runs it close; the 13th Earl died ten years before Spryng, so it may be a few years earlier, but the two were clearly wrought by the same hand – the idea of two contemporary carvers of such quality is almost inconceivable.

As well as the two chantries, there are also two chapels off the east end – the Branch Chapel to the north and the Spryng Chapel to the south. Their dates are 1500 and 1525 respectively. The Branch Chapel clearly replaced an earlier building; on the outside, the buttresses are built up against the plinth rather than bonded into it, so it must have been already there. The Spryng Chapel – now the Lady Chapel – is, however, the more interesting of the two, if only on account of the windows, which are of painted glass and look, at first sight, to be seventeenth-century Flemish; they are in fact early nineteenth-century, but they compare most favourably with the windows in the chancel or, for that matter, the four-light west window in the tower.

And now, rather than end a description of this glorious church on such a note of criticism, let me direct you to the only part of it that I have not yet mentioned: the little, low vestry extending east of the chancel, the gift of Thomas Spryng II in 1444, and in particular the marvellous resurrection brass of himself, his wife and his children now set into the wall – he and their four sons on one side, she and their six daughters on the other, all naked but for their shrouds. What a shame that a work of this quality should be kept in the vestry, which is all too often locked: how much better if it were replaced in the body of the church for everyone to see; for the Spryngs were a good and generous family, and Lavenham owes them much.

## Little Wenham

*36; 7 miles SW of Ipswich off A12*

An astonishing survival indeed, LITTLE WENHAM HALL is a fortified hall house of about 1270, beautifully set in a private garden and looking almost exactly as it must have looked when first it was built. Despite its battlements and somewhat formidable appearance, it is emphatically *not* a castle – the size and shape of many of its windows are sufficient evidence of that – but in the turbulent thirteenth century the builder of any considerable house had to give thought to its defence. The plan is L-shaped, with the east–west range rather higher than the north–south one, and a stair turret in the re-entrant angle rising higher still. All three elements are embattled. The base of the walls is of flint-faced rubble, and stone is used for the buttresses (much rebuilt by J.S. Corder for F.A. Crisp earlier this century) and dressings; but the body of the house is of brick, and whereas a little of this is of Roman origin, by far the greater part is locally made and of the date of the building – one of the earliest examples of post-Roman brick anywhere in the country, and certainly the first appearance of that white brick which was later to become something of a Suffolk speciality. Even when brick became widespread, its use was to be restricted to ecclesiastical buildings until well into the fifteenth century; in this respect Little Wenham seems to be some two centuries before its time.

The entire ground floor is occupied by a great rib-vaulted undercroft, from which a narrow spiral staircase leads up to the Chapel and the Great Hall – though the

*Holy Trinity Church, Long Melford.*

latter can also be reached by an outside wooden stairway. The Hall is a magnificent room by any standards, with a splendid old floor of red tiles and four two-light windows with plate tracery; the only two features which speak plainly of a later date are the timber roof – whose carved beams are probably of the sixteenth century – and the curious little piscina-like recess just to the left of the entrance door, whose Perpendicular surround cannot be much earlier than 1400.

Just off the north-east corner of the Hall lies the Chapel: vaulted, with its deeply moulded ribs resting on corbels, two of which are carved with stiff-leaf. The broad eastern arch frames an exquisite three-light window with more plate tracery, pierced with quatrefoils. A capacious angle piscina cuts into the splay of the south window, its arches gently cusped – the eastern one is now slightly askew – and is reflected on the north side by an aumbry with heavy hood-mould. The stone-flagged floor has a single shallow step to mark the 'chancel'; there is no other division.

From the junction of Hall and Chapel the spiral stair from the undercroft – the earliest domestic stairway in the county – winds up to a solar. Small and square, it is lit by a pair of two-light windows with Y-tracery. Above this is only the roof, from which there is a marvellous view down to the moat on the south side, the church to the north, the old farm buildings (which include a fine sixteenth-century timber-framed TITHE BARN) and the Suffolk countryside beyond.

ALL SAINTS' CHURCH is principally of flint, though the tower was topped with brick in Henry VIII's day. Its date is about 1300 – just the moment when Early English was giving way to Decorated – but its pride is the series of remarkably well-preserved contemporary paintings, covered over during the Reformation and uncovered only by chance by Mr Crisp in the 1890s. Those on the east wall – of the Virgin and Child, saints and angels – are of quite outstanding quality for a simple parish church. The Virgin and Child are repeated on the north wall, on a larger scale; but although this latter painting is about 150 years later than the others it has proved rather less durable.

Finally I have been asked to emphasise that Little Wenham Hall is private property and *not* open to the public. All Saints' church is now looked after by the Redundant Churches Fund; it is normally kept locked, but a notice in the porch states where the key may be found.

## Long Melford*

*37; 7 miles E of Clare on A1092*
*Includes Melford Hall* (*NT*)

Seen in the ensemble, the village of Long Melford is not, perhaps, as satisfying as Lavenham; it is too spread out, for one thing – well over a mile from Melford Place (rebuilt after a fire in 1967) at its southern end to the village green and the church, and even there it does not really end. But there are any number of fine houses, timber-framed, seventeenth-century and Georgian, down the whole length of the High Street, while the vast, sloping green itself – dotty little Victorian school at the bottom, high pepper-pot turrets of Melford Hall with its octagonal brick garden pavilion and the neighbouring Trinity Hospital at the top, and the greatest parish church of Suffolk towering behind – provides a superb climax of a kind to which intimate, pretty Lavenham, for all its charm, could never aspire.

Let us take the church first. HOLY TRINITY is an immensely opulent wool church of the later fifteenth century in the manner of Lavenham's, but considerably longer: twelve bays in the aisles and eighteen in the clerestory. It is better proportioned, too, since St Peter and St Paul always looks a little dwarfed by its tower, while that of Holy Trinity harmonises with it perfectly. (The fact that it was built by G.F. Bodley in 1903 – replacing an earlier brick one which had in turn replaced the original, struck by lightning in the reign of Queen Anne – hardly seems to matter.) It has its defects; the chapels at the eastern ends of the aisles break the rhythms of the fenestration for no apparent reason, as do the tall windows to each side of the chancel, and the extraordinary Lady Chapel of 1496 with its three parallel pitched roofs quite destroys the effect of the east window. But that great march of tall, transomed window shafts, extending at two levels down the length of the church, makes an unforgettable impression – and, incidentally, demonstrates the glory of the Perpendicular style at its best. There is also – on the south (show) side, a bravura display of flushwork decoration, as fine as any to be seen in the county.

On entering – through a surprisingly restrained south porch – you may notice that the piers of the five western bays are of a different shape from the rest. These are all that remains of the earlier fourteenth-century church before its remodelling after the Wars of the Roses. Thanks to a quantity of inscriptions we know a good deal about this remodelling; what is interesting about it is that, whereas Lavenham was built largely at the expense of two families, in Long Melford there was a whole group of rich clothiers and wool merchants, all willing and ready to make their contributions – the Sparrows, the Cowpers and the Smiths; the Cutlers, the Ellises and the Moriells. The greatest benefactors of all seem to have been the Cloptons; but more of them anon.

It is a noble nave, nine bays long, with broad, beautifully moulded arches and blank panelling in the space between them and the clerestory windows. It is not particularly broad – its dimensions are in fact identical with those of the aisles – but there is no feeling of constriction, only of light and space. The light is due largely to the fact that most of the enormous windows are now glazed with plain glass; what stained glass has survived is, however, of the same date as the church and of marvellous quality; the best of it is in the north aisle – particularly the west windows and the east window. Over the north door is the tiny but celebrated rabbit window, depicting three rabbits in a triangle, the left ear of each serving also as the right ear of its neighbour; it is probably a symbol of the Trinity, but the rabbit imagery is, to say the least, unusual. Not far off, and also on the north wall, is an alabaster relief of the Adoration of the Magi, dating from *c.*1350; it is said to have been discovered in the eighteenth century, beneath the floor of the chancel. A beautiful piece, and curiously touching; note the ox and the ass, poking their heads drowsily out from under the drapery of the Virgin's bed.

At the east end of the north aisle is the Clopton Chapel, rich in monuments and brasses to Melford's wealthiest merchant family; and beyond this, again to the east, is the Clopton Chantry Chapel – a completely separate room with a fireplace and seven-light east window, in the centre of which is inserted what is surely the most beautiful piece of medieval glass in all Suffolk: a white lily on a deep blue background, with the almost ghostly image of the crucified Christ superimposed upon it. The south wall is taken up by the tomb of John Clopton, who died in 1497, delicately carved with shields within quatrefoils above and below. In the canopy above and within the arch of the adjacent door leading into the chancel are contemporary paintings, including a fine one of the risen Christ carrying a staff surmounted by a cross. Higher still runs a frieze of empty canopied niches, and then a long poem by John Lydgate, a monk of Bury, painted on a carved scroll, with a design of coiled rope and foliage between the pages.

And so to the chancel. Its central feature is a huge carved reredos – a representation in Caen stone of Dürer's *Crucifixion*, given in 1879 by the rector's mother. This, however, pales into insignificance beside the great monument which occupies almost the entire south side. It commemorates Sir William Cordell, Master of the Rolls, who died in 1581. He it was who built Melford Hall – where, in 1578, he entertained Queen Elizabeth. He lies, a knight in armour, on a loosely rolled mat, in a pure Renaissance setting of Corinthian columns and deep niches from which the four cardinal Virtues gaze down on him with solicitous eyes. This magnificent conceit, which is surmounted by a huge strapwork crest with the Cordell coat of arms, is almost certainly the work of Cornelius Cure, Master Mason to the Crown, who was also responsible for the tomb of Mary Queen of Scots in Westminster Abbey.

Almost obscured by the Cordell monument, a little low door just to the right of the altar leads into the priest's vestry and thence into the Lady Chapel. From the outside, as we have seen, this late fifteenth-century addition to the church – it too was partly endowed by John Clopton – seemed an unnecessary excrescence, if not actually an eyesore; inside, one becomes in some degree reconciled. It proves to be a three-bay sanctuary surrounded by a sort of ambulatory, or processional way. The arcades to north and south have blank panels and empty niches above, and a beautiful cambered timber roof; the ambulatory, lit with pretty stepped three-light windows within four-centred arches, has an even prettier roof, supported on carved corbels. There may be other Lady Chapels in England of similar design, but I cannot think of any.

Between the church and the green, Sir William Cordell's TRINITY HOSPITAL comes, it must be said, as something of a disappointment. Of red brick, with projecting wings and an embattled centre topped by a cupola, it was built in 1573 for twelve poor men of the village; alas, it was given a thorough going-over in 1847 and has never really recovered. Its neighbour, MELFORD HALL (NT), is on the other hand very splendid indeed. Built by Sir William as early as *c.*1555, it is an E-shaped house of red brick, facing east – that is, with its back to the village green – with two long wings embracing a broad courtyard. (An eastern range, which would have turned the courtyard into a completely enclosed quadrangle, was demolished in the seventeenth century.) Two of the polygonal turrets with their ogival caps, which are such a feature of the house, spring up rather oddly, not from the ends of these wings but from about three-quarters of the way along them; four more are placed, equally oddly, along the west front overlooking the garden. From the east, the house appears to be two-storeyed throughout, though there are pretty little elliptical attic windows in the gable ends of the projecting wings; from the garden, however, one sees that a second floor has been added at the west end of these wings behind their pitched roofs and again between the two central towers. The east-facing windows have retained their original mullions and transoms; nearly all the rest are sashed.

Though the exterior of Melford Hall has been relatively little touched, little of the Elizabethan work remains within. The two-storey hall now has a pair of Doric columns where the screen used to be, an eighteenth-century stone fireplace and nineteenth-century panelling; south of it, in place of the old buttery and pantry, we now find what is probably the most memorable feature of the present house: the long Greek Revival staircase inserted in 1813 by Thomas Hopper. It rises in a single sweep, broken only by a broad half landing but with no corners or returns, and flanked by side galleries of Ionic columns supporting a coffered ceiling in the form of a shallow barrel vault.

Of the principal rooms of the house, several – including the Adam Saloon – were destroyed in a fire which gutted the north wing while the building was occupied by the military in 1942. A number remain, however, and very fine they are, with pictures, furniture and porcelain fully worthy of them. The most distinguished of all is Hopper's Library, which is properly speaking two connecting rooms linked by a broad depressed arch slightly Soanian in feeling, before which is a screen formed by two Ionic columns in scagliola. Both ends are apsed. It is a most unusual composition, necessitated by the fact that the smaller room occupies the space between the two inner turrets on the west side – one of which is actually supported by the columns. But it is no less satisfying or impressive on that account. Like most of the other rooms, it is rich in naval pictures and other memorabilia of the Hyde Parker family, a long line of admirals – the second of whom, at the battle of Copenhagen in 1801, gave the signal on which Nelson put his telescope to his blind eye.

To the north of Long Melford village and at the end of a mile-long avenue of lime trees stands KENTWELL HALL. It too is a massive Tudor manor house of red brick, built by William Clopton (great-grandson of John) only five years or so after Melford. It stands within a broad moat and has, like the latter, two long projecting wings with pepper-pot towers. It too was remodelled by Hopper, though not till after a bad fire in 1822. But thereafter the resemblance between the two houses ceases abruptly. Where Melford remained the home of a single relatively wealthy family, Kentwell suffered no fewer than ten occupants, all unrelated to each other, between 1822 and its purchase by the present owner in 1971. He and his wife are struggling determinedly to restore the house to something of its former glory, but the task is Herculean and when I was there in 1982 they still had a long way to go.

*Melford Hall, Long Melford.*

## Mildenhall*

*38; 11½ miles NW of Bury St Edmunds on A1101*

ST MARY'S is another of those staggering Suffolk churches; it is, however, of a completely different character from those of Lavenham or Long Melford. It is a good deal older, for one thing; for another, it stands not on a hill above the village but right in the middle of it; for a third, it is a church of considerable eccentricity – you have only to look up at the great east window from the High Street to see that. It could, I suppose, be described as a Decorated window of seven lights – except that the design of the tracery is totally unlike any other Decorated window I have ever seen, and the seven lights in fact resolve themselves into a pattern of two subdivided lancets clasping a mandorla-like pointed ellipse between them in the spandrels, the whole thing being framed by a continuous band which forms additional lights at the sides but in the curve of its arch breaks into a series of quatrefoils. To north and south, the other chancel windows alternate between plain intersecting tracery and another unusual design of stepped lancets in threes, with tentative suggestions of tracery at the top between the sides and the centre. There is a theory that this is meant to symbolise the Trinity; something very like it is to be found at Fountains Abbey.

Despite these windows, which must be of about 1300, the chancel is (with its adjoining vestry) the best part of a century older, and indeed the oldest part of the church. This becomes clear when we go inside. The remaining parts of the exterior are virtually all of the fifteenth century – though the buttresses along the north aisle look as though they may come from the earlier church and are thus re-used. The north has obviously always been the principal entrance side: so much is clear from the immense north porch of two bays and two storeys, buttresses with niches, traceried windows, battlements decorated with two tiers of panels and a tierceron vault within. The south porch, by comparison, is a distinctly modest affair. The tower, too, is Perpendicular; its bottom stage has a fine fan-vaulted ceiling, and it also boasts a huge six-light west window. Its great height – 120 feet – is subtly emphasised by the attached shafts with crocketed pinnacles which seem to climb up its broad angle buttresses; until a century and a half ago it was higher still, since it carried a wooden spire with an illuminated lantern – see the old engraving that hangs in the vestry.

On entering, one is struck first of all by that extraordinary east window – somehow the design seems a good deal more convincing from the inside – and the exquisite Early English chancel arch that frames it, its capitals adorned with lovely stiff-leaf and tiny carved heads. The nave arcades, some two centuries later in date, are very nearly as high; then comes a generous clerestory, its windows renewed; and, finally, the roof. The Mildenhall roof is, with those of Lakenheath and Needham Market, the finest in Suffolk; indeed, it is among the top half dozen in England. Tie-beams and hammer-beams alternate: the tie-beams are supported on traceried arched braces, and carry queenposts which have yet more tracery between them; the horizontal bases of the hammer-beams are carved with huge angels whose spreading wings, though peppered with buckshot by the Puritans, somehow managed to survive intact – for the most part at least. And then there are the roofs of the north and south aisles, which are even finer than that of the nave. They too have hammer-beams – carved not only with angels, prone people and couchant animals and monsters but also with biblical and mythological scenes: St George and the dragon, the Annunciation, Abraham and Isaac and many others. The detail is sometimes hard to make out from the ground; but if you climb into the former Lady Chapel on the first floor of the north porch you will see one or two of the carvings close up, in all their glory.

And so, finally, to the vestry, which you enter through the door in the north wall of the chancel. Originally a chapel, it is of the same date as the chancel arch, built – entirely of limestone instead of the generally prevailing flint – around 1220, very probably by one of the masons from Ely. Its two bays are elegantly rib-vaulted, its east window of three lancets, only very slightly stepped, in splayed recesses and shafted inside with very slender colonnettes in Purbeck marble, with a ring halfway down and some good stiff-leaf at the top.

Before you leave, take note of the floor – lovely old flagstones interspersed with huge black ledger slabs. This is a church to remember – and to return to again and again.

## Nayland*

*39; 9 miles SE of Sudbury on A134*

The architectural highlight of this typical and charming Suffolk village is unquestionably ALSTON COURT. It stands proudly at the end of Church Street – or, strictly speaking, at the point where it turns sharply left towards the church – and is immediately recognisable by the flamboyant double-transomed nine-light window, ostensibly of the early fifteenth century, and the rather inappropriate-looking Queen Anne doorway just to the right of it. It is gabled, and partly timber-framed. The impression given is that of a fine Tudor manor house; only when you get inside do you realise that it is something considerably more: a building whose origins probably go back as far as the thirteenth century, and one which conceals a wealth of fine carving which, for its size, must be considered one of the richest in all East Anglia.

The house seems to have begun its history as an aisled hall, running on a north–south axis at the west end of the present Hall. Then, probably in the late fourteenth century, a new open Hall was built out from this to the east, with a cross passage (there were probably no screens) at its east end and solar above. Finally, in about 1471 – an ER inscription seems to relate to Edward IV – a further wing was added, running northward from the east end. The present Hall is consequently of 1380 or thereabouts, though its two principal windows – there is a similar one to that on the entrance front, opposite it on the south side, looking over the courtyard – spectacular as they are, seem likely to be later insertions of indeterminate date. The Hall has kept its timber roof, with a tie-beam on arched braces and a kingpost; but it is the magnificently carved solar above – now a principal bedroom – that finally emerges as the *pièce de résistance* of the house. Here the arched braces supporting the roof are even more extravagantly carved, and rest on massive corbels in the shape of human heads. A great pendant boss dominates the centre.

The house in its present form completely encloses the rectangular courtyard; and there is scarcely a room from whose exposed timbers more of its long history cannot be traced. Here, by any standards, is an astonishing survival, on which much research remains to be – and is being – done.

## Needham Market

*40; 3½ miles SE of Stowmarket on B1115*

Until 1907, the CHURCH OF ST JOHN THE BAPTIST was a chapel of ease dependent on nearby Barking. Thus it stands halfway along the main street in a row of ordinary houses, without churchyard or tower, for all the world like a non-conformist meeting house. It was actually built around 1470, but at first sight you could be forgiven for thinking 1870 a likelier date. (The idiotic little porch does in fact date from 1883.)

Inside, at a lower level, there is little to prompt a revision of such an opinion; the church remains plain and characterless – until you raise your eyes. The roof has been described as 'the culminating achievement of the English carpenter', which is exactly what it is. No matter that most of the timber below the tie-beams had to be renewed in Victorian times; it is the design that counts here, and the design is unquestionably exactly as it was in the fifteenth century – a masterpiece of architectural joinery unparalleled in this country or anywhere else.

The church consists in essence of a broad, aisleless nave; the achievement of the roof builder was to provide the aisles at an upper level and thus, through sheer technical virtuosity, to give the church clerestory windows within the roof itself. This he managed to do by an inspired variant of the hammer-beam principle in which tall storey posts rise up from the ends of the hammers, linked by carved tie-beams to each other both longitudinally and latitudinally across the church until they are firm enough to support rafters sloping up from the walls like a lean-to roof. Above this runs the line of the clerestory, and above that the very slightly canted roof itself. This basic structure is then magnificently adorned with angels – renewed, but remarkably well done – against the ends of the hammers, their wings alternately swept upward and outstretched.

It is no good pretending that this roof will give you the aesthetic pleasure that you will find at Mildenhall, or even at Lakenheath. The rest of the building militates too strongly against it, destroying the atmosphere; and perhaps it lacks poetry anyway. Thus, although it will catch your breath, it is unlikely to bring tears to your eyes, and I am accordingly withholding – after some hesitation – the accolade of a star. But it remains, if not ultimately a great work of art, at least a dazzling *tour de force* that should not be missed.

*The roof, St John the Baptist, Needham Market.*

## Norton

*41; 6 miles E of Bury St Edmunds on A1088*

You could well be excused, on seeing LITTLE HAUGH HALL for the first time, if you did not give it a second glance. That long, relatively unadorned façade of grey brick is agreeable enough in its late Georgian way, but there is nothing about it remotely out of the ordinary. On going round to the garden front, you notice at once from the Baroque doorway and the Venetian window above it that the house is perhaps 100 years or so older than it looked from the entrance side; still, there are literally hundreds of English manor houses of which so much could be said.

Then enter the house – and prepare for a shock. On the inside, Little Haugh Hall reveals itself as the most magnificent early seventeenth-century house in Suffolk. It was in fact the house of Cox Macro, DD, chaplain to George II, one of the most eminent antiquarians and dilettanti of his day. When he first acquired it, it was a simple Jacobean three-storey building of red brick; there is a painting of it by Peter Tillemans in the Entrance Hall. Macro, however, lost no time in having his home thoroughly modernised, and expense seems to have been no object. What he did to the outside – apart from the west doorway and that Venetian window – we do not know, since the building was again remodelled in the 1830s, losing its top floor in the process. The interior he made very grand indeed.

What is left of Macro's work consists in essence of the Entrance Hall, staircase and first-floor landing, together with two rooms leading off, one above the other. The Hall is decorated with paintings by Tillemans (obviously a personal friend, since he is known to have died at Little Haugh in 1734) in panels over the chimneypiece and above the door. This leads directly to the staircase – a spectacular conception by any standards, lit by the Venetian window and by an oval lantern set in a deeply coved ceiling, with paintings by Francis Hayman. The stairs are richly carved, below the flights as well as above, with three shapely balusters to each tread. The mural paintings on the staircase walls, by the local painter Thomas Ross, have unfortunately gone; but the general effect remains so fine that one hardly feels like complaining.

The staircase leads up to the first-floor landing – not, usually, a major architectural feature of a house. But Little Haugh is an exception. In the centre is a niche in which Rysbrack's bust of Tillemans once stood, surrounded by superbly carved garlands and flanked by fluted Corinthian pilasters supporting an ornate broken pediment. To each side of this magnificent centre are two fine doorways, with rich carving above them and more garlands. Round the corner in the right-hand wall is a third door, equally grand, topped this time by a high triangular pediment. The workmanship throughout is of the highest quality imaginable, and one would love to know who was responsible; Norman Scarfe attributes all the carving to Thomas Ross; if he is right, Ross emerges as one of the greatest wood carvers of eighteenth-century England.

Of the two smallish rooms that have come down to us from Macro's day, the Tapestry Room on the first floor is something of a misnomer, having no tapestry. It does however possess more, equally assured, wood carving, especially over the chimneypiece and around the doorcases. Yet more of the same adorns the Dining Room immediately below, which has the additional attraction of a sumptuous stucco ceiling. This is by a certain Mr Burrough, an unidentified relative of James Burrough, the amateur Cambridge architect who was once Master of Caius.

## Orford

*42; 9 miles E of Woodbridge on B1084*

Once Orford was a prosperous sea port and a considerable town to boot, with three churches and its own parliamentary representation. Now the sea has receded and it has become a quiet village on the way to nowhere, with the remains of a great royal castle and of a church that must have been every bit as magnificent. Of the CASTLE, only the keep survives; built for Henry II in 1165–7, it is the earliest accurately datable castle in the kingdom for which documentary evidence exists. What is more important, however, is the fact that it is probably the first keep whose designers abandoned the old square or rectangular plan in favour of something more militarily sophisticated. In this instance they chose a roughly circular shape – to be precise, it is an irregular polygon – with the addition of three rectangular turrets, battlemented and rising some 90 feet: considerably higher than the main tower itself. It is built principally of the local septaria; but higher-quality freestone is used for the great rugged plinth on which it stands, the quoins, string-courses and dressings for windows and doors. One of the turrets contains a beautifully built spiral staircase which rises the entire height of the keep. On the south side there is a fore-building which contains, at first-floor level, the main entrance, with a basement below and the little Chapel above. The Hall occupies the centre of the first and second floors – circular, with a stone bench running round the wall, a vast fireplace (original, but much altered) and three great windows with double round-headed lights.

The CHURCH OF ST BARTHOLOMEW, like the castle, gives only an intimation of its former splendour. Once it possessed a broad late Norman chancel of five bays, with aisles; but of this only a few broken columns remain, to the east of the present church. What is interesting about these columns, however, is their decoration: bold geometrical designs of the kind that one sees in Durham Cathedral or, less spectacularly, at Norwich – except that here the designs are raised above the surface of the column as opposed to being incised in it, a far more difficult and time-consuming operation and a significant indication of just how grand the church must have been.

*Orford Castle.*

St Bartholomew's as we see it today was built in the fourteenth century on the site of the western part of the old church, of which the only part remaining within the present structure is the big Norman arch with zigzag decoration leading from what is now the north chancel aisle into the former north transept. The rest, apart from a Perpendicular and most disagreeably rendered south porch, is all good Suffolk Decorated, with nice tracery of various designs in the windows. Inside, the church is strikingly broad, with a south aisle as wide as, if not wider than, the nave and a north aisle only very little narrower. They are separated by fine five-bay arcades. For obvious structural reasons there is no chancel arch, only a carved screen – modern, but of excellent quality – running the breadth of the church. The only other item of furniture worth special mention is the font – fourteenth-century, and for once not bashed about.

Finally we come to the tower. If it looks a bit odd this is because the top stage fell off in 1830. It remained truncated for 130 years and its restoration was completed only at the end of 1971. Alas, there were insufficient funds for the bell openings – which explains its somewhat blank appearance.

## Otley Hall★

*43; 10 miles N of Ipswich off B1077*

It was in about 1450 that the moated manor of Otley was acquired by John Gosnold, whose family was to be associated with the house for the next 250 years. At that time it probably consisted only of what is now the south wing, with perhaps the short eastward projection towards the moat; but in 1485 or thereabouts John's son Robert built himself a splendid new wing to the west, with a magnificent timbered Hall as its centre, a service range beyond the screens passage and, at the dais end, a Parlour covered with linenfold panelling of the highest quality. The service range has gone, but the Hall and Parlour remain and form the nucleus of the present house.

Entrance is no longer from the north, as was originally planned, but – since 1910 – from the south side, where a space formerly filled by a staircase now provides a small vestibule. The north door, however, still bears the initials R.G. in the spandrels of its four-centred arch, and inside the open timber screen is still in place. The Hall itself, one storey high, has deeply moulded beams and joists and a chimneypiece with a really tremendous bressummer, also heavily moulded and crested with a trefoil pattern. The large transomed window of eight lights in the north wall which now provides the principal illumination for the room is in fact a later addition, of about 1600; in Robert Gosnold's day the light came from the windows to the left – now a single row only, the lower row having been blocked in when, after the destruction of the service range, the front door was moved a few feet to the east. The Parlour beyond, which also faces north, has an even larger window – fourteen lights above the transom, eight below. This too is a Jacobean addition, the room having originally been lit from the south by a window which was blocked when a new corridor was built to run along the outside of the south wall.

Seen from the north-west, this Hall and Parlour range gives the impression of the perfect late Elizabethan manor house, with a jetty overhanging the heavily glazed ground floor, the first-floor windows with their heavy sills rising up to the eaves, high gables to north and west, brick nogging between the closely placed studs and magnificent decorative brick chimneys towering above. Then, to the left, a rather more modest-looking range projects northward – cement-rendered, with on the ground floor a timber loggia, formerly open but now filled in. This was intended as a Banqueting Hall range and was added about 1600 by another Robert, brother of that Bartholomew Gosnold who pioneered the direct route to New England in 1602 and named Martha's Vineyard after his daughter. The Banqueting Hall itself, on the first floor, has walls charmingly painted to represent wainscot panelling, with fanciful caryatids in the Jacobean style, wild men and coats of arms.

Finally the south wing. Although – indeed, perhaps because – it is the oldest, it has less original work than the rest. It now contains a two-storey Dining Hall – looking, in fact, considerably more like a medieval one than Robert Gosnold's – kitchen and bedrooms.

The house is surrounded by beautiful gardens and is occasionally open to the public. It is also used for concerts, for which I can imagine no more perfect setting.

## Southwold

*44; 19 miles S of Lowestoft on A1095*

This is the best, by a considerable margin, of the Suffolk seaside towns. Aldeburgh has its charming but much-restored Moot Hall and a certain Peter Grimes romance, Felixstowe a few sad vestiges remaining from its Edwardian heyday; of Lowestoft, the less said the better. Only Southwold has real character and architectural distinction. This lies not so much in any individual building – though there are pretty houses throughout the town, especially around SOUTH GREEN – as in the ensemble: nothing spectacular, nothing pretentious, but a quiet unambitious serenity everywhere. Brick and pantile prevail, but there are plenty of delightful colour-washed fishermen's cottages and a perfectly splendid 1890s' LIGHTHOUSE. This effectively marks the northern limit of the old town; don't bother to go any further. Since Southwold stands on a clifftop, there are wonderful views across the North Sea and over the marshes.

ST EDMUND'S CHURCH is magnificent, its 100-foot flat-topped tower a landmark for miles around. It was built all of a piece between 1430 – after a fire had destroyed its predecessor on the same site – and about 1460; the style is accordingly Perpendicular throughout. Clearly, at that time, there was plenty of money around: few churches in East Anglia are richer in flushwork, and nowhere is it of a higher quality. It rises up the buttresses, it runs all around the base and along the parapet of the tower, it flanks the west door (invoking St Edmund just above it), it crowns the west window, it covers almost every inch of the great two-storeyed south porch. A further happy touch is the delicate little *flèche* that rises about halfway along the roof of the nave.

That nave, on the inside, seems at first sight a little narrow for its great height, though the broad aisles prevent any feeling of real constriction. It is surmounted by a hammer-beam roof, so well done that one scarcely minds its being a Victorian rebuilding, with nice big angels reaching out from each side. It is brilliantly painted over the chancel, but left bare of colour over the nave. Above the screen there is a ceilure, quite a rarity in Suffolk.

But now drop your eyes to the screen itself, for this is the church's chief pride. It too dates from the later fifteenth century, and is lavishly decorated in gilded gesso. It runs the entire width of the church, but the sections across the aisles are rather less elaborate and clearly by a different hand. They too, however, like the central part, carry painted figures in the dado panels. They have been cleaned but never retouched, and have preserved a surprising amount of their original colour. As for the rest of the furniture, there are some fine stalls and a lovely pulpit, wineglass-stemmed and recently repainted. The huge font cover is a 1935 replacement of one destroyed nearly 300 years before by the Puritans. A final curiosity is the 'Clock Jack', a mechanical figure standing against the wall just to the north of the tower arch. In his right hand he holds a battle axe, with which he strikes a bell to mark the beginning of the service. He dates from 1470 and provides us with fascinating evidence of what an English man-at-arms would have been wearing at the time of the Wars of the Roses.

The east window is by Sir Ninian Comper, 1954. A good deal more interesting, however, is the north chancel window of engraved glass, by John Hutton, presented by Sir Charles Tennyson (who died in 1977 aged ninety-seven) in memory of his wife.

## Stoke-by-Nayland

*45; 8 miles N of Colchester on B1087*

Set high on a ridge above the Stour barely half a mile from the Essex border, ST MARY'S CHURCH with its tremendous west tower makes a very considerable landmark. It is, moreover, an unusually fine tower, 120 feet high, with a frieze of shields around the base, a generous four-light west window and, below it, a magnificent west door with more shields, stylised foliage and lions' heads. Its huge diagonal buttresses – which have buttresses of their own, and canopied niches to boot – give it an unusual and not altogether attractive silhouette, tapering up through five stages to the battlemented top with its stubby pinnacles; but the detailing is a delight, and its beauty is further enhanced

*The lighthouse, Southwold.*

by the introduction into the prevailing flint and freestone of a very pale red brick, causing it to blush a wonderful warm apricot in the afternoon sun. More of this brick appears in the Tudor north porch; the south porch, however, is a considerably more elaborate affair, two-storeyed and with Decorated windows – a surprising feature since virtually all the rest of the building is of the mid-fifteenth century. It must therefore have been part of the earlier church on the site, together with the little St Edmund's Chapel which extends outwards from the north aisle. For the rest, the St Mary's that we see today has a tall, six-bay nave and a clerestory of thirteen two-light windows, embattled everywhere. It is, in short, a grand Suffolk church – of the kind, one feels, that Constable might have painted; and it comes as no surprise to discover that in fact he did – though in his day the clerestory was still unbuilt.

Enter, then, through the rib-vaulted south porch, taking care not to miss the carved bosses and corbels – nor indeed the door itself, its thick oak carved with canopied niches and what remains of the original figures within them. In the nave, the first thing that strikes you is the enormously tall – though surprisingly narrow – tower arch, which provides a dramatic backdrop to the octagonal font, centrally placed on three steps. The arcades are predictably less tall, but are beautifully proportioned and intricately moulded. Above the clerestory is a rather plain timber roof on arched braces resting on stone corbels (some of which are carved), while a pretty frieze of angels with outstretched wings runs along the top of the arcade on each side. The high nineteenth-century clerestory windows – which continue in the chancel – flood the church with light, though it would be lighter still without the horrible Victorian glass. There are two particularly fine tombs: that of Lady Anne Windsor, who died in 1615, in the south chapel, and that of Sir Francis Mannock of Giffords Hall, who died in 1634, in the north; the latter is probably by Nicholas Stone.

Just west of the church, in School Street, are the two other most interesting buildings of the village: the MALTINGS and the GUILDHALL, both timber-framed and of the early sixteenth century. There are, however, plenty of more modest dwellings of similar date in the streets nearby. Finally, if you are driving south towards Nayland, you should not miss the charming little eighteenth-century FISHING LODGE overlooking the lake. It is all that remains of the Tendring Hall estate, in which the great house by Sir John Soane was, alas, demolished in 1955.

## Stutton

*46; 7 miles S of Ipswich on B1080*

Standing at the end of a long straight drive, STUTTON HALL has on its north entrance front a lovely Tudor walled garden with a brick Gatehouse very much on the lines of that at Erwarton (*q.v.*), only on a slightly smaller scale and with four pinnacles instead of nine. The south side has marvellous views down to the Stour estuary. Built by Sir Edmund Jermy in 1553, it is not in any sense a classically beautiful house, more a commodious residence suitable for a comfortable but unambitious country gentleman. Originally it was entirely timber-framed, with three tall chimneystacks each having four ornamental chimneys. Only around the turn of the present century were the walls rebuilt in brick. Later still, in 1912, an extension was added to the west end (with a gable and two more similar chimneystacks for reasons of symmetry), together with a new porch and a new north front incorporating an inner passageway running the length of the house.

The interior, too, has seen many changes; the original Hall, for example, has vanished almost without trace. But nearly all the downstairs rooms have retained their original plaster ceilings and fine friezes with pine cones and pomegranates; there are also some splendid sixteenth-century chimneypieces and, upstairs, a really spectacular Great Chamber. This has a six-bay ceiling on pilasters; in each bay there is a central pendant, from which lovely curved ribs sweep outwards to form interlaced patterns. The effect is grand without being in any way pompous or even formal, and does not therefore detract from the pervading atmosphere of happy domesticity that remains the hallmark of the house.

A mile or so to the east, and similarly sited over the estuary, is a building of a very different but equally fascinating kind: CROWE HALL. It was built some time in the second quarter of the seventeenth century, but this fact is not, at least to the unsuspecting visitor, immediately apparent; for a Mr George Reade, acquiring the house in 1821, commissioned a local architect, one Richard Beales of Lawford, Essex, to clothe it in an impenetrably Gothick disguise. Crowe Hall thus emerges as Suffolk's answer to Strawberry Hill.

The entrance front, which faces north, has kept its square sash windows, though some have been enriched with hood-moulds to add period flavour. The five eastern bays are of two storeys, the two western ones of three. To the three in the centre, however, Beales added a three-bay porch with four-centred arches, at the same time embattling – together with his porch – the roof line above and adding a series of crenellated turrets and buttresses wherever the opportunity arose. On the garden front, he was considerably more ambitious, throwing out a new wing towards the river and ending it in a deep bow with huge transomed Gothic windows. This bow consists of a single storey on a high basement, from which there projects another deep porch with its own little turrets.

Inside, Beales's two best rooms are the ground-floor Dining Room and the Drawing Room which occupies the great bow just described. The Dining Room forms a further eastward extension, ostensibly of two storeys but in fact of one, since it has a high coved ceiling; the upper windows are consequently blank. It is oval in shape, the ceiling rising above a deep Gothic frieze of vines and crockets. At the far end a stone chimneypiece in similar style supports a projecting, embattled chimneybreast; the claret-coloured wallpaper and mahogany furniture complete the effect. The Drawing Room, however, was Beales's *tour de force*. It boasts a most ornate Gothic chimneypiece of carved wood with its original iron grate and fender, and the entrance door is also richly adorned with side panels, carved spandrels, a crocketed frieze and pinnacles; but the over-riding element in the decorative scheme is the astonishing plaster ceiling, a shallow barrel vault apsed at one end, divided by delicate ribs into countless narrow panels which lead the eye upward to three central pendants, the central one surrounded by quadrant evocations of fan vaulting. It is said to be based deliberately on Henry VII's Chapel in Westminster Abbey; at all events, one would love to know the name of the craftsmen responsible; they seem most unlikely to have come from a local firm.

To me, however, the best room in the house is neither of these. It is a bedroom in the west wing, facing south, and Beales seems to have ignored it. It boasts a plasterwork ceiling still more memorable than that of the Drawing Room, though of a very different style. There, on each side of a central oval framed by garlands of fruit emerging from the mouths of what I take to be lions, are two figures, very nearly life-size, their feet projecting several inches from the ceiling only a yard or so from the sleeper below. Presumably angels – they are winged, long-haired and clean-shaven – they wear loose robes tied with neat bows at the waist; with their outside arms, they brandish wreaths above their heads, while holding in their other hands rings apparently connected to the central oval. What can it all mean? And who can have done it? There are obvious affinities with the plasterwork on Sparrowe's House in Ipswich (*q.v.*) and it could be by the same hand – not of a genius, perhaps, but surely of a visionary.

## Ufford

*47; 3 miles NE of Woodbridge off A12*

The CHURCH OF THE ASSUMPTION dates back to Norman times and perhaps even before: look at the herringbone courses of ironstone in the north wall, and the massive round pier between the two eastern bays. The chancel is probably of about 1200. Later the church seems to have been extended towards the west, the piers changing in shape from circular to octagonal. The four-stage west tower, lavishly flushworked south porch and the four-centred nave arcades are all Perpendicular.

But at Ufford it is not the architecture that matters so much as the contents. First and foremost comes the font cover, the most sensational in England if not the world, 18 feet high, carved into the most delicate of filigrees and dating from about 1450. Somehow it was protected from the attentions of Dowsing and his vandals: he mentions it in his diary, likening it typically to 'the Pope's triple crown', but though he tore the angels from the roof, mutilated the bench ends and smashed the two organs and the stained glass, he left the greatest masterpiece of them all unharmed. It is, incidentally – among its less obvious virtues – telescopic: the upper half collapses into the lower.

Note, too, the benches. Despite Dowsing, several have survived, bearing *inter alia* the figures of St Catherine and St Margaret of Antioch (both near the font), the usual mythical and heraldic beasts and a charming couple in fifteenth-century costume. There are splendid stalls, too, in the chancel; and below the ancient rood-beam the dado of the screen, its panels painted with figures of the virgin martyrs.

The single hammer-beam roof has had its angels meticulously replaced; crenellated tie-beams alternate. The roof of the chancel is quite different: collars, with long arched braces interrupted by pendants. Anglo-Catholicism rules throughout.

## Walsham-le-Willows

*48; 10 miles NE of Bury St Edmunds off A143*

ST MARY'S is a church of great beauty, if somehow lacking any strong character. It resembles so many of those fine Suffolk Perpendicular churches, with plentiful flushwork, especially around the main porch – here it is the north one – a stalwart tower, and a tall clerestory with close-set windows and more flushwork between them. The date is probably around 1440.

The interior boasts a fine nave roof, arch-braced tie-beams and hammer-beams alternating. Once there were angels a-plenty, but they have all gone now, when and whither nobody knows. Once, too, the entire roof was painted vermilion; traces of the colour still remain. The rood-screen, dated 1441, has retained all its original coving; in one of the panels is the head of a wolf, the symbol of St Edmund, and the dado is prettily painted with flowers. A curiosity, on the south side of the nave, is a pendant memorial on one of the piers. It commemorates one Mary Boyce, who died in 1685 at the age of twenty, and is known as a 'Virgin's Crant', from which other, more fortunate, maidens would from time to time hang garlands.

*The church of the Assumption, Ufford.*

## Westhall

*49; 6 miles S of Beccles off B1124*

If ST ANDREW'S CHURCH has no star, it may well be only because I was unable to get inside and see it for myself; alas, I could only look at it longingly from the churchyard. The south-west tower, the lovely Decorated windows of the chancel and the Perpendicular ones of the south aisle and the north wall of the nave (there is no north aisle) suggest that the whole building is of the fourteenth and fifteenth centuries; in fact, however, the south aisle is essentially the nave of a Norman church, to which a tower was added in about 1300 and the present nave and chancel immediately to the north some half a century later. At that time, too, the old apsed chancel of the Norman church was pulled down – presumably to allow more south light to its successor.

The original west door of the Norman church still exists within the tower; it looks magnificent in photographs. There is also said to be a fine screen and seven-sacrament font and a good timber roof. Why are so many vicars still so reluctant to tell one where to apply for the church key?

## Wingfield

*50; 7 miles SE of Diss off B1118*

The three principal claims to our attention here are a castle, a collegiate church and – perhaps the most interesting of all from the architectural point of view – the old secular College, until recent years almost impenetrably disguised as a modest Georgian mansion.

Let us take the CASTLE first. It was built by Michael de la Pole, 2nd Earl of Suffolk, who received his licence to crenellate from Richard II in 1384. Most of what we see today is in fact Tudor, of about 1545; but the fourteenth-century south front is still virtually complete, with its fine three-storey Gatehouse in the centre with stout polygonal turrets, and its original door, carved with blank tracery. From this Gatehouse walls extend to left and right, ending in corner towers, equally well preserved.

The CHURCH OF ST ANDREW proclaims itself at once as something special. It is exceptionally high, for one thing, with unusually tall aisle windows and lofty clerestories above them, both for the nave and – surprisingly – for the chancel, where the three-light windows are set so closely together as to be almost touching. All these features, together with the west tower, are in High Decorated style and date from the complete rebuilding of the church at the time when Sir John de Wingfield founded his College in June 1362. (The foundation was actually posthumous, Sir John – who had distinguished himself at the battle of Poitiers and was a close personal friend of the Black Prince – having unfortunately succumbed to the Black Death in the previous year.) His tomb stands against the north wall of the chancel, where he lies in full armour, hands together as in prayer, beneath a huge ogee gable, cusped and crocketed. His funeral, and perhaps his tomb also, was paid for by the Black Prince. Immediately to the east, a similarly canopied door leads into the Wingfield Chantry Chapel – a curiously shaped chamber in that the western part is divided horizontally into two, each level being separated from the undivided part by a parclose screen.

Sir John's only surviving child, his daughter Katherine, married in 1360 that Michael de la Pole who, while already possessor of considerable lands in his native Yorkshire, was to build Wingfield Castle some quarter of a century later. By this time he had become Earl of Suffolk and Chancellor of England; and it was his son, another Michael and the 2nd Earl, who built the exquisite chapel south of the chancel, from which it is separated by a three-bay arcade. Beneath the easternmost arch, which is decorated with the wings of the Wingfields, the leopards' heads of the de la Poles and the knots of the Staffords, lie the wooden effigies of himself and his wife. He died in the year of Agincourt, 1415, where he would have fought if he had not previously fallen victim to dysentery at Harfleur, a few months before. At this date, one would have expected the chapel to be purely Perpendicular in style; the Decorated tracery in the windows can only have been a deliberate archaism to harmonise with that of the south aisle. The true Perpendicular parts of the church – notably the south porch, double-transomed east window and clerestory – are probably the work of William, 1st Duke of Suffolk (whose effigy is at Wingfield, although that of his wife, the granddaughter of Chaucer, is one of the chief glories of Ewelme in Oxfordshire (*q.v.*)), or of his son John, who married the sister of Edward IV. Their tomb is to the north of the chancel, east of the chantry door.

Finally, the old COLLEGE itself. From the outside the impression it gives is that of a long, low Georgian house, in a style that might best be described as village Palladian; thus the outsize pediment is unsupported by columns or pilasters, and there are no steps, rustications or the slightest suggestion of a *piano nobile*. The proportions, too, of eleven bays but only two low storeys (with two small attic dormers), belong more to vernacular architecture than to that of Palladio's *Quattro Libri dell'Architettura*. Perhaps for this very reason, however, the façade with its slightly overblown doorcase and its two unexpected Venetian windows is one of considerable charm. It certainly gives not the faintest indication of what lies behind.

This proves to be nothing less than the Great Hall of the Wingfields, dating from the early fourteenth century and thus several decades older than the College of which it was to become a part. Only in the 1970s, when the house was bought by its present young owner, were the eighteenth-century false ceilings and floors stripped away to reveal it in all its splendour – a magnificent timber roof with tie-beam (a Tudor insertion), a collar-beam supported on immense arched braces, and a carved kingpost. The contrast between this majestic chamber and the charming little Georgian rooms along the west front could hardly be more complete.

Wingfield College (it keeps its old name, occasionally confusing visitors who arrive expecting to find an academic institution) and its pleasant gardens are open regularly in summer, when there is also a season of concerts: a lovely way to spend an August evening.

## Woolpit*

*51; 6 miles NW of Stowmarket off A45*

In 1852 the tower and spire of ST MARY'S CHURCH was struck by lightning and crashed to the ground. The rebuilding that we see today is the work of R.M. Phipson and a good deal better than might have been expected: the S-shaped flying buttresses are a particularly nice touch. The rest of the church is mid-fifteenth-century Perpendicular, except for the south aisle and chancel which must be about a century older and were thus clearly retained when everything else was remodelled. The most noteworthy features of the exterior are the clerestory, with its extraordinary flushwork decoration, and the south porch, which was erected between 1430 and 1455. Its ashlared front is intricately panelled, its crocketed ogee arch topped with shields. On the upper level are five canopied niches of varying heights; all, alas, lack their statues. There is some fine openwork quatrefoil cresting along the top.

The interior has a pleasant five-bay Perpendicular arcade; but one hardly notices it. What counts here – and what earns the church its star – is the timber roof. Double hammer-beamed throughout, with angels on both rows of hammers, below the canopied figures on the bases of the wall posts and above the crested collar-beams along the central ridge, it is one of the most spectacular in Suffolk. Still more angels adorn the two-tiered wall plates and the aisle roofs, every bit as richly carved as that of the nave. A further most unusual embellishment is the coved rood-canopy, presumably from some other church, set high on the east wall of the nave just below its little three-light window. The church's own screen is fifteenth-century, but the eight painted figures are modern replacements. The date 1750 on the top, referring to minor alterations at that time, can safely be ignored.

The other – though lesser – pride of Woolpit is the splendid collection of carved benches and chancel stalls, lovingly peopled with saints and animals and a variety of traceried patterns. In many another church these alone would attract visitors and impress themselves on the memory, but here they have little chance; that great roof dominates all.

## Worlingham Hall

*52; 1½ miles E of Beccles off A146*

Standing in its park just outside Beccles on the Lowestoft road, Worlingham Hall is a fascinating house, and at the same time a strangely enigmatic one. As we see it today it is a radical remodelling of an older, probably late seventeenth-century, house of which we know nothing – undertaken by its owner, one Robert Sparrow, in 1785. In that year he commissioned the young John Soane, recently returned from Italy, to make plans; Soane complied with enthusiasm, and quickly produced no fewer than five sets of alternative designs, but to no avail. Sparrow had apparently lost interest and took no action, either on the building or on Soane's bill, which remained unpaid for the next eleven years.

It was not until 1800 that Sparrow again thought of remodelling his house. This time he seems to have called in the local – though originally Irish – architect Francis Sandys, at that time working on Ickworth (*q.v.*). Admittedly, there is no documentary evidence for this, but Sandys exhibited a drawing of the house in that year at the Royal Academy and copied the façade almost exactly when he came to build the Assembly Rooms at Bury St Edmunds a few years later. Thus it is to him that Worlingham is invariably – and on the whole correctly – attributed. Yet as one goes round the house one feels conscious, again and again, of the unmistakable hand of Soane. Sparrow, so far as we know, never relinquished those plans – for which, after all, he finally paid – and it is hard to believe that he did not put them at the disposal of Sandys, who had never received any formal training, who certainly found himself faced with a number of difficult problems, and who would probably have been only too pleased to take advantage of them.

Worlingham is not large; the entrance front shows us only two storeys and seven bays – though the central one is given a tripartite treatment and is consequently a good deal broader than the rest. The bays to each side of it are flanked by giant pilasters, which support an entablature slightly higher than the parapet which surmounts the end bays. Is some Soane influence already perceptible here? Possibly, but we cannot be sure. It is only when we get inside the house that the impression becomes impossible to ignore. Take, for example, the Entrance Hall, with its shallow segmental tunnel vault, always one of Soane's hallmarks. Here already, the architect – whoever he was – ran up against a problem. He had to keep the staircase well of the old house, but this was unfortunately not quite central. The solution here is wonderfully ingenious: two adjacent doors, rather than one central one, appear to lead through to the staircase. Together, united by a high semi-circular pediment, they close off the Entrance Hall symmetrically and satisfactorily; but the way through is by the right-hand door only, the left-hand one leading to nothing more than a cupboard. There are what appear to be several more doors along each side, similarly grouped together under pediments (triangular this time); only one, however, is genuine, the others being all sham. The composition taken as a whole is not entirely convincing, and one feels something less than a sense of mastery; but Soane was still a young man of little practical experience, and it is anyway more likely that Sandys was using his drawings only for the occasional idea and not following them slavishly.

The Staircase Hall is the pride of the house – the only example in English architecture of a double, 'imperial', staircase – in other words beginning with one central flight, which then splits into two, rising up opposite sides – built into an octagonal hall. At the top of the first flight, dominating the whole Hall from its central position, is a majestic-looking doorcase, suggesting the existence of some opulent saloon behind it; alas, it proves to be only another broom cupboard. Above it to each side, tall round-headed arches offer tantalising glimpses into other parts of the house – including the back stairs, which prove to be almost as elegant as the front ones. A pair of half landings are used to surmount another difficulty – the fact that the upper-floor rooms are on different levels. One of the landings thus gives access to the lower series of rooms, the other once again to a cupboard; the higher rooms are reached from the top landing, above which the octagon begins to curve inward through a pattern of shallow coffering to the lantern above.

This difference in first-floor levels – an awkward legacy of the old house – greatly affects the proportions of the ground-floor rooms. Whereas the Dining Room and Saloon on the left of the staircase are as lofty as one might reasonably expect, the Library and Drawing Room to the right seem almost uncomfortably low. The Drawing Room has a screen of two Ionic columns rising almost to the line of the ceiling; a strange mistrust of architraves is another idiosyncrasy of Worlingham, manifesting itself in all the principal rooms. The Library is odder still. Both its longer sides are bowed, and these curves are echoed in the shallow segmental tunnel vaults which cover both ends. These are separated from the centre – where the ceiling, now horizontal, carries an enormous filleted oval in plasterwork and nothing else – by columns and pilasters, one of each, arranged in pairs: another wilful eccentricity, far more easily attributable to Soane than to the normally rather unimaginative Sandys. Add to all this the arcaded, groin-vaulted passages, the sudden unexpected vistas, the whole astonishing display of spatial imagination that characterises this most remarkable house – and the case for Soane looks strong indeed. Worlingham Hall is a relatively little-known building, on which not much research has yet been done. Will no young architectural historian take up the challenge?

---

# Short List

## Badingham

*53; 6 miles W of Yoxford off A1120*

The CHURCH OF ST JOHN THE BAPTIST is built on quite a steep incline from west to east and has a rather splendid porch of 1486 in flint flushwork. The nave is Early English, with Decorated and Perpendicular alterations. The two best features are the exquisite seven-sacrament font, also late fifteenth-century, which has retained its beauty despite the attentions of Dowsing and his men, and the superb hammer-beam roof – from which Dowsing has recorded the beating-down of 'sixteen superstitious cherubims'.

## Barsham

*54; 1½ miles W of Beccles on A1116*

HOLY TRINITY CHURCH has a round tower with a Norman window to the west; but what gives it a place here is its quite extraordinary east wall and window. They must be taken together since they both form part of a single design – a diagonal trellis-like grid, in flushwork on the wall, continuing in tracery across the window. It is not beautiful, but unforgettable, and so unique that it cannot be stylistically dated. My guess is the fifteenth century, but it could be any period between the fourteenth and seventeenth.

## Bramfield

*55; 3 miles SE of Halesworth on A144*

ST ANDREW'S is an enchantingly pretty thatched church with a free-standing Norman round tower. The main building is Decorated, but not aggressively so. The simple whitewashed interior emphasises the delicacy of the best late medieval screen in Suffolk (though only five of the figures painted on the dado are left). The ledger slab to the memory of Bridgett Applewhaite is the funniest I know anywhere.

## Bungay

*56; 6 miles W of Beccles on A1116*

This agreeable little town possesses two medieval churches and the remains of a fine castle. ST MARY'S was once the nave of a Benedictine nunnery, whose ruined choir – destroyed by fire in 1688 – can still be seen to the east. It has a magnificent south-west tower of 1470 or thereabouts, and a north porch with most enjoyable carving in the spandrels. HOLY TRINITY nearby has an early Norman round tower with herringbone masonry. Of the CASTLE there is little left; but you can still see the mining galleries dug in 1174 which would have brought the whole building down if it had not surrendered in the nick of time.

## Cavendish

*57; 3 miles W of Long Melford on A1092*

The beauty of Cavendish lies in its village green, surrounded as it is with charming houses and cottages of many different periods. On the north side, ST MARY'S CHURCH dominates: of the fourteenth and fifteenth centuries, Decorated and Perpendicular. Behind it is the Tudor, timber-framed NETHER HALL FARMHOUSE, beautifully restored, as is the pink-washed group of CHURCH COTTAGES to the south-west.

## Cotton

*58; 4½ miles N of Stowmarket off B1113*

ST ANDREW'S CHURCH has a west tower with a giant arch on the west side running up the height of two normal stages. The church itself looks a bit dilapidated with its rendered walls; but there are some fine Decorated windows – particularly the chancel five-lighter – and a lovely south porch with flushwork. Flushwork can also be seen between the windows of the Perpendicular clerestory. Inside are a nice brick floor and a double hammer-beam roof with angels; pleasant but unexciting.

## Crowfield

*59; 4½ miles NE of Needham Market off A1120*

ALL SAINTS' CHURCH possesses a unique oddity for Suffolk: a timber-framed chancel. The timber is exposed inside and out, in a modest vernacular style which accords strangely with the hammer-beam roof and carved wall plate. The general effect is quaint rather than beautiful, but memorable in a dotty sort of way.

## Erwarton Hall

*60; 6½ miles SE of Ipswich off B1456*

The Elizabethan brick manor house looks much as it should on the outside, despite much inner remodelling. The important thing is the fantastic little Gatehouse which predates it by a quarter of a century, having been built *c.*1549. It too is of brick, tunnel-vaulted and with no fewer than nine circular brick pinnacles, three down each side which stem from circular buttresses and three more, parallel to them, sprouting from the keystones of the tunnel.

## Framsden Hall

*61; 2½ miles SE of Debenham off B1077*

Originally a hall house, built probably *c.*1480, Framsden Hall has been much altered, but the great timber roof of the Hall can still be seen in some of the bedrooms and – best of all – in the attic. It has kingposts, and great diagonal struts which broaden out in the middle to make room for pierced quatrefoils. There is also a deep wall plate of angels, their wings outstretched – rare indeed in a secular building – and a quantity of fine carvings of heads, portrait and grotesque, on bosses and corbels.

## Freston Tower

*62; 4 miles SE of Ipswich off B1456*

The tower was built about 1550 as a look-out across the Orwell estuary. Though the country around has been largely taken over by the suburban industry of Ipswich, the tower is still a dramatic sight, rising up through six storeys of diapered red brick, its angle buttresses topped with polygonal pinnacles above an openwork parapet, with an embattled stair turret going higher still. The more important windows are pedimented and, on the top floor, transomed as well.

## Ixworth Priory

*63; 4½ miles NE of Bury St Edmunds on A143*

The old Augustinian priory has been much built over and now possesses Georgian fronts to north and west and partly to the east as well. But a surprising amount remains, including almost the whole dormitory range with its beautifully vaulted thirteenth-century undercroft, the slype (converted into a chapel in the seventeenth century) and the timber-framed prior's lodging of about 1470. It is a fascinating example of the way in which monastic buildings were adapted for secular life during the centuries that followed the Dissolution.

## Leiston

*64; 4 miles E of Saxmundham on B1119*

E.B. Lamb was a Victorian architect of wild originality, seldom shown to greater effect than at ST MARGARET'S CHURCH. Most of the space is taken up by the timber roof. You may hate it; I think it's marvellous. LEISTON ABBEY, in the shadow of the nuclear power station at Sizewell, was once a house of the Premonstratensians; there are considerable ruins, now in the care of the Historic Buildings and Monuments Commission.

## Little Saxham

*65; 4 miles W of Bury St Edmunds off A45*

ST NICHOLAS'S CHURCH has the most extraordinary Norman round tower in Suffolk, its top stage consisting of a round-headed arcade; there are four bell openings of deeply recessed twin arches, with pairs of blank arches filling the diagonals. If the rest of the church maintained this standard, it would be in the main list, with a star to boot. But it doesn't, so it isn't.

## Parham

*66; 2 miles SE of Framlingham on B1116*

Half a mile outside the village to the south-east, MOAT HALL is, when seen from the north, quite ridiculously picturesque. It was built around 1490 by the Willoughbys, and descends on this side sheer into the moat. The two canted bays (their gables are later additions) and the tall chimneybreast next to them have beautiful diapered brickwork; Their mullioned and transomed windows were probably all arch-headed originally, as some still are. There is a fine gateway with wild men in niches. CHURCH FARM is nice, too.

## Peasenhall

*67; 3 miles W of Yoxford on A1120*

NEW INN, some 125 yards north-east of the Angel, is a small hall house going back almost certainly to the fifteenth century. Timber-framed and plastered, it has a kingpost roof and part of an original three-light window upstairs. It is now owned – and regularly leased – by the Landmark Trust.

## Polstead

*68; 6 miles SW of Hadleigh off A1071*

A pretty enough little church, but you would never know from the outside of ST MARY'S that it went back to the twelfth century. Inside, all is revealed by the Norman piers and arches – the latter being, most surprisingly, of brick. The bricks may well be the oldest surviving English – as opposed to Roman – ones. Sadly the interior, for all its architectural interest, lacks charm.

## Rougham

*69; 3½ miles SE of Bury St Edmunds off A45*

ST MARY'S CHURCH (formerly St John's) has a splendid Perpendicular tower with good flushwork, traceried windows and inscriptions, and an impressive south porch with a roof of 1632. The inside is mostly Decorated. The single hammer-beam roof must have been a treat, but its angels have all lost their heads to Dowsing and his thugs.

## Shrubland Hall

*70; 6 miles NW of Ipswich off A45*

A mile or so south of Coddenham, Shrubland Hall is now a health clinic. The nucleus of the house is by James Paine and dates from 1770, but it was largely remodelled in 1830–2 by J.P. Gandy-Deering and, twenty years later, by Sir Charles Barry. His is the Italianate overlay – notably the tower; his, too, the glorious terraced gardens, inspired by the Villa d'Este at Tivoli. The style here is very much that of Cliveden or even Osborne. OLD HALL, in the grounds, has two quite remarkable three-light windows, genuine Italian Renaissance this time since they date from *c.*1525. The opulent designs in terracotta are almost certainly the work of craftsmen from Layer Marney (*q.v.*).

## Somerleyton Hall

*71; 7 miles NW of Lowestoft off B1074*

You would never guess from the flamboyantly Victorian–Jacobean–Italianate exterior that the house had a real seventeenth-century core, which still survives in one or two rooms and contains some superb wood carvings in the Grinling Gibbons style. The rest was built by the unfortunately named John Thomas during the ten years after 1844, for Sir Morton Peto, the celebrated builder-entrepreneur and MP. Lovers of High Victoriana should not miss it.

## Stowupland

*72; 1½ miles NE of Stowmarket on A1120*

COLUMBINE HALL, half a mile north-west of the village, is a medieval manor house with a continuous jetty running along two sides, and a moat – once all-embracing – which still laps its walls along three. It is exceedingly pretty and undeniably romantic.

## Stratford St Mary

*73; 9 miles SW of Ipswich off A12*

Another of those big Perpendicular flushwork churches, ST MARY'S is relegated to this list only because of much Victorian restoration. This was however by Woodyer, who is never dull: look, for example, at the 'Decorated' window in the north porch. Among the original flushwork decoration is an entire alphabet – why? The interior furniture includes, equally unaccountably, a bassoon.

## Thornham Parva

*74; 7 miles SW of Diss off A140*

Not only is ST MARY'S CHURCH itself thatched; the tower is too, its thatching descending right down to the ridge of the nave roof. The doorways to south and north are Norman, as is one of the windows on the south side; the little round west window is thought to be Saxon. The great pride of the church – though not strictly architectural – is the famous retable, dating from *c.*1300 – a Crucifixion with eight saints, apparently emanating from the royal workshops of Edward I, and marvellously well preserved.

## Walpole

*75; 2 miles SW of Halesworth on B117*

The CONGREGATIONAL CHAPEL was built in 1607 and converted to religious purposes forty years later. It is all wonderfully evocative of Civil War days – the pulpit as the focal point, scrubbed wooden pews and galleries all around.

## Woodbridge

*76; 9 miles NE of Ipswich off A12*

One of the prettiest small towns in Suffolk, Woodbridge achieves its effect more through the ensemble than because of any individual building. ST MARY'S CHURCH would deserve a place in the main list if the standards set by the tower and the north porch were maintained elsewhere; both provide quite remarkable displays of flushwork, much prominence being given to monogrammed initials. The most interesting secular building is the SHIRE HALL, its core of 1575 (the darker red brick with the stone dressings) but the rest, given its hipped roof, outside double staircases and shaped Dutch gables, a century or so later. There are further good buildings to be seen in SECKFORD STREET and the THOROUGHFARE.

# Surrey

In the seventeenth century, Thomas Fuller compared Surrey to 'a cynamon tree, whose bark is far better than the body thereof. For the skirts and borders bounding this shire are rich and fruitful, whilst the ground in the inward parts thereof is very hungry and barren, though, by reason of the clear air and clean waves, it is full of many gentle habitations.' Inevitably, after 300 years, this statement needs some modification, especially the bit about the air. As for the habitations, it might be argued that in parts of the county at any rate there are now all too many, and that they tend to be not so much gentle as genteel. But this is to do Surrey an injustice. Suburban sprawl has certainly taken its toll, yet there are still vast expanses of unspoilt countryside, over a tenth of which is still woodland, with many a small town and village that has sacrificed little or none of its character to the march of progress.

But character is not the same as architectural excellence, and it must be admitted that, in strictly architectural terms, the county has comparatively little to offer. (Still less since 1965, when several of its brightest jewels, such as Richmond, Ham, Petersham and Kew, were snatched by a voracious Greater London Council and incorporated into the Great Wen.) The reasons for this mediocrity have been variously given: paucity of good building materials, the soggy clay on both sides of the North Downs and their westward extension the Hog's Back, the lack of adequate communications by road or river with London. None of these explanations, however, seems to me entirely satisfactory. In the south, at least, there has never been any shortage of building stone; Reigate stone, or firestone as it was often called, may not be up to Cotswold standards but it was thought good enough for Westminster Abbey and Windsor Castle; Bargate stone, of which there were many small quarries around Guildford and Godalming, was used in the twelfth century for the keep of Guildford Castle, much of which is still standing today. Then there was chalk from the Downs and the Hog's Back, and with chalk, as always, abundant quantities of flint. Wood was everywhere. The clay admittedly presented transportation problems, but the Portsmouth Road was a much-used thoroughfare, at least from the seventeenth century onwards. In any case East Anglia had far less stone than Surrey and was far more cut off from the capital, and East Anglia's medieval church architecture is the best in the country. By contrast, you will find only eight medieval Surrey churches listed below; two – Burstow and Compton – owe their inclusion more to their eccentricity and charm than to any perfection of style, while another three – Wisley, Pyrford and Farleigh – are included merely because any unspoilt Norman church deserves to be, however modest.

Whatever the cause, the fact remains that throughout the Middle Ages Surrey was, of all the counties near London, the most ignored and neglected. To the Normans and the Plantagenets, the Houses of York and of Lancaster, this wild, sparsely inhabited region of hills and forests was a superb hunting ground but very little else. True, it possessed one or two monasteries of some renown including, at Waverley, the first Cistercian abbey in all England; but this is now only a few picturesquely scattered fragments in a water-meadow beside the Wey, while its principal rival, the seventh-century Benedictine foundation at Chertsey, was demolished by Cardinal Wolsey to provide stone for Hampton Court.

Just about the same time as that great palace began to rise across the river in Middlesex, however, another of Henry VIII's closest advisers was planning for himself a country house which, though on a far more modest scale, was destined to prove almost as important a milestone in English secular architecture. It was at Sutton Place that Surrey was first touched by the breath of the Renaissance, and Sutton Place remains, externally, unchanged and still looking much as it always did. Would that the same could be said of Nonsuch, the fabulous prodigy palace that Henry began in 1538, calling in artists and artisans from all over Western Europe to make it the most sumptuous and sophisticated building England had ever seen. Alas, Nonsuch lasted little over a century. It was pulled down in 1687 – perhaps, with the destruction of the City of London in 1940–1, the most tragic architectural loss in our history.

The seventeenth and eighteenth centuries saw a gradual improvement in the situation. As Surrey slowly blossomed as a result of new agricultural prosperity, building in both town and country took on a fresh impetus. Both Guildford and Farnham bear witness to how distinguished the new urban architecture could be, and already by the 1630s small country houses were springing up everywhere – particularly in the north of the county, where London was more accessible and the Thames helped communications. Most of these houses were very much what one might have expected, but there is one smallish group that deserves a special mention, and that is the houses built around 1630–50 in the style which Sir John Summerson has called 'Artisan Mannerism'. This had its roots in the City of London, where the leading craftsmen – and above all the bricklayers, since it was essentially a brick style – developed a handsome new idiom which drew something from Jacobean Renaissance and something from the current fashions in the Low Countries, with Dutch gables, pediments (triangular, segmental or even broken), columns, pilasters and elaborate architraves, all executed in virtuoso brickwork. The style spread through the Home Counties and East Anglia, but it is in Surrey more than anywhere that it has survived at its best. Now that Kew Palace can no longer be included, the masterpieces of the genre are to be found at West Horsley and Slyfield Manor; there are lesser examples everywhere.

But Artisan Mannerism, for all its potential elegance, has a homely touch about it. What Surrey lacks is palaces, showpieces, really great houses of splendour and magnificence. Squires and landed gentry were two a penny, yet somehow the nobility tended to keep away. Of the only two notable exceptions, it is worth noting that the Duke of Newcastle was still a commoner, Thomas Pelham, when he bought Claremont from Vanbrugh in 1714; while the barony of Lord Onslow, the builder of Clandon, was of still more recent creation. And even before their respective elevations, neither the Pelhams nor the Onslows could claim any long associations with the county. Newcastle's was particularly short-lived: his wife sold Claremont in 1768 to Lord Clive, who immediately demolished it, leaving Kent's island temple in the park and the Vanbrugh pew in Esher church as the only tangible memorials of his passing. The Onslows did better. Clandon, like Sutton, survives intact and, thanks to Leoni's Marble Hall, can contest with Sutton pride of place among Surrey buildings.

And yet, paradoxically, it is only with the nineteenth century that the county really comes into its own. Few rural counties can boast more, or better, Victorian architecture per square mile. Among the churches, despite much noble work by Pugin, Pearson, Butterfield, Bodley and Burges, it is the comparatively obscure name of Henry Woodyer that forces itself upon the memory. (Mrs Watts at Compton is, needless to say, in a class by herself.) On the domestic front, in face of stiff competition from Philip Webb, Norman Shaw and C. F. A. Voysey, it is the young Lutyens who, in the last years of Victoria's reign, carries all before him, pointing new ways for the new century which, alas, his successors never seemed quite able to follow; post-Edwardian Surrey architecture is miserable indeed.

---

## Burstow

*1; 4 miles N of Crawley off B2037*

The point about ST BARTHOLOMEW'S CHURCH is the tower and slender broach spire, in which everything, including the four pointed pinnacles at the corners, is made of wood: weatherboarding below, shingles above, like an Essex belfry. The shingling, presumably eighteenth-century though on a fifteenth-century frame, is admirably done, though the general effect is, perhaps, more curious than beautiful. The interior of the tower is equally interesting, with six dangling bell ropes and much campanological paraphernalia. It makes one wonder that such a fragile-looking structure can be strong enough for a peal of six. The rest of the church is mainly fifteenth-century, though a few Norman details have survived; it is pretty enough, but unremarkable. John Flamsteed, the first Astronomer Royal, is buried in the chancel.

## Clandon Park

*NT; 2; 3 miles E of Guildford off A248*

It is not at first sight an attractive house. There is something distinctly uncompromising about that great static block of red brickwork, a heaviness that the pedimented three-bay stone centrepiece does little if anything to lighten. Ignore, insofar as you can, the atrocious Victorian vestibule and *porte-cochère*, erected in a moment of aberration by the 4th Earl of Onslow in 1876; I have no doubt that the National Trust would remove it if they could ever afford to. There is still little enough in those frowning façades – a strange mixture of Baroque and Palladian styles with French, English and Italian motifs – to redound to the credit of Clandon's putative architect, Giacomo Leoni.

I say 'putative' not because there is any doubt about Leoni's involvement with the house, but because there is enough conflicting evidence about the dating (probably 1729–33) to make it uncertain whether he had control of the building from the very start or, if he did, whether later alterations have not blurred his original design. Despite the fact that he was a Venetian *émigré* who had published the first adequate English edition of Palladio's *Quattro Libri dell'Architettura* in 1715–20, Leoni's other work in England – at Lyme Park in Cheshire, for example – shows that he was never a doctrinaire Palladian like Colen Campbell or Lord Burlington; nonetheless one cannot help feeling that he was a more sensitive architect than the exterior of Clandon suggests and that, left to himself, he would have done a better job.

Why, then, include the house in this book? Because, once we enter, the whole scene changes. Suddenly we find ourselves in the purest Palladian atmosphere, in a great Marble Hall of which that of Houghton in Norfolk is the only rival. Here is Leoni at his breathtaking best.

Clandon Park.

Like Kent at Houghton, he seems to have intended a deliberate contrast between the cool whiteness of the Hall and the rich colour of the state rooms beyond. Like Kent, too, he owes an immense debt to three outstanding artists who worked in both houses: the sculptor Rysbrack, whose two fireplaces and overmantels are both major works of art in their own right, and the two stuccoists Artari and Bagutti who again indulge in one of their favourite conceits – figures, full-blown men this time and not just *putti*, breaking out over the cornice and dangling their legs over the space below. At Clandon, however, the plasterwork is far more adventurous, with feats of foreshortening and perspective never attempted at Houghton.

In the Saloon, which is predictably the grandest of the state rooms after the Hall itself, the two Italians have kept their exuberance rather more in check, though neither the ceiling nor their marbled overmantel could ever be described as restrained. The Saloon is interesting for another reason too, however; when the National Trust restored the room in 1968–9, John Fowler's careful cleaning and exploratory scrapes revealed the original colour scheme. The decoration therefore now looks essentially as it must have looked in the 1730s. The other state rooms maintain a high standard, particularly the Palladian Room with its flock wallpaper of *c.*1780 and the Green Drawing Room with more plasterwork by Artari and Bagutti, and provide a splendid setting for the outstanding collection of furniture and ceramics left to the Trust by Mrs David Gubbay in 1968.

## Claremont

*3; ½ mile SE of Esher on A244*
*Includes Claremont Landscape Garden (NT)*

Few houses of its size are more awe-inspiring to the new arrival than Claremont. Of cream brick with stone dressings, it stands detached on all sides, squarely on top of a hill. Pity the poor little schoolgirls who, on the first evening of their first term, climb the twenty-two steps to that gigantic portico, suitcase clutched in clammy palm. One can only hope that their faith in Christian Science – the persuasion to whose principles Claremont School is dedicated – sustains them.

It was not always so. Sir John Vanbrugh described the square battlemented house that he built for himself on the estate in 1708 as 'a very small box'; but that was demolished in 1769 by Lord Clive, recently returned from India. Clive fortunately left Vanbrugh's mock medieval Belvedere on a mound to the south-west, his White Cottage and his massive red-brick garden walls, but he decided on a brand-new house; and to build it, on a higher, drier and (he thought) healthier site, he commissioned Lancelot 'Capability' Brown. Work began in 1771, Brown working in close association with the young Henry Holland, who thenceforth became a sort of unofficial partner and two years later married Brown's daughter, Bridget. About this time, too, Holland in his turn took on an assistant, his nineteen-year-old pupil John Soane, who was later to claim responsibility for the beautiful elliptical Entrance Hall, the most distinguished room in the house – though the classical reliefs, the main doorways and the inlaid floor, echoing the design of the ceiling, were probably borrowed by Holland from Robert Wood's *Ruins of Palmyra*, published twenty years before. By 1774 the work was done, but in that same year Clive committed suicide at his house in Berkeley Square and it is uncertain whether he ever moved in. On the other hand the Rev Francis Kilvert, visiting Claremont on 18 January 1871, wrote in his diary of how he was shown Lord Clive's bedroom: 'When the S.W. gales blew and rattled the windows Lord Clive used to get up in the night to wedge them tight and guineas being more plentiful with him than anything else he always used them. The housemaids used to transfer these guineas to their own pockets in the morning and prayed with reason for a S.W. storm.'

The design of the house owes much to the advanced ideas of Lord and Lady Clive, which must have seemed highly eccentric to their contemporaries. The extraordinarily high basement, for example, was the result of Lady Clive's view that normal basements were too damp and unhealthy for the servants. Hers too seems to have been the decision to appropriate the western half of the main floor as a separate private suite. Clive himself insisted on the provision, under the south portico, of a vaulted bathroom with a sunken marble bath big enough – just – to swim in. Other conveniences were water closets, and a separate kitchen block connected with the main house by an underground tunnel to preserve the simple elevations on all four sides. The state rooms themselves, apart from the Entrance Hall, are not particularly memorable; but the quality of decoration –

*The Entrance Hall, Claremont.*

varying as it does between Brown's Palladian style and the more delicate neo-classicism of Holland and Soane – maintains a generally high level. One is therefore not totally surprised to learn that Claremont was a royal residence from 1816 – when it was bought by Princess Charlotte, daughter of the Prince Regent, and her husband Prince Leopold of Saxe-Coburg, later King of the Belgians – until 1922. Queen Victoria often stayed there as a child and in the first years of her reign, and in 1848 it became the refuge of the French King Louis-Philippe and Queen Marie-Amélie, both of whom died in the house.

CLAREMONT LANDSCAPE GARDEN (NT) is one of the earliest and most important in the country. Begun by Vanbrugh, it was continued by Henry Bridgeman (who was probably responsible for the unique turf amphitheatre), then by Kent and afterwards, naturally enough, by Brown himself. Since 1949 it has been the property of the National Trust, who have recently completed a brilliant restoration.

## Compton*

*4; 4 miles SW of Guildford off A3*

Few small churches anywhere in the country have more character than ST NICHOLAS'S, Compton. As you walk up the hill towards it, its charm is already evident with the three little flat-topped dormers marking the tiny clerestory, behind them the squat stone and flint Saxon tower of *c.*970 with a fourteenth-century shingled broach spire above, and two of the most magnificent cedars in England providing the backdrop. A closer look at the tower reveals quantities of broken red tiles, almost certainly from some neighbouring Roman villa. There is also a finely ornamented Norman south doorway.

But none of this really prepares you for the surprise that awaits within. First of all, the whiteness of the arcades, made of hardened chalk, or 'clunch', from the Hog's Back; the piers round and very Norman – 1180 or so – with scalloped or foliated capitals, the arches just beginning to show a tentative point. Eastward along these the eye travels, under the chancel arch (a nineteenth-century copy in stone of the original arch), with very rare twelfth-century painted lozenge decoration above it, to Compton's unique feature, its double sanctuary dating from around 1170. For reasons which remain a mystery, the sanctuary proper has been given a very low rib vault, above which is a completely separate chamber, open to the western part of the chancel like a deep gallery. Along the front of it runs a wooden balustrade cut from a single gigantic plank – one of the earliest pieces of Norman woodwork still surviving. Rarer and still more wonderful is the sliver of stained glass in the Norman east window: a Virgin crowned, with Child, dating at the very latest from the beginning of the thirteenth century. There is other glass of this date at Canterbury and York, but little – very little – anywhere else in England.

This church alone would be worth the drive out from London. But Compton has another treat in store – the MORTUARY CHAPEL to the painter G.F. Watts, designed by his widow in 1896 and erected in the years following by her and a team of villagers she had trained, with no professional assistance but that of the local builder and blacksmith. Surrey may have plenty to show more fair, but nothing, surely, more monumentally dotty. 'It looms', writes Wilfrid Blunt, curator of the Watts Gallery nearby, 'excessively red on its green hillside, strident like a London bus that has strayed down a country lane. Of this defect . . . Mary Watts was acutely aware: "I always hoped", she once said, "that it would *tone down.*" Alas! it never did.' Its style is difficult to define; there are suggestions of Tuscan vernacular, southern Romanesque, Bavarian Rococo, Bentleyesque Byzantine, Celtic Revival and Norman-Viking of the school of Kilpeck, all rather uncertainly held together via a decorative scheme by the Arts and Crafts movement out of *art nouveau* and itself pregnant with symbolism.

But it is with the interior that Mrs Watts has gone, as it were, to town. Here *art nouveau* has triumphed, though Celtic Revival has clearly fought a spirited rearguard action before fleeing from the field. And what a field! The ground plan being that of 'The Circle of Eternity run through by the Cross of Faith', the impression is that of a high, curiously vaulted, circular chamber with four stubby transepts radiating from it, every single square inch of which is literally encrusted with the gesso ornamentation. (Mary Watts called it 'glorified wallpaper'.) At the lower level a row of vaguely Burne-Jonesian angels stands sentinel; above them, cherubim and seraphim; around them Trees of Life, writhing and twining their tendrils in endless convolutions of golden toothpaste. The whole Chapel glows with colour and richness and – one is surprised to note – a certain reverential joy which ultimately disarms criticism. We may not find it beautiful in the conventional sense; we may not even manage to take it altogether seriously; but we cannot withhold admiration for the sheer creative energy that gave it being.

## Dunsfold*

*5; 8 miles S of Guildford off B2130*

William Morris called ST MARY AND ALL SAINTS 'the most beautiful country church in all England'. Not quite, perhaps; but the detailing of this lovely little Early English church is quite exceptionally fine – it was almost certainly built by royal masons – and the overall design is well-nigh perfect. In any case, a church that has survived essentially unchanged for over seven centuries is always worth a visit, and the quiet and unassuming modesty of Dunsfold only adds to its charm. The chancel arch, it must be admitted, was renewed and heightened in 1882, and the east window was restored at the same time. The shingled bell turret is probably of the fifteenth century. For the rest, the church looks much as it must have in about 1300 when the lovely west window was added. Even the benches are original, among the oldest in England, and very beautiful they are too.

## East Horsley Towers

*6; 7½ miles NE of Guildford off B2039*

The Compton Mortuary Chapel was hard enough to describe; East Horsley Towers is impossible. The first sight of that tremendous Neo-Norman two-storey entrance lodge is enough to send your car into the ditch; but it is the palest reflection of what is to come. Eschew this main lodge, turn left, then after a few hundred yards go in at the next, smaller, lodge. You pass under an arch, then through a long curved tunnel into, of all things, a horseshoe-shaped cloister in patterned flint and polychrome brick; thence a horseshoe arch brings you out by a huge round tower to the main entrance. No house in England can provide a more sensational approach; so outlandish are the forms, so violent the designs, so strident the colours that you are visually punch-drunk long before you reach the front door.

This wonderfully awful place is the creation of the 1st Earl of Lovelace, Byron's son-in-law. It has as its core a rather boring, rectangular, mock Tudor house by Barry, but soon after inheriting it Lovelace began the programme of 'improvements' which he was to continue, on and off, until his death in 1893. He was quite an accomplished amateur engineer – the curved trusses of the Great Hall he built in 1847 were bent by a steam process of his own invention – but as he proceeded his fantasies grew wilder and wilder. The over-riding idiom seems to be a vaguely Italianate Gothic, but in reality East Horsley is like nothing but itself, a grotesque Victorian Disneyland which has to be seen to be believed – and may not be even then. Worse still, the infection has somehow spread all over the estate; south along the A246 and north as far as Ockham, in houses, cottages, lodges, even in schools, those dread symptoms appear again and again, with undiminished virulence, until one has fears for one's sanity. Unlike virtually all the other entries in this book, therefore, this one is not a recommendation: it is a warning.

*St Nicholas's Church, Compton.*

## Egham

*7; 18 miles SW of London on A30*

The sight of ROYAL HOLLOWAY COLLEGE, whether distant on the skyline or in all its glory at close quarters, invariably has the same effect on me – an effect which can but be compared to that of a triple whisky and soda. Despite its gigantic size – it is considerably larger than Hampton Court – it was built in only eight years, from 1879 to 1887, at the behest of Thomas Holloway who, having amassed a huge fortune through Holloway's Pills, decided to found what was to be one of the first women's colleges in the country. For his model he chose, rather surprisingly, the Château de Chambord, and for his architect W.H. Crossland, who spent two years doing fieldwork on the banks of the Loire before building began. The finished work now stands, a dazzling extravaganza on a French Renaissance theme, red-brick, bristling like some gargantuan pincushion with towers and turrets, cupolas and tall, segmental-headed chimneys; never pompous like Waddesdon, but full of life and movement and *joie de vivre*. The best of the inside features are the Chapel and the Art Gallery, the latter being of particular interest since nearly all the paintings were bought between 1881 and 1883, thus representing the height of informed artistic taste at that precise moment.

About a mile away to the south is Crossland's companion piece, HOLLOWAY SANATORIUM, as Flemish as the College is French. Long, low wings, topped with crow-stepped gables such as you might find at Ghent or Bruges, run off each side of a Great Hall, arcaded at ground level, behind whose steep hipped roof rises a pinnacled tower which is palpably England's answer to the Cloth Hall at Ypres. The whole design is informed with the same energy and vitality as the College, and a self-assurance that leaves one gasping.

*St George's Church, Esher.*

## Esher

*8; 15 miles SW of London on A3*

ST GEORGE'S CHURCH is conveniently situated just behind the Bear Hotel. Stone-built in the mid-sixteenth century, its weatherboard bell turret capped with a pyramid roof, it looks pretty enough but not especially exciting. Go in regardless, for the sake of the two surprises: one is the double-tiered gallery at the west end, the lower tier nicely bow-fronted and supported on slender fluted columns of indeterminate style; the other is the so-called family pew, designed in 1725 by Vanbrugh for the Duke of Newcastle, to whom, ten years before, he had sold his house at nearby Claremont (*q.v.*). This is in fact not so much a pew as a separate chapel set into the south wall; from the nave it appears as a gallery with an elegant temple front, its high triangular pediment supported on two Corinthian columns and two matching angle pillars. You enter by a separate door – the key is kept in the little office adjoining the church – to find two large box pews, each furnished with its own fireplace, in which the Duke, his family and their guests could certainly have made themselves very comfortable, pleasantly protected from the common gaze and sustained when necessary from the Bear across the way.

A little to the west of the London road, beyond the green, stands a grand early Tudor GATEHOUSE. This is all that remains of Esher Place, the great mansion built for himself around 1475–80 by William of Waynflete, Bishop of Winchester and founder of Magdalen College, Oxford. Three-storeyed, but flanked with four-storeyed polygonal towers, its façade of blue-diapered red brick is imposing enough; in its original form, however, it could not have competed with that of Oxburgh in Norfolk – its almost exact contemporary – or the slightly later Layer Marney in Essex. What makes it unique is the work done on it in the early 1730s by William Kent, who was commissioned by Henry Pelham, the Duke of Newcastle's younger brother, to incorporate it into a new country house. The result (together with Kent's other Gothicising gatehouse in the Clock Court at Hampton Court) marks the first tentative beginnings of the Gothic Revival as we know it. The big quatrefoil openings, the straight Tudor labels over the faintly ogival arches – both these features are hallmarks of Kentian Gothick, which is feeling its way to a lightness and delicacy far removed from the heavy, monumental sort of medievalism attempted by Wren at Christ Church or Hawksmoor at Westminster Abbey. Whether it is successful in its context is another matter; it remains an architectural milestone, even if it is of the eighteenth century rather than the fifteenth.

## Farnham

*9; 10 miles SW of Guildford on A3*

The CASTLE was built largely in the twelfth century, at which time it served a purely military purpose; then, in the following century, it was given a lower domestic court and became a principal residence of the Bishops of Winchester during their constant progresses through their diocese. One of these, William of Waynflete, endowed it with an extraordinary brick tower in about

*Farnham Castle.*

1470 – shortly before he started work on his Gatehouse at Esher – which, architecturally speaking, is the most remarkable feature of the entire castle. Its original windows were alas replaced with segmental-headed ones in the eighteenth century, but all the rest is as Waynflete left it, including the entrance arch which has been deliberately set off-centre and even cuts through a corner of one of the flanking turrets. The rooms inside have decoration of *c.*1670. After the Waynflete Tower, little seems to have been done to the castle till the Civil War when, like so many other medieval castles up and down the country, it had to be hurriedly readapted for military purposes. The work cannot have been outstandingly successful; Farnham was forever being taken and retaken, suffering considerable damage in the process. With the Restoration an extensive programme of rebuilding was begun, and it is from this period that we get the undistinguished brick front to the Great Hall and the beautiful Chapel of about 1680, its panelling embellished with wood carvings by Grinling Gibbons.

In the eighteenth century, emphasis shifted from the castle to the town. Farnham is still pre-eminently Georgian in spirit, and WEST STREET and CASTLE STREET are both justly famous. The end of West Street where the two converge is called THE BOROUGH, and it is here that the character of Farnham is best seen – in particular the virtuoso brickwork which is used for columns, capitals, niches, garlands, even carved bowls of flowers. Too much of the Georgian is, it must be admitted, of the 'Neo' variety; there is a slight self-consciousness in the air that can prove irritating to spirits more sensitive than mine. For all that, Farnham remains an unusually pleasant place which is further enhanced by the perpetual contrast between castle and town, stone and brick, feudalism and the age of elegance.

## Guildford

*10; 28 miles SW of London on A3*

According to William Cobbett, Guildford was 'the prettiest, and taken altogether the most agreeable and most happy-looking town that I ever saw in my life'. It began, as its name implies, as a ford, the place where the east–west road running along the high chalk ridge dropped steeply down to cross the River Wey, then rose still more steeply up again to follow the continuation of that ridge – what we know as the Hog's Back. The eastern approach to the ford is now the High Street, and Guildford has remained a linear town. One looks in vain for a central square, a market place or any other focal point. Guildford has a backbone but no heart.

Fortunately that backbone, the HIGH STREET, is a very good one indeed. Despite the bypass, the weekday traffic is appalling; but a Sunday morning walk is full of rewards. Start from the eastern end of the High Street. The first building of interest is on the left, the stone-gabled quadrangle of the GRAMMAR SCHOOL. It was founded in 1509 – the year of Henry VIII's accession – and was completed by 1586. There is no real architectural distinction, but few better examples exist of town grammar schools of Tudor times. Now walk on as the High Street begins to fall away – the hill grows steeper as it gets nearer the river – keeping on the left-hand side. This is important, as from now on all the best buildings are on the right (the sunny side) and only from the opposite pavement will you be able to see them properly. They start off with a considerable bang, in the shape of the towering red-brick ABBOT'S HOSPITAL. It is a deceptive building, a conscious archaism, aping as it does the great early Tudor gatehouses such as Esher or Hampton Court, whereas it was actually built in 1619–22. But it is none the worse for that, and the quadrangle within,

*The High Street, Guildford.*

formed by the almshouses founded by George Abbot, Archbishop of Canterbury, is a model of its Jacobean kind – simple and straightforward, but beautifully proportioned. It has also been lucky enough to keep nearly all its original furnishings and fitments – especially in the Dining Room and Chapel. The Duke of Monmouth was held here on his way back to London after the battle of Sedgemoor in 1685.

Just beyond at No. 155 is GUILDFORD HOUSE, of 1660, though the bow-fronted shop windows are a century or so later. Then comes LLOYDS BANK, with a marvellously unexpected ground floor of pilasters and columns and round-headed windows and some splendid plaster *fioritura* in the spandrels of the door; and so to the climax of the High Street, the GUILDHALL. This is the centre of Guildford, if anything is. The façade is a remodelling of 1683; its three-bay first floor is projected on caryatid brackets over the street, and above this is a strange trapezoidal pediment, on whose flat top is perched an octagonal lantern with weathervane, and from whose front projects – to an extent that makes one tremble for the entire building's centre of gravity – the Town Clock. This, also of 1683, is a work of art in itself, as are the great gilded beam and the elaborate wrought-iron ties that suspend it with exhibitionist bravado over the road.

Apart from these buildings – and many others of considerable distinction but lesser importance – Guildford also boasts a castle and a cathedral. Alas, neither is really up to scratch. The CASTLE consists of little more than the outer shell of its tower keep, now open to the sky; the CATHEDRAL – on Stag Hill, half a mile away to the north-west – is the work of Sir Edward Maufe, built between 1936 and 1961. It is better than it looks; but when you think of what Giles Gilbert Scott was achieving in Liverpool at the same time it is difficult to summon up much enthusiasm.

## Hascombe

*11; 6 miles S of Godalming on B2130*

Here is a rarity indeed. Nearly all the best Victorian churches are in cities and towns; when an architect had to design a church for a small village, he tended not to bother very much. Hascombe, however, is an exception. Henry Woodyer is not generally considered to be in the front rank of nineteenth-century architects, but at ST PETER'S he produced a church of real distinction. It was built, of Bargate stone, in exactly a year – between June 1863 and June 1864 – at a cost of £3,100. The design is simple enough, with a nave (supporting a shingled bell-cote and short broach spire), an apsed chancel and a separately roofed Lady Chapel to the south, all in simplified late thirteenth-century style. Within this small space there is any amount to admire: the decorative scheme of the nave, based on the post-Resurrection miracle of St Peter's net; the composition of chancel arch, ornate rood-screen beneath (fifteenth-century, but heavily restored in 1864) and immense rood above, backed by the cusped and gilded woodwork of the chancel roof, its rafters radiating around the curve of the apse; both of these are as unusual as they are unforgettable. Stranger still is the east window, a single, slender lancet set within a buttress, yet somehow giving the eye just the degree of focus it needs. The interior decoration throughout, including the glass, is by Hardman and Powell; their names too deserve to be remembered.

HOE FARM, to the west, has a Dining Room wing and staircase added by Sir Edwin Lutyens, who was also responsible for HIGH HASCOMBE HOUSE (in vernacular style) nearby.

## Hatchlands

*NT; 12; 3 miles NE of Guildford off A246*

The modest Palladian house of vermilion brick was built at the edge of the village of East Clandon by Admiral Edward Boscawen in 1757. 'Palladian,' one says lightly; but what would Palladio have said of a house that had three storeys on its western elevation and two to the south? At one point there is yet another horizontal sub-division, with the result that this rather prim-looking eighteenth-century house actually functions at seven different levels, all conveniently connected by ingeniously arranged staircases. Strangely enough this does not seem to matter, either inside or out; the eye instantaneously adjusts, if indeed it notices at all. Yet the question remains: what professional architect would have permitted himself such a design? The answer is, surely, none; the architects, in all probability, were the admiral himself – who, as a seaman, knew all there was to know about the economical use of space – and his brilliant and talented wife.

In 1759 they took the step which, for later generations, put their house firmly on the map by placing the interior decoration in the hands of Robert Adam, then aged thirty-one and just returned from Italy and Dalmatia. This was his first commission and is, not surprisingly, still a little tentative; his hand is plainly recognisable in several of the rooms, particularly the Library and Drawing Room, but anyone looking for a showpiece like Osterley or Syon will be disappointed. The most ostentatious room in the house is in fact the Music Room, added by Sir Reginald Blomfield in 1903. The Garden Hall and the flat pilastered frontispiece on the west front are by Joseph Bonomi, who also turned the first-floor Saloon into a bedroom at the end of the eighteenth century.

Hatchlands is at present let by the National Trust to tenants who use it as a finishing school. It is not, in consequence, looking its best. It is, on the other hand, open to the public, and it possesses considerable architectural and decorative interest. I would only suggest that, if you are going to Clandon Park on the same day, you should see Hatchlands first, not afterwards.

## Kew Gardens

See London section.

## Kew Palace

See London section (Kew Gardens).

## Kingswood

*13; 3 miles N of Reigate on A217*

The CHURCH OF ST SOPHIA in Lower Kingswood is, with the Watts Mortuary Chapel at Compton, the biggest architectural surprise that Surrey has to offer. Built in 1891 by Sidney Barnsley at the behest of the Byzantine scholar Dr Edwin Freshfield, it represents a true enthusiast's tribute to Byzantium. Already the Greek cupola strikes a bizarre note in its Betjemanesque environment, but the interior is more unexpected still. The chancel continues directly from the nave; its walls are faced entirely with marble and it ends in a mosaic apse, dominated by a cross almost certainly inspired by that in a similar position in St Irene, Istanbul. Moreover, distributed around the church are no fewer than nine Byzantine capitals brought back from the east by Dr Freshfield; they include two from St John of Studium at Istanbul, two from the imperial palace at Blachernae, and three from St John at Ephesus. Speaking strictly architecturally, this church may be no great shakes; but its curiosity value is high indeed.

## Lingfield

*14; 7½ miles NE of Crawley on B2028*

The CHURCH OF ST PETER AND ST PAUL, built in 1431, is Surrey's only important Perpendicular church – and very fine it is too. Because the north aisle is the same length and breadth as the nave and continues into an east chapel of the same dimensions as the chancel (the south aisle being considerably shorter and ending in a vestry), the initial impression is that of a double-naved church – which, since it was originally intended to serve as a collegiate as well as a parish church, it may well have been. There is everywhere a feeling of airiness, lightness and space, accentuated by the huge five-light east window and an agreeable absence of clutter; and, as bonuses, Lingfield offers you stalls with splendid misericords, a superb set of tombs – especially those of the Cobhams – and the finest brasses in the county.

## Loseley House*

*15; 2½ miles SW of Guildford off B3000*

An inscription over the inner door of the Entrance Hall reads '*Invidiae claudor, pateo sed semper amico*' – 'I am closed to envy, but open always to a friend.' This glorious Elizabethan house of greenish Bargate stone is indeed open to the public, but it is hard not to feel envious. It was started in 1562 and completed in 1568, at a total cost of £1,640 19*s* 7*d*, by Sir William More, one of Queen Elizabeth's most trusted advisers and a direct

*Loseley House.*

ancestor of the present owner. He seems to have been his own architect, and a competent one too: the main front (to the north) is not spectacular – Loseley has no pretensions to being a prodigy house – but with its pattern of advancing bays in an undulating 1–2–3–2–3–2–1 rhythm it has plenty of movement and shows due respect for the laws of symmetry, which were assuming increasing importance as the century progressed. Oddly, this symmetry does not extend to the fenestration; in no two units is the window arrangement repeated. Elegance was all very well, but this is a house in which practical considerations obviously came first. (The main doorway of Portland stone is an addition of *c.*1689.)

Inside, Loseley is one delight after another. The lofty Great Hall with its flat beamed ceiling is dominated by a glorious painting of Sir More Molyneux and his family in 1739, obviously intended for its present position; otherwise the Hall is essentially of the date of the house, with a grand Elizabethan overmantel and plenty of good panelling – including some false perspectives carved in brilliant *trompe-l'oeil* – which was brought to Loseley from Henry VIII's great palace of Nonsuch, demolished in the late seventeenth century. There is more good panelling in the Library (Jacobean but with a pronounced Victorian accent) and, in the Drawing Room beyond, a beautiful ceiling, gilded for the visit of James I, to say nothing of the most sensational fireplace in the house, a grandly exuberant composition of columns and caryatids, strapwork and coats of arms, garlands and vermiculated rustication, all hewn by some genius of an Elizabethan mason from a single block of snow-white clunch. The upstairs bedrooms, too, are as good as you might expect. Everything is lovingly maintained, by a family to whom it has belonged for over 400 years and who know and cherish every inch of it. If he could see the house he created today, old Sir William would be proud indeed.

## Lowfield Heath

*16; 2 miles N of Crawley off A32*

This village has now been completely swallowed up in Gatwick Airport. Should you, however, find yourself stranded at the airport – and who doesn't, sooner or later? – one of the best ways to cheer yourself up is to make a quick visit to ST MICHAEL'S CHURCH, just opposite the modern Gatwick Hikmet Hotel. It was built in 1867 by that most eccentric and enjoyable of Victorian architects, William Burges. Ian Nairn has written that 'Burges's sense of fun got closer to the original childlike spirit of Early Gothic invention than did either piety or historical accuracy.' I am not sure that this is strictly true, but it is certainly arguable; at any rate Burges is always worth looking at, and St Michael's is well up to his form. There is a very jolly rose window (a wheel really, with columnar spokes) over the lean-to porch, which is quite a feature in itself – neither Arts-and-Craftsy nor *art nouveau*, being too early for either of them, but with an indefinable something of both. The stained glass in the east end is in the same idiom, whatever it is.

## Munstead

*17; 1½ miles SE of Godalming off B2130*

Not so much a village, more a way of life, this wooded region above Godalming is really a shrine to that remarkable *fin-de-siècle* partnership, Gertrude Jekyll and Sir Edwin Lutyens. Miss Jekyll's first residence, MUNSTEAD HOUSE, is not by Lutyens, though he made subsequent alterations to it and added the Orangery; but between 1891 and 1900 he produced, within a square mile or two, at least a dozen houses, cottages or pavilions of one kind or another. To one of them, MUNSTEAD WOOD, Miss Jekyll shortly removed; for nearly all of them, she designed the garden. Pilgrims to the shrine can do a circuit of MUNSTEAD PLACE, MUNSTEAD WOOD, MUNSTEAD WOOD HUT, THE QUADRANGLE, THUNDER HOUSE, MUNSTEAD ORCHARD and LITTLE MUNSTEAD – though they should be warned that none of these houses is normally open to the public; if, however, they have the time and energy for one only, I would suggest ORCHARDS, in Munstead Heath Road. The approach is quietly dramatic, past a long projecting wing running parallel with the drive, buttressed, creeper-hung and with, on the first two bays, tiny slit windows only; then under a high arch with a totally useless dormer window above it – a typical Lutyens joke – and so into the inner quadrangle, facing the entrance. Look carefully at the continuous line of high windows, carrying on round the projecting porch almost as if it didn't exist; at the way in which the chimneys are arranged, asymmetrically but nonetheless perfectly balanced; at the loggia to the right, its three semi-circular arches decorated with the same motif of radiating tiles that he was to use again at Tigbourne Court; this is Lutyens at his most characteristic and inventive.

## Ockham

*18; 3 miles NW of East Horsley on B2039*

Let the visitor beware: if he is a lover of country churches he will be all too familiar with the frustration of finding a church locked, and the subsequent relief when he runs to earth the vicar or churchwarden who produces the key. He will realise, of course, that in certain areas where vandalism and thefts are common, churches *must* be kept locked, and will accept the situation philosophically. But has he ever found a vicar who, at three o'clock on a Saturday afternoon, politely but categorically refuses to hand that key over? This happened to me, for the first and only time in my life, at ALL SAINTS, Ockham. Proofs of identity, and offers of credit cards, driving licence, watch and wallet as security for my good behaviour and the key's safe return were alike in vain. In consequence, while I have admired the church's seven-lancet east window – a phenomenon equalled in England only by Blakeney in Norfolk – from the outside, I have never seen the interior. But everyone tells me it is the finest Early English church in the county, and since good medieval churches are all too rare in Surrey I am including it here.

## Petersham

See London section (Sudbrook Park).

## Polesden Lacey

*NT; 19; 3 miles NW of Dorking off A246*

Not a great house, but an immensely agreeable one, Polesden Lacey is a delightful place in which to spend a sunny summer afternoon. The early seventeenth-century house bought by Richard Brinsley Sheridan is no more; its place has been taken by an unpretentious Neo-Grecian villa of 1824 by Cubitt, much enlarged by Ambrose Poynter in 1906. Cubitt's is the centre of the south front – the four bays covered by the eight-columned portico and one additional bay on each side – and Poynter's all the rest. The interior is unabashedly Edwardian, and recaptures as well as any house I know the atmosphere of the years before the First World War when all London society from the King down would descend on Polesden Lacey at the invitation of Mrs Ronald Greville. Here too King George VI and Queen Elizabeth spent part of their honeymoon in 1923. The pictures, furniture and works of art – to say nothing of the glorious gardens – amply make up for any lack of architectural distinction.

## Richmond

See London section (Asgill House; Ham House).

*All Saints' Church, Ockham.*

## Slyfield Manor

*20; 2 miles NW of Leatherhead off A245*

There seem to be three principal dates in the building history of Slyfield, though only the last of them is known with very great accuracy. The first was probably some time in the middle or later fifteenth century, when the house was first built, around a courtyard, with its entrance on the north side. The second comes some time between 1614, when it was bought by one George Shiers, and 1642 when he died. And the last was 1743, when the north-eastern and south-western parts were demolished. What is left is the south-east corner, to which Shiers added a further extension towards the east, the two together now constituting the present house; and an L-shaped block which comprises roughly half the former northern and western ranges and which is now Slyfield Farm. All parts of the old house were, however, largely rebuilt by Shiers, and the architectural impression it gives today is almost wholly of King Charles I's time.

The house itself faces south, framed by splendid old cedars. It is of two storeys and seven bays, the latter being separated by bulgy brick pilasters with spreading capitals and badges – likewise carved in the brick – halfway up. This text-book example of the Artisan Mannerist school is finished off to the left (where the south-east corner of the courtyard would originally have been) by a huge Dutch gable, beneath which is a four-light window whose segmental head breaks through the cornice. At first glance this might seem to be a later insertion to give more light to the master bedroom within; in fact it dates, like the rest of this main front, from Shiers's time – as becomes clear when we go inside. The gable marks the end of the existing house to the west; when the rest of the south range was demolished, however, the lower courses of the outer wall were left, to a height of some 7 or 8 feet, presumably to divide the old courtyard from the garden. It too has pilaster articulation, but the pilasters here are a good deal smaller and simpler than on the house itself.

The surviving north-west corner seems always to have been the service wing of the house, and is consequently rather less ornate. The lower floor here is of flint, and in the frieze below the lower cornice there is a band of flint and brick chequerwork. Above the brick upper floor is a continuous hood-mould of quite complicated section; but the only brick pilasters to be seen are an isolated pair at the eastern corner, which probably formed the right-hand side of the main gateway.

The entrance to the present house is now on its west side, formerly within the courtyard. It leads directly into a stone-flagged Hall, on the left of which, behind a timber screen, is the present 'Great' Hall – the original one was demolished – and on the right the Parlour, perhaps the prettiest room in the house with its panelled walls, its fluted wood pilasters decorated with masks of lions and its enchanting plaster ceiling featuring the Goddess of Plenty with basket and cornucopia. At the end of the Entrance Hall is the staircase, another considerable pleasure: everything is rusticated, including the charming dog-gate at the foot of the stairs and the

*The Long Gallery, Sutton Place.*

newel-posts with their wooden urns. There are open-work panels instead of balusters, as at Eltham or Ham; but here the workmanship is far less sophisticated, confining itself to strapwork designs which must have seemed a little old-fashioned by the 1630s and 1640s. The designs are echoed in panels carved in relief running up the inside wall.

At the end of the first-floor landing is the Great Chamber; it is here that we realise the large segmental-headed window to be original, since the Chamber is barrel-vaulted, the vault exactly fitting the curve of the window. Here again is an extravaganza of plasterwork with swags and birds and monsters and playfully cavorting *amorini*, all set against a strapwork background.

There are plaster ceilings in two other first-floor bedrooms, but they are flat, more restrained and probably a little later in date. Their designs are a good deal more geometrical, with ovals inside rectangles. If, as seems likely, the Great Chamber dates from about 1625, these rooms might be the work of George Shiers's son Robert in 1660 or so. The figure of Peace in the centre of one of them could well symbolise the blessings of the Restoration. (It is true that Robert received in 1657 a special writ of Privilege and Exemption from Oliver Cromwell; but he would not have been the only Englishman to experience a sudden change in his political sympathies on the return of the King.)

It is impossible not to regret the demolition of so much – including the Great Hall and, presumably, several other rooms no less sumptuous than those which have remained. Yet the house as it stands has a charm and intimacy which might well have been absent in a building more than twice the size and seems, in some strange way, sufficient unto itself; so perhaps it is churlish to complain.

## Sudbrook Park

See London section.

## Sutton Place

*21; 4 miles N of Guildford off A3*

It was in 1521 that Henry VIII granted the manor of Sutton, near Guildford, to one of the most trusted and influential members of his Court, Sir Richard Weston. Sir Richard started building at once, and by the end of the decade his house was ready, a magnificent two-storey building of rich red diapered brick round a square courtyard. The south range was dominated by the Great Hall, the north by the usual high gatehouse. Within a year or so of its completion the King was a regular visitor, and there is a tradition that it was here, in 1530 or 1531, that he first met Anne Boleyn. It would have been better for the Westons had he not done so: in 1536 Sir Richard's son Francis was accused at Anne's trial of having been one of her lovers, and was beheaded on Tower Hill.

The north range with its gatehouse was pulled down in 1786; the rest of the exterior, however, looks almost exactly as its owner knew it, and very intriguing it is. First of all, it is one of the first English manor houses to be built without any regard for defence. Secondly, it makes effective use of a new decorative enrichment which had just been introduced from Italy – terracotta. This had first appeared in England, at Hampton Court, in 1521, and within the next few years was to show itself at Layer Marney in Essex and at East Barsham in Norfolk; but Sutton is probably its second earliest manifestation. Here it takes the form of small moulded plaques. The majority, on the quoins, alternate Sir Richard's initials, R.W., with representations of a tun – his somewhat inadequate rebus. But in the middle of the north front, in one long row beneath the parapet and two shorter ones above the central door, are representations of winged, dancing *amorini* which lend a welcome touch of playfulness to what is otherwise a distinctly forbidding façade and show, beyond all doubt, that the Renaissance was on its way.

Another precocious feature about the elevation of all three surviving ranges is the rigid symmetry everywhere. At Loseley, built some forty years later, symmetry is applied to the mass only; fenestration and detail were left to arrange themselves as best they might. At Sutton, every pane of glass has its opposite number; the big, two-storeyed bay that lights the Hall is echoed by another that serves no useful purpose at all. And these bays themselves, incidentally, are well in advance of their time. Windows so large, regular and plentiful are much more a hallmark of the late Elizabethan age than the Henrician. Sutton may not quite be described as 'more glass than wall'; but it is closer to Hardwick, still three-quarters of a century away, than is many a house of the 1540s or 1550s.

It was presumably this passion for symmetry that led the unknown architect to make his principal entrance into the Great Hall from the centre of the north front, rather than from a screens passage at one end – a unique arrangement at this date. Ian Nairn has suggested that the Hall was originally smaller, and ended only just west of the existing door. If he is right, it must have been a mean affair indeed; I prefer to think that Sutton was, in this respect too, in advance of its time, and that the area of the Hall is unchanged. It is a proud and impressive conception, with a minstrels' gallery at each end, a noble fireplace given by Catherine of Aragon (the pomegranates are her crest), much of the original panelling and, best of all, some glorious heraldic stained glass in the windows, as old as the house and possibly even older.

Of the other state rooms, the most important are the Dining Room in the west wing and the two Long Galleries, one above the other, in the east. None, alas, is in its original form, though two marvellous oak trestle tables in the Dining Room figure in Sir Richard's original inventory. The east wing was gutted by fire in 1571, after which it lay semi-derelict for 300 years; it is now largely a nineteenth-century reconstruction by Norman Shaw. Whether it always contained a Long Gallery is unknown; the original drawings are lost. If so, Sutton would once again have been well ahead of the fashion. Be that as it may, the present upper Gallery is spectacularly successful by any standards.

Sutton Place has recently been bought by an American, Mr Stanley Seeger, and made the subject of a charitable trust. As such it now houses a remarkable collection of pictures and is also used for special exhibitions and concerts. The grounds are, at the time of writing, being magnificently re-landscaped – including the provision of a lake – by Sir Geoffrey Jellicoe.

## Tigbourne Court

*22; 1½ miles S of Witley on A283*

Set back only a few yards from the Milford–Petworth road stands one of Lutyens's very best and most individual houses. As with all his early work – it was built between 1899 and 1901 – it is difficult, if not impossible, to describe: one could call it a free variation on an Elizabethan theme, with three very pointed gables, a recessed porch and lower side wings running forward to enclose a small forecourt, each of them ending in a gigantic pair of Tudor-style chimneys. One could try to give a feeling of its extraordinary colour and texture: yellow rough-cut stone, yellow brick and red brick all play their part, with courses of herringbone tiles and rather ostentatious galleting, that curious practice of sticking little slivers of flint into the mortar between the stones. One could point to the characteristic quirks – the celebrated Lutyens puckishness – like the way he has given his windows brick mullions but stone transoms. Yet nothing, not even photographs, can altogether

*Tigbourne Court.*

express the impact of a house like this, which relies for its effect on its solid geometry and the movement of the beholder around it.

The inside is full of surprises and good things. There is a beautifully thought-out staircase, straight but broken by two separate landings and lit by hexagonal windows on each side, another window which is actually oval (not elliptical), and an extraordinary coved Music Room with what was once a musicians' gallery and a huge pedimented chimney corner. But these are details; it is the ensemble that counts, the product of one of the most fertile architectural imaginations of our century.

### West Horsley Place

*23; 4½ miles NE of Guildford off A3*

Since Kew was lost to London, West Horsley Place is the best example in Surrey of that curious but attractive style known as Artisan Mannerism. The style has been briefly described in the introduction to this county, but the best description is given by the house itself – or rather by the south front, built around 1630 on to the medieval manor house that goes rambling off behind. Here are all the hallmarks of the Mannerist style: the shaped Dutch gable, the pilasters and cornices and elaborate entablature, the square wooden window frames that made mullions and transoms things of the past. The east wing was truncated in the eighteenth century, and it was probably then also that its western counterpart was given that distinctly inappropriate Venetian window and the same semi-circular lunette above – echoed, alas, in the central gable; but this has not appreciably detracted from the sense of comfortable domesticity which seventeenth-century English architecture, whatever its style, so effortlessly creates.

## Short List

### Albury

*24; 4 miles SE of Guildford on A248*

The much altered ALBURY PARK was finally and depressingly done over by Pugin and his son Edward in the 1850s, but retains an elegant staircase by Sir John Soane and two chimneypieces of about 1690. It has been converted into flats by the Mutual Households Association. In the park is the old disused CHURCH OF ST PETER AND ST PAUL. The tower is Saxon below and Norman above, finished with a seventeenth-century cupola. The thirteenth-century chancel is roofless, but the south transept was decorated by Pugin in 1839 in glowing red, blue and gold.

### Bletchingley

*25; 4½ miles E of Reigate on A2*

BREWER STREET FARMHOUSE is an impressive timber-framed hall house, with a two-bay hall between jettied and gabled wings. It has a Horsham slate roof and dates from the fifteenth century, of whose vernacular architecture it is a splendid example. Pendell House, just north of the village, is described separately.

### Chaldon

*26; 3 miles N of Redhill off B2031*

The small flint twelfth- and early thirteenth-century CHURCH OF ST PETER AND ST PAUL hides a unique treasure, a twelfth-century Doom painting of *c.*1200 covering the entire west wall – one of the most important English wall paintings in existence. Iconographically somewhere between a Ladder of Salvation and the Last Judgement, it is called the Purgatorial Ladder and is strangely grotesque.

### Farleigh

*27; 4 miles SE of Croydon off B269*

An extraordinary survival: an almost unspoilt village right next to Croydon, it boasts the delightful little Norman ST MARY'S CHURCH consisting of just an aisleless nave and a chancel – the latter lengthened and given lancet windows in Early English times (*c.*1250). Miraculously, there have been no major alterations since.

### Great Tangley Manor

*28; 3 miles SE of Guildford off A281*

A most impressive house of 1584, it has ornate timbering on the three-gabled upper storey, using curved braces round square panels to form a star shape. The gables are of unequal size and all have a double overhang. The house contains simple panelled interiors, and the rooms at the east and west ends are by Philip Webb, though subsequently altered. Unaltered is his covered way from the entrance drive across the moat.

### Haslemere

*29; 12 miles SW of Guildford on A286*

NEW PLACE was built by C.F.A. Voysey in 1897 and is an excellent and typical example of his work – rough-cast, slate-roofed, and melting into its woodland setting.

### Limpsfield

*30; 8 miles E of Redhill on A25*

In the centre of the village, just opposite the Bull, is DETILLENS. The early Georgian front is a fraud; it conceals something far more interesting, a fifteenth-century hall house substantially altered in the sixteenth century but remarkably little since. The hall itself has been divided both vertically and horizontally, but the gigantic tie-beam and kingpost are preserved *in situ* in what is now an upstairs bedroom.

The composer Frederick Delius is buried in ST PETER'S churchyard.

### Pendell House

*31; ¾ mile NW of Bletchingley*

Dated 1636, Pendell House has been ascribed to Inigo Jones. Outside, it is restrained Artisan Mannerist with a hipped roof. There is fine brickwork in English bond, with panels like reversed pilasters between all the main windows. Inside, the staircase is like the smaller one in the Queen's House at Greenwich.

## Peper Harow

*32; 3 miles SW of Godalming off B3001*

Sir William Chambers's brick cube was never very inspired, and was certainly not improved by the addition of a third storey in 1913. The five-bay east and west fronts were originally identical, with their big Venetian windows on the ground floor, to either side of the three-bay projecting centre; but the former has now to contend with a two-storey porch, its two storeys being of different dates and conflicting styles. Inside, things are a little better: there is an elegant staircase and some plaster ceilings that look excellent in photographs, but I have not seen the actual interior.

## Pyrford

*33; 3 miles E of Woking on B367*

Another simple little Norman church, ST NICHOLAS'S is quite unspoilt – though the shingled bell turret and broach spire are obviously later additions – and utterly unassuming apart from an uncertainly ambitious north door. Remains of wall paintings can be seen on the south wall of the aisleless nave. It was restored – and probably preserved for us – by Sir Thomas Jackson in 1869, so sensitively that you would scarcely notice.

## Ranmore

*34; 1 mile NW of Dorking*

ST BARTHOLOMEW'S is a splendidly typical church by Sir George Gilbert Scott, uncompromisingly of its date (1859), with an octagonal central tower and a spire with dormers. It is faced overall with round flint cobbles. The interior is a bit heavy, but has some fine thirteenth-century-inspired details; note especially the crossing, with its cornucopia of foliage capitals and friezes and its multiple shafts. The glass is by Clayton and Bell.

## Reigate Priory

*35; 21 miles S of London on A217*

The priory is now a school, its Tudor origins hidden under late eighteenth-century stucco elevations. Inside, however, are two treasures. First comes the so-called Holbein fireplace in the Hall, with its huge wooden surround and overmantel with the Royal Arms and Tudor roses intertwined in strapwork. This is flanked by pairs of Corinthian columns and two seats with three-stage canopies above – an early Renaissance masterpiece. Then there is the Staircase Hall of 1702, the walls and ceiling all painted with classical scenes (they are attributed to Verrio). The staircase itself, with elegant twisted and fluted balusters, rises to a landing with Corinthian columns.

## Shere

*36; 6 miles SE of Guildford off A25*

The CHURCH OF ST JAMES is large and impressive, with a big Norman central tower, tall single bell openings and a shingled broach spire, a very satisfactory composition. There is a Norman south door with zigzag and foliage. The rest of the church is mainly thirteenth-century with a fourteenth-century chapel. The window tracery repays close study; there are also fine timber roofs.

## Wisley

*37; 7 miles NE of Guildford on A3*

How many people visit the Royal Horticultural Society gardens, all oblivious of the simple little Norman CHURCH (apparently undedicated) only a minute or two away? Reminiscent of its near neighbour at Pyrford, it is only slightly more altered: the east window and the twin-light nave windows are of 1627, the west wall windows and the north door of 1872.

# Sussex

I spent nearly all my childhood summers in Sussex – in a late eighteenth-century, pebble-dashed, unpretentiously Gothicising house from which you could hear the waves. That house, a few miles from Bognor Regis, is now lost beyond recall; but Sussex remains the one county in which I always feel a sense of homecoming. My Sussex was a place of high shingly beaches with endless expanses of oatmeal-coloured sand when the tide was out, and of long garden walls of knapped flints; always, along the northern horizon, there ran the line of the Downs, misty in fine weather, menacingly clear when rain was on the way. To a child's eye they looked immeasurably far distant; but on sunny weekends we would drive to Halnaker or Bignor for picnics, and gaze down from the high places and across the flat plain below to the spire of Chichester Cathedral and the distant sea.

That is very much a West Sussex recollection; the Downs meet the sea around Brighton and it is only to the west of that point that there is any alluvial plain worth speaking of; to the east, the cliffs begin and immediately introduce a very different feeling to the landscape. Even the Downs feel different – somehow they are more domesticated in the west, and far more thickly wooded. Architecturally, however, the two halves of the ancient Kingdom of the South Saxons share a common heritage. Inevitably there are minor differences in materials: the greenish sandstone from the Petworth area (used to such subtle effect on Petworth House itself) is unknown in the east. But the Conqueror made sure that each of his six Rapes of Sussex had its own castle, and that of Arundel still remains – on the outside – as romantically beautiful as any in England. Sussex, both East and West, also has its full quota of exquisite Saxon and Norman churches, some of them splendidly enlarged in the Decorated style when, in the fourteenth century, sheep farming on the Downs brought the county a new prosperity. As for country houses, there are perhaps fewer of the first league than one might expect to find, though the quality is there all right: no county that can boast a Petworth or a Parham, a Firle or an Uppark, can be considered underprivileged. Then there is Chichester Cathedral – exactly right for Sussex – and the show-stopper of all time in the almost unbelievable phenomenon of the Brighton Pavilion.

Inevitably, modern tourism has wrought its usual havoc, especially along the coast, where the innumerable excruciatingly sited caravan parks and uncontrolled developments like Shoreham and Peacehaven are – or should be – object lessons to us all. But the Downs conceal many a little village and combe where the old generation of Sussex-lovers – Belloc and Chesterton and Kipling and their friends – would still feel at home.

# East Sussex

### Ashburnham

*1; 4½ miles SE of Battle off B2204*

Capability Brown's Ashburnham Park, and Robert Adam's gates on the eastern side, promise great things; ASHBURNHAM PLACE itself does not, alas, fulfil them. Its position, looking down across a chain of lakes to clumps of noble trees climbing up the green hillside opposite, could hardly be improved upon; but there is little left of the once-great house of the seventeenth and eighteenth centuries, and what there is has been largely ruined in the nineteenth and twentieth – most recently by a nasty new block added in the 1960s when the house became a Christian conference centre.

ST PETER'S CHURCH, however, has been spared. It looks at first glance to be medieval, and the tower is indeed of the early fifteenth century; but the rest is that rare phenomenon, an English Gothic church of 1665 – not self-consciously Gothicising as Wren was to do at Christ Church, Oxford, nearly twenty years later, but simply built in the old traditional style because it seemed the natural, sensible thing to do. Inside, it shows itself for what it is – a beautiful example of its period with box pews, a commodious west gallery supported on endearingly crude Ionic columns, a tremendous painted Decalogue and a very high chancel raised on seven steps. The glass of the big five-light east window is plain – a pity, if only because it now reveals an excessively dreary modern roofscape which must be (in the phrase with which a long-suffering vicar once described the organ-playing of Penelope Betjeman) destructive of devotion.

In the side chapel to the north of the chancel are the tombs of John and William Ashburnham, the two brothers who rebuilt the house and the church. One is static late medieval, the other all swirling, attitudinising Baroque. The first is of 1671, the second of 1675, yet whole centuries lie between.

## Battle Abbey

*2; 6 miles NW of Hastings on A2100*

The great abbey of Battle was founded, according to ancient if unsubstantiated tradition, by William the Conqueror as a thank-offering after his victory of 1066, with its high altar marking the spot where King Harold fell. It was complete by 1094, and consecrated in the presence of William Rufus; of the abbey church itself, however, scarcely one stone is left on another. Remains of the monastic outbuildings are still plentiful, but by far the most impressive monument in Battle today is the magnificent Gatehouse, towering above Market Square and controlling the entry into the abbey precincts. It dates from 1338; to the right of it, seen from the square, is part of the original Norman wall, but the rather longer range to the left is of the mid-sixteenth century, after the Dissolution of the Monasteries, when Henry VIII had given the abbey to his Master of Horse, Sir Anthony Browne.

Beyond the Gatehouse, nothing is quite so good again. It is agreeable enough to wander through what remains of the monastic outbuildings – the dorter and rere-dorter, guest house and infirmary – but there is too little of them left to give any real impression of abbey life and, as so often on such occasions, one finds oneself simply brooding on the hatefulness of Henry VIII, the tragedy of the Dissolution and the magnitude of our loss. For the rest, there is only the Abbot's House, converted by Sir Anthony into a residence for himself, reconverted in 1857 into a Neo-Gothic mansion (making good use of a piece of thirteenth-century cloister arcading), rebuilt after a fire in 1932 and now a school. It is not open to the public. I personally prefer, at this point, to forget about architecture, head for the west end of the lower terrace – where Harold drew up the right wing of his line – and look out across the now tranquil playing fields where, in a few nightmare hours, all English history was changed.

## Bishopstone

*3; 1½ miles E of Newhaven off A259*

ST ANDREW'S CHURCH is not only a pleasure to behold, with its flint walls so typical of Sussex, its tiled roof all yellow with lichen, and its sturdy four-stage tower topped by a shingled pyramidal cap; it is also of considerable architectural importance, having kept a south porch and a nave which date back to the early tenth century and possibly even a little earlier. The porch, as was the custom in Saxon times, originally did duty as a chapel in its own right; its inner door, leading into the church, was deliberately built to one side so as to leave room for a small altar along the east wall. In the gable above the outer door is a Saxon sundial, inscribed with the word 'EADRIC' – presumably the donor's name. The tower is Norman, twelfth-century, its four stages receding very slightly as they rise towards the corbel table, a pretty little bestiary of carved monsters.

Inside, the surprise is the broad Norman north aisle – its small round-headed windows looking unaccountably earlier than the north arcade which cannot have been built before about 1200 – and a very distinct choir, Norman again, with big, gently pointed arches to east and west, and blank arcading along the north and south walls. Beyond is a small sanctuary with Victorian vaulting – a pity, but not a disaster. St Andrew's remains a lovely little downland church that is not easily – or quickly – forgotten.

*Battle Abbey.*

*Bodiam Castle.*

## Bodiam Castle*

*NT; 4; 3 miles S of Hawkhurst off A229*

One's first sight of Bodiam seems almost too good to be true – everybody's idea of the perfect medieval castle, not large perhaps, but impressive and totally symmetrical, set in a broad moat and in a quite astonishing state of preservation. Its strategic purpose is less immediately apparent, but this too becomes clear when one remembers that in the 1380s, when it was built by Sir Edward Dalyngrygge, the Hundred Years' War was going full blast and French raiding parties from across the Channel were a constant menace. The River Rother, more navigable then than now, enabled them to penetrate deep into the hinterland; Rye and Winchelsea had both been burnt to the ground in the previous decade. Fortunately, by the time the castle was finished, England had regained control of the Straits; Bodiam in fact saw no fighting until 1655, when it was successfully besieged by the Parliamentarians and suffered a good deal of damage. The admirable restoration, together with the landscaping of the surrounding parkland, is largely the work of Lord Curzon, who bought the property in 1916 and on his death bequeathed it to the National Trust.

Outwardly, the castle is of the French pattern – Sir Edward must have seen plenty of prototypes during his service in France under Edward III – and distinctly old-fashioned for its date: its rectangular plan, with round angle towers, a square tower in the centre of each flank and imposing gatehouses to front and rear, was already being superseded. The interior, on the other hand, must have been considered the *dernier cri* – far more luxurious and sophisticated than those of earlier times, with splendid suites for the family, separate quarters (without communicating doors) for the hired mercenaries, a chapel, two kitchens and plenty of modern conveniences: Lord Curzon, during his restoration work, counted thirty-three fireplaces and twenty-eight lavatories, all with proper drainage. Thus, although one of the noblest examples of medieval military architecture in Britain, Bodiam is also a reminder that by Richard II's reign the great age of castle building was drawing to its close; that of the fortified manor house was at hand.

## Brighton

*5; on coast 53 miles S of London on A23*

*Includes Royal Pavilion* and St Bartholomew's Church**

Before the middle of the eighteenth century, no one could have guessed the glorious future that awaited the modest little fishing village of Brighthelmstone. It was only in the 1750s that a certain Dr Richard Russell published his *Dissertation concerning the Use of Sea Water in Diseases of the Glands* and settled in the village with a devoted following of fashionable valetudinarians. From that moment its fame began to spread; and the first of many visits by the Prince of Wales in 1783 provided just the additional impetus it needed. In 1798 work began on Royal Crescent, and for the next forty years building continued apace, with row after row of elegant 'Regency' houses springing up to give the town that aristocratic *cachet* which, despite the efforts of modern developers, it has still not entirely lost.

To mention specific streets or houses in this context would be invidious, and is anyway unnecessary; it is the ensemble that counts, and the Regency architecture of Brighton, like the Palladian architecture of Bath, not only should not, but cannot, be missed. The town also possesses, however, another architectural complex of a very different character – famous too in its way, but needing rather more seeking out. This is the area bounded by East, North and West Streets which conceals that rabbit warren of alleyways and narrow passages known as THE LANES. These are virtually the only remnants of the old Brighthelmstone days and – though few if any predate the seventeenth century – seem almost like a relict of the Middle Ages. On hot sticky afternoons of high summer they also approximate more closely than anywhere I know in England to an oriental *souk*. They are nowadays inevitably self-conscious and somewhat chi-chi, and the bric-à-brac that is their stock-in-trade is often ridiculously over-priced; but Brighton would be a poorer place without them.

Of individual monuments in the town there is one that, as everybody knows, stands in a class by itself. For me, the ROYAL PAVILION★ is one of the half dozen most purely enjoyable buildings in the kingdom – a building that lifts the spirit in such a way that you always leave it feeling more elated than when you went in. When the twenty-four-year-old Prince of Wales first leased it in 1786 it was a perfectly respectable gentleman's farmhouse, nothing more; then Henry Holland was called in. He almost trebled it in size, gave it a central rotunda and turned it into a noble Palladian villa, with no loss of respectability. His royal patron, however, was still unsatisfied. By 1802 he was replacing Holland's restrained decorations with wildly fanciful *chinoiserie*, and a few years later he decided to go the whole hog. His first choice to remodel the extension was Humphry Repton; but Repton's carefully thought out drawings for an Indian pavilion were too scholarly to win favour and it was not until 1815 that John Nash came up with what was required.

The result was a triumph. Nowhere in Europe, perhaps nowhere in the world, is there a royal fantasy palace combining such sheer exuberance with such fine workmanship, all achieved with grace, humour and a lightness of touch that sets it on a completely different plane from the other buildings with which it is occasionally compared, notably the heavy-handed, lunatic conceits of King Ludwig II of Bavaria. Once again, it is almost impossible to pick out individual gems from such a treasure house; I suppose I would award my personal palm to the Banqueting Room, were it not for the fact that four of them were already supporting the ceiling of the Great Kitchen and another two that of the South Drawing Room; and that Messrs Grace & Sons, the Prince's decorators, had already filled the dome of the Banqueting Room with a gigantic banana plant, some of whose leaves actually project from the ceiling in three-dimensional painted copper. Beneath this hovers a great silver dragon, holding in its claws a 30-foot-high gasolier encircled with open lotuses.

A similar exoticism informs the Pavilion's other great *tour de force*, the Music Room – almost destroyed by a demented arsonist a few years ago but, as these words are being written, rapidly approaching the end of a long and meticulous restoration. Here the dome is a myriad of golden fish-scales, the walls painted with Chinese landscapes in red and gold. Snakes, dragons and pagodas abound; and the general impression is that of the most marvellously imaginative and sumptuous oriental extravaganza ever mounted. But all this is only a beginning; there are a dozen other rooms equally memorable, any one of which would be worth a visit to Brighton to see.

Not surprisingly, the Brighton churches are almost all Victorian; even the old parish church of Brighthelmstone, ST NICHOLAS'S, is scarcely an exception, having been remorselessly restored in the 1850s to the point where only the glorious Norman font and the fourteenth-century tower remain as they have always been. Connoisseurs should not miss Pearson's ALL SAINTS, Hove, and will also enjoy comparing the two churches by Sir Charles Barry, ST PETER'S in Victoria Gardens (the present parish church) of 1824–8, and ST ANDREW'S, in Waterloo Road, Hove, of 1827–8. Both are early works, built when Barry was about thirty; but whereas St Peter's is Gothic – its soaring, pinnacled west end facing unliturgically south to the sea – St Andrew's is Renaissance, Barry's first excursion into the style for which, above all, he was to become famous.

If, however, you have the time or inclination for one church only, go unhesitatingly to ST BARTHOLOMEW'S★, Ann Street, which is by an architect you have almost certainly never heard of – I hadn't – called Edmund Scott. He built it between 1872 and 1874 for Father Arthur Wagner, an immensely rich High Anglican who paid for no fewer than five churches in the poorer parts of the town. Of the five, this one is far and away the most exciting – for me one of the supreme Victorian churches of England. You can see it right across Brighton; and very awesome it looks, with its brick walls towering above the surrounding houses, almost unrelieved except for a huge rose window at the liturgical west end (which, like St Peter's, actually faces south). This first impression of austerity and height is confirmed when you go in; at night the roof – which, at 135 feet, is considerably higher than that of Westminster Abbey – is virtually lost to view; the great brick walls, now punctuated by giant pointed-arch recesses, a triforium of three slit lancets per bay and tall clerestory windows above, seem to rise up for ever into the darkness. No aisles, no mouldings, no carvings, nothing cushions the shock. I suppose it is Gothic more than anything else; but Gothic was never like this before.

Now turn towards the altar. The style changes. Gothic becomes Byzantine. And yet, inexplicably, the mood remains the same. The flat east wall – Scott's intended apsed chancel was never built – is divided horizontally halfway up. The upper half is dominated by a huge cross in low relief, glittering gold against the brick, the

St Bartholomew's Church, Brighton.

unexpected richness of its texture contrasting with the plainness of its outline and its sheer scale to produce an impact that I can only compare with that of the rough painted cross in the whitewashed apse of the sixth-century church of St Irene at Istanbul. Beneath it, this contrast is continued in a high, arched *baldacchino* and a plethora of polychrome marble and Arts and Crafts metalwork: a brilliantly successful combination and conception, the work of one Henry Wilson between 1895 and 1910. It is flanked by mosaics by Hamilton Jackson – not great works of art in themselves, but utterly right here.

With the Pavilion, St Bartholomew's is Brighton's greatest masterpiece; but no town in England displays more eloquently, or more enjoyably, the wealth and infinite variety of nineteenth-century architecture.

## Charleston Manor

See Westdean.

## Eastbourne

*6; on coast 63 miles from London on A22*

The Belgravia of Sussex, Eastbourne is a piece of superbly aristocratic property development by a single landowner. Though known as a bathing place since the early nineteenth century, it was scarcely more than a village before its lord of the manor, William Cavendish, later the 7th Duke of Devonshire, got to work on it in 1851. Because of this – and also because of the superior *cachet* of Brighton, which was a little too close for comfort – it possesses few really memorable buildings, unless you count the WISH TOWER, one of the line of Martello towers constructed between 1805 and 1810 as a defence against Napoleon. Its distinction comes rather from its 3 miles of sea front, self-conscious with more than a hint of pomposity – no shop is allowed anywhere along its length – and from the occasional set-piece like GRAND PARADE, based on the misguided assumption that anything Nash could do in Regent's Park, Eastbourne could do better. The churches, too, are disappointing: not a patch on Brighton's, though Street's ST SAVIOUR'S is worth a visit. (It is better inside than out.)

At the edge of the town, and serving now as a finishing school for young ladies from overseas, stands COMPTON PLACE, from which the Duke could direct the progress of his development operations. It seems to have begun Jacobean, but after two extensive remodellings – the first by Colen Campbell in the 1720s, the second around 1800 – little of the original style remains. The real splendour of the house lies in the State Bedroom and its immediate neighbours, all of which are stuccoed to within an inch of their lives; the plasterwork of the ceiling includes an excellent portrait in relief of Campbell himself – almost certainly a posthumous tribute, since he died in 1729.

## Etchingham

*7; 4 miles SW of Hawkhurst on A265*

When a very grand church arises out of a very small village there are only two likely explanations: either the village has dwindled and grown poorer, or else there was some rich private patron. In the case of ST MARY AND ST NICHOLAS it was the latter. Sir William de Echyngham raised this noble collegiate church in the 1360s and, apart from the now-vanished moat, it remains largely as he left it – one of the proudest and purest examples of the Decorated style in Sussex. The tower, over the crossing, gives a tremendous impression of massiveness and strength, making a notable contrast with the delicate filigree of the window tracery below – particularly that of the chancel, which is longer, as well as lower, than the nave. Sir William himself is commemorated in brass (unfortunately minus his head) on the chancel floor. Nearby is another brass, better preserved, to his son, grandson and daughter-in-law.

## Firle Place*

*8; 5 miles SE of Lewes off A27*

Of all the great houses of Sussex, Firle is the one which, given the means for its upkeep, I should most like to own. It is not a house of any outstanding architectural distinction; we are not even sure who the architect was. It is grand, but not so grand as Petworth; old, but without the unspoilt unity of Parham; beautiful, but lacking the formal perfection of Uppark. Gently secluded below the steep northern slopes of the Downs, with the 700-foot Firle Beacon towering high above it to the south-east, it strives for no particularly dramatic impact, inspires no awe. With its two and a half storeys, its hipped roof, dormers and mellow lichened stone, it is approachable, serene and welcoming.

As you drive up through the park and see the house for the first time against the backdrop of wooded hillside, it looks completely of the eighteenth century – an impression strengthened by the Venetian window above the heavily rusticated entrance arch on the east front. It is only on the south side that it betrays its Tudor origins – in the westernmost of the three gables, which survived the mid-Georgian rebuilding of about 1745. This is part of the old Tudor house built – quite possibly on the site of an earlier medieval manor – by Sir John Gage in the middle of the sixteenth century. Inside, there are other survivals, notably the Great Hall, which fills virtually the whole central range of the outer courtyard, opposite the entrance arch. This was superficially Georgianised, but if you look hard at the eighteenth-century coving round the ceiling you will see ghostly white traces of the great hammer-beams which are still in position behind it; and in the Staircase Hall to the left stands a fine Tudor doorway, rediscovered only after the First World War.

Apart from this single feature the Staircase Hall is pure Palladian and, with its fine, almost Rococo, plasterwork panels and broad staircase, one of the glories of Firle. Sophisticated and utterly assured, neither it nor the splendid Sitting Room leading off it, which is divided into three with screens of Ionic columns, seem to show any of the slightly naïve touches which, elsewhere in the house, appear to indicate the hand of a local architect – probably that of John Morris of Lewes who, from 1750 onwards, is known to have been heavily involved with Glynde Place (*q.v.*). The inference is that for these two showpieces – as Mr Arthur Oswald puts it in his quite admirable guide-book – 'a London man was called in'. William Kent himself has been suggested, though for both stylistic and chronological reasons he seems unlikely; his disciples John Vardy or Henry Flitcroft might be better bets. The plasterwork of the staircase, together with that of the Library, is attributed to William Wilton, who achieved similar splendours at Stanmer close by.

On the first floor the most interesting room, architecturally speaking, is the Long Gallery, which stretches the full length of the entrance front. An eighteenth-century Long Gallery seems to be almost a contradiction in terms; even by the 1650s such things were becoming obsolete, and though they were inevitably to make something of a comeback with the Gothic Revival there is not a hint of Gothic at Firle. It is a lovely room nonetheless – and made lovelier, as is the whole house, by the superb collection of pictures, furniture and porcelain for which, more than for its architecture, Firle is famous – a collection that can be matched, south of London, only by that of Petworth. Yet Firle has an intimacy about it that Petworth lacks. It is not a palatial house; it is, quite simply, everything that an English country house at its best ought to be.

*Firle Place.*

## Forest Row

*9; 3½ miles SE of East Grinstead on A22*

A little over a mile north-east of the village stands ASHDOWN HOUSE, one of the only two surviving English works of Benjamin Latrobe. (The other is Hammerwood, *q.v.*) Latrobe, a pupil of S.P. Cockerell and an architect of international significance, emigrated in 1796 to America, where he built Baltimore Cathedral and, in Washington, the south wing of the Capitol – thereby, incidentally, transforming American architecture. Ashdown, now a school, is a gem of a house, built just before Latrobe left England. Ashlar-faced, it is only three bays wide, with a lovely little Ionic bow portico which is really the front half of a circular porch. Inside, the staircase with its elegant ironwork banisters has obviously been altered, since it suddenly changes from timber to stone and cuts across a rather beautiful door; it leads up to three little tripartite doorways, each featuring a pair of columns with vaguely Egyptian capitals. On the attic floor are some rather curious semi-circular rooms which are, bafflingly, not reflected on the exterior.

## Glynde Place

*10; 4 miles SE of Lewes off A27*

It started off as a typical, medium-sized Elizabethan courtyard house, built of Caen stone and the local Sussex flint for one William Morley; the completion date, 1569, is carved above the old entrance arch in the central courtyard. The exterior is still essentially Elizabethan; but the house could not altogether escape alterations when the Rev. Richard Trevor, later to become Bishop of Durham, inherited it in the 1750s and completely remodelled it inside, simultaneously shifting the main entrance front from the west to the east. Thus, though the old west front with its three Dutch gables remains more or less unchanged, that to the east is now a rather puzzling mixture of styles – the more so after a not entirely successful attempt in the nineteenth century to restore it to its former Tudor purity.

One wonders why they bothered, since once inside the Entrance Hall the atmosphere is Georgian through and through – and very formal Georgian at that, with its screens of coupled Tuscan columns at each end. It leads through to a broad staircase with a fireplace on the half landing – the Bishop obviously liked his comfort – and, at the top, a much broader landing, almost a room in itself, giving directly on to the Long Gallery that runs along the east range above the Hall. This is a really lovely room, richly panelled, with elaborate woodcarvings *à la* Gibbons above the chimneypiece framing the two principal portraits. Beyond it, a small Dining Room has kept its original Tudor floor, composed not of planks but of half pine logs laid out in a chevron pattern. Tudor too (or conceivably Jacobean) is the secondary staircase outside it – an interesting contrast to the far grander one at the other end.

Glynde Place is not, by any stretch of the imagination, a great house; but it is a remarkably pleasant one to visit and can be comfortably – and most agreeably – combined with Firle on a summer afternoon. While there, you should not miss seeing the pretty little Palladian CHURCH OF ST MARY built for the Bishop by his friend Sir Thomas Robinson, with its charming contemporary box pews, west gallery, communion rail and pulpit. Only the horrid Victorian screen and glass spoil the effect; could not the former, at least, be removed?

*Glynde Place.*

*Herstmonceux Castle.*

## Hammerwood

*11; 3 miles E of East Grinstead on A264*

Ashdown House at Forest Row has already been described; Latrobe's other creation, HAMMERWOOD HOUSE, built in the early 1790s and his first commission, is not so easy to find, standing as it does at the bottom of a long winding lane to the west of the church. The first view of the ashlar-faced house, from the back, was gloomy indeed when the whole place was entirely derelict, as it was when I visited it in 1978; it has since been saved in the nick of time and is now being restored. Anyway, the front tells another story. Where Ashdown is all Ionic, feminine grace, Hammerwood is Doric, stalwart masculinity – no porch to the central block, just four engaged giant pilasters framing the three middle bays; only the angle pavilions have plain, uncompromising tetrastyle porticoes with pediments – the columns, derived from Paestum, tapering sharply as they rise and fluted only at the very top, another faint whisper from the Nile just as we had at Ashdown. From the centre a broad flight of ornamental steps leads down in two flights to the garden, whence there is a glorious prospect of Ashdown Forest directly to the south.

Next to the house and towards the main road is the big timber-framed, fifteenth- to sixteenth-century BOWER FARM HOUSE, and near that is a house known simply as HAMMERWOOD, built in 1872 by Norman Shaw with a diapered brick ground floor and a tile-hung upper one. They form an extraordinary trio for so tiny and remote a village; but of the three styles represented Latrobe's is far and away the most important – an architectural milestone and a key work (like Ashdown) in the early history of the Greek Revival.

## Herstmonceux

*12; 9 miles NE of Eastbourne on A271*

Only sixty years and twelve miles separate Herstmonceux (nobody seems too sure how to spell it) from Bodiam, but between these two grandest moated castles in Sussex there is all the difference in the world. Bodiam Castle, of the 1380s, was built for defence, a serious stronghold on a strategic site; HERSTMONCEUX CASTLE, of the 1440s, was designed for gracious living. This is not to say that moat, battlements and watch towers were intended purely for decoration – life in England during the Wars of the Roses did not permit that sort of self-indulgence – but they were never thought of as anything more than sensible precautions. Anyway, the brick walls of Herstmonceux are far too thin to withstand any but the most desultory siege.

Brick – that is the other most intriguing feature about this glorious castle. As a building material it had existed in England since Roman times, but it was only in about 1440 – the very moment, in fact, when the King's Treasurer, Sir Roger de Fiennes, was given licence to crenellate Herstmonceux – that it became fashionable to use it for grand and important buildings. This was one of the first; others, more or less contemporary, are Tattershall in Lincolnshire, Caister in Norfolk and Eton College.

Of course it has been restored. More of the exterior is original than one might imagine, but the building was largely gutted in the 1770s by Sir Robert Hare, who was then employing Samuel Wyatt to enlarge his more up-to-date residence at Herstmonceux Place nearby. It owes its salvation above all to two twentieth-century benefactors, Sir Claud Lowther and Sir Paul Latham, who did for it what Lord Curzon did for Bodiam. The interiors mainly date from their time or, like the staircases, have been brought in from other houses. But much credit should also go to the Astronomer Royal and the staff of the Royal Observatory, who moved here from smog-polluted Greenwich in 1957. No building in England looks less like a government scientific establishment; only the outbuildings in the surrounding park, which is open to the public in summer, give the game away.

HERSTMONCEUX PLACE, half a mile out of the village to the north-west, began life in about 1720. This is the date of the present entrance front. It has three rather cramped storeys, and gives the impression of fussiness more than anything else – as if the architect, almost certainly a local man, was desperately keen to make a show but not quite sure how to do it. Around the corner to the left, however, things improve considerably: this marks the point at which Samuel Wyatt was brought in, in 1777. He knew precisely what he was doing, so could afford to be relaxed. In the same height into which his predecessor had crammed three storeys, he was content with two, spacing his windows out horizontally in proportion, giving his front a separately quoined three-bay pedimented centre and placing Coade stone plaques below a strongly emphasised string-course running immediately under the first-floor windows. These last two features are continued on the garden side, where he provided a five-bay centre flanked by generous three-bay semi-circular bows, rising the full height of the house to shallow domes – the insides of which we see in the oval rooms beneath them. This garden front he was to repeat almost exactly at Belmont in Kent (*q.v.*) some fifteen years later.

*The Barbican, Lewes.*

## Lewes

*13; 9 miles NE of Brighton on A27*

A hill town, Lewes is dominated by the remains of the great flint CASTLE built on the summit by William de Warenne, whose wife Gundrada may have been – but probably wasn't – a daughter of William the Conqueror. Most unusually, de Warenne gave it two artificial mounds rather than one; on the south-western stand the ruins of the keep, strengthened in the thirteenth century by two projecting octagonal turrets. (These now possess delightful little Gothick windows, dating from the eighteenth century when the owner converted the keep into a summer-house.) But the most impressive surviving feature of the castle is the tremendous BARBICAN, in its time – the early fourteenth century – one of the mightiest in the kingdom; it had to be, if the French were to be kept in their place.

For the rest of the town, what one remembers best is the warren of steep little streets, with red-roofed Georgian houses tumbling higgledy-piggledy down them – none of outstanding individual distinction, but making a splendid impression in the ensemble. The churches are rather disappointing. ST MICHAEL'S has one of the three Sussex round towers (see Southease) but not much else; ST ANNE'S has another Norman tower and a good south arcade of the late twelfth century; ST JOHN THE BAPTIST in Southover High Street contains, in a simply awful pseudo-Norman chapel of 1847, Gundrada's magnificent tomb slab of black marble, and the two lead caskets that held her bones and those of her husband. ST JOHN'S was once the hospice of Lewes PRIORY, a Warenne foundation and the first Cluniac house in England; its church alone was bigger than Chichester Cathedral. But it fell on evil days and had already suffered many vicissitudes before its final vindictive demolition by Henry VIII. The ruins, such as they are, can be seen among the playing fields behind Southover High Street; they are not an edifying sight.

## Poynings

*14; 4½ miles N of Brighton off A281*

HOLY TRINITY is, like St Mary and St Nicholas at Etchingham (*q.v.*), a church of unexpected grandeur for a small village. This time the benefactor was Michael of Poynings, who died in 1369 and left money for it to be built after his death. His executors, however, were either a bit slow or very avant-garde; for whereas Etchingham, built in the 1360s, is Decorated through and through, Poynings is essentially Perpendicular. Unusually, it is built on a rough Greek cross pattern, with a good firm embattled crossing-tower, supported within on four more or less identical arches. Nave and chancel extend the same distance; the transepts, themselves unequal, are very slightly shorter. There are no aisles. Apart from a good Jacobean pulpit and a lovely oak screen in the south transept, the furniture is a little disappointing; but, despite the rough vernacular flint of which it is built, this is an aristocrat among the Sussex village churches.

## Rye

*15; 9 miles NE of Hastings on A259*
*Includes Lamb House (NT)*

Proud of its venerable history, Rye has been a Royal Borough since 1289 and one of the Cinque Ports since 1336. It can also boast any number of excellent timber-framed and Georgian houses that make it one of the showpieces of Sussex. Perhaps, indeed, it is a little too pretty; for though it has avoided – or almost avoided – the taint of the quaint, it has inevitably acquired that slight degree of self-consciousness that manifests itself with a plethora of antiques, boutiques and small shops selling almost unbearably sensitive hand-made pottery. But though it contains much that is bogus, the beauty is real enough. As in so many beautiful towns, the whole is greater than the sum of its parts: one should obviously mention the thirteenth-century YPRES TOWER (formerly a prison, now a museum); PEACOCK'S SCHOOL (1636) with its Dutch gables and giant pilasters, among the earliest appearances in England for both features; the fifteenth- and sixteenth-century OLD HOSPITAL and of course LAMB HOUSE (NT), a sternly august building of the early eighteenth century which is a literary shrine twice over, having been inhabited first by Henry James and later by E.F. Benson. But one could add any number of others, all fitting neatly and appropriately into the general scheme of things, which is Rye itself.

At the top of the hill, just round the corner from the mid-eighteenth-century arcaded TOWN HALL, stands ST MARY'S CHURCH – very large and matriarchal with its low battlemented crossing-tower. It is a pleasant fusion of styles, the transepts originally Norman (don't be deceived by the huge Perpendicular window dominating Lion Street along the side of the Town Hall), the nave Early English, and has a splendid gilded clock of 1760 whose mechanism is in fact two centuries older – the oldest in England still in working order, with a 14-foot pendulum swinging away inside the church itself.

## Sheffield Park

*16; 10 miles N of Lewes on A275*
*Includes Sheffield Park Garden (NT)*

Originally a Tudor house, Sheffield Park was completely remodelled (and much enlarged) by James Wyatt in 1776–7 and is one of the very first houses of its size to have been built in a serious, scholarly Gothic style – an idiom far removed from the Rococo Gothick of Strawberry Hill or Lacock Abbey. There is no light-hearted dilettantism here, of the kind shown by gentlemen amateurs such as Chute or Walpole, Sanderson Miller or Thomas Prowse; Wyatt, for all those unbusinesslike habits that so infuriated his patrons and bedevilled his career, was a professional who knew his stuff. This did not debar him, however, from the occasional flight of

*Sheffield Park.*

fancy; he would not otherwise have made one of the principal features of the east front a huge traceried six-light window big enough for a small cathedral, made of solid Honduran mahogany, but serving no interior purpose whatever – though it does provide a splendid focal point from the lakes below. Nor, ten years later, would he have added battlements and turrets. (The house now looks a little uncertain whether it is a church or a castle.) Inside, the most impressive room is the Staircase Hall, galleried at first-floor level, with a circular lantern on pendentives, the whole design infused with a marvellous airy weightlessness – Wyatt at his best. The same spirit reappears in the Drawing Room, which has a broad semi-circular apse at one end, set with smaller apsed niches, and a big tripartite window looking out on to the gardens.

And what gardens! SHEFFIELD PARK GARDEN (NT) is the work of Capability Brown and Humphry Repton and covers nearly 150 acres, including five lakes at different levels. Whether the original designers would have approved of the seasonal explosion of azaleas and rhododendrons – a Victorian innovation – is an open question; but on a sunny May afternoon one is scarcely in the mood to cavil.

## Southease

*17; 3 miles S of Lewes on A275*

The PARISH CHURCH of Southease appears to have no dedication, which is rare; it also possesses a Norman round tower, which is rarer still, there being only three in all Sussex. (The other two are at St Michael's, Lewes, and Piddinghoe.) It has a shingled conical roof and traces of more windows than there are today. Inside, it is as simple as can be, with a *wooden* chancel arch – you can't get much simpler than that. The north and west walls show vestiges of thirteenth-century wall paintings, alas too faded to give any pleasure to most of us, and there is a Jacobean altar rail with a few box pews to match. Does all this sound just a little dull? Probably. There is little at Southease to compel our admiration; but there is much to love.

## Westdean*

*18; 5 miles W of Eastbourne off B2109*

King Alfred had a residence here, and after eleven centuries there are still few more delectable corners of England than this remote combe set deep in the Downs. ALL SAINTS' CHURCH, with its curious gabled west tower, is basically Norman, with early fourteenth-century

*Charleston Manor, Westdean.*

St Thomas's Church, Winchelsea.

additions and some good monuments, including busts of Lord Waverley by Epstein and of Sir Oswald Birley, the painter, by Clare Sheridan. The flint and brick RECTORY next door has been inhabited since about 1220; it has preserved its Hall and a solar opening off it, with a garderobe – latrine – projecting off the end wall.

But the pearl of Westdean is CHARLESTON MANOR, half a mile away to the north-west. The house, beautifully restored by W.H. Godfrey for Sir Oswald Birley, has a south wing of the twelfth century – one of the few examples of Norman domestic architecture still in existence. On to this was grafted a small Tudor block and, finally, a perfect little Georgian front. The ravishing garden contains a medieval dovecot full of doves, to say nothing of the enormous barns, now run together into one, where Sir Oswald had his studio and his widow used to run a festival of music, horticulture and gastronomy – a festival which has been revived by the present owner.

## Winchelsea

*19; 7 miles NE of Hastings on A259*

The history of Winchelsea is that of one disaster after another. Originally a thriving port on the Rother estuary, it was largely washed away by a freak storm in 1288. A new town was built some 2 miles off on higher ground, but soon fell victim to a still more disagreeable enemy – the French, who raided and pillaged it seven times between 1337 and 1459, destroying the larger part of St Thomas's church. Demoralised and dispirited, the inhabitants gradually drifted away; the harbour silted up; and Winchelsea, with its present winter population of only a few hundred, is now something of a ghost town – in sharp (and peaceful) contrast to bustling, tourist-ridden, pub-thumping Rye.

ST THOMAS'S, truncated though it is, is still beautiful and awesomely grand, with a richness of decoration that would do credit to a cathedral. The only part remaining is the early fourteenth-century chancel with its side chapels, so that it gives the feeling of being far broader than it is long; and even here there has been much inevitable restoration, not all of it over-sensitive. The 1850 tracery in the east window is a good example – what a contrast to the fourteenth-century splendour on each side! All the glass – except a little in the north window of the chancel – is modern, by Douglas Strachan; over-fussy and, to my eye at least, distinctly mawkish. More interesting by far are the tombs. The three black marble effigies in the north aisle are obviously much older than the church, and are consequently thought to have been removed from the earlier town, now submerged. Their hugely ornate, rather oppressive, canopies, on the other hand, can only be afterthoughts – the Decorated style at its least sensitive. Would that prostrate crusader in his chain mail really have wanted quite so flatulent a surround? The two tombs against the south wall are thought to be those of Gervase and Stephen Alard, successive Admirals of the Cinque Ports, the head stops being those of Edward I and Edward II and their queens, respectively. Here the workmanship is on a level with the best that this extraordinary building has to offer, which is to say very fine indeed.

# Short List

## Alfriston

*20; 3 miles NE of Seaford on B2108*
*Includes Clergy House (NT)*

The CLERGY HOUSE (NT), a timber-framed and thatched building of the late fourteenth century, was the first building ever to be bought by the National Trust, who got it for £100 in 1896. The village also boasts two magnificent medieval inns, the GEORGE and the STAR, both of the fifteenth century, also timber-framed with admirably close studding. The Star in particular is most exuberantly carved. ST ANDREW'S CHURCH, which stands some little distance away from the rest of the village, dates from about 1370: Decorated, just shading into Perpendicular, it is a tall and impressive structure, with a crossing-tower.

## Bateman's

See Burwash.

## Berwick

*21; 7½ miles SE of Lewes off A27*

ST MICHAEL AND ALL ANGELS is a simple enough country church from the outside. What makes it special are the wall paintings by Duncan Grant, Vanessa Bell and Quentin Bell who lived in a nearby farmhouse at Charleston. These were commissioned by Bishop Bell of Chichester (no relation) and carried out in 1941–3; the biblical scenes are set in the surrounding countryside, and the Bishop and the local rector are depicted on the right-hand side of the chancel arch. It forms a worthy memorial to Bloomsbury where one would least expect to find it.

## Burwash

*22; 6 miles SW of Hawkhurst on A265*
*Includes Bateman's (NT)*

BATEMAN'S (NT) was built by a local ironmaster in 1634. It is a straightforward Jacobean house of local dressed stone, designed in a conventional E-shape, though the north wing has now disappeared. Fine provincial craftmanship can be seen in the details of the windows, the panelling of the hall and the contemporary staircase with turned balusters. Rudyard Kipling spent the last thirty years of his life here, and the rooms remain much as he left them.

## Great Dixter

See Northiam.

## Hassocks

*23; 6 miles N of Brighton on B2116*

DANNY has two main fronts, the east one of 1582–93, the south one of 1728; both are handsome in their different ways. The Elizabethan one, of diapered brick, is on a monumental scale, with two projecting wings and canted bay windows, those of the Hall rising two storeys with three transoms. The Hall remains, though the decoration is of the eighteenth century, as is the main staircase.

## Mayfield

*24; 7½ miles S of Tunbridge Wells on A267*

The remains of Mayfield Palace, which once belonged to the Archbishops of Canterbury, are now incorporated into the CONVENT OF THE HOLY CHILD JESUS. The school Chapel was the spectacular early fourteenth-century Hall of the Palace; it is enormous (68 feet by 34 feet) with three pointed stone arches, rising from huge grotesque corbels which support the timber roof. The Gatehouse, giving on to the main street, is Tudor.

## Michelham Priory

*25; 7½ miles NW of Eastbourne off A2108*

The red ironstone house is approached through a broad fourteenth-century Gatehouse, the most obvious survival of a priory of Augustinian canons who came here in the thirteenth century. The other remains, incorporated into the Tudor house, include an elaborately vaulted Parlour with carved stone bosses and, above it, the Prior's Room with original window and fireplace.

## Northiam

*26; 8 miles NW of Rye off A28*

GREAT DIXTER is interesting as the creation of Nathaniel Lloyd, the architectural historian. He bought a superb, if somewhat dilapidated, timber-framed fifteenth-century hall house, and employed Lutyens to restore and extend it. His is the tile-hung left half of the main front, the bay windows of the magnificent Hall to the right of the porch and the staircase to the solar. At the back, another closely studded timber-framed house – brought from Benenden in Kent – was attached by Lutyens to the existing buildings. The halls of both houses have kingpost trusses; the Dixter house also has a unique combination of hammer-beams alternating with tie-beams, and another kingpost in the solar. The ensemble may not be authentic, but it is certainly spectacular.

## Penhurst

*27; 3 miles E of Battle off B2204*

The seventeenth-century gabled manor house, duck-pond, farm buildings and church make an unforgettable group. The church, ST MICHAEL'S, was built between 1340 and 1500 of Wealden sandstone, with a nice stocky tower firmly buttressed and crowned with the pyramidal 'Sussex cap'. Inside, such restoration as there may have been is discreet to the point of invisibility. Oaken screen of the fifteenth or even fourteenth century, box pews, a wooden roof with a kingpost in the nave: nothing is individually outstanding, but the ensemble quietly, unassumingly right.

## Stanmer House

*28; 3 miles NE of Brighton off A27*

Now the music school of Sussex University, Stanmer House is a classical house of fine ashlar built in 1722–7 by Nicholas Dubois, and the only country house he is known to have designed. It is of brick, partly refaced with re-used stone, and incorporates an older house on the north side. There is a pedimented porch with classical details, and a fine plaster ceiling in the former Dining Room.

# West Sussex

## Amberley

*1; 4 miles SW of Pulborough on B2139*

The village is far greater than the sum of its parts – architecturally mediocre but, thanks to its clustered cottages, its perfect setting in the Arun gap, its Norman church and its romantic castle, everybody's idea of the perfect Sussex village for a sunny summer evening. ST MICHAEL'S is one of those lovely little churches in which the county is so unbelievably rich, with a towering late Norman chancel arch (though the zigzag ornament is decidedly overdone) and, behind it, an almost perfect thirteenth-century chancel with three separate lancets at the east end. In some counties it would be a show church: here it is scarcely more than typical.

But what makes Amberley is the CASTLE. It is almost exactly contemporary with Bodiam and was built by Bishop Rede of Chichester in the 1370s, also as a defence against the marauding French. The Bishop enlarged the old manor house with a great rectangular curtain wall rising sheer from the river. The old building still survives in the south-east corner, and includes a rich late Norman door of the same date as the chancel arch of the church – though it may not be *in situ*. Signs of a thirteenth-century upper hall are also evident. The house, however, was still not impressive enough for Bishop Rede, who turned part of it into a Chapel and built a grand Gatehouse with semi-circular towers and a new Hall. Half of this Hall is in ruins but the two southern bays, restored and altered, now make up the northern part of the present house. The southern part contains the chamber and solar of the old Hall range, though all fourteenth-century work has gone. The existing house also includes some early sixteenth-century windows and a simple staircase of the late seventeenth century. It has a cheerful lived-in atmosphere and is one of those houses that one would love to own.

## Arundel

*2; 9 miles W of Worthing on A27*

The further away you get from ARUNDEL CASTLE, the better it looks; this is because, like Windsor and Alnwick, it is largely a grandiose nineteenth-century reconstruction. Little more than the Gatehouse remains of the original fortress, built within a few years of the Norman Conquest; nearly everything else was destroyed by the Roundheads in the Civil War, and what we now see is largely the work of one of the most insensitive and ham-fisted of all Victorian architects, C.A. Buckler. As for the interior – well, Augustus Hare's description of the monumental state apartments as 'the climax of discomfort as well as of ugliness' may be a slight exaggeration, but not much of one. Some of the castle, however, is better than Hare suggests; one could cite the Library of 1801, built entirely of mahogany and planned like a complete hall church, or again the Duke's private Chapel in 'Early English style', all Purbeck marble columns and striped stone vaulting and with some acceptable Hardman glass. There is a genuine Norman undercroft with a round tunnel vault underpinning this megalomanic display.

A good deal more interesting is ST NICHOLAS'S CHURCH, built all of a piece at the end of the fourteenth century: not just because it is one of the comparatively few outstanding Perpendicular churches in Sussex but because it is really two churches in one, and of two different denominations at that. The eastern half, originally the chapel of a college of secular priests, was sold by Henry VIII after the Dissolution of the Monasteries to the Earl of Arundel, while the western end continued as the parish church; and this is the situation which in essence prevails today, with the Earl's descendants, the Roman Catholic Dukes of Norfolk, still retaining what is now known as the Fitzalan Chapel – to which the only entry is through the castle grounds – for their private use. Fortunately, however, the ecumenical spirit is having its effect: a brick separating wall has been removed and a plate-glass screen substituted over the original iron grille, through which the Chapel with its tombs and its great seven-light east window may – from a respectful distance – once again be viewed. The fourteenth-century wall paintings in the church are faded but not impossibly so.

Almost incredibly, the 15th Duke of Norfolk seems not to have thought the Fitzalan Chapel entirely adequate to his needs, and so, to celebrate his coming of age in 1868, he built at his own expense the gigantic CHURCH OF ST PHILIP NERI, which towers over the town and even dwarfs the castle. Architect – J.A. Hansom; style – French Gothic, 1300; taste – dubious.

*The church of St Philip Neri, Arundel.*

## Balcombe

*3; 3 miles NW of Haywards Heath on B2036*

The glory of Balcombe is its VIADUCT, one of the most magnificent in England. Built in 1839–41 to carry the Brighton line over the Ouse valley, its thirty-seven towering brick arches extend 500 yards. Go right up to it if you have the time, and examine it closely: each pier has its own, transverse, arch with an inverted one, reflecting it as it were, at the bottom. If you stand underneath, there are marvellous disappearing vistas of these arches diminishing, like the railway lines above them, into infinity.

## Barnham

*4; 4½ miles N of Bognor Regis off A29*

A beautiful house of 1640 or thereabouts, BARNHAM COURT was carried out with vision and much virtuosity entirely in brick – which is used for pilasters, capitals, pediments, metopes, triglyphs, modillions and just about everything else except the windows themselves. The whole is crowned by three brave gables and four ranges of tall square chimneys set diagonally. In style it is so like the Dutch House at Kew that Ian Nairn and Pevsner suggest it must be by the same unknown architect; but London had many such houses at the time, so we can never be sure.

ST MARY'S CHURCH is pretty as a picture, small and rustic, basically Norman, with tall Early English lancets at the east end.

*The church of St Mary and St Blaise, Boxgrove.*

## Bosham★

*5; 3 miles SW of Chichester off A27*

Pronounced Bozzum, Bosham is traditionally where King Canute conducted his experiment with the waves; one of its streets is still regularly flooded at high tide. It also appears, mentioned by name, in the Bayeux Tapestry. It is hardly surprising, then, that this modest little seaside village should possess HOLY TRINITY, one of the most stunning churches in all Sussex. With its squat stone Saxon tower topped with a stubby broach spire, and its lovely uninterrupted expanse of lichened tiles spreading across the high-pitched nave roof and the slightly lower (but equally long) chancel, it looks beautiful from the outside but scarcely outstanding; only when you step inside is its full majesty revealed. The Saxon chancel arch, horseshoe-shaped and with unique capitals, is quite simply tremendous. It makes a perfect frame for the glorious thirteenth-century east lancet, whose five lights are separated by tall, thin, free-standing columns of much elegance.

The nave – in which Canute's little daughter is buried – was rebuilt and enlarged in the thirteenth century. From this period, too, dates the curious little crypt, half under and half over the south aisle, which was probably intended as a charnel house, a repository for the bones of defunct canons.

## Boxgrove

*6; 4 miles NW of Chichester off A22*

The present very grand parish church, dedicated to ST MARY AND ST BLAISE, is basically the crossing, transepts and chancel of an important priory, founded in about 1115 from Lessay in Normandy. Look first at the ruins of the nave and, a few yards away to the north-west, some strangely evocative vestiges of Cloister, Chapter House and other monastic buildings; all are lovely in their setting. Then go inside, walk direct to the font, stand behind it and look straight down the axis of the church to the east window. The impact of this magnificent Early English building (only the crossing and transepts date from the original foundation) immediately makes itself felt. Some *cognoscenti* may complain at the way round and pointed arches have been combined, but the general effect is happy and, to my eye at least, not inharmonious. The same goes for the light-hearted ceiling painting of the mid-fifteenth century, and even for the Victorian glass of the east window, which is a good deal better than likely – O'Connor of London, 1862.

*The Market Cross, Chichester.*

## Chichester*

*7; 12 miles E of Portsmouth on A27*

THE CATHEDRAL AND IMMEDIATE ENVIRONS

Chichester may not be one of the very greatest of English cathedrals, but there is none more welcoming or more lovable. It inspires no awe, as Durham or Lincoln do; it is not coldly, unapproachably, beautiful like Salisbury. It is exactly what it ought to be: a homely, comfortable cathedral in a sunny little English county town, dominating the buildings around it but only in the gentle way that a beloved old grandmother might dominate her grandchildren. It is Sussex through and through.

Its twelfth-century proportions are so good that it looks marvellous from every angle: away in the distance from the Downs, the big central tower rising up across the cornfields as you approach, reassuring and protective from Cloister or Close. And, once you are safely through the unfortunate modern plate-glass doors at the west end, the interior is just as satisfying. It begins with a considerable bang in the shape of the south-west tower, three storeys high, the lower two setting the style of sturdy Romanesque which pervades the whole building. (The top storey is Early English only because its Norman predecessor was blown down by a storm in 1210.) On cloudless summer afternoons this tower seems to be literally flooded with sunshine. From here the nave marches up in a balanced and reasonable way – its rather low arcades, massive piers, and twin arches under the main arches of the tribune all recalling Winchester – to the fifteenth-century screen. This was replaced in 1960 after a century's oblivion – not perhaps altogether wisely, since its row of blank niches gives it a faintly top-heavy appearance and its late Perpendicular clashes discordantly with the surrounding Romanesque.

As a style, Chichester Romanesque is quieter than that of Norwich or Ely. Even after the fire of 1187 the rebuilders stuck to the Norman design, though they embellished it with Purbeck marble shafts and string-courses, and provided a quadripartite vaulted roof. Only in the two-bay eastward extension of the choir were they more adventurous; and this, perhaps more than anywhere else in England, marks the point where Romanesque gives way to Gothic. The Gothic note is sounded, but softly and harmoniously, with the pointed arches of the gallery set within an embracing round arch as if to ensure their acceptance, like a proud father introducing his children into grown-up society. At ground level there is further joy to be had from the design of the piers – the central shaft of Purbeck marble supporting the walls themselves, surrounded by four more slender columns to carry the arches and vaults. Here is grace indeed.

A few feet to the north of the west end of the nave stands a detached BELL TOWER – the only cathedral one remaining in England. In the precinct proper the two outstanding buildings are the early thirteenth-century BISHOPS' CHAPEL and the great KITCHEN. The former is not as easy of access as it should be; the efforts required may be considerable, but the rewards are great – the interior is as good as anything in Chichester. Many of the details can be compared with those of ST RICHARD'S PORCH, through which one enters the Cloisters from the cathedral, which is of the same date. The Kitchen is easier to visit and equally rewarding. It is a huge four-square room designed for a central flue – a problem solved by a system of double hammer-beams of breathtaking complexity. What makes it more interesting still is that if it dates, as seems most likely, from about 1300, these are among the earliest of their kind in England.

THE CITY

Elsewhere in the city, the minor felicities are too numerous to list. The octagonal MARKET CROSS of 1501, lushly ornate, is now heavily restored; we can only be grateful that the city centre was pedestrianised before it disappeared altogether. More interesting to my mind is the Palladian COUNCIL HOUSE built of brick and stone by Roger Morris in 1731–3, obviously in a light-hearted, devil-may-care mood which his master, the austere Lord Burlington, would in no wise have approved. A bit of a joke if you like, but a deliberate one and none the worse for that. The rather more Burlingtonian Council Chamber on the first floor was beautifully redecorated by the late John Fowler – his last important work.

The area of the city known as the PALLANTS, to the south-east of the Market Cross, is well worth a visit: almost a little town in itself, and a piece of lovely early eighteenth-century town planning with *all* the houses listed as buildings of special architectural or historical interest. Note particularly PALLANT HOUSE of 1712, an outstanding example of eighteenth-century brickwork. Then, if you continue along North Pallant across East Street and keep straight on for 200 yards, you will come to the most extraordinary building Chichester has to offer. This is the medieval HOSPITAL OF ST MARY. The present building – the unique survivor of a style common in the Middle Ages – dates from 1290. Its overall design is roughly that of an aisled church, with a chancel-like Chapel at the east end, separated from the rest by a fine contemporary oak screen – one of the best in the country. Instead of a nave, however, there is a long passage, running beneath a tremendous beamed and timber-framed roof and between two rows of low partitions. Behind these partitions were originally beds for the sick; but in Henry VIII's time the infirmary became an almshouse, and in the 1660s the bed space was ingeniously converted into eight minute two-room flats, with four colossal chimneys serving the eight fireplaces. These are still there, and still occupied; several, within the specified times, are open to visitors. Here is an astonishing – and moving – example of a medieval pattern of life still being happily lived, with remarkably few modifications, after more than seven centuries.

## Clayton

*8; 4½ miles N of Brighton on A273*

Seen from the outside, ST JOHN THE BAPTIST is just another pretty little Sussex church – very old (it is mentioned in the Domesday Book) and with a delightfully squat shingled bell-cote sticking straight up above the roof like a glorified chimney, but not outstandingly memorable. Inside, it is a different story. The chancel arch dominates all, just as its brothers do at Bosham or Worth, grandly uncompromising in its starkness. For the Saxon masons who gave it its shape, brave, manly mouldings were all right, but frippery capitals were not: a square chamfered slab would do just as well.

A couple of generations later, around 1100 as far as we can guess, Clayton received its other benison – a cycle of wall paintings depicting the Last Judgement, probably the most complete anywhere for their date and, thanks to a recent grant from the Pilgrim Trust, quite astoundingly well preserved. They are also far more sophisticated than most other medieval English wall paintings, the work not of local artists or even of journeymen, but of top-calibre professionals who had studied in southern France and (I would suspect) Norman Sicily, and really knew their stuff.

Just across the road from the church is the irresistibly dotty entrance to CLAYTON RAILWAY TUNNEL, which the trains enter through a pointed arch framed by two brick embattled turrets and topped by a small house whose inhabitants, if such there be, cannot possibly get any sleep at all.

*St Mary's Church, Climping.*

## Climping*

*9; 1½ miles W of Littlehampton off A259*

ST MARY'S CHURCH starts with oddness and continues with beauty. Odd – very odd indeed – is the late Norman lower part of the tower: it possesses both a first-floor window and a west door which are unlike any others in the country. The window, a pointed lancet (the date must be well before 1200), is somehow scooped out of a flat, central buttress and then given a heavy zigzag moulding all the way round, which lends it an indescribably raffish appearance; the door, the inner arch of which has been exuberantly trefoiled, is crowned with more zigzag and dogtooth and flanked by – of all things – zigzag columns. To each side there is a blind niche, the left one surmounted by a roundel, the right by a lozenge. Eccentricity could hardly go further.

Beautiful is the church. It is all-of-a-piece thirteenth-century, controlled to the point of austerity but with proportions so perfect as to make decoration unnecessary. Such restoration as has been done has shown similar restraint; the church today still looks very much as it must have done the day it was finished. It was, and is, a gem.

## East Grinstead

*10; 10 miles W of Tunbridge Wells on A264 and A22*
*Includes Standen (NT)**

A pleasant country town, East Grinstead has much in it to admire – if only the relentless traffic would allow one to do so. How one longs for a bypass! The best thing in it is SACKVILLE COLLEGE, dated 1619 but founded two years earlier by the 2nd Earl of Dorset. Behind the long, low stone frontage with its three widely separated gables and tall chimneys lies a beautiful, square, near-symmetrical quadrangle like that of an Oxford or Cambridge college, around which are the almshouses, still used for their original purpose. The actual private accommodation is not shown to the public as it is at the Hospital of St Mary, Chichester; but the Hall is worth a visit (especially for the sake of the screen at its west end) and so, in its Victorian way, is the Chapel, now largely the work of William Butterfield in 1850. (His work was commissioned by the Warden of the time, J.M. Neale, who wrote 'Good King Wenceslas'.) The two styles blend more harmoniously than might have been expected.

ST SWITHUN'S CHURCH is by James Wyatt, but not particularly distinguished. More interesting are the several fine timber-framed houses of the fifteenth and sixteenth centuries, notably CROMWELL HOUSE, opposite the College.

Only 2 miles from East Grinstead to the south-west – along the B2110 – lies STANDEN (NT)* built in 1891–4 by Philip Webb, the friend and close associate of William Morris, as the country house of a London solicitor named James Beale. In many ways it is the antithesis of Victorian taste. There is nothing stuffy here; everything is light, airy and flooded with sunshine, with glorious views over the Medway valley to Ashdown Forest. Nor is there any pompousness. Webb was trying hard to distil his style, ridding it of all ostentation, until it reached a sort of quintessence of pure architecture. Purity, however, did not mean plainness; if anything, it seems to have led Webb into an extraordinary eclecticism. At one outside corner of the house there are no fewer than four different building materials, all within a few feet of each other – brick, pebble-dash, tile and stone. In another, there suddenly rises up a curious sort of pele tower, which accords oddly with the five gables on the south front and the old farm buildings comfortably grouped round a small green.

Inside, Standen preserves many of its original furnishings, supplemented by more of a similar kind provided by the National Trust and by the tenants, Mr and Mrs Arthur Grogan, whose superb collection of late Victorian pictures, furniture and works of art suits the house to perfection. For any student of William Morris and his circle – indeed, for anyone interested in the history of interior decoration at all – here is a treasure house not to be missed.

## Goodwood

*11; 3½ miles NE of Chichester off A285*

James Wyatt, but not alas at his best – GOODWOOD HOUSE, built for the Duke of Richmond between 1790 and 1800, is one of his few dull designs. If he had been allowed to complete his original neo-classical plan, which seems to have been to incorporate a modest 1720 brick house into an irregular octagon, with domed circular turrets at each corner, the house might have been more successful. As it is, the three sides which stand today give the building a curious sprawly look which not even the two-storey columned central portico does much to redeem. Moreover the use of unknapped flint and stone, a combination forced on Wyatt by the Duke, creates a low-key vernacular effect not at all in keeping with the grandiose scale of the house. Inside, too, the rooms, though impressive enough, tend to lack Wyatt's usual decorative brilliance. Only the Tapestry Room, built to an earlier design of his, shows him at the top of his form with a typically elegant plaster ceiling in which the colour scheme of pink, green and gold is superbly handled.

The stable block, built by Sir William Chambers in 1757–63, is a good deal more distinguished than the house; here, by contrast, the architect is at his very best. It is a wonderfully controlled design, a quadrangle as big as the house, and the use of beautifully knapped flint with stone dressings has much to do with its effect. The coffered central triumphal arch would have been grand enough for the house itself.

The park and setting are lovely, with ravishing views – including a marvellous one along a specially designed avenue to the spire of Chichester Cathedral. North of the house on a hillside is CARNE'S SEAT, built in 1743 and a more elaborate edition of the Council House at Chichester.

## Lancing College

*12; 4 miles E of Worthing on A27*
*Includes Lancing College Chapel**

Gloriously sited on a high eminence above the Adur, Lancing College commands a breathtaking view of Portslade power station, the seemingly endless ribbon development of Old and New Shoreham and apparently uncontrolled proliferation of seaside bungalows, and a busy civil airfield. It was founded in 1848 by the Rev. Nathaniel Woodard, whose dream was for not one but a whole series of inexpensive and classless public schools, united within a single philanthropic corporation. Lancing was the first – and most ambitious – of the ten he founded before his death; there are now thirty.

The College is dominated by its tremendous CHAPEL*, which is open to the public every day of the year; but before visiting it, most people will find it well worth strolling through the two main quadrangles behind. The chief architect was R.C. Carpenter, on whom I cannot do better than to quote Ian Nairn. Carpenter, he writes, 'was almost the only person in England who could design Gothic buildings with the right mixture of competence, sincerity and common sense. Pugin and Butterfield would have been too fanatical, the rank-and-file would not have cared enough. Because Carpenter initiated no twist of style and produced no decorative fireworks, he is passed over too often, yet he more than anyone else could have made the Gothic Revival work. His death at forty-three was as great a loss as Pugin's.' The first, lower, quadrangle is almost entirely his. It has a Cloister running round the north, west and south sides, with broad, rather squat window openings – their height determined by the floor level of the Library and old Chapel on the first floor of the western, gabled, range. (Carpenter, one feels, would have despised tricks of the kind Wren employed for the Library of Trinity College, Cambridge.)

The upper quadrangle is rather less successful, lacking as it does the unity of the lower. Carpenter had died in 1855, only a year after building at the College had begun, and his work was carried on by his son, R.H. Carpenter, and his partner William Slater. Theirs are the north, south and east ranges: Carpenter Jun.'s School Hall on the north must be considered, by any standards, a bit of a disaster. The quadrangle remained open to the west until just before the First World War, when it was added by Maxwell Ayrton: worthy, but dull.

And so to the Chapel. It is R.H. Carpenter's work, and his masterpiece. Elsewhere in the College his work is often less than impressive; here, the effect is stunning. The Chapel began as an act of faith, first because of the shifting sand and clay that had to be dug through to an average depth of 55 feet before reaching the chalk in which the foundations could be set – those foundations alone took three years to complete – and secondly because there was no building fund and only twenty years' output of far from well-to-do old boys to whom to appeal. For all that, Woodard was projecting the biggest church to be built in England since St Paul's Cathedral and the biggest Gothic one since King's College Chapel. Knowing that, even if it were ever to be finished, he would not be there to see it, he entrusted the work to his son Billy, whose faith and determination were equal to his own – but devoted all his money and labour to raising the apse immediately to its full height, thus ensuring that the plans would not be scrapped in favour of something less ambitious. He laid the topmost stone himself.

And the work *was* finished – in 1978, just 110 years after it began. Admittedly, it was never possible to build the 350-foot tower of which Woodard had dreamed, from the top of which, in times of storm, the choir would sing hymns for those at sea. Admittedly, too, there are still plans for a vast ante-chapel which will link the Chapel with the other College buildings and provide its principal entrance. But the basic edifice is complete – one of the great architectural *tours de force* of the past hundred years.

One must, of course, avoid the word *modern*. Lancing College Chapel is of the purest French Gothic. It is not without inconsistencies: in *The Buildings of England*, Ian Nairn has pointed out that, while the proportions are those of the Flamboyant period of the late fifteenth century, the detail is of the thirteenth: in our own terms, the equivalent would be a combination of Early English and Perpendicular. But this, after all, is only what the best Victorian ecclesiastical architects were doing again and again; and there are few medieval parish churches in England – and no medieval cathedrals – in which two, or even three or four, styles are not happily combined. What takes one's breath away at Lancing is in any case not the detailing, fine as it is; it is the sheer soaring height of the building, the clustered shafts shooting up like rockets into the roof, the immensely high clerestory continuing right round the polygonal apse. The nave itself is of nine bays, divided on the exterior by doubled flying buttresses; below it is a tall, rib-vaulted crypt with a beautiful octagonal chapel at the east end.

The west end was, as always, the last part of the chapel to be completed. The westernmost bay of the nave and the narthex with its painted wooden ceiling are the work of Stephen Dykes Bower. The western wall now contains the largest rose window in England, 32 feet across, its glass being the coats of arms of all the colleges in the Woodard Corporation and their respective dioceses.

Seen from afar – and it is an unmistakable landmark for miles around – the Chapel loses, perhaps (as many of its French prototypes lose), from the absence of a tower; even its pinnacles do not rise above the roof ridge. Seen from close quarters, on the other hand, there is so much good detail that one does not feel inclined to complain: the beautiful treatment of the eastern chevet, a rarity in English architecture; the exquisitely judged foliated tracery there, and also in the eastern turrets and the clerestory and aisle windows; even the flying buttresses, set so close together that when seen from the west end they seem to form two superimposed tunnels on each side of the rose window. This memorable building is indeed an almost miraculous achievement, but it is also a superb work of art – and incidentally, more likely than not, the last great Gothic building in the world.

## New Shoreham

See Shoreham.

## Newtimber

*13; 7 miles N of Brighton off A23*

Although there was a house at Newtimber recorded in the Domesday Book, what we see today is a moated manor house, modest but wonderfully unspoilt, of the sixteenth and seventeenth centuries. The main front shows how well local materials can harmonise: the doughty Sussex flint of the walls, the stone quoins and plinth course, the two-coloured brickwork of the window dressings, the roofing of Horsham slabs. The moat, fed from a natural spring, surrounds it completely, on one side literally washing the wall.

Inside the house, the most interesting feature is the Entrance Hall, with eighteenth-century wall paintings inspired by Greek and Etruscan vases and quite possibly the work of Biagio Rebecca. They are not beautiful, but they do lend an extraordinary character to the room. Nothing else in the house quite matches this for impact, but there is a lovely small garden with views out in all directions on to countryside as unspoilt as the house itself. (Newtimber Hill, opposite, is owned by the National Trust.) Neither seems to have changed for the past three centuries; how much longer can they last?

## Old Shoreham

See Shoreham.

## Parham

*14; 4 miles SE of Pulborough on A283*

On 28 January 1577 the foundation stone of Parham was laid by one Thomas Palmer, aged two and a half; and the grey stone house we see today, apart from some sensitive modern restoration, is still essentially the one he knew. Despite its considerable size, it is a comfortable, unostentatious sort of house, with no fireworks. It is built on a typical Elizabethan E-plan, with gabled wings on either side and a central porch on the south front. Apart from the Hall windows, the others on this front are post-Tudor or modern restorations. Inside, there is a glorious Great Hall with, instead of a minstrels' gallery, a steward's room with two interior windows from which he could look down and make sure that all was well down below. The ceiling is probably only a nineteenth-century copy, but the oak panelling is original, and very fine it is too. The Great Parlour and Great Chamber were restored in this century, and the Saloon was remodelled about 1790. The other grand *pièce de résistance*, apart from the Hall, is the Long Gallery – at 160 feet it is one of the longest in England – which benefits hugely from having windows on both sides as well as at both ends. The ceiling may strike the unsuspecting visitor as a bit overdone; it was designed and painted, with its twined and twirling tendrils, by Oliver Messel in the 1930s. But many an Elizabethan painter-decorator might have indulged himself in much the same way given the chance, and to my eye at least it works quite remarkably well. Here, and indeed all over the house, the pictures, furniture and – a Parham speciality – the embroideries and stumpwork are a joy to behold.

On the south lawn is the CHURCH, basically of the sixteenth century but remodelled with great charm around 1820. The north transept is totally given over to the squire's pew, complete with fireplace. The pretty plaster roof makes much play with those curious hooked corbels that are such a feature of New Shoreham (*q.v.*).

## Petworth

*15; $5\frac{1}{2}$ miles E of Midhurst on A272*

*Includes Petworth House* and Park (both NT)*

Here is one of those rare English examples of a phenomenon which is much more frequent in France – town, park and mansion so closely linked with each other as to be virtually inseparable, forming a trinity of almost Athanasian complexity in which each element sparks off the other two, now attracting, now repelling, setting up a chain of tensions and counterbalances that somehow results in a perfect, or near-perfect, equipoise.

The town, were it not for the fearsome traffic, would be a delight to wander in. Practically all the streets grouped around Market Square have their treasures – especially LOMBARD STREET with its misleadingly named TUDOR HOUSE of 1629, and NORTH STREET with the adjoining SOMERSET HOSPITAL and SOMERSET LODGE; the latter is a real joy, dated 1653. All would be well worth a perambulation, even if PETWORTH HOUSE* (NT) didn't exist. But it does, so here goes.

Viewed, as it should be, from PETWORTH PARK (NT), this splendid mansion shows no external traces of the early fourteenth-century house which still forms its core. What we see today is the complete remodelling undertaken by the 6th Duke of Somerset in 1688–93 in what seems to be a distinctly French idiom: so French, in fact, that its design has been tentatively ascribed to Daniel Marot, who is known to have worked for William III at Hampton Court and Kensington Palace. One hundred and seven yards long but only two and a half storeys high, this western, show, front has been known to strike first-time observers as a little dull; there are, however, two points to remember. The first is that the centre was originally crowned with what was described in 1690 as a 'sirculer roofe' – almost certainly the dome over the three-bay centre which appears in an old picture of the house (now at Belvoir Castle) but was destroyed in a disastrous fire of 1714. This dome, together with the separate hipped roofs which formerly crowned the three-bay projections at each end (and which, incidentally, must have made it look more French than ever) would have pulled the whole composition together and given the eye rather more of an anchorage. The second point is that, as with so many French exteriors of the date, the façade is a good deal more subtle than appears at first sight. Thus the three central bays are distinguished, not by anything so obvious as a portico or pediment, but with rustication and blind balustrades and by the use throughout of Portland stone – which, in the rest of the house, is reserved for the dressings only, to set off the value of the green Sussex sandstone. The two outer wings are also given their own special character, this time by the continuation of the window reveals between the upper and lower storeys and the filling of the resultant recesses with busts and stone eagles. The whole thing is so controlled, so restrained, that it takes a little time to sink in; but after a while you begin to realise that you are looking at a quite beautifully judged architectural composition which, given only that dome, would be well-nigh perfect of its kind. The one thing that spoils it – though only from the

*Petworth.*

middle distance and beyond – is the top of the tower of St Mary's church, poking up asymmetrically and faintly ridiculously from the roof. One cannot but regret the addition of its top stage by Barry in 1827 – while, however, being heartily thankful for the removal of his spire as recently as 1947. The effect of tower and spire together must have been odder still – as can be seen in the enchanting picture by W.F. Witherington which hangs in the North Gallery and is reproduced on the cover of the National Trust's excellent guide-book.

Apart from the effects of the fire, the only appreciable change to the west front since the house was built has been the addition of this Gallery to the north end in about 1780. It is of one storey only, and has little effect on the general ensemble. It does of course make nonsense of the north front, but this was never of much importance. Since the east, entrance, front is also surprisingly unassuming and the south is a safe reconstructon by Salvin in 1869–72, it follows that Petworth is in essence a one-front house – another most unusual characteristic for its date.

Historically speaking, the earliest of the main reception rooms – we shall come to the Chapel later – is the Marble Hall, which occupies the centre of the west front. It is in fact the only room to have survived both the fire of 1714 and the major interior redecorations in the early nineteenth century. Like the front itself, it has a number of French Baroque features and – still more interestingly – several Dutch ones: notably the gargantuan frieze and the two huge overmantels with their broken segmental pediments, virtually identical with those which Marot was to add to the audience chamber of the Binnenhof at The Hague a few years after Petworth was built. Immediately to the left of this is the so-called Beauty Room, whose focus of interest is not architectural but sculptural: the famous Leconfield Aphrodite of the fourth century BC, which is confidently attributed to Praxiteles himself. The rooms to the south of this – which include the White and Gold Room with its Rococo plasterwork of about 1760 – are not normally open to the public; immediately to the east, however, is the Grand Staircase, painted by Louis Laguerre around 1720 – a few years after the fire, to which the scenes from the story of Prometheus on the lower part may or may not be a reference. On the main south wall, by contrast, the 6th Duchess of Somerset is to be seen riding in a triumphal chariot, escorted by angels, winged *putti*, her children and her dog. The rather heavy balustrade is a pity; it seems to have been inserted by Barry – why, I cannot imagine.

Beyond the Marble Hall to the north, the Little Dining Room has a marvellous carved frieze by a brilliant local craftsman, John Selden; but even this is quickly forgotten when we pass into the next room, which is the great *tour de force* of Petworth. The Carved Room was originally two rooms, which were thrown together by the 3rd Lord Egremont in the early nineteenth century to form what is effectively a gallery. Here is more superb carving by Selden and by his successor at Petworth, Jonathan Ritson; but it is overshadowed by the masterpieces along the long east wall, which could be by one hand only – that of Grinling Gibbons himself. Obviously they were not designed for the room, which did not exist in Gibbons's day; equally obviously, however, they were commissioned for the house, since they include the coronet and crest of the 6th Duke of Somerset – the 'Proud Duke' – and his Garter star. Of all the surviving work of the greatest wood carver that ever lived, that at Petworth is the best: a near-miraculous transmogrification of plain limewood into all the animals and flowers of the forest.

The room next door to the north is similarly dominated by another genius: J.M.W. Turner, who was a close friend of the 3rd Lord Egremont and who practically lived at Petworth during the 1830s, having a studio in the old Library above the Chapel. Thirteen of his pictures hang in this room, including two radiant ones of the lake in the Park, and there are another half dozen in the North Gallery beyond. This is a plain, almost undecorated space added at the end of the eighteenth century by that same 3rd Earl (who ruled at Petworth for sixty-five years, having succeeded at the age of twelve) and enlarged with a deep north bay in about 1824, with the express purpose of housing the paintings and sculptures collected by his father and himself. It was described by Christopher Hussey as 'the finest surviving expression of early nineteenth-century taste', and indeed the sculpture is just the sort of collection that a wealthy young dilettante might have amassed on his Grand Tour, leavened with a few neo-classical pieces by such artists as Flaxman and Westmacott. The paintings in the Gallery – in contrast to the breathtaking international collection elsewhere in the house – are, somewhat surprisingly, all English.

And so, finally, to the Chapel, east of the Turner Room. It is set oddly askew, for it is a survival – the only one, apart from the cellars – of the Percys' medieval manor house. The Early English window arcades with their Purbeck marble columns are clearly of this period, as is some of the tracery. All the rest, however – the tunnel-vaulted plasterwork ceiling and the splendid wooden furnishings – date from the Duke of Somerset's time, between 1685 and 1692. Even the Proud Duke must have been satisfied by his family pew: it takes the form of a splendid west gallery, topped by a vast *trompe-l'oeil* curtain – actually made of carved and painted wood – on which a pair of angels bear aloft the ducal arms, topped by a simply enormous coronet.

Capability Brown's Park and Pleasure Grounds are as beautiful as the house and a perfect complement to it. No higher praise can be given.

## Selham

*16; 3 miles E of Midhurst off A272*

ST JAMES'S is a really extraordinary little church, Saxon in its proportions, Norman in its herringbone walling and regular (as opposed to long and short) quoins. Pevsner and Nairn suggest a Saxon mason working in the twelfth century. If they are right, he must have used some earlier Saxon pieces in his chancel arch, which is one of the oddest in England. The two sides are quite different. The northern jamb consists of an attached column ending in a capital with a rather crude design of volutes; above it is an abacus with the familiar Saxon motif of interlaced cords, and on top of that an impost block with Norman moulding and foliage. On the southern side the capital has interlaced snakes and an animal's head, marvellously strong and barbaric, perhaps tenth-century or even earlier. Above, there is Norman-looking foliage on the abacus and Saxon coils on the impost. As one looks, one becomes more and more chronologically cross-eyed; but the panache compels admiration.

## Shoreham

*17; 3 miles W of Brighton off A27*

There are really two Shorehams, the New and the Old, and both possess astonishing churches. That of New Shoreham, ST MARY DE HAURA (the same word as in the French Le Havre, or the English 'haven'), has lost almost all its nave, which was destroyed either in a French raid in 1628 or in the Civil War. Even now it looks enormous for a small village, with its massive square tower of which the upper stage has its round-arched openings enclosed in taller, pointed arches – just the opposite to what goes on in the Chichester retrochoir, but every bit as effective. It is obviously half a century or so later than the lower stage: presumably 1180 or thereabouts. The choir alone is larger than many a whole church, its five broad bays supported by flying buttresses bridging the low side aisles.

Inside, this choir is grander still, giving an overwhelming impression of luxury and lavishness, but without ever becoming pompous or heavy. So rich is the detail and the decoration everywhere that one doesn't at first notice the disparity between the north and south arcades, which exists not only at ground level – the north is composed of alternate round and octagonal piers, while the less satisfactory south is of clustered shafts not quite sufficiently demarcated – but up to triforium and clerestory as well. It is when one starts to look at these differences that one is struck by another curious fact: whereas most churches of different periods tend to progress from one to the next horizontally, St

*The church of St Mary de Haura, Shoreham.*

Mary de Haura does so vertically. Admittedly the transepts are earlier than the choir, and Norman through and through; but the choir, in its chronological progression, was heightened rather than lengthened: late Norman/Transitional at the bottom level, Early English above. This means that the corresponding levels of the two sides, disparate as they may be, were built at very much the same time, making the phenomenon odder still.

There are plenty of other points of interest, like the beautiful round arches striding around the outside walls of the aisles, or the strange hook corbels, their stems turning inward into the wall like drainpipes, which are far commoner in France than in England. But here it is the ensemble, rather than the detailing, that one remembers.

In Old Shoreham the CHURCH OF ST NICHOLAS, seen from the outside, has a sturdy squat Norman tower just as appealing as that of its neighbour down the road; the remainder is less exciting. To enter it is to have this first impression confirmed. Much of the church is a nineteenth-century restoration, by J.M. Neale – he of East Grinstead (*q.v.*) and 'Good King Wenceslas' – and J.C. Buckler (not, fortunately, C.A., who ruined Arundel) for the chancel. What counts here is the crossing – four terrific Norman arches, one on each side of the central square, with nice sculpted corbels: those on the north are thought to represent King Stephen and his Queen. Note the old tie-beam over the west arch. The billet moulding strongly suggests that it is original Norman timber. If so it is almost unique in England.

## Sompting

*18; 1½ miles NE of Worthing off A27*

Its tower is the claim to fame of ST MARY'S CHURCH, Sompting. Topped with a gabled pyramidal cap – the so-called 'Rhenish helm' common enough along the Rhine and elsewhere in Germany – it has no fellow anywhere in the British Isles. It cannot date from much later than AD 1000 – early even for Sussex – and is supported inside by a crudely carved but splendidly robust arch. (Incredibly, the local descriptive leaflet fails to mention the tower. This sorry publication, which wins my 'Worst in West Sussex' prize, is the more regrettable in that it has supplanted one which, according to Alec Clifton-Taylor, recorded an eighteenth-century vicar as having written a poem entitled 'Laugh and Lye Down; or, a pleasant but sure remedy for the Gout'.)

The north transept, with its two-bay vaulted eastern aisle, and the odd excrescence to the south which looks like a transept but was in fact closed off from the inside of the church until the last century, are both the work of the Knights Templars, who held the church from 1154 until their dissolution in 1306.

## Standen

See East Grinstead.

## Steyning

*19; 9 miles NW of Brighton on A283*

In the Norman churches of Shoreham it was respectively the choir and the crossing that counted; at Sompting the tower; here at ST ANDREW'S in Steyning it is the nave. Few moments of Sussex sightseeing are more exciting than that when you open the south door and, before even passing the threshold, catch your first glimpse of those tremendous late Norman round piers, their manifold, exuberantly carved arches soaring and plunging above, culminating in a chancel arch that goes up like a rocket. In terms of imaginative splendour, this nave is unbeatable in any parish church in the county – though New Shoreham runs it close. Alas, the rest of the church is a sad disappointment, nearly all seventeenth- and nineteenth-century restoration. But after such richness it seems positively churlish to complain.

The village has much to admire. CHURCH STREET in particular is a tiny treasure chest.

*Church Street, Steyning.*

St Andrew's Church, Steyning.

## Thakeham

*20; 4½ miles E of Pulborough off B2139*

Three-quarters of a mile out of the village to the south stands LITTLE THAKEHAM, the house by Sir Edwin Lutyens that he himself described as 'the best of the bunch'. The outside, like so much of his earlier work (it dates from 1902–3) is Tudor in style; unlike Tigbourne Court or Marsh Court, however, which respectively precede and follow it, it is strictly symmetrical on both the entrance and the garden fronts. Both are basically E-plan; on the entrance side the stubby wings have few windows and end in massive chimneybreasts surmounted by tall brick stacks, diagonally set, and the centre has Lutyens's trademark of an almost uninterrupted row of small windows running on each side of the porch immediately beneath the eaves. There are tiny dormers in the roof. The porch projection rises the whole height of the house and is surmounted by a gable that curves slightly outwards at the bottom – a faintly oriental, or possibly even toytown, touch. The garden front has two projecting gables, the centre consisting of a big polygonal bay – lighting the Hall – with three transoms, and a tall gabled section on each side. The whole thing is built in the marvellously mellow-looking local sandstone.

Inside, the main living room is a vast two-storey Hall, entered through a sort of screens passage which does not, however, run straight in from the front door but opens off a transverse corridor. It is lined, with the same Sussex stone that we saw on the outside, to some two-thirds of its height; the rest, including the ceiling, is of plain white plaster. Opposite the immense bay, which is framed by a massive stone arch, is a broad fireplace, with a balcony above and a door behind it (where does the smoke go?), while to the side two most portentous doors with heavily rusticated surrounds and high segmental pediments lead into the screens passage. Across this, opposite the Hall, is the principal staircase, which leads up to a gallery over the passage whence an iron balcony looks down over the Hall. The stairs then continue up another short flight to a bedroom, outside which another identical balcony, immediately behind the first one, encloses a small landing. There are plenty of other illustrations of Lutyens's irrepressible playfulness, including cavernous inglenooks (in the parlour, the outer fireplace arch actually touches the ceiling) and, in the ante-room to the nursery, a special little window from which Nanny could look down to make sure that the children were behaving themselves.

## Up Marden*

*21; 7½ miles NW of Chichester off B2146*

For Ian Nairn, ST MICHAEL'S CHURCH possesses 'one of the loveliest interiors in England'; and he is right. It has stood, 500 feet up on a ridge of the Downs, with its endearing triangular chancel arch, virtually untouched since the thirteenth century; but the date is immaterial, for at Up Marden time stands still. This tiny church whispers only of eternity, and peace, and sunlit serenity. It has nothing to do with architecture, but if I left it out then this book itself would have no meaning.

## Uppark

*NT; 22; 5 miles SE of Petersfield on B2146*

It is a curiosity of Uppark that its two most celebrated residents lived there in unexpected capacities. Emma Hart – better known by her later name of Hamilton – a fifteen-year-old unmarried mother who had been discovered by Sir Harry Fetherstonhaugh while dancing at the 'Temple of Aesculapius' in the Aldwych, was brought there in 1780, effortlessly re-seduced, and set up briefly as his *maîtresse en titre*. A century later H.G. Wells spent thirteen years there below stairs while his mother was housekeeper and loved to tell, in later years, how he had goosed the kitchenmaids in the scullery passage, laying the foundations of those techniques of which in later life he was to make such copious and energetic use.

The house itself, however, breathes an air of civilised serenity and restraint. Built between 1685 and 1695 by William Talman at one of the highest points of the South Downs, in a lovely mellow brick with stone dressings, its hipped roof and graceful pediment on the south front give it a faintly Dutch air – which Repton's Doric colonnade of 1812 to the north does little to diminish. Inside, the sumptuous state rooms date from the third quarter of the eighteenth century, just when the high Palladian manner was about to give way to the gentler, more graceful, neo-classical. (The designer is not known; Henry Keene and James Paine have both been suggested.) It is a fascinating exercise to trace the rooms chronologically, starting with the Palladian Red Drawing Room and Small Drawing Room, both of 1755 or

*Uppark.*

thereabouts, through the Saloon (perhaps ten years later) and on to the Little Parlour, where the neo-classical has quite obviously arrived and which cannot have taken its present form before the 1770s. Finally, by way of an epilogue, comes the Dining Room, still preserving Talman's Corinthian pilasters – and the great dining table on which Emma danced – but rejuvenated by Repton until it speaks of the Regency and little else.

Below stairs – even if you forget H.G. Wells – the kitchen and other offices are a museum in themselves; and the early eighteenth-century dolls' house in the service lobby, authentic even down to the hallmarks on the silver, is a unique historical document.

## Wakehurst Place

*NT; 23; 5 miles N of Haywards Heath on B2028*

Although this magnificent E-shaped house, built in 1590 by Sir Edward Culpeper, is the property of the National Trust, it is leased to the Ministry of Agriculture and occupied by staff of the Royal Botanic Gardens, who maintain its own gardens as an offshoot of Kew. It is consequently not open to the public – a pity, since despite much interior remodelling it still contains some fine chimneypieces, strapwork ceilings and woodwork. Among later additions of the 1870s is a Chapel with windows by Kempe and, *pace* Pevsner, 'a room painted by a Japanese artist whom the Mikado had sent to Paris to study'.

What we can enjoy, forming as it does a spectacular backdrop to the gardens, is the show front to the south – originally part of the north range of an inner courtyard. It is grand and noble, but in no way awe-inspiring; rather the reverse, thanks to the series of small gables, each one enclosing two little columns on either side of the window, and decorated with finials and bobbles galore. They give it a gay, even exuberant, air. The frontispiece forming the short central bar of the E is of stone, with distinctly Renaissance touches including a rather naïve little triangular pediment on Ionic columns. How sad that it can no longer be in private hands.

The gardens, needless to say, are a dream.

## Worth

*24; 3 miles SE of Crawley on B2110*

When you first stand before the CHURCH OF ST NICHOLAS you must ignore, if you can, Salvin's nineteenth-century tower and broach spire; fix your gaze instead on the semi-circular apse, with its conical roof and lesenes – those intriguing if unlovely vertical pilaster strips around the outer walls that constitute one of the surest trademarks of a Saxon church. Then go inside, for this is where the real impact is made – by the height and breadth of the tremendous chancel arch and its transeptal brothers, by the proportions of the nave, by the titanic, unadorned four-squareness of it all. The semi-circular chancel, lit by three narrow round-headed lancets, is in fact largely rebuilt – at least on the inside; but it follows the original plan. The windows in the nave are virtually untouched. The church is probably of the eleventh century and radiates a tremendous sense of power, an awesome, primitive masculinity; not an easy church to love, perhaps, but a splendid one in which to tremble.

## Short List

### Bramber

*25; 8½ miles NW of Brighton on A283*

The house known as ST MARY'S is probably the eastern range of a courtyard building dating from the fifteenth century which housed the wardens of old Bramber bridge. It is timber-framed, with an overhanging first floor on the east and north sides. Inside is a plain sixteenth-century staircase, and on the first floor a room with early seventeenth-century wall paintings of landscapes, framed by arched panels in false perspectives.

### Castle Goring

*26; 1½ miles W of Worthing on A27*

This house, 50 yards off the A27, is worth a guinea a minute. It was designed in 1790 or so by Biagio Rebecca for Sir Bysshe Shelley, the poet's grandfather; he certainly got value for money. Of the three sections on the entrance side, the left wing is Perpendicular (its windows framed, with superb *insouciance*, in Norman dogtooth decoration), the central part vaguely castellated baronial, the right wing reminiscent of a slightly dottier Carcassonne. All this is odd enough; but it becomes odder still when, on the other side, you are confronted with a rather splendid Palladian–neo-classical.

When I was last there in June 1978 it looked sadly derelict. Alas, I failed to get in.

### Charlton

*27; 6 miles N of Chichester off A286*

FOX HALL is a tiny hunting lodge, built at the edge of the village (as part of the Goodwood estate) by Lord Burlington in about 1730. Outside, only the windows hint at its noble origins, but the room occupying virtually the whole of the first floor is of a pomposity and splendour which seem faintly ridiculous for so small a building, particularly in view of its place and purpose. The house as a whole is not beautiful, and never could have been, but is worth including for its curiosity value. It now belongs to the Landmark Trust.

### Cowdray House

*28; 1 mile N of Midhurst off A272*

A ruin but a tremendous one, Cowdray House was being built throughout the first half of the sixteenth century, and was gutted by fire in 1793. The Gatehouse still survives in relatively good shape, Gothicly overgrown around the battlements; most of the rest is little more than an empty shell, but somehow the majesty remains.

### Cuckfield Park

*29; 3 miles W of Haywards Heath off A272*

A charming brick Gatehouse of *c.*1570, with mullioned windows and four polygonal angle turrets, raises one's hopes; but they are dashed again at the first sight of the house, which was altered almost beyond recognition in 1848–51, when the Tudor east front was rendered and regularised and all its windows sashed. At the same time a new south range was built and adorned with hideous dormers. Only the north range betrays the house's Elizabethan origins. Inside there are one or two good plaster ceilings and fireplaces and a vast screen of 1581, no longer in its original position.

### Hardham

*30; 1 mile S of Pulborough on A29*

The small, primitive, eleventh-century CHURCH OF ST BOTOLPH with simple kingpost roofs is whitewashed and very attractive. It is famous for its early twelfth-century wall paintings, alas much faded.

### North Stoke

*31; 6 miles N of Littlehampton off B2139*

Here is a delightful CHURCH (of uncertain dedication), which is cruciform with a Norman nave, Early English chancel (with some charming foliage corbels), late thirteenth-century transepts and a complex early fourteenth-century chancel arch.

### South Harting

*32; 4 miles SE of Petersfield on B2146*

ST MARY AND ST GABRIEL is an unusually large cruciform church mainly of the early fourteenth century (the east end dates from 1858). A fire of 1576 resulted in new tower arches and, more important, some new and spectacular Elizabethan roofs. That of the chancel is particularly fine, and well worth coming to see.

### Stoughton

*33; 6 miles NW of Chichester off B2147*

This remote, still unspoilt village lies deep in the Downs. ST MARY'S CHURCH is revealed inside as a fine Saxon–Norman building. A towering chancel arch frames an east window rather oddly enlarged in the thirteenth century with rere-arches and narrow ringed shafts.

### Tillington

*34; 1 mile W of Petworth on A272*

ALL HALLOWS' CHURCH is worth mentioning for the tower with its 'Scots crown' – an unashamed eye-catcher for the benefit of Petworth. Local tradition claims it as the work of J.M.W. Turner, who trained as an architect.

### Warminghurst

*35; 9 miles N of Worthing off B2133*

The CHURCH OF THE HOLY SEPULCHRE has a numinous interior, cool and whitewashed, a unified nave and chancel culminating in a three-light window of about 1300. All this harmonises perfectly with the seventeenth- and eighteenth-century furnishings, notably the three-arched wooden screen, three-decker pulpit and box pews. William Penn lived at Warminghurst Place; if I had had this as my parish church, I should never have become a Quaker – or emigrated.

### Yapton

*36; 3 miles NW of Littlehampton on B2233*

ST MARY'S is a perfect example of what a rustic Sussex church looked like at the time of Magna Carta. It has a tie-beam roof with kingposts, and tiny little aisles, the outer walls of which are only about 5 feet off the ground. The east window is later, but the atmosphere is unspoilt.

# Wiltshire

In the earliest times, the area we know as Wiltshire seems to have been considered the centre of England. No other region is anything like so rich in prehistoric remains – indeed it has few rivals in all Europe. Today it possesses only one major town, Swindon, and even that is tucked away in the extreme north-east, near the Berkshire border. Of the rest, Salisbury is still mercifully small – with well under 50,000 inhabitants – yet is more than twice the size of any of the others. Here, then, is a county of little towns and villages, nearly all tucked away in the river valleys that furrow their way through the high downland, or in the broad vale of Pewsey that separates the Marlborough Downs from the vast – though now sadly desecrated – expanses of Salisbury Plain. (In marked contrast, the Neolithic and Bronze Age Wiltshiremen all seem to have preferred to live on the colder and unsheltered Downs; I have often wondered why this should be.)

But what towns and villages many of them are! Salisbury itself is an architectural treasure house, all too often overlooked; how many people, when they have finished with the cathedral, think of passing on to St Thomas's, with its tremendous Doom painting over the chancel arch? Of the smaller towns, Bradford-on-Avon, Devizes and Malmesbury are all outstanding, while among villages the justly celebrated Lacock and Castle Combe are closely rivalled by the lesser-known Steeple Ashton, Urchfont and any number of others. Driving through the county, one is struck over and over again not just by the beauty of these villages but by their variety – a variety that stems above all from the wide choice of building materials available. There are two superb local limestones, the golden Bath stone in the north-west and the cooler, whiter product of the Chilmark and Tisbury quarries in the south. There is sandstone, thanks to the great sarsens of the Marlborough Downs. There is chalk, obviously, in abundance, used both as a building stone and 'pugged', or powdered; and where there is chalk there is also flint. In the north-east, brick takes over. But there are no hard dividing lines, and Wiltshire builders loved to use two or more different materials, in bands, chequerwork or still more intricate patterning.

Ecclesiastical architecture must start with the eighth-century church of St Lawrence at Bradford-on-Avon, advancing through the Norman of Malmesbury and Devizes to the glorious Early English of Potterne, Bishops Cannings and of course Salisbury Cathedral itself, so inspiring from a distance, so disappointing from the front and within. Of the Decorated style, Wiltshire has surprisingly little to offer, apart from its greatest showpiece of all, the cathedral spire; my own favourite is Bishopstone. But by the second half of the fourteenth century, thanks to the Flemish weavers brought over by Edward III, the broadcloth industry was gathering momentum; wealth was flowing in; and the result was an explosion of sumptuous Perpendicular, beginning at Edington – where Decorated is still much in evidence – and finding its apogee at places like Lacock, Steeple Ashton, and St Thomas's, Salisbury. Credit was given where credit was due: in the moulding of the west window at Seend, pairs of sheep shears have been lovingly carved; while a rich mill-owner of Corsham has his tomb inscribed with the comfortable words:

*The labouring poor he never did contemn,*
*And God enriched him by the means of them.*

But it is in domestic architecture that Wiltshire really comes into its own. Here is richness indeed. First consider the manor houses: Great Chalfield, South Wraxall and Westwood above all, but there are others like Norrington (near Alvediston), Woodlands (near Mere) and Sheldon (near Chippenham) which, even if space has denied them separate entries in this book, are yet remarkable – and precious – survivals of the Middle Ages. Marvellous barns exist, too, at Tisbury and Bradford. With the sixteenth century comes the first grand prodigy house, Longleat, followed by Longford, Littlecote and, at the very end of the century, Stockton. The seventeenth brought Charlton, the Hall at Bradford, Newhouse (near Whiteparish) and that other great showstopper, Wilton, going on in the age of Wren to Urchfont, Mompesson and the perfection of Ramsbury. With the Georges come Campbell's Stourhead; Wyatt's Bowden Park; Lydiard Tregoze and Trafalgar, probably by Roger Morris; Adam's contributions to Bowood; and the crowning if somewhat austere glory of Paine's Wardour. Nor must we forget the gay Gothick of Lacock. If only Fonthill could be added to the list . . . .

The early nineteenth century carried on where the eighteenth left off, with Philipps House, Dinton and Pyt House, Newtown. After that there is little enough to merit a detour, with the possible exceptions of St Mary and St Nicholas at Wilton and Pugin's curiously endearing St Marie's Grange at Alderbury, with its medieval privy tower. (Victorian Gothic was all very well; but here, one wonders, was he not pushing things a little too far?) Our own century has made little architectural contribution to Wiltshire; on the other hand it has done it little permanent harm. The Ministry of Defence has, admittedly, a lot to answer for; but the huts and the hangars and the housing estates will one day disappear and leave Salisbury Plain undiminished. The M4 has saved far more in the towns and villages than it has destroyed in the countryside. Wiltshire is still one of the pleasant places of the earth.

---

## Amesbury

*1; 8 miles N of Salisbury on A345*

The abbey CHURCH OF ST MARY AND ST MELOR (and what is that obscure Breton youth doing here anyway?) has had its nave shortened at some time or other, but still looks noble enough with its sturdy square crossing-tower, its long chancel in which two brave fourteenth-century windows, richly traceried, interrupt the sequence of tall single lancets, and its great south transept, set with three more lancets at the end, advancing almost threateningly towards the road. Inside, the general air of nobility is preserved; if the church seems somehow a little devoid of character, much of the fault probably lies with William Butterfield, who was let loose on it in 1853. His east and west windows spoil the view in both directions; his hideous tiles on the east wall have, however, been decently obscured by curtains.

On the site of AMESBURY ABBEY itself – demolished soon after the Dissolution – there now rises a huge and stately Palladian mansion built in the 1830s by Thomas Hopper, on the site of and on similar lines to an earlier one by John Webb. The high hexastyle portico over a rusticated *porte-cochère* and the giant attached porticoes on each side are monumentally impressive, as is the central hall, with its tiers of arcaded galleries rising to the lantern of the tower. But the house has now been converted into flats, and sadly depersonalised in consequence.

## Avebury*

*2; 6½ miles W of Marlborough on A361*

Lying within the greatest megalithic stone circle in Europe, Avebury is greater far than Stonehenge and – though less immediately assimilable to the eye – to me a good deal more impressive. Four thousand years ago, it was probably one of the most important places in all England, and its immense upstanding sarsen stones still lure tourists – and the occasional pilgrim – in formidable numbers. But this is a book about architecture, not ancient history, and for me the beauty of Avebury, as opposed to its mystery and magic, lies in the church and the manor, standing lovingly next to each other in a perfect and quintessentially English composition.

ST JAMES'S CHURCH is originally Saxon, and still preserves two small Saxon windows – possibly five if we include the three circular ones in the north clerestory. Norman are the south door and font, fifteenth-century Perpendicular the tower. As for AVEBURY MANOR, stone-built and gabled, I know few more desirable small country houses anywhere. Begun in about 1557 on the site of a small foundation of Benedictines and enlarged some forty years later when the south range containing the Great Hall and Great Chamber was added, the house from the outside still looks much as it must have looked in the first years of the seventeenth century. Inside, nearly all the principal rooms, with their rich panelling and decorated chimneypieces, maintain the impression; the Great Hall, however, was split horizontally in two in the early eighteenth century – traditionally in preparation for a visit by Queen Anne, though Pevsner suggests a date of 1730, by which time she had been dead for sixteen years – and the resultant Dining Room and bedroom above are of that period. They are lovely rooms in their way; but one cannot help regretting their presence in what is otherwise so perfect a late Elizabethan setting.

*Avebury Manor.*

*Biddesden.*

## Biddesden

*3; 1½ miles W of Ludgershall off A342*

Here is as quirkish and lively a Queen Anne house as can be seen anywhere. The architect who built it for General John Webb in 1711 is unknown, which is sad because this building must have been his masterpiece. It is full of individuality, with its perfectly judged segmental pediment and its three-bay projection containing windows of different shapes at each level – including the three ravishing round ones that give more light to the two-storey Entrance Hall, and, incidentally, to the colossal portrait of Webb around which the Hall was probably designed. But what gives Biddesden another, special, fillip is the gloriously unexpected and supremely inappropriate turret, round and castellated, that pops up at the north-east corner – barely visible from the south front – apparently constructed to house a bell brought home by Webb from Lille as a trophy. And even that is not all: on the east and west sides the blank windows are light-heartedly painted in *trompe-l'oeil* by Roland Pym and Dora Carrington respectively.

## Bishops Cannings*

*4; 3 miles NE of Devizes off A361*

ST MARY'S is a beautiful cruciform church, whose profusion of perfectly proportioned lancets proclaims its Early Englishness – though the windows of the aisles and clerestory are obviously a couple of centuries later, as is the spire. The interior, scraped though it is, comes as no disappointment; indeed, the scalloped capitals beneath the pointed arches suggest that the body of the church is even a little earlier than it looks from the outside. There is a gloriously high crossing arch and the crossing itself is suitably monumental, leading to a long, vaulted chancel which would be lovely if only it were a very little higher. (A mark on the side of the tower shows that it originally was.) There is a very splendid view back from the altar towards the west, with the centrally placed font beneath a triple lancet, all beautifully lit – though the Victorian glass is horrid.

One final bonus: note the Penitential Seat just inside the doorway, surmounted by a huge hand painted with various depressing reminders of sin and death. Here is the seventeenth century at its gloomiest.

## Bishopstone*

*5; 4½ miles SW of Salisbury off A354*

ST JOHN THE BAPTIST is a sumptuous church for a small village, cruciform and almost all early fourteenth-century, with lovely, flowing, Decorated tracery in its windows. Halfway along the south wall there is a curious little two-bay extrusion, arcaded and vaulted, covering a tomb; and just beyond this towards the east, a lovable if faintly ridiculous priest's door of extreme pomposity – its cusped and ogeed canopy far too heavy for its size, supported to the west on curious brackets which snake back into the wall at right-angles to each other. Although the underside of this canopy is only 2 feet broad, it is *vaulted*, with three ribs on each side and a large boss in the middle. Was this some medieval joke? It made me laugh aloud.

The interior is no disappointment. There is more rib vaulting – equally ornate but a good deal better justified – in the chancel and southern transept, where a splendidly virtuoso monument by Pugin does its successful best to compete with the immense wall tomb opposite in the northern one. Here and in the chancel, grotesque figures crouch in the corbels. The sedilia and piscina are splendid, and naturally vaulted too. This church is worth going a long way to see.

## Bowden Park

*6; 4 miles SE of Chippenham off A342*

A ravishing Georgian house by James Wyatt with crisp clear-cut masonry, Bowden Park was completed in 1796 and commands a superb view to the west over the Avon valley and Lacock. Perhaps because of this, Wyatt has put the main emphasis on to the narrow west front rather than the much longer south one, giving it a central bow of four giant Ionic columns and, to each side, a single broad window flanked by a niche. Within the bow is an elliptical Music Room, with a lovely circular bedroom above it. Wyatt's original decoration, including a frieze of bucrania running through both these rooms and the Staircase Hall, is perfectly preserved thanks to the present owners, who have spared no expense to restore the whole house to immaculate condition. There is a pretty shell grotto in the garden to the south-east. Bowden is one of the very few remaining houses by Wyatt in the classical idiom and, like Heaton House (Lancashire), Aston Hall (Shropshire) and Dodington House (Gloucestershire), exemplifies all the salient features of his domestic style.

## Bowood*

*7; 5 miles SE of Chippenham off A342*

Less, as somebody once said, is more; and however much one may regret the demolition in 1955–6 of the 'Big House', begun by Sir Orlando Bridgeman in 1725 and enlarged by Henry Keene and Robert Adam, it cannot be denied that the surviving 'Little House' by these last two architects, its south range now open to the lake and to the morning sun, must be a far pleasanter place to live in. This 'Little House' began life as two courtyards by Keene, intended principally for stable and kitchens, which had been left open on the south side. In 1768, however, the 1st Marquess of Lansdowne – whose father had bought the property fourteen years before – commissioned Robert Adam to close them off. His original idea was to do so with a range of greenhouses, but what actually took shape was something a good deal more grandiose: a 100-yard-long Orangery with a fine pedimented central portico, and two unpedimented sub-porticoes respectively a quarter and three-quarters of the way along it. It is a fine composition indeed, exquisitely judged and not, it must be said, really needing the vaguely Italianate clock tower which Sir Charles Barry saw fit to plonk on the roof.

The purpose of this clock tower is to call attention to C.R. Cockerell's neo-classical Chapel which lies beneath it, stretching back at right-angles to the Orangery in the range separating Keene's two courtyards. Cockerell worked at Bowood from 1822 to 1824, supplying it with a splendid Library at the far end of the Orangery. His too is the decoration of the so-called 'Laboratory', in which Joseph Priestley discovered oxygen in 1770. The east side, by Keene, originally intended as nurseries, has two pedimental angle pavilions with a two-storey, seven-bay block between them.

Bowood boasts grounds and a park as glorious as any in England – lake and cascade, temples and grottoes,

*Bowood.*

Capability Brown at his virtuoso best. Architecturally, however, they contain only one building that must be mentioned here – the Mausoleum built by Robert Adam between 1761 and 1765, in other words well before he started work on the house proper. It is square, with a Doric portico, very short projections on each side and a central dome. Inside, all is very pure, and the projections are revealed as being tunnel-vaulted recesses for the tombs themselves. The only mystery is how the dome is supported, since there are no squinches or pendentives, merely flat horizontal panels between the circular rim and the four corners of the square.

## Boyton

*8; 5½ miles SE of Warminster off A36*

ST MARY'S is a pretty village church of the thirteenth and fourteenth centuries; it would, however, hardly have merited inclusion but for its south chapel of about 1280. This seems to have been built by Walter Giffard, Archbishop of York, and his brother Godfrey, Bishop of Worcester, in memory of a third brother, Alexander, 'hero of the battle of Mansourah in Eygpt, 1250'. The tomb, with effigy – the feet are resting on an otter – is presumably, though not unquestionably, Sir Alexander; but even this point is of subordinate interest. The glory of Boyton, over-riding all else, is the chapel's west window, a show-stopper if ever there was one. It is circular, 12 feet across, with an intricate design of convex triangles, circles and quatrefoils; during a recent restoration it was discovered that the smallest circles were designed to rotate, in special grooves, within the larger ones. More incredible still, this is among the earliest examples of bar tracery in England, which possesses no other church window remotely like it.

BOYTON MANOR, overlooking the churchyard, dates from 1618 and has a two-storeyed porch on the east side, with Ionic columns below, Corinthian ones above. The south side has a doorway of 1700, the staircase behind it a fine plaster ceiling.

*The church of St Lawrence, Bradford-on-Avon.*

## Bradford-on-Avon*

*9; 2½ miles NW of Trowbridge on A363*

'The praty clothinge towne on Avon . . . made all of stone': thus did John Leland describe Bradford in 1542. I would go further. To me, Bradford is not just pretty; it is one of the loveliest small towns in England. In essence, it appears as a smaller, more intimate Bath – without any of the great civic showpieces, perhaps, but built of that same magical stone and breathing the same air of serene and measured prosperity. Its central focus is the TOWN BRIDGE, which still keeps two of its thirteenth-century arches, though it was largely rebuilt 400 years later. The little Chapel on it is also essentially medieval, though the roof and finial – supporting a Bradford gudgeon in copper gilt – date only from the seventeenth century, by which time it was being used as a lock-up. Its two cells are still *in situ*, their iron bedsteads vainly awaiting the next occupants.

The view from the bridge encapsulates the whole spirit of Bradford. Along the riverside are the cloth factories and mills of the industrial revolution, admirable buildings in their own right which in no way detract from the picture – rather the reverse, since they give it character and point. Then, to the north, the best vista of all: those wonderful stone houses, street after street of them, climbing and clustering one above the other up the steep river bank, beautifully proportioned every one, and including several free-standing small town mansions of real distinction. One of the best, just above Holy Trinity church, is the LITTLE CHANTRY, which is in fact part of a larger house behind it, the CHANTRY, in which Byron's friend Hobhouse was born; above it again lies BARTON ORCHARD, an eighteenth-century terrace of much charm.

HOLY TRINITY CHURCH is not particularly exciting, despite its 20-foot squint, the longest in England; but, just opposite, the tall yet tiny Anglo-Saxon CHURCH OF ST LAWRENCE is an extraordinary survival indeed. It was rediscovered only in 1871, when it was identified with a fair degree of certainty as the 'Ecclesiola' built by St Aldhelm in about AD 700. The chancel, higher than it is long, has been beautifully and sensitively restored, with a few remnants of an old Saxon cross and altar frontal nicely incorporated into the restoration. Notice too the pair of Byzantinesque sculpted angels, soaring high above the chancel arch.

But in Bradford it seems invidious to pick out individual streets or buildings; better far to buy the admirable town guide produced by the local Chamber of Commerce and follow the itineraries it suggests. You need not turn back when you reach the gates of THE HALL, at the end of Woolley Street on the right: it is not open to the public, but the owner, Mr Alex Moulton – inventor of the Moulton bicycle and much else besides – kindly grants permission to enter the garden to those who call first at the lodge. Once in the garden, you are face to face with a Jacobean country house of real magnificence, possessing to the south a show front that can be compared with those of Hardwick or Longleat. It is true that it was very largely refaced in 1848, but this hardly matters: even where the stonework is not

*The Hall, Bradford-on-Avon.*

original, every detail has been scrupulously copied, and after a century's weathering it now looks, surely, as fine as ever. So elaborate is this front, so immense the area of glass in the windows, so impressive the height of each of the two main storeys, that one suspects the hand of Robert Smythson himself. By the time the Hall was built he had left Wiltshire; but many of his Longleat masons were still about and would have had no difficulty in interpreting any plans or sketches he might have sent them. At all events, whether he designed it or not, here is a house of which he might well have been proud.

South-east of the town, at BARTON FARM, is a fourteenth-century TITHE BARN, one of the most monumental in the country. The GRANARY next to it is almost as old and very nearly as impressive.

BALCOMBE COURT to the west has additions of 1734 by the elder John Wood, in particular the Palladian villa at the south-west corner which forms the frontispiece to the main part of the house and was built for Walter Yerbury, a local clothier who made a fortune from inventing a new type of cloth. It looks as though it had strayed across the border from Bath; indeed Wood himself said it had 'the best tetrastyle frontispiece in square pillars [of the Ionic order] yet executed in or about Bath'. The pillars are in fact giant pilasters and carry a pediment, as do the ground-floor windows. The west side has a shallow bay window with a tripartite window above. There is an enchanting octagonal Study whose ceiling has exquisite plasterwork – a central basket overflowing with fruit and flowers encircled by cherubs and with swags of leaves, grapes and roses hanging down the coved wall.

## Charlton Park

*10; 2 miles NE of Malmesbury on B4040*

This great Jacobean prodigy house was very largely remodelled on the inside – and to some extent on the outside too – by Matthew Brettingham the Younger between 1772 and 1776. For the past few years it has been undergoing equally drastic alteration as a result of the decision to divide it up into flats. This work, however, is being quite magnificently and sensitively done, and the house still fully deserves its place in this book.

The entrance front, to the west, is much as it has always been. It is E-shaped, with two projecting side wings and a central porch, behind and to each side of which runs an open loggia. In the inner angles of the E are tall four-storey turrets with ogee caps; two more opposite them mark the corners on the east side. The composition might well sound a bit heavy; that it is not so is principally due to the exuberance of the strapwork cresting running round the top.

Brettingham reworked the south and east fronts, but his principal alteration was to cover in the vast interior court. The resulting great Central Hall has been retained and redecorated and looks marvellous – a lovely classical composition in pale green and white, with big apses to east and west and, to the sides, galleries on two floors, supported on the ground floor by Ionic and on the upper by Corinthian columns. There is much fine plasterwork: medallions, decorative panels, and deep coffering in the apses. Still more plaster enriches the elliptical lantern above, and the splendid Saloon that forms the centre of the east range. Here the decoration is said to be by Wyatt, though I can find no confirmation of this.

The relatively modest staircase – tucked away in a corner, with its own top lighting – leads up to the Long Gallery of the Jacobean house. This was retained by Brettingham, but the present conversion work has necessitated dividing it up both vertically and horizontally. Fortunately this has not involved the destruction of the glorious strapwork ceiling with its frieze of monsters and mythological animals; parts of it, still in their original position, now embellish several of the new rooms looking out over the porch to the west.

## Corsham

*11; 4½ miles SW of Chippenham off A4*

A fine village, Corsham has more really good houses in it than any other in Wiltshire – most of them a good deal better than the great house that attracts the visitors. They are nonetheless right to come, since CORSHAM COURT possesses a remarkably fine collection of pictures and eighteenth-century furniture; but architecturally the house has been altered so often in ill-advised attempts to keep up with changing fashions that most of its personality has been lost. Starting Elizabethan in 1582, when it was built of local stone by Thomas Smythe, a haberdasher, it was partly Palladianised in 1749 and gently neo-classicised in the 1760s by Capability Brown – who, however, retained the exterior Elizabethan character of the south façade. The east wing he converted into a suite of state rooms, of which the finest is the long Picture Gallery, with its curiously coved ceiling executed by Thomas Stocking of Bristol. Then – after a furious row with James Wyatt whose designs were rejected – Corsham was disastrously Gothicised by Nash after 1800. The disaster was not so much aesthetic as structural; within a few years of completion the foundations were collapsing under loads for which they were never intended, several rooms were being flooded whenever it rained, and dry rot was rampant. In 1840 Nash's work was almost totally demolished and Corsham given yet another face, pseudo-Jacobean this time, by a third-rate Victorian architect, Thomas Bellamy. All that remains of the Gothic dream are a few bits of furniture, a mantelpiece or two, some decorative mouldings, and Nash's enchanting little Dairy. No wonder the *Quarterly Review* in 1826 published the following verse:

*Augustus at Rome was for building renown'd,*
*And of marble he left what of brick he had found;*
*But is not our Nash, too, a very great master?*
*He finds us all brick and he leaves us all plaster.*

THE GROVE, an attractive eighteenth-century house with a fine staircase is, at the time of writing, open by appointment with the Corsham Estate Office.

*St John's Church, Devizes.*

## Devizes

*12; 7 miles SE of Melksham on A361*

Here is another of those lovely Wiltshire towns, like Bradford, in which walking is a real pleasure. The CASTLE, where it all began, was completely destroyed by Cromwell and now exists only as a rather jolly Victorian affair; but the MARKET PLACE and the neighbouring streets are full of good things. Once again one hesitates to mention individual buildings; the ensemble is what matters. Of secular joys, there is the admirable bow-fronted TOWN HALL in St John Street (by Thomas Baldwin of Bath, 1806) and, only a few yards away facing the Market Place, the NEW HALL – formerly the Cheese Hall – of 1750–2, largely ruined by the fascia of the Cheltenham and Gloucester Building Society, which ought to know better. In the Market Place itself, both parts of the eighteenth-century BEAR HOTEL (which was once kept by Sir Thomas Lawrence's father) are good, the 1857 CORN EXCHANGE – crowned by Ceres – irresistible, and there is a really beautiful early eighteenth-century brick house at No.17, whose panelled rooms with stuccoed ceilings on the first floor can be visited by appointment. Best of all the houses in the town, however, is BROWNSTON HOUSE, dated 1720, near the Castle Hotel in New Park Street.

Devizes can boast two churches of considerable importance, both built in about 1130 by Bishop Roger of Salisbury: ST JOHN'S for the castle and garrison, ST MARY'S for the people of the town. Of the two, he clearly took more trouble over the former. Outside, its most notable features are the massive Norman crossing-tower and the later fifteenth-century south chapel, inescapably reminiscent of Bromham. Inside, all eyes must turn eastward where, beyond the great crossing (whose north and south arches are precociously pointed), the rib-vaulted chancel is a riot of interlaced blind arcading with bold zigzag decoration. Behind it the stone wall is carved in fish-scales. The effect is only slightly spoilt by some wonderfully nasty Victorian glass – including a severed

*Philipps House, Dinton.*

head of John the Baptist, with a carving knife above to make sure everybody gets the point – in the north and east windows.

The sister church of St Mary has a similar vaulted Norman chancel, but more tentative and without the fish-scales. (The east wall is in any case a restoration.) Otherwise it is now largely fifteenth-century and, after St John's, something of an anti-climax.

## Dinton

*13; 8 miles W of Salisbury on B3089*
*Includes Philipps House (NT)*

PHILIPPS HOUSE is a serene, unadventurous, neo-classical house by Jeffrey Wyatt, completed in 1816, eight years before he changed his name to Wyatville. (Can it have been inspired by Pyt House, completed eleven years before and only 10 miles or so away at Newtown? The two are suspiciously alike.) There is a particularly attractive approach, through a small park, so that one's first view of the house is oblique, from the south-east. It is built of local Chilmark limestone, very finely jointed, with a plain nine-bay front and a dominating Ionic portico. The details are restrained and stylised, the proportions perfect. Inside, though the decorative features are of high quality, it strikes one as faintly disappointing – except, perhaps, for the great staircase, lit from a central circular lantern and surrounded by screens of Ionic columns at first-floor level. The principal state rooms are good but unmemorable; one finds oneself wishing that a house as distinguished as this would stop playing quite so safe.

## Edington

*14; 4 miles NE of Westbury on B3098*

ST MARY, ST KATHERINE AND ALL SAINTS is quite a dedication, but this majestic church, so four-square and embattled that it looks more like a small castle, fully lives up to it. Built all of a piece as a chantry between 1352 and 1361, it is also the perfect illustration of how the Decorated style turned into the Perpendicular. The east window first tells the story: see how the two central mullions shoot straight up to the arch, oblivious of the flowing tracery around them. The west window repeats it, just as clearly but in slightly different language. The aisle windows, on the other hand, are still untouched by the wind of change.

There is a high, beautifully proportioned chancel with exquisite canopied niches framing the east window (no Perpendicular threats here either). The white plaster ceiling of 1789 provides a nice contrast between Gothic and Gothick and here at least, it must be admitted, the combination works beautifully. I feel a good deal less happy about the fussy seventeenth-century pink and white decoration of the vaults in the nave and crossing; the dark, heavily restored rood-screen is also a pity. In fact, the whole western part of the church strikes me as strangely lacking in charm. Individual features are excellent; quality and craftsmanship are high throughout; but the atmosphere seems cold and unwelcoming. Edington is undoubtedly one of the great churches of Wiltshire, just as Salisbury is one of the great cathedrals of England; my loss, perhaps, but I cannot love either of them.

*Great Chalfield Manor.*

## Great Chalfield

*15; 2½ miles NE of Bradford-on-Avon on B3107*
*Includes Great Chalfield Manor (NT)*

Thomas Tropnell was a rich and ambitious landowner who after thirty years of remorseless litigation eventually succeeded, in 1467, in acquiring the manor of Great Chalfield and at once set about building himself a new house of yellowish grey Corsham stone on the ancient site. This is in all essentials the house we see today as we approach GREAT CHALFIELD MANOR (NT) across the moat on its northern side. The general design is vaguely symmetrical, the Great Hall being flanked by gabled wings with elaborate oriel windows; but it is not slavishly so. (The cult of perfect symmetry was still a century away in the future.) The two oriels, for example, are of quite different shapes, and the huge chimney-breast just left of centre, marking the position of the Hall hearth, looks strangely incongruous to the modern eye – though it is unlikely to have bothered Tropnell much. The windows are finely detailed and there are intricately carved stone figures on the gable ends.

Inside the Great Hall itself, perhaps the most remarkable feature is the trio of stone masks above the Hall bays and in the gallery, through the pierced eyes and mouths of which the ladies, or perhaps the steward, could watch how things were going down below. Another oddity is the absence of a dais, or indeed any trace of one; by the time Great Chalfield was built, local lords had largely given up the old tradition of dining in the Hall with their retainers, and it looks as though Tropnell from the very first took his meals in a private Dining Room beyond the screens passage. It was only comparatively recently that part of the sixteenth-century panelling in this room was removed to reveal, under a thick layer of whitewash, a forceful wall painting which is almost certainly a portrait of the man himself – and gives him five fingers as well as the thumb on each hand.

Upstairs, the North Bedroom behind the right-hand oriel still has its original roof timbers and even a fragment of the fifteenth-century glass. Behind the other oriel, however, the solar is largely a reconstruction and on the south side there is all too little that Tropnell would recognise. This is a pity, but we cannot grumble: enough of Great Chalfield still remains to give it character and atmosphere in plenty, as well as the distinction of being one of the most valuable surviving examples of the late medieval English manor house at its best.

The little parish church, ALL SAINTS, only a few yards away, is originally fourteenth-century, but was added to first by Tropnell (who built his own chapel) and then again in the eighteenth century. There is a fine three-decker pulpit and a delightful little organ in the Italian Gothic style, painted with exemplary talent by a Miss Maurice in 1880.

## Lacock*

*NT; 16; 3 miles S of Chippenham off A350*

This ravishing village is entirely the property of the National Trust. Every century is represented from the fourteenth onwards, but somehow everything coalesces, effortlessly and harmoniously. There are not even any television aerials, since the Trust built a single communal one on a neighbouring hillside, resulting in the removal of one of the worst of twentieth-century eyesores and, incidentally, far better reception all round. The CHURCH OF ST CYRIAC is as good as the rest. A Perpendicular building (though the transepts are earlier), its lofty nave is dazzlingly lit by huge clerestory windows. Its pride and glory, however, is the north-east chapel of about 1430, lierne-vaulted with stone pendant, and containing, in the tomb of Sir William Sharington, one of the most important early Elizabethan monuments in England.

And so to LACOCK ABBEY. The original convent, for Augustinian canonesses, was founded in 1232 and continued to prosper until its dissolution in 1539. A good deal of the medieval building has survived, notably the fourteenth- to fifteenth-century Cloister and several rooms leading off it, including a vaulted Chapter House and Warming Room. All this is interesting enough, but there are plenty of better examples around the country; what makes Lacock unique is what happened to it after it was bought by Sharington in 1540 and entered a new phase of its existence, this time as a country house. Sharington gave it the octagonal tower in the south-east corner; more of his additions can be seen in the Stone Gallery and Brown Gallery. (He used as mason one John Chapman, who had a good knowledge of Renaissance detail; the tower chamber is vaulted in a most original way.)

At this point I cannot resist quoting John Aubrey:

> Dame Olave a Daughter and coheir of Sir Henry Sharington of Lacock being in Love with John Talbot (a younger Brother of the Earle of Shrewsbury) and her Father not consenting that she should marry Him: discoursing with Him one night from the Battlements of the Abbey-Church; said shee, *I will leap downe to you*: her sweet Heart replied, He would catch Her then: but he did not believe she would have done it: she leap't downe and the wind (which was then high) came under her coates: and did something breake the fall: Mr Talbot caught her in his armes, but she struck him dead; she cried out for help, and he was with great difficulty brought to life again: her father told her that since she had made such a leap she should e'en marrie him.

But it was in the eighteenth century that the fun really began. By then Lacock had passed to the Talbot family and in 1753 John Ivory Talbot commissioned the gentleman-architect Sanderson Miller to rebuild his Hall in the Gothick taste.

The result of Miller's work is by far the most memorable room in the house, outside as well as in. The two huge mullioned and transomed windows with their heavy

*The village street, Lacock.*

ogival hood-moulds, the star decoration between them like a Hindu caste mark, and the polygonal corner turrets are the most arresting features of the west front, but even this is inadequate preparation for what lies within. All over the walls, in highly ornate, canopied niches, stand terracotta statues and busts which make up one of the most curious collections of Baroque sculpture in any English country house. They are the work of an Austrian named Sederbach, of whom absolutely nothing is known except that he was said to be 'easy and not expensive'. He was obviously no great master; but he had energy and imagination in plenty, and even if his figures were occasionally apt to get a bit out of control – some of them, in their frenzied lunging and plunging, seem to be on the point of hurling themselves bodily from their niches – they make perfect foils for Miller's conception.

Lacock's final claim to fame is as the birthplace of photography. The small oriel window on the south front – one of three inserted in about 1830 – was photographed by William Henry Fox Talbot in 1835, resulting in the world's first negative. The sixteenth-century barn at the entrance to the abbey has now been converted by the National Trust into a fascinating Fox Talbot Memorial Museum.

*Lacock Abbey.*

## Littlecote

*17; 3 miles NW of Hungerford off A419*

Though parts of the fabric go back to the fifteenth century, Littlecote is for all practical purposes an E-shaped Elizabethan house, with its long front of rich red brick with stone dressings – it is the only important brick mansion in the county – stretching out along the valley of the Kennet. It was at one time the property of Elizabeth's Lord Chief Justice of England, Sir John Popham; but the house now whispers far more insistently of the days of the Civil War, when Sir John's grandson, Col. Alexander Popham, commanded the local Parliamentary forces. Not only their arms and armour but also their jerkins of thick yellow felt hang around the walls of the Great Hall, and strangely evocative they are.

Once through the Great Hall, the most perfect of the seventeenth-century rooms is the Brick Hall with its carved oak panelling, its ancient pewter and its brick floor which was till recent years regularly strewn with rushes from the neighbouring water-meadows. The most eccentric is the Dutch Parlour with its painted ceiling and walls, one of the latter covered with Dutch genre scenes, their frames, ribbons and even hanging nails painted in *trompe-l'oeil*. The most interesting and important, however, is unquestionably the Cromwellian Chapel, with screen and gallery of turned wooden balusters and a high-roofed pulpit where the altar would normally be. This is said to be the most complete example of such a chapel still extant.

Littlecote is gruesomely haunted, as a result of a dreadful incident in 1575 when an unwanted new-born baby was hurled into a fire. The fireplace is still shown, as is the bed – with its original hangings – in which the baby was born and the unknown mother died. A guide in the 110-foot Long Gallery told me that she, and many of her colleagues, had often heard the heavy footfalls of Roundhead soldiers tramping about on the floor above, and more in the Cromwellian Guard Room below.

## Longford Castle*

*18; 4 miles SE of Salisbury off A338*

Sir Thomas Gorges, who built Longford Castle between 1578 and 1591, was a religious mystic; his tomb in Salisbury Cathedral is scattered about with astrological and cabbalistic signs, and the great house which he erected a few miles away on the banks of the Avon is surely the strangest of all those that have survived from the sixteenth century. Like Sir Thomas Tresham's famous lodge at Rushton in Northamptonshire – though on an infinitely grander scale – Longford was designed on a triangular plan, its three round towers at the corners symbolising Father, Son and Holy Ghost; its architect seems to have been John Thorpe the Elder – arguably the first English architect whose name has come down to us – some of whose drawings for it have been preserved in his sketch-book, now in Sir John Soane's Museum. There have admittedly been many alterations over four centuries: the house suffered considerable damage during the Civil War, when it became first a Royalist and later a Parliamentarian stronghold; the interior was Georgianised in the 1730s and 1740s and then returned

*The Central Hall, Longford Castle.*

to something approaching its original style by Anthony Salvin, at the cost of much rebuilding. The outside, however, looks relatively unchanged, the corner towers and the garden front having preserved the distinctive chequer pattern of stone and flint that constitutes another memorable feature of the house.

The great entrance front, which runs so magnificently between the northern and western towers, lacks this pattern, being built of stone throughout. It is in fact a remodelling by Salvin, who moved the flanking three-bay pedimented wings one bay nearer the centre and recessed the second-floor section above the loggia; but he preserved and re-used the original materials whenever possible, and the result is still instantly recognisable from Thorpe's original elevation. The central feature – unusually early for its date – is a five-bay loggia on two floors, with four-centred arches at ground level and round-headed ones above; the lower ones are supported on rather squat, tapering columns standing on high plinths; the upper on fluted half columns set into piers. Above this the recessed second storey, its cross windows separated by a line of caryatids, supports a central segmentally pedimented crest carved with a figure of Neptune sitting, uncharacteristically, in a boat. This is traditionally believed to represent an Armada galleon – which, however, it in no way resembles – wrecked in 1588 off Hurst Castle, of which Gorges was at that time Governor. By then, work at the still unfinished Longford had left him practically penniless; fortunately the wreck was awarded to him by the Queen, and subsequently found to contain 'Silver barrs as well as Iron ones and such a vast though concealed Treasure as served . . . to compleate their pile at Langford [*sic*]'. To each side of the loggias rises a three-bay wing, the middle bay being narrower than its neighbours and carrying niches rather than windows, and the bays being separated by heavily ornamented pilasters on the two lower storeys and more caryatids above. They also support pedimented crests, with niches identical to those below. Beyond these wings is a slightly recessed, nondescript bay born of Salvin's remodelling; then come the corner towers with their shaped battlements, tall chimneys and pinnacles.

The garden front, to which Salvin added gabled projections, and the north-east side which he entirely transformed, need not detain us for long; we can now enter the house, through the centre of the loggia. This was originally a screens passage, with the Hall opening off it to the right, in what is now the Billiard Room. It leads directly through to what in Gorges's day would have been an interior court but is now covered over to form a central Hall with circular staircases in the corners. Of the grand reception rooms the two most important are those which run the length of the garden front, on the ground and first floors respectively – the upper one forming the gallery in which the best of Longford's staggering collection of pictures are splendidly displayed. The most delightful, however, if only

*Longford Castle.*

because of their shape, are the circular rooms in the corner towers. One remembers in particular the Green Drawing Room, its walls and upholstery still covered in the original dark green Genoa velvet, and its superb portraits by Holbein and Quentin Matsys; the Study in the ground floor of the west tower, where the decorative Renaissance panelling must be contemporary with the house itself, together with the tremendous Elizabethan chimneypiece framing a relief of Venus and Mars and rising to the intricately patterned ceiling; and, immediately above it, the astonishing former Chapel; its ribbed Gothicising vault and outsize central pendant of solid stone also go back to the time of Gorges, as do the ten Corinthian columns of Purbeck marble which carry it.

Wiltshire possesses, at Wilton and Longleat, two of the most famous country houses in England. They are both larger than Longford, and more palatial; but neither, to my mind, is as fascinating – nor as spectacular. The house is not normally open to the public, but groups may be admitted by special appointment.

## Longleat

*19; 3 miles SW of Warminster on A362*

You approach Longleat from above. The drive winds slowly up a gentle hill, over its crest, and then, suddenly, in a distant but glorious prospect, the house is revealed, standing four-square in Capability Brown's setting of park and lake and woodland, neither dominated by it nor dominating, quietly secure in its splendour.

So magnificent is the sight, so harmonious the marriage of art and nature, that the originality of the concept is easily forgotten. Half a century before John Thynne acquired the land from the Carthusians in 1541, for a rich man to have chosen such a place for his country seat would have been unthinkable. Though scenically superb, strategically it was disastrous, and in medieval England the first requirement for any major non-religious building was a good defensive position; an Englishman's home was of necessity, literally as well as figuratively, his castle. But Henry VII had changed all that. Perhaps for the first time since Roman days, he had brought serenity to the land, and great houses began to be built for pleasure and display rather than for impregnability. As the sixteenth century progressed, walls grew thinner, windows higher, and façades adopted more and more Renaissance motifs – superimposed columns, for instance, or busts of the Roman Emperors in circular niches. Of this new style, which was to develop into what for want of a better name we might call the High Elizabethan, Longleat is the prototype. Sir John Thynne – he had been knighted on the battlefield of Pinkie in 1545, while still bleeding from his wounds, and was thereafter allowed to quarter on his arms the Scottish lion with its tail twisted – was not only a compulsive builder but a perfectionist, and from 1547 till his death in 1580 he never allowed Longleat a moment's peace. One of his neighbours actually wrote a satire in which the house itself complained of its exhausting life: 'But now see him that by these thirtie yeares almost with such turmoyle of mynd hath byn thinking of me, framing and erecting me, musing many a tyme with great care and now and then pulling downe this or that parte of me to enlardge sometyme a foote or some few inches, upon a conceyt, or this or that man's speech. . . .'

In fact, thanks to the remarkably complete records and building accounts which survive, we can see that Thynne effectively rebuilt the house twice before it was destroyed by fire in 1567, and twice more afterwards; its present appearance with the pilastered bow windows in three stages, Doric, Ionic (endearingly referred to in the accounts as 'Dorrick and Yonk') and Corinthian, dates only from the last decade of his life. During this period he had as his master masons – working the beautiful stone that he had dragged here from a quarry he owned near Bath – the *émigré* Frenchman Allen Maynard and the greatest name in Elizabethan architecture, Robert Smythson; but architects in the modern sense – designers rather than artificers – were still unknown in England, and if any one man can be said to be the architect of Longleat, that man is unquestionably Thynne himself. His, too, was the idea of building the little square pavilions on the roof to serve as 'banketting houses' – a mystifying description until one learns that in the sixteenth century 'banquet' simply meant 'dessert'; Thynne and his guests would stroll up in twos and threes to the roof after dinner to sip a final glass or two of wine and watch the sun go down behind the Mendip Hills.

Inside the house, only the Great Hall has remained fundamentally unchanged since Sir John's day, with its hammer-beam roof (flattened in the late seventeenth century when the Library was built above) and the tremendous fireplace, almost certainly carved by Maynard. The rest, magnificent as it is, has been altered beyond recognition. The most interesting room remaining, the library built for Bishop Ken in the 1690s, is frustratingly not open to the public; the others mostly bear the stamp either of Sir Jeffrey Wyatville, who was turned loose on the house from 1801 to 1811, or of the Italian decorators and plasterers imported in the 1860s. Their craftsmanship was faultless, but the over-riding effect is one of gloom. It is a relief to emerge once more into the sunshine, to see the house again as it should be seen and as it was originally conceived – the first truly Renaissance house to be built in England, a milestone in the history of our architecture.

## Lydiard Tregoze*

*20; 5 miles W of Swindon off A420*

Here is another of those beautiful compositions of house, church and park, all setting each other off to perfection. The house was built in the 1740s, of finest Bath stone ashlar, by an unknown architect (probably Roger Morris) on the site of an earlier, medieval building, parts of which can still be seen at the back. It is a fine Georgian edifice with its three-bay pediment on the south-west front and corner towers *à la* Wilton, very restrained and perhaps just the tiniest bit dull. There is beautiful decoration in the state rooms, especially in the Library, which has preserved all its original bookcases: a really lovely room. The whole place is admirably maintained by the Borough of Thamesdown, who run it as a conference centre.

Nonetheless, there are any number of houses all over the country every bit as good as this one, and had it stood by itself it might well never have found its way into this book. But it does not stand by itself. ST MARY'S CHURCH next to it is unique in Wiltshire, almost in England, for the wealth and splendour of its contents, and effortlessly earns for Lydiard its star. Basically a thirteenth-century building, it was rebuilt and enlarged in the early fifteenth by one Oliver St John, the first of a family line which was to hold the manor for the next 500 years. By then it was already rich in wall paintings, several of which still survive in various states of preservation – notably the poignant Risen Christ on the second pier of the south arcade; but it was the St Johns, and they alone, who made the church the treasure house it is.

The most extraordinary single object is a gigantic family triptych, a good 15 feet high, consisting of a number of painted panels, some hinged, some completely detachable. This was begun by Sir John St John in 1615 to commemorate his parents, who are depicted on the central inner panel; but it was added to at various times throughout the century and into the next. Meanwhile Sir John had built a simply stunning tomb for himself and his two wives – their recumbent effigies lie on a slightly lower level than his own – a screen, pulpit and reredos, and an extraordinary gilded memorial statue to his son Edward, killed at Newbury during the Civil War. Other monuments were to follow, including a fine one by Rysbrack to the 2nd Viscount St John who rebuilt the house. This is not even to mention the exuberantly wrought Italian communion rails (also gilded), the sun, moon and stars on the chancel roof, the helms and the hatchments, the fifteenth-century glass, the sheer vitality and colour that knocks the unsuspecting visitor sideways. Here is a church worth going a long way to see.

## Malmesbury

*21; 9½ miles N of Chippenham on A429*

A truncated masterpiece, MALMESBURY ABBEY now consists of the nave and the south porch of what was once one of the grandest and richest abbeys in the West Country. The nave dates from the middle of the twelfth century; its already slightly pointed arches are among the earliest anywhere (though St John's, Devizes, has even earlier ones) but the massive cylindrical piers and the splendid bounding triforium – interrupted at one point by a curious little stone box of uncertain purpose – give it a thoroughly Romanesque flavour which not even the fourteenth-century clerestory and lierne-vaulted roof can dispel.

The best of Malmesbury Romanesque is, however, not in the nave at all but in the south porch. Here is genius indeed, in the form of relief sculptures as fine as any in the country. Many of the smaller carvings on the tremendous eight-order arch are sadly worn, though their beauty is by no means gone; but no one, surely, could be left unmoved by the Apostles in the two opposing lunettes just beyond, six a side, with angels hovering dangerously low above their heads.

The town has any number of good seventeenth- and eighteenth-century buildings. It also boasts a memorable MARKET CROSS of about 1500, over 40 feet high, vaulted and flying-buttressed. Leland wrote that its purpose was 'for poore folkes to stande dry when rayne cummeth'. There must have been an easier way of achieving such a purpose; but none, surely, more sensational.

*The carved south porch arch, Malmesbury Abbey.*

## Mildenhall*

*22; 1½ miles E of Marlborough off A4*

Pronounced, and sometimes actually written, Minal, Mildenhall boasts two buildings of real distinction. The first, which appears almost at once on a hill to the right of the road as you enter from the east, is the Gothick SCHOOL HOUSE, built by Robert Abraham in 1823. It has an octagonal central Hall, topped by a lantern, from which spread four radiating wings – an enchanting design and, provided the school had no more than four classes, an eminently practical one.

At the further, south-west, end of the village stands the little CHURCH OF ST JOHN THE BAPTIST, another gem. Its origins are old indeed – the double window in the lower stage of the tower is indisputably Saxon and the rest is mostly twelfth- and thirteenth-century – but what counts here is the quality and completeness of its late Georgian Gothick furnishings. As Sir John Betjeman once put it, 'you walk straight into a Jane Austen novel'. There is a semi-circular west gallery, two pulpits straight out of Strawberry Hill, box pews and, in the panelled chancel, two tiny settees for, presumably, the very smallest choirboys. All of this, according to an inscription, went up at the expense of the parishioners in 1816; they made it one of the loveliest village churches in England, and so it remains today.

## Mompesson House

See Salisbury.

## Newtown

*23; 6 miles NE of Shaftesbury off A350*

PYT HOUSE, OR PYTHOUSE, was built in 1805 by its owner, John Benett, 'from his own designs'. He is also said to have 'supervised the execution of them ... rising at 5 o'clock every morning for that purpose'. Apart from a little Gothic chapel in the grounds, now much ruined, this elegant house with its noble Ionic portico marks the sum total of Benett's architectural achievement; surprisingly, since it is remarkably assured and, with those giant recessed loggias on each side, even a good deal more adventurous than it looks at first sight. Note, for example, the staircase, rising in one flight to the half landing and then returning in two, the single, central arm being supported on iron colonnettes. The house has now been converted into flats, but the main rooms are open to the public on certain summer afternoons.

## Old Wardour Castle

See Wardour Old Castle.

## Philipps House

See Dinton.

## Potterne

*24; 2 miles SW of Devizes on A360*

Like Salisbury Cathedral, ST MARY'S CHURCH was built all of a piece in the second quarter of the thirteenth century and consequently has a marvellous unity about it. As at Salisbury, too, this unity is broken in one important respect. In the fourteenth century, the crossing-tower of

*Pyt House, Newtown.*

Salisbury was given its spire, which worked triumphantly; in the fifteenth, that of Potterne received its pinnacles and embattled top storey, which did not. This, however, is a minor blemish; St Mary's remains, with its soaring trios of lancets, a building of real beauty – Wiltshire Early English at its purest. The font is Anglo-Saxon, comfortably predating the Conquest.

There are several remarkable timber-framed houses, of the late fifteenth century, still standing in the High Street. The finest is PORCH HOUSE which, despite the appalling traffic, has even managed to keep much of its original glass.

## Ramsbury Manor*

*25; 4½ miles NW of Hungerford off A419*

Of all the houses built in the second half of the seventeenth century – arguably the high point of English domestic architecture – Ramsbury Manor is the one in which, had I the means comfortably to do so, I should most like to live. It stands on a beautiful, unspoilt site just a mile or two across the border from Berkshire, overlooking an artificial arm of the River Kennet; its proportions are exquisite, its detailing a constant joy; its interior decoration has not been touched in any appreciable way since the days of George III.

This superb house was built for Sir William Jones, the Attorney-General who in 1678 successfully prosecuted Titus Oates, and was begun about 1680 – too late, alas, for its owner to enjoy it, since he died two years later, aged only fifty-one, while it was still little more than half completed. The architect was until recently unknown; Howard Colvin has, however, now established as 'virtually certain' that it was Robert Hooke, the associate of Wren, who must have been working on it simultaneously with Ragley Hall in Warwickshire. The style is, fundamentally, that which was introduced by Inigo Jones and further developed by Sir Roger Pratt at Coleshill; the material, a mellow red brick with copious stone dressings. The entrance front is to the east. It has two principal storeys on a semi-sunken basement (which looks as though it may have served for the previous house on the site) and a row of dormers along the hipped roof; nine bays altogether, with a three-bay centre, slightly projecting and with its own quoins, its pediment containing an ornate coat of arms with garlands. There are modillions in the pediment and in the continuous cornice that encircles the house. The flat of the roof has no balustrade; there is a cupola but – and this seems to me one of the few defects of Ramsbury – it is set in a shallow declivity and is so small as to be practically invisible from the ground. The west front is almost identical; north and south fronts, however, come as something of a surprise. First of all, they have an even number of bays – six – which means the absence of a strong centre. To the north, this problem has been solved by grouping the two middle bays together under a small pediment and setting them against an ashlar ground. To the south, the difficulties are aggravated by the fact that the land shelves away steeply, necessitating an extra storey on this side of the house; but here too a similar solution (though without the ashlar) has been adopted – the pediment now covering three storeys instead of two –

with a similar degree of success. The windows are all sashed, with properly close-set glazing bars; they have charming little masks in the keystones of their square, stone frames.

A flight of ten steps leads up to the front door – tall but surprisingly narrow, with a high segmental pediment raised on brackets – and through to the noble Entrance Hall, wainscoted from floor to ceiling with huge bolection-moulded panels. From here a magnificent doorway on the same central axis, surmounted by another segmental pediment – broken this time – opens into the Saloon. This too is richly panelled; but now we see for the first time some signs of late eighteenth-century redecoration: the delicate plaster ceiling, for example, and the Adam-style chimneypiece. Above this, by contrast, the virtuoso display of wood carving – flowers and foliage, fruit, vegetables and ears of corn – can be by one hand only, that of Grinling Gibbons.

On the east side of the ground floor, flanking the Entrance Hall, are the Library and the Dining Room. The latter occupies the south-east corner of the house, but the two south-facing windows have been blocked – presumably in 1775, to accommodate the magnificent mahogany sideboard which was obviously designed specially to fit them. On the west side, leading off the Saloon, is a Breakfast Room and, towards the north, two small interconnecting rooms with remarkably pretty eighteenth-century Chinese wallpaper.

Occupying the centre of the north and south ends of the house are its two staircases, of which only the southern one is original. Having been intended from the start as the subsidiary staircase, it is not particularly grand, though quite massive and somehow satisfying in a seventeenth-century way. It possesses one unusual feature, however, that adds much to its character: at first-floor level, as well as rising up in the normal way to the second floor, it also includes a gangway going straight back across the stairwell to a gallery opposite, giving direct access to the two rooms at the west end. The northern staircase is odder still, for though it was – and is – the principal one, rising up a fine and generous well, the balustrading is quite unworthy of it, being simply unshaped vertical bars. The most likely explanation is that Sir William Jones had originally intended something suitably sumptuous, perhaps with carved floral panels in the style of Eltham Lodge, Ham House or Sudbury Hall, but that this had been countermanded on his death. The well would then have remained empty for some time – there was always the south staircase to use – and then, in the following century, the present stairs could have been inserted, perhaps even as a temporary measure. The effect is more curious still in that the two little independent flights from the half landing are quite nicely turned and set three to a tread.

The bedrooms upstairs are fully up to the standards set by the reception rooms below. All have kept their original doorways, and their oak doors with splendid brass fittings; and all, it need hardly be said, enjoy marvellous views over the gardens and the park. Here there are two outbuildings particularly deserving of mention. To the south, backing the eighteenth-century service quadrangle and looking out over the 'improved' Kennet, is a delightful Orangery dated 1775 and consisting of five tall round-headed windows grouped closely together under a pediment. The designer is unknown. Unknown too is the architect of the quite remarkable stable block a few hundred yards west of the house. Nine bays long, it has a single-bay pedimented centre and, to each side, four very large *oeil-de-boeuf* windows, elliptical, set vertically, with keystones at top and bottom. A similar one, horizontal this time, surmounts the door. Above is a row of dormers in a pitched roof.

These few paragraphs of bald description are as accurate as I can make them, but they do not do anything like justice to the house. For at Ramsbury it is not the detail that matters, but the ensemble. Here, in short, is one of the most beautiful houses in England. The only sad thing about it is that, at the moment of writing, it is also among the most difficult to get permission to see.

*Ramsbury Manor.*

*Salisbury Cathedral.*

## Salisbury

*26; 14½ miles SW of Stockbridge on A30*
*Includes Mompesson House (NT)*

THE CATHEDRAL AND IMMEDIATE ENVIRONS

I suppose I had better come clean right away: I cannot love Salisbury Cathedral. I admire it, naturally; I find its setting superb, its proportions perfect, its distant prospect incomparable. Its spire, as everybody knows, is the best in England. On the other hand, while its ground plan is if anything just a little too tidy, its west front seems to me a meretricious mess that allows neither rest to the eye nor satisfaction to the spirit; while its interior, surely the most soulless of any ancient cathedral in the land, chills me to the marrow. It would be perverse to deny it a place in this book; but it will get no star from me.

Salisbury was begun and completed in a single reign – that of King Henry III, who had already been four years on the throne when Bishop Poore laid the foundation stone in 1220 and who lived to attend the consecration in 1258. The west front took another few years, after which, except for the upper stages of the tower and the spire, which were added in the 1330s, the main body of the cathedral looked much the same as it does today; and it is the speed of the construction and the absence of any important later work that gives the building its quite remarkable unity, making it, even more than Wells, the paradigm of the Early English style. As such, it must be admitted that, seen from any other direction than due west – and possibly due east – it cannot fail to please. It is when you get inside that the disappointment sets in.

Why should this be? First, I think, it is a matter of the light. Salisbury has kept scarcely any of its old glass – a good deal of it was scrapped by James Wyatt in his disastrous restoration of the 1790s – and the consequent excess of light somehow robs it of all its mystery. A further misfortune has been the use, for many of the shafts in the arcade piers, of a Purbeck marble which has been deliberately darkened to make a more striking contrast to the pale grey Chilmark stone. As a result these dark shafts, with their inverted bell capitals, look like nothing so much as drainpipes. Then there is the question of the perspectives down the nave. The length is impressive, the arcading lovely; but the effect is spoilt by a particularly strident dark string-course running below the gallery, just across the points of the arches. If only there were the occasional tall shaft to break that harsh, remorseless line; alas, there is none. Finally, the great procession of nave and choir leads to no visual climax, merely to the five modest lancets of the Lady Chapel, seen through the three arches of the eastern end of the choir – an unsuccessful trio at the best of times since there is not really room for two side ones, which are so squashed that their points have been pushed up a little higher than their broader, central, companion. The perspective in the opposite direction is still more unhappy, since neither of the two horizontals of the inner west wall matches up with those of the nave.

Outside the cathedral proper but within its precincts, the best things are the Chapter House and the Cloister. The CHAPTER HOUSE is a mixed delight: the particularly nasty painting on the vault and even nastier glazed floor give it a Victorian atmosphere which takes the edge off one's enjoyment of the structure itself: a pity, since this is of the late thirteenth century and very fine indeed – a close copy, incidentally, of that of Westminster Abbey, and a good deal less altered than its exemplar. The centre pier soars up, tall and slender, before spreading out like a palm tree into the sixteen branches that support the vault. The windows themselves, their great octofoiled circles rising above pairs of smaller circles with quatrefoils, are lovely (though their present glass is unworthy of them) and there is much enjoyable and imaginative carving, especially in the capitals and mouldings of the blank arcading round the walls. The frieze of Old Testament scenes just above it has been sadly over-restored, but is still worth looking at.

And so to the CLOISTER. What a pleasure it is, after so much carping, to say that here at last is something quite unspoilt and utterly magnificent. Only that of Gloucester can hold a candle to it; but Salisbury's is larger, as well as being older by a century and a half. The important thing to notice here is that the light enters not, as in earlier cloisters, through arcades, but through *windows* – unglazed, perhaps, but windows just the same – and that these windows mark the first appearance on a large scale of bar tracery at Salisbury: indeed, are among the first in England. Bar tracery was the herald of the Decorated period; and there could hardly be a greater contrast between these great broad openings and the narrow Early English lancets that had gone before. The design may seem to be still a little crude, but it is subtler than it looks: how many people, I wonder, notice that the huge cart-wheel roundels in the apex of each window are alternately cinquefoiled and sexfoiled?

*The north aisle, Salisbury Cathedral.*

Emerging from the Cathedral, we can now turn our attention to the Close. Here is another feature of which Salisbury can be justly proud. No cathedral in England has a lovelier one – a huge expanse of green, around which there is scarcely a single building that does not possess real architectural distinction. There is no space here to speak of them all; I shall therefore single out only the best – which, being the property of the National Trust, has the additional merit of being open to the public. This is MOMPESSON HOUSE. It stands on Choristers' Green, in the north-west corner, its smooth ashlar face distinguishing it immediately from its brick neighbours. Of two and a half storeys and seven bays, it is modest in scale; with its broken segmental pediment and scroll decoration framing the window above, it is dignified without being austere.

This façade dates from about 1700; the rainwater heads are actually dated 1701. Inside, however, apart from the beautiful staircase and some of the panelling, most of the interior decoration – plaster ceilings, fireplaces and overmantels – is Palladian and Baroque, which puts it at 1740 or thereabouts. The contrast is in itself a subtle and delightful one; I know of no smallish town house that better conveys the grace and elegance of the eighteenth century, or one in which I should be happier to live. The view alone would be worth the rent.

#### THE CITY

While not, perhaps, of the standard of Bradford-on-Avon or Devizes, Salisbury has preserved a remarkable number of buildings from the fourteenth century onwards. ST THOMAS'S CHURCH is distinguished by any standards, and provides the additional bonus of a dark and dynamic Doom painting over the chancel arch. There are two good medieval GUILD HALLS (as well as the GUILDHALL itself, designed by Sir Robert Taylor in 1788) and several lovely old inns, notably the PHEASANT (fifteenth-century) and the OLD GEORGE – now partially occupied by the Bay Tree Restaurant. ALMSHOUSES and hospitals are another Salisbury speciality. The best of the former are in BEDWYN STREET; ST NICHOLAS'S HOSPITAL, of the thirteenth century, is in St Nicholas Road and TRINITY HOSPITAL, of the eighteenth (though of fourteenth-century origin), in Brown Street. But this is only a start; buy a city guide and wander about – there is no other way of discovering all that this fine old city has to offer.

*South Wraxall Manor.*

## South Wraxall Manor

*27; 3 miles N of Bradford-on-Avon off B3109*

The quintessential old English manor house, South Wraxall was probably begun by Robert Long, a rich clothier who became Member of Parliament for the Shire in 1433; and the Gatehouse through which one enters the courtyard is much as he left it, with its pretty double-transomed canted oriel, the individual lights round-headed and cusped. Above it rises a steep gable, with a surprisingly tall chimney ascending from one side; below, the gateway itself has a flat lintel with rounded corners and a heavy angular hood-mould. Once inside the courtyard you find the porch to your right, diagonally buttressed and with a little two-light Perpendicular window above. The old Hall is immediately inside to the left. It is rather high in relation to its length, and is surmounted by a good timber roof with arched braces, collar-beams and queenposts.

In this part of the house the medieval atmosphere is still strong; it is interesting to see how closely, in the fifteenth century, domestic architecture of this kind still continues to follow the ecclesiastical: windows with Perpendicular tracery, buttresses with set-offs, even gargoyles. Then, a few paces to the north, the mood changes. We enter that part of the house that was built – or very substantially remodelled – in the years around 1600. The showpiece of this period must rank as one of the major Jacobean rooms in all England. Standing on a shallow basement, its floor is a few feet higher than that of the Hall, which it infinitely surpasses in splendour. It is barrel-vaulted, the ceiling richly ornamented with swirling plasterwork and pendants. The afternoon sun streams in through a gigantic window which occupies the entire west end of the room, with eight lights and two transoms, and continuing with another three lights towards the south. There is a similar window at the other end, and between the two a colossal stone chimneypiece rises to the roof – a work of the greatest possible fantasy and exuberance. Curious coupled figures, half column, half caryatid, support the high entablature, which consists, after several stages of variegated decoration, of the god Pan standing naked in the centre, flanked by figures in niches representing Prudence and Justice, Arithmetic and Geometry. Opposite this prodigious conceit there emerges a curious projection from the wall, its lower level having fluted Ionic columns and shell niches – possibly intended as seats – its upper filled with fine panelling. It is considerably more sophisticated than the chimneypiece and, at least where its decoration is concerned, must date from the best part of a century later.

There are several other magnificent rooms in the house, of much the same style and with similarly prominent chimneypieces, though none can match that of the Drawing Room for imaginative vigour. A particularly fine one dominates the Dining Room, with big strapwork cartouches, in which are inscribed improving aphorisms. Another, surmounted by a sort of shaped gable in strapwork, carries the date 1598.

Beyond the screens passage, a little Jacobean cloister runs out towards the east, supporting a single timber-framed storey on a little row of columns. Within this is the so-called Raleigh Room, where Sir Walter Long and his friend Sir Walter Raleigh are said to have sat smoking together; by tradition this is the first smoking room in England. It has good linenfold panelling but is not otherwise remarkable. South Wraxall is a rambling house, in which wing has been added to wing in a haphazard and totally unselfconscious way; yet it possesses a remarkable unity of its own, so strong that even the sudden appearance of a Tuscan loggia hardly comes as a shock. It is a house that breathes self-confidence, a house that still seems part and parcel of Shakespearean England.

## Steeple Ashton

*28; 3 miles E of Trowbridge off A350*

The village is a bit of a misnomer since the spire of ST MARY'S CHURCH was struck by lightning in 1670 and never re-erected; but the church, one suspects, is none the worse for that. It is a tremendous building, late Perpendicular of about 1500 (the tower, from a previous church, is rather earlier) and very, very rich – pinnacles everywhere, even in relief on the buttresses; broad, four-light windows, even in the clerestory, where they are as big as those in the aisles; gigantic gargoyles, lunging and leering at both levels. The general effect is startling and utterly unforgettable.

According to the original plan, the interior was to be vaulted throughout in stone; alas, the nave vaulting is in wood only, with particularly unfortunate results on the shafts where one material takes over from the other. Whether this wood is original or whether it dates from the fall of the spire is uncertain; still, the chancel (rebuilt in 1853 with a hideous east window), chapels and aisles are all lierne-vaulted in stone to various intricate designs with splendid bosses, and this is rare enough. The aisles were paid for by two local clothiers, one of them Robert Long of South Wraxall (*q.v.*); a more telling illustration of the wealth of the Wiltshire wool trade in the late Middle Ages could scarcely be imagined. That to the north contains a Lady Chapel said to be of superb quality; its blocking by a huge and hideous Victorian organ is all the more unforgivable. Could not this dreadful instrument now be removed?

The centre of the village – as opposed to its distinctly depressing outskirts – is a delight. There are plenty of good buildings around and about the pretty, triangular green, including an octagonal LOCK-UP actually on it. The MANOR HOUSE of 1647 with its gabled three-bay front, and, on the right, a late seventeenth-century long brick GRANARY with two-light windows, are also well worth looking at.

## Stockton

*29; 12 miles NW of Salisbury off A36*

There is a good Norman church at Stockton – though, as usual, with later additions – with that extremely rare and not altogether satisfactory feature, a solid wall dividing nave from chancel. (Since the beginning of this century it has had a tall screen as well.) ST JOHN BAPTIST contains some most interesting monuments, including that of John Topp and his wife. He died in 1640, so it was probably his father who built STOCKTON HOUSE – a fine, four-square house of about 1600, faced with alternating bands of stone and flint. It is totally symmetrical on the entrance front, and has a high – three-storeyed – frontispiece rising almost to the gabled roof with a proud strapwork cresting. The windows on this front are all properly mullioned and transomed. The other fronts are similarly unspoilt. A seventeenth-century Chapel stands a few yards away and is connected to the house by a short link. It too is faced with flint and stone, but chequered rather than striped.

Even after the promise of the exterior, the inside of the house does not disappoint. True, there is a rather inappropriate and somewhat complicated staircase inserted around 1800, possibly by James Wyatt or Wyatville, but elsewhere the Tudor atmosphere is remarkably well preserved. The Hall has unfortunately lost its plasterwork, but the Parlour adjoining has a frieze of strapwork with masks, and an intricate, geometrically patterned ceiling; it also boasts a towering stone and plaster chimneypiece with a coat of arms above. Upstairs, another fine overmantel features a stucco relief of the three men in the Burning Fiery Furnace, with caryatids below. Yet another bears, in a strapwork cartouche, the Arms of James I; oddly enough, the ceiling of that same room has ER monograms, so it looks as though this room received its decoration at the moment of James's succession, 1603.

The *pièce de résistance* of Stockton is, however, unquestionably the Great Chamber, which occupies the centre of the house on the first floor. Here too is another of those tremendous chimneypieces, with two detached heads, one male, one female, in the overmantel. And above is one of the most fantastic explosions of Jacobethan plasterwork that I have seen for a very long time. The artist has let his imagination run riot, picking out his design of swirling flowers, framed within richly decorated ribs, with animals real and mythical, including one prodigiously large butterfly sitting on the back of an elephant. Surely one could never be really unhappy in a room like this.

## Stourhead

*NT; 30; 10 miles S of Frome off B3092*
*Includes landscape garden**

When a rich banker, Henry Hoare, decided to build himself a new country house in 1718 and commissioned Colen Campbell as his architect, he knew exactly what he was getting. Ever since Campbell's publication of *Vitruvius Britannicus* in 1715, he had been the leading champion of the new English Palladian style. In this style he had already built Burlington House in London for his patron Lord Burlington, and Houghton in Norfolk for the Prime Minister, Sir Robert Walpole. For Mr Hoare something on a slightly smaller scale was required; and Campbell turned to Palladio's Villa Emo at Fanzolo, near Vicenza, for his model.

Stourhead has been altered in several respects since it was completed in 1724 – the two side wings were added in 1793 and Campbell's attached portico was replaced with a projecting one in 1840 – but it still presents a fine Palladian appearance. The state rooms within it are also well up to standard, splendidly decorated (and carefully restored after a fire in 1902) and containing a remarkably catholic collection of pictures and furniture, much of the latter made by the Chippendales, father and son, for the house – and in particular for the magnificent Library and Picture Gallery in the wings, which were untouched by the fire.

But as everybody knows, the real glory of Stourhead is that it possesses the finest landscape garden in England. Here, even more successfully accomplished than at Stowe, was the ideal, 'educated' nature, just as it had been in the pictures of Claude and Poussin. The

The gardens at Stourhead.

principal creator of this extraordinary achievement was not one of the famous landscape gardeners of the time – Kent or Brown, Bridgeman or Repton – but was Henry Hoare the Younger, son of the builder of the house. The best of the temples and pavilions, including the Pantheon, the Temple of Flora and the Temple of Apollo (this last inspired by the original at Baalbek) are by Henry Flitcroft, but Hoare's was the overall conception; and to him more than to anyone else must go the credit for this breathtaking realisation of the eighteenth-century English gentleman's vision of paradise.

## Trafalgar House

*31; 7 miles SE of Salisbury off B3080*

Though the house was named after the battle, it is pronounced differently, with the stress on the last syllable. Until it was bought by the nation in 1814 as a thank-offering to the memory of Nelson and a home for his successors, it was always known as Standlynch. It was begun in 1733 for a rich businessman of Netherlandish extraction called Sir Peter Vandeput, whose sister was married to the architect Roger Morris; and though there is no firm documentary evidence, it seems reasonable to credit Morris with the designs for the central block. Perhaps the most notable feature of it, architecturally, is the fact that it bears not the slightest exterior trace of Palladian influence, despite having been built when Palladianism was at its height. The west front has a pediment, admittedly, but no columns: to the east there is not even that. (The neo-classical porch is a later addition, as we shall see.) Morris – if Morris it was – was still working firmly in the old William and Mary/Queen Anne tradition. One is left with only one nagging doubt: could that tradition, splendid as it was, really cope with a house this size? This gigantic block of brick, with its stone dressings and rather heavy Gibbs surrounds to the windows, looks, at least on a grey autumn evening, formidable rather than elegant, forbidding rather than welcoming.

The impression is mercifully mitigated by the two wings. Though each is itself the size of a considerable country house, they give the ensemble a horizontality which seems to reduce the mass rather than the reverse. They were built by John Wood the Younger for Henry Dawkins, who had bought Standlynch after Vandeput's death. At much the same time Dawkins commissioned Nicholas Revett, a fellow member of the Society of Dilettanti (whose stay in Athens from 1751 to 1753, surveying the ancient monuments with 'Athenian' Stuart, had been largely financed by Dawkins's brother James), to add the Grecian portico on the entrance front. This is a copy of the unfinished Temple of Apollo on Delos – hence the curious columns, without bases and fluted only for a couple of inches at top and bottom.

On entering the house one immediately becomes aware that the Palladian influence, so conspicuously lacking outside, is not altogether absent after all. The Hall, rising two storeys, is a perfect cube – apart from its coved ceiling – and actually commemorates Inigo Jones, the first English apostle of Palladianism, with a relief bust in the place of honour on the overmantel. (Above, in the centre of a broken pediment, is a free-standing bust of Nelson.) Much of the plaster decoration on the walls is also of Jonesian inspiration, though the ceilings – which include several by Revett – tend to be rather more neo-classical or even Rococo.

After its presentation to the Nelson family in 1814 the house became a remarkable treasure house of Nelson relics. Most of these were removed when the Nelsons sold it after the Second World War; the Ganges Room on the top floor, however, still contains wooden pilasters and panelling from HMS *Ganges*, one of the ships of the line at Trafalgar.

## Urchfont*

*32; 4½ miles SE of Devizes on B3098*

A lovely village, Urchfont is centred on a green and a duckpond and a great cedar tree, with pretty Georgian houses grouped around them: one of those archetypal English villages in which Agatha Christie tended to set her murders. It is dominated, as all such villages should be, by its church, ST MICHAEL'S – long and low, with big broad transepts, and over the chancel a marvellous roof of lichened stone with crockets like fleurs-de-lis set along the ridge. Within, the chancel is even better than it looks outside. Framed in an absolutely glorious broad Early English arch, it was rebuilt in the early fourteenth century, as Decorated was gathering momentum, and with its stone lierne vault, intricate yet assured, seems determined to prove just what the new style could do. The bosses and corbel heads are a particular joy. There is more glorious Decorated work in the south aisle.

Half a mile away lies URCHFONT MANOR, a really beautiful smallish William and Mary house of 1680 or thereabouts. According to the director of the residential college which now occupies it, a dozen or so years after its construction it was substantially altered by William Talman, who gave it a new eastern elevation, moving the stone porch with its segmental pediment from its original position on the south front and adding a three-bay central projection with sash windows, which were just then coming into fashion. (It is only fair to add that neither Howard Colvin in his *Biographical Dictionary of British Architects* nor the *Victoria County History* makes any mention of Talman's connection with Urchfont, though it is certainly not improbable.) The theory is to some extent borne out by the fact that the brick on this projection is of a slightly lighter colour, and also by an agreeably crude contemporary painting, now in the Library, depicting the house's new look and showing the central window wide open – as if to prove to the world that this exciting invention really worked.

## Wardour Castle

*33; 4 miles NE of Shaftesbury off A30*

Privileged indeed are the young ladies of Cranborne Chase School; for they inhabit one of the noblest Palladian houses in the kingdom, the masterpiece of James Paine. Paine, it must be admitted, was not the most exciting of Palladian architects; but he was certainly the most successful of the second generation, and from 1735 until about 1776 – when he completed Wardour Castle for the 8th Lord Arundell – his reputation stood above all others. Wardour makes a fitting climax to a distinguished career. At first glance it may seem a little forbidding, with its austere entrance front marked only by a Venetian window beneath a pediment – though the quadrant links to the two flanking pavilions cheer things up a bit; the real impact of the house comes only when one enters the Central Hall. Here is splendour indeed – a huge rotunda, 60 feet high from the floor to the top of its glassed and coffered dome, and some 50 feet in diameter, around whose walls a cantilevered double staircase soars up to a circular gallery marked by eight tall Corinthian columns.

*The Central Hall, Wardour Castle.*

The principal rooms are predictably fine – the Music Room in particular has a magnificently decorated ceiling – though their present academic functions scarcely allow them to be shown off to their best advantage. No visitor should leave, however, without seeing the Chapel, just beyond the western pavilion. It was built as a Catholic Chapel – the Arundells never wavered in their devotion to Rome – and Catholic it has remained, quite separate from the school. It impresses, above all, by the richness of its decoration. Just compare it with Paine's equally beautiful but far less ornate Protestant Chapel at Gibside; nothing could more clearly illustrate the difference between the Churches of England and of Rome. But here, unlike everywhere else at Wardour, Paine was not left to himself. Virtually all the interior decoration is by the Venetian Giacomo Quarenghi, while only a dozen years after its completion the building was further enlarged by the young John Soane. He it was who added the crossing with its oval vault, the two stubby transepts and the apsed chancel. Can such an enlargement have been really necessary, one wonders, to a family chapel already the size of a modest parish church? Yes, because it was a family chapel in name only. In the eighteenth century free-standing Roman Catholic places of worship were still forbidden; it was only thus that the Arundells were able to cater for the spiritual needs of well over 500 of their co-religionist retainers, neighbours and tenants – the largest Catholic congregation outside London.

## Wardour Old Castle

*34; 3½ miles NE of Shaftesbury off A30*

When John, Lord Lovel of Titchmarsh, obtained a licence in 1393 to crenellate his house – and used it to build himself an entirely new one – it is unlikely that he had any serious military purpose in mind. Though the castle was magnificently placed on a high spur, its location was hardly strategic; besides, Lovel was a retired soldier who had no political ambitions, and few barons and squires of Richard II's time had any cause to think in terms of self-defence. But the era of the country house was not yet come; an Englishman's home was still a castle, even if it were rather more comfortably appointed than in stormier days gone by. Where Lovel broke with tradition was in building his in the shape of a hexagon, with a roughly hexagonal bailey around it and a hexagonal courtyard within. Whether or not he was remembering the Château of Concressault in France – its closest parallel – we shall never know; but the plan of Old Wardour is certainly unique in England.

Though the castle was to pass through many hands in the next two centuries, it remained more or less unchanged until 1578, when Sir Matthew Arundell, who had bought it a few years earlier, decided to bring the whole thing up-to-date and called in the best architect of his time, Robert Smythson. Smythson made no alterations to the basic structure; but he managed to give the building a vaguely Renaissance air by adding classical doorcases to the main entrance and the first-floor approach to the Hall and by replacing Lovel's narrow slits with two- and three-light mullioned windows. These windows are particularly interesting for two reasons: first, Smythson was clearly determined to group them symmetrically – so determined, indeed, that some of them are actually false, with chimney flues behind them; second, they were designed by an architect who had just been working on the huge nine- and twelve-light windows of Longleat, and who can have reverted to the old-fashioned design only because he felt it to be more in keeping with a medieval castle. They are thus both modish and archaic at the same time.

All too little, alas, survives of Old Wardour today. Ironically enough, three-quarters of a century after the last military pretences had been dropped, the castle found itself actually besieged. For six heroic days in 1643 old Lady Arundell and a handful of retainers defended it against 1,300 of Cromwell's men, submitting only after Roundhead sappers mined the vaults. Six months later, after a far longer siege, her son regained it for the Cavaliers, but by then it was a ruin, and a ruin it remains. Yet this is not quite all: this looming pile, medieval in origin yet overlaid with Elizabethan fantasy, precisely captured the late eighteenth-century fashion for the picturesque. The surroundings were landscaped; behind the yews to the south there appeared a rocky, romantic grotto; down by the lake, on the site of the old Gatehouse, rose a charming Gothick Pavilion and nearby, painted and panelled, an irresistible three-seater closet.

*Wardour Old Castle.*

*Westwood Manor.*

## Westwood Manor

*NT; 35; $1\frac{1}{2}$ miles SW of Bradford-on-Avon off B3109*

Another one of those lovely old Wiltshire manor houses – part medieval, part early Tudor, part Jacobean, all three periods fusing together in a single entity, utterly unpretentious – Westwood Manor has all the mellow serenity of a house that has been lived in and cherished uninterruptedly for some 500 years. There is, admittedly, not much remaining fifteenth-century work – only a single window and a few beams in the central block; but Thomas Horton, the well-to-do cloth merchant who bought Westwood in about 1515, has left us much to remember him by – above all the Dining Room (which he would have thought of as the solar) whose fireplace still bears his initials, and the little panelled bedroom above it. These two rooms share the two-storey bay window, which still contains in its upper half some of the original stained glass, including the owner's rather primitive rebus – a barrel ('TUN') surmounted by the letters 'HOR' which he understandably, if regrettably, thought it wiser not to illustrate.

Just a century after Horton's arrival the last of his descendants sold Westwood to his brother-in-law John Farewell. He it was who divided the fifteenth-century Great Hall horizontally to create the Great Chamber, now the Music Room, giving it a shallow coved ceiling with big pendants and plenty of that fine and endlessly inventive Jacobean plasterwork which is a feature of the house. Downstairs, the so-called King's Room is still more exuberantly plastered; though it must in fairness be pointed out that the frieze of royal portraits was brought from nearby Keevil Manor in 1910.

The charming garden is rich in topiary, with one particularly pretty conceit – an entire cottage clipped in yew, almost life-size, with a front door you can walk through.

## Whiteparish

*36; 7 miles SE of Salisbury on A27*

Two and a half miles south-west of Whiteparish – and by no means easy to find – stands NEWHOUSE, as curiously conceived a house as any in Wiltshire. It was built as a hunting lodge some time before 1619 by Sir Edward Gorges, then the owner of Longford Castle, and like Longford reflects his penchant for odd plans. The ground plan of Newhouse is a hexagon with wings projecting from every second side, forming the letter Y. (Only one other house of this shape, the coincidentally named Newhouse Farm in Hereford and Worcester, is known to be still standing.) All this is Jacobean; but in the mid-eighteenth century the wings were considerably lengthened, and two of these three additions remain today. As at Trafalgar nearby there is a strong Nelsonian connection, the daughter of the house, Harriet Eyre, having married the Admiral's nephew. In the Parlour hangs a most extraordinary picture of the triumph of hares (Eyres?) over men: phantasmagorical and not a little sinister.

## Wilbury House

*37; $4\frac{1}{2}$ miles E of Amesbury and 1 mile N of Newton Tony off A338*

The architect and first owner of Wilbury House was William Benson, MP, who was later to engineer the dismissal of the eighty-six-year-old Sir Christopher Wren from the post of Surveyor-General of the King's Works in his own favour. His tenure of the office was not, however, a success. He antagonised everybody in sight, including the entire House of Lords, whom he informed – wrongly – that their Chamber was in imminent danger of collapse; after only fifteen months he was forced to resign, having, as Hawksmoor put it, 'got more in one year (for confusing the King's Works) than Sr. Chris. Wren did in 40 years for his honest endeavours'.

Wilbury, the only major building that can be attributed to this unalluring figure, was built in 1710, but was radically remodelled some thirty years later. As Benson designed it – and as it was depicted in the first volume of Colen Campbell's *Vitruvius Britannicus* in 1718 – it was of one storey only over a half basement, having on the south front a pedimented portico above which rose a hipped roof crowned with a balustraded belvedere. It was, in fact – apart from the number of storeys – modelled almost slavishly on John Webb's Amesbury Abbey (of 1661) some 5 miles away. Oddly enough, this fact gives the house greater rather than lesser importance. The Inigo Jones interpretation of Palladianism – of which Webb, Jones's nephew or son-in-law, had been a principal exponent – had never really found favour in England outside Court circles; throughout the last thirty-five years of the seventeenth century and the first decade of the eighteenth, the style of Roger Pratt and of Wren had carried all before it. Benson's choice of a Jonesian model for his new house of 1710 thus marks the very beginning of the fashion for Palladianism that was to dominate English architecture for well over half a century.

It was probably around 1740, when Wilbury was bought by the Fulke Grevilles, that it was given the appearance that, essentially, it still has today. An upper floor was added, pediment and belvedere were swept away, and although the portico itself was retained its columns were subtly repositioned to increase the distance between the two in the centre. The only important subsequent alterations to the exterior were the additions of two single-storey wings in 1775 or so, and of a bow to the west in the nineteenth century.

The showpiece of the interior is the great South Hall behind the portico. It has a high ceiling, deeply coved, with elaborate plasterwork dating almost certainly from Benson's time. There are further splendid stucco decorations on the walls and over the fireplace, but these probably date from the 1740 or 1775 alterations. Somewhat unexpectedly the floor is of scagliola, laid in a bold oval design that vaguely – but only vaguely – echoes that of the ceiling. The main Entrance Hall and the smaller rooms to the east and west of the South Hall are treated in similar, if rather more modest, fashion. In the south-west wing there is a most beautiful Library, with its original bookcases of 1775.

From the front door on the north side of the house one looks up a long avenue to a small column surmounted by an urn and commemorating Queen Victoria's Diamond Jubilee; and from here another similar avenue ends in a little artificial hill from which rises a remarkably pretty octagonal domed summer-house with a grotto. This, we can be quietly confident, is also Benson's work. Obviously, he was an insufferable character; conceivably, he was also a crook – there is evidence to suggest that the false alarm about the House of Lords was part of a plot by him and his deputy, Colen Campbell, to demolish the old Houses of Parliament and erect new and splendid Palladian ones in their place. But for all that he must have been a man of sensibility and taste, with ideas well in advance of his time. It is a pity he did not design more.

## Wilton★

*38; 2½ miles W of Salisbury on A30*

'King Charles the First', wrote John Aubrey, 'did love Wilton above all places: and came thither every Sommer.' As one wanders through glorious WILTON HOUSE on a sunlit June afternoon, there sometimes comes a suspicion that he has never really left; and it seems more than ever appropriate that there should be here enshrined, in one of the noblest suites of rooms ever built in England or anywhere else, the supreme monument to Stuart splendour.

Essentially, it must be said, Wilton dates not from the Stuarts but from Tudor times; the tower in the centre of the east front, with its lantern and oriel windows, has been preserved almost unchanged from the middle of the sixteenth century. Much of the rest, however, was rebuilt of Chilmark stone in the twenty-five years between 1630 and 1655; and although the precise extent of his involvement is still argued by the *cognoscenti*, the controlling vision behind the rebuilding was indubitably that of King Charles's greatest architect, Inigo Jones.

At this time Wilton had recently come into the possession of Philip Herbert, Earl of Pembroke and Montgomery, after the death of his brother William – with whom, incidentally, he had been the joint dedicatee of Shakespeare's First Folio. Philip was Charles's Lord Chamberlain and, in addition, a close personal friend; and Inigo Jones would thus have been not only well known to him but also the obvious choice for the radical transformation he had in mind. Jones, however, was fully occupied with the house at Greenwich – still called the Queen's House (*q.v.*) – which he was building for Henrietta Maria. He seems to have simply sketched out a rough plan of the work proposed, and then left the details to his associate, the Frenchman Isaac de Caux. According to a drawing of the south front by de Caux that has survived, this original idea was for a house twice the size of the present one, with a great Corinthian portico flanked by eight bays on each side; but as a result, probably, of the outbreak of the Civil War – during which the Earl vacillated from one side to the other, finally throwing in his lot with the Parliamentarians – only the proposed east wing was ever built.

In 1647, like some divine retribution for his betrayal, Philip saw his new house gutted by fire. Undaunted, he immediately began the rebuilding; and Inigo Jones, who was by now less fully occupied – he was after all seventy-five years old – set to work on those magnificent rooms which are still the chief of Wilton's glories. Neither he nor his patron lived to see them completed; this time the work devolved on his successor John Webb. But conception and designs alike are virtually all Jones's own, planned and executed with an exuberance belied by the house's comparatively restrained exterior. He once wrote that 'outwardly every wise man carries a gravity, yet inwardly has his imagination set on fire and sometimes licentiously flies out'. At Wilton, more than anywhere else, he showed that he was no exception.

But it was a seventeenth-century licentiousness. In all six of the celebrated state rooms – and particularly in the

*Wilton House.*

grandest of them all, the Double Cube – Jones's swags and garlands, his bunches of fruit and flowers, have a weight and solidity, a feeling of quintessential Englishness about them utterly different from the more tenuous refinements that Robert Adam and his followers were to import from the Continent in the century to come. It is fascinating to see, in this same room, how brilliantly Kent and Chippendale, working 100 years later, adapted their furniture to his style.

Jones had another collaborator too, one whose contribution is greater far than that of Webb or de Caux, Kent or Chippendale. Sir Anthony Van Dyck had painted his superb series of portraits of the Herbert family between 1634 and 1636; and for these portraits, culminating in the tremendous conversation piece that dominates the west wall, the Double Cube was specifically designed. There are few rooms, anywhere, in which paintings on canvas – as opposed to frescoes – combine so effortlessly with gilding and plasterwork to form a single, completely satisfying, decorative whole. If only Philip Herbert could have seen it in time, one feels he might have remained a Royalist; but in any case the ghost of King Charles, if it ever passes this way, must surely have forgiven him.

It may prove more reluctant to forgive James Wyatt, who in 1801 was called in to make improvements and promptly pulled down the west and north fronts, including the Great Hall and the two northern towers. Wyatt's additions, notably the Gothic Entrance Hall and Cloister, are harmless enough in themselves but a poor substitute for the Caroline splendour which he destroyed.

In the town, the CHURCH OF ST MARY AND ST NICHOLAS is a phenomenon indeed: a totally unexpected and, in a small English country town, wonderfully inappropriate explosion of the *Rundbogenstil*, the 'round arch' style which was imported from Germany in the 1840s. Though the work of two English architects – T.H. Wyatt and David Brandon – this gigantic pile is clearly inspired by South Italian Romanesque. The columns supported on crouching beasts, the wheel window with twisted columns for spokes, the free-standing *campanile* – we might well be in Tuscany or Apulia, but we are certainly a far cry from Wiltshire.

The interior is equally tremendous, with its arcade set on tall columns, their capitals decorated in a free and original style of much virtuosity. More columns, of black marble, mark the division of nave and chancel, beyond which the apse carries in its conch a majestic mosaic of the enthroned Christ. Other, smaller, mosaics glisten below and in the side apses, as does the rich – and sometimes genuine – Cosmati-work on the floor and the high pulpit. The small barley-sugar columns on the upper level of this pulpit come from the famous thirteenth-century Shrine of Capoccio in Rome. They previously formed part of the collection of Sir William Hamilton, who presented them to Horace Walpole at Strawberry Hill. All is immensely opulent and un-English; only the ubiquitous inscriptions in Victorian Gothic lettering and some particularly nasty stained glass give the show away.

But not all the glass is nasty. There is marvellous quality to be found in the central and northern apses – French, of the twelfth and thirteenth centuries – with the added advantage that much of it is at eye level: a rare privilege indeed.

All this, and much else that there is alas no space to describe, we owe to Ekaterina Voronzov, the daughter of the Russian Ambassador in London who married the 11th Earl of Pembroke as his second wife in 1808, and to her son Sidney Herbert, Secretary for War during the Crimean campaign, friend and champion of Florence Nightingale. It was apparently at the Countess's request that the church was given a north–south axis according to the normal practice in Russia, where Jerusalem lies roughly to the south.

This is by no means the most beautiful church in Wiltshire, but it is unquestionably the oddest and the most ornate. The thousands of tourists who visit Wilton House and then pass by the church without a second glance can have no idea what an experience they are missing.

# Short List

## Aldbourne

*39; 6½ miles NW of Hungerford on A419*

ST MICHAEL'S is a large church with a fine stepped Perpendicular tower, an Early English chancel and thirteenth-century arcades. There are excellent Perpendicular roofs with moulded beams throughout the church and a lovely irregularly tiled and stone-flagged floor.

## Alderbury

*40; 3 miles SE of Salisbury on A36*

ST MARIE'S GRANGE was built by Pugin for himself in 1835 after his marriage. It was enlarged in 1841 after he had left, but it is still possible to see the diapered red-brick house as an example of the Victorian medieval Gothic dream. The original house had two towers (there are now three) and a two-storey Chapel. Pugin's second-floor bedroom has a garderobe in the turret – which is carrying the idea of medievalism, it might be thought, a little too far.

## Bromham

*41; 4½ miles E of Melksham off A342*

ST NICHOLAS'S CHURCH would scarcely merit inclusion were it not for the late fifteenth-century Tocotes and Beauchamp Chapel at its south-east corner, marked by three gigantic five-light windows surmounted by angels. The east window of the church is by Burne-Jones, and the poet Thomas Moore is buried in the churchyard.

## Compton Chamberlayne

*42; 7 miles W of Salisbury off A30*

Beautifully set overlooking its lake, COMPTON PARK is mostly of the seventeenth century but hiding behind a Georgian ashlared and embattled façade. The panelled Drawing Room contains some quite superb seventeenth-century wood carving very much in the Grinling Gibbons tradition.

## The Courts

See Holt.

## Durnford

*43; 7 miles N of Salisbury off A345*

ST ANDREW'S CHURCH has two Norman doorways with tympana of green and white stone, a Norman chancel arch and wall paintings of the thirteenth century. There is some fine furniture, including a Jacobean family pew and a west gallery on columns.

## East Knoyle

*44; 10½ miles S of Warminster on A350*

ST MARY'S CHURCH contains one unique and fascinating feature – the plasterwork 'inventions' on the chancel walls, devised by the rector – the father of Sir Christopher Wren – in 1539. The east wall shows us Jacob's Ladder, the west the Ascension of Christ, and the south the Sacrifice of Isaac.

## Enford

*45; 6½ miles N of Amesbury on A345*

ALL SAINTS AND ST MARGARET'S, a fine church of flint and stone, has impressive Norman arcades and chancel arch. There is a most curious north wall in the chancel, with deeply cut thirteenth-century blank arcading of alternately tall and short pointed arches.

## Farley

*46; 5 miles E of Salisbury off A36*

ALL SAINTS is a classical church, probably built around 1690 by Alexander Fort, who also built the local almshouses. Christopher Wren may have helped with the design. It is brick with stone dressings, and the plan is that of a Greek cross. The tower has urn pinnacles, and the windows are round-headed. The proportions are satisfying both inside and out, the interior is simple with plaster vaults, and many original furnishings remain.

## Holt

*47; 2½ miles NE of Bradford-on-Avon on B3107*
*Includes The Courts (NT)*

THE COURTS looks like a town house which has found itself transported to the country. It has an exuberant early eighteenth-century front, possibly by a Bradford or Bristol master mason. Plain open triangular pediments and open scrolly ones compete over the windows, and there is an elaborate central feature – more lively than grammatical – using both motifs.

## Inglesham

*48; 9 miles NE of Swindon off A361*

ST JOHN THE BAPTIST has an inscription saying 'This church was repaired in 1888–9 through the energy and with the help of William Morris who loved it'. It is indeed lovable, with its late thirteenth-century double bell-cote and its charming interior, mostly dating from *c.*1200. There are Perpendicular screens, Jacobean box pews, an Elizabethan pulpit, and even a late Anglo-Saxon sculpture of the Virgin and Child.

## Manningford Bruce

*49; 7½ miles SE of Devizes off A345*

ST PETER'S is an apsed Norman church splendidly preserved. It was well restored in 1882 by J.L. Pearson, who was responsible for the unusual herringbone timber ceiling of chancel and apse.

## Mere

*50; 7 miles NE of Wincanton off A303*

ST MICHAEL'S is a large and quite splendid church with a mainly fourteenth-century exterior, but a Perpendicular tower and interior. There are magnificent stalls with misericords, seventeenth-century benches and exceptionally good screens. WOODLANDS MANOR, half a mile to the south-east, has a fourteenth-century Chapel and Hall, the Chapel on the upper floor with a wagon roof, the Hall superbly timbered with arched braces up to collar-beams and three tiers of cusped wind-braces. The ground-floor room below the Chapel has a plaster ceiling of *c.*1570 and a fine stone chimneypiece.

## Norrington Manor

*51; 4½ miles SE of Shaftesbury off B3081*

Of the original late fourteenth-century house, Hall and porch survive. The Hall windows are of two lights, transomed and with a touch of tracery, while the porch has a finely moulded arch and vault. The small vaulted undercroft of the solar wing also remains, but the wing itself was rebuilt during the course of the seventeenth century.

## Sheldon Manor

*52; 1½ miles W of Chippenham off A420*

An attractive small stone manor house, mainly dating from the 1660s, it has typical tall gables and mullion and transom windows. What makes it special is an amazing late thirteenth-century porch, which stands two storeys high and is heavily rib-vaulted on the ground floor. There is also a detached small fifteenth-century Chapel.

## Stratford sub Castle

*53; 1½ miles N of Salisbury off A345*

ST LAWRENCE'S CHURCH has a charming interior with bossed wagon roofs, fine woodwork of *c.*1711 and a Jacobean pulpit. There are box pews and a west gallery of *c.*1800.

## Tisbury

*54; 12 miles W of Salisbury off B3089*

A very large cruciform church, ST JOHN THE BAPTIST is mainly of the Decorated and Perpendicular periods – though the crossing is late twelfth-century and the north porch early thirteenth-century. The high nave has a wagon roof and three pairs of hammer-beams with angels; the aisles have sixteenth-century panelled ceilings. PLACE FARM is a fourteenth- and fifteenth-century house with two gatehouses, once a grange of a medieval nunnery. The adjacent fifteenth-century BARN, nearly 200 feet long, is the largest in England. It is a tremendous building, splendidly raftered and heroically thatched.

# *Bibliography*

The books listed below have general application to all parts of the country. Titles relating to individual counties and districts are not included as they are too numerous to mention. However the *Shell Guides* – in those counties for which they exist – form excellent introductions to the architecture of specific areas of England.


Betjeman, John (Ed.). *The Collins Pocket Guide to English Parish Churches*, 2 vols, London, 1968.

Bony, Jean. *The English Decorated Style: Gothic Architecture Transformed, 1250–1350*, Wrightsman Lectures, London, 1979.

Braun, Hugh. *An Introduction to English Medieval Architecture*, London, 1951.

Clifton-Taylor, Alec. *The Cathedrals of England*, London, 1967.

*The Pattern of English Building*, revised edn, London, 1972.

*English Parish Churches as Works of Art*, London, 1974.

Colvin, Howard. *A Biographical Dictionary of British Architects, 1600–1840*, London, 1978.

Cook, Olive. *The English Country House*, London, 1974.

Downes, Kerry. *Hawksmoor*, London, 1969.

Fawcett, Jane (Ed.). *Seven Victorian Architects*, London, 1976.

Fedden, Robin, with John Kenworthy-Browne. *The Country House Guide*, London, 1979.

Gascoigne, Christina and Bamber. *Castles of Britain*, London, 1975.

Girouard, Mark. *Robert Smythson and the Architecture of the Elizabethan Era*, London, 1966.

*Life in the English Country House*, London, 1978.

*The Victorian Country House*, London, 1979.

Harris, John. *William Talman, Maverick Architect*, London, 1982.

Hutton, Graham, with Olive Cook. *English Parish Churches*, London, 1976.

Joekes, Rosemary (Ed.). *The National Trust Guide*, revised edn, London, 1984.

O'Neill, Daniel. *Lutyens: Country Houses*, London, 1980.

Pevsner, Nikolaus. *The Buildings of England*, London, various dates, and in constant revision.

Robinson, John Martin. *The Wyatts: An Architectural Dynasty*, London, 1979.

Service, Alastair (General Editor). *The Buildings of Britain*.

*Anglo-Saxon and Norman*, by Alastair Service, London, 1982.

*Tudor and Jacobean*, by Malcolm Airs, London, 1982.

*Stuart and Baroque*, by Richard Morrice, London, 1982.

*Regency*, by David Watkin, London, 1982.

Stanton, Phoebe, *Pugin*, London, 1971.

Summerson, John. *Architecture in Britain, 1530–1830*, London, 1953.

Watkin, David. *Athenian Stuart, Pioneer of the Greek Revival*, London, 1982.

Webb, Geoffrey. *Architecture in Britain: The Middle Ages*, London, 1956.

Whinney, Margaret. *Wren*, London, 1971.

**BEDFORDSHIRE**
1 Ampthill
2 Chalgrave
3 Dunstable Priory
4 Eaton Bray
5 Elstow
6 Felmersham
7 Luton Hoo
8 Marston Morteyne
9 Southill
10 Toddington
11 Turvey
12 Woburn Abbey
13 Wrest Park
14 Wymington
15 Chicksands Priory
16 Clapham
17 Haynes
18 Mogerhanger Park

**BERKSHIRE**
1 Avington
2 Basildon Park
3 Bear Wood
4 Donnington
5 Eton College
6 Farley Hill
7 Langley Marish
8 Ockwells Manor
9 Padworth
10 Shottesbrooke
11 Sonning
12 Swallowfield Park
13 Tidmarsh
14 Warfield
15 Windsor
16 Hurley
17 Hurst
18 Lambourn
19 Monkey Island
20 Newbury
21 Sandleford Priory
22 Shaw House
23 Sulhamstead
24 Theale
25 Wickham

**BUCKINGHAMSHIRE**
1 Amersham
2 Beaconsfield
3 Bledlow
4 Chequers
5 Chetwode
6 Chicheley Hall
7 Claydon House
8 Cliveden
9 Denham Place
10 Dorney
11 Dropmore
12 Gayhurst
13 Hartwell House
14 Hillesden
15 Mentmore
16 Nether Winchendon
17 Notley Abbey
18 Stewkley
19 Stowe
20 Tyringham House
21 Waddesdon Manor
22 West Wycombe
23 Willen
24 Wing
25 Winslow Hall
26 Wotton Underwood
27 Ascott
28 Boarstall Tower
29 Chenies
30 Dinton
31 Fawley Court
32 Fingest
33 Gerrards Cross
34 Hanslope
35 Harleyford Manor
36 High Wycombe
37 Hughenden Manor
38 Ivinghoe
39 Long Crendon
40 Maids' Moreton
41 Marlow Place
42 North Marston
43 Twyford

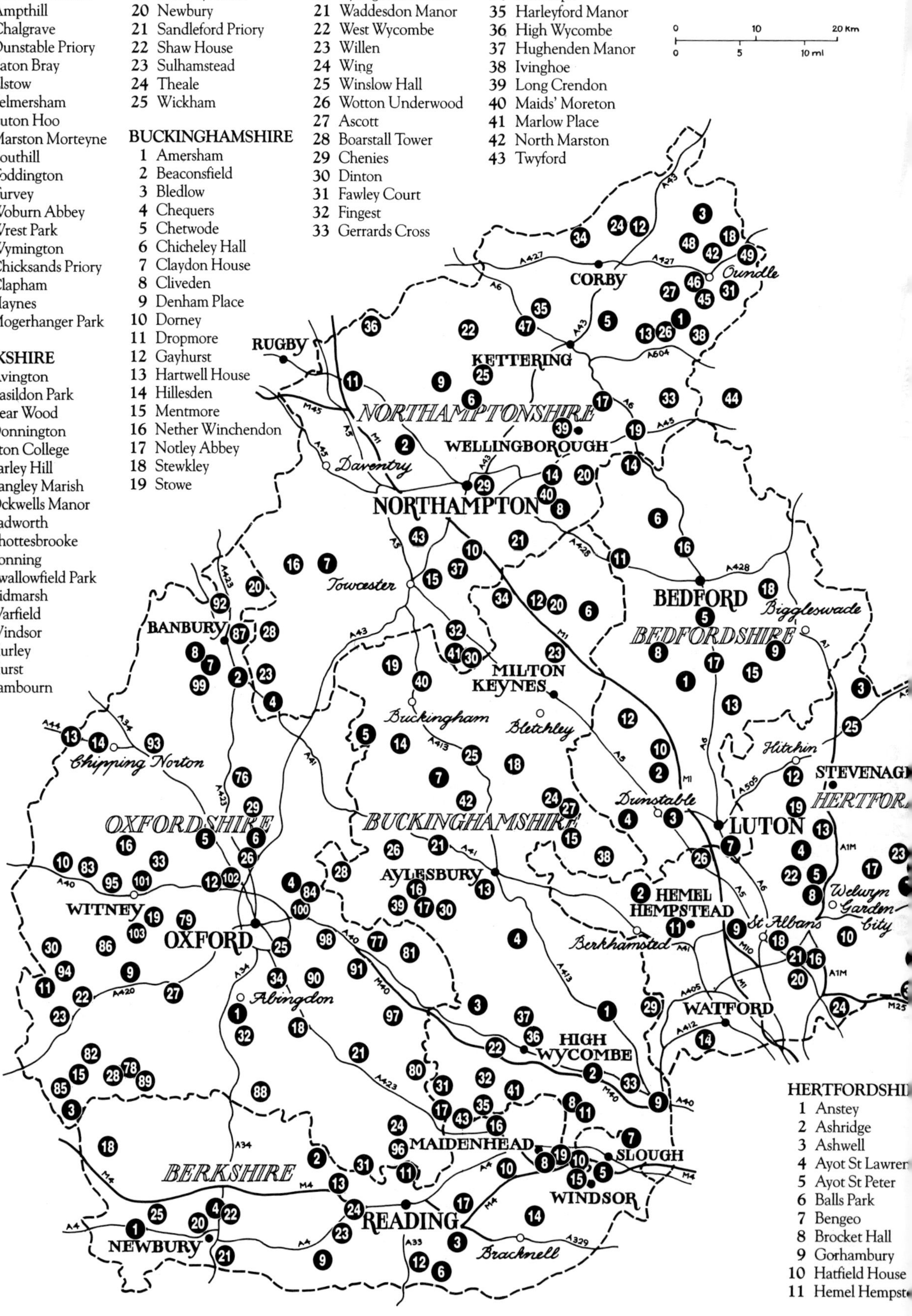
0 10 20 Km
0 5 10 ml
RUGBY
CORBY
Oundle
KETTERING
NORTHAMPTONSHIRE
WELLINGBOROUGH
Daventry
NORTHAMPTON
Towcester
BEDFORD
Biggleswade
BEDFORDSHIRE
BANBURY
MILTON KEYNES
Buckingham
Bletchley
Chipping Norton
Hitchin
STEVENAG
HERTFOR
OXFORDSHIRE
BUCKINGHAMSHIRE
Dunstable
LUTON
AYLESBURY
HEMEL HEMPSTEAD
Welwyn Garden City
WITNEY
OXFORD
St Albans
Berkhamsted
Abingdon
WATFORD
HIGH WYCOMBE
MAIDENHEAD
SLOUGH
BERKSHIRE
WINDSOR
READING
NEWBURY
Bracknell

**HERTFORDSHI**
1 Anstey
2 Ashridge
3 Ashwell
4 Ayot St Lawren
5 Ayot St Peter
6 Balls Park
7 Bengeo
8 Brocket Hall
9 Gorhambury
10 Hatfield House
11 Hemel Hempst

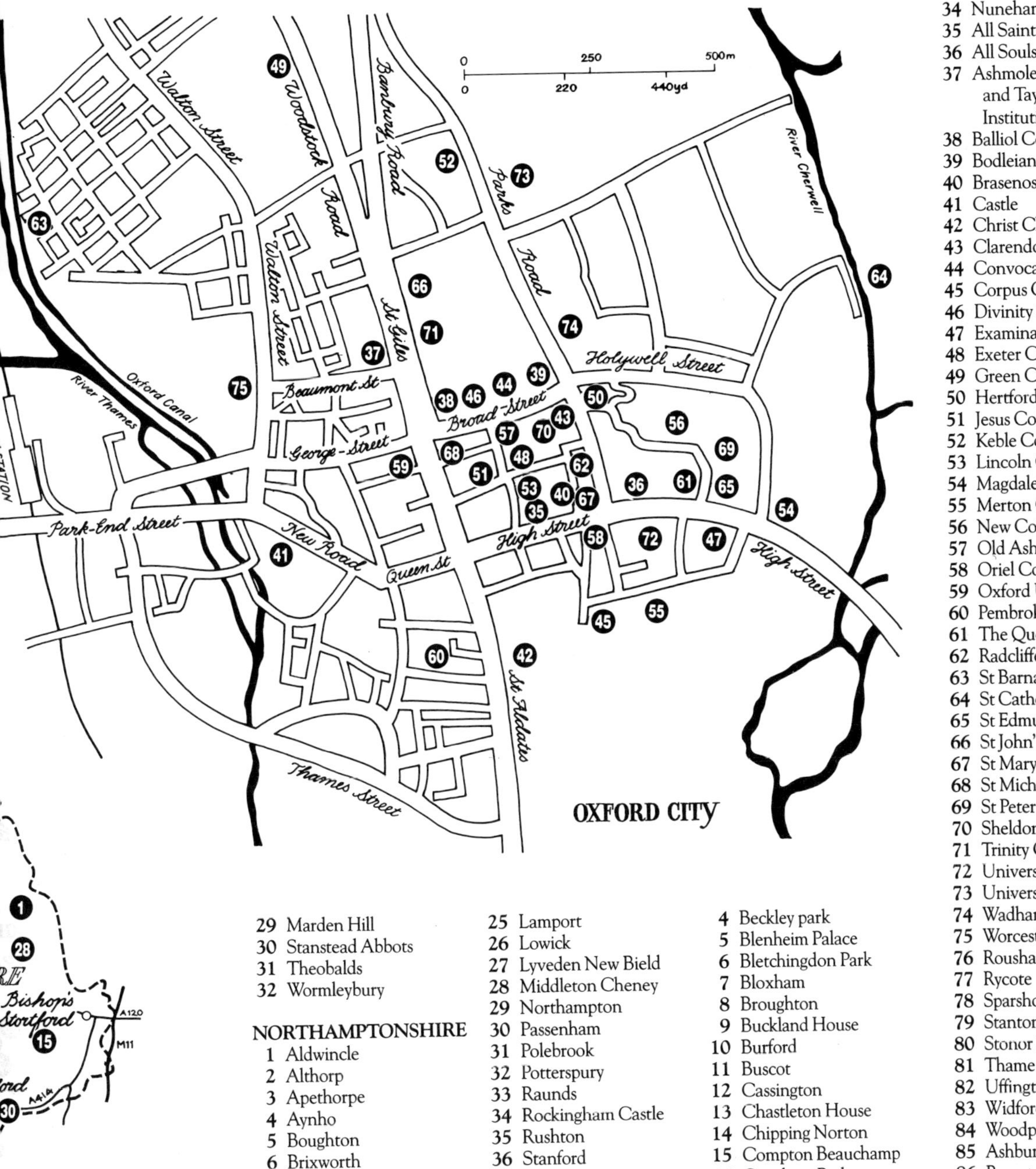


12 Hitchin
13 Knebworth
14 Moor Park
15 Much Hadham
16 North Mymms House
17 Queen Hoo Hall
18 St Albans Cathedral
19 St Pauls Walden
20 Salisbury Hall
21 Tyttenhanger
22 Wheathampstead
23 Woodhall Park
24 Wrotham Park
25 Baldock
26 Beechwood
27 Haileybury
28 Little Hormead
29 Marden Hill
30 Stanstead Abbots
31 Theobalds
32 Wormleybury

NORTHAMPTONSHIRE

1 Aldwincle
2 Althorp
3 Apethorpe
4 Aynho
5 Boughton
6 Brixworth
7 Canons Ashby
8 Castle Ashby
9 Cottesbrooke Hall
10 Courteenhall
11 Crick
12 Deene Park
13 Drayton House
14 Earl's Barton
15 Easton Neston
16 Eydon
17 Finedon
18 Fotheringhay
19 Higham Ferrers
20 Hinwick House
21 Horton
22 Kelmarsh
23 Kings Sutton
24 Kirby Hall
25 Lamport
26 Lowick
27 Lyveden New Bield
28 Middleton Cheney
29 Northampton
30 Passenham
31 Polebrook
32 Potterspury
33 Raunds
34 Rockingham Castle
35 Rushton
36 Stanford
37 Stoke Bruerne
38 Titchmarsh
39 Wellingborough
40 Whiston
41 Wicken
42 Cotterstock
43 Gayton
44 Hannington
45 Lilford Hall
46 Oundle
47 Rothwell
48 Southwick Hall
49 Warmington

OXFORDSHIRE

1 Abingdon
2 Adderbury
3 Ashdown House
4 Beckley park
5 Blenheim Palace
6 Bletchingdon Park
7 Bloxham
8 Broughton
9 Buckland House
10 Burford
11 Buscot
12 Cassington
13 Chastleton House
14 Chipping Norton
15 Compton Beauchamp
16 Cornbury Park
17 Ditchley Park
18 Dorchester Abbey
19 Ducklington
20 Edgcote House
21 Ewelme
22 Faringdon
23 Great Coxwell Barn
24 Greys Court
25 Iffley
26 Kidlington
27 Kingston Bagpuize
28 Kingstone Lisle House
29 Kirtlington Park
30 Langford
31 Mapledurham House
32 Milton Manor
33 North Leigh
34 Nuneham Courtenay
35 All Saints
36 All Souls College
37 Ashmolean Museum and Taylorian Institution
38 Balliol College
39 Bodleian Library
40 Brasenose College
41 Castle
42 Christ Church
43 Clarendon Building
44 Convocation House
45 Corpus Christi College
46 Divinity School
47 Examination Schools
48 Exeter College
49 Green College
50 Hertford College
51 Jesus College
52 Keble College
53 Lincoln College
54 Magdalen College
55 Merton College
56 New College
57 Old Ashmolean
58 Oriel College
59 Oxford Union Society
60 Pembroke College
61 The Queen's College
62 Radcliffe Camera
63 St Barnabas
64 St Catherine's College
65 St Edmund Hall
66 St John's College
67 St Mary the Virgin
68 St Michael
69 St Peter-in-the-East
70 Sheldonian Theatre
71 Trinity College
72 University College
73 University Museum
74 Wadham College
75 Worcester College
76 Rousham Park
77 Rycote
78 Sparsholt
79 Stanton Harcourt
80 Stonor Park
81 Thame Park
82 Uffington
83 Widford
84 Woodperry
85 Ashbury
86 Bampton
87 Banbury
88 Blewbury
89 Childrey
90 Chislehampton
91 Great Haseley
92 Hanwell
93 Heythrop House
94 Kelmscott Manor
95 Minster Lovell Manor
96 Rotherfield Peppard
97 Shirburn Castle
98 Shotover Park
99 South Newington
100 Stanton St John
101 Witney
102 Yarnton
103 Yelford Manor

**CAMBRIDGESHIRE**
1 Alconbury
2 Barnack
3 Bottisham
4 Burghley House
5 Burwell
6 Christ's College
7 Clare College
8 Corpus Christi College
9 Downing College
10 Emmanuel College
11 Fitzwilliam Museum
12 Gonville and Caius College
13 Holy Sepulchre (The Round Church)
14 Jesus College
15 King's College
16 Magdalene College
17 Old Schools
18 Pembroke College
19 Peterhouse
20 Queens' College
21 St Bene't's
22 St Catharine's College
23 St John's College
24 St Mary the Great
25 Senate House
26 Sidney Sussex College
27 Trinity College
28 Trinity Hall
29 St Mary the Less
30 St Mary Magdalene, Barnwell
31 St Peter's
32 Castor
33 Cherry Hinton
34 Conington (1)
35 Conington (2)
36 Elm
37 Ely
38 Etton
39 Fenstanton
40 Fordham
41 Great Paxton
42 Hail Weston
43 Hemingford Grey
44 Histon
45 Ickleton
46 Kimbolton
47 Kirtling
48 Leighton Bromswold
49 Leverington
50 Little Gidding
51 Longthorpe
52 March
53 Milton
54 Over
55 Peterborough
56 Ramsey
57 St Ives
58 St Neots
59 Soham
60 Somersham
61 Sutton-in-the-Isle
62 Thorney
63 Thorpe Hall
64 Willingham
65 Wimpole Hall
66 Wisbech
67 Wittering
68 Yaxley
69 Anglesey Abbey
70 Bluntisham
71 Buckden
72 Duxford
73 Godmanchester
74 Hinchingbrooke House
75 Isleham
76 Keyston
77 Madingley Hall
78 Northborough
79 Stow Longa
80 Swaffham Prior

**ESSEX**
1 Audley End
2 Beeleigh Abbey
3 Blackmore
4 Boreham
5 Bradwell-Juxta-Mare
6 Castle Hedingham
7 Coggeshall
8 Colchester
9 Copford
10 Dedham
11 Faulkbourne Hall
12 Finchingfield
13 Fingringhoe
14 Great Bardfield
15 Great Bromley
16 Great Waltham
17 Great Warley
18 Greensted-Juxta-Ongar
19 Havering-Atte-Bower
20 Ingatestone
21 Kelvedon Hatch
22 Lawford
23 Layer Marney
24 Little Dunmow
25 Little Leighs
26 Maldon
27 Moyns Park
28 Saffron Walden
29 St Osyth
30 Terling Place
31 Thaxted
32 Tilty
33 Waltham Abbey
34 Bobbingworth
35 Bradwell-Juxta-Coggeshall
36 Clavering
37 Cressing
38 Gosfield Hall
39 Great Braxted
40 Great Leighs
41 Hadleigh
42 Hatfield Broad Oak
43 Little Coggeshall Abbey
44 Little Maplestead
45 Margaretting
46 Mistley
47 Pentlow
48 Tolleshunt D'Arcy Hall
49 Tolleshunt Major

**NORFOLK**
1 Attleborough
2 Barnham Broom Hall
3 Barningham Winter
4 Beeston-next-Mileham
5 Beeston St Laurence
6 Binham Priory
7 Blakeney
8 Blickling Hall
9 Castle Acre
10 Castle Rising
11 Cawston
12 Cley-next-the-Sea
13 East Barsham
14 East Harling
15 Felbrigg Hall
16 Fritton
17 Great Cressingham
18 Great Walsingham
19 Gunton
20 Hales
21 Heydon
22 Holkham Hall
23 Houghton Hall
24 Hoveton
25 King's Lynn
26 Knapton
27 Langley Park
28 Mannington Hall
29 Melton Constable
30 Norwich
31 Oxburgh Hall
32 Rainthorpe Hall
33 Raynham Hall
34 Redenhall
35 Salle
36 Shelton
37 Sheringham Hall
38 Shotesham Park
39 South Creake
40 South Lopham
41 Swaffham
42 Terrington St Clement
43 Thompson
44 Tilney All Saints
45 Trunch
46 Upwell
47 Walpole St Peter
48 Walsoken
49 West Walton
50 Wolterton Hall
51 Worstead
52 Wymondham
53 Breccles Hall
54 Caister Castle
55 Elsing
56 Emneth
57 Great Snoring
58 Haddiscoe
59 Heckingham
60 Holt
61 Kimberley Hall
62 Narford Hall
63 Necton
64 North Runcton
65 Pulham St Mary
66 Ryston Hall
67 Saxlingham
68 Snettisham
69 Wiggenhall St Germans
70 Wiggenhall St Mary
71 Wiggenhall St Mary Magdalene
72 Wiggenhall St Peter
73 Wilby

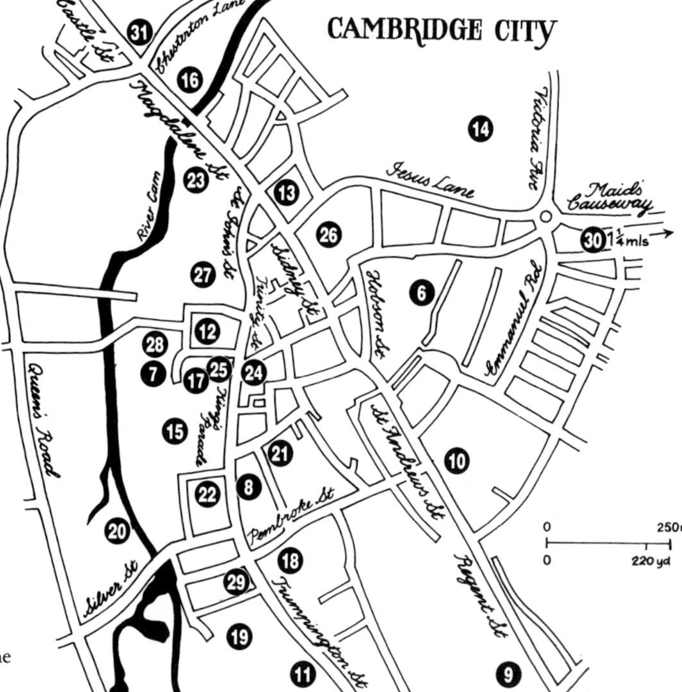

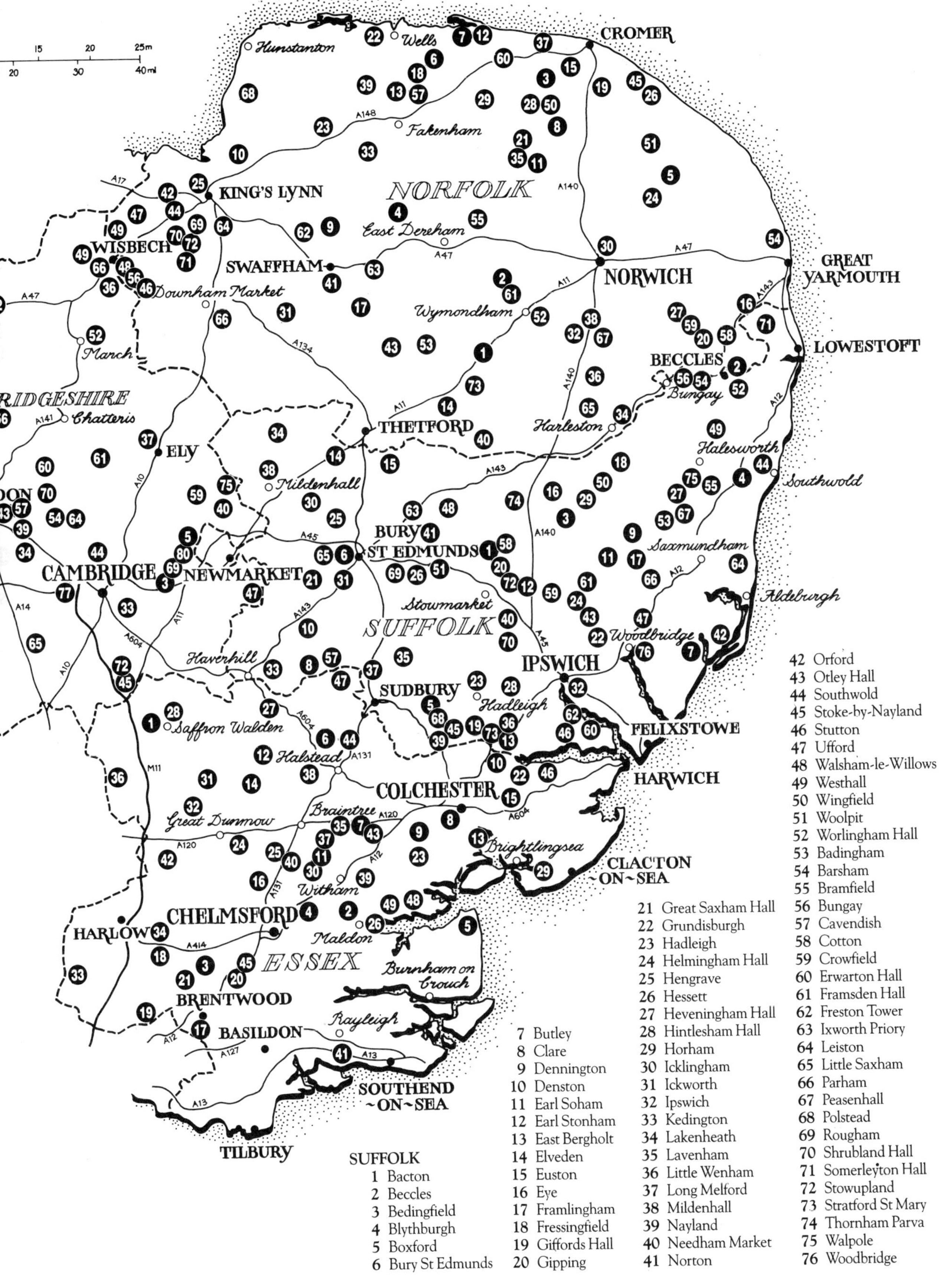

15 20 25m
20 30 40ml
Hunstanton
Wells
CROMER
Fakenham
NORFOLK
KING'S LYNN
East Dereham
WISBECH
SWAFFHAM
Downham Market
NORWICH
GREAT YARMOUTH
Wymondham
March
LOWESTOFT
BECCLES
Bungay
RIDGESHIRE
Chatteris
THETFORD
Harleston
ELY
Mildenhall
Halesworth
Southwold
BURY ST EDMUNDS
Saxmundham
CAMBRIDGE
NEWMARKET
Aldeburgh
Stowmarket
SUFFOLK
Woodbridge
IPSWICH
Haverhill
SUDBURY
Hadleigh
FELIXSTOWE
Saffron Walden
Halstead
HARWICH
COLCHESTER
Braintree
Great Dunmow
Brightlingsea
CLACTON ~ON~SEA
Witham
CHELMSFORD
Maldon
HARLOW
ESSEX
Burnham on Crouch
BRENTWOOD
Rayleigh
BASILDON
SOUTHEND ~ON~SEA
TILBURY
A17
A47
A148
A140
A11
A134
A141
A10
A45
A143
A12
A14
A604
M11
A131
A120
A414
A127
A13
SUFFOLK
1 Bacton
2 Beccles
3 Bedingfield
4 Blythburgh
5 Boxford
6 Bury St Edmunds
7 Butley
8 Clare
9 Dennington
10 Denston
11 Earl Soham
12 Earl Stonham
13 East Bergholt
14 Elveden
15 Euston
16 Eye
17 Framlingham
18 Fressingfield
19 Giffords Hall
20 Gipping
21 Great Saxham Hall
22 Grundisburgh
23 Hadleigh
24 Helmingham Hall
25 Hengrave
26 Hessett
27 Heveningham Hall
28 Hintlesham Hall
29 Horham
30 Icklingham
31 Ickworth
32 Ipswich
33 Kedington
34 Lakenheath
35 Lavenham
36 Little Wenham
37 Long Melford
38 Mildenhall
39 Nayland
40 Needham Market
41 Norton
42 Orford
43 Otley Hall
44 Southwold
45 Stoke-by-Nayland
46 Stutton
47 Ufford
48 Walsham-le-Willows
49 Westhall
50 Wingfield
51 Woolpit
52 Worlingham Hall
53 Badingham
54 Barsham
55 Bramfield
56 Bungay
57 Cavendish
58 Cotton
59 Crowfield
60 Erwarton Hall
61 Framsden Hall
62 Freston Tower
63 Ixworth Priory
64 Leiston
65 Little Saxham
66 Parham
67 Peasenhall
68 Polstead
69 Rougham
70 Shrubland Hall
71 Somerleyton Hall
72 Stowupland
73 Stratford St Mary
74 Thornham Parva
75 Walpole
76 Woodbridge

## AVON

1 Badminton
2 Bath
3 Blaise Hamlet
4 Bristol
5 Clevedon Court
6 Clifton
7 Combe Hay Manor
8 Compton Martin
9 Dodington Park
10 Dyrham Park
11 Kings Weston
12 Little Sodbury Manor
13 Redland
14 Thornbury
15 Wrington
16 Yatton
17 Abbotsleigh
18 Hinton Charterhouse
19 Horton Court
20 Long Ashton
21 Midford Castle
22 Newton St Loe
23 Saltford Manor

## CORNWALL

1 Altarnun
2 Antony House
3 Blisland
4 Caerhays Castle
5 Cotehele
6 Cury
7 Falmouth
8 Godolphin House
9 Ince Castle
10 Kilkhampton
11 Lanhydrock
12 Launcells
13 Launceston
14 Lostwithiel
15 Morwenstow
16 Pencarrow House
17 Penfound Manor
18 Prideaux Place
19 Probus
20 St Buryan
21 St Columb Major
22 St Germans
23 St Ives
24 St Mawes Castle
25 St Michael's Mount
26 St Neot
27 Tintagel
28 Trelowarren
29 Trematon Castle
30 Trerice
31 Truro
32 Carnanton
33 Fowey
34 Mullion
35 Penzance
36 Pendennis Castle
37 St Winnow
38 Trelissick

## DEVON

1 Arlington Court
2 Ashton
3 Bradley Manor
4 Branscombe
5 Buckland Abbey
6 Cadhay
7 Castle Drogo
8 Castle Hill
9 Compton Castle
10 Cullompton
11 Dartington
12 Dartmouth
13 Exeter
14 Exmouth
15 Hartland
16 Holcombe Rogus
17 Kenton
18 Kings Nympton
19 Knightshayes Court
20 Littlehempston
21 Luscombe Castle
22 Mamhead
23 Molland
24 Ottery St Mary
25 Plymouth
26 Plympton
27 Powderham Castle
28 Saltram
29 Sharpham
30 Sidmouth
31 Swimbridge
32 Sydenham
33 Tawstock
34 Tiverton
35 Totnes
36 Ugbrooke
37 Bicton House
38 Bradninch
39 Chittlehampton
40 Coldridge
41 Collacombe Barton Manor
42 Crediton
43 Culmstock
44 Flete
45 Great Fulford
46 Harberton
47 Lapford
48 Luppitt
49 Puslinch
50 Shute Barton
51 Tavistock
52 Torbryan
53 Weare Giffard Hall
54 Youlston Park

## DORSET

1 Abbotsbury
2 Athelhampton Hall
3 Beaminster
4 Bere Regis
5 Bettiscombe
6 Bingham's Melcombe
7 Blandford Forum
8 Bridport
9 Bryanston
10 Cattistock
11 Cerne Abbas
12 Charborough Park
13 Charminster
14 Chettle House
15 Christchurch
16 Church Knowle
17 Corfe Castle
18 Cranborne
19 Crichel House
20 Eastbury
21 Encombe House
22 Forde Abbey
23 Horton
24 Kingston
25 Kingston Lacy
26 Lulworth
27 Mapperton
28 Melbury Sampford
29 Milton Abbas
30 Moreton
31 Purse Caundle
32 Sandford Orcas
33 Sherborne
34 Studland
35 Trent
36 Warmwell House
37 Weymouth
38 Whitchurch Canonicorum
39 Wimborne
40 Wimborne St Giles
41 Winterborne Came
42 Winterborne Tomson
43 Woodsford Castle
44 Worth Matravers
45 Bothenhampton
46 Bradford Abbas
47 Brownsea Island
48 Canford Magna
49 Chalbury
50 Chantmarle
51 Clifton Maybank
52 Creech Grange
53 Dewlish
54 Folke
55 Hanford House
56 Iwerne Courtney (or Shroton)
57 Iwerne Stepleton
58 Kingston Maurward
59 Kingston Russell
60 Lyme Regis
61 Puddletown
62 Smedmore
63 Toller Fratrum
64 Wareham
65 Winterborne Anderson
66 Winterborne Clenston
67 Winterborne Herringston
68 Yetminster

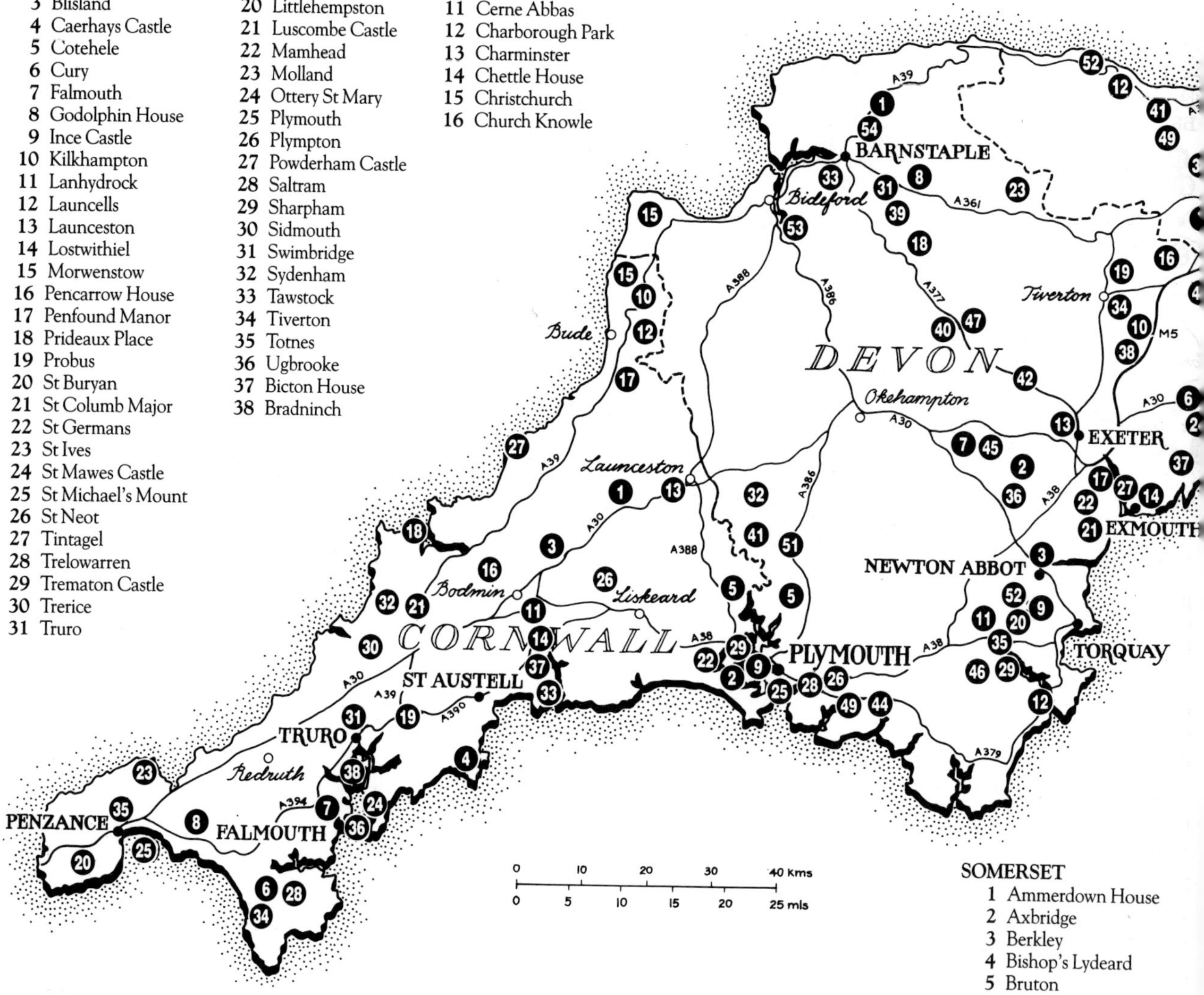

## SOMERSET

1 Ammerdown House
2 Axbridge
3 Berkley
4 Bishop's Lydeard
5 Bruton

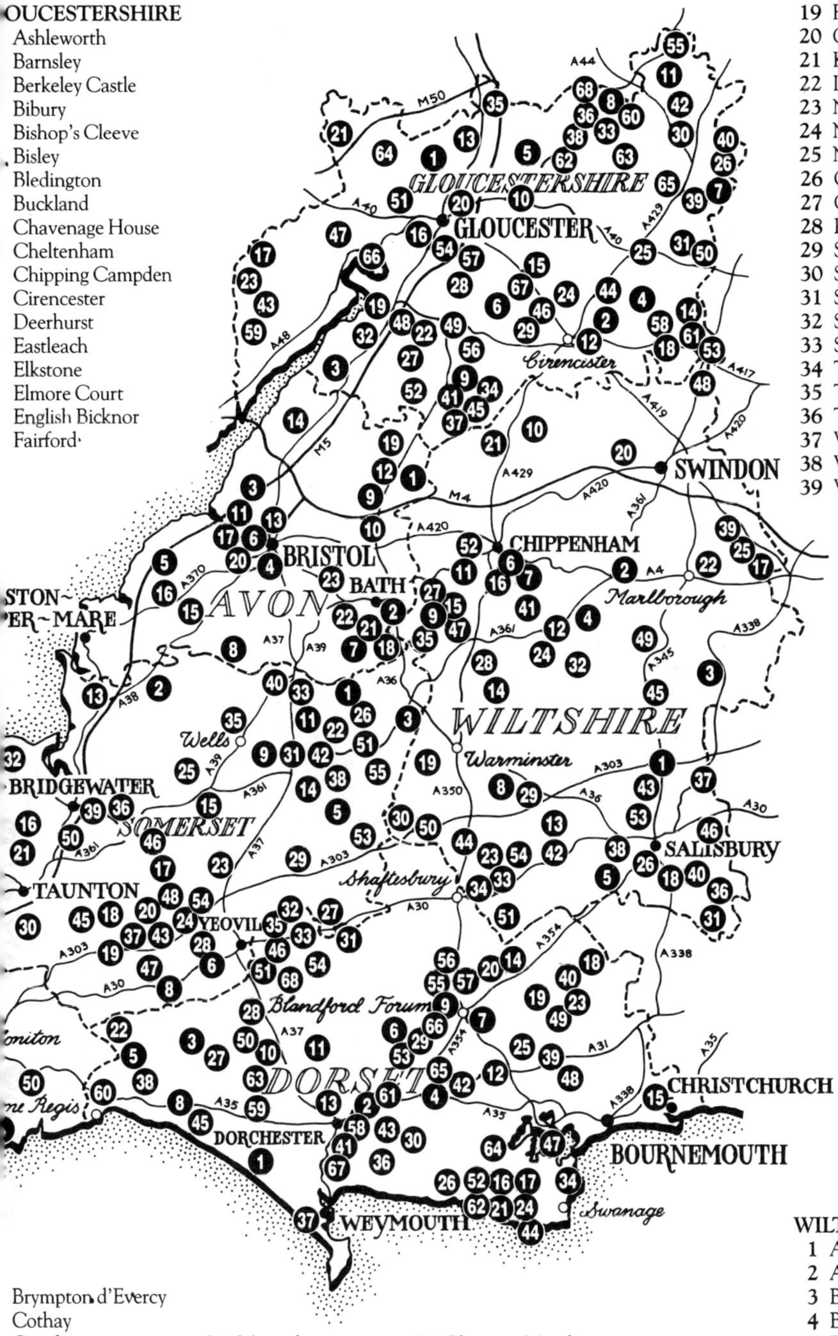

M50
A44
GLOUCESTERSHIRE
GLOUCESTER
A40
A429
A48
Cirencester
A417
A419
A420
M5
SWINDON
A429
M4
A420
A361
A420
CHIPPENHAM
BRISTOL
A370
BATH
A4
AVON
Marlborough
A37
A39
A36
A338
A38
A345
WILTSHIRE
Wells
A39
Warminster
A303
BRIDGEWATER
A350
A36
A361
SOMERSET
A30
A37
A303
SALISBURY
Shaftesbury
TAUNTON
A30
YEOVIL
A303
A354
A338
A30
Blandford Forum
A37
A354
A31
A35
DORSET
CHRISTCHURCH
A35
A338
A35
DORCHESTER
BOURNEMOUTH
WEYMOUTH
Swanage


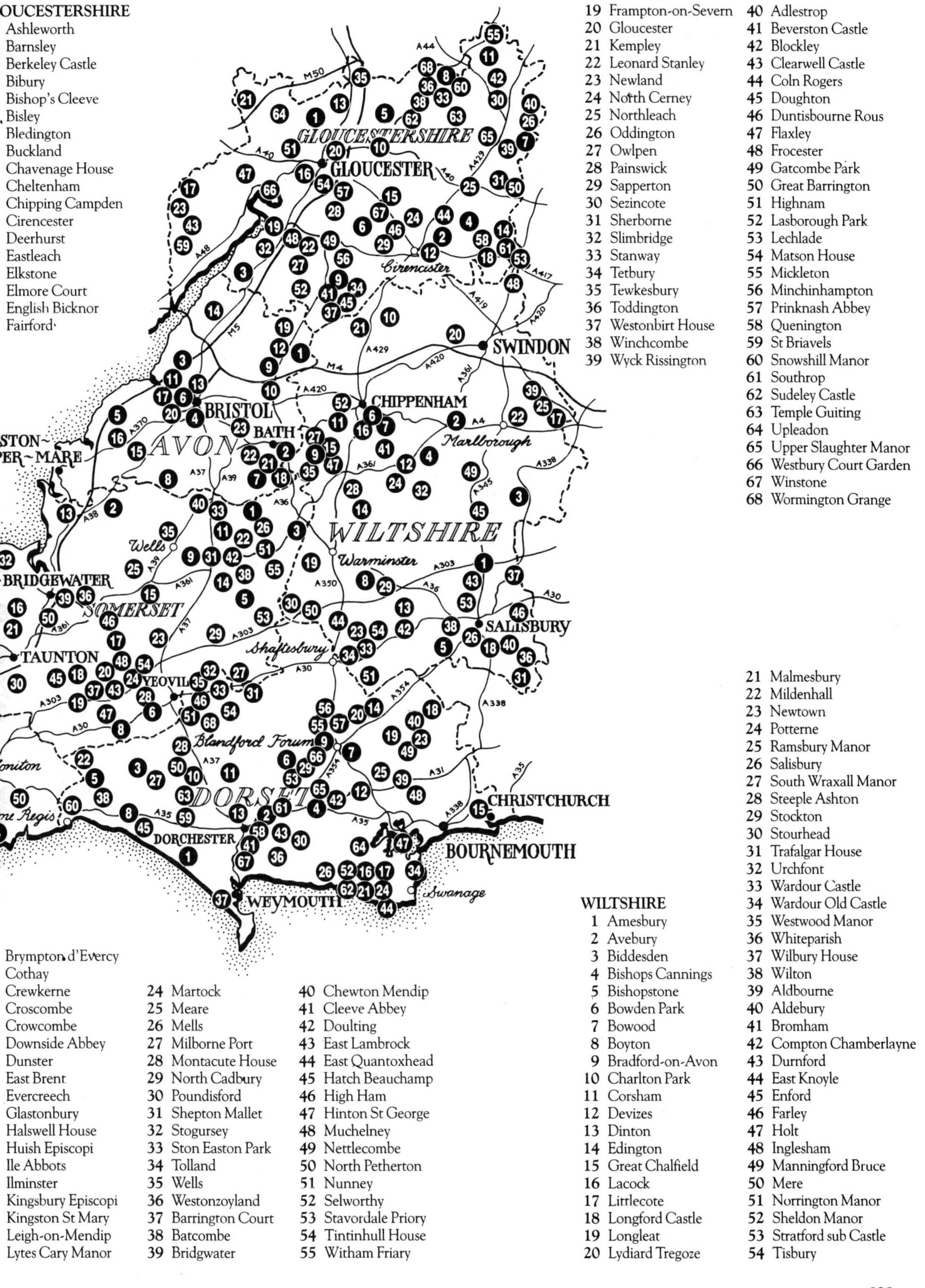

## OUCESTERSHIRE

Ashleworth
Barnsley
Berkeley Castle
Bibury
Bishop's Cleeve
Bisley
Bledington
Buckland
Chavenage House
Cheltenham
Chipping Campden
Cirencester
Deerhurst
Eastleach
Elkstone
Elmore Court
English Bicknor
Fairford

19 Frampton-on-Severn
20 Gloucester
21 Kempley
22 Leonard Stanley
23 Newland
24 North Cerney
25 Northleach
26 Oddington
27 Owlpen
28 Painswick
29 Sapperton
30 Sezincote
31 Sherborne
32 Slimbridge
33 Stanway
34 Tetbury
35 Tewkesbury
36 Toddington
37 Westonbirt House
38 Winchcombe
39 Wyck Rissington

40 Adlestrop
41 Beverston Castle
42 Blockley
43 Clearwell Castle
44 Coln Rogers
45 Doughton
46 Duntisbourne Rous
47 Flaxley
48 Frocester
49 Gatcombe Park
50 Great Barrington
51 Highnam
52 Lasborough Park
53 Lechlade
54 Matson House
55 Mickleton
56 Minchinhampton
57 Prinknash Abbey
58 Quenington
59 St Briavels
60 Snowshill Manor
61 Southrop
62 Sudeley Castle
63 Temple Guiting
64 Upleadon
65 Upper Slaughter Manor
66 Westbury Court Garden
67 Winstone
68 Wormington Grange

Brympton d'Evercy
Cothay
Crewkerne
Croscombe
Crowcombe
Downside Abbey
Dunster
East Brent
Evercreech
Glastonbury
Halswell House
Huish Episcopi
Ile Abbots
Ilminster
Kingsbury Episcopi
Kingston St Mary
Leigh-on-Mendip
Lytes Cary Manor

24 Martock
25 Meare
26 Mells
27 Milborne Port
28 Montacute House
29 North Cadbury
30 Poundisford
31 Shepton Mallet
32 Stogursey
33 Ston Easton Park
34 Tolland
35 Wells
36 Westonzoyland
37 Barrington Court
38 Batcombe
39 Bridgwater

40 Chewton Mendip
41 Cleeve Abbey
42 Doulting
43 East Lambrock
44 East Quantoxhead
45 Hatch Beauchamp
46 High Ham
47 Hinton St George
48 Muchelney
49 Nettlecombe
50 North Petherton
51 Nunney
52 Selworthy
53 Stavordale Priory
54 Tintinhull House
55 Witham Friary

## WILTSHIRE

1 Amesbury
2 Avebury
3 Biddesden
4 Bishops Cannings
5 Bishopstone
6 Bowden Park
7 Bowood
8 Boyton
9 Bradford-on-Avon
10 Charlton Park
11 Corsham
12 Devizes
13 Dinton
14 Edington
15 Great Chalfield
16 Lacock
17 Littlecote
18 Longford Castle
19 Longleat
20 Lydiard Tregoze

21 Malmesbury
22 Mildenhall
23 Newtown
24 Potterne
25 Ramsbury Manor
26 Salisbury
27 South Wraxall Manor
28 Steeple Ashton
29 Stockton
30 Stourhead
31 Trafalgar House
32 Urchfont
33 Wardour Castle
34 Wardour Old Castle
35 Westwood Manor
36 Whiteparish
37 Wilbury House
38 Wilton
39 Aldbourne
40 Aldebury
41 Bromham
42 Compton Chamberlayne
43 Durnford
44 East Knoyle
45 Enford
46 Farley
47 Holt
48 Inglesham
49 Manningford Bruce
50 Mere
51 Norrington Manor
52 Sheldon Manor
53 Stratford sub Castle
54 Tisbury

**HAMPSHIRE**
1 Avington Park
2 Beaulieu Abbey
3 Bramshill
4 Breamore
5 Broadlands
6 Cranbury Park
7 East Meon
8 Farnborough
9 Hartley Wintney
10 Highclere
11 King's Somborne
12 Lyndhurst
13 Micheldever
14 Minstead
15 Mottisfont Abbey
16 Northington
17 Nursling
18 Pamber Priory
19 Portchester Castle
20 Romsey Abbey
21 Stratfield Saye
22 The Vyne
23 Winchester
24 Boarhunt
25 Bramley
26 Burghclere
27 Eaglehurst
28 Easton
29 Eversley
30 Fordingbridge
31 Hale Park
32 Hartley Wespall
33 Highcliffe Castle
34 Milford-on-Sea
35 Odiham
36 Portsmouth
37 Titchfield
38 Wolverton

**KENT**
1 Barfreston
2 Belmont
3 Boughton Monchelsea Place
4 Brasted Place
5 Brook
6 Brookland
7 Broome Park
8 Canterbury
9 Charing
10 Chartham
11 Chevening
12 Cobham
13 Dover
14 Godinton Park
15 Goudhurst
16 Graveney
17 Groombridge
18 Hadlow Tower
19 Hever Castle
20 Hildenborough
21 Hythe
22 Ightham Mote
23 Ivychurch
24 Knole
25 Leeds Castle
26 Lees Court
27 Lullingstone
28 Mereworth Castle
29 Minster-in-Thanet
30 New Romney
31 Old Romney
32 Patrixbourne
33 Penshurst Place
34 Ramsgate
35 Rochester
36 St Clere
37 St Margaret's at Cliffe
38 St Mary in the Marsh
39 Saltwood Castle
40 Sandwich
41 Scotney Castle
42 Sissinghurst Castle
43 Stelling
44 Stone
45 Sutton-at-Hone
46 Tunbridge Wells
47 Westerham
48 Westwell
49 Alkham
50 Allington Castle
51 Bishopsbourne
52 Bonnington
53 Bredgar
54 Chilham Castle
55 Deal Castle
56 Godmersham Park

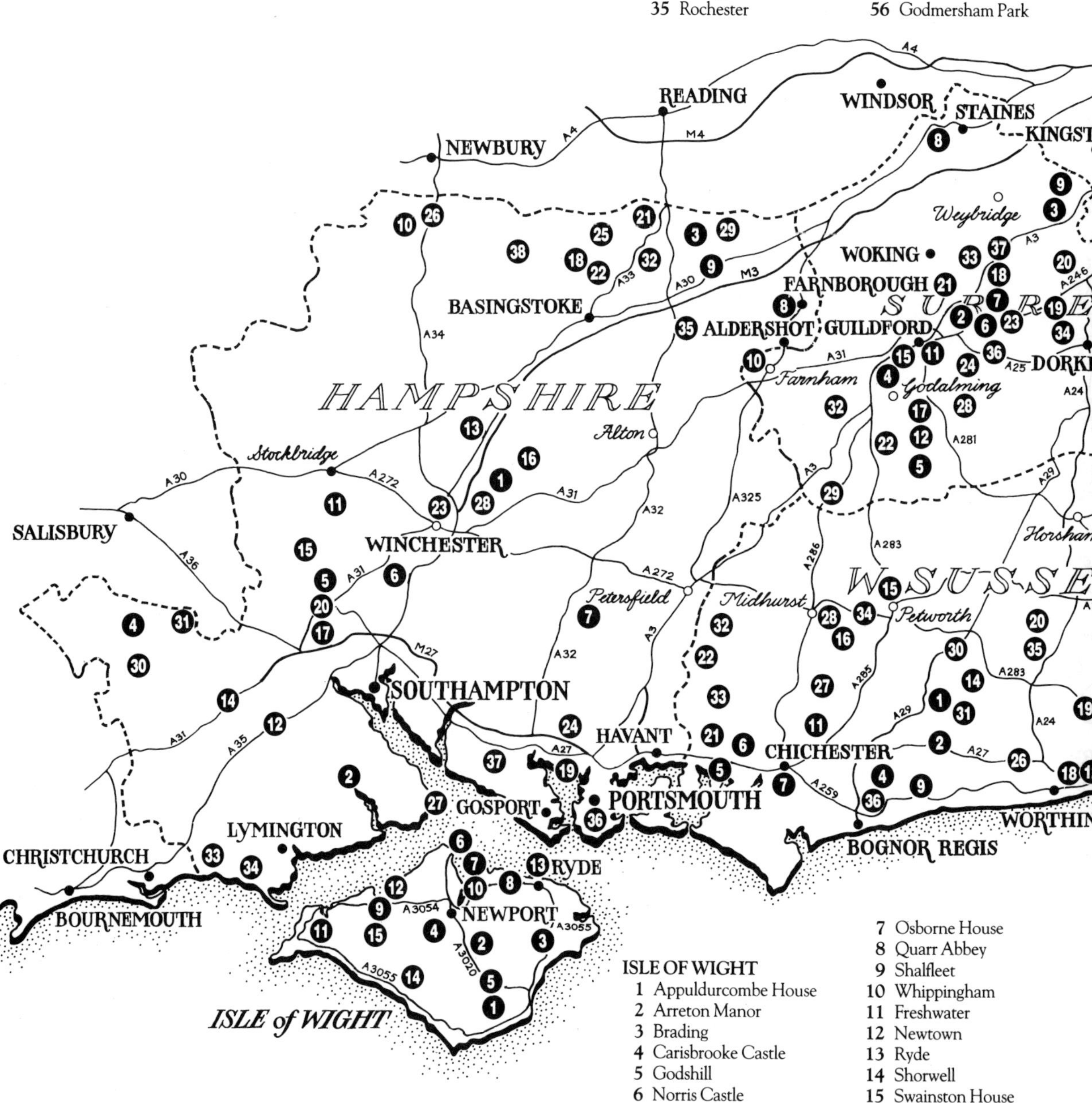


**ISLE OF WIGHT**
1 Appuldurcombe House
2 Arreton Manor
3 Brading
4 Carisbrooke Castle
5 Godshill
6 Norris Castle
7 Osborne House
8 Quarr Abbey
9 Shalfleet
10 Whippingham
11 Freshwater
12 Newtown
13 Ryde
14 Shorwell
15 Swainston House

57 Kilndown
58 Larkfield
59 Linton Park
60 Lympne
61 Maidstone
62 Mersham le Hatch
63 Newington next Sittingbourne
64 Nonington
65 Otham
66 Plaxtol
67 Ruckinge
68 St Nicholas at Wade
69 Smallhythe
70 Smarden
71 Somerhill
72 Sundridge
73 Tenterden
74 West Farleigh Hall
75 Woodchurch

**SURREY**
1 Burstow
2 Clandon Park
3 Claremont
4 Compton
5 Dunsfold
6 East Horsley Towers
7 Egham
8 Esher
9 Farnham
10 Guildford
11 Hascombe
12 Hatchlands
13 Kingswood
14 Lingfield
15 Loseley House
16 Lowfield Heath
17 Munstead
18 Ockham
19 Polesden Lacey
20 Slyfield Manor
21 Sutton Place
22 Tigbourne Court
23 West Horsley Place
24 Albury
25 Bletchingley
26 Chaldon
27 Farleigh
28 Great Tangley Manor
29 Haslemere
30 Limpsfield
31 Pendell House
32 Peper Harow
33 Pyrford
34 Ranmore
35 Reigate Priory
36 Shere
37 Wisley

**EAST SUSSEX**
1 Ashburnham
2 Battle Abbey
3 Bishopstone
4 Bodiam Castle
5 Brighton
6 Eastbourne
7 Etchingham
8 Firle Place
9 Forest Row
10 Glynde Place
11 Hammerwood
12 Herstmonceux
13 Lewes
14 Poynings
15 Rye
16 Sheffield Park
17 Southease
18 Westdean
19 Winchelsea
20 Alfriston
21 Berwick
22 Burwash
23 Hassocks
24 Mayfield
25 Michelham Priory
26 Northiam
27 Penhurst
28 Stanmer House

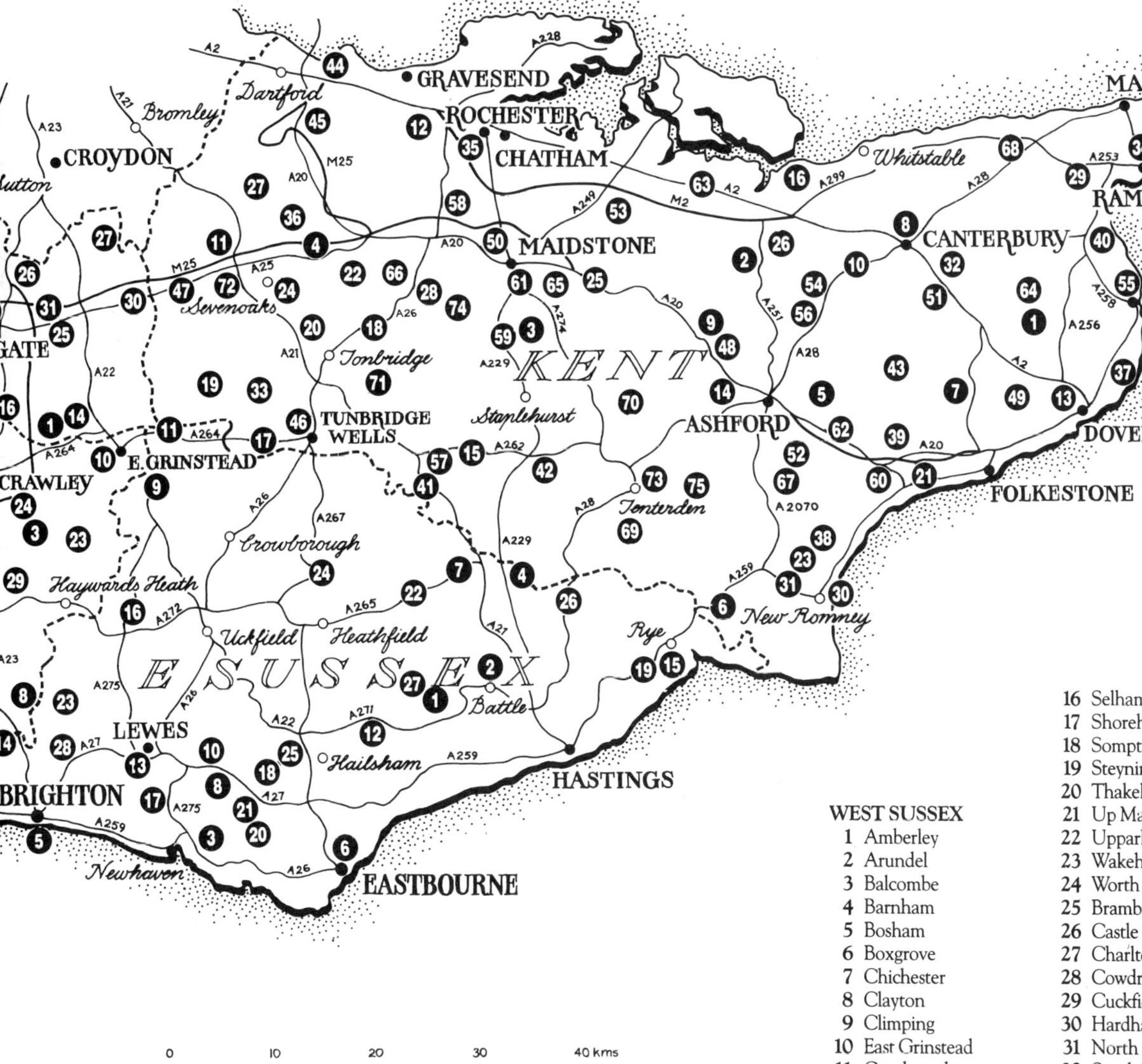

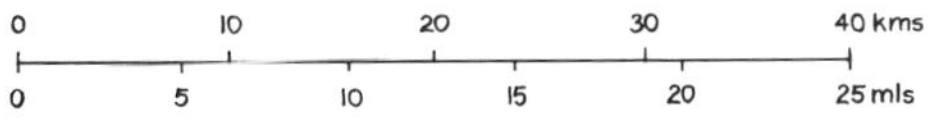

**WEST SUSSEX**
1 Amberley
2 Arundel
3 Balcombe
4 Barnham
5 Bosham
6 Boxgrove
7 Chichester
8 Clayton
9 Climping
10 East Grinstead
11 Goodwood
12 Lancing College
13 Newtimber
14 Parham
15 Petworth
16 Selham
17 Shoreham
18 Sompting
19 Steyning
20 Thakeham
21 Up Marden
22 Uppark
23 Wakehurst Place
24 Worth
25 Bramber
26 Castle Goring
27 Charlton
28 Cowdray House
29 Cuckfield Park
30 Hardham
31 North Stoke
32 South Harting
33 Stoughton
34 Tillington
35 Warminghurst
36 Yapton

LONDON

1 All Hallows, London Wall
2 All Saints, Margaret Street
3 All Souls, Langham Place
4 Asgill House
5 Banqueting House
6 Bexleyheath
7 Blewcoat School
8 British Museum
9 Buckingham Palace
10 Chiswick House
11 Christ Church, Spitalfields
12 Dulwich Picture Gallery
13 Eltham
14 Forty Hall
15 Greenwich
16 Ham House
17 Hampton Court Palace
18 Holy Trinity, Marylebone
19 Kensington Palace
20 Kenwood
21 Kew Gardens
22 Lambeth Palace
23 Law Courts
24 Mansion House
25 Marble Hill House
26 Natural History Museum
27 The Octagon, Orleans House
28 Osterley Park
29 Palace of Westminster
30 Pitshanger Manor
31 Royal Albert Hall
32 Royal Hospital, Chelsea
33 St Anne's, Limehouse
34 St Augustine's, Kilburn
35 St Bartholomew's Hospital
36 St Bartholomew the Great
37 St Benet, Paul's Wharf
38 St Botolph, Aldersgate
39 St Bride's, Fleet Street
40 St Clement Danes
41 St George-in-the-East
42 St George's, Bloomsbury
43 St George's, Hanover Square
44 St James's, Garlickhythe
45 St James's Palace
46 St James's, Piccadilly
47 St John's, Clerkenwell
48 St John's, Smith Square
49 St Katherine Cree
50 St Lawrence Jewry
51 St Lawrence Whitchurch
52 St Magnus the Martyr
53 St Margaret's, Westminster
54 St Martin-in-the-Fields
55 St Martin within Ludgate
56 St Mary Aldermary
57 St Mary at Hill
58 St Mary-le-Bow
59 St Mary-le-Strand
60 St Mary's on Paddington Green
61 St Mary Woolnoth
62 St Pancras Station and Hotel
63 St Pancras, Upper Woburn Place
64 St Paul's Cathedral
65 St Paul's, Covent Garden
66 St Paul's, Deptford
67 St Stephen's, Walbrook
68 Sir John Soane's Museum
69 Somerset House
70 Southwark Cathedral
71 Strawberry Hill
72 Sudbrook Park
73 Syon House
74 Temple Church
75 Tower of London
76 Westminster Abbey
77 Westminster Cathedral
78 Westminster Hall

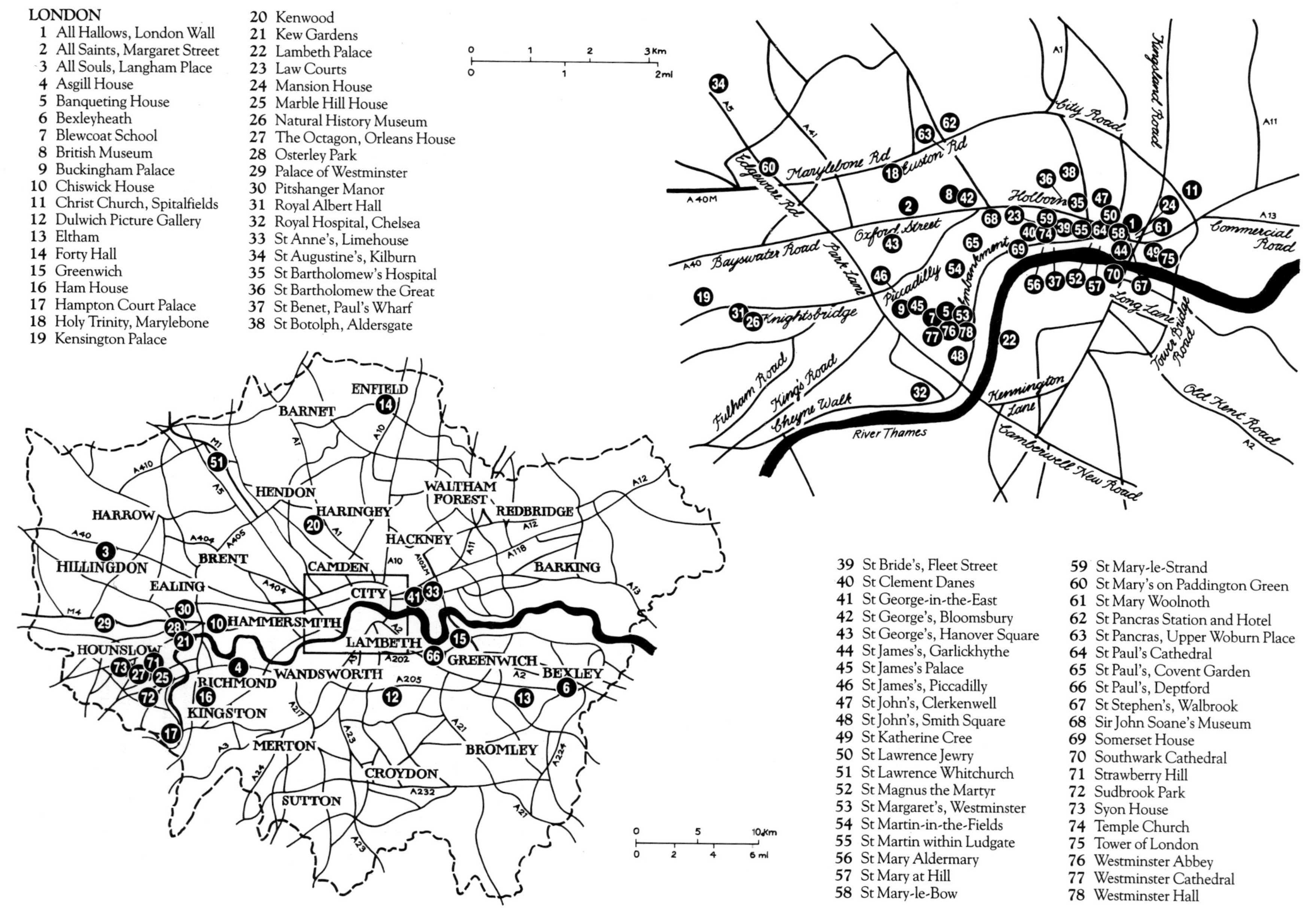

# Glossary

**abacus** flat slab on top of a *capital*
**achievements** (heraldic) a complete display of armorial bearings
**acroterion** a foliage-carved block on the end or top of a classical *pediment*
**aedicule** the framing of a window or door by columns and a *pediment*
**ambulatory** a semi-circular or polygonal aisle enclosing an *apse*
**amorino** a cherub; a popular motif in Renaissance art
**angel roof** a timber roof decorated with carved wooden figures of angels
**apse** a vaulted semi-circular or polygonal end of a *chancel* or chapel
**arcade** a range of arches supported on *piers* or columns, free-standing or blind, i.e. attached to a wall
**architrave** the lowest of the three main parts of an *entablature*; also, more loosely, the moulded frame surrounding a door or window
**Artisan Mannerism** a term coined by Sir John Summerson to define a style of the best London craftsmen – particularly bricklayers – which flourished in England between 1615 and 1675.
**aumbry** a cupboard or recess in which to keep sacred vessels
**baldacchino** a canopy supported on columns
**ball-flower** a globular three-petalled flower enclosing a small ball, a decoration used in the first quarter of the fourteenth century
**barrel vault** see **tunnel vault**
**basket arch** an arch whose curve resembles that of the handle of a basket, formed by a segment of a large circle continued right and left by two segments of much smaller circles
**bas-relief** a shallow carving or sculpture on background, raised less than half its full depth
**beak-head** a Norman decorative motif consisting of a row of birds' or beasts' heads, with beaks usually biting into a roll moulding
**belvedere** a raised turret from which to view the surrounding scenery
**blank arcading** a range of arches supported on *piers* or columns attached to a wall
**blank arch** an arch attached to a wall; also known as a blind arch
**blind arcading** see **blank arcading**
**blind arch** see **blank arch**
**bolection moulding** a projecting moulding used to cover the joint between two members with different surface levels
**boss** an ornamental knob or projection covering the intersection of ribs in a *vault* or ceiling; often carved with foliage or other decoration
**braces** diagonal subsidiary timbers strengthening the frame of a roof and connecting either a *tie-beam* with the wall below or a *collar-beam* with the rafters above; they may be straight or arched
**bressummer** a beam in a timber-framed building which supports the (usually) projecting superstructure; a massive beam spanning any wide opening, especially a chimneypiece
**broach spire** a spire, usually octagonal in plan, placed on a square tower with each of the angles of the tower not covered by the base of the spire filled with an inclined mass of masonry or broach, built into the oblique sides of the spire to effect the transition from the square to the octagon
**bucrania** a favourite motif in antique architecture, consisting of a row of ox skulls, usually garlanded
**campanile** a bell-tower, usually separate from the main building
**cap-à-pie** from head to foot
**capital** the top part of a column
**cartouche** a tablet with an ornate frame, usually enclosing an inscription
**caryatid** a sculpted female figure used as a supporting column
**celure** a panelled and adorned part of a *wagon roof* above the *rood* or altar
**chancel** the part of the east end of the church in which the altar is placed; usually applied to the whole continuation of the *nave* east of the crossing (though not to the eastward extensions of cathedrals, etc.)
**chevet** the French term for the east end of a church, consisting of *apse* and *ambulatory* with or without radiating chapels

**cinquefoil** see **foil**
**clerestory** the upper storey of the nave walls of a church, pierced by windows above the roofs of the aisles
**clunch** a hard chalk used as building stone
**Coade stone** artificial (cast) stone invented by Mrs Eleanor Coade in the 1770s and widely used in the late eighteenth and early nineteenth centuries for all types of ornamentation
**coffering** recessed square or polygonal panels forming a decoration on a ceiling or *vault*
**Composite** a classical *order* whose *capital* combines the foliate bell of the *Corinthian* with the *volutes* of the *Ionic*
**console** an ornamental bracket with a compound curved outline
**corbel** a projecting block, usually of stone, supporting a beam or other horizontal member
**Corinthian** a classical *order* featuring an intricately moulded *capital* with acanthus leaves
**cornice** in classical architecture, the top projecting section of an *entablature*; also any projecting ornamental moulding along the top of a building, wall, arch, etc. finishing or crowning it
**cottage orné** a deliberately rustic or romantic building, usually of asymmetrical plan and often thatched; a product of the late eighteenth- and early nineteenth-century cult of the Picturesque
**cove/coving** a large concave moulding, particularly where wall and ceiling meet
**crocket/crocketing** a decorative feature carved in various leaf shapes and projecting at regular intervals from the angles of spires, pinnacles, canopies, gables etc. in *Gothic* architecture
**crownpost** a vertical timber standing centrally on a *tie-beam* and supporting a collar *purlin*
**cruck** a big curved wooden beam supporting both walls and roof of a building
**cupola** a small polygonal or circular domed turret crowning a roof
**cusp** a projecting point formed at the intersections of circles or arches (*foils*) in *Gothic* architecture
**dado** a decorative covering of the lower part of a wall
**Decorated** a historical division of English *Gothic* architecture covering the period from *c.*1290 to *c.*1350
**dentil** a small, square block used series as a decoration for a classical *cornice*
**diaper** a surface decoration, usually of brickwork, made up of repeated small squares, rectangles or lozenges
**Diocletian window** a semi-circular window divided vertically by two mullions; much used in Palladian architecture and named after the Baths of Diocletian in Rome. Also known as a thermal window
**Doom painting** a painting of the Last Judgement, usually facing west over the *chancel* arch of a church
**Doric** a classical *order*, primarily distinguished by the *triglyphs and metopes* in its *frieze*
**Early English** a historical division of English Gothic architecture covering the period from *c.*1180 to *c.*1280
**encaustic tiles** glazed and decorated tiles of earthenware, much used in the Middle Ages and in Victorian churches for flooring
**enceinte** in military architecture, the main enclosure of a fortress surrounded by a curtain wall
**enfilade** a system of aligning internal doors in sequence so that a vista can be obtained through a series of rooms
**entablature** in classical architecture, the horizontal elements of an *order* supported by the columns, comprising the *architrave*, the *frieze* and the *cornice*
**entasis** a slight convex deviation from a straight line; used on Greek columns and sometimes on spires to prevent an optical illusion of concavity
**fan vault** a late medieval *vault* composed of inverted concave cones overlaid with numerous ribs of the same curve and length, radiating at equal angles from one *springer*, thus giving a fan-like pattern
**fenestration** the arrangement of the windows in a building
**finial** a formal ornament at the top of a gable, pinnacle or canopy
**flèche** a slender wooden spire rising from the centre of a roof; also called a spirelet
**flushwork** the decorative use of knapped flint in conjunction with dressed stone so as to form patterns of tracery, initials etc.
**fluted** having shallow concave vertical channels in the shaft of a column
**flying buttress** an arch or half arch transmitting the thrust of a *vault* or roof from the upper part of a wall to an outer support or buttress
**foil** a lobe- or leaf-shaped curve formed by the *cusping* of a circle or an arch; the number of foils involved is shown by the prefix, i.e. trefoil, quatrefoil, cinquefoil
**frieze** in classical architure, the central part of the *entablature*; otherwise, the decorated band along the upper part of an initial wall, immediately below the *cornice*
**galilee** a chapel or vestibule usually at the west end of a church; sometimes called a *narthex*
**gargoyle** a waterspout projecting from a roof, or the parapet of a wall or tower, carved into a grotesque human or animal shape
**garth** an enclosed open space, as in a cloister
**Gothic/Gothick** Gothic is the architecture of the pointed arch, the *rib vault*, the *flying buttress*, the walls reduced to a minimum and spacious *clerestory* windows; the style started about 1130 in England and continued until the end of the sixteenth century. Gothick is used to decribe the early part of the Gothic Revival, in the mid-eighteenth century, started by Horace Walpole at Strawberry Hill and characterised by a light-hearted, almost *Rococo* decoration; it continued into the first quarter of the nineteeth century
**green man** a wild man of the woodland; also called a jack-in-the green
**grisaille** a way of painting in grey monochrome
**ha-ha** a sunken ditch to keep livestock out of gardens and eliminating the need for a fence or wall
**hammerbeam** a horizontal roof bracket projecting at

the level of the base of the rafters to carry arched *braces* and struts

**hood mould** a moulding, projecting from round an arch, doorway or window, or from a wall, to keep the rain off

**impost** a bracket in a wall, usually formed of mouldings, on which the end of an arch appears to rest

**in antis** a term used to describe a *portico* when it recedes into a building and the columns range with the side walls

**Ionic** a classical *order* characterised by the *volutes* of its *capital* and the *dentils* in its *cornice*; the shaft is generally *fluted*

**jack-in-the-green** see **green man**

**Jesse window** a window in which the tracery represents the branches of the tree of Jesse, a genealogical tree showing the ancestors of Christ ascending from the root of Jesse

**jetty** the projection of an upper storey in a timber-framed building beyond the storey below, made by the beams and joists of the lower storey oversailing the external wall

**keystone** the central stone of an arch or *rib vault*, sometimes carved

**kingpost** a vertical timber standing centrally on a *tie-beam* or *collar-beam* and rising to the apex of the roof to support the ridge

**label stop** a decorative *boss* at either end of a *hood mould*

**lancet** a slender pointed-arched window, characterising the *Early English* style

**lantern** a small circular or polygonal turret, with windows all round, crowning a roof or dome

**lesene** a **pilaster** without base and capital, also called a pilaster strip; usually found on exteriors of later Anglo-Saxon and early Romanesque churches

**lierne vault** a tertiary rib, i.e. one which springs neither from one of the main *springers* nor from a central *boss*

**linenfold** Tudor panelling ornamented with a conventional representation of a piece of linen laid in vertical folds

**long-and-short work** Saxon *quoins* consisting of long stones on end between flat ones, all bonded into the wall

**louvre** an opening, often with a *lantern* over, in the roof of a hall to let out the smoke from a central hearth

**lucarne** a small opening in an attic or spire, originally to let in light but often purely decorative

**lunette** a *tympanum* or semi-circular opening; the term can also be applied to any flat, semi-circular surface

**machicoulis/machicolation** a projecting gallery on brackets built on the outside of castle towers or wall, with openings in the floor through which to drop missiles

**mandorla** an upright almond shape, found chiefly in medieval art, to enclose a figure of Christ enthroned; also known as a *vesica*

**mathematical tiles** small yellowish-white facing tiles, the size of brick headers, popularised by Henry Holland and very much used, especially in the South of England, between *c.*1780 and *c.*1840

**merlon** the raised portion of the battlement of a castle or house

**metope and triglyph** the *frieze* of a *Doric* order; triglyphs are the blocks separating the metopes or square space between. They have two vertical grooves, or glyphs, in the centre and half grooves at the edges

**meurtrière** in military architecture, a small loophole, large enough for the barrel of a gun or musket

**misericord** a bracket, often elaborately carved, placed on the underside of a hinged choir-stall seat, which, when turned up, gave support to the occupant when standing during long services

**modillion** a small bracket of which a series (modillion *frieze*) is often placed below a *cornice*

**motte and bailey** the usual post-Roman and Norman defence system, consisting of an earthen mound (the motte) topped with a wooden tower eccentrically placed, with a bailey (open space) surrounded by an enclosure ditch and palisade

**mouchette** a curved dagger-like motif in curvilinear *tracery*, popular in the early fourteenth century

**mullion** a vertical post or other upright dividing a window into 'lights'

**narthex** see **galilee**

**nave** the part of a church west of the crossing, often flanked by aisles

**newel-post** the central post in a circular or winding staircase; also the principal post where a flight of stairs meets a landing

**nogging** the name given to brickwork used to fill the spaces between the timbers in a timber-framed building

**oculus window** a circular opening in a wall or at the apex of a dome

**oeil-de-boeuf** a small round or oval window

**ogee/ogival** a double-curved line made up of a convex and a concave part; an ogee arch is pointed and uses this compound curve. It was introduced *c.*1300 and is also called a keel arch

**opus Alexandrinum** a form of wall or pavement mosaic composed of small pieces of coloured marble and gilded tesserae

**oriel** a bay window on an upper storey or storeys of a building

**ormolu** a gold-coloured alloy of copper, zinc and tin; gilded bronze or lacquered brass. Widely used in French cabinet-making for furniture ornaments in the seventeenth and eighteenth centuries

**order** in classical architecture an order comprises a column, with or without a base, a shaft, *capital* and *entablature*, decorated and proportioned in one of the accepted modes: *Doric, Tuscan, Ionic, Corinthian* or *Composite*

**pantile** a roofing tile of curved S-shaped section

**parclose screen** a screen, usually of wood or iron, separating a chapel or tomb from the body of a church

**pargetting** exterior plastering of timber-framed buildings, usually modelled with ornamental patterns or figures, popular in the sixteenth and seventeenth

centuries, especially in East Anglia
**pediment** a low-pitched gable above a **portico** or above doors, windows etc.; it may be straight-sided or curved segmentally. A broken pediment has a gap in the upper moulding
**pele tower** a term used in northern England and Scotland, signifying a small tower or house suitable for sudden defence
**pendentive** a concave *spandrel* leading from the base of a dome to the angle of two supporting walls
**Perpendicular** the style of English Gothic architecture succeeding the Decorated. First appearing *c.*1330 and continuing throughout the fifteenth century, it is characterised by the strong vertical lines of its *tracery*
**piano nobile** the principal storey of a house, usually above ground level, containing the main reception rooms
**pier** a solid masonry support
**Pietà** a devotional type of the suffering Virgin bearing the dead Christ on her knees
**pilaster** a shallow *pier* or rectangular column projecting only slightly from a wall
**piscina** a shallow basin with a drain, in which Communion or Mass vessels are washed; generally placed in a niche in the south wall of the chancel
**poppy-head** the ornamental *finial* of a church pew, often carved with ornamental patterns or figures; the name is derived from *poupée*, doll, and has nothing to do with the flower
**porphyry** a kind of rock with crystals embedded in a red or other ground mass
**porte-cochère** a porch large enough to admit wheeled vehicles
**portico** a roofed space, open or partly enclosed, forming the entrance and centrepiece of a house or church; often with classical detached or attached columns and a *pediment*
**prodigy house** extravagant country house built *c.*1570–*c.*1620, many of them designed primarily to entertain Queen Elizabeth and her court; examples are Longleat, Wollaton, Hardwick, Burghley, Audley End and Hatfield
**pulpitum** a screen, usually of stone, in a major church, erected to shut off the choir from the *nave*
**putto** a little boy, often winged, developed from the god Eros, and a frequent motif of decorative art in the classical, post-classical and Renaissance periods
**purlin** a longitudinal timber of a roof laid parallel with the wall plate and apex, usually at one-third or two-thirds interval up the slope of the roof
**pyx** a vessel in which the Host is reserved during Mass
**quadripartite vault** a rib *vault* in which two diagonal ribs divide each bay into four compartments
**quatrefoil** see **foil**
**queenpost** pairs of vertical or near-vertical timbers placed symmetrically on a *tie-beam* and supporting side *purlins*
**quoins** the dressed stones at the corners of buildings, usually laid so that their exposed faces are alternately large and small
**Red Book** a book specially produced by Humphry Repton for each of his more important clients, containing watercolours of their existing house and grounds with ingenious lift-up flaps showing his suggested improvements
**repoussé** decoration of metalwork by relief designs, formed by beating the metal from the back
**rere-arch** the inner arch or a window or door opening, when it differs in size or form from the original (outer) arch
**reredorter** a privy, situated at the back of the dormitory in a convent or monastery
**reredos** a wall or screen, usually of wood or stone and often decorated, rising behind an altar
**respond** a half pier bonded into a wall and carrying one end of an arch
**reticulated** a form of tracery typical of the early fourteenth century, consisting entirely of circles drawn at top and bottom into *ogee* shapes, giving a net-like appearance
**retrochoir** the space behind the high altar in a major church
**rib vault** a system of cross-vaulting in which the groins are replaced by arched ribs constructed across the sides and diagonals of the vaulted bay to act as a framework or support for the infilling
**rocaille** originally the stone or shell decoration for artificial grottoes; later used to describe *Rococo* decoration of any work
**Rococo** a form of decoration developed from the late Baroque but lighter and more elegant; fashionable in England in the mid-eighteenth century
**Roman cement** Parker's Roman Cement, patented in 1796, was made from burnt septaria; it surpassed all previous stuccos for durability and imperviousness to damp, and is said to have made Nash's architecture possible
**rood** a cross, usually wooden or painted on the *chancel* arch, at the east end of the *nave*
**rood-screen** a screen at the west end of the chancel, separating *nave* and choir and below the rood-loft
**rose window** a circular window with patterns of concentric or radiating *tracery*
**rotunda** a building circular in plan and often domed
**roundel** a circular panel, disc or medallion; also a similarly shaped panel in a stained-glass window
**rustication** masonry cut in massive blocks separated from each other by deeply recessed joints and often with a roughened surface; see also *vermiculated*
**sarcophagus** a stone coffin
**scagliola** imitation marble, composed of cement or plaster and marble chips or colouring matter, often used for columns and in interior decoration in eighteenth-century classical architecture
**scissor-braces** a pair of *braces* which cross diagonally between pairs of rafters or principals
**screens passage** the entrance passage of a medieval house separating the hall screen from the kitchen, buttery and pantry
**sedilia** a series of seats (usually three) on the south side of the *chancel* for the use of the clergy. Often recessed into the wall at three different levels and linked

decoratively with the *piscina*
**sexpartite vault** a form of vaulting in which each bay is divided into six parts by two diagonal ribs and one transverse rib
**shell keep** a circular or oval wall surrounding the inner portion of a castle
**solar** a parlour or private room in medieval and Tudor manor houses, usually at first-floor level, approached by a stair from the dais end of the hall
**spandrel** the triangular surface between one side of an arch, the horizontal line taken from its apex and the vertical drawn from its springing (see *springer*); also the surface between two adjacent arches and the horizontal moulding above them; also the surface of a *vault* between two adjacent ribs
**spirelet** see **flèche**
**springer** the point at which an arch rises from its support
**squinch** a small arch or series of concentric arches built across the angle of a square or polygon to support a superstructure, i.e. a dome or spire
**stiff-leaf** a late twelfth-century and early thirteenth-century type of sculptured foliage, found chiefly on *capitals* and *bosses*
**strainer arch** an arch inserted across a *nave* or aisle to prevent the walls from leaning inwards, or to support a superstructure
**strapwork** decoration originating in the Netherlands *c.*1540 and popular in Elizabethan and Jacobean England, consisting of interlaced bands similar to fretwork or cut leather; generally executed in plaster or stone on ceilings, screens or parapets
**sub-arch** one of a small group of arches (usually a pair) enclosed within a single embracing arch
**tester** the horizontal board or canopy over a pulpit; also called a sounding-board
**tie-beam** a beam spanning the space from wall plate to wall plate of a timber roof, preventing the wall from spreading
**tierceron** a secondary rib of a *vault* which springs from one of the main *springers* and leads to a place on the ridge-rib
**tracery** ornamental intersecting work in the upper part of a window, screen or panel, or used decoratively in *blank arches* and *vaults*
**transepts** the transverse arms of a cruciform church
**Transitional** a term usually referring to the transition from the Norman to the Early English style of architecture in the late twelfth century
**transom** a horizontal bar of stone or wood across the opening of a window
**trefoil** see **foil**
**tribune gallery** the upper storey above an aisle in a church, with arches to the *nave*
**triforium** the arcaded wall passage, or *blank arcading*, facing the *nave* at the height of the aisle roof and below the *clerestory* windows
**trompe-l'oeil** a style of painting which, through precise draughtsmanship and a careful placing of shadows, attempts to deceive the eye by producing a three-dimensional effect
**trumeau** a vertical stone mullion supporting the *tympanum* of a wide doorway
**tunnel vault** an uninterrupted *vault* of semi-circular or pointed section, the simplest form of vault; also called barrel vault or wagon vault
**tympanum** the space between the lintel of a doorway and the arch above it, or the space between the enclosing mouldings of a *pediment*
**undercroft** a vaulted chamber, sometimes wholly or partly underground, below a church, chapel or hall
**vault** an arched ceiling or roof of stone or brick, sometimes imitated in wood or plaster
**Venetian window** a tripartite window, with an arched central opening higher and wider than the side openings, which have flat heads
**vermiculated** a form of masonry decoration in which the stone is scored with irregular shallow channels like worm tracks
**vesica** see **mandorla**
**volute** a spiral scroll, the distinctive feature of the *Ionic* capital, used in modified form in *Corinthian* and *Composite* capitals and in *consoles* and brackets
**voussoir** one of a series of wedge-shaped stones or bricks used to form an arch
**wagon roof** a roof formed by closely set rafters with arched braces and often panelled or plastered; so called because it looks like the stretched canvas roof of a wagon
**wagon vault** see **tunnel vault**
**water-leaf** a leaf shape used in later twelfth-century *capitals*, with a broad, unribbed, tapering leaf curving up towards the angle of the *abacus* and turned in at the top
**wild man** see **green man**
**wind-brace** a diagonal timber *brace*, usually curved, crossing the rafters to stiffen the roof longitudinally; sometimes decorated with *cusping*

Definitions of other architectural terms, and illustrations of some of those given above, can be found in *The Penguin Dictionary of Architecture* by John Fleming, Hugh Honour and Nikolaus Pevsner.

# Index

Page numbers in *italic* refer to the illustrations